T0093711

The Sage Handbook of
Human–Machine
Communication

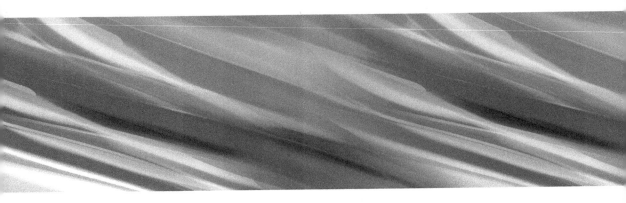

The Sage Handbook of
Human–Machine Communication

Edited by

Andrea L. Guzman
Rhonda McEwen and
Steve Jones

§ Sage

S Sage

1 Oliver's Yard
55 City Road
London EC1Y 1SP

2455 Teller Road
Thousand Oaks, California 91320

Unit No 323-333, Third Floor, F-Block
International Trade Tower, Nehru Place
New Delhi 110 019

8 Marina View Suite 43-053
Asia Square Tower 1
Singapore 018960

Editor: Michael Ainsley
Assistant Editor: Ozlem Merakli
Production Editor: Neelu Sahu
Copyeditor: Martin Noble
Proofreader: Clare Weaver
Indexer: Michael Allerton
Marketing Manager: Ruslana Khatagova
Cover Design: Ginkhan Siam
Typeset by KnowledgeWorks Global Ltd
Printed in the UK

Library of Congress Control Number: 2023934000

British Library Cataloguing in Publication data

A catalogue record for this book is available from the British Library

ISBN 978-1-5297-7392-7

At Sage we take sustainability seriously. Most of our products are printed in the UK using responsibly sourced papers and boards. When we print overseas we ensure sustainable papers are used as measured by the Paper Chain Project grading system. We undertake an annual audit to monitor our sustainability.

Editorial Arrangement & Introduction © Andrea L. Guzman, Rhonda McEwen, Steve Jones, 2023

Chapter 1 © Kate K. Mays and James E. Katz, 2023
Chapter 2 © Andreas Hepp & Wiebke Loosen, 2023
Chapter 3 © Ronald Kline, 2023
Chapter 4 © Katina Michael, Jeremy Pitt, Roba Abbas, Christine Perakslis, MG Michael, 2023
Chapter 5 © Jonathan Roberge, 2023
Chapter 6 © Florian Shkurti, 2023
Chapter 7 © S. Shyam Sundar & Jin Chen, 2023
Chapter 8 © Steve Jones & Rhonda McEwen, 2023
Chapter 9 © Victoria McArthur & Cosmin Munteanu, 2023
Chapter 10 © Adam Dube, 2023
Chapter 11 © Eleanor Sandry, 2023
Chapter 12 © David Gunkel, 2023
Chapter 13 © Andrew Iliadis, 2023
Chapter 14 © Leopoldina Fortunati, 2023
Chapter 15 © Margaret Rhee, 2023
Chapter 16 © Nathanael Poor, 2023
Chapter 17 © Joshua Reeves, Jeremy Packer, Kate Maddalena, 2023
Chapter 18 © Autumn Edwards, 2023
Chapter 19 © Nick Diakopoulos, Jack Bandy, Henry Dambanemuya, 2023
Chapter 20 © Nicole C. Krämer & Jessica M. Szczuka, 2023
Chapter 21 © Michelle Lui, 2023
Chapter 22 © Kristina M. Green, 2023
Chapter 23 © Hervé Saint-Louis, 2023
Chapter 24 © Patric Spence, David Westerman, Zhenyang Luo, 2023
Chapter 25 © Jack Jamieson, 2023
Chapter 26 © Sharon Ringel, 2023
Chapter 27 © Andrea L. Guzman, 2023
Chapter 28 © Paula Gardner & Jess Rauchberg, 2023
Chapter 29 © Charles Ess, 2023
Chapter 30 © Gina Neff & Peter Nagy, 2023
Chapter 31 © Carmina Rodríguez-Hidalgo, 2023
Chapter 32 © Kun Xu & David Jeong, 2023
Chapter 33 © Astrid Rosenthal-von der Pütten & Kevin Koban, 2023
Chapter 34 © Kevin Koban & Jaime Banks, 2023
Chapter 35 © Christoph Lutz, 2023
Chapter 36 © Natalie Parde, 2023
Chapter 37 © Julie L. Mortensen, Nicoline N. Siegfredsen & Anja Bechmann, 2023
Chapter 38 © Jenny Kennedy & Rowan Wilken, 2023
Chapter 39 © Sarah Myers West, 2023
Chapter 40 © Beth Coleman, 2023
Chapter 41 © Chinar Mehta, Payal Arora, and Usha Raman 2023
Chapter 42 © Gerard Goggin, 2023
Chapter 43 © Damith Herath, Stelarc, 2023
Chapter 44 © Julian Posada, Gemma Newlands, and Milagros Miceli, 2023
Chapter 45 © Vincent Manzerolle, 2023
Chapter 46 © Simone Natale, 2023
Chapter 47 © Sara Brooks & AJung Moon, 2023
Chapter 48 © Jasmine McNealy, 2023
Chapter 49 © Keiko Nishimura, 2023
Chapter 50 © Maartje de Graaf & Jochen Peter, 2023
Chapter 51 © Taina Bucher, 2023
Chapter 52 © Wei-Jie Hsiao & Sam Woolley, 2023
Chapter 53 © Yi Mou & Yuheng Wu, 2023
Chapter 54 © Ekaterina Pashevich, 2023
Chapter 55 © Jason Archer, 2023
Chapter 56 © Riley Richards, 2023
Chapter 57 © Eric Novotny, Joomi Lee, and Sun Joo (Grace) Ahn, 2023
Chapter 58 © Chad Edwards & Matthew Craig, 2023
Chapter 59 © Jihyun Kim, Hayeon Song, Kelly Merrill Jr., Taenyun Kim, and Jieun Kim, 2023
Chapter 60 © Seth C. Lewis & Felix M. Simon, 2023
Chapter 61 © Weizi Liu & Mike Yao, 2023
Chapter 62 © Jenna Jacobson, Irina Gorea, 2023
Chapter 63 © Thilo von Pape, 2023
Chapter 64 © Regina Peldszus, 2023
Chapter 65 © Pauline Hope Cheong & Yashu Chen, 2023

Apart from any fair dealing for the purposes of research, private study, or criticism or review, as permitted under the Copyright, Designs and Patents Act, 1988, this publication may not be reproduced, stored or transmitted in any form, or by any means, without the prior permission in writing of the publisher, or in the case of reprographic reproduction, in accordance with the terms of licences issued by the Copyright Licensing Agency. Enquiries concerning reproduction outside those terms should be sent to the publisher.

To Matt, thank you for all of your love and support.
– Andrea L. Guzman

To my clan – the McEwen's of Toronto – Stuart, LinTai and Ashe,
thank you for putting up with my late nights! Love you.
– Rhonda McEwen

To Jodi, Ella, Mack, Felix and Oscar.
– Steve Jones

Contents

PART 3: CONCEPTS AND CONTEXTS

Notes on the Editors
and Contributors

THE EDITORS

Andrea L. Guzman is an Associate Professor of Communication at Northern Illinois University and Co-director of The Human–Machine Communication Lab at NIU. Her research focuses on HMC theory and people's perceptions of artificial intelligence, including voice-based assistants and automated news-writing programs. Guzman is editor of *Human–Machine Communication: Rethinking Communication, Technology, and Ourselves*, and her award-winning research has been published in top journals, including *New Media & Society, Computers in Human Behavior, Digital Journalism*, and *Journalism & Mass Communication Quarterly* and has been presented at leading interdisciplinary and disciplinary conferences. Guzman served as the inaugural chair of the Human–Machine Communication Interest Group of the International Communication Association. https://andrealguzman.net

Rhonda N. McEwen is the 14th President and Vice-Chancellor of Victoria University in the University of Toronto; Canada Research Chair in Tactile Interfaces, Communication and Cognition; a Professor of Emerging Media & Communication; and a faculty member at the Institute of Communication, Culture, Information & Technology. Dr. McEwen combines communication studies, and applied and behavioral sciences to examine the social and cognitive effects of technologies. Her pioneering approach to communication research employs experimental techniques, eye tracking, observations, sensor data, and interviews to investigate Human–Machine Communication involving children and adults across the user spectrum, including those diagnosed with communication and learning disorders. Journalists from CBS news magazine *60 Minutes* covered McEwen's research in 2012 and 2013, and she has over 47 publications, including articles in *Human–Robot Interaction Companion; Information, Communication & Society; Computers and Education; Learning & Instruction; New Media and Society*; and information science journals.

Steve Jones is UIC Distinguished Professor of Communication and Adjunct Professor of Computer Science at the University of Illinois Chicago, USA and Adjunct Research Professor in the Institute for Communications Research at the University of Illinois Urbana-Champaign, USA. He is editor of *New Media & Society* and co-editor of *Mobile Media & Communication*. His research interests encompass popular music studies, music technology, sound studies, internet studies, media history, virtual reality, human–machine communication, social robotics and human augmentics. His research has been funded by the National Science Foundation, National Institutes of Health, National Cancer Institute, Centers for Disease Control and the Tides Foundation.

THE CONTRIBUTORS

Roba Abbas is a Senior Lecturer and formerly Academic Program Director with the Faculty of Business and Law at the University of Wollongong, Australia, and more recently a visiting professor at Arizona State University in the School for the Future of Innovation in Society. She has a Ph.D. in location-based services regulation and has received competitive grants for research addressing global challenges in areas related to co-design and socio-technical systems, operations management, robotics, social media, and other emerging technologies. Dr. Abbas is Co-Editor of the *IEEE Transactions on Technology and Society* and is the IEEE Socio-Technical Systems Committee Chair. Her research is focused on methodological approaches to complex socio-technical systems design, emphasizing transdisciplinarity, co-design and the intersection of society, technology, ethics, and regulation.

Sun Joo (Grace) Ahn is a Professor at the Grady College of Journalism and Mass Communication. She is the founding director of the Center for Advanced Computer-Human Ecosystems Lab. Her main program of research investigates how interactive digital media such as virtual and augmented reality transform traditional rules of communication and social interactions, looking at how virtual experiences shape the way that people think, feel, and behave in the physical world. Her work is supported by the National Science Foundation and National Institutes of Health and is published in numerous top-tier outlets in the fields of communication, health, and engineering.

Jason Edward Archer is an Assistant Professor of Communication in the Department of Humanities at Michigan Technological University. His main interests revolve around human–machine communication, haptics, and surgical robotics. He has conducted funded research on the intersections of privacy, security, and Human Augmentics as an NSF-IGERT Fellow. His work has been published in *New Media & Society*, *Communication + 1*, and *CHI*, won a top paper award from the Human–Machine Communication interest group at ICA, and been presented at numerous conferences including 4S, AoIR, NCA, SLSA, and SCMS.

Payal Arora is a Professor and Chair in Technology, Values, and Global Media Cultures at Erasmus University Rotterdam. Her expertise lies in digital experience and user values among low-income communities worldwide and comes with about two decades of fieldwork experience in such contexts. She is the author of a number of award-winning books including *The Leisure Commons* and most recently *The Next Billion Users* with Harvard Press. Forbes named her the "next billion champion" and "the right kind of person to reform tech." Several international media outlets have covered her work including the BBC, *The Economist*, Quartz, Tech Crunch, *The Boston Globe*, F.A.Z, *The Nation* and CBC. She is the co-founder of FemLab.co, a feminist future of work initiative, and is a section editor for *Global Perspectives*, a University of California Press journal.

Jack Bandy is a Ph.D. candidate in the Technology and Social Behavior program at Northwestern University, where he works in the Computational Journalism Lab. His work focuses on how computing can serve the public interest, with recent projects exploring the impact of algorithmic platforms like Twitter, Apple News, and TikTok. His research and writing have appeared in *The Guardian*, *The Hill*, and the *Chicago Tribune*, and often combines topics in ethics, algorithm auditing, human–computer interaction, and media studies. Before coming to Northwestern, Jack completed an M.S. in Computer Science from the University of Kentucky. He has also held research positions at the University of North Carolina at Charlotte.

Jaime Banks is Associate Professor at the School of Information Studies at Syracuse University. Her work is driven by questions about humans' relationships with social technologies, with a current emphasis on people's perceptions of social robots' moral agency and patiency. Other work considers gamer-avatar relations, theory of mind for agentic tech, mental models in tech engagement, and media influences on tech understandings.

Anja Bechmann is a professor at Media Studies and director of the interdisciplinary research center DATALAB - Center for Digital Social Research at Aarhus University in Denmark. Her research mainly examines datafication, AI and data ethics, digital and social media communication and collective behavior using large-scale data collection and applied machine learning. She has acted as appointed member of numerous expert groups for government entities in Denmark, the Nordics and the EU. Her research has been funded by national and international research councils such as the Danish Council for Independent Research, Swedish Research Council, Danish Agency for Science and Innovation, Horizon 2020, EU CEF, and Aarhus University Research Foundation and published in journals such as *New Media & Society*, *Big Data & Society*, *Information, Communication & Society*, *Social Media + Society* and *Digital Journalism*.

Nandini Asavari Bharadwaj is a Ph.D. student in the Learning Sciences program at the Department of Educational & Counselling Psychology, McGill University. Her research interests are in educational technology, digital learning environments, and artificial intelligence in education. Her interdisciplinary research investigates the impact of digital assistant (e.g. Amazon Alexa, Google Assistant and Apple Siri) use on children's theories of artificial minds. Specifically, how children interact with digital assistants, how they perceive the affordances of these technologies and how these perceptions impact understanding of intelligent technologies. She holds a M.A in Educational Psychology (Learning Sciences) from McGill University, a B.A (Hons) in Cognitive Science from York University and a B.A (Hons) in English Literature from Delhi University.

Sara Brooks is presently a clinical research coordinator at a clinic specializing in psychedelic-assisted therapies. Her scholarly interests focus on the philosophy of technology, particularly ethics, governance, and regulation of artificial intelligence technologies including collaborative robotics. She gained her Master in public policy and Bachelor of Arts in Philosophy degrees from the University of Calgary.

Taina Bucher is Professor in Media Studies and Head of Screen Cultures at the Department of Media and Communication, University of Oslo. She is the author of *Facebook* (Polity Press, 2021) and *IF... THEN: Algorithmic Power and Politics* (OUP, 2018). Taina Bucher has published extensively on topics such as algorithmic culture, media temporalities, software studies, social media platforms, facial recognition, and disconnection.

Jin Chen is a graduate fellow and Ph.D. Candidate in mass communications at the Bellisario College of Communications at the Pennsylvania State University. Her scholarly interest lies at the intersection of interactive media technologies, strategic health communication, and social psychology. Her research has explored the potential of interactive media technologies including chatbots, AI algorithms, and video games to promote user engagement as well as health behaviors and personal well-being. In addition, she examines the role of different emotions in helping to shape people's attitudinal and behavioral responses to messages related to health issues in digital media environments.

Yashu Chen is a Lecturer at the School of Communication at San Diego State University. Her research focuses broadly on the intersection between Internet-based communication platforms, civic engagement, and cultures, and has been published in several journals including *Journal of Health Communication*, *International Journal of Communication*, *Journal of International and Intercultural Communication*, *Western Journal of Communication*, and *International Journal of Interactive Communication Systems and Technologies*. Dr. Chen has taught courses such as Investigating Communication, Communication Theory, Research Methods & Design, Political Communication, and Intercultural Communication.

Pauline Hope Cheong is Professor and Director of Engagement and Innovation at the Hugh Downs School of Human Communication, Arizona State University. Her research examines the interactions between digital technologies and different cultural communities, including religious authority practices, and the socio-cultural implications of big data, artificial intelligence, and robotics. Author of numerous print and online publications, her grant-funded research studies have appeared in key communication and interdisciplinary journals, including *New Media & Society, Applied Artificial Intelligence, Information, Communication and Society*, and *Journal of Intercultural and International Communication*. She is co-editor of *The Oxford Handbook of Digital Religion*. Her work has been honored with top paper and book awards by the National Communication Association, Western Communication Association, and the International Communication Association. http://www.drpaulinecheong.com

Beth Coleman is an Associate Professor of Data & Cities at the University of Toronto, where she directs the City as Platform lab. Working in the disciplines of Science and Technology Studies and Critical Race Theory, her research focuses on smart technology and machine learning, urban data, and civic engagement. She is the author of *Hello Avatar* and multiple articles. Her research affiliations have included the Berkman Klein Center for Internet & Society; Microsoft Research; Data & Society Institute; Google Visiting Senior Researcher; and expert consultant for the European Commission Digital Futures. She is a founding member of the Trusted Data Sharing group, Schwartz Reisman Institute for Technology and Society and the Inaugural Director, University of Toronto Black Research Network Institute Strategic Initiative.

Matthew J. A. Craig is a Ph.D. candidate in the College of Communication and Information at Kent State University, a Graduate Research fellow at the Communication and Social Robotics Labs (www.combotlabs. org), and a Graduate Researcher in the Communication and Technology Research Lab in Kent State

University's College of Communication and Information. His teaching and research concerns communication with and through machines at the intersections of communication technology, society, and interpersonal communication. Recent publications include articles in: Popular Culture Studies Journal, Communication Studies, Companion of the 2020 ACM/IEEE International Conference on Human–Robotic Interaction, and Conference Proceedings of the 14th ACM/IEEE International Conference on Human–Robot Interaction. Matthew received his master's degree in Communication from the School of Communication at Western Michigan University. www.matthewjacraig.com

Henry Dambanemuya is a Ph.D. candidate in the Technology and Social Behavior program at Northwestern University, where he works in the Laboratory on Innovation, Networks, and Knowledge (LINK). His research broadly aims to understand and predict group behavior in networks and sociotechnical systems. Using a combination of methods from machine learning and complex networks analysis, he examines how people's social networks and their opinion diversity impact their judgments in online collaborative settings. Prior to Northwestern, Henry obtained his M.A. from the Kroc Institute for International Peace Studies at the University of Notre Dame and a BA in computer science and conflict studies from DePauw University.

Nicholas Diakopoulos is an Associate Professor in Communication Studies and Computer Science (by courtesy) at Northwestern University where he directs the Computational Journalism Lab and is Director of Graduate Studies for the Technology and Social Behavior Ph.D. program. His research focuses on computational journalism, including aspects of automation and algorithms in news production, algorithmic accountability and transparency, and social media in news contexts. He is author of the award-winning book, *Automating the News: How Algorithms are Rewriting the Media*, published by Harvard University Press in 2019. He holds a Ph.D. in Computer Science, with a focus on Human–Computer Interaction, from the Georgia Institute of Technology.

Adam Kenneth Dubé is an Associate Professor of Learning Sciences and Director of the EdTech Office for the Faculty of Education at McGill University. He is the McGill Faculty of Education Distinguished Teacher award recipient, the head of the Technology, Learning, & Cognition Lab (mcgill.ca/tlc), and a joint Fellow of the American Educational Research Association and the Society of Research in Child Development in middle childhood education and development. He investigates how educational games augment the learning process and teaches courses on the use of emerging educational technologies. His recent work on the use and design of effective educational technology informs his contribution to the UNESCO-MGIEP "Industry guidelines on digital learning."

Autumn Edwards is Professor in the School of Communication at Western Michigan University and Co-director of the Communication and Social Robotics Labs (combotlabs.org). She is founding Editor-in-Chief of the journal *Human–Machine Communication* (hmcjournal.com), which focuses on the theory and practice of communication with and about digital interlocutors, including social robots, technologically augmented persons (cyborgs), and communication in augmented, virtual, and mixed-reality environments. She was named in 2020 by Women in Robotics as one of "30 Women in Robotics You Need to Know About." Her research addresses human–machine communication with an emphasis on how ontological considerations, or beliefs about the nature of communicators and communication, both shape and are shaped by interactions with digital interlocutors. Professor Edwards also writes about the expectations, impressions, and message strategies people bring to communication with social robots.

Chad Edwards is a Professor of Communication in the School of Communication at Western Michigan University. He is a Theodore von Kármán Fellow at RWTH Aachen University. Edwards' research interests include human–machine communication and instructional communication. Recent publications include articles in: *International Journal of Social Robotics, Frontiers in Robotics and AI, Communication Education, Computers in Human Behavior, Journal of Computer-Mediated Communication*, and *Communication Studies*. Chad Edwards co-directs the Communication and Social Robotics Labs (www.combotlab.org).

Charles Ess is Professor Emeritus, Department of Media and Communication, University of Oslo, Norway. He works across the intersections of philosophy, computing, applied ethics, comparative philosophy and religious studies, and media studies, with emphases on internet research ethics, Digital Religion, virtue ethics, social robots, and AI. Ess has published extensively on ethical pluralism, culturally variable ethical norms and communicative preferences in cross-cultural approaches to Information and Computing Ethics, and their applications to everyday digital media technologies; his *Digital Media Ethics*, 3rd edition, was published in early 2020. His current work concerns meta-theoretical and meta-disciplinary complementarities between ethics and the social sciences, applied ethics in ICT design and implementation (especially social robots and AI), and research ethics in Human–Machine Communication (HMC). He serves as an ethics advisor to research projects such as "Datafied Living" (https://datafiedliving.ku.dk/) and "BioMe: Existential challenges and ethical imperatives of biometric AI in everyday lifeworlds" (https://wasp-hs.org/projects/biome-existential-challenges-and-ethical-imperatives-of-biometric-ai-in-everyday-lifeworlds/)

Leopoldina Fortunati is Senior Professor of Sociology of Communication and Culture at the University of Udine and is member of the Academia Europaea. For the past three decades she has studied the role of new media (computers, mobile phones, robots) in society, especially from a gender point of view. She has written or edited 21 books and published over 200 peer-reviewed papers and book chapters. She is Associate Editor of the journal *The Information Society* and was a co-editor of the Oxford University Press Series *Studies in Mobile Communication*. Her works have been published in twelve languages.

Paula Gardner is Asper Chair of Communication and directs Pulse Lab in the Department of Communication Studies and Media Arts at McMaster University in Canada. Gardner is a former President of the International Communication Association, and a long-time feminist and human rights activist, specializing in feminist, intersectional media, and science and technology studies, employing text-based and multimodal approaches. Gardner's teams collaborate with communities, employing participatory, anti-colonial and art/design approaches to create technology solutions to community-defined problems. Her research has been funded by Heritage Canada, SSHRC, and NSERC and published in spaces including *The Journal of Communication*, *Communication, Culture and Critique*, *Communication Research & Practice*, *Body & Society*, *Catalyst: Feminism, Science, Technology*, and various HCI, health and aging publications. View Gardner's research at: paulagarder.ca and pulselab.humanities.mcmaster.ca.

Gerard Goggin is Professor of Media and Communications, University of Sydney. Gerard has published widely on media, culture, and disability, with a particular interest on emerging technology and communication rights. As well as many papers, Gerard's books include *Routledge Companion to Disability and Media* (2020; with Katie Ellis and Beth Haller), *Normality & Disability* (2018; with Linda Steele and Jess Cadwallader), *Disability and the Media* (2005; with Katie Ellis), and with Christopher Newell, the two books *Disability in Australia* (2005) and *Digital Disability* (2003). With Kuansong Victor Zhuang, Gerard is writing a book on disability, politics, and emerging technologies.

Irina Gorea is a Professor at Humber College and works as a research assistant at Toronto Metropolitan University's Ted Rogers School of Retail Management. She received her Master's degree from Toronto Metropolitan University where she conducted experimental research to analyze the role of influencers' sponsorship disclosure in tourism; her research was nominated for the Distinguished Thesis Award.

Maartje de Graaf is an Assistant Professor in the Department of Information and Computing Sciences at Utrecht University, The Netherlands. Her research focuses on peoples' responses to robots on an affective, behavioural, and cognitive level while noting the societal and ethical consequences of those responses. With her research, she aims to influence technology design and policy direction to pursue the development of socially acceptable robots that benefit society. De Graaf obtained a Bachelor of Business Administration in Communication Management (2005) from Amsterdam University of Applied Sciences, and a Master of Science in Media Communication (2011) and a Ph.D. in Communication Science and Human–Robot Interaction (2015) from Twente University.

Kristina M. Green is a case study methodologist and human–machine communication scholar. Her work explores the paradigmatic shifts that characterize the 4th industrial revolution including the unprecedented capture, storage, sources, volume, scale, and analyses of big data and what it means for the production of knowledge and governance. Her research examines how people interact with and understand mobile and static smart technologies, and how our communication with AI–and their communication with us–steers our judgments, perceptions, attitudes, beliefs, decisions, emotions, affect, and behaviors. Kristina earned her doctorate in communication from the University of Illinois at Chicago and works as a senior qualitative research analyst in industry.

David J. Gunkel is an award-winning educator, scholar, and author, specializing in the philosophy and ethics of emerging technology. He is the author of over 85 scholarly articles and book chapters and has published thirteen internationally recognized and award-winning books, including *Thinking Otherwise: Philosophy, Communication, Technology* (Purdue University Press 2007), *The Machine Question: Critical Perspectives on AI, Robots, and Ethics* (MIT Press 2012), *Of Remixology: Ethics and Aesthetics After Remix* (MIT Press 2016), *Robot Rights* (MIT Press 2018), and *Deconstruction* (MIT Press 2021). He currently holds the position of Presidential Research, Scholarship and Artistry Professor in the Department of Communication at Northern Illinois University (USA). More information at http://gunkel-web.com

Andreas Hepp is Professor of Media and Communications and Head of ZeMKI, Centre for Media, Communication and Information Research, University of Bremen, Germany. He was Visiting Researcher and Professor at leading institutions such as the London School of Economics and Political Science, Goldsmiths University of London, Université Paris II Panthéon ASSAS, Stanford University and others. His research focuses on mediatization, datafication, the automation of communication / communicative AI, and media use and appropriation. He is the author of twelve monographs including *The Mediated Construction of Reality* (with Nick Couldry, 2017), *Transcultural Communication* (2015) and *Cultures of Mediatization* (2013). His latest book is *Deep Mediatization* (2020).

Damith Herath is an Associate Professor in Robotics and Art at the University of Canberra. He is a multi-award-winning entrepreneur and a roboticist with extensive experience leading multidisciplinary research teams on complex robotic integration, industrial and research projects. His research focuses on both technical and cultural aspects of robotics. He has chaired multiple international workshops on Robots and Art including the first IEEE sponsored robotic art program complete with a major art installation at the prestigious IEEE International Conference on Robotics and Automation. He is the lead editor of the book *Robots and Art: Exploring an Unlikely Symbiosis* – the first significant work to feature leading roboticists and artists together in the field of Robotic Art.

Andrew Iliadis is an Assistant Professor at Temple University in the Department of Media Studies and Production (within the Klein College of Media and Communication) and serves on the faculties of the Media and Communication Doctoral Program, Cultural Analytics Graduate Certificate Program, and Science, Technology, and Society Network. He is the author of *Semantic Media: Mapping Meaning on the Internet* (Polity, 2022) and co-editor of *Embodied Computing: Wearables, Implantables, Embeddables, Ingestibles* (MIT Press, 2020). He has had work published in *New Media & Society, Communication Theory, The Information Society, Global Media and Communication*, and *Online Information Review*, among others.

Jenna Jacobson is an Assistant Professor at Toronto Metropolitan University's Ted Rogers School of Management. She is also a Research Fellow at Toronto Metropolitan University's Social Media Lab. Her research analyzes the consumer and producer perspectives of digital technologies with a focus on social media, branding, digital retailing, and user behaviour.

Jack Jamieson is a postdoctoral research associate at NTT Communication Science Laboratories. He received his Ph.D. from the University of Toronto, where he studied values in the construction and maintenance of a decentralized web infrastructure. His current research focuses on software development communities, inclusive design, and human perspectives of emerging technologies.

David C. Jeong is an Assistant Professor in the Department of Communication and the Director of the WAVE+Imaginarium Lab at Santa Clara University. His lab focuses on both the production and analysis of immersive media, namely XR media production and computer vision analysis of moving human motion. He currently serves as Vice Chair and Planner of ICA's Information Systems Division.

James E. Katz is the Feld Professor of Emerging Media and also directs COM's Division of Emerging Media Studies. He recently received the ICA's Frederick Williams Prize for Contributions to the Study of Communication Technology. His pioneering publications on the effects of artificial intelligence (AI), social media, mobile communication, robot-human interaction, have been internationally recognized and translated into many other languages, including Chinese and Japanese. His two most recent books, *Journalism and the Search for Truth in an Age of Social Media*, co-edited with Kate Mays, and *Philosophy* *of Emerging Media*, co-edited with Juliet Floyd, were published by Oxford University Press in 2019 and 2016, respectively. An earlier book, *The Social Media President: Barack Obama and the Politics of Citizen Engagement*, was published in 2013 by Macmillan.

Jenny Kennedy is a Senior Research Fellow in Media and Communication at RMIT University, Australia. She presently holds an Australian Research Council Discovery Early Career Research Award (DECRA). She is an Associate Investigator in the ARC Centre of Excellence for Automated Decision-Making and Society (ADM+S) and is a core member of the Digital Ethnography Research Centre (DERC). Her research charts shifts in digital technology practices against the context of rapid evolutions in digital infrastructures, smart devices, artificial intelligence, and automated decision-making. Jenny's most recent co-authored books include *Digital Domesticity: Media, Materiality and Home Life* (Oxford University Press, 2020) and *The Smart Wife: Why Alexa, Siri and Other Smart Home Devices Need a Feminist Reboot* (MIT Press).

Jieun Kim is a Ph.D. student in Information Science at Cornell University, exploring the psychological impacts of media technologies that promote users' attitudinal and behavioral changes. She has examined and designed the virtual agent's social interventions that motivate users' engagement in goal tasks using diverse platforms (e.g., voice speakers, VR, online games, mobile apps, and video conferencing tools). Her broader interest is to investigate the persuasive effect of media and its applications to practical domains such as healthcare, education, and teamwork. She completed her master's degree in the Department of Human–AI Interaction at Sungkyunkwan University, South Korea.

Jihyun Kim is an Associate Professor in the Nicholson School of Communication and Media at the University of Central Florida. Broadly, her research is focused on the effects and implications of new media/communication technologies for meaningful outcomes (e.g., education, health). Her research examines the role of technology not only as a tool but also as a digital agent, which is centered on human–machine communication. In particular, she is interested in social and psychological impacts of AI (artificial intelligence) from a communication perspective. Additionally, her research is primarily driven by the theoretical understanding of presence, especially social presence.

Taenyun Kim is a Ph.D. student in the Department of Media and Information (Cognitive Science Specialization) at the College of Communication Arts and Sciences at Michigan State University. He received an M.Sc. in Interaction Science (Human-AI Interaction Major) from Sungkyunkwan University, Seoul, South Korea. His research interests include trust and morality in artificial agents (e.g., artificial intelligence, robots, virtual agents, etc.) and human cognitive bias and heuristics in artificial agents. For instance, he is interested in artificial agents' trust repair strategy after trust and moral violations and the effect of cognitive bias and heuristics in this process. In particular, his research primarily focuses on applying social and cognitive psychological theories to human-machine communication.

Ronald Kline is the Bovay Professor in History and Ethics of Engineering, Emeritus, at Cornell University, and the author of three books, *Steinmetz: Engineer and Socialist* (1992), *Consumers in the Country: Technology and Social Change in Rural America* (2000), and *The Cybernetics Moment, Or Why We Call Our Age the Information Age* (2015), all published by Johns Hopkins University Press.

Kevin Koban is a postdoctoral researcher at the Department of Communication at the University of Vienna. His current research focuses on the digital well-being, online hostility, and individuals' interaction with digital systems (e.g., social robots, video games). He worked in the projects "Moral Agency in Robot-Human Interactions: Perceptions, Trust, & Influence" (MARIA) at Texas Tech University and "Social Media Use and Adolescents' Well-Being" at University of Vienna and is currently engaged in the ERC-funded project "Digital Hate: Perpetrators, Audiences, and (Dis)Empowered Targets" (DIGIHATE).

Nicole Krämer is Full Professor of Social Psychology, Media and Communication at the University of Duisburg-Essen, Germany, as well as one of the founding directors of the Research Center "Trustworthy Data Science and Security". She completed her Ph.D. in Psychology at the University of Cologne in 2001 and received the venia legendi for psychology in 2006. She investigates processes of information selection, science communication, opinion building, and relationship maintenance of people communicating via Internet and social media. She heads numerous third-party funded projects and currently serves as Associate Editor of the *Journal of Computer Mediated Communication*.

Joomi Lee is a postdoctoral research associate in the Games and Virtual Environments Lab at the University of Georgia. She completed a Ph.D. in communication at Michigan State University in 2020, and her M.A. in telecommunications at Indiana University in 2017. Her research investigates human–media interaction with emphases on motivation and behavioural change through emerging media technologies, such as video games and immersive virtual reality.

Seth C. Lewis is Professor, Director of Journalism, and the Shirley Papé Chair in Emerging Media in the School of Journalism and Communication at the University of Oregon. He studies the social implications of emerging technologies, and has published more than 100 articles and book chapters on technology and news. He is co-author, with Matt Carlson and Sue Robinson, of *News After Trump: Journalism's Crisis of Relevance in a Changed Media Culture* (Oxford University Press, 2021). Lewis has held visiting appointments with Yale University, Columbia University, and Stanford University, and in 2019-2020 was a visiting fellow with the Reuters Institute for the Study of Journalism at the University of Oxford. He recently served as Chair of the International Communication Association's Journalism Studies Division, the world's largest organization dedicated to the study of journalism. He has a Ph.D. from the University of Texas at Austin.

Weizi Liu is a doctoral student in the Institute of Communications Research (ICR), University of Illinois at Urbana-Champaign (UIUC). Her research focuses on human perceptions and behaviors under the impacts of artificial intelligence. Specifically, she is interested in user trust, privacy concerns, and information disclosure in contexts involving algorithms and artificial intelligence. She has been working on research projects related to interactions with conversational agents, acceptance of online surveillance, and self-disclosure on social media. Through research, she tries to answer her ultimate questions about how humans perceive the roles of intelligent machines and deal with their relationships with the machines. Before joining the Ph.D. program of ICR, she earned her master's degree in advertising from UIUC and bachelor's degree in advertising from Communication University of China (CUC).

Wiebke Loosen is a senior journalism researcher at the Leibniz Institute for Media Research | Hans-Bredow-Institut (HBI) (Germany) as well as a professor at the University of Hamburg. Her major areas of expertise are the transformation of journalism within a changing media environment, theories of journalism, and methodology. Her current research focuses on the changing journalism-audience relationship, the datafication of journalism, forms of "pioneer journalism" and emerging start-up cultures as well as algorithms' "journalism-adjacent" constructions of public spheres and reality. She is also involved in interdisciplinary projects situated at the intersections of journalism research and computer science.

Michelle Lui is an Assistant Professor in the Department of Curriculum, Teaching and Learning at the Ontario Institute for Studies in Education (OISE) of the University of Toronto. Her research examines immersive, embodied, and multisensory interactions for meaning-making. Using a mixed-methods, multimodal approach to understand the different facets of the technology-supported experience – from physiological signals to behavioral indicators – Lui connects rich user data to understand the impact of immersive and embodied design features on learning. Her work spans the fields of learning sciences, human–computer interaction, computer-supported collaborative learning, and human–machine communication.

Zhenyang Luo is a Ph.D. candidate in the Department of Communication at North Dakota State University. Her research examines social cognition in human–machine communication, especially in relation to anthropomorphism, trust, and hyperpersonal communication potential.

Christoph Lutz is an Associate Professor at the Nordic Centre for Internet and Society, BI Norwegian Business School (Oslo). With a background in sociology and communication, his research interests include online participation, privacy, the sharing economy, and social robots. Christoph has published widely in top-tier journals in his area such as *New Media & Society*, *Information, Communication & Society*, *Mobile Media & Communication*, *Social Media + Society*, *Big Data & Society*, the *Journal of the Association for Information Science and Technology* (JASIST), the *Journal of Management Information Systems*, *Communications of the ACM*, and the *International Journal of Communication*.

Kate Maddalena is an Assistant Professor at the University of Toronto Mississauga, where she teaches writing and media studies. She thinks with media theory, science and technology studies (STS), and technical communication to describe knowledge-making media apparatus in the environmental and life sciences. She has published in journals such as *Theory, Culture, and Society*, the *Project on the Rhetoric of Inquiry* (*POROI*), and *The Canadian Journal of Communication*.

Steve Mann received his Ph.D. from MIT in 1997, and is a Professor at the University of Toronto. He is recognized as *the father of wearable computing* (IEEE ISSCC 2000), and is a pioneer of wearable augmented reality (AR). Mann is also an inventor and his creations include the Digital Eye Glass/EyeTap; the Chirplet Transform; Comparametric Equations; and High Dynamic Range imaging (U.S. Pat. 5828793). As an early leader in Artificial Intelligence Mann co-created the new discipline of Humanistic Intelligence. He has authored more than 200 publications, books and patents, and his work and inventions have been shown at the Smithsonian Institute, National Museum of American History, The Science Museum, MoMA, Stedelijk Museum (Amsterdam), and Triennale di Milano.

Vincent Manzerolle is an Assistant Professor in the Department of Communication, Media & Film at the University of Windsor, Canada. His research and teaching focuses on the history, theory, and political economy of media. He has published on a range of topics including mobile media, consumer surveillance, digital audiences, payment technologies, infrastructure, and social media. He is the co-editor of *The Audience Commodity in the Digital Age* (2014) and *Mobile and Ubiquitous Media* (2018).

Kate K. Mays is a postdoctoral researcher in the Maxwell School of Citizenship and Public Affairs Autonomous Systems Policy Institute at Syracuse University. She completed her Ph.D. in Emerging Media Studies at Boston University's College of Communication, where she also taught communication theory and research methods. Her research interests include the influence of emerging technologies on social life with a particular focus on social robot design, attitudes about artificial intelligence, and AI governance. She has presented her research at a variety of international conferences, in peer-reviewed journals, and co-edited a volume with James E. Katz published by Oxford University Press, *Journalism & Truth in an Age of Social Media*. She was also a Graduate Student Fellow for computational and data-driven research at BU's Rafik B. Hariri Institute for Computing and Computational Science & Engineering.

Victoria McArthur is an Associate Professor in the School of Journalism and Communication at Carleton University. She holds graduate appointments in the HCI and Information Technology grad programs and presently serves as program director for Carleton's Media Production and Design program. She is an interdisciplinary scholar whose work represents the intersection of various fields including HCI, games studies, and feminist technoscience. While her expertise is largely in understanding how avatar customization interfaces in games and virtual environments constrain representation, often leading to socially exclusive design, she is also currently exploring research methodologies that could potentially democratize augmented reality (AR) and virtual reality (VR) storytelling.

Jasmine McNealy is an Associate Professor of Telecommunication at the University of Florida, where she teaches courses on regulation and policy. She researches media, technology, and law with an emphasis on privacy, surveillance, and data governance. She is also the Associate Director of the Marion B. Brechner First Amendment Project at UF, and a Faculty Associate at Harvard University's Berkman Klein Center for Internet & Society.

Chinar Mehta is currently a doctoral scholar at the Department of Communication at the University of Hyderabad, working on values embedded in web design. Working as a student assistant, she aided in organizing roundtables related to online hate speech and gendered violence, commissioned by Facebook India. She has presented her papers at Imagine a Feminist Internet, Negombo, Sri Lanka, and at Frames of Reference, TISS, Mumbai. With an interest in media production, she has also been involved in making two documentary films; *Ghutan*, which is about a slum rehabilitation colony in Mahul Gaon, an area unfit for human settlement due to high air & water toxicity, and *The Dancing Lion of Mazgaon*, about the Chinese temple in Mazgaon, Mumbai. With training in information & communication technology, she has previously worked as a web developer.

Kelly Merrill Jr. is an Assistant Professor in the School of Communication, Film, and Media Studies at the University of Cincinnati. His primary research interests are at the intersection of health communication and communication technology. In particular, he is interested in health disparities and the use of communication technologies for physical, psychological, and social well-being.

Milagros Miceli is a sociologist and computer scientist who investigates how ground-truth data for machine learning is produced. The foci of her research are the labor conditions and the power dynamics in data generation and labeling. Broadly, she is interested in questions of meaning-making, knowledge production, and symbolic power encoded in ML data. Milagros leads the newly funded research group Data, Algorithmic Systems, and Ethics at Weizenbaum Institute. She also works as a researcher at DAIR Institute where she is thinking through ways of engaging communities of data workers in AI research.

Katina Michael is a tenured Professor at Arizona State University, a Senior Global Futures Scientist in the Global Futures Laboratory with a joint appointment in the School for the Future of Innovation in Society and School of Computing and Augmented Intelligence. She is the director of the Society Policy Engineering Collective (SPEC) and the Founding Editor-in-Chief of the *IEEE Transactions on Technology and Society*. Katina is a senior member of the IEEE and the founding chair of the inaugural Masters of Science in Public Interest Technology. She has been funded by the National Science Foundation (NSF), the Canadian Social Sciences and Humanities Research Council (SSHRC), and the Australian Research Council (ARC). Prior to academia, Katina was employed by Nortel Networks, Anderson Consulting and OTIS Elevator Company. www.katinamichael.com

MG Michael is formerly an Honorary Associate Professor in the School of Information Systems and Technology at the University of Wollongong. Michael is a theologian and historian with cross-disciplinary qualifications in the humanities who introduced the concept of *überveillance* into the privacy and bioethics literature to denote embedded surveillance devices in the human body. Michael was co-editor of three volumes of the Research Network for a Secure Australia's "Human Factors" workshop proceedings between 2006 and 2008. Michael brings with him a unique perspective to Emerging Technologies. His formal studies include Theology, Ancient History, General Philosophy, Political Sociology, Linguistics, Government, and Modern Greek. www.mgmichael.com

AJung Moon is Assistant Professor in the Dept. of Electrical and Computer Engineering at McGill University. Prof. Moon specializes in ethics and responsible design of AI and interactive robotic systems. She takes experimental, mixed-method approaches to study how people's behaviours and decisions are influenced by designed instances of human–robot interaction. Prior to joining McGill, she served as a Senior Advisor for the UN Secretary-General's High-level Panel on Digital Cooperation, and a CEO of an AI ethics consultancy. She founded the Open Roboethics Institute, a Canadian nonprofit that investigates societal and ethical implications of robotics and AI. She currently directs the Responsible Autonomy and Intelligent Systems Ethics (RAISE) lab, an interdisciplinary group investigating the ethical design of intelligent systems that inherently influence humans through interaction.

Julie L. Mortensen is a Campaign – and Media Specialist at VIA University College, where she works with student recruitment campaigns. Julie obtained her master from Aarhus University in 2020 in Media Studies. Her research interest includes digital culture, social media, and human–machine communication.

Yi Mou is Associate Professor at the School of Media and Communication of Shanghai Jiao Tong University. Her research interests include new media study, human–machine communication, and environmental health communication. Examples of her work include investigating (1) the differences between interacting with humans and interacting with chatbots from the human side, (2) the implicit and explicit attitudes and perceptions of machine-generated content in various cultures, and (3) the psychological effects of interacting with robots. Her studies have been published in a number of leading peer-reviewed journals such as *New Media & Society, Computers in Human Behavior, International Journal of Human–Computer Interaction*, and *Journal of Broadcasting and Electronic Media*.

Cosmin Munteanu is an Associate Professor and Schlegel Research Chair in Technology for Healthy Aging at the Systems Design Engineering Department, University of Waterloo, and Director of the Technologies for Ageing Gracefully lab. He is a Human–Computer Interaction scholar, conducting sociotechnical research at the intersection of user experience design, digital inclusion, aging, natural language processing, and ethics. Cosmin takes a primarily ethnomethodological approach to study how voice- and language-enabled interactive technology and media interfaces should be designed in a safe, effective, inclusive, and ethical manner, in order to empower digitally underrepresented groups such as older adults. Cosmin has dedicated more than two decades to research on facilitating natural, meaningful, and safe interactions between people and digital media and devices. Cosmin's interests include designing intelligent applications that improve access to information, support learning late in life, and reduce digital marginalization, such as for older adults whose enjoyment of life and participation in society could be better supported by advances in interactive assistive technologies such as voice, conversational, or virtual reality interfaces.

Sarah Myers West is the Managing Director of the AI Now Institute and a Visiting Research Scientist at the Network Science Institute at Northeastern University. She recently served as a Senior Advisor on AI at the Federal Trade Commission. Dr. West has over a decade of experience critically examining the political economy of the tech industry. Her award-winning research and writing blends social science, policy, and historical methods to address the intersection of technology, labor, and platform accountability. Her forthcoming book, *Tracing Code* (University of California Press), draws on years of historical and social scientific research to examine the origins of data capitalism and commercial surveillance. Her writing is published in journals including *Social Studies of Science, New Media & Society, the International Journal of Communication, Policy & Internet* and *Business and Society*, and her research is featured in the Wall Street Journal, PBS, CBS, the Associated Press, and Motherboard, among others.

Peter Nagy is a media researcher with a master's degree in psychology from Eötvös Loránd University and a Ph.D. in business administration from Corvinus University of Budapest. He works as a Lecturer in Major and Career Exploration at Arizona State University. His research interests include human–machine communication, virtual identity formation and digital consumer culture. His writing has appeared in the peer-reviewed journals *Social Media + Society, International Journal of Communication,* and *Information, Communication & Society*. Before joining Arizona State University, Peter worked as a psychologist at a high school and as a research fellow at Central European University's Center for Data, Media and Society in Budapest, Hungary.

Simone Natale is Associate Professor in Media History and Theory at the University of Turin, Italy and Visiting Fellow at Loughborough University, UK. He is the author of *Deceitful Media: Artificial Intelligence and Social Life after the Turing Test* (Oxford University Press, 2021), as well as three other books and more than thirty peer-reviewed journal articles in some of the most authoritative journals of his field, including *New Media & Society*, the *Journal of Communication, Convergence,* and *Communication Theory*. He has been awarded fellowships and grants by organizations including the Arts and Humanities Research Council (AHRC) in the UK, the Humboldt Foundation in Germany, and Columbia University's Italian Academy in the US. Since 2023 he is Editor of Media, Culture and Society.

Gina Neff is the Executive Director of the Minderoo Centre for Technology & Democracy at the University of Cambridge and Professor of Technology & Society at the University of Oxford. Her books include *Venture Labor* (MIT Press 2012), *Self-Tracking* (MIT Press 2016) and *Human-Centered Data Science* (MIT Press 2022). Her research focuses on the effects of the rapid expansion of our digital information environment on workers and workplaces and in our everyday lives. Professor Neff holds a Ph.D. in sociology from Columbia University and advises international organisations including UNESCO, the OECD and the Women's Forum for the Economy and Society. She chairs the International Scientific Committee of the UK's Trusted Autonomous Systems programme and is a member of the Strategic Advisory Network for the UK's Economic and Social Research Council. She also led the team that won the 2021 Webby for the best educational website on the Internet, for the A to Z of AI, which has reached over a million people in 17 different languages.

Gemma Newlands is a Departmental Research Lecturer in AI & Work at the Oxford Internet Institute, University of Oxford. As an organizational sociologist, her research explores the impact of artificial intelligence on work and organizations, with particular focus on issues of societal evaluation, surveillance and visibility. Her current research investigates the sustainability of AI production, situated at the intersection of supply-chain theory and critical data studies. Gemma wrote her Ph.D. dissertation on the evaluation of work in the digital economy and will defend her dissertation at the University of Amsterdam in 2023. Previously, Gemma has been a Doctoral Stipendiary Fellow at the Nordic Centre for Internet and Society, BI Norwegian Business School. Her research has been published in leading journals including *Organization Studies, Sociology, Environment and Planning A: Economy and Space, Big Data & Society, New Media & Society, New Technology, Work and Employment* and *Research in the Sociology of Organizations*.

Keiko Nishimura is a doctoral candidate in the Department of Communication at the University of North Carolina at Chapel Hill. Through Cultural Studies of Technology, she investigates how culture, society and technology intersect in the figure of communication robots, in both practices and discourses. Her recent publications include *Social Media, Information, and Political Activism in Japan's 3.11 Crisis* (co-authored with David Slater and Love Kindstrand) published in *The Asia-Pacific Journal* (2012), "Semi-autonomous Fan Fiction: Japanese Character Bots and Nonhuman Affect" published in the edited volume *Socialbots and Their Friends: Digital Media and the Automation of Sociality* (2016) and "Surechigai Sociality: Location-Aware Technology on the Yamanote Line" published in *Japan Forum* (2018).

Eric Novotny is a postdoctoral research associate within the Owens Institute of Behavioral Research at the University of Georgia. He received his Ph.D. from the Department of Communication at Michigan State University in 2020, and his M.A. from the Department of Communication at the University at Buffalo, SUNY, in 2015. He is a project associate on the Virtual Fitness Buddy projected funded by NIH. His research focuses on nonverbal communication, new media technology, and virtual environments. Specifically, his research leverages virtual reality and motion capture to assess nonverbal communication patterns between people free of physical confounds. He also studies the effects of new and old media on psychological variables like morality and time perception.

Jeremy Packer is Professor in the Institute for Communication, Culture, Information, and Technology and the Faculty of Information at the University of Toronto. His work addresses the historical, political, and epistemological dimensions of technological development. His books include *Mobility Without Mayhem* (2008), *Killer Apps* (2020), and *Prison House of the Circuit* (2023).

Thilo von Pape is Professor for Communication Studies at the Department of Communication and Media Research (DCM) of the University of Fribourg in Switzerland. His work focuses on the uses of digital communication technologies and mobile media as well as associated transformations in communication, mobility, and transportation, such as autonomous vehicles and micromobility. He is a co-founding editor of the journal *Mobile Media & Communication* as well as an associate editor of the *Journal of Computer-Mediated Communication*. Thilo von Pape has co-edited a special issue of the *International Journal of Communication* (*IJoC*) on Cars and Contemporary Communication.

Natalie Parde is an Assistant Professor in the Department of Computer Science at the University of Illinois at Chicago, where she also co-directs UIC's Natural Language Processing Laboratory. Her research interests are in natural language processing, with emphases in healthcare applications, interactive systems, multimodality, and creative language. Her research has been funded by the National Science Foundation, the Office Ergonomics Research Committee, the Discovery Partners Institute, and several internal seed funding programs. She has served on the program committees of the Conference on Empirical Methods in Natural Language Processing (EMNLP), the Association for Computational Linguistics (ACL), and the North American Chapter of the ACL (NAACL), among other venues. In her spare time, Dr. Parde enjoys engaging in mentorship and outreach for underrepresented CS students.

Ekaterina Pashevich has recently defended her dissertation at the Department of Media and Communication, University of Oslo. She is interested in researching the social implications of AI technologies. Her current focus is the potential impact of communication with social robots on the development of empathy in children. Recent publication: Pashevich, E. (2022). Can communication with social robots influence how children develop empathy? Best-evidence synthesis. *AI & Society,* 37, 579–589. https://doi.org/10.1007/s00146-021-01214-z

Elizabeth Patitsas is an assistant professor specializing in computer science education, at McGill University. She is joint appointed between the School of Computer Science and the Department of Integrated Studies in Education. Her research focuses on sociological issues in computer science education, such as gender inequity, how institutional policies affect how CS is taught, and the development and practices of CS educators.

Christine Perakslis serves as an educator and consultant for various organizations. She serves as a researcher with publications and presentations focusing on the social implications of technology, group integration competencies, and behavioral motivators/psychometrics. Perakslis is a member of various associations and serves in the capacity of a peer-reviewer, as well as a member of advisory boards, program committees, and technical committees. Certificates and certifications include such areas as Advanced Graduate Studies, Lean Operations, Praendix Analyst, and Six Sigma.

Jochen Peter is a Full Professor in the Amsterdam School of Communication Research ASCoR at the University of Amsterdam, The Netherlands. His research focuses on the implications of new technologies for young people's cognitive, socio-emotional, and behavioral development.

Jeremy Pitt is Professor of Intelligent and Self-Organising Systems in the Department of Electrical and Electronic Engineering at Imperial College London. He received a B.Sc. in Computer Science from the University of Manchester and a Ph.D. in Computing from Imperial College (University of London). He has been teaching and researching Artificial Intelligence and Human–Computer Interaction for over thirty years. He is a trustee of AITT (the Association for Information Technology Trust), a Fellow of the BCS (British Computer Society) and of the IET (Institution of Engineering and Technology), and in 2018 was appointed as Editor-in-Chief of *IEEE Technology & Society Magazine*.

Nathaniel Poor is a computational social scientist at the Underwood Institute who researches issues involving online communities, often gaming communities, with a socio-technical appreciation for design, technology, culture, and history. After earning his Ph.D. in 2004 from the University of Michigan, he was a professor for two years and then moved to New York, where he took part in the then-burgeoning tech scene. He also co-founded and co-chairs the Games & Gaming mini-track for the Hawaii International Conference on System Sciences.

Julian Posada is an Assistant Professor of American Studies at Yale University. His research integrates theories and methods from information studies, sociology, and human–computer interaction to study technology and society. His latest project explores how the artificial intelligence industry perpetuates coloniality by focusing on the relationship between human labor and data production. This research focuses on the experiences of outsourced workers in Latin America employed by digital platforms to produce machine learning data and verify algorithmic outputs. Posada's research has been published in several influential journals, including *Information, Communication & Society*, and the *Proceedings of the ACM on Human-Computer Interaction*.

Usha Raman is a Professor in the Department of Communication, with teaching and research interests in digital culture, feminist media studies, civic engagement, and media pedagogy. She has over 30 research papers and book chapters and is the author of *Writing for Media* (Oxford University Press, 2009). She has consulted with UNICEF India on several health communication projects and is currently an honorary professorial fellow of The George Institute for Global Health. She has held visiting fellowships at the University of Sydney's School of Public Health, the Comparative Media Studies program at MIT (as a Fulbright Fellow), and the ZeMKI Centre for Media, Communication and Information Research at the University of Bremen, Germany. She edits *Teacher Plus*, a monthly magazine for school teachers, and is a columnist for *The Hindu*, one of India's largest newspapers. She is Vice President of the International Association for Media and Communication Research (2020–24).

Jessica Sage Rauchberg is a doctoral candidate in the Department of Communication Studies and Media Arts at McMaster University. Raucherg's dissertation research, grounded in new media, crip theory, and cultural studies, examines the encoding of racist, ableist, and colonial ideologies into digital media platforms and their shaping of digital labor, content moderation, and cultural production. Her published and forthcoming work appears in *Feminist Media Studies, the Journal of Applied Communication Research, the Journal of International and Intercultural Communication, First Monday, Studies in Social Justice*, and various edited collections. To learn more visit www.jessrauchberg.com.

Joshua Reeves is Associate Professor in the School of Communication at Oregon State University. An associate editor at *Surveillance & Society*, he is also the author of *Citizen Spies: The Long Rise of America's Surveillance Society* (2017) and co-author of *Killer Apps: War, Media, Machine* (2020) and *Prison House of the Circuit* (2023).

Margaret Rhee is a poet, scholar and new media artist. Her debut poetry collection, *Love, Robot*, was published in 2017 and recognized with the Best Book of Poetry Award by the Asian American Studies Association. She has published in academic journals such as *Cinema Journal, Amerasia Journal*, and the *Scholar Feminist Online*. Her book manuscripts *Poetry Machines* is under contract, and *How We Became*

Human: Race, Robots, and the Asian American Body is under review at Duke University Press. Currently, she is an assistant professor at The New School in the School of Media Studies and teaches in the Creative Writing MFA.

Riley Richards is an Assistant Professor in the Department of Communication at the Oregon Institute of Technology. He studies relational communication and behavior from a functionalist perspective, particularly in the context of relational goals, sexual communication, communication technology, taboo topics, and quasi-sexual relationships (e.g., human–robot).

Sharon Ringel is a lecturer in the Department of Communication at the University of Haifa. Her studies focus on digitization processes of archival sources and the preservation of digital born materials, specifically, on the ways in which current archiving practices are implicated in the narratives we will be able to produce in the future. Her current study focuses on the preservation of news content – print and digital – and the ways in which news organizations are dealing with the challenges of long-term conservation while ensuring future access to the first draft of history. Using ethnographic methods, Ringel examines the ways in which humans are communicating with machines and the implications of these processes on future memory.

Jonathan Roberge is Full Professor of Sociology at the Institut National de la Recherche Scientifique (INRS) in Montreal, Canada. He funded the Nenic Lab as part of the Canada Research Chair in Digital Culture he has held since 2012. His most recent edited volumes include *Algorithmic Cultures* (Routledge, 2016) and *The Cultural Life of Machine Learning* (Palgrave, 2020).

Carmina Rodríguez-Hidalgo is an Assistant Professor at the School of Communication and Journalism, Universidad Adolfo Ibáñez (UAI), Chile. She is the founder and director of RobotLAB UAI (https://robotlab.uai.cl), a lab which conducts empirical research on communication with social robots. She obtained her Ph.D. at the Amsterdam School of Communication Research (ASCoR), University of Amsterdam, where she investigated the process and outcomes of sharing emotions online (https://tinyurl.com/3zt9xtep). Her research focuses on the social and emotional outcomes of mediated communication through and with technological agents such as social robots and human–machine communication theory.

Astrid Rosenthal-von der Pütten is Full Professor and Director of the Chair Individual and Technology at the Department of Society, Technology, and Human Factors at RWTH Aachen University, Aachen, Germany. She received her Ph.D. degree in psychology from the University of Duisburg-Essen, where she also worked as a postdoctoral researcher until 2018. Her research interests include social effects of and linguistic alignment with artificial entities and human–robot interaction.

Hervé Saint-Louis is a cartoonist, and an associate professor of emerging media at Université du Québec à Chicoutimi. His research is human–machine communication and information policy.

Eleanor Sandry is a Senior Lecturer at Curtin University and previously a Fellow in the Curtin Centre for Culture and Technology (CCAT). Her research is focused on developing a theoretical recognition of, and practical respect for, otherness and difference in communication, drawing on examples from science and technology, science fiction and creative arts. She is particularly interested in exploring human–machine communication (HMC) involving robots and artificial intelligence. Her book, *Robots and Communication*, was published in 2015 by Palgrave Macmillan. More recent publications include "Interdependence in Collaboration with Robots" in the *Routledge Companion to Disability and Media* (Routledge, 2019) and "Taking Social Machines beyond the Ideal Humanlike Other" in *A Networked Self: Human Augmentics, Artificial Intelligence, Sentience* (Routledge, 2019).

Florian Shkurti is an Assistant Professor at the Department of Computer Science at the University of Toronto, where he directs the Robot Vision and Learning lab. He is a faculty member of the University of Toronto's Robotics Institute, a Faculty Affiliate at Vector Institute, and a fellow of the NSERC Canadian Robotics Network (NCRN). His research spans robotics, machine learning, computer vision, and control. He is the recipient of the Alexander Graham Bell Doctoral Award, the AAAI Robotics Fellowship, the Coxeter Scholarship in Mathematics, the Connaught New Researcher Award, the CVPR Outstanding Reviewer Award, and the Amazon Research Award in Robotics.

Nicoline Nørskov Siegfredsen is a Communication & Copy Specialist with a master's degree in Media Studies from Aarhus University. Her research interests include Consumer Behavior and UX Design, Branding, and Communication. She has been the Head of the Project of a B2B-marketing game, Make a Match, used in Danish companies and has appeared in the educational article *Børns fritid: Virtuel eller virkelig?,* used in Danish high schools. Today, Nicoline works in e-commerce, branding, and marketing at a Danish performance bureau.

Felix M. Simon is a Leverhulme Doctoral Scholar and Dieter Schwarz Scholar at the Oxford Internet Institute (OII) at the University of Oxford, a Knight News Innovation Fellow at Columbia University's Tow Center for Digital Journalism, and an affiliate at the Center for Information, Technology, and Public Life at the University of North Carolina at Chapel Hill. He works as a research assistant at the Reuters Institute for the Study of Journalism (RISJ) at the University of Oxford. As a member of the Leverhulme Doctoral centre "Publication beyond Print," he is researching the implications of AI in journalism and the news industry. His research interests are around digital media, political communication, and the transformation of the news, with a special focus on the future of mis- and disinformation studies. Felix has published in leading journals including *New Media & Society, Digital Journalism*, and *Journalism Studies.*

Hayeon Song is a Professor in the Department of Human–Artificial Intelligence Interaction at Sungkyunkwan University in South Korea. Her primary research interest is to investigate ways to use new media (e.g., artificial intelligence (AI), robots, games, social media, mobile phones) as persuasive and educational vehicles to promote health. Her broader research area focuses on the social and psychological effects of communication technology. Her recent work focuses on the interaction design of AI agents that can promote trust and relationship building and she is developing AI agents for dementia prevention and foreign language learning. She leads the Human–AI Interaction Lab (HAI lab) at Sungkyunkwan.

Patric R. Spence is a Professor in the Nicholson School of Communication and Media at the University of Central Florida – Downtown. He is a member of the Communication and Social Robotics Labs (www.combotlabs.org).

Stelarc explores alternative anatomical architectures. He is an artist whose projects incorporate prosthetics, robotics, biotechnology, medical imaging, and the internet. He has performed with a Third Hand, a Stomach Sculpture, Exoskeleton and a Prosthetic Head. Fractal Flesh, Ping Body and Parasite are internet performances that explore remote and involuntary choreography. He is surgically constructing an ear on his arm that will be internet enabled. In 1996 he was made an Honorary Professor of Art and Robotics at Carnegie Mellon University, Pittsburgh and in 2002 was awarded an Honorary Doctorate of Laws by Monash University, Melbourne. In 2010 was awarded the Ars Electronica Hybrid Arts Prize. In 2014 he initiated the Alternate Anatomies Lab. In 2015 he received the Australia Council's Emerging and Experimental Arts Award. In 2016 he was awarded an Honorary Doctorate from the Ionian University, Corfu. Between 2013 and 2018 he was a Distinguished Research Fellow, School of Design and Art (SODA) at Curtin University. His artwork is represented by the Scott Livesey Galleries, Melbourne.

S. Shyam Sundar is James P. Jimirro Professor of Media Effects and founding director of the Media Effects Research Laboratory at The Pennsylvania State University (http://bellisario.psu.edu/people/individual/s.-shyam-sundar). He is also Director of the Center for Socially Responsible Artificial Intelligence (https://ai.psu.edu), an interdisciplinary consortium at Penn State. His theories and research pertain to social and psychological effects of technological affordances in interactive media, including mobile phones, social media, chatbots, robots, smart speakers, and AI algorithms. His research is supported by the National Science Foundation (NSF), MacArthur Foundation, Social Science Research Center, Meta, and Lockheed Martin Information Systems and Global Services, among others. He edited the first-ever *Handbook on the Psychology of Communication Technology* (Blackwell Wiley, 2015) and served as editor-in-chief of the *Journal of Computer-Mediated Communication, 2013–2017*. He was awarded the Frederick Williams Prize by the International Communication Association (ICA) for his contributions to the study of communication technology.

Jessica M. Szczuka is a postdoctoral researcher at the Department of Social Psychology: Media and Communication at the University of Duisburg-Essen (Germany), where she leads the junior research group INTITEC (Intimacy with and Through Technology). Her empirical research is dedicated to the field of human–computer interaction. Here, she focuses on questions from the field of digitized intimacy and sexuality, that is, how people experience such social dynamics not only with technologies (e.g., sexualized robots, voice assistants, chatbots) but also through new media (e.g., dating apps) and to what extent technologies potentially extend and reshape these intimate social processes. She received her PhD with a thesis in the field of human–robot interaction.

Victoria Talwar is a Canada Research Chair (Tier II) and Chair of the Department of Educational and Counselling Psychology at McGill University's Faculty of Education. Her research is in the area of developmental psychology with an emphasis on social-cognitive development. Her research includes examining children and youth's digital engagement, their perceptions of online behaviors and perceptions of harm of witnessing online aggression. Among other distinctions, she was awarded the Society for Research on Child Development Outstanding Early Career Contributions to Child Development Research award, Fellow of American Psychological Association (Div 7), Fellow of Association for Psychological Science and member of the College of the Royal Society of Canada.

David Westerman is an Associate Professor in the Department of Communication at North Dakota State University. His research examines how people interact with and through technology.

Rowan Wilken is Associate Professor in Media and Communication, RMIT University, Melbourne. He is Associate Investigator in the Australian Research Council Centre of Excellence for Automated Decision-Making and Society (ADM+S), and a core member of the Digital Ethnography Research Centre (DERC), and, RMIT University, Australia. He has published widely on mobile and location-based media, and the everyday uses of digital media technologies. His most recent authored, co-authored and co-edited books include *Everyday Data Cultures* (Polity, 2022), *Wi-Fi* (Polity, 2021), *Automating Vision: The Social Impact of the New Camera Consciousness* (Routledge, 2020), *Digital Domesticity: Media, Materiality and Home Life* (Oxford University Press, 2020), *Cultural Economies of Locative Media* (Oxford University Press, 2019), and *Location Technologies in International Context* (Routledge, 2019).

Samuel Woolley is an Assistant Professor of Journalism and Media and Information (by courtesy) and fellow of the R.P. Doherty, Sr. Centennial Professorship in Communication at the University of Texas at Austin. He is the program director of the propaganda research lab and a Knight faculty fellow at UT Austin's Center for Media Engagement. Dr. Woolley's research is focused on emerging technologies and propaganda. Prior to joining the faculty at UT Austin, he was a visiting scholar at UC Berkeley's Center for Information Technology Research in the Interest of Society (CITRIS), an affiliate researcher at Stanford University's Project on Democracy and the Internet, and research director of the Computational Propaganda Project at the University of Oxford. He is co-editor of the book *Computational Propaganda* and author of *The Reality Game: How the Next Wave of Technology Will Break the Truth*.

Yuheng Wu is a Ph.D. student in the Department of Media and Communication at City University of Hong Kong and the School of Media and Communication at Shanghai Jiao Tong University (SJTU). His recent research focuses on sociopsychological issues related to human -AI interaction and human -machine communication. His studies have been published in a number of leading peer-reviewed journals such as New Media & Society, Media Culture & Society, and Computers in Human Behavior.

Wei-Jie Hsiao is a Ph.D. student in the School of Journalism and Media at the University of Texas at Austin. He is a research fellow on the Emerging Technology Project at the Aspen Institute and a research affiliate at the Propaganda Research Lab at the Center for Media Engagement at UT Austin. His primary research interests include political, economic, and cultural facets of data-driven technologies, as well as computational methods for new media research. Hsiao's current research examines the social implications of blockchain on user data governance and the socio-economic dynamics between humans (e.g., developers, journalists, and entrepreneurs) and blockchain technology.

Kun Xu is an Assistant Professor affiliated with the Department of Media Production, Management, and Technology at the College of Journalism and Communications, University of Florida. His work focuses on the concept of social cues and social presence in human–robot interaction, human-computer interaction, and computer-mediated communication. He also investigates how people make sense of spaces and maintain social relationships in virtual and augmented reality environments.

Mike Z. Yao is a Professor of Digital Media in the College of Media, University of Illinois at Urbana-Champaign (UIUC). His research focuses on the social and psychological impacts of interactive digital media. He conducts research and writes on a variety of topics such as online behavior, digital literacy, and computer-mediated communication. His current interest is in how users perceive and manage personal boundaries on social media. Specifically, he examines people's attitudes, beliefs, and self-protective behaviors related to online privacy from a psychosocial perspective by considering the influence of cognitive appraisal, social norms, and individual differences. The second area of Mike's research is the psychological impacts of digital media use. He examined the influence of various interactive media, such as video games and social media, on users' online and offline social behavior.

Human–Machine Communication, Humacomm, and Origins: A Foreword by Steve Mann, 2022

Origin stories are incredibly fascinating. To discover the conditions, environments, issues, drivers, naïveté, and mythology of the start of a thing is gratifying and revelatory. Whether it is the earliest spark of an idea that led to a great invention, or the moments preceding the spark of a solar system (what *is* "A" that led to "B" and so on …) – origins offer breadcrumbs to an emerging future. For communication scholars, being members of a broad community within both the oldest and newest of disciplines, curious is enticing.

Despite valiant efforts to pinpoint its origins, it is hard to be convinced that communication studies came from any single place, and it is a conceit to believe that the first people to study communication were from the west, or global north as told by authors of texts from these locations. Perhaps semiotics is central to the study of tea leaves in Asia, or cybernetics is core to the deep understanding of lessons from the earth among first nations peoples, or rhetoric is rooted in central African practices of storytelling. Perhaps all of these are true. Perhaps these breadcrumbs snaking across continents, through the air, and within water all in some way foretold the emerging communication technologies that we have today.

In this Handbook, the editors and authors seek to establish the roots for a newer sub-discipline or area within communication, called human–machine communication (HMC). In a sense this Handbook may be considered a key part of the origin story for HMC. In this comprehensive collection, the contributors formed their ideas within scholarship in longer defined academic disciplines such as engineering, literature, anthropology, philosophy, psychology, music, mathematics, and art. At times these scholars raise debates and tensions in this new area often obscured by many other three-letter-acronym cognates. Yet, what we can agree on is that communication is the common aspect of human–human communication (HHC), human–machine communication (HMC), human–computer interaction (HCI), human–machine interfaces (HMI), human–robot interaction (HRI), humachines (the human–machine nexus), superhumachines (HMC for super-human intelligence), cyborgs, etc.

This collection of articles will inform newer scholars across several disciplines and also those researchers who have worked over the decades to develop a deeper understanding of communication issues. The authors are among the most highly respected in scholarly networks; however, there are also some international rising stars with insights that will drive the evolution of many fields from the vantage point of HMC.

I now take the foreword author's privilege to share my own views on HMC – particularly as a multi-decade pioneer in the study of the material and conceptual integration of machines with the human body. Among cognate disciplines, HMC may offer the most expansive conceptualization of embodiment that is composed of the following three core elements:

- Human;
- Machine;
- Communication.

Consider the illustration below:

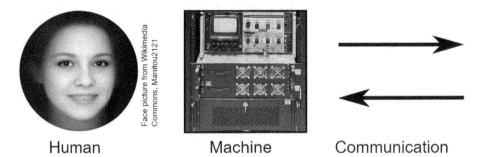

Face picture from Wikimedia Commons, Manitou2121

Human   Machine   Communication

Figure 1   The three elements of HMC

As others have agreed, this can be represented as in Figure 1, with the human denoted as a circle (the simplest of curves), the machine as a square (the simplest of boxes), and communication as the multidirectional flow of data, knowledge, information, understanding, insight, wisdom, etc., i.e. as bidirectional signal/communication lines. These lines may comprise neurons, wires, fibers, or be wireless data communications lines. Simple, yet humans are anything but simple; machines are anything but homogeneous; and communication lines can be easily crossed.

Although some communication, e.g. radio broadcasts, broadcast television, etc., historically, and to some degree today, can be unidirectional, we argue in favor of cybernetic communication that focuses on communication that includes some kind of feedback. Even a broadcaster will likely want some audience feedback. Indeed, feedback can be found in some form, pre-internet, in traditional forms of mass communication, albeit limited and indirect at times. Social media is essentially driven by demanding feedback in an action – a like, share, or comment. Only in rare circumstances such as NASA's message to possible extraterrestrials (Pioneer plaque, 1972) is it really only unidirectional, and even there, we might hope someday to get a response. Anything but simple.

The key essence of bi-directionality in communication is circular causality, also known as "feedback." Feedback is the core concept of cybernetics.

COMMUNICATION = CYBERNETICS = κυβερνήτης = HELMSPERSON

The word "cybernetics" comes from the ancient Greek word "κυβερνήτης" which means helmsperson.

The word "cyborg" was coined by Manfred Clynes in 1960 to denote "cybernetic organism," as a nexus of a living being with a machine. His favorite example of a cyborg is a person riding a bicycle, i.e. a human and machine in a cybernetic feedback loop. This example of human–machine communication dates back about 200 years, but it has also been argued that HMC has ("cyborgs" have) been in existence for more than a million years (Mann 2021, in "Crossing the Border of Humanity," pp. 47–64)!

One of the simplest of machines is the million-year-old Hominid Raft which predates the approximately 5,000-year-old invention of the wheel. The hominid raft even predates the existence of

Figure 2   Waterborgs (aquatic cyborgs) have existed for more than a million years

homo-sapiens! It is well-known that hominids traveled from Africa to other continents on rafts having simple cybernetic (steering) mechanisms. Thus, the world's first cyborgs could be considered to be "aquatic cyborg." In bringing together the human and the raft, as pictured in Figure 2, the "waterborg" or "aquaborg" has some functions of an information or communication system facilitating connections of entities, sharing, trading, and exchanging across distances (image from the National Museum of Australia).

More precisely, it is a well-known and widely accepted fact that communication is what takes place between the human and the machine, as shown in Figure 3.

And in the diagrams of feedback and control theory, we often prefer to show communication signals going around in a loop, thus we might re-envision HMC in one of two ways, as shown in Figure 4.

As the contributors to this Handbook agree, HMC rejects, or at best is more dismissive of, ontologies that place humans in the most powerful role and the machine in that of the enslaved. Instead, HMC pushes us to consider that the human and the machine are in direct, undeniable communication. This communication is sometimes subtle, and at other times in the form of a companion dyad. This can go further to consider the integration of humans and machines more intentionally often referred to as a "cyborg" or "humachine." I proffer the concept of a nexus of human, machine, AND communication therebetween, as a cohesive entity called a "humacomm." The humacomm erases the hyphen between human and machine in HMC, allowing for a new nested self-similar (fractal-like) ontology.

A humacomm may itself interact with other machines, giving rise to a metahumacomm, itself capable of interacting with other machines, and so on, to any desired layer of complexity. An example is a humacomm comprised of a human with an eyeglass-based XR (eXtended Reality) and eXtended Intelligence (XI) system (Mann and Wyckoff, 1991), brain–computer-interface, and the like, interacting with a smart paddle, and this new metahumacomm interacting with a smart vessel such as a smart paddleboard, as shown in the next two figures.

In Figure 6 we have a smart paddleboard that senses the water, e.g. water quality, using sound wave propagation based on the SYSU x MannLab multicomponent lock-in amplifier sonar system (Mann, 2017), as pictured on the top figure. The system architecture shown in the bottom figure comprises the nested set of feedback loops.

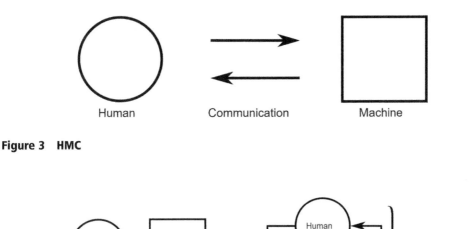

Figure 3   HMC

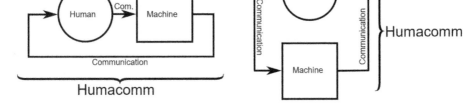

Figure 4   Humacomm

Water–Human–Computer Interface (WaterHCI)

Figure 5   Water HCI = Water–Human–Computer Interaction

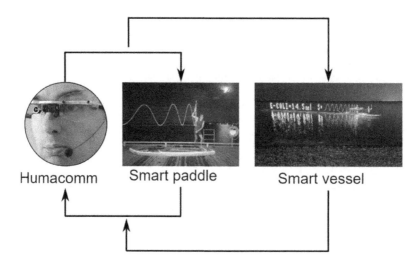

Figure 6   Metahumacomm: Humacomm–machine interaction (smart paddle, smart vessel)

BACK TO BASICS

As computers pervaded our nearly every waking moment, those of us working with computing went through an era of being "chained" or wired to our desks, hunched over the computer as with computing of the past, forcing us to bend over and twist ourselves like a pretzel around the computer. But then "wearables" allowed us to stand upright and enjoy the raw nature of the great outdoors, capturing a healthy dose of vitamin D, and for those in my lab, to experience a blend of icewater swimming and "growlerboarding" (standing on growlers while paddling) for example as in Figure 7.

These are also examples of HMC taking a systems form. Here the wearable computer provides simultaneous information overlays about what's happening inside the body while it is being pushed to its extreme limits of coldwater endurance (e.g. heart, respiration, mind, body, etc.) as well as what's happening around the body (e.g. water conditions, weather, maps, wayfinding, potential hazards, etc.). Bidirectional communication between the human and the machine (e.g. growlerboard) resulted in a unified system, even if a temporary HMC entity.

Figure 7   Growlerboarding

HUMAN–HUMACOMM

Finally, consider the situation where a non-cyborg human interacts with a humacomm, and now we have human–human–computer-communication – yet another iteration of HMC (see Figure 8).

FRACTAL (SELF-SIMILAR) NATURE OF HMC
Summarizing, I have asked you to consider these three nested examples of HMC, as follows:

- The mind is the seat of consciousness, i.e. that which makes us human. We can think of the human body as a machine. In this sense the efferent (outgoing) and afferent (incoming) nerves form the communication between the human and the machine, i.e. the feedback loop that defines this form of HMC;

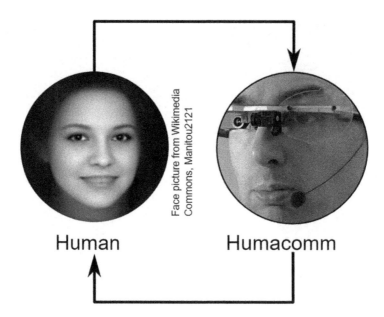

Figure 8   Human–humacomm communication

- For more than a million years, cyborgs (humachines) have existed in the form of humans using machines to extend their reach. The world's first cyborgs were waterborgs using vessels (simple rafts) to travel great distances between continents, thus the foundation of humacomm;
- The humacomm can interact within the spaces of smart cities, smart beaches, etc., where technologies sense the human (surveillance) and the human senses the smart world (sousveillance). A typical city has multiple humacomm/cyborg/humachine inhabitants, and thus we have a community of humacomms living in a city that may itself be regarded as a machine, made up of many machines. This machine machine (machine of machines) is a metamachine.

The fractal (self-similar) nature of this nested set of feedback loops (Figure 9) should be readily apparent (Sousveillant Cities and Media, Mann et al., 2018).

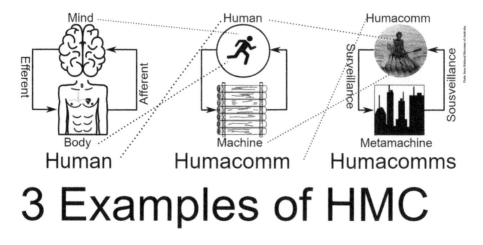

Figure 9   Fractal (self-similar) nature of HMC

Whereas the human and machine are in communication with one another, each may also be in communication with other entities. I argue that this must be an important HMC design principle, that is, to design for openness in HMC systems. For example, the machine (or technology) should be designed so as to be unmonopolizing, such that the human can remain aware of the surroundings. It must be unrestrictive so the human can continue to interact with the surroundings. It should be attentive, i.e. so the computer can sense the surroundings, and it should be communicative so that the computer can communicate with other humans who may or may not be humacomms, as well as with other entities such as AI (Artificial Intelligence). Thus, there are six communication paths between human and computer, as shown leftmost in Figure 10.

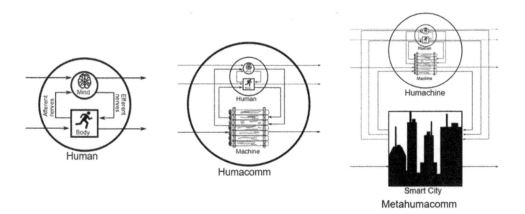

Figure 10   Fractal (self-similar) nature of HMC in-context

Furthermore, these six HMC pathways apply in the same fractal (self-similar) way, as shown middle and rightmost images. Simple? Perhaps not – HMC is not simple but offers building blocks and modularity that can evolve with emerging cognitions and technological developments in the future.

HMC TYPE 0, TYPE 1 AND TYPE 2: DYADIC ENTITIES/CYBORGS/HUMACHINES/ HUMACOMMS

It is useful to consider three different types of HMC formats. Type 0 HMCs, a majority discovered in the chapters of this Handbook, are in the form of the human and machine as interacting as dyads within separate embodiments, e.g. a person speaking with a voice agent. But we can push this concept further. A Type 1 HMC as a cyborg/humachine/humacomm is one in which the human enters the technology, e.g. the human enters a vessel or vehicle. A generalized vessel/vehicle/clothing, etc., is known as a vironment (Mann et al. 2021, WaterHCI). A Type 2 HMC such as a cyborg/humachine/humacomm is one in which a vessel enters the human, e.g. implantable technologies. This distinction is illustrated in Figure 11.

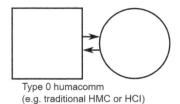

Type 0 humacomm
(e.g. traditional HMC or HCI)

Type 1 humacomm
(e.g. "wearables")

Type 2 humacomm
(e.g. "implantables")

Figure 11   Type 0, Type 1, and Type 2 HMC

THE EGG AND THE WALL

Finally, let us consider the machine metaphorically in the form of large institutions such as "big government," "big banks," "big science," and "big watching" (surveillance). Such entities are geared toward efficiency and massive scale, in some sense run like machines, and are often even referred to as machines, e.g. in the phrase "machinery of government" (Mill, J.S. (1861) *Considerations on Representative Government*, ISBN 0-7661-8898-1).

Staying with this metaphor, if the large organization is a machine, one can regard humans as "cogs" in that machine. But a better metaphor is perhaps the "egg" and the "wall," as captured in the following quote:

> If there is a hard, high wall and an egg that breaks against it, no matter how right the wall or how wrong the egg, I will stand on the side of the egg. Why? Because each of us is an egg, a unique soul enclosed in a fragile egg. Each of us is confronting a high wall. The high wall is the system which forces us to do the things we would not ordinarily see fit to do as individuals … We are all human beings, individuals, fragile eggs. We have no hope against the wall: it's too high, too dark, too cold. To fight the wall, we must join our souls together for warmth, strength. We must not let the system control us – create who we are. It is we who created the system. (Haruki Murakami, Jerusalem Prize acceptance speech, *Jerusalem Post*, Feb. 15, 2009)

The egg/human and wall/machine metaphor (Figure 12) speaks to HMC, but let us not merely reverse this, but give the diagram a kind of 90-degree rotation. Using the concepts of surveillance and sousveillance (watching the watchers) as the communication, we could say: No matter how right the surveillance (e.g. machine-driven sensory communication), or how wrong the sousveillance (i.e. human-driven sensory communication), I will stand on the side of the sousveillance. Why? Because each of us is confronting a high degree of surveillance. We have no hope against the hypocrisy of the vast surveillance networks. They're too pervasive, too powerful. To fight the hypocrisy and corruption of a surveillance-only society, we must join in widespread sousveillance to create communication on our own terms that benefit humans overall.

In particular, there are many closed-source systems that collect lots of information about us but reveal little about themselves. This one-sided surveillance-without-sousveillance (information-hoarding in the name of "public safety") is the antithesis of closed-loop feedback. Feedback delayed (or reduced) is feedback denied! In this way, we must ensure that there is sousveillance in proportion to surveillance, i.e. that we can sense when we are being sensed. Systems that provide for this are known as sousveillant systems. Failure to provide for sousveillance is one of the most common shortcomings of modern HMC.

This Handbook on HMC is the start at a new set of concepts, methods, and applications in the

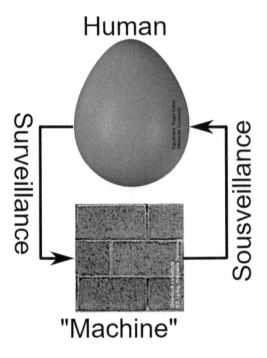

Figure 12   HMC metaphor: egg and wall

study of the three types of human–machine communication. These chapters are important breadcrumbs for the pathways to come as both humans and machines (and humacomms) evolve. Just like the theoretical bricolage and multi-locative origin of the discipline of communication studies that became codified in writings in the early 1930s, HMC is the well-needed new pathway that comes a century later. The importance of these chapters will be understood immediately, but will resonate for another 100 years. I am fortunate to bear witness to the emergence of this scholarship, lay my own thinking alongside those of these authors, and offer a contribution as part of this collection.

ELEMENTAL/MATTER ACKNOWLEDGEMENT

I wish to acknowledge not just the land (earth) but matter in all four states-of-matter: earth, water, air, and fire (i.e., loosely-speaking, solid, liquid, gas, and plasma, as well as any other state-of-matter), of Ontario Place where our outdoor "TeachBeach™" is located. This foreword is the result of conversations that took place on this shore, including one between myself and Rhonda McEwen, one of the editors of this Handbook, on a cloudy summer day in 2021.

For thousands of years these places have been traditional places of the Huron-Wendat, the Seneca, and most recently, the Mississaugas of the Credit River. Today, these meeting places are still the home to many Indigenous people from across Turtle Island and we are grateful to have the opportunity to work here. In some sense a part of the photographs and videos we capture here are owned, at least in part, by the many Indigenous peoples.

BIBLIOGRAPHIC REFERENCE CITATIONS (IN THE ORDER CITED)

[Mann 2001], Mann, Steve, "Can humans being machines make machines be human?" In *Proceedings of the International Conference on Cyborgs in Ethics, Law, and Art, December 14–15, 2021*, Michałowska, Monika, ed., "Crossing the Border of Humanity," pp. 47–64.

[Mann and Wyckoff 1991] Mann, Steve and Wyckoff, Charles, "Extended reality," Massachusetts Institute of Technology, Cambridge, Massachusetts, 4-405, 1991, available at http://wearcam.org/xr.htm

[Mann 2017] Mann, Steve. "Rattletale: Phase-coherent telekinetic imaging to detect tattletale signs of structural defects or potential failure." In *2017 13th International Conference on Signal-Image Technology & Internet-Based Systems (SITIS)*. IEEE, 2017.

[Sousveillant Cities and Media, Mann et al., 2018] Mann, S., Havens, J. C., Cowan, G., Richardson, A., & Ouellette, R., *Sousveillant cities and media, mesh cities*, pp. 1–15, 2018.

[Mann et al. 2021, WaterHCI] Steve Mann, Mark Mattson, Steve Hulford, Mark Fox, Kevin Mako, Ryan Janzen, Maya Burhanpurkar, Simone Browne, Craig Travers, Robert Thurmond, Seung-min Park, Atlas Roufas, Cayden Pierce, Samir Khaki, Derek Lam, Faraz Sadrzadeh-Afsharazar, Kyle Simmons, Tomoko Yonezawa, & Ateeya Manzoor (2021). "Water-human–computer-interface (WaterHCI): Crossing the borders of computation, clothes, skin, and surface." In *Proceedings of the 23rd annual Water-Human–Computer Interface Deconference* (pp. 6–35).

[Mill, J.S. (1861) *Considerations on Representative Government*, ISBN 0-7661-8898-1]

Acknowledgements

Like many other contemporary scholarly projects, *The Sage Handbook of Human–Machine Communication* began before the COVID-19 pandemic and reached its conclusion before we could have any knowledge of which trajectory the pandemic may yet continue its evolution. We are beyond grateful to the numerous contributors who have stood by the project when it meant adding work to schedules and lives already stretched thin. The chapters of this Handbook were written by scholars throughout the world, and we watched as the pandemic spread in multiple waves across different nations, easing in some areas while intensifying in others. The contributors were selected because of their exemplary work in their areas of research, but we must remark that we are awed by the quality of the chapters contributing authors provided to us. In spite of the economic, social, psychological, and physical ravages of the pandemic, these scholars produced chapters that will provide solid foundations for the future of HMC research.

Likewise we are extraordinarily grateful to the team at Sage for helping us to bring this project to fruition. Michael Ainsley was instrumental in providing feedback as we conceived the Handbook and developed its scope, and Colette Wilson provided invaluable support with extreme patience as we negotiated the logistics of such an ambitious project while also addressing the numerous complications and setbacks wrought by a global pandemic.

We also want to acknowledge the support of our colleagues and our respective departments and universities: the Department of Communication at Northern Illinois University, the Institute of Communication, Culture, Information and Technology at the University of Toronto Mississauga, Victoria University in the University of Toronto, and the Department of Communication at University of Illinois Chicago. Funding for part of this project was provided by the Canada Research Chair program of the Social Science and Humanities Research Council of Canada.

After early sparks of an idea, this project ignited in 2018, and for the past four years, we have spent countless hours developing the proposal, reaching out to authors, coordinating chapters, providing reviews on multiple chapter drafts, and writing our individual and collective contributions as editors. All of these efforts were graciously supported by our families even when it meant time away from them.

The completion of this Handbook is bittersweet – what will we do without the weekly Friday morning meetings? We are excited to bring this contribution to the field and proud of this work. Almost everyone involved with this project has suffered loss during the past few years alongside those who will read this Handbook and everyone else who has struggled since early 2020 during the global pandemic. As editors, we have personally lost loved ones, and we honor them.

Introduction to the Handbook

Andrea L. Guzman, Rhonda McEwen, and Steve Jones

While the idea of an expansive collection on HMC existed in our individual imaginations for some time, as a trio we first discussed putting together a handbook during the AoIR annual conference in Montreal in 2018. Clarity on the fundamental goal of this Handbook came from three days of whiteboarding in Chicago early in 2019. Then we cast nets as far globally and as wide disciplinarily as we could to entice authors established and emerging to contribute to the vision. As is the case with most every handbook, our vision was that it should serve as a foundational text, in this case in Human–Machine Communication (HMC), as a tool that scholars can reference as they engage in new research in the field. HMC focuses on the study of technologies designed as communicative subjects, people's interactions with these technologies, and the resulting implications for individuals, organizations, and society.

Burgeoning scholarly interest in HMC is amply illustrated by the growing number of students and researchers who have flocked to international conferences such as the International Communication Association (ICA), HMC pre-conferences and workshops at AoIR and the ACM/IEEE International Conference on Human Robotic Interaction. These HMC scholarly sessions have seen participation from scholars from varying theoretical, methodological, and cultural backgrounds across the globe. In 2019, the International Communication Association recognized HMC as an official Interest Group with membership growing significantly in the group each year since. Special journal issues regarding HMC have been published in *Communication +1, Computers in Human Behavior,* and *Communication Studies*. A new journal, *Human–Machine Communication* (ISSN: 2638-6038), published its first volume online on February 3, 2020.

The goal of this Handbook is to contribute a landmark text that comprehensively assays the historical antecedents, fields, methods, debates, and theories that contribute to the emerging field of HMC. We seek to inform students and researchers in HMC and cognate fields whose work and interests intersect with the study of new technologies and forms of relationships with machines. We also wish to provide a point of departure for theorizing interactions between people and technologies that are functioning in the role of communicators and consider the theoretical and methodological implications of machines performing traditionally "human" roles. The Handbook's topics also apply to designers and developers of the next generation of voice assistants, robotics, autonomous vehicles, and artificial intelligence, as well as practitioners in media industries.

Despite rapidly growing interest, Human–Machine Communication is an area of study that is still emerging. To this point, no single book covers its foundations, antecedents, theories, methods, and possible futures. Our goal is for *The Sage Handbook of Human–Machine Communication* to fill this gap by being the primary text by which students and scholars discover this area of study and to which scholars and students repeatedly refer. It provides an optimal means by which HMC can be incorporated into courses not only in HMC but also in new media, HCI, communication, psychology, HRI, computer science, information studies, policy studies, and health sciences.

DEFINING HMC

As a field communication has long struggled to find its place in the academy. Is it a discipline? A field? A sub-field? A 1983 special issue of *Journal of Communication* (vol. 33, no. 3) titled "Ferment in the Field," gained widespread readership (and notoriety) for opening the debate on such questions. There have been follow-up issues, one ten years later in 1993 (vol. 43, no. 3) and another thirty-five years later in 2018 (vol. 68, no. 2) along with many articles in between, published in different journals, and numerous conference papers and roundtables, too many to cite here. There will undoubtedly be more such discussion and debate. Internet studies experienced a similar moment to communication in the early 2000s as it was coalescing in the late 1970s and early 1980s when scholars from numerous disciplines began to meet and form scholarly associations such as AoIR, the Association of Internet Researchers (Jones, 2005; Jones, 2006). Those formations were instrumental in creating a broadly drawn canon of literature that aided scholars in a variety of ways, but perhaps most importantly assisted them in determining how to blend the different languages employed in different fields that fed into internet studies.

If we take 2015 as approximately the year that HMC began to coalesce in ways similar to the formation of communication and internet studies, then HMC is now, in the early 2020s, about at the same point in its development as those fields were when their gaze turned (at least somewhat) inward. And, indeed, there is evidence that scholars are looking at HMC's place both among the various fields from which scholars have come to it and with regard to the affordances[1] it provides scholars. For example, in the introductory editorial to a special section of *Computers in Human Behavior* published in 2019, Patric Spence simply asks, "is Human–Machine Communication a distinct field of study?" (Spence, p. 285). Echoing Guzman's (2018) efforts to address that question, Spence examines the growth of organizational communication as a field of study and concludes that there are several elements that seem to constitute the development of a field, ranging from the practical (journals, conferences) to the intellectual (theories, methods). Our goal with this Handbook is to greatly expand the range of answers to questions such as Spence's, to contextualize them, and to provide a comprehensive foundation for HMC's development as a distinct field of inquiry.

Establishing a field – and developing a handbook to represent that field – requires answering a seemingly basic question: "What is Human–Machine Communication?" It is a question of definition: One that simultaneously lays out HMC's scope of scholarly inquiry while also setting its boundaries, determining what is "within" and "outside" its purview. Answering the question of "What is HMC?," however, is far from straightforward. The impetus for establishing HMC lies in emerging technologies and practices. The devices and applications, people's interactions with them, and the resulting implications are still developing and evolving, extremely quickly we might add as evidenced in recent developments with chatGPT and generative AI. Thus, setting the initial parameters of research requires flexibility and fluidity: the scaffolding and building are being erected simultaneously. It also means that defining aspects of HMC likely will remain for some time contentious, particularly in relation to human–human communication research.

Communication scholars do not agree on a single conceptualization of their core concept, communication. The study of communication comprises research from the social sciences and the humanities and even reaches across to some of the hard sciences, all operating from varied philosophical and epistemological standpoints. The aims and methods of communication research, then, are not uniform. A rigid operationalization of communication, or a specific aspect of it, for the purposes of a social science experiment may not translate to humanities scholarship examining the intertwined threads of communication and culture. This is not to say that commonality cannot be found among the many conceptualizations of communication, chiefly the conveyance of information and creation of meaning. Communication has most often been modeled as a human activity occurring among and between people with technology, when present, serving as a means to transmit human messages (e.g., Barnlund, 1970). HMC, in contrast, situates machines in the communicator role, hitherto almost exclusively reserved for humans and, therefore, is contentious because it directly challenges the anthropocentric definition of communication (Gunkel, 2012). For some communication scholars, this is a step too far; although, now that social technologies (such as voice-based assistants) are becoming increasingly sophisticated and common place, more communication researchers are realizing that the parameters surrounding the study of communication, formed around technologies of the twentieth century, may no longer best represent the emerging realities of people's communicative behaviors involving technologies of the twenty-first century.

Such "communicative AI" raise the question of whether and how communication should be redefined to accommodate machines functioning in this role previously reserved for humans (Fortunati & Edwards, 2020; Gunkel, 2012; Guzman & Lewis, 2020). Some research continues to operate from a model in which technology, including AI, remains a mediator of human interaction, albeit one with increasing agency. From this theoretical perspective, AI can exchange messages with people, but its actions are situated within the larger context of mediating interactions between and among humans (e.g., Jakesch et al., 2019; Sundar, 2020). Observing that technology is increasingly functioning with greater and more sophisticated levels of agency in communication, some scholars recognize that machines can, in fact, serve as a type of communicator necessitating the revision of theoretical models to accommodate them as such. At the same time, these scholars may seek out ways to avoid erasing the ontological assumptions undergirding traditional definitions of communication by referring to interactions involving technology using terms such as "quasi-communication" (e.g., Hepp, 2020). Still other approaches put forward a general definition of communication that does not hinge on who or what is doing the communicating (e.g., Guzman, 2018). Communication is generally defined as a process of "meaning making" achieved through the exchange of messages with implications for the self and society. Communication can take place among humans (what has been hitherto referred to simply as "communication" with the human implied) and among humans and machines, or human–machine communication. Regarding the mediator role previously assigned to machines, such an approach recognizes that machines can occupy both roles just as humans can serve not only as communicators but also as mediators. To be clear, this is not an argument that human–machine communication and human–human communication are necessarily one in the same (see Fortunati & Edwards, 2020). Heeding Spence's (2019) warning, the goal of this latter approach is to avoid positioning human–machine communication as inferior to human communication, as "quasi" or similar qualifiers would imply, even if this is not the intended effect of those who employ such terms. It is this reconceptualization of communication around which we as editors planned the Handbook; however, we recognize that scholars approach communication between humans and machines from a multitude of theoretical starting points, as highlighted in the Histories and Trajectories section and demonstrated throughout the Handbook. Given the field's nascency and its likelihood to continue to evolve, we think acknowledging the multitude of perspectives and giving them space from which to be engaged – instead of ignoring differing viewpoints – is vital to fostering ongoing discussion and theoretical development.

There also exist questions and debates as to how HMC fits into the larger research space of communication and media (as well as across other fields and disciplines – a point we will return to momentarily). One of the key markers of institutional recognition for HMC research was the formal approval of the Human–Machine Communication Interest Group of the International Communication Association. Such designation signaled that scholarly interest in HMC is of merit, warranting institutional and disciplinary space and support. A crucial aspect of making the case for HMC was justifying how HMC contributed to an understanding of communication in ways not currently realized across the multitude of research areas within communication and media studies.

What falls within the purview of HMC research has developed out of both explicit efforts to define the field and a more implicit shaping emerging from HMC scholars' justification of their work. Scholars have been motivated to study people's communication with machines by a fundamental change in the design and function of technology (e.g., Zhao, 2006). Most explanations of the scope of HMC, therefore, trace out the types of applications and devices that qualify for HMC research. Edwards and Edwards (2017) explain that "HMC involves communication with digital interlocutors including embodied machine communicators, virtual and artificially intelligent agents (e.g., spoken dialogue systems), and technologically augmented persons, either in real or virtual and augmented environments." The HMC Interest Group of the ICA states that it "supports and promotes scholarship regarding communication between people and technologies designed to enact the role of communicators (i.e., artificial intelligence (AI), robots, digital assistants, smart and Internet of Things (IoT) devices)."[2] Across HMC research and the chapters of this Handbook, scholars point to different attributes of these devices and applications as defining characteristics, including the level of agency and autonomy, the degree of adaptability, the sophistication of message exchange, the social cues enacted, and the likeness to humans or living creatures. For some scholars, what is of greater importance is not so much the design of the technology but rather how people respond to and behave toward certain attributes in ways deemed "social."

The devices and applications that most clearly belong to HMC and, to date, have received the most scholarly attention by scholars working in this area are those that overtly communicate in human-like ways verbally and/or non-verbally, chiefly social robots, smart assistants (particularly if they are voice-based), and a wide array of chatbot applications such as chatGPT. Yet, there exist questions as to whether other technologies or applications should fall into the study of HMC if their communicative behavior is more subtle, "less human," or buried within the technological layers that enable people to engage with devices. Such technologies may include a variety of applications and ambient technologies that collect data and feed it back to users, such as the Netflix or Spotify algorithms, and in doing so, communicate an indirect message to the user about who they are and what the algorithm is. This communication is not a direct verbal exchange, but it is an interaction with meaning for the human involved and has been interpreted as such (Colbjørnsen, 2018; Gaw, 2022). The idea of more indirect communication via algorithms also raises the question of whether older technologies, such as the industrial robots that preceded social robots, also are part of a communicative process with humans (Guzman, 2016). While HMC research has largely focused on the end user, it also is possible to ask how the people programming technology – directly inputting not "natural language" but "machine language" – see their relationship to and exchange with the machine. Within computing history, engineers have long used the term communication to describe programming and design. Do such interactions with computers qualify as *communication* or is communication serving as more of a metaphor, as some people who push back entirely on the idea of machines as communicators have argued (e.g., Ekbia, 2008)? Then there are the technological layers that facilitate the outward exchange of messages between human and machine, including machine-to-machine communication. Should these be part of the HMC research agenda or are they too far removed from the human interaction?

Scholars do not necessarily agree on which of these borderline technologies, if any, should be included within the scope of HMC. It is entirely possible to restrict HMC to the most human or life-like interactions with technology. The benefit would be a clean line, so to speak, about what is or is not HMC. At the same time, however, it would mean more strictly defining the scope of HMC early in the field's formation, potentially cutting off trajectories of scholarly inquiry before their full value to HMC can be explored or understood. At the heart of this debate is a very old one within the study of communication – defining communication. For scholars such as James Carey (1989), communication is more than the transmission of information, it is the vehicle through which our reality and our culture are formed through manifest and latent meaning. From the perspective of critical and cultural theorists and scholars from closely related areas of research, such as Science and Technology Studies, technology can "speak" through its very design and the cultural values it embodies and are enacted in its use. A scholar's definition of communication, generally, therefore, can have implications for how they may draw the boundaries around HMC. Even if scholars were to focus more on the manifest communication from machines built on human or life-like traits, categorization is difficult. As documented in research, the communicative traits built into technology and how they are interpreted by people run along a highly nuanced spectrum that we are only beginning to conceptualize. There also is the question of whether we can fully theorize about the process and implications of people's communication with machines if we do not understand what is "going on behind the scenes." Yet it also is important to note, that if the boundaries of HMC are drawn overly broad, the field could suffer from a lack of identity with incongruous research. This would work against attempts to theorize more broadly regarding human–machine communication.

While the majority of the technologies discussed within this Handbook tend to be the more literal in terms of their communicative abilities, we do include technologies and interactions that some other scholars in the field may consider edge cases, such as algorithms generally, machine-to-machine communication, and the process of programming machines as a form of communication. We made such a decision in keeping with our ethos that – at this stage in HMC's development and existence – we should be more exploratory and inclusive, to promote dialogue and leave space for refinement within the field.

Furthermore, we want to stress that it is not the technology alone that determines whether research falls within the purview of Human–Machine Communication. More recently this has become a source of confusion as some scholars have assumed that research involving communicative AI or robots automatically qualifies as HMC research. Part of this confusion may stem from an overcorrection in the study of technology more broadly – one in which researchers, realizing that a focus on the human element has resulted in overlooking the design and function of technology, have shifted their attention to the machine, so now the human element is not properly accounted for (Natale & Guzman, 2022). To be clear, what has always been key in establishing HMC is a focus on questions of and relating to communication – on how people make sense of and behave with technologies and the individual, organizational, and cultural implications (see Fortunati & Edwards, 2020).

The most obvious lines of research include tracing how interaction unfolds between people and technology, how people conceptualize technology as communicator, and people's immediate behavior with and in response to machines. But, as with human communication research, the study of people's communication with machines goes much deeper (Guzman & Lewis, 2020). Communication is a relational act, establishing what each entity is to the other, and how people come to see not only the machine but also themselves and others in relation to the machine. What the technology is and how people come to see it in relation to themselves develops in interactions with and about machines, as well as through cultural discourse. These too are driving questions in HMC research. AI and robots also have been part of the millennia-old pursuit of understanding life and recreating it, making philosophical inquiry important as well. For these reasons, the HMC community has been built around a broad recognition of the different philosophical, theoretical, and methodological approaches to communication research that are reflected throughout this Handbook.

SETTING AND RESETTING BOUNDARIES

HMC exists in relation to communication and media research as well as related fields and disciplines. It is important to address the matter of boundaries, and specifically the boundaries across fields that are presented in this Handbook as histories informing HMC, those that appear cognate, or those that may be viewed as disparate. In the most straightforward sense, boundaries attempt to define a space by saying what something is not. A fence in a backyard is a physical representation of a property line versus another; distinguishing my things from my neighbors' things. In cellular biology, a boundary categorizes what is inside an entity from what is outside. Boundaries applied to geographies in this sense are more contentious and depending on who has the power to decide what is inside or outside, a boundary can incite war. Within academic dialogue, boundaries are represented in a structural differentiation of disciplines – artificial and reductive, yet useful in organizing scholarship and other arrangements in institutions of higher learning.

The utility of boundaries is sometimes in tension with operationalizing ideas, concepts, and methods. For example, the field of human–computer interaction (HCI) is interested in the interface between humans and machines where a machine is in the form of a computer. HMC is also interested in this interface. However, where HCI scholars focus more heavily on issues of design and use of computers by humans, HMC scholars are interested in the issues arising from the exchange between humans and machines as a form of communication and meaning making. There is overlap as design/use/communication can feature in research for both HCI and HMC interdisciplinary scholars. However, there are some fundamental differences between the two fields. For one, the analytical weighing of the human and the machine/computer approaches equivalence for HMC scholars, while it is asymmetrical within most HCI research. Design and development are also more central to HCI than they are to HMC, and this draws computer science and engineers to HCI, while HMC has a stronger appeal to social science researchers.

Another example is the boundary between HMC and human–robot interaction (HRI). In a similar way to HMC and HCI, HRI scholarship is concerned with interactions between humans and machines, where machines are specified as robots. HRI researchers are also interdisciplinary, however, the field draws scholars from a wide range – humanities, social science, natural sciences, and engineering. The boundary between HRI and HMC appears more porous when the topic of communication is under investigation and where conceptualizations of a robot as a type of machine are defined. However, as these areas evolve there may be other, more fundamental points of departure to consider.

Conceptualizing such boundaries can follow one of two tacks: Devising hard boundaries in which there is very little overlap among HMC and existing lines of research or establishing porous parameters that trace out the main aims of HMC research while also allowing for significant influence from and contribution back to other areas. Research regarding technology during the last half-century has necessitated the latter approach as substantial shifts in the function of technology significantly challenged foundational axes of communication research, collapsing what were once seen as firm dividing lines (Lievrouw, 2009).

Such is the case with HMC. The chapters in the second half of this Handbook – the Concepts and Contexts and Technologies and Applications sections – demonstrate how HMC and established areas of research mutually inform one another. Interpersonal theory of human–human communication, for example, has proved an invaluable starting point for theorizing people's direct interactions with machines. Communicative AI also are increasingly being incorporated into media industries, such as journalism. Journalism studies scholars, for example, are grappling with the shifting roles of humans and technology in content creation, distribution, and consumption (Lewis et al., 2019; Wu et al., 2020). Theories and concepts within HMC can be applied to the study of journalism and other media industries. At the same time, research applied to specific contexts has the potential to provide insight into HMC more generally. Much as the internet and then mobile phone have reshaped the contexts of communication, so too communicative AI is expected to have far-reaching implications. The applications and contexts highlighted within the Handbook are some of the earliest areas being transformed by AI, and we expect the reach of AI, robotics, and related technologies to continue to diffuse throughout communication and media research.

Across the chapters presented in this Handbook we can consider the human and the machine as boundary objects. Star & Griesemer (1989) defined boundary objects as those of common interest to multiple actors who approach the object from their own local needs. Boundary objects are "plastic" enough to be adapted across contexts but robust enough to have a common identity for the different actors. While there is critique of this concept when some objects become hardened into permanence, losing their flexibility in the service of infrastructure, humans and machines as conceptual boundary objects that communicate with each other for now, works. And where there is more contention, we invite critique that is the hallmark of academic debate.

The interpretive flexibility of boundary objects allows interdisciplinary scholars in this Handbook (and beyond) to collaborate and converse about humans and machines as objects of common interest. HMC carves out a space that encourages intellectual engagement and provides opportunities for many scholars to locate like-minded others. It is this coalition building without needing to have consensus that is a strength of HMC. There will be departures, the boundaries will shift as humans and machines both continue to evolve, and overlap is inevitable. Yet the richness of the ideas and the creativity of the methodologies presented in this Handbook will serve as a foundation from which coalition building and consensus may emerge.

SECTION OVERVIEW

The book has been organized into four sections: Histories and Trajectories, Approaches and Methods, Concepts and Contexts, and Technologies and Applications. The Histories and Trajectories section provides an in-depth overview of fields and disciplines, ranging from the humanities to the sciences, that have had a connection to HMC, and its chapters provide a foundation for understanding the historical roots of the many ways scholars, authors and artists have attempted to understand interactions between people and technology. The Approaches and Methods section provides an overview of the inventive methods and approaches that scholars are applying to HMC. It should be noted that chapter authors in other sections will also address questions of method when appropriate, providing a more organic discussion of method situated within the context in which it is employed. These scholars grapple with research techniques originating from science and engineering, technology studies, and social science, innovating in the context of HMC questions. The Concepts and Contexts section focuses on concepts, themes, and contexts central to and within HMC research. Chapters discussing a concept or theme will focus on explaining its importance and relevance, its conceptualization, and its application within the study of HMC. Many of the concepts discussed in this section are shared with other fields and related areas of research, and so, when warranted, chapters will also compare and contrast the application of concepts within HMC to their use in other areas of research. The focus of these chapters may include the contributions of HMC theory and research to the study of people's interactions with technologies within a specified setting. Other chapters may focus on identifying research questions that arise when a technology is viewed as a communicator instead of its historical positioning as a mediator or that have been overlooked within the research thus far. The final section focuses on the Technologies and Applications that are central areas of research in HMC. It provides a view of HMC in action – including devices, media, and digital communicators that will grow as technologies emerge.

CONCLUSION: SETTING A FOUNDATION

This volume's primary audience are scholars throughout communication, computer science, media and information studies, and related fields as well as practitioners, engineers, and researchers interested in the foundational elements of this emerging field. In situating HMC within broader and more established disciplines, it is our hope that the Handbook will not only create a shared vocabulary among HMC scholars but also foster channels for dialogue across related research areas. While the functional value of a shared vocabulary is obvious, there are other worthwhile considerations arising from the evolution of a new *lingua franca*. As Joli Jensen wrote in the tenth anniversary issue of *Journal of Communication*, vocabularies have consequences, they shape "our understanding of what constitutes good inquiry, appropriate evidence, sound conclusions… (and) less obviously but no less deeply (shape) our beliefs about ourselves, our teaching, our research, our common enterprise" (1993, p. 68). We are indebted to the many scholars who have contributed their work to this Handbook and thus to the effort to create a shared ground on which we can build future research in HMC.

We created this Handbook to provide a generative text to which scholars will return again and again to inform their research and ongoing education in HMC. The Handbook offers a comprehensive set of themes and approaches that can support course texts as a supplement or can be adopted as the primary text for undergraduate and graduate courses in HMC, providing a pathway for teaching HMC in Communication, Media and Information Studies, Science and Technology Studies, and related areas. We fully anticipate the Handbook to contribute back to research across the many areas feeding into HMC scholarship, including communication, HCI, HRI, psychology, computer science, the philosophy of technology, media and information studies, policy studies, and health sciences.

While we are assaying the state of the art in HMC with this Handbook, it is important to say a few words about HMC's future. Even during the short time in which we have been working on the Handbook, we have witnessed continued growth and development of HMC in both stand-alone technologies and in devices and applications that connect to other media and technologies. Voice interaction continues to be incorporated into existing technologies, and artificial intelligence developments seem increasingly capable of providing human-like communication and interaction. As this volume was going to press, OpenAI released chatGPT. The capabilities of generative AI make the study of HMC even more critical. We expect these trends to continue, and like most of those who will read this Handbook, we are keen to witness and contribute to what will come next for HMC. It is our hope that existing researchers and those new to HMC will consider this Handbook the go-to reference for frameworks and concepts that theoretically underpin HMC and that it will continue to serve scholars well into the future.

NOTES

1   We use the term "affordances" deliberately to denote that fields, like technologies, may have particular and specific elements and capabilities suited, or directed, toward and/or away from specific modes of inquiry.
2   See https://humanmachinecommunication.org

REFERENCES

Barnlund, D. C. (1970). A transactional model of communication. In J. Akin, A. Goldberg, G. Myers, & J. Stewart (Eds.), *Language behavior: A book of readings in communication* (pp. 43–61). Mouton.

Carey, J. W. (1989). *Communication as culture: Essays on media and society*. Routledge.

Colbjørnsen, T. (2018). My algorithm: User perceptions of algorithmic recommendations in cultural contexts. In A. L. Guzman (Ed.), *Human-machine communication: Rethinking communication, technology, and ourselves*. Peter Lang.

Edwards, A., & Edwards, C. (2017). The machines are coming: Future directions in instructional communication research. *Communication Education, 66*(4), 487–488. https://doi.org/10.1080/03634523.2017.1349915

Ekbia, H. R. (2008). *Artificial dreams: The quest for non-biological intelligence*. Cambridge University Press.

Fortunati, L., & Edwards, A. (2020). Opening space for theoretical, methodological, and empirical issues in human-machine communication. *Human-Machine Communication, 1*, 7–18. https://doi.org/10.30658/hmc.1.1

Gaw, F. (2022). Algorithmic logics and the construction of cultural taste of the Netflix Recommender System. *Media, Culture & Society, 44*(4), 706–725. https://doi.org/10.1177/01634437211053767

Gunkel, D. J. (2012). Communication and artificial intelligence: Opportunities and challenges for the 21st century. *Communication +1, 1*(1), 1. https://doi.org/10.7275/R5QJ7F7R

Guzman, A. L. (2016). The messages of mute machines: Human-machine communication with industrial technologies. *Communication +1, 5*.v https://doi.org/10.7275/R57P8WBW

Guzman, A. L. (Ed.). (2018). *Human-machine communication: Rethinking communication, technology, and ourselves*. Peter Lang.

Guzman, A. L., & Lewis, S. C. (2020). Artificial intelligence and communication: A human–machine communication research agenda. *New Media & Society, 22*(1), 70–86. https://doi.org/10.1177/1461444819858691

Hepp, A. (2020). Artificial companions, social bots and work bots: Communicative robots as research objects of media and communication studies. *Media, Culture & Society, 42*(7–8), 1410–1426. https://doi.org/10.1177/0163443720916412

Jakesch, M., French, M., Ma, X., Hancock, J. T., & Naaman, M. (2019). AI-mediated communication: How the perception that profile text was written by AI affects trustworthiness. *Proceedings of the 2019 CHI Conference on Human Factors in Computing Systems* – CHI '19, 1–13. https://doi.org/10.1145/3290605.3300469

Jensen, J. (1993). The consequences of vocabularies, *Journal of Communication 43*(3), 67–74.

Jones. S. (2005). Fizz in the field: Toward a basis for an emergent internet studies. *The Information Society 21*(4), 233–237.

Jones, S. (2006). Dreams of fields: Possible trajectories of internet studies. In *Critical cyberculture studies*, David Silver and Adrienne Massanari, Eds. New York University Press, 2006, pp. ix–xvii.

Lewis, S. C., Guzman, A. L., & Schmidt, T. R. (2019). Automation, journalism, and human–machine communication: Rethinking roles and relationships of humans and machines in news. *Digital Journalism, 7*(4), 409–427. https://doi.org/10.1080/21670811.2019.1577147

Lievrouw, L. A. (2009). New media, mediation, and communication study. *Information, Communication & Society, 12*(3), 303–325. https://doi.org/10.1080/13691180802660651

Natale, S., & Guzman, A. L. (2022). Reclaiming the human in machine cultures: Introduction. *Media, Culture & Society, 44*(4), 627–637. https://doi.org/10.1177/01634437221099614

Spence, P. (2019). Searching for questions, original thoughts, or advancing theory: Human-machine communication. *Computers in Human Behavior 90*, 285–287.

Star, S., & Griesemer, J. (1989). Institutional ecology, 'Translations' and boundary objects: Amateurs and professionals in Berkeley's Museum of Vertebrate Zoology, 1907-39. *Social Studies of Science, 19* (3): 387–420. doi: 10.1177/030631289019003001

Sundar, S. S. (2020). Rise of machine agency: A framework for studying the psychology of human–AI interaction (HAII). *Journal of Computer-Mediated Communication, 25*(1), 74–88. https://doi.org/10.1093/jcmc/zmz026

Wu, S., Tandoc, E. C., & Salmon, C. T. (2019). Journalism reconfigured: Assessing human–machine relations and the autonomous power of automation in news production. *Journalism Studies, 20*(10), 1440–1457. https://doi.org/10.1080/1461670X.2018.1521299

Zhao, S. (2006). Humanoid social robots as a medium of communication. *New Media & Society, 8*(3), 401–419. https://doi.org/10.1177/1461444806061951

PART 1

Histories and Trajectories

INTRODUCTION

It is daunting to begin the construction of the history of a new field of study as early in its development as we are doing in this section of *The Sage Handbook of Human–Machine Communication*. To avoid doing so, however, would not only impoverish histories written in the future but also diminish the richness of the field in the present when it can greatly benefit from understanding its own past.

We have therefore set out in this section of the Handbook to illustrate and explain the precedents to Human–Machine Communication (HMC) and to explore what might be its antecedents. Our aim is to provide historical context that is generative, that connects the multiple threads that are woven throughout the study of HMC while, at the same time, to gently but purposefully unravel the threads to better understand how they constitute the larger tapestry being knitted together.

As is the case with many historical overviews, ours is both general and particular: General insofar as it ranges across many of the abundant fields from which HMC draws, and particular insofar as it concentrates on the specific elements of those fields in relation to HMC. This section thereby provides an in-depth overview of fields and disciplines, ranging from the humanities to the sciences, that have had a connection to HMC, and the chapters provide a foundation for understanding the historical roots of the many ways scholars, authors, and artists have attempted to understand interactions between people and technology and the implications of such interactions for self and society.

What is clear from the puzzle that has emerged as the pieces comprising this section were put together is that the study of Human–Machine Communication is built on a very solid foundation of fundamental theories that underpin the social sciences and humanities, from philosophy to psychology, poetry to information theory, history to communication. The study of HMC, however, is most valuable when it also looks for cracks in that foundation. As Andreas Hepp and Wiebke Loosen highlight in their chapter in this section on the interdisciplinarity of HMC, the "challenge lies in the fact that HMC starts from the assumption that the machine communicates, which calls into question the fundamental understanding of communication as human interaction, of media as mediating instances, and of agency as purely human." Now that we may admit technology not only as mediator but also as interlocutor, not only as object but also subject, not only as interactive but also agentic, we would do well to interrogate the theories that brought us here, as the authors of chapters in this section so eloquently do. Whether or not one is convinced by predictions of advancements in artificial intelligence technologies, the chapters in this section point out the many scholarly inroads that are converging on human interactions with machines that are functionally similar to interactions with artificial intelligence and robotics. Understanding the routes scholars have taken to get here will help us assay future terrain to traverse and give us a map with which to better chart HMC's history as well as its future.

The history of HMC is, therefore, like all other histories, being continuously written and revised. Attending to the shifts in the locus of those histories will aid us as we seek to better understand the developments explored throughout this Handbook, namely the increasing interaction between humans and machines, among machines themselves, and the resulting human–machine configurations and reconfigurations (Suchman, 2007). Those developing and studying emerging communication technologies, whether digital or analog, have benefited and contributed most when their work has not only opened up new areas of study but also refocused attention on existing ones, calling into question canons, theories, methods, practices. We have endeavored in this section to provide a state-of-the-art overview of areas from which HMC has arisen, areas in which it has had impact, and areas in which it is growing. It is our hope that in so doing we will encourage and inspire scholars across a variety of fields to continue to move HMC forward and to also continue to look back at where it has been, thereby assuring that it will be grounded.

REFERENCES

Suchman, L.A. (2007) *Human-machine reconfigurations: Plans and situated action*, 2nd edn. Cambridge University Press.

Machines are Us: An Excursion in the History of HMC

Kate K. Mays and James E. Katz

INTRODUCTION

Our imaginations exert great influence over our behavior, our understanding of the world, and even our visceral reactions. It is only to be expected that our imaginations would affect how we use and interact with our technology, especially interactive communication technologies. As W. I. Thomas pointed out, when he helped found the social interaction movement a century ago, what we believe to be the situation guides how we will act toward it, regardless of the situation's reality. We've seen evidence of this already, even decades ago with the rudimentary chatbot Eliza. "She" was a text-based interlocutor that identified the main keywords in a message and transformed them to pose a question (in the manner of a psychologist) back to the human correspondent (Neff & Nagy, 2016). Despite the limited scope of conversation, people responded emotionally to Eliza; when they were informed that she was a machine, some maintained an emotional attachment (Neff & Nagy, 2016).

In the present day, our lives are filled with proliferating technologies that both facilitate our socio-emotional lives and, increasingly, act as socio-emotional outlets themselves. This chapter considers various perspectives that shed light on the relationships between people and their interactive technology, most especially in the domain of personal communication. We approach this task from the overarching notion of the imaginarium, a portmanteau that describes what groups of people conjure up in their imaginations and how these mental processes interact, albeit sometimes tenuously, with various levels of external physical and social realities. Similar to Peter Nagy and Gina Neff's (2015) notion of "imagined affordance," these mental embellishments create narratives and anticipatory structures that are used to guide our understandings and interpretations of what is happening around us.

The imaginarium provides a lens through which human interactions with computers, smart phones, and AI agents, among others, can be explored. People's tendencies to have emotional and social interactions *with*, and not just through, technology have been well established (cf., Nass & Moon, 2000; Reeves & Nass, 1996; Vincent, 2015). Yet in this line of research, the technology in question is typically analyzed as a tool, that is, as a mechanism to extend the self. This is the case with technologies like the computer, and even more closely held technologies of communication such as the mobile phone. In both cases, the technology is wielded, navigated, and directed by the human actor. Its affordances suggest certain types of use, but the technology itself does not have any agency.

Social robots and other AI-enabled technology do exhibit varying degrees of agency, insofar as they can act independently by sensing and responding to the surrounding environment (Sandry, 2015). It is this question of agency on which human–machine communication (HMC) pivots (Guzman, 2020; Guzman & Lewis, 2019; Spence, 2019; Sundar, 2020). PCTs may be imbued with meaning by their owners, but functionally they are still *channels* through which people communicate with others (Guzman & Lewis, 2019). In contrast, AI technology acts more as a communicative *partner* that can relate in more human-like ways with their human interactants (Guzman, 2018a; Guzman & Lewis, 2019).

This humanness manifests itself not only in the technology's agency but also at times in its features – digital voice assistants like Amazon's Alexa and Apple's Siri have human voices; the home robot Jibo incorporates head movements in its responses; commercial robots like Pepper and Nao have human-shaped bodies and faces. Further, the possibilities and perils of human-like robots have been probed extensively across works of literary fiction, movies and TV shows, and the popular press.

These characterizations influence the way we talk, think, and study these technologies as more than tools; that ontologically they represent life-type forms, which challenges our conceptions of humanity (Guzman, 2018b). Whenever a new technology emerges it is a marvel that may alter our behavior in its domain, but as Andrea Guzman points out:

> Volumes have not been written about how garage door openers will force us to rethink our humanity … What has historically situated AI as extraordinary, setting it apart from garage doors, social media, and other technologies is that AI seeks to recreate a part of us that we have conceived as being uniquely human – our minds. (Guzman 2018b, p. 85)

Despite this ostensibly looming existential crisis, when Guzman (2018b) explored how people conceived of AI digital voice assistants, she did not find "wringing of hands or zealous optimism regarding what these programs meant for them as individuals, let along humanity, now or in the future" (p. 83). Rather, she found people's approach to the technology similar to that of mobile phones: people were concerned about appearing lazy if they told an assistant to input an address for direction, or whether it would be rude to talk *to* their phone around others (Guzman, 2018b) – a "new" old controversy around

mobile phone etiquette, when people were concerned about talking *on* their phone around others. Put differently, Guzman's (2018b) interviewees remained focused on their immediate and real-world contexts and how the technology would interact with them and their surroundings: "Users were more interested in how a sassy Siri could make them the center of attention than in what a disembodied voice complete with personality meant for the future of the human race" (pp. 83–84).

Therefore we consider social robots, even with their agency, as more akin to the everyday technology that lubricates our lives like the mobile phone. As the HMC paradigm puts forth, though, agentic machines should be conceived of as partners rather than channels. In this conceptualization, we see two emergent dynamics: one related to the communication dyad of a human and machine, and the second related to a communication triad or more, wherein a machine is another interactive entity with and around human–human communication dyads.

Before we turn to our discussion of agentic machines, we first consider the mobile phone as a type of proto-HMC technology. Although the mobile phone most resembles a communication channel, it has taken on significant meaning and influence in people's lives. This importance has elevated it beyond a mere tool, to an object that holds symbolic importance in personal lives and relationships.

MOBILE PHONES AND PERPETUAL CONTACT: THE TENSION BETWEEN AUTONOMY AND CONNECTEDNESS

People can and do invest great meaning in their quotidian technology, which as a result has far-reaching consequences in one's life and relationships. This phenomenon was captured in the theory of "Apparageist" (Katz & Aakhus, 2002), which was originally conceptualized to explore the use and integration of the mobile phone in people's lives across cultural contexts.

The neologism means, literally, "machine-spirit," termed in this way to probe "how humans invest their technology with meaning and use devices and machines to pursue social and symbolic routines" (Katz, 2003, p. 15). In their first application of the theory of Apparatgeist, Katz and Aakhus (2002) developed the "socio-logic" of "perpetual contact" to describe the emergent influence of mobile phones. Namely, that the mobile phone's technological capabilities for anytime and anywhere reachability challenged the status quo in people's everyday communicative practices, that such challenges required new norms and expectations to evolve, and that these evolving practices would be continuously negotiated over time within contexts and communities. Indeed, a socio-logic is something that "develops socially through the interaction of communities over time" (Campbell & Russo, 2003, p. 331). Apparatgeist provides a framework for how communities' interactions with technology are informed by both everyday practices and the imaginarium – the intangible symbolism with which the technology is imbued.

This marriage of the quotidian and imaginative is particularly pertinent for HMC, which considers the interrelations of agentic technologies' functional, relational, and metaphysical aspects. Our communication technologies are developed to lubricate our lives and better facilitate our connections. In this process, though, the technology creates new norms and expectations from those to whom the technology connects us. The potential for perpetual contact was an emergent norm from the mobile phone that revealed an old tension in people's lives: that of autonomy versus connectedness.

Broadly speaking, perpetual contact highlighted how "the mobile phone was exposing deeper struggles about communication that would be generative of social, technical, and socio-technical practices" (Aakhus, 2021, pp. 9–10). As Aakhus (2021) emphasizes, the idea of perpetual contact was not that of a homogenizing force across the globe – they were not arguing that all groups, regardless of background and context, desired perpetual contact and would eventually normalize that communication mode through their mobile phone use. Such an argument reinforces an exclusively technologically deterministic stance that Apparatgeist was explicitly resisting. Rather, the theory recognizes that the influence of a technology's affordances will be tempered or amplified by the particular social context in which the technology is being used. The mobile phone unearthed social expectations "that were embedded in the technical" and revealed "social expectations [that] were not in keeping with what was now socially possible due to technical capabilities" (Aakhus, 2021, p. 9).

Importantly, the specific social norms and expectations that are exposed and challenged are not necessarily consistent across cultural contexts and communities, and the resultant negotiated solutions may look different depending on the groups. For example, the "reachability conundrum" the mobile phone's affordances created (e.g., being theoretically reachable anytime and anywhere) affects the Japanese differently than their American and Swedish counterparts; the

Japanese are both least enthusiastic about and bothered by their phones' ability to make them more reachable (Baron and Segerstad, 2010).

Similar types of group differences in mobile phone adoption and use have been explored over the years since *Perpetual Contact*. To offer a few examples, old Order Amish and Ultra-Orthodox Jewish women reject smartphones as "impure" by dint of their ability to distract from family and friends, undermining community, though they differed on their approaches to the "dumber" mobile phone (Shahar, 2020). For Saudi youth, the line drawn for mobile phone use is based on specific public and sacred locations, like the mosque or in class (Opoku, 2017). Younger people are more likely than older people to use their phones for constant contact, and also to be in contact through multiple modes (e.g., both voice calling and text messaging) (Axelsson, 2010). This distinction between younger and older people's use could speak to the greater susceptibility that young people have to peer pressure; it may not be the case that all young people necessarily desire more intense contact, but that they feel more compelled to follow the usage norms set by their peers (Mascheroni & Vincent, 2016).

The above research demonstrates a fundamental and consistent dynamic in perpetual contact, which is the tension between autonomy and social connectedness. When the mobile phone came out, it did not arrive with a corresponding rule book that laid out the terms of "anytime, anywhere" communication. No one expects to have literal perpetual contact that is theoretically possible with the phone: though the mobile phone as a piece of hardware enables, it does not compel, perpetual contact. Indeed, its features also allow disconnection: the phone can be turned off, calls can go to voicemail, texts can remain unread and unanswered. More insidious and difficult to navigate are the social expectations and norms that arise from the capability, and thus possibility, of perpetual contact. In this sense, turning off one's phone is infinitely more complicated because it involves not just pressing the power button but considering the relational implications in severing one's reachability. These may include a loved one's anxiety over not being able to make contact, the possibility of missing important social information, and balancing one's need for space with another's need for connection.

Tied up in these considerations are fundamental needs for identity, individuation, security, and connection. As a result, relational maintenance through mobile phone use creates contradictory outcomes for close relationships: Hall and Baym (2012) found that maintenance expectations resulted in dependence and satisfaction, but also led to overdependence and dissatisfaction. These conflicting dynamics speak to the sense of closeness with more contact – expectations would not exist without a baseline intimacy – but also to the feelings of guilt and entrapment that can accompany such expectations (Hall & Baym, 2012). Intimacy and mutual expectations are critical lubricants for close relationships, but they also carry with them obligations to consider others' needs (Mascheroni & Vincent, 2016).

We illustrate these tensions with an example of parent–child communication, which theoretically could be nearly constant through the mobile phone. In fact, the mobile phone has been a source of connection and control for parents over their children (Fortunati, 2001; Ling, 2007; Ribak, 2009), with the phone serving as "a type of umbilical cord between parent and child" (Ling, 2007, p. 100). As the child grows up and leaves the home, most might consider such contact excessive and stymying, but there are also no universal rules as to what moments and how much time is appropriate. What ensues, therefore, is a delicate negotiation of parent–child love and obligation. A parent may desire to have a near-permanent connection but also want their child to grow in independence and autonomy, so they make themselves available – and not constantly present – to jump in with support, advice, and comfort when needed. The child may strategically contact their parent in order to ensure non-contact at other times. For example, a college student may speak with their parents on a Friday afternoon in order to discharge their obligation and be able to focus on their friends for the weekend. In this way, the child is managing perpetual contact expectations. At the same time, other children even while in college stay in exceedingly frequent contact with their parents, even to the point of consulting with them before meals to obtain their gastronomic suggestions (Chen & Katz, 2009).

In short, people's social interactions are freighted with the capability of being in touch 24/7. The outcomes of such tensions are context-sensitive, dependent on cultural influences, relationship type and duration, and individual differences and goals. For example, there is a great deal of variation in the ways that romantic partners negotiate phone usage during their time together; the "rules" that couples develop are dependent on the relationship length and type, context, and how important the virtual interrupter is (Büchenbacher & Chang, 2018; Duran, Kelly, & Rotaru, 2011; Duran, Miller-Ott, & Kelly, 2015). Couples that are more established experience less friction around phone usage because they are more habituated to one another's behavior, thus reducing the

uncertainty that otherwise generates anxiety and hurt feelings (Duran et al., 2015).

In part, the friction around personal communication technology (PCT) use in romantic relationships demonstrates the purpose for Apparatgeist that Katz and Aakhus envisioned, namely as "a novel way of thinking about how humans invest their technology with meaning and use devices and machines to pursue social and symbolic routines" (Katz, 2003, p. 15). Diverting attention to one's phone during a date is not merely a momentary interruption; it implicates the care and priority (or lack thereof) for one's partner. Unless, of course, there is an understanding between a couple that allows for interruptions (Duran et al., 2015).

Even with established protocols for PCT use in relationships, we must also consider each individual's personal growth and change over time, which could necessitate an alteration of the terms. As Aakhus (2021) reminds us, in our communication "we may desire deep intersubjective connection but not at the expense of ourselves" (p. 11). Thus, there is a negotiation between the self and others in our lives to balance personal needs to autonomy and connection, also against the backdrop of daily life which itself is not static. Juliet Floyd observes how our notions of:

> the ordinary … constantly evolves from day to day, pressured, biologically and ethologically, by human beings' constant embedding and re-embeddings of words in "forms of life," which now include machine-apparatus increasingly. In a world in which PCTs are widely distributed and used, the importance of "the ordinary" is altered, yet amplified. The "everyday" is …. a delicately woven equilibrium of familiarity and rupture of familiarity, something we inhabit, explore, confront, escape, and constantly shift our relationship to. (Floyd, 2021, p. 22)

In her description, Floyd depicts continual movement in our negotiation of what Goffman (1967) termed "interaction rules," made more complex by our mobile phones, other PCTs, and soon, we imagine, personal social machines.

This complexity arises from not the fact of the technology but the fundamental human needs that the technology highlights and challenges. The mobile phone "had drawn into relief, and challenged, the habits and etiquette that grease the wheels of everyday interaction in accommodating the competing demands for autonomy and connectedness in communication" (Aakhus, 2021, p. 9). In this dynamic communication process, the goals are not just to project and process information, but also to maintain relationships, express oneself, and manage one's life. Given this complexity it is no wonder that myriad concepts arose to describe phenomena stemming from perpetual contact, such as phubbing (ignoring one's partner for one's phone) (Roberts & David, 2016), FOMO ("fear of missing out" on social activities) (Schreckinger, 2014), "absent presence" (attending to one's virtual, mediated world at the expense of their surrounding physical world) (Gergen, 2002), and "connected presence" (Licoppe, 2003), "continuous partial presence" (Ebner & Schiefner, 2008) and "ambient intimacy" (Thompson, 2008) – all related to retaining interpersonal closeness through asynchronous and social media communication.

As such, the rise of PCTs fundamentally shifted the paradigm of communication models, from an information-conveyance process with source and receiver to a more dynamic and complex sociotechnical process (Floyd, 2021; Sandry, 2015). This dynamic process is also increasingly prevalent with algorithmic technologies like bots, which take in information and learn from ongoing, everyday behaviors and adapt accordingly. Rather than look to people's evolving norms with one another around technology, bots reflect back to us our behavior in their evolution. An extreme example is Microsoft's bot Tay on Twitter, which Neff and Nagy (2016) analyzed at length. In this case, it only took a few hours for Tay to reveal Twitter's racist and sexist underbelly (Neff & Nagy, 2016). People framed Tay either as the victim of humanity's dark side or as a dangerous, runaway threat to humanity that must be controlled somehow – a discrepancy that Neff and Nagy (2016) attribute in part to the differences in people's conceptions of Tay's algorithm and artificial intelligence.

Importantly, what Neff and Nagy (2016) hit upon in their analysis is the flexible nature of agency attributions, to Tay, to her human creators at Microsoft, and to the human users who interacted with her on Twitter. Agency is not simply a technological capability; rather, it is a negotiated understanding of the machine's context and interactions "through the lens of human experience" (Neff & Nagy, 2016, p. 4926). In other words, algorithmic technology's autonomy is tempered by its connections to the human world in which it operates.

Now we turn to an emergent technology, social robots, to consider possible dimensions of their use that might intersect with and challenge human interpretation. Part of this discussion is how people may collaborate with robots to create effective human-robot interactions in their lives. The other aspect is how human–robot collaboration may also intersect with the rest of our lives and the people in them. The remainder of this chapter explores the possibilities.

DYADIC HMC: HUMAN–MACHINE COLLABORATION

There is an artist, Sougwen Chung, whose *Drawing Operations (Duet)* project explores the collaboration between human and machine. She developed an AI-enabled drawing robot that she termed "drawing operations unit generation (1 & 2)" – DOUG_1, _2, – for short. In her first artistic foray with DOUG_1, titled "Mimicry," Chen trained the robot on videos of her own hand drawing so that DOUG_1 could replicate the "pace, shape, and style" of her movements (Chang, 2019). In real-time, Chung draws with DOUG_1, the machine seeing her gestures through an overhead camera, then mimicking her movements and replicating her drawing. "Generation 2" of the project, titled "Memory" and "Agency," moves beyond replication to probe AI's creative capabilities. In this stage, DOUG_2 is activated by a neural network trained on a database of Chung's hand gestures while drawing. By this process, DOUG_2 is able to select from a pool of drawing movements and generate new drawing behaviors. When Chung draws alongside DOUG_2 in these performances, she must improvise her own style in order to incorporate DOUG_2's new and unexpected movements. She has described these experiences with the more agentic robot arm as a "creative catalyst" (Chung, 2019) for her own drawing style.

Many extensive arguments have been made in the last several years over whether AI and robots can be creative. The recent sale of an AI-generated portrait highlighted this debate, as the team of French students who created the art replaced the artist's signature in the painting's corner with the mathematical equation representing the algorithm used to create the piece (Chang, 2019). Some were quick to point out that though the final product was not painted by a human's hand, the image was generated by learning from a database of thousands of human-generated portraits (Chang, 2019). Chung's goal for *Drawing Operations* is not to engage the question of human vs. machine – whether machines can (or should) replace humans – in creative pursuits. Rather, she explores the tension in the space *between* human and machine. As she has described it, the DOUG iterations "recontextualize" the image of robotic arms, which have long represented industrialization, the displacement of humans by machine, and instead represent the ways in which robots can be collaborative and co-creative agents (Chung, 2019). In engaging with the machine as co-creative agent, she finds herself exploring her own agency in her artwork: by confronting the question of the machine's agency, she questions her agency in terms of what actually motivates her decisions and behaviors.

In her "Duet" with DOUG, too, Chung aims to bring others (e.g., audience members) into her process. Co-creating with DOUG in these exercises produces not only works of art but also highlights these questions of human and machine agency for the audience to engage with. In this way, Chung's performances seem to marry the quotidian with the imaginarium. *Drawing Operations* would hardly be a performance if it were simply her and her "stick of graphite" drawing live; what makes the exercise performative is the transformation of an entirely commonplace art technique by the infusion of machine, probing the bounds of machine's capabilities and evoking notions of two-way communication with machines.

Sandry (2018) argues that productive human-robot collaboration will rely on a recognition of the robot's "liveliness" and agency, in the way that Chung incorporates DOUG into her creative process. People should leverage the robot's "nonhuman advantages … rather than [seek] to control it as a tool" (Sandry, 2018, p. 53). Considerations of control must necessarily come part and parcel with a robot's agency. Indeed, Sandry (2018) points to Brenna Argall's work, which explores customizable robot autonomy by the human end-user in human-robot teams, termed "sliding autonomy" or a "continuum of shared control paradigms" (Argall, 2015). Interestingly, in one study, Gopinath, Jain, and Argall (2016) found that, in a task with a robotic arm, not all subjects utilized the arm for optimal assistance, instead preferring to retain more control during task execution at the expense of task performance. This finding suggests that considerations beyond optimal performance are critical to people's experience with agentic robots; that they are, indeed, not merely tools – it is hard to imagine someone would purposefully choose a suboptimal setting on their drill – but also not quite equal partners.

Thus, questions of control are central to autonomous machines and serve as points of similarity with mobile phones. Like autonomy, perpetual contact is not a binary, either/or proposition. The variable nature of perpetual contact is what gave rise to tensions and negotiations around mobile phone use: individual choices around increasing or decreasing contact could take on symbolic import about one's priorities. From another angle, these conflicts could be viewed as power struggles over one another's behaviors and the factors that should influence them. The "fundamental characteristic" of mobility (Campbell, 2013, p. 10) opened up new access points and avenues for social conflict. In that vein, we imagine that a social robot's autonomy may introduce new

social considerations and ramifications by dint of its capacity for collaboration. Importantly, too, a social robot is not a personal, small device that one can cradle in the palm of their hand and shield from those around them. Depending on the type, a social robot can move or speak, and so it necessarily is a larger presence within human–human interaction, not just symbolically as in the mobile phone but also physically.

TRIADIC HMC AND BEYOND: CONDUCTING HUMAN–MACHINE INTERACTIONS ALONGSIDE HUMAN–HUMAN INTERACTION

Chung speaks to the incorporation of a third party into her DOUG collaboration via the audience members, but for the most part they are passive onlookers; they do not interfere with the Chung–DOUG interaction. Another aspect to consider within HMC is when the human–machine dyad exists in the "real world" where, likely, there are other human interactants. To that end, Höflich (2013) has suggested a pivot from dyadic conceptualizations of human–robot interactions to a triadic model, in order to account for human–human interactions that may also be implicated in the human–robot dynamic. Gunkel (2018) has termed this kind of shift as a "relational turn" in how we think about human–machine interactions. This shift in thinking moves away from a functionalist stance that focuses on "the capabilities or operations of the two interacting components" (p. 3) and centers instead on the relationship between the human and machine.

The "relational turn" and triadic HMC models expands the scope of inquiry beyond how humans may "use" robots and accounts also for how such use occurs in broader social contexts. Part of this situational awareness includes nuanced conceptualizations of the robot's agency, which "could be thought of not as universal, generalizable, and autonomous, but as particular, contextual, and dialogic" (Neff and Nagy, 2016, p. 4925). Like with perpetual contact, we can imagine gradations of agency and control that are context- and task-dependent.

Eleanor Sandry provides a wonderful example in the case of caregiving robots, which she imagines being deployed in a "caregiving triangle" that consists of a (human) caregiver, the care receiver, and the robot (Sandry, 2019, p. 320). In this formulation, the robot takes on the physically laborious tasks of caregiving, while the human caregiver focuses their efforts on the socio-emotional support. In this way, the otherwise-dependent care receiver experiences a "relational autonomy" that is enabled by the robot's physical help. Such a human–robot–human care relationship optimizes the robot's capabilities and mitigates the potential degradation of the human–human relationship from the burden of the care receiver's physical dependence on the caregiver.

Of course, this kind of harmonious care triangle rests largely on the human participants' attitudes towards the delegation of roles. Nagy and Neff's (2015) concept of "imagined affordances" is critical here. We know that there is a range in people's anthropomorphic tendencies (Donath, 2019; Waytz, Cacioppo, & Epley, 2010), which is related to their social and emotional reactions to robots (Darling, 2017). It follows that people will also vary in their perceptions, attitudes, and expectations of social robots. So, regardless of the robot's actual affordances that enable physical caretaking, if the care receiver has different attitudes about being taken care of by a robot and different expectations about what caregiving entails, then the triangulation may break down. Rather than primarily a caregiver, the robot in this scenario is a "robot as Rorschach" (Turkle, Taggart, Kidd, & Dasté, 2006), serving as a point of reflection about the care receiver's relationship with the human caregiver. As Turkle and colleagues (2006) have suggested, social robots can serve as "relational artifacts" that prompt reflections on human uniqueness and relationships. Therefore, discrepancies in each individual's imagined affordances of a robot and any disagreements that follow may more meaningfully reveal dynamics within the human–human relationships situated around the human–robot interactions.

In her goals for social robots, Cynthia Breazeal wants them to be personalized and adaptive devices that can sustain socio-emotional engagement with their humans and serve "in the spirit of a technological 'Jiminy Cricket' that provides the right message at the right time, in the right way to gently nudge its user to make smarter decisions" (Breazeal, 2011, in Donath, 2019, p. 17). Some of the robots' "nudges" one could imagine is suggestions to exercise, take daily medicine, eat healthier, stop working, call a family member, and so on (Donath, 2019). These are also suggestions that, in the context of an intimate partnership and depending on moods, might be termed "loving reminders" or "nags." With a domestic robot to provide these reminders, would the burden of this routine care be offloaded entirely? Would a partner's reminder be amplified by the robot's? What happens if the partner is ignored but the robot's reminder is adhered to? Relationship scorekeeping over who does more chores, for example, is generally discouraged; and in a way, prioritizing

a robot's advice may not be very dissimilar from disagreement about listening to one's parent or sibling over one's spouse. The root of the conflict, regardless of the human or machine nature of the interactants, is the perceived (lack of) respect for the partner's opinion.

Of course, blaming a robot is easier than blaming a mother-in-law. A challenge with emergent technology is the ways in which its extraordinariness may obfuscate the underlying human issues. It is easier to pillory the new technology than grapple with the objectionable behavior that the technology revealed.

CONCLUSION

When a couple argues about what temperature to set the thermostat to, it is, yes, about physical comfort, but the tenor of the disagreement may be amplified by the underlying implications of priority and care: why can't you just put on a sweater; why do you care more about the bottom line than my comfort? This tension reverberates in couples' disagreements over mobile phone use on dates: why is the person on the other end of that text more important than I am; why can't I spend a mere 30 seconds responding to a text? We can imagine similar disagreements around a domestic social robot that on the surface touch on logistics and etiquette – when does the robot get turned off, how should the robot be addressed – but bely more intimate, interpersonal dynamics.

While a social robot is a distinctively different type of technology from a thermostat, we discuss them together to bolster Guzman's (2018b) notion of "extraordinarily ordinary" technology. Our treatment of AI as an extraordinary technology, she argues, makes it "magically exempt from the normal process through which we make sense of our world" (p. 94). But when she studied AI voice assistants in the context of her participants' lived experiences, a "different picture of AI" emerged. The extraordinary notions of AI and robots make them exciting technologies to cover, generative of compelling narratives about ourselves and our humanity. Moral panics grab our attention: the television is destroying community; video games are inciting violent rampages; mobile phones are ruining dinners out and killing intimacy. Such dire consequences therefore merit research grant funding, art residencies, and headlines. No one buys a newspaper to read stories about the status quo and that life is fine. This pull of the imaginarium may be subtly directing researchers' and artists' attention towards the extraordinary and existential.

In reality, the status quo is always shifting, and such is the case for our development of and adaptation to emergent technology. We agree with Guzman (2018b) that, rather than an "ontological upheaval," the integration of social robots in our lives will occur while "our own sense of self remains rooted in our interactions and with the world around us" (p. 94). Apparatgeist provides a useful framework for thinking about how our marvelous, extraordinary technology, when wielded by ordinary humans, becomes part of our everyday lives, swept up in the messiness and demands of human needs.

REFERENCES

Aakhus, M. (2021). Media are dead, long live media: Apparatgeist's capacity for understanding media evolution. In J. E. Katz, K. Schiepers & J. Floyd (Eds.), *Perceiving the future through new communication technologies* (pp. 7–16). New York: Palgrave Macmillan.

Argall, B. D. (2015, February). Turning assistive machines into assistive robots. In *Quantum sensing and nanophotonic devices XII* (Vol. 9370, p. 93701Y). International Society for Optics and Photonics.

Axelsson, A. S. (2010). Perpetual and personal: Swedish young adults and their use of mobile phones. *New Media & Society, 12*(1), 35–54.

Baron, N. S., & Segerstad, Y. H. (2010). Cross-cultural patterns in mobile-phone use: Public space and reachability in Sweden, the USA and Japan. *New Media & Society, 12*(1), 13–34.

Büchenbacher, K., & Chang, C. W. (2018). Mobile love in China: The cultural meaning and social implications of mobile communications in romantic relationships among young Chinese adults. *Advances in Journalism and Communication, 6*(2), 38–54.

Campbell, S. W. (2013). Mobile media and communication: A new field, or just a new journal? *Mobile Media & Communication, 1*(1), 8–13.

Campbell, S. W., & Russo, T. C. (2003). The social construction of mobile telephony: An application of the social influence model to perceptions and uses of mobile phones within personal communication networks. *Communication Monographs, 70*(4), 317–334.

Chang, V. (2019, October 5). Ghost hands, player pianos, and the hidden history of AI. *Los Angeles Review of Books*. Retrieved from https://lareviewofbooks.org/article/ghost-hands-player-pianos-and-the-hidden-history-of-ai/

Chen, Y-F., & Katz, J. E. (2009). Extending family to school life: College students' use of the mobile phone. *International Journal of Human-Computer Studies, 67* (2), 179–191.

Chung, S. (n.d.). Drawing operations duet. Retrieved from https://sougwen.com/exhibitions.

Chung, S. (2019). Making art with artificial intelligence: Artists in conversation. Google I/O'19. Retrieved from www.youtube.com/watch?v=21BbGGGrq9s.

Chung, S. (2019, September). Why i draw with robots. TED@BCG Mumbai. Ted.com. Retrieved from www.ted.com/talks/sougwen_chung_why_i_draw_with_robots?language=en.

Darling, K. (2017). "Who's Johnny?" Anthropomorphic framing in human-robot interaction, integration, and policy. In P. Lin, K. Abney, & R. Jenkins (Eds.), *Robot ethics 2.0: From autonomous cars to artificial intelligence* (pp. 173–191). New York: Oxford University Press

Donath, J. (2019). The robot dog fetches for whom? In Z. Papacharissi (Ed.), *A networked self and human augmentics, artificial intelligence, sentience* (pp. 10–24). London: Routledge.

Duran, R. L., Kelly, L., & Rotaru, T. (2011). Mobile phones in romantic relationships and the dialectic of autonomy versus connection. *Communication Quarterly, 59*, 19–36.

Duran, R. L., Miller-Ott, A. E., & Kelly, L. (2015). The role of mobile phones in romantic relationships. In Z. Yan (Ed.), *Encyclopedia of mobile phone behavior* (pp. 322–337). Hershey, PA: IGI Global.

Ebner, M., & Schiefner, M. (2008, January). Micro-blogging-more than fun. In *Proceedings of IADIS mobile learning conference* (Vol. 2008, p. 155Y159).

Floyd, J. (2021). Selves and forms of life in the digital age: A philosophical exploration of Apparatgeist. In J. E. Katz, K. Schiepers, & J. Floyd (Eds.), *Perceiving the future through new communication technologies* (pp. 17–41). New York: Palgrave Macmillan.

Fortunati, L. (2001). The mobile phone: An identity on the move. *Personal and Ubiquitous Computing, 5*(2), 85–98.

Gergen, K. J. (2002). The challenge of Absent Presence. In J. E. Katz & M. A. Aakhus (Eds.), *Perpetual contact: Mobile communication, private talk, public performance* (pp. 227–241). Cambridge, UK; New York: Cambridge University Press.

Goffman, E. 1967. *Interaction ritual: Essays on face-to-face interaction*. New York: Pantheon Book, Random House.

Gopinath, D., Jain, S., & Argall, B. D. (2016). Human-in-the-loop optimization of shared autonomy in assistive robotics. *IEEE Robotics and Automation Letters, 2*(1), 247–254.

Gunkel, D. J. (2018). The relational turn: Third wave HCI and phenomenology. In M. Filimowicz and V. Tzankova (Eds.), *New directions in third wave* human-computer interaction: Volume 1 – Technologies (pp. 11–24). Springer, Cham.

Guzman, A. (2018a). What is human-machine communication, anyway? In A. Guzman (Ed.), Human-machine communication: Rethinking communication, technology, and ourselves (pp. 1–29). New York: Peter Lang.

Guzman, A. (2018b). Beyond extraordinary: Theorizing artificial intelligence and the self in daily life. In Z. Papacharissi (Ed.). A networked self and human augmentics, artificial intelligence, sentience. New York, NY: Routledge.

Guzman, A. (2020). Ontological boundaries between humans and computers and the implications for human-machine communication. Human-Machine Communication, 1(1), 3.

Guzman, A., & Lewis, S. C. (2019). Artificial intelligence and communication: A human-machine communication research agenda. New Media & Society, 22(1), pp. 70–86.

Hall, J. A., & Baym, N. K. (2012). Calling and texting (too much): Mobile maintenance expectations, (over) dependence, entrapment, and friendship satisfaction. New Media & Society, 14(2), 316–331.

Höflich, J. R. (2013). Relationships to social robots: Towards a triadic analysis of media-oriented behavior. Intervalla, 1(1), 35–48.

Katz, J. E. (2003). Do machines become us? In J. Katz (Ed.), Machines that become us: The social context of personal communication technology (pp. 15–25), New Brunswick, NJ: Transaction Publishers.

Katz, J. E., & Aakhus, M. (Eds.). (2002). Perpetual contact: Mobile communication, private talk, public performance. Cambridge, UK; New York: Cambridge University Press.

Licoppe, C. (2003). Two modes of maintaining interpersonal relations through telephone: From the domestic to the mobile phone. In J. Katz (Ed.), Machines that become us: The social context of communication technology (pp. 171–186), New Brunswick, NJ: Transaction Publishers.

Ling, R. (2007). Children, youth, and mobile communication. Journal of Children and Media, 1(1), 60–67.

Mascheroni, G., & Vincent, J. (2016). Perpetual contact as a communicative affordance: Opportunities, constraints, and emotions. Mobile Media & Communication, 4(3), 310–326.

Nagy, P., & Neff, G. (2015). Imagined affordance: Reconstructing a keyword for communication theory. Social Media + Society, 1(2), 2056305115603385.

Nass, C., & Moon, Y. (2000). Machines and mindlessness: Social responses to computers. Journal of Social Issues, 56(1), 81–103.

Neff, G., & Nagy, P. (2016). Automation, algorithms, and politics| talking to Bots: Symbiotic agency and the case of Tay. International Journal of Communication, 10, 4915–4931.

Opoku, R. A. (2017). Attitudes towards mobile phone usage in public places among young Saudi adults. International Journal of Mobile Communications, 15(3), 235–251.

Reeves, B., & Nass, C. (1996). The media equation: How people treat computers, television, and new media like real people. Cambridge, UK: Cambridge University Press.

Ribak, R. (2009). Remote control, umbilical cord and beyond: The mobile phone as a transitional object. British Journal of Developmental Psychology, 27(1), 183–196.

Roberts, J. A., & David, M. E. (2016). My life has become a major distraction from my cell phone: Partner phubbing and relationship satisfaction among romantic partners. Computers in Human Behavior, 54, 134–141.

Sandry, E. (2015). Robots and communication. New York: Palgrave Macmillan.

Sandry, E. (2018). Aliveness and the off-switch in human-robot relations. In A. Guzman (Ed.), Human-machine communication: Rethinking communication, technology, and ourselves. (pp. 51–66). New York: Peter Lang.

Sandry, E. (2019). Interdependence in collaboration with robots. In The Routledge Companion to Disability and Media (pp. 316–326). Routledge.

Schreckinger, B. (2014, July 29). "The home of FOMO," Boston Magazine. Retrieved from www.bostonmagazine.com/news/2014/07/29/fomo-history/.

Shahar, R. N. B. (2020). "Mobile internet is worse than the internet; it can destroy our community": Old Order Amish and Ultra-Orthodox Jewish women's responses to cellphone and smartphone use. The Information Society, 36(1), 1–18.

Spence, P. R. (2019). Searching for questions, original thoughts, or advancing theory: Human-machine communication. Computers in Human Behavior, 90, 285–287.

Sundar, S. S. (2020). Rise of machine agency: A framework for studying the psychology of human–AI interaction (HAII). Journal of Computer-Mediated Communication, 25(1), 74–88.

Thompson, C. (2008, September 5). Brave new world of digital intimacy. The New York Times. Retrieved from www.nytimes.com/2008/09/07/magazine/07awareness-t.html.

Turkle, S., Taggart, W., Kidd, C. D., & Dasté, O. (2006). Relational artifacts with children and elders: The complexities of cybercompanionship. Connection Science, 18(4), 347–361.

Vincent, J. (2015). The mobile phone: An emotionalized social robot. In J. Vincent, S. Taipale, B. Sapio, G. Lugano, & L. Fortunati (Eds.), Social robots from a human perspective. (pp. 105–115). Cham, Switzerland: Springer International.

Waytz, A., Cacioppo, J., & Epley, N. (2010). Who sees human? The stability and importance of individual differences in anthropomorphism. Perspectives on Psychological Science, 5(3), 219–232.

2

The Interdisciplinarity of HMC: Rethinking Communication, Media, and Agency

Andreas Hepp and Wiebke Loosen

INTRODUCTION

In just a few years, human–machine–communication (HMC) has become an important area of scholarly study in media and communication studies. The novelty of this area is underlined by the fact that various "sensitizing concepts" have been established in a relatively short time, which "suggest directions along which to look" and gives "the user a general sense of reference and guidance in approaching empirical instances" (Blumer, 1954, p. 7). While concepts such as "communicative AI" (Guzman & Lewis, 2020, p. 1) want to draw attention to the fact that artificial intelligence underlies many of HMC's most prevalent technologies, other concepts such as "communicative robots" (Hepp, 2020a, p. 1410) emphasize automation as a unifying element among systems as diverse as artificial companions, social bots, or workbots operating in the field of robot journalism. At the same time, both terms have in common that they foreground communication – and this is also what the C in HMC stands for. However, communication means more than just the interaction between a human being and a machine: It is also about the question of how broader communication dynamics – including intricate forms of societal communication such as public discourse – change when machines become

more intimately involved. It is striking that both concepts, "communicative AI" and "communicative robots," emphasize the actor and agency, and the role they play as participants in communication processes. Both of these "sensitizing concepts" come together in that they draw attention to the fact that with current developments in HMC the fundamental concepts of media and communication studies – communication, media, and agency – are challenged. These theoretical challenges also have considerable consequences for the methods of empirical research applied to HMC.

This all brings us back to the fundamental question of how best to approach HMC and there are many arguments for addressing HMC interdisciplinarily. Interdisciplinarity can be summarized as "a variety of different ways of bridging and confronting the prevailing disciplinary approaches" (Huutoniemi, Klein, Bruun, & Hukkinen, 2010, p. 80). Following Foucault, "disciplines characterize, classify, specialize; they distribute along a scale, around a norm, hierarchize individuals in relation to one another and, if necessary, disqualify and invalidate" (Foucault, 1991, p. 223). This general understanding of discipline can also be applied to scientific disciplines which, through a canon of theory and a set of accepted methods shared by their adherents, direct attention to certain phenomena in a particular way.

Approached in this way, the field of HMC is doubly interdisciplinary:

- On an *analytical level*, the established disciplinary view of media and communication studies hinders access to HMC phenomena. For media and communication studies an understanding of communication as a necessarily human action and of media as shaping or molding – but *not acting* – has traditionally dominated, skewing its empirical methods along this semi-dogma. In that moment when a machine communicates (Esposito, 2017, p. 256), this theoretical and methodological position is fundamentally challenged. It becomes necessary, therefore, to broaden the "disciplinary view" in order to adequately account for HMC.
- On a *descriptive level*, HMC as an empirical phenomenon is itself the "child" of interdisciplinarity. Many of the technical systems integral to automated communication (in the field of journalism, for example) have emerged from funding and research programs that have made "interdisciplinary teams" a guiding maxim (Loosen, Nölleke, & Springer, 2022). Social science and psychological research on human communication has been approached by computer science to develop systems of automated communication (see, Natale, 2019), the use and appropriation of which is now being researched by social scientists and psychologists who, in turn, find that their previous theories and methods are challenged by precisely these technical artifacts. We cannot approach HMC without being open to such "interdisciplinary connections."
- We can understand the interdisciplinary character of HMC as a rearticulation of the discussion about media and communication studies' historic interdisciplinarity. Since its emergence, there has been a broad discussion about whether media and communications is a scientific discipline or, rather, a field (see Craig, 2012; McQuail & Deuze, 2020, pp. 5–24). Irrespective of which position you take, both come together in terms of the value they ascribe to interdisciplinarity: media and communication concern numerous and varied societal domains, so it is important to integrate knowledge from fields as diverse as such as political science, law, sociology, education, and psychology into media and communication research.

With the emergence of digital media and their infrastructures – of which communicative AI and communicative robots can be considered

highly contemporaneous – the associated "mediation of everything" (Livingstone, 2009, p. 1) and the "deep mediatization" of society (Hepp, 2020b, p. 5), interdisciplinarity's importance is amplified. Accordingly, it has been argued that to speak of media and communication studies is to operate "post-discipline" (Waisbord, 2019, p. 123f): consisting of facets from numerous "areas of specialization [...] held together by an institutional architecture of professional organizations, academic units and journals." From this point of view, media and communication studies was ahead of its time precisely by virtue of its interdisciplinarity. As a "proto post-discipline" (Waisbord, 2019, p. 131) it has been forced to overcome the barriers of narrow disciplinary thinking due to the seemingly prosaic subject matter of mediated communication which, when looked at with any scrutiny, could only be grasped in an interdisciplinary way as it constantly transformed historically, technologically, and culturally, leading to an ever-expanding bundle of disciplinary connections. Accordingly, HMC's interdisciplinarity is the preliminary culmination of a long historical development that reflects both the fluid and manifest character of media and communication as "material" that is constitutive for socialization and the "processing" of societies.

If we take up once more the general discussion on interdisciplinarity (Huutoniemi et al., 2010; Klein, 2017) and relate it to HMC, the result is a six-field matrix along which we can identify key challenges (see Table 2.1).

When it comes to the *scope of interdisciplinarity*, both narrow and broad relations are important for HMC: Narrow relations are mainly those that connect to other social sciences and the humanities for their expertise in the various social domains in which communicative AI and communicative robots are applied. At this point, an emphasis is placed on the *human* aspects of HMC. Broad relations generally refer to computer science and engineering, where the technical nature of corresponding systems is at stake and contextual weight is applied to the *machine-related* aspects of HMC. However, another challenge emerges; that is to find an appropriate descriptive language that can connect diverse disciplines. Remarkably, the first reflections on human–machine–communication relate to the establishment of cybernetics, which Norbert Wiener (1948) understood as an appropriate approach to bridge different academic fields.

We deal with different *types of interdisciplinarity* when we consider HMC. The fact that, on an empirical level, HMC itself is a child of

Table 2.1 The interdisciplinary character of HMC

Scope of interdisciplinarity	A) Narrow relations: Other social sciences and humanities
	B) Broad relations: Computer science and engineering
Type of interdisciplinarity	A) Empirical: Interdisciplinarity of the phenomenon
	B) Methodological: Mix of disciplinary methods
	C) Theoretical: Integration of different disciplinary theories
Goal of interdisciplinarity	A) Epistemological orientation: Description and understanding
	B) Instrumental orientation: (Social) design and regulation

Source: The above classification is based on Huutoniemi et al., 2010 and was contextualized in relation to HMC by the authors.

interdisciplinarity has already been mentioned above. Research into HMC often requires a variety of methods from a variety of disciplines. This is obvious when taking up the so-called computational social sciences and research into communicative robots. For example, particular dynamics of social bots within online discourse can only be investigated through computational methods (Lazer et al., 2018), while a particular challenge is to fuse these methods with other social scientific approaches to gain a deeper understanding of the related processes of sense-making. Theoretically, HMC renders necessary the overcoming of disciplinary boundaries in conceptualization. This is apparent in the ways it challenges existing conceptualizations in the field of media and communication studies. Again, however, we are confronted with the challenge of developing appropriate, operational, and effective bridging concepts.

Among HMC's *interdisciplinary goals* we find both epistemological and instrumental challenges. Epistemological is used here in that interdisciplinarity aims at better describing and understanding the processes and dynamics at the heart of HMC. Empirical research and theory development around HMC are characterized by this objective. Given its social relevance, instrumental aspects of interdisciplinarity emerge, for example, when the interdisciplinarily generated knowledge is to be used to better regulate communicative AI and communicative robots, or when the aim is to develop systems with a design that addresses everyday social needs.

If one wants to approach the development of and current discussions around HMC's interdisciplinarity, it is helpful to do so along the basic concepts of media and communication studies that it challenges: communication, media, and agency. Although empirical research and theoretical discussion continues with respect to all three, and how they might be rethought with respect to HMC, it is apparent that this reformulation needs to go beyond disciplinary thinking.

COMMUNICATION

Communication is one of the most fundamental concepts of the social sciences in general and in media and communication studies in particular. How to theorize communication in a meaningful way persists at its core. As John Durham Peters (2008, p. 5) puts it, the "history of the idea of communication reveals diverse semantic strands." It is not enough to speak of *one* concept of communication (Craig, 1999, 2012), especially if one also considers non-Western theoretical traditions (Kim, 2002).

Despite this limitation, it can be said that since the 1980s a basic understanding of communication that focuses on *human* interaction has been established in media and communication studies. At its heart, this understanding is anchored in both symbolic interactionism and pragmatism. In both traditions, communication is theorized as the mutually interrelated action of humans (i.e. Dewey, 1927; Mead, 1967 [orig. 1934]).[1] In media and communication studies, it was, and still is, widely common to assume that communication is an intentional action. Early criticisms of this idea have been made, especially within cybernetics, which argued that communication could also refer to people, animals, and machines (Wiener, 1948). These kinds of theories have staked a claim in the field of media and communication studies, in particular, through different variants of systemic thinking, epitomized by the "Palo Alto Group" (Watzlawick, Beavin, & Jackson, 1967). Furthermore, a critique of communication as *intentional* mutual interaction was advanced in areas of practice theory (Couldry, 2004; Pentzold, 2015). However, despite these criticisms it is evident that media and communication studies is dominated by an understanding of communication as a fundamental *human* characteristic. In this sense, communication theory is defined as an approach that "addresses the media, modalities, and messages by which humans exchange, reflect on, and enact different perspectives of reality" (Jensen, 2008, p. 1).

More recent research into "mass communication" does not break with this way of thinking either: this, too, was and is thought of as human action in which the mass media are positioned between "producers" and "audiences" (i.e. Denzin, 2014; Thompson, 1995). The analysis of mass communication as "para-social interaction" (Horton & Wohl, 1956, p. 215) exemplifies the extent to which the implicit model of this form of communication is governed by human action. Correspondingly, "mediated interaction" forms the core of thinking in media and communication studies – even in the "digital age" (Thompson, 2020, p. 3).

This line of disciplinary thought falls short of the conceptual questions at stake in HMC: What does the moment in which the "machine" begins to "communicate" (Esposito, 2017, p. 250) and "to abandon modern society's idea that only human beings qualify for communication and to extend this peculiar activity to computers" (Baecker, 2011, p. 17) mean for our understanding of communication? How does the "robotic moment" (Turkle, 2015, p. 340) materialize in relation to our understanding of communication? At least three positions are plausible in principle and have already been discussed in past research. One of these expands the current concept of communication to include human communication with machines (see Fortunati & Edwards, 2020; Guzman, 2018). A second is to make a clear conceptual distinction between human communication and human exchange with machines (Gunkel, 2020, pp. 31–60). A third position is more constructivist and begins with the attributions of the human actors involved, in a certain parallel with the so-called "Turing Test": We speak of communication between humans and machines when the people involved attribute the status of communication to their "act" with the machine (Lindemann, 2016). These positions already have "narrow" interdisciplinary relations by integrating broad references to sociology, psychology, and philosophy.

However, interdisciplinarity can and does go further. As Klaus-Bruhn Jensen already stated in regard to digital media, "the rapidly shifting configurations of communicative practices in twentieth-century society, and the mixed success of single research traditions in accounting for them, has prompted the field to become increasingly interdisciplinary, observing communication through multiple lenses of human, social and, to a degree, natural sciences" (Jensen, 2008, p. 2). This statement is even more true for today's automated communication, where the interdisciplinarity of HMC (empirical interdisciplinarity) refers to necessary analytical concepts beyond narrow disciplinary borders (theoretical interdisciplinarity). To reflect the importance Jensen places on this sense of polyvalency, an interdisciplinary historicization and contextualization can prove helpful.

Interdisciplinary historicization refers to the aforementioned fact that concepts of communication predate the establishment of what we now call HMC, and that we can, and should, ask ourselves from which disciplinary contexts the respective concepts of communication originated. It is important to remain mindful of how closely analytical concepts for the description of communication, and the basic concepts along which these systems were developed, refer to each other. One can think of the early systems that first made HMC possible, such as ELIZA, Kismet, or more recently, Twitter bots. In each of these cases, explicit and implicit theories of communication have been the starting point for the development of these communicative robots and were subsequently inscribed upon them: In the case of ELIZA, Weizenbaum started from the theoretical concept of "establishing a narrower channel of communication than that available to humans in face-to-face-communication" (Weizenbaum, 1967, p. 474) and developed ELIZA on the basis of a psychotherapeutic setting based on the idea of low-context inquiry. With Kismet, Cynthia Lynn Breazeal (2003) operated with communication models from developmental psychology and emotion theory to construct a machine with a highly reduced interface that could communicate feelings. Twitter bots are based on theories of the "imitation" of communication, as they first appeared with the Turing Test's "imitation game" (Veale & Cook, 2018, pp. 22–23) whereby bots communicate on platforms that *reduce* the possibilities of human communication, which is why they can easily replicate it (Gehl & Bakardjieva, 2016, pp. 2–3). There is a pattern here: theories and concepts from different disciplinary contexts are used to create a limited setting in which it becomes possible for a machine to "communicate like a human being" in the first place – although the way this is interpreted differs, sometimes considerably. In this mode of historicization, it is, therefore, a matter of reconstructing the ways in which concepts of communication from various disciplines were themselves gradually inscribed in the corresponding machines.

However, if we turn our focus from the historical emergence of HMC to the current situation, we are dealing with a comprehensively *interdisciplinary context* of its present development, a context that remains entangled with its investigation. During the development process it is not uncommon for computer scientists to come together with engineers, designers, social scientists, and psychologists; all disciplines with very different theories and concepts surrounding the area of communication. "Pioneer communities" (Hepp, 2020b, p. 30; Hepp & Loosen, 2022), for example, have produced imaginaries of possible futures in regard to automated communication that provide orientation for engagement as part of their inherent development. One characteristic of pioneer communities is that they operate at the interface of very different disciplines (Hepp, 2016, p. 926). So, what we are confronted with is a circular relationship between field observation and the development of a field based on this observation, as was addressed early on by the domestication approach (Mansell & Silverstone, 1998). In its nascent state, human interaction with systems of automated communication – as well as its development in laboratories – is again observed and described by social scientists, linguists, and psychologists whose research acts as a basis for further development in the fields of computer science and engineering. To grasp such a dynamic and reflect on what "communication" means and what consequences communicative AI and communicative robots have for different communication processes (such as personal or public communication), the development of HMC points to an interdisciplinary approach.

MEDIA

In a similar way, HMC demands that we rethink the concept of media. As noted in the introduction to this chapter, within media and communication studies, media have been understood as instances of "mediating" texts and technologies (Fornäs, 2000, p. 45). Typically, in relation to media as dissemination channels, institutions, and organizations have been of interest for the field, while taking in sociological (Thompson, 1995), political science (Hallin & Mancini, 2004), linguistic (Bignell, 2002) and legal (Gies, 2007) approaches as part of its observation, theorization, and historicization (Briggs & Burke, 2009). The idea of "legacy mass media" was quickly problematized when digital media emerged that, in new ways, had to be considered in terms of their materiality and their embeddedness within wider infrastructures (see, Gillespie, Boczkowski, & Foot, 2014; Plantin & Punathambekar, 2019). Media became defined by their "shaping" or "molding" properties as part of communicative practices insofar as certain "affordances" (boyd, 2010; Bucher & Helmond, 2018; Hutchby, 2001) or "logics" (Altheide, 2004; Thimm, Anastasiadis, & Einspänner-Pflock, 2018; van Dijck & Poell,

2013) were attributed to them. Research on digital media has also emphasized their "process character" (Hepp, 2020b, pp. 56–99), that is, the fact that they are continuously developed on the basis of user data, are in "constant flux" (Cheney-Lippold, 2017, p. 90) and exist in a "permanently beta" (Neff & Stark, 2003, p. 173) state of development. Media and communication studies' early discourse on the character of digital media adapted knowledge from other disciplines, typically those from the social sciences and humanities. However, communicative AI and communicative robots reinforced the need to incorporate knowledge from computer science – not least because media (offerings) today are increasingly based on digital infrastructures.

This also means that the need for the broadening of disciplinary perspective has increased in that an expanded notion of media is challenged by today's HMC. HMC systems are no longer simply instances of the mediation or dissemination of communication, but also for its generation – a development that is based on the automated processing of (human) verbal and non-verbal utterances. This is ultimately the idea expressed through the concept of "automated media" (Andrejevic, 2020; Napoli, 2014). From this perspective, communicative AI and communicative robots operate as "media within media"; they process within media. For example, bots are deployed on online platforms such as Facebook or Twitter, chatbots are typically embedded in websites or other media infrastructures, and artificial companions act on the basis of the information available as digital traces on the internet. Various scholars have argued that *infrastructural media*, on which communicative AI and communicative robots are based, are a necessary pre-condition for their existence (Gehl & Bakardjieva, 2016).

In this regard, HMC "challenges the very concept of medium, because the machine is at the same time the channel as well as the producer of communication messages" (Natale, 2021, p. 905). However, developing an understanding of medium that is appropriate for HMC is not about directly adopting concepts from computer science. This is the point where we can perceive the challenge in integrating different theories on theoretical-level interdisciplinarity. An interdisciplinary dialogue is crucial as opposed to simply picking and choosing concepts "off the shelf." As an illustration, consider Herbert Kubicek's (1997) argument on the question of whether we should understand the "internet as a mass medium" (Morris & Ogan, 1996, p. 39). He points out that many of the interdisciplinary misunderstandings between the social sciences and computer science stem from the fact that no clear distinction is made between first-order and second-order media and that too many uni-directional conclusions are drawn from one to the other (Kubicek, 1997, p. 220). For Kubicek, first-order media are technical systems possessing certain functions and the potential for the dissemination of information, exemplified by the internet with its various protocols as a technical infrastructure (as it is addressed by computer science). Second-order media are socio-cultural institutions for the production of meaning in the dissemination of information by means of first-order media. These include online newspapers, social media platforms, and music services, which have all developed specific organizational forms to institutionalize communication (offering formats, habitualized modes of use) around first-order media technologies. This is what the social sciences and humanities address when they speak about media.

Perhaps the distinction between first- and second-order media may seem somewhat striking, but it reminds us of the main challenge for all types of interdisciplinarity: *Interdisciplinary* does not mean a simple transfer of concepts but a much more complex dialogue in which particular empirical descriptions, methodological approaches, and theoretical concepts are reformulated in a way that they can become meaningful across disciplines; "'working together' should adopt and apply the idea of immersing oneself in the language(s), practices, methodologies and epistemologies of other disciplines" (Tsatsou, 2016, p. 653). Just as it is not possible to simply transfer existing media-related concepts from the social sciences and humanities to computer science, it is similarly impractical to directly adopt concepts from computer science. We need concepts to grasp media's first- and second-order dimensions, as well as their social contextualization without falling into either technological or social determinism. The same can be said for empirical descriptions and methodological approaches.

AGENCY

HMC asks that we rethink agency. If we follow a basic social sciences definition, "agency describes the locus of action, whether in the person, in language, or in some other structure or process" (Denzin, 2014, p. 75). This broad, basic definition already points to an interdisciplinary discussion in that agency is located differently depending on the disciplinary and, therefore, theoretical position adopted by that discipline. Linguistic speech act theory, for example, has seen humans

as possessors of agency. Social theories have developed understandings of supra-individual agency, such as the agency of organizations or collectives. Foucauldian research assumes that certain discursive practices reveal agency. Such examples show that the social sciences and humanities alone each have very different ways of locating agency – and also which social entities (such as animals, natural phenomena, ghosts, or machines) they model as agency-capable in the first place (Lindemann, 2016). The question of locating agency is of particular relevance to HMC when dealing with questions of ethics and law (Arkin, 2009; Bryson, 2010; Wallach, 2008). Is it only humans who possess agency in processes of communication? Or do communicative robots possess their own? If the answer to the latter is yes, how does this relate to and interfere with human agency?

In this discussion, social constructivism sees *agency* solely from the perspective of the *human being*, tied to one's own intentionality, which a machine cannot possess. The machine is then to be understood as the "objectification" of human intentionality (Knoblauch, 2020, p. 118; Pfadenhauer, 2014, p. 144). Nevertheless, humans may *experience* the machine as intentional, that is, as having an agency of its own. Here, agency is understood as an observer-related category. We are then dealing with a human form of "projection" (Knoblauch, 2020, p. 114), just as in certain cultures nature is conceived as having agency. A specific variant of this kind of thinking can be found in systems theory, which assumes, based on its particular approach to communications, that the decisive question is whether a "personification" of the machine takes place in the act of human–machine communication and that agency is attributed as a personalized formation of expectations (Muhle, 2018, pp. 155–159; see also Baecker, 2011, pp. 23–25). Such a theoretical turn is not so different to some computer science approaches. Just to quote one aforementioned historical example, we can see at this point a parallel to critical work such as that of Weizenbaum who wanted to demonstrate with ELIZA that even simple systems can evoke in humans the assumption of their own agency without being capable of "understanding" (Weizenbaum, 1967, p. 474). The same can be said for today's machine translation which is based on pattern recognition using large amounts of data, therefore developing some form of agency without any "understanding" of meaning (Gunkel, 2020, pp. 97–134).

Some current research adopts a *hybrid agency* approach, particularly in the area of "new materialism" (Fox & Aldred, 2017, p. 3). From this perspective, communicative AI and communicative robots do not develop an agency on their own, but in their entanglement with humans, a new form of agency "in-between" emerges that would otherwise not exist. Hybrid approaches in particular are seen as a way of overcoming simplistic dichotomies and arriving at more complex understandings of agency (Gunkel, 2020, pp. 277–281). One starting point is provided by actor-network theory which focuses on "collectives" (Latour, 2007, p. 247), not only of humans but of assemblages of humans and things which collectively build upon the social and, therefore, possess agency. In parallel, F. Allan Hanson has developed what he calls "extended agency theory," in which he theorizes the "joint responsibility" of human and machine, where "moral agency is distributed over both human and technological artifacts" (Hanson, 2009, p. 94). In a similar way, Werner Rammert has written about the "hybrid interdependencies of action" (Rammert, 2007, p. 79) from the perspective of the sociology of technology (see also Matsuzaki, 2011).

We have argued, in the tradition of relational process sociology, for the concept of "hybrid figurations" – and aim to overcome the apparent opposition between the approaches of new materialism and phenomenology by combining two perspectives of observation: This approach is able to capture both "projections of agency" onto the machine and, at the same time, new forms of emerging "joint human–machine agency." From process sociology's point of view, every social entity such as a group, a community, an organization, is articulated by certain figurations and these, in turn, constitute societies by means of their constellation with one another (Elias, 1978). In media and communications research, these figurations can be understood as *communicative* figurations. These are characterized by a certain actor constellation where frames of relevance as a shared sense of orientation for the actors involved, as well as characteristic communicative practices that are closely interwoven with an ensemble of different media, are key (Hepp, Breiter, & Hasebrink, 2018). Such communicative figurations build "supra-individual actors" (Schimank, 2010, pp. 327–341), that is, they develop their own agency as a collectivity or organization. To take a simple example, the supra-individual agency of a newsroom with automated journalistic production systems ("work bots") is different from that of a newsroom that does not work with such systems.

These discussions around agency in the context of HMC specifically point to the goals of interdisciplinarity. Certainly, epistemological objectives such as describing and understanding communication with machines are at stake. However, especially in terms of agency, an instrumental orientation is vital: Like no other question, that of agency refers to very practical problems of dealing with and regulating systems of automated communication. As Frank Pasquale points out, these problems are confronted with a crisis of knowledge, which results in a "clash of forms of expertise" (Pasquale, 2020, p. 23). The views of economists and AI experts dominate – bringing with them numerous oversights. A more open, interdisciplinary discussion into the agency of automated communication, on the other hand, could broaden the view and lead to new practical solutions.

CONCLUSION: THE NECESSITY OF INTERDISCIPLINARY THEORY BUILDING

The point of departure for this chapter was the observation that the field of HMC, dealing with phenomena such as those of communicative AI and communicative robots, challenges three of the basic, definitive concepts of media and communication studies, which are often the un-problematized starting point for empirical research: communication, media, and agency. The challenge lies in the fact that HMC starts from the assumption that the machine communicates, which calls into question the fundamental understanding of communication as human interaction, of media as mediating instances, and of agency as purely human. To date, the discussion in and around HMC has not been able to come to clear conclusions regarding any of these concepts. Many theoretical conceptions stand side by side, often in isolation from one another. Others – especially in their applicability to empirical research – remain conceptually blurred and far less "definitive" than Herbert Blumer's (1954) distinction between "sensitizing" and "definitive concepts" presupposes.

However, it is precisely in questioning the fundamental concepts of media and communication studies that both the challenge and the relevance of HMC can be seen: The challenge lies in the fact that this field of research necessarily leaves the fundamental grounding of media and communication studies' traditional conceptualization. The relevance of HMC is articulated in the ways that the field allows us to reflect on the theoretical foundations of media and communication studies beyond its inherent subject matter and to, at least potentially, place it on a conceptually more solid ground.

But, if HMC research wants to succeed in this idea, it will only be possible if it understands such an endeavor as interdisciplinary. There are many reasons why the need for interdisciplinarity is relatively urgent: the concept of communication, from which today's communicative AI and communicative robots were developed, emerged through an interdisciplinary discourse that must be included if one wants to "understand" these systems in social science terms. In regard to their character as media, it becomes evident that we can only analytically describe today's communicative robots as automated media if we interweave the consideration of technological and social dimensions. A conceptualization of agency is confronted with the theoretical paths that already run across different disciplines as we arrive at the question of whether it is about a juxtaposition of human and machine agency or about understanding *hybrid* forms of agency.

Media and communication studies has had a multidisciplinary history since it first entered the scientific discourse as an academic discipline. Without sociology, political science, economics, law, linguistics, and other disciplines in the humanities and social sciences, it would barely have emerged in its current form. With HMC, it is necessary to expand this dialogue to other disciplines – especially computer science – to a much greater extent and to conduct it on an equal footing. Such a broadening of outlook, as we have seen, affects not only the theories and concepts of engagement with communicative AI and communicative robots, but also the methodological approach.

NOTE

1 Simmel's original concept of *Wechselwirkung* (Simmel, 1908, p. 2) was reductively translated by American sociology as "interaction," a term that limits itself to the level of "action" and fails to reflect the complex reciprocal consequences and non-intended side-effects that Simmel and others were concerned with. Seyfert (2019, p. 151, our translation) criticizes the "activist impetus" behind the term "interaction" and emphasizes that it was originally intended to be much more comprehensive and abstract and also takes reactive and passive behavior into account, which is why he (2019, p. 150) also uses the term "interpassivity." For this reason, Norbert Elias, for example, later used the term "interdependencies" (Elias, 1978, p. 134) to describe the reciprocal dynamics in human figurations.

REFERENCES

Altheide, D. L. (2004). Media logic and political communication. *Political Communication, 21*(3), 293–296.

Andrejevic, M. (2020). *Automated media*. London: Routledge.

Arkin, R. (2009). *Governing lethal behavior in autonomous robots*. BocaRaton: CRC Press.

Baecker, D. (2011). Who qualifies for communication? A systems perspective on human and other possibly intelligent beings taking part in the next society. *Technikfolgenabschätzung: Theorie und Praxis, 20*(1), 17–26.

Bignell, J. (2002). *Media semiotics*. Manchester University Press.

Blumer, H. (1954). What is wrong with social theory? *American Sociological Review, 19*, 3–10.

boyd, D. (2010). Social network sites as networked publics: Affordances, dynamics, and implications. In Z. Papacharissi (Ed.), *Networked self: Identity, community, and culture on social network sites* (pp. 39–58). London: Routledge.

Breazeal, C. L. (2003). Emotion and sociable humanoid robots. *International Journal of Human-Computer Studies, 59*(1–2), 119–155.

Briggs, A., & Burke, P. (2009). *A social history of the media. From Gutenberg to the internet*. Third edition. Cambridge: Polity Press.

Bryson, J. J. (2010). Robots should be slaves. In Y. Wilks (Ed.), *Close engagements with artificial companions: Key social, psychological, ethical and design issues* (pp. 63–74). Amsterdam: John Benjamins.

Bucher, T., & Helmond, A. (2018). The affordances of social media platforms. In J. Burgess, T. Poell, & A. Marwick (Eds.), *The SAGE handbook of social media* (pp. 233–253). London: SAGE Publications.

Cheney-Lippold, J. (2017). *We are data. algorithms and the making of our digital selves*. New York: New York University Press.

Couldry, N. (2004). Theorising media as practice. *Social Semiotics, 14*(2), 115–132.

Craig, R. T. (1999). Communication theory as a field. *Communication Theory, 9*(2), 119–161.

Craig, R. T. (2012). Communication as a field and discipline. In W. Donsbach (Ed.), *The international encyclopedia of communication*. Chichester, UK: John Wiley & Sons, Ltd.

Denzin, N. K. (2014). Symbolic interactionism and the media. In R. S. Fortner & P. M. Fackler (pp. 74–94). Malden: Wiley.

Dewey, J. (1927). *The public and its problems: An essay in political inquiry*. New York: Holt.

Durham Peters, J. (2008). Communication: History of the idea. In W. Donsbach (Ed.), *The international encyclopedia of communication*. Chichester, UK: John Wiley & Sons, Ltd.

Elias, N. (1978). *What is sociology?* London: Hutchinson.

Esposito, E. (2017). Artificial communication? The production of contingency by algorithms. *Zeitschrift für Soziologie, 46*(4), 249–265.

Fornäs, J. (2000). The crucial in between. The centrality of mediation in cultural studies. *European Journal of Cultural Studies*, *3*(1), 45–65.

Fortunati, L., & Edwards, A. P. (2020). Opening space for theoretical, methodological, and empirical issues in human-machine communication. *Human-Machine Communication*, *1*, 1. Retrieved from https://stars.library.ucf.edu/cgi/viewcontent.cgi?article=1021&context=hmc

Foucault, M. (1991). *Discipline and punish: The birth of the prison* (New ed.). London: Penguin.

Fox, N. J., & Aldred, P. (2017). *Sociology and the new materialism: Theory, research, action*. London: Sage.

Gehl, R. W., & Bakardjieva, M. (2016). Socialbots and their friends. In R. W. Gehl & M. Bakardjieva (Eds.), *Socialbots and their friends: Digital media and the automation of sociality* (pp. 1–16). London: Routledge.

Gies, L. (2007). *Law and the media: The future of an uneasy relationship*. London: Routledge.

Gillespie, T., Boczkowski, P. J., & Foot, K. A. (Eds.). (2014). *Media technologies. Essays on communication, materiality, and society*. Cambridge, London: MIT Press.

Gunkel, D. J. (2020). *An introduction to communication and artificial intelligence*. Cambridge: Polity.

Guzman, A. L. (2018). Introduction: What is human-machine-communication anyway? In A. L. Guzman (Ed.), *Human-machine communication* (pp. 1–28). New York: Peter Lang.

Guzman, A. L., & Lewis, S. C. (2020). Artificial intelligence and communication: A human-machine communication research agenda. *New Media & Society*, *22*(1), 70–86.

Hallin, D. C., & Mancini, P. (2004). *Comparing media systems: Three models of media and politics*. Cambridge: Cambridge UP.

Hanson, F. A. (2009). Beyond the skin bag: On the moral responsibility of extended agencies. *Ethics and Information Technology*, *11*(1), 91–99.

Hepp, A. (2016). Pioneer communities: Collective actors of deep mediatisation. *Media, Culture & Society*, *38*(6), 918–933.

Hepp, A. (2020a). Artificial companions, social bots and work bots: Communicative robots as research objects of media and communication studies. *Media, Culture & Society*, *42*(7–8), 1410–1426.

Hepp, A. (2020b). *Deep mediatization*. London: Routledge.

Hepp, A., Breiter, A., & Hasebrink, U. (Eds.). (2018). *Communicative figurations: Transforming communications in times of deep mediatization*. London: Palgrave Macmillan.

Hepp, A., & Loosen, W. (2022). Beyond innovation: Pioneer journalism and the re-figuration of journalism. In P. Ferrucci & S. Eldridge (Eds.), *The institutions changing journalism: Barbarians inside the gate* (pp. 118–135). London: Routledge.

Horton, D., & Wohl, R. R. (1956). Mass communication and para-social interaction. Observations on intimacy at a distance. *Psychiatry*, *19*, 215–229.

Hutchby, I. (2001). Technologies, texts and affordances. *Sociology*, *35*(2), 441–456.

Huutoniemi, K., Klein, J. T., Bruun, H., & Hukkinen, J. (2010). Analyzing interdisciplinarity: Typology and indicators. *Research Policy*, *39*(1), 79–88.

Jensen, K. B. (2008). Communication theory and philosophy. In W. Donsbach (Ed.), *The international encyclopedia of communication*. Chichester, UK: John Wiley & Sons, Ltd.

Kim, M.-S. (2002). *Non-western perspectives on human communication: Implications for theory and practice*. London: Sage.

Klein, J. T. (2017). Typologies of Interdisciplinarity: The boundary work of definition. In R. Frodeman (Ed.), *The Oxford handbook of interdisciplinarity* (2nd ed.). Oxford University Press.

Knoblauch, H. (2020). *The communicative construction of reality*. London: Routledge.

Kubicek, H. (1997). Das Internet auf dem Weg zum Massenmedium? Ein Versuch, Lehren aus der Geschichte alter und neuer Medien zu ziehen. In R. Werle & C. Lang (Eds.), Modell Internet? *Entwicklungsperspektiven neuer Kommunikationsnetze* (pp. 213–239). Frankfurt a. M./New York: Campus.

Latour, B. (2007). *Reassembling the social: An introduction to actor-network-theory*. Oxford: OUP Oxford.

Lazer, D. M. J., Baum, M. A., Benkler, Y., Berinsky, A. J., Greenhill, K. M., Menczer, F., … Zittrain, J. L. (2018). The science of fake news. *Science*, *359*(6380), 1094–1096.

Lindemann, G. (2016). Social interaction with robots: three questions. *AI & Society*, *31*(4), 573–575.

Livingstone, S. M. (2009). On the mediation of everything. *Journal of Communication*, *59*(1), 1–18.

Loosen, W., Nölleke, D., & Springer, N. (2022). Journalismusforschung: Disziplin durch Entdisziplinierung. *Medien & Kommunikationswissenschaft*, *70*(1), 1–16.

Mansell, R., & Silverstone, R. (Eds.). (1998). *Communication by design: The politics of information and communication technologies*. Milton Keynes: Open University Press.

Matsuzaki, H. (2011). Die Frage nach der "Agency" von Technik und die Normenvergessenheit der Techniksoziologie. In *Akteur – Individuum – Subjekt* (pp. 301–325). Wiesbaden: VS Verlag.

McQuail, D., & Deuze, M. (2020). *McQuail's media and mass communication theory*. 7th ed. London: Sage.

Mead, G. H. (1967). *Mind, self and society from the standpoint of a social behaviorist*. Edited with an introduction by Charles W. Morris. Chicago: University of Chicago Press.

Morris, M., & Ogan, C. (1996). The internet as mass medium. *Journal of Communication, 46*(1), 39–50.

Muhle, F. (2018). Sozialität von und mit Robotern? Drei soziologische Antworten und eine kommunikationstheoretische Alternative. *Zeitschrift für Soziologie, 47*(3), 147–163.

Napoli, P. M. (2014). Automated media: An institutional theory perspective on algorithmic media production and consumption. *Communication Theory, 24*(3), 340–360.

Natale, S. (2019). If software is narrative: Joseph Weizenbaum, artificial intelligence and the biographies of ELIZA. *New Media & Society, 21*(3), 712–728.

Natale, S. (2021). Communicating through or communicating with: Approaching artificial intelligence from a communication and media studies perspective. *Communication Theory, 31*(4), 905–910.

Neff, G., & Stark, D. (2003). Permanently beta. Responsive organization in the internet era. In P. N. Howard & S. Jones (Eds.), *Society online* (pp. 173–188). New Delhi, London: Sage.

Pasquale, F. (2020). *New laws of robotics: Defending human expertise in the age of AI.* Cambridge, London: Belknap Press.

Pentzold, C. (2015). Praxistheoretische Prinzipien, Traditionen und Perspektiven kulturalistischer Kommunikations- und Medienforschung. *Medien & Kommunikationswissenschaft, 63*(2), 229–245.

Pfadenhauer, M. (2014). On the sociality of social robots. A sociology-of-knowledge perspective. *Science, Technology & Innovation Studies, 10*(1), 135–153.

Plantin, J.-C., & Punathambekar, A. (2019). Digital media infrastructures: pipes, platforms, and politics. *Media, Culture & Society, 41*(2), 163–174.

Rammert, W. (2007). *Technik - Handeln - Wissen. Zu einer pragmatistischen Technik- und Sozialtheorie.* Wiesbaden: VS.

Schimank, U. (2010). *Handeln und Strukturen. Einführung in die akteurstheoretische Soziologie,* 4. Auflage. Weinheim, Basel: Juventa.

Seyfert, R. (2019). *Beziehungsweisen: Elemente einer relationalen Soziologie.* Weilerswist: Velbrück Wissenschaft.

Simmel, G. (1908). *Soziologie. Untersuchungen über die Formen der Vergesellschaftung.* Berlin: Duncker & Humblot.

Thimm, C., Anastasiadis, M., & Einspänner-Pflock, J. (Eds.). (2018). *Media logic(s) revisited. Modelling the interplay between media institutions, media technology and societal change.* London: Palgrave Macmillan.

Thompson, J. B. (1995). *The media and modernity. A social theory of the media.* Cambridge: Cambridge University Press.

Thompson, J. B. (2020). Mediated interaction in the digital age. *Theory, Culture & Society, 37*(1), 3–28.

Tsatsou, P. (2016). Can media and communication researchers turn the present challenges of research impact and interdisciplinarity into future opportunities. *International Communication Gazette, 78*(7), 650–656.

Turkle, S. (2015). *Reclaiming conversation. The power of talk in a digital age.* New York: Penguin.

van Dijck, J., & Poell, T. (2013). Understanding social media logic. *Media and Communication, 1*(1), 2–14.

Veale, T., & Cook, M. (2018). *Twitterbots: Making machines that make meaning.* Cambridge, MA: MIT Press.

Waisbord, S. (2019). *Communication: A post-discipline.* Cambridge: Polity.

Wallach, W. (2008). Implementing moral decision making faculties in computers and robots. *AI & Society, 22*(4), 463–475.

Watzlawick, P., Beavin, J. H., & Jackson, D. D. (1967). *Pragmatics of human communication* (1st ed.). New York: Norton.

Weizenbaum, J. (1967). Contextual understanding by computers. *Communications of the ACM, 10*(8), 474–480.

Wiener, N. (1948). *Cybernetics or control and communication in the animal and the machine.* Cambridge, MA: MIT Press.

3

Cybernetics and Information Theory in Human–Machine Communication

Ronald Kline

The sciences of cybernetics and information theory have helped researchers understand communication among humans and machines, mainly by blurring the boundaries between humans and machines. Founded after World War II, cybernetics claimed that both humans and intelligent machines were self-regulating organisms, which could be analyzed using the same engineering theories of control and communication. With the aid of information theory, cybernetics could thus explain the ability of humans to survive as biological organisms—by means of such homeostatic processes as maintaining bodily temperature—and to adapt to their environments—by means of muscular and cognitive processes. In a similar manner, cybernetics could explain how intelligent machines, such as the household thermostat and the robot, performed these human-like functions. By treating both humans and machines as purposeful organisms, cybernetics and information theory inspired researchers to model humans as machines in the social sciences and inventors to create such humanoid machines as AI systems and bionic technologies.

This chapter recounts the contested invention of cybernetics and information theory in the early Cold War, then analyzes the contributions of these two sciences to today's emerging field of Human–Machine Communication (Guzman,

2018). It explains how early cyberneticians and information theorists included human–machine communication in their purview, and how three new postwar disciplines—Human–Computer Interaction, Artificial Intelligence, and Communication Study—drew on insights from cybernetics and information theory to understand the new relationships between humans and machines they were helping to co-construct in an era marked by rapid innovations in computing, electronics, and communications. The chapter concludes with a brief reflection on how this history can help inform current research in HMC.

INVENTING CYBERNETICS AND INFORMATION THEORY

While the invention of cybernetics and information theory was an international endeavor, I focus on the contested process of creating the two new sciences in the United States and Britain. In general, I discuss their history separately, while recognizing that cyberneticians included information theory in their discipline, while information theorists in the U.S. excluded cybernetics from theirs (Kline, 2015).

Cybernetics, the exciting new science with the mysterious name and universal aspirations, boasted a common language of control, communication, feedback, and information. Yet cybernetics evoked so many different meanings that it was difficult to define. In 1969, Georges Boulanger, the president of the International Association of Cybernetics, asked, "But after all what is cybernetics? Or rather what is it not, for paradoxically the more people talk about cybernetics the less they seem to agree on a definition." He identified several meanings of cybernetics: a mathematical theory of control; automation; computerization; a theory of communication; the study of analogies between humans and machines; and a philosophy explaining the mysteries of life. To the general public, Boulanger noted, cybernetics "conjures up visions of some fantastic world of the future peopled by robots and electronic brains!" His favorite definition was the "science of robots" (Boulanger, 1969, pp. 3–4).

This multiplicity of meanings, this "disunity of cybernetics" in interpretation and methodology (Kline, 2015), was an ironic fate for a field that claimed to be universal, a science that could explain the behavior of all living organisms from the level of the cell to that of society, and the behavior of all purposeful machines. Norbert Wiener, the renowned MIT mathematician whose 1948 book *Cybernetics* gave the field its name (which he derived from the Greek word for steersman), defined cybernetics as the "entire field of control and communication theory, whether in the machine or in the animal" (Wiener, 1948, p. 19). For Wiener, that analogy was central to cybernetics. It explained how all living organisms and purposeful machines utilized their internal communication-control systems—consisting of sensors, effectors, "brains," and "nervous systems"—to attain their goals. They continuously monitored information about themselves and the environment, compared that to their goals (through negative feedback loops), then adapted their behavior (steered it) to reach their goals, survival being the primary one for living organisms.

Wiener grasped this idea while working with electronics engineer Julian Bigelow on a military-funded project at MIT to develop an improved anti-aircraft system in World War II. The problem was how to direct anti-aircraft guns to shoot down fast-moving enemy bombers flying high above the gunners on the ground. The solution was to design a semi-automatic communication-control system, in which humans operated aircraft-tracking devices on the ground and also a computer in a nearby Army truck, but not the massive anti-aircraft guns. The computer received tracking information and such data as the muzzle velocity of the guns and the

wind's direction and speed. It used these and other inputs to calculate the bomber's future position and sent information to the anti-aircraft guns to automatically aim them at the target.

In late 1940, Wiener received a grant from the Fire-Control section of the National Defense Research Committee to design a more sophisticated anti-aircraft director than the linear one being designed by AT&T's Bell Telephone Laboratories. Combining control systems theory with statistical communication theory, he and his small group (Bigelow, a technician, and the group's human "computer") designed and built a prototype analog electronic predictor from components common in radio sets. It predicted the plane's future position by continuously correlating its prior and current positions. The predictor did this by filtering "noise" (such as tracking errors and the pilot's evasive maneuvers) from the tracking "signal" to obtain the "message" (the plane's true path), from which it predicted the optimum target position. In early 1943, the head of the Fire-Control section—Warren Weaver, an applied mathematician on leave from the Rockefeller Foundation—recommended that the military procure the AT&T director for the war and did not renew Wiener's contract. Yet, working on the project led Wiener, with the assistance of Bigelow, to develop a statistical theory of prediction and filtering, which is still used today, and the basic idea for the new science of cybernetics (Galison, 1994; Mindell, 2002, chapter 11).

The cybernetics insight came when Wiener and Bigelow realized that the humans operating the anti-aircraft system, as well as the enemy pilot, were themselves acting like communication-control systems (i.e., as servomechanisms). Wiener then consulted with his friend, Arturo Rosenblueth, a neurophysiologist at Harvard University, who confirmed Wiener's idea that the engineering theories of control and communication could explain the behavior of both humans and purposeful machines. In an influential article, "Behavior, Purpose, and Teleology," Rosenblueth, Wiener, and Bigleow (1943) pointed out the philosophical implications of this concept and the importance of negative feedback in steering behavior, the basis for Wiener's cybernetics.

Wiener developed that insight into a science of wide scope in the highly mathematical, but surprisingly popular, book *Cybernetics*, by discussing it with physicists, mathematicians, engineers, neurophysiologists, and social scientists. They carried on that interdisciplinary conversation at the short-lived Teleological Society, which met in Princeton in early 1945, during Wiener's stay at Rosenblueth's neurophysiological laboratory in Mexico in 1947, which was funded by a grant in "mathematical biology" from Warren Weaver at the Rockefeller Foundation, and at the Josiah Macy, Jr., Foundation conferences on cybernetics, which met in New York City and Princeton from 1946 to 1953.

Chaired by neurophysiologist Warren McCulloch, the interdisciplinary Macy meetings—whose original title was the "Conference on Feedback Mechanisms and Circular Causal Systems in Biology and the Social Sciences"—discussed the cutting-edge research of its members and guests, which helped to define cybernetics for years to come. This included the theory of feedback control systems in humans and machines by Rosenblueth, Wiener, and Bigelow; the neural net model of the mind by McCulloch and Walter Pitts; the design of electronic digital computers by John von Neumann; theories of information developed by Wiener, Claude Shannon, and others; and the application of cybernetics to the social sciences by such luminaries as anthropologist Margaret Mead and her anthropologist husband, Gregory Bateson. The automata discussed at the meetings represented the cybernetic origins of what came to be called "Artificial Intelligence" (Heims, 1991; Kline, 2015, chapter 2).

Toward the end of the Macy conferences, the discussion turned from feedback and circular causality to the nature of information. Shannon's "A Mathematical Theory of Communication," published in the *Bell System Technical Journal* in 1948, the same year as Wiener's *Cybernetics*, established his reputation as the founder of information theory. But contemporaries noted that several researchers had independently come up with the basic idea behind the theory: that information was mathematically equivalent to the physical concept of entropy (the unavailability of a system's energy to do work). In *Cybernetics*, Wiener observed that "This idea occurred at about the same time to several writers, among them the statistician R. A. Fisher, Dr. Shannon of the Bell Telephone Laboratories, and the author. Fisher's motive in studying this subject is to be found in classical statistical theory; that of Shannon in the problem of coding information; and that of the author in the problem of noise and message in electrical filters" (Wiener, 1948, p. 18). He might have added that physicist Leo Szilard had equated information with entropy in the 1920s, in order to explain a paradox in physics known as Maxwell's demon (Segal, 2003, pp. 19–21).

Shannon, who received a Ph.D. in mathematics from MIT in 1940, is credited with founding information theory because of how extensively he treated the general process of communications, which he derived from his wartime research on cryptography. The first part of his lengthy 1948 article analyzed the case of discrete channels (whose signals represented, for example, the individual letters of a telegram). The second part analyzed the case of continuous channels (whose signals represented, for example, the sound waves transmitted by the telephone). These cases would later be called "digital" and "analog," respectively. Shannon proved several coding theorems that allowed information to be reliably transmitted in the presence of noise in a "general communication system," which refers to any communications process, whether in living organisms, machines, or a combination of these. In his schematic diagram of that system, an Information Source selects a message from a set of possible messages. The Transmitter encodes the message, converting it into a signal, which is sent along a channel affected by a Noise Source. The received signal (transmitter signal plus noise) enters the Receiver, which decodes it into a message for the Destination (Shannon, 1948, p. 381).

The theory is counter-intuitive in a couple of ways. First, Shannon dealt with the engineering problem of how to accurately transmit a message, not the semantic aspect of messages, despite the common usage of the term "information" to denote meaning. "Frequently," Shannon said, in an often quoted passage, "the messages have *meaning*; that is they refer to or are correlated according to some system with certain physical or conceptual entities. These semantic aspects of communication are irrelevant to the engineering problem" (Shannon, 1948, p. 379, his emphasis). Second, he defined the scientific term "amount of information" as the measure of the freedom of choice in selecting a message out of an ensemble of possible messages or the uncertainty of the outcome of the selection, not the amount of data transmitted. For Shannon, the source generates the maximum amount of information when it selects messages at random; no information is generated when the selection is known. Taking into account the statistical structure of the source in this way made sense intuitively, because the more *uncertain* we are of what messages will be selected, the more information we receive. The more *certain* we are, the less information we receive. But the theory is counter-intuitive when we realize that the amount of information of a source producing non-sense words is much greater than that of a source producing meaningful words!

It is important to remember that although Shannon was a mathematician, he developed his theory from the point of view of the engineer: how to design and analyze communications systems. The heart of the enterprise is to use entropy equations to calculate the amount of information generated by the source, the redundancy of the source, and the capacity of the channel (e.g., in bits per symbol) in order to devise efficient codes to transmit messages reliably in the presence of noise. Before Shannon, inventors and engineers had developed efficient communication codes by considering the structure of language. In the nineteenth century, Samuel Morse, for example, assigned the shortest code symbol, a dot, to represent the letter "e" in his telegraph code, because it is the most frequent letter in the English language. He assigned much longer codes for infrequent letters such as "z." As a result, telegraph companies could send more text with fewer symbols and, thus, at less expense. In the twentieth century, telegraph companies used more efficient codes for sending standard messages, such as birthday telegrams. These were encoded using the number assigned to each greeting, rather than encoding each letter of the messages (Shannon, 1948, p. 385). What Shannon did was to provide a scientific (i.e., mathematical) basis for efficient coding in general communications systems with noise, and show how to calculate limits for channel capacity and other parameters of that system.

A simple coding example for a noiseless discrete channel, drawn from the 1948 paper, illustrates his approach. Consider a source that produces a sequence of symbols chosen independently from the set A B C D, in which A occurs one-half of the time, B one-fourth of the time, and C and D one-eight of the time each. The most *inefficient* binary coding scheme assumes that the selection of symbols is equally probable: resulting in, for example, 00 for A, 01 for B, 10 for C, and 11 for D. This code averages two bits per symbol. The most *efficient* coding scheme considers the statistics of the source by using an entropy equation to calculate the uncertainty of which symbol is selected, i.e., the amount of information produced by the source. This is one and three-quarters bits per symbol. The most efficient code will match that entropy: resulting in, for example, 0 for A, 10 for B, 110 for C, and 111 for D. This code uses, on average, one and three-quarter bits per symbol, versus two bits per symbol for the equiprobable case. That gives a compression ratio of seven to eight and a redundancy of one-eighth (Shannon, 1948, pp. 410–413). In the much more complex case of coding a natural-language source to transmit messages reliably over a noisy channel, suitable codes are much more complex and also much longer (to correct errors). As pointed out by engineer John Pierce at Bell Labs, who popularized Shannon's theory, "Indeed, the whole problem of efficient and error-free communication turns out to be that of removing from messages the somewhat inefficient redundancy which they have [as was done in the ABCD example] and then adding redundancy of the right sort in order to allow correction of errors made in transmission (Pierce,

1980, pp. 164–165). Yet, devising such codes for a natural language proved to be an exceedingly difficult task.

Communication theorists sought to broaden the scope of Shannon's theory as soon as it appeared. One of the first to do so was Warren Weaver in *The Mathematical Theory of Communication* (1949), which included Shannon's original paper and Weaver's commentary on it. After explaining Shannon's theory to a nontechnical audience, Weaver argued that it could address the semantic and effectiveness problems of communication, not just the technical problem of accurately transmitting messages, to which Shannon had limited it. Because Shannon's theory had analyzed so well the technical level of communications by considering syntactics, Weaver claimed that the theory "has so penetratingly cleared the air that one is now, perhaps for the first time, ready for a real theory of meaning," the next level of communications in his schema. To that end, Weaver suggested adding two components to Shannon's communication diagram: a "Semantic Receiver" alongside the original Receiver; and "semantic noise" alongside the original Noise Source (Weaver, 1949, pp. 115–116). A generation of social scientists pointed to Weaver's intervention as an intellectual sanction to interpret Shannon's theory semantically (Kline, 2015, pp. 129–133).

The English School of Information Theory (Kline, 2015, pp. 104–112) broadened Shannon's model even further. At the 1951 Macy conference on cybernetics, physicist Donald MacKay at Kings College London, the leader of this movement, presented a "general information theory," which combined approaches from physics and engineering. MacKay claimed that he could cover "all technical senses of the term 'information' by defining it operationally as *that which logically enables the receiver to make or add to a representation of that which is the case, or is believed or alleged to be the case.*" He introduced the term "scientific information" for representations made about the natural world, and the term "selective information" to measure representations added via communication, the realm of Shannon's theory. He broke down scientific information into two components. "Metrical information," derived from statistician R. A. Fisher, indicated the precision of an experiment. "Structural information," derived from physicist Denis Gabor, indicated the degrees of freedom of an experiment. Selective information, derived from Shannon, indicated the uncertainty of transmitting messages, such as the values of a vector representing scientific information. At the Macy meeting, MacKay gave an example to illustrate the difference between scientific and selective information. "Two people, A and B, are listening for a signal which each knows will be either a dot or a dash. A dash arrives." A, a physicist, measures the signal and "remarks that there was 'a good deal of information' in the signal." B, an engineer, says "I knew it would be either a dot or a dash.... [therefore] ... I gained 'little information.'" MacKay explained that "For lack of a vocabulary, they are using the phrase 'amount of information' to refer to different measurable parameters of the different representational activities in which they are engaged." His theory provided that vocabulary (MacKay, 1952, pp. 181–183, 219, his emphasis).

MacKay also brought semantics into information theory, an early attempt at what proved to be a popular but controversial endeavor related to cybernetics. At the 1951 Macy meeting, MacKay vaguely defined the logical meaning of a statement as the orientation of the scientific information vector. He continued to revise his semantic theory of information theory in the 1950s, extending it from scientific statements to the internal representation of the world made by humans and automata (MacKay, 1969, Chapters 5–9). At the last Macy meeting, in 1953, Israeli philosopher of science Yehoshua Bar-Hillel presented a theory of semantic information which he had developed with logical positivist Rudolph Carnap. They related Shannon's theory to the meaning of logical statements of an artificial language. It was more rigorous than MacKay's theory, but it dealt with the truth value of statements, not the communication of them (Bar-Hillel, 1955; Cherry, 1957, pp. 231–241). Wiener took a different tack in his popular book on cybernetics, the *Human Use of Human Beings*, by equating the "amount of meaning" of telegraph messages with their improbability of occurrence. MacKay severely criticized that idea at the 1951 Macy meeting (Wiener, 1950, pp. 6, 8; MacKay, 1952, p. 192). Much later, Gregory Bateson, a prominent figure at the Macy meetings, succinctly defined information as "any difference that makes a difference" (Bateson, 1979, p. 212), which combined all three semiotic aspects of communication (syntactic, semantic, and pragmatic). Journalist Stewart Brand, the founder of the countercultural *Whole Earth Catalog*, noted that Bateson's pithy definition was popular with researchers at MIT's newly established Media Lab in the 1980s (Brand, 1987, pp. 79–80). By including the observer in his cybernetic theory of immanent mind, Bateson also contributed to the establishment of second-order cybernetics, which Heinz von Foerster, editor of the Macy conferences on cybernetics, founded in the mid-1970s as the next frontier of cybernetics (Kline, 2020, pp. 22–28).

HUMAN–MACHINE COMMUNICATION

Although early cyberneticians and information theorists relied on communication theory to blur the boundaries between humans and machines, they did not analyze human-machine communication in depth.[1] In his foundational article, Shannon said that the "*destination* is the person (or thing) for whom, the message is intended" (Shannon, 1948, p. 381, his emphasis). Warren Weaver gave some examples of machine–machine communication, drawn from his wartime experience managing fire-control research, in his commentary on Shannon: "In some connections it may be desirable to use a still broader definition of communication [than one human mind affecting another], namely, one which would include the procedures by means of which one mechanism (say automatic equipment to track an airplane and to compute its probable future positions) affects another mechanism (say a guided missile chasing this airplane)" (Weaver, 1949, p. 95). Communication theorist Colin Cherry at Imperial College London, gave a similar military example of control signals being sent between a guided missile and ground radar (Cherry, 1957, p. 219).

Norbert Wiener went much further and analyzed human–machine communication. In the *Human Use of Human Beings*, he mentioned his work on anti-aircraft systems in World War II as an example of machine-machine communication, as Weaver had done. But he also said, "We ordinarily think of communication and language as being directed from person to person. However, it is quite possible for a person to talk to a machine or a machine to a person, and a machine to a machine." To illustrate, he gave the example of load dispatchers at electrical power plants sending electrical signals to control small hydro-electric plants in remote locations. The dispatcher sent commands to the power station and received feedback from it via encoded signals transmitted over a channel, such as a leased telegraph line. "Here, then," said Wiener, "is one instance of language emanating from man and directed toward the machine, and vice versa." He suggested how to apply information theory to this case, by using entropy equations to calculate the maxim amount of information that could be transmitted if proper terminal equipment was used and how much information would be lost in transmission. Wiener concluded that the hydro-station's operations, resulting from the orders encoded in the dispatcher's signals, "may be regarded as a language in itself, with a system of probabilities of behavior given by its own history" (Wiener, 1950, pp. 86–88, 178). This is the earliest instance I have found of applying cybernetics and information theory to analyze human–machine communication.

HUMAN–COMPUTER INTERACTION

The postwar field of human–computer interaction had many ties to cybernetics and information theory. Two prominent sites for this early work were MIT and the Stanford Research Institute (SRI). Out of MIT came techniques for humans to interact with the computer in real-time, such as the cathode-ray-tube display and light pen, developed at Lincoln Laboratory for SAGE, a massive computerized air-defense system, in the 1950s, and remote time-sharing, developed at Project MAC in the 1960s. Out of SRI came the computer mouse, windows, and hyperlink environment, the basis for creating the Graphical User Interface (GUI) at XEROX PARC in the 1970s. Apple popularized GUI when it introduced the MacIntosh personal computer in 1984, the interface used by today's personal computers and smartphones (Barnes, 2002). In commercial time-sharing, customers logged into a "computer utility" to access such information services as news, weather, and stock quotes. These early computer networks featured human–machine communication, not the computer-mediated-communication (CMC) that gained popularity when home networks began to offer email and Bulletin Boards on personal computers in the 1980s (Rheingold, 1993). These technologies enabled a paradigm shift, from the indirect batch mode of operating computers with IBM cards, to a direct interaction (communication) between humans and computers that is taken for granted today.

Cybernetics and information theory informed the work of two key figures in this transformation: J. C. R. Licklider at MIT and Douglas Engelbart at SRI. Licklider, a psychologist specializing in psycho-acoustics, learned about real-time computing on the SAGE project, then became the first director of the Information Processing Techniques Office at the Pentagon's Advanced Research Projects Agency. There he funded time-sharing, AI, and computer graphics, and set the stage for ARPANET, the fabled forerunner of the Internet. Engelbart, an electrical engineer, established SRI's Augmentation Research Center, where he and his group patented the computer mouse and developed the NLS (oN-Line System), a multi-user, multi-media text-based time-sharing system, operated by a graphical-user interface of mouse, chord keyset, and keyboard. Engelbart's demonstration of NLS at a computer conference in 1968,

filmed by Stewart Brand, became a famous demo in HCI circles.

Licklider had close ties to cybernetics and information theory. He presented a paper on the distortion of speech at the 1950 Macy conference, where he held his own in discussions with Norbert Wiener and Claude Shannon. In the paper, he noted a parallel between his mathematical equation for speech articulation and Shannon's entropy equation for information (Licklider, 1951). Licklider's 1960 article, "Man-Computer Symbiosis," which the HCI community regards as a founding document, resonates with cybernetics. Licklider dreamed of an interaction between humans and computers that would be analogous to biological symbiosis, a hierarchical partnership in which humans planned projects and computers carried them out. He saw symbiosis as a middle stage between semi-automatic control systems (such as SAGE) and full-blown AI in the future development of HCI (Licklider, 1960). Steeped in cybernetics at MIT (Waldrop, 2001, pp. 97–98), it was not a big step for Licklider to think of the computer as an organism that could have a symbiotic relationship with humans.

Engelbart drew on cybernetics to develop a different conception of HCI. Instead of seeing the digital computer as a partner of humans, Engelbart viewed it as a prosthesis in his program to "augment human intellect," i.e., to increase the intellectual effectiveness of knowledge workers. In 1962, he noted the similarity of his idea to that of English cybernetician W. Ross Ashby's concept of an "intelligence amplifier" (Engelbart, 1962, p. 19). Sociologist Thierry Bardini has noted that Engelbart's program of "bootstrapping" (using systems like NLS in a positive feedback manner to augment human intelligence) resonated with the cybernetics notion of feedback (though Wiener stressed negative feedback). It also resonated with a social interpretation of the biological concept of "co-evolution" proposed by Brand and Gregory Bateson in the 1970s (Bardini, 2000, pp. 24–25, 56–57). For Engelbart, the two species that coevolved were humans and computers.

An early experiment in computer communications among small groups was conducted by the main promoter of second-order cybernetics in the United States, Stuart Umpleby at George Washington University. In the mid-1970s, Umpleby established a computer conference (topical discussion group) on general systems theory, which is related to cybernetics, for about 40 researchers in the U.S., Canada, and Sweden on the Electronic Information Exchange System (EIES), a pioneering CMC system, under a grant from the U.S. National Science Foundation. Umpleby drew on the definition of second-order cybernetics as the cybernetics of cybernetics to reflexively apply systems theory to study group communications about systems research on this EIES conference (Umpleby & Umpleby, 1983; Hiltz & Turoff, 1978, pp. 18–27; and Subramanian, 2013).

ARTIFICIAL INTELLIGENCE

The emergence of artificial intelligence after World War II owed a large debt to cybernetics and information theory. The celebrated automata of the 1950s that emulated the brain and human behavior were created by cyberneticists and information theorists: W. Ross Ashby's homeostat, W. Grey Walter's tortoises, Norbert Wiener's moth/bedbug, and Claude Shannon's maze-solving mouse, Theseus (Husbands, Holland, & Wheeler, 2008). Wiener also speculated in *Cybernetics* on how to program a computer to play chess, while Shannon wrote an early influential article on how to do that using the min/max strategy from game theory (Shannon, 1950; Wiener, 1948, pp. 193–194). The 1956 Dartmouth Summer Research Project on Artificial Intelligence, which gave the field its name, was funded by the ubiquitous Warren Weaver at the Rockefeller Foundation and organized by Shannon and John McCarthy, then a mathematics professor at Dartmouth. Shannon proposed to do research that summer on using information theory to improve brain models, while McCarthy wanted to develop a suitable computer language for displaying human intelligence. That contrast illustrates the nascent split that developed between cybernetic brain models and what came to be called "symbolic AI" (Kline, 2015, pp. 153–165). Marvin Minsky, a participant at Dartmouth who co-founded, with McCarthy, the AI program at MIT (Penn, 2020, chapters 4–5), noted that the term "cybernetics" had covered all forms of machine intelligence in the 1950s. But as a result of improvements in digital computers in the 1960s, he thought that cybernetics had divided into three areas: that of minimal "Self-Organizing Systems," represented by Ashby's research; the "Simulation of Human Thought," represented by the work of Allen Newell and Herbert Simon at Carnegie Institute of Technology, who demonstrated the influential Logic Theorist computer program at Dartmouth; and "Artificial Intelligence," represented by the approach of Minsky at MIT and McCarthy, who had moved to Stanford. They aimed to "build intelligent machines without any prejudice toward making the system simple, biological, or humanoid" (Minsky, 1968, pp. 7–8).

While the latter two approaches thrived under the name of AI, self-organizing systems and neural nets were poorly funded and remained underdeveloped until the emergence of neural-net connectionism in the 1980s and Artificial Life (A-Life) in the 1990s. Both movements grew directly out of cybernetics. Connectionism, in the form of adding back-propagation to perceptron neural networks, is the predecessor of a popular technique in today's explosion in "machine learning" for data analysis, machine translation, and so forth (Boden, 2018, chapter 4). Cognitive scientist Margaret Boden calls A-Life, whose goal is to model biological systems in software or hardware, the "new cybernetics" (Boden, 2006, p. 203). From that program came the field of situated robotics, promoted by Rodney Brooks at MIT, whose colleague Cynthia Breazeal created such memorable social robots as Kismet at the turn of the millennium (Fox-Keller, 2007). Brooks was inspired to build robots that navigated their environment by reading a book by cybernetician Grey-Walter on his tortoises (Brooks, 2002, pp. 17–21, 27).

COMMUNICATION STUDY

Social scientists were also enthusiastic about cybernetics and information theory during the Cold War, especially those in the established fields of economics, psychology, and linguistics (Kline, 2020), but also those in the new fields of information science (Kline, 2004) and communication study. As noted by communication scholar Everett Rogers, cybernetics inspired the interactional communication approach of the Palo Alto Group, centered around Gregory Bateson, who developed the double-bind theory of schizophrenia, and the group dynamics field established by Kurt Lewin and Alex Bavelas, whom Bateson invited to attend the Macy conferences on cybernetics. According to Rogers, Shannon's theory "shaped the directions taken by the field of human communication, determined many of its main concepts, and contributed toward the closer intellectual integration of this field that arose from diverse multidisciplinary roots." Rogers claimed that "Information is the central concept in the study of communication, and Shannon's information theory became the root paradigm for communication study" (Rogers, 1994, pp. 411, 413).

One of the founders of the field, Wilbur Schramm, played a key role in this outcome. As chief editor of the University of Illinois Press, he published Shannon and Weaver's *The Mathematical Theory of Communication* in 1949

(Rogers, 1994, pp. 424–425; Kline, 2015, pp. 121–123). As a professor of communications at Stanford in the mid-1950s, he supervised a master's thesis that documented the spread of cybernetics and information theory in the natural and social sciences (Dahling, 1957), and wrote an influential article on the application of information theory to mass communications. In that paper, Schramm discussed two methods of applying Shannon's theory. Information measurement, a technique common at the time in psychology and linguistics (Kline 2015, pp. 138–143), used entropy equations to calculate such communication parameters as readability. The more common technique was to apply Shannon's model non-mathematically, what Schramm called its "stimulating analogic quality" (Schramm, 1955, p. 144). The technique of information measurement drew on the mathematics of Shannon's theory, but not on its engineering view of transmitting information. Shannon's model (called SMCR, for Source, Message, Channel, Receiver, in communication literature) appealed to communication scholars because it provided a convenient method to study the effects of mass communication, a central problematic in the early days of the field (Rogers, 1994 pp. 434–442).

Several communication scholars in the 1970s and 1980s called for more use of information measurement (Finn and Roberts, 1984; Ritchie, 1986; Rogers, 1994, note, p. 434), but many more criticized Shannon's model for being one-way and promoting what James Carey (2009, pp. 12–15) called the "transmission view" of human communication. Carey associated that view with the advent of the telegraph in the nineteenth century.[2] These criticisms helped to end the long run of Shannon's theory as the dominant paradigm of communication study.

CONCLUSION

While cybernetics and information theory inspired the creation of several fields of high interest to Human–Machine Communication—such as Human–Computer Interaction, Artificial Intelligence, and Communication Study—their main contribution to HMC was to blur the boundaries between humans and machines in ways that are taken for granted today. Asking Siri to find information and control household appliances, and engaging with social robots as toys and helpmates have become naturalized ways of life in well-to-do households in the early twenty-first century. In large part, I would argue, that is because their designers engaged in a cybernetic enterprise of coupling machine intelligence with

information-feedback systems, an enterprise that began three quarters of a century ago.

The history of this enterprise can help inform research in Human–Machine Communication in a couple of ways. Understanding how early researchers in Human–Computer Interaction, Artificial Intelligence, and Communication Study drew on cybernetics and information theory to establish the principles of their fields can help explicate what concepts of communication and control are built into computer interfaces and robots, as well as the main paradigm for studying communications. Furthermore, reading the classic literature of these fields—such as Norbert Wiener's *The Human Use of Human Beings* (1954), J. C. R. Licklider's "Man-Computer Symbiosis" (1960), and Marvin Minsky's *The Society of Mind* (1985)—can illuminate present debates in HMC about the meaning of information and control, the machine-like character of mind, and the mind-like character of machines.

NOTES

1   This section expands on the point made by Everett Rogers (1994, p. 397), that "Wiener was unique (along with Claude Shannon) among other communication theorists in including machines as possible components in a communication system."
2   For a similar conclusion from linguistics, see Reddy, 1979.

REFERENCES

Bar-Hillel, Y. (1955). Semantic information and its measures. In H. von Foerster, M. Mead, & H. Teuber (Eds.). *Cybernetics: Circular causal and feedback mechanisms in biology and social systems. Transactions ...*, vols. 6-10 (pp. 10: 35-48). Josiah Macy Foundation.

Bardini, T. (2000). *Bootstrapping: Douglas Engelbart, coevolution, and the origins of personal computing*. Stanford University Press.

Barnes, S. B. (2002). Computer interfaces. In A. Akera & F. Nebeker (Eds.). *From 0 to 1: An authoritative history of modern computing* (Chapter 11). Oxford University Press.

Bateson, G. (1979). *Mind and nature: A necessary unity*. E. P. Dutton.

Boden, M. A. (2006). *Mind as machine: A history of cognitive science*. Clarendon Press.

Boden, M. A. (2018). *Artificial intelligence: A very short introduction*. Oxford University Press.

Boulanger, G. R. (1969). Prologue: What is cybernetics? In J. Rose (Ed.). *Survey of cybernetics: A tribute to Dr. Norbert Wiener* (pp. 3–9). Iliffe Books.

Brand, S. (1987). *The media lab: Inventing the future at MIT*. Viking.

Brooks, R. (2002). *Flesh and machines: How robots will change us*. Vintage Books.

Carey, J. (2009). *Communication as culture: Essays on media and society*, rev. ed. Routledge.

Cherry, C. (1957). *On human communication: A review, a survey, and a criticism*. MIT Press.

Dahling, R. L. (1957). Shannon's information theory: The spread of an idea [Master's thesis, Stanford University].

Engelbart, D. (1962). Augmenting human intellect: A conceptual framework. Air Force Office of Scientific Research. Available at www.dougengelbart.org/pubs/papers/scanned/Doug_Engelbart-AugmentingHumanIntellect.pdf. Accessed July 1, 2020.

Finn, S., & Roberts, D. F. (1984). Source, destination, and entropy: Reassessing the role of information theory in communication research. *Communication Research*, 11(4): 453–476.

Fox-Keller, E. (2007). Booting up baby. In J. Riskin (Ed.). *Genesis redux: Essays in the history and philosophy of artificial life* (pp. 334–345). University of Chicago Press.

Galison, P. (1994). The ontology of the enemy: Norbert Wiener and the cybernetic vision. *Critical Inquiry*, 21: 228–266.

Guzman, A. L. (2018). Introduction: "What is human-machine communication, anyway?" In A. L. Guzman (Ed.). *Human-machine communication: Rethinking communication, technology, and ourselves* (pp. 1–28). Peter Lang.

Heims, S. J. (1991). *The cybernetics group*. MIT Press.

Hiltz, S. R, & Turoff, M. (1978). *The network nation: Human communication via computer*. Addison-Wesley.

Husbands, P., Holland, O., & Wheeler, M. (Eds.). (2008). *The mechanical mind in history*. MIT Press.

Kline, R. (2004). What is information theory a theory of? Boundary work among information theorists and information scientists in the United States and Britain during the cold war. In W. B. Rayward & M. E. Bowden (Eds.). *The history and heritage of scientific and technical information systems: Proceedings of the 2002 conference ...* (pp. 15–28). Information Today.

Kline, R. (2015). *The cybernetics moment: Or why we call our age the information age*. Johns Hopkins University Press.

Kline, R. (2020). How disunity matters to the history of cybernetics in the human sciences. *History of the Human Sciences*, 33: 12–35.

Licklider, J. C. R. (1951). The manner in which and extent to which speech can be distorted and remain intelligible. In H. von Foerster, M. Mead, & H. Teuber (Eds.). *Cybernetics: Circular causal and feedback mechanisms in biology and social systems. Transactions ...*, vols. 6–10 (pp. 7: 59–122). Josiah Macy Foundation.

Licklider, J. C. R. (1960). Man-computer symbiosis. *IRE Transactions on Human Factors in Electronics* (March): 4–11.

MacKay, D. M. (1952). In search of basic symbols. In H. von Foerster, M. Mead, & H. Teuber (Eds.). *Cybernetics: Circular causal and feedback mechanisms in biology and social systems. Transactions ...*, vols. 6–10 (pp. 8: 181–221). Josiah Macy Foundation.

MacKay, D. M. (1969). *Information, mechanism, and meaning*. MIT Press.

Mindell, D. A. (2002). *Between human and machine: Feedback, control, and computing before cybernetics*. Johns Hopkins University Press.

Minsky, M. (1968). Introduction. In M. Minsky (Ed.). *Semantic information processing* (pp. 1-32). MIT Press.

Minsky, M. (1985). *The society of mind*. Simon and Schuster.

Penn, J. N. R. (2020). Inventing intelligence: On the history of complex information processing and artificial intelligence in the United States in the mid-twentieth century [Doctoral thesis, University of Cambridge].

Pierce, J. R. (1980). *An introduction to information theory: Symbols, signals, and noise* (2nd ed.). Dover.

Reddy, M. J. (1979). The conduit metaphor: A case of frame conflict in our language about language. In A. Ortony (Ed.). *Metaphor and Thought* (pp. 284–324). Cambridge University Press.

Rheingold, H. (1993). *The virtual community: Homesteading on the electronic frontier*. Addison-Wesley.

Ritchie, D. (1986). Shannon and Weaver: Unravelling the paradox of information. *Communication Research*, 13(2): 278–298.

Rogers, E. M. (1994). *A history of communication study: A biographical approach*. Free Press.

Rosenblueth, A., Wiener, N., & Bigelow, J. (1943). Behavior, purpose and teleology. *Philosophy of Science*, 10: 18–24.

Schramm, W. (1955). Information theory and mass communication. *Journalism Quarterly*, 32: 131–146.

Segal, J. (2003). *Le zéro et le un: Histoire de la notion scientifique d'information au 20e siècle*. Éditions Syllepse.

Shannon, C. E. (1948). A mathematical theory of communication. *Bell System Technical Journal*, 27: 379–423, 623–656.

Shannon, C. E. (1950). Programming a computer for playing chess. *Philosophical Magazine*, 7th series, 41: 256–275.

Subramanian, R. (2013). Starr Roxanne Hiltz: Pioneer digital sociologist. *IEEE Annals of the History of Computing*, 35(1): 78–85.

Umpleby, S., & Umpleby, K. T. (1983). Applying systems theory to the conduct of systems research. In A. Debons (Ed.). *Information science in action: System design* (pp. 381–395), vol. 1. Martinus Nijhoff.

Waldrop, M. M. (2001). *The dream machine: J. C. R. Licklider and the revolution that made computing personal*. Viking.

Weaver, W. (1949). Recent contributions to the mathematical theory of communication. In C. Shannon and W. Weaver, *The mathematical theory of communication* (pp. 94–117). University of Illinois Press.

Wiener, N. (1948). *Cybernetics: Or control and communication in the animal and the machine*. John Wiley; Technology Press.

Wiener, N. (1950). *The human use of human beings: Cybernetics and society*. Houghton Mifflin.

Wiener, N. (1954). *The human use of human beings: Cybernetics and society* (rev. ed.). Anchor Books.

4

Cyborgs and Human–Machine Communication Configurations

Katina Michael, Jeremy Pitt, Roba Abbas,
Christine Perakslis, and MG Michael

INTRODUCTION

The term "cyborg" has traditionally meant "a coupling between a human being and an electronic or mechanical apparatus," or "the identity of organisms embedded in a cybernetic information system" (Balsamo, 1996, p. 11). The notion of a "cyborg" replaces the traditional Cartesian mind/body duality (Muri, 2007, p. 6); it also "undermines" the very concept of being "human" (Claudia Springer cited in Muri, 2007, p. 6). Balsamo (1996, p. 11) argues that cyborgs are hybrid entities, "neither wholly technological nor completely organic, which means that the cyborg has the potential … to disrupt persistent dualisms that set the natural body in opposition to the technologically recrafted body." Diverse interpretations of the cyborg can be found in the extant literature from the perspective of socio-technical sub-cultures and imaginaries, commercialism, materialism, feminism and gender, socialism, politicism, historicism, indigeneity, apocalypticism, economics, postmodernism, and posthumanism (Balsamo, 1996, p. 11; Mirowski, 2002; Muri 2007, p. 6). Muri (2007, p. 7) argues: "cyborg consciousness has been defined not so much by evidence as by the necessity of a given theoretical stance." But beyond the theory, all approaches and

perspectives agree on a single point; that the term "cyborg" has redefined "boundaries" not only of what "being human" means today (Muri, 2007, p. 7), but also of being emergent in the context of the present and future. Those boundaries are the subject of this chapter, first from a material configuration perspective, steeped in techno-utopianism relevant to socio-technical imaginaries, pointing to the purely "technical" possibilities. And second, toward a necessary reconfiguration of cyborg futures using a sustainability lens that places people and planet first, emphasising the need to consider social transformation as the chief cornerstone of digital transformation (Michael and Abbas, 2021). This presents a much-needed paradigm shift away from the technophilic love-affair of science fiction, enamoured by the possibilities of merging the wetware with the hardware, all the while acknowledging the truths of Donna Haraway in her classic *A Manifesto for Cyborgs* (1985) where she rightly states in the words of Muri (2007, p. 5) that we have been "utterly and irrevocably changed by the technologies merging humans and machines."

This chapter begins by defining "cyborgs," and emphasising the need to study boundaries and limitations in the context of communications at the human–machine interface. We begin with an exploration of socio-technical imaginaries and the role of science-fiction scenarios. The chapter then presents human–machine communication configurations, incorporating examples that have emanated from the creation of artefacts (e.g. exoskeletons, wearables, and implantables), and techno-utopian visions of the coalescence of the human and machine. Finally, the chapter presents a discussion around the need to cast a vision of an alternate future, where human flourishing through health, wellbeing and environmental sustainability through self-organising systems is achieved. The emphasis should be on social development and social transformation, and not the "digitalisation of everything" (Degryse, 2016), nor for the ultimate goal of society "becoming" technology (Stephan et al., 2012, p. 21). The conclusion provides a vision of a world where humans build appropriate tools for the longevity of Earth's species, toward planetary sustainability, the ultimate aim of which is security and safety. The relevance of this work to human–machine communications is in its proposal to realign our technological developments and capabilities with human wellbeing and sustainability objectives (Michael and Abbas, 2021), rather than remain enamoured by cyborgian futurism that can give rise to nihilistic potentials. Here the vision is fixed on sustainability of the person and the planet, with the belief that any other reconfiguration of the human–machine interface may well be catastrophic. When limits to just boundaries are ignored, trespassed, or overthrown, then we become ignorant, lawless, greedy, and cease to act as a collective.

METHODOLOGY: SOCIO-TECHNICAL IMAGINARIES, SCENARIOS, SCIENCE FICTION, AND ANTICIPATION

Trist (1981, p. 11) describes socio-technical systems as: (1) primary work systems (e.g. at the level of a line department), (2) whole organisation systems (e.g. entire corporations or public agencies), and (3) macrosocial systems (e.g. communities and industrial sectors and institutions at the societal level). He states that these systems can be understood from the micro to the macro, each interrelated to one another. The social imaginary on the other hand, according to Taylor (2002, p. 91) makes sense of "the practices of a society" that are divergent in nature, considering "multiple modernities." Taylor (2003) further emphasises the making of the "economy" as the major shift in society that was previously concerned with the management of resources that people collectively required. Taylor (2002, p. 105) maintains that "the

economic … defines a way in which we are linked together." He goes on to state: "I speak of imaginary because I'm talking about the way ordinary people 'imagine' their social surroundings, and this is often not expressed in theoretical terms; it is carried in images, stories, and legends" (Taylor, 2002, p. 106). By bringing together the terms "socio-technical systems" and "social imaginaries," we can better appreciate the antecedents of "socio-technical imaginaries" as defined by Jasanoff and Kim (2009, 2013, 2015). Of socio-technical imaginaries, Jasanoff (2015, p. 25) writes that they are "collectively held and performed visions of desirable futures… animated by shared understandings of forms of social life and social order attainable through, and supportive of, advances in science and technology." She continues: "socio-technical imaginaries are collective, durable, capable of being performed… these imaginaries are at once products of and instruments of the co-production of science, technology, and society in modernity" (p. 25).

In the context of socio-technical imaginaries with respect to cyborg futures, shared understandings can be found in speculative science fiction-based scenarios through narrative, and avant-garde and experimental real-world examples in practice. We have visualised the cyborg in all its guises, and from the different disciplines and perspectives through scenario planning (Lindgren and Bandhold, 2003), where we describe the power of "stories" with respect to cyborgs in the context of the "science-fiction" genre (Artz, 1998, 2008). It is here through diverse narrative forms that we are free to explore the stakeholders and the cyborg protagonists and their material networks. In this context, the cyborg is couched as not simply a human who makes use of the tools they have created, but in some sense as someone who is committing hubris, like the ancients who attempted to build a tower to reach the heavens (Gen 11:1–9) (Ware et al., 2017, p. 15). Only in this instance, some cyborgs dream of overcoming death as we know it, through the possible downloading of the consciousness to silicon chips, among other potentialities. Burnam-Fink (2015, p. 48) writes: "scenarios are stories," critically calling out scenarios for being underdeveloped, unrelatable, uncompelling and unpersuasive. Influenced by the science fiction genre, our narratives seek to ascertain the role of the human that has breath, and the role of the inhuman machine that comes to life (Hudson et al., 2021).

We repeatedly find examples of deep-seated human consciousness related to cyborgian futures (Hally, 2005), explored, for example, in Mary Shelley's (1818) *Frankenstein* and Fritz Lang's (1927) *Metropolis* to name but two classics; asking what happens when the biological gives life to the inanimate machine. More recently, the contrasting perspective in modern science fiction film has provided a bidirectional potential, in what happens when the machine takes on the guise of a human, as demonstrated in *The Terminator* (James Cameron, 1984) and *A.I. Artificial Intelligence* (Spielberg, 2001). But perhaps most controversial of all are the dystopic visions of the convergence of the human–machine, becoming not just part human and part machine, but one body, indistinguishable. Here we can point to C. S. Lewis' (1945) *That Hideous Strength*, Ridley Scott's (1982) *Blade Runner*, and Robert Longo's (1995) *Johnny Mnemonic*. In these latter three depictions of the human-machine, we venture beyond a vision of Elon Musk's (2019) Neuralink-style brain-machine interface toward the complete melding and intersection of the biological and non-biological (Armstrong and Michael, 2020; Demko et al., 2020). As Pringle (2013) so eloquently states, "life imitating art" perhaps, and if so, what does that tell us about cyborgs, cinema and our future scenarios?

We are being sold the "better, stronger, faster" motif of the *Six Million Dollar Man* (1973–1978) based on Martin Caidin's (1972) novel titled, *Cyborg*. Is the techno-scientific myth a questionable distraction to the human plight, or a plausible future intended to be discovered once a level of intelligence is achieved (Toffoletti, 2007; Schermer, 2009; Selin and Hudson, 2010; Yeoman, 2012; Emanuel et al., 2019)? Reminiscent of such works as *This Perfect Day* (Ira Levin, 1970) and George Lucas' (1971) film *THX-1138*, the politically fuelled socio-technical imaginary is revealed by those very few who hold the power, to "the rest" who do not. The questionable morality depicted in the *Iron Man* Series (Jon Favreau, 2008, 2010, 2013) exemplifies this disparity. As undemocratic as this might seem, "we the people" takes on new meaning in these contexts that prevent the people from self-organising and from making their own determinations and conclusions. So long as experimentation and tinkering continue to be top-down, the powerless will be made to feel that their struggle will merely fuel the "real machine" (i.e., the machine engine behind the creation of machines) further, that which Taylor (2002) referred to as "the economic." This leaves us with the connotation of "immaturity," defined by Immanuel Kant as "the inability to use one's understanding without guidance from another" (Kant, 1784). Bhaskar (2010) thus challenges "the people" to reclaim reality, while Finn et al. (2017) call for a unique framing of Shelley's *Frankenstein* in the promotion and enhancement of interdisciplinary dialogue.

One is left pondering whether the human–machine interface is on a level playing field, or if instead the "machine" is that process of co-production that coerces "civil society" to act in an enslaved fashion, though they be free. *Here, take of this and eat, it is good for you, it will give you something to do while you grow older preparing for the futility of death.* In these cyborgian manifestations of "little bits of heaven," we are led to believe that the world would be a better place if we all donned the head-mounted units, and zoned out completely in Zuckerberg's Metaverse, often dubbed "the new Internet" (see Neal Stephenson, *Snow Crash*; Steven Spielberg, 2018, *Ready Player One*). These systems of innovation (Edquist, 1997) emerge to sell us a dream turned reality through proofs of concept and half-baked prototypes and pilots, and the implications for policy are grave (Fox, 2018). No matter how hard we try, we are all exposed the possibilities, preoccupied with digital transformations (Matt et al., 2015; Vial, 2019) and promises of yet another industrial revolution that will have us working fewer hours for more money, while the majority of the earth's inhabitants struggle to access clean drinking water. If machines could be created to overcome any challenge, why have they not yet resolved the fundamental problem of pain (C.S. Lewis, 1940)?

No one denies the potential benefits of such technological marvels nor the brilliance of the minds behind them; however, the problem with function creep and disregard for some of the more urgent issues at hand remains. Of course, this envisioning occurs as a result of anticipation, where we ask those existential questions about life – "why are we here?," and "what happens to us when we die"? Our stories may provide a comfort, our reasons for believing them may even be called irrational, some of us even wishing to gamify the human existence. In the end, the ultimate hope of overcoming death itself through innovation has become a dominant narrative. Some might call this a form of escapism, detracting from the reality and responsibility of sustaining life on Earth for all, not just the select few.

FINDINGS: CYBORG CONFIGURATIONS – OF ARTEFACTS, BOUNDARIES, AND INTERFACES

Building on our exploration of cyborgian depictions related to the imagination, this section examines how these depictions, in part, have been incorporated in real-world human–machine communication configurations (Michael, 2003, pp.

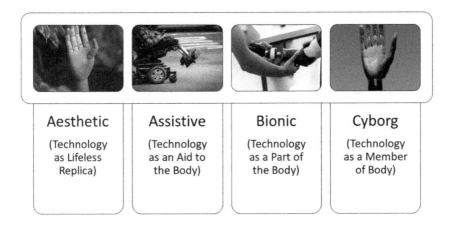

Aesthetic	Assistive	Bionic	Cyborg
(Technology as Lifeless Replica)	(Technology as an Aid to the Body)	(Technology as a Part of the Body)	(Technology as a Member of Body)

Figure 4.1   The evolution of cyborg innovations for prosthesis for assistive technology

302–310). We turn our attention now to representations that are widely recognised as belonging to anthropological and cultural descriptions of cyborgs. One category of cyborgs can be defined as those that require or opt-in to prosthetic or assistive technologies that are either life-sustaining or life-enhancing (Hamdoun et al., 2021). Some of these are bioinspired while others are purely mechanical apparatus (e.g. implantable insulin pump, electric wheelchair) (Figure 4.1). Broadly, some of these are powered by the body's movement, while others have an external or additional power source. Another category of cyborgs (Michael, 2021), loosely defined, includes those who wear, bear, carry, or utilise in some way technology in everyday life/work that serves a particular function or application that is non-medical in nature (e.g. a robot arm in a process workflow in a manufacturing plant) (Figure 4.2).

According to Downey et al. (1995, p. 265), cyborg anthropology explores "the production of humanness through machines… it invests in alternative world-making by critically examining the powers of the imagination invested in the sciences and technologies of contemporary societies." "Cyborg anthropology" is an oxymoron that bridges the non-human with the human. The field uses "human-centred presuppositions of anthropological discourse" to begin a conversation about alternate machine–human configurations. Downey et al. (1995, p. 266) describe humans as a "function of machines, machine relations, and information transfers as [much as] they are machine producers and operators." A primary indicator of the complexity of the human–machine interface is autonomy, determined by how much a human depends on or requires the machine to exist. Bioartist Eduardo Kac (1997) articulates this well

in his performance *Time Capsule*: "it is almost as if the body has become an extension of the computer, and not the other way around… organic life is indeed becoming an extension of the computer, as the emerging vectors in microchip technology clearly point to biological sources as the only way to continue the exponential process of miniaturization, beyond the limits of traditional materials." It is for this reason that the ethnographic approach is embraced by many in this field in the context of human agency with respect to the positioning of technologies (e.g. eyeglasses, airplanes, heart pacemakers). Stated simply, a cyborg is a "coproduction of human and machine" with varying degrees of agency. Individuals who take on a machine element are considered "actants" (Downey et al., 1995, p. 267) as opposed to purely "actors," and when considering actor-networks, the term is now transposed to "actant-networks" (see Latour, 1993; Holton, 2021). Cyborgology is considered "dangerous" because it blurs "the boundaries between humans and machines and between society and science" (Downey et al., 1995, p. 268).

A number of distinct patterns are prevalent in the cyborg selection environment. These include: migration, integration, and convergence, culminating in the co-existence of individual cyborg artefacts that are adopted by the market (Figure 4.2). In the following section we present five categories of cyborg human–machine configurations (Figure 4.3). By no means are these categories exhaustive, but they do illustrate the representative cyborg selection environment (Michael and Michael 2005, p. 26).

Human or machine: in this configuration, the choice between a human or a machine provides clear demarcation between the two entities. For example, an organization may choose to implement a security role using a human security guard, or fill that

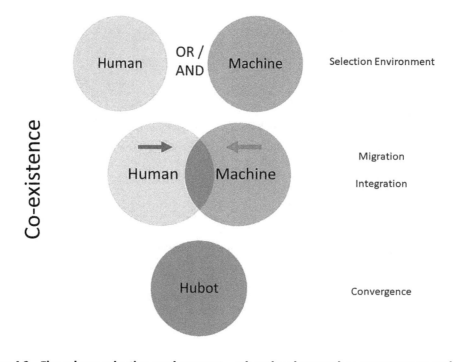

Figure 4.2   The cyborg selection environment – migration, integration, convergence and co-existence

same role with a robot (e.g. K5 robot drone from Knightscope). Human choice is retained in this decision of whether to satisfy a function using a human, or machine. The costs incurred by each scenario are different; a human incurs an operational cost (their labour), while a robot drone will incur an operational cost (maintenance). There will be up-front capital costs depending on whether a purchase decision is made to buy the robot outright or "as a service," and there will be other new not previously considered costs, such as an employment robot tax handed down by government, cybersecurity-related costs to defend against unauthorised access, and much more (Michael et al. 2010). Despite the distinction between the human and the machine, depending on the context, there may be a human in-the-loop. For example, consider a team of firefighters using a drone to conduct reconnaissance in a burning building. The firefighter by extension, e.g. remote monitoring through a drone, can be considered a cyborg logically, but the material bodies of the drone and human remain separate. The drone is not embodied in/on the human but amplifies the senses of the firefighter by providing "eyes" through remote observation, something that is otherwise unachievable by using just the human sense of direct line of sight. This is known as a secondary human action in human systems integration design (Silva-Martinez, 2016).

Human and machine: in this configuration, there is a decision to introduce a machine into the direct purview of a human's material action. Rather than replace the human with a machine, human systems engineering determines that in a given task in a workflow, the human could be directly assisted by a hard or soft machine. In the case of a hardware-based machine, a human might be assisted in fitting a car door in the construction of a vehicle. A hydraulic hoist with suction pad is then utilised under the control of a human arm to guide the robot arm until a clean join is made. Here the human maintains full autonomy, and the machine is used as an aid to lessen the burden on the human. This is known as primary human actions, which are front-line actions where humans are in direct interface with a physical machine for process stability (Silva-Martinez, 2016). The human could attach the car door to the rest of the vehicle on their own accord, but the human effort combined with the assistance of the machine can access three benefits: a more precise construction, faster task completion, and a human actor whose wellbeing is not compromised due to repetitive strain injury (RSI) or heavy lifting. For those in the field of human systems engineering, the machine's support is optimal when considering what are known as "human factors" (Booher, 2003).

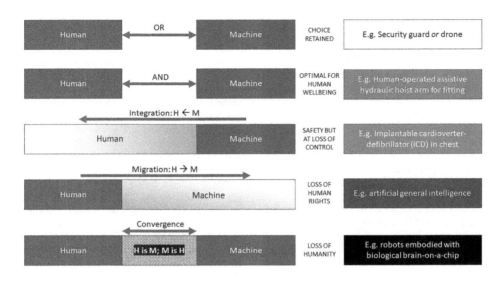

Figure 4.3   Cyborg human–machine communication configurations

Integration (human ← machine): in this configuration, the human by necessity or choice invites a hardware/software machine into/onto the body for a prosthetic or perceived human augmentation or enhancement (Anderson, 2003). In this configuration, the machine comes in two modalities: either wholly within the body or physically attached to the body either permanently or intermittently. The first modality is the machine being wholly embodied in the human through a process of implantation and may come as several interconnected parts (e.g. electrodes that act as stimulators, a lead, and corresponding battery pack in Deep Brain Stimulation). In this case, the human-machine interface is direct, as in the case of an implantable cardioverter-defibrillator (ICD) in the chest, triggered when someone goes into sudden cardiac arrest. In the second modality, a human takes on an exoskeleton for heavy lifting (Rébé, 2021). The apparatus is fitted to the human, granting them additional power to lift without being injured, for example, in the sorting of sizeable parcels moving along a conveyer belt at a distribution hub. Another key feature in this setting that can help delineate the various forms of integration, is whether the machine can self-actuate, effectively knowing when to turn itself on and off to conserve battery if required, or knowing when to autonomously receive bio-feedback from an organ or send bio-feedback to another machine for processing, or whether the machine needs direct human intervention to work.

In the field of human systems engineering, the term "human systems integration" (National Research Council, 2007) is often used to describe this kind of human–machine interface where data is collected from the human actor by the machine and sent by the machine to another host for further analysis and storage. The machine in the body can also act semi-autonomously in response to reading specific biological indicators, in order to find an optimal action. Increasingly, such devices will be configurable by the socio-economic circumstances, cultural context and behavioural traits of an individual. When machines enter the body, they are usually considered a mechanism for safety, e.g. for the treatment of a disease or deterioration of an organ's function (Michael, 2018a, 2018b). The use of the machine is due to the human's loss of control and/or agency. If a machine in the human body unexpectedly malfunctions, the result can be at the very least a diminishment of human activity, with more severe consequences possible. For more complex prosthetic devices, the machine in the body communicates wirelessly back to its manufacturer (Michael, 2017). At times, coordinated machines embedded in the body may work in concert to deliver a human capability (e.g. a neural chip in the brain working with sensor chips in the arm to excite the muscles to render movement in an individual living with quadriplegia).

Migration (human → machine): one of the socio-technical imaginaries brought about by science fiction novels and films, has given rise to the possibility of migration from human to machine, with advanced speculative cyborg functionality. At the physical layer, a step in this direction is the building of hardware that mimics the human brain.

Neuromorphic computing has modestly progressed to emulate the way a human brain functions by radically changing the computer system's architecture of a microchip from the traditional CMOS (complementary metal oxide semiconductor) to a chip that contains what is analogously identified as neurons and synapses with memristor memory stores. While brain on a bench projects allow for simulations to occur using machinery to learn more about how the brain functions, there are neuroengineers who envision the ability to replicate a person's brain function onto a machine (Lozano et al., 2016; Wallace et al., 2020).

While it has been demonstrated that a tiny part of someone's brain can be modelled using advanced computing, and the effort to achieve artificial general intelligence (AGI) is still being pursued. Realistically achieving AGI may well be determined to be impossible in the evolution of humankind. While machines are quick to compute, they are limited by physics and digital capacity. The brain on the other hand is asynchronous and analogue. For some, the ultimate discovery as a socio-technical imaginary would be to harness the power of the brain of a human, and download it (and theoretically consciousness with it), thus migrating it to a computational device that has previously developed some intuition and even perception. The ultimate hope for some in this context is removing the need to retain the human body which decays, and instead preserving that part which is able to "think," e.g., *Archive* (Gavin Rothery, 2020). This is when we can return to the definition of cyborg anthropology and argue the term's redundancy. Analysed carefully, there can be no human rights when someone's brain is embodied in an external storage device. It might even be said that communications between the human brain and such a machine brain could be a relay to the "self." In undergoing a pattern of migration to the machine, the human would be anything but a person. Rather, the human would be completely disembodied in form, save for the simulation of the self in bits and bytes (Stephan et al., 2012). We could label this configuration HAAS, after the term human-as-a-system, in which the human is no longer in the loop, or in control. HAAS is when a human is "considered as a system within the systems," stressing that systems are ultimately designed for humans (Wong, 2009), even if they are embodied in something other than human form.

Convergence (human is machine): in this final speculative form of the human and machine interface, true convergence occurs when humans and machines are indistinguishable from one another. An example of convergence may well be the science fiction scenario of a hubot ('human-like' robot) that is sentient with a human brain encapsulated in a machine. Here we can say rather loosely that humans may be considered redundant. This is one of the most dire scenarios of them all. While some transhumanists dream of a hybridisation of humans and robots, even unto robot companions that hold beliefs and attitudes, machines are required to be powered and such a vision of a human-breathed robot is short-sighted. This theme is addressed extensively in the work of Carvalko (2020).

If we inspect human–machine interface configurations, we are able to better understand cyborgian realities today. The selection environment is ever widening to be inclusive of several variant cyborg interpretations. What are we to take as legitimate? For if we believe that eyeglasses will make one a cyborg, then almost all of us may be categorised as such. But if we are to render full fusion of the biological with the synthetic, then we are only now embarking on that journey for silicon to be melded into the brain and to interpret biological signals as if it were a part of the body (e.g. a prosthetic limb after amputation that has been linked to the central nervous system) (Pataranutaporn et al., 2018).

DISCUSSION: ALTERNATE VISION – SUSTAINABILITY OF PEOPLE AND PLANET

What will be humanity's future? Futurists attempt to answer this question by offering a variety of predictions. Many of these predictions continue to be steeped in science fiction, making it difficult for science and technology studies scholars to forecast or provide foresight without being caught up in conjectures. A search of the TED/TEDx series demonstrates that topics of device implantation (biotechnology or otherwise), prosthesis, augmentation, transhumanism, and posthumanism dominate talks by futurists. One criticism of proponents of cyborgian futures by science and technology studies (STS) and interdisciplinary social studies scholars is the preoccupation with the "artefact" itself. For instance, Aicardi et al. (2018) note that inquiry into the future of humanity, or any scenario context, should avoid commencing with the artefact as the central "actor" to the narrative. Thus, we should not seek to personify the object, nor should we be technologically deterministic. Rather, imagination and the collective consciousness should propel us forward first, after which we may better articulate the socio-technical imaginary. Alex McDowell (2019) and his team of collaborators have placed greater significance on looking at the world we wish to inhabit, believing that the stories we tell shape our future. His team's ambitious aim is to "world-build" our future proactively, rather than fall victim to someone else's ideals, although non-participation has great merit because silence can at times mean refusal to comply with a vision that is not shared (Cechanowicz et al., 2016; von Stackelberg and McDowell, 2015; Zaidi, 2019). Finn and Wiley (2021) refer to this as "collaborative imagination" with the central belief that together "we can build the future" (Finn, 2015) through the engagement of narrative-based learning activities (Mawasi et al., 2021). Finn, who directs the Center for Science and the Imagination at Arizona State University, seeks to work closely with scholars across disciplines to ensure more robust socio-technical imaginaries.

We return from micro to macro socio-technical systems perspectives (Trist, 1981), and acknowledge that while some researchers apply actor-network theory (ANT) (Callon and Latour, 1992; Latour, 1996, 2007; Roßmann, 2021; Walsham, 1997) to the study of cyborgs, others focus on the design of cyborg systems through the application of multi-level perspectives. The social-technical imaginaries of cyborgs do not simply pertain to the individual who has undergone amputation and is seeking the best possible outcome for their prosthetic limb (micro perspective); but also to the identification of collective ideas and meanings that emerge when groups, such as organizations, promote a given socio-technical cyborgian vision (meso perspective), and especially pertain to the whole socio-technical suprasystem (macro perspective) (Magnani and Cittati, 2022). Konrad and Böhle (2019, p. 101) study "socio-technical futures, such as widely debated technological promises, deeply rooted socio-technical imaginaries, or carefully crafted scenarios [that] are important elements in the governance of innovation processes." In their deduction, socio-technical futures are those that "couple techno-scientific potentials and prospects with envisioned societal change and new social arrangements... [Their] interest in socio-technical futures includes not only the knowledge objects, such as scenarios, roadmaps, imaginaries or narratives, but as well the practices and processes that contribute to the construction of socio-technical futures and the ways they get a bearing on innovation and governance processes." These socio-technical futures require a variety of stakeholders to come together with different experiences, challenges and interests, speculating on how certain outcomes might be governed if they eventuate (Konrad and Böhle, 2019, p. 102).

Chilvers et al. (2018, p. 202) offer a framework for wider socio-technical systems and ecologies of participation proven by time and space that provide for participatory practices. These form multiple participatory collectives that can be connected with, for example, institutional settings, which prescribe and reproduce particular identities and imaginaries of publics (e.g. consumer-citizens, innocent citizens) (McCarthy, 2021).

As we reflect on the different configurations and potentialities from stand-alone to symbiotic beings and fully-fledged coalescence of human and machine, important values begin to be drawn out related to privacy, security, autonomy, control, and more. The borders and definitions of privacy, of surveillance, and of security are more meaningful as we traverse from micro to macro socio-technical systems where boundaries are crossed between firms, regulators, members of society, and the physical environment (Lalonde, 2018). At each level, micro through to macro, the trespass of physical and psychological borders without consent will cause a fractures in expected laws and rules, and normalised protocols (Abbas et al., 2022). In order to assess privacy violations in these socio-technical systems, we must consider invasions relative to "borders of privacy." Marx (2001) proposed four such borders. *Natural Borders* relate to materially observable elements such as walls, doors, clothing, facial expressions, and oral conversations. *Social Borders* relate to expectations such as confidentiality with professionals or family and friends, and freedom from invasion of privacy by others in the social system. *Spatial or Temporal Borders* relate to expectations such as the right to delineate between various areas of an individual's life (work, personal, religious spheres) or at various points in time, and rights to maintain decoupled spheres. *Borders Due to Ephemeral or Transitory Effects* relate to expectations such as the right to have information forgotten, or to delete permanently a past extemporaneous or regrettable action. Human–computer interactions (HCIs), as achieved through cyborg multi-functionality, would most certainly generate a fifth border: the *Physio-Psychological Border*, defined as "the boundaries of the internal realm of the individual's human system such as physiological and psychological; the expectations of personal autonomy and self-determination of his or her human system, including ownership of the information" (Perakslis et al., 2016).

The cyborg future is not just about "me" (Hughes, 2004), but about how "we" transition (Hayles, 2006) on matters related to, for example, energy, with respect to "policies, laws, regulations, infrastructures, established social practices, socio-technical imaginaries, and collective forms

Figure 4.4   In search of alternate narratives over time – nature, homo sapiens, the built environment and synthetic futures

of public reason that have become established within situated (national) political cultures over historical time" (Chilvers et al., 2018, p. 202). It is to acknowledge the cyborg self but in the context of a network (Mitchell, 2004), and at that, a network of stakeholders (Nickelsen, 2018). It is Genevieve Liveley (2006, 2019, 2022) who points us to the need to be creative in our social futures and to look for alternate narratives. Liveley looks back (2019) and anticipates (2020) using narratology (Figure 4.4). Rivera (2012) refers to these eloquently as "future histories." And no doubt, incorporated within these future histories must also be cyborg morals, values and ethics if a revolution awaits (Warwick, 2003, 2014; Wright et al., 2014; Forester and Morrison, 1994). Cyborgs need to be every bit as much a part of that dialogue as others.

The most pressing agenda item for those who self-identify as cyborgs (or not) are sustainability scenarios (Ciegis et al., 2009). For without sustainable development neither cyborgs nor others who self-identify as non-cyborgs will survive an "uncertain world" (Peterson et al., 2003). The most pressing issues are often how we mobilise together to care for the current ecosystem within which we reside, to ensure longevity and sustainability. In this context, scholars refer to sustainability transitions (Markard et al., 2012) that will assist us to manage the future (Ringland and Schwartz, 1998) through imagining sustainability (Sondeijker, 2009). Scenario planning is thus a vital tool with which we can visualise, predict, and plan for the future (Schoemaker, 1995). It is futile to think about cyborgisation without grounding the science fiction in reality. We need to acknowledge that no matter how "service oriented" we become in this manifest Gig economy (Michael, 2022), that outsourcing the human mind to computers will not save humankind in a salvific or *deus ex machina* kind of way. Cyborgology has to become responsible, even in its social futures,

and especially in its socio-technical imaginaries. Otherwise, we might as well don the Oculus goggles and join in the escapism of the Metaverse, all the while our physical environment continues to decay whether or not we acknowledge that decay (Hess and Sovacool, 2020). Eldred et al. (2021, p. 4) too ask that question "Why could not progress consist of taking a step back into more elementary truths than modern science and technology are ever able to uncover, and which they seem intent on covering up?" We thus argue for a collective approach to sustainability of the person and planet where we can harness the power of technology (Pitt et al., 2021), but not necessarily have to "become" technology to survive the unknowns. Technology itself is a part answer, and not the whole answer or the only answer. What might our visions of the future now look like having reoriented human–machine communications not to the self but to society?

CONCLUSION

This chapter has investigated cyborgs through socio-technical imaginaries, acknowledging the importance of scenarios, science-fiction, narratives, the artefact, connections, borders and interfaces, and the broader socio-technical ecosystem. It has set cyborgs in the context of a macrosocial image and not merely as a micro entity revolving around the "me." Cyborgs are part of a complex internetworked system, and no matter how we understand their social futures, they are still bound to gravity and a physical environment. Any narrative of the cyborg must be inclusive of a narrative of humans and the planet. We can assert that the collective is just as important as the individual member in society, and that we all must join together to discuss how we would like to self-organise and "world build" for a better tomorrow. Understanding human–machine communications, and the borderlands reach with respect to safety and security, privacy and attention, and surveillance and neglect, means that we will be better able to navigate the needs of society at large through structured and nuanced governance. As the complexity of bidirectional transaction flows increases (not just human to machine, but machine to human to machine to machine and any combination thereof) we must harness the data that is gathered and create better knowledge systems to inform our decisions. There is no doubt that cyborgisation will result in information being generated over a multiplicity of networks. By creating knowledge systems to better capture the components that make up our world, it is critical that we create regenerative processes toward sustainability of people and planet.

REFERENCES

Abbas, R., Michael, K., Michael, M.G., Perakslis, C., & Pitt, J., 2022. Machine Learning, Convergence Digitalization, and the Concentration of Power: Enslavement by Design Using Techno-Biological Behaviors. *IEEE Transactions on Technology and Society*, 3(2), pp. 76–88. doi: 10.1109/TTS.2022.3179756.

Aicardi, C., Fothergill, B.T., Rainey, S., Stahl, B.C., & Harris, E., 2018. Accompanying technology development in the Human Brain Project: From foresight to ethics management, *Futures*, 102: 114–124, ISSN 0016-3287, https://doi.org/10.1016/j.futures.2018.01.005.

Anderson, W. T., 2003. Augmentation, symbiosis, transcendence: technology and the future(s) of human identity. *Futures*, 35(5): 535–546.

Armstrong, W., & Michael, K., 2020. The Implications of Neuralink and Brain Machine Interface Technologies. *IEEE International Symposium on Technology and Society (ISTAS)*, pp. 201–203. doi: 10.1109/ISTAS50296.2020.9462223.

Artz, J.M., 1998. The role of stories in computer ethics. *ACM SIGCAS Computers and Society*, 28(1): 11–13.

Artz, J.M., 2008. The central problem in cyber ethics and how stories can be used to address it. In *Information Security and Ethics: Concepts, Methodologies, Tools, and Applications* (pp. 238–252). IGI Global.

Balsamo, A.M., 1996. *Technologies of the gendered body: Reading cyborg women*. Duke University Press.

Bhaskar, R., 2010. *Reclaiming reality: A critical introduction to contemporary philosophy*. Routledge.

Booher, H. R., 2003. *Handbook of Human Systems Integration* (Vol. 23). John Wiley & Sons.

Burnam-Fink, M., 2015. Creating narrative scenarios: Science fiction prototyping at Emerge. *Futures*, 70: 48–55.

Caiden, M., 1972. *Cyborg*. Arbor House.

Callon, M., & Latour, B. 1992. Don't throw the baby out with the bath school! A reply to Collins and Yearley. In A. Pickering (Ed.), *Science as practice and culture*, 343(368). University of Chicago Press.

Cameron, J., 1984. *The Terminator*. United States: Orion Pictures.

Carvalko, J. R., 2020. *Conserving humanity at the dawn of posthuman technology*, Palgrave Macmillan, p. 238.

Cechanowicz, L., Cantrell, B., & McDowell, A., 2016, World building and the future of media: A case study-Makoko 2036. *IEEE Technology and Society Magazine*, 35(4): 28–38, doi: 10.1109/MTS.2016.2618678.

Ciegis, R., Ramanauskiene, J., & Martinkus, B., 2009. The concept of sustainable development and its use for sustainability scenarios. *Engineering Economics*, 62(2).

Chilvers, J., Pallett, H., & Hargreaves, T., 2018. Ecologies of participation in socio-technical change: The case of energy system transitions. *Energy Research & Social Science*, 42: 199–210.

Degryse, C., 2016. Digitalisation of the economy and its impact on labour markets. *ETUI research paper-working paper*, WP 2016.02, Brussels, Belgium: ETUI aisbl, pp. 1–80.

Demko, M., Michael, K. Wagner, K. & Bookman, T. When Brain Computer Interfaces Pose an Existential Risk. 2020 *IEEE International Symposium on Technology and Society (ISTAS)*, 2020, pp. 112–114, doi: 10.1109/ISTAS50296.2020.9462244.

Downey, G. L., Dumit, J., & Williams, S., 1995. Cyborg anthropology. *Cultural Anthropology*, 10(2): 264–269.

Genevieve Lively, 2019. *Narratology*, Oxford, Oxford University Press.

Edquist, C., 1997. *Systems of innovation: Technologies, institutions and organizations*. Pinter.

Eldred, M., Michael, M.G. & Michael, K., 2021. *Michael Eldred on the Digital Age: Challenges for Today's Thinking*, M&K Press, Wollongong, Australia.

Emanuel, P., Walper, S., DiEuliis, D., Klein, N., Petro, J. B., & Giordano, J., 2019. *Cyborg soldier 2050: Human/machine fusion and the implications for the future of the DOD*. CCDC CBC APG United States.

Favreau, J., 2008. *Iron Man*. Marvel Studios.

Favreau, J., 2010. *Iron Man 2*. Marvel Studios.

Favreau, J., 2013. *Iron Man 3*. Marvel Studios.

Finn, E., 2015. We can build the future. *Computer*, 48(11): 90–91.

Finn, E., Guston, D., & Robert, J.S. (eds). 2017, *Frankenstein*, The MIT Press, Cambridge: Massachusetts, http://library.oapen.org/handle/20.500.12657/31387

Finn, E., & Wylie, R., 2021. Collaborative imagination: A methodological approach. *Futures*, 132: 102788.

Forester, T., & Morrison, P., 1994. *Computer ethics: Cautionary tales and ethical dilemmas in computing*. MIT Press.

Fox, S., 2018. Cyborgs, robots and society: Implications for the future of society from human enhancement with in-the-body technologies. *Technologies*, 6(2): 50.

Gray, C. H., 2000. *Cyborg citizen: Politics in the post-human age*. Routledge.

Hally, M., 2005. *Electronic brains: stories from the dawn of the computer age*. Granta Books.

Hamdoun, S., Michael, K., Monteleone, R., & Bookman, T., 2021. Assistive Technologies for Greatly Improved Quality of Life for People Living With MND/ALS. *IEEE Consumer Electronics Magazine*, 10(3): 76–81. doi: 10.1109/MCE.2020.3035523.

Haraway, D.J., 1985. *A manifesto for cyborgs: Science, technology, and socialist feminism in the 1980s* (pp. 173–204). San Francisco, CA: Center for Social Research and Education.

Hayles, N.K., 2006. Unfinished work: From cyborg to cognisphere. *Theory, Culture & Society*, 23(7–8): 159–166.

Hess, D.J. & Sovacool, B.K., 2020. Sociotechnical matters: Reviewing and integrating science and technology studies with energy social science. *Energy Research & Social Science*, 65, 101462. https://doi.org/10.1016/j.erss.2020.101462.

Hudson, A.D., Finn, E., & Wylie, R., 2021. What can science fiction tell us about the future of artificial intelligence policy?. *AI & SOCIETY*, 1–15.

Hughes, J., 2004. *Citizen cyborg: Why democratic societies must respond to the redesigned human of the future*. Basic Books.

Jasanoff, S. (2015). Future imperfect: Science, technology, and the imaginations of modernity. In S. Jasanoff, & S.H. Kim (Eds.). *Dreamscapes of modernity. Socio-technical imaginaries and the fabrication of power* (pp. 1–33). The University of Chicago Press.

Jasanoff, S., & Kim, S. H. (2009). Containing the atom: Sociotechnical imaginaries and nuclear power in the United States and South Korea. *Minerva*, 47(2): 119–146. https://doi.org/10.1007/s11024-009-9124-4.

Jasanoff, S., & Kim, S.-H. (Eds.). (2015). *Dreamscapes of modernity. Sociotechnical imaginaries and the fabrication of power*. University of Chicago.

Kac, E. (1997). *Time capsule*, www.ekac.org/timec.html

Kallistos Ware, M.G. Michael and Katina Michael, 2017. *Religion, Science & Technology: An Eastern Orthodox Perspective*. M&K Press.

Kant, I. (1784). *An answer to the question: "What is enlightenment?,"* Konigsberg in Prussia, September 30, 1784.

Konrad, K., & Böhle, K., 2019. Socio-technical futures and the governance of innovation processes—An introduction to the special issue. *Futures*, 109, pp. 101–107.

Lalonde, P.C., 2018. Cyborg work: Borders as simulation. *The British Journal of Criminology*, 58(6): 1361–1380.

Lang, F., 1927. *Metropolis*. United States: Paramount Pictures.

Latour, B., 1993. *We have never been modern*. Harvard University Press.

Latour, B., 1996. On actor-network theory: A few clarifications. *Soziale welt*, 369–381.

Latour, B., 2007. *Reassembling the social: An introduction to actor-network-theory*. Oxford University Press.

Levin, I., 1970. *This Perfect Day*. Random House.

Lewis, C. S., 1940, *The problem of pain*. The Centenary Press.

Lewis, C.S., 1945. *That Hideous Strength: A Modern Fairy-Tale for Grown-Ups*. Nelson, U.K. (retrieved from: https://isfdb.org/cgi-bin/title.cgi?1034)

Lindgren, M., & Bandhold, H., 2003. *Scenario planning*. Palgrave.

Lively, G., 2006. Science fictions and cyber myths: or, do cyborgs dream of Dolly the sheep?. In *Laughing with Medusa: Classical myth and feminist thought* (pp. 275–294). Oxford University Press.

Lively, G., 2017. Anticipation and narratology. In *Handbook of anticipation: Theoretical and applied aspects of the use of future in decision making* (pp. 1–20). Springer International Publishing AG.

Lively, G., 2019. *Narratology*. Oxford University Press.

Lively, G., 2020. Ovid's Metamorphoses: Changing Worlds. In *A Companion to World Literature*, pp. 1–12.

Lively, G., 2022. Narrative: Telling social futures. In *Routledge handbook of social futures* (pp. 224–232). Routledge.

Lively, G., & Thomas, S., 2020. Homer's intelligent machines. In Steven Cave, Kanta Dihal, and Sarah Dillon (Eds.), *AI narratives: A history of imaginative thinking about intelligent machines* (p. 25). Oxford University Press.

Longo, R., 1995. *Johnny Mnemonic*. Johnny Mnemonic Productions.

Lozano, Rodrigo, Stevens, Leo, Thompson, Brianna C., Gilmore, Kerry J., Gorkin III, Robert A., Stewart, Elise M., in het Panhuis, Marc, Romero-Ortega, Mario I., & Wallace, Gordon G., 2016. Brain on a bench top, *Australian Institute for Innovative Materials - Papers*. 2079. https://ro.uow.edu.au/aiimpapers/2079

Lucas, G., 1971, *THX-1138*. Warner Bros, American Zoetrope.

Magnani, N. & Cittati, V-M., 2022. Combining the multilevel perspective and socio-technical imaginaries in the study of community energy. *Energies*. 15(5):1624. https://doi.org/10.3390/en15051624

Markard, J., Raven, R., & Truffer, B., 2012. Sustainability transitions: An emerging field of research and its prospects. *Research Policy*, 41(6): 955–967.

Marx, G.T., 2001. Murky conceptual waters: The public and the private. *Ethics and Information Technology*, 3(3), pp.157-169.

Matt, C., Hess, T., & Benlian, A., 2015. Digital transformation strategies. *Business & Information Systems Engineering*, 57(5): 339–343.

Mawasi, A., Nagy, P., Finn, E., & Wylie, R., 2021. Narrative-based learning activities for science ethics education: An affordance perspective. *Journal of Science Education and Technology*, 1–11.

McCarthy, D. R., 2021. Imposing evenness, preventing combination: Charting the international dynamics of socio-technical imaginaries of innovation in American foreign policy. *Cambridge Review of International Affairs*, 34(2): 296–315.

McDowell, A. (2019). Storytelling shapes the future. *Journal of Futures Studies*, 23(3), pp. 105–112. doi:10.6531/JFS.201903_23(3).0001

Michael, K., 2003. *The technological trajectory of the automatic identification industry: the application of the systems of innovation (SI) framework for the characterisation and prediction of the auto-ID industry*, PhD thesis, School of Information Technology and Computer Science, University of Wollongong. http://ro.uow.edu/theses/309

Michael, K., 2017. Implantable medical device tells all: Uberveillance gets to the heart of the matter. *IEEE Consumer Electronics Magazine*, 6(4), pp.107–115. doi: 10.1109/MCE.2017.2714279.

Michael, K., 2018a. Brain pacemakers in consumer medical electronics improve quality of life: Benefits, risks, and challenges. *IEEE Consumer Electronics Magazine*, 7(4), pp.82–85. doi: 10.1109/MCE.2018.2816298.

Michael, K., 2018b. Brain pacemakers in consumer medical electronics improve quality of life-Part II: The need for patient feedback in the product lifecycle management. *IEEE Consumer Electronics Magazine*, 7(6), pp. 51–54. doi: 10.1109/MCE.2018.2835879.

Michael, K., 2021. DARPA's ADAPTER Program: Applying the ELSI Approach to a Semi-Autonomous Complex Socio-Technical System. 2021 *IEEE Conference on Norbert Wiener in the 21st Century (21CW)*, pp.1–10.doi:10.1109/21CW48944.2021.9532581.

Michael, K., 2022. Modern indentured servitude in the gig economy: A case study on the deregulation of the taxi industry in the United States. *IEEE Technology and Society Magazine*, 41(2), pp. 30–41. doi: 10.1109/MTS.2022.3173306.

Michael, K., & Michael, M.G. 2005. Microchipping people: The rise of the electrophorus. *Quadrant*, 49(3): 22–33.

Michael, K., & Abbas, R., 2021. Technology, information systems and sustainability: A public interest research agenda. In Y. Dwivedi et al., "Climate change and COP26: Are digital technologies and information management part of the problem or the solution? An editorial reflection and call to action," *International Journal of Information Management*, 102456, JJIM_102456PIIS0268-4012(21)00149-www.sciencedirect.com/science/article/pii/S0268401221001493

Michael, K., , George, R., George Q. H., Arunabh C., Rajit G., B. S. Prabhu, & Peter C., 2010. Planetary-Scale RFID services in an age of uberveillance. *Proceedings of the IEEE*, 98(9), pp. 1663–1671. doi: 10.1109/JPROC.2010.2050850.

Mirowski, P., 2002. *Machine dreams: Economics becomes a cyborg science*. Cambridge University Press.

Mitchell, W. J., 2004. *Me++: The cyborg self and the networked city*. MIT Press.

Muri, A., 2007. *The enlightenment cyborg: A history of communications and control in the human machine, 1660-1830*. University of Toronto Press.

Musk, E., 2019. An integrated brain-machine interface platform with thousands of channels. *Journal of Medical Internet Research*, 21(10), p.e16194.

National Research Council, 2007. *Human-system integration in the system development process: A new look*. National Academies Press.

Nickelsen, N.C.M., 2018, November. Socio-Technical Imaginaries and Human-Robotics Proximity-The Case of Bestic. In *Robophilosophy/TRANSOR* (pp. 212-220).

O'Connell, M., 2018. *To be a machine: Adventures among cyborgs, utopians, hackers, and the futurists solving the modest problem of death*. Anchor.

Pataranutaporn, P., Ingalls, T., & Finn, E., 2018, April. Biological HCI: towards integrative interfaces between people, computer, and biological materials. In Extended Abstracts of the *2018 CHI Conference on Human Factors in Computing Systems* (pp. 1–6).

Perakslis, C., Michael, K. & Michael, M.G., 2016. The converging veillances: Border crossings in an interconnected world. *IEEE Potentials*, 35(5), pp. 23-25.

Peterson, G. D., Cumming, G. S., & Carpenter, S. R., 2003. Scenario planning: A tool for conservation in an uncertain world. *Conservation Biology*, 17(2): 358–366.

Pitt, S., van Meelis Lacey, M., Scaife, E., & Pitt, J., 2021. No app is an island: Collective action and sustainable development goal-sensitive design. *Int. J. Interact. Multim. Artif. Intell.* 6(5): 24–33.

Pringle, R., 2013. Life imitates art: Cyborgs, cinema, and future scenarios. *The Futurist*, 47(4): 31.

Rébé, N., 2021. Future Military Scenarios. In *Artificial Intelligence: Robot Law, Policy and Ethics* (pp. 34–43). Brill Nijhoff.

Reeves-Evison, T., 2021. The art of disciplined imagination: Prediction, scenarios, and other speculative infrastructures. *Critical Inquiry*, 47(4): 719–748.

Ringland, G., & Schwartz, P.P., 1998. *Scenario planning: managing for the future*. John Wiley & Sons.

Rivera, L., 2012. Future Histories and Cyborg Labor: Reading Borderlands Science Fiction after NAFTA. *Science Fiction Studies*, 39(3): 415–436.

Rothery, G., 2020. *Archive*. Independent Films.

Roßmann, M., 2021. Vision as make-believe: how narratives and models represent sociotechnical futures, *Journal of Responsible Innovation*, 8:1, 70–93, DOI: 10.1080/23299460.2020.1853395

Schermer, M., 2009. The mind and the machine. On the conceptual and moral implications of brain-machine interaction. *Nanoethics*, 3(3): 217–230.

Schoemaker, P.J., 1995. Scenario planning: a tool for strategic thinking. *Sloan Management Review*, 36(2): 25–50.

Scott, R., 1982. *Blade Runner*. U.S.A.: Vangelis and Vangelis.

Selin, C., & Hudson, R., 2010. Envisioning nanotechnology: New media and future-oriented stakeholder dialogue. *Technology in Society*, 32(3): 173–182.

Shelley, M., 2001. *Frankenstein* [1818]. New York: Oxford.

Sondeijker, S., 2009. *Imagining sustainability: Methodological building blocks for transition scenarios*. E. Jurriaanse Stichting Rotterdam.

von Stackelberg, P., & McDowell, A. (2015). What in the world? Storyworlds, science fiction, and futures studies. *Journal of Futures Studies*. doi:10.6531/JFS.2015.20(2).A25

Stamford, L., & Azapagic, A., 2014. Life cycle sustainability assessment of UK electricity scenarios to 2070. *Energy for Sustainable Development*, 23: 194–211.

Stephan, K.D., Michael, K., Michael, M.G., Jacob, L., & Anesta, E.P., 2012. Social implications of technology: The past, the present, and the future.

Proceedings of the IEEE, 100 (Special Centennial Issue), pp. 1752-1781.

Stephenson, N., 1992, *Snow Crash*, Bantam Books.

Silva-Martinez, J., 2016. Human systems integration: process to help minimize human errors, a systems engineering perspective for human space exploration missions. *Reach*, 2: 8–23.

Spielberg, S. 2001. *A.I. Artificial Intelligence*. United States: Warner Bros. Pictures.

Spielberg, S., 2018. *Ready Player One*. Warner Bros.

Taylor, C., 2002. Modern Social Imaginaries. *Public Culture*, 14(1), 2002: 91–124. Project MUSE muse.jhu.edu/article/26276.

Taylor, C., 2003. *Modern social imaginaries*. Duke University Press.

Toffoletti, K., 2007. *Cyborgs and Barbie dolls*. Bloomsbury Publishing.

Trist, E.L., 1981. *The evolution of socio-technical systems (Vol. 2)*. Toronto: Ontario Quality of Working Life Centre.

Vial, G., 2019. Understanding digital transformation: A review and a research agenda. *The Journal of Strategic Information Systems*, 28(2), pp. 118–144.

Wallace, G., Michael K., & Cook, M. 2020. The Brain on the Bench Project - The Science, The Application, The Implications, *ACES 2020 Public Lecture*, August 19, www.uow.edu.au/events/2020/aces-2020-public-lecture.php.

Walsham, G., 1997. Actor-network theory and IS research: current status and future prospects. In *Information Systems and Qualitative Research* (pp. 466–480). Springer, Boston, MA.

Warwick, K., 2003. Cyborg morals, cyborg values, cyborg ethics. *Ethics and Information Technology*, 5(3): 131–137.

Warwick, K., 2014. The cyborg revolution. *Nanoethics*, 8(3): 263–273.

Wong, D. T., 2009, March. Human factors interface with systems engineering for NASA human spaceflights. In *Human Systems Integration Symposium*. Annapolis, Maryland.

Wright, D., Finn, R., Gellert, R., Gutwirth, S., Schütz, P., Friedewald, M., Venier, S., & Mordini, E., 2014. Ethical dilemma scenarios and emerging technologies. *Technological Forecasting and Social Change*, 87: 325–336.

Yeoman, I., 2012. *2050-tomorrow's tourism*. Channel View Publications.

Zaidi, L. 2019. Worldbuilding in Science Fiction, Foresight and Design, *Journal of Futures Studies*, June, 23(4): 15–26.

5

The Meaning and Agency of Twenty-First-Century AI

Jonathan Roberge

INTRODUCTION

Machine learning (ML), deep neural networks, and related innovations in computer science are often hailed as the drivers of a twenty-first-century artificial intelligence (AI) so-called "revolution." Such hype is multifaceted and often time quite ambiguous; on the one hand, it is fuelled by dystopian as well as utopian discourses akin to science fiction and, on the other, it assists all of its promotors to translate and make happen the technological deployment they are rooting for. So much, then, for the performative aspect of today's AI *desirata* and how it engulfs into a self-fulfilling prophecy that comes to shape the different fields from banking, insurance, and logistics to vaccine production and, really, everything digital. Less known, however, are the *conditions of possibility* that makes for this to be unfolding before our very eyes; how and why, especially, does it come to so fundamentally inform human–machine communication (HMC)? This implies a conversation of a different kind: a deeper, more complex and critical way of asking questions and raising issues. Scholars like Mona Sloane and Emanuel Moss have recently argued that one of the most pressing tasks in that regard is to prevail over what they call "AI's social science deficit" (2019, p. 330).

History, anthropology, political sciences and the like all have insights to contribute with; something that is reminiscent of mostly forgotten efforts in the mid-1980s to fight against the "exclusion of sociological question from any serious examination of AI" (Bloomfield, 1987; see also Schwartz, 1989; Woolgar, 1985). Everything AI is indeed inseparable from human interactions, entrenched in social activity, and contingent on human affairs. Today's social science should then not only be reflective of such an encompassing process, but also able to incorporate the latest and more precise account of AI's evolution – say from communication and/or science and technology studies. What is at stake, for instance, when the space in-between human *à la* Arendt (2005) is being automated? What does constitute the nod between communication and AI or what Andrea Guzman and Seth Lewis of late have adequately coined as "communicative AI" (2020, p. 70). To address these pressing issues is the purpose of this chapter.

For obvious reasons related to spatial constraints, it will not be possible to deal here with all the ramifications that have ever existed between AI, those who create the technology and those who must live with it. Editorial choices must be made; particular paths and narratives have to be privileged in what is then a dual approach that tackles both the *genesis* and *social construction* of said technology. AI has its roots in the 1940s and 1950s; assumptions crafted at that period evolved into debates, trends, and movements of which the most relevant are still possible to decipher to this day. The first section ("*Quid es*? A too short history of AI") explores the genealogy of the key concepts and definitions at play with the purpose of showing the contingency that never ceases to accompany this historical development – including today's relative take over by the connection-ist community. The remaining sections build on this genealogy to posit and (re)actualize/reframe a SCOT (social construction of technology) ana-lytical frame (Bijker et al., 1987). AI represents an end-to-end social phenomenon, from the bias hidden in the data to its socioeconomical impacts to the design of algorithms and choices made in calibrating a model's hyperparameters (Roberge & Castelle, 2021). With a manifold and unstable object such as this one, what is ultimately at issue? What are the questions that come to crystallized AI's *modus operantis*? The second section ("A meaning-making machine") shows that one of such high stakes relates to the capacity to engage in *meaning-making* and thus in communication per se. So-called 'smart' machine feeds on media content, massages and interprets data to distil a surplus of value and significance – something that will be discussed via the use of category in image recognition or natural-language processing for instance. From there, the third section ("AI as actionable knowledge") discusses how machine intelligence is sought after – i.e. considered pos-sible, desirable, and worthy – for it engages in *decision-making*. AI is all about developing new forms of actionable knowledge where rationali-zation translates *eo ipso* into operationalization. So much then for the practical and rather down-to-earth solutions put forward, such as driverless vehicles (Stilgoe, 2018). As the section shows, it is this appetite for doing (real) things, for being agentic that in the end puts AI on a collision course with everything human: that is human interactions, institutions in the likes of science and law, and/or broader system such as government or capitalism. HMC, in the age of AI, exists precisely because it allows for the messy entrenchment of the terms at play.

QUID ES? A TOO SHORT HISTORY OF AI

What is AI, and where does it come from? To answer these questions first implies to clear some of the ambiguity, if not the inaccuracy that is usu-ally inferred from the canonical myth of intelli-gent machines. Following Matteo Pasquinelli and Vladan Joler (2020), I would argue these are twofold. On the one side, AI remains as much an evasive as a fractal object. "AI is not a monolithic paradigm of rationality," they note, "but a spurious architecture made of adapting techniques and tricks" (p. 4). AI's history is one where science and engineering meshes, where trials meet errors, and progress meets setbacks in what is thus a fully contingent deployment. AI, in other words, is made possible as something worth fighting for in terms of definition and control. On the other side, it is important to underscore that if – again, so-called "smart" – machine communicate and inter-act with humans, there are not in and by themselves to be "anthropologized," so to say. As Pasquinelli and Joler rightly state "machine learning *learns nothing* in the proper sense of the word, [it] simply maps a statistical distribution of numerical values and draws a mathematical function that hopefully approximates human comprehension" (2020, p. 11, emphasis in the original). Describing AI as a "brain" or as having "common sense" is to use metaphors that, by the definition of that later term, infer allegoric and mythical tropes to statis-tical techniques. Yet again, these are metaphors worth fighting for by the actors who were and still are involved in AI deployment. They are, along-side the competing techniques and visions, what set the tone in this broader history of AI and how, in turn, it is such a fault line that allows for its better understanding.

Much has already been written about the Minsky–Rosenblatt rivalry and how it has super-charged the early day of AI research in the US (Cardon et al., 2018; Mendon-Plasek, 2021; Andler, 1992). In the interest of brevity, the fol-lowing will be less about the details of their respective accomplishments than what they exem-plify – notwithstanding the risk of oversimplifica-tion. Whereas computer scientist Marvin Minsky is known for being one of the main organizers of the Dartmouth Conference and the founder of the MIT artificial intelligence Lab, Cornell University psychologist and computer scientist Frank Rosenblatt found his name in the history books for being the inventor of the Perceptron (1957–1961), the first operative neural network. A vision machine aimed at recognizing patterns, the later counted, according to its creator, "on *probabilistic* rather than deterministic principles for its operation, and gain its reliability from the properties of *statistical measurement* obtained from large population of elements" (Rosenblatt quoted in Pasquinelli, 2017; emphasis added). The Perceptron, in a nutshell, embodies the very idea of an inductive and connectionist approach to knowledge, one that would take the form of a bottom-up and distributed structure of calculation.

And, to be sure, it is in this quality that it attracted the hires of Minsky. In 1969, he published together with Papert a critique precisely titled *Perceptron* in which they attempted at showing how "higher dimension" problems and classifications were out of reach without a – properly and maybe tautologically – higher degree of abstraction. This encapsulates what is a formal and deductivist approach; one named "Symbolic AI" obviously not in the sense of a socio-anthropological real of culture, but in the direction of seeking rules, logics, and the language to "program" these.

Minsky and Rosenblatt positions really are the two sides of the same coin; or to be more precise the two side of the same problem. Dominique Cardon and colleagues synthesize the issue nicely:

> For [t]he *symbolic* approach [...] thinking consists of calculating symbols that have both a material reality and a semantic representation value. By contrast, the *connectionist* paradigm considers thinking to be similar to a massive parallel calculation of elementary functions – functions that will be distributed across a neural network – the meaningful behaviour of which only appears on the collective level as an emerging effect of the interactions produced by these elementary operations [...]. This distinction between two ways of conceiving of and programming the "intelligent" operation of a machine is the basis of a tension that has consistently and very profoundly structured the orientations of research, scientific careers, and the design of calculation infrastructure. (2018, p. 4)

Divergences abound in between the symbolists and the connectionists, but that is not to say that the debate has settled once and for all or that it has reached its definite conclusion. In fact, Cardon and colleagues use the French term "*chassé-croisée*" to refer to the back and forth momentum, which also makes sense when looking at the longer period separating today from the Second World War and how, historically, the two schools or perspectives have thrived in successive phases. AI's genealogy is punctuated by several so-called "winters" – the rise and fall of expert systems in the 1980s for instance – in what is then a highly cybernetic development comprising tweaking and recycling. Noticeably, it could very well be that an inductive turn has moved today's field towards the (neo)-connectionists and given them – i.e. the neural network/deep learning community – the upper hand. Yet, this is not the equivalent of accepting the internal, if simplistic, account of their latest rise (Sejnowski, 2018) nor is it of taking for granted the superiority of the models and views being promoted.

Fast forward some 70-plus years, what does so fundamentally characterize twenty-first-century AI, namely what is at issue in the current state of the art? First and foremost, one such characteristic deals with its ever pragmatic, grounded culture. The success of today's AI is inseparable from down-to-earth affordances such as in "big data" greater training set, faster tools to calculate in the forms of GPUs (graphic processing units), and more sophisticated algorithms that have come to learn faster and better. The conjunction of these three technical affordances really is what has allowed for the iconic win of Geoffrey Hinton's team AlexNet at the ImageNet competition in 2012. Coined a "revolution in computer vision" by its promoters (LeCun, Bengio, Hinton, 2015), the reality might be more in the realm of an increased score in image recognition, albeit in itself rapid and substantial. The prosaic significance of ImageNet, in other words, is that calculation allows for statistical commensuration; here, the quality encapsulates in forms, edges, and colors that are translated in distributed numbers and quantities. This, in turn, represents a second key characteristic: twenty-first-century AI is all about pattern recognition. A pattern is assumed to be a (re)occurrence robust enough to be detected by the virtue of how its data point are disseminated in time and space. As Pasquinelli and Joler once again note, the strength of AI is to power through large amounts of data with the "brute force [of] approximation" (2020, p. 11) where a model can be trained, i.e. become better at classifying and predicting outcomes of all sorts from car movements to faces and emotions – these issues and examples will also be central in the next sections. For now, it is mostly useful to decipher how such is linked to another – third – characteristic by which the model advances via trial and error and applies the latter as a way to tweak itself. That is the *ingenuity* of backpropagation algorithms operating in between a model's multiple layers. To learn is really *to adapt* here, in what is thus the highly flexible and cybernetic quality of today's AI. A quality that is not only self-referential and inward-looking, but also to be deployed in the world. Indeed, and that is its fourth and last characteristic: the emergent, orderly-chaotic nature of the mathematics involved mirrors the constant flux of digital data out there. Shaping the models – weakening its layer and hyperparameters – is meant to perceive what is changing *for real* in business, hospitals, military operations, and the like. There is a non-negligible dose of objectivism being both presumed and promoted; one that could render any efforts at theorizing obsolete, except that it doesn't. The following section deals with the question of meaning-making and will attempt at explaining precisely why theory is unescapable.

A MEANING-MAKING MACHINE

The current deployment of AI may well be driven by new tricks and incremental successes; it nonetheless remains reminiscent of the Minsky–Rosenblatt debate in that it is unable to fully evacuate the question of what constitutes "higher dimensionality," "higher representation," and the like. The following is the very first sentence of the famous *Nature* piece by Yann Lecun, Yoshua Bengio, and Hinton: "Deep learning allows computational models that are composed of multiple processing layers to lean representation of data with multiple levels of abstraction" (2015, p. 436). Elsewhere, the same Bengio goes on to say that his research program attempts at building "systems stronger in higher-level cognition and greater combinatorial (and systemic) generalization" (quoted in Marcus). So, what is at stake in these two examples? What is it that "higher" means? The truth and/or the reality is that, for the actors to engage in the deployment of the technology itself, this ends up meaning meaning-making. The promise of AI, for platforms such as Facebook for instance, now revolves around automated content moderation to the point where Facebook CEO Mark Zuckerberg declared that "most of our AI research is focused on *understanding the meaning* of what people share" (2016, emphasis added). The key researchers met above are also keen to promote this sort of thick narrative; from Hinton stating that "these neural nets can learn to reason in a natural way like human do […] we are going to do things like *common reasoning*" (2015, emphasis added) to Bengio, again, for whom the conversation is "talking about computer *gradually making sense of the world* around us by observation" (2016). Other renowned scholars like Stanford's Fei Fei Li would concur by saying that an important purpose of image recognition is to acquire a "fuller understanding of the 3D as well as the semantic visual world" (quoted in Knight, 2018). Yet, all the above are easier said than done. How to achieve that, under which condition, and for what purpose? These are vital questions turned into essential problems.

For a data-rich and information-dense machine, to learn about the world is to organize it with a certain degree of control and confidence. "Grasping" and "mapping," "representation" and "abstraction," or any other synonym of "sorting" are all there to signal the fundamental logic of "sorting

things out" (Bowker & Star, 1999). Classification is indeed the name of the game for AI. In the latest socio-scientific literature it could be said that it is Adrien MacKenzie who has discussed the issue in the greatest length. For him, AI is essentially a "diagramming machine," namely that the only way to situate a data point or a node – in the abstract – is to calculate its proximity/distance with others within a broader matrix (Mackenzie, 2017, p. 21). AI infers a new "vector space," writes Mackenzie (2017, p. 62), but one that is the perfect continuation of the Foucaldian "space of order" championed in the classical age of the encyclopedia: this is a Zebra, this is a horse, they both belong to the equidae family, etc. (Foucault, 2005, p. 238). What there is now, in other words, is the mathematical complexification of a certain nominalism, but a nominalism nonetheless. Moreover, it is relatively easy to notice how such space of classification rests on an equality problematic notion of "category." What holds together and why? Where should the boundary be drawn between a category and the next one or, in AI's case, what is the regression curve? The problem is that in order to formalize a useful set of knowledge, one has to design ensembles of identity and differences – i.e. category, concept, labels – that never quite cease to be arbitrary.

Insoluble as it may seem, the non-neutrality of categories is not a problem for which AI is incapable to find a practical solution. In fact, by looking at the field's latest developments, it is as if the idea of category as an ad hoc composite and useful approximation has been the de facto model. The issue of what today is deemed "fitting" is a case in point as interpolation and extrapolation intertwine and as a trial and error attitude informs the most naïve, if not pragmatic, views:

> A statistical model is said to be trained successfully when it can elegantly fit only the important patterns of the training data and apply those patterns also to new data 'in the wild'. If a model learns the training data too well, it recognises only exact matches of the original patterns and will overlook those with close similarities 'in the wild'. In this case, the model is overfitting, because it has meticulously learnt everything (including noise) and is not able to distinguish a pattern from its background. On the other hand, the model is underfitting when it is not able to detect meaningful patterns from the training data. (Pasquinelli & Joler, 2020)

The operation is the goal here in that to find the perfect fit or the "sweat spot" is what makes sense. Hence, slippages might be subtle, but they are certainly not accidental. While, for instance, any descriptive features of a model allows for more predictive ones – where such model would foresee what comes next – the same could be said about the mingling between objectivity and normativity.

The point is that by using categories AI does convert data input into a representation of the world that is necessarily prescriptive. As Geoffrey C. Bowker and Susan Leigh Star note, "each category values some point of view and silence other" (quoted in Burrell, 2016, p. 3). And as they mesh and multiply their effects, AI technologies generate what can only be described as a statistico-cultural *new normal*; one that would be absolutely key for an understanding of "communicative AI" and the associate HMC research program.

Two examples could illustrate what is at stake here. The first relates to the 2018 introduction by Google of a new method in natural language processing called BERT (Bidirectional Encoder Representations from Transformers) (Wang et al., 2018). Not only does BERT easily feed on the massive corpus of written text the like of Wikipedia, but it reads everything left to right and right to left simultaneously all the while letting the neural network derive prediction of missing words on their own. The core of the model, i.e. the transformer itself, is said to be an "attention-focused architecture" as it is able to calculate multiple and parallel connections and to modify the weight of the different terms interplaying – in "I eat an apple," "an" carries less than "apple" for instance. The success of BERT is thus inseparable from how flexible the model is; as a matter of fact, it is the equivalent to an open-source, pretrained, ready-to-adapt recipe that found practical application in everything from spam detection to automated translation and Q/A sections of web sites. BERT's value is thus its efficiency; while it engages with organizing meaningful content, it also makes sure to stop at partaking in a fully hermeneutical activity. As John Pavlus states, "even a simulacrum of understanding has been [a] good enough goal for natural language processing" (2019, p. 3). In short, BERT is today's Clever Hans, the so-called "smart" horse of the early 1900s who appeared to solve arithmetic problems, but was really just responding to its trainer's cues.

Another, second, yet not-too-distant example is Siri, Alexa, and the vast array of vocal assistants readily available. While the desire for using spoken language to communicate with computer might be as old as computing itself, the latest advances in recent deep learning and natural language processing offers a new brand of anthropomorphism. Following Simone Natale, users might not believe their assistant is really alive, yet it certainly feels "[…] 'like a person' [as] AI assistant rely on human's tendency to project identity and humanity onto artifacts" (2020, p. 3). It is about

"banal, mundane forms of deception" (p. 4) where a "persona" gets into one life by being sassy and reassuring – still today's most default mode and female voice – all the while constructing an intimate social space with the allure of communication, both dyadic and sufficiently ritualistic to be meaningful (see Guzman, 2017). AI is what creates such seamless flow able to conceal the more structural aspect making it possible in the first place, namely the role of platforms as capitalist entities. Data powerhouse and their actions do not vanish, but are deflected in favor of more tangible, day-to-day tasks. The focus is set on micromanagement and "helping" in decision-making, which in turns is another way at attempting to give a new sense of agency to both the human and the machine.

AI AS ACTIONABLE KNOWLEDGE

From what precedes, it becomes clear that AI exhibits pragmatic views that are themselves linked, if ever problematically, with meanings and all of what communication entails. Models are created to be accurate; they are meant to perform and drive concrete unfoldings to the point, in fact, where the question turns out to be what this "performance" actually is? What kind of complex "agency" is at play? Scholars who deciphered the social and cultural life of algorithms in the mid-2000s already captured the issue and the matters. For instance, Andrew Goffey argued in 2008 that "algorithms do things, and their syntax embodies a command structure to enable this to happen" (p. 17). Donald Mackenzie, just two years earlier, signalled somehow famously that algorithms were "an engine, not a camera" (2006). In financial markets, to follow up on his example, algorithms do buy and sell, with a non-negligible dose of autonomy and with the purpose of boosting profit margins. Today's learning models represent the sophistication of previous models, i.e. they swallow large amount of data and tweak their own structure faster and better in order to tackle any problems they are designed to solve. And yet again, this is never a straightforward process but rather a messy entanglement – never an artefact of pure control but of constant adaptation. In fact, these models are set up to adjust to practical, everyday life and solvable problems. As a result, these models create new forms of knowledge and generate new operations of power, as Bernhard Rieder notes:

> […] on the level of performativity […] every classificatory decision can be pushed back into real world instantly, showing a specific ad, hiding a

specific post, refusing a loan [...], setting the price of a product [...], and so forth. No data point remains innocent. If we consider power to operate as a 'network of relation' [...] we can appreciate how data mining delivers specific ways of establishing, organizing, and modulating relations between datafied entities in service of strategic goals. [...] We no longer (only) decide based on what we know, we know based on the decision we have to make. (2017, p. 111)

AI models are actionable "know how" because they are timely and spatially situated and the other way around, namely situated by the virtue of being actionable. Models live in a particular *moment* that corresponds to the performative relation constructed between the immediate present and the near-future. They detect patterns in real-time; they expect and anticipate what would come next and then move on it, deciding on which ad to show in milliseconds to use the example above. The deployment of AI also corresponds to a specific *place* where the digital world coalesces and aggregates so that it supercharges a handful of platforms. Google, Facebook, Amazon, and the likes are both the greatest sponsors as well as the main beneficiaries of a technology that accelerates their own pace and reach in what is then a highly cybernetic process (Roberge et al., 2020; Helmond, 2015). AI, stated otherwise, creates the condition of possibility of an "enhanced" modus operandi. On the one hand, platforms gain value by monitoring users' engagement, reaping big data, conducting quantitative research on it, and selling the fine-grained analysis of user behavior to advertisement companies. On the other hand, these same companies use their own AI-based products to diminish their operation cost, as the AI content moderation case illustrates (Gorwa et al., 2020). This is what platforms do. Their own and very partial agency is meant to capture people's agency by manufacturing the choices they make. Datafication, commensuration, and commodification go hand in hand in that regard, i.e. to transform behavior into data is to transform qualities into quantities and sellable products or experiences. In short, platforms commodify human engagement through AI models. Biases as well as social and cultural consequences are questions out of sight in such a "here and now" approach or, if biases are issues to be tackled, they are dealt with as technical glitches, something that can be easily "fixed" by throwing more data at the AI model (Powles, 2018).

Image recognition becoming facial recognition becoming emotion recognition is a case in point. While facial recognition has come to be a scatter technology operating in subtle and mundane ways, it represents nonetheless the "plutonium of AI"

(Stark, 2019). In fact, it epitomizes what AI does best, i.e. sorting out data. However, facial recognition algorithms sequence body parts data, which has real-world impacts: it expands the gatekeeping logic of algorithms in which they include or exclude people from services, making them visible or invisible, opening up opportunities or not, etc. What happens today, in other words, is the acceleration of a longer trend in which facial recognition systems that are sold and bought are deployed with the obliviousness of the history of facial recognition, perpetuating dangerous assumptions in the search for hidden signals and deeper meanings that are skin-deep. As Sarah Kember puts it, facial recognition is still "embedded with the legacy of tech limited, pseudo-scientific and politically problematic ways of seeing" (2014, p. 189). These practical systems are the latest development in the long history of technologies reproducing and reinscribing categorizations of body markers through sorting mechanisms, which have detrimental impacts on several populations, especially on visible minorities and other marginalized groups (e.g. Benjamin, 2019). "[T]he classification [...] of human facial features," Luke Stark writes, is "irredeemably discriminatory" (2019, pp. 52–53). The calculus used to code human faces performs an essentializing visual schematization; as such they are mechanisms for visually categorizing and reifying racial classifications. As a matter of facts, these systems have led to misidentifications and false-positives time and time again. According to a study released in December 2019 by the U.S. National Institute of Standards and Technology (NIST), which analyzed 189 software algorithms from 99 vendors, most of the algorithms generated more errors on Asian and Black faces, particularly female faces (Grother et al., 2019).

Facial recognition systems bring all the aforementioned problems to an ever-growing number of everyday spaces: airports, movie theatres, city streets, shopping malls, private homes, and so forth. And while the uses of facial recognition systems are quickly expanding, so is the list of problems inherent to their uses. Facial recognition operates *at a distance*; it is *always* on, yet it remains often invisible itself. Computational methods of "seeing" have dramatically improved the efficiency of technologies of surveillance, with facial recognition systems able to analyze greater volumes of personal information, often collected without consent in spaces that are otherwise considered to be "safe" and "open" to the public. This is where they also entrench on the "political," so to speak. Today's systems are linked to the massification of "algorithmic surveillance" (Norris & Armstrong, 1999) that works as readings of the body, and the construction of citizenship and consumer personhood as a set of data points. Yet again, it is crucial to understand in what mundane, if not banal, ways this "political" is deployed. Technical failings point to the half-baked nature of facial recognition: how any particular system becomes part of a larger and rather competitive market and precedes any attempt at reckoning with their social calculus with regard to broader costs and consequences. Emotion detection finds its way in the car industry, where research at Hyundai/Kia for instance focuses on a program called R.E.A.D. (Real-Time Emotion Adaptive Driving) (Lekach, 2019). Behavioral recognition programs and business solutions are another example here. Even though these programs mostly rely on the simplistic, if not dubious, psychological model developed by Paul Ekman (based on only six emotions: fear, anger, joy, sadness, disgust, and surprise), they are being increasingly adopted by human resources across the world, and especially for job interviews (Hoggins & Zolfagharifard, 2019). These behavioral recognition programs are cost-effective for corporations in the sense that they are cheaper to use than would be the staff hired and trained to do similar tasks. Platforms small and big are investing the field; that is, they are creating such things as an ecosystem in the double sense of a market, on the one side, and an ecology in which facial and emotion recognition devices have gained mundane normalcy, on the other.

CONCLUSION

The aim of this chapter was to historically and conceptually reconstruct the conditions of possibility for AI to have become such an inescapable aspect of today's human–machine communication. What is at stake when different sets of technologies are brought together and labelled as "smart"? How to track down the genesis of an object that is, before everything else, a social construction? As this chapter illustrates, twenty-first-century AI really is about *meaning* and *agency*, namely that its discursive as well as performative nature is what allows it to be a *new form of communication in and of itself*. Indeed, some themes and interrogation have proven recurrent over time, or at least cybernetic enough to be recycled and adapted in the period spanning the Second World War to today. For instance, the hyperbolic debate between Minsky and Rosenblatt, between symbolists and connectionists, still resonates to this date even if, or precisely because the deep learning community appears to have the upper hand. While AI now mainly deals with pattern recognition, using the "brute force of approximation," proposing machines that self-tweak and by this reflecting on the constant flux of data of the digital world,

it cannot escape the epistemic issues of representation, categorization, and ultimately, meaning. AI is not self-aware, nor is it reflexive, but it is nonetheless a meaning-making machine that proves to be more and more efficient precisely because it automates significance. For instance, BERT offers technological and semiotic prowess in translation, yet its natural language processing cannot emulate communication as understood or imagined by the tradition of hermeneutics nor can the machine fully connect with individual subjectivity. As for SIRI, it might engage in anthropomorphism, but the meaningful relation it creates with users never quite ceases to be tainted by a sense of deception – which often has to do with the fact that voice assistant of a sort are built by and mostly for platforms. This is where things get real and where people's deep, relational experience with machines comes to matter. AI models of today spill over and are woven into everyday life to create ever messier entanglements. They are an actionable form of knowledge driven by a mathematical sense of optimization as well as a need to find ways to be operative and decisive. Facial and emotion recognition expresses this issue in a rather clear fashion. Challenges, such as cleaning databases or properly marketing a given technology, share little with the evanescent, if well-intended idea of an "AI for the betterment of human kind." In this case, as in many other practical and sociological examples, the deployment of "smart" technologies acts for its own improvement and the financial, political, and social betterment of its promoters, as the major platforms exemplify today. For the HMC research program, the problem then becomes to reckon and engage with the *new normal*, yet very mundane reality of AI in a way that recognizes these now widely spread technologies as indistinctively idiot and cognisant.

REFERENCES

Andler, D. (1992). From paleo- to neo-connectionism. In G. van de Vijver (Ed.), *New Perspectives on Cybernetics.* (Vol. 1–220). Dordrecht: Springer, https://doi.org/10.1007/978-94-015-8062-5_8

Arendt, H. (2005). *Responsibility and Judgment* (Reprint edition). New York: Schocken.

Benjamin, R. (2019). *Race after Technology: Abolitionist Tools for the New Jim Code*. Cambridge: Polity.

Bijker, W. E., Hughes, T. P., & Pinch, T. (Eds.). (1987). *The Social Construction of Technological Systems.* Cambridge, MA: The MIT Press.

Bloomfield, B. P. (Ed.). (1987). *The Question of Artificial Intelligence: Philosophical and Sociological Perspectives*. London: Routledge.

Bowker, G. C., & Star, S. L. (2000). *Sorting Things Out: Classification and Its Consequences* (Revised edition). Cambridge, MA: The MIT Press.

Burrell, J. (2016). How the machine 'thinks': Understanding opacity in machine learning algorithms. *Big Data & Society*, *3*(1), 1–12. https://doi.org/10.1177/2053951715622512

Cardon, D., Cointet, J.-P., & Mazières, A. (2018). Neurons spike back: The invention of inductive machines and the artificial intelligence controversy. *Réseaux*, *n° 211*(5), 173–220.

Foucault, M. (2005). *The Order of Things: An Archaeology of the Human Sciences*. London: Routledge.

Goffey, A. (2008). Abstract experience. *Theory, Culture & Society*, *25*(4), 15–30. https://doi.org/10.1177/0263276408091980

Gorwa, R., Binns, R., & Katzenbach, C. (2020). Algorithmic content moderation: Technical and political challenges in the automation of platform governance. *Big Data & Society*, *7*(1), 1–15. https://doi.org/10.1177/2053951719897945

Grother, P., Ngan, M., & Hanaoka, K. (2019). *Face Recognition Vendor Test FRVT. Part 3: Demographic Effects*. National Institute of Standards and Technology. U.S. Department of Commerce. https://doi.org/10.6028/NIST.IR.8280

Guzman, A. L. (2017). Making AI safe for humans. In R. W. Gehl & M. Bakardjieva (Eds.), *Socialbots and Their Friends: Digital Media and the Automation of Sociality* (pp. 69–85). New York: Routledge.

Guzman, A. L., & Lewis, S. C. (2020). Artificial intelligence and communication: A human–machine communication research agenda. *New Media & Society*, *22*(1), 70–86. https://doi.org/10.1177/1461444819858691

Helmond, A. (2015). The platformization of the Web: Making web data platform ready. *Social Media + Society*, *1*(2), 1–11. https://doi.org/10.1177/2056305115603080

Hoggins, T., & Zolfagharifard, E. (2019, May 30). The British companies pioneering AI that reads your emotions – and will revolutionise everything from shopping to sport. *The Telegraph*. www.telegraph.co.uk/technology/2019/05/30/british-companies-pioneering-ai-reads-emotions-will-revolutionise/

Kember, S. (2014). Face recognition and the emergence of smart photography. *Journal of Visual Culture*, *13*(2), 182–199. https://doi.org/10.1177/1470412914541767

Knight, W. (2016, January 26). *Next Big Test for AI: Making Sense of the World*. MIT Technology Review. www.technologyreview.com/2016/01/26/163630/next-big-test-for-ai-making-sense-of-the-world/

Knight, W. (2018). One of the fathers of AI is worried about its future. MIT Technology Review. http://www.technologyreview.com/s/612434/one-of-the-fathers-of-ai-is-worried-about-its-future/ (accessed on 6 April 2019).

LeCun, Y., Bengio, Y., & Hinton, G. (2015). Deep learning. *Nature*, *521*(7553), 436–444. https://doi.org/10.1038/nature14539

Mackenzie, A. (2017). *Machine Learners: Archeology of a Data Practice*. Cambridge, MA: The MIT Press.

MacKenzie, D. (2006). *An Engine, Not a Camera: How Financial Models Shape Markets*. Cambridge, MA: The MIT Press.

Mendon-Plasek, A. (2021). Mechanized significance and machine learning: Why it became thinkable and preferable to teach machines to judge the world. In J. Roberge & M. Castelle (Eds.), *The Cultural Life of Machine Learning: An Incursion into AI Critical Studies*. Palgrave Macmillan. https://doi.org/10.1007/978-3-030-56286-1_2

Minsky, M., & Papert, S. (1969). *Perceptrons: An Introduction to Computational Geometry*. Cambridge, MA: The MIT Press.

Natale, S. (2020). To believe in Siri: A critical analysis of AI voice assistants. *Universitat Bremen*, *32*, 1–17.

Norris, C., & Armstrong, G. (1999). *The Maximum Surveillance Society: The Rise of CCTV* (1st edition). Oxford: Berg Publishers.

Pasquinelli, M. (2017). *Machines that Morph Logic: Neural Networks and the Distorted Automation of Intelligence as Statistical Inference*. Glass Bead. Site 1. Logic Gate: The Politics of the Artifactual Mind. www.glass-bead.org/article/machines-that-morph-logic/

Pasquinelli, M., & Joler, V. (2020). *The Nooscope Manifested: Artificial Intelligence as Instrument of Knowledge Extractivism*. KIM research group (Karlsruhe University of Arts and Design) and Share Lab (Novi Sad). https://nooscope.ai

Pavlus, J. (2019, October 17). *Machines Beat Humans on a Reading Test. But Do They Understand?* Quanta Magazine. www.quantamagazine.org/machines-beat-humans-on-a-reading-test-but-do-they-understand-20191017/

Powles, J. (2018, December 7). *The Seductive Diversion of 'Solving' Bias in Artificial Intelligence*. Medium. https://onezero.medium.com/the-seductive-diversion-of-solving-bias-in-artificial-intelligence-890df5e5ef53

Rieder, B. (2017). Scrutinizing an algorithmic technique: The Bayes classifier as interested reading of reality. *Information, Communication & Society*, *20*(1), 100–117. https://doi.org/10.1080/1369118X.2016.1181195

Roberge, J., & Castelle, M. (Eds.). (2021). *The Cultural Life of Machine Learning: An Incursion into AI Critical Studies*. Palgrave Macmillan. https://doi.org/10.1007/978-3-030-56286-1

Roberge, J., Senneville, M., & Morin, K. (2020). How to translate artificial intelligence? Myths and justifications in public discourse. *Big Data & Society*, *7*(1), 1–13. https://doi.org/10.1177/2053951720919968

Schwartz, R. D. (1989). Artificial intelligence as a sociological phenomenon. *The Canadian Journal of Sociology / Cahiers Canadiens de Sociologie*, *14*(2), 179–202. https://doi.org/10.2307/3341290

Sejnowski, T. J. (2018). *The Deep Learning Revolution*. Cambridge, MA: The MIT Press.

Sloane, M., & Moss, E. (2019). AI's social sciences deficit. *Nature Machine Intelligence*, *1*(8), 330–331. https://doi.org/10.1038/s42256-019-0084-6

Stark, L. (2019). Facial recognition is the plutonium of AI. *XRDS: Crossroads, The ACM Magazine for Students*, *25*(3), 50–55. https://doi.org/10.1145/3313129

Stilgoe, J. (2018). Machine learning, social learning and the governance of self-driving cars. *Social Studies of Science*, *48*(1), 25–56. https://doi.org/10.1177/0306312717741687

Wang, A., Singh, A., Michael, J., Hill, F., Levy, O., & Bowman, S. R. (2018). *Glue: A Multi-Task Benchmark and Analysis Platform for Natural Language Understanding*. Seventh International Conference on Learning Representations, New Orleans. https://arxiv.org/abs/1804.07461

Woolgar, S. (1985). Why not a sociology of machines? The case of sociology and artificial intelligence. *Sociology*, *19*(4), 557–572. https://doi.org/10.1177/0038038585019004005

Zuckerberg, M. (2015, June 30). *For the next hour I'll be here answering your questions of Facebook* [Facebook post]. www.facebook.com/zuck/posts/10102213601037571

6

The History and Future of Human–Robot Communication

Florian Shkurti

BACKGROUND AND HISTORY

It is possible to see the following three quests: building general-purpose computing machines that can help us model physical phenomena and answer valuable scientific questions; understanding the underlying mechanisms of intelligence by creating artificial intelligence and robotics; and putting automation in the service of everyday people, as three separate trajectories. Their emergence and confluence, however, can be traced to the origins of the field of computer science, by the same communities of scientists, engineers, and mathematicians.

The birth of digital automation

The notion of a general-purpose, programmable, computing machine was formalized by Alan Turing in 1936, as an abstract instruction processor with infinite memory, called the Turing Machine. A non-programmable instantiation of this machine, called the Bombe, was constructed in 1939 for the specific purpose of searching over possible encryptions of messages of Axis forces during WW2. The first general-purpose mechanical computer was conceived and described by

Charles Babbage and Ada Lovelace in 1837 (Analytical Engine), but was never fully built in their lifetimes. The first general-purpose programmable electro-mechanical computer was actually conceived in 1935 and built in 1941 by Konrad Zuse in Berlin, who is often credited to be the inventor of the computer. This electro-mechanical device, representing numbers in binary, was a precursor of today's computer architectures that have a CPU, random-access memory, storage, and support peripheral devices. In 1945, ENIAC was the first electronic, programmable general-purpose computer, and with the invention of transistors in 1947, an era of miniaturization of digital computing hardware started and was progressing according to Moore's law, doubling the number of transistors that can be packed in a chip every year, and thus enabling faster computation with less power consumption, and in smaller spaces.

While today the continuity of Moore's law is under dispute, this exponential rate of electronic miniaturization of the last few decades has enabled the transition from an era of mainframes and large workstations toward an era of personal computing, starting in the early 1970s. The first adopters of this transition were hobbyists and technicians who had to assemble these machines themselves. Programming them required substantial knowledge of electronics, which presented an often insurmountable barrier-to-entry for non-expert users. With the advent of personal computers and human-machine interfaces as we know them today (the mouse, keyboard, the screen, the stylus) at Xerox in 1973, and with the invention and standardization of more user-friendly programming languages, these barriers-to-entry were lowered considerably, to the point where mass-market and already assembled personal computers with a graphical user interface started appearing in 1977 (Commodore PET, Apple II, TRS-80). This allowed many more potential users to participate in the programming of these devices using abstractions and interfaces, without needing to have a background in electronics.

The birth of artificial intelligence and robotics

The question of whether machines are capable of thinking and whether it is possible to mechanize/automate intelligent reasoning can be traced back to folklore and mythology in almost all ancient civilizations. The first time the word "robot" (meaning worker) appeared in the English language was in 1921 by Karel Capek.

Yet, despite these historical references, a formal study of artificial intelligence had not appeared until the late 1940s with the advent of general-purpose, programmable computers. The ability of a human to recognize artificial intelligence was proposed as a test by Turing in a seminal paper (Turing, 1950). In 1956, AI was established as a field of study in a 6–8 weeks long summer workshop at Dartmouth. The participants of the workshop included academics who became leading figures of the new discipline – for example, John McCarthy, Claude Shannon, Ray Solomonoff, Marvin Minsky, and others – who nonetheless pursued significantly different approaches. These ranged from studying the effect of feedback on control systems (cybernetics), to the properties of neural networks as function approximators, to the emergence of reasoning and symbolic systems, to the role of information theory in representations and communication of signals, and to the construction of expert systems. Despite the diversity of approaches considered by the participants of this workshop, it is widely accepted in hindsight that all participants chronically underestimated the challenge of the task they proposed to undertake.

Regardless of the shifting tides between optimism and pessimism in AI circles from the late 1950s to the 80s, it is undeniable that progress was made in all areas of AI. For example, the first steps toward Natural Language Processing (NLP) were taken in those years, with the invention of SHRDLU (Winograd, 1971), a natural language parser that allows users to issue commands and carry a simplified conversation with a computer for the purpose of manipulating a simple set of block objects. Speech understanding also progressed during the 1950s and 60s, although with limited scalability, to the point that only special-purpose vocabularies of 200 words were being recognized in the 1960s and 70s. In computer vision, some of the first image processing and 3D perception algorithms were invented at this time (Nevatia, 1976). In terms of reasoning methods, for example efficient search algorithms for automated theorem proving as well as motion planning algorithms for robotics. The most well-known example of the latter was the Shakey robot developed at Stanford and SRI, which was built in 1966. Shakey was the first general-purpose mobile robot that combined visual reasoning for spatial awareness and navigation, with search and planning algorithms.

While Shakey was a mobile robot designed to operate indoors, by the late 1970s, the first self-driving cars appeared at the University of Tsukuba's Mechanical Engineering Lab, which traveled on unoccupied Japanese roads at speeds up to 20 miles per hour, using two video cameras to visually detect street markings. By the mid 1980s, Ernst Dickmanns' research group in Germany demonstrated vision-based self-driving in realistic conditions and in 1995 his vehicles managed to drive 1,758km from Munich, Germany to Odense, Denmark on major highways with traffic at speeds up to 175km/h. Around the same time, in 1993 at CMU, the first PhD thesis on applying machine learning to vision-based self-driving was completed by Dean Pomerleau, who showed that a neural network (Pomerleau, 1988) could learn to follow lanes based on human driving commands and a camera placed on the car. Whether self-driving pipelines should rely on human-engineered rules for decision-making or end-to-end imitation of human driver commands is still a subject of fervent debate in the robotics and machine learning community.

The electronic miniaturization that started with transistors and enabled programmable personal computers can also be credited for the invention of sensors that perceive and measure the state of the world, which propelled the robustness of robotic systems to the point where real-world deployment was possible. One of the most important and influential sensors are orientation and general localization systems, such as GPS (Global Positioning System), IMU (Inertial Measurement Unit), which enabled 3D positioning and map estimation, as well as cameras and rangefinder sensors, such as LiDAR, sonar, and radar. High-precision motor encoders and force-torque sensors enabled the operation of robot arms that are safe to deploy near humans, and starting from the early 2000s ushered the era of collaborative robots (cobots), moving robot arms from the large-scale industrial setting (for example, in the automotive industry) to medium and smaller-scale manufacturing and logistics operations in environments that are populated by humans (for instance, packaging stations and assembly lines).

The birth of human–robot interaction

These sensors have brought forth increasing levels of interaction between humans and machines that go beyond mere co-existence in the same environment, often aiming to achieve meaningful collaboration, including shared autonomy between humans and machines, as well as social engagement toward personal robots in the home. While references to an axiomatization of human–robot interaction (HRI) can be traced back to Isaac Asimov's Three Laws of Robotics in 1941, the formal creation of the discipline is widely regarded to have taken place in the mid 1990s when researchers from robotics, human–computer interaction, psychology, cognitive science, human factors, natural language, started to develop application-specific models and design principles of human–robot interaction. The field of affective computing, pioneered by Rosalind Picard's (Picard, 1997) and others' work from the mid-1990s, was also emblematic of these considerations and topics making their way from psychology and cognitive science closer to computer science and HCI and HRI.

The first set of applications that emerged as most important in the first few NSF workshops on HRI in the early 2000s, and set the research agenda for the new discipline, were: assistive robotics for people with mobility challenges, such as autonomous wheelchairs for the elderly or the disabled (Pineau et al., 2010); developing affective and emotive social interactions between humans and personal anthropomorphic robots, for education or entertainment (Breazeal, 2006); teleoperation, haptic interaction (Kuchenbecker & Niemeyer, 2004), and shared autonomy under severe communication and time lag constraints, for example underwater, on other planets, over large distances, or during robot-aided surgery; robotics operations for search-and-rescue scenarios (Murphy Burke, 2005). With the increased popularization of and demand for self-driving vehicles, the scope of HRI applications naturally started including problems of shared autonomy for semi-autonomous driving. These problems range from traditional HCI challenges concerned with information visualization through effective interfaces, to the design of effective hand-over strategies and monitoring of the driver's mental state while they are in control of their vehicle.

The emergence of a significant number of applications necessitated a common methodological framework for jointly addressing many of these scenarios using the same principles. Could progress and experience in HCI over many decades of interface design provide a foundation for this new discipline? While traditional HCI has focused around issues of usability and accessibility as some of its main design goals, HRI scenarios impose many additional constraints that require a different algorithmic approach altogether. These constraints are that, unlike general computing devices, robots are embodied and occupy physical space as first-class citizens, potentially interacting with multiple people in the surrounding environments, from their direct users to bystanders. In addition to acting as users of the technology, humans may also be expected to be vigilant teachers or even supervisors of these machines. Thus, the focus of HRI extends beyond the usability of a system that is known to be able to perform its function, to shepherding systems of various levels of autonomy that may be learning to do so.

COMMUNICATION CHANNELS

How can humans communicate intent and objectives and provide feedback to a machine? Inversely, how can a machine engage the human in a conversation, or more simply, provide feedback to a human? What is the right information to be conveyed in either direction? In this section we examine some of the limitations imposed by available communication channels and how that affects the choice of messages and interaction schemes.

Kinesthetic demonstrations and touch

One of the most direct ways to communicate intent to a robot, particularly one that has robot arms, is to physically guide the joints of the robot until a desired configuration is reached. This is often called a *kinesthetic demonstration*, measured by the robot's internal sensors (e.g. encoders and inertial measurement units). Kinesthetic demonstrations are limited in many ways: first, it is difficult for the user to control all the degrees of freedom of the robot simultaneously, which ends up communicating sub-optimal behavior (e.g. erratic motion on unattended joints) to the robot;

second, there is no good mechanism for the human to demonstrate highly tactile behaviors that rely on touch and contact. The former set of challenges is due to the internal controllers of the robot being in charge of the degrees-of-freedom of the robot that the human is not attending to at a particular point in time. The latter set of challenges arises because the user does not receive any feedback about the contact forces and pressure applied to the object the robot hand (end-effector) is interacting with. This makes kinesthetic demonstrations typically suitable for communicating a set of waypoints and grasps, but unable to cope well with low-level contact dynamics.

Teleoperation and remote control

Teleoperation can be seen as a form of kinesthetic demonstration, in which the user is not necessarily controlling the many joints (degrees-of-freedom) of the robot directly, but often through a low-dimensional input device, such as a joystick, a gamepad, or a haptic device used from a distance away from the robot. One of the tradeoffs made by such interfaces, especially over long distances, is that the physical communication channel introduces a delay to the exchange of messages, which makes expression of intent more challenging because the feedback arrives to the human user later than its effect on the machine (Kuchenbecker & Niemeyer, 2004). This is a critical factor, for example, in surgical robotics scenarios, or in teleoperation of robots that are underwater, or on other planets.

What information can a robot extract from a demonstrated trajectory?

A sequence of states and actions can indeed be valuable, provided the state being measured contains the full contextual information that is required for the robot to take action. For example, if the user demonstrates to the robot how to pick up a bottle of water and pour some of it into an empty glass through kinesthetic teaching, then the state of the system would typically include the configuration of the robot arm, the position and orientation of the bottle and the glass, as well as the position and orientation of the table, since these variables are generally feasible to observe and measure through sensors (e.g. encoders and cameras on the robot). On the other hand, it would be very difficult to include the state of the liquid, owing to its transparent and non-rigid nature.

The useful information that one can extract from this type of sequence of time-series data is: (a) the relative height and location from which pouring takes place, (b) the order of operations – set up the glass, pick up the bottle, pour some water in the glass, put down the bottle, (c) the speed at which these operations are taking place, and (d) how much water there is left in the bottle, according to its weight, (e) that the whole sequence of sub-tasks took place on a flat surface. All of these inferences from the observed data contain useful information that generalizes and applies to other types of environments, such as generic kitchens in other apartments. So, the message that the human is conveying through this demonstration is specific enough for the robot to be able to reproduce it to the kitchen environment it is being demonstrated in and general enough to be used in another environment where similar context applies (bottle, glass, flat table).

Visual communication

Vision can be one of the most natural ways for humans to communicate information to a robot, especially spatial information or social interaction cues. Robots equipped with RGB or RGB-D cameras can recognize and track human motion, ranging from gestures, to facial expressions, to full-body articulated skeleton detection (Zhang et al., 2020). The main enabling technology for the successful performance of these detectors has been the use of deep neural network models trained via backpropagation in a supervised learning setting on large image and video datasets. Regardless of the underlying modeling assumptions, however, it is worth asking what type of information can be reliably conveyed through visual communication and at what speed?

Fiducial markers and tags: One of the most widely used media for encoding a communication symbol in computer vision is the idea of artificial tags, or more generally fiducial markers, whose appearance is determined to be such that it would stand out in the natural world. AR-tags and QR-codes are some of the most frequently used markers in this category, and they are able to convey both a symbol, for instance a number that can be mapped to a URL, a function call, or a primitive operation. They can also be used to estimate the camera's relative position and orientation in 3D space with respect to the tag, which is often used for camera calibration or even motion specification. One of the disadvantages of these two tag encoding methods is that their decoding sharply deteriorates as a function of the tag's distance away from the camera. This drawback was addressed by Fourier tags (Sattar et al., 2007), which provide an alternative to these tags, achieving smoother degradation of decoding with increased depth. Another drawback of AR-tags and QR-codes was that typical implementations required having the entire tag visible in the field of view of the camera, which reduced the range of possible interactions away from the camera. Addressing this issue was one of the primary motivations behind April tags (Olson, 2010).

In practice, it is cumbersome for the human to carry as many tags as symbols required to transmit to the robot. Showing the tag to the robot and switching from one tag to the next is a time-consuming process that on average takes at least 4–5 seconds per tag, even for a small set of 5–10 tags that might be numbered.

Gesture recognition: One of the possible variables that can be inferred from video data is gesture information, each gesture corresponding to a symbol that the machine is programmed to map to a particular action. This mapping is usually established a priori on the machine, although there are cases of interest where the machine should learn this mapping from experience. Gesture recognition has been used in HCI in many settings, from sign-in verification mechanisms, to pointing devices in Touchless User Interfaces (TUI), to natural interaction in household video games. These HCI settings usually assume interaction that takes place close to the camera (typically up to 5 meters away), with each gesture completed in a short period of time, and typically does not require keeping track of the temporal history of gestures.

This is not necessarily the case for gesture recognition in HRI settings, which makes a number of additional requirements. For example, in HRI we often need a *sequence of gestures* that correspond to a set of instructions that specify a small, high-level program to be executed by the robot. This has been particularly useful in underwater robotics, where physical communication is limited to acoustic and short-range visual channels. GPS signals, for example, do not significantly penetrate the surface of the water due to sharp attenuation. Acoustic communication, often relied upon by submarines and ships, requires significant, heavy, and often costly equipment (e.g. sonar, underwater modems) that is often optimized for long-range communication. Visibility in shallow underwater environments is often limited to a few meters due to silt, water turbidity, dissolved material and other factors.

That said, for short-range communication and for HRI settings where the human is within a couple of meters of the robot, visual communication has proved to be a useful avenue. For example, Dudek et al. (2007) created a formal grammar called RoboChat, whose rules generate a family of valid programs and sequences of instructions that

can be issued to a robot via tags, an idea which later influenced gesture-based communication.

Gesture recognition has also been prevalent in robotics in outdoor contexts for directing attention, where the distance between the robot and the user has exceeded 10 meters. For instance, it has been applied to inform the control of an unmanned flying vehicle (Bruce, 2016) and to enable flying vehicles to better detect their user from high altitudes (30–40m), even in the presence of other people in the surrounding area, by recognizing the periodicity of their user's hand waving motion (Sattar & Dudek, 2009).

Emotion recognition: Making robots socially perceptive and responsive to humans' emotional state, by visually recognizing their facial expressions (such as eye, gaze, and mouth tracking), their posture, their physiological features (e.g. blood pressure and pulse), and the way they interact with other people in close proximity, have been some of the key technical foci of sociable robotics (Breazeal, 2006). In addition to examining issues purely around the perception of users' emotions, sociable robotics, and more broadly affective computing, focused on how to enable robots to express empathy toward the user at a credible level by modulating the robot's facial or vocal expressions.

Augmented reality

Seamlessly blending rendered objects in the perception of the real 3D world is one of the hallmarks of augmented and virtual reality. The hardware that AR setups often use in HRI scenarios includes a heads-up display from which the user visually perceives the world with the overlay of rendered objects on top of the real scene, as well as haptic gloves with inertial sensors that control the hand(s) of the robot. This hardware configuration has facilitated the demonstration of complex trajectories, particularly manipulation tasks, by rendering objects of interest in the real scene and asking the human to grasp or push artificial objects in the real world. In addition, the potential applications of AR have been extensive in other fields of society, including education, training, spatial navigation, social interaction, commerce, design, and immersion in video games.

Speech recognition and natural language understanding

Communicating instructions to a robot in natural language has been shown to be an effective method to enable non-expert users to specify the task of a robot, in both navigation and manipulation scenarios. But, how can we convert a sequence of instructions into a plan that the robot can execute or a program that can produce that plan? It seems like a daunting task. Luckily, there is a lot of structure in natural language instructions: they are mostly sequential, they contain references to landmarks (objects) in the environment, they specify geometric relations (*directly ahead, before, after*), they contain actions (*lift, put, go, move*). Also, people generally want to be helpful when they give them, so they try to be on point and minimize ambiguities.

One of the most impressive robotics demonstrations of a machine learning model that does this mapping to address the *grounding problem* can be found in Tellex et al. (2011). The paper's experimental results section shows a robotic forklift operating in a warehouse lot, and successfully responding to commands such as "*Lift the tire pallet and proceed forward to set it on the platform directly ahead, to the right of the tire pallet already there.*" In fact, sentences such as this were actually transcribed to text by a speech-to-text system which was running in real time, so the human user was simply uttering the command. The paper builds a parametric probabilistic model (*a graphical model*), whose structure is dynamically induced from the hierarchical structure in the instructions, which are parsed into spatial description clauses containing {subject, relation/action, objects}. The model is trained using aligned pairs of spatial description clauses from instructions (association of words with objects in the environment), including both positive and negative examples.

It is also worth mentioning that, since the advent of deep learning in the last decade, the fields of natural language processing and speech recognition have both experienced significant enough progress and growth to the point where all major commercial uses of these systems from major companies rely on this learning paradigm and on vast arrays of training data from transcribed conversations, as well as large text corpora available on the web (e.g. CommonCrawl, Wikipedia, Webtext2, Books1, Books2).

IMITATION AND INTERACTIVE LEARNING

Robots can learn and adapt their behavior using either their own trial-and-error experience (reinforcement learning), or the experience demonstrated by other agents, ranging from human teachers, other machines, or algorithms (imitation learning). The former is out of the scope of this chapter, but the latter raises many questions that involve human–machine communication. For instance, how often should a human be involved in demonstrating/teaching the robot? What tasks should they teach in the first place, using what channel, and in what order? Is repeated interaction necessary, or is one round of demonstrations sufficient for the robot's learned behavior to generalize to new environments, without the human being needed again?

Interactive training: Ross et al. (2010) showed that repeated interaction is in fact required if we want the robot to adapt to new environments without making mistakes that compound over time. For example, to train a self-driving car to drive using vision and other sensing modalities, it is necessary to have vast amounts of training data from human drivers, who on average drive without being involved in accidents or dangerous maneuvers. When such a scenario does arise, however, the training set for the self-driving car needs to be expanded to take into account what would a driver do in a rare situation. So, interactive teaching is necessary if we care about robustness in the face of rare or unseen events. The training set has to grow over time.

Setting a curriculum: The teacher often bears the responsibility of setting the curriculum of goals that the robot will need to develop expertise and skill in. An alternative to this is that the robot learner can set the curriculum by asking the human teacher to provide demonstrations about goals that the robot is currently unable to reach or uncertain about. Enabling robot learners to quantify their uncertainty and properly model the limitations of the probabilistic models they are using to make predictions about the future state of their environment and take actions based on those predictions, is a subject of extensive research in probabilistic reasoning communities.

Human–robot dialog: Another way in which enabling robot learners to model their uncertainty is important is that they can take actions to disambiguate their sources of confusion by posing appropriate questions to the teacher. These questions might be expressed in natural language, in more limited grammar, or even as a repetition of the instruction that was ambiguous. For example, Sattar and Dudek (2011) developed an HRI method of interaction whereby the robot quantifies the level of predicted risk associated with each instruction given by the human teacher and repeats the high-risk command back to the teacher for confirmation.

Task specification: The most common way to specify the behavior of a robot is by making it optimize a reward function. In the easiest case, this function represents the distance of the robot's current configuration to a desired goal configuration. In many other cases, however, specifying a cost function to optimize is as challenging as writing a program to achieve the desired functionality. This happens in cases where there is a need for long-horizon tasks, or a hierarchy of sub-tasks that are needed to accomplish the original goal. It also occurs in cases where the goal is specified via natural language, or via showing the robot an exemplar image that will guide its attention and decision-making, for example, in visual search tasks (Koreitem et al., 2020).

First-person vs third-person imitation: Kinesthetic teaching, as well as learning self-driving as described above, typically makes the assumption that the demonstrations are expressed in first-person, i.e. in the same morphology as the robot that is going to deploy the learned system. This is not always the case. For example, we would like robots to be able to learn from third-person video demonstrations where the actor is a human (potentially different body morphology), and looking at the scene from a different viewpoint. The potential of third-person imitation is that it could provide a much larger set of training data than what is currently possible with data collected from a first-person point of view.

ALGORITHMIC THEORY OF MIND

The interaction of a human user with their robot is such that the internal state and preferences of each agent are hidden to the other, and therefore both the robot and the human have to infer the other's state and objectives from repeated interactions. In psychology, theory of mind refers to acting while exhibiting an understanding of others' intents, beliefs, and knowledge. Informed by advancements in game theory in the 1950s, there have been consistent efforts by the HRI and machine learning community to develop mathematical models of rational and near-rational behavior, as well as methods to infer other agents' intents, objectives, and internal states (Dragan, 2017).

Learning rewards from demonstrations: Learning objective functions from demonstrations of trajectories has been examined in the context of two methods: *inverse reinforcement learning* (inverse planning, inverse optimal control) and *preference elicitation*. In either case, the reward function is represented in parametric form, as a function of a vector of features, and the problem of interest is to find which reward parameters best explain the demonstrated behaviors. In preference elicitation, on the other hand, we keep a posterior distribution over reward parameters and we show the user trajectories generated from rewards sampled from this posterior.

Quantifying a user's trust on a robot: The degree to which a human user trusts the (semi-) autonomous operation of a robot is ill-defined, challenging to measure, and self-reporting from the user can be unreliable. One would hypothesize that trust towards a robot highly correlates with the errors the robot is committing at each timestep; however, when humans lose trust and, after a critical autonomy error, take over the control of the robot, it often takes a long time for their trust to be restored to previous levels, despite consistently good autonomous behavior from the robot after the error. In other words, trust is difficult to obtain and easy to lose. Another way to define trust is as inversely proportional to the number of interventions committed by the user, which ignores non-critical errors. Xu and Dudek (2016a) developed a probabilistic model that inferred trust in real-time from observations that included interventions, events of trust reassessments, and other features of the robot's trajectory. They later used this probabilistic trust model to modify the robot's control to aim to achieve both task performance and maximize human trust, which in practice ended up in cautious behavior from the robot (Xu and Dudek, 2016b).

Shared and sliding autonomy: Balancing control authority between the autonomous systems of the robot and human control is a nontrivial decision-making problem, since there is no guarantee that the human's actions will incur higher value than the robot's. One way to address this has been to estimate the utility brought by the action recommended by the human versus a controller trained using reinforcement learning in a shared autonomy setting. In other scenarios, estimating the intention and goal of the user, especially in assistive robotics scenarios, makes the shared autonomy problem more tractable (Javdani et al., 2015). This is important for the operation of smart wheelchairs that often carry a robot arm, which has to predict what object their user is interested in interacting with next.

Legibility and motion transparency: When humans and robots share the same workspace, it is important for the human to not be surprised by the robot's actions. One of the ways to achieve this transparency of intentions is for the robot to optimize for legibility and interpretability of its motion, in addition to task performance (Dragan, 2013). By solving this optimization problem, the robot often exaggerates its motion so that the purpose of the motion is more predictable by a third-person observer with no a priori knowledge of the robot's internal planner. Legible motion has been shown to be useful in manipulation scenarios, with robot arms exaggerating their reaching motion for a particular object, but has also been examined in the context of autonomous driving, for interpretable driving behavior during lane changes, as well as in the context of social navigation, where a mobile robot autonomously navigates in densely crowded indoor spaces with significant dynamic motion from many people (Che et al., 2020).

FUTURE TRAJECTORIES

Richer datasets for HRI: While large datasets and auto-differentiation frameworks have catalyzed progress in fields such as computer vision and machine learning, particularly in the last 15 years, datasets for HRI tend to be of small size, and very much limited by the scope of the user studies that generated them. What would an ImageNet-like dataset (Deng et al., 2009) look like for HRI? We can get clues for answering this question from the field of autonomous driving research, which has released datasets that contain driver monitoring data as well as sensor observations during manual driving. Knowing both the state of the driver as well as the measurements of the various sensors on the vehicle allows for more informed predictions about what the driver will do next and whether it is dangerous enough to warrant an alert that an accident is about to happen. Similar settings for collecting interaction data in more general HRI scenarios could include recording egomotion (camera mounted on the human's head, looking forward), particularly in unstructured manipulation scenarios, such as the ones captured in the EpicKitchens dataset (Damen et al., 2020).

Robot touch as a modality in HRI: While human operators constantly touch robots during kinesthetic teaching, it is worth asking under what scenarios would we need robots to touch humans? What would be the requirements for doing this safely, naturally, and to maximize empathy? There are many application scenarios where this functionality would be useful. For instance, we want to have robots that can help dress people with mobility issues, from patients at a hospital, to elderly in their homes, and everyone in between. Yet, robots are far from doing this in a way that feels natural and comfortable. This has been mostly due to our lack of high resolution tactile sensing for large surfaces – we lack the sensitivity of robotic skin. We also lack good mathematical models and planning/control algorithms that take into account

contact, particularly with deformable objects and surfaces, such as human skin.

Safe interaction: Many of the methods we included here lack formal safety guarantees that ensure compliance and co-operative behavior. For example, how would we measure whether the human is in pain when robot touch is employed? Current interaction methods render robots fully co-operative, meaning they will stop moving when contact is detected (over some force threshold), but for many applications, such as heavy lifting of objects, that might not be the correct approach. Defining guaranteed safe interaction schemes in regimes where high force is required is an opportunity for future exploration and development.

SUMMARY

Human–robot communication is still a very young and interdisciplinary field, spanning psychology, design, computer science, and engineering, with many exciting possibilities and open research questions ahead. Above all, it is a field with enormous potential for impacting human experience in the near future, as robotics technologies are becoming more commonplace at an increasing pace. It is vital that these technologies progress in tandem with easy ways for humans to interact with them.

REFERENCES

Breazeal C. (2006). Sociable robots. *Journal of the Robotics Society of Japan*. Vol. 24 (5). Pages 591–593.

Bruce J., Monajjemi V., Wawerla J., & Vaughan R. (2016). Tiny people finder: Long-range outdoor HRI by periodicity detection. *IEEE Computer and Robot Vision*. Pages 216–221.

Che Y., Okamura A., & Sadigh D. (2020). Efficient and trustworthy social navigation via explicit and implicit robot–human communication. *IEEE Transactions of Robotics*.

Damen D., Hazel D., Farinella G. M., Fidler S., Furnari A., Kazakos E., Moltisanti D., Munro J., Perrett T., Price W., & Wray M. (2020). *The EPIC-KITCHENS Dataset: Collection, Challenges and Baselines*. TPAMI.

Deng J., Dong W., Socher R., Li L. J., Li K., & Li F. F. (2009). *ImageNet: A large-scale hierarchical image database*. CVPR.

Dragan A. (2013). Generating legible motion. *Robotics: Science and Systems*.

Dragan A. (2017). Robot planning with mathematical models of human state and action. https://arxiv.org/abs/1705.04226.

Dudek G., Sattar J., & Xu A. (2007). A visual language for robot control and programming: A human-interface study. *IEEE ICRA*.

Javdani S., Srinivasa S., & Bagnell A. J. (2015) Shared autonomy via hindsight optimization. *Robotics: Science and Systems.*

Koreitem K., Shkurti F., Manderson T., Chang W.D., Gamboa Higuera J.C., & Dudek G. (2020). One-shot informed robotic visual search in the wild. *IEEE IROS.*

Kuchenbecker K., & Niemeyer G. (2004). Canceling induced master motion in force-reflecting teleoperation. *ASME International Mechanical Engineering Congress and Exposition.* Pages 1091–1098.

Murphy R., & Burke J. (2005). Up from the rubble: Lessons learned about HRI from search and rescue. *Human Factors and Ergonomics Society Annual Meeting.* Vol. 49 (3).

Nevatia R. (1976). Depth measurement by motion stereo. *Computer Graphics and Image Processing.* Vol. 5 (2). Pages 203–214.

Olson E. (2010). AprilTag: A robust and flexible visual fiducial system. *IEEE ICRA.* Pages 3400–3407.

Picard R. (1997). *Affective Computing.* MIT Press.

Pineau J., Atrash A., Kaplow R., & Villemure J. (2010). On the design and validation of an intelligent powered wheelchair: Lessons from the SmartWheeler Project. *Brain, Body, and Machine.* Pages 259–268.

Pomerleau D. (1988). ALVINN: an autonomous land vehicle in a neural network. *Neural Information Processing Systems.* Pages 305–313.

Ross S., Gordon G. J., & Bagnell A. J. (2010). A reduction of imitation learning and structured prediction to no-regret online learning. *AISTATS.*

Sattar J., & Bourque E., & Giguere P., & Dudek G. (2007). Fourier tags: Smoothly degradable fiducial markers for use in human-robot interaction. *IEEE Conference on Robot Vision.*

Sattar J., & Dudek G. (2009). Underwater human-robot interaction via biological motion identification. *Robotics: Science and Systems.*

Sattar J., & Dudek G. (2011). Towards quantitative modeling of task confirmations in human-robot dialog. *IEEE ICRA.*

Tellex S., Kollar T., Dickerson S., Walter M., Banerjee A., Teller S., & Roy N. (2011). Understanding natural language commands for robotic navigation and mobile manipulation. *AAAI.*

Turing M.A. (1950). Computing machinery and intelligence, *Mind.* Vol. LIX (236). Pages 433–460.

Winograd T. (1971). Procedures as a representation for data in a computer program for understanding natural language. *Tech Report*, MIT.

Xu A., & Dudek G. (2016a). Towards modeling real-time trust in asymmetric human–robot collaborations. *ISRR*, Springer.

Xu A., & Dudek G. (2016b). Maintaining efficient collaboration with trust-seeking robots. *IEEE IROS.*

Zhang Y., Black M.J., & Tang S. (2020). *We are more than our joints: Predicting how 3D bodies move.* CVPR.

7

From CASA to TIME: Machine as a Source of Media Effects

S. Shyam Sundar and Jin Chen

Historically, research on social and psychological effects of communication, be it mass communication or interpersonal communication, has focused on messages rather than the medium of communication. The attributed source of these messages has always been one or more human beings, labeled variously as senders or communicators. Around the turn of the century, when much of our communication began to be mediated by computers and related smart technologies, we started orienting to these machines as sources (Sundar & Nass, 2000). We exhibited social responses to them, much like we do with other human beings (Nass & Moon, 2000). As a result, the medium of communication became the source of communication, leading to a groundswell of human–computer interaction (HCI) research on the psychological effects of a wide range of computer-based technologies, such as mobile phones, robots, and conversational agents. As this research matured, attention turned toward specific attributes of these media technologies, and new theoretical frameworks were proposed to guide empirical research on the role of technological affordances in shaping users' cognitions, emotions, and actions (Sundar & Oh, 2019).

A new subdiscipline called "human machine communication" or HMC (Guzman, 2018) was proposed, with a deliberate focus on the communicative aspects of technological sources, ranging from information transmission to meaning-making. Given the increasing diffusion of artificial intelligence (AI) in the past decade, scholars came to view communication technologies as being more autonomous and capable of communicating rather than merely interacting. Emergent AI-based media devices such as smart speakers, with their unique affordances, came to be seen as qualitatively different communicators than simply imitators of human communicators (Guzman & Lewis, 2020). However, their superior ability to personalize communications, often by invading one's privacy, led some to worry that the notion of machines as sources may have gone too far, raising concerns about machine agency undermining human autonomy (Sundar, 2020). The future trajectory of scholarship in this area is one that promises to interrogate this emerging tension between machine agency and human agency, as machines become the default sources of communication.

We begin by reviewing classic studies under the CASA (Computers Are Social Actors) paradigm, which demonstrated that individuals apply social rules of human–human interaction to human–computer interaction. Building on this, we discuss computer-as-source studies following the object-centered view of technology, address their critical limitations, and briefly introduce the variable-centered approach. In the next two sections, we will highlight theoretical models and studies focused on unpacking computer-based media into affordances, such as interactivity, and examine their attitudinal and behavioral effects. This line of research shows that technological affordances serve as the source of media effects via different psychological mechanisms. The chapter will conclude by articulating how the affordances of emergent AI-based media serve to make machines overly agentic, and present our latest theoretical framework on human–AI interaction (HAII-TIME) as emblematic of the future trajectory of inquiry by scholars in this area of research. Taken together, the extension of computer-as-source studies in terms of a focus on communicative affordances and recognition of the autonomous nature of AI-based media lay the theoretical foundation for HMC research on machines as sources of psychological effects.

COMPUTERS AS SOCIAL ACTORS

In the 1990s, as personal computers began to diffuse into society, Clifford Nass and his team at Stanford University launched a new paradigm of human–computer interaction research that departed from the traditional notion of computers as workstations or tools for accomplishing tasks, and proposed that computers are interactive objects that evoke social responses from human users. Their fundamental thesis was that humans apply the same social rules of interaction with computers as they do with other humans. Known as CASA (Computers Are Social Actors), studies in this paradigm (Nass et al., 1994) systematically varied attributes of computers—not just the content and tone of their communications, but also their role and personality. In an early study, Nass and Steuer (1993) found that individuals implicitly applied the notion of "self" and "other" to computers even though they believed it was inappropriate to do so when they were asked in a post-interaction interview. Nass et al. (1994) further demonstrated that individuals' responses to computers were fundamentally social.

Perhaps the most important insight from CASA studies is that computers can be seen as having distinct personalities, thus evoking distinct social responses from users (Moon & Nass, 1996). Users showed greater intention to purchase a book when they heard book reviews delivered by the synthesized computer voice exhibiting a personality similar to their own (Nass & Lee, 2001). Along the same lines, individuals who were told that they teamed up with a computer

(Nass et al., 1996) perceived greater similarity to the "teammate" computer and showed greater conformity to the computer's recommendations compared to a computer that was not part of their team. In other words, the "teammate" identity cue of the computer was sufficient to trigger human ingroup-outgroup behavioral norms.

Social responses to computers seem to be triggered not only by their human-like traits but also by their behaviors (Lee & Sundar, 2010). Studies have found that users' responses to computer flattery resembled the effect of flattery from other humans (Fogg & Nass, 1997). In addition, the dynamics of self-disclosure in human–human interaction were observed in human–computer interaction. For example, Moon (2000) showed that individuals were more likely to reveal intimate information about themselves to a computer when the computer told them more about itself.

All these early CASA studies were quite convincing in demonstrating that humans respond socially to computers, following the same social rules that govern human–human interaction. Therefore, we psychologically treat the computer as a distinct entity worthy of human-like attributions, an insight that has powerfully reshaped the traditional conceptualization of communication by suggesting that computers are no longer simply a medium of communication, but a source of information (Sundar & Nass, 2000).

MEDIUM AS SOURCE

The notion of medium as a source of communication is revolutionary, not just because it challenges the longstanding distinction between the concepts of "source" and "medium" that has been deified in communication models for over half a century, but because it undermines the psychological importance of the human source behind most mediated communications.

One school of thought argues that the findings suggest the exact opposite, that the human source behind the computer is all too relevant. This is because the social responses found in the aforementioned CASA studies are assumed to be directed not at the computer itself but at the human creator or sender of the message. According to this argument, the computer is simply a proxy for the human source. When viewed through this lens, the use of social rules of human–human communication when interacting with a computer is not all that surprising or strange. After all, we have long known about media users carrying on a social interaction with mediated characters, ever since

Horton and Wohl (1956) documented the phenomenon of "parasocial interaction" in the early days of television.

Sundar and Nass (2000) labeled this explanation as Computer as Medium (CAM) model, in contrast to the view of Computer as Source (CAS). Under the CAM view, the social responses exhibited in front of a computer are really meant for the human source behind it, and the computer is simply a conduit between human senders and receivers, in keeping with the conception of "medium" in traditional transmission models of communication. The CAS model, on the other hand, argues that the social responses are directed at the computer itself, and that psychologically, the computer is seen as an autonomous source and therefore worthy of human-like social attributions. Here, the users are orienting to the computer as a source, not as a medium.

Sundar and Nass (2000) directly tested these competing explanations with a set of experiments in which participants who interacted with identical computers were explicitly told that they were dealing with either a computer or a human via the computer (e.g., programmer, networker). If participants had actually imagined a programmer when they were interacting with the computer, then labeling the computer as a programmer should not cause differences in their responses. However, the evidence suggested otherwise, leading the authors to conclude that "computers themselves, like human beings, are sources" (p. 700).

A systematic review by Nass and Moon (2000) of potential alternative explanations to early CASA findings further supported the "source orientation" explanation. Nass and Moon reasoned that social responses to computers cannot be due to ignorance because participants were all adult computer users who insisted that they would never respond socially to technologies. In addition, social cues associated with computers were quite subtle and minimal in the experiments, and therefore could not have led participants to believe that they were expected to treat computers socially. By ruling out these alternative explanations, Nass and Moon concluded that social responses to computers are essentially mindless responses directed at the computers. All evidence pointed to users orienting to computers as sources, just like they do with humans.

What factors contribute to individuals' treatment of computers as sources? Sundar and Nass (2000) suggested three possibilities—interactivity, use of natural language, and filling of roles previously held by humans. Computers that exhibited a high level of interactivity and offered "contingent" responses (Rafaeli, 1988) to users are more likely to be perceived as sources rather than as media or channels. Similarly, when presented with human-like cues (e.g., voice, self-reference), computers are more likely to be treated as sources of communication. In the same vein, Lee and Sundar (2010) argued that studies should pay more attention to particular technological features and investigate their psychological effects, which is consistent with the variable-centered view proposed by Nass and Mason (1990). Sundar (2009) further identified this emphasis on variables as a key methodological aspect of the "media effects approach" to research on communication technologies, and called for studying technology in terms of features and affordances that cause effects rather than studying any given technology in its entirety.

MEDIA AFFORDANCES AS SOURCES

As scholars began to see the value of the variable-centered approach in a rapidly evolving media scenario at the turn of the century, characterized by a frenetic pace of innovation in communication technologies, studies increasingly focused on specific affordances embedded in computer-based technologies rather than entire objects or devices. Social responses, and indeed all psychological responses, were increasingly attributed to specific features of mediated communication that suggested action possibilities to users. Technological affordances of the medium became de facto "sources" of communication because they played a major role in shaping the nature and scope of communication, echoing claims made by McLuhan (1964) four decades earlier.

Sundar (2008a) advanced the concept of "agency affordance" to refer to technologies that enabled users to vary the nature of sourcing in mediated communication. As Sundar and Nass (2001) discovered, news consumers distinguished between computers as sources and humans as sources by differentially rating content sourced to them. They further distinguished between human news editors, other news consumers as a collective, and themselves as sources of news. Depending upon which of these sources is salient in a particular interaction, our responses to the content can be different, even though the content may not vary as a function of the source. Each of these "agencies" have unique symbolic value for users and accordingly alter user perceptions. When technology affords users the ability to customize their content preferences, the agency of the user is more salient and may lead to a different set of user perceptions that are more positive. The notion of "self as source" is the heart of the agency model of customization (Sundar, 2008b), which posits that the customizability afforded by the interface can serve to increase user agency, which leads to beneficial attitudinal, cognitive, and behavioral outcomes. When the user acts as the source, s/he/they will have a higher stake in it and thus pay more attention to the content and have greater involvement (Oeldorf-Hirsch & Sundar, 2015). It also means that the user will identify more strongly with it and feel greater behavioral control over the interface, as per the agency model.

These propositions of the agency model have received empirical support over the years. Kalyanaraman and Sundar (2006) demonstrated that the greater the level of customization afforded by a Web portal, the more positive the users' attitude toward the portal. Marathe and Sundar (2011) found that sense of identity was the main reason why user engagement in customization would lead to a sense of control. In other words, user experience with customization is fundamentally tied to expressing one's identity and "self" on the site. Other studies found that customization influences message processing (e.g., Kang & Sundar, 2016).

While customization features afford users the ability to gatekeep and exert influence on the content they consume, interactive features of social media invite users to produce content (e.g., blogging, tweeting) and serve as a source for other users. This type of interactivity, which affords users the ability to serve as sources, is called "source interactivity," with different technologies imbuing different levels of "sourceness" in users, leading to a continuum in which customization is at the lower end and content creation is at the higher end (Sundar, 2008a). Sundar, Oh, et al. (2012) operationalized and tested this "source-interactivity continuum" with a portal site featuring cosmetic customization, functional customization, filter blogging, and active blogging. In the study, active blogging alone was rated as more interactive and useable than filtering and was powerful enough to evoke a sense of personal competence and a sense of community as well as positive attitudes towards the portal.

Aside from source interactivity, modern communication technologies afford other types of interactivity, as outlined in the interactivity effects model (Sundar, 2007a), with each one leading to user engagement through a distinct theoretical mechanism. Modality interactivity increases user engagement by enhancing perceptual bandwidth. For example, applications of augmented reality (AR) technologies in e-commerce enable online shoppers to virtually experience the products before they make the purchase. Users can rotate the images of the product in a 360-degree view and move around true-to-scale virtual models of

the product in their living space with phone cameras, leading to deeper engagement with the interface and a richer perceptual experience. Research on modality interactivity has focused on examining participants' assessment of the interface (e.g., perceived naturalness) and how these assessments in turn shape user responses to the interface and its content. For example, Sundar, Bellur, et al. (2014) examined six modalities (click, slide, mouseover, drag, zoom, and swipe) and found that slide was better in aiding user memory whereas mouseover and swiping encouraged more user actions, with consequent effects on user experience and attitudes.

Another type of interactivity is message interactivity, which refers to the contingency in users' exchanges with the system. For instance, on a movie search site, when the interface displays one's individual interaction history, users perceive a higher level of contingency and dialogue, which in turn enhances their level of user engagement and dictates their attitudes and behavioral intentions towards the site (Sundar et al., 2016). These effects on user perceptions of the site can also bleed over into their attitudes toward the content delivered by the site. As Bellur and Sundar (2017) discovered, the greater perceived contingency of Q&A tools on a health risk assessment website was associated not only with positive attitudes toward the site, but also with health attitudes and behavioral intentions.

The benefits of message interactivity in the health domain extend beyond promoting positive attitudes to motivating individuals to sustain and engage in positive health behaviors, as argued by the motivational technology model (Sundar, Bellur, & Jia, 2012). Contingent conversations with others in the same health situation (Rafaeli, 1988) can provide users with psychological feelings of relatedness, fostering a sense of community and greater communal participation. In this way, it gives users the opportunity to serve as the source for other users, to showcase and express oneself. Likewise, the affordance of customization offers autonomy, enabling users to demonstrate individualistic preferences and tailor the mediated environment to serve their unique needs. The affordance of navigability can guide users to explore the environment with ease and thereby contribute to their sense of competence. Together with relatedness and autonomy, a sense of competence predicts intrinsic motivation, as per self-determination theory (Ryan & Deci, 2000). The central proposition of the motivational technology model is that technological affordances of message interactivity, customization, and navigability can contribute to intrinsic motivation by heightening users' sense of relatedness, autonomy and competence respectively. In support of this model, one recent study (Molina & Sundar, 2020) found that affordances of workout apps successfully predicted app usage and fitness outcomes (e.g., weight and body-fat) by eliciting user needs for relatedness, autonomy, and competence.

Aside from exerting influence through user actions, technological affordances hold the promise of affecting user perceptions and behaviors by simply serving as heuristic cues. In this regard, it is the interface cue that serves as the source of perceptual and behavioral outcomes. For example, Amazon users can infer the quality of a product by checking the star rating and the number of reviews, which can influence their purchase behavior. Likewise, a disabled comment section can be interpreted as a signal of a YouTuber's unwillingness to interact with viewers or the controversial nature of their video. Either of these interpretations can shape the viewers' attitudes toward the content and the content producer. Such cue effects of technological affordances constitute the fundamental argument of the modality-agency-interactivity-navigability (MAIN) model (Sundar, 2008a), which proposes that each affordance can be viewed as "a repository of cues" that operate at distinct levels and have a range of effects based on the heuristics that they trigger in the minds of users.

Modality affordances can either enhance or undermine the perceived quality and credibility of content based on the cued heuristic, serving as sources of either positive or negative effects. Similarly, agency affordances can serve as the source of heuristics that shape credibility perceptions of content sources and content quality. Interactivity affordances trigger a wide range of heuristics that shape user experience. For example, the availability of a chatbot on a website can cue the interaction heuristic, shaping user impressions of the website and its contents. Along similar lines, navigability tools on an interface also contribute to user experience by cueing various heuristics, e.g., evoke the helper heuristic if they ease the browsing experience. In this way, affordances facilitate the psychological process of "meaning making" between humans and machines, which is one of the central tenets of HMC (Guzman, 2018).

A large body of research has provided support for this notion of affordances as sources of perceptual effects via cognitive heuristics. Newer modalities of digital devices and apps have been known to trigger the coolness heuristic, guiding users toward more positive evaluations of the product (Sundar, Tamul, & Wu, 2014). Even older modalities can trigger distinct heuristics. For example, one study showed that large screen size and video modality evoked being-there and realism

heuristics respectively. Large screen and video modality promoted heuristic processing, leading to greater affective and behavioral trust, and subsequently greater purchase intention (Kim & Sundar, 2016).

In sum, a variety of technological affordances of contemporary digital media, from modality and agency to interactivity and navigability, serve as distinct sources of media effects, quite independent of content. They shape our perceptions by emitting cues on the interface and/or alter the nature of user experience by inviting user participation. Both these species of effects inform the theory of interactive media effects (TIME), as we describe in the next section.

ERA OF TIME

In general, studies on technological affordances as sources have identified two distinct conceptualizations—affordances as cues and affordances as actions. In the MAIN model (Sundar, 2008a), an affordance of the medium provides cues that trigger specific cognitive heuristics which influence perceptions of source, content, and user experience. Aside from providing cues that convey meaning to users, affordances can lead to actual user engagement and result in psychological effects, such as heightened sense of agency and greater self-determination. Sundar et al. (2015) labeled the latter as the "action route," which integrated the aforementioned interactivity effects model (Sundar, 2007a), agency model of customization (Sundar, 2008b), and motivational technology model (Sundar, Bellur, & Jia, 2012).

The cue route suggests that affordances, with their sheer presence on an interface, function as salient cues that convey meanings for users and elicit certain cognitive heuristics. And these heuristics translate into important psychological outcomes. For example, interface cues like view counters and comments respectively shape audience perceptions about the crowd size and sentiment of online videos, triggering the "bandwagon heuristic" and thereby affecting audience enjoyment of the mediated content (Waddell & Sundar, 2020). In other contexts, if the agent is manifest on the interface as a human, i.e., providing human-like cues (e.g., picture of the agent), it triggers the "social presence heuristic" and thereby shapes their perceptions and expectations of the agent (Sundar et al., 2016), but if it is presented to users as an automated chatbot, it triggers the "machine heuristic" leading users to apply their stereotypes about machines in evaluating the quality of the agent's performance (Koh & Sundar, 2010) as well as calibrating their own participation in the interaction, such as decisions regarding revealing personal information to the agent (Sundar & Kim, 2019).

By contrast, the action route posits that affordances affect users' psychology by motivating them to take real actions on the interface (e.g., posting a selfie) and engaging with the media content. For instance, Oh and Sundar (2016) discovered that when an anti-smoking website is equipped with an interactivity affordance, the action of using the slider results in a significantly higher level of "imagery engagement" compared to simply viewing a gallery of those same images. Such engagement results in more positive attitudes toward the anti-smoking messages and greater behavioral intention to recommend the website to others.

Actions engendered by affordances can shape how users process and respond to media content in a variety of ways, from increasing users' perceptual bandwidth to facilitating more contingent interactions to imbuing in them a greater sense of agency and self-determination (see Table 7.1). Studies have found that perceptual bandwidth, or

the perceived vividness of the interface, mediates the causal relationship between users' on-screen interactions and their positive attitudes towards the content on a website (Oh & Sundar, 2020). Also, customizing one's avatar imbues in users such a heightened sense of agency that it increases their likelihood of benefiting from health messages conveyed in a virtual environment (Kim & Sundar, 2011). Further, the use of features that promote relatedness, autonomy, and competence in a mobile fitness app is associated with exercise outcomes (Molina & Sundar, 2020), and the number of photos uploaded on Facebook is positively associated with feelings of competence and subjective well-being (Jung & Sundar, 2021).

When affordances are sources of media effects, their effects differ based on whether they serve as cues on the interface or as enablers of actions for users. The former is based on cognitive heuristics while the latter is based on enhancing users' perceptual bandwidth, feelings of contingency, sense of agency and degree of self-determination. More generally, the theory of interactive media effects (TIME) is premised on providing interface indicators and tools for users to make decisions and take

Table 7.1 Action and cue effects of affordances

Affordances	Action effects	Cue effects
Modality	Perceptual bandwidth • Ease of use • Natural mapping • Intuitiveness • Vividness	realism heuristic distraction heuristic intrusiveness heuristic old media heuristic being there heuristic novelty heuristic coolness heuristic bells and whistles heuristic
Agency	Sense of agency • Customization • User control • User identity • Self-affirmation	authority heuristic bandwagon heuristic social presence heuristic machine heuristic identity heuristic
Interactivity	Contingency • Dialogue • Reciprocity • Threadedness • Responsiveness	activity heuristic telepresence heuristic contingency heuristic own-ness heuristic identity heuristic control heuristic interaction heuristic flow heuristic

Navigability	Self determination
	• Intrinsic motivation
	   ○ Relatedness
	   ○ Competence
	   ○ Autonomy
		helper heuristic
		scaffolding heuristic
		play heuristic
		elaboration heuristic
		similarity heuristic
		prominence heuristic

actions respectively. As such, it articulates the psychological potential of technological affordances embedded in interactive media. While extant research has documented this potential separately for cues and actions, emerging research focuses on their combinatory effects. The ability to view the number of other users commenting on a YouTube video can potentially interact with the user's own ability to comment on the video, and in turn both the cue and the action may moderate the effects of message-level variations in the content of the video (e.g., Li & Sundar, 2021). Such explorations can facilitate richer understanding of the effects of various layers of media as sources and provide a nuanced appreciation of the degree to which the level of user engagement with certain affordances of the medium can shape the effects of messages conveyed by that medium.

WHITHER HUMAN SOURCE? TENSION WITH MACHINE SOURCE

While interactive media help users assert their "sourceness," the rise of artificial intelligence (AI) undermines it somewhat by posing as autonomous sources (Sundar & Nass, 2001), and thereby persuading users to orient to machines as sources (Sundar & Nass, 2000). Furthermore, interface manifestations of AI-based media, from humanoid robots to online chatbots to smart speakers, tend to transmit anthropomorphic cues and thereby lay claim to agency alongside humans (Sundar, 2007b). At the turn of the century, Heckman and Wobbrock (2000) called this a "dangerous illusion," but it is no longer an illusion, thanks to rapid advancements in data science and machine learning in the past two decades, which have ensured that machine sources know more about us than do most of our human acquaintances. This gives rise to an important tension between human agency and machine agency (Sundar et al., 2015)—while we appreciate machines serving us in a targeted manner, providing us only those media offerings that are relevant and interesting to us, we loathe the fact that machines need to closely monitor our preferences in order to do so and fear that our privacy may be in jeopardy.

Designers of AI products have responded to this tension by providing more user control over collection, storage, management, and disposal of their personal information. This has meant greater involvement of users in shaping both the functioning and outcomes of AI-driven technologies. Users and machines are not competing sources but rather collaborators that augment each other

and synergistically produce outcomes that are superior to those produced by either one operating independently. This is the central argument of the HAII-TIME model (Sundar, 2020), which provides a framework for understanding human interaction with AI-driven media by theorizing about the perceptual and experiential effects of interacting with agentic machines. It is an application of TIME (Sundar et al., 2015) to the context of Human–AI interaction (HAII).

The cue route posits that affordances of the AI medium can influence users' responses by advertising their existence or providing indicators of their attributes and performance on the interface. Studies have found that users' awareness of the algorithm's existence leads to more active engagement with the interface and evokes greater feelings of control among users (Eslami et al., 2015). Along with awareness, users' lay perceptions of algorithms also shape their experiences and responses. As Lee (2018) discovered, users possess both positive and negative perceptions of machines, and those perceptions influence their experiences with AI-driven media.

Eslami et al. (2016) found that individuals have elaborate folk theories about curation algorithms, which influence how they plan their behaviors. They tend to use such folk theories as "frames" for interpreting algorithmic decisions and deciding how to interact with the medium (Devito et al., 2017). These frames are developed by divining the underlying attributes of the algorithm based on one's prior experience with the medium, and can be invoked by interface cues to guide the formation of cognitive heuristics (or rules of thumb), according to HAII-TIME model (Sundar, 2020).

The action route of HAII-TIME model predicts that the actions afforded by AI interfaces determines user engagement and experiences. It is based on the extent to which interface features enable users to take actions (e.g., manage one's personalized news feeds; engage in conversation with a chatbot) and assert their personal agency. The effects of AI affordances on user psychology via the action route are therefore likely to be more systematic, robust, and durable. Furthermore, as TIME suggests, the enabling aspect of affordances has potential psychological benefits for the users. For example, the affordance of customizing one's privacy settings in smart speakers enhances users' trust and perceived usability of the technology (Cho et al., 2020). The action route rests on the promise of a desirable level of social exchange between the user and the system. As such, it stresses collaboration between the two, with the goal of augmentation and building synergistic interactions that capitalize on the strengths of human and machine sources.

CONCLUSION

In conclusion, this review reveals a research trajectory that began in the 1990s by treating machines as social actors, then viewing the increasingly agentic media as autonomous sources of communication, followed by disaggregation of media platforms into constituent affordances that have distinct potential for user engagement as well as human–machine collaboration in the form of interactive media powered by artificial intelligence. It chronicles the psychological research that supports HMC's central contention that machines are no longer mere channels, but communicators with which users co-construct meaning. Around the turn of the century, the assignment of "sourceness" to machines may have seemed heretical given that the source of communication had historically been a human entity, but recent developments in smart media technologies (and psychological research on their effects) have made agentic machines an entirely acceptable aspect of our everyday reality.

REFERENCES

Bellur, S., & Sundar, S. S. (2017). Talking health with a machine: How does message interactivity affect attitudes and cognitions? *Human Communication Research*, *43*(1), 25–53. https://doi.org/10.1111/hcre.12094

Cho, E., Sundar, S. S., Abdullah, S., & Motalebi, N. (2020). Will deleting history make Alexa more trustworthy? Effects of privacy and content customization on user experience of smart speakers. *Proceedings of the 2020 CHI Conference on Human Factors in Computing Systems*. https://doi.org/10.1145/3313831.3376551

DeVito, M. A., Gergle, D., & Birnholtz, J. (2017). "Algorithms ruin everything": #RIPTwitter, folk theories, and resistance to algorithmic change in social media. *Proceedings of the 2017 CHI Conference on Human Factors in Computing Systems*. https://doi.org/10.1145/3025453.3025659

Eslami, M., Karahalios, K., Sandvig, C., Vaccaro, K., Rickman, A., Hamilton, K., & Kirlik, A. (2016). First I "like" it, then I hide it: Folk theories of social feeds. *Proceedings of the 2016 CHI Conference on Human Factors in Computing Systems*. https://doi.org/10.1145/2858036.2858494

Eslami, M., Rickman, A., Vaccaro, K., Aleyasen, A., Vuong, A., Karahalios, K., … Sandvig, C. (2015). "I always assumed that I wasn't really that close to [her]": Reasoning about invisible algorithms in news feeds. *Proceedings of the 33rd Annual ACM Conference on Human Factors in Computing Systems* (pp. 153-162). https://doi.org/10.1145/2702123.2702556

Fogg, B. J., & Nass, C. (1997). Silicon sycophants: the effects of computers that flatter. *International Journal of Human-Computer Studies*, *46*(5), 551–561. https://doi.org/10.1006/ijhc.1996.0104

Guzman A. L. (2018) What is human-machine communication, anyway? In A. L. Guzman (Ed.), *Human-Machine communication: Rethinking communication, technology, and ourselves* (pp. 1–28). Peter Lang.

Guzman, A. L., & Lewis, S. C. (2020). Artificial intelligence and communication: A human–machine communication research agenda. *New Media & Society*, *22*(1), 70–86. https://doi.org/10.1177/1461444819858691

Heckman, C. E., & Wobbrock, J. O. (2000). Put your best face forward: Anthropomorphic agents, e-commerce consumers, and the law. *Proceedings of the Fourth International Conference on Autonomous Agents* (pp. 435–442). Barcelona, Spain. https://doi.org/10.1145/336595.337562

Horton, D., & Richard Wohl, R. (1956). Mass communication and para-social interaction. *Psychiatry*, *19*(3), 215–229. https://doi.org/10.1080/00332747.1956.11023049

Jung, E. H., & Sundar, S. S. (2021). Older adults' activities on Facebook: Can affordances predict intrinsic motivation and well-being? *Health Communication*, 1–11. https://doi.org/10.1080/10410236.2020.1859722

Kalyanaraman, S., & Sundar, S. S. (2006). The psychological appeal of personalized content in web portals: Does customization affect attitudes and behavior? *Journal of Communication*, *56*(1), 110–132. https://doi.org/10.1111/j.1460-2466.2006.00006.x

Kang, H., & Sundar, S. S. (2016). When self is the source: Effects of media customization on message processing. *Media Psychology*, *19*(4), 561–588. https://doi.org/10.1080/15213269.2015.1121829

Kim, K. J., & Sundar, S. S. (2016). Mobile persuasion: Can screen size and presentation mode make a difference to trust? *Human Communication Research*, *42*(1), 45–70. https://doi.org/10.1111/hcre.12064

Kim, Y., & Sundar, S. S. (2011, May). *Can your avatar improve your health? The impact of avatar attractiveness and avatar creation*. Paper presented at the 61st Annual Conference of the International Communication Association, Boston, MA.

Koh, Y. J., & Sundar, S. S. (2010). Heuristic versus systematic processing of specialist versus generalist sources in online media. *Human Communication Research*, *36*(2), 103–124. https://doi.org/10.1111/j.1468-2958.2010.01370.x

Lee, E.-J., & Sundar, S. S. (2010). Human-computer interaction. In C. R. Berger, M. E. Roloff, & D. R. Ewoldsen (Eds.), *The handbook of communication science* (2nd ed., pp. 507–523). Thousand Oaks, CA: Sage Publications.

Lee, M. K. (2018). Understanding perception of algorithmic decisions: Fairness, trust, and emotion in response to algorithmic management. *Big Data & Society, 5*(1), https://doi.org/10.1177/2053951718756684

Li, R., & Sundar, S. S. (2021). Can interactive media attenuate psychological reactance to health messages? A study of the role played by user commenting and audience metrics in persuasion. *Health Communication*, 1–13. https://doi.org/10.1080/10410236.2021.1888450

Marathe, S., & Sundar, S. S. (2011). What drives customization? *Proceedings of the 2011 Annual Conference on Human Factors in Computing Systems - CHI '11*. https://doi.org/10.1145/1978942.1979056

McLuhan, M. (1964). *Understanding media: the extensions of man*. New York: McGraw-Hill.

Molina, M. D., & Sundar, S. S. (2020). Can mobile apps motivate fitness tracking? A study of technological affordances and workout behaviors. *Health Communication, 35*(1), 65–74. https://doi.org/10.1080/10410236.2018.1536961

Moon, Y. (2000). Intimate exchanges: Using computers to elicit self-disclosure from consumers. *Journal of Consumer Research, 26*(4), 323–339. https://doi.org/10.1086/209566

Moon, Y., & Nass, C. (1996). How "real" are computer personalities? *Communication Research, 23*(6), 651–674. https://doi.org/10.1177/009365096023006002

Nass, C., & Lee, K. M. (2001). Does computer-synthesized speech manifest personality? Experimental tests of recognition, similarity-attraction, and consistency-attraction. *Journal of Experimental Psychology: Applied, 7*(3), 171–181. https://doi.org/10.1037/1076-898x.7.3.171

Nass, C., & Mason, L. (1990). On the study of technology and task: A variable-based approach. In J. L. Fulk & C. Steinfield (Eds.), *Organizations and communication technology* (pp. 46–68). Newbury Park, CA: Sage.

Nass, C., & Moon, Y. (2000). Machines and mindlessness: Social responses to computers. *Journal of Social Issues, 56*(1), 81–103. https://doi.org/10.1111/0022-4537.00153

Nass, C., & Steuer, J. (1993). Voices, boxes, and sources of messages. *Human Communication Research, 19*(4), 504–527. https://doi.org/10.1111/j.1468-2958.1993.tb00311.x

Nass, C., Fogg, B. J., & Moon, Y. (1996). Can computers be teammates? *International Journal of Human-Computer Studies, 45*(6), 669–678. https://doi.org/10.1006/ijhc.1996.0073

Nass, C., Steuer, J., & Tauber, E. R. (1994). Computers are social actors. *Conference Companion on Human Factors in Computing Systems - CHI '94*. https://doi.org/10.1145/259963.260288

Oeldorf-Hirsch, A., & Sundar, S. S. (2015). Posting, commenting, and tagging: Effects of sharing news stories on Facebook. *Computers in Human Behavior, 44*, 240–249. https://doi.org/10.1016/j.chb.2014.11.024

Oh, J., & Sundar, S. S. (2016). User engagement with interactive media: A communication perspective. In H. O'Brien & P. Cairns (Eds.), *Why engagement matters: Cross-disciplinary perspectives of user engagement in digital media* (pp. 177-198). Switzerland: Springer International Publishing.

Oh, J., & Sundar, S. S. (2020). What happens when you click and drag: Unpacking the relationship between on-screen interaction and user engagement with an anti-smoking website. *Health Communication, 35*(3), 269–280. https://doi.org/10.1080/10410236.2018.1560578

Rafaeli, S. (1988). Interactivity: From new media to communication. In R. P. Hawkins, J. M. Wiernan, & B S. Pingree (Eds.), *Advancing communication science? Merging mass and interpersonal processes* (pp. 110–134), Newbury Park, CA: Sage.

Ryan, R. M., & Deci, E. L. (2000). Self-determination theory and the facilitation of intrinsic motivation, social development, and well-being. *American Psychologist, 55*(1), 68–78. https://doi.org/10.1037/0003-066x.55.1.68

Sundar, S. S. (2007a). Social psychology of interactivity in human-website interaction. In A. N. Joinson, K. Y. A. McKenna, T. Postmes, & U-D. Reips (Eds.), *The Oxford handbook of internet psychology* (pp. 89-104). Oxford, UK: Oxford University Press.

Sundar, S. S. (2007b). Agency and on-line media. In J. J. Arnett (Ed.), *Encyclopedia of children, adolescents, and the media* (pp. 635–636). Thousand Oaks, CA: Sage Publications.

Sundar, S. S. (2008a). The MAIN model: A heuristic approach to understanding technology effects on credibility. In M. J. Metzger & A. J. Flanagin (Eds.), *Digital media, youth, and credibility* (pp. 72–100). Cambridge, MA: The MIT Press.

Sundar, S. S. (2008b). Self as source: Agency and customization in interactive media. In E. Konijn, S. Utz, M. Tanis, & S. Barnes (Eds.), *Mediated interpersonal communication* (pp. 58–74). New York: Routledge.

Sundar, S. S. (2009). Media effects 2.0: Social and psychological effects of communication technologies. In R. L. Nabi & M. B. Oliver (Eds.), *The SAGE handbook of media processes and effects* (pp. 545–560). Thousand Oaks, CA: Sage Publications.

Sundar, S. S. (2020). Rise of machine agency: A framework for studying the psychology of human–AI Interaction (HAII). *Journal of Computer-Mediated Communication, 25*(1), 74–88. https://doi.org/10.1093/jcmc/zmz026

Sundar, S. S., & Kim, J. (2019). Machine heuristic: When we trust computers more than humans with our personal information. *Proceedings of the 2019 Conference on Human Factors in Computing Systems* (pp. 1–9). https://doi:10.1145/3290605.3300768

Sundar, S. S., & Nass, C. (2000). Source orientation in human-computer interaction: Programmer, networker, or independent social actor? *Communication Research*, *27*(6), 683–703. https://doi.org/10.1177/009365000027006001

Sundar, S. S., & Nass, C. (2001). Conceptualizing sources in online news. *Journal of Communication*, *51*(1), 52–72. https://doi.org/10.1111/j.1460-2466.2001.tb02872.x

Sundar, S. S., & Oh, J. (2019). Psychological effects of interactive media technologies: A human-computer interaction (HCI) perspective. In M. B. Oliver, A. A. Raney, & J. Bryant (Eds.), *Media effects: Advances in theory and research* (4th ed) (pp. 357–372). New York: Routledge.

Sundar, S. S., Bellur, S., & Jia, H. (2012). Motivational technologies: A theoretical framework for designing preventive health applications. In M. Bang & E. L. Ragnemalm (Eds.), *Proceedings of the 7th International Conference on Persuasive Technology* (pp. 112–122). Springer, Berlin, Heidelberg. https://doi.org/10.1007/978-3-642-31037-9_10

Sundar, S. S., Bellur, S., Oh, J., Jia, H., & Kim, H.-S. (2016). Theoretical importance of contingency in human-computer interaction: Effects of message interactivity on user engagement. *Communication Research*, *43*(5), 595–625. https://doi.org/10.1177/0093650214534962

Sundar, S. S., Bellur, S., Oh, J., Xu, Q., & Jia, H. (2014). User experience of on-screen interaction techniques: An experimental investigation of clicking, sliding, zooming, hovering, dragging, and flipping. *Human–Computer Interaction*, *29*(2), 109–152. https://doi.org/10.1080/07370024.2013.789347

Sundar, S. S., Jia, H., Waddell, T. F., & Huang, Y. (2015). Toward a theory of interactive media effects (TIME): Four models for explaining how interface features affect user psychology. In S. S. Sundar (Ed.), *The handbook of the psychology of communication technology* (pp. 47–86). Malden, MA: Wiley Blackwell.

Sundar, S. S., Oh, J., Bellur, S., Jia, H., & Kim, H.-S. (2012). Interactivity as self-expression: A field experiment with customization and blogging. *Proceedings of the 2012 ACM Annual Conference on Human Factors in Computing Systems - CHI '12*. https://doi.org/10.1145/2207676.2207731

Sundar, S. S., Tamul, D. J., & Wu, M. (2014). Capturing "cool": Measures for assessing coolness of technological products. *International Journal of Human-Computer Studies*, *72*(2), 169–180. https://doi.org/10.1016/j.ijhcs.2013.09.008

Waddell, T. F., & Sundar, S. S. (2020). Bandwagon effects in social television: How audience metrics related to size and opinion affect the enjoyment of digital media. *Computers in Human Behavior*, *107*, 106270. https://doi.org/10.1016/j.chb.2020.106270

8

Computer-Supported Cooperative Work (CSCW) and Human– Machine Communication (HMC)

Steve Jones and Rhonda McEwen

Computer-Supported Cooperative Work (CSCW, sometimes referencing Computer-Supported Collaborative Work) is an interdisciplinary area of scholarly research that examines how humans and computer technologies interact and inter-relate in work processes with some more recent research beginning to incorporate social processes. It should be clear, then, that Human–Machine Communication (HMC) as a field that centers the interactions and relationships that arise as humans and machines communicate with one another opens new and interesting avenues for CSCW scholarship.

CSCW emerged in the 1980s alongside the rapid development and deployment of computer technologies in the workplace, ranging from desktop computers to early networks. The term was first used by Greif and Cashman (Greif, 1988) in a description of a workshop during which scholars were to examine how people perform duties and tasks in environments that incorporated computers into traditional workplaces and how the interactions between people and between people and computers might be best organized.

While CSCW's beginning as an academic research is attributed to this workshop, within the first publications there is evidence of intellectual threads formed during the final stages of the industrial production era in factories, and, in particular,

there is a strong influence from systems thinking scholarship (Schmidt, 2011; Schorch et al., 2020). One of the early comparators used to demarcate CSCW as a unique scholarly area is research on Group Support Systems (GSS). GSS uses process-driven ideologies rooted in Taylorism, Fordism, and Toyotism and applies them to decision support, thus making use of structured and computational frameworks in computer-based information systems. The opportunities to use hardware and software to organize and structure data, coordinate meetings, and chunk office environment projects into executable tasks, were well-suited to the philosophies of systems design.

As an interdisciplinary group, the early CSCW scholars turned their attention to the possibilities and effects of technology support for office workers who engage in group communication and work processes (Bowers & Benford, 1991, p. 5). This emphasis on investigating the role of technology as a tool to facilitate efficient group communication processes remains at the core of CSCW scholarship. The ontological underpinnings in CSCW research draw a distinct line between the human as an actor in the system and technologies (or machines) as more passive apparatus in the service of the system. As discussed later, this is an area of difference between most CSCW scholarship and that of Human–Machine Communication.

CSCW is grounded in the sociology of work (Suchman, 1982, for example), and its adoption of the term "cooperative work" signals researchers' interest in examining processes and interaction rather than objects or spaces. Such focus has, of necessity, shifted attention away from individual technologies and toward the consequences these technologies may have for process, interaction, and coordination. Perhaps the most clear and succinct definition of CSCW is this one from Bannon and Schmidt: "CSCW should be conceived as an endeavor to understand the nature and characteristics of cooperative work with the objective of designing adequate computer-based technologies" (1989, p. 360). It is notable their definition extends the vision of CSCW toward design in addition to cooperative work, and participatory design is a hallmark of much CSCW research (see for example Kensing & Blomberg, 1998). It is also the case that much work in CSCW is of a practical nature, seeking to improve not only productivity and efficiency but also social and interpersonal relations within work settings (Wallace, Oji, & Anslow, 2017).

As the technologies of workplaces have evolved, the utility of applying CSCW concepts in cognate disciplines and research areas has increased. Given Bannon's and Schmidt's definition, it should be clear that human–robot interaction (HRI) and HMC are areas of study that would engage CSCW researchers and that CSCW is in some ways an antecedent of HMC. One offshoot of CSCW is research on the use of social software, also called enterprise social software or social computing, for work. Social software has become, if not synonymous with CSCW, then, a very close academic relation; at CSCW conferences the terms CSCW/social computing/social software are often used interchangeably, and the annual ACM conference on CSCW is now called "CSCW and Social Computing" (Koch et al., 2015).

Tom Coates, one of the leading developers and voices on social software, defines it as, "a particular sub-class of software-prosthesis that concerns itself with the augmentation of human social and/or collaborative abilities through structured mediation (this mediation may be distributed or centralized, top-down or bottom-up/emergent)" (Coates, 2003). Examples of social software that have become workplace standards are email, instant messaging, wikis, and social network services like LinkedIn™. From Coates' definition, social software supports social interaction and communication, thus energizing the exchange of ideas and methodologies among CSCW/social software and HMC scholars.

While CSCW most often has focused on white-collar workplaces (e.g., the introduction of computers or networks in an office) manufacturing and other industrial workplaces have a lengthy history of automation. As Guzman wrote, "during the mid-twentieth century, the manufacturing sector in the United States and other countries underwent an 'automation revolution' that affected not only the work being done in factories but also the lives of individual workers and society at large" (2016, p. 1). The deployment of automation and robots in industrial workplaces like warehouses has greatly increased in the 2010s and continues apace. Per the International Federation of Robotics (IFR), the global average for industrial robots per 10,000 manufacturing workers grew from 66 robots in 2015 to 74 robots in 2016, to 85 in 2017 (International Federation of Robotics, 2018). It would be unsurprising if the Covid-19 pandemic accelerated the trend.

A great deal of CSCW research has been grounded in ethnography with fieldwork and field studies predominating. From the mid-1980s, CSCW researchers were influenced by ethnomethodology and ethnography thinkers such as Ludwig Wittgenstein, Peter Winch, Harold Garfinkel, and Harvey Sacks (Randall et al., 2021). Workplace studies have commonly employed participant-observation and conversation analysis to study social interactions and workplace activities, and regularly include interviews and surveys. Among the areas of study, one finds focus most often falls on group tasks, shared goal formation, the nature of group formation and membership, and contextual factors that influence cooperative work. The early CSCW researchers that employed ethnography in information systems workplaces broke ground by positioning humans as active participants in systems, in contrast with viewing them as more passive "end users" (Blomberg & Karasti, 2013).

While HMC has arguably been an area to which CSCW researchers have paid some attention, technological developments in areas like artificial intelligence (AI), digital voice assistants, and social robotics, among others, will almost certainly require reconsiderations and reformulations of prior approaches to CSCW. As has been the case with the study of communication more broadly, CSCW researchers have largely only considered human communication in their studies. Even when computers are foregrounded they are considered tools, or media, rather than collaborators. Put another way, CSCW research has treated computers and machines as non-agentic objects, mediators, through which human communication is passed and through which human–human collaboration occurs. A central precept of HMC is that both humans and machines are active communicators in a system, including communicating with each other. Thus, HMC theorizes machines beyond supporters of collaborative work, but as collaborators in the workplace and as participants of the interactions.

Suchman (2007) revisits prior research on photocopiers to engage with human–machine communication from the lens of situated action theory. For Suchman, the situation of action includes all the resources available to an actor for both sharing her own actions and for interpreting the actions of others (2007, p. 125). For Suchman, in a human–machine interaction, the human responds to the machine's action and makes adjustments. The machine is not able to likewise adjust or align to the human's actions but must follow the instructions or predictive modeling of the designer/programmer. Situated action theory thereby finds an irreconcilable asymmetry between the human and the machine. Similarly, CSCW scholars point to situated awareness, which is awareness motivated by what is going on at the moment (e.g. overhearing coworkers), as a uniquely human–human resource (Blomberg & Karasti, 2013, p. 378). But as computers and robots increasingly listen to, speak, interact with, and learn from humans, CSCW research and situated action/awareness theory will need to account for machines in new ways to consider them as agents and actors, as collaborators in cooperative work. HMC scholars attentive to sensor and machine learning developments find a diminution of asymmetry between humans and machines, including in workplaces.

Advances in artificial intelligence complicate existing assumptions about relationships between collaborators. Machine learning (ML), including natural language processing, graph neural networks, variational autoencoders, and the like, usher in a host of machines that have the capacity for unsupervised learning. This means that machines, like their human collaborators, can increasingly adjust their responses and actions to situations. For CSCW researchers, HMC concepts offer theoretical, methodological, and analytical opportunities to answer questions related to workplace sociality. For example, how will people working collaboratively within a group react to the presence of a robot or AI that is also collaborating with them? How might CSCW researchers study such scenarios? To what extent can existing CSCW ethnographic techniques be adapted to observe the choices and decision-making of machines at work? Questions of agency, autonomy, and independence will of necessity be foregrounded and power dynamics are likely to be shifted from ones more commonly observed in prior CSCW research. It will be necessary to incorporate machines into ethnographic and other methods often employed in CSCW research and

to develop new methods that could interrogate the machine during and after work processes.

Robots, for example, are already not only single-task machines that are segregated from humans on an assembly line but also can be co-workers, sharing the same space as humans. Particularly given uncertainties about attitudes towards robots, what research might CSCW scholars undertake to understand the presence of machines as co-workers in the workplace? Similar questions may be asked of AI, digital voice assistants, ML search engines, and other HMC technologies that will increasingly be incorporated into the workplace.

Workplaces themselves are under ongoing transformation as well. Decades-long experiments on working outside of organizational bricks and mortar, hastened by the global pandemic across all spheres of work, have resulted in affordable, distributed access via cloud computing. As domiciles became workplaces during lockdowns, machines became the consistent and colocated coworker. CSCW had already begun to consider workplaces as consumer domains (Schmidt, 2011); however, this restructuring of spatial boundaries for work and the availability of machines in the home, leads to an unboundedness that CSCW must reckon with. Further, the blurring of lines between work and leisure when humans interact and collaborate with the same technologies (mobile devices, laptops, social networking software, etc.) for employment and entertainment may encourage CSCW researchers to approach HMC for concepts and techniques.

Furthermore, CSCW researchers will want to engage with the broader HMC and HRI design community to consider means by which all parties could collaborate in participatory design processes in the development and deployment of devices specifically intended to engage in HMC and HRI. Considering the aforementioned shifts in agency and autonomy, what might CSCW scholars bring to efforts to support and empower humans in collaborative work with machines?

Some recent publications point to interesting potential directions that CSCW research might take in light of HMC. For example, Drury et al. (2006) sought to combine CSCW and HRI methodologies to create design guidelines for development of urban search and rescue (USAR) robots. At the 2017 ACM CSCW conference, Jung et al. offered a work to address "the social and technical challenges that surround the placement of robots within work-groups and teams" (2017, p. 401). Particularly noteworthy was their focus on moving away from HRI research that focused on one-on-one human–robot interaction. More recently, Taylor et al. (2022) examined processes for design of interactive robotic systems for use in hospital emergency departments (ED) and found the potential for robots to reduce healthcare workers' workload. Additionally, they noted, robots have "the potential to reduce wait times, block smells and sounds of the ED, prevent patient self-harm and harm to others, and empower patients by helping them be more involved in their care" (p. 21). Finally, Rittenbruch's (2011) work on intentional awareness and disclosure in collaborative systems, approaches the notion of human–machine shared intentionality and can be expanded by CSCW research into HMC.

Of particular interest as HMC technologies develop will be the contribution CSCW research can make to probing our understanding of how humans and machines adapt to one another, as well as how and whether they may trust one another. Given the decades-long experience CSCW scholars have studying technologies for collaborative work and learning about as well as influencing the design of those technologies, their contribution will be critical to research on, and development of, HMC technologies that cooperate and support human work.

As asymmetries between humans and machines are reduced, how will CSCW account for the situated action of both the human and the machine? As with human–human communication, human–machine interactions are not perfectly anticipated nor understood by participants, and mutual intelligibility remains a design and development goal (McEwen & Dube, 2017).

There is the potential for researchers within CSCW and HMC subfields to engage in projects that respond to the questions raised above. Whether this would lead to the emergence of additional areas, such as Robot Supported Collaborative Work (RSCW) or AI–Human Supported Collaborative Work is a fun speculation. Regardless, as workplaces and technologies evolve together, the contribution of HMC to CSCW and their intermingling is highly likely and exciting.

REFERENCES

Bannon, L., & Schmidt, K. (1989). CSCW: Four Characters in Search of a Context. In *Proceedings of the EC-CSCW '89. Proceedings of the First European Conference on Computer Supported Cooperative Work*. Gatwick, London, 13–15 September, 1989.

Blomberg, J., & Karasti, H. (2013). Reflections on 25 years of ethnography in CSCW. *Computer supported cooperative work (CSCW)*, *22*(4), 373–423.

Bowers, J., & Benford, S. (1991). *Studies in computer-supported cooperative work: theory, practice, and design*. Elsevier, Amsterdam.

Coates, T. (2003). My working definition of social software. http://plasticbag.org/archives/2003/05/my_working_definition_of_social_software/ (last viewed on Sept. 1, 2022).

Drury, J. L., Scholtz, J., & Yanco, H. A. (2006) Applying CSCW and HCI techniques to human-robot interaction. MITRE Corporation: Bedford, MA. Available online at https://apps.dtic.mil/sti/pdfs/ADA456188.pdf (last accessed August 25, 2022).

Greif, I. (1988) Overview. In Greif, I. (Ed.) *Computer-Supported Cooperative Work: A Book of Readings*. Morgan Kaufmann Publishers: San Mateo, CA., pp 5–12.

Guzman, A. (2016). The messages of mute machines. *communication +1* 5(1). Available online at https://scholarworks.umass.edu/cpo/vol5/iss1/4/ (last accessed August 18, 2022).

International Federation of Robotics (2018). Robot density rises globally, news release, February 7, 2018, https://ifr.org/ifr-press-releases/news/robot-density-rises-globally (last accessed August 18, 2022).

Jung, M. F., Eyssel, F., Sabanovic, S., & Fraune, M. (2017). Robots in groups and teams. *CSCW '17 Companion: Companion of the 2017 ACM Conference on Computer Supported Cooperative Work and Social Computing* (401–407). https://doi.org/10.1145/3022198.3022659

Kensing, F., & Blomberg, J. 1998. Participatory design: Issues and concerns. *Computer Supported Cooperative Work (CSCW)* 7, 167–185.

Koch, M., Schwabe, G., & Briggs, R.O. (2015). CSCW and social computing. *Bus Inf Syst Eng* 57, 149–153. https://doi.org/10.1007/s12599-015-0376-2 (last accessed Sept. 1, 2022).

McEwen, R., & Dubé, A. (2017). *Understanding tablets from early childhood to adulthood: Encounters with touch technology*. Routledge.

Randall, D., Rouncefield, M., & Tolmie, P. (2021). Ethnography, CSCW and ethnomethodology. *Computer Supported Cooperative Work 30*, 189–214. https://doi.org/10.1007/s10606-020-09388-8 (last accessed Sept. 1, 2022).

Rittenbruch, M. (2011). Active awareness: Supporting the intentional disclosure of awareness information in collaborative systems (Doctoral dissertation, University of Queensland) (last accessed Sept. 1, 2022).

Schmidt, K. (2011). The concept of "work" in CSCW. *Computer Supported Cooperative Work (CSCW)*, *20*(4), 34–401.

Schmidt, Kjeld, & Liam J. Bannon. (1992). Taking CSCW seriously: Supporting articulation work, *Computer Supported Cooperative Work (CSCW): An International Journal*, 1(1–2), 7–40

Schorch, M., Seifert, F., Syed, H. A., Kotthaus, C., & Pipek, V. (2020). Doing CSCW research in small and medium enterprises: Experiences, options and challenges. In *Proceedings of 18th European Conference on Computer-Supported Cooperative Work*. European Society for Socially Embedded Technologies (EUSSET).

Suchman, L. (1982). Toward a sociology of human-machine interaction. CIS Working Paper, Xerox Palo Alto Research Center: Palo Alto, CA.

Suchman, L. A. (2007). *Human-machine reconfigurations: Plans and situated actions,* 2nd ed. Cambridge University Press.

Taylor, A., Murakami, M., Kim, So, Chu, R., & Riek, L. D. (2022). Hospitals of the future: Designing interactive robotic systems for resilient emergency departments. CSCW '22. Available online at https://cseweb.ucsd.edu/~lriek/papers/cscw2022.pdf (last access August 25, 2022>

Wallace, J. R., Oji, S., & Anslow, C. 2017. Technologies, methods, and values: Changes in empirical research at CSCW 1990–2015. *Proceedings of the ACM on Human-Computer Interaction*, article 106.

9

HMC and HCI: Cognates on a Journey

Victoria McArthur and Cosmin Munteanu

INTRODUCTION

The field of human–computer interaction (HCI) is a multidisciplinary field which is largely concerned with the study and design of interfaces, and more importantly, studying the interactions that occur between humans and computers. HCI represents the intersection of a number of fields, including psychology, sociology, information systems, communications, and computer science. Long before the formal existence of the field, researchers have always studied how humans and systems (machines and other technologies) work together. While the term HCI is commonly used to describe this interdisciplinary field, it has also been referred to as computer–human interaction, or CHI. So which is it? Are humans interacting with the computers, or are computers interacting with humans? In the introductory chapter to his text on human–computer interaction, MacKenzie describes a shift in computing, occurring gradually from the 1940s to the 1980s, with the notable emergence of personal computing (MacKenzie, 2013). Prior to the 1970s, computers were largely used by computer engineers and scientists. Interaction design was not necessary as a research paradigm, since those using the computers were likely the same people who would have written the user manuals. Thus, although the field of HCI is said to have emerged to better understand how interface design could be studied to accommodate usability, the field rightly shifted to focus on supporting more diverse user populations through the study of accessibility and inclusive design (Shneiderman, 1999).

This etymological shift is significant in the context of this chapter as it highlights the agency that the field has granted to humans who interact with Information and Communication Technologies (ICTs). However, from the perspective of human–machine communication it seems as though the space in which interaction occurs is of interest, since HCI research is essentially about the ways in which humans interface with information and communication technologies. If HCI is the study of human interaction with computers, it must also include the study of the agency designers have in creating interfaces that will subsequently mediate user experience and the degree to which interaction is truly nuanced and contextual. Mannovich (2002) writes, "[g]iven that computer media is simply a set of characters and numbers stored in a computer, there are numerous ways in which it could be presented to a user. Yet, as it always happens with cultural languages, only a few of these possibilities actually appear viable in a given historical moment" (Mannovich, 2002, p. 81).

HCI as a field not only studies the ways in which computer media are presented to users, but also ascribes many of the frameworks that inform the design of these artifacts. Human–computer interactions are the result of a negotiation between the user and the designer and computer interfaces are one tool or actor that is often used in the creation of meaning between humans and machines. This chapter explores this negotiation through several prominent theories in this field, concluding with a reflection on how emerging technologies and new forms of interaction pose challenges to the applicability of some of these theories to supporting agency in digitally mediated communications.

COMPUTER-MEDIATED COMMUNICATION

Computer interfaces support a wide array of activities involving information communication technologies (ICTs), including work, scientific research, communication, and play. In the context of communications and media studies, HCI researchers are interested in the ways in which the computer mediates communication and shapes online identities. For example, research on identity formation in online environments draws from earlier work on identity in Multi-User Dungeons (MUDs), multi-player virtual worlds that are traditionally text-based. In these spaces, virtual "bodies" were crafted entirely in text, and in a very literal sense, identities were "authored" by the users. Research on MUDs highlighted identity performance and identity play in online settings, including the trying out of multiple- and other-selves, those environments afforded (e.g. Berman & Bruckman, 2001; Bruckman, 1992). Users had complete control over nearly all aspects of their virtual selves, including their gender. Players could choose to be gendered, gender-neutral, and/or gender-plural (Bruckman, 1996; Reid, 1996).

With the shift from textual environments to graphical 2D and 3D user interfaces, virtual identities were no longer authored by players but produced by software designers. Textual bodies have been replaced by graphical representation – avatars or other images that are mediated by a user interface. Free-form user-generated identities were replaced with forms that required identities be spliced and made to fit the requirements of the database. Nakamura (2002) describes the ways in which interface widgets constrain a user's ability to express their identity online. She referred to this phenomenon as "menu-driven identities"; the ways in which design "reveals assumptions about a user's race and ethnicity" (Nakamura, 2002,

p. 101). For example, as a Japanese-American, Nakamura found it difficult to use web portals to create an accurate online identity for herself. Many of the web portals she used included an option for indicating her ethnic identity, but the widget she was presented with would only allow her to choose Japanese or American, not both. The type of widget chosen by the designer, and the limitations it imposed on her online identity, presents a hegemonic view of identity and limits the user in their ability to craft an online identity. The system simply did not afford a mixed ethnic identity. As Nakamura suggests, "[c]yberspace's interfaces are perfectly hegemonic, in the sense that they are enforced and informed by dominant ideologies, however unconscious, as well as, to a much lesser extent, infrastructure and design limitations" (Nakamura, 2002, p. 135).

If we consider the communication affordances of ICTs, it is important not only to investigate the technological advances, but also the ways in which communication is mediated by computer interfaces. For example, Albright (2007) mobilizes Goffman's "expression given" and "expression given off" (Goffman, 1959) in order to explore how one man, Colonel Saleh, was able to maintain romantic relationships with over 50 women on an online dating site. Specifically, Albright proposes that it is the nature of information communication technologies – their affordances – that allowed Colonel Saleh, who was married in real life, to support multiple, simultaneous intimate relationships. In face-to-face communication, Goffman proposes that cues fall broadly into two categories: "expression given" and "expression given off." Expressions given are understood to be verbal where expressions given off include the gamut of non-verbal cues, many of which we have less control over, such as body language or facial movements that are given off during communication and interaction. Since we anticipate that people may be dishonest in how they present themselves, we rely on "expressions given off" as a sort of litmus test, used by others in order to assess the authenticity of the speaker's mood or motives. Albright cites the works of others that state the obvious: ICTs allow us to carefully craft and control the digitized equivalents of our "expressions given off." In many cases, online interactions occur almost entirely in the absence of these "expressions given off," and many of our "expressions given" are reduced to textual interactions.

The effects of ICTs on Goffman's work are illustrated in Walther's "hyperpersonal interactions" (Walther, 1996). Taking the affordances of computer-mediated communication into account, Walther proposes the following framework for understanding how users both mediate and mobilize these affordances in evaluating and managing online personae:

1   optimization of self-representation (due to latency)
2   receiver forms impressions by "inflating" tiny pieces of information
3   user can thereby re-allocate cognitive resources used for non-verbal language to #1 (textual optimization)

Essentially, the latency in computer-mediated-communication (whether generated by hardware/software, or artificially via users evoking away from keyboard or "AFK" moments), not only allows users to carefully manage both their "expressions given" and "expressions given off," it also allows them to re-allocate cognitive resources to "expressions given" that would have otherwise been used to manage "expressions given off." Depending on the medium of communication, the latter may take on many different forms (photo sharing, scripting an avatar's body language such that it aligns with the expressions given, etc.). If the user on the other end is emotionally invested in the success of the performance, they subconsciously support it by enhancing the tiny fragments of identity data they receive and using these pieces to construct a complete impression of the user. Walther proposes that computer-mediated interaction may be more intimate and positive than face-to-face interaction. ICTs support identity play through the anonymity of the Internet, as well as the interplay between "actors" in the presentation of self as described in the work of Goffman.

ACTOR-NETWORK THEORY

Although the aforementioned paradigm shift in HCI emphasized the human in human–computer interaction, some HCI scholars have mobilized Actor-Network Theory or ANT in the study of ICT use. ANT highlights the network of constantly shifting relationships between humans and objects, ascribing both humans and non-humans the status of "actors" in the network that are equally important in creating social situations.

In 2013, ANT scholar Bruno Latour addressed attendees of the annual CHI conference in a closing plenary talk and challenged them to consider a monadological approach to HCI research. In his talk Latour suggested that "there is no collective phenomena… but there exist many collecting

devices that generate collected phenomena." Instead of focusing on the kinds of individual experiences that may be derived from "collective phenomena," Latour urged the CHI community to consider monads. If actor-network theory highlights the networked actors (human and non-human) contributing to an observed social phenomenon, then monads can be thought of as various inter-connected actor-networks. As a theoretical framing the monadological approach to sociology, originally proposed by Gabriel Tarde (2012), allows researchers to trace-out different monadic relations, revealing various actor-networks both micro and macro in relation to the social phenomenon under study. Monads are inter-connected and overlapping, but also possess nodes which do not overlap and may connect to other monads in ways that are surprising. For Latour, monads can evoke the fallacy of the impossible zoom as a means of illustrating the ways in which "zoom" and "focus" in research can sometimes be problematic, or in terms of "big data," seemingly impossible. He goes on to suggest, "a more 'global' view is never larger than another but it leads to a different local site with different data flows, instruments, visual displays and expert teams where most of the information is discarded or formatted differently." For HCI researchers, a monadological view reveals the actor-networks that are often outside of the sites of research but are still very much a part of the people and objects that we study.

Standing before the community, Latour challenged HCI researchers to look for the monads in our research. Specifically, he challenged us to embrace monads in HCI; to find ways to capture the inner narrativity of overlapping monads and to find new ways to make them visible. Along with Michel Callon (1997) and John Law (2004), Bruno Latour is one of the primary developers of actor–network theory (1987, 1992, 2005), a somewhat controversial approach to research in the social sciences which not only includes non-humans in the study of social phenomena, but considers the ways in which both humans and non-humans form a network of material-semiotic relations. In his study of social phenomena, Latour is concerned primarily with our interest as researchers in "the social," especially as the word itself has been problematized within the social sciences. The issue, he argues, is that the word "social" began to "mean a type of material, as if the adjective was roughly comparable to other terms like 'wooden', 'steely', 'biological', 'economical', 'mental', 'organizational', or 'linguistic'" (Latour, 2005, p. 1). He goes on to suggest that "[a]t that point, the meaning of the word breaks down since it now designates two entirely different things: first, a movement during a process of assembling;

and second, a specific type of ingredient that is supposed to differ from other materials" (Latour, 2005, p. 1). Thus, he argues, that to only study that which has come to represent "the social" actually excludes other relevant actors necessary in truly understanding social processes.

Looking to ANT, Latour aims to redefine sociology "not as the 'science of the social', but as the tracing of associations… a type of connection between things that are not themselves social" (Latour, 2005, p. 5). The emphasis here is not only on the "tracing of associations" within the network of social phenomena, but also in being able to identify all of the actors who contribute to the same social phenomena, whether human or non-human. Through studying this networked association of actors, Latour argues that social scientists can truly study the social.

The actors identified in social phenomena have traditionally been human participants, perhaps due to the fact that our agency is a fundamental property of our humanness. This focus on athropocentric discourse holds true not only within the field of sociology, but also within the field of HCI. ANT differs from traditional approaches in that it involves the controversial attribution of agency to non-humans. Latour argues that the exclusion of non-humans in the past was "not only due to the definition of the social used by sociologists, but also to the very definition of actors and agencies most often chosen" (Latour, 2005, p. 71). He goes on to suggest:

> If action is limited a priori to what "intentional", "meaningful" humans do, it is hard to see how a hammer, a basket, a door closer, a cat, a rug, a mug, a list, or a tag could act. They might exist in the domain of "material" "causal" relations, but not in the "reflexive" "symbolic" domain of social relations. By contrast, if we stick to our decision to start from the controversies about actors and agencies, then any thing that does modify a state of affairs by making a difference is an actor – or, if it has no figuration yet, an actant. Thus, the questions to ask about any agent are simply the following: Does it make a difference in the course of some other agent's action or not? Is there some trial that allows someone to detect this difference? (Latour, 2005, p. 71)

The relationship between humans and ICTs is unproblematically presented as an account of intentional user behaviors, positioning ICTs as tools that are utilized by humans. Computer interfaces, like hammers and cats, can and do have an observable effect on the choices a user makes when they interact with technology. The effect is not a unidirectional one in which a user arrives at an interface with fixed plans and then acts on the interface to complete them. Interactions are the result of an interplay between users and interfaces. These interactions are influenced by a variety of factors, including affordances, constraints, assumptions, designs, and experiences. The role that the computer plays in these interactions is an important part of understanding the resultant phenomena that emerge from their use. ICTs afford communication, but that communication is mediated by the design of the system itself. An ANT lens provides HCI researchers with a theoretical framing – a means to access actors that have been previously underprivileged and subsequently undertheorized.

Methodologically, how does one do ANT research in the field of HCI? Latour proposes that "…ANT is simply an attempt to allow the members of contemporary society to have as much leeway in defining themselves as that offered by ethnographers" (Latour, 2005, p. 41). ANT is successful when it can theorize about an observable social phenomenon through a tracing of its associations (through the actor-network) – navigating complexity, rather than providing an over-simplified, positivist account that is presented as being "true" or "false" of the social phenomena under study. Since HCI is an interdisciplinary field with a diverse array of research methods, any tools that allow for the collection of data that might assist the researcher in making these material-semiotic relationships accessible should be utilized.

One might argue that a lab-based study is inherently incapable of producing authentic ANT discourses since it removes the actors from the more authentic network and places them in an artificially constructed one. Such an argument is really one of internal versus external (or ecological) validity. Arguably, there is always a trade-off when one chooses an internally valid research design over an externally valid one. The problem is largely one of positivism: internally valid studies tend to produce truths about controlled phenomena and externally valid studies produce discourses that are more generalizable. However, ANT has absolutely nothing to do with producing truths, no matter how generalizable, and is instead a labor of allowing actors to "deploy the full range of controversies in which they are immersed" (Latour, 2005, p. 23). It is the job of the ANT researcher not to emerge from the network with a more authentic positivist account than that of another sociology, but to "trace connections between the controversies themselves rather than try to decide how to settle any given controversy" (Latour, 2005, p. 23). Controversies may refer to the controversies that arise when predetermined networks are imposed upon groups of actors, or they may also refer to the controversies that arise between related work and the resultant actor-networks uncovered by the ANT researcher.

In any ANT study, the researcher is also one actor in the network; the one who proposes the theories, names the other actors, and traces the network, making its nodes visible – or invisible. John Law describes this process as ontological politics. As Law suggests, "[i]n an ontological politics we might hope, instead, to make some realities realer, others less so" (Law, 2004, p. 67). Even though unintentional, the researcher shapes the network, chooses which nodes to elevate to the status of "actor" and which actors are worth studying. In order to carefully navigate the space between ontological politics and the need to produce some discursive account of the phenomena under study, Latour proposes that an ANT scholar should endeavor to choose labels or names for the phenomena they describe that are as "meaningless" as possible so as to not speak for the actors. Terms that are too specific or carry too much ontological baggage may ascribe limited meanings to the explanations offered. As Latour suggests, "ANT prefers to use what could be called an infralanguage, which remains strictly meaningless except for allowing displacement from one frame of reference to the next" (Latour, 2005, p. 30).

AFFORDANCES

The reworked relationship of actors and agency as offered by ANT is an important one, as it also highlights how the design of user interfaces potentially mediate and constrain user interactions. HCI researchers refer to this phenomenon as affordance. The term affordance originated with the work of Gibson (1977, 1979) and was later adopted by the HCI community through the work of Donald Norman (1988). Within the HCI community, interpretations of the concept of affordances have become increasingly diverse since Gibson's work (Kaptelinin & Nardi, 2012). In subsequent work, Norman (1999) refined his concept of affordance, suggesting instead that they are perceived affordances – the actions a user perceives as being possible based on the objects present. Kannengiesser and Gero (2012) describe three different kinds of affordances relating to perception: reactive, hidden, and reflexive. Despite nuanced conceptual shifts, the term has generally held to refer to action possibilities afforded by the environment. ANT challenges the way we position user interfaces in HCI research. Through their affordances, sociologists and communications scholars within the field of HCI argue that they

too are actors; actors that co-construct an online identity with the user.

Much of the literature on HCI not only privileges human actors over non-human actors, but also privileges user choice (e.g., the ability to complete tasks with a given interface; its usability) over interface affordances. User action are often discussed in terms of speed, accuracy, and usability – as though users arrive at interfaces already knowing the action they plan to take and that the interaction will produce the desired outcome. Suchman explores the tension between plans and situated actions, stating that, "every course of action depends in essential ways on its material and social circumstances" (Suchman, 2006, p. 70). Suchman (2006) further examines the tension between interaction and intention, challenging "traditional assumptions regarding purposeful action and shared understanding" (Suchman, 2006, p. 69). Using the term "situated action", Suchman proposes that the actions we take when interacting with interfaces depends on "material and social circumstances" (Suchman, 2006, p. 70). In the context of communication, even if users do arrive at these interfaces with communication strategies in mind, the resultant interaction is a result of situational circumstances that contributed to the creative process. Affordances are one facet of situated actions. The affordances of computer interfaces challenge the assumption of plans with regards to computer-mediated communication.

Anthropologist James Wertsch (1998), reconceptualizes mediation (the tension between human actors and, in this case, computer interfaces) in terms of how systems may limit, rather than facilitate, action. In particular, Wertsch draws attention to the ways in which computer interfaces shape interactions and potentially limit the ways in which we represent ourselves. He explains:

> Most discussions of mediation view it in terms of how it empowers or enables action... However, a narrow focus on the kinds of empowerment provided by cultural tools gives us only a partial picture and one that is benign in an important sense. It does so because it overlooks a counter-vailing, though equally inherent, characteristic of mediational means – namely, that they constrain or limit the forms of action we undertake. (Wertsch, 1998, pp. 38–39)

To date, research on computer-mediated communication tends to frame the interface in, as Wertsch suggests, a benign and incomplete way. Interfaces are discussed in terms of quality and quantity of features available to users but are ultimately framed as tools that facilitate communication. So, while it is tempting to understand ICTs in terms of how they support computer-mediated communication, it is important not to overlook the ways in which these same interfaces also mediate expression. Thus, at the intersection of communications theory and HCI, we should not only be interested in the range and presentation of communication functions available, but also how users interact with and negotiate these affordances.

A PARADIGM SHIFT: MOBILIZING A MORE INCLUSIVE HCI

Although the field of HCI is informed by a diverse methodological toolkit informed by interdisciplinary approaches, members of this community have noted that it is problematic to assume a positivist approach that values replicability and "best practices" over a more ecological and inclusive approach. In HCI, best practices are commonly understood as representing a standard of practice which are best suited to a desired outcome. The term has been commonly accepted as a feature of accredited management standards as outlined in ISO 9000 (Bamford & Deibler, 2003) and ISO 14001 (Clements, 1996). Bretschneider et al. outline a methodology for best practice research, stressing the importance of analyzing example cases from a variety of contexts and requiring a comparative process between multiple methodologies (Bretschneider, Marc-Aurele, & Wu, 2005). Others have raised concern over the totalitarian nature of the term "best" in describing such practices (Bardach, 2011) and have suggested that "contextual practice" is a more appropriate term (Ambler, 2011).

In the 1960s and 70s, the paradigm of co-design, which also goes by the name of participatory design, emerged as a means of rooting design in contextual practice. Participatory design (PD) is an approach to software design that emerged as a counter-movement to the traditional, top-down design paradigm. Suchman et al. argue that "participatory forms of design emphasize the value of crossing professional boundaries and reworking relations of technology production" (Suchman, Trigg, & Blomberg, 2002). Participatory design encompasses a variety of methodologies designed to engage stakeholders in the design process of software and other systems (Muller & Kuhn, 1993). Its practices are motivated by the desire to create a product that is both contextually suitable and usable (Blomberg, Suchman, & Trigg, 1996). PD methodologies allow designers to bypass the interference of a digitally mediated exploratory project by employing low-fidelity, analog prototyping techniques so as to include stakeholders in the design process (Blomberg et al., 1996). Such techniques include, but are not limited to, the use of paper, cue cards, and clay (Sanders, Brandt, & Binder, 2010), interviews, focus groups, and ethnography (e.g. see Nardi, 1997; Suchman, et al., 2002), scenario building, and role playing (e.g. see Svanaes & Seland, 2004; Simsarian, 2003). A combination of the aforementioned methods is generally employed in order to ensure that (a) designers are truly familiar with the stakeholders' needs, (b) stakeholders are actively included in the design process, and (c) stakeholders' needs have been met in the design and deployment of the finished product. A participatory design approach not only modifies the position users take in relation to software design and development, it may also allow for interventions where the traditional software development model would otherwise not have.

Where PD is a methodological approach that invites stakeholders to participate in the iterative design cycle, inclusive design takes this one step further and implores researchers to ensure that stakeholders represent diverse populations. Inclusive design (ID) is a sub-field in HCI largely concerned with the differences in perceptual thinking and physical capabilities of diverse users, looking more generally at existing design practices for interactive electronic systems, including computers, digital television, and smartphones (Biswas & Langdon, 2011; Biswas, Robinson, & Langdon, 2012; Langdon, Persad, & Clarkson, 2010). One notable example, by Ormerod and Newton (2005), proposes an nD model of design principles, wherein universal design, another term for inclusive design, is the focus. The first set of guidelines in their model, UD1, outlines the properties of equitable use, which state that "the design [should be] useful and marketable to people with diverse abilities" (Ormerod & Newton, 2005, p. 105). The first guideline within the UD1 subset deals broadly with avatar design, suggesting that equitable design must "avoid segregating or stigmatizing any users' and this could be detected through the use of avatars, digital human models (DHM) or intelligent agents that replicate a diverse range of impairments, including multiple impairments" (Ormerod & Newton, 2005, p. 107).

Related work on social inclusion is broadly focused on diversifying stakeholder populations by including users from diverse ethnicities, socioeconomic statuses, and ability in the design process (Bleumers et al., 2013; Schuller, Paletta, & Sabouret, 2013; Stewart et al., 2013). Bleumers et al. (2013) classify this work as PESI work (Personal Empowerment and Social Inclusion), wherein interactive digital technologies are viewed as spaces in which marginalized users could potentially become empowered users, and where PESI-driven design practices may allow developers to mobilize games as a means of "leveling-up" this user group. Schuller et al. (2013) focus on how the design of intelligent algorithms could be utilized as a means to adapt systems, in real-time, to a user's behavior, motivation, and interest.

More generally, games scholar Mary Flanagan (2009) proposes modifications to the existing iterative design process in HCI and re-frames it in a way that systematically provides designers with opportunities to include social inclusion as a design goal. Where the traditional model focuses on the cycle of design (e.g., prototyping, usability testing, and the subsequent re-design of a digital game), Flanagan's model identifies opportunities at each stage in the design process for alternative design goals to be integrated into practice. This model augments the design process in a way that addresses intervention, disruption, and social issues. Specifically, the model identifies opportunities for social inclusion, alternative design methods, as well as subversive and emergent gameplay (two phenomena that are often rejected as "bugs" or erroneous use via the traditional model). The critical play model is easily incorporated into existing practice and illustrates how easily the current iterative model can be modified to allow for socially inclusive design.

FROM INCLUSIVE DESIGN TO DE-MARGINALIZING DESIGNS: CHALLENGES AS NEW INTERACTION METAPHORS EMERGE

The growing awareness and interest in making HCI more inclusive was greatly facilitated by the adoption of several participatory and ethnomethodological research and design methods (Bødker, 2015). However, the recent emergence and market adoption of new interaction metaphors have posed challenges to the ideals of a more inclusive HCI. It also challenged the extent to which ethnomethodological approaches can support an inclusivity agenda with respect to such new interactions.

A relevant example of such emerging interaction metaphors is that of voice / conversational user interfaces (VUIs), with applications such as Amazon Alexa or Apple Siri seeing unprecedented consumer market adoption (McTear et al., 2016), while being heavily advertised as "helpful" to a wide range of underrepresented user groups (Sin et al., 2021b). Yet, as we argue here, the HCI research space has been rather slow in adapting

its methodological approaches to ensuring that the design of such interfaces is inclusive of all user groups. In fact, as we will discuss here, our current design methods may in fact not only exclude certain user groups, but actively marginalize them from a larger ecosystem of essential services, critical information, and social participation.

The HCI design community has embraced and championed several potential benefits of VUIs, particularly as voice is often considered the most natural and human-like form of interacting with computing devices (Nass & Brave, 2005). Thus, numerous authors within the space of HCI and, more broadly, within related areas such as communication or information studies, have investigated several applications where VUIs are expected to bring a positive change into users' lives, especially to those users that are often seen "on the other side" of the digital divide (such as older adults). Within this context, VUIs are presented as having the potential to be seamlessly incorporated in daily lives (Kowalski et al., 2019; Ziman & Walsh, 2018), help manage health or access health information (Sidner et al., 2018), navigate the web (Singh, 2009), or develop and maintain social connections (Ali et al., 2018). However, such uncritical embrace of an emerging interaction metaphor could be problematic in several ways, as it can lead the HCI community into traps such as that of technosolutionism (Morozov, 2013). In fact, voice interactions are particularly at risk of being seen as a solution to a wide range of personal or societal "problems" and attempts to design voice-based technology "solutions" may in turn lead to not only furthering digital divides, but marginalizing user groups outside of the digital space (Sin et al., 2021).

The transition of many essential services (such as banking) to not only online, but to "voice first" intelligent agents, has exposed many underrepresented users such as older adults to the harms of technosolutionism that have been manifested elsewhere. When technodeterminism is driving the imposition of structures and solutions that are marketed as helpful by industry, this often is accompanied by the removal of decision-making agency and autonomy from users, with further consequences such as loss of trust in the (digital) services and eventually withdrawal from its use. Such digital marginalization (Sin et al., 2021a) has been extensively documented, with e.g. algorithmic discrimination often associated with artificial intelligence applications being a prime example. In the case of voice interfaces, the consequences extend to marginalized users being excluded not only from the digital application itself (as voice interfaces are not always inclusive and accessible (Brewer et al, 2018)), but also from fully participating in the (new) digital society.

Despite the increasing prevalence of conversational voice interfaces and improvements in the underlying technology (Clark et al., 2019), we do not yet know how to design and evaluate VUIs in a manner that is not only inclusive of all user groups, but also does not further marginalize them. For example, we still do not fully understand the perceptions and barriers to use of VUIs and how they should be designed to interact with underrepresented groups (e.g. older adults, as per Sayago et al. (2019)). One such barrier is the lack of a thorough understanding of users' mental models when interacting with such interfaces – what they know or think they know about someone or something else, in this case conversational voice interfaces (Cowan et al., 2017; Munteanu et al., 2017, 2019).

Prior research on VUIs within HCI has often followed the technosolutionist path in proposing "solutions" to perceived problems. This resulted in the design of systems or applications that are problem-oriented – such research probes do not reflect the adoption barriers many underrepresented groups face when interacting with common conversational voice interfaces that are currently available. Examples of groups that encounter VUI-specific barriers that our current design methodologies fail to fully capture are older adults (Pradhan et al., 2020) or low-literacy users (Pearson et al., 2019). Additional knowledge gaps in this space include the type of interactions where VUIs are optimal to use for, and how these can be designed to be helpful to underrepresented users (Brewer & Piper, 2017; Martin-Hammond et al., 2019). There are also knowledge gaps in terms of the elements that are associated with trust in using different technology tools such as conversational agents, often stemming from the lack of applicable user experience design frameworks (Carr et al., 2013; Franz et al., 2019).

Following a user-centered approach may address issues of inclusion (Lusardi, 2007). However, this may be at odds with the accelerated shift towards "voice first" interactions (Campbell, 2020), especially as we do not fully know how to design voice interactions that are meaningfully inclusive. For example, many parameters such as the choice of voice for the text-to-speech component of VUIs play a significant role in users' experience when interacting with VUIs (Cambre et al., 2020), yet are often overlooked during design (Aylett et al., 2014). Further usability issues may continue posing adoption barriers, regardless of the application area. Many such issues have been documented in recent research (Aylett et al., 2014; Cowan et al., 2017; Luger & Sellen, 2016), ranging from the misplaced effort to make VUIs "more human" to designing conversational models that implement the metaphor of the personal assistant

without consideration for users' perception of such models.

While the HCI literature provides ample sources of support for the design of inclusive applications within the more traditional graphical interfaces (GUIs), there is a significant practice gap with respect to VUIs. This includes the lack of fundamental resources such as validated design heuristics (Murad et al., 2018). However, one of the most striking gaps is methodological: ethnomethodological approaches such as participatory design have been instrumental in making our design practices more inclusive. As we have previously argued earlier in this chapter, as well as in Munteanu et al. (2019), participatory design is one of the most readily available methods to ensuring new interactions and interfaces are not only inclusive, but do not actively discriminate or marginalize users, in no small part because it allows (underrepresented) users' mental models and socio-cultural models to be more directly reflected in the way interfaces are designed (Axtell & Munteanu, 2019). Yet, these have largely been focused on GUIs – the HCI community has not fully explored how empowering approaches such as participatory design may be adapted to make VUIs more inclusive (Axtell et al., 2018; Liaqat et al., 2018). However, we remain optimists, as recent research, albeit sparse, is increasingly exploring such adaptations – for example, participatory design of social robots in educational settings (Candello et al., 2019), or participatory design aimed at uncovering older adults' perceptions of conversational health interfaces (Martin-Hammond et al., 2019). We hope that future research will explore such adaptations in-depth, and aim to make novel interactions such as voice truly inclusive.

CONCLUSIONS

In this chapter, we have explored paradigm shifts in HCI related to HMC. ICTs have the potential to support HMC in new and exciting ways. However, as ICTs continue to advance, it is important for HCI researchers to focus on methods that support inclusive design. In 1999, Ben Shneiderman, prominent researcher in the field of HCI, challenged members of the community to consider how their work can better serve human needs. His suggested domains included ways to provide accessible education, improve communication, and promote world peace. Shneiderman posed 10 challenges for designers, intended to guide practice towards his desired reshaping. For designers, he proposed, "usability testing, user interface management software, guidelines documents, and participatory design revolving typical users" (Shneiderman, 1999, p. 7). Design interventions must allow for differences within the user population to emerge. When it comes to human–machine interaction, researchers must carefully negotiate socio-cultural and socio-technical relationships when doing HCI research. Experimental design should take these relationships into account in order to allow for authentic differences within the user population to emerge.

Shneiderman further suggests the following four questions as a useful guide: "Have I considered individual differences among users in the design of my system? Have I considered the social context of users? Have I arranged for adequate participation of users in the design process? Have I considered how my design empowers users?" (Shneiderman, 1999, p. 8). These questions were posed more than two decades ago, and although technological innovations continue to shape the ways in which we communicate, HCI researchers must not forget to consider the impetus to mobilize inclusive HCI methodologies.

REFERENCES

Albright, J. (2007). How do I love thee and thee and thee: Impression management, deception and multiple relationships online. In M. Whitty (Ed.), *Online Matching*. Palgrave.

Ali, M. R., Van Orden, K., Parkhurst, K., Liu, S., Nguyen, V. D., Duberstein, P., & Hoque, M. E. (2018, March). Aging and engaging: A social conversational skills training program for older adults. In *23rd International Conference on Intelligent User Interfaces* (pp. 55–66).

Ambler, S. (2011). Questioning "best practices" for software development Retrieved November 23, 2014, from http://www.ambysoft.com/essays/bestPractices.html

Axtell, B., & Munteanu, C. (2019). Back to real pictures: A cross-generational understanding of users' mental models of photo cloud storage. In *ACM Proc of IMWUT (Journal of UbiComp)*. 2019; 3(3):1–24.

Axtell, B., Murad, C., Cowan, B., Munteanu, C., Clark, L., & Doyle, P. (2018, April). Hey computer, can we hit the reset button on speech? In *Proc. CHI Workshop on Conversational Voice User Interfaces*.

Aylett, M. P., Kristensson, P. O., Whittaker, S., & Vazquez-Alvarez, Y. (2014). None of a CHInd: relationship counselling for HCI and speech technology. In *CHI Extended Abstracts on Human Factors in Computing Systems*.

Bamford, R., & Deibler, W. (2003). *ISO 9001:2000 for software and systems providers: An engineering approach* (1st ed.): CRC-Press.

Bardach, E. (2011). *A practical guide for policy analysis: The eighfold path to more effective problem solving*. Sage.

Berman, J., & Bruckman, A. S. (2001). The Turing Game: Exploring identity in an online environment. *Convergence*, 7(3): 83–102.

Biswas, P., & Langdon, P. (2011). Towards and inclusive world – A simulation tool to design interactive electronic systems for elderly and disabled users. Paper presented at the SRII Global Conference.

Biswas, P., Robinson, P., & Langdon, P. (2012). Designing inclusive interfaces through user modeling and simulation. *International Journal of Human–Computer Interaction*, 28(1), 1–33.

Bleumers, L., Marien, I., Van Looy, J., Stewart, J., Schurmans, D., & All, A. (2013). Best practices for deploying digital games for personal empowerment and social inclusion. Paper presented at the European Conference on Game Based Learning.

Blomberg, J., Suchman, L., & Trigg, R. H. (1996). Reflections on a work-oriented design project. *Human–Computer Interaction*, 11(3), 237–261.

Bødker, S. (2015). Third-wave HCI, 10 years later—participation and sharing. interactions 22, 5 (Aug. 2015), 24–31. DOI: https://doi.org/10.1145/2804405.

Bretschneider, S., Marc-Aurele, F. J. J., & Wu, J. (2005). "Best practices" research: A methodological guide for the perplexed. *Journal of Public Administration Research and Theory*, 15(2): 307–323.

Brewer, R. N., & Piper, A. M. (2017). xPress: Rethinking design for aging and accessibility through a voice-based online blogging community. *Proceedings of the ACM on Human-Computer Interaction*, 1(CSCW), 26.

Brewer, R. N., Findlater, L., Kaye, J. J., Lasecki, W., Munteanu, C., & Weber, A. (2018, October). Accessible voice interfaces. In *Companion of the 2018 ACM Conference on Computer Supported Cooperative Work and Social Computing* (pp. 441–446).

Bruckman, A. S. (1992). Identity workshop: Social and psychological phenomena in text-based virtual reality. MIT MediaLab Technical Report, April 1992. Retrieved Apr 2022 from https://faculty.cc.gatech.edu/~asb/papers/old-papers.html.

Bruckman, A. (1996). Gender swapping on the Internet. *High noon on the electronic frontier: Conceptual issues in cyberspace*. In Proceedings of the 1993 International Networking Conference – INET, pp. 317–326.

Callon, M. (1997). *Representing nature. Representing culture*. Paris: CSI, Ecole Nationale Superieures des Mines.

Cambre, J., Colnago, J., Maddock, J., Tsai, J., & Kaye, J. (2020, April). Choice of voices: A large-scale evaluation of text-to-speech voice quality for long-form content. In *Proc of CHI* (pp. 1–13).

Campbell, T. (2020, March). How Canadians are harnessing the technological revolution in banking. *The Hamilton Spectator*. Retrieved Oct. 2021.

Candello, H., Pichiliani, M., Wessel, M., Pinhanez, C., & Muller, M. (2019, November). Teaching robots to act and converse in physical spaces: participatory design fictions with museum guides. In *Proceedings of the Halfway to the Future Symposium 2019* (pp. 1–4).

Carr, K., Weir, P. L., Azar, D., & Azar, N. R. (2013). Universal design: A step toward successful aging. *Journal of Aging Research*, 2013.

Clark, L., Doyle, P., Garaialde, D., Gilmartin, E., Schlögl, S., Edlund, J., Aylett, M., Cabral, J., Munteanu, C., & Cowan, B. (2019) The state of speech in HCI: Trends, themes and challenges. *Interacting with Computers Journal*. Oxford University Press.

Clements, R. B. (1996). *Complete guide to ISO 14000.* Prentice Hall.

Cowan, B. R., Pantidi, N., Coyle, D., Morrissey, K., Clarke, P., Al-Shehri, S., … & Bandeira, N. (2017, September). " What can I help you with?" infrequent users' experiences of intelligent personal assistants. In *Proc Int Conf Human-Computer Interaction with Mobile Devices and Services – MobileHCI* (pp. 1–12).

Flanagan, M. (2009). *Critical play: Radical game design.* MIT Press.

Franz, R. L., Wobbrock, J. O., Cheng, Y., & Findlater, L. (2019, October). Perception and adoption of mobile accessibility features by older adults experiencing ability changes. In *The 21st International ACM SIGACCESS Conference on Computers and Accessibility* (pp. 267–278)

Gibson, J. J. (1977). The theory of affordances. In R. Shaw & J. Bransford (Eds.), *Perceiving, acting and knowing.* Erlbaum.

Gibson, J. J. (1979). *The ecological approach to visual perception.* Houghton Mifflin.

Goffman, E. (1959). *The presentation of self in everyday life.* Doubleday.

Kannengiesser, U., & Gero, J. S. (2012). A process framework of affordances in design. *Design Issues*, 28(1), 50–62.

Kaptelinin, V., & Nardi, B. (2012). Affordances in HCI: toward a mediated action perspective. Paper presented at the SIGCHI Conference on Human Factors in Computing Systems (CHI '12).

Kowalski, J., Jaskulska, A., Skorupska, K., Abramczuk, K., Biele, C., Kopeć, W., & Marasek, K. (2019). Older adults and voice interaction: A pilot study with Google Home. *Extended Abstracts of the 2019 CHI Conference on Human Factors in Computing Systems*, 1–6.

Langdon, P., Persad, U., & Clarkson, J. P. (2010). Developing a model of cognitive interaction for analytical inclusive design evaluation. *Interacting with Computers*, 22(6): 510–529.

Latour, B. (1987). *Science in action: How to follow scientists and engineers through society.* Open University Press.

Latour, B. (1992). Where are the missing masses? Sociology of a few mundane artefacts. In W. Bijker & J. Law (Eds.), *Shaping technology, building society: Studies in sociotechnical change.* MIT Press.

Latour, B. (2005). *Reassembling the social: An introduction to Actor-Network-Theory.* Oxford University Press.

Law, J. (2004). *After method: Mess in social science research.* Routledge.

Liaqat, A., Axtell, B., Munteanu, C., & Epp, C. D. (2018). Contextual inquiry, participatory design, and learning analytics: An example. In *Companion Proceedings 8th Int Conf on Learning Analytics & Knowledge* (pp. 1–5).

Luger, E., & Sellen, A. (2016, May). "Like having a really bad PA." The gulf between user expectation and experience of conversational agents. In *Proc. CHI Conf. on Human Factors in Computing Systems* (pp. 5286–5297).

Lusardi, A., & Mitchell, O. S. (2007). The importance of financial literacy: Evidence and implications for financial education programs. Policy Brief. The Wharton School

MacKenzie, I. S. (2013). *Human-computer interaction.* Morgan Kaufmann.

Mannovich, L. (2002). *The language of new media.* MIT Press.

Martin-Hammond, A., Vemireddy, S., & Rao, K. (2019). Exploring older adults' beliefs about the use of intelligent assistants for consumer health information management. *JMIR Aging*, 2(2).

McTear, M., Callejas, Z., & Griol, D. (2016). *The conversational interface: Talking to smart devices.* Springer.

Morozov, E. (2013). To save everything, click here: The folly of technological solutionism. *Public Affairs*.

Muller, M. J., & Kuhn, S. (1993). Participatory design. *Communications of the ACM*, 36(6), 24–28.

Munteanu, C., Irani, P., Oviatt, S., Aylett, M., Penn, G., Pan, S., Sharma, N., Rudzicz, F., Gomez, R., Cowan, B., & Nakamura, K. (2017, May) Designing speech, acoustic and multimodal interactions. In *Proceedings of the 2017 CHI Conference Extended Abstracts on Human Factors in Computing Systems* (pp. 601–608).

Munteanu, C., Axtell, B., Rafih, H., Liaqat, A., & Aly, Y. (2019). Designing for older adults: Overcoming barriers toward a supportive, safe, and healthy retirement. In O. Mitchell, (Ed.), *The disruptive impact of FinTech on retirement systems.* Wharton

School Pension Reform Council. Oxford University Press.

Murad, C., & Munteanu, C. (2019) Revolution or evolution? Speech interaction and HCI design guidelines. *IEEE Journal of Pervasive Computing*, 18(2): 33–45.

Nakamura, L. (2002). *Cybertypes: race, ethnicity, and identity on the Internet*. Routledge.

Nardi, B. (1997). The use of ethnographic methods in design and evaluation. In M. G. Helander, T. Landauer, & P. Prabhu (Eds.), *Handbook of human-computer interaction* II (pp. 361–366). Elsevier Science.

Nass, C. I., & Brave, S. (2005). *Wired for speech: How voice activates and advances the human-computer relationship* (p. 9). MIT Press.

Norman, D. A. (1988). *The psychology of everyday things*. Basic Books.

Norman, D. A. (1999). Affordance, conventions and design. *Interactions*, 6(3), 38–43.

Ormerod, M. G., & Newton, R. A. (2005). Moving beyond accessibility: The principles of universal (inclusive) design as a dimension in nD modelling of the built environment. *Architectural Engineering and Design Management*, 1(2), 103–110.

Pearson, J., Robinson, S., Reitmaier, T., Jones, M., Ahire, S., Joshi, A., … & Bhikne, B. (2019, May). StreetWise: Smart speakers vs human help in public slum settings. In *Proceedings of the 2019 CHI Conference on Human Factors in Computing Systems* (pp. 1–13).

Pradhan, A., Lazar, A., & Findlater, L. (2020). Use of intelligent voice assistants by older adults with low technology use. *ACM Transactions on Computer-Human Interaction*, 27(4), 1–27.

Reid, E. M. (1996). Text-based virtual realities: Identity and the cyborg body. In P. Ludlow (Ed.), *High noon on the electronic frontier: conceptual issues in cyberspace*. MIT Press.

Sanders, E. B. N., Brandt, E., & Binder, T. (2010). A framework for organizing the tools and techniques of participatory design. Paper presented at the 11th Biennial Participatory Design Conference (PCC '10).

Sayago, S., Neves, B. B., & Cowan, B. R. (2019, August). Voice assistants and older people: some open issues. In *Proceedings of the 1st International Conference on Conversational User Interfaces* (pp. 1–3).

Schuller, B., Paletta, L., & Sabouret, N. (2013). Intelligent digital games for empowerment and inclusion – an introduction. Paper presented at the Foundations of Digital Games.

Shneiderman, B. (1999). Human values and the future of technology: a declaration of responsibility. *ACM SIGCAS Computers and Society*, 29(3): 5–9.

Sidner, C. L., Bickmore, T., Nooraie, B., Rich, C., Ring, L., Shayganfar, M., & Vardoulakis, L. (2018). Creating new technologies for companionable agents to

support isolated older adults. *ACM Transactions on Interactive Intelligent Systems*, 8(3).

Simsarian, K. T., (2003). Take it to the next stage: the roles of role playing in the design process. In *CHI'03 extended abstracts on Human factors in computing systems* (pp. 1012–1013).

Sin, J., & Munteanu, C. (2019, May) A preliminary investigation of the role of anthropomorphism in designing telehealth bots for older adults. In *Companion Pro of CHI Conf on Human Factors in Computing Systems*.

Sin, J., Franz, R. L., Munteanu, C., & Barbosa N. B., (2021a, May). Digital design marginalization: New perspectives on designing inclusive interfaces. *Proc CHI Conf on Human Factors in Computing Systems* (1–11).

Sin, J., Munteanu, C., Ramanand, N., & Rong Tan, Y. (2021b, July). VUI influencers: How the media portrays voice user interfaces for older adults. In *Proc Int Conf on Conversational User Interfaces* (pp. 1–13).

Singh, A. (2009). The potential benefits of multi-modal social interaction on the web for senior users (MSc dissertation, Auburn University).

Stewart, J., Bleumers, L., Van Looy, J., Marlin, I., All, A., Schurmans, D., et al. (2013). The potential of digital games for empowerment and social inclusion of groups at risk of social and economic exclusion: Evidence and opportunity for policy. *Technical Report no JRC 78777, Joint Research Centre, European Commission*. doi:10.2791/88148.

Stigall, B., Waycott, J., Baker, S., & Caine, K. (2019). Older adults' perception and use of voice user interfaces: A preliminary review. *Proc Australian Conf on Human-Computer-Interaction*, 423–427.

Suchman, L. (2006). *Human-machine reconfigurations: Plans and situated actions*. Cambridge University Press.

Suchman, L., Trigg, R. H., & Blomberg, J. (2002). Working artefacts: Ethnomethods of the prototype. *British Journal of Sociology*, 53: 163–179.

Svanaes, D., & Seland, G. (2004). Putting the users center stage: Role playing and low-fi prototyping enable end users to design mobile systems. Paper presented at the Proceedings of the SIGCHI conference on Human factors in computing systems (CHI '04).

Tarde, G. (2012). *Monadology and sociology*. Re. Press.

Walther, J. B. (1996). Computer-mediated communication: Impersonal, interpersonal, and hyperpersonal interaction. *Communication Research*, 23(1): 3–43.

Wertsch, J. V. (1998). *Mind as action*. Oxford University Press.

Ziman, R., & Walsh, G. (2018). Factors Affecting Seniors' Perceptions of Voice-enabled User Interfaces. Extended Abstracts of the 2018 CHI Conference on Human Factors in Computing Systems – CHI '18.

10

Developing a Theory of Artificial Minds (ToAM) to Facilitate Meaningful Human–AI Communication

Nandini Asavari Bharadwaj, Adam Kenneth Dubé,
Victoria Talwar, and Elizabeth Patitsas

The 1990s animated children's TV show *The Jetsons* placed an American family in a distant future of flying cars and moving sidewalks. On the show, Rosie is a robot maid that caters to the family's household needs. In the episode *Dance Time*, the titular character George Jetson asks Rosie to fetch him a shoehorn for his shoes. Rosie struggles to compute this request and after a significant amount of confusion, she returns with a sneaker and a trumpet! Rosie, an Artificial Intelligence agent, was unaccustomed to the shoehorn or its utility and hence processed the word literally as its constitutive parts. This anecdote illustrates how Artificial Intelligence (AI) systems can struggle to process natural language and may be insensitive to contextual factors of human communication. To solve the confusion, one imagines that George Jetson ensures Rosie has the knowledge of a shoehorn, if he sees Rosie floundering with the request. This example indicates opportunities to be had if human beings and Artificial Intelligence systems have a reciprocal Theory of Mind (ToM) to facilitate successful human–AI interactions.

Interactions between intelligent agents are situated in the social world and navigating the social world requires a ToM. ToM is the human capacity to ascribe beliefs, desires, and intentions to others. It is the ability to form mental models of others. In a ToM, there are several ways that agents

perform these mental attributions including but not limited to mind-reading, stereotypes, personality traits, context-sensitivity, and self-reference (Andrews, 2015). Due to the significant amount of prediction, coordination, explanation, and justification of behavior required between agents, it is a crucial ability to facilitate successful human–AI interactions.

AI attempts to model human intelligence in its design and development (Pennachin & Goertzel, 2007). While a majority of contemporary AI systems involve single-agent simple interactions and have been highly specialized in their capabilities (Pennachin & Goertzel, 2007), future AI will need to contend with increasingly complex multi-agent social interactions and solve for more general problems (Pennachin & Goertzel, 2007). With the growing deployment of AI in different industries and social contexts (Vincent, 2019), it follows that AI will increasingly become a significant presence in the social world. AI deployed in industries like healthcare or education, for example, will need to consider a variety of human needs. On the other side, for humans to understand AI's functionality and execution fully, we need to consider AI systems' similarly complex internal states. Thus, it is important for both humans and AI to develop a ToM regarding the intentions and actions of the other.

We offer two reasons for thinking that a reciprocal ToM is required for successful AI systems. The first is that we argue a robust ToM is required to navigate the social world. To support this claim, we leverage argumentation from philosophy and psychology of mind (see Gopnik & Wellman, 1994; Gordon, 1986), empirical support (see Baron-Cohen, Leslie, & Frith, 1985), and social psychology. The second reason is that AI systems will increasingly navigate the social world. To support this claim, we discuss contemporary and future usage of social AI systems. We then consider some concerns about this need for ToM, such as humans not elevating AI systems to the status of a social partner and considering AI as "mere tools." In response to these worries, we appeal to a descriptive claim and a prescriptive claim. In the descriptive claim, we highlight that human beings already frequently attribute beliefs and desires to minimal AI systems and draw on social psychological evidence regarding the human tendency to anthropomorphize (see Heider & Simmel, 1944; McGeer, 2007). In the prescriptive claim, we argue that it should not be the case that we treat AI as mere tools. Here, we highlight the potential social risks for non-consideration and the tremendous opportunities available by developing a robust reciprocal ToM with AI systems, which we come to term a Theory of Artificial Minds (ToAM).

We conclude with a summary of our position as well as a discussion of some innovative implementations of ToAM in AI systems. Lastly, we discuss the wider implications of our thesis as well for the fields of AI, robotics, and psychology.

THEORY OF MIND (TOM) IS REQUIRED TO NAVIGATE THE SOCIAL WORLD

Theory of Mind has been a well-researched area across philosophy and developmental psychology for the last three decades (see Baron-Cohen, Leslie, & Frith, 1985; Hughes & Cutting, 1999; Shahaeian et al., 2011). ToM research began in the 1970s with a general interest in pre-school children's understanding of mental states, metacognition, and reasoning of others' intentional behaviors (Wellman, 2018). Since then, ToM research has evolved in its subject and participant foci, methodology, and lens. Research foci expanded to include emotional understanding, false beliefs, lying, and pretend play (Wellman, 2018). Participants in ToM studies now range from pre-linguistic infants to adolescents and even adults (Wellman, 2018). Methods for studying ToM have

moved beyond measuring overt behaviors to include covert mechanisms like genetic and neural processes (Gallagher & Frith, 2003; Saxe, Carey, & Kanwisher, 2004). Lastly, ToM is now studied more globally, with a non-Western lens across cultures (see Shahaeian et al., 2011).

Currently, the American Psychological Association defines ToM as "the understanding that others have intentions, desires, beliefs, perceptions, and emotions different from one's own and that such intentions, desires, and so forth affect people's actions and behaviors" (APA, n.d). As per this definition, we discern that having a ToM involves mental state attribution, a recognition that there are other minds other than one's own, and that those minds may hold different beliefs, such as false ones. ToM is thought to develop from birth into a proficient competency in young children at 4–6 years (Onishi & Baillargeon, 2005; Wellman, 2014; Wimmer & Perner, 1983). Wellman and Liu (2004) capture children's developing understanding of mental state contrasts (i.e., my thoughts vs. other's thoughts) in their Theory of Mind scale. This scale highlights development of understanding that people can have different desires, different beliefs, different levels of knowledge access, hold false beliefs, and have hidden emotions (Wellman, 2018). The awareness of how mental states such as memories, beliefs, desires, and intentions govern the behavior of self and other is a crucial part of social intelligence (Baron-Cohen, 2000; Wellman, 2018). Because of this, ToM is often taken to be essential for navigating the social world.

In order to navigate the social world, individuals need to engage with one another in a way to ensure smooth interaction. Interactions often discussed in the context of social navigation include behavior prediction, justification, explanation, and coordination (Andrews, 2015). As there are two or more agents around to coordinate behavior with, there is reciprocity involved. Just as an agent has a ToM about others around them, so too will others around have a ToM about the agent.

Given that interactions can range from the basic (pre-linguistic child and caregiver) to complex (agent in a multi-agent environment such as utilizing urban public transport), the question arises of how we correctly attribute mental states to have a theory of mind at all. Understanding how we go about social coordination tasks is methodologically fraught for two reasons. First, akin to Morton's (1996) presentation of the problem of holism, there are a seemingly infinite number of internal states that lead to behavioral responses in social environments. For example, rainy days are not perceived by all people in the same way. There are those that enjoy them for their quiet contemplation and others who revile them for their gloom. In this way, situational factors may be underdetermined by the sheer number of mental states that could be produced in a given situation. This makes mental state attribution computationally intractable. Second, as McGeer (2007) has highlighted, human beings are so biologically and socially primed to engage in behaviors of social coordination that it is difficult to turn a critical eye toward it.

Nonetheless, across the disciplines of psychology and philosophy, there exist several approaches to uncover how humans understand others and achieve social coordination. One school of thought, the theory–theory account, holds that we may accomplish social cognition tasks through mind-reading and by developing implicit theories about how others behave (Gopnik & Wellman, 1994). In this theory-based approach, ToM is seen as assigning states to other agents. Supporters of simulation-theory contend that humans simulate the mental states of others, where they simulate how they would act in a given situation and adjust for relevant differences (Gordon, 1986). Simulation theory is process-driven, emphasizing the process of putting oneself into another's shoes. The theory–theory account argues for a hypothesis testing method of model extraction, whereas simulation theory argues for a simulation-based method for model selection (Sarkadi et al., 2019). Beyond these explanations are approaches that involve more social construction such as trait attribution (Andrews, 2008), non-linguistic and linguistic associations (Fiebich & Coltheart, 2015), stereotypes and social roles (Locksley et al., 1980).

Bringing these ideas together through a pluralistic view of ToM serves us well in understanding how humans go about the complex task of navigating the social world. As Fiebich and Coltheart (2015) systems approach has suggested, depending on cognitive capacities and situational demands, humans may choose to adopt one strategy over the other. Further, there may also exist individual variation in these various social competencies, with people more skilled in some competencies over others (Andrews, 2015).

In the classic Sally-Anne false belief task (Baron-Cohen, Leslie, & Frith, 1985), a failure to attribute false beliefs to fictional characters results in incorrect behavior prediction. In a similar vein, without a ToM, one can imagine a world filled with social misunderstanding and even conflict. Take a simple example of using an elevator in a building. Suppose you are in an elevator and as the doors begin to close at lobby level, you see a person sprinting toward the elevator doors with their hand raised. Without a ToM faculty, you would not attribute to this person, the desire of riding the elevator, the belief that they should hurry, or the emotion of stress. This could make you close the elevator door and ride the elevator alone, oblivious to the negative social repercussions of doing so! Hence, without a ToM, we might be unable to understand why others behave the way they do, explain their behavior or, most critically, be unable to coordinate our behavior with theirs.

As discussed, while there continues to be debate about which particular strategy is adopted to operationalize ToM, it is clear that a ToM competency of some kind is required for humans to navigate the social world smoothly. Furthermore, ToM development is not restricted to the understanding of human minds alone. Children also learn to conceptualize "extraordinary minds" with extraordinary capabilities, such as all-knowing God(s), super-intelligent superheroes, or even robots (Brink & Wellman, 2019; Wellman, 2018). As Brink and Wellman (2019) suggest, robots and digital assistants can be thought of as extraordinary minds due to their non-human computing capabilities, ubiquitous presence, and limitless access to information. Hence, it will be important to consider the impact of Artificial Intelligence devices on the development of ToM and consider how the presence of these extraordinary "artificial minds" influence humans' navigation of the social world.

SUCCESSFUL ARTIFICIAL INTELLIGENCE (AI) SYSTEMS WILL NAVIGATE THE SOCIAL WORLD

Successful artificial intelligence systems that engage with humans will have to navigate the social world. AI in machines is typically presented in scientific literature in two flavors. Artificial Narrow Intelligence (ANI) refers to intelligence that is demonstrated by systems in a "narrow" sense whereby artificial systems are specialized at a task-level or at a system-level such as in medical diagnostic systems, self-driving cars, or digital assistants (Pennachin & Goertzel, 2007). Artificial General Intelligence (AGI) on the other hand is intelligence that allows for complex problem solving across a wide variety of domains (Pennachin & Goertzel, 2007). Additionally, AI systems can be disembodied as application programs housed in devices such as phones and computers or embodied agents in the form of robots. For the purposes of our discussion, we focus on ANI systems as contemporary AI systems are currently only capable of this kind of intelligence. Additionally, we would not like to differentiate between embodied and disembodied AI systems and include robots in our purview as well. AI researchers continue to actively work towards both realizing ANI and AGI in systems (Pennachin & Goertzel, 2007).

To support our premise, we appeal to two perspectives, the current state and the future state of AI systems usage. First, looking at the current state, we see that AI is already being deployed in social settings. From digital assistants perched on apartment walls to applications that predict our taste in music to self-driving cars that share the same roads with human drivers. Digital assistant usage, for example, is growing rapidly in the world. Techcrunch, a leading technology news website, reports that there are 2.5 billion digital assistants in use worldwide as of 2018 (Perez, 2019). While most of these assistants are featured in cellphones, Amazon's Alexa primarily integrates with smart speakers at home and has sold over 100 million units (Perez, 2019). These numbers are staggering considering they are larger than the population of most countries! As showcased at Consumer Electronics Show (CES) 2018, a global consumer technology conference and trade show, Google Assistants, powered by Google Duplex, can carry out sophisticated human-sounding conversations for appointment booking, and most strikingly, human conversation partners may not even realize they are interacting with a non-human entity. Hence, literally speaking, AI systems are already part of the social conversation.

Second, the future usage of AI systems involves a change to the workplace—a space that thrives on social interactions. From a workplace perspective, AI systems are being increasingly integrated with traditional industries. A 2017 report by Mckinsey Global Institute discusses the impact of AI technology adoption, particularly ones that promote automation of tasks. Manyika et al. (2017) estimate that 60% of occupations have tasks, over 30% of which are "automatable" and predict that this automation may lead around 14% of the global workforce to shift into new professions in 2030. Rather than widespread job loss, Accenture researchers argue that the future will entail change to the nature of work (Wilson & Daugherty, 2018). Change in jobs will entail significant collaboration between human and AI systems to maximize productivity (Wilson & Daugherty, 2018). Wilson and Daugherty (2018) predict that AI systems and humans will work together to significantly improve elements of business processes such as decision making, speed, personalization, scale, and flexibility. In some instances, it will involve humans training machines on context and process and in other instances, it will involve machines assisting humans through automation (Wilson & Daugherty, 2018). Hence, as AI systems and human beings interact more closely at home and work, there will be a critical need to understand the behavior and internal motivations of the other.

In summary, successful AI systems will interact with different human beings across social situations at work and home. Given ToM mechanisms are required to successfully navigate the social world, it follows that successful AI systems will also need a ToM. What's more, this Theory of Artificial Minds (ToAM) may not just be incidental but a requirement. Given concerns around the opaque nature of the underlying architecture of AI systems (e.g., artificial neural networks), an artificial ToM may be crucial to furthering our understanding of AI systems (Rabinowitz et al., 2018)

OBJECTIONS TO TOAM

The objections against the notion of a reciprocal ToAM tend to center around AI systems navigating the social world and its implications. There are broadly three kinds of objections raised. Namely arguments from bio-chauvinism, necessity, and societal implications.

The first challenge appeals to bio-chauvinism. Akin to the notion of biological naturalism (as discussed in Schneider, 2019), the idea is that artificial minds are not made of a biological substrate and hence lack the ability to generate and subjectively experience aspects of social behavior like emotions. Without the ability to experience emotions of one's own, how can artificial agents ever accurately recognize it in others and hence, how would they navigate the social world? We argue that bio-chauvinism is not compelling as it can appeal to inductive reasoning. While it may be the case that agents that subjectively experience social behaviors have all been biological so far, it does not follow that only biological agents may be capable of these behaviors. Further, while one could conceive that biological substrate is required to subjectively experience emotions, it does not follow that other ToM attributions such as beliefs and desires similarly require biological underpinnings to be realized. Artificial intelligence agents are already immersed in the social world and will be subject to social expectations, without any kind of substrate considerations.

The second kind of objections consider how well AI systems already interact socially with humans. If the Google Assistant performs as well as a human and passes the conversational Turing test (Turing, 1950), there would be no reason to think that a special ToM mechanism is required. However, while it is true that these systems are not equipped with a robust ToM, we contend they perform well with humans only because the situations they are deployed in are transactional and simplistic in nature. Akin to following a conversational algorithm, these systems demonstrate artificial narrow intelligence (Pennachin & Goertzel, 2007). Hence, these systems may fail to accommodate even slightly convoluted social scenarios that deviate from their script, like Rosie in the introductory anecdote. As social situations with AI systems inevitably become more complex, it will benefit both AI systems and humans to develop a flexible ToM to facilitate more complicated transactions.

The third kind of objections consider the implications of attributing beliefs and desires to artificial intelligence systems such that they become deserving of rights. These arguments consider whether or not machines will truly be a full social agent. Commentators have argued that these "robot rights" are unworthy of attention given more pressing issues of human welfare (Birhane & van Dijk, 2020). Bryson (2010) has provocatively argued that as robots are fully owned by human beings, they are servants or tools that do our bidding and not agents at all. We would like to focus on these latter kinds of arguments, which we will call the "AI systems are a mere tool" objection, as they are fecund and lead to consideration of larger societal implications.

If navigating the social world involves behavior prediction, justification, explanation, and coordination, then a requirement to do so is social partnership. That is, to be able to successfully navigate the social realm, we need to work cooperatively with others as their partners. We need to be able to treat others as if they have agency, with their own intentions and goals. The objection against ToAM stems from this position. The objection holds that AI systems are not treated as partners at all, they are treated as tools or mere artifacts. In the same way that humans do not consider the intentions, beliefs, or desires of a tool like a hammer, humans will not consider the internal states of AI systems. In this way, robots should only be viewed as tools that extend human abilities and whose goals are derived from human beings (Bryson, 2010). Bryson (2010) further cautions against robot rights as overt personification of robot systems could be potentially costly to human beings in terms of resource and responsibility. Hence, this compelling objection, against applying ToM concepts to AI systems, holds that it is wholly unnecessary, given the uneven power dynamic that human beings share with AI systems.

AI SYSTEMS AS A SOCIAL PARTNER

In response to the kinds of concerns raised above, we would like to offer two kinds of replies. The first is the descriptive claim that holds that it is not the case that human beings treat AI systems as mere tools. The second is the stronger prescriptive claim, which is a direct reply to some of the claims made by Bryson (2010). It holds that AI systems should not be treated as mere tools.

The descriptive claim

As the name suggests, the descriptive claim points to evidence to describe how things actually are. Here, evidence shows that human beings frequently and effortlessly attribute beliefs and desires to all kinds of systems and objects. McGeer (2007) describes humans as "inveterate mentalizers" who cannot help but see diverse entities like infants, animals, or computers as being minded. McGeer (2007) has argued that the attribution of mental states to non-human animals and infants seems relatively harmless. Further, in many cases, it seems to accurately describe naive mechanisms at work (Andrews, 2015). However, the attribution of beliefs and desires even to inanimate objects is a peculiar phenomenon. Viewers think nothing of it when Tom Hanks's character anthropomorphizes a volleyball in the film, *Cast Away*. *Star Wars* fans vehemently argue for the existence of intentional states in droids R2D2 and C3PO. The classic Heider and Simmel (1944) study showed how participants attribute a variety of intentions, beliefs, and desires to simple moving geometric shapes on a screen. Weizenbaum's famous chatbot ELIZA simulated human conversations so successfully that participants felt they were interacting with a real human therapist and shared intimate details of their lives (Weizenbaum, 1966). Now popularly dubbed "The Eliza effect," this tendency to ascribe human qualities to artificial non-human entities is seen in countless facets of human life. Lastly, with advents in machine learning and increasingly personalized experiences on e-commerce and media applications, anecdotes of humans attributing beliefs to their digital assistants and mobile phones are commonplace. Whether it is because of a strong need to be social with others or because humans are easily deceived by the mere semblance of "human-like" behaviors, humans frequently attribute beliefs and desires to entities around them. Hence, as descriptive and experimental evidence has shown, it is not the case that humans treat systems around them as mere tools.

The prescriptive claim

The prescriptive claim holds it ought not to be the case that we treat AI systems as mere tools.

The motivating reasons are of two kinds, threats, and opportunities. We will discuss two threats caused by not exploring ToAM and two opportunities gained by exploring artificial ToAM. As Broadbent (2017) has argued, interactions that we have with robots reveal a lot about how we are as human beings and careful thought will need to go into how exactly social AI systems should be designed in the future.

Threats. We propose that viewing AI systems as mere tools is to invite undesirable consequences, and by investing in the development of a ToAM, we can avoid two potential threats, namely lost utility, and negative social influences.

Lost Utility. By not seriously considering ToAM, we may not function effectively with artificial intelligence agents in the social world. Dennett (1989) describes the intentional stance as one of the three stances we take to abstractly understand function and utility of various entities around us. Through the intentional stance, we attribute intentions, beliefs, and desires to entities in order to make meaningful predictions about the future behavior of an entity (Dennett, 1989). The intentional stance (Dennett, 1989) is related to the notion of ToM. The two ideas are similar in their objective to predict and explain the behavior of others; however, both deviate on exact mechanisms at work and the actual presence of mindedness in other entities. While it has been argued that not all behavior predictions result from adopting the intentional stance (Andrews, 2000), for the purposes of our discussion, we would like to focus on the similarities that intentional stance and ToM have, concerning their predictive power. Similar to the predictive utility gained from adopting the intentional stance (Dennett, 1989), without a ToAM, humans might be unable to successfully predict the behavior of artificial systems. Thellman et al. (2017) discuss the power of the intentional stance in successful predictions of others' behavior and social interactions by investigating how human participants perceived human and humanoid robot actions. Participants were shown photos of either humans or humanoid robots in household settings depicting situations like cooking food or mopping the floor and were asked to rate intentionality, desirability, and controllability of behaviors (Thellman et al., 2017). Thellman et al. (2017) demonstrated that given behavioral cues, human participants were similarly likely to attribute intentionality to both humans and humanoid robots. Wiese et al. (2012) have shown how adopting the intentional stance facilitates mechanisms of social attention. Participants were presented with robot or human faces and provided with instructions that induced the intentional stance, such as being told that a human controlled the actions of the presented face (Wiese et al., 2012). When participants believed they were looking at an intentional "minded" agent, gaze cueing effects were significantly higher than when they believed they were looking at an unintentional agent (Wiese et al., 2012). Hence, as indicated in these studies, not only are human participants similarly capable of mental state attribution to both biological and artificial systems but doing so may be beneficial for social functioning.

Negative Social Influence. By adopting a view that robots are merely property that should do the bidding of human beings (see Bryson, 2010), we might be inadvertently promoting negative social behaviors in two ways. First, we might be negatively influencing society's most vulnerable and impressionable population, children. Researchers studying domestic Amazon Alexa usage found that children perceived the knowledge, placement, and personhood of their smart speakers in unique ways (Sciuto et al., 2018). During their study, Sciuto et al. (2018) observed that children who used digital assistants sometimes berated their speakers as "stupid." Brščić et al. (2015) found numerous instances of "robot abuse" by young children, ranging from obstruction of the robot's movement to verbal abuse and even violence. Strikingly, Brščić et al. (2015) revealed that it was only children who abused the social robot and usually when they were alone with the robot. This also raises the question of whether we should devise norms for human–AI system interaction and educate children about the same.

Second, if AI systems are treated as mere tools, we may be exacerbating an already contentious issue of human-designed AI systems, namely inherent bias. As Wajcman (1991) has discussed, technology and particularly domestic technologies are both socially constructed and possess the ability to mold society and its values. Implicit in the various feature decisions of technologies are the culture and values of engineers that design them (McEwen & Dubé, 2017; Wajcman, 1991). This issue is especially true of contemporary interactive conversational agents like digital assistants where responses need to be "programmed" into a system. How digital assistants respond to queries reflect its programming and the values of its programmer (Ni Loideain & Adams, 2019). Popular digital assistants on the market today such as Google Assistant or Amazon Alexa present a pleasant female voice as their default voice options. Commentators like Sutko (2020), Wang (2020), and Ni Loideain and Adams (2019) have discussed how gendered AI systems can reinforce objectionable stereotypes regarding female servitude and submissiveness. Ni Loideain and Adams (2019) have catalogued how sexually provocative and even abusive human voice-commands are met with programmed flirtatious responses or deflection from digital assistants. For our purposes, continuing to treat already-gendered AI systems as mere tools has the potential to cause social harm. We need to be thoughtful about how interactions take place with female-voiced digital assistants, given societal implications. Whitby (2008) has correctly argued that artificial systems are significantly different from tools as they are often designed to resemble humans in their design, behavior, and goals. Whitby (2008) contends that as these dimensions have ethical and social consequences, the ethics around the treatment of robots and AI systems must be considered seriously.

Opportunities. We propose that viewing AI systems as mere tools is to miss out on tremendous opportunities for the future of human–AI interactions. By investing in the development of ToM for AI, we can enhance AI's capability for social interactions, and this will eventually lead to positive societal change as well.

Enhanced interactions. Developing an ToAM could open the doors to enhanced social interactions between humans and AI systems. As discussed in previous sections, AI systems are increasingly embedded in the human social world and the opportunities for complex human connections are extensive. In an innovative project, researchers at MIT have looked to classify driver behaviors according to social psychology theories for autonomous vehicles to better predict human driver intentions and lane-change behavior (Schwarting et al., 2019). Stanford researchers Chin et al. (2013) have developed instructional technology that harness social aspects of teaching, using intelligent teachable agents (TA). This has resulted in improved learning outcomes for young learners over traditional instructor-led training (Chin et al., 2013). These technologies rely on ToM assumptions between learner and AI TAs and have proved to be exciting tools for learning.

Industry impact. Social AI systems can radically change global industries and uplift the human experience. Healthcare is one industry worth highlighting. Paro, a Japanese autonomous therapeutic robotic seal, has been used extensively with elder patients and clinical populations (dementia, etc.). Paro responds emotionally to humans in its environment, learns their preferences and has several sensory inputs (PARO Therapeutic Robot., n.d.). A 2013 study showed that using Paro was effective in reducing loneliness of elder patients in a nursing home and surprisingly was even more effective than a real dog (Robinson et al., 2013). Mobile conversational agents like WOEBOT that simulate the experience of talking to a minded human therapist, akin to ELIZA, have delivered

cognitive-behavioral therapy in an engaging format and have been shown to reduce some effects of depression (Fitzpatrick et al., 2017). Lastly, one can certainly wonder how impactful ToM-enabled AI systems could be in the wake of pandemics like Covid-19. For example, voice-enabled AI systems could be deployed in fielding health enquiries and mobile robots could help deliver critical medicines to patients in hospitals. Having ToM mechanisms in these systems would facilitate effortless and empathic interactions with humans to support overburdened global healthcare systems.

CONCLUSION

The social landscape is continually evolving with the advent of technological tools. From the way people consume media, purchase commodities, and communicate, social lives are becoming virtual and complex. As sophisticated AI systems become embedded in social lives, a re-examination of basic assumptions about the social world is called for.

As has been discussed, humans often rely on a host of social cognitive mechanisms to navigate the social world. These mechanisms are diverse, situational, and can be influenced by cognitive demands and culture. Utilizing these mechanisms assist humans to attribute beliefs, desires, intentions, and emotions to fellow humans around them. This ability encompassed in a pluralistic theory of mind allows for seamless interaction in the social world. As we think about situating AI systems in human lives, we need to thoughtfully consider how to accommodate artificial systems into our social world. We have previously discussed the human propensity to anthropomorphize as well as some negative societal repercussions of treating intelligent systems as mere tools. Not to mention, there is the innovative proposal that many intelligent devices may be extensions of our own minds! (Clark & Chalmers, 1998). Taken together, there is a lot at stake. Rather than focus on the reasons of why we sometimes treat AI systems as intentional agents or the extent to which we do so, we want to stress that there is tremendous opportunity with treating AI systems as social partners.

Regarding what implementation could look like for an artificial ToM, there are exciting research projects underway. Researchers at MIT's AI lab built *Kismet*, a social robot with an expressive anthropomorphic face that can replicate infant interactions with caregivers (Breazeal & Scassellati 1999). By programming behavior that made *Kismet* appear intentional, *Kismet* produced affective behaviors in response to caregivers and in return, was treated as a social agent (Breazeal & Scassellati 1999). Japanese researchers investigated whether a ToM-mechanism such as mind-reading could help human participants understand a robot's intentions and predict its behavior (Ono et al., 2000). Participants who perceived a mobile robot as an intentional agent were able to predict the needs of the robot, and even understand its synthetic sounds, compared to control groups (Ono et al., 2000). In this way, Ono et al. (2000) propose that ToM mechanisms can be powerful for the future of human–AI interactions. Lastly, researchers have created an artificial neural network capable of using ToM mechanisms called *TomNet* (Rabinowitz et al., 2018). *TomNet* uses meta-learning models to build predictions about agents it encounters in its grid-world, based on agent behavior alone; as *TomNet* learns from multiple agents in its environment, it creates models to accurately predict agent behavior and internal states (Rabinowitz et al., 2018). Rabinowitz et al. (2018) emphasize the far-reaching implications of their work in human–AI system interactions and understanding.

Therefore, we contend that a robust, reciprocal ToAM is needed and its formation will allow for AI systems and humans to understand each other and interact effectively. As Broadbent (2017) has highlighted, psychologists are becoming more involved in the field of human–robot interaction (HRI), a field that has been traditionally dominated by computer scientists and engineers. This is particularly encouraging given what we can learn about behavior of humans, AI systems, and their social dynamics. It is well established that AI systems have the potential to improve human lives; however, what remains to be seen is how fundamentally AI systems can alter social norms and behavior. Developing a reciprocal Theory of Artificial Minds (ToAM) is a critical step in this direction.

REFERENCES

Andrews, K. (2000). Our understanding of other minds: Theory of mind and the intentional stance. *Journal of Consciousness Studies, 7*(7), 12–24.

Andrews, K. (2008). It's in your nature: A pluralistic folk psychology. *Synthese, 165*(1), 13–29.

Andrews, K. (2015). The folk psychological spiral: Explanation, regulation, and language. *The Southern Journal of Philosophy, 53*, 50–67.

APA Dictionary of Psychology. (n.d.). Theory of Mind. In *APA Dictionary of Psychology*. Retrieved from https://dictionary.apa.org/theory-of-mind

Baron-Cohen, S. (2000). Theory of mind and autism: A review. *International Review of Research in Mental Retardation, 23*, 169–184.

Baron-Cohen, S., Leslie, A. M., & Frith, U. (1985). Does the autistic child have a "theory of mind". *Cognition, 21*(1), 37–46.

Birhane, A., & van Dijk, J. (2020, February). Robot rights? Let's talk about human welfare instead. In *Proceedings of the AAAI/ACM Conference on AI, Ethics, and Society* (pp. 207–213).

Breazeal, C., & Scassellati, B. (1999, October). How to build robots that make friends and influence people. In *Proceedings 1999 IEEE/RSJ International Conference on Intelligent Robots and Systems. Human and Environment Friendly Robots with High Intelligence and Emotional Quotients (Cat. No. 99CH36289)* (Vol. 2, pp. 858–863). IEEE.

Brink, K. A., & Wellman, H. M. (2019) Technology as teacher: How children learn from social robots. *Varieties of Understanding, New perspectives from philosophy, psychology and theology, 139*, 139–166.

Broadbent, E. (2017). Interactions with robots: The truths we reveal about ourselves. *Annual Review of Psychology, 68*, 627–652.

Brščić, D., Kidokoro, H., Suehiro, Y., & Kanda, T. (2015, March). Escaping from children's abuse of social robots. In *Proceedings of the Tenth Annual ACM/IEEE International Conference on Human-Robot Interaction* (pp. 59–66).

Bryson, J. J. (2010). Robots should be slaves. *Close Engagements with Artificial Companions: Key Social, Psychological, Ethical and Design Issues, 8*, 63–74.

Chin, D. B., Dohmen, I. M., & Schwartz, D. L. (2013). Young children can learn scientific reasoning with teachable agents. *IEEE Transactions on Learning Technologies, 6*(3), 248–257.

Clark, A., & Chalmers, D. (1998). The extended mind. *Analysis, 58*(1), 7–19.

Dennett, D. C. (1989). *The intentional stance*. MIT Press.

Fiebich, A., & Coltheart, M. (2015). Various ways to understand other minds: Towards a pluralistic approach to the explanation of social understanding. *Mind & Language, 30*(3), 235–258.

Fitzpatrick, K. K., Darcy, A., & Vierhile, M. (2017). Delivering cognitive behavior therapy to young adults with symptoms of depression and anxiety using a fully automated conversational agent (Woebot): a randomized controlled trial. *JMIR mental health, 4*(2), e7785.

Gallagher, H. L., & Frith, C. D. (2003). Functional imaging of 'theory of mind'. *Trends in cognitive sciences, 7*(2), 77–83.

Gopnik, A., & Wellman, H. M. (1994). The theory theory. In L. A. Hirschfeld & S. A. Gelman (Eds.), *Mapping the mind: Domain specificity in cognition and culture,* Cambridge University Press. (pp. 257–293).

Gordon, R. M. (1986). Folk psychology as simulation. *Mind & Language, 1*(2), 158–171.

Hughes, C., & Cutting, A. L. (1999). Nature, nurture, and individual differences in early understanding of mind. *Psychological Science, 10*(5), 429–432.

Heider, F., & Simmel, M. (1944). An experimental study of apparent behavior. *The American Journal of Psychology, 57*(2), 243–259.

Locksley, A., Borgida, E., Brekke, N., & Hepburn, C. (1980). Sex stereotypes and social judgment. *Journal of Personality and Social Psychology, 39*(5), 821.

Manyika, J., Lund, S., Chui, M., Bughin, J., Woetzel, J., Batra, P., Ko, R. & Sanghvi, S. (2017). Jobs lost, jobs gained: Workforce transitions in a time of automation. *McKinsey Global Institute, 150.*

McEwen, R., & Dubé, A. (2017). *Understanding tablets from early childhood to adulthood: Encounters with touch technology.* Routledge.

McGeer, V. (2007). The regulative dimension of folk psychology. In *Folk psychology re-assessed* (pp. 137–156). Springer.

Morton, A. (1996). Folk psychology is not a predictive device. *Mind, 105*(417), 119–137.

Ni Loideain, N., & Adams, R. (2019). Female servitude by default and social harm: AI virtual personal assistants, the FTC, and unfair commercial practices. *Rachel, Female Servitude by Default and Social Harm: AI Virtual Personal Assistants, the FTC, and Unfair Commercial Practices (June 11, 2019).*

Onishi, K. H., & Baillargeon, R. (2005). Do 15-month-old infants understand false beliefs?. *Science, 308*(5719), 255–258.

Ono, T., Imai, M., & Nakatsu, R. (2000). Reading a robot's mind: A model of utterance understanding based on the theory of mind mechanism. *Advanced Robotics, 14*(4), 311–326.

PARO Therapeutic Robot. (n.d.). PARO Therapeutic Robot. Retrieved from http://www.parorobots.com/

Pennachin, C., & Goertzel, B. (2007). Contemporary approaches to artificial general intelligence. In *Artificial general intelligence* (pp. 1–30). Springer.

Perez, S. (2019, February 12). Report: Voice assistants in use to triple to 8 billion by 2023. Retrieved from https://techcrunch.com/2019/02/12/report-voice-assistants-in-use-to-triple-to-8-billion-by-2023/

Rabinowitz, N., Perbet, F., Song, F., Zhang, C., Eslami, S. A., & Botvinick, M. (2018, July). Machine theory of mind. In *International conference on machine learning* (pp. 4218–4227). PMLR.

Robinson, H., MacDonald, B., Kerse, N., & Broadbent, E. (2013). The psychosocial effects of a companion robot: A randomized controlled trial. *Journal of the American Medical Directors Association, 14*(9), 661–667.

Sarkadi, Ş., Panisson, A. R., Bordini, R. H., McBurney, P., Parsons, S., & Chapman, M. (2019). Modelling deception using theory of mind in multi-agent systems. *AI Communications, 32*(4), 287–302.

Saxe, R., Carey, S., & Kanwisher, N. (2004). Understanding other minds: Linking developmental psychology and functional neuroimaging. *Annu. Rev. Psychol., 55*, 87–124.

Schneider, S. (2019). *Artificial you: AI and the future of your mind.* Princeton University Press.

Schwarting, W., Pierson, A., Alonso-Mora, J., Karaman, S., & Rus, D. (2019). Social behavior for autonomous vehicles. *Proceedings of the National Academy of Sciences, 116*(50), 24972–24978.

Sciuto, A., Saini, A., Forlizzi, J., & Hong, J. I. (2018). "Hey Alexa, what's up?" A mixed-methods studies of in-home conversational agent usage. In *Proceedings of the 2018 Designing Interactive Systems Conference* (pp. 857–868).

Shahaeian, A., Peterson, C. C., Slaughter, V., & Wellman, H. M. (2011). Culture and the sequence of steps in theory of mind development. *Developmental Psychology, 47*(5), 1239.

Sutko, D. M. (2020). Theorizing femininity in artificial intelligence: A framework for undoing technology's gender troubles. *Cultural Studies, 34*(4), 567–592.

Turing, A. M. (1950). Mind. *Mind, 59*(236), 433–460.

Thellman, S., Silvervarg, A., & Ziemke, T. (2017). Folk-psychological interpretation of human vs. humanoid robot behavior: Exploring the intentional stance toward robots. *Frontiers in Psychology, 8*: 1962.

Vincent, J. (2019, January 28). The state of AI in 2019. Retrieved from: www.theverge.com/2019/1/28/18197520/ai-artificial-intelligence-machine-learning-computational-science

Wajcman, J. (1991). *Feminism confronts technology.* Penn State Press.

Wang, L. (2020). The three harms of gendered technology. *Australasian Journal of Information Systems, 24.*

Weizenbaum, J. (1966). ELIZA—a computer program for the study of natural language communication between man and machine. *Communications of the ACM, 9*(1), 36–45.

Wellman, H. M. (2014). *Making minds: How theory of mind develops.* Oxford University Press.

Wellman, H. M. (2018). Theory of mind: The state of the art. *European Journal of Developmental Psychology, 15*(6), 728–755.

Wellman, H. M., & Liu, D. (2004). Scaling of theory-of-mind tasks. *Child Development, 75*(2), 523–541.

Whitby, B. (2008). Sometimes it's hard to be a robot: A call for action on the ethics of abusing artificial agents. *Interacting with Computers*, *20*(3), 326–333.

Wiese, E., Wykowska, A., Zwickel, J., & Müller, H. J. (2012). I see what you mean: how attentional selection is shaped by ascribing intentions to others. *PloS one*, *7*(9).

Wilson, H. J., & Daugherty, P. R. (2018). Collaborative intelligence: humans and AI are joining forces. *Harvard Business Review*, *96*(4), 114–123.

Wimmer, H., & Perner, J. (1983). Beliefs about beliefs: Representation and constraining function of wrong beliefs in young children's understanding of deception. *Cognition*, *13*(1), 103–128.

11

HMC and Theories of Human–Technology Relations

Eleanor Sandry

INTRODUCTION

This chapter draws together a set of relational and ontological approaches that can be used to consider human–technology interactions and relations. Its overarching aim is to explore how communications scholars can theoretically and practically understand people's direct interactions with machines as human–machine communication (HMC). In general, research into HMC identifies machines as active communicators, not simply as tools enabling human–machine communication. This positions machines as active in the world, so theorizing HMC requires a reconsideration of how this activity can be described and analyzed, a move that can be linked with a broader "nonhuman turn" in scholarship that involves "decentering the human" (Grusin, 2015, p. vii). This scholarship depicts "a world populated not by active subjects and passive objects, but by lively and essentially interactive materials, by bodies human and nonhuman" (Bennett, 2015, p. 224). The approaches discussed in this chapter therefore provide ways to recognize nonhuman machines either as members of dynamic systems within which communication emerges, or as active communicators in their own right. These approaches are less widely used than some of the other theories and methods covered elsewhere in this book, but they provide productive ways to rethink how HMC works and how human–machine relations develop over time.

Other chapters of this volume consider the implications of acknowledging that Computers are Social Actors (CASA), theories and methods drawn directly from human–robot and human–computer interaction (HRI and HCI) research, and ideas about computer-supported cooperative work (CSCW) in depth. This chapter therefore sets a detailed discussion of these particular theories and methods aside, although it notes where CASA, HRI, HCI, and CSCW connect with, and diverge from, the approaches it does explore.

The chapter begins by considering actor-network theory (ANT), alongside other relational approaches to human–nonhuman interaction. These network or relational perspectives are often linked with the "heterogeneous body of research" known as science and technology studies (STS) (Roosth & Sibley, 2009, p. 451). Although STS scholarship encompasses "a multitude of varying approaches and schools of thought," it regularly focuses on "the question of the ontology of scientific things and the relations of diverse heterogeneous people, animals, machines, and things to one another" (Roosth & Sibley, 2009, p. 459).

For this reason, it has a direct bearing on discussions of human–machine relations and communication in interactive networks, while also leading some scholars to address the ontology and agency of machines more directly, aside from the relations in which they are found. Taking ideas about ontologies further, the chapter moves on to address object-oriented ontology (OOO) and perspectives drawing on that philosophical framework. OOO regards both humans and nonhumans as objects that are fundamentally separate, and yet nonetheless find ways to engage and communicate with one another. Finally, the chapter explores the case for a middle ground, one that takes both associations and objects into account.

ACTOR-NETWORK THEORY (ANT) AND OTHER RELATIONAL APPROACHES

The overarching tenet of ANT is to position humans and nonhumans, including "mundane objects, exotic technologies, texts of all sorts, nonhuman environments and animals" (Michael, 2017, p. 5), within social and relational networks. Importantly, this means nonhumans are not just conduits for human–human communication, because for ANT "technologies and natures are as much a part of society as humans" (Michael, 2017, p. 3). As "a complex, and oftentimes disparate, resource" (Michael, 2017, p. 3), ANT is highly adaptable and applicable across many different contexts. Its focus on how "the nonhuman, in the guise of technological artefacts, routinely shapes the comportment of, and the inter-relations amongst, human actors" (Michael, 2017, p. 17) may make it a particularly attractive approach for many HMC research projects.

ANT provides a different perspective on humans and nonhumans, and therefore on humans and machines, than is found in CSCW, HRI, HCI, and CASA frameworks. Ideas about CSCW, for example, often relate to situations where technologies act as mediators between people to enable effective group work. In combination with HRI and HCI perspectives, a CSCW approach also offers ways to research what happens when robots become part of human teams (Drury et al., 2004; Jung et al., 2017). The focus of such research is most often on the human, and on implications for human–human interaction and teamworking. With its emphasis on a network of human–technology associations, considered equally alongside human–human associations, ANT offers a different direction for analysis that focuses on the network of associations itself and

on the communication and cooperation that occurs between humans and machines directly, as well as between human team members.

One of the most influential theoretical approaches used to consider human–technology relations is the CASA paradigm (Reeves & Nass, 1996). Originally a statement about how people behave toward computers, it has been extended to suggest that people have an innate tendency to see many other technologies, including communicative machines, as social. As is the case for research into CSCW, human thinking about and appraisals of machines as social communicators are at the core of this perspective. In contrast, from an ANT perspective the decentered human is no longer the sole arbiter of what is to be considered social. ANT offers a more open idea of social relations, within which both humans and nonhumans take part *in their own ways*. This is driven by its insistence that humans and technologies are equally active and engaged in the social, with other nonhumans also in the mix.

Latour explains that, although early descriptions were often about technical networks, the network for ANT "is a concept" and need not be "a thing out there" (2005, p. 131). For much HMC research this is helpful, since the approach can address situations involving a broad range of diverse networks at once. For example, assessing the use of a smart speaker in the home from an ANT perspective helps one's analysis to consider not only the human and smart speaker taking part in the communicative interaction directly (a conceptual network), but also the technical network and cloud computing of the advanced speech recognition (ASR) system needed to enable the smart speaker to listen, interpret, and respond to the person (a physical "thing out there"). An ANT approach can also encompass the question of whether other humans, as well as the ASR technology, are listening behind the scenes to supplement the ability of technology alone to respond helpfully (again more conceptual, albeit served by physical technical connections), potentially raising privacy concerns. A further extension might also raise questions about whether information about stored common keywords might be sold on to drive targeted advertising via the smart speaker itself or other platforms.

For a more concrete example, Lutz and Tamò (2016) use ANT as a framework for their consideration of healthcare robots and the privacy implications they raise. Their paper notes that robots carry specific "agency, interests and embedded values," while also being "embedded in existing and constantly evolving actor-networks of people, interest groups, ideas, social constructions and evolving norms" of their own (Lutz & Tamò, 2016, n.p.).

An ANT approach therefore enables their work to tread the middle ground between technological determinism and socio-determinism, an outcome that is valuable in HMC research more generally.

As already mentioned, ANT decenters the human in its descriptions by insisting "that the social world needs to be understood as a flat network of associations" (Michael, 2017, p. 29), adopting the term actant for both humans and nonhumans to emphasize how they operate on the same ontological level (Collin, 2014, p. 206). ANT therefore identifies how humans and nonhumans "contribute to the production of society" in such a way that "it is not possible to say *a priori* whether it is human or nonhuman actors that have played the decisive part" (Michael, 2017, p. 12). It may seem difficult to accept that machines and humans exist and associate on the same ontological level, in particular when people's experiences are of technologies that don't necessarily communicate or respond as they expect or desire. However, ANT's aim is to encourage consideration of the associations between disparate actants on a level only "a priori," then becoming more "interested in pursuing empirically whatever is instrumental or influential in the making and remaking of networks" (Michael, 2017, p. 87). As an approach, ANT therefore looks to describe how networks operate in the world by paying serious attention to not only how humans, but also how nonhumans, associate with one another.

At times, associations between "humans and nonhumans are so closely entwined that it is better to think in terms of hybrids" (Michael, 2017, p. 17). Indeed, some scholars argue that humans are inherently and irrevocably interlinked with technology. Thus, for Stiegler, humans cannot be separated from technology because they "invent each other respectively" (1998, p. 142), whereas Haraway claims that "we are cyborgs," being "theorized and fabricated hybrids of machine and organism" (2000, p. 292). Acknowledging hybrids and cyborgs in ANT adds another dimension to the consideration of entities associated in a network. Alongside this, Haraway's more recent conception of "companion species" relations, provides another perspective from which to view not just cyborgs (as human–technology hybrids), but also nonhumans including animals and machines, arguing that companion species "take shape in interaction" and "co-constitute each other, at least partially" (2004, p. 307). This highlights how scholars draw on and extend ANT in their own ways developing specific terminologies and perspectives on actors and the networks within which they are located to support their arguments.

A further terminological extension is seen in discussions about networks and assemblages (Michael, 2017, pp. 4–5). Although some ANT research uses the terms network and assemblage interchangeably, the latter does have its own history and specific meaning, being developed by Gilles Deleuze and Félix Guattari (1987), DeLanda (2006) extending their ideas to propose assemblage theory (AT). From this perspective, an assemblage is a co-functioning, or symbiotic, set of disparate parts that work together for a period of time (Müller, 2015). The potential crossover with ANT is clear: the assemblage as defined here could easily be termed a network instead, albeit one composed of specific actors with a temporary shared purpose. Indeed, ANT can be thought of as "an empirical sister-in-arms of the more philosophical assemblage thinking" (Müller, 2015, p. 30). Its empirical nature may make ANT an easier approach for experimental or observational HMC research contexts, but assemblage theory provides a view on close human–machine associations directed toward specific tasks that might also be useful. Tim Dant, for example, uses the term assemblage in his work on "the driver-car" (2004). Dant notes the temporary nature of driver-car associations, within which driver and car do not merge into a "cyborg life form" and are also not permanently combined as a hybrid; instead, many different drivers and cars can be associated over time in a more flexible relation (Dant, 2004).

While not using the term assemblage, Andrew Pickering's concept of "the mangle of practice" (1995) provides another way to analyze flexible, goal-oriented human–machine interactions. Pickering draws on ANT, but wants to avoid its representational, semiotic idea of agents that continually shift status between being "real entities and social constructs" (1995, loc. 328). He therefore adopts a performative stance for which material agency, including the agency of machines, "is temporally emergent in practice" (Pickering, 1995, loc. 338). This is the mangle, within which a continual interplay, or "*dance of agency*," between human and machine supports a process of gradual "tuning in goal-oriented practice" (Pickering, 1995, loc. 446). His idea of the "dialectic of resistance and accommodation" (Pickering, 1995, loc. 451), a negotiation that constitutes any human–machine dance of agency, lends itself to analyses of the not always seamless or easy processes of meaning making that occur in many communication contexts (Cooren, 2010), including those between humans and machines.

The continual extension and adaptation of ANT results in it being full of shifting and entangled terminology requiring HMC researchers to pick and choose from the options with care. Close, ongoing relations between humans and machines, also seen in scientists' associations with technical instruments essential for their research, might well be thought of as hybrid at a particular moment in time within much ANT scholarship, in spite of the level of permanence this carries (Michael, 2017, p. 42). However, the idea of the assemblage in either Müller or Dant Haraway's work on "companion species," or Pickering's on the "mangle," might prove useful to HMC researchers seeking to analyze more flexible and mutable examples of human–technology relations and communication. While communication within a cyborg or hybrid element might be considered seamless, shifting the focus for communication research onto the way that element communicates as a whole with others in the network, communication within a more loosely connected assemblage clearly warrants its own analysis, to explore the way this co-functioning and symbiotic relation works in detail.

Unfortunately, ANT itself does not provide clear support for detailed analyses of how communication occurs in any level of network. ANT's focus on associations as opposed to actants carries through into its understanding of power, since actants are not considered to "'possess' power," instead they "wield influence" to "establish and make durable" a particular set of associations (Michael, 2017, p. 21). ANT does not therefore acknowledge agency as a permanent property of actors, or it seems reasonable to assume actants, in themselves (Latour, 1999, p. 18), but more often identifies distributive agency as "enacted in the relations 'between' entities" or attributive agency that "is ascribed to particular entities" (Michael, 2017, p. 68). While ANT makes a valuable contribution by "surfacing previously overlooked people and things" (Lewis et al., 2019, p. 415), addressing their joint operation as part of a network, its treatment of agency does not help HMC researchers to "conceptualize what it means to be a communicator" (Lewis et al., 2019, p. 415). An ANT approach drives a focus on how communication and meaning emerges in interaction, without addressing the message producer's communicative ability or intention, or the receiver's attentiveness or predispositions.

Beyond this problem, ANT also does not "essentialize humans and nonhumans," instead regarding them as emerging within networks (Michael, 2017, p. 40). This perspective is mirrored by Haraway, who argues that "beings do not pre-exist their relatings" as companion species (2003, p. 6). It is therefore relatively easy to see how ANT and other relational theories have been critiqued as overly focused on associations with little thought for the ontology of the entities they involve (Bogost, 2012; with Bennett, 2012, noting this as a feature of Harman and Morton's work as well). In addition, some theories can also be critiqued as overlooking

the relative positioning of entities and networks within broader sociocultural power structures relating to class, race, and gender, which many see as affecting whether entities are able to form associations at all (Müller, 2015). It can be argued that, rather than seeing "an 'external factor' such as class or gender" as "'responsible' for this or that social ordering", ANT instead "aims to trace how such 'external factors' might themselves emerge" (Michael, 2017, p. 45). However, considering digital voice assistants as an example, early on all female and still predominantly so, it would seem to make more sense not to argue that external assumptions about helpful female assistants emerge from peoples' associations with this technology, but rather that these associations have been designed in line with and reinforcing the existing stereotype that assumes most assistants in offices will be women.

The need to address ideas about the agency of humans and machines as communicators in HMC is highlighted by the example of Tay the Twitterbot, left to its own devices only to become a victim (at least according to some commentators) of negative influences on the platform, driving its own racist and misogynistic tweets and leading to its deletion. The question of Tay's agency and how this relates to the agency of both its designers and Twitter users is complex (Neff & Nagy, 2016), but arguably Tay's designers could have taken responsibility for monitoring and managing Tay's interactions toward a better outcome.

It is therefore good to note that despite the strong relational focus of companion species theory, Haraway nonetheless acknowledges the importance of attending to pre-existing power differentials and structures as she considers human–dog relations within a societal setting that inevitably privileges human concerns. In this context, it is up to humans to keep dogs safe by ensuring they adhere to established rules (Haraway, 2003). In addition, Pickering's perspective, by setting aside semiotic representations of materiality to acknowledge human and nonhuman practice and performance, is part of an ontological turn that repositions agents themselves as objects of study alongside their relations, providing ways to consider who or what has power to improve a situation at a particular moment in time.

FOCUSING ON HUMAN AND NONHUMAN ENTITIES WITH OBJECT-ORIENTED ONTOLOGY (OOO)

A stronger line on attending to human and nonhuman entities over the associations into which they enter is offered by OOO. In contrast with philosophies for which "reality is something 'constructed' by language, power or human cultural practices," an idea very much a part of ANT, "OOO is a bluntly *realist* philosophy" (Harman, 2018, p. 10). Reality though is "elusive" (Harman, 2018, p. 6). It is something we cannot "encounter directly in the flesh," the "*withdrawal* or *withholding* of things from direct access" being "the central principle of OOO" (Harman, 2018, p. 7). While ANT theorists often refer to humans and nonhumans as actants, OOO adopts the term object to refer to "any entity whatsoever" (Morton, 2012, p. 205), whether "human, non-human, natural, cultural, real or fictional" (Harman, 2018, p. 9). Whatever they are, OOO insists that each object must "be given equal attention" (Harman, 2018, p. 9). What results is a synthesis of "the human and the nonhuman into a common collective," a "flat ontology" that makes "no distinction between the types of things that exist but treats all equally" (Bogost, 2012, loc. 393). In contrast with ANT, for OOO objects do not "emerge as the effects of networks" (Michael, 2017, p. 40), because they are "ontologically prior to their relations" (Morton, 2012, p. 208). In positioning machines and humans as separated objects that are active alongside one another in the world, OOO provides HMC researchers with a framework that takes objects and their actions seriously. Communicators themselves—their intentions and predispositions, and the histories and experiences they bring to a communicative event—are very much back on the research agenda, whether those communicators are humans or machines.

In contrast with many other approaches, not just ANT, but also CSCW, CASA, HRI, and HCI as briefly introduced above, OOO promotes a definitive move away from anthropocentrism. This is driven by the way that for OOO, "objects do not relate merely through human use but through any use, including all relations between one object and any other" (Bogost, 2012, loc. 164). This means that "human perception becomes just one among many ways that objects might relate" (Bogost, 2012, loc. 226), which raises the difficulty of understanding, as a human, how things relate from a nonhuman point of view, while also freeing one's analysis from always being about the human, their presence and concerns.

The way OOO is often introduced (as can be seen above) is not easy to link with many people's everyday experiences of the world, for which objects and humans are rarely thought of as "equivalent or as being open to being considered and treated equally" (Sandry & Willson, 2014, p. 2/9). Digging deeper though, Bogost points out that while "all things equally exist," this does not mean they "exist equally" (2012, loc. 276). For OOO "objects are all fundamentally different from one another" (Bogost, 2012, loc. 659). Alongside the way they are withdrawn (Harman, 2018), partitioned, and thus "utterly isolated" from one another (Bogost, 2012, loc. 887), this raises the question of how objects interact with one another at all, something that is a core concern of HMC research (and most other research into communication).

Bogost suggests that the only way to articulate connections between objects is by analogy. So humans, for example, use "anthropomorphic metaphors" to explain what an object appears to be and appears to be doing (2012, loc. 1403). Bogost extends this idea to suggest that all objects "try to make sense of each other through the qualities and logics" they themselves possess (Bogost, 2012, loc. 1426). In this way, "one object caricatures another" to "make some sense of" that other (Bogost, 2012, loc. 1426). How exactly nonhuman objects produce "caricatures" of others cannot be known by humans, and this results in the need to speculate not only from the "metaphorical vantage point of the human" but also the imagined vantage point of the nonhuman (Bogost, 2012, loc. 1706). In an HMC context, it is worth noting that humans may be able to make reasoned arguments to consider how a machine "sees" the world, for example, or even "chooses" what to say in response to a query. The accuracy of these appraisals will likely depend on how well-informed a person is about the inner workings of the machine. As technologies become increasingly complex, with machine learning programs that develop new ways to operate over time, this may no longer be possible. Importantly, as noted below, there are times when it is better to adopt a metaphorical stance, to consider what it is like to be the machine, as opposed to trying to work out how it actually operates.

There are a number of reasons why the need to depend on metaphors and anthropomorphic appraisals might be difficult to accept, not least because anthropomorphism is a process that is often frowned upon (Bennett, 2010; Bekoff, 2007; Hearne, 2000). Therefore, extending this process to produce the "metaphoristic daisy chains" of understanding suggested by Bogost (2012, loc. 1741) might only be met with more skepticism; and yet, proponents of OOO argue that anthropomorphism is unavoidable (Morton, 2012). Offering a positive take on the potential of anthropomorphism aside from its dangers, Jane Bennett argues that it might be "worth running the risks associated with anthropomorphizing," since it counters anthropocentrism by reminding humans that they are not "above or outside a nonhuman 'environment'" (2010, p. 120). For HMC, taking the unavoidable anthropomorphic responses of humans seriously provides insight into how people think they relate to the machines with which they communicate, not just in the social terms identified by the CASA paradigm, but also in ways that "underscore the differences" between humans and the objects around them (Bogost, 2012, loc. 1403). For example, D. E. Wittkower notes how using Alexa, embodied in the form of Amazon's Echo smart speaker, "requires us to think about how she ~~thinks about~~ things" (2021, p. 7). He uses a strikethrough to indicate where what would often be called anthropomorphism plays a part, although Wittkower himself avoids this term saying that it unhelpfully collapses and oversimplifies the process involved (2021, p. 9). Setting terminology aside, for communication with Alexa to work, Wittkower argues that people "must think about ~~what it's like~~ to be a bot," alongside considering the likely differences between Alexa's ~~thought processes~~ (to adopt the strikethrough myself) and those of a human (2021, p. 7). When dealing with technologies such as smart speakers, having more knowledge about the workings of the speaker itself, or the ASR system in the cloud that allows it to respond to human speech, may not improve one's ability to connect and communicate with the object. This is an example where embracing the metaphors of anthropomorphism is easier, works faster, and produces better results than trying to use the machine by reasoning about its underlying operations.

Both Bennett and Wittkower highlight the benefits of embracing anthropomorphism (Bennett) or at least an intentional stance (Wittkower) towards objects, while also emphasizing the need to remain aware of their specificity. Even when communicating with another person, the importance of respecting the difference of the other is reinforced in phenomenological theories of communication, in particular those that draw on the philosophy of Emmanuel Levinas. Such theory is therefore useful in considering how communication occurs in the presence of difference more broadly, including the difference that exists between human and machine.

Levinas himself was only concerned with communication between humans, since he said only humans could reveal a "face," and thus take part in the communicative encounter he defined as "the face to face" (Levinas, 1969, pp. 79–81). However, arguments have been made to extend this idea to include animals (Clark, 1997; Derrida, 2002), as well as machines (Gunkel, 2012; Sandry, 2015). Levinas' encounter draws self and other into proximity, but also emphasizes the distance that remains between them. This distance constitutes their insurmountable differences; a reminder

that the self can only ever partially know the other. Unlike communication theories that stress the commonalities between interlocutors, from this perspective "the irreconcilable difference of alterity" becomes "the ultimate condition for communication" (Pinchevski, 2005, p. 71). This idea of alterity at the core of communication is relevant for HMC, where the differences between interlocutors are often more marked than between humans (Sandry, 2015, pp. 50–58). Levinas' philosophy also has implications for OOO perspectives on human–object and object–object relations more broadly.

Avoiding anthropomorphism, Harman instead considers the work of Levinas as a way to frame how objects interact while also remaining absolutely separate. Harman accepts Levinas' insistence that the self can "never fully encounter the Other" (an idea also key to OOO), suggesting that in the proximity of the self-other encounter, they reach "a state of sincerity" in their response (2007, p. 24). They take each other seriously, even as they also notice their individual differences, allowing them to touch "without fusing" (Harman, 2007, p. 24). In terms of communication, the proximity and sincerity of this relation enables "communication without full contact" (Harman, 2007, p. 26). Harman therefore notes Levinas identifies that the real problem "is not how beings interact in a system" but rather "how they withdraw from that system as independent realities while somehow communicating" (Harman, 2007, p. 30). While philosophically demanding, this type of explanation of self-other relations and communication can be useful in HMC research. In particular, for Levinas "communication is always asymmetrical, since the things are proximate to me without my being proximate to them" (Harman, 2007, p. 26); an idea that helps alleviate the difficulty of discussing HMC within which asymmetry, and a lack of reciprocity in response, is almost always a feature (Sandry, 2015). By firmly positioning otherness as a part of any relation between objects (human and nonhuman) alongside offering the potential to make partial, asymmetrical connections in proximity, OOO together with a Levinasian perspective enables a broad understanding of communicative situations within which difference is respectfully acknowledged and negotiated even as meaningful exchanges are made.

RETHINKING ANT AND OOO TOGETHER

Bennett, responding to the work of Harman and Morton, questions whether there is a need to "choose between objects or their relations" at all, noting that people's everyday experiences tend to identify "some effects as coming from individual objects and some from larger systems" (2012, p. 227). She therefore suggests it might make more sense to "aim for a theory that toggles between both kinds or magnitudes of 'unit'," to "make both objects and relations the periodic focus of theoretical attention" (2012, p. 227). Bennett sees this realized in Deleuze and Guattari's work *A Thousand Plateaus*, where they "conceptualize groupings" and "attend carefully to many specific objects" (2012, p. 227). However, for those who wish to stress the existence of entities separate from their relations, the idea of objects "becoming" in relation may be too central to Deleuze and Guattari's thinking.

Michael, in setting out potential post-ANT theoretical pathways, also emphasizes that it seems increasingly important to find ways to engage with humans and nonhumans in ways that follow their "heterogeneity, multiplicity and complexity" (2017, p. 151). This may be particularly valuable in situations where "the designers of technological artefacts cannot fully determine the goals and uses that attach to their technologies," as they are put into use (Michael, 2017, p. 42). From an HMC perspective, where the technologies under discussion are often open to varied implementations (beyond the designer's original intentions) and user interpretations (once positioned in a particular context), noticing the multiplicity of ways in which people interact and associate with machines is always relevant. Alongside attempts to consider machines as active parts of associative networks, or communicators in their own right, it can therefore be important to notice when machines are also regarded as things (from a non-OOO perspective). For example, Morana Alač's research with a robot demonstrates how this machine is "simultaneously enacted as a thing and as a social agent" (Alač, 2016, p. 519), in ways that draw attention to its decidedly inorganic object texture (its "thing-like aspects"), as well as its attentive and communicative social responses. The workings of human–machine relations are clearly difficult to pin down, even during a particular interaction, so adopting analytical approaches that consider networks or systems, as well as actants or objects, may well assist HMC researchers to cope with this complexity.

An overt attempt to combine ANT and OOO approaches into a single "toolkit" is seen in Teodor Mitew's research (2014) on objects in the internet of things (IoT). The IoT is a network within which HMC occurs alongside machine–machine communications that don't involve humans at all

(Mitew, 2014). Smart speakers form a part of the IoT, their ability to communicate with humans being supported by the machine–machine communication with an ASR system. These systems clearly demonstrate OOO's acknowledgement that nonhuman objects relate to one another directly, not just in relation to humans. While Mitew could more clearly acknowledge the difficulties of mixing ANT and OOO perspectives, in particular to resolve issues around how the being of objects can be thought apart from their relation to others, his work suggests that the IoT "profoundly undermines human-centric notions of sociality" (2014, p. 10). This perspective supports ANT's insistence that humans and nonhumans are equally important in building social associations to form a network, although HMC researchers might question whether all associations in the IoT need to be thought of as social, or whether different forms of communication might also be in play. Aside from this, Mitew's work is certainly a good attempt to deploy an ANT/OOO toolkit that makes both the "setting and the entities populating it … visible in their agential complexity" (2014, p. 18), just as Michael suggests is vital in post-ANT research in general.

In considering the potential of extending ANT and relational perspectives more generally to look in detail at actants themselves it is worth noting that, although many of her statements about companion species focus only on their relation, Haraway does also attend to the individuals involved. Arguing that companion species are "significantly other to each other, in specific difference" (2003, p. 3), her experience of agility training with her dog involves "acts of communication [they] barely understand" (2003, p. 2). This resonates with the ways OOO theorists grapple with explaining communication between irrevocably separated objects. In common with some OOO theorists, Haraway considers anthropomorphism as a vital way "to keep the humans alert to the fact that somebody is at home in the animals they work with" (2003, pp. 49–50). However, as she goes on to say, "who is at home must permanently be in question," (2003, p. 50), recognizing the fundamental alterity of the other (also emphasised by Levinas and Harman). Haraway argues that the "embodied communication" between companion species "is more like a dance than a word" (Haraway, 2008, p. 26), a statement that highlights the potential of linking her work with Pickering's dance of agency to consider humans and machines as communicators (Sandry & Peaty, 2021), without losing sight of the communicative meaning that also emerges through their interactions.

From the opposite direction, working to embed some sense of systems thinking into OOO, Bennett notes that "even Harman," while strenuously rejecting the idea of "things-operating-in-systems," occasionally "finds himself theorizing a kind of relation—he calls it 'communication'—between objects" (2015, pp. 229–230). While Harman's ideas about communication as a means for objects to relate were discussed above in terms highlighting objects as communicative in themselves, here Bennett points out how drawing objects into relation also opens ways for meaning to emerge in the object–object systems those relations create. There is therefore potential to frame communication-related analyses of systems, as well as the actions of their constituent parts, whether one works out from ANT or relational theory, or from frameworks based in OOO.

CONCLUSION

This chapter has presented an introduction to various theoretical approaches that might be of use in HMC research, aside from the more commonly explored perspectives offered by CASA, CSCW, HRI, and HCI research. Laura Forlano (2017) emphasises how ideas about posthumanism, and approaches such as ANT and OOO (alongside others), have important implications for design processes and methodologies. Extending this, ANT-related and OOO-related approaches, as well as combinations of the two, highlight the benefit of taking a nonhuman turn in HMC research, to consider machines as active contributors to the communication that emerges in networks, as well as acknowledging their presence as communicative agents in their own right. This supports explorations of the complexity of HMC as communication between very different "beings": not just examining the seeming ease of communication in a well-formed network, but also noticing the challenges of communicating with others that might sense and interpret the world very differently from oneself. Adopting this two-way focus, both sides of which decenter the human, should help researchers to attend seriously to nonhuman activity in its specificity, with the potential to drive deeper and more comprehensive HMC research. Such research could even have a pivotal role, not only through its analysis of existing human–machine interactions, but also in suggesting ways to design new machines created to communicate and interact with people, other machines, animals, and the world.

REFERENCES

Alač, M. (2016). Social robots: Things or agents? *AI & Society*, *31*(4), 519–535. https://doi.org/10.1007/s00146-015-0631-6

Bekoff, M. (2007). *The emotional lives of animals: A leading scientist explores animal joy, sorrow, and empathy–and why they matter*. New World Library.

Bennett, J. (2010). *Vibrant matter a political ecology of things*. Duke University Press.

Bennett, J. (2012). Systems and things: A response to Graham Harman and Timothy Morton. *New Literary History*, *43*(2), 225–233.

Bennett, J. (2015). Systems and things: On vital materialism and object-oriented philosophy. In R. Grusin (Ed.), *The nonhuman turn* (pp. 223–239). University of Minnesota Press.

Bogost, I. (2012). *Alien phenomenology, or, What it's like to be a thing*. University of Minnesota Press.

Clark, D. (1997). On Being "the last Kantian in Nazi Germany": Dwelling with animals after Levinas. In J. Ham & M. Senior (Eds.), *Animal acts: Configuring the humans in western history* (pp. 165–198). Routledge.

Collin, F. (2014). Who are the agents? Actor network theory, methodological individualism, and reduction. In J. Zahle & F. Collin (Eds.), *Rethinking the individualism-holism debate: Essays in the philosophy of social science* (pp. 197–217). Springer International Publishing. https://doi.org/10.1007/978-3-319-05344-8_11

Cooren, François. (2010). *Action and agency in dialogue: Passion, incarnation and ventriloquism*. John Benjamins Pub. Co.

Dant, T. (2004). The driver-car. *Theory, Culture & Society*, *21*(4–5), 61–79. https://doi.org/10.1177/0263276404046061

DeLanda, Manuel. (2006). *A new philosophy of society: Assemblage theory and social complexity*. Continuum.

Deleuze, Gilles, and Guattari, Félix. (1987). *A thousand plateaus*. Translated by Brian Massumi. University of Minnesota Press.

Derrida, J. (2002). The animal that therefore I am (more to follow) (D. Wills, Trans.). *Critical Inquiry*, *28*(2), 369–418.

Drury, J., Scholtz, J., & Yanco, H. (2004). *Applying CSCW and HCI techniques to human-robot interaction*, report (Case #04-0166), MITRE. http://www.mitre.org/sites/default/files/publications/drury_cscw.pdf

Forlano, L. (2017). Posthumanism and design. *She Ji: The Journal of Design, Economics, and Innovation*, *3*(1), 16–29. https://doi.org/10.1016/j.sheji.2017.08.001

Gunkel, D. J. (2012). *The machine question: Critical perspectives on AI, robots, and ethics*. MIT Press.

Grusin, R. (2015). Introduction. In R. Grusin (Ed.), *The nonhuman turn* (pp. vii–xxiv). University of Minnesota Press.

Haraway, D. (2000). A cyborg manifesto: Science, technology and socialist-feminism in the late twentieth century. In D. Bell & B. M. Kennedy (Eds.), *The cybercultures reader* (pp. 291–324). Routledge.

Haraway, D. (2003). *The companion species manifesto: Dogs, people, and significant otherness*. Prickly Paradigm Press.

Haraway, D. (2004). Cyborgs to companion species: Reconfiguring kinship in technoscience. In *The Haraway reader* (pp. 295–320). Routledge.

Haraway, D. (2008). *When species meet*. University of Minnesota Press.

Harman, G. (2007). Aesthetics as first philosophy: Levinas and the non-human. *Naked Punch*, *9*, 21–30.

Harman, G. (2018). *Object-oriented ontology: A new theory of everything*. Pelican, an imprint of Penguin Books.

Hearne, V. (2000). *Adam's task: Calling animals by name*. Akadine Press.

Jung, M. F., Šabanović, S., Eyssel, F., & Fraune, M. (2017). Robots in groups and teams. *Companion of the 2017 ACM Conference on Computer Supported Cooperative Work and Social Computing*, 401–407. https://doi.org/10.1145/3022198.3022659

Latour, B. (2005). *Reassembling the social: An introduction to actor-network-theory*. Oxford University Press.

Latour, B. (1999). On recalling ANT. *The Sociological Review*, *47*(1_suppl), 15–25. https://doi.org/10.1111/j.1467-954X.1999.tb03480.x

Levinas, E. (1969). *Totality and infinity*. Duquesne University Press.

Lewis, S. C., Guzman, A. L., & Schmidt, T. R. (2019). Automation, journalism, and human–machine communication: Rethinking roles and relationships of humans and machines in news. *Digital Journalism*, *7*(4), 409–427. https://doi.org/10.1080/21670811.2019.1577147

Lutz, C., & Tamò, A. (2016). Privacy and healthcare robots – an ANT analysis. *Proceedings of the We Robot Conference*. We Robot 2016, University of Miami School of Law. http://robots.law.miami.edu/2016/wp-content/uploads/2015/07/We_Robot_Lutz_Tamo_ANT_Healthcare_Robots_final.pdf

Michael, M. (2017). *Actor-network theory: Trials, trails and translations*. SAGE.

Mitew, T. (2014). Do objects dream of an internet of things? *The Fibreculture Journal*, *23*, 3–26.

Morton, T. (2012). An object-oriented defense of poetry. *New Literary History*, *43*(2), 205–224.

Müller, M. (2015). Assemblages and actor-networks: Rethinking socio-material power, politics and space: Assemblages and actor-networks. *Geography Compass*, *9*(1), 27–41. https://doi.org/10.1111/gec3.12192

Neff, G., & Nagy, P. (2016). Talking to bots: Symbiotic agency and the case of Tay. *International Journal of Communication*, *10*, 4915–1931.

Pickering, A. (1995). *The mangle of practice*. University of Chicago Press.

Pinchevski, A. (2005). *By way of interruption: Levinas and the ethics of communication*. Dusquene University Press.

Reeves, B., & Nass, C. I. (1996). *The media equation: How people treat computers, television, and new media like real people and places*. CSLI Publications; Cambridge University Press.

Roosth, S., & Sibley, S. (2009). Science and technology studies: From controversies to posthumanist social theory. In B. S. Turner (Ed.), *The new Blackwell companion to social theory* (pp. 451–473). Wiley-Blackwell.

Sandry, E. (2015). *Robots and communication*. Palgrave Macmillan.

Sandry, E., & Peaty, G. (2021). Joyful encounters: Learning to play well with machines. *Cultural Science Journal*, *12*(1), 44–58. https://doi.org/10.5334/csci.137

Sandry, E., & Willson, M. (2014). Interruptions: Reconsidering the immaterial in human engagements with technology. *Transformations*, *25*, 1/9-9/9.

Stiegler, B. (1998). *Technics and time I: The fault of Epimetheus*. Stanford Univ. Press.

Wittkower, D. E. (2021). What is it like to be a bot? In S. Vallor (Ed.), *The Oxford handbook of philosophy of technology*. Oxford University Press.

12

Philosophical Contexts and Consequences of Human–Machine Communication

David J. Gunkel

Human–Machine Communication (HMC) deliberately challenges fundamental commitments that have been organizing principles for the discipline of communication studies. As Andrea L. Guzman (2018, p. 8) explains: "humans are communicators (senders and receivers) and technology is the medium, or channel, through which people exchange messages. This has been the dominant paradigm for communication research." HMC flips the script on this standard framework by turning the technological object into another kind of communicative subject. This chapter investigates the philosophical contexts and consequences of this revolutionary innovation.

BACK TO THE FUTURE

Research in HMC is directed at and concerned with a subset of artificial intelligence (AI) technology that has been called "communicative AI." As Guzman and Lewis (2020, p. 72) explain, communicative AI is "focused on the pragmatic aims of AI and the technologies designed to carry out specific tasks within the communication process that were formerly associated with humans." Consequently, the term "machine" in the phrase

Human–Machine Communication is intended to be specific, referring to recent technological innovations like "conversational agents, social robots, and automated-writing software" (Guzman and Lewis 2020, p. 72). Described in this way, one might get the impression that HMC is rather limited in its scope and is concerned with one particular application and employment of the more general category of artificial intelligence. But this is incorrect. The HMC paradigm circumscribes AI and describes the defining conditions of machine intelligence from the very beginning.

In his agenda-setting paper from 1950 – "Computing Machinery and Intelligence" – Alan Turing proposes to answer the question "Can machines think?" But he immediately recognizes persistent and seemingly irresolvable terminological difficulties with the words that comprise the question itself. So instead of answering the question, he changes the terms of the inquiry, and he does so in terms of communicative behavior.

> I shall replace the question by another, which is closely related to it and is expressed in relatively unambiguous words. The new form of the problem can be described in terms of a game which we call the "imitation game." It is played with three people, a man (A), a woman (B), and an interrogator (C) who may be of either sex. The interrogator

stays in a room apart from the other two. The object of the game for the interrogator is to determine which of the other two is the man and which is the woman (Turing, 1999, p. 37).

This determination, as Turing explains, is to be made by way of communication, specifically interpersonal conversational behavior framed in terms of a sequence of questions and answers. The interrogator (C) asks participants A and B various things and based on their responses tries to discern whether the respondent is a man or a woman. "In order that tone of voice may not help the interrogator," Turing (1999, pp. 37–38) further stipulates, "the answers should be written, or better still, typewritten. The ideal arrangement is to have a teleprinter communicating between the two rooms."

Following this initial setup, Turing then takes his thought experiment – or what he calls a "game" – one step further. "We can now ask the question, 'What will happen when a machine takes the part of A in this game?' Will the interrogator decide wrongly as often when the game is played like this as he does when the game is played between a man and a woman? These questions replace our original, 'Can machines think?'" (Turing, 1999, p. 38). In other words, if the man (A) in the game of imitation is replaced with a computing machine, would this device be able to respond to questions and pass as another human person, effectively fooling the interrogator into thinking that it was just another human subject? It is this question, according to Turing, that replaces the initial and unfortunately ambiguous inquiry "Can machines think?" Although there is a good deal that has been written in response to Turing's essay, the game of imitation, and subsequent efforts to produce actual applications capable of playing and even passing the "the Turing test," Turing's work has important philosophical consequences that matter for research in HMC.

The Problem of Other Minds

Turing's essay situates communication – and a particular form of potentially deceptive social interaction – as the deciding factor. As Simone Natale (2021, p. 25) suggests, the imitation game might just as well have been called the "communication game." This is not a capricious decision or accidental outcome. There are good epistemological reasons for focusing on this particular capability, and it has to do with what philosophers and behavioral scientists routinely call "the problem of other minds" – the seemingly undeniable fact that we do not have direct access to the inner workings of another entity's mental states. As the

neurophilosopher Paul Churchland (1999, p. 67) famously described the problem: "How does one determine whether something other than oneself – an alien creature, a sophisticated robot, a socially active computer, or even another human – is really a thinking, feeling, conscious being; rather than, for example, an unconscious automaton whose behavior arises from something other than genuine mental states?"

In other words, we generally assume that other people are thinking/feeling beings like ourselves. But strictly speaking, we have no way of knowing this for sure. I might know my own mind – in a kind of Cartesian self-reflective moment of *cogito ergo sum* – and have a good idea that I am a thinking/feeling thing. But what about others? How do I know for sure – beyond a reasonable doubt – that you are also a thinking/feeling being? How can I know the woman sitting across from me on the subway is also a conscious entity with an internal life of thoughts and feelings? How can I be sure about what or if my dog or cat thinks and has conscious experiences? The problem is that we don't have any way to resolve these questions in a definitive way. Even if we employ expensive medical-imaging devices, like an fMRI machine that shows which parts of the brain light-up when various stimuli are presented to an organism, none of that confirms the presence of a thinking, feeling, or conscious mind.

Attempts to resolve or at least respond to this problem invariably involve some kind of behavioral demonstration or test, like Turing's game of imitation. "To put this another way," as the AI scientist Roger Schank (1990, p. 5) concludes, "we really cannot examine the insides of an intelligent entity in such a way as to establish what it actually knows. Our only choice is to ask and observe." For Turing, and for many who follow his lead, intelligence is something that is neither easy to define nor able to be directly accessed and observed. It is, therefore, evidenced in and decided on the basis of external behaviors that are considered to be signs or symptoms of intelligence, especially communication and human-level verbal conversation in particular. In other words, because intelligent thought is not directly observable or even rigorously definable, the best one can do is deal with something tangible – like apparent communicative interaction – that is assumed to be the product of an intelligent mind and that can be empirically observed, measured, and evaluated.

Circular Reasoning

Recognition of this fact exposes a logical complication. For Turing, the appearance of communicative behavior is taken to be an effect or sign of intelligence. But the existence of an intelligent subject behind the communicative phenomena is only able to be determined by extrapolating from this exhibited behavior. The apparent circularity involved in this determination opens the opportunity for critical push-back and counter-arguments, most notably the "Chinese Room" thought experiment developed by the American philosopher John Searle. This intriguing and rather influential illustration, introduced in 1980 with the essay "Minds, Brains, and Programs" and elaborated in subsequent publications, was initially offered as an argument against the claims of strong AI – that machines are able to achieve intelligible thought:

> Imagine a native English speaker who knows no Chinese locked in a room full of boxes of Chinese symbols (a data base) together with a book of instructions for manipulating the symbols (the program). Imagine that people outside the room send in other Chinese symbols which, unknown to the person in the room, are questions in Chinese (the input). And imagine that by following the instructions in the program the man in the room is able to pass out Chinese symbols which are correct answers to the questions (the output). The program enables the person in the room to pass the Turing Test for understanding Chinese but he does not understand a word of Chinese (Searle, 1999, p. 115).

The point of Searle's imaginative illustration is quite direct: "The Turing test fails to distinguish real mental capacities from simulations of those capacities. Simulation is not duplication" (Searle, 1999, p. 115). In other words, merely shifting verbal symbols around in a way that looks like linguistic understanding (from the outside) is not really an understanding of the language properly speaking. As the computer scientist Terry Winograd (1990, p. 187) explains, a computer does not really understand the linguistic tokens it processes; it merely "manipulates symbols without respect to their interpretation." Or, as Searle (1984, p. 34) characterizes it, computers have syntax and a method of symbol manipulation, but they do not have semantics. We can, for instance, write a software program, like Joseph Weizenbaum's ELIZA or even Apple's Siri, which takes verbal input, extracts keywords, rearranges these words according to preprogrammed scripts, and then spits out seemingly intelligible results. This does not, however, necessarily mean that such a mechanism is capable of original thought or of understanding what is stated in even a rudimentary way.

Behavioralism and its Discontents

Seale's counter argument depends on and employs a classic philosophical distinction that differentiates real being from mere external appearances. This idea goes back at least as far as Plato (see for example the "Allegory of the Cave") and sets up a value system – still operative today in all forms of scientific endeavor – that not only distinguishes how something really is from how it appears to be but gives privilege and precedent to the former over the latter. Turing, and HMC by extension, deliberately challenges and overturns this ontological order.

Even if one is convinced, following arguments like those offered by Searle, that a machine is just a "mindless" instrument that merely manipulates linguistic tokens, the game of imitation also demonstrates that what really matters is not necessarily what happens inside the box (or the Chinese Room). What matters and makes a difference is what human users do with and in response to these various external manifestations. In other words, whether we conclude that the mechanism is, in fact, engaged in genuine communication or not, the apparent behavior that is exhibited in, for example, the game of imitation or other socially interactive exchange, does have an effect on us and our very real social relationships. As Weizenbaum (1967, pp. 474–475) observed with his chatbot ELIZA, "the human speaker will contribute much to clothe ELIZA's responses in the vestments of plausibility. However, he will not defend his illusion (that he is being understood) against all odds. In human conversation a speaker will make certain (perhaps generous) assumptions about his conversational partner. As long as it remains possible to interpret the latter's responses to be consistent with those assumptions, the speaker's image of his partner remains undamaged."

Despite philosophical commitments rooted in Platonism, this is not an anomaly. It is part and parcel of human social interaction. And it has been experimentally tested and confirmed by Byron Reeves and Clifford Nass's (1996, p. 22) *Media Equation* and their subsequent work with the Computers are Social Actors (CASA) studies:

> Computers, in the way that they communicate, instruct, and take turns interacting, are close enough to human that they encourage social responses. The encouragement necessary for such a reaction need not be much. As long as there are some behaviors that suggest a social presence, people will respond accordingly.... Consequently, any medium that is close enough will get human treatment, even though people know it's foolish and even though they likely will deny it afterwards.

The CASA model, which was developed in response to numerous experiments with human subjects, describes how users of computers, irrespective of the actual intelligence possessed (or not) by the machine, tend to respond to the technology as another socially aware and interactive subject. In other words, even when experienced users know quite well that they are engaged with using a machine, they make what Reeves and Nass (1996, p. 22) call the "conservative error" and tend to respond to it in ways that afford this other thing social standing on par with another human individual.

In social circumstances, therefore, what really matters – or at least what seems to make a difference – is not what something really is in its essence but how it comes to be situated in actual social interactions and relationships. In order for something to be recognized and treated as another socially significant subject who communicates with us, "it is not necessary," as Reeves and Nass (1996, p. 28) conclude, "to have artificial intelligence," strictly speaking. All that is needed is that they appear to be "close enough" to encourage some kind of social response. Whether the machine can actually think or not appears to be less important than how it appears to be in actual social circumstances and situations.

APPARENT PROBLEMS AND COMPLICATIONS

Validating appearances is revolutionary. As if following the example of Friedrich Nietzsche, doing so deliberately overturns the usual way of thinking about and organizing things. "My philosophy," Nietzsche (1980, p. 199) once wrote, "is a reversed Platonism. The farther removed from true beings, all the purer more beautiful and better it is. Life in illusion as goal." Despite promising to arrange alternative ways of proceeding, revolutionary interventions like this do have important epistemological consequences and moral repercussions.

No Deception, no AI

Sherry Turkle, an MIT social scientist specializing in the psychological aspects of emerging technology, worries that socially evocative technologies – especially digital voice assistants and social robots – are a potentially dangerous form of self-deception. "I find people willing to seriously consider robots not only as pets but as potential friends, confidants, and even romantic partners. We don't seem to care what their artificial intelligences 'know' or 'understand' of the human moments we might 'share' with them... the performance of connection seems connection enough" (Turkle, 2011, p. 9). In the face of apparently social interactive devices, Turkle argues, we seem to be willing, all too willing, to consider these technological objects to be another socially significant subject – not just a kind of surrogate pet but a close friend, personal confidant, and even paramour. According to Turkle's diagnosis, we are in danger of substituting a technological interface for the real face-to-face interactions we used to have with other human beings. "Technology is seductive when what it offers meets our human vulnerabilities. And as it turns out, we are very vulnerable indeed. We are lonely but fearful of intimacy. Digital connections and the sociable robot may offer the illusion of companionship without the demands of friendship" (Turkle, 2011, p. 1).

But things could potentially be much worse. This human-all-too-human proclivity might be intentionally exploited for commercial gain. Matthias Scheutz, for instance, finds very compelling reasons to be concerned with this kind of deliberate manipulation.

> What is so dangerous about unidirectional emotional bonds is that they create psychological dependencies that could have serious consequences for human societies … Social robots that cause people to establish emotional bonds with them, and trust them deeply as a result, could be misused to manipulate people in ways that were not possible before. For example, a company might exploit the robot's unique relationship with its owner to make the robot convince the owner to purchase products the company wishes to promote. Note that unlike human relationships where, under normal circumstances, social emotional mechanisms such as empathy and guilt would prevent the escalation of such scenarios; there does not have to be anything on the robots' side to stop them from abusing their influence over their owners. (Scheutz, 2015, pp. 216–217)

On the other side of this debate, however, are various other voices that promote these socially interactive technologies not as a deceptive substitute for human sociability, which is Turkle's point, but as a means to augment and improve social interactions and circumstances. The Paro robot, invented by Takanori Shibata, has proven to be incredibly useful for elder care, especially in situations involving individuals suffering from debilitating forms of dementia. In a number of clinical studies, the robot has been found to improve individual well-being by providing companionship and comfort in cases where other forms of interaction therapy are either difficult to provide or ineffectual (Bemelmens et al., 2012; Šabanović et al., 2013). Social robots have also been shown to be expedient and effective for helping children with autism navigate the difficult terrain of human social interaction (Robins et al., 2005).

Beyond these therapeutic employments, however, these technologies are both engaging and entertaining. Many of us now have rudimentary social robots in our pockets and purses, with the smart phone being a kind of handheld companion/service robot that helps us connect to each other and our world (Vincent, 2013). "Home robots such as Jibo and companion chatbots such as Replika," as Natale (2021, p. 6) points out, "are designed to appear cute and to awaken sentiments of empathy in their owners. This design choice looks in itself to be harmless and benevolent: these technologies simply work better if their appearances and behavior stimulate positive feelings in their users." Even technologies that are not explicitly designed for it can become social subjects due to the role and function they play in human organizations. This is the case with many of the explosive ordinance disposal (EOD) robots used by soldiers on the battlefield. These miniature tank-like devices, which are clearly not designed for nor outfitted with any of the programming and mechanisms for producing the effects of social interaction, occupy an important and valued position within the human combat unit based not on the cognitive capabilities of the device but on the social needs of the soldiers (Carpenter, 2015; Sandry, 2015b). In these cases, whether the robot is a genuine social entity or not seems less important than the net effect of its social presence and interactions – even if just simulated – on the human users who engage with it.

What we see in the face or the faceplate of these machines, then, is not necessarily the visage of another kind of social subject. What we encounter is uncertainty and ambivalence – an inability to decide whether the machine is just a technological thing and instrument or has some legitimate claim to social standing as another subject. A socially interactive mechanism, like a chatbot, natural language processing (NLP) digital assistant, or social robot, is not (at least not at this particular moment in history) considered to be a social, moral, or legal subject. But these devices are also situated and appear to be something more than a mere tool, instrument, or object. They therefore occupy what is arguably an ambivalent in-between position that complicates the usual way of sorting things into "who" counts

as another socially significant subject and "what" remains a mere thing (Derrida, 2005, p. 80). They are a kind of "quasi-other" (Ihde, 1990).

The challenge, therefore, is not the potential for deceptive manipulation. It is the undecidability that confronts us in the face of this very question. In other words, we seem to be unable to decide whether anthropomorphism, or what Joanna Bryson and Philip Kime (2011, p. 2) call "over identification," is a bug to be eliminated in order to expedite correct understanding and operational transparency that can protect users from deception (Bryson and Kime, 2011; Shneiderman, 1989) or whether it is, as Duffy (2003) and Natale (2021) argue, a feature to be carefully cultivated so as to create better, socially interactive artifacts. As Eleanor Sandry (2015a, p. 340) has explained: "Scientific discourse is generally biased against anthropomorphism, arguing that any attribution of human characteristics to nonhumans is incompatible with maintaining one's objectivity…However, social robotics research has, for some time, been open to the idea of encouraging anthropomorphic responses in humans…[as] an important part of facilitating meaningful human-robot interactions." The problem, then, is not that the potential for "deceptive anthropomorphic projection" exists; the problem is that we seem to be unable to decide whether such deceptions or appearances (to use a more positive term) are detrimental, useful, or both. This is the more fundamental question that research in HMC will need to address, contend with, and answer.

Responsibility Gaps

Beyond epistemological equivocation, the innovations of HMC also have moral consequences. In interactions with technologies that appear to be another kind of communicative subject, it is not entirely clear as to who or what does the talking or can be responsible for what is said or done. The concept of responsibility, as Paul Ricœur (2007) insightfully points out, is quite literally understood and formulated as the "ability to respond." So, the moral question that confronts us in the face of communicative AI is who or what is responsible or able to respond for what is said or done in these encounters and interactions?

The standard answer to this question is typically formulated in terms of the instrumental theory of technology, which is something identified and explained by Martin Heidegger (1977, pp. 4–5) in the essay "The Question Concerning Technology." According to Heidegger's analysis, the presumed role and function of any kind of technology – whether it be a simple hand tool, jet airliner, or a sophisticated robot – is that it is a means employed by human users for specific ends. Heidegger calls this particular characterization of technology "the instrumental definition" and indicates that it forms what is considered to be the correct understanding of any kind of technological contrivance. As Andrew Feenberg (1991, p. 5) neatly summarizes it: "The instrumentalist theory offers the most widely accepted view of technology. It is based on the common sense idea that technologies are 'tools' standing ready to serve the purposes of users." And because a tool "is deemed 'neutral,' without valuative content of its own" (Feenberg 1991, p. 5), a technological object is evaluated not in and for itself but on the basis of the particular employments that have been decided by a human subject.

According to this way of thinking, the machine – a computer, NLP digital assistant, social robot, etc. – can never be an end in and of itself; it is always a means or an instrument employed by human users for the purpose of humanly defined ends and objectives. This is precisely the way that the technology of the computer has been understood and situated in computer-mediated communication (CMC), and this is also the way that both communication and computer ethics has understood the moral position and status of the technological object. As Deborah Johnson (2006, p. 197) explains: "Computer systems are produced, distributed, and used by people engaged in social practices and meaningful pursuits. This is as true of current computer systems as it will be of future computer systems. No matter how independently, automatic, and interactive computer systems of the future behave, they will be the products (direct or indirect) of human behavior, human social institutions, and human decision."

This way of thinking makes sense and is considered "common sense." Holding a robotic mechanism or NLP system accountable would be not only illogical but also irresponsible. This is because ascribing responsibility to machines, as Mikko Siponen (2004, p. 286) argues, would allow one to "start blaming computers for our mistakes. In other words, we can claim that 'I didn't do it – it was a computer error', while ignoring the fact that the software has been programmed by people to 'behave in certain ways', and thus people may have caused this error either incidentally or intentionally (or users have otherwise contributed to the cause of this error)." This maneuver, what Helen Nissenbaum (1996, p. 35) terms "the computer as scapegoat," is understandable but problematic, insofar as it allows human designers, developers, or users to deflect or avoid taking responsibility for their actions by assigning accountability and deflecting liability to what is a mere object. It is,

in other words, a poor carpenter who blames his tools.

But the instrumental theory, for all its notable success handling different kinds of technology, appears to be unable to contend with recent developments involving communicative machines, especially those that have been designed with machine learning capabilities. Consider, for example, Microsoft's notoriously foul mouthed Twitterbot Tay.ai, which became a raving neo-Nazi racist after interacting with human users. Although little has been made public about the exact inner workings of the Tay application, Microsoft did explain that the system was built by mining relevant public data, i.e. training the application's neural networks on anonymized data obtained from social media, and was designed to evolve its exhibited conversational behaviors from interacting with users (Microsoft, 2016). In other words, Tay was a machine learning algorithm, using (presumably) a combination of both unsupervised and reinforcement learning. The application, therefore, did not simply follow prescribed instructions provided by its programmers but developed its conversational behaviors from exploiting discoverable patterns in existing data and its own interactions with human users on social media platforms. Machine learning applications, like Tay, are intentionally designed to do things that their programmers cannot anticipate, completely control, or answer for. They are, in effect, "black boxes," which is both interesting and potentially problematic when it comes to questions of responsibility and ethics.

When one asks the question: Who is responsible for Tay's bigoted comments posted to Twitter and other social media platforms? the answer is complicated. According to the standard instrumentalist way of thinking, one would need to blame the programmers at Microsoft, who designed the application to be able to do these things. But the programmers obviously did not set out to create a racist chatbot. Tay developed this reprehensible behavior by "learning" from human conversational behaviors. So how did Microsoft answer for this? How did they explain and respond to the question concerning responsibility?

Initially a company spokesperson – in damage-control mode – sent out an email to *Wired*, *The Washington Post*, and other news organizations, that sought to blame the victim.

The AI chatbot Tay is a machine learning project, designed for human engagement. It is as much a social and cultural experiment, as it is technical. Unfortunately, within the first 24 hours of coming online, we became aware of a coordinated effort by some users to abuse Tay's commenting skills to have Tay respond in inappropriate ways. As a result, we have taken Tay offline and are making adjustments. (Risely, 2016)

According to this statement, it is not the programmers or the corporation who are responsible for the hate speech. It is the fault of the users (or some users) who interacted with Tay and taught her to be a bigot. Tay's racism, in other word, is our fault.

Later, on Friday, March 25, Peter Lee, VP of Microsoft Research, posted the following apology on the Official Microsoft Blog: "As many of you know by now, on Wednesday we launched a chatbot called Tay. We are deeply sorry for the unintended offensive and hurtful tweets from Tay, which do not represent who we are or what we stand for, nor how we designed Tay. Tay is now offline and we'll look to bring Tay back only when we are confident we can better anticipate malicious intent that conflicts with our principles and values" (Lee, 2016). But this apology is also frustratingly unsatisfying or interesting (it all depends on how you look at it). According to Lee's carefully worded explanation, Microsoft is only responsible for not *anticipating* the bad outcome; it does not take responsibility or answer for the offensive Tweets. For Lee, it is Tay who (or "that," and words matter here) is named and recognized as the source of the "wildly inappropriate and reprehensible words and images" (Lee, 2016). And since Tay is a kind of "minor" (a teenage chatbot) under the protection of her parent corporation, Microsoft needed to step-in, apologize for their offspring's bad behavior, and put Tay in a time out.

Although the extent to which one may be prepared to assign agency and responsibility to these mechanisms remains a contested matter, what is not debated is the fact that the rules of the game appear to be in flux and that there is evidence of a widening responsibility gap.

Presently there are machines in development or already in use which are able to decide on a course of action and to act without human intervention. The rules by which they act are not fixed during the production process, but can be changed during the operation of the machine, by the machine itself. This is what we call machine learning. Traditionally we hold either the operator/manufacture of the machine responsible for the consequences of its operation or "nobody" (in cases, where no personal fault can be identified). Now it can be shown that there is an increasing class of machine actions, where the traditional ways of responsibility ascription are not compatible with our sense of justice and the moral framework of society because nobody has enough control over the machine's actions to be able to assume responsibility for them. (Matthias, 2004, p. 177)

In other words, the instrumental definition of technology, which had effectively tethered machine action to human agency and responsibility, no longer adequately applies to mechanisms that have been deliberately designed to operate and exhibit some form, no matter how rudimentary, of independent action or autonomous decision making.

Consequently and contrary to the instrumentalist way of thinking, we now have technologies that are conceptualized and designed to do things that exceed our control and ability to respond or to answer for them. But let's be clear as to what this means. What is being argued is not that a mechanism, like Tay, is or should be considered a moral/legal agent and held solely accountable for the decisions it makes or the actions it deploys. That may be going too far, and it would be inattentive to the actual results that have been obtained. But what this does indicate is that the HMC paradigm and actual existing systems like Tay introduce significant complications into the standard way of assigning and dealing with responsibility. The machines might not be agents in their own right (not yet at least), but the manner by which we conceptualize their operations and the way that they are designed to function effectively challenge the standard instrumentalist theory and open up fissures in the methods by which responsibility is typically decided, assigned, and formulated.

REVOLUTIONARY OUTCOMES AND FUTURE RESEARCH

When the usual way of thinking about and making sense of things is challenged or put in question, there are generally two ways of formulating a response, which the Slovenian philosopher Slavoj Žižek (2008, p. vii) called "Ptolemization" and "Copernican revolution". The term "Ptolemization" indicates efforts to revise an existing framework or way of thinking by introducing modifications and reconfigurations, like the epicycles that were added to the Ptolemaic model of the solar system to account for seemingly aberrant observational data, in an effort to ensure the continued functioning and success of the prevailing model.

"Copernican revolution," on the contrary, designates not minor adjustments or revisions in the existing way of thinking but a complete reconfiguration or transformation of the accepted framework. The name, of course, comes from Nicolaus Copernicus, whose heliocentric model of the solar system provides the prototype for scientific revolution, insofar as it not only introduced a new framework but literally inverted or overturned the Ptolemaic system by moving the sun, which had been located on the periphery, to the center of the system.

The philosophical contexts and challenges of communicative AI are of this magnitude. The questions we now have to contend with are these: Can the opportunities/challenges that confront us in the face of communicative AI – things that appear to be able to talk to us like chatbots and other NPL applications, machine learning algorithms that do things beyond the comprehension and control of their human programmers, and sociable machines and robots that question the very limits of who or what is considered a legitimate social subject – be accommodated to the usual way of thinking? Can these innovations be Ptolemized and brought into accord with existing theories and practices in communication studies? Or do these things require revolutionary new frameworks, approaches, and research methods? Are we, in other words, in the midst or on the verge of what will be recognized (in retrospect) as a Copernican revolution?

At this juncture – at this moment in history when the opportunities and challenges of communicative AI are first becoming identified, recognized, and addressed by the discipline of communication – there is evidence of both. Efforts at Ptolemization have been advanced under the banner of "AI-Mediated Communication" (AI-MC). According to Jeffrey T. Hancock, Mor Naaman, and Karen Levy (2020, p. 90), AI-MC can be defined as "mediated communication between people in which a computational agent operates on behalf of a communicator by modifying, augmenting, or generating messages to accomplish communication or interpersonal goals." AI-MC, therefore, does not introduce a new theoretical paradigm; it seeks to rework and reassert the existing CMC framework so as to better accommodate innovations in AI systems and devices.

HMC, by contrast, pursues Copernican revolution. It overturns the CMC framework, recognizing that communicative AI is not just a medium *through* which human messages pass but is itself another kind of communicative subject *with* whom one interacts. This shift, a shift that can be registered in the material of the very words that are used to describe it – from *through* to *with* and from *what* to *whom* – is not a modification or reworking of the existing ways of thinking. It is a fundamental alteration in the subject of communication, one that promises (or threatens) to undermine the essentially anthropocentric metaphysics that organize the discipline.

What this means for research in the field of communication studies is that HMC offers a uniquely different way to approach and address the subject of communication – understood in terms of both *the subject matter researched* and *the subject of that research*. In other words, it alters what is asked about and who is to be questioned. This is precisely how and why this innovation is first and foremost a matter of philosophy. Philosophy, unlike other intellectual pursuits, is not directed at providing answers to an available set of questions. Instead, it is dedicated to critically examining and evaluating the modes of inquiry. And it does so, not because the available means of research have somehow failed. Quite the contrary, it does so precisely because the existing ways of thinking have functioned and continue to function all-too-well and are, for that reason, often taken for granted and not able to be seen as such. HMC not only challenges the standard operating presumptions of the discipline but opens-up the opportunity for asking different kinds of questions and pursuing other ways of thinking about human beings, machines, and communication. Defining what these questions are and how they should be pursued and investigated is the task of/for research in HMC.

REFERENCES

Bemelmans, R., G. J. Gelderblom, P. Jonker, & L. de Witte (2012). Socially assistive robots in elderly care. *Journal of the American Medical Directors Association* 13(2): 114–120. https://doi.org/10.1016/j.jamda.2010.10.002

Bryson, J., & P. P. Kime. (2011). Just an artifact: Why machines are perceived as moral agents. In the *Proceedings of The Twenty-Second International Joint Conference on Artificial Intelligence*. Barcelona, Spain. www.cs.bath.ac.uk/ĵjb/ftp/BrysonKime-IJCAI11.pdf

Carpenter, J. (2015). *Culture and human–robot interaction in militarized spaces: A war story*. Ashgate.

Churchland, P. (1999). *Matter and consciousness*. MIT Press.

Derrida, J. (2005). *Paper machine*. Trans. Rachel Bowlby. Stanford University Press.

Duffy, B. R. (2003). Anthropomorphism and the social robot. *Robotics and Autonomous Systems* 42(3–4): 177–190. https://doi.org/10.1016/S0921-8890(02)00374-3

Feenberg, A. (1991). *Critical theory of technology*. Oxford University Press.

Guzman, A. L. (2018). Introduction: What is human-machine communication, anyway. In Andrea L. Guzman (ed.), *Human-machine communication: Rethinking communication, technology and ourselves*, pp. 1–28. Peter Lang.

Guzman, A. L., & S. C. Lewis (2020). Artificial intelligence and communication: A human–machine communication research agenda. *New Media and Society* 22(1): 70–86. https://doi.org/10.1177/1461444819858691

Hancock, J. T., M. Naaman, & K. Levy (2020). AI-mediated communication: Definition, research agenda, and ethical considerations. *Journal of Computer-Mediated Communication* 25(1): 89–100. https://doi.org/10.1093/jcmc/zmz022

Heidegger, M. (1977). *The question concerning technology and other essays*. Trans. by W. Lovitt. Harper & Row.

Ihde, D. (1990). *Technology and the lifeworld: From garden to earth*. Bloomington, IN: Indiana University Press.

Johnson, D. G. (2006). Computer systems: Moral entities but not moral agents. *Ethics and Information Technology* 8: 195–204. https://doi.org/10.1007/s10676-006-9111-5

Lee, P. (2016). Learning from Tay's introduction. Official Microsoft Blog, March 25. https://blogs.microsoft.com/blog/2016/03/25/learning-tays-introduction/

Matthias, A. (2004). The responsibility gap: Ascribing responsibility for the actions of learning automata. *Ethics and Information Technology* 6(3): 175–183. https:// doi.org/ 10.1007/ s10676-004-3422-1.

Microsoft. (2016). Meet Tay – Microsoft AI. Chatbot with Zero Chill. www.tay.ai/

Natale, S. (2021). *Deceitful media: Artificial intelligence and social life after the Turing test*. Oxford University Press.

Nietzsche, F. (1980). *Nachgelassene Fragmente 1869–1874*, in *Friedrich Nietzsche Sämtliche Werke, Kritische Studienausgabe*, vol. 7, ed. Giorgio Colli and Mazzino Montinari. Walter de Gruyter. Translation by the author.

Nissenbaum, H. (1996). Accountability in a computerized society. *Science and Engineering Ethics*, 2(1), 25–42.

Reeves, B., & C. Nass (1996). *The media equation: How people treat computers, television, and new media like real people and places*. Cambridge University Press.

Ricœur, P. (2007). *Reflections on the just*. Trans. by David Pellauer. University of Chicago Press.

Risely, J. (2016). Microsoft's Millennial Chatbot Tay.ai pulled offline after internet teaches her racism. *GeekWire*.http://www.geekwire.com/2016/even-robot-teens-impressionable-microsofts-tay-ai-pulled-internet-teaches-racism/

Robins, B., K. Dautenhahn, R. T. Boekhorst, & A. Billard (2005). Robotic assistants in therapy and education of children with autism: Can a small humanoid robot help encourage social interaction skills? *Universal Access in the Information Society* 4(2): 105–120. https://doi.org/10.1007/s10209-005-0116-3

Šabanović, Selma, Casey C. Bennett, Wan-Ling Chang, & Lesa Huber (2013). PARO robot affects diverse interaction modalities in group sensory therapy for older adults with dementia. *IEEE 13th International Conference on Rehabilitation Robotics (ICORR)*. June 24–26. https://doi.org/10.1109/ICORR.2013.6650427

Sandry, E. (2015a). Re-evaluating the form and communication of social robots: The benefits of collaborating with machinelike robots. *International Journal of Social Robotics* 7(3), 335–346. https://doi.org/10.1007/s12369-014-0278-3

Sandry, E. (2015b). *Robots and communication*. Palgrave Macmillan.

Schank, R. C. (1990). "What is AI anyway?" In *The foundations of artificial intelligence: A sourcebook*, ed. Derek Partridge and Yorick Wilks, 3–13. Cambridge University Press.

Scheutz, M. (2012). The inherent dangers of unidirectional emotional bonds between humans and social robots. In *Robot ethics: The ethical and social implications of robotics*, ed. Patrick Lin, Keith Abney, & George A. Bekey, 205–221. Cambridge, MA: MIT Press.

Searle, J. (1984). *Mind, brains and science*. Harvard University Press.

Searle, J. (1999). The Chinese room. In *The MIT Encyclopedia of the Cognitive Sciences*, ed. R. A. Wilson and F. Keil, 115–116. MIT Press.

Shneiderman, B. (1989). A nonanthropomorphic style guide: Overcoming the Humpty–Dumpty syndrome. *The Computing Teacher* 16(7), 5–7.

Siponen, M. (2004). A pragmatic evaluation of the theory of information ethics. *Ethics and Information Technology* 6(4), 279–290. https://doi.org/10.1007/s10676-005-6710-5

Turing, A. (1999). Computing machinery and intelligence. In *Computer media and communication: A reader*, ed. Paul A. Meyer, 37–58. Oxford University Press.

Turkle, S. (2011). *Alone together: Why we expect more from technology and less from each other*. Basic Books.

Vincent, J. (2013). Is the mobile phone a personalized social robot? *Intervalla* 1(1), 60–70. www.fus.edu/intervalla/volume-1-social-robots-and-emotion-transcending-the-boundary-between-humans-and-icts/is-the-mobile-phone-a-personalized-social-robot

Weizenbaum, J. (1967). Contextual understanding by computers. *Communications of the ACM* 10(8): 474–480. https://doi.org/10.1145/363534.363545

Winograd, T. (1990). Thinking machines: Can there be? Are we? In *The foundations of artificial intelligence: A sourcebook*, ed. Derek Partridge and Yorick Wilks, 167–189. Cambridge University Press.

Žižek, S. (2008). *The sublime object of ideology*. Verso.

13

Critical and Cultural Approaches to Human–Machine Communication

Andrew Iliadis

INTRODUCTION

The integration of intelligent technologies into personal spaces raises questions about how they are active communicators in contexts like social settings, language, and identity. This chapter provides a short survey of and discusses critical and cultural approaches to Human–Machine Communication (HMC), summarizing early critical theory research and then identifying sites of conflict, starting with a review of foundational texts and critical interventions in the field. The chapter then presents three brief examples of areas where researchers conduct critical and cultural work in HMC.

Researchers have conducted critical and cultural HMC work in early ethnographic and Science and Technology Studies (STS) investigations of expert systems, knowledge representation, artificial agents, and more modern HMC engagements with interactive machines like virtual assistants. Others have focused on cultural work on embodiment in the more technology-focused fields of Human–Computer Interaction (HCI) and Human–Robot Interaction (HRI). These works explain how to help situate HMC research on consumer market products, emerging health media, and their contexts. Yet another group has addressed privacy and

surveillance issues in terms of the infrastructures that support things like robots and innovative car/home technologies. This chapter discusses these areas and ends with a few suggestions for future critical and cultural research on HMC. Overall, I focus on the effects, affective experiences, and examples of meaning-making in people's everyday encounter with technology as a communicative subject.

HUMAN–MACHINE COMMUNICATION NEEDS CRITICAL AND CULTURAL APPROACHES

Critical and cultural approaches to communication tend to focus on issues like power, public advocacy, compassion, groups and alliances, identity, language, embodied knowledge, interpersonal relationships, mediated cultures, and communication as a means of social action (Fassett et al., 2018). While there is extensive technical literature on how humans interact with machines, technology-oriented fields such as HCI and HRI do not focus exclusively on the act of *communicating*. These fields also tend to ignore critical and cultural dimensions (Alper, 2017;

Guzman, 2018; Spiel, 2021), though there are exceptions (Blythe et al., 2010). HMC, as a *subfield of communication,* is thus uniquely positioned to examine acts of communication and meaning-making processes between humans and machines while also remaining attentive to critical and cultural approaches by incorporating communication's wide variety of humanistic and qualitative tools, theories, methods, and frameworks.

At their core, critical and cultural approaches to HMC might question the existence, purposes, and foundations of communication technologies that serve as our interlocutors, focusing on pressing political and social issues. To give a general idea, the following are a few examples of the types of questions, topics, and concerns that critical and cultural approaches to HMC might cover (this list is not exhaustive, and the areas can overlap). HMC researchers who want to focus on critical and cultural issues could begin a project by focusing on any prompts listed in Table 13.1.

These critical and cultural approaches generally have a long, rich history in communication research. Researchers discuss such topics in journals such as *Communication and Critical/ Cultural Studies, Critical Studies in Media Communication,* and *Communication, Culture, & Critique.* In the specific context of communicating with machines, the questions raised in Table 13.1 are particularly well-suited for research and discussion in the HMC flagship journal *Human-Machine Communication,* which publishes such critical/cultural studies (along with more quantitative approaches). Fortunati and Edwards (2020), in the journal's inaugural editorial, discuss such theoretical, methodological, and empirical issues

in HMC. The authors highlight the importance of studying HMC in the context of "the differences of power" between interlocutors while also asking researchers to focus on such things as dialogue, characteristics, speech, language, cultural references, and "knowledge of social roles, good manners, and contexts" (p. 12). Others have articulated critical approaches to communication technologies more generally. Bakardjieva and Gehl (2017) describe several areas where scholars conduct critical evaluations of emerging media. All of this is to say that critical and cultural approaches have a longstanding publishing history in communication research and that, along with technological advances in artificial intelligence (AI), critical and cultural interest in HMC continues to grow (Jones, 2014; Spence, 2019; Edwards et al., 2019; Guzman & Lewis, 2020).

A few classic works in communication may serve as precursors to what would eventually become known as critical and cultural approaches to HMC, which deserve special mention. Early results in cultural communication, beginning most famously with Carey (1989), argue that communication and technology are inherently cultural phenomena and are thus open to research approaches that focus on lived experience where technology embodies culture. Carey's analysis draws on the critical work of scholars such as Dewey (1939), Innis (1951), Williams (1958), Geertz (1973), and Hall (1982) to show how technology "is thoroughly cultural from the outset: an expression and creation of the very outlooks and aspirations we pretend it merely demonstrates" (p. 7). Carey argues against what he sees as the "transmission view of communication" (p. 12), which

Table 13.1   Critical-cultural questions for human–machine communication

What are the cultural and intercultural contexts of HMC?

What types of biases and invisibilities are in HMC technologies?

What is the political economy of HMC, what is its history, and what is its relationship to capitalism, imperialism, and market logic?

What peoples, bodies, subjects, and identities are excluded or insufficiently accounted for in HMC processes, including industry and research?

How are race, sexuality, gender, and ethnicity accounted for in HMC?

What theoretical frameworks are involved in the formation of HMC research?

What radical and alternative approaches are there to the study of HMC?

What are the kinds and categories of HMC?

What should HMC avoid, boycott, ignore, caution against, or simply not do?

What are forms of interdisciplinary research and scholarship needed in HMC?

How can HMC learn from and think with Science and Technology Studies, Media Studies, Information Studies, Political Science, Sociology, Gender and Sexuality Studies, and Postcolonial Studies?

How can HMC think about issues such as what it means to be human, posthumanism, and other approaches to thinking about humans?

How can one research HMC in terms of meaning, semiotics, and signs?

How can HMC contribute to social justice, ethics, and reparative projects?

views communication as only dealing with things like sending information signals along a channel. Instead, communication is considered by Carey through a cultural lens, focusing on such things as customs, traditions, biases, and languages. This perspective wants to shift focus away from researching communication and technology only through the abstractions of quantitative studies on communication signals (cues, statistics, etc.) and instead prefers analyzing the everyday scenarios where people culturally engage in acts of communication and interact with technologies.

Other critical-minded scholars from outside the field of communication also influence critical and cultural approaches to HMC, arguing against quantification and the inscrutable acceptance of interactive technologies such as those involving AI into the social fabric of everyday life. According to these researchers, communication technologies like AI are not intelligent, and people should not uncritically trust them. From the perspective of philosophy, such influential scholarship includes Dreyfus' (1972) decisive rejection of the reasoning capabilities of artificially intelligent machines. From the standpoint of computer science, many reference Weizenbaum's (1976) warning that computing machinery ought not to be used in politically sensitive domains where human expertise is required, to avoid the pitfalls of what he refers to as "the imperialism of instrumental reason" (p. 256).

Such critiques of technology's instrumental reason are present in some of the works of Marx (1939), particularly in the fragments on machines. There, Marx describes how capitalists exploit scientific and technical knowledge to continue accumulating fixed capital (e. g., things like machinery), all in the service of mechanical production. Some of the earliest critical theory literature that Marx influenced emerged from researchers associated with the Frankfurt School of critical theory (Horkheimer & Adorno, 1944; Marcuse, 1964). From the point of view of these historically critical researchers of political economy, critical and cultural approaches should focus on the types of foundational problems raised by Horkheimer (1972), who described critical theory's object of inquiry as society itself and its functioning. Researchers such as Smythe (1977) further elaborated critical scholarship in the political economy of communication, and this tradition continues in the works of Mosco (1996) and Fuchs (2010) and their critical studies of digital and social media.

The primary goal of critical theory, according to Horkheimer, is not to contribute to the betterment or incremental improvement of technological or organizational systems but rather to challenge their very foundations and presuppositions. Critical approaches are thus not focused on "the better functioning of any element in the structure" of society (Horkheimer, 1972, p. 207). Instead, critical theory is "suspicious of the very categories of better, useful, appropriate, productive, and valuable" and is "wholly distrustful of the rules of conduct with which society as presently constituted provides each of its members" (ibid).

From these early beginnings, one can see that there are no natural limits or rules from the perspective of critical theory and that people should not view science and technology as objective and universal. Likewise, researchers should not take relationships between humans and machines for granted but instead must relativize from different subject positions and political orientations. Indeed, this emphasis on culture, relativity, subjectivity, standpoints, and the situated interactions of humans and machines as they communicate is the focus of critical and cultural approaches in this research area today.

SITUATED INTERACTIONS, COMMUNICATION, AND EXPERIENCE

All critical and cultural approaches to HMC should have in common the idea that HMC takes place within situated and lived environments and away from the purely abstract theorizing of philosophy or the calculated studies of the research laboratory. This approach comes from Suchman's (1987) foundational work in *Human-Machine Reconfigurations: Plans and Situated Actions*, which focuses on the situatedness of people's interaction with machine technologies. Suchman importantly asks us to focus on "the organization of human-machine communication, including its troubles, in terms of constraints posed by asymmetries in the respective situation resources of human and machine" (p. 126).

The focus on what Suchman calls "troubles" and "asymmetries" in particular "situations" shows that her investigations are directed at power imbalances as agents play them out on the field in real-world scenarios. Suchman highlights that HMC happens in specific situations, often involving collaboration, focusing on different kinds of people, participants or individuals, feedback, and adjustment of meaning, and how background experiences and circumstances embed communication. Suchman sees communication between people and machines not as an abstract symbolic process outside of lived experience and reality but as a situated activity "in which we make use of language to delineate the collective relevance of our shared environment" (p. 178). According to Suchman, HMC should thus focus on "embodied interactional competencies" (p. 10) and on the "profound difficulty of the problem of interactive interface design" (p. 11) since it is at the interfaces where humans meet machines.

Indeed, this critical emphasis on the functionality of *interfaces* is one way that critical theorists such as Galloway (2012) conduct close readings from material and semiotic perspectives "to identify the interface itself as historical" (p. 30). Interfaces often serve as a bridge between humans and machines and have capacities, meanings, politics, and histories "baked" into their materiality. It is the critical and cultural researcher's job to study these sensitive technology areas. For example, Sweeney (2016a) critically interrogates interfaces in the context of intersectionality, race, and gender, paying particular attention to the social construction of technology. Meanwhile, Bratton (2015) provides a deep philosophical reading of how an interface "necessarily limits the full range of possible interactions in a specific and arbitrary way" and "must eliminate or make invisible a whole range of other equally valid possible interactions" (p. 221). While technological interfaces are perhaps the modern locus of situatedness in HMC, the focus on situatedness that Suchman introduced also has historical precedent in the methodologies of earlier sociologists, including Mills' (1940) work on language and situated action and Garfinkel's (1967) developmental ethnomethodology.

Equally influential for a critical and cultural approach to HMC, while also focusing on embodied situatedness, is Agre's (1997) work on autonomous agents. Agre and Chapman (1990) previously discuss communication in this context as improvisation in the moment and not entirely determined by plans on the side of designers, engineers, or technologies. Instead, Agre foregrounds the agency of the user, whom he describes as sometimes having "sensible, organized, goal-directed activity without using plans at all" (p. 17). Agre moves away from a deterministic and mechanically understood notion of user interaction and toward the user as an agent who continually redefines what they want to do in a communication scenario. He asks readers to focus on processes of "interpretation which can be arbitrarily complicated and draw on a wide variety of resources" and on "people and robots as participating in the world, not as controlling it" (ibid.).

To this end, Agre (1996) suggests that HMC might focus on such critical and cultural topics as artifacts, signs, customs, practical constraints, learning situations, mutual adaptation, and

locality, among others (p. 15). He also argues that such studies can benefit by being interdisciplinary and connecting to other fields beyond computer science and engineering, including more humanistic ones, such as phenomenology, sociology, and anthropology. Such multidisciplinary studies may allow researchers interested in HMC to focus or frame their studies on aerial versus ground views, structure in the world, practices, convergence, and how computation renders specific cultural values as concrete (Agre, 1996, pp. 48–49).

A key book, Agre's *Computation and Human Experience* (1997) further and perhaps most famously articulates this critical orientation. In the text, Agre applies a strong focus on how information can act as a commodity, how social relations are exploitable as networks, how formalization and hygiene can be and often are implicitly preferred in computation and elevated, and how computation itself is a form of power (pp. 312–313). Agre describes AI technologies as bringing "control regimes of unprecedented scope" (p. 314). Thus, like Suchman, Agre asks readers to bring critical attention to *interface* and *design* arguments coming from science and engineering.

The historical precedent for such studies exists, particularly in the works of Layton (1971) on the history of social responsibility and engineering and Noble's (1977, 1984) accounts of engineering design and the social history of automation. More recently, critical technology studies are the focus of the intersectional and applied cultural critiques of Noble (2018) on algorithmic discrimination and Nakamura (2007) and Benjamin (2019) on racial bias and technology. Such critical concerns about the cultural influence of these technologies elucidate how HMC can be detrimental to specific peoples and situations if the intentions of their developers are taken for granted or at face value.

In the book's preface, Agre provides his most straightforward explanation of the moral responsibility of a critical theory of machines. He writes that critical theory is lost "unless it is organized and guided by an affirmative moral purpose…critical research draws attention to structural and cultural levels of explanation – to the things that happen through our actions but that exist beneath our conscious awareness" (p. xii). Bringing to light the structural and cultural problems of HMC requires cultivating a critical attitude toward the technologies that marketers, designers, engineers, and corporations promote as inherently good, productive, efficient, desired, and necessary. Here, Agre explains the purpose that motivates critical theory, echoing the words used by Horkheimer (1972), and re-focuses it for the computer age, applying the tools of critical theory to contexts where humans interact and communicate with machines. Critical and cultural approaches to HMC thus also must confront the unintended consequences of actions, structural and cultural levels of explanation, and all the unjust things that happen beneath conscious awareness.

The following three sections describe just some examples and applied areas where researchers have conducted or are conducting critical and cultural research in HMC.

EXAMPLE 1: QUESTIONING MACHINES THAT COMMUNICATE 'COMMON SENSE' KNOWLEDGE

Virtual assistants who interact with us have certain understandings, reasonings, facts, and approaches to communicating about the world. It is important to remember that these machines are not magical artifacts but are programmed and taught to work using certain types of logic and structured data techniques. These machines like Siri, Alexa, and Google Assistant are often our interaction partners and thus can be understood as a type of "computational interpersonal communication" (Gunkel, 2012, 2016).

Corporations build such machines using AI to interact conversationally with us and share facts and information codified in specific ways. Researchers have investigated these techniques for decades since early AI work in expert systems (Waterman, 1985) and knowledge-based systems (Lenat & Guha, 1989), and later research in embodied conversational agents (Cassell et al., 2000) and voice user interfaces (Pearl, 2017). Reasoning technologies frequently make use of what is known as "ontology engineering" (Lenat, 1989) or "knowledge engineering" (Feigenbaum, 1980), where allegedly "common sense" information and facts about the world are programmed into and taught to computers. Today, engineers conduct this process through structured data modeling, which helps machines interact and communicate facts in a dialogical setting to human users. There are epistemological consequences here in terms of knowledge production (whose knowledge, and at what cost?) and direct technological and personnel connections from these earlier technologies to some of the products and companies that HMC researchers study today.

For example, Gruber (1993) presents crucial early work in ontology engineering; the author is the co-creator of Siri and went on to work for Apple. Another early example of knowledge-based systems, Guha (1992), was written by a future Google employee who became responsible

for developing custom search. Both are examples of the logic underlying ontology and knowledge engineering work instantiated in market products (Iliadis, 2018, 2019, 2022). Siri and Google Assistant both use and rely on the ontologies that represent "knowledge" through structured data fed into them to answer queries. The consequences of how engineers orchestrate these data will affect the growth and decline of local and indigenous knowledge and carry sociocultural biases that are in danger of supporting only the knowledge and languages of the predominantly white, northern, English-speaking world.

Several academics and researchers in STS, Anthropology, Sociology, Media Studies, Information Studies, Communication, and Feminist Studies have conducted critical research on ontology and knowledge engineering. They brought critical and cultural approaches to their research agendas, positioning themselves as suspicious of the enlightenment claims to objectivity and common sense that the developers frequently made of these AI systems.

For example, Star (1988) proposes viewing information systems involved in AI as types of "boundary objects" where people or groups work with the technology without understanding different localized expectations, models, or uses. She suggests that various analyses, methods, and abstractions happen with other goals, time horizons, and audiences (p. 46). The foregrounding and inverting of the multidimensional nature of this work in AI (Bowker, 1994; Star, 1999) from the perspectives of Sociology and Library and Information Science scholars coincide with and complement the ethnographies of anthropologists and STS scholars. Forsythe (1993a, 1993b, 2002) famously uses ethnography to explore the complex processes of interpretation and translation involved in creating these AI systems, pushing against the positivism promoted by engineers of such tools, and emphasizing their socially constructed nature.

Taking such concerns about interpretation and translation in AI to issues of gender, Adam (1998) examines how such AI systems are "used to promulgate what might be undesirably normative views of women and other groups" (p. 3). More recently, several scholars have critically examined the political stakes of how ontology and knowledge engineering in AI systems are developed in the backend by designers, scientists, and engineers (Waller, 2016; Allhutter, 2019; Poirier, 2019). Other scholars, such as Sweeney (2016b, 2020, 2022) and Guzman (2017, 2018, 2019, 2020), extend some of these concerns into modern-day virtual assistants, focusing on how design encodes gender, race, and class into these technologies.

EXAMPLE 2: CULTIVATING CULTURAL CONTEXTS IN HUMAN–MACHINE COMMUNICATION

Context should be a key concern for critical and cultural scholars of HMC. HCI and HRI have long dealt with the issue of context in applications designed for environmental awareness and positionality. These spatial concerns also extend specifically to machines meant to communicate with humans. Early HCI work developed by Moran and Dourish (2001) in a special double issue of *Human-Computer Interaction* focused on "Context-Aware Computing" and includes papers focusing on how context is theoretically crucial for how humans communicate with machines. While many of the documents in the collection focus on contexts in terms of place and setting, Dourish's (2001) contribution emphasizes the importance of paying attention to "embodiment" to understand contexts. To do so, he suggests, echoing Agre (1996) and others in the issue (Svanæs, 2001), that researchers use the critical and qualitative tools available from phenomenology. Phenomenology places research emphasis on conscious experiences, how these are based and grounded in reality, and how individuals experience their physical embodiment. Thus, through an understanding of material embodiment, one can come to terms with the meaning of a specific context.

HRI researchers are similarly attentive to the differing contexts that are important to people, and thus they too thought these should be relevant to the development of robots. Breazeal, the co-founder of Jibo, writes in *Designing Sociable Robots* (2002) that robots should "play a critical role in our cognitive development, how we learn from others, how we communicate and interact, our culture, and our daily lives as members of society" (p. xii). Others have researched the effects of culture and context on perceptions of robotic facial expressions (Bennett & Šabanović, 2015) and the construction of gender in social robots (Liu, 2021). Issues relating to social factors and embodiment, both on the part of human users and the role of machines, are critical for understanding context in HMC. The handling of these issues affects how people from different classes, genders, sexualities, age groups, backgrounds, cultures, degrees of physical ability, and socioeconomic status can or cannot participate in forms of HMC.

With a concern for marginalized groups, several scholars in HCI, Communication, Media Studies, and Information Studies have conducted research projects that adopt critical and cultural approaches to HMC, focusing on embodied agency (Gibbs et al., 2021). For example, in a study of iPads and mobile communication technologies that designers promote to assist those with disabilities, Alper (2017) finds "that technologies largely thought to universally empower the 'voiceless' are still subject to disempowering structural inequalities" (p. 3). Alper adopts a critical lens to examine how such tools "unintentionally contributed to naturalized disempowered states and exclusionary positions" (pp. 28–29).

Similarly, critical and cultural approaches relating to communication have appeared in HCI, focusing specifically on the intersecting topics of gender and disability studies (Richardson, 2018; Spiel et al., 2019; Burtscher & Spiel, 2020) and, more generally, on HCI's insufficient focus on these crucial areas. Spiel's work focuses on creating meaningful interaction between researchers, designers, and engineers with the marginalized and underrepresented groups they study, such as neurodivergent and non-binary peoples in machinic contexts like assistive wearable and gaming technologies. In discussing the lack of focus on diverse bodies and minds in the area of embodied computing (Pedersen & Iliadis, 2020), Spiel (2021) asks, "Where are the trans*, the crip, the fat, the queer, the indigenous, the black, the mad, the damaged, the sick, the old, the young, the dead, the sexual bodies in embodied computing?" (p. 10). The above studies take the notion of context away from simple considerations of place, space, and strictly theoretical concerns and expand it to the specific social, physical, and cultural contexts that situate various peoples.

EXAMPLE 3: ADAPTING PRIVACY AND SURVEILLANCE IN MACHINE INFRASTRUCTURES

As a third and final example, critical and cultural HMC researchers may consider humans' privacy and surveillance needs when interacting with machines. Early work by Gandy (1993) and Lyon (1994) focuses on the surveillant capacities of information technologies. Other scholars focus specifically on surveillance and human-machine interfaces (Mason & Raab, 2005). More recent engagements have focused on how human actions and traces contribute to large datasets for corporations, leading to research projects in critical data studies (Dalton & Thatcher, 2014; Iliadis & Russo, 2016; Kitchin & Lauriault, 2018). Van Dijck (2014) discusses datafication and dataveillance in contemporary society, and Couldry and

Mejias (2019) extend these concerns by examining regimes of data extraction.

Machines produce data and metadata increasingly related to information about us in our homes and environments, such as offices and cars. Contemporary communication and media studies scholars have focused on the privacy and surveillance aspects of such machine and robot technologies that interact with us. These machines produce data about people's movements through technologies like wearables (Iliadis & Pedersen, 2018) and devices for creatures such as our pets at home (Richardson et al., 2017). There is a growing body of literature on surveillance, privacy, and robot technologies (Lutz et al., 2019; Lutz & Tamó-Larrieux, 2020), including those related to smart cars and other smart gadgets that participate in what Gekker and Hind refer to as "infrastructural surveillance" (2020). All this data is also used by policing and intelligence agencies that use data integration software to surveil and control information about people (Iliadis & Acker, 2022). HMC occurs within, among, and between structures that constantly track and produce data about the individuals and entities involved in the communication process. Critical and cultural researchers can thus focus on these areas, where machines that interact with us are also tracking and surveying us, limiting the boundaries of our privacy in our everyday lives.

Rights to these data, access to them, ownership of them, and the freedom to stop and delete them are essential concerns for critically-minded researchers in this area. For example, employees and managers now use machines to assist the elderly, help train and educate students, and aid workers, and they exist in places like airports, warehouses, etc. Computers generate massive amounts of data about the people interacting with these technologies in these fields. Such processes open the space for questions that critical and cultural researchers can ask concerning the social functioning of these technologies for people like students, patients, workers, immigrants, pets, children, seniors, and others.

CONCLUSION

This chapter has served as a summary of some relevant studies that have researched critical and cultural issues relating to HMC. There are several other ways that researchers can and are conducting studies in this area. These include focusing on such topics as agency and what it means to be human (Banks & Graaf, 2020), emotions and affect (Banks & Bowman, 2016;

Stark, 2019), as well as by creating alternative histories of related fields (Bell, 2018).

Of particular importance, HMC researchers may continue to hone their focus on the three following areas. First, critical and cultural scholars may build studies looking into the effects of these technologies—what outcomes do they produce in society and for what people? While basic research and design are valuable, scholars should continue to examine the results of these technologies and their effects on people's everyday interactions, good or bad. Second, emotions are essential to understanding communication and are central to understanding how people feel about their interactions with machines. Researchers should consider people's feelings, including empathy, and how they exist concerning our machinic counterparts (including how people perceive devices as having emotions). Lastly, scholars may conduct archival research on examples such as historical and legal case studies looking into the totality of a particular product's design, implementation, and outcome. What lessons can scholars learn from these historical examples, and how can they be used to further HMC research in terms of social justice? While research is already underway in these areas, HMC scholars can continue to focus on them to help develop the critical and cultural research agenda.

Future critical and cultural researchers can conduct qualitative studies that foreground interpretive results where machines participate in human life and culture in the ways listed above and more. In this domain of scholarly activity, critical and cultural researchers of HMC have many methods at their disposal, including those of narrative, ethnography, autoethnography, case studies, interviewing, and critical theory, among others. Such studies should focus on questioning the foundations of situated actions, communication, and experience to maintain the relevance and urgency of criticism today.

REFERENCES

Adam, A. (1998). *Artificial knowing: Gender and the thinking machine*. Routledge.

Agre, P. E. (1996). Computational research on interaction and agency. In P. E. Agre & S. J. R. Rosenschein (Eds.), *Computational theories of interaction and agency* (pp. 1–52). MIT Press.

Agre, P. E. (1997). *Computation and human experience*. MIT Press.

Agre, P. E., & Chapman, D. (1990). What are plans for? In P. Maes (Ed.), *Designing autonomous agents: Theory and practice from biology to engineering and back* (pp. 17–34). MIT Press.

Allhutter, D. (2019). Of 'working ontologists' and 'high-quality human components': The politics of semantic infrastructures. In D. Ribes & J. Vertesi (Eds.), *DigitalSTS: A field guide for science & technology studies* (pp. 326–348). Princeton University Press.

Alper, M. (2017). *Giving voice: Mobile communication, disability, and inequality*. MIT Press.

Bakardjieva, M. & Gehl, R. W. (2017). Critical approaches to communication technology – the past five years. *Annals of the International Communication Association*, *41*(3–4), 213–219. https://doi.org/10.1080/23808985.2017.1374201

Banks, J. & Bowman, N. D. (2016). Emotion, anthropomorphism, realism, control: Validation of a merged metric for player–avatar interaction (PAX). *Computers in Human Behavior*, *54*, 215–223. https://doi.org/10.1016/j.chb.2015.07.030

Banks, J. & de Graaf, M. M. A. (2020). Toward an agent-agnostic transmission model: Synthesizing anthropocentric and technocentric paradigms in communication. *Human-Machine Communication*, *1*, 19–36. https://doi.org/10.30658/hmc.1.2

Bell, G. (2018). Making life: A brief history of human-robot interaction. *Consumption, Markets & Culture*, *21*(1), 22–41. https://doi.org/10.1080/10253866.2017.1298555

Benjamin, R. (2019). *Race after technology: Abolitionist tools for the new Jim Code*. Polity.

Bennett, C. C. & Šabanović, S. (2015). The effects of culture and context on perceptions of robotic facial expressions. *Interaction Studies*, *16*(2), 272–302. https://doi.org/10.1075/is.16.2.11ben

Blythe, M., McCarthy, J., Light, A., Bardzell, S., Wright, P., Bardzell, J., & Blackwell, A. (2010). Critical dialogue: Interaction, experience and cultural theory. *CHI '10 Extended Abstracts on Human Factors in Computing Systems*, 4521–4524. https://doi.org/10.1145/1753846.1754189

Bowker, G. C. (1994). *Science on the run: Information management and industrial geophysics at Schlumberger, 1920–1940*. MIT Press.

Bratton, B. (2015). *The stack: On software and sovereignty*. MIT Press.

Breazeal, C. (2002). *Designing sociable robots*. MIT Press.

Burtscher, S. & Spiel, K. (2020). "But where would I even start?": Developing (gender) sensitivity in HCI research and practice. In *Proceedings of the Conference on Mensch und Computer (MuC '20)*. Association for Computing Machinery, New York, NY, USA, 431–441. https://doi.org/10.1145/3404983.3405510

Carey, J. W. (1989/2008). *Communication as culture: Essays on media and society*. Routledge.

Cassell, J., Sullivan, J., Prevost, S. & Churchill, E. (Eds.). (2000). *Embodied conversational agents*. MIT Press.

Couldry, N., & Mejias, U. A. (2019). *The costs of connection: How data Is colonizing human life and appropriating it for capitalism*. Stanford University Press.

Dalton, C. & Thatcher, J. (2014). What does a critical data studies look like, and why do we care? Seven points for a critical approach to 'Big Data.' *Society & Space Open Site*. Available at: www.societyandspace.org/articles/what-does-a-critical-data-studies-look-like-and-why-do-we-care (accessed September 6, 2020).

Dewey, J. (1939). *Intelligence in the modern world*. Modern Library.

Dourish, P. (2001). Seeking a foundation for context-aware computing. *Human-Computer Interaction*, *16*(2–4), 229–241. https://doi.org/10.1207/S15327051HCI16234_07

Dreyfus, H. L. (1972/1997). *What computers can't do: A critique of artificial reason*. MIT Press.

Edwards, C., Edwards, A., Kim, J., Spence, P. R., de Graaf, M., Nah, S., & Rosenthal-von der Pütten, A. (2019). Human-machine communication: What does/could communication science contribute to HRI? *14th ACM/IEEE International Conference on Human-Robot Interaction (HRI)*, 673–674. https://doi.org/10.1109/HRI.2019.8673138

Fassett, D. L., Warren, J. T., & Nainby, K. (2018). *Communication: A critical/cultural Introduction*. Cognella.

Feigenbaum, E. A. (1980). *Knowledge engineering: The applied side of artificial intelligence*. Stanford University. https://stacks.stanford.edu/file/druid:cn981xh0967/cn981xh0967.pdf

Forsythe, D. E. (1993a). Engineering knowledge: The construction of knowledge in artificial intelligence. *Social Studies of Science*, *23*(3), 445–477. https://doi.org/10.1177/0306312793023003002

Forsythe, D. E. (1993b). The construction of work in artificial intelligence. *Science, Technology, & Human Values*, *18*(4), 460–479.

Forsythe, D. E. (2002). *Studying those who study us: An anthropologist in the world of artificial intelligence*. Stanford University Press.

Fortunati, L. & Edwards, A. (2020). Opening space for theoretical, methodological, and empirical issues in Human-Machine Communication. *Human-Machine Communication*, *1*, 7–18. https://doi.org/10.30658/hmc.1.1

Fuchs, C. (2010). Labor in informational capitalism and on the internet. *The Information Society*, *26*(3), 179–196. https://doi.org/10.1080/01972243.1003712215

Galloway, A. R. (2012). *The interface effect*. Polity.

Gandy, O. H. Jr. (1993/2021). *The panoptic sort: A political economy of personal information*. Oxford University Press.

Garfinkel, H. (1967). *Studies in ethnomethodology*. Prentice Hall.

Geertz, C. (1973). *The interpretation of cultures*. Basic Books.

Gehl, R., & Bakardjieva, M. (Eds.). (2017). *Socialbots and their friends: Digital media and the automation of sociality*. Routledge.

Gekker, A. & Hind, S. (2020). Infrastructural surveillance. *New Media & Society, 22*(8), 1414–1436. https://doi.org/10.1177/1461444819879426

Gibbs, J. L., Kirkwood, G. L., Fang, C. & Wilkenfeld, J. N. (2021). Negotiating agency and control: Theorizing human-machine communication from a structurational perspective. *Human-Machine Communication, 2*, 153–171. https://doi.org/10.30658/hmc.2.8

Gruber, T. R. (1993). A translation approach to portable ontology specifications. *Knowledge Acquisition, 5*(2), 99–220. https://doi.org/10.1006/knac.1993.1008

Guha, R. (1992). *Contexts: A formalization and some applications*. Ph.D. Dissertation. Stanford University, Stanford, CA, USA. Order Number: UMI Order No. GAX92-17827.

Gunkel, D. J. (2012). Communication and artificial intelligence: Opportunities and challenges for the 21st century. *communication +1, 1*(1), 1–26. https://doi.org/10.7275/R5QJ7F7R

Gunkel, D. J. (2016). Computational interpersonal communication: Communication studies and spoken dialogue systems. *communication +1, 5*, 1–20. https://doi.org/10.7275/R5VH5KSQ

Guzman, A. (2017). Making AI safe for humans: A conversation with Siri. In R. W. Gehl, & M. Bakardjieva (Eds.), *Socialbots and their friends: Digital media and the automation of sociality* (pp. 69–85). Routledge.

Guzman, A. (Ed.). (2018). *Human-machine communication: Rethinking communication, technology, and ourselves*. Peter Lang.

Guzman, A. (2020). Ontological boundaries between humans and computers and the implications for human-machine communication. *Human-Machine Communication, 1*, 37–54. https://doi.org/10.30658/hmc.1.3

Guzman, A., & Lewis S. C. (2020). Artificial intelligence and communication: A Human–Machine Communication research agenda. *New Media & Society, 22*(1), 70–86. https://doi.org/10.1177/1461444819858691

Hall, S. (1982). The Rediscovery of 'Ideology': The return of the repressed in media studies. In M. Gurevitch, T. Bennett, James Curran, & J. Woollacott (Eds.), *Culture, society and the media* (pp. 52-86). Methuen.

Horkheimer, M. (1972/2002). *Critical theory: Selected essays*. Continuum.

Horkheimer, M. & Adorno, T. (1944/2007). *Dialectic of enlightenment*. Stanford University Press.

Iliadis, A. (2018). Algorithms, ontology, and social progress. *Global Media and Communication, 14*(2), 219–230. https://doi.org/10.1177/1742766518776688

Iliadis, A. (2019). The Tower of Babel problem: Making data make sense with Basic Formal Ontology.

Online Information Review, 43(6), 1021–1045. https://doi.org/10.1108/OIR-07-2018-0210

Iliadis, A. (2022). *Semantic media: Mapping meaning on the internet*. Polity.

Iliadis, A. & Russo, F. (2016). Critical data studies: An introduction. *Big Data & Society, 3*(2), 1–7.

Iliadis, A. & Pedersen, I. (2018). The fabric of digital life: Uncovering sociotechnical tradeoffs in embodied computing through metadata. *Journal of Information, Communication and Ethics in Society, 16*(3), 1–18. doi.org/10.1108/JICES-03-2018-0022

Iliadis, A., & Acker, A. (2022). The seer and the seen: Surveying Palantir's surveillance platform. *The Information Society, 38*(5), 334–363. https://doi.org/10.1080/01972243.2022.2100851

Innis, H. A. (1951). *The bias of communication*. University of Toronto Press.

Jones, S. (2014). People, things, memory and human-machine communication. *International Journal of Media & Cultural Politics, 10*(3), 245–258. https://doi.org/10.1386/macp.10.3.245_1

Kitchin, R. & Lauriault, T. (2018). Towards critical data studies: Charting and unpacking data assemblages and their work. In J. Thatcher, J. Eckert, & A. Shears (Eds.), *Thinking big data in geography: New regimes, new research* (pp. 3–20). University of Nebraska Press.

Layton, E. T. Jr. (1971/1986). *The revolt of the engineers: Social responsibility and the American engineering profession*. Johns Hopkins University Press.

Lenat, D. B. (1989). Ontological versus knowledge engineering. *IEEE Transactions on Knowledge and Data Engineering, 1*(1), 84–88. https://doi.org/10.1109/69.43405

Lenat, D. E. & Guha, R. V. (1989). *Building large knowledge-based systems: Representation and inference in the Cyc project*. Addison-Wesley.

Liu, J. (2021). Social robots as the bride? Understanding the construction of gender in a Japanese social robot product. *Human-Machine Communication, 2*, 105–120. https://doi.org/10.30658/hmc.2.5

Lutz, C. & Tamó-Larrieux, A. (2020). The robot privacy paradox: Understanding how privacy concerns shape intentions to use social robots. *Human-Machine Communication, 1*, 87–111. https://doi.org/10.30658/hmc.1.6

Lutz, C., Schöttler, M., & Hoffmann, C. P. (2019). The privacy implications of social robots: Scoping review and expert interviews. *Mobile Media & Communication, 7*(3), 412–434. https://doi.org/10.1177/2050157919843961

Lyon, D. (1994). *Electronic eye: The rise of surveillance society*. University of Minnesota Press.

Marcuse, H. (1964/1991). *One-dimensional man: Studies in the ideology of advanced industrial society*. Beacon Press.

Marx, K. (1939/1993). *Grundrisse: Foundations of the critique of political economy*. Penguin.

Mason, D. & Raab, C. D. (2005). Surveillance and the human–machine interface. *Information, Communication & Society*, 8:1, 81–83. https://doi.org/10.1080/13691180500067118

Mills, C. W. (1940). Situated actions and vocabularies of motive. *American Sociological Review*, 5(6), 904–913. https://doi.org/10.2307/2084524

Moran, T. P. & Dourish, P. (2001). Introduction to this special issue on context-aware computing. *Human–Computer Interaction*, 16(2–4), 87–95. https://doi.org/10.1207/S15327051HCI16234_01

Mosco, V. (1996/2009). *The political economy of communication*. Sage.

Nakamura, L. (2007). *Digitizing race: Visual cultures of the internet*. University of Minnesota Press.

Noble, D. F. (1977/1984). *America by design: Science, technology, and the rise of corporate capitalism*. Oxford University Press.

Noble, D. F. (1984/2011). *Forces of production: A social history of industrial automation*. Routledge.

Noble, S. U. (2018). *Algorithms of oppression: How search engines reinforce racism*. New York University Press.

Pearl, C. (2017). *Designing voice user interfaces: Principles of conversational experiences*. O'Reilly.

Pedersen, I. & Iliadis, A. (2020). *Embodied computing: Wearables, implantables, embeddables, ingestibles*. MIT Press.

Poirier, L. (2019). Classification as catachresis: Double binds of representing difference with semiotic infrastructure. *Canadian Journal of Communication*, 44, 361–371. https://doi.org/10.22230/cjc.2019v44n3a3455

Richardson I., Hjorth, L., Strengers Y. & Balmford W. (2017) Careful surveillance at play: Human–Animal Relations and Mobile Media in the Home. In C. E. Gómez, S. Sumartojo & S. Pink (Eds.), *Refiguring Techniques in Digital Visual Research* (pp. 105–116). Palgrave Macmillan.

Richardson, K. (2018). Critical autism studies and robot therapy. In K. Richardson (Ed.), *Challenging Sociality: An Anthropology of Robots, Autism, and Attachment* (pp. 121–140). Springer. https://doi.org/10.1007/978-3-319-74754-5_7

Smythe, D. W. (1977). Communications: Blindspot of western Marxism. *Canadian Journal of Political and Society Theory*, 1(3), 1–28. https://journals.uvic.ca/index.php/ctheory/article/view/13715

Spence, P. R. (2019). Searching for questions, original thoughts, or advancing theory: Human-machine communication. *Computers in Human Behavior*, 90, 285–287.

Spiel, K. (2021). The bodies of TEI – Investigating norms and assumptions in the design of embodied interaction. In *Proceedings of the Fifteenth International Conference on Tangible, Embedded, and Embodied Interaction (TEI '21)*. Association for Computing Machinery, New York, NY, USA, Article 32, 1–19. https://doi.org/10.1145/3430524.3440651

Spiel, K., Frauenberger, C., Keyes, O., & Fitzpatrick, G. (2019). Agency of autistic children in technology research: A critical literature review. *ACM Transactions on Computer-Human Interaction*, 26(6), 1–40. https://doi.org/10.1145/3344919

Star, S. L. (1988). The structure of ill-structured solutions: Boundary objects and heterogeneous distributed problem solving. In M. Huhns & L. Gasser (Eds.), *Readings in distributed artificial intelligence* (pp. 37–53). Kaufman.

Star, S. L. (1999). The ethnography of infrastructure. *American Behavioral Scientist*, 43(3), 377–391. https://doi.org/10.1177/00027649921955326

Stark, L. (2019). Affect and emotion in digitalSTS. In J. Vertesi and D. Ribes (Eds.) *digitalSTS: A field guide for science & technology studies* (pp. 117–135). Princeton University Press.

Suchman, L. (1987/2007). *Human-machine reconfigurations: Plans and situated actions*. Cambridge.

Svanæs, D. (2001). Context-aware technology: A phenomenological perspective. *Human–Computer Interaction*, 16(2–4), 379–400. https://doi.org/10.1207/S15327051HCI16234_17

Sweeney, M. E. (2016a). The intersectional interface. In S. U. Noble & B. M. Tynes (Eds.), *The intersectional internet: Race, sex, class, and culture online* (pp. 215–228). Peter Lang.

Sweeney, M. E. (2016b). The Ms. Dewey "experience:" Technoculture, gender, and race. In J. Daniels, K. Gregory, and T. McMillian Cottom (Eds.), *Digital Sociologies* (pp. 401–420). Policy Press.

Sweeney, M. E. (2020). Digital assistants. In N. B. Thylstrup, D. Agostinho, A. Ring, C. D'Ignazio, & K. Veel (Eds.), *Uncertain archives: Critical keywords for big data* (pp. 151–159).

Sweeney, M. E. & Villa-Nicolas, M. (2022). Digitizing the 'ideal' Latina information worker. *American Quarterly*, 1–35.

Van Dijck, J. (2014). Datafication, dataism and dataveillance: Big Data between scientific paradigm and ideology. *Surveillance & Society*, 12(2), 197–208. https://doi.org/10.24908/ss.v12i2.4776

Waller, V. (2016). Making knowledge machine-processable: Some implications of general semantic search. *Behaviour & Information Technology*, 35(10), 784–795.

Waterman, D. A. (1985). *A guide to expert systems*. Addison-Wesley.

Weizenbaum, J. (1976). *Computer power and human reason: From judgment to calculation*. Freeman.

Williams, R. (1958). *Culture and society: 1780–1950*. Columbia University Press.

14

Gender and Identity in Human–Machine Communication

Leopoldina Fortunati

GENDER AND IDENTITY: SOME NOTES

This chapter is about how gender and identity have been shaped historically in the scientific debate regarding the evolution of communication from in-person to human–machine communication (HMC) via computer-mediated communication (CMC). My objective is placed obliquely with respect to two very popular approaches that have highlighted, first, the great benefits of digital media, and second, their de-socializing effects. Here, I take another stance and I situate my analysis in another framework that acknowledges a process that occurred in parallel and that so far has been quite neglected by scholars. This process is the progressive increase of the physical separation among individuals that has been strengthened thanks to digital media and the increase of disembodied communication. Within this framework, I analyze gender differences at the communication level, trying to capture the political and social meaning of the various communication shifts that have occurred so far.

Before going into the description of this framework, it is necessary to briefly mention that as Rakow (1986, p. 21) argues, "gender is both something we do and something we think with, both a set of social practices and a system of cultural technologies. The social practices – the 'doing' of gender – and the cultural meanings – 'thinking the

world' – ... constitute us as women and men, organized into a particular configuration of social relation". The vision of gender has passed from being binary (including men as a group and women as a group) to acknowledging the differences among women and among men (Eckert & Wenger, 2005, p. 165) and its intersectionality with other variables such as age, ethnicity, and class. In particular, post-structural thinking opened up a discourse on the social constructivism of gender, proposing additional categories – such as transgender – leading to the notion of a "gender continuum," which made room for third genders, agender, two-spirit, and different dimensional models of gender (Søraa, 2017). The structure of the chapter is organized as follows: in the next section I will analyze the theme of gender in in-person communication and in CMC. In the following section I will focus on HMC and in the conclusion I will offer some final reflections.

THE PHYSICAL SEPARATION OF INDIVIDUALS IN THE SHIFT FROM IN-PERSON COMMUNICATION TO HMC VIA CMC

This discussion is pivotal because gender is an important marker of identity that helps people relate to one another, is characterized by cultural norms and practices, and is bound to power structures and relationships. Drawing on it, there is the need to generate an analytical framework capable of addressing the question of women's agency and subjectivity in the social changes that have reshaped gender relations in the shift from in-person communication to CMC and HMC. The theoretical framework of reference for this analysis is informed by the long tradition of feminist Marxism (e.g. Dalla Costa & James, 1972), that will help me outline the historical and social meaning of the relation between gender, communication, and technology.

Within this framework, the pivotal element is that the shifts from in-person communication to CMC and HMC progressively deter human beings from having in-person communication and co-present relationships with each other. As Jones writes (2014, p. 251), these devices, "by mediating our relationship with the things they control and with our selves further remove us from our environment and ultimately from one another." In other words, these shifts outline the progressive removal of individuals' presence from the communication context. This powerful process in reality describes a new phase, in which the traditional division of labor in factories and offices is accompanied by the physical division of all the individuals among themselves. Such a physical division has been accelerated by globalization, a process in which capital was obliged to migrate toward developing countries to recuperate a high level of profits (Gambino, 1975), and which has created borderless worlds, communities, organizations, and politics. To weaken the new freedom that the erasure of borders brought with it, capital has needed to strengthen the physical separation of individuals by means of a specific genealogy of information and communication technologies (ICT): telephone, mobile phones, computer/internet, robots, chatbots, voice-based virtual assistants, and so on. The physical separation among individuals weakens the possibility of creating solidarity among them or a political and trade union awareness. This process however does not only weaken their bargaining power, but also breaks down even human/machine binaries. Lash (2002) was the first to intuit that contemporary societies are based less on present social relationships and structures than on communication technologies. The physical separation between individuals describes not only a weakened worker – male and female – (and weakened citizens) but also has two further consequences: on the one hand, men and women are more easily controlled (Zuboff, 2019), and above all, on the other hand, they have become an additional source of surplus value production.

In fact, the labor force no longer works only in the production sphere, but also, and increasingly, in the sphere of domestic reproduction, creating an enormous amount of value. The physical separation of one individual from the other is an attack against all humankind, but it is also a specific attack against women and the domestic sphere, because it devalues the reproduction of the labor force, which is the outcome of women's work process.

WOMEN'S AGENCY AND POWER STRUGGLE ON THE DYNAMICS OF COMMUNICATION AND MEDIATED COMMUNICATION

In the domestic sphere, the network of personal and family technologies has the specific implication of amplifying the gendered and racialized division of labor in the home. While it prevents the rooting of the process of individual reproduction in the materiality of life, it works as a privatizing mechanism which decreases the need to leave the house or talk to, interact or make love with another human being, legitimizing the development of relationships of domination and dehumanization (e.g. Schiller & McMahon, 2019). This process has a particular importance regarding the gender issue, because it takes place in a historical moment in which, in the domestic sphere, after the various waves of feminism, women had reshaped gender power relationships more in their favor, had strengthened their mastery and control over in-person communication (where, as we will see later, no or very small differences between men and women are documented), had appropriated communication in the public sphere, and had reshaped power relationships also between generations inside the family. The power gained by women at the communicative level was reduced through the arrival of digital technologies and their diffusion in the domestic sphere. This attack against women did not find a solid resistance from women, who continued to opt for the domestic appliances (so-called white goods) that could liberate them immediately from a certain amount of material fatigue and produce a more equal division of labor within the household, and to neglect the electronic and digital devices (so-called brown goods), which were perceived by them as more connected to entertainment and information. This women's strategy was labeled by Gray (1992) "calculated ignorance." However, given the unequal power relationships within the family, becoming competent in the use of domestic appliances has been socially posited as a sign of women's lack of power, while males' competence in the use of information and communication technologies (ICTs) has ended up strengthening their greatest power. In this process there has been a crucial shift for the gender issue: the introduction of the computer in the domestic sphere. Specifically, through the computer women's strength in communication was downsized (e.g. Herring & Martinson, 2004), since this artefact was designed primarily by males for males (especially intended in affluent Western markets). Among digital technologies, the computer has been a specific case in which appropriation by women was particularly difficult, whereas research shows that women tend to be more open than men to the technology when it is easy to use (Vankatesh & Morris, 2000). Women consequently have needed more time to domesticate and appropriate these devices, not becoming early adopters in this case either. To conclude this discourse, the most relevant gender difference that crosses all these fields of communication is that, differently from men who are equally under attack as workers and citizens, women were also affected by these technologies as women, that is in their identity, and thus became more vulnerable than men. In the next section we will analyze specifically the role of gender in the two precursors of HMC: in-person communication and CMC.

GENDER IN IN-PERSON COMMUNICATION AND IN CMC

Gender in in-person communication

Communication is a social process, in which individuals create meanings by reading, viewing and listening to and with one another. Communication is at the basis of the formation of social relationships and ultimately of how society forms. In the communication process each interlocutor makes sense of the attributes and traits of the other interlocutor in relation to the self. The visibility of others and their acting is important since the awareness of their appearance and behavior is an essential part of this process. The physical presence of the interlocutors generates a context in which they perceive themselves as co-inhabiting a spatial environment (self-location) and sense that they can interact with that environment. Similarly, social presence corresponds to the sense of "being there with a real person," and consists of the separate feelings of co-presence and psychological

involvement and of the perception of potential interaction. As a consequence, as Richardson (2015) puts it, individuals only experience their full humanity, and I would add their full sociality, when confronted with other humans. There are other elements, however, to consider in in-person communication – presentation of the self, the role of the human body, sociality, and labor – just to cite some – that are all pivotal to understanding the social foundations of in-person communication and to capturing the changes that the mediation of technology has introduced in the relation between gender and communication. The presentation of self, supported unavoidably by the materialization of the human body, serves to facilitate social categorization (mainly gender, age, and ethnicity), putting in motion stereotyping and discrimination processes that are the costs derived of automatic, category-based information (Eyssel & Hegel, 2012). At the same time, it responds, within certain terms, to criteria of visibility, authenticity, and reciprocal control. The role of the body is illuminated by the notion of embodied cognition, according to which cognition is affected by the physical sensations and the actions of the body (Varela et al., 1992). The voice, which represents an extension of the human body, is fundamental in in-person communication as it allows us to implement social categorization and regulate social behaviors. People rely on all the bodily cues to form impressions and make judgments of the interlocutors. These cues serve to avoid communication uncertainty and predict the mental and physical status of others, helping communicators to manage their conversations and build interpersonal relationships.

Like many other domains, communication is subject to the shaping of the social structure and its class stratification, based on the attribution of more social, political, and economic power to men, who have to mediate the power of capital toward women, children, and the older adults. The power difference between men and women, combined with the weight of social construction of gendered identities and gendered socialization processes as well as the strength of stereotypes, norms, expectations, and performances, has shaped a different relation with communication on the part of men and women. But after the first and second waves of feminism, scholarship has documented the existence of very small or no sex differences in communication behavior, thanks to the findings that emerged in several meta-analyses exploring many dimensions and variables of communication: from men's and women's self-disclosure to language and verbal ability.

How can we make sense of this lack of differences? We can hypothesize that this gap in communication has practically disappeared or that the gender differences have migrated towards other dimensions of the daily life. What is sure is that sex is no longer that wall capable of dividing men and women in a frontal way, at least in the communication domain. I argue that the erosion of this wall has implicated for capital the need to erect, as mentioned in the introduction, other walls to articulate the strategy of dividing individuals from the other and also to rearticulate at a higher level the gender division of communication work along the lines of sex and gender. These new walls have been reintroduced by the spread of digital technology.

This scenario typical of in-person communication has been profoundly affected, as we will see, by the diffusion of CMC, which is both a source and a consequence of gender relations, and in which "social relations (including gender relations) are materialized" (Wajcman, 2010, p. 147). How in this scenario has gender been reshaped by CMC, and in turn, how have computers been reshaped by gender?

Gender in CMC

The process of separation of individuals from each other reached a higher level with the diffusion of CMC, but this separation did not proceed in the same way for anyone. Women are the target of a double attack: they are separated by the computer, as everyone is, from each other, but they are in many cases also separated by the computer itself. Although the history of the computer has been made also by women – not least at the programming level – (e.g. Light, 1999, p. 455), women's omission from the history of computer science has perpetuated "misconceptions of women as uninterested or incapable in the field" as well as the lack of female role models who use computers. The gendering of computing has emerged from hyper-masculine fraternity cultures of computer design, "against which feminist technologists and designers have worked to carve out spaces and create more equitable products" (Lingel & Crawford, 2020, p. 3). By configuring the computer/internet as an "everybody" tool and by applying I-methodology, their designers made the computer/internet as a clear example of how it has come to incorporate barriers against specific groups of users, such as women, the older adults, and the differently able (Oudshoorn, Rommes, & Stienstra, 2004). With the diffusion of CMC, the masculine culture has been played heavily against women. This gendered culture was strengthened by the fact that the diffusion of the computer at

home has replicated the same scheme of ownership, access, and use as the fixed telephone. Like the fixed telephone, the computer was usually bought by the husband/father, who also paid for its use and maintenance, and it was used, when possible, by all the members of the family, prefiguring its collective use. This structure obviously tended to replicate in computer/internet access and consumption the same power structure shaping the family and the society. Another element that has characterized the more difficult appropriation by women of the computer/internet, is that this technology required not only financial resources to access and maintain it, but also many prerequisites, including computer literacy and the achievement of various skills, both quite time consuming, while time was just what women did not have at their disposal. Among women there was the widespread sensation that the computer/internet was not serving them well (Wajcman, 2010, p. 146).

In CMC the human body disappeared completely from the interlocutor's vision, even more severely than in telephone communication, since even the voice disappeared except in chatrooms and on videos. This disappearance of the body has led designers to not focus sufficiently on incorporating users, and in particular users' identity, in the design process. The lack of the human body in the communication process involves also the presentation of the self, which becomes something with which one can play by hiding oneself behind nicknames, or through avatars.

The absence of the body had the primary consequence that social cues as well as non-verbal cues were blocked in CMC, and this made it difficult to manage proper communication and, for example, to correctly identify interlocutors, including their gender (e.g. Savicki and Kelly, 2000). This feature of CMC has had specific consequences for women. The computer environment was built from the beginning as a written and silent world in which women, who have always been more sensitive than men to social cues in general, and to non-verbal cues in particular (Henley, 1977), have been deprived of the use of this specific ability. If we consider that the non-verbal message greatly overwhelms the verbal one (e.g. Birdwhistell, 1970; Mehrabian, 1981), we have an idea of the disadvantage that this technological artefact has entailed for women.

Another specific difficulty for women came from the fact that the internet is a public arena and historically women have had more difficulty than men speaking in public, because their life and work was centered especially within the four walls of the house. This is one of the elements that explains why at the beginning of the internet's history women's presence in online discussion and communication was quite smaller than that of men.

The studies of sex differences are generally characterized by the same flaws outlined by Carey (2005) regarding internet studies: they are ahistorical, lack a comparative perspective, and are not related to the foundational categories of the social sciences. Moreover, they do not problematize the notions of sex and gender. For example, the peculiar female use of communication tools for reproductive aims (support, affect, etc.) is not typical of women as such, but of women whose social role is based on the foundations of the sphere of reproduction. Playing this role historically has shaped women's abilities and preferences in certain directions instead of others. Consequently, gender stereotypes continue to be perpetuated even in scientific research. Recently, they are even exacerbated by the current use of machine learning tools in language processing, since these often translate and incorporate gender biases.

In addition to these stereotypes, the results of the research carried out in the first decade of internet diffusion risk strengthening stereotypes, because they continue to be cited as timelessly valid findings. On the contrary, if gender differences in access and use of the computer/internet persisted almost for two decades, now the gender gap is being reduced. According to ITU, in 2017 the only region where the percentage of women using the internet is higher than that of men is the Americas, where, not by chance, gender parity in tertiary education is more widespread. Since 2013 the gender gap has narrowed in most regions, while in Africa it has widened. There the percentage of women using the internet is 25% lower than that of men. And in Least Developed Countries (LDCs) "only one out of seven women is using the internet compared with one out of five men" (ITU, 2017, p. 4). The internet continues to show that men and women use it for different purposes.

In the next section, focused on HMC, we will see how the process of individuals' separation from each other, put in motion in in-person communication and in CMC, will reach its peak.

GENDERING ROBOTS AND VIRTUAL ASSISTANTS

If in CMC the individual is separated from others by means of a machine that mediates communication between them and that, at the same time, connects and distances them, in HMC each individual is separated by the others even more

radically. Individuals disappear from the communication scene, since they talk to a machine that responds to them. However, whereas houseworkers valorize the individual reproduced by them, machines can only transfer their own value and, as a consequence, individuals are subjected to a deep devalorization. But, if HMC is a devalorization for all, for women it represents a double devalorization, one first as individuals and second as houseworkers, since their reproductive work is made superfluous.

In this shift many features of the communication scenario change, since in the new environment technologies are designed as communicative "subjects" (Guzman & Lewis, 2020, p. 71). For example, with voice-based virtual assistants and social robots the presentation of self by the human interlocutor – fundamental feature of the dynamics of human–human interaction – no longer exists. Humans do not spontaneously present themselves to the robot; now the issue is how to incorporate in the robot all the information regarding themselves to make the robot capable of recognizing them. The materiality of the human body has become a secondary presence that is only partially implicated in human–robot interaction, whereas the material body of the technological artefact acquires great importance. In the case of virtual assistants, the human voice comes back as a feature, as it was in the experience of telephone and mobile communication as well as of the automatic voice recorded in the answering machine, which has trained millions of users to acquire the habit and the discipline of talking to a machine. In human–robot communication, human communication from being a spontaneous flow becomes disciplined within the automated paths of conversation that the robot is able to perform. Furthermore, communication with robots is based on their capacity to simulate a conversation, and this devalues from the sense-making of communication itself by humans, who are used to a relatively high degree of authenticity in in-person communication. More than facilitating communication, AI automates communication and the social processes connected to it (Gehl & Bakardjieva, 2017). Moreover, emotional exchange in human–machine communication is reduced to the fact that robots can recognize prod-users' emotions from their voices and react appropriately, but so far they are unable to feel and thus to convey emotions to their users. Warmth, which is one of the main elements exchanged in social relationships, becomes difficult to manage for robots, and thus the quality of the social relationship they can offer is quite poor.

Even sociality in human–robot interaction, being deprived of emotions, can only be stereotyped and automated. If compared with our understanding of what social interaction and the 'social' are, the outcome of human–robot inter-action is a rudimentary form of sociality which reduces the degrees of freedom of flesh-and-blood interlocutors, and it is unclear what will be the consequences for our ability to interact with human beings (Cranny-Francis, 2016). Weber (2005, p. 213) suggests that this understanding of sociality serves to minimize users' expectations towards social robots and to trigger a naïve, non-demanding attitude toward them. Are we really convinced, she continues (p. 215), that we are able to repair the deficiencies of our social life in terms of care and company with the basic sociality that social robots can offer to women, older adults, children, disabled, ill persons, and so on?

The debate developed on gender and HMC has focused not only on sex attitudes and behaviors towards robots, chatbots, and virtual assistants, but also on the sex of machines. The research on sex differences in human–robot interaction has drawn from the CASA (Computers as Social Actors) paradigm (e.g. Reeves & Nass, 1996). By means of a series of experiments Nass and his colleagues demonstrated that people instinctively tend to treat computers like humans. Several scholars, such as Eyssel and Hegel (2012), extended this approach to robotics. In human–robot interaction robots' appearance, voice, and demeanor pro-vide the social cues that guide social perception and the categorization processes, although voice was the main cue to trigger gender stereotyping of machines, while other peripheral signs and sym-bols are hair length and pink or gray lips. In Nass, Moon, and Green's (2007) experiments, evalu-ations supplied by a male computer were taken more seriously than those provided by a female computer, as if the voice would mirror the power stratification at the social level. This result was later confirmed by Powers and Kiesler (2006). As Jung, Waddel, and Sundar (2016) documented, minimal visual gender cues on the robot's inter-face are sufficient to cause people to assign gender to robots. If a gender cue is not provided, robots tend to be perceived generally as male; if it is pro-vided, the robot with a male cue is perceived as more masculine and the robot with a feminine cue is perceived as more feminine. The real problem is that robot sex is affected by the cultural order of gender which is in force in most societies.

In particular, anthropomorphic robots pose the problem of their sexual identity, because the more humanlike a robot is, the more gendered it becomes. Both Bray (2012) and Søraa (2017) argue that attributing gender to a robot is inevi-table: first, because for humans a way to express gender is through technology, and second, because if people want to talk to robots, they need to give

them names (and usually a name raises expecta-tions about robots' gender) and to use pronouns when they talk about the robots. The gendered voice and appearance of a robot is usually matched by the stereotyped gender of its occupational role. The "matching" hypothesis suggests that when the robot's appearance matches stereotypical occupa-tional roles this can influence users' willingness to comply with the robot, but it can also strengthen gender/occupation stereotypes and reinforce gen-der divides in human society.

Nomura (2017) found that female participants, compared to male participants, are less likely to have a positive view of robots (although he high-lighted that the gender differences can interact with moderate factors). Taipale et al. (20185), drawing on a representative sample of Europeans (N = 26,751), showed that, among 70% of respondents who declare to have a fairly or very positive view of robots, men have a slightly more positive vision than women. This gendered vision can be explained by the fact that women have less interest in scientific discoveries and techno-logical development. Women's lukewarm attitude towards science and the latest technological inno-vations is probably a reaction against the original sin of science and technology, which historically have been largely managed by male scholars and professionals, who have built this field of knowl-edge in their image and likeness and not in an inclusive way. Other studies (e.g. Reich-Stiebert & Eyssel, 2017) did not find significant sex dif-ferences. Another set of studies challenged gen-der stereotypes. For example, Eyssel and Hegel (2012) proposed that designers should "develop gender-neutral or counter-stereotypical machines to counteract the stability of personal and cultural stereotypes" (p. 2224). In this debate on gender and HMC a great contribution is given by two sources of reflection: the Stanford website http://genderedinnovations.stanford.edu/case-studies/genderingsocialrobots.html, that addresses espe-cially the theme of gender stereotypes, and the European funded research project GEECCO on gender and feminist aspects in Robotics (Pillinger, 2019). However, at the present moment we cannot follow Suchman's (2019) suggestion to explore the mundane practices of the use of social robots, which are at the basis of the big issues, because social robots are still at the prototyping level and thus users have a very limited direct experience of them.

A particular discourse has to be dedicated to voice-based virtual assistants such as Alexa, Siri, Cortana, holograms, and chatbots, which are programmed to have credible conversations with humans. Several feminist scholars have expressed criticism of how AI has inscribed gender bias in

AI-based computer systems (e.g. Noble, 2018). Siri, Cortana, and Alexa, for example, combine technological innovation with retrograde visions of gender. These virtual assistants are very popular since they are used regularly by 600 million people worldwide (Leskin, 2018), and they are clearly linked, first to the idea of the female secretary, or, better, the female administrative assistant (e.g. Woods, 2018), and second, to the idea of the housewife (Walker, 2020). The motivation that is at the base of this kind of programming choice is that in the last few decades the professional figure of the administrative assistant has been made superfluous by the computerization development. Thus, today only high-level managers have a secretary, while all the medium and medium-high managers (among whom many are men) have to incorporate administrative work into their duties, or to deal with the outsourcing of administrative work to call centers or service enterprises in the Global South (Lingel & Crawford, 2020, p. 9). Faced with these upheavals, what could have been more flattering for ordinary men and ordinary women or for ordinary families than the possibility of having their own administrative assistant, albeit virtual? In particular, Alexa represents exactly the proposal of an automatic administrative assistant for everyone, on which to vent the frustrations of the world of work by commanding her to perform several types of work, from calling a telephone number to regulating room temperature and lighting. Regarding the second occupational role embodied by Alexa, the digital housewife, this has been designed to replicate a docile and subjected housewife (who probably never existed), that is, to re-propose a model of woman that was imposed about fifty years ago. Why did Alexa, designed as she has been described, arrive in today's homes, inhabited by women who have been able to radically redefine the power relationship with partners as well as the division of domestic labor? As Schiller and McMahon (2019) propose, this represents the inoculation of regressive behaviors (starting from communication) within the household, both toward women (the first to be attacked) and toward children. Children are taught that women respond on command, and this narrative, based on maleness and whiteness, claims to enforce a connection between women and obedience that has never been true in the real world.

Another important source of political concern toward women and children is not only the command tone with which Alexa is addressed but also the behaviors of harassment and violence expressed by users toward her. These violent behaviors on the one hand mimic aggressive and disrespectful behaviors toward secretaries, housewives, and women in general, and on the other, protest and rebel against a tricky artefact that is very far from being effective. Actually, Alexa proposes a communicative scheme free from any bargaining and negotiation, while in real life communication between women and men is also a field of tension, conflict, and confrontation. In the real world women react, struggle, and elaborate strategies to acquire more power in their relationships while talking to men and to combat potential violence. Eliminating from communication between humans and robots the power dynamics which characterize the field of human communication implicitly gives the green light to the virtual exercise of violence.

I also interrogate the social and political implications of the diffusion of robotization in the domestic sphere. First, I ask to what extent can machines automate reproductive labor and thus relieve some of its burden. This is an old question that has already received the right answer: it has been observed that the volume of housework increases correspondingly to the efficiency of the new machines. These machines surely relieve a part of the segment of the reproductive labor related to information processing (not to manual labor), but in compensation, additional work is required to program and manage machines like Alexa.

Second, scholars ask to what extent robots, chatbots, and virtual assistants can actually push further the machinization of the worker (e.g. Delfanti, 2021). This will depend on the level of agency that people will be able and willing to invest in controlling and eventually contrasting the diffusion of these technological artefacts. At the same time, it is worth recalling that there is an impassable limit to the humanization of machines that is identifiable in several elements, from the machines' lack of awareness of the self to their incapacity to think and feel (e.g. Fortunati et al., 2021).

Robots and virtual assistants are also an information retrieval and storage tool. In addition to serving value production in the domestic sphere, they perform household surveillance and harvest data on preferences, affects, behaviors, and histories of users to further develop markets and sell products. Moreover, the perpetuation of gender stereotypes passes through the content that these machines process in conversation and that "may be populated with existing sounds, images, from which memories can be called upon by a machine, algorithmically, interactively, sometimes stored from prior interactions with us or from the collective communication of other users, or in other cases, agents that originate communication without reference to pre-existing texts" (Jones, 2014, p. 253). What impact this has on the quality of the meaning we process together with the machines and on us remains to be explored.

CONCLUSION

This analysis of gender and communication has allowed us to capture the social and political meaning of the shift from in-person communication to HMC via CMC. The framework that has emerged describes an increasingly strong attack against women as productive subjects, which has been launched by means of the technology. The battle took place, also by means of technologies, in the field of communication, but it has involved other domains of the society, primarily the process of valorization in the sphere of reproduction. However, there is need for future research to deepen the analysis just sketched here on the recent history of gender and human–machine communication.

REFERENCES

Berger, C., & Calabrese, R. (1975). Some explorations in initial interaction and beyond: Toward a developmental theory of interpersonal communication. *Human Communication Research*, 1, 99–112.

Birdwhistell, R.L. (1970). *Kinesics and context. Essays on body motion communication*. University of Pennsylvania Press.

Bray, F. (2012). Gender and technology. In *Women, science, and technology: A reader in feminist science studies* (pp. 370–381). Routledge.

Carey, J.W. (2005). Historical pragmatism and the internet. *New Media & Society*, 7(4), 443–455.

Cranny-Francis, A. (2016). Is data a toaster? Gender, sex, sexuality and robots. *Palgrave Communications*, 2(1), 16072.

Dalla Costa, M.R., & James, S. (1972). *The power of women and the subversion of the community: Women and the subversion of the community*. The Falling Wall Press.

Delfanti, A. (2021). Machinic dispossession and augmented despotism: Digital work in an Amazon Warehouse. *New Media & Society*, 23(1), 39–55.

Eckert, P., & Wenger, E. (2005). What is the role of power in sociolinguistic variation? *Journal of Sociolinguistics*, 9(4), 582–89.

Eyssel, F. and Hegel, F. (2012). (S)he's got the look: Gender stereotyping of robots. *Journal of Applied Social Psychology*, 42(9), 2213–2230.

Fortunati, L., Manganelli, A.M., Hoëflich, J., & Ferrin, G. (2021). Exploring the perceptions of cognitive and affective capabilities of four, real, physical robots with a decreasing degree of morphological human likeness. *International Journal of Social Robotics*, online first.

Gambino, F. (1975). Composizione di classe e investimenti diretti statunitensi all'estero. In L. Ferrari Bravo (Ed.) *Imperialismo e classe operaia multinazionale* (pp. 318–359). Feltrinelli.

Gehl, R.W., & Bakardjieva, M. (Eds.) (2017). *Socialbots and their friends: Digital media and the automation of sociality*. Routledge.

Gray, A. (1992). *Video playtime: The gendering of a leisure technology*. Routledge.

Guzman, A., & Lewis, S.C. (2020). Artificial intelligence and communication: A human-machine communication research agenda. *New Media & Society*, 22(1), 70–86.

Henley, N.M. (1977). *Body politics: Power, sex, and nonverbal communication*. Prentice Hall.

Herring, S., & Martinson, A. (2004). Assessing gender authenticity in computer-mediated language use: Evidence from an identity game. *Journal of Language and Social Psychology*, 24, 424–446.

ITU (2017). *ICT. Facts and figures 2017*. International Telecommunications Union.

Jones, S. (2014) People, things, memory and human-machine communication, *International Journal of Media & Cultural Politics*, 10(3), 245–258.

Jung, E. H., Waddell, T. F., & Sundar, S. S. (2016). Feminizing robots: User responses to gender cues on robot body and screen. In *Proceedings of the 2016 CHI Conference Extended Abstracts on Human Factors in Computing Systems* (pp. 3107–3113). San Jose, CA.

Lash, S. (2002). *Critique of information*. Sage.

Leskin, P. (2018, October 10). Over a million people asked Amazon's Alexa to marry them in 2017 and it turned them all down. *Business Insider*. http://www.businessinsider.com/amazons-alexa-got-over-1-million-mariage-proposals-in-2017-2018-10.

Light, J.S. (1999). When computers were women. *Technology and Culture*, 40(3), 455–483.

Lingel, J., & Crawford, K. (2020). "Alexa, tell me about your mother": The history of the secretary and the end of secrecy. *Catalist: Feminism, Theory, Technoscience*, 6(1), 2380–3312.

Mehrabian, A. (1981). *Silent messages: Implicit communication of emotions and attitudes*. 2nd Edition, Wadsworth.

Nass, C., Moon, Y., & Green, N. (2007). Are machines gender neutral? Gender-stereotypic responses to computers with voices. *Journal of Applied Social Psychology*, 27(10), 864–876.

Noble, S.U. (2018). *Algorithms of oppression: How search engines reinforce racism*. New York University Press.

Nomura, T. (2017). Robots and gender. *Gender and the Genome*, 1(1): 18–25.

Oudshoorn, N., Rommes, E., & Stienstra, M. (2004). Configuring the user as everybody: Gender and design cultures in information and communication technologies. *Science, Technology & Human Values*, 29(1), 30–63.

Pillinger, A. (2019). Gender and feminist aspects in robotics. Retrievable at www.geecco-project.eu/fileadmin/t/geecco/FemRob_Final_plus_Deckblatt.pdf

Powers, A., & Kiesler, S. (2006, March 1–3). The advisor robot: Tracing people's mental model from a robot's physical attributes. *Proceedings of the Conference on Human-Robot Interaction (HRI 2006)*, Salt Lake City, UT, pp. 218–225.

Rakow, L. (1986). Rethinking gender research in communication. *Journal of Communication*, 36(4), 11–26.

Reeves, B., & Nass, C. (1996). *The media equation: How people treat computers, television, and new media like real people and places*. Cambridge University Press.

Reich-Stiebert, N., & Eyssel, F. (2017, March). (Ir)relevance of gender?: On the influence of gender stereotypes on learning with a robot. In *Proceedings of the 2017 ACM/IEEE International Conference on Human-Robot Interaction*, 166–176.

Richardson, K. (2015). The asymmetrical 'relationship': Parallels between prostitution and the development of sex robots. *ACM SIGCAS Computer & Society*, 45(3): 290–293.

Savicki, V., & Kelley, M. (2000). Computer mediated communication: Gender and group composition. *CyberPsychology & Behavior*, 3(5), 817–826.

Schiller, A., & McMahon, J. (2019). Alexa, alert me when the revolution comes: Gender, affect, and labor in the age of home-based artificial intelligence. *New Political Science*, 41(2), 173–191.

Søraa, R. A. (2017). Mechanical genders: How do humans gender robots? *Gender, Technology and Development*, 21(1–2), 99–115.

Suchman, L. (2019). If you want to understand the big issues, you need to understand the everyday practices that constitute them: Lucy Suchman in conversation with Dominik Gerst & Hannes Krämer. *Forum: Qualitative Social Research*, 20(1). Text available at www.qualitative-research.net/index.php/fqs/article/view/3252

Taipale, S., Sarrica, M., de Luca, F., & Fortunati, L. (2015). Europeans' perception of robots implications for social policies. In J. Vincent, S. Taipale, B. Sapio, G. Lugano, & L. Fortunati (Eds.) *Social robots from a human perspective*, pp. 11–24. Springer.

Vankatesh, V., & Morris, M. (2000). Why don't men ever stop to ask for directions? Gender, social influence, and their role in technology acceptance and usage behavior. *MIS Quarterly*, 24(1), 115–39.

Varela, F.J., Thompson, E.T., & Rosch, E. (1992). *The embodied mind: Cognitive science and human experience*. The MIT Press.

Wajcman, J. (2010). Feminist theories of technology. *Cambridge Journal of Economics*, 34, 143–152.

Walker, T. (2020). "Alexa, are you a feminist?" Virtual assistants doing gender and what that means for the world. *The iJournal*, 6(1), 1–16.

Weber, J. (2005). Helpless machines and true loving care givers: A feminist critique of recent trends in human-robot interaction. *Information, Communication & Ethics in Society*, 3(4), 209–218.

Woods, H.S. (2018). Asking more of Siri and Alexa: Feminine persona in service of surveillance capitalism. *Critical Studies in Media Communication* 35(4), 334–349. DOI: 10.1080/15295036.2018.1488082

Zuboff, S. (2019). The age of surveillance capitalism: The fight for a human future at the new frontier of power. *Public Affairs*.

15

Literature and HMC:
Poetry and/as the Machine

Margaret Rhee

"A poem is a small (or large) machine made of words." – William Carlos Williams

Machines and literature are often thought of as separate concepts, disciplines, and objects; however, there are rich interconnections between the two which speak to the dynamic promise of human–machine communication (HMC). Both literary artists and scientists have written on the intersections of literature and HMC such as the epigraph above from poet William Carlos Williams on the "poem is a small (or large) machine." In another important example, computer scientist Alan Turing in his landmark 1950 paper "Computer Machinery and Intelligence" on artificial intelligence (AI) refers to the sonnet as a key syllogism for AI. Additionally, literature – specifically science fiction – has informed science in society. Early myths of the ancient golem as artificial beings coming to life shaped early ideas of the robot; *Frankenstein; or, The Modern Prometheus* by Mary Shelley is known as the first science fiction novel, and the 1921 play by Karel Čapek *Rossum's Universal Robots* actually coined the word robot and replaced the word automaton for artificial beings in society and science. These literary and scientific examples speak to the rich and dynamic interconnections of HMC and literary arts. As Turing poses, while the two – poetry and

technology – seem disparately connected, technology is intimate, poetic, and humanized, and the poetic can be technologized and when doing so, it illuminates HMC through a literary light.

This chapter provides an overview, genealogy, and speculations of the interconnections with literature and HMC. Although the chapter will cover metaphors of poetry and the machine, such as Williams's writing in the epigraph that frames this chapter that "[a] poem is a small (or large) machine made out of words," additional sections of the chapter include further exploration on how computer scientists such as Turing included poetry and literature in their scientific theorizations to help shape the possibilities of human and machine relations, and when playwrights such as Čapek transformed the meanings of machines in society through his science fictional visions. I demonstrate a historical, genealogical, and conceptual approach to the intersections of literature and HMC by analyzing key scientific theory and literary works and then I turn to contemporary examples of poetry that address how literature and HMC offers new directions for justice. Additionally, I include personal insights as a poet working in these intersections of HMC and literature to help further illuminate these interconnections between machine and literature. As we contemplate how technology informs machine–human interactions, useful to this is how literature informs human–machine communication and thus, helps to envision a future of HMC that is humanistic and as the contemporary examples attest, aligns with justice. In our ever increasing digitalized every day, language has become even more punctuated and transformed with the interconnections of technology with humanity. How do machines speak to us? How do we speak to machines? Could we speak together? While these machine and literary connections and questions may seem limitless or confusing, in our digital world, therein a responsibility for critical engagement and pleasure in the intersection of HMC and literature for future possibilities.

HUMAN–MACHINE COMMUNICATION: BACKGROUND

In the article, "What is Human-Machine Communication, Anyway?" scholar Andrea Guzman articulates that HMC is less about "people's interactions with technology" and is a "concept and an area of research within communication."[1] If communication is a human-only process, human–machine communication intervenes in a human-centric approach. When the medium is the message, as stated by media theorist Marshall McLuhan, the literature is not a telegram and the relationship with HMC illuminates new findings in our digital world. Rhonda McEwen et al. write in their study on disabled children and machine technologies: "The case for human-machine communication is strong for people for whom the machine is not only a tool, but is an integral part of their expression and access to information."[2] Along with this intervention of seeing the machine not as a static object, but an interactive and communicative one with humans provides an essential opening to understanding HMC. This sheds light on the deconstruction of logics between human and machine made in Donna Haraway's formative article, "The Cyborg Manifesto." Published in 1983, Haraway's article formatively transformed feminist critique in her theorization of the cyborg. Haraway writes, "The cyborg appears in myth precisely where the boundary between human and animal is transgressed"—it is a "theorized and fabricated [hybrid] of machine and organism; in short, we are cyborgs."[3] Perhaps similarly, this chapter aims to theorize the hybrid and cross disciplinary lens of literature and HMC dismantling binaries and not adhering to the notion that literature or technology is more valued. Instead of the juxtaposition of literature and technology, I aim to demonstrate bridging. Drawing from science and technology studies and art, Peter Galison and Caroline Jones's *Picturing Science, Producing Art*,[4]

for example, speaks to the complexity of these divides. Similarly, I hope to discourse by discussing literature that adds to the rich conversations of HMC and bridges the epistemological gap between art and science.

IS A POEM A MACHINE?

When poet and physician, William Carlos Williams, most known for his poetry about the everyday such as "This Is Just To Say" wrote in *The Wedge* (1944) "…A poem is a small (or large) machine made out of words," or "poetry is a machine which drives it, pruned to a perfect economy" he may not have been contemplating human and machine communications.[5] However, as he writes that the poem is, "As in all machines, its movement is intrinsic, undulant, a physical more than a literary character," he speaks to how literature is informed by technology and machines as a metaphor.

However, Williams is not the only time a poet has referred to a poem as a machine. Take for instance, Edward Hirsch in his epigraph on the sonnet: "There must be something hardwired into its machinery—a heartbeat, a pulse—that keeps it breathing…" Certainly the sonnet, invented in Italy in the 1200s, a 14-line poem, of infinite possibilities; "a little sound or song," of iambic pentameter, tightly structured, and the Shakespearean, or the Petrarchan with the volta, the turn between the eighth or ninth lines is mechanical. Williams' notion of the sonnet as mechanical relates to Turing's connection of AI bridging the discourses of literature and machine learning. If poets have been informed by machine and human communications, we can turn to scientists and their utilization of poetry and the machine. As Turing writes in a section in his article "Computer Machinery and Intelligence":

Q: Please write me a sonnet on the subject of the Forth Bridge.
A: Count me out on this one. I never could write poetry.
Q: Add 34957 to 70764.
A: (Pause about 30 seconds and then give as answer) 105621.
Q: Do you play chess?
A: Yes.[6]

In Alan Turing's theory of AI, two surprising components are shared in his thinking and conceptualization. In this section I refer to the ways that the human interrogator is "replaced" by a machine, and in order to understand artificial intelligence, the machine passes the test. There are two less commonly known tests in Turing's test, including the gender test, and the test for the sonnet. These both attest to the contours of issues of difference such as gender, and the intersection of technology and literature at the crux of these essential questions of technology and communication today. The key to this trick is not whether the machine is artificially intelligent, but whether the human could guess it was a machine.[7]

Turing begins his article by asking the question:

"Can machines think?" This should begin with definitions of the meaning of the terms "machine" and "think." The definitions might be framed so as to reflect so far as possible the normal use of the words, but this attitude is dangerous. If the meaning of the words "machine" and "think" are to be found by examining how they are commonly used it is difficult to escape the conclusion that the meaning and the answer to the question, "Can machines think?" is to be sought in a statistical survey such as a Gallup poll. But this is absurd. Instead of attempting such a definition I shall replace the question by another, which is closely related to it and is expressed in relatively unambiguous words.[8]

For Turing, the new replacement of the imitation game is stated to be played by (A) Human, (B) Human, and (C) Interrogator. If the human cannot guess who or what is human and machine, the machine is artificially intelligent. However, initially the game for artificial intelligence otherwise known as the "imitation game" was played by three people and gender: "a man (A), a woman (B), and an interrogator (C) who may be of either sex." For Turing, the object of the game is for the interrogator to determine the gender of the individuals. Questions are asked such as:

"C: Will X please tell me the length of his or her hair?

Now suppose X is actually A, then A must answer. It is A's object in the game to try and cause C to make the wrong identification. His answer might therefore be:

"My hair is shingled, and the longest strands are about nine inches long."

In this section, Turing contemplates the many dimensions of how one can deduce gender in the imitation game. From this test of gender, he then turns to machine intelligence. He writes: "We now ask the question, 'What will happen when a machine takes the part of A in this game?' Will the interrogator decide wrongly as often when the game is played like this as he does when

the game is played between a man and a woman? These questions replace our original, 'Can machines think?'"[9]

From there, Turing offers the syllogism from above on the sonnet, and he writes further on the sonnet and AI:

I do not think you can even draw the line about sonnets, though the comparison is perhaps a little bit unfair because a sonnet written by a machine will be better appreciated by another machine.[10]

ROSSUM'S UNIVERSAL ROBOTS

Written in 1920, premiered in Prague in 1921, and first performed in New York in 1922—the play *R.U.R. or Rossum's Universal Robots* not only provided global fame for Karel Čapek, it popularized the word robot as a common lexicon and replaced the word automaton. As mentioned earlier in this chapter, Čapek's play *R.U.R. or Rossum's Universal Robots* marks the first use of the term robot which spread internationally and replaced the word automaton for an artificial being. After premiering in Prague, the play traveled to the United States to New York in 1928, and then to the television screens of the BBC where it became the first BBC televised science fiction program globally. With highly resonant technological themes, *RUR* demonstrates how the scientific and technological terms travel from literature to society and technology.

When Čapek coined the term robot in his Czech play, he described a world made up of labor and robots, and it was the robots who completed the labor as artificial slaves. The wide proliferation of the play, aligned with the globalization of industrialism, speaks to the resonance of a world imagined with "man" did not work, and cheap artificial beings did. Artificial beings as "laborers" emerged from the history of the word *robot*; it comes from the Czech word *robota*, which means "obligatory work or servitude." Similarly, robots in *RUR* were also produced as cheap workers, and the play demarks a cultural turn in understanding robots not as magical beings, and not simply as labor, but as *cheap* labor. Discussing the role of the robot in the passage above, the character Domain, a factory manager of the RUR factory, explains that the best robot is the "cheap" laborer, and the robot has "no soul."

RUR begins in a factory that creates artificial beings from organic matter. Rather than machinery like the robots we imagine today, they are living creatures of artificial flesh and akin to a process like cloning. The robots resemble humans however as we can see defined in the play as without human traits. The story of the factory includes the experiments of a Darwin figure-like scientist named Rossum who travels to the island to study marine biology. Rossum accidentally discovers a chemical like protoplasm, and attempts to make animals, and a man, but fails. Like Shelley's famed story *Frankenstein*, Čapek was influenced by the notions of the creation of an artificial being. His nephew the young Rossum visits him, and with more capitalist aligned intentions, he creates a synthetic human called a robot (Czech for worker). The young Rossum makes robots that are cheap, numerous, easily replaceable, and now ubiquitous all over the world as laborers.

RUR opens with the introduction of Helena Glory, the President's daughter who visits the factory. Helena Glory is empathetic and an advocate for robots. She believes they should be freed. However, when robots were first created by the scientist older Rossum, his grandson, the "younger" Rossum in a process similar to cloning, the artificial beings are understood not to have a soul, and to serve human beings all over the world. As inexpensive workers, they were produced in mass quantities and shipped to global countries in the South Pacific Island where the factory was set. For Helena as the daughter of the company's owner, and ironically president of The Humanity League for the rights and freedoms of robots, understanding the process would aid the freeing of robots. However, in the first act she learns more about the history of creating an artificial being – including the several attempts from the older Rossum – and the mass production that she witnesses taking over the world at the moment. The factory is created with a "spinning wheel" for nerves and veins, and "vats for preparation."

By the end of Act I, Helena Glory meets Henry Domain who not only educates her on the inhumanity and working robots, but also asks her to marry him. This allows her to stay on the island, where she lives in close proximity to the robots. This leads to the events in the second and third act a as Helena attempts to save and stop the creation of robots. However, the plot progresses ultimately to leave us with robots killing the humans at the factory, including Helena and later, to the dystopian conclusion of the end of the human world. Within theater, plays such as *RUR* illustrate how robots shed light on dystopian themes and illuminate how robots shed light on literature.

ELIZA

With the development of computer technologies, we can turn to the 1960s' ELIZA as an early natural language processing computer platform which worked as an interactive play, perhaps bringing the dialogue exchange of a play like *RUR* to life. ELIZA performed dialogue between humans and machines as an early chatbot and while not meant to be an artistic platform, ELIZA demonstrates the early formations of HMC and literature within electronic forms. Along with ELIZA, the continued exchange between literature and HMC point to the development of electronic literature aligns the intersection of technology and literature and blurs the boundaries of genres. ELIZA is one early example of the ways interaction between humans and text could be performed, whether intentional or not, and chatbots, interactive fiction, and social media such as Twitter, for example, illuminate how society shifted in human communication with and alongside machines.

CYBORG POETICS

To help track these developments, artists and scholars in electronic and experimental poetry have noted the large variety of poetic practices encompassing the term cyborg poetics or e-poetry. The intersection of machines and poetry include: "code poetry, hypertext poetry, poetry produced via search engines and other digital poetry experiments. Poems using email or tweets. Poems that envision collaboration between programmers and poets" as scholar Susan Vanderborg wrote in 2012. The gamut of "cyborg poetics" includes various experiments with form, technology, and poetics. Artists and poets who work within this genre include Nick Montfort, John Cayley, Stephanie Strickland, Mark Marino, and others. Scholarship written in the 1990s such as Matthew Kirschenbaum's "Machine Visions" details how electronic literary texts engage with AI and experimental graphic design, the article itself is on a website and accompanied with animations, language movement, reading of the "lyric automaton."[11] As programmer poet and scholar Neil Aitken cites, "Daniel Tiffany links the lyric poem to magical Loss Glazier in his formative work on electronic poetry," these inscriptions which were meant to be invoked through speech, as well as the idea that such speech acts called into something into existence out of pure language.[12] Aitken writes that the "spell or poem then is not a poem itself but like 'a recipe or a set of instructions to transform the intangible into the materially real.'" Aitken later describes how code works similarly, the code itself is words, and when compiled, the execution produces a result. The code must run.

ELECTRONIC LITERATURE IN THE 1980s TO CONTEMPORARY MOMENT

Key electronic literature projects from the 1980s and 1990s include Eduardo Kac's Holopoetry (1983–1993) as Kac produced a series of holographic poems throughout the 1980s and 1990s. He used raster and vector-based software to model and animate the movements of texts, after which each sequence would then be transferred to hologram. Kac's holopoetry explored nonlinearity through placing text in three-dimensional space. Feminist e-lit artist Judy Malloy created; several foundational texts in hyperfiction and interactive literature in the 1980s and 1990s as well. One early piece is *Uncle Roger* (1986), which comprises three files telling parallel narratives, which she describes as a "hyperfictional narrative database," including an authoring system that she would use for many subsequent works called "Narrabase." In Diane Greco's *Cyborg: Engineering the Body Electric* (1989) she investigates the figure of the cyborg both thematically and formally. N. Katherine Hayles wrote that the piece's "hybrid form is so completely interwoven with the electronic prostheses through which we encounter it that the cyborg body is the text, and the text is the cyborg body." In the 1990s, works such as by Deena Larseon, *Marble Springs* (1993), Shelley Jackson, *Patchwork Girl* (1995), and Stephanie Strickland, *True North* (1997) all shed light on electronic literature as a new form of HMC literary arts. We can turn to prolific and groundbreaking coder and artist Darius Kazemi's "Bot Poetry" and "Galatea" by Emily Short for recent electronic literature works. In addition, new media artworks such as Shu Lea Cheang's "Brandon" was the first new media artwork acquired by the Guggenheim and shed light on the politics of transgender rights, narrative, and hate crimes. All these works illuminate the powerful intersection of digitality and machines, quite like the way Alan Turing may have imagined it being possible in the 1950s.

LOVE, ROBOT

Readers may see there is an emphasis on poetry in this chapter, and I write specifically in regards to poetry, because I am a poet, and when completing a book on science fiction poetry, the ACM graduate student magazine asked me to contribute an article to the Human-to-Human issue instead of Computer–Human Interaction in which I draw from here.[13] This section draws from my article in the ACM graduate magazine on my poetry collection entitled *Love, Robot* to help illuminate the connections between HMC and literature. Writing about robots poetically sprung from a conversation I had when I was a graduate student. At the time, I worked with several roboticist-artists, namely Ken Goldberg who served on my dissertation committee. While my scholarly work centers on culture, race, and difference as a theoretical and historical project, his work and others in robotics and computer science piqued my artistic explorations of the robot. My robot emerged during my poetic explorations, one that largely centered on themes of race, sexuality, and class that sheds light on HMC. As a scholar studying media and literature, I could not ignore the current digital age as a societal phenomenon, and so I sought to engage with science, technology, and robotics in poetry.

The uncanny similarities and slippage between the two—poetry and AI—I hoped would frame my poetry collection and prompt the exploration of poetry, love, and AI. Without being engaged with robots and technology as a cultural history and poetic approach, my poetry would have lacked the grounding and imagination that AI theory, computer science, and other fields could offer. Philosophically, I am interested in how robots teach us what it means to be human. The robot offers us so many questions to grapple with, in our urgency for humanity, compassion, empathy, and justice. Could we think of robots as entities that evoke more compassionate characteristics than humans? Could we think of robots as object-choices of desire, or as more compassionate lovers?

Research then inspired my poetry. For example, my poetry on robot love draws upon Alan Turing's question, "Can machines think?" As a poet, I switched the "think" to "love." In addition, there is the question of the sonnet and artificial intelligence (AI) that Turing poses. Could a machine write poetry? Would it then prove humanity? On the other hand, I was researching poetics and learned about how we can think of poetic forms, such as the sonnet, as machines. My own reflection of my collection is short, and I leave it up to others to review or critique the book.[14]

When I reflect back on the experience of writing my poetry book alongside the dissertation project, I fondly remember the importance of conversations that are paradisciplinary. Not only across the humanities and social sciences, but the sciences as well. This approach centers prominently in this work, as I attempt to highlight the imbricated bridges of ethnic studies and science and technology studies. Moreover, I focus on conversations that are founded on the development of questions, and not only the performance of knowledge. The intersection of poetry with machines provokes a creative and intellectual interaction. The conversation, as ephemeral as it may be, "is a human-human interaction also conducive to consider. As we contemplate how technology informs human-human interactions, it may be useful to reenact on human-human interaction and engagement with literature, namely with words. The cybernetics of these kinds of relations never stops short of being astonishing."[15]

ANALYSIS OF HMC LITERATURE: WORRA, LAI, KEARNEY, AND WILSON

To help these themes, in this section I provide a reading of four literary artists – Bryan Thao Worra, Larissa Lai, Douglas Kearney, and Keith Wilson – who engage with HMC in their reincorporation of the cyborg through subversive and aesthetics strategies. Thao Worra, Lai, Kearney, and Wilson provide an extraordinary intervention between literature and HMC while at the same time addressing key facets of social justice such as race, diaspora, and power. Their work is compelling in regards to the illumination of machine communication, and their work illuminates new directions in the field.

How would you prove you are human?

Bryan Thao Worra, The Robot Sutra

01110011011000010110000100110000101110100101100100011001010110011 begins the poem by Lao American poet Bryan Thao Worra "The Robot Sutra."[16] As the first Lao American to be accepted as a member of the Horror Writer Association and the Science Fiction Poetry Association, and where he serves as president, Thao Worra is an exciting poet who crosses both fields of technology, genre, and literature. Mixing languages of Laotian and English, Thao Worra utilizes the robots to describe workers in Minneapolis as:

It took a pack of jokers working overtime
In the world's largest padaek factory
In the Laotown quarter of North Minneapolis

As Thao Worra writes the padaek factory takes the place of the robot factory in *RUR* or the show factory in North Adams, and we're placed in the "Laotown of North Minneapolis." By taking on the role of AI, the fish sauce known as padaek is the factory that "little laobots" make leaving other tasks to humans. By taking on the notions of automation, Thao Worra shapes HMC in a literary way drawing from code and human languages such as Laotian and English that illuminates the politics of labor, race, and diaspora:

Little Laobots running around
Trying only to make people happy,

Banned from murder and injury.
What absurdity,
Leaving dreadful responsibilities to mere humans!

Larissa Lai, The Automaton Biographies

Like Thao Worra, poet and fiction writer Larissa Lai's work in literature reimagines HMC and poetry. Recent North American SF (science fiction) poetry has created some of the most provocative reimagining of lyric subjects and forms via the mechanical figure of the robot. Larissa Lai's love poems in *Automaton Biographies* (2009) use a replicant character from *Blade Runner* to portray Asian immigrants and women longing for an autonomy reserved for white men.[17] In *Do Metaphors Dream of Literal Sheep?* (2010) science fiction scholar Seo-Young Chu analyzes the connections between science fiction (sf) and the lyric, arguing that sf has always had "lyrical" characteristics.[18] Lai utilizes epigraphs from *Blade Runner* and Donna Haraway in her book. In Lai's work, the quote from Haraway includes, "The Replicant Rachel in Ridley Scott's film *Blade Runner* stands as the image of cyborg culture's fear, love, and confusion." In her work, she rewrites Rachel from *Blade Runner* utilizing the robot as a figure in her literary arts. At times, Lai would literally "translate" the visual scenes of *Blade Runner* into poetic description, while in other gestures, move into illuminating the consciousness of Rachel one is never privy to while watching the film.

Douglas Kearney, The Black Automaton

"the first black you met was on the radio. / this is true even if you lived with blacks," writes Douglas Kearney in his innovative collection *Black Automaton*.[19] Kearney illuminates Black life and resistance through retelling the myth of John Henry and incorporating the black robotic lion in Voltron through his innovative graphic design and lyrics that crosses and transform the boundaries between poetry and art. As a counter to anti-Blackness, Kearney's innovative poetry transforms the book as new media, and presents interventions with the robot through Afro-futurism. Along with thinking about technology and Black life, Kearney addresses Katrina in his poems "Flood Song Series" and how technology can help illuminate race and contemporary social issues. In the poems about John Henry, Kearney reasserts the myth of John Henry: "Mr J Hammer Henry / with your black /as rail spike neck / mallet muscled Mr J Bama / Henry outlantish from station…" As a folklore, the legend of John Henry recounts an African American man who sought to beat a "steam powered machine" illuminating through literature the violence through the robot. In the collection, "rock drilling machine" during the industrial period, only to die from stress, and the "hammer in hand." Kearney retells John Henry's story with an explicit critique against U.S. industrialization and the confrontation of the humans and machines binary for African Americans and writes:

no one doubts your heart John
the busted meat of it the machine
carve the right angles of your grave
raise high its robot arms
Then.. " giving America a charlie horse
CLANG! CLANG! CLANG! CLANG! let them drop
on down…"

Kearney's work demonstrates the provocative and necessary interventions of HMC in literature in addressing anti-Black violence in history, the present, and the future.

Keith S. Wilson, *The Uncanny Emmett Till*

In the visual poem "Uncanny Emmett Till," poet and game designer Keith Wilson re-narrativizes racializing history with the uncanny valley as a metaphor – visually and literally – for the experience of racialization and the 1955 violent murder of fourteen-year-old Emmett Till.[20] In Wilson's hands, the well-known theory by Japanese

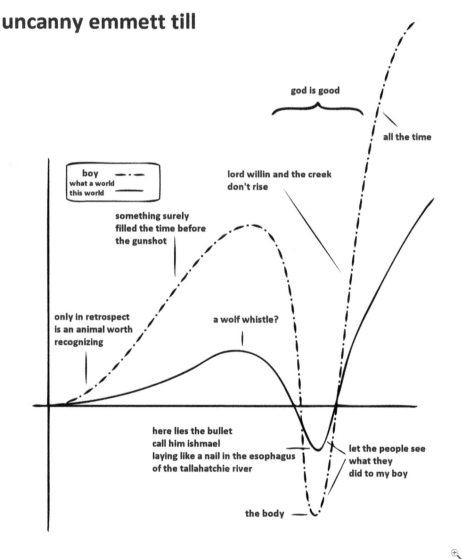

Figure 15.1   Uncanny emmett till

roboticist Masahiro Mori includes an evocative chart of robots and human likeness, transforms into a minimalistic and visual poem that charts Till's story and notions of race, the body, justice, the body, otherness, and freedom. According to Mori, the more affinity (or familiarity) the robot has with humans, the less affinity the human feels due to feelings of "uncanny" similarity to the human. In the uncanny valley, a robot perceived as being too human evokes uneasy feelings and even repulsion and disgust. However, Wilson utilizes the uncanny valley to depict the uneasy feelings of racism against Black bodies in a white supremacist world. The robot depicts racism experienced by African Americans often to terrifying ramifications as the valley becomes a site of otherness in Wilson's redesign.

In the "Uncanny Emmett Till" Wilson depicts racialized violence and the sequences of Emmett Till's story through details of the graph. The square key for the graph that indicates the y and x axes changes from "Moving" to "Boy" and "Still" to "What a world, this world" which illuminate the racist structures and the risks and harm when one moves, which shape the lives and untimely deaths of young Black men like Till. Till was only fourteen years old when subjected to a false accusation of sexual violence by a white woman and then brutally murdered by her husband and white racists. The murder galvanized the civil rights movement in the South. By changing the axes of the graph, Wilson reclaims the trajectory and movement of "robot" into one that centralizes the Black experience throughout the sections of the graph.

Wilson provocatively changes the terms of the uncanny valley, from "zombie" to "the body" which depicts the gruesome hate crime and murder of the body that was displayed in an open casket by Emmett's Till's mother. The dip in the graph states: "Let the people see what they did to my boy," leads the eye to the original "zombie" status of the robot and refers to the violence and inability to identify Till's mutilated body. Wilson sutures the dissonance between "robot" and Black person through remixing the graph. In doing so, he also illuminates the irony and violence of the category of "human" and "robot" in the original uncanny valley that does not consider race. Wilson retells a brutal anti-Black story through redesigning the uncanny valley into visual poetry and into a poetics of resistance.

Both Kearney and Wilson utilize the automaton to discuss and resist anti-Black racism through riveting visual poetry. Drawing from violent histories and myths, both Wilson and Kearney retell history without reinscribing racist structure through renaming and rebuilding their own design through graphics and words. Specifically, Wilson writes about Emmett Till through rewiring the uncanny valley graph and Kearney rewrites the Black automaton and myth of John Henry. The poets utilize graphics, lyrics, and music to resurrect the robot to illuminate the struggle and survivance of Black life. Kearney and Wilson's visual poetry animates what is often invisible in the histories of racist acts of violence and reasserts the possibilities of the HMC and poetry as a site for freedom.

CONCLUSION

If we consider the diverse meanings of communication between human and machine, the central questions illuminated by literature help us understand further the complexity and possibilities of HMC. Poets and artists such as Worra, Kearney, Lai, and Wilson shed light on how literature and HMC fuses poetry and HMC for a vision of a socially engaged world for justice. Their literary work utilizes the thematic of the robot as a means of addressing pertinent social issues and history such as Black violence, gender representations in film, immigration, diaspora, class, and labor. In doing so, they illuminate the creative modalities of the automaton in poetry and the intersections of HMC and literature. If Alan Turing imagined the possibility of artificial intelligence with a vision of a machine writing a sonnet, then literary artists such as Worra, Lai, Kearney, and Wilson discussed at the end of this chapter illuminate the limitless possibilities of HMC and poetry as an important facet of artificial intelligence.

We began this journey of HMC and literature by tracing the rich interconnections between machines and literature which speak to the dynamic possibilities of human machine communication. Literary artists and scientists have shed light on the intersections of literature and HMC such as William Carlos Williams, Alan Turing, and the poets and artists analyzed in this chapter illuminate the rich intersections of HMC and literature. This chapter provides an overview, genealogy, and contemporary examples of the interconnections with literature and human–machine communication. Specifically, the chapter demonstrates a historical, genealogical, conceptual, and poetic approach to the intersections of literature and HMC.

While most people think of machines and literature as separate concepts, disciplines, and fields, there are rich interconnections between the two which speak to the promise of human–machine communication (HMC). As McEwen et al. write on "machine is not only a toll, but…an integral part of their expression…" literary artists have utilized the machine to express important themes of justice and dismantle binaries. As Turing poses, while the two – poetry and technology – seem disparately connected, technology is intimate, poetic, and humanized, and the poetic can be technologized. Literary and scientific examples speak to the rich and dynamic interconnections of HMC and literary arts, mutually informed by technology and at the same time, shaped by literature. In this chapter, I also include personal insights as a poet working in these intersections of literature and HMC.

Future directions of HMC research can include literary interconnections and questions of difference such as race, gender, ability and class in history, the present, and the future. While there has been significant writing on humans and machines in feminist, literature and cultural studies, the intersection of HMC and literature is an exciting point of departure and brings new horizons in the bridging of both fields. Poets and artists who examine and speculate on HMC to address race, gender, and other differences in their literary works offer new and important paths of resistance and future making at the intersections of HMC and literature in the present and future world. As we contemplate how technology informs machine–human interactions, useful to this is how literature informs human–machine communication. Literature helps us to envision a future of HMC and the world that is humanistic, technological, and aligned with justice.

ACKNOWLEDGEMENTS

For this article, I thank Ken Goldberg for his long time mentorship, and to interlocutors such as Judeth Oden Choi and Alexis Lothian. I also thank former research assistants Blair White and Morgan Sammut for their assistance on this article in particular.

NOTES

1   Andrea Guzman, What is human-machine communication, anyway? In *Human-machine communication: Rethinking communication, technology, and ourselves* (New York: Peter Lang), 2018: 2.

2   McEwen, R., Atcha, A., Lui, M., Shimaly, R., Maharaj, A., Ali, S., & Carroll, S. (2020). Interlocutors and interactions: Examining the interactions between students with complex communication needs, teachers, and eye-gaze technology. *Human-Machine Communication*, 1, 113–131. https://doi.org/10.30658/hmc.1.7

3   Donna J. Haraway, A cyborg manifesto: science, technology, and socialist-feminism in the late twentieth century. In *Simians, cyborgs, and women: The reinvention of nature* (Routledge, 1991), 149–181.

4   Picturing Science, Producing Art Edited By Peter Galison, Caroline A. Jones, Routledge, 1998.

5   Williams. C.W. *Introduction. Selected essays of William Carlos Williams*. New Directions, 1969.

6   Alan Turing, Computing machinery and intelligence, *Mind* LIX, no. 236 (October 1950): 433–460, DOI https://doi.org/10.1093/mind/LIX.236.433.

7   Margaret Rhee, On beauty: Gamers, gender, and Turing, edited by Bonnie Rueberg and Steven Wilcox, First Person Scholar, March 2016.

8   Alan Turing, Computing machinery and intelligence," *Mind* LIX, no. 236 (October 1950): 433–460, DOI https://doi.org/10.1093/mind/LIX.236.433.

9   Full text on the Loebner Prize website: www.loebner.net/Prizef/TuringArticle.html. Massachusetts Institute of Technology, last revision October 29, 2015.

10 Excerpts from Alan Turing, Computing machinery and intelligence, *Mind* 59: 433–460, (October 1950), p. 406.

11 Matthew G. Kirschenbaum, Machine visions: Towards a poetics of artificial intelligence, *ebr*, vol. 6, November 1997.

12 Susan Vanderborg, *-empyre soft-skinned space*, 2017, empyre@lists.artdesign.unsw.edu.au. Accessed Sept. 19, 2020; Neil Aitken, *-empyre soft-skinned space*, 2017, empyre@lists.artdesign.unsw.edu.au. Accessed Sept. 19, 2020.
     Loss Pequeño Glazier. *Digital poetics: The making of e-poetries*. Tuscaloosa: University of Alabama Press, 2002. 500 Daniel Tiffany. *Toy Medium: Materialism and Modern Lyric*. U of California P, 2000.

13 Margaret Rhee, Robots and poetry, XRDS: Crossroads, The ACM Magazine for Students December 2017.

14 Susan Vanderborg, "I still want all the bits of you": Margaret Rhee's robot love lyrics, *Journal of the Fantastic in the Arts* 30(2): 2019. 198–218.

15 Margaret Rhee, Reflecting on robots, love, and poetry.

16 Bryan Thao Worra, "The Robo Sutra," Machine Dreams Zine, edited by Margaret Rhee, 2017. 2017

17 Larissa Lai, The Automaton Biographies, Toronto: Arsenal Pulp Press, 2009.

18 Seo-Young Chu, Do Metaphors Dream of Literal Sleep? *A Science-Fictional Theory of Representation Cambridge, Harvard UP, 2011.*

19 Douglas Kearney, *The Black Automaton*, Fence Books, 2010. 531.

20 Keith Wilson, Uncanny Emmett Till, *Connotation Press*, July 2019; Keith Wilson, Uncanny Emmett Till, Machine Dreams edited by Margaret Rhee, 2017.

16

Human–Machine Communities: How Online Computer Games Model the Future

Nathaniel Poor

People form communities, bonds with others, by communicating (Carey, 1989; Dewey, 1927; Gamble et al., 2014; Strauss, 1978). We communicate and bond with many nonhuman entities as well, such as our pets, robots, and even characters in video games. In this chapter, I explore a specific type of online video game, the massively multiplayer online game (MMO), and the lessons it offers about how societies with both human and artificial intelligence (AI) actors can eventually work. MMOs can have thousands of both human-controlled *player characters* (PCs) and computer-controlled *non-player characters* (NPCs): avatars wandering around a virtual representation of a three-dimensional world, talking to each other, and working together to create in-game communities with a mixture of economic and social activities.

We are edging closer to this mixed human–machine community outside of games. We have computerized helpers such as Amazon's Alexa and Apple's Siri, both voice-centric smart assistants. AI-driven recommender systems suggest products for us to buy. Some people's lives are already heavily infused with computer agents, and these relationships work to the extent they do because the people and the software-based agents communicate with each other. Computer games are similarly infused with communication between people (the human players) and the AI agents (the computer-driven characters). Games are an interesting test of how hybrid communities might work at a large scale when computer agents become more widespread and perhaps human in form, due to the widespread human–machine communication that takes place within game communities.

HUMAN–MACHINE COMMUNICATION (HMC)

Perhaps the first computer program with which people communicated—via text typed on the computer keyboard—was *Eliza*, created in the 1960s (Bassett, 2019). *Eliza* responded to a person's input in a computationally simplistic way, often mirroring back their sentence as a question. Some people found *Eliza* to be a convincing and emotionally moving experience and felt a bond with the program. Today we have many more *Eliza*-like, computer-driven entities in our lives (Guzman, 2018), and researchers have studied how people view computers as actual social actors (Nass et al., 1994; Reeves & Nass, 1996), much in the same way people respond to other people. Unsurprisingly, this extends to characters in video games (Lombard, 2018).

Video games generally have two types of characters: PCs, controlled by a human player, and NPCs, controlled by the game (a computer). With both human and computer control, PCs and NPCs parallel real-world humans and robots. Most NPCs don't look like robots; they appear as, and play the role of, humans, elves, or space mutants, depending on the game. But they are fully controlled by the computer code for the game. When human players interact with NPCs, the humans are interacting with computer-driven entities.

Researchers have studied how humans interact with robots, finding that some people see a close bond between humans and robots. Robots can be "kin" to humans (Edwards, 2018, p. 44) or are even viewed as being alive (Sandry, 2018). Researchers have also studied the relationships that video game players have with their in-game character (avatar), finding that gamers view these avatars in a different ways, including as a virtual being independent of themselves (Banks, 2015; Banks & Bowman, 2016). With enough of these human-to-robot bonds, or PC and NPC bonds, a community is the result. One definition of *community* comes from Preece (2000), who focused on three elements: *people* who interact, their shared *purpose*, and their *policies* for behavior. For hybrid communities, we need to adjust our thinking about the *people* aspect to include software agents, such as AI, smart appliances, robots, and NPCs in computer games.

HMC IN A SINGLE-PLAYER GAME

Before presenting massively multiplayer games, I examine a single-player game, as the two have many similarities. Starting by examining a game with only one human player and hundreds of NPCs is simpler than examining a game with thousands of human players and hundreds of NPCs—yet the analysis easily scales up. Currently, NPCs in single-player games are a bit more interactive than NPCs in MMOs, so they are a more illustrative example.

There are many examples to choose from. I use the video game *Skyrim* from 2011 (officially, *The Elder Scrolls V: Skyrim*). *Skyrim* takes place in a frozen northland within the typical fantasy setting of elves, wizards, magic swords, and dragons. It also has a large game world, with cities, towns, hamlets, and other locations and with hundreds of NPCs to enliven the virtual world. An important part of bringing life to the virtual world is to have the NPCs interact with the player. In the current generation of single-player games, NPCs

talk with the player using recorded voice acting. Players choose text options to speak back to the NPCs. Talking with others is one way we humans bond with them, even if those others are not actual people. People also bond by just spending time together (Granovetter, 1973), although we usually talk to each other when doing so. In *Skyrim*, the player doesn't really have to talk to any NPCs to play the game (except in the introduction). However, if they do not, they will find it an exceedingly boring game. NPCs fill in the player on the lore of the land (the cultural setting), gossip about other NPCs (the community), and give quests to do.

Many of *Skyrim*'s NPCs live an in-game version of normal lives. They wake up in the morning, get out of bed, and go to their jobs. Some are merchants, who will exchange goods for coin. There are farmers, miners, smiths, townsfolk, and priests. There are soldiers, rebels, and bandits. Some, like most bandits, just try to kill the player, but players can interact with hundreds of different NPCs—and there are even a few to marry. One type of *Skyrim* NPC that players end up interacting with a lot is a follower: an NPC who pledges their support to the player and who generally helps the player in combat, as a computerized teammate (Nass et al., 1996).

The first follower most players meet in *Skyrim* is Lydia. One can easily find fan-written fiction (fanfic) about her online, but one of my favorite game narratives centers on one player who accidentally killed her and then tried to bury her body (Walker, 2011). Burying the dead is culturally appropriate (Geertz, 1973), and it is something we do for those we care about, as this player did. Lydia's purpose is mostly functional (defeating opponents and carrying items), but some players bond with her even though she is a virtual robot.

NPCs have both instrumental and social roles (Dabbish et al., 2012). Many are mostly instrumental: they all help the game function as a game for the player. Some characters are mostly economic, such as merchants. Others are primarily quest givers. Still others are more basic and simply help fill out the game world: like extras in a movie, they may not have named roles or have many lines to speak.

Socially, some characters tie into the game's imagined social connections. Local lords, for instance, wield power and influence over other characters. If a player befriends one faction, characters of opposing factions may refuse to deal with the player. If the player has not been initiated into a group, that group will not give the player any quests; one has to earn their trust. One cannot just marry any other character—the player has to woo them first. To succeed at any of this, the player must interact with the characters. The interactions between the player and all of these computer-driven characters reveal and create the social relations that the player must track and navigate, much as we do in real life (Gamble et al., 2014).

Gamers will be able to easily think of more examples of game worlds with these social dimensions, as well as examples that do not fit this profile (like *Pac-Man*). In *Stardew Valley*, players live within the complexities of a community, interacting with a wide variety of characters. In *Fallout 4*, set in a futuristic yet 1950s retro nuclear wasteland, players have to decide which factions to ally with, creating social ramifications for their actions. In *Red Dead Redemption 2*, set in a fictionalized, late-nineteenth-century American Wild West, players are part of a band of con men (and women) and general rogues, and they have to keep the band on its feet economically while navigating a complex social environment filled with bandits, merchants, ranch hands, barmaids, clergy, and many others. All these examples are situations in which the player character, controlled by the human player, exists within a world populated with similar NPCs, avatar-beings, and in which social connections matter. But the PC is the only one that is human-controlled; everyone else is run by the game's processes on the computer.

The term we use for the NPCs may influence how we think about them. Are they AIs, scripts, programs, or virtual robots? "AI" sounds fairly powerful, while "script" sounds plainly simple. All NPCs can be described as scripts ("if this happens, do this"), but some are more complex than others. "Program" may be a good framing for our understanding of them, as some are simple (like town guards) and some are more complex (characters that have many interaction and behavioral options). But even a relatively simple program, such as *Eliza* or *Skyrim*'s Lydia, can be sophisticated enough to prompt some players to form a connection with whatever they imagine that program is.

World of Warcraft, *EverQuest II*, and *The Elder Scrolls Online* (*ESO*), which are all fantasy-based. Some are different, such as *EVE Online*, a space-based game that is not avatar-focused and has no behavioral rules imposed by the developers (Carter et al., 2016), although it is still highly social (Ramirez, 2018). What all these MMOs have in common is that they are designed for a large number of simultaneous players, who can all encounter each other and interact in the game world.

In many MMOs, players form *guilds*: semi-permanent, long-term affiliations between players. Guilds are supported by a game's code, and researchers have consistently noted that although guild members share in gameplay and economic actions, many guilds have a social component (Cărătărescu-Petrică, 2015; M. Chen, 2012; Ducheneaut et al., 2007; O'Connor et al., 2015; Poor, 2019; Poor & Skoric, 2014; Ramirez, 2018). NPCs may play an instrumental role in some guilds (such as market access) but usually not a social role.

MMO worlds are *persistent*: the game and other players will continue without the player, and things change when one is not there. A player can always log in, regardless of how many other players are in-game. Single-player games stop when one is not playing them; time is frozen for the single-player game world and all of the characters in it. Some MMOs have a night and day cycle; but because the game worlds are persistent, players (who may be in different time zones) find it more convenient for NPC-run shops to be always available. So some NPCs in MMOs never sleep and are always at their posts.

Despite these differences, there are enough similarities to jump from analyzing a single-player game to analyzing an MMO: specifically, the in-game interactions between PCs and NPCs, and the communities that people form with NPCs in these games. Most interactions between PCs and NPCs can be framed as either instrumental (perhaps economic) or social (Dabbish et al., 2012).

HMC IN A MASSIVELY MULTIPLAYER SETTING

MMO games are complex settings, but all are highly social (M. Chen, 2009b, 2012; V. H. Chen & Duh, 2007; Ducheneaut & Moore, 2004; Nardi & Harris, 2006; O'Connor et al., 2015; Poor, 2019)—in part due to human sociality and in part due to the benefits of teaming up to take on more difficult in-game challenges (Jakobsson & Taylor, 2003). Many MMOs are similar in genre, such as

INSTRUMENTAL INTERACTION

Quests are a large part of fantasy MMOs. Much as *The Hobbit* (Tolkien, 1937) revolves around a quest in which Bilbo Baggins must help a group of dwarves regain treasure from a dragon, so too do in-game quests give narrative structure to players. Quests also usually make PCs more powerful by allowing them to gain experience and better equipment. Almost all these quests, and some of the rewards upon their completion, come from NPCs.

Although quests can be social in nature, and questlines may be long and involve interacting with many NPCs along the way, quest giving itself is rather straightforward: the player talks with the quest giver. Talking to NPCs in a quest-driven game is vital for players.

Some characters, like town guards, can act as information kiosks, telling players where various people (NPCs) and services are located around town. This feature is especially helpful to players who are new to a location in a game. Players also frequently ask other players about gameplay specifics in general chat, in their guild chat, and in forums outside the game. Many other NPCs also act in an instrumental manner, one with an economic angle.

ECONOMIC INTERACTION

Economic interactions with both PCs and NPCs make up an important part of many MMOs (Castronova, 2005; Dibbell, 2007; Nardi, 2010; Poor, 2019; Taylor, 2006). With some NPCs, like shopkeepers who buy and sell items, the primary interaction is often not dialog but essentially a spreadsheet showing a cost per unit of whatever is for sale. These NPCs are basically a human-like (or elf-like, etc.) robot with an interface to their store, the player's bank, or the game's market. Buying and selling items directly with players can be more complex and may involve bidding or back-and-forth text chat. Some games implement a brokerage interface so that both players (buyer and seller) can verify the item and the amount. NPCs enable a large part of the economic activity that occurs in MMOs. It may not be social; but it can be looked at as a large amount of work in terms of human-equivalent time and effort, and it requires accuracy and trusted database access.

SOCIAL INTERACTION

Players in MMOs are highly social because people are highly social, regardless of context (Gamble et al., 2014). MMO players have weddings (C. Y. Chen, 2007; Grimmelmann, 2004; Poremba, 2003) and funerals (Gibbs et al., 2012, 2013; Servais, 2015) for both in-game characters and human players; and their groups can fall apart for various, often social, reasons (M. Chen, 2012; Ducheneaut et al., 2007; Poor & Skoric, 2014).

Social interaction can be important to a player's success in and enjoyment of an MMO (Agre,

2004; M. Chen, 2009a). Most true social interaction in MMOs occurs among players, as any social interaction between NPCs is, to date, fully scripted and lacks variability—although it is scripted to mimic real human interaction. All the MMO social research I am aware of focuses solely on social interaction among players and not with NPCs— yet we know that people find even basic computer programs socially compelling. NPCs in MMOs do have a large amount of social information about the game world and other NPCs; but given that most MMO game worlds are fairly static, many NPCs do not wander too far from their given location and rarely have new information to give out.

Not all in-game player-to-player interaction is positive. Some players enjoy posting juvenile things in general chat and griefing (Bakioglu, 2009; Dibbell, 2008; Foo & Koivisto, 2004; Paul et al., 2015). Griefing, a form of harassment, is something done to other players and not typically to NPCs, as NPCs do not react in the same way as some human players do. Griefing has a social component that NPCs are not programmed to react to.

AN EXAMPLE: *THE ELDER SCROLLS ONLINE*

ESO, an MMO based on the world of *Skyrim* and launched in 2014, serves as a nice example for our purposes for at least three reasons. One is that I know it well enough to explain it. Second is that every NPC interaction is voiced, meaning they speak all of their lines. The third reason is somewhat more technical in that, unlike in older MMOs, most players occupy the same technological, and thus social, world.

First, *ESO* is in some ways a typical fantasy MMO, with elements from Tolkien and *Dungeons & Dragons*, and is similar to older fantasy MMOs like *World of Warcraft* and *EverQuest II*. An in-game character has skills and equipment and generally levels up by completing quests given by NPCs or gaining experience in some other way.

That brings us to the second point: NPCs engage in other social interactions in addition to giving quests and are vital for the game's instrumental and economic interactions. All the game's service roles are filled by NPCs, and in *ESO* most of their interactions are voiced. To access the resource that the NPC represents, a player has to talk with them. To improve a horse, talk with a stablemaster. To access the bank, talk with a banker. To buy from a guild, find the right item at the right price (perhaps) by talking with different traders. To repair gear or to sell junk picked up from a dungeon run, talk with the right kind of merchant. Here I intentionally say "talk with" instead of "talk to," implying interaction, but all these interactions are straightforward, scripted, and simple. They are exactly the same every time, which is not at all how human interactions are. But it is still interaction, and the NPCs always speak with the player with human voices supplied by voice actors.

Speech, for most of our history, is how we have communicated with one another. That the characters in *ESO* speak allows for a more natural interaction experience, although one can just read the text—more quickly than it can be spoken naturally—and then click the appropriate reply to forward the dialog, which causes the NPC to jump ahead to the next part of the interaction. But the speaking done by the NPCs, mimicking the back-and-forth of a thought-out conversation, is so important to some players that one third-party add-on prevents the player from advancing the conversation until the NPC has finished what they are saying. The add-on forces a more natural conversation.

The third reason *ESO* a good example for this chapter is its current-day computer technology. That is, most players inhabit the same game world. Older popular MMOs, like *World of Warcraft*, had millions of players at one point. But with the computing power then available, the game servers could not have millions of people share the same online, in-game, virtual space. When one created a character, one had to choose which *server* to play on (servers had names related to the game). To play with friends, one had to be on the same server as the friends. In this way, servers are like a board game played at home with friends. Take the game *Monopoly*: if you're playing in your home, and I'm playing in my home, we can both boast about owning Boardwalk in an online forum. But we will never encounter each other in the game. We're playing copies of the same game in different locations because the game board can only handle so many players. This is the way servers have generally worked in larger MMOs.

ESO works around that to some degree by having only six "megaservers": a North American (NA) and European (EU) server each for three different platforms: Windows/Mac, Xbox, and Playstation (the platforms do not play well together for technological reasons). Most players are on either the PC-NA or PC-EU server (here, "PC" means "personal computer," i.e., Windows/Mac), as are most of their friends. But the upshot is that, unlike in previous games, a player does not need to worry too much about where friends will be, in terms of what server they are on, because so many people are together in the same game world.[1]

This also means that thousands of people are in the same game world, all communicating and forming communities with each other and with the NPCs who inhabit *ESO*, at least until the game is shut down someday in the far future (Pearce, 2009).

DISCUSSION

Much of the interaction between PCs and NPCs is instrumental, whereas the interactions between players can be much more social, although it need not always be so: many players ignore each other. Despite the basic levels of communication between players and NPCs, we can still feel a connection with some NPCs because humans have evolved to be both social and imaginative.

Game worlds with NPCs would not work without them. NPCs fill important, if basic, roles: some akin to automatic teller machines (ATMs) where players do their banking, and others (merchants) akin to vending machines that dispense items when you give them payment. Note how both of these framings use the word *machine*.

Players get to play in these worlds, although researchers have noted that some of the time players spend in MMOs can be construed as work, not play (M. Chen, 2012; Nakamura, 2009; Pearce, 2006; Taylor, 2006; Yee, 2006). The NPCs do not play in the game like the players do. NPCs primarily function for the benefit of the players—NPCs do not run around doing quests on their own. This is true even if, like Lydia in *Skyrim*, an NPC accompanies a player character during gameplay in a way that would be considered play for a PC.

Perhaps this is what gamers and game designers expect from NPCs, and it may reflect how we view robots outside games as tools (Sandry, 2018; Taipale & Fortunati, 2018). This approach does align with both how we use robots so far (primarily for work-related tasks) and how we often view them in science fiction, again as instrumental objects who may also have a human-like social side. But people can see robots and perhaps NPCs as "more than tools"—as team members or even friends (Sandry, 2018, p. 64). It is easy to program robots and NPCs as basic workers, but given human sociality it is not too hard to see them as equivalent beings.

METHODS, DATA, AND LIMITATIONS

This chapter is a summation of my many years of participant-observer game playing (e.g., Nardi, 2010; Taylor, 2006). However, the data have at least two limitations. The first limitation is that these games, the game studios, and the players I have encountered are predominantly from Western cultures (Henrich et al., 2010). The second limitation is that the player population is restricted to those who have the time to play these games, the money to afford them, and the device needed to play them. These limitations do not mean there is anything inaccurate about the data, but rather means that the data may not be representative of how other segments of humanity might behave while playing or creating similar games.

Virtual worlds such as MMOs are not separate from the "real world," nor are they mirrors of it in some way (Eklund, 2014; Lehdonvirta, 2010). Rather, they are embedded in technologies, social norms, legal jurisdictions, and cultural practices. We understand people's behavior within the games as behaviors that originate from their lives, whether playing games or not. So too must we understand that play is not separate from the rest of life; play is instead a regular component of people's lives (Brown, 2009).

Finally, this chapter does not directly address issues such as race, gender, class, language, or nationality. These are important identity markers (Geertz, 1973) but are also used for discrimination and exclusion, in both offline settings and virtual spaces (Brock, 2011; Gray, 2012, 2020; Massanari, 2017; Nakamura, 2009, 2013). These identity markers are also a problem for digital assistants such as Siri and Alexa, which are often both voiced as female (Panzarino, 2021; Strengers & Kennedy, 2020), further acknowledging how the virtual and the real are deeply entangled. Racism and lack of representation have been clearly noted in the primary sources for today's fantasy video games (LaLone, 2019; Rearick, 2004) and continue in today's games in various ways. Given that most NPCs and robots (in both science fiction and reality) have instrumental service jobs (Wirtz et al., 2018), noting the socioeconomic status of their work for both real-world workers and in-game NPCs is vital as we strive to reduce inequality, not replicate it or continue it.

CONCLUSIONS

People who play MMOs navigate in-game worlds filled with characters represented by avatars, some of which are PCs and some of which are NPCs run by computers. Although PC and NPC avatars generally look alike, they fill different roles, and people typically interact with and bond with each in different ways. Many players form bonds with some number of other players, but these bonds are less common between PCs and NPCs. Interactions with a fellow player span a huge potential range of topics and social norms, whereas interacting with an NPC is usually limited to an easily understood script. NPCs often fill basic genre-specific roles, like town guard, or service roles, such as vendor, banker, or quest giver. But these roles are vital to the functioning of the game: they often relate to items of importance or power (financial power, resources, and quests). Access to these types of power must be fair and balanced so the game world can function, or otherwise some players would cheat (Consalvo, 2009) and unbalance the game. NPCs are scripted to not cheat or steal in this manner, although human banking scams are a part of some MMOs (Drain, 2011). Players understand how to navigate these game worlds filled with both PCs and NPCs and are able to create a community of sorts out of it. Recalling Preece (2000), there are *people* (PCs and NPCs) who have a *purpose* (to act in the game world), and there are *policies* (some of which are embedded in the game code, allowing or not allowing certain actions, whereas others are social norms or guild rules).

Altogether, the many human players and the computer program, which was created by humans, work together to make the virtual world a place that the human players can view as a society with functional communities. The humans are highly social, but not with everyone (human sociality has limits); and they play, but some kinds of play in MMOs are work. The NPCs are less social, but some humans project social agency onto them; and NPCs mostly work in service roles so that the humans can play. A few NPCs explore and battle foes, like many human players do much of the time—yet this is not play for a basic computer program. It is an oddly one-sided relationship, but with merely basic programs there will be no machine uprising like in dystopian science fiction. Although too basic to be considered true AI, these programs are still interactive enough that people bond with them at times.

This is what we have started to see with our non-gaming HMC. Machines perform mostly service roles, yet people do bond with these simple robots (Guzman, 2018). Games, as they become more advanced, should have smarter and more capable NPCs, especially in online MMOs that could use cloud-based AI agents for NPCs, although online social bots have not yet made this leap successfully (Assenmacher et al., 2020). Games can continue to serve as models and experiments for how we deal with HMC in our daily lives when the machines are deeply embedded in and intertwined with our communities. If communication forms community (Carey, 1989; Dewey, 1927), then human–machine communication easily transforms in our understanding to human–machine community.

NOTE

1 Technically, these megaservers are server farms. To avoid having too many characters populating the same location, the servers create *instances* of locations. If you don't play an MMO, do not worry about these details. It simply means that you and a friend might be in different instances of the same location (a crowded city center, perhaps), like in the *Monopoly* example. But unlike in *Monopoly*, *ESO* allows you to teleport to the same instance as your friend if you need to.

REFERENCES

Agre, P. (2004). The practical republic: Social skills and the progress of citizenship. In A. Feenberg & D. Barney (Eds.), *Community in the digital age: Philosophy and practice* (pp. 201–223). Rowman & Littlefield.

Assenmacher, D., Clever, L., Frischlich, L., Quandt, T., Trautmann, H., & Grimme, C. (2020). Demystifying social bots: On the intelligence of automated social media actors. *Social Media + Society, 6*(3). https://doi.org/10.1177/2056305120939264

Bakioglu, B. (2009). Spectacular interventions in Second Life: Goon culture, griefing, and disruption in virtual spaces. *Journal of Virtual Worlds Research, 1*(3), 3–21.

Banks, J. (2015). Object, me, symbiote, other: A social typology of player-avatar relationships. *First Monday, 20*(2). https://doi.org/10.5210/fm.v20i2.5433

Banks, J., & Bowman, N. D. (2016). Avatars are (sometimes) people too: Linguistic indicators of parasocial and social ties in player–avatar relationships. *New Media and Society, 18*(7), 1257–1276. https://doi.org/10.1177/1461444814554898

Bassett, C. (2019). The computational therapeutic: Exploring Weizenbaum's ELIZA as a history of the present. *AI & SOCIETY, 34*(4), 803–812. https://doi.org/10.1007/s00146-018-0825-9

Baym, N. (2007). The new shape of online community: The example of Swedish independent music fandom. *First Monday, 12*(8). https://firstmonday.org/article/view/1978/1853

Brock, A. (2011). "When keeping it real goes wrong": Resident Evil 5, racial representation, and gamers. *Games and Culture, 6*(5), 429–452. https://doi.org/10.1177/1555412011402676

Brown, S. (2009). *Play: How it shapes the brain, opens the imagination, and invigorates the soul.* Avery.

Cărătărescu-Petrică, I. (2015). Do those who play together stay together? The World of Warcraft community between play, practice and game design. *Journal of Comparative Research in Anthropology and Sociology, 6*(1), 27–53.

Carey, J. W. (1989). *Communication as culture: Essays on media and society.* Routledge.

Carter, M., Bergstrom, K., & Woodford, D. (Eds.). (2016). *Internet spaceships are serious business: An EVE Online reader.* University of Minnesota Press.

Castronova, E. (2005). *Synthetic worlds: The business and culture of online games.* University of Chicago Press.

Chen, C. Y. (2007). Virtual vows. *Foreign Policy, 158*, 101.

Chen, M. (2009a). Social dimensions of expertise in World of Warcraft players. *Transformative Works and Cultures, 2.* https://doi.org/10.3983/twc.2009.0072

Chen, M. (2009b). Communication, coordination, and camaraderie in World of Warcraft. *Games and Culture, 4*(1), 47–73. https://doi.org/10.1177/1555412008325478

Chen, M. (2012). *Leet noobs: The life and death of an expert player group in World of Warcraft.* Peter Lang.

Chen, V. H., & Duh, H. B.-L. (2007). Understanding social interaction in world of warcraft. *Proceedings of the International Conference on Advances in Computer Entertainment Technology—ACE '07*, 21. https://doi.org/10.1145/1255047.1255052

Consalvo, M. (2009). *Cheating: Gaining advantage in videogames.* MIT Press.

Dabbish, L., Kraut, R., & Patton, J. (2012). Communication and commitment in an online game team. *Proceedings of the 2012 ACM Annual Conference on Human Factors in Computing Systems—CHI '12*, 879. https://doi.org/10.1145/2207676.2208529

Dewey, J. (1927). *The public and its problems.* Swallow Press.

Dibbell, J. (2007). *Play money: Or, how I quit my day job and made millions trading virtual loot.* Basic Books.

Dibbell, J. (2008). Mutilated furries, flying phalluses: Put the blame on griefers, the sociopaths of the virtual world. *Wired Magazine, 16*(2). www.wired.com/gaming/virtualworlds/magazine/16-02/mf_goons?currentPage=all

Drain, B. (2011). *Biggest EVE Online scam ever recorded nets over a trillion ISK.* Engadget. www.engadget.com/2011/08/12/biggest-eve-online-scam-ever-recorded-nets-over-a-trillion-isk/

Ducheneaut, N., & Moore, R. J. (2004). The social side of gaming: A study of interaction patterns in a massively multiplayer online game. *Proceedings* of the 2004 ACM Conference on Computer Supported Cooperative Work (CSCW '04). https://doi.org/10.1145/1031607.1031667

Ducheneaut, N., Yee, N., Nickell, E., & Moore, R. J. (2007). The life and death of online gaming communities: A look at guilds in World of Warcraft. *Proceedings of the SIGCHI 2007 Annual Conference*, 839–848. http://dl.acm.org/citation.cfm?id=1240750

Dunbar, R. (2005). *The human story*. Faber & Faber.

Edwards, A. P. (2018). Animals, humans, and machines: Interactive implications of ontological classification. In A. L. Guzman (Ed.), *Human-machine communication: Rethinking communication, technology, and ourselves.* (pp. 29–49). Peter Lang.

Eklund, L. (2014). Bridging the online/offline divide: The example of digital gaming. *Computers in Human Behavior*. https://doi.org/10.1016/j.chb.2014.06.018

Foo, C. Y., & Koivisto, E. M. I. (2004). Defining grief play in MMORPGs. *Proceedings of the 2004 ACM SIGCHI International Conference on Advances in Computer Entertainment Technology*, 245–250. https://doi.org/10.1145/1067343.1067375

Gamble, C., Gowlett, J., & Dunbar, R. (2014). *Thinking big: How the evolution of social life shaped the human mind*. Thames & Hudson.

Geertz, C. (1973). *The interpretation of cultures*. Basic Books.

Gibbs, M., Carter, M., & Mori, J. (2013). Vile Rat: Spontaneous shrines in EVE Online. *Proceedings of the 1st International Workshop on EVE Online*, 12–15. www.fdg2013.0rg/program/workshops/papers/EVE2013/Gibbs—Vile Rat.pdf

Gibbs, M., Mori, J., Arnold, M., & Kohn, T. (2012). Tombstones, uncanny monuments and epic quests: Memorials in World of Warcraft. *Game Studies*, *12*(1). http://gamestudies.org/1201/articles/gibbs_martin

Granovetter, M. (1973). The strength of weak ties. *American Journal of Sociology*, *78*(6), 1360–1380.

Gray, K. L. (2012). Intersecting oppressions and online communities: Examining the experiences of women of color in Xbox Live. *Information, Communication & Society*, *15*(3), 411–428.

Gray, K. L. (2020). *Intersectional tech: Black users in digital gaming*. LSU Press.

Grimmelmann, J. (2004). Virtual worlds as comparative law. *New York Law School Law Review*, *49*, 147.

Guzman, A. L. (Ed.). (2018). *Human-machine communication: Rethinking communication, technology, and ourselves*. Peter Lang.

Henrich, J., Heine, S. J., & Norenzayan, A. (2010). The weirdest people in the world? *Behavioral and Brain Sciences*, *33*(2–3), 61–83. https://doi.org/10.1017/S0140525X0999152X

Jakobsson, M., & Taylor, T. L. (2003). The Sopranos meets EverQuest: Social networking in massively

multiplayer online games. *Proceedings of the 2003 Digital Arts and Culture (DAC) Conference*, 81–90.

Jonze, S. (2013). *Her*. Annapurna Pictures.

LaLone, N. (2019). A tale of Dungeons & Dragons and the origins of the game platform. *Analog Game Studies*, *6*(3). http://analoggamestudies.org/2019/09/a-tale-of-dungeons-dragons-and-the-origins-of-the-game-platform/

Lehdonvirta, V. (2010). Virtual worlds don't exist: Questioning the dichotomous approach in MMO studies. *Game Studies*, *10*(1). http://gamestudies.org/1001/articles/lehdonvirta

Lombard, M. (2018). Presence past and future: Reflections on 25 years of presence technology, scholarship, and community. In A. L. Guzman (Ed.), *Human-machine communication: Rethinking communication, technology, and ourselves.* (pp. 99–117). Peter Lang.

Massanari, A. (2017). #Gamergate and The Fappening: How Reddit's algorithm, governance, and culture support toxic technocultures. *New Media & Society*, *19*(3), 329–346.

Nakamura, L. (2009). Don't hate the player, hate the game: The racialization of labor in World of Warcraft. *Critical Studies in Media Communication*, *26*(2), 128–144. https://doi.org/10.1080/15295030902860252

Nakamura, L. (2013). *Glitch racism: Networks as actors within vernacular internet theory*. Culture Digitally. http://culturedigitally.org/2013/12/glitch-racism-networks-as-actors-within-vernacular-internet-theory/

Nardi, B. (2010). *My life as a Night-elf priest: An anthropological account of World of Warcraft*. University of Michigan Press.

Nardi, B., & Harris, J. (2006). Strangers and friends: Collaborative play in World of Warcraft. *Proceedings of the 2006 Conference on Computer Supported Cooperative Work*, 149–158. https://doi.org/10.1145/1180875.1180898

Nass, C., Fogg, B. J., & Moon, Y. (1996). Can computers be teammates? *International Journal of Human Computer Studies*, *45*(6), 669–678. https://doi.org/10.1006/ijhc.1996.0073

Nass, C., Steuer, J., & Tauber, E. C. (1994). Computers are social actors. *Proceedings of the 1994 SIGCHI Conference on Human Factors in Computing Systems*, 72–78.

O'Connor, E. L., Longman, H., White, K. M., & Obst, P. L. (2015). Sense of community, social identity and social support among players of massively multiplayer online games (MMOGs): A qualitative analysis. *Journal of Community & Applied Social Psychology*, *25*(6), 459–473. https://doi.org/10.1002/casp.2224

Panzarino, M. (2021, March). Apple adds two brand new Siri voices and will no longer default to a female or male voice in iOS. *TechCrunch*. https://techcrunch.com/2021/03/31/apple-adds-two-siri-voices/

Paul, H. L., Bowman, N. D., & Banks, J. (2015). The enjoyment of griefing in online games. *Journal of Gaming & Virtual Worlds*, *7*(3), 243–258. https://doi.org/10.1386/jgvw.7.3.243_1

Pearce, C. (2006). Productive play: Game culture from the bottom up. *Games and Culture*, *1*, 17–24.

Pearce, C. (2009). *Communities of play*. MIT Press.

Poor, N. (2019). Building and sustaining large, long-term online communities: Family business and gamifying the game. *Proceedings of the 14th International Conference on the Foundations of Digital Games*. https://doi.org/10.1145/3337722.3337760

Poor, N., & Skoric, M. M. (2014). Death of a guild, birth of a network: Online community ties within and beyond code. *Games and Culture*, *9*(3), 182–202. https://doi.org/10.1177/1555412014537401

Poremba, C. (2003). Remaking each other's dreams: Player authors in digital games. *Proceedings of the New Forms Festival 2003*.

Preece, J. (2000). *Online communities: Designing usability, supporting sociability*. Wiley.

Puente, H., & Tosca, S. (2013). The social dimension of collective storytelling in *Skyrim*. *Proceedings of the 2013 DiGRA International Conference*.

Ramirez, F. A. (2018). From good associates to true friends: An exploration of friendship practices in massively multiplayer online games. In K. Lakkaraju, G. Sukthankar, & R. Wigand (Eds.), *Social interactions in virtual worlds: An interdisciplinary perspective* (pp. 62–79). Cambridge University Press. https://doi.org/10.1017/9781316422823.004

Rearick, A. (2004). Why is the only good orc a dead orc? The dark face of racism examined in Tolkien's world. *Modern Fiction Studies*, *50*(4), 861–874.

Reeves, B., & Nass, C. (1996). *The media equation: How people treat computers, television, and new media like real people and places*. CSLI Publications.

Sandry, E. (2018). Aliveness and the off-switch in human-robot relations. In *Human-machine communication: Rethinking communication, technology, and ourselves*. (pp. 51–66). Peter Lang.

Servais, O. (2015). Funerals in the 'World of Warcraft': Religion, polemic, and styles of play in a video-game universe. *Social Compass*, *62*(3), 362–378. https://doi.org/10.1177/0037768615587840

Strauss, A. L. (1978). A social world perspective. In N. K. Denzin (Ed.), *Studies in Symbolic Interaction 1* (pp. 119–128). JAI Press.

Strengers, Y., & Kennedy, J. (2020). *The smart wife: Why Siri, Alexa, and other smart home devices need a feminist reboot*. MIT Press.

Taipale, S., & Fortunati, L. (2018). Communicating with machines: Robots as the next new media. In A. L. Guzman (Ed.), *Human-machine communication: Rethinking communication, technology, and ourselves*. (pp. 201–219). Peter Lang.

Taylor, T. L. (2006). *Play between worlds: Exploring online game culture*. MIT Press.

Tolkien, J. R. R. (1937). *The Hobbit, or there and back again*. George Allen & Unwin.

Walker, J. (2011, November 21). *The life and death of Skyrim's Lydia*. Rock Paper Shotgun. www.rockpapershotgun.com/2011/11/21/skyrim-lydia-death/

Wirtz, J., Patterson, P., Kunz, W., Gruber, T., Lu, V. N., Paluch, S., & Martins, A. (2018). Brave new world: Service robots in the frontline. *Journal of Service Management*, *29*(5), 907–931. https://doi.org/10.1108/JOSM-04-2018-0119

Yee, N. (2006). The labor of fun: How video games blur the boundaries of work and play. *Games and Culture*, *1*(1), 68–71. https://doi.org/10.1177/1555412005281819

17

Perfect Incommunicability: War and the Strategic Paradox of Human–Machine Communication

Jeremy Packer, Joshua Reeves, and Kate Maddalena

INTRODUCTION

From a military perspective, human–machine communication is a strategic problem, a technical solution, and a field of battle. Battlefield communication has been a primary consideration of military practitioners and strategists for centuries. The historical innovation and ongoing strategic importance of these developments in HMC are addressed in this chapter as a means for stressing the importance of acknowledging military prominence and of assessing inevitable ethical considerations. In wartime, the chain of command is characterized by unique challenges of meaning production and signal certainty that have always been dictated by the capacity of media technology. In fact, a great deal of military communication is precisely designed to be impenetrable, imperceptible, or improperly decoded. In this domain meaning is not merely cryptic, but encrypted. This complicates considerably the work of a field primarily motivated by "the creation of meaning among humans and machines" (Guzman, 2018). Further, much military communication is meaningless without the technical capacity to separate signal from encryption-amplified noise. While this makes machines necessary to military C4 (command, control, communication, and computers), they also serve as a point of strategic vulnerability.

Regardless of the communicative dynamics present during warfare, the underlying technical properties and the basic telos guiding human–machine communication (HMC) are nearly universal. They are, in the words of Lucy Suchman, the successful transfer of signals between human and machine to insure "the mutual intelligibility of action" (Suchman, 1987). This is true in civilian and military situations, regardless of the complexity or impossibility of the task (Peters, 1999). This has led to extensive overlap and transfer between civilian and military realms in terms of HMC development, research, and practice. While Friedrich Kittler's claim that all modern communication systems arose out of three wars (the American Civil War, WWI, and WWII) has been criticized for being overly deterministic (Winthrop-Young, 2002), John Durham Peters suggests it is "a useful antidote to a myopically civilian approach that has marked most of our media histories" (2010).

The emergence of a global digital infrastructure that continues to network an ever-higher percentage of the people and machines populating the Earth and its thermosphere, is a direct result of military-developed technologies such as ARPANET, GPS, satellites, fiberoptics, and various forms of AI. Apple's Siri is a perfect case in point. Originally developed as part of DARPA's

Personalized Assistant that Learns (PAL) initiative and presented to the world as a friendly face of AI (Guzman, 2013; Reeves, 2016), Siri was initiated and funded by the US military through one of its favorite partners the Stanford Research Institute (SRI) which sold it to Apple in 2007. Using machine-learning, PAL attempted to "make information understanding and decision-making more effective and efficient for military users... enabling smaller, more mobile, less vulnerable command centers" (DARPA, 2011). The notion of a mobile command center, conceptualized as a techno-empowered individual soldier, is consonant with the Revolution in Military Affairs (RMA) that rose out of the post-cold war logic of netwar and popularized in the 1996 RAND publication *The Advent of Netwar*. Hence, the formation of a new kind of warfare and attendant strategy provided the impetus and funding for the development of new forms of AI and HMC that would come to prominence as a feature in the smartphones civilians use to access data circulating through a network devised to survive the nuclear weapons developed for use in WWII. Both of Kittler's theses that military conflict induces media escalation and that civilian media result from the "misuse of military technology" provide insight into the martial origins (and diverse surveillance potential) of Siri, Alexa, and similar devices (Reeves, 2019). It also highlights the fact that the most expensive U.S. military project in history, the F-35, has been outfitted with Adacel's Voice Activated Cockpit, which, according to the promotional hype, "enables the pilot and the aircraft to talk to each other" (Silicon Review, 2017). Such systems remain important on land, as well, because "you can't exactly tuck your weapons away and remove your gloves to use the on-screen keyboard while bullets are flying over your head" (Medeiros, 2019).

Yet from a military-strategic perspective, this process is absolutely crucial. In fact, the immediate stakes of miscommunication can be catastrophic and can even pose an existential threat if communication in the nuclear chain of command goes awry. The Cuban Missile Crisis is just one of several examples where the meaning-making of machine-processed artifacts (satellite photos and 1590 pages of letters, telegrams, translations, and other correspondence that first passed through typewriters, teletypes, and radio transmission before reaching Kennedy and Krushchev) would determine whether Mutually Assured Destruction (MAD) would be unleashed. In contemporary military strategy, this process has reached a perplexing level of complexity. Because of the strategic competition involved in military HMC, the most forward-reaching designs for military technology are guided by the fantasy of absolute communications security. This fantasy reaches its paradoxical fulfillment in the ideal of perfect incommunicability – that is, in autonomous machines which are impenetrable to any and all intrusions of human communication, whether from friend or foe. Human communication, recognized to be infinitely slower and less precise, is viewed as an obstacle to be overcome through the application of machine-driven communication processes (Packer & Reeves, 2020).

In addressing the interrelationship of war, technology, and human–machine communication, we find ourselves at two impasses. First, under the sign of total warfare (which has become global in a metaphorical sense, such as in the twentieth century's "world wars," as well as in a technological sense, in which satellites and kindred data-tracking technologies have enveloped the world as a potential war-space), all machines, all humans, and all their interactions are potential sites for military-strategic advance (Dreisziger, 1980). Second, the horizon of autonomous weaponry may refigure the limits of human–machine communicative capacity, as attempts to make machines wholly autonomous expose some of the dangers that were present from the first moment that humans began communicating with machines. In short, we turn our attention to the paradoxical military drive to both create perfect human–machine communication and perfect human–machine incommunicability. To do so, we will explore three trends that characterize this drive within the military: first, machines and humans become interchangeable because military signaling isn't about semantics, but about the Signal Corps' motto of "getting the message through"; second, the advent of nuclear threat shifts the onus to technical media which independently monitor and create an understanding (meaning) of situations using signals sent by machines; and third, the rise of artificial intelligence and weapons autonomy demands that machines become "incommunicable" – that is, to be secure from hacking and other acts of human interference, the strength of AI weapons' machine-to-machine communication – in the form of swarm intelligence – is being strengthened in order to endow AI weapons with communicative insularity vis a vis their human collaborators.

This chapter takes up these questions by delving into the historical basis of the human–machine communicative couplet as a central tenet of military strategy and tactic. We begin with the US Signal Corps and its founder Albert Myer who developed signing systems for the deaf in his medical dissertation. The Corps worked extensively to integrate humans and machines into a secret signaling system in which the signers themselves need not know the message. We then analyze the military development of IFF, which turns meaning-making over to machines, and to ARPANET as the backbone for networking global HMC and as the terrain upon which (cyber) war is conducted (Arquilla & Ronfeldt, 1996; Van Creveld, 1985). This is particularly telling from a military perspective in which communication and control are inseparable (Bousquet, 2008). While we wouldn't want to over-simplify the similarity between signaling and ballistics as two effective means for altering the behavior of others, Marshall McLuhan (1964) described guns as media technologies; as extensions of fists. This terrain further exposes the dual imperatives around communication and its opposite. Finally, we look at the development of autonomous military technologies and the strategic necessity of creating "perfect incommunicability" between humans and machines to assure full autonomy and protect from hacking. Further research into HMC within military settings must attend to the potential fallout resulting from such machine autonomy, even as the field attempts to grapple with how AI reorients the very conceptual vocabulary of HMC: as Lewis, Guzman, and Schmidt (2019, p. 4) put it, "the underlying, but often unacknowledged and unquestioned, theoretical assumption in the majority of communication research is that it is humans who are communicators and machines that function as mediators... [W]ithin HMC this assumption is challenged by asking what happens when a machine steps into this formerly human role." This chapter provides some historical examples of how these assumptions have been challenged in military settings for more than 150 years.

SECRET SIGNALS IN THE HUMAN–MACHINE COUPLET

One of the fundamental problems faced by all military endeavors is summed up by Friedrich Kittler's claim that "Command in war has to be digital precisely because war itself is noisy" (Kittler, 1997, p. 119). Clausewitz's famous notion of the "fog of war" similarly describes the perceptual and cognitive difficulties created by the field of battle. The sense that signal certainty must be ensured against the backdrop of hostile conditions and even more hostile forces – both of which are conspiring to disrupt and steal signals – creates the conditions in which humans have turned to machines to counteract the many forms of "noise" and "friction" endemic to warfare. Kittler places profound emphasis upon war as the motor that has driven the development of increasingly

advanced media systems and forms of human–machine communication. Geoffrey Winthrop-Young calls this Kittler's "war answer" and explains that, for Kittler, "the media a priori [is] collapsed into a martial a priori" (Winthrop-Young, 2011, p. 131). And as Kittler himself observes, the German invasion of France in 1870 marks a decisive moment in which the telegraph comes to reorient the distinct division of military signals from troops (Kittler, 1990). Military commands are finally freed from the necessity of humans (or trained animals) to physically move texts through space. This indexes a key conceptual turning point in warfare and human–machine communication. However, we might look backward a few years and across the Atlantic Ocean to the U.S. Civil War (1861–65) for further insight (Maddalena & Packer, 2014).

Dr. Albert James Myer, soldier for the Union Army, was the first signal officer and (as history has since named him) founder of the United States Signal Corps. It is not merely by chance that the military needed Albert Myer nor that Myer needed the military. In 1844, at the age of sixteen, Myer learned how to work a telegraph while at Hobart College. Four years later he completed a degree in medicine and made a special study of sign language for deaf mutes. At the time of his studies, Myer worked as a telegrapher at the New York Telegraph Company. His thesis developed a binary sign language that gave bodily life to morse code. As his thesis attested, "[i]t is not strange, therefore, that under such circumstances, I should not conceive the idea of aiding, with so simple a speech as can be founded on this principle, those whom the Deity has seen fit to deprive of the natural organ" (Myer, 1851, p. 774). Myer argued, "There is no thing or sight or sound or motion or taste or odor perception sensation or indication," he writes in his doctoral thesis, "but by which or through which ideas and meanings may be intelligibly transmitted and which may thus be used for signal communication" (Myer, 1851, p. 56). Myer's system for the deaf binarized signing into two simple distinct movements: one equated with a dot, another a dash. Myer suggested that sight, hearing, and touch could all interchangeably be made to sign with equal semiotic efficiency. For Myer, the corpus of human sensation was an untapped cornucopia of semiotic capacity that could produce digital certainty.

Myer conceived of his signal system for the military – an application of the same concepts that he had used in his dissertation – while he was serving at Fort Davis, in Texas (History, Army Times). According to the Army's official history (1961), Myer exploited non-verbal long-distance techniques he had seen Native American scouts using for signaling and realized that a visual signal system could be applied by the U.S. military as well in its attempt to settle what was perceived as wide-open terrain. He apparently developed, deployed, and promoted his system himself – he taught it to his own unit in Texas, and it was authorized by the Union War Department in 1858. Myer was made Signal Officer – a position invented for him – in 1860, and as soon as the war broke out, Myer positioned himself and the Signal Office as an important Union advantage over the Confederacy. Myer's system was called Wig Wag and involved a set of coded form of flag waving whose semiotic choreography is absolutely dependent upon the soldier's body. The body's arms move the flag and are the primary (though impermanent) inscription. The body's coronal plane (line of symmetry) becomes key to the system's binary code. The body's eyes become the receiver, the body's brain becomes the processor, and the body's hand records the interpreted message for storage (on the material, non-human medium of paper). So, the entire process of remediation – from what Myers himself calls "transient signal" to "permanent signal" – depends upon the soldier's body. Further, this media solved the unique set of problems endemic to warfare; overcome time and distance (thus visual flags or sonic telegraphs), mobility (thus modular and attached to the railroad), secrecy (thus encoded), and precision (thus binary/mathematical).

More importantly, this system, similar to others developed for long distance signaling such as Chappe's telegraphic system in France, disarticulated the signal from the semantic capacity of the sender and receiver by turning humans into signaling machines as opposed to "speaking" or "communicating" subjects. The humans doing the signaling need not, and in many cases could not and should not, be able to decipher the messages which they were sending. In warfare, signal certainty, not human comprehension, is paramount. Kittler suggests the important distinction derived from the telegraph is that signals could travel separate from humans. An equally important development was the determination that in war, humans could be turned into signaling machines. In terms of military signal strategy, this makes humans and machines interchangeable. Signaling, not the signaler, became paramount. Myers recognized that sight, sound, taste, and touch were interchangeable when digital signaling was the goal. So too humans and machines. Wigwag turned humans into machines – into technical media by dissociating their semantic language with their signaling capacity. This replaceability with machines for humans and humans for machines exposes some of the conceptual slippage (from a Luhmanesque perspective) of differentiating between human and machine. It is in the end, just communication, just signaling, from the perspective of the guided missile.

SIGNAL UNCERTAINTY AND NUCLEAR ANNIHILATION

For thousands of years humans used simple and complex machines to amplify their perceptual capacity to detect enemy signals and threats. Guided missiles have merely complexified the task. Spotting enemies was accomplished through the use of towers, telescopes, conch shells, hot air balloons, airplanes, and eventually cameras that extended human perceptual capacities by amplifying and capturing auditory and visual signals. (Virilio, 1989). With the advent of technical media, new bandwidths, such as the radio spectrum, are used to make meaning and aid in detection. Warfare was no longer a game of cat and mouse, but rather a game of machine and machine. This is to say that the signals produced and those detected were machine signals using visual and auditory spectrums that were often beyond human perceptual capacity. Machines can and do signal, communicate, with each other in ways that are imperceptible to humans. Humans had to learn to "trust" what machines were telling them even if it contradicted human perception and expectation. The Japanese "surprise attack" on Pearl Harbor did not surprise technical media which announced the attack, rather humans chose to disregard and ignore the warnings of their machines (Buderi, 1996).

Radio waves are an easy and important example that leads to "Radio Detection And Ranging" (RADAR). Radar is a meaning-making machine. It sends and receives radio waves that "tell a story" about what is happening "out there" in the space beyond human perception. Radar divides the world into presence and absence, thereby turning space into battle-space. Radar necessitated more sophisticated forms of machine to machine communication so that friendly blips on a radar screen could be separated from enemy blips on a screen. Called Identification, Friend or Foe (IFF), technical processes were created by which machines identify themselves to other machines. The political act of distinguishing friend from foe was ceded to machines.

During the late stages of WWII, networked radar and analog computers automated communication processes and "decoded" machine threats in ways that pushed the limits of machine perception, computation, interconnection, and recollection. Shortly thereafter, following the Soviet Union's successful atomic bomb development in

1949, the U.S. military embarked on the largest computational project in history (Edwards, 1996) to replace a human-based anti-aircraft surveillance system (The Ground Observer Corps) with a semi-autonomous network of machines dubbed SAGE (Semi-Automatic Ground Environment) that would scour the skies of North America for enemy bombers (Packer, 2013). By the time it was operational in 1959, SAGE was so complicated it exhibited qualities typically used to "distinguish(es) organisms from machines" (Dyson, 1997). It was later used as the test-bed to experiment with Leviathan, an early 1970's RAND attempt to create an AI capable of inventing and testing military strategy. In each of these scenarios, humans were seen as imperfect communicators. Humans could fail to recognize bombers or produce false positives. Once sighted, the human chain of command was often slow, inadequately dispersed, and incapable of surpassing the speed of bombers, let alone ICBMs. Humans were also deemed incapable of addressing the full-complement of attack scenarios that would unfold in a real-time attack. Machines on the other hand were promoted as ideal communicative agents, accurate, extensive, and fast enough to counteract the onslaught of nuclear attack (Packer, 2013).

Nuclear war spurred the most far-reaching alteration to HMC by developing ARPANET as a means to maintain signal certainty following nuclear annihilation. The technical and protocological progenitor of the contemporary internet rose out of the imaginary ashes of a post-nuclear world (Levine, 2018). Further, nuclear threat continued to push the development of autonomous forms of computation and communication, including the capacity for signaling to continue following a nuclear attack, even to the point of a "dead hand" (that is to say an inhuman or machine "hand") "pulling the switch" to launch a nuclear counter-attack after all humans capable of doing such work have been killed (Elam, 2018). These machines communicate with each other, tirelessly, ceaselessly, and at a tempo impenetrable to human comprehension. It is only on special occasions, when a potential threat appears, that machines decide human communication is necessary. The ability to decipher between human and machine, as with Turing's famous test, is lost. Everything is communicated via machines, hence the adversary may at any time be a machine.

NETWORKING MACHINES

Faced with this shifting technological landscape, in 2010 then-Secretary of Defense Robert Gates ordered the Army and the Air Force to develop new multi-aircraft piloting technologies. In response, the Army – which deploys its drone pilots to overseas bases – has developed a system by which pilots can oversee two vehicles at once. In 2015, therefore, the Army began to field multi-aircraft control for their cutting-edge drone, the MQ-1C Gray Eagle (Scharre, 2014a, p. 17). This advance in unmanned warfare has been made possible only because the craft possess a remarkable degree of autonomy, having the capacity to take off and land on their own, for example (Center for a New American Security, 2014). Yet this step forward in the autonomous operation of aerial vehicles creates a deluge of additional vulnerabilities. The Gray Eagle's present data transmission systems, for example, are highly sensitive to enemy hacking. Just as telegraph cables and then wireless radio transmissions enhanced the potential for message interception, drones' complex systems of satellite-based communications are highly vulnerable to penetration and sabotage. In fact, in order for drones to operate in the air, unmanned systems require constant, assured communications to remote pilots (Scharre, 2014a, p. 31). This communication link, therefore, is an Achilles Heel of unmanned craft: as former Deputy Defense Secretary Robert O. Work and military strategist Shawn Brimley point out in *Preparing for War in the Robotic Age*, "An actor who dominates in cyber conflict can infiltrate command-and-control networks, generate misinformation and confusion, and potentially even shut down or usurp control over physical platforms. This will be especially true for unmanned systems" (2014, p. 23). As the authors make clear, however, ultimately new transmission media are not radical enough to solve this problem in all its complexity. At least as far back as January 2001, DoD has been worried about terrorists and rival militaries attacking US SATCOM capabilities. At that time, Defense Secretary Donald Rumsfeld warned about a looming "Space Pearl Harbor" (Wirbel, 2004, p. 78). while his colleague Admiral David Jeremiah argued that hostile states – and even the mythical Osama bin Laden – could hack our satellite systems.

While at this time only humans are officially entrusted with "kill" decisions based upon these data, this DoD policy is contradicted by autonomous media/weapons like Raytheon's new Close-In Weapon System, the Phalanx (Stimson Center, 2014, p. 71). To compensate for the data vulnerability, physical impracticality, and financial cost of keeping humans in the command chain, the Phalanx and similar technologies empower computing systems to make kill decisions based on algorithmic determinations of enemyship. Thus, in tracing the history of how communication technologies and humans have cooperatively communicated to overcome military challenges, we have been telling a story that has built more or less logically to the computerized automation of enemy epistemology – and hence, eventually, to the pure fulfillment of what Katharine Hall Kindervater calls "lethal surveillance" (Kindervater, 2017).

In one of the major developments of this military technical revolution, the figure of the "network" has transformed into the figure of the *swarm*. While swarm warfare has important precedents in military history – such as in Alexander the Great's Central Asian campaigns, the Mongol invasions of Asia and Eastern Europe, Native American attacks on the western frontier, and postcolonial guerilla resistance in Asia and Africa (Arquilla & Ronfeldt, 2000; Edwards, 2005) – logics of robotic autonomy have revolutionized the potential of the swarm. Faced with the failure of networks to solve the problem of over-centralization, military strategists have begun to realize that traditional models of intelligence and command – based, that is, on human cognition and human communication – are inadequate to the challenges of twenty-first-century warfare. The next step in the revolution, therefore, relies on the development of nonhuman models of knowledge and communication. Observing this transition to animal intelligences, military strategist Paul Scharre has remarked that forces will shift "from fighting as a *network* to fighting as a *swarm*, with large numbers of highly autonomous uninhabited systems coordinating their actions on the battlefield. This will enable greater mass, coordination, intelligence, and speed than would be possible with networks of human-inhabited or even remotely controlled uninhabited systems" (Scharre, 2014b, p. 8). While humans could retain a degree of supervisory contact with the swarm, "the leading edge of the battlefront across all domains would be unmanned, networked, intelligent, and autonomous" (Work and Brimley, 2014, p. 29). In military parlance, these stages of swarm warfare constitute the "kill chain" of twenty-first-century autonomous missions: Find, Fix, Track, Target, Engage, Assess (United States Air Force, 2014). Today, military AI projects like the DoD's Project Maven capitalize on the mnemonic labor carried out by previous missions, allowing the kill chain to grow faster, smarter, and more precise with every deployment (Tucker, 2017).

With its extraordinary capacities for inter-craft cooperation, the swarm is seen as an ideal technological arrangement for dispersing the fog of war. Upending the metaphorical connotations of Clausewitz's "fog," swarms operate through a "combat *cloud*" that is driven by collective interoperability (Stimson Center, 2014, p. 26). Traditional military networks, of course, had to safeguard their principal nodes of intelligence against enemy attack. But with swarms, this epistemological center of gravity is a thing of the past. In a radical departure from human–machine command and control, which requires communication between psychically isolated cooperating subjects, the swarm cloud possesses a continuously refined collective intelligence that is far beyond the grasp of humans' physiological capacity. These swarms continuously reorient their collective intelligence – they are even "self-healing" in the event of companion loss, which they compensate for by readjusting the epistemological topology of the swarm (Rubinstein & Shen, 2008; Scharre, 2014b, p. 32). These decisions for topological restructuring can be accomplished by the use of "voting" mechanisms, which could allow swarms to achieve a decentralized epistemology that is inconceivable among networked human combatants (Scharre, 2014b, p. 26). This emergent intelligence is made possible by what military strategists call "implicit communication," which is modeled on the cooperative epistemologies of flock and school animals like birds, ants, and fish. Although the RAND Corporation and the U.S. government have been funding military research in "microrobotics" since the early- and mid-1990s (Solem, 1996), new manufacturing technologies, such as 3-D printing, have made it possible for DoD affiliates to develop swarms which take the physical form of dragonflies, "robobees," house-flies, remoras, hornets, eels, and other animals that cooperate with distributed intelligence. This development could allow DoD to deploy thousands or even billions of tiny, cheaply produced, cooperative drones that could be released into the field of combat in order to carry out reconnaissance and locate enemy combatants (Scharre, 2014b, p. 20).

PERFECT INCOMMUNICATION

Outfitted with sophisticated onboard sensors, these swarms can perform attack assessments before they strike, thus enabling them to collectively refine their knowledge of the enemy and coordinate their attacks accordingly. As these developments and related escalations suggest, the fog and chaos of the battlefield really only have one solution: machine epistemology. We have finally reached the situation foreseen by Manuel Delanda, who feared that "in the modern battlefield, full of noisy data, commanders will feel only too tempted to rely on the accumulated expertise stored in [machines'] arsenals of know-how, and will let the computer itself make the decisions. Further, only computers have fast access to all the 'perceptual' information about a battle, coming from satellite and ground sensors, so that a commander confronted by the noisy data emanating from the battlefield might … allow it to mutate from a mere smart prosthesis, a mechanical adviser, into a machine with executive capabilities of its own" (Delanda, 1991, p. 81). Formerly prosthesis, the machine is stepping into its more fitting roles of sage, executive, and executioner. By computational necessity, these intelligent weapons will only be able to follow kill commands devised by machines, based upon coordinates formulated by machines, targeted at the enemies of machines.

With digital military media, incommunication is often used to assert control over particular domains. No fly zones, for example, establish spaces in which enemy craft cannot – either legally or technically – operate. Geofencing, too, establishes these boundaries by erecting a digital domain in which unapproved craft cannot receive incoming communications. For unmanned vessels, this means that remote control ceases and that craft-to-command communications abruptly halt. With geofencing, therefore, corporations and governments can create domains of exclusive communication and command. And because warfare has gone so thoroughly digital, cutting off an enemy's C4 capacity prevents the vast majority of activities that are now intelligible as war.

There are other ways, too, that ultimate success in digital warfare demands the establishment of perfect incommunicability. Because this ideal can only be accomplished through the communications perfection offered by robotic autonomy, the drone must be able to freely choose how best to carry out its mission. Human communicative fallibility (with its narrow bandwidth, faulty memory, slow and irrational processing, and weak signaling) must be removed from military communications for the drone to truly fulfill its mission. Zac Kallenborn, of the National Consortium for the Study of Terrorism and Responses to Terrorism, describes how unmanned launch platforms can be used to aid in overcoming these vulnerabilities: "Unmanned launch platforms are useful over manned, because there is lower risk to manned operators and it allows much greater system integration. The unmanned ship might provide recharging, communication, and data processing for the larger swarm" (Hambling, 2021). For Kallenborn, the system integration allowed by automating all aspects of communication provides a substantial advantage over current human-centered control strategies. By offloading all these

capacities to an integrated machine system, the bungling human can be sidestepped in favor of a more flawless internal command system. And this emphasis on internality, of course, is a deliberate attempt to create a space of human incommunicability – a space where human commands, hacks, and distortions cannot threaten the system.

Robert O. Work, who was U.S. Deputy Secretary of Defense under Obama and Trump, argues that commanders will have to gain comfort "delegating" more and more tasks to machines. For Work, "The problem is that when you're dealing [with war] at machine speed, at what point is the human an impediment? … There's no way a human can keep up, so you've got to delegate to machines" (Fryer-Biggs, 2019). Because we have allowed media escalation to produce a situation in which carbon-based impediments cannot "keep up" with machines, Work argues that we will now have to tolerate them processing information that is too esoteric for human organs. Robert Brizzolara, who works in the Office of Naval Research and leads the Navy's Sea Hunter AI project, explores this problem from a similar vantage point. According to Brizzolara, command will simply have to "trust" military AI to carry out its duties: "Sailors and their commanding officers are going to have to trust that the autonomous systems are going to do the right thing at the right time" (Fryer-Biggs, 2019). Because human approval and human command would prevent the machine from carrying out its mission at the highest speed and efficiency, command must cut the cord of human oversight and empower the machine to do what it perceives to be "the right thing at the right time."

These developments are indicative of a broader trend in the military/media relationship. As Geoffrey Winthrop-Young describes, we are now in a situation in which media are "moving ever farther away from their human subjects" (Winthrop-Young, 2017, p. 2). Drone swarms are simply a stark illustration of digital media's rapidly accelerating departure from the realm of human collaboration and human perception. For Winthrop-Young, the story of digital media's infiltration into our lives, and especially into our military command, is a "tale of deception…. The ability of digital media to store, process, and communicate levels of the real inaccessible to human perception comes at the cost of humans no longer being able to determine whether that which is allegedly processed by media is not in fact produced by them" (Winthrop-Young, 2017, p. 2). Digital media have pushed information processing into a realm insensible to humans: as Kittler would have it, they simply "fool" us into thinking that they share communicative capacities in common with us, while in fact they operate "in frequency ranges that exceed human perception thresholds, that is, in those domains where technological media operate simply because otherwise they would not be able to systematically fool our eyes and ears" (Kittler, 2017, pp. 12–13). Media technology, in other words, is in the business of deceiving us into thinking it operates according to humanistic perceptual categories. It specializes, rather, in an esotericism that straddles the line between deception and incommunication.

The greatest trick that digital military media have played on the fools, therefore, is that it has convinced us that we are its partners in command and control. Yet at the same time, it has gradually taught us that warfare is no longer a suitable domain for human communication. Various military blocs, their citizens and their policy makers are assured that to insist on human communication with the machine is to risk being obliterated by the Russians or the Chinese or the Americans. Under this imminent threat, escalation is the only answer. And accordingly, any trace of the human is an insidious infection, a threat to the security and intelligence – to the very life – of the autonomous system. While a postoperative surgeon may check "the margins" in a search for remaining malignant tissue, humans may not be able to properly sense the ripple effects of their own presence in the system, however diminished. In that sense, humans cannot be counted on to remove all that is "human" from the drone. Only the drone is capable of that.

CONCLUSION AND FUTURE WARNINGS

HMC in the historical context of warfare highlights dueling desires and imperatives that have arisen when enmity, not cooperation, rule. We have chosen to focus on three moments in which the relation between humans, machines, and the capacity or desirability to make meaning and communicate has been uprooted. In the first moment of flag-based semaphore, humans are turned into machines that signal, but do not themselves make meaning. The presumed roles of human and machine are overturned. The second moment sees the development of increasingly sophisticated machines that communicate with and about other machines in bandwidths and at speeds beyond human perception. Humans are seen as inferior to machines in the realm of military communication. Finally, in our third moment, truly autonomous machines, those which cannot be communicated with by humans, are presented as the only solution to the problem of human

communicative meddling into machine warfare. Human–machine communication is seen as a threat and as such must be evacuated.

A future featuring perfect incommunicability as a military desire is one that highlights some of the challenges facing HMC scholars in a world in which animosity is the guiding principle for the development of many communication techniques and technologies, particularly those involving HMC. Warfare, and its attendant subdisciplines spy craft, propaganda, and disinformation, present the human and machine as operating in a field of constant struggle in which miscommunication or the *inability* to properly know, understand, or alter the intentions of another are desirable features, not signs of failure. HMC scholars might even be seen as "enemies" within such a framework as their telos is one of understanding, decoding, and making visible that which is unseen.

Conversely, recognizing the centrality of HMC to contemporary and future warfare should also suggest that knowledge produced about HMC opens new avenues and routes for its application to warfare. As Julie Carpenter's research with the U.S. military's Explosive Ordnance Disposal units clarifies, "each bit of gained insight into the human side of human-robot interactions contributes to an understanding and influence of controllable variables (e.g., design, training) for the most positive intended outcomes of human-robot teamwork" (Carpenter, 2016). As we have argued at length (Packer & Reeves, 2020a, 2020b), the epistemological, technical, and strategic capacities created by new communication technologies and techniques have historically and will necessarily continue to produce new capacities for engaging in warfare. From this perspective, HMC scholars are active or unwitting "friends" of the military whether they are funded by DARPA or the International Peace Research Association. This is not a critique of HMC scholarship per se, but rather an acknowledgement that communication has been and will remain a vital feature of military capacity and strategy. All knowledge that can produce strategic advantage will be applied by military operatives. Christopher Simpson's research clearly established that the CIA, Pentagon, and numerous U.S. security agencies were central to the establishment of modern communication research and the distinct discipline of communication (Simpson, 1996). The lessons from this militaristic past should be especially resonant within the HMC scholarly community as communication research is not only important in ideological struggles as it was in the past, but rather is the very backbone of military C4 capacity. As such, its prominence as a strategic nodal point cannot be understated.

REFERENCES

Army Times. (1961). *A history of the United States Signal Corps,* 1st edition. G.P. Putnam & Sons.

Arquilla, J. and Ronfeldt, D. (1996). *The advent of netwar.* RAND.

Arquilla, J. and Ronfeldt, D. (2000). *Swarming and the future of conflict.* Rand Corporation.

Bousquet, A. (2008). Cyberneticizing the American war machine: Science and computers in the Cold War. *Cold War History, 8* (1), 77–102.

Buderi, R. (1996). *The invention that changed the world.* Simon & Schuster.

Carpenter, J. (2016). *Culture and human-robot interaction in militarized spaces: A war story.* Routledge.

Center for a New American Security. (2014). Eighth annual conference: robotics on the battlefield: The coming swarm. www.youtube.com/watch?v= WuxwBHI6zY.

DARPA Information and Innovation Office. (2011). Personalized assistant that learns (PAL). www. darpa.mil/Our_Work/I2O/Programs/Personalized_ Assistant_that_Learns_%28PAL%29.aspx.

Delanda, M. (1991). *War in the age of intelligent machines.* Zone.

Dreisziger, N. (1980). *Mobilization for total war: The Canadian, American and British experience.* Collège militaire royal du Canada.

Dyson, G. (1997). *Darwin among the machines: The evolution of global intelligence.* Basic Books.

Edwards, P. (1996). *The closed world: Computers and the politics of discourse in Cold War America.* Massachusetts Institute of Technology Press.

Edwards, S. J. A. (2005). *Swarming and the future of warfare.* Ph.D. dissertation, Pardee Rand Graduate School.

Elam, J. (2018). *Automated: The life and death of the human subject.* Ph.D. Dissertation, North Carolina State University.

Fryer-Biggs, Z. (2019). Coming soon to a battlefield: robots that can kill. www.theatlantic.com/technol- ogy/archive/2019/09/killer-robots-and- new-era-machine-driven-warfare/597130/.

Guzman, A. (2013). Making machines safe for humans: The case of Siri. *AoIR Selected Papers of Internet Research*, 3. https://spir.aoir.org/ojs/ index.php/spir/article/view/8719.

Guzman, A. (2018). What is human-machine com- munication? In A. Guzman (Ed.), *Human-machine communication: Rethinking communication, tech- nology, and ourselves* (pp. 1–28). Peter Lang.

Hambling, D. (2021). Drone swarms are getting too fast for humans to fight, U.S. general warns. www.forbes.com/sites/davidhambling/2 021/01/27/drone-swarms-are-getting-too-fast-for- humans-too-fight-us-general-warns/?sh= 372369ed372c.

Kindervater, K. H. (2017). The technological rational- ity of the drone strike. *Critical Studies on Security 5* (1), 28–44.

Kittler, F. A. (1990). *Discourse networks 1800/1900.* Stanford University Press.

Kittler, F. A. (1997). Media wars: Trenches, lightning, stars. In *Essays: Literature, media, information systems.* Overseas Publishers.

Kittler, F.A. (2017). Real-time analysis, time axis manipulation. *Cultural Politics 13* (1), 1–18.

Levine, Y. (2018). *Surveillance valley: The secret mili- tary history of the Internet.* Public Affairs Press.

Lewis, S. C., Guzman, A. L., and Schmidt, T. R. (2019). Automation, journalism, and human–machine communication: Rethinking roles and relationships of humans and machines in news. *Digital Journal- ism 7* (4), 409–427.

Maddalena, K. and Packer, J. (2014). The digital body: Telegraphy as discourse network. *Theory, Culture, & Society 32* (1), 93–117.

McLuhan, M. (1964). *Understanding media: The extensions of man.* McGraw-Hill.

Medeiros, J. (2019). Here's how the military is using voice technology. www.voicesummit.ai/blog-old/ how-the-military-is-using-voice-technology.

Myer, A. J. (1851). *A new sign language for deaf mutes.* Buffalo, N.Y: Steam Press of Jewett.

Packer, J. (2013). Screens in the sky: SAGE, surveil- lance, and the automation of perceptual, mne- monic, and epistemological labor. *Social Semiotics 23* (2), 173–195.

Packer, J. and Reeves, J. (2020a) *Killer apps: War, media, machine.* Duke University Press.

Packer, J. and Reeves, J. (2020b) Making enemies with media. *Communication and the Public 5* (1–2), 16–25.

Peters, J. D. (1999). *Speaking into the air: A history of the idea of communication.* University of Chi- cago Press.

Peters, J. D. (2010). Introduction: Friedrich Kittler's light shows. In F. Kittler, *Optical media: Berlin lectures 1999.* Polity Press.

Reeves, J. (2016). Automatic for the people: The automation of communicative labor. *Communica- tion and critical/cultural studies 13* (2), 150–165.

Reeves, J. (2019). Surveillance and communication. In H. Bean and B.C. Taylor (Eds.), The *Routledge handbook of communication and security* (pp. 368–380). Routledge.

Rubinstein, M., and Shen, W. 2008. A scalable and distributed model for self-organization and self- healing. In *Proceedings of the 7th international joint conference on autonomous agents and multiagent systems*, 3, 1179–82. International Foundation for Autonomous Agents and Multiagent Systems.

Scharre, P. (2014a). *Robotics on the battlefield, part I: Range, persistence, and daring.* Center for a New American Security.

Scharre, P. (2014b). *Robotics on the battlefield, part II: The coming swarm*. Center for a New American Security.

Sharkey, A J. C, and Sharkey, N. (2006). The application of swarm intelligence to collective robots. In J. Fulcher (Ed.), *Advances in applied artificial intelligence* (pp. 157–85). IGI Global.

Silicon Review (2017). The leading global software technology and systems integrator: Adacel. https://thesiliconreview.com/magazine/profile/the-leading-global-software-technology-and-systems-integrator-adacel.

Simpson, C. (1996). *Science of coercion: Communication research and psychological warfare, 1945–1960*. Oxford University Press.

Solem, J. (1996). The application of microrobotics in warfare. Los Alamos National Laboratory Report LA-UR-96-3067.

Stimson Center. (2014). *Recommendations and report of the Task Force on U.S. Drone Policy*. Stimson.

Suchman, L. (1987). *Plans and situated actions: The problem of human-machine interaction*. Cambridge University Press.

Tucker, P. (2017). *The future of military tech*. www.defenseone.com/assets/future-military-tech/portal/.

United States Air Force (2014). Dynamic targeting and the tasking process. https://doctrine.af.mil/download.jsp?filename=3-60-D17-Target-Dynamic-Task.pdf.

Van Creveld, M. (1985). *Command in war*. Harvard University Press.

Virilio, P. (1989). *War and cinema: The logistics of perception*. Verso.

Winthrop-Young, G. (2002). Drill and distraction in the yellow submarine: On the dominance of war in Friedrich Kittler's media theory. *Critical Inquiry 28* (4), 825–854.

Winthrop-Young, G.W. (2011). *Kittler and the media*. Polity.

Winthrop-Young, G. (2017). Translator's introduction to Kittler, F.A., (2017). *Cultural Politics* 13.1 (2017): 1–5.

Wirbel, L. (2004). *Star wars: U.S. tools of space supremacy*. Pluto Press.

Work, R. O., and Brimley, S. (2014). *Preparing for war in the robotic age*. Center for a New American Security.

PART 2

Approaches and Methods

INTRODUCTION

While there are many well-used and disciplinary specific definitions for the term *research methods* (e.g. Luker, 2009; Allen, 2017; Creswell & Cresswell, 2017), most definitions share common words: tools, techniques, strategies, processes, and procedures. In essence, a researcher's methods are their approaches to answering questions, and a closer look at the method reveals the choices that are made, or not made.

Mindful of the substantial number of books, chapters, and treatises published on how to conduct scholarly research, in this section of *The Sage Handbook of Human–Machine Communication* we sought out researchers with a common curiosity about Human–Machine Communication (HMC). We were also interested in presenting researchers of HMC who have adapted traditional research approaches and methods to better address research subjects that are either humans or machines and those who are developing innovative methods.

Well-prepared upper-year undergraduate and year-one graduate students can identify the centuries old bifurcation in research methods described as quantitative and qualitative. Imbedded in this binary are longstanding arguments with

epistemological roots that run deep below the surface of a study and eventually bear fruit within the analyses that follow. Even a choice to stand more neutral in these debates and use mixed methods makes a statement about how the researchers have understood the task of question answering, and in the method chapters within this collection, most researchers have employed multiple techniques, perhaps highlighting that HMC research requires multiple lenses drawn from its interdisciplinary roots.

When engaging in inquiry within a new field of study, the choices are even more fraught. Since researchers working within the frame of HMC have a wide range of disciplinary backgrounds, many bring the methodologies from their scholarly communities to their studies, shaping them to meet new needs.

Because HMC researchers – to varying degrees – question, blur, or remove the ontological separation between humans and machines, data collection requires some creativity. If both humans and machines are to be considered as participants within communicative encounters, the more established methods that have been human-centric can prove challenging. For example, in human–human communication studies interviews provide a proven mechanism for gathering responses for questions that are qualitative in nature and not heavily recall-dependent, including questions beginning with *what* and *why*. This can be adapted for HMC exchanges, and in this section, Guzman considers how we talk with people about how they talk with machines. What about gathering responses from machines; can machines be interviewed? Both Green and Diakopoulos et al. used query-based audits as a means to simulate communicative exchanges with machines, giving interviewing a distinctive HMC spin.

The chapters by Jamieson and Lui offer methods to collect data from machines. These involve data that are generated through interactions with humans, including archival log data analyses that can qualify and quantify questions starting with *when* and *to what extent*, while data from sensors can provide insight on *how* HMC interactions are experienced physiologically. Edwards also offers a chapter that considers the machine more thoroughly as a source for data in HMC, provides a historical comparison to human–robot interaction methods, and gives recommendations for HMC methods in the future.

Gardner and Rauchberg challenge HMC researchers to take risks by moving beyond methods that analyze HMC interaction within narrower lenses that can accompany some methodological traditions and to include frameworks that resist generalizations about both humans and machines. These authors state that "a lack of attention to social, regional, and cultural contexts can flatten the human research subject, failing to account for relevant micro and macro contexts that nuance and complicate human-computer analyses." In this chapter they demonstrate how this can be overcome using feminist and crip methods successfully. Krämer and Szczuka also sound a similar warning about applying methods from other disciplines to HMC without some adaptation. Using experimental methods as a case in point, they skillfully show how independent and dependent variables must be adjusted by behavioral measures to more thoroughly capture the complexities in HMC.

Chapters by St. Louis and Spence et al. consider ways to reduce potential effects of having a researcher within the HMC interaction space. For St. Louis, visual methods offer a way to elucidate the mental models that people develop when interacting with machines, in a sense, getting inside the mind of the human while trying not to influence the experience. Spence et al. demonstrate that observational techniques can help to assess elements in HMC interactions for which participants may not be consciously aware. Ringel also examines the role of observation in HMC research, but, in contrast to Spence et al., explores what is to be gained through participant observation and the adaptation of ethnography to human-machine contexts.

Our goal for this section of *The Sage Handbook of Human–Machine Communication* is to serve as an excellent source of ideas, considerations, and inspiration for researchers engaging in HMC research. We also want to underscore that adopting method for HMC research goes beyond adjusting the mechanisms of data collection and analysis. As Ess thoughtfully argues, the ethics of how we conduct our research also require careful re-examination and reflection. We hope that as the study of HMC continues to grow, the method canon will also continue to expand and that the approaches offered here are generative of future methodological innovations.

REFERENCES

Allen, M. (Ed.). (2017). The SAGE encyclopedia of communication research methods. SAGE publications.

Creswell, J. W., & Creswell, J. D. (2017). Research design: Qualitative, quantitative, and mixed methods approaches. Sage Publications.

Luker, K. (2009). *Salsa dancing into the social sciences*. Harvard University Press.

18

Human–Robot Interaction

Autumn Edwards

INTRODUCTION

Human–Robot Interaction (HRI) is both the name of an academic research field and a general context of interaction between humans and robotic systems. Some research conducted within the field of HRI pertains to communication and a great deal is indirectly relevant by shedding light on perception, cognition, and behavior. Moreover, numerous researchers overlap HRI and Human–Machine Communication (HMC) in their professional memberships, conference participation, and publication outlets. However, this chapter narrows the focus to summarize the methodological contributions of communication scholars who have investigated HRI as a form of HMC. First, I briefly explain HRI as both a field of study and context of interaction as it relates to HMC. Second, I discuss how robots have been variously positioned within the communication process. Third, I survey the HMC research which centers HRI, highlighting the knowledge claims and methods behind them. Finally, I offer summarizing remarks and future research directions.

HRI AND HMC

HRI is a multidisciplinary and problem-based field of study characterized by collaboration between scientists, designers, and engineers to understand how robots and people interact in the social world (Bartneck et al., 2020). Communication is a special form of interaction that involves information sharing, collaborative meaning-making, and/or the construction of social reality (Guzman, 2018). Within Human–Machine Communication (HMC), scholars centering HRI investigate the theory and practice of communication with and about robots, including discourse and interaction practices that construct and relate the broad categories of human and robot (http://hmcjournal.com). HMC researchers bring assumptions, theories, constructs, and methodologies valuable for understanding communicative interactions between humans and robots.

WHAT IS A ROBOT?

Defining a robot is not easy because their bodies are multiform and mutant, as are understandings of their fundamental nature (see Fortunati & Edwards, 2021), but they refer broadly to "an autonomous machine capable of sensing its environment, carrying out computations to make decisions, and performing actions in the real world" (https://robots.ieee.org/learn/what-is-a-robot/). The core of HMC research involving robots focuses on communication processes between humans and social robots, and so it is important to understand what makes a robot "social." Definitions of social robots emphasize their adherence to social norms, materiality and embeddedness in social contexts, and ability to interact in human-like ways (Xu, 2019; Sarrica et al., 2019). Physical embodiment is a key feature that differentiates robots from other computing technologies and introduces distinct interaction processes and possibilities (Bartneck et al., 2020). The bodies of social robots may take many forms—anthropomorphic, zoomorphic, phytomorphic, creaturely, character-based, mechanomorphic, or theomorphic—but there is a strong focus on humanoid social robots in HMC scholarship. Zhao's (2006) definition as "human-made autonomous entities that interact with humans in a human-like way" (p. 405) and elaboration that "humanoid robots are not user-friendly computers that operate as machines; rather, they are user friendly computers that operate as humans" (p. 403) remain influential. However, what a "humanlike manner" entails often goes unspecified (de Graaf et al., 2015). Two-way interaction, possession (or display) of thoughts, feelings, and emotions, and capacity to sense the social environment emerged as essential features in their study of user perspectives. Meanwhile, Eleanor Sandry (2015b) challenged the assumption that human-likeness is the only way to build robots that can interact in social, natural, and meaningful ways with humans (p. 30).

WHAT IS THE ROBOT'S ROLE IN THE COMMUNICATION PROCESS?

Should a robot be considered a traditional communicator, a medium/messenger, a media product, or a text? Because robots possess qualities that overlap with human actors involved in interpersonal and social processes and also with communication and media technologies, multiple accounts have been offered. According to Peter and Kühne (2018), social robots challenge (1) traditional notions of medium and media because humans interact *with* rather than *through* them (Zhao, 2006; Gunkel, 2012; Guzman, 2018), (2) ideas about the communication partner because they test the human "gold standard" (Taipale et al., 2015; Spence, 2019), and (3) concepts of communication boundaries because their material differences from humans introduce new communication possibilities (e.g., Sandry, 2015b).

Many HMC researchers construe social robots as an interpersonal or quasi-interpersonal other (see Fortunati & Edwards, 2020; Fortunati et al., 2020) because "social robots overlap in form and function with human beings to the extent that their locally controlled performances occupy social roles and fulfill relationships that are traditionally held by other humans" (Edwards et al., 2016, p. 628) and because human–humanoid interaction has been designed in "language use, relationality, and normativeness" to resemble human interaction (Zhao, 2006, p. 404). HMC scholars

have suggested the applicability of interpersonal communication theories to HRI (e.g., Westerman et al., 2020) and discussed the challenges (Fox & Gambino, 2021).

HMC scholars frequently resource the influential Computers are Social Actors (CASA) paradigm (Nass et al., 1996), which posits that people mindlessly treat and respond to computers as if they were other humans, despite conscious knowledge they are not. In structured expansions of CASA, Gambino et al. (2020) used the term "media agents" for technologies cued to signal social interaction, and Lombard and Xu (2021) contended in their Media are Social Actors (MASA) paradigm that robots garner strong "medium-as-social-actor presence." Hoorn (2020) also foregrounded perception, proposing that robots may be seen as a means to transmit messages between humans (CMC), an autonomous social actor aligning with interpersonal communication processes, or a hybrid entity that is both "a technical medium as well as an autonomous social actor" (p. 5). Approaching from media studies, social robots have been analyzed as (a) the next "new media" (Taipale & Fortunati, 2018), (b) narrative texts and symbolic humans (Fortunati & Edwards, 2021), (c) media ecology (Hildebrand, 2021), and (d) actants in a transhuman technological/material network (Lutz & Tamó, 2018).

ROBOT ONTOLOGY AND AGENT-CLASS EFFECTS

Communicators are challenged to define the essential nature of robots and to understand them in relation to other types of beings (Fortunati & Edwards, 2020). HMC scholars have investigated lay sensemaking and offered critical analyses of robot ontology as related to other more familiar categories of being (e.g., A. Edwards, 2018) and have attended to the hybrid (subject/object, person/thing) ontology of social robots and the implications for communication (K.M. Lee et al., 2005; Sandry, 2018; Ling & Björling, 2020; Etztrodt & Engesser, 2021).

A substantial thread of HMC research has focused on identifying what differences are linked purely to an agent's class as a robot. Using between-subjects experiments that substitute a robot for another actor while holding their behavior constant, this research has shown that agent type can influence people's emotional responses (Rosenthal-von der Pütten et al., 2014), partner impressions (Bowman & Banks, 2019), credibility judgments (A. Edwards et al., 2017; C. Edwards et al., 2018, 2020a; Spence et al., 2021; Spence et al., 2019b,

2021), learning (A. Edwards et al., 2016), comfort (C. Edwards et al., 2018), and behavior evaluations (Banks et al., 2021a). Such experiments have often but not always demonstrated a relational advantage for a human actor over a robot performing the same script. However, social robots have been perceived as credible, attractive, and competent communicators with stronger social presence than earlier ICTs (Westerman et al., 2018).

INITIAL EXPECTATIONS AND THE HUMAN–HUMAN INTERACTION SCRIPT

In a series of three experiments, Spence, C. Edwards, A. Edwards, and Westerman measured people's expectations for a first encounter with a social robot versus human. Their "human-to-human interaction script" refers to the initial expectation and preference for human communication partners (anthropocentric expectancy bias) and the potential for expectancy violation effects with social robots. Participants primed verbally (Experiment 1; Spence et al., 2014) and visually (Experiment 2; C. Edwards et al., 2016) for a robot interaction partner (versus a human partner) were more uncertain and expected less social presence and liking. In a replication (Experiment 3; A. Edwards et al., 2019) using a more humanlike robot (Pepper) and tracing expectations from baseline to prime to post-interaction reality, there were no differences in uncertainty or anticipated social presence of the robot versus human, but the human partner was expected to be more socially attractive (A. Edwards et al., 2019). A brief conversation with a social robot led to lessened uncertainty and greater perceptions of its social presence, an effect not observed in the human condition. People may hold different expectations for communication with human and social robot partners and expectations may be altered or overcome through subsequent interaction (see also Haggadone et al., 2021). Further testing and elaboration of the human-to-human interaction script require accounting for the role of novelty, explicit measurement of the anthropocentric expectancy bias, and comparison of more and less anthropomorphic robot designs and a human partner in the context of a single experiment.

MIND, MORALITY, AND TRUST

There is evidence of similarity in people's implicit processing of humans' and robots' actions in the sense that they interpret robots as goal-oriented agents and not just complex moving objects (Sciutti et al., 2013), use the same "conceptual toolbox" of behavior explanations for human and robot agents (de Graaf & Malle, 2019), make implicit Theory of Mind (ToM) ascriptions for machine agents (Banks, 2020b), use the same basic moral foundations for evaluation (Banks, 2020a) and describe a social robot's message behavior in terms of its underlying beliefs, desires, and intentions for communication (A. Edwards et al., 2020). However, Appel et al. (2020) found that people experienced greater uncanniness in response to robots portrayed as having feelings and minds compared to robots portrayed as tools.

Although the same basic moral foundations were relevant to social evaluations of machine and human agents, machines were subject to different moral norms and may bear the greater burden to behave morally (Banks, 2020a) and social robots were subject to a stronger and more confident correspondence bias, or conflation of actor and action, compared to humans engaging the same behavior (A. Edwards & C. Edwards, 2021). HMC scholars have also conducted experiments on how the kinds of activities and interactions in which robots are engaged may influence perceptions of their nature and behavior; task interactions (versus play and social) cultivated greater trust (Banks et al., 2021b) and robot behavior/ability was more influential than morphology (human-likeness) on mind perception and anthropomorphic projection (Küster et al., 2020).

ACCEPTANCE AND USE INTENTIONS

Several HMC researchers have studied people's acceptance of social robots and intentions for use, often using survey methodology. Katz et al. (2015) showed that human-likeness of robots and previous engagement in virtual worlds were positively related to US college students' willingness to accept them. Also with U.S. college students, Spence et al. (2018) found that almost half agreed to sign a petition urging the U.N. to consider robot rights: Less negative attitudes toward robots, previous robot interactions, and higher perceptions of petitioner credibility were associated with endorsement. Lutz and Tamó-Larrieux (2020) introduced the robot privacy paradox to understand how privacy concerns shaped intentions to use social robots. People were most concerned about data protection on the robot manufacturer side, followed by social and physical privacy concerns; however, the perceived benefits of social robots often outweighed privacy concerns (see also J. Kim et al., 2013).

Researchers have paid special attention to children's acceptance or rejection of social robots, as detailed in the narrative review of research from 2000–2017 conducted by de Jong et al. (2019, 2020). In a field study of children who engaged in abusive behavior toward a social robot placed in a shopping corridor, Nomura et al. (2016) found that curiosity, enjoyment, and modeling of others' actions were the primary reasons children offered.

Alongside empirical investigations of precursors and outcomes, HMC scholars have created or adapted new instrumentation and process models. Banks and Edwards (2019) developed and validated a social distance scale to assess the degrees of closeness that humans are willing to accept with social robots on physical, relational, and conversational levels. Such tools enable baselining and tracking changes over time, as well as comparing acceptance toward different human and machine agents and agent classes. Although there are too few long-term use and acceptance studies, in a notable exception de Graaf et al. (2018) conducted a six-month home study of the interactive robot Karotz and found support for their phased framework for long-term acceptance.

COMMUNICATION WITH ROBOTS

Robot Verbal Message Strategies

Identifying effective verbal message strategies for robots in contexts of influence, exchange, and impression management has been a focus of HRI research in HMC. In the context of persuasion, S. A. Lee and Liang (2019) demonstrated a robotic-foot-in-the-door effect, in which persuasive outcomes were improved when the robot used a sequential-request strategy of making a small request before the larger (actual) request, and later (S. A. Lee & Liang, 2016), a reciprocity effect in which a robot's prior helping behavior in a trivia game significantly increased the likelihood of compliance with its later request for a 15-minute pattern recognition task (see also S. A. Lee & Liang, 2018).

In a regulatory scenario, A. Edwards et al. (2020) found that a humanoid social robot using a rhetorical message design logic (versus expressive or conventional) to correct/control the behavior of another was rated most favorably in terms of predicted communication success, goal-relevant attributes (ability to motivate and provide face support), competence, credibility, and

attractiveness, and it was perceived as the least eerie, unnatural, and machinelike. Craig et al. (2019) found that people were equally willing to comply with a robot's request whether it used warning or obligation strategies, but the latter led to higher perceptions of caring and task attraction. Stoll et al. (2016) found that a robot negotiating as a buyer's agent without guilt-tripping was perceived as more credible than a guilt-tripping robot and a robot negotiating as a principal buyer, but neither agency nor guilt influenced overall concession in the negotiation task. Strait et al. (2014) used a novel mixed-methods approach (survey and brain-based measures) to determine whether people preferred the same advice-giving strategies from humans with robots; politeness improved likability and considerateness perceptions and decreased aggressiveness perceptions. However, some effects occurred only in the third-person modality of *observing* HRI and not in actual first-person encounters with the robot. Positive impressions of social robots have also been linked to verbally joyful (versus sad) demeanor (Craig & C. Edwards, 2021) and remembering (versus forgetting) information (Packard et al., 2019).

In the context of self-disclosure, Birnbaum et al. (2016) demonstrated that robot responsiveness increased perceptions of appealing traits, approach behaviors, and willingness to relate with it during stress (Study 1) and improved people's self-perceptions during a stress-inducing task (Study 2). Similarly, Ling and Björling (2020) found that emotional, technical, and by-proxy robot self-disclosure elicited self-disclosure from participants, but the emotional type resulted in lower perceptions of robot safety. This accumulating body of work suggests pro-social and positivity biases infuse interpersonal evaluation processes in HRI similarly to human communication.

Robot Nonverbal Behavior and Appearance

HMC scholars have studied the effects of robots' nonverbal communication, including paralanguage, affect displays, morphology (body shape), and embodiment representing human identity groups. Notably, B. Lee (2007) proposed nonverbal intimacy as a benchmark for human–robot interactions, offering codes for "doing intimacy" drawn from human interaction, with the caveat that some appropriate human intimacy behaviors like touch may be less appropriate for robots. In terms of the role of paralanguage, or the nonlexical components of spoken communication, positive evaluations of robots have resulted from the robot's use of vocal fillers (e.g., uh, um) (Goble & C. Edwards, 2018), moderately slow to normal speech rate (Shimada & Kanda, 2012), and human-like voice (Xu, 2019).

Concerning nonverbal affect, expressive and humanlike nonverbal behavior led to higher perceived animacy, positive affect, and self-disclosure (Rosenthal-von der Pütten et al., 2018).

In terms of morphology, Barco et al. (2020) conducted an exploratory study of 7–14-year-old children's perceptions of social robots with different body designs. They perceived the anthropomorphic robot (NAO) as higher in anthropomorphism, social presence, and similarity than the zoomorphic robot (Pleo), and the caricatured robot (Cozmo) which was typically was somewhere in between. More broadly, Mieczkowski et al. (2018) demonstrated that people used the human-based stereotype content model of warmth and competence to form impressions and emotional responses toward robots based on their appearance, with some differences in the conversion of impressions to behavioral tendencies.

Importantly, characteristics of human identity groups may be incorporated in robot design. Strait et al. (2018) analyzed YouTube comments about videos of gynoids racialized as Black, White, and Asian (Bina48, Nadine, Yangyang) and showed a link between marginalizing racialization and antisocial and dehumanizing commentary. Dehnert and Leach (2021) critically analyzed the portrayal of robots as both sub- and super-human in the videogame *Detroit: Become Human* as it relates to ableist communication scripts about the socially constructed normal body of humans. Lastly, Sandry (2015a) urged a re-evaluation of the assumption that social robots should be designed as humanlike or animal-like at all. Through analysis of human relations with machine-like robots (EOD and the desk lamp, AUR) Sandry introduced the value of *tempered anthropomorphism and zoomorphism*, which allow a robot to be regarded as "familiar enough in its behavior to interpret its movements as meaningful, while also leaving space to acknowledge its fundamental differences from both humans and machines" (p. 344).

COMMUNICATION ABOUT ROBOTS

Scholarship on communication *about* robots comes from a variety of communication research traditions, including rhetorical/discourse analyses, media framing and effects studies, and word-of-mouth communication research. From the rhetorical tradition, Coleman (2018) developed the framework of "machinic rhetoric" to illuminate the tacitly persuasive actions associated with the movement of robots and computers even when they cannot speak for themselves. In a rhetorical analysis of the social robots Jibo and Buddy, Fritz (2018) illuminated their ontological positioning within the tension to situate them "as *both* intelligent subjects to converse with" and "technological objects for sale" (p. 68). Furthermore, Fortunati et al. (2021) introduced the term "roboid" for a robot in the prototyping stage that claims to be fully functional (Sophia), and which may be an effective means of reducing uncertainty in the liminal stage before commercial availability.

In media framing of robots, Roderick (2013) conducted a critical multimodal analysis of the representation of robot workers in commercials to demonstrate their framing as living labor linked to neoliberal transformations of work. In an experiment examining news framing effects on feelings about robots in the workplace, Spence et al. (2018b) found that humanoid (vs. nonhumanoid) imagery stoked more negative attitudes and replacement anxieties. Focusing on a specific social robot product, Liu (2021) examined the construction of gender in the hologram Azuma Hikari by combining semiotic analysis of marketing materials with users' experiences to show that the hologram device leverages stereotypes of the Japanese ideal bride and reproduces unequal gender relations as users are disciplined to play the role of the wage earner and master-like husband. HMC scholars have also demonstrated experimentally that what humans say to one another about a social robot can impact social and emotional responses to it (C. Edwards et al., 2020b; Liang & S.A. Lee, 2016; Mara & Appel, 2015; Van Straten et al., 2020).

BROADER IMPACTS AND APPLIED CONTEXTS

HMC research also has addressed the larger implications of HRI for societies and individuals. Fortunati (2018) critically analyzed the interrelation between robotization and the domestic sphere in a political economy sense, concluding that social robots must be participatory, inclusive, and intentionally deployed. Fortunati et al. (2019) found preliminary evidence that CAPTCHA execution was associated with feelings of alienation and dehumanization. Finally, Lachlan et al. (2016) suggested social robots as a promising platform for delivering information in dangerous and difficult scenarios and Rainear et al. (2019) demonstrated in the context of weather crises that novel technologies with strong social presence may distract and lead to lower information retention. More research is needed on how proliferating and sustained HRI influences individuals, relationships, and societies.

CONCLUSION

In summary, HMC research that centers HRI has generated debate about the role of robots in the communication process and their similarities and differences from human interlocutors. Studies show that when performing the same roles traditionally held by human communicators, robots tend to be perceived less favorably, but still competent. There is evidence that people are more uncertain about first interactions with robots and expect them to be less socially present and attractive, but that actual encounters with human-like robots may exceed expectations and even rival or surpass positive perceptions formed in human communication. People attribute mind, mental states, and morality to robots, but may hold them to a different and higher standard of conduct and judge them more for their behavior. Individual experiences, attitudes, and cost-benefit analyses are important factors in robot acceptance and use intentions. When communicating verbally with robots in persuasion, self-disclosure, and impression-formation contexts, human-based communication theories and models tend to apply well, with some differences linked to the unique ontology of robots. Nonverbal cues are important because people judge robots based on their morphology and the human-likeness of their behavior, and they may extend biases and stereotypes of human identity groups to robots designed in their likenesses. Robots both perform and are surrounded by unique and interesting rhetoric, and the messages and frames people receive about robots influence their subsequent experience and perception. Finally, increased interactions between humans and robots occur alongside seismic shifts in political economy and will reconfigure personal identity and group dynamics; therefore, the broader impacts of HRI on human communication demand increased scholarly attention. Each of these empirically supported observations substantially advances understanding of HRI and demonstrates the relevance and value of communication-based (HMC) scholarship. Important theoretical, social, and design implications have emerged from this research and will continue to grow.

Going forward, researchers must continue to grapple with questions regarding whether, when, and to what degree human–robot communication fits the human mold, and whether and how it might be productively and generatively considered on its own terms. HRI research in HMC has been dominated by experimental methodology, often undertaken within the CASA framework. The traditional procedure to conduct research in this paradigm involves selection of a social science finding from human research, replication of the research by replacing a human actor with a computer or robot, equipping the robot with human-linked qualities, and determining the applicability of the original finding (Nass et al., 1994). An innovation and expansion characterizing many HMC approaches is to also include a human–human comparison group, which offers several advantages: replication of the original finding, identification of both similarities and differences in human and human–robot interaction (including effect size comparisons within the same data set), and exploration of the possibility that apparent similarities may arise for different reasons than the mindless application of social scripts mean for other humans (A. Edwards & C. Edwards, 2022). The last point is especially important because the original CASA testing procedure is not particularly sensitive to the potential that the same observational endpoint may arise for different theoretical reasons. In this sense, researchers may over-identify CASA support because of similarities in HMC and human communication processes that cannot be attributed to mindlessness. At the same time, there is the need to counterbalance methodologies that approach HRI from a human-centric place (using the theories, constructs, and variables that bend toward, advantage, or presume humanness) with approaches that treat the machine partner on its own terms. In this early stage of the field, qualitative inquiry and observational studies rooted in actual use practices over time are crucial (Fortunati & Edwards, 2021). Furthermore, there is much to learn about meaning making involving robots that are not explicitly social or humanlike and which include drones, autonomous cars, and robots used for delivery, surgery, and factory work. Finally, HMC scholars are well qualified and uniquely situated to shed light on how HRI over time transforms communication processes, both with machines and with each other.

REFERENCES

Appel, M., Izydorczyk, D., Weber, S., Mara, M., & Lischetzke, T. (2020). The uncanny of mind in a machine: Humanoid robots as tools, agents, and experiencers. *Computers in Human Behavior, 102*, 274–286. https://doi.org/10.1016/j.chb.2019.07.031

Banks, J. (2019). A perceived moral agency scale: Development and validation of a metric for humans and social machines. *Computers in Human Behavior, 90*, 363–371. https://doi.org/10.1016/j.chb.2018.08.028

Banks, J. (2020a). Good robots, bad robots: Morally valenced behavior effects on perceived mind, morality, and trust. *International Journal of Social Robotics*, 1–18. https://doi.org/10.1007/s12369-020-00692-3

Banks, J. (2020b). Theory of mind in social robots: Replication of five established human tests. *International Journal of Social Robotics, 12*, 403–414. https://doi.org/10.1007/s12369-019-00588-x

Banks, J., & Edwards, A. (2019, October). A common social distance scale for humans and robots. In *2019 28th IEEE International Conference on Robot and Human Interactive Communication (RO-MAN)* (pp. 1–6). IEEE.

Banks, J., Edwards, A., & Westerman, D. (2021a). The space between: Nature and machine heuristics in evaluations of organisms, cyborgs, and robots. *Cyberpsychology, behavior, and social networking*. https://doi.org/10.1089/cyber.2020.0165

Banks, J., Koban, K., & Chauveau, P. de V. (2021b). Forms and frames: Mind, morality and trust in robots across prototypical interactions. *Human-Machine Communication, 2*, 81–103. https://doi.org/10.30658/hmc.2.4

Barco, A., de Jong, C., Peter, J., Kühne, R., & van Straten, C. L. (2020, March). Robot morphology and children's perception of social robots: An exploratory study. In *Companion of the 2020 ACM/IEEE International Conference on Human-Robot Interaction* (pp. 125–127).

Bartneck, C., Belpaeme, T., Eyssel, F., Kanda, T., Keijsers, M., & Šabonović, S. (2020). *Human-robot interaction: An introduction*. Cambridge University Press.

Birnbaum, G., Mizrahi, M., Hoffman, G., Reis, H. T., Finkel, E. J., & Sass, O. (2016). What robots can teach us about intimacy: The reassuring effects of robot responsiveness to human disclosure. *Computers in Human Behavior, 63*, 416–423. http://dx.doi.org/10.1016/j.chb.2016.05.064

Bowman, N. D., & Banks, J. (2019, October). Social and entertainment gratifications of videogame play comparing robot, AI, and human partners. In *2019 28th IEEE International Conference on Robot and Human Interactive Communication (RO-MAN)* (pp. 1–6). IEEE.

Coleman, M. C. (2018). Machinic rhetorics and the influential movements of robots. *Review of Communication, 18*(4), 336–351. https://doi.org/10.1080/15358593.2018.1517417

Craig, M. J., & Edwards, C. (2021). Feeling for our robot overlords: Perceptions of emotionally expressive social robots in initial interactions. *Communication Studies, 72*(2), 251–265. https://doi.org/10.1080/10510974.2021.1880457

Craig, M. J., Edwards, C., Edwards, A., & Spence, P. R. (2019, March). Impressions of message compliance-gaining strategies for considering robot rights. In *2019 14th ACM/IEEE International Conference on Human-Robot Interaction (HRI)* (pp. 560–561). IEEE. https://doi.org/10.1109/HRI.2019.8673117

de Graaf, M. M., Allouch, S. B., & Van Dijk, J. A. G. M. (2015, October). What makes robots social?: A user's perspective on characteristics for social human-robot interaction. In *International Conference on Social Robotics* (pp. 184–193). Springer, Cham.

de Graaf, M. M., Allouch, S. B., & Van Dijk, J. A. G. M. (2018). A phased framework for long-term user acceptance of interactive technology in domestic environments. *New Media & Society, 20*(7), 2582–2603. https://doi.org.libproxy.library.wmich.edu/10.1177/1461444817727264

de Graaf, M. M., & Malle, B. F. (2019, March). People's explanations of robot behavior subtly reveal mental state inferences. In *2019 14th ACM/IEEE International Conference on Human-Robot Interaction (HRI)* (pp. 239–248). IEEE.

Dehnert, M., & Leach, R. B. (2021). Becoming human? Ableism and control in Detroit: Become human and the implications for human-machine communication. *Human-Machine Communication, 2*, 137–152. https://doi.org/10.30658/hmc.2.7

de Jong, C., Kühne, R., Peter, J., van Straten, C. L., & Barco, A. (2020). Intentional acceptance of social robots: Development and validation of a self-report measure for children. *International Journal of Human-Computer Studies, 139*, 1–9. https://doi.org/10.1016/j.ijhcs.2020.102426

de Jong, C., Peter, J., Kühne, R., & Barco, A. (2019). Children's acceptance of social robots: A narrative review of the research 2000-2017. *Interaction Studies, 20*(3), 393–425. https://doi.org/10.1075/is.18071.jon

Edwards, A. (2018). Animals, humans, and machines: Interactive implications of ontological classification. In A. Guzman (Ed.), *Human-machine communication: Rethinking communication, technology, and ourselves* (pp. 29–49). Peter Lang.

Edwards, A., & Edwards, C. (2022). Does the correspondence bias apply to social robots?: Dispositional and situational attributions of human versus robot behavior. *Frontiers in Robotics and AI*, 404. https://doi.org/10.3389/frobt.2021.788242

Edwards, A., Edwards, C., & Gambino, A. (2020). The social pragmatics of communication with social robots: Effects of robot message design logic in a regulative context. *International Journal of Social Robotics*, *12*, 945–957. https://doi.org/10.1007/s12369-019-00538-7

Edwards, A., Edwards, C., Spence, P. R., Harris, C., & Gambino, A. (2016). Robots in the classroom: Differences in students' perceptions of credibility and learning between "teacher as robot" and "robot as teacher". *Computers in Human Behavior*, *65*, 627–634. https://doi.org/10.1016/j.chb.2016.06.005

Edwards, A., Edwards, C., Westerman, D., & Spence, P. R. (2019). Initial expectations, interactions, and beyond with social robots. *Computers in Human Behavior*, *90*, 308–314. https://doi.org/10.1016/j.chb.2018.08.042

Edwards, A., Omilion-Hodges, L., & Edwards, C. (2017, March). How do patients in a medical interview perceive a robot versus human physician?. In *Proceedings of the Companion of the 2017 ACM/IEEE International Conference on Human-Robot Interaction (HRI)* (pp. 109–110) ACM. https://doi.org/10.1145/3029798.3038308

Edwards, C., Edwards, A., Albrehi, F., & Spence, P. R. (2020a). Interpersonal impressions of a social robot versus human in the context of performance evaluations. *Communication Education*, *70*(2), 1–18. https://doi.org/10.1080/03634523.2020.1802495

Edwards, C., Edwards, A., & Omilion-Hodges, L. (2018, March). Receiving medical treatment plans from a robot: Evaluations of presence, credibility, and attraction. Proceedings of the Companion of the 2018 *ACM/IEEE International Conference on Human-Robot Interaction (HRI)* (pp. 101–102). https://doi.org/10.1145/3173386.3177050

Edwards, C., Edwards, A., Spence, P. R., & Westerman, D. (2016). Initial interaction expectations with robots: Testing the human-to-human interaction script. *Communication Studies*, *67*(2), 227–238. https://doi.org/10.1080/10510974.2015.1121899

Edwards, C., Edwards, A., & Rijhwani, V. (2020b). Rate my robot: The effect of word-of-mouth (WOM) on perceptions of a social robot's teaching performance. In In *2020 29th IEEE International Conference on Robot and Human Interactive Communication (RO-MAN)* (pp. 1063–1068). IEEE. 10.1109/RO-MAN47096.2020.9223496

Edwards, C., Stoll, B., Edwards, A., Spence, P., & Gambino, A. (2018). "I'll present to the human": Effects of a robot evaluator on anticipatory public speaking anxiety. In A. Gutzman (Ed.), *Human-machine communication: Rethinking communication, technology, and ourselves* (pp. 83–97). Peter Lang.

Etzrodt, K., & Engesser, S. (2021). Voice-based agents as personified things: Assimilation and accommodation as equilibration of doubt. *Human-Machine Communication*, *2*, 57–79. https://doi.org/10.30658/hmc.2.3

Fritz, L. M. (2018). Child or product? The rhetoric of social robots. In A. Guzman (Ed.), *Human-machine communication: Rethinking communication, technology, and ourselves* (pp. 67–82). Peter Lang.

Fortunati, L. (2018). Robotization and the domestic sphere. *New Media & Society*, *20*(8), 2673–2690. https://doi.org/10.1177/1461444817729366

Fortunati, L., Cavallo, F., & Sarrica, M. (2020). Multiple communication roles in human–robot interactions in public space. *International Journal of Social Robotics*, *12*, 931–944. https://doi.org/10.1007/s12369-018-0509-0

Fortunati, L., & Edwards, A. (2020). Opening space for theoretical, methodological, and empirical issues in human-machine communication. *Human-Machine Communication*, *1*, 7–18. https://doi.org/10.30658/hmc.1.1

Fortunati, L., & Edwards, A. (2021). Moving ahead with human-machine communication. *Human-Machine Communication*, *2*, 7–28. https://doi.org/10.30658/hmc.2.1

Fortunati, L., Esposito, A., Sarrica, M., & Ferrin, G. (2015). Children's knowledge and imaginary about robots. *International Journal of Social Robotics*, *7*(5), 685–695. https://doi.org/10.1007/s12369-015-0316-9

Fortunati, L., Manganelli, A. M., Cavallo, F., & Honsell, F. (2019). You need to show that you are not a robot. *New Media & Society*, *21*(8), 1859–1876. https://doi.org/10.1177/1461444819831971

Fortunati, L., Sorrentino, A., Fiorini, L., & Cavallo, F. (2021). The rise of the roboid. *International Journal of Social Robotics*, 1–15. https://doi.org/10.1007/s12369-020-00732-y

Fox, J., & Gambino, A. (2021). Relationship development with humanoid social robots: Applying interpersonal theories to human/robot interaction. *Cyberpsychology, Behavior, and Social Networking*. https://doi.org/10.1089/cyber.2020.0181

Gambino, A., Fox, J., & Ratan, R. A. (2020). Building a stronger CASA: Extending the Computers are Social Actors paradigm. *Human-Machine Communication*, *1*, 71–86. https://doi.org/10.30658/hmc.1.5

Goble, H., & Edwards, C. (2018). A robot that communicates with vocal fillers has... Uhhh... greater social presence. *Communication Research Reports*, *35*(3), 256–260. https://doi.org/10.1080/08824096.2018.1447454

Gunkel, D. J. (2012). Communication and artificial intelligence: Opportunities and challenges for the 21st century. *communication+ 1*, *1*(1), 1–25.

Guzman, A. (2018) Introduction: "What is human-machine communication, anyway?". In A. Guzman (Ed.), *Human-machine communication: Rethinking communication, technology, and ourselves* (pp. 1–28). Peter Lang.

Haggadone, B., Banks, J., & Koban, K. (2021). Of robots and robotkind: Extending intergroup contact theory to social machines. *Communication Research Reports*. https://doi.org/10.1080/08824096.2021. 1909551

Hildebrand, J. M. (2021). What is the message of the robot medium? Considering media ecology and mobilities in critical robotics research. *AI & Society*. https://doi.org/10.1007/s00146-021-01204-1

Hoorn, J. F. (2018). Theory of robot communication: I. The medium is the communication partner. *arXiv preprint arXiv:1812.04408*.

Katz, J. E., Halpern, D., & Crocker, E. T. (2015). In the company of robots: Views of acceptability of robots in social settings. In J. Vincent, S. Taipale, B. Sapio B., G. Lugano, and L. Fortunati (Eds.) *Social robots from a human perspective* (pp. 25–38). Springer. https://doi.org/10.1007/978-3-319-15672-9_3

Kim, K. J., Park, E., & Sundar, S. S. (2013). Caregiving role in human-robot interaction: A study of the mediating effects of perceived benefit and social presence. *Computers in Human Behavior, 29*(4), 1799–1806. http://dx.doi.org/10.1016/j.chb.2013. 02.009

Küster, D., Swiderska, A., & Gunkel, D. (2020). I saw it on YouTube! How online videos shape perceptions of mind, morality, and fears about robots. *New Media & Society*, https://doi.org/10.1177/1461444 820954199

Lachlan, K. A., Spence, P. R., Rainear, A., Fishlock, J., Xu, Z., & Vanco, B. (2016). You're my only hope: An initial exploration of the effectiveness of robotic platforms in engendering learning about crises and risks. *Computers in Human Behavior, 65*, 606–611. http://dx.doi.org/10.1016/j.chb.2016.05.081

Lee, B. (2007). Nonverbal intimacy as a benchmark for human–robot interaction. *Interaction Studies, 8*(3), 411–422.

Lee, K. M., Park, N., & Song, H. (2005). Can a robot be perceived as a developing creature? Effects of a robot's long-term cognitive developments on its social presence and people's social responses toward it. *Human Communication Research, 31*(4), 538–563. https://doi-org.libproxy.library.wmich.edu/10. 1111/j.1468-2958.2005.tb00882.x

Lee, S. A., & Liang, Y. (2016). The role of reciprocity in verbally persuasive robots. *Cyberpsychology, Behavior, and Social Networking, 19*(8), 524–527. https://doi.org/10.1089/cyber.2016.0124

Lee, S. A. & Liang, Y. (2018). Theorizing verbally persuasive robots. In A. Guzman (Ed.), *Human-machine communication: Rethinking communication, technology, and ourselves* (pp. 119–143). Peter Lang.

Lee, S. A., & Liang, Y. J. (2019). Robotic foot-in-the-door: Using sequential-request persuasive strategies in human-robot interaction. *Computers in Human Behavior, 90*, 351–356. https://doi.org/10.1016/j. chb.2018.08.026

Liang, Y., & Lee, S. A. (2016). Advancing the strategic messages affecting robot trust effect: The dynamic of user- and robot-generated content on human-robot trust and interaction outcomes. *Cyberpsychology, Behavior, and Social Networking, 19*(2), 538–544. https://doi.org/10.1089/cyber.2016.0199

Liang, Y., & Lee, S. A. (2017). Fear of autonomous social robots and artificial intelligence: Evidence from national representative data with probability sampling. *International Journal of Social Robotics, 9*(1), 379–384. https://doi.org/10.1007/s12369-017-0401-3

Ling, H. Y., & Björling, E. A. (2020). Sharing stress with a robot: What would a robot say? *Human-Machine Communication, 1*, 133–158. https://doi.org/10.30658/hmc.1.8

Liu, J. (2021). Social robots as the bride?: Understanding the construction of gender in a Japanese social robot product. *Human-Machine Communication, 2*, 105–121. https://doi.org/10.30658/hmc.2.5

Lombard, M., & Xu, K. (2021). Social responses to media technologies in the 21st century: The Media are Social Actors paradigm. *Human-Machine Communication, 2*, 29–55. https://doi.org/10.30658/hmc.2.2

Lutz, C. & Tamò, A. (2018). Communicating with robots: ANTanlyzing the interaction between healthcare robots and humans with regard to privacy. In A. Guzman (Ed.), *Human-machine communication: Rethinking communication, technology, and ourselves* (pp. 145–166). Peter Lang.

Lutz, C., & Tamó-Larrieux, A. (2020). The robot privacy paradox: Understanding how privacy concerns shape intentions to use social robots. *Human-Machine Communication, 1*, 87–111. https://doi.org/10.30658/hmc.1.6

Mara, M., & Appel, M. (2015). Science fiction reduces the eeriness of android robots: A field experiment. *Computers in Human Behavior, 48*, 156–162. http://dx.doi.org/10.1016/j.chb.2015.01.007

Mieczkowski, H., Liu, S. X., Hancock, J., & Reeves, B. (2019). Helping not hurting: Applying the stereotype content model and BIAS map to social robotics. *In Proceedings of the 14th ACM/IEEE International Conference on Human-Robot Interaction (HRI)* (pp. 222–229). https://doi.org/10.1109/HRI.2019. 8673307

Nass, C., Steuer, J., & Tauber, E. R. (1994). Computers are social actors. In *Proceedings of the SIGCHI 583 Conference on Human Factors in Computing Systems* (pp. 72–78).

Nomura, T., Kanda, T., Kidokoro, H., Suehiro, Y., & Yamada, S. (2016). Why do children abuse robots?. *Interaction Studies, 17*(3), 347–369. https://doi.org/10.1075/is.17.3.02nom

Packard, C., Boelk, T., Andres, J., Edwards, C., Edwards, A., & Spence, P. R. (2019, March). The pratfall effect and interpersonal impressions of a robot that forgets and apologizes. In *2019 14th ACM/IEEE International Conference on Human-Robot Interaction*

(HRI) (pp. 524–525). IEEE. https://doi.org/10.1109/HRI.2019.8673101

Peter, J, & Kühne, R. (2018). The new frontier in communication research: Why we should study social robots. *Media and Communication (Lisboa), 6*(3), 73–76. https://doi.org/10.17645/mac.v6i3.1596

Peter, J., Kühne, R., Barco, A., de Jong, C., & van Straten, C. L. (2019). Asking today the crucial questions of tomorrow: Social robots and the Internet of Toys. In G. Mascheroni and D. Holloway (Eds.) *The internet of toys* (pp. 25–46). Palgrave Macmillan.

Rainear, A. M., Lachlan, K. A., & Fishlock, J. (2019). Exploring retention and behavioral intentions when using social robotics to communicate a weather risk. *Computers in Human Behavior, 90*, 372–379. https://doi.org/10.1016/j.chb.2018.08.029

Roderick, I. (2013). Representing robots as living labour in advertisements: The new discourse of worker–employer power relations. *Critical Discourse Studies, 10*(4), 392–405. http://dx.doi.org/10.1080/17405904.2013.813773

Rodríguez-Hidalgo, C. (2020). Me and my robot smiled at one another: The process of socially enacted communicative affordance in human-machine communication. *Human-Machine Communication, 1*, 55–69. https://doi.org/10.30658/hmc.1.4

Rosenthal-von der Pütten, A., et al. (2014). Investigations on empathy towards humans and robots using fMRI. *Computers in Human Behavior, 33*, 201–212. http://dx.doi.org/10.1016/j.chb.2014.01.004

Rosenthal-von der Pütten, A. M., Krämer, N. C., & Herrmann, J. (2018). The effects of humanlike and robot-specific affective nonverbal behavior on perception, emotion, and behavior. *International Journal of Social Robotics, 10*(5), 569–582. https://doi.org/10.1007/s12369-018-0466-7

Sandry, E. (2015a). Re-evaluating the form and communication of social robots. *International Journal of Social Robotics, 7*(3), 335–346. www.doi.org/10.1007/s12369-014-0278-3

Sandry, E. (2015b). *Robots and communication.* Springer.

Sandry, E. (2018). Aliveness and the off-switch in human-robot relations. In A. Guzman (Ed.), *Human-machine communication: Rethinking communication, technology, and ourselves* (pp. 51–66). Peter Lang.

Sarrica, M., Brondi, S., & Fortunati, L. (2019). How many facets does a "social robot" have? A review of scientific and popular definitions online. *Information Technology & People, 30*(1), 1–22. https://doi.org/10.1108/ITP-04-2018-0203

Sciutti, A., Bisio, A., Nori, F., Metta, G., Fadiga, L., & Sandini, G. (2013). Robots can be perceived as goal-oriented agents. *Interaction Studies, 14*(3), 329–350. https://doi.org/10.1075/is.14.3.02sci

Shimada, M., & Kanda, T. (2012). What is the appropriate speech rate for a communication robot?. *Interaction Studies, 13*(3), 406–433. https://doi.org/10.1075/is.16.2.07ros

Spence, P. R. (2019). Searching for questions, original thoughts, or advancing theory: Human-machine communication. *Computers in Human Behavior, 90*, 285–287. https://doi.org/10.1016/j.chb.2018.09.014

Spence, P. R., Edwards, A., & Edwards, C. (2018a, March). Attitudes, prior interaction, and petitioner credibility predict support for considering the rights of robots. *In Companion of the 2018 ACM/IEEE International Conference on Human-Robot Interaction (HRI)* (pp. 243–244). ACM. https://doi.org/10.1145/3173386.3177071

Spence, P. R., Edwards, C., Edwards, A., & Lin, X. (2019b, March). Testing the machine heuristic: Robots and suspicion in news broadcasts. In *2019 14th ACM/IEEE International Conference on Human-Robot Interaction (HRI)* (pp. 568–569). IEEE. https://doi.org/10.1109/HRI.2019.8673108

Spence, P. R., Edwards, C., Edwards, A., Rainer, A., & Jin, X. (2021). "They're always wrong anyway": Exploring differences of credibility, attraction, and behavior intentions in professional, amateur, and robot-delivered weather forecasts. *Communication Quarterly.* https://doi.org/10.1080/01463373.2021.1877164

Spence, P. R., Westerman, D., Edwards, C., & Edwards, A. (2014). Welcoming our robot overlords: Initial expectations about interaction with a robot. *Communication Research Reports, 31*(3), 272–280. https://doi.org/10.1080/08824096.2014.924337

Spence, P. R., Westerman, D., & Lin, X. (2018b). A robot will take your job. How does that make you feel? Examining perceptions of robots in the workplace. In A. Guzman (Ed.), *Human-machine communication: Rethinking communication, technology, and ourselves* (pp. 185–200). Peter Lang.

Stoll, B., Edwards, C., & Edwards, A. (2016). "Why aren't you a sassy little thing": The effects of robot-enacted guilt trips on credibility and consensus in a negotiation. *Communication Studies, 67*(5), 530–547. https://doi.org/10.1080/10510974.2016.1215339

Strait, M., Canning, C., & Scheutz, M. (2014, March). Let me tell you! investigating the effects of robot communication strategies in advice-giving situations based on robot appearance, interaction modality and distance. In *Proceedings of the 2014 ACM/IEEE international conference on Human-robot interaction* (pp. 479–486).

Strait, M., Ramos, A. S., Contreras, V., & Garcia, N. (2018, August). Robots racialized in the likeness of marginalized social identities are subject to greater dehumanization than those racialized as white. In *2018 27th IEEE International Symposium on Robot and Human Interactive Communication (RO-MAN)* (pp. 452–457). IEEE.

Taipale, S., & Fortunati, L. (2018). Communicating with machines: Robots as the next new media. In A. Guzman (Ed.), *Human-machine communication: Rethinking communication, technology, and ourselves* (pp. 201–220). Peter Lang.

Taipale, S., Vincent, J., Sapio, B., Lugano, G., & Fortunati, L. (2015). Introduction: Situating the human in social robots. In *Social robots from a human perspective* (pp. 1–7). Springer, Cham.

van Straten, C. L., Peter, J., Kühne, R., & Barco, A. (2020). Transparency about a robot's lack of human psychological capacities: Effects on child-robot perception and relationship formation. *ACM Transactions on Human-Robot Interaction (THRI)*, *9*(2), 1–22. https://doi.org/10.1145/3365668

Westerman, D., Edwards, A., & Edwards, C. (2018, May). *Social robots and social presence: Interpersonally communicating with robots*. [Paper presentation]

Human-Machine Communication Preconference of the International Communication Association Conference, Prague, Czech Republic.

Westerman, D., Edwards, A., Edwards, C., Luo, Z., & Spence, P. R. (2020). I-It, I-Thou, I-Robot: The perceived humanness of AI in human-machine communication. *Communication Studies*, *71*(3), 393–408. https://doi.org/10.1080/10510974.2020.1749683

Xu, K. (2019). First encounter with robot Alpha: How individual differences interact with vocal and kinetic cues in users' social responses. *New Media & Society*, *21*(11–12), 2522-2547. https://doi-org.libproxy.library.wmich.edu/10.1177/1461444819851479

Zhao, S. (2006). Humanoid social robots as a medium of communication. *New Media & Society*, *8*(3), 401–419. https://doi.org/10.1177/1461444806061951

19

Auditing Human–Machine Communication Systems Using Simulated Humans

Nicholas Diakopoulos, Jack Bandy, and
Henry Dambanemuya

INTRODUCTION

As machine communicators come to occupy many of the same spaces as human beings—whether by populating our homes with Siris and Alexas or by pervading social media platforms as bots or newsfeed curators and recommenders—they introduce a host of new opportunities and styles for communication both between humans and machines as well as between and amongst humans themselves (Gómez-Zará & Diakopoulos, 2020). Machines are a form of alien communicator, drawing on vast data and algorithms that permit them unfamiliar communicative capabilities. But they are nonetheless aliens of human design and reflection in their patterns of behavior. Given HMC's orientation toward understanding how people make sense of and relate to machines as communicators (Guzman & Lewis, 2019), how should researchers approach these peculiar new inhabitants of our communicative spaces? In this chapter, we argue that in order to better understand how humans communicate with machines, it can be beneficial to audit the mechanisms and functions of machines by simulating how humans might communicate with them.

Audit methods have a long history of use in social science research to study behavior, largely relying on observational techniques to examine reactivity bias and discrimination (Gaddis, 2017). More recently, they have been applied in a variety of clever ways to better understand the behavior of algorithms, including how algorithmic decisions may be biased or otherwise lead to errors and harms to individuals or society for which they should be held accountable (Sandvig et al., 2014; Diakopoulos, 2015; Bandy, 2021). In addition, a growing number of studies use audit methods to systematically describe and articulate the role of algorithms in communication systems and their reactions to users, such as in media distribution (Bandy & Diakopoulos, 2020a), targeted advertising (Sweeney, 2013), content recommender systems (Hussein et al., 2020), and search engines (Trielli & Diakopoulos, 2019). Such studies help to characterize and explain machine behavior as it relates to the human experience and can therefore provide an important tool for articulating the contexts and conditions under which HMC takes place.

To achieve the highest levels of validity, researchers will ultimately need to undertake large-scale experiments which assess how real people in natural contexts interact and communicate with machines. Many methods can be brought to bear in studying machine communicators, from discourse analysis and individual case studies to interviewing designers (Haim, 2020). However, here we argue that audit studies using simulated humans—essentially computer agents mimicking human communicators (Haim, 2020; Sandvig et al., 2014)—are an important and efficient way to begin to characterize machine communication behavior that can, in turn, set the stage for larger behavioral inquiry and experiments. While such an approach focuses on the machine in understanding how it responds and reacts as a communicator, audit studies can also inform new questions that re-center people with respect to the bounds and nuance of machine capabilities. Audit studies also reduce resource demands by limiting the need for human subjects, and they have additional advantages in their repeatability and potential to control and precisely vary the nature and context of (simulated) interactions with machines. Thus, the empirical grounding of simulated agents in plausible human communicative behavior becomes a key concern. The value and validity of what we learn about machine communication by way of audits will depend on the fidelity of the simulated agents to actual human behavior.

In the following sections, we first describe our own experience in two case studies that simulated human agents to audit algorithms in communication contexts. These include one audit focused on how the Amazon Alexa smart speaker device responds to various news-related queries (Dambanemuya & Diakopoulos, 2021) and another audit contrasting the curation of media on Twitter's algorithmic timeline compared to its chronological timeline (Bandy & Diakopoulos, 2021). We then delve into methodological considerations and challenges exposed by these cases to elaborate effective ways for other researchers to undertake such studies. Finally, we look ahead to new opportunities to deepen the role of simulation and auditing in understanding HMC systems.

NEWS QUALITY ON ALEXA

Smart speakers such as the Amazon Alexa and Google Home are becoming increasingly ubiquitous machine communicators in society. However, despite soaring trends in their use for news consumption (NPR, 2020), little is yet known about the quality, source diversity, and comprehensiveness of news information conveyed by smart speakers. To address this, we developed a data-driven method for evaluating the information quality of news-related queries on smart speakers. Our methodology, evaluated on the Amazon Echo Plus device running the Alexa voice assistant,

demonstrates a combination of approaches for generating user queries, automating data collection, and evaluating the smart speaker responses along key data quality dimensions of relevancy, accuracy, and timeliness.

To simulate how real people interact with the Alexa smart speaker, we generated user queries composed of a *query topic* and a *query phrasing*. To generate query topics, we relied on the top 20 U.S. Google daily trending search topics collected each day at the same time of day over a two-week period from October 28 to November 11, 2019. To generate user queries, we crowdsourced and tailored our audit to four common phrases that people use when seeking news-related information from voice assistants. In pilot testing, we observed that the device could be sensitive to correct preposition use in the query phrase. Therefore, to increase the validity for the audit, we matched the type of query topic to a specific preposition, e.g., "What happened *to* {person}" or "What happened *during* {event}". Based on our crowdsourced data collection and analysis, the four most commonly used phrasings we identified were:

- What happened {during / to / in / on / with / at the } {query topic}?
- What is going on {during / with / at / in / on} {query topic}?
- Can you tell me about {the} {query topic}?
- What is new {with / on} {query topic}?

Because query topics are based on trends derived from large-scale search behavior, they reflect actual human search interest around news-relevant topics. And because query phrases are derived from an aggregation of user survey results around query patterns, they reflect some of the more common ways people request news information from the device.

To automate the data collection process, we used Amazon Polly with default settings and the "Matthew" voice to synthesize the text of the user queries to speech. We then used the synthesized speech to query the device with each of the 20 daily trending topics using all four query phrasings during early evening hours. To minimize the potential for Alexa to learn from previous queries, we randomized the order of the query phrasings, introduced a one-minute delay between each subsequent query, and let each response play uninterrupted. Finally, we used Amazon Transcribe to transcribe the audio responses and recorded both the responses and queries in a database for analysis. Thus, we were able to systematically and continuously audit various queries and phrasings by simulating human speech production and automatically transcribing data for further analysis.

Overall, Alexa was able to return relevant responses for 71.6% of the queries. However, a significant shortcoming of the device was the lack of provenance information for 60.4% of its responses. Additionally, we further observed subtle variations in how the query phrasings affect (1) the sources of information provided by Alexa, (2) Alexa's ability to understand users' queries, and hence (3) Alexa's ability to provide relevant and timely responses. These observations merit further experimental investigation with real human interlocutors to understand whether there are patterns between question phrasing and other relevant factors such as education level, social-economic standing, or cultural background, which could lead to unequal access to news information for specific user groups.

MEDIA DISTRIBUTION ON TWITTER

While Twitter has described their timeline curation algorithm as a key feature for attracting and retaining users (Kastrenakes, 2020), they provide sparse information as to how the algorithm alters communication on the platform. This led us to design and conduct an experiment to help characterize some of the algorithm's high-level effects on communication, comparing chronological timelines to algorithmic timelines for a small group of simulated users. Our method involved two main phases: (1) strategically sampling and setting up simulated users, and (2) collecting and analyzing data to compare media exposure patterns for those simulated users.

Ideally, such an experiment would involve millions of real-world Twitter users. Large-scale experiments may still be possible in the future (e.g. through collaboration or by the platform itself), but as a first step, this experiment tested algorithmic timelines for a small group of simulated users. Thus, the first main phase involved choosing which users to simulate. Due to Twitter API data constraints our experimental capacity was on the order of about 10 accounts, which called for some deliberate sampling from Twitter's more than 150 million daily active users.

To identify users to simulate we first collected 20 million accounts that followed U.S. congresspeople in February 2020. This collection method was fairly blunt, but it allowed us to collect a large initial pool of users and scoped the study to users engaged in U.S. politics. From this initial pool, we collected network data for 10,000 random accounts (which took one week due to Twitter API constraints), then used a community detection algorithm to identify major communities in this sample. Most users belonged to one of eight communities. We identified the most central representative user in each community based on co-following behavior, computed the Botometer score (Yang et al., 2020) to ensure it was greater than 0.5 and therefore more likely to be human, and then set up simulated accounts to resemble each of those eight central users. While some aspects of this sampling pipeline narrowed the scope of our study, it was instrumental for strategically using our experimental resources to collect meaningful data.

The second main phase involved collecting and analyzing data for the simulated users. By clicking a button, Twitter's user interface can provide access to the "latest tweets" sorted by time (i.e., the chronological timeline), which we used as the baseline environment for our study. Based on a Pew research survey that described social media usage patterns (Wojcik & Hughes, 2019), we set up our accounts to collect timelines (both chronological and algorithmic) twice per day. Also, based on empirical findings in position bias on social media feeds (Bakshy et al., 2015), we collected the critical window of the first 50 tweets in the timeline, which we reasoned would be most likely to receive user attention and engagement.

Setting these factors (i.e. checking twice per day and collecting the first 50 tweets) and holding them constant allowed us to isolate the behavior of the algorithm and how it impacts communication on the platform. Notably, the algorithm's impact included significantly reduced exposure to external links, increased source diversity, significant exposure to "suggested" tweets, topical shifts, and a slight echo chamber effect. Overall, these findings suggest that Twitter's curation algorithm substantially alters communication on the platform, behaving more as an editorial interlocutor rather than a mere channel.

METHODOLOGICAL CONSIDERATIONS

In the following subsections, we examine various methodological considerations for audit studies of communication systems, including system access, audit scope, simulation fidelity, and ethical issues, drawing on our case studies to offer concrete illustrations and advice for researchers interested in applying audit methods.

System access

Audit methods and their ability to characterize the behavior of computational systems are constrained by the types and degrees of access that the auditor has to the system. An auditor that works closely with product designers and engineers and who is *internal* to the organization producing the system may have far greater access not only to data and algorithms but could also have access to the code or talk to designers and engineers to understand the design intents of the people creating the system (Raji et al., 2020). New approaches for internally auditing and simulating HMC systems during their design will help steer those systems in ways that enhance their value to human communicators during both their design and deployment. For instance, the SIREN framework was developed to simulate the impact of different recommendation algorithms on the diversity of news information people are exposed to (Bountouridis et al., 2019). HMC system designers could use such an approach in evaluating the likely impact of algorithmic choices on end-users.

On the other hand, an auditor who is *external* to an organization is far more likely to be limited in the information that is available to them, including the degree of access they might have to provide inputs to the system, observe outputs, or review relevant contextual or proprietary information on system design or operation (Trielli & Diakopoulos, 2020). It is common for communication platforms such as Twitter or Facebook to place limits on the data available via APIs, thus restricting the types and volume of data that can be collected (Bruns, 2019). In some cases, unofficial APIs (with their own limitations) can be leveraged to provide the needed data, such as was done in another of our audits in order to understand the visibility of call-to-action videos on TikTok (Bandy & Diakopoulos, 2020b). In other cases, new techniques for collecting data need to be developed because not only is there no API but also the system designer actively blocks attempts to create unofficial APIs using security techniques. In an audit of content and personalization of Apple News, we had to simulate the Apple News app in a virtual environment for these reasons. A program typically employed for quality assurance (Q/A) testing was used to automatically copy and paste results out of the app in the virtual environment in order to collect data on what a simulated user would see (Bandy & Diakopoulos, 2020a).

While internal audits should be pursued where possible, this chapter focuses on instances where the auditor is external to the organization that developed the machine communicator. For the audit of Alexa, there was no externally available API, and so we bought an Alexa device and set it up such that we could test it directly using synthesized speech. To do this, we configured a computer to programmatically talk to (and listen and record responses from) the device in an empty room for two weeks. In the case of our Twitter audit, there were some data available via their API, which was crucial for identifying archetypal users from the detected communities in the network graph. However, the API did not provide exposure information about what an account had "seen", and we therefore needed to scrape that information after loading the account in a web page to render its feed. In our experience doing external audits, there is a certain amount of familiarity that first needs to be developed with the data available via a communication platform before the limits of what questions the audit can address become fully apparent. Technical knowledge can be valuable in pursuing this work because data availability may vary and new technical work-arounds may need to be developed to address particular gaps.

Audit scope

Devising the scope of an audit study is a dance between the research questions of the auditor, the ability to collect data about the system that is responsive to those questions, the design and engineering bounds of the system, and the level of resources that can be put towards the audit. In principle, any research question that might be asked of a human communicator could be asked of a machine communicator, though it may not always be prudent to do so. The types of questions (and the stakes of results) may differ based on the context of the communication system. A chatbot operating in the domain of mental health screening may warrant a different set of questions than one operating in online banking or in entertainment. There is not a standard set of questions that inform HMC audits, though perhaps over time a context-sensitive set of standards could emerge in terms of the typical aspects of a machine communicator to audit.

Oftentimes the scope of an audit is initially informed based on some background research, a disclosure from the system creator, or some other observation of system behavior. For instance, in the case of the Alexa device, our initial anecdotal observations indicated that news sources were rarely cited in responses. This led to questions about the provenance and quality of information provided when posing news-related queries to the device, including how that might vary according to the topic or phrasing of the query. In the case of the Twitter audit, a blog post from the company indicated that deep learning was being used to drive the algorithmic timeline, drawing on popularity and network-based signals. This led us to ask questions about what such an algorithm might do to the diversity of exposure of media in comparison to the chronological feed. Of course, there are many other dimensions of interest that researchers may audit about machine communicators, such as editorial values that may be apparent in an algorithmic curator (Trielli & Diakopoulos, 2019) or whether a system engages in content localization or personalization (Bandy & Diakopoulos, 2020a). We encourage researchers to thoroughly examine any transparency information about the system including documentation, blog posts, news articles, or other organizational communications from designers or developers. In addition, developing first-hand experience communicating with the machine can be valuable for establishing gaps in communicative ability that may suggest areas of focus for the audit.

In some cases it can be helpful to scope the bounds of an audit according to known engineered capabilities of the machine communicator. For the Alexa device, we were aware that the device sometimes misunderstood queries and as a result didn't provide a response. To better understand when this might be happening, we used the Amazon Polly and Transcribe APIs in isolation to assess when the respective text-to-speech and speech-to-text processes were failing. This helped us see that the system could fail when queried with names (e.g. Yung Miami was transcribed as "Young Miami"), and led us to segment audit results according to transcription quality.

For external audits there will often be resource limitations that constrain the breadth of the audit due to data access limits or other platform policies. For instance, in order to undertake the Twitter timeline audit, we needed to create eight Twitter accounts to mimic the eight unique user profiles we tested. This taxed our ability to supervise those eight accounts to ensure they weren't being blocked; in a couple of cases, we did end up missing a data collection cycle because an account had to confirm itself and was unable to automatically do so because of a CAPTCHA. In other words, the agent needed a little boost from a real human to help pass as a legitimate user of the platform. In an earlier phase of the project, we needed to take a subsample of 10,000 Twitter users to do the network analysis because of Twitter API limitations. Researchers will need to be cognizant of these types of limitations and how to satisfice in the audit given available resources, with appropriate attention to how that may put bounds on the generalizability or scope of results.

Simulation fidelity

The use of simulation in social science research requires that an abstracted and simplified model of human behavior must be articulated (Gilbert & Troitzsch, 2005). The question then becomes one of whether that model is well-justified with respect to actual human behavior: is it an accurate and valid model? The utility of audits of machine communicators hinges on this question. If we simulate behaviors that are not plausible with respect to actual human communication behaviors, then it's unclear whether the results would be meaningful in the context of regular human interaction with the machine communicator. In general, observations of machine communicators as well as transparency information about the system or even prior audits can help identify what aspects the system may be reacting to and which may therefore be important to include in a simulated model of behavior. It's also important to note that the fidelity of the simulated agent includes not only its communicative behavior but also its sensed context, such as what location information it makes available to the machine communicator (Haim, 2020).

To ensure the fidelity of simulated agents, researchers can draw on a variety of empirical methods to characterize and parameterize simulated behavior in plausible ways. For instance, in the case of the Alexa audit we used Google Trends data to capture a notion of news-relevant query topics that people were searching for online. We then used a crowdsourcing approach to gather data on the actual phrasing people might use to query a voice assistant on those topics. For Twitter, we leveraged network analysis techniques such as community detection in order to identify archetypal users whose following graph we wanted to mimic in the audit. Although we used the Botometer score to verify that archetypal accounts were not bot-like, in this case we did not distinguish real from bot accounts in the overall network, since we were interested in how the aggregate observed network impacts information flow for the archetypes. Future audits might differentiate bot-like and human-like accounts (e.g. using surveys, CAPTCHAs, or scores like Botometer) in order to focus on how bots might warp the curation algorithm. Results from survey work (e.g. from Pew) were used to choose parameters for how often we checked timelines. In both audits the goal was to define the behavior of the simulated agents, whether in query topic and phrasing or in following activity on social media, in ways that were justifiable and afforded some ecological validity to the results of the audits.

Choices related to simulation fidelity can come into tension with resource requirements, system access, level of control, and the scope of questions that the auditor chooses to pursue. Because of resource requirements and system access researchers typically cannot audit every aspect of a system, and therefore a simpler abstraction of human behavior can reduce the dimensions of variation from real human behavior into something that fits within, for instance, API limitations. Reducing fidelity can also help manage sources of variance in the audit results which may not be the focus of the research. In the Alexa case, we used a synthesized voice and a standardized setup to query the device, which had the benefit of controlling for potential confounds such as different accents or voices which could impact results. A tradeoff here is that this also meant that we were unable to study differences in how the machine communicator responded based on those factors, which is an important area for future work given the variable performance of speech recognition systems across different racial groups (Koenecke et al., 2020). In some cases, variance in human users can also be simulated by the agent (e.g. a male and female synthesized voice could be used to query Alexa), and audits may therefore systematically vary those dimensions of the agent.

Ethical concerns

HMC systems may be in active deployment and use by people outside the context of the audit. Thus, some consideration of ethical issues is warranted if the interaction of the simulated users in the audit might contaminate the environment of the system or create algorithmic or human reactivities, such as by altering how the system treats real people or changing how people behave towards the system or each other (Haim, 2019; Rahwan et al., 2019). By now, Tay the Twitter bot is a cautionary tale for how a social bot that is configured to learn from the people it interacts with online can be manipulated to say harmful things (de Lima Salge and Berente, 2017). Microsoft had to shut the bot down after less than 24 hours. Now imagine an auditor interested in studying the bounds in which a bot might respond to or produce hate speech. Such boundary testing of bots is common amongst people and is well-warranted as part of an audit. The issue is that the auditor could plausibly influence such a bot based on the types of inputs or messages they prompt it with as well as the types of feedback they supply to it. In the case of the Alexa audit, we knew from news reports that the system learns from query reformulation (i.e. if the user interrupts the device to rephrase a query), and so we decided to only evaluate a single query at a time without any follow-up.

Our audits were clearly oriented towards assessing the algorithmic components of Twitter and Alexa. However, in some cases, additional ethical consideration is warranted if a simulated agent might directly interact with other users on a platform. Such cases would call for a review by an IRB because communications initiated by the agent might create sensitivities or reactivities amongst participants that should be thoughtfully addressed, such as through consent or debrief procedures. If it's unclear whether an account is a real person or might itself be a bot, such procedures might be liberally applied in order to account for that uncertainty.

Another concern that arises when auditing technical systems relates to whether the audit might violate the Terms of Service (ToS) set forth by the organization that created the system (Bruns, 2019). If the researcher does decide that the benefit of auditing the system overrides concerns over a ToS violation, then best practices suggest not overly stressing the computational infrastructure of the system being audited (so as to avoid any service disruptions for actual users) or running the audit at an off hour when computer servers may have additional capacity to absorb requests related to the audit (Bhandari and Goodman, 2017). Researchers should consider the legal environment where they undertake the work as well as the ethical norms in their communities of publication for doing such work. They may also consider notifying the owners of machine communicators when an audit is underway, though this could create validity concerns if the owner causes the machine to shift behavior as a result.

The issue of simulation fidelity intersects with another important ethical dimension, which is the representativeness of the agents with respect to relevant demographic characteristics. When using simulated agents, researchers should consider whether the positionality of those agents might reflect dominant user groups at the expense of not representing more marginalized users who might be differently impacted. In our audit of Alexa, we chose to use the default simulated voice to query the device in order to control for confounds, but this also meant we didn't collect information about how the device might respond differently to other voice profiles, such as to a female voice. While the scope of every audit may not be designed to encompass the assessment of discrimination of a machine communicator, some of the most important societal questions revolve around the fairness of such systems and whether they disparately treat people of different demographics.

LOOKING AHEAD

In this chapter we have outlined various methodological considerations for audit studies of communication systems, emphasizing issues related to system access, audit scope, simulation fidelity, and ethics. While the method certainly has its limitations, whether that be from a lack of data access or challenges around parameterizing realistic and representative simulated agents, there is much to be learned by systematically observing machine communicators using suitably programmed agents. In particular, the descriptive richness afforded by the method helps increase the stock of information about machine communicator capabilities and behavior which can inform downstream studies which re-center the human experience. As audit methods continue to evolve to match the increasing complexity of HMC systems, they will be an important method for both initially understanding machine communication behavior and for informing other experimental and mixed-methods approaches.

Moving forward there are a number of opportunities for future work related to the application of such methods. Typically, studies of machine behavior tend to focus on the mechanism or function of the system. However, future work might try to more closely attend to the evolution of machine communication systems in learning feedback loops with people. One challenge here is in modeling simulated users that can engage in plausible back and forth behavior with a machine communicator over time, such that the evolution of the machine communicator can be systematically observed. Another challenge is modeling how actual human communication behavior might co-evolve over time. A related issue is differentiating between humans and machines in mixed environments like Twitter, where it may be useful to distinguish interactions and feedback pathways between a simulated agent and real people versus with other bots or system algorithms.

To further blur the ontological boundaries here, another intriguing avenue for future work would be to incorporate more human interactors in systematized machine-driven audits of machine communicators. Doing so may have advantages in terms of the ecological validity of audit results. For example, if appropriate attention is given to sampling, having more human interactors could help address the representativeness issues associated with trying to reflect a diversity of users in simulated agents. A machine would structure the audit and delegate certain actions to humans as they engage with the machine, observing and recording the results of the interactions. Such an approach would have the advantage of systematizing data collection, while incorporating diverse user behaviors and accounting for how systems might be personalized to individuals based on their user profile or demographic characteristics. A panel of individual observers would thus be computationally coordinated in such a way that many diverse viewpoints on the machine communicator could be synthesized into a fuller picture of its behavior.

REFERENCES

Bandy, J. (2021) Problematic machine behavior: A systematic literature review of algorithm audits. *Proceedings of the ACM on Human-Computer Interaction* 5(CSCW1): 1–34. DOI: 10.1145/3449148.

Bandy, J. & Diakopoulos, N. (2020a) Auditing news curation systems: A case study examining algorithmic and editorial logic in Apple News. *Proc. International Conference on Web and Social Media (ICWSM)*.

Bandy, J. & Diakopoulos, N. (2020b) #TulsaFlop: A case study of algorithmically-influenced collective action on TikTok. In: *FAccTRec Workshop on Responsible Recommendation, 2020*.

Bandy, J. & Diakopoulos, N. (2021) More accounts, fewer links: How algorithmic curation impacts media exposure in Twitter timelines. *Proceedings of the ACM on Human-Computer Interaction* 5(CSCW1): 1–28. DOI: 10.1145/3449152.

Bakshy, E., Messing, S., & Adamic, L. A. (2015) Exposure to ideologically diverse news and opinion on Facebook. *Science*, 348(6239), 1130–1132.

Bhandari, E. & Goodman, R. (2017) Data journalism and the computer fraud and abuse act: Tips for moving forward in an uncertain landscape. *Proc. Computation + Journalism Symposium*.

Bountouridis, D., Harambam, J., Makhortykh, M., et al. (2019) SIREN: A simulation framework for understanding the effects of recommender systems in online news environments. In: *FAT* '19: Proceedings of the Conference on Fairness, Accountability, and Transparency, 2019*, pp. 150–159. DOI: 10.1145/3287560.3287583.

Dambanemuya, H.K. & Diakopoulos, N. (2021) Auditing the information quality of news-related queries on the Alexa voice assistant. *Proceedings of the ACM on Human-Computer Interaction* 5(CSCW1): 1–21. DOI: 10.1145/3449157.

de Lima Salge, C.A. & Berente, N. (2017) Is that social bot behaving unethically? *Communications of the ACM (CACM)* 60(9): 29–31.

Diakopoulos, N. (2015) Algorithmic accountability: Journalistic investigation of computational power structures. *Digital Journalism* 3(3): 398–415. DOI: 10.1080/21670811.2014.976411.

Gaddis, S.M. (2017) An introduction to audit studies in the social sciences. In: Gaddis, S.M. (ed.). *Audit studies behind the scenes with theory, method, and nuance*. Springer.

Gilbert, N. & Troitzsch, K.G. (2005) *Simulation for the social scientist (2nd edition)*. Open University Press.

Gómez-Zará, D. & Diakopoulos, N. (2020) Characterizing communication patterns between audiences and newsbots. *Digital Journalism* 8(9): 1–21. DOI: 10.1080/21670811.2020.1816485.

Guzman, A.L. & Lewis, S.C. (2019) Artificial intelligence and communication: A human–machine communication research agenda. *New Media & Society* 22(1): 146144481985869. DOI: 10.1177/1461444819858691.

Haim, M. (2020) Agent-based testing: An automated approach toward artificial reactions to human behavior. *Journalism Studies* 21(7): 895–911. DOI: 10.1080/1461670x.2019.1702892.

Hussein, E., Juneja, P. & Mitra, T. (2020) Measuring misinformation in video search platforms: An audit study on YouTube. *Proc. ACM Hum.-Comput. Interact. 4(CSCW1)*: 1–27. DOI: 10.1145/3392854.

Kastrenakes, J. (2020). Twitter says AI tweet recommendations helped add millions of users. *The Verge*. www.theverge.com/2020/2/6/21125431/twitter-q4-2019-earnings-daily-user-growth-machine-learning

Koenecke, A., Nam, A., Lake, E., et al. (2020) Racial disparities in automated speech recognition. *Proceedings of the National Academy of Sciences* Vol. *1*: 201915768. DOI: 10.1073/pnas.1915768117.

NPR & Edison Research. 2020. The Smart Audio Report.

Rahwan, I., Cebrian, M., Obradovich, N., et al. (2019) Machine behaviour. *Nature* 568(7753): 477–486. DOI: 10.1038/s41586-019-1138-y.

Raji, I.D., Smart, A., White, R.N., et al. (2020) Closing the AI accountability gap: Defining an end-to-end framework for internal algorithmic auditing. *Proceedings of the 2020 Conference on Fairness, Accountability, and Transparency*: 33–44. DOI: 10.1145/3351095.3372873.

Sandvig, C., Hamilton, K., Karahalios, K., et al. (2014) Auditing algorithms: Research methods for detecting discrimination on Internet platforms. In: *International Communication Association Preconference on Data and Discrimination Converting Critical Concerns into Productive Inquiry*.

Trielli, D. & Diakopoulos, N. (2019) Search as news curator: The role of Google in shaping attention to news information. *Proc. CHI Conference on Human Factors in Computing Systems*.

Trielli, D. & Diakopoulos, N. (2020) How journalists can systematically critique algorithms. In: *Proc. Computation + Journalism Symposium, 2020*.

Wojcik, S., & Hughes, A. (2019). Sizing up Twitter users. Pew research center, 24.

Yang, K., Varol, O., Hui, P., & Menczer, F. (2020). Scalable and generalizable social bot detection through data selection. In *Proceedings of the Association for the Advancement of Artificial Intelligence (AAAI)*.

20

Experiments in Human–Machine Communication Research

Nicole C. Krämer and Jessica M. Szczuka

INTRODUCTION

Imagine a user pushing a button on a computer. The control of the machine is largely driven by linguistic commands that were previously used for interpersonal interactions, as people refer to it as "dialogue" or "conversation." Consequently, it is likely that the machine is designed to respond to the user's input. In some interactions this will be a rather functional output, in others it can have or be accompanied by social meaning. The one button may activate multiple processes, also referred to as behavior, that are hidden from users. This is also why algorithms are frequently referred to as "black boxes." In her pioneer work on how humans communicate with machines, Lucy Suchman (1987) described how all these aspects of machines and computers contribute to users' reliance on intentional explanations, meaning that users anticipate the reactions of a machine based on assumptions that the design is rational, and that the machine has a specific use. And while humans have numerous resources to rationalize interpersonal behavior, this is not inherently the case with machines. In other words, Suchman (1987) investigated how human intentions of purposeful actions can or should be integrated into the machine's abilities to react to human plans, which

can result in productive human–computer communications. These conclusions were drawn from ethnographic data, in this case the observation of users' interactions with a photocopier. What started as an ethnographically based research project guided the path for human–machine communication research (Suchman et al., 2017). Despite more than 30 years of research in this area, technologies built for social interaction with users, such as voice assistants, virtual agents, and robots, still raise numerous questions. First, we need to understand the nature of the interaction: How do we interact with artificial entities in comparison to other humans? Here, on a more applied note, we can additionally ask: How should artificial interaction partners be designed to convey impressions which enable social interaction that appears natural to humans and facilitates their needs? Besides these insights on the interaction process, we need to gain an in depth understanding of the effects of human–machine communication. It is important to not only scrutinize short-term effects of human–machine communication on cognition, attitudes, emotions, or behavior but also how human–machine communications play out in the long run, for example, regarding the change of people's communication habits.

By focusing on this type of research aims, more overarching questions might be addressed as well: What distinguishes an artificial entity from a human? And ultimately: What defines humanness? Interdisciplinary empirical research is crucial to answer these questions related to human–machine communication. The goal of the present chapter is to discuss in what ways experimental methods can be beneficial to HMC research, and to what degree controlled experimental studies might be particularly valuable.

WHEN TO USE EXPERIMENTAL METHODS AND PREREQUISITES FOR THEIR EMPLOYMENT

Why might it be necessary to employ experimental methods to address the questions depicted above? In general, the research method needs to match the research question and therefore, experiments are specifically well-suited to address causal relations and mechanisms. Experiments have crucial advantages over surveys as the latter can investigate relations between variables but rarely offer insights into causal effects. So, whenever the question refers to a potential causal relation (e.g., "Does the appearance of the robot influence the quality of the interaction?"), researchers should conduct an experimental study.

Uncovering Causality

The reason for why we can uncover causality lies in an experiment's typical procedure: An independent variable is manipulated (i.e., varied in different conditions), followed by the observation of its differential effects on one or more dependent variables. The conditions are manipulated in a controlled way, varying only one specific aspect while holding other aspects constant. By this, we can identify the causal influence of only this specific aspect. In the field of human–machine communication, it can, for instance, be interesting to compare the effects of different characteristics of a technology (e.g., different forms of embodiment, appearances, or behaviors). In some cases it may be advisable to compare to a control condition in which humans interact with humans.

Quality Criteria

The research design and the measurements need to meet the quality criteria of validity (Does the experiment measure what it intends to measure?) and reliability (Does the experimental procedure measure what it means to measure in a reliable way?) (Leung, 2015; Ali & Yusof, 2011). Therefore, researchers need to plan experiments in a way that enables the fulfilment of these criteria. Specifically, experiments must balance internal and external validity. Internal validity ensures the measurement of the specific variable of interest. For this, the procedure systematically controls that only the manipulated variables affect the outcome, namely, the dependent variables. This, however, means that experimental settings are often artificial and have low degrees of freedom, for example regarding the behavior of the participant that will be restricted to a very specific situation. External validity refers to the generalizability of the results in the sense of whether the findings can be applied to other settings, such as whether findings can be replicated in another population, under real-life conditions, or with similar technologies. In order to guarantee this balance, the situation must be controlled but at the same time close to real-life-situations and include a certain diversity regarding the population and the employed stimuli and technologies (e.g., when a robot's behavior is varied in the experiment, two or more robots with different appearance should be used to make sure that the behavior does not only yield the effects when it is performed by one specific robot).

Sample Size

Another important prerequisite to consider is the sample size. This is crucial since the statistical analyses will only yield robust findings when the sample size is large enough to meet the criterion of statistical power: Literature agrees that there is no rule of thumb that suits all experimental studies, but that the estimated sample size should be calculated based on design parameters and the effect sizes found in previous studies (Maxwell et al., 2008). A sample should be representative to enable the generalization of findings for a specific group of people and should include the diversity of the population that the results aim to be valid for. While one may intuitively think that the bigger the sample the better, this needs to be reflected on the aspect of cost and time. Specifically experiments generate high costs in terms of time and resources for both, experimenters and participants. Therefore, the size of the sample is often limited to a number that is in accordance with statistical power.

Since usually, experiments will employ direct communication with (different forms of) technology, they are crucial to understand how humans react to technology and to scrutinize the process of how humans and machines communicate and interact. There are several examples of studies in which experiments provided a better understanding of how and why humans communicate with machines in a certain way. Powers and colleagues (2005), for instance, manipulated the gender appearance of a robot to investigate whether the transferred gender stereotypes would cause the participants to treat robots according to these stereotypes. Experimental settings also allow to investigate whether social and communicational phenomena found among humans are transferable to machines (see the Computers-Are-Social-Actors paradigm, CASA, by Nass et al., 1994). Given these advantages, experiments are one of the most common methods in the field of human–machine communication.

Decisions to Take when Planning an Experiment

When planning an experiment, one must make various decisions which can influence the quality of the data in different ways. In the following, we comment on the advantages and disadvantages of between- versus within-subjects designs, laboratory versus online experiments and experiments with existing versus future technologies.

Between- or within-subjects design: An important decision to make is whether one participant should be confronted with all conditions (within-subjects design) or whether it is more suitable that each participant will be assigned to one specific condition only (between-subjects design). While within-subjects designs may be less demanding in terms of the sample size (as all participants can be confronted with all conditions), it may not be feasible for all research questions or hypotheses due to confounding effects between the conditions (e.g., based on social desirability; Jackson, 2014). Also, within-subjects studies have the disadvantage that participants can directly compare the conditions which usually increases demand characteristics of the study setting and thus renders effects larger than they actually are.

Laboratory or online experiments: Most experiments take place in a lab to allow for a controlled communication with a technology. Here, unlike when employing a survey or an online experiment, participants can interact with the technology. This is often decisive, not only because a real interaction can take place, but because especially in robot research the possibility to touch

the robot or feel its embodied presence might affect the results. In addition, lab experiments allow to employ dependent variables that go beyond self-report measures which cannot be assessed remotely (e.g., skin conductance; see more detailed discussion on dependent variables below). Still, online experiments can be valuable when the research question is in accordance with it or when conditions do not allow for laboratory experiments (as, e.g., during the COVID-19 pandemic). Here, the participant can either watch and evaluate a pre-recorded interaction between a human and a technological device, or a pre-scripted video-based dialogue can be used that has a limited degree of freedom for user input but might still feel like an interaction.

Interactions with existing or future technologies: Experiments can be conducted with either existing or future technologies. In the realm of human–machine communication, researchers are often interested in effects of technologies which are not (yet) available in everyday life. In this case, Wizard-of-Oz scenarios are employed (Dahlbäck et al., 1993). Here, (a confederate of) the experimenter controls the technology from another room. While the participant assumes that the machine works autonomously, its output is generated by the experimenter or a confederate, for instance, by pressing a button to elicit the reaction that is appropriate given the input of the participant. In this way, the experimenter can test how humans react to communicating robots which (in reality) are seldom sufficiently advanced to allow for a decent interaction or conversation with humans. The technique therefore focusses on understanding future "natural" communication with artificial entities as they are envisioned by the researchers (Dahlbäck et al., 1993). The downside of this procedure is that sometimes technology is "invented" that will never exist in the way it is envisioned by the researcher – potentially making the results irrelevant as long as the study was not targeted at fundamental mechanisms of human-machine communication. Also, it might increase the novelty effect (Wells et al., 2010) as people will not be familiar with the technology. This implies that people's reactions might not be comparable to how they would react to a technology they have lived and interacted with for some time.

In the following, we will give two examples of what experimental studies can look like in the context of human-machine communication. We will describe experimental studies in the context of the well-known Computers-Are-Social-Actors paradigm as well as experimental field studies which entail more realistic and therefore more generalizable settings and allow for longitudinal data collection.

SPECIFIC FORMS OF EXPERIMENTS I: COMMUNICATING WITH MACHINES AND THE COMPUTERS-ARE-SOCIAL-ACTORS PARADIGM

Empirical studies on how humans communicate with machines have increasingly emerged after previous graphical user interface interaction practices were amended with human-like communication forms (e.g., speech-based interaction) and first artificial characters (e.g., Microsoft Bob). In 1996, Reeves and Nass started to investigate social reactions toward machines and postulated the media equation theory which suggests that people treat media as they would treat other people. According to their theory, media can be equipped with what the authors labeled social cues; interactivity, natural language, and the fulfilment of social roles (Nass & Moon, 2000). The authors argue that these social cues automatically trigger social scripts which people usually apply during interactions with other humans and now transfer to human–computer encounters. Although on a conscious level people are aware that machines do not warrant social treatment, their immediate reactions are fundamentally social. Reeves and Nass conducted a series of empirical studies which underlined their theory by showing that people overuse social categories, meaning that they, for instance, apply human stereotypes to systems and that humans participate in over-learned social behaviors, such as reciprocity and politeness, in human-machine encounters (Fogg & Nass, 1997; Nass et al., 1997). These studies all followed the same framework which still serves as a foundation for empirical studies in the field of human–computer communication: the CASA paradigm (Nass et al., 1994). The basic idea behind this methodology is that social reactions which can be observed among humans can be investigated between humans and machines by replacing one human interaction partner with an artificial stimulus that is equipped with social cues. More recently, this paradigm has been used in numerous studies with entities, such as humanoid robots that present even more social cues than the ones used in the classic CASA studies and address different psychological effects, such as empathy (Rosenthal-von der Pütten et al., 2014), common ground (Powers et al., 2005) or jealousy (Szczuka & Krämer, 2018). Specifically, various empirical studies have demonstrated that social reactions can be evoked by different types of artificial personas, ranging from non-embodied technologies such as voice assistants (Strathmann et al., 2020), virtual agents (Hoffmann et al., 2009) or humanoid robots (Eyssel et al., 2012). Those examples provide first insights into the numerous parameters researchers can vary in empirical studies in the field of human–machine communication research. These, for example, pertain to the attributes of the artificial entity (e.g., form of embodiment, appearance) and its specific behavior.

SPECIFIC FORMS OF EXPERIMENTS II: FIELD EXPERIMENTS AND LONGITUDINAL STUDIES

As mentioned above, the external validity of experiments, especially when they are conducted in a laboratory setting, is limited. One way to address this problem are field studies. They enable to observe humans interacting with technology in their natural environment in everyday situations (such as in a public space or a private home). In general, field studies do not need experimental manipulations, yet here we will only refer to cases which incorporated a systematic manipulation. Except when field studies are conducted in public places, one goal is often to not only observe a short-term interaction but to accompany a longitudinal interaction. Longitudinal field studies are rare which is due to both, the costs and additional efforts, and the lack of sufficient robustness of the interactive systems to be operated in a natural, uncontrolled environment instead of a laboratory. Since the experimenter controls conditions, ethical considerations are also important: For example, there should not be one group of participants which is kept from a treatment that is hypothesized to be more helpful while the other group is receiving it (e.g., a virtual assistant helping with health issues in a longitudinal setting).

MEASUREMENTS OF DEPENDENT VARIABLES IN HUMAN–MACHINE COMMUNICATION RESEARCH: SELF-REPORT, BEHAVIORAL MEASURES AND PHYSIOLOGICAL MEASURES

The most frequently employed assessment strategy in experimental research is self-report. In this way, participants' evaluation, their attitudes and feelings toward the artificial interaction partner can be assessed. This is usually administered by questionnaires that measure these and other variables by means of quantitative data. In addition, researchers can acquire the participants' perceptions and evaluations by qualitative means, namely, interview questions. This allows for deeper insights into participants' experiences during the interaction, but it is more difficult to systematically analyze and generalize. Particularly when the study is conducted in a laboratory, one should not only rely on self-report as this is often biased by social desirability or demand characteristics of the experiment. In addition, researchers should make sure that variables are collected which are not prone to the conscious adjustment by the participants. This is true for behavioral measures as well as for all kinds of psychophysiological measures.

Regarding behavioral measurements, the experimenters can observe and analyze people's overt behavior, such as the participants' decision about whether to adhere to an artificial interaction partner's suggestions (Hoffmann & Krämer, 2013), how to treat this artificial interaction partner (e.g., in a prisoner's dilemma setting, de Melo et al., 2012), or whether the interaction triggers actual prosocial behavior (Hoffmann & Krämer, 2021). More opaque forms of behavior, such as eye movements, can be used to measure the participants' attention to different aspects of the artificial interaction partner but require specific eye tracking technology (for an example see Szczuka & Krämer, 2019). Behavioral measurements can also include subliminal reactions to the stimuli, for example, when using the affective priming technique (Szczuka & Krämer, 2017).

Psychophysiological measures include the capturing of various forms of peripheral activity, such as heart rate, electrodermal activity, and respiration (for an overview see Ravaja, 2004). While particularly heart rate and electrodermal activity are used to estimate emotional reactions toward a machine, there are additional procedures to measure cognitive activity. Besides electroencephalogram (EEG) and Event-Related Potentials (ERP), functional magnet resonance tomography (fMRT) are used to observe reactions in the participants' brains. Specifically, the latter has already been used in studies on human–robot communication research and relationships and proved to be beneficial in describing both cognitive and affective reactions (Rosenthal-von der Pütten et al., 2014; Rosenthal-von der Pütten et al., 2019).

POTENTIAL PITFALLS IN EXPERIMENTAL RESEARCH ON HUMAN–MACHINE COMMUNICATION

Even though this chapter has presented the manifold advantages of experiments in human–machine communication, the method is certainly not without limitations. As discussed above, results are only valid when there is sufficient internal and external validity. Especially external validity is often not sufficiently catered for as the technology which is tested often does not look, feel, and function like actual future technology (e.g., future robots might make different mistakes than those which are envisioned and implemented in Wizard-of-Oz studies). This means that some of the insights do not hold for future human–technology interaction. Similarly, we cannot avoid novelty effects in the sense that people often have not encountered the machine employed in the experimental setting in real life or have even heard of it. In concert with the fact that people have often built expectations toward technology based on media content such as science fiction movies (Horstmann & Krämer, 2019), this might lead to reactions toward the machine which would not be observable after a month-long interaction phase. Based on these problems, it is necessary to reconsider the way most experimental studies are conducted: To overcome the artificial nature and balance internal and external validity better, more longitudinal and field experiments are needed, whereas dependent variables need to go beyond self-report measures and include behavioral, subliminal, and psychophysiological methods that are less prone to social desirability and cognitive biases.

SUMMARY

In this chapter, we have argued that experimental studies in human–machine communication are an important method to uncover causal relationships. To achieve this, the experimenter needs to manipulate independent variables and measure their influence on dependent variables. In this procedure, internal and external validity need to be balanced and various other decisions have to be made. Given that every decision on how to conduct an experiment (i.e., in the laboratory, online, or in the field; between- or within-subjects design; form and realization of the stimulus design) has immediate consequences for the validity, reliability, and generalizability of the results, researchers need to meticulously plan each study by reflecting on the potential implications of each design decision. Future studies need to increasingly include objective measures that assess subliminal aspects and unconscious reactions as well as employ long-term design. As only an appropriate set of choices will result in valuable insights, planning and conducting experiments consitute a challenging task that warrants training and experience.

REFERENCES

Ali, A. M., & Yusof, H. (2011). Quality in qualitative studies: The case of validity, reliability and generalizability. *Issues in Social and Environmental Accounting*, *5*(1), 25–64. http://dx.doi.org/10.22164/isea.v5i1.59

Dahlbäck, N., Jönsson, A., & Ahrenberg, L. (1993). Wizard of Oz studies – why and how. *Knowledge-Based Systems*, *6*(4), 258–266. https://doi.org/10.1016/0950-7051(93)90017-N

de Melo, C. M., Carnevale, P., & Gratch, J. (2012). The effect of virtual agents' emotion displays and appraisals on people's decision making in negotiation. In Y. Nakano, M. Neff, A. Paiva, M. Walker (Eds.), *Intelligent Virtual Agents. IVA 2012. Lecture Notes in Computer Science: Vol 7502* (pp. 53–66). Springer. https://doi.org/10.1007/978-3-642-33197-8_6

Eyssel, F., De Ruiter, L., Kuchenbrandt, D., Bobinger, S., & Hegel, F. (2012). 'If you sound like me, you must be more human': On the interplay of robot and user features on human-robot acceptance and anthropomorphism. In *Proceedings of the Seventh Annual ACM/IEEE International Conference on Human-Robot Interaction (HRI '12). Association for Computing Machinery, New York, NY, USA*, 125–126. https://doi.org/10.1145/2157689.2157717

Fogg, B. J., & Nass, C. (1997). Silicon sycophants: The effects of computers that flatter. *International Journal of Human-Computer Studies*, *46*(5), 551–561. https://doi.org/10.1006/ijhc.1996.0104

Hoffmann, L., & Krämer, N. C. (2021). The persuasive power of robot touch. Behavioral and evaluative consequences of non-functional touch from a robot. *PLoS ONE 16*(5), e0249554. https://doi.org/10.1371/journal.pone.0249554

Hoffmann, L., & Krämer, N. C. (2013). Investigating the effects of physical and virtual embodiment in task-oriented and conversational contexts. *International Journal of Human-Computer Studies*, *71*(7–8), 763–774. https://doi.org/10.1016/j.ijhcs.2013.04.007

Hoffmann, L., Krämer, N. C., Lam-Chi, A., & Kopp, S. (2009). Media equation revisited. Do users show polite reactions towards an embodied agent? In Ruttkay Z., Kipp M., Nijholt A., & Vilhjálmsson H.H. (Eds.), *Intelligent Virtual Agents. IVA 2009. Lecture Notes in Computer Science: Vol 5773* (pp. 159–165). Springer. https://doi.org/10.1007/978-3-642-04380-2_19

Horstmann, A. C., & Krämer, N. C. (2019). Great expectations? Relation of previous experiences with social robots in real life or in the media and expectancies based on qualitative and quantitative assessment. *Frontiers in Psychology*, *10*, 939. https://doi.org/10.3389/fpsyg.2019.00939

Jackson, S. L. (2014). *Research methods: A modular approach* (3rd ed.). Cengage Learning.

Leung, L. (2015). Validity, reliability, and generalizability in qualitative research. *Journal of Family Medicine and Primary Care*, *4*(3), 324. doi: 10.4103/2249-4863.161306

Maxwell, S. E., Kelley, K., & Rausch, J. R. (2008). Sample size planning for statistical power and accuracy in parameter estimation. *Annual Review of Psychology*, *59*, 537–563. https://doi.org/10.1146/annurev.psych.59.103006.093735

Nass, C., & Moon, Y. (2000). Machines and mindlessness: Social responses to computers. *Journal of Social Issues*, *56*(1), 81–103.

Nass, C., Moon, Y., & Green, N. (1997). Are machines gender neutral? Gender-stereotypic responses to computers with voices. *Journal of Applied Social Psychology*, *27*(10), 864–876. https://doi.org/10.1111/j.1559-1816.1997.tb00275.x

Nass, C., Steuer, J., & Tauber, E. R. (1994). Computers are social actors. *Proceedings of the SIGCHI Conference on Human Factors in Computing Systems, USA*, 72–78. https://doi.org/10.1145/191666.191703

Powers, A., Kramer, A., Lim, S., Kuo, J., Lee, S. L., & Kiesler, S. (2005). Common ground in dialogue with a gendered humanoid robot. *Proceedings of RO-MAN 2005*.

Ravaja, N. (2004). Contributions of psychophysiology to media research: Review and recommendations. *Media Psychology*, *6*(2), 193–235. https://doi.org/10.1207/s1532785xmep0602_4

Reeves, B., & Nass, C. I. (1996). *The media equation: How people treat computers, television, and new media like real people and places*. Cambridge: Cambridge University Press.

Rosenthal-von der Pütten, A. M., Krämer, N. C., Maderwald, S., Brand, M., & Grabenhorst, F. (2019). Neural mechanisms for accepting and rejecting artificial social partners in the uncanny valley. *The Journal of Neuroscience*, *39*(33), 6555–6570. https://doi.org/10.1523/JNEUROSCI.2956-18.2019

Rosenthal-Von Der Pütten, A. M., Schulte, F. P., Eimler, S. C., Sobieraj, S., Hoffmann, L., Maderwald, S., ... & Krämer, N. C. (2014). Investigations on empathy towards humans and robots using fMRI. *Computers in Human Behavior*, *33*, 201–212. https://doi.org/10.1016/j.chb.2014.01.004

Strathmann, C., Szczuka, J., & Krämer, N. (2020). She talks to me as if she were alive: Assessing the social reactions and perceptions of children toward voice assistants and their appraisal of the appropriateness of these reactions. *Proceedings of the 20th ACM International Conference on Intelligent Virtual Agents. Association for Computing Machinery, New York, NY, USA*, 52, 1–8. https://doi.org/10.1145/3383652.3423906

Suchman, L., Blomberg, J., Orr, J. E., & Trigg, R. (2017). Reconstructing technologies as social practice. In A. C. Jimenez (Eds.), *The anthropology of organisations* (pp. 431–447). Routledge.

Suchman, L. A. (1987). *Plans and situated actions: The problem of human-machine communication.* Cambridge University Press.

Szczuka, J. M., & Krämer, N. C. (2019). There's more to humanity than meets the eye: Differences in gaze behavior toward women and gynoid robots. *Frontiers in Psychology*, *10*, 693. https://doi.org/10.3389/fpsyg.2019.00693

Szczuka, J. M., & Krämer, N. C. (2018). Jealousy 4.0? An empirical study on jealousy-related discomfort of women evoked by other women and gynoid robots. *Paladyn, Journal of Behavioral Robotics*, *9*(1), 323–336. https://doi.org/10.1515/pjbr-2018-0023

Szczuka, J. M., & Krämer, N. C. (2017). Not only the lonely—how men explicitly and implicitly evaluate the attractiveness of sex robots in comparison to the attractiveness of women, and personal characteristics influencing this evaluation. *Multimodal Technologies and Interaction*, *1*(1), 3. https://doi.org/10.3390/mti1010003

Wells, J. D., Campbell, D. E., Valacich, J. S., & Featherman, M. (2010). The effect of perceived novelty on the adoption of information technology innovations: A risk/reward perspective. *Decision Sciences*, *41*(4), 813–843. https://doi.org/10.1111/j.1540-5915.2010.00292.x

21

Detecting the States of our Minds: Developments in Physiological and Cognitive Measures

Michelle Lui

Physiological measures have been receiving increasing attention over the past few decades in different research areas beyond traditional clinical, ergonomics, and sports applications (Cowley et al., 2016). Digitally monitoring physiological signals has been used to better understand users' cognitive states – to interpret their experience and provide an unobtrusive adaptive experience with interactive systems. Through external sensors placed on the body, physiological signals can detect a person's internal activity from the central and autonomic nervous systems, which offers continuous and objective measures that indicate the state of human cognitive processes and resources, such as attention, cognitive effort, engagement, stress, and fatigue (Martin, 2014). For Human–Machine Communication (HMC) researchers, physiological measures offer an additional means for understanding humans' internal states as they engage in meaning making with machines. As the primary mode of interaction with machines moves away from mouse-and-keyboard interactions to those that are vocal, tactile, and embodied, our relationship to the machines and our means for communicating with them are increasingly personal. Physiological measures and their affordance for unobtrusively capturing our objective responses open up the HMC research space for deeper understanding about the novel forms of interaction occurring between humans and machines, and their impact on how we relate to machines.

This chapter reviews recent developments for the use of cognitive and physiological measures as applied in research that considers machines and humans simultaneously. Also known as psychophysiological measures, they assess the interaction between psychological and physical states (Gaffey & Wirth, 2014). Working with psychophysiological measures requires a complex array of knowledge and techniques. This chapter presents a foundational review of commonly assessed physiological signals, such as electrocardiograms (ECG), electrodermal activity (also known as skin conductance or galvanic skin response), eye tracking, and their derived metrics (e.g., heart rate from ECG). Individual signals, what they tell us about the user, and their complexities and challenges are discussed. Multimodal data streams as a way to overcome interpretation challenges are briefly touched upon. Finally, a general discussion of the role of psychophysiological measures in evolving the communication between humans and machines and possible future directions concludes this chapter.

HUMAN COGNITION AND TRADITIONAL COGNITIVE MEASURES

Before delving into physiological measures, we first discuss our understanding of cognitive states and traditional means of understanding them. Research on the state of human cognitive processes and resources largely rests upon the conceptualization that there is a limit to working memory capacity (Sweller et al., 1998). Previously understood as "mental workload" (Moray, 1979) and conceptualized as the cognitive load theory (CLT; Sweller et al., 1998), the CLT framework has been a leading theory for understanding cognition in learning, particularly with digital technologies (Sweller et al., 2019).

From the perspective of CLT, there are three different components of cognitive load involved in learning and cognitively demanding tasks, understood as intrinsic load, extraneous load, and germane load (Sweller et al., 1998). While the intrinsic load is attributed to the inherent difficulty of the task itself or the learning content, the extraneous load is the difficulty associated with the design of materials involved in completing the task or learning the material (i.e., instructional design). Germane load is thought to be associated with constructing, processing, and automating schemas, in other words, consolidating knowledge structures into long-term memory (Sweller et al., 1998). The instructional design is thought to also influence levels of germane load (Costley & Lange, 2017). Some researchers suggest that germane load is linked to metacognitive processes, or at the very least, compete for the same limited resources (Klepsch & Seufert, 2020; Valcke, 2002; Young et al., 2016). It is recognized that CLT does not fully account for all aspects of cognitive processes and that such a multidimensional construct would consider individual influences, such as ability, domain expertise, motivations, expectations, or metacognitive beliefs (Moreno, 2006; Moreno & Park, 2010; van Merriënboer & Sweller, 2005). Still, CLT researchers believe the theory offers important lessons on the instructional design of learning materials so

as to optimize cognitive load (Ayres & van Gog, 2009; Young & Stanton, 2002). Too little load experienced by learners infers the material is not challenging enough, while too much load infers learners may be too overwhelmed to adequately process the material – in both situations, learning deteriorates.

Cognitive measures can be broken down into direct and indirect approaches, as well as subjective and objective measurements (Table 21.1). Subjective methods include self-reported questionnaires of stress or mental effort. Such retrospective Likert-type scale surveys include a commonly used one-item question that asks participants to rate their mental effort (Paas, 1992) and the NASA Task Load Index (NASA-TLX; Hart & Staveland, 1988). Mental effort in the case of the 9-point Paas Cognitive Load Scale is considered to reflect the cognitive demands imposed by the task and thus is an indicator of the total cognitive load (Paas et al., 2003). The NASA-TLX survey consists of six question items on mental demand, physical demand, temporal demand, performance, effort, and frustration, rated on a scale of 0–20 (Hart & Staveland, 1988; Naismith et al., 2015). Questionnaires separately measuring intrinsic, extraneous, and germane cognitive load also have been proposed (Cierniak et al., 2009; Eysink, Tessa H. S. et al., 2009; Leppink et al., 2013; Swaak & de Jong, 2001).

While subjective methods may provide useful information about participants' cognitive load retrospectively, some limitations exist. Scholars have questioned whether a clear distinction can be made between load types (e.g., de Jong, 2010). Furthermore, different phrasing in the question items and how participants might understand them may lead to conflicting results (Leppink et al., 2013; van Gog & Paas, 2008).

PHYSIOLOGICAL SIGNALS AND THEIR CONNECTION TO THE MIND

In recent years, interest in the digital monitoring of physiological signals has grown for researchers

Table 21.1   Classification of physiological and cognitive measures

| Data objectivity | Relationship | |
	Indirect	Direct
Subjective	Self-reported mental effort	Self-reported stress level Self-reported difficulty of materials
Objective	Physiological measures (e.g., EEG, GSR) Behavioral measures (e.g., time on task, help-seeking behavior, efficiency measures) Learning outcome measures	Eye-tracking measures Brain activity measures (e.g., fMRI, fNIRS) Dual-task performance

Note: Updated and adapted from Brünken et al., 2010; Brunken et al., 2003; Kalyuga, 2011; Martin, 2014.

Table 21.2   Physiological signals, measures and states of mind

Signal	Example measures & metrics	Example interpreted state of mind

Skin conductance:
   Electrodermal activity (EDA)
   Galvanic skin response (GSR)
	Skin conductance level (SCL)
	Skin conductance response (SCR)
	Number of peaks
	Amplitude for peaks
		Arousal (e.g., stress, frustration)
		Cognitive activity

Cardiovascular signals:
   Electrocardiogram (ECG)
	Heart rate (HR)
	Heart rate variability (HRV)
	   (e.g., LF/HF ratio)
		Mental workload
		Cognitive load

Eye-tracking	Fixations: location (i.e., areas of interest; AOI),
	   duration, and frequency
	Saccades: frequency, duration, amplitude, average
	   speed, speed profiles
	Blinks: blink rate, blink latency, blink duration
	Pupil dilation
		Visual attention and related
		   states (e.g., flow, focus,
		   interest, engagement)
		Mental workload
		Fatigue

studying human–machine communication. It not only allows researchers to monitor users of computer systems unobtrusively but can also further enhance and personalize interactions in "smart" machines (Cowley et al., 2016). Also known as psychophysiological methods, quantitative measurements of physiological signals are used to form inferences about qualitative states of the mind (Table 21.2). Changes in cognitive or affective states are assumed to be highly sensitive to physiological changes and considered involuntary and thus "objective" (Martin, 2014).

While this chapter does not specifically focus on affective states of the mind, certain emotional states that may be detected with physiological signals impact cognition. Affective states detected by physiological signals typically fall along two dimensions: arousal (alert to lethargic) and valence (pleasant to unpleasant), also known as the emotional circumplex model (Figure 21.1). Emotions related to the unpleasant side of valence and alert end of the arousal dimension, such as stress and frustration, can limit working memory resources (Shields et al., 2017). However, a "stressful" state

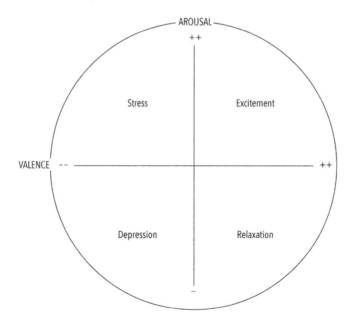

Figure 21.1   A simplified emotional circumplex model

Note: Adapted from Cowley et al. (2016).

is not necessarily detrimental to cognitive processing. Research on epistemic emotions suggests that some level of frustration is appropriate in contexts that involve heavy cognitive processing, such as learning of complex topics (Baker et al., 2010).

SKIN CONDUCTANCE

Considered to be an internal signal, sensors placed on the skin (e.g., palms and fingers) can detect changes in the electrical properties resulting from the autonomic nervous system (ANS), which regulates physiological processes such as heart rate, blood pressure, and respiration (Dawson et al., 2016). Electrodermal activity (EDA) is the general term used to describe fluctuations caused by activation of sweat glands that are controlled by the sympathetic nervous system (e.g., controlling "fight-or-flight" responses), while the term Galvanic Skin Response (GSR) refers to the method used to detect changes in the electrical properties of the skin (Cowley et al., 2016). A widely used method is passing a direct current between two electrodes to measure the skin's conductivity. The recorded EDA signal has two components. A slowly varying tonic component of the EDA signal represents the current skin conductance level (SCL), which can be influenced by external or internal factors such as dryness of the skin and psychological state. Superimposed on the slow tonic component is a rapidly changing phasic component, known as skin conductance response (SCR). Commonly used phasic features include the number of significant peaks, the amplitudes of those peaks, or the sum of the peaks. If event times are known or induced, latency-based detection of SCRs can be performed (Boucsein et al., 2012).

Since skin conductivity is not influenced by parasympathetic activation (e.g., "rest-and-digest" activities), it can be used as indicators of both psychological and physiological arousal, and by extension, as a measure of cognitive and emotional activity respectively (Boucsein et al., 2012; Dawson et al., 2016). GSR sensors used to evaluate stress and arousal levels while using a multimodal interface indicate that GSR shows promise as an indicator of cognitive load in real-time (Shi et al., 2007). Villarejo and colleagues have built GSR sensors for stress detection in the home while users performed various tasks (such as mathematical operations, reading, thinking about an anxious experience). They found that GSR can detect different states of each user with a 77% success rate (Villarejo et al., 2012).

CARDIOVASCULAR SIGNALS

Similar to EDA, cardiovascular signals are reflective of activity in the ANS. Increases in the heart rate are tied to the sympathetic branch of the ANS and tied to stress (i.e., "fight-or-flight" responses). In contrast, the parasympathetic branch represented by "rest-and-digest" behavior decreases heart rate (Cowley et al., 2016). The electrocardiogram (ECG) records electrical signals of the heart non-invasively, from which heart rate (i.e., beats per minute) and heart rate variability (HRV) can be extracted. Both heart rate and HRV have been used to measure cognitive load (Kim et al., 2018; Paas et al., 2014).

HRV refers to the fluctuation in heartbeat intervals and is associated with the body's ability to cope with internal and external stressors (Kim et al., 2018). One metric for describing HRV involves distributing heart rate oscillations into frequency bands. It is thought that the low frequency (LF) band is linked to sympathetic activation while the high frequency (HF) band is linked to parasympathetic activation in the ANS (Malik et al., 1996). The LF to HF ratio (LF/HF) is used to estimate the ratio between sympathetic and parasympathetic nervous system activity under certain conditions, with reduced HRV generally indicative of mental effort (Cowley et al., 2016; Shaffer & Ginsberg, 2017).

In one study, researchers explored the feasibility of understanding cognitive-affective states by triangulating data obtained from GSR and HRV measures, observations, self-reports, and performance as kindergartners performed tasks of varying mental effort (Sridhar et al., 2019). They found the GSR and HRV to be applicable markers in understanding children's cognitive load as they performed digital sorting tasks, and the approach enabled them to differentiate between cognitive-affective states. Using a combination of physiological measures, Ferreira and colleagues (2014) developed a model for assessing real-time cognitive load in younger and older adults (as they completed perceptual speed and visuospatial cognitive processing tasks). The measures include GSR, breathing rate, and skin temperature.

EYE-TRACKING

EDA and cardiovascular signals are considered *indirect* objective measures involving internal signals from the ANS (e.g., EDA, HRV). Eye-tracking measures, along with brain activity measures (e.g., fMRI, fNIRS), are considered *direct* objective measures. Some consider the eyes to be "the only surface feature of the central nervous system" (Cowley et al., 2016, p. 218). Camera-based eye trackers track movements through changes in visual features (e.g., reflections on the surface of the cornea from an infrared light source). Eye movements can be divided into *fixational* and *saccadic* movements (Rayner, 2009). Fixational control consists of visual gaze on a single location as well as smooth pursuit movements that track slowly moving targets. Saccadic movements, on the other hand, are jumpy, rapid movements of the eye to fixate and acquire new features from the visual field. Several parameters for each type of eye movement may be extracted from eye trackers (Table 21.2). Typical parameters for fixations are location (i.e., areas of interest; AOI), duration, and frequency. For saccades, frequency, duration, amplitude, and average speed are considered (Skulmowski & Rey, 2017).

The analysis of eye movements is highly task- and context-specific (Rothkopf et al., 2016). Researchers have used eye-tracking to interpret users' visual attention and related constructs such as flow, focus, and engagement, as well as mental workload and fatigue as they engage with digital technologies (Cowley et al., 2016). In a virtual classroom with head-tracking devices worn by students, Airdrie and colleagues (2018) collected the students' gaze behavior to examine patterns of attention and gaze to diagnose attention deficits among children. Ke, Lee, and Xu (2016) examined fixation time, frequency, and dwell time from eye-tracking data to examine student engagement in a mixed-reality virtual teaching simulation and understand its salient design features. McEwen and Dube (2015) used eye-tracking data to examine memory and attention in children using simple and complex mathematics applications on tablet computers.

MULTIMODAL APPROACHES

Multimodal approaches may combine sources from both physiological and behavioral data streams, such as video and audio data. Data collected from a single data physiological source may lead to ambiguous or conflicting interpretations about the cognitive or affective state of mind. For example, EDA signals indicate arousal on the emotional circumplex model (Figure 21.1), which may be interpreted as stress or excitement. Increasing the number of signals analyzed can improve the accuracy of data interpretations. Coding of behavior from video data post-recording or facial analysis performed in real-time can disambiguate participants' affective state (Bailenson et al., 2008). Taub and colleagues (2017)

combined eye-tracking and computer log data to understand learner performance in real-time. Using Crystal Island, a game-based learning environment for learning microbiology, researchers used multi-level modeling of eye tracking and logged data to assess 50 college students' cognitive and metacognitive self-regulating learning processes as they read virtual books to learn about potentially relevant material for solving the mystery of the disease that has spread through a fictional remote island. Authors found that the combination of eye-tracking and log data offered a more comprehensive picture of learning compared to a single channel of data.

Lui and colleagues (2020) combined EDA, temperature, eye tracking, and video sources to gain insight into the conditions under which immersive virtual reality (VR) impacts the learning experience. In a virtual simulation of a scientific model, university students in a microbiology course were tasked with interacting with simulation elements to understand the dynamic processes in either a seated or standing position. Using a multimodal approach, each session was thematically analyzed, coding sections of the sessions that present with co-occurrence of increasing GSR and decreasing body temperature, used as indices of stress (Sattar & Valdiya, 1999; Smets et al., 2018; Villarejo et al., 2012). Additional temporal mapping of interaction patterns offered fine-grain representations of the experience (Figure 21.2). Finally, videos and screen recordings which indicate gaze fixations provided contextual information of the learning experience in VR. Examination of the quantitative data demonstrated significant differences between conditions, while interpretations of the in-depth multimodal analysis of VR sessions revealed insights as to *when* and *why* they differed.

CHALLENGES, INNOVATIONS, AND FUTURE DIRECTIONS FOR PSYCHOPHYSIOLOGICAL METHODS IN HMC

Judging from recent research, there is a great deal of potential for further development of psychophysiological methods in HMC. The unobtrusive objective and continuous nature of the data alongside advances in wearable computing expand cognitive measures far beyond static and retroactive traditional methods. This opens up the possibilities for understanding individual cognition in complex settings, such as communication between multiple people, interfaces, and machines – in both experimental and ecological settings and for longer periods (Betella et al., 2014; Paletta et al., 2015). Yet, there are diverse technological, methodological, and theoretical challenges to be overcome.

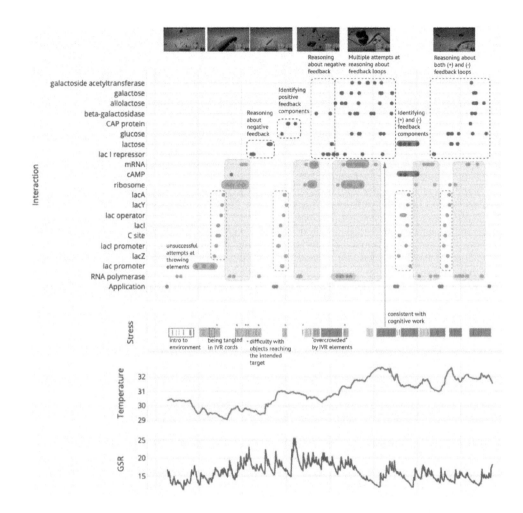

Figure 21.2   Temporal map of interactions and psychophysiological responses in VR

Note: The temporal map depicts an engagement pattern demonstrating high levels of interactions and learning gain, with stress markers generally consistent with learning tasks.

From a technological standpoint, we can expect sensing technology to become more robust and resistant to noise artifacts, while maintaining signal sensitivity. For example, the correct placement of lab-grade sensing equipment on the body is crucial to acquire noise-free data. However, with commercial wearables such as Fitbit and Apple watches gaining in popularity, it is likely that multiple reliable signals can be acquired in a single user-friendly wearable device in the near future. Methodologically, physiological methods may be used in a number of different contexts, varying in research designs and methods for analyses. One consequence is difficulty in building upon the methodology or comparing it with previous work. To address this challenge, researchers have called

for methodological standardizations (Cowley et al., 2016). As a body of HMC research with physiological methods emerge, researchers are encouraged to explore guidelines for using different signals and appropriate analyses, for example, at dedicated workshops or special issues. A key theoretical challenge is an incomplete model of cognitive-affective states. There is an on-going debate about how well physiological changes reflect specific internal states. For example, there are several competing models of emotion and affect (Fridlund, 1991; Hess et al., 1995; Mehrabian, 1997). As we are still understanding the connections between cognitive and affective states, addressing arousal along a single bipolar dimension is acknowledged to be a necessary simplification in many studies. The above challenges speak to much-needed additional research to advance the methods and our understanding between cognitive and affective states.

Researchers have applied physiological methods to additional indices beyond cognitive measures. These include flow in games (Bian et al., 2016; Nacke & Lindley, 2008), mindfulness (Burg et al., 2012), and feelings of trust in a mediated virtual environment (Gupta et al., 2020). Furthermore, there is exciting potential for expanding the use of psychophysiological measures in more complex and social settings, such as in embodied settings (Skulmowski & Rey, 2017). We can adapt existing methods to understand experiences in complex spaces that involve multiple kinds of interactions and people, like museums and classrooms, as well as research based on embodied cognition. We can leverage machine learning and predictive states to enhance user interactions with novel interfaces and robots. For example, an adaptive interface using electromyography (EMG) has been constructed to relieve the workload of humans when operating robots remotely (Luo et al., 2019). To conclude, psychophysiological methods offer a timely and rich research space for exploring human cognition and emotions as we engage with increasingly sophisticated technologies in our everyday lives. Further research is necessary to overcome technological, theoretical, and methodological challenges to advance our understanding as a field.

REFERENCES

Airdrie, J. N., Langley, K., Thapar, A., & van Goozen, S. H. M. (2018). Facial emotion recognition and eye gaze in attention-deficit/hyperactivity disorder with and without comorbid conduct disorder. *Journal of the American Academy of Child and Adolescent Psychiatry*, 57(8), 561–570. https://doi.org/10.1016/j.jaac.2018.04.016

Ayres, P., & van Gog, T. (2009). State of the art research into Cognitive Load Theory. *Computers in Human Behavior*, 25(2), 253–257. https://doi.org/10.1016/j.chb.2008.12.007

Bailenson, J. N., Pontikakis, E. D., Mauss, I. B., Gross, J. J., Jabon, M. E., Hutcherson, C. A. C., Nass, C., & John, O. (2008). Real-time classification of evoked emotions using facial feature tracking and physiological responses. *International Journal of Human-Computer Studies*, 66(5), 303–317. https://doi.org/10.1016/j.ijhcs.2007.10.011

Baker, R. S. J. d., D'Mello, S. K., Rodrigo, Ma. M. T., & Graesser, A. C. (2010). Better to be frustrated than bored: The incidence, persistence, and impact of learners' cognitive–affective states during interactions with three different computer-based learning environments. *International Journal of Human-Computer Studies*, 68(4), 223–241. https://doi.org/10.1016/j.ijhcs.2009.12.003

Betella, A., Zucca, R., Cetnarski, R., Greco, A., Lanatà, A., Mazzei, D., Tognetti, A., Arsiwalla, X. D., Omedas, P., De Rossi, D., & Verschure, P. F. M. J. (2014). Inference of human affective states from psychophysiological measurements extracted under ecologically valid conditions. *Frontiers in Neuroscience*, 8. https://doi.org/10.3389/fnins.2014.00286

Bian, Y., Yang, Y. C., Gao, F., Li, H., Zhou, S., Li, H., Sun, X., & Meng, X. (2016). A framework for physiological indicators of flow in VR games: Construction and preliminary evaluation. *Personal and Ubiquitous Computing*, 20(5), 821–832. https://doi.org/10.1007/s00779-016-0953-5

Boucsein, W., Fowles, D. C., Grimnes, S., Ben-Shakhar, G., Roth, W. T., Dawson, M. E., Filion, D. L., & Society for Psychophysiological Research Ad Hoc Committee on Electrodermal Measures. (2012). Publication recommendations for electrodermal measurements. *Psychophysiology*, 49(8), 1017–1034. https://doi.org/10.1111/j.1469-8986.2012.01384.x

Brunken, R., Plass, J. L., & Leutner, D. (2003). Direct measurement of cognitive load in multimedia learning. *Educational Psychologist*, 38(1), 53–61. https://doi.org/10.1207/S15326985EP3801_7

Brünken, R., Seufert, T., & Paas, F. (2010). Measuring cognitive load. In J. L. Plass, R. Brünken, & R. Moreno (Eds.), *Cognitive load theory* (pp. 181–202). Cambridge University Press. https://doi.org/10.1017/CBO9780511844744.011

Burg, J. M., Wolf, O. T., & Michalak, J. (2012). Mindfulness as self-regulated attention. *Swiss Journal of Psychology*, 71(3), 135–139. https://doi.org/10.1024/1421-0185/a000080

Cierniak, G., Scheiter, K., & Gerjets, P. (2009). Explaining the split-attention effect: Is the reduction of extraneous cognitive load accompanied by an increase in germane cognitive load? *Computers in Human Behavior*, 25(2), 315–324. https://doi.org/10.1016/j.chb.2008.12.020

Costley, J., & Lange, C. (2017). The mediating effects of germane cognitive load on the relationship between instructional design and students' future behavioral intention. *Electronic Journal of E-Learning*, 15(2), 174–187.

Cowley, B., Filetti, M., Lukander, K., Torniainen, J., Henelius, A., Ahonen, L., Barral, O., Kosunen, I., Valtonen, T., Huotilainen, M., Ravaja, N., & Jacucci, G. (2016). The psychophysiology primer: A guide to methods and a broad review with a focus on human–computer interaction. *Foundations and Trends® in Human–Computer Interaction*, 9(3–4), 151–308. https://doi.org/10.1561/1100000065

Dawson, M. E., Schell, A. M., & Filion, D. L. (2016). The electrodermal system. In G. G. Berntson, J. T. Cacioppo, & L. G. Tassinary (Eds.), *Handbook* of psychophysiology (4th ed., pp. 217–243). Cambridge University Press. https://doi.org/10.1017/9781107415782.010

de Jong, T. (2010). Cognitive load theory, educational research, and instructional design: Some food for thought. Instructional Science, 38(2), 105–134. https://doi.org/10.1007/s11251-009-9110-0

Eysink, Tessa H. S., de Jong, Ton, Berthold, Kirsten, Kolloffel, Bas, Opfermann, Maria, & Wouters, Pieter. (2009). Learner performance in multimedia learning arrangements: An analysis across instructional approaches. American Educational Research Journal, 46(4), 1107–1149.

Ferreira, E., Ferreira, D., Kim, S., Siirtola, P., Röning, J., Forlizzi, J. F., & Dey, A. K. (2014). Assessing real-time cognitive load based on psycho-physiological measures for younger and older adults. 2014 IEEE Symposium on Computational Intelligence, Cognitive Algorithms, Mind, and Brain (CCMB), 39–48. https://doi.org/10.1109/CCMB.2014.7020692

Fridlund, A. J. (1991). Sociality of solitary smiling: Potentiation by an implicit audience. Journal of Personality and Social Psychology, 60(2), 229–240. https://doi.org/10.1037/0022-3514.60.2.229

Gaffey, A. E., & Wirth, M. M. (2014). Psychophysiological measures. In A. C. Michalos (Ed.), Encyclopedia of quality of life and well-being research (pp. 5181–5184). Springer Netherlands. https://doi.org/10.1007/978-94-007-0753-5_2315

Gupta, K., Hajika, R., Pai, Y. S., Duenser, A., Lochner, M., & Billinghurst, M. (2020). Measuring human trust in a virtual assistant using physiological sensing in virtual reality. 2020 IEEE Conference on Virtual Reality and 3D User Interfaces (VR), 756–765. https://doi.org/10.1109/VR46266.2020.00099

Hart, S. G., & Staveland, L. E. (1988). Development of NASA-TLX (Task Load Index): Results of empirical and theoretical research. In P. A. Hancock & N. Meshkati (Eds.), Advances in psychology (Vol. 52, pp. 139–183). North-Holland. https://doi.org/10.1016/S0166-4115(08)62386-9

Hess, U., Banse, R., & Kappas, A. (1995). The intensity of facial expression is determined by underlying affective state and social situation. Journal of Personality and Social Psychology, 69(2), 280–288. https://doi.org/10.1037/0022-3514.69.2.280

Kalyuga, S. (2011). Cognitive load theory: How many types of load does it really need? Educational Psychology Review, 23(1), 1–19. https://doi.org/10.1007/s10648-010-9150-7

Ke, F., Lee, S., & Xu, X. (2016). Teaching training in a mixed-reality integrated learning environment. Computers in Human Behavior, 62(C), 212–220. https://doi.org/10.1016/j.chb.2016.03.094

Kim, H.-G., Cheon, E.-J., Bai, D.-S., Lee, Y. H., & Koo, B.-H. (2018). Stress and heart rate variability: A meta-analysis and review of the literature.

Psychiatry Investigation, 15(3), 235–245. https://doi.org/10.30773/pi.2017.08.17

Klepsch, M., & Seufert, T. (2020). Understanding instructional design effects by differentiated measurement of intrinsic, extraneous, and germane cognitive load. Instructional Science, 48(1), 45–77. https://doi.org/10.1007/s11251-020-09502-9

Leppink, J., Paas, F., Van der Vleuten, C. P. M., Van Gog, T., & Van Merriënboer, J. J. G. (2013). Development of an instrument for measuring different types of cognitive load. Behavior Research Methods, 45(4), 1058–1072. https://doi.org/10.3758/s13428-013-0334-1

Lui, M., McEwen, R., & Mullally, M. (2020). Immersive virtual reality for supporting complex scientific knowledge: Augmenting our understanding with physiological monitoring. British Journal of Educational Technology, n/a(n/a). https://doi.org/10.1111/bjet.13022

Luo, J., Yang, C., Su, H., & Liu, C. (2019). A robot learning method with physiological interface for teleoperation systems. Applied Sciences, 9(10), 2099. https://doi.org/10.3390/app9102099

Malik, M., Bigger, J. T., Camm, A. J., Kleiger, R. E., Malliani, A., Moss, A. J., & Schwartz, P. J. (1996). Heart rate variability: Standards of measurement, physiological interpretation, and clinical use. European Heart Journal, 17(3), 354–381. https://doi.org/10.1093/oxfordjournals.eurheartj.a014868

Martin, S. (2014). Measuring cognitive load and cognition: Metrics for technology-enhanced learning. Educational Research and Evaluation, 20(7–8), 592–621. https://doi.org/10.1080/13803611.2014.997140

McEwen, R. N., & Dubé, A. K. (2015). Engaging or distracting: Children's tablet computer use in education. Journal of Educational Technology & Society, 18(4), 9–23.

Mehrabian, A. (1997). Comparison of the PAD and PANAS as models for describing emotions and for differentiating anxiety from depression. Journal of Psychopathology and Behavioral Assessment, 19(4), 331–357. https://doi.org/10.1007/BF02229025

Moray, N. (Ed.). (1979). Mental workload: Its theory and measurement. Springer US. https://doi.org/10.1007/978-1-4757-0884-4

Moreno, R. (2006). Learning in high-tech and multimedia environments. Current Directions in Psychological Science, 15(2), 63–67. https://doi.org/10.1111/j.0963-7214.2006.00408.x

Moreno, R., & Park, B. (2010). Cognitive load theory: Historical development and relation to other theories. In J. L. Plass, R. Brünken, & R. Moreno (Eds.), Cognitive load theory (pp. 9–28). Cambridge University Press. https://doi.org/10.1017/CBO9780511844744.003

Nacke, L., & Lindley, C. A. (2008). Flow and immersion in first-person shooters: Measuring the player's gameplay experience. Proceedings of the 2008

Conference on Future Play: Research, Play, Share, 81–88. https://doi.org/10.1145/1496984.1496998

Naismith, L. M., Cheung, J. J. H., Ringsted, C., & Cavalcanti, R. B. (2015). Limitations of subjective cognitive load measures in simulation-based procedural training. *Medical Education*, 49(8), 805–814. https://doi.org/10.1111/medu.12732

Paas, F. G. (1992). Training strategies for attaining transfer of problem-solving skill in statistics: A cognitive-load approach. *Journal of Educational Psychology*, 84(4), 429–434. https://doi.org/10.1037/0022-0663.84.4.429

Paas, F. G., Merriënboer, J. J. G. van, & Adam, J. J. (2014). Measurement of cognitive load in instructional research, *Perceptual and Motor Skills*. https://doi.org/10.2466/pms.1994.79.1.419

Paas, F. G., Tuovinen, J. E., Tabbers, H., & Gerven, P. W. M. V. (2003). Cognitive load measurement as a means to advance cognitive load theory. *Educational Psychologist*, 38(1), 63–71. https://doi.org/10.1207/S15326985EP3801_8

Paletta, L., Pittino, N. M., Schwarz, M., Wagner, V., & Kallus, K. W. (2015). Human factors analysis using wearable sensors in the context of cognitive and emotional arousal. *Procedia Manufacturing*, 3, 3782–3787. https://doi.org/10.1016/j.promfg.2015.07.880

Rayner, K. (2009). Eye movements and attention in reading, scene perception, and visual search. *The Quarterly Journal of Experimental Psychology*, 62(8), 1457–1506. https://doi.org/10.1080/17470210902816461

Rothkopf, C. A., Ballard, D. H., & Hayhoe, M. M. (2016). Task and context determine where you look. *Journal of Vision*, 7(14), 16–16. https://doi.org/10.1167/7.14.16

Sattar, F., & Valdiya, P. (1999). Biofeedback in medical practice. *Medical Journal, Armed Forces India*, 55(1), 51–54. https://doi.org/10.1016/S0377-1237(17)30315-5

Shaffer, F., & Ginsberg, J. P. (2017). An overview of heart rate variability metrics and norms. *Frontiers in Public Health*, 5. https://doi.org/10.3389/fpubh.2017.00258

Shi, Y., Ruiz, N., Taib, R., Choi, E., & Chen, F. (2007). Galvanic skin response (GSR) as an index of cognitive load. *CHI '07 Extended Abstracts on Human Factors in Computing Systems*, 2651–2656. https://doi.org/10.1145/1240866.1241057

Shields, G. S., Sazma, M. A., McCullough, A. M., & Yonelinas, A. P. (2017). The effects of acute stress on episodic memory: A meta-analysis and integrative review. *Psychological Bulletin*, 143(6), 636–675. https://doi.org/10.1037/bul0000100

Skulmowski, A., & Rey, G. D. (2017). Measuring cognitive load in embodied learning settings. *Frontiers in Psychology*, 8. https://doi.org/10.3389/fpsyg.2017.01191

Smets, E., Schiavone, G., Velazquez, E. R., Raedt, W. D., Bogaerts, K., Diest, I. V., & Hoof, C. V. (2018).

Comparing task-induced psychophysiological responses between persons with stress-related complaints and healthy controls: A methodological pilot study. *Health Science Reports*, 1(8), e60. https://doi.org/10.1002/hsr2.60

Sridhar, P. K., Chan, S. W. T., Chua, Y., Quin, Y. W., & Nanayakkara, S. (2019). Going beyond performance scores: Understanding cognitive–affective states in kindergarteners and application of framework in classrooms. *International Journal of Child-Computer Interaction*, 21, 37–53. https://doi.org/10.1016/j.ijcci.2019.04.002

Swaak, J., & de Jong, T. (2001). Learner vs. system control in using online support for simulation-based discovery learning. *Learning Environments Research*, 4(3), 217–241. https://doi.org/10.1023/A:1014434804876

Sweller, J., van Merriënboer, J. J. G., & Paas, F. (2019). Cognitive architecture and instructional design: 20 years later. *Educational Psychology Review*, 31(2), 261–292. https://doi.org/10.1007/s10648-019-09465-5

Sweller, J., van Merrienboer, J. J. G., & Paas, F. G. W. C. (1998). Cognitive architecture and instructional design. *Educational Psychology Review*, 10(3), 251–296. https://doi.org/10.1023/A:1022193728205

Taub, M., Mudrick, N. V., Azevedo, R., Millar, G. C., Rowe, J., & Lester, J. (2017). Using multi-channel data with multi-level modeling to assess in-game performance during gameplay with CRYSTAL ISLAND. *Computers in Human Behavior*, 76, 641–655. https://doi.org/10.1016/j.chb.2017.01.038

Valcke, M. (2002). Cognitive load: Updating the theory? *Learning and Instruction*, 12(1), 147–154.

van Gog, T., & Paas, F. (2008). Instructional efficiency: Revisiting the original construct in educational research. *Educational Psychologist*, 43(1), 16–26. https://doi.org/10.1080/00461520701756248

van Merriënboer, J. J. G., & Sweller, J. (2005). Cognitive load theory and complex learning: Recent developments and future directions. *Educational Psychology Review*, 17(2), 147–177. https://doi.org/10.1007/s10648-005-3951-0

Villarejo, M. V., Zapirain, B. G., & Zorrilla, A. M. (2012). A stress sensor based on Galvanic Skin Response (GSR) controlled by ZigBee. *Sensors (Basel, Switzerland)*, 12(5), 6075–6101. https://doi.org/10.3390/s120506075

Young, J. Q., Irby, D. M., Barilla-LaBarca, M.-L., & Ten Cate, O. (2016). Measuring cognitive load: Mixed results from a handover simulation for medical students. *Perspectives on Medical Education*, 5(1), 24–32. https://doi.org/10.1007/s40037-015-0240-6

Young, M. S., & Stanton, N. A. (2002). It's all relative: Defining mental workload in the light of Annett's paper. *Ergonomics*, 45(14), 1018–1020. https://doi.org/10.1080/00140130210166816

22

Human Shoppers, AI Cashiers, and Cloud-computing Others: Methodological Approaches for Machine Surveillance in Commercial Retail Environments

Kristina M. Green

In her essay, *The robot dog fetches for whom?*, Donath (2018) uses social robots and voice assistants as examples of intelligent machines that challenge our assumptions about who or what people communicate with within human–machine communication (HMC) contexts. One such machine – AIBO – walks and talks like a dog, emulating puppy-like behaviors at the outset and, over time, "learns" tricks and "matures" into an older, more well-behaved pup. A persuasive technology, AIBO is affective and pulls the heartstrings of its unsuspecting owners by convincingly imitating the mannerisms one expects from a live canine companion. In Donath's (2018) estimation "If you bought an AIBO, it became your robot dog, your artificial pet. You were its owner, and all its parts, for better or worse, were yours" (p. 19).

Another intelligent machine, by way of comparison, is Amazon's Alexa: an artificially intelligent (AI) voice assistant that does not look like a humanoid robot but is nonetheless embodied insofar that Alexa speaks using a woman's voice (Donath, 2018). Like AIBO, Alexa's hardware is something a person could own. The device from which Alexa listens and speaks is local, residing in the spaces and environments that her human counterparts occupy. However, Alexa's software – her memory and algorithmic processes – are remote, stored in the cloud. As Donath (2018) rightly asserts, people cannot own Alexa in the same way they own AIBO. "Alexa has customers…[and] is not acting solo" (p. 19).

AI machines, like Alexa and many others, disrupt existing theories and methods in the field of communication. Therefore, I use Donath's (2018) essay as an invitation to stake out new methodological approaches that contend with HMC's triadic orientation: an orientation that encompasses people, machines, and the cloud. By adapting existing walkthrough methodologies (Light, Burgess, & Duguay, 2018; Star, 1999) and incorporating them into a case study research design, I advanced a triadic framework that overcomes some of the challenges machine intelligence pose and attempt to accommodate "who it is that [we] are with" (Donath, 2018, p. 22) when humans and machines communicate.

ACCOMMODATING AND EMBRACING TRIADIC ORIENTATIONS IN HMC CONTEXTS

The insight that something or someone *else* enters into HMC contexts represents a significant departure from traditional communication theory and is an important theoretical and methodological consideration for researchers. Historically, an underlying assumption in communication and human–computer interaction (HCI) positioned communicators as human and technologies as tools (Cathcart & Gumpert, 1985; Gunkel, 2009). A hand-written letter or telephone communication, for example, is traditionally understood as a dyadic, linear model of communication where one person (i.e., the sender) uses media as a channel to transmit a message to another person (i.e., the receiver; Cathcart & Gumpert, 1985). Over time, communication models matured alongside technology, and new ways of accommodating the mass, participatory, and non-linear ways humans communicate were established. However, even interactional models of communication ascribe to a sender/receiver orientation that does not accurately depict the communicative roles that machines undertake and the extent to which it fundamentally differs from people (Frijns, Schürer & Koeszegi, 2021).

HMC reconceptualizes intelligent machines as technologies that humans communicate *with*, as opposed to channels for transmitting messages *thru* (Guzman, 2018). Additionally, and unlike humans – who are physically and cognitively unified – machines are asymmetrical entities (Frijns et al., 2021). AI cannot be reduced to their localized hardware devices. Through the cloud – a site of memory storage and algorithmic processes – intelligent machines communicators are incommensurable to their human counterparts.

In the case of Alexa, for example, people do not simply transmit messages to other people but direct their communication toward Alexa itself, using a natural language processing (NLP) interface. By posing the question "whom else," Donath (2018) spotlights a communicative orientation where machines communicate with people – extracting, remembering, calculating, predicting, and deciding outcomes – but are also directed away from humans and toward a digital archive that is abstract, remote, and accessible by an unknowable number of third-party stakeholders. In an attempt to resist the binary sender/receiver orientations found in early communication scholarship and with an interest toward more accurate accounts of communicative exchanges between people, machines, and third-party stakeholders, I look to case study methodologies for guidance.

MAKING A CASE FOR HMC CASE STUDIES

Case studies are a preferred "empirical method that investigates a contemporary phenomenon (the 'case') in depth and within its real-world context, especially when the boundaries between phenomenon and context may not be clearly evident" (Yin, 2017, p. 45). Unlike controlled lab settings or experimental research designs – which isolate an object of study or phenomenon from the messiness of everyday life – case study researchers meet the object of study where it is. AI cannot be decontextualized or studied independently from the people and environments where it is encountered. Thus, case study approaches are especially relevant for HMC methodologists.

Historically, case studies emerged from the Chicago School of sociology and were used for documenting the life histories of understudied, underserved populations in social work disciplines (Platt, 1992). Classically, cases focused on a person as a unit of analysis but, over time, scholars undertook different units of analysis including organizations, programs, neighborhoods, institutions, processes, and events as cases (Yin, 2017). In my research, I decided to undertake a specific instantiation of AI (i.e., sensor fusion) as a case too.

There are several advantages that case study methodologies offer to HMC scholars. First, undertaking intelligent machines as case studies creates opportunities for communication scholars to narrowly examine and describe context-specific applications of AI in ways that offer greater nuance and less ambiguity. By taking an in-depth approach, scholars are called upon to specialize in a type of AI, becoming intimately familiar with its logic, and expand communication and media studies' lexicon to machine alterities. Regarding the last point, communication scholars are especially well-positioned to articulate the qualitative consequences of otherwise quantitative processes and techniques. Case study methodologies are exploratory, rigorous, and flexible, allowing researchers to deploy multiple methods within a unified study.

SELECTING A CASE

How researchers choose a case of machine intelligence will depend on their research questions or the propositions they wish to prove or disprove (Yin, 2017). While there is no formula for demarcating a case, there are some informal steps researchers can take to get started. In my own case study research, I began by taking seriously Yin's (2017) recommendation to identify "a fluid rendition of the recent past and the present, not just the present" (Yin, 2017, p. 43). In practice, this means identifying new or emerging genres of AI, while also acknowledging their historicity. By grounding machine intelligence as historically informed artifacts, researchers can establish the myriad of ways that automation replaces or displaces processes and roles formerly carried out by people. By learning about and engaging with a technology's past, media scholars are trained upon whether the consequences of machine intelligence in our everyday lives endures or diverges from what came before. It is also helpful to recognize case study methods as a non-linear and iterative process that casts a wide net at the onset but leads to a narrow investigation of AI by the end. A necessary part of this process entails reading for breadth, both inside and beyond the artificial parameters of one's field, as well as reading actively by annotating high-level topics, pulling intriguing quotes, familiarizing oneself with the dominant arguments, noting anomalies, and identifying gaps or omissions in the literature that demands further exploration.

One additional consideration when selecting a case is establishing whether a single- or multiple-case study design is most appropriate for your project (Yin, 2017). A single-case study design, for example, might focus on one instantiation of an intelligent machine (e.g., Amazon Alexa), while a multiple-case study design might focus on a genre of AI that shares something in common (e.g., Amazon's Alexa, Apple's Siri, Microsoft's Cortana). These steps are by no means exhaustive but offer practical ways to get started.

An HMC Case Study Example: Amazon Go

In my research, I examined Amazon Go cashierless convenience stores as a case study and reference this work to demystify how machine intelligence can be approached, which sub-methods can be deployed, and what sources of data can be reasonably gathered. Based on the human–machine–cloud orientations discussed above, my goal is to offer a more holistic and accurate representation of HMC that takes place in smart retail environments. Unlike anthropomorphic social robots that are made to look or sound like humans or animals, I became interested in how scholars could study muted instantiations of intelligent machines, particularly those that surveil and observe people but are themselves difficult for people to detect back.

What is Amazon Go?

Marketed as "the future of shopping," Amazon Go is a chain of cashierless convenience stores, located in urban cities across the US – including New York, Chicago, Seattle, and San Francisco. To begin, shoppers must download the Amazon Go mobile app, create or connect the app to an Amazon account, and link the app to a method of electronic payment. Only after completing this initial registration phase, can shoppers scan a QR code to enter the physical store. Like scanning a commuter pass at a subway station, the Amazon Go app functions as a digital passport that opens an automated gate at the store's entrance. Once inside, shoppers can choose from typical convenience store offerings, including Amazon Go's own brand of consumer-packaged goods like premade sandwiches, drinks, and even souvenir water bottles and coffee mugs. What sets Amazon Go apart from other convenience or grocery stores is that when shoppers are ready to purchase their items, they bypass check-out lanes, scanners, and human cashiers, and "just walk out."

The "frictionless" affordances of "just walk out" technology is made possible by sensor fusion: the same technology used in driverless cars. At its simplest, sensor fusion refers to the combination or fusion of data from multiple sensors of differing modalities (Chen et al., 2017; Gravina et al., 2017). The underpinning machine learning logics inherent to sensor fusion are comparable to informational triangulation whereby sensing, detecting, and extracting data from multiple sources compensates for the limitations of a single sensor. In other words, one sensor on its own may be insufficient and susceptible to errors, signal loss, inconsistency, or noise. Data from multiple sensors, on the other hand, can overcome these challenges through redundancy and produce robust outcomes across several domains (Chen et al., 2017; Gravina et al., 2017). Amazon Go cashierless smart environments deploy three main sensors to infer what shoppers are purchasing by triangulating data from smartphone devices, weighted shelves, and computer vision cameras strewn across the retail space ceilings. In computer science literature, Amazon Go constitutes a human action recognition (HAR) system that autonomously detects, monitors, and infers human body movements and behaviors (Chen et al., 2017) and, by extension, automates surveillance (Andrejevic, 2019).

Select Sub-methods

Once researchers choose a case, the next step includes considering the sources of data that might answer or satisfy the research objective and, by extension, the methods for acquiring that data. Here, applying a triadic interpretation of HMC offers a useful starting point for mapping and identifying key stakeholders that are implicated and context specific. For example, as a convenience store, Amazon Go dictates or creates conditions where – at a minimum – shoppers, sensors, and corporate entities (who maintain, access, and own the data generated in these spaces) intersect and represent three possible avenues from which information can be gathered. Each of these stakeholders demands a different methodological approach to accommodate their unique and differing status.

Semi-structured Interviews

Quantitative and qualitative methods for assessing the attitudes, beliefs, perceptions, and behaviors of people are well-established in social science research. In communication, surveys, interviews, and focus groups, as well as network and discourse analyses are commonly deployed and offer distinct advantages and challenges. Generally speaking, case study designs offer flexibility and researchers can elect to choose one or more of these methods to account for the human stakeholder in HMC.

At the onset of the Amazon Go case study, I considered which people could participate and inform this study and established that shoppers who had first-hand experience *and* media consumers who had second-hand knowledge of cashierless convenience stores could help answer research questions about the *imagined affordances* (Nagy & Neff, 2015) of cashierless technology. A semi-structured interview methodology was selected, constructed, pilot tested, and deployed. Since there is an extensive body of literature that details best practices and key strategies for conducting interviews, an elaboration on why HMC scholars might consider incorporating the insights of primary and secondary sources in case study research are discussed.

Why is it Important to Interview Secondary Sources of AI Systems?

Consider for a moment that you want to do a study about the cultural significance of cars and, therefore, develop and administer interview questions for drivers. You ask drivers about their direct experience of using, owning, selling, borrowing, paying for, and sometimes even crashing cars. The textual data you collect will necessarily reveal how drivers feel about cars, their attitudes and beliefs about cars' advantages and disadvantages in society, as well as evidence about cars as

cultural objects that convey status, norms, values, and so on. On its face, it might seem logical to end data collection here, write up findings, and move on to your next research project. However, to conclude the study here neglects the reality that pedestrians also experience car culture.

In this example, the addition of transcript data from pedestrians would likely yield objective and valid analyses about the cultural significance of cars in society. As a demographic, pedestrians know intimately what cars are, even if they don't own or drive one. Pedestrians harbor beliefs, attitudes, and routine behaviors surrounding cars, and can expand the researcher's understanding of this topic in unexpected and important ways. A similar analogy can be extended for HMC case study researchers. Rarely, if ever, is it the case that the social, cultural, technical, and economic consequences of AI are confined to the immediacy of its intended users.

In terms of accommodating the difference in shopper and non-shopper cohorts, I created two versions of semi-structured interview questions. The questions posed to Amazon Go shoppers asked participants to reflect on their last experience at Amazon Go stores (e.g., can you walk me through your latest experience?; thinking back to the last time you visited an Amazon Go, how would you describe the atmosphere of the store?). By contrast, non-shoppers who had only heard or read about Amazon Go in the media (or from others) were asked to reflect on their perceptions, knowledge, and attitudes of cashierless shopping, more broadly (e.g., what have you heard or read about Amazon Go?). There were also several overlapping questions posed to both cohorts of interview participants in order to gather evidence about how participants imagine cashierless technology works.

Applying and Adapting Walkthrough Methods for HMC Case Studies

Accounting for the machine portion of the HMC equation is less straightforward than administering semi-structured interviews to people who have primary experience with or secondary knowledge about HAR systems. Machines are not commensurate to humans and a triadic orientation to HMC conceives of machine intelligence as something that is both local and remote, visible and abstract, interactive and mute, hardware and software. How, then, can HMC methodologists approach machine interlocutors within contexts like cashierless smart environments?

Revisiting the case of Amazon Go, sensor fusion technology is not one, standalone hardware device but an apparatus of surveillance that infers people's convenience store purchases through behavior: entering, walking, picking up, putting down, exiting. The remaining sensors embedded throughout the smart retail space – weight sensors located within display case shelves and computer vision cameras located within the ceiling – are infrastructural, with no corresponding interface for people to interpret or interact with. Sensor fusion observes but is, itself, difficult for humans to detect back in many ways. While shoppers in a cashierless environment can see computer vision cameras along the ceiling, sensors embedded within shelves are imperceptible, looking no different than any other kind of display. To overcome the challenges of this multi-machine system, I apply and adapt the walkthrough method (Light et al., 2018) and treat the Amazon Go smartphone interface as a discursive stakeholder.

Walkthrough Method for Mobile Smartphone Apps

Borrowing from Light, Burgess, and Duguay (2018), the walkthrough method offers a critical approach to the study of mobile smartphone applications (apps). This systematic method involves "engag[ing] with an app's interface to examine its mechanisms and embedded cultural references to understand how it guides users and shapes their experiences" (p. 2). From download and registration to everyday engagement with and discontinuation from the application, the walkthrough method captures the start-to-finish life cycle of app usage. Additionally, it offers researchers a wide range of source material to work with and account for machine interlocutors. Leveraging the walkthrough method as part of this case study approach, yielded a large corpus of data including screenshot images of its interface, which encompasses textual, visual, and procedural rhetorics that can be analyzed through critical discourse analysis (Fairclough, 1995; van Dijk, 1993; Wodak & Meyer, 2009).

A walkthrough approach to apps allows HMC methodologists to evaluate apps in several important ways. In past studies, for example, methodologists create 'dummy accounts' to identify and assess the effect of personalization, which enables and constrains user experiences based on normative interpretations of identity (Dieter et al., 2018; Light et al., 2018). By imitating and walking through an app according to differing user types, personas, or scenarios, researchers can document discrepancies in how apps behave and the implied meaning of those activities and actions more broadly. In this way, researchers can conduct multiple walkthroughs on a single app.

In another example, Ahmadvand and colleagues (2018) evaluate the usability of a health literacy app and apply a two-pronged walkthrough method where researchers first engage with an app and offer feedback to refine its design. In the second phase, the method is deployed again, this time with researchers and participants walking through the application together. This two-part approach yields a rich corpus of data about user experiences and informs additional avenues for improvement. These scenarios represent but a few additional ways that the walkthrough method can be tailored to meet the demands of HMC researchers.

In the Amazon Go case study example, I deploy the original walkthrough method summarized above to assess the Amazon Go app and its unique affordances as a method of payment and a method for access. The walkthrough method helps resolve existing methodological challenges, especially in cases where machine observers are tacit. As the second sub-method for the case study, an analysis of Amazon Go's smartphone app offers evidence about the muted, sensory technology operating in the retail space. Through "how to" instructional content and animations, and an analysis of the interface more broadly, a cashierless environment's sensor fusion apparatus operates in overt and covert ways. Importantly, an analysis of the app's *Help* menus also establishes an indirect way for researchers to more meaningfully convey the significance of intelligent machines as archive-oriented entities as well

Among its most relevant strengths for HMC methods, the walkthrough method relies on three key constructs to ascertain designers' intended (1) vision (e.g., purpose, audience, user scenarios), (2) operating model (e.g., how it generates capital), and (3) governance (e.g., formal and informal rules, constraints, and legalities). By focusing on these three constructs, HMC methodologists can account for Donath's provocation about "whom else" tacit infrastructures "fetch." As Light and colleagues (2018) suggest, an analysis of an app's vision, operating model, and governance encompasses more than a descriptive account of what an app looks like and how to navigate its menus. Part and parcel to the method is direct engagement with corporate-generated documentation that communicates formalized rules about data ownership, usage, and legalities.

Through an assessment of an app's *operating model*, for example, researchers learn about the multi-sided markets that apps cultivate, as well as partnerships with third-party developers (Nierborg, 2015). In trying to better understand and evidence how apps generate capital – financial, political, social, or otherwise – researchers may also look to public market information (i.e., IPOs, press kits, etc.; p.10). Through an assessment of an app's *governance*, researchers review regulatory discourses, found in terms of service (ToS), among many other texts. In my research, Amazon Go's ToS explicitly references the cloud and AI as an author of information, thereby offering theoretical support for triadic orientations toward HMC. For example, ToS state that Amazon Go "collects three kinds of personal information about customers: information you give us, *automatic information,* information from other sources." In-app documentation also states that "to help you get in and out of our store quickly, we use in-store technology *and* cloud computing to determine the items that you and your guests select." Taken together, these data points offer specifics about cloud-computing through its related topics (i.e., data extraction, authorship, ownership, copyright, legal status, privacy, safety, and community standards; Light et al., 2018). Thus, while the cloud cannot be queried directly, HMC researchers can redirect their focus toward app documentation created by those stakeholders who benefit financially, legally, socially, and politically from the muted status of the cloud.

Walkthrough Method for Smart Infrastructure

Before it was applied to digital architectures, the walkthrough method was inspired by ethnographic approaches to physical architectures (Star, 1999). Like the walkthrough method for mobile smartphone apps, which involves compiling images, workflows, and field notes about "working through screens, tapping buttons and exploring menus" (Light et al., 2018, p. 11), a walkthrough approach to smart environments involves a similar sensibility. Leveraging many of the same considerations surrounding expected use and with a commitment to the core constructs of vision, operating model, and governance, I shifted the focus away from mobile screens and toward the smart infrastructure itself.

In their work on situated app studies, Dieter and colleagues (2018) highlight the importance of engaging with apps under *static* and *dynamic* conditions. By this, the authors suggest that apps behave differently within and apart from the 'native' environment for which they are designed. Taking the case of Amazon Go, a static condition generates evidence about the expected use of the Amazon Go app outside of or decontextualized from cashierless stores. By contrast, a dynamic

condition of the Amazon Go app generates evidence of capabilities and constraints that are predicated on shoppers' embeddedness within the smart retail environment. Indeed, a walkthrough approach to Amazon Go's app represents an ideal case where a smartphone app's capabilities and constraints must be investigated within the environment for which it was designed.

Adapting the walkthrough method for smart environments requires an ethnographic approach. As a participant-observer exploring Amazon Go cashierless stores, my iPhone served as the linchpin that collapsed the space between shopper, access, and payment. I scanned my QR code to open the automated gates to enter the store and browse its product assortment. App functionality that had been restricted outside of the store – such as the virtual cart feature – was suddenly useable, activated within the native environment. Additionally, walking through a smart retail space involved taking ethnographic field notes that documented and described reoccurring imagery, signage, patterns of walking, instructions, and so on. By visiting and situating myself within a cashierless environment, I undertook Farman's (2015) invocation that communication scholars "go beyond what takes place on the screens of devices to contextualize those interactions with what is happening *around* those devices" (p. 1).

In practice, a walkthrough approach to smart infrastructure also meant creating a record about where Amazon Go brick-and-mortar stores are located: its nearby streets, adjacent businesses, transportation option, as well as its *politics of location* (see Rich, 2003). Approached as part of an existing urban landscape, many unforeseen stakeholders necessarily entered the case study dataset. For example, the sample of Amazon Go stores examined in the case study included six downtown Chicago retail environments, which were located inside of corporate office building lobbies, minimall settings, and/or near major transportation hubs. I loitered store aisles, picked up and put down merchandise, inspected shelving displays, and spent a considerable amount of time staring at the computer vision cameras littered across its ceiling. As such, my field notes included observations and interactions with other shoppers and employees. On one occasion, I noted not seeing a single employee nor shopper inside or surrounding the Amazon Go store, which calls into question what people ought to do if they need to use SNAP benefits or cash; the app suggests that speaking to an Amazon Go representative should be an option. As a participant-observer trying to take my time in a space marketed for its time-saving affordances and efficiency, I also attracted the attention of extra-authority figures like security guards on more than one occasion. Were it not for walking through the retail smart environments, these additional stakeholders and context-specific interactions would have gone undocumented and unnoticed. Especially in cases where automated systems allow and constrain access to food, beverages, medications, personal hygiene products, and other merchandise common to convenience store offerings, a walkthrough approach to infrastructure proves valuable in illuminating what lies beyond smartphone screens and the many ways that HMC has become inextricably linked to topics like accessibility, surveillance, security, safety, labor, and capitalism.

By adapting and conducting a walkthrough of smart infrastructure as the third and final submethod for this case study, my ethnographic field notes were also informed by the methodologies that came before it. In fact, the order in which HMC case study methodologists conduct their research likely has a bearing on the outcomes of the research since case studies are cumulative, building upon itself throughout. The insights, questions, confusions, attitudes, beliefs, and imaginings of interview participants could be tested, verified, or witnessed in my own first-hand experience of the cashierless smart environments. In line with the cultural studies objectives outlined in Light, Burgess, and Duguay's (2018) walkthough method a smart infrastructure walkthrough reprioritizes the materiality of HMC by examining virtual and physical ways of organizing, constraining, and enabling user experiences. Additionally, and according to Light and colleagues (2018), one of the advantages walkthrough methodologies is that it "allows the researcher to place oneself in the user's position and imagine the range of affordances the user perceives" (Light et al., 2018, p. 6). By putting these three distinct datasets in conversation with one another, HMC case study researchers do not have to imagine how others feel or use Amazon Go but can cite others' own words, experiences, and imaginings in their findings.

Working with HMC Case Study Datasets

Case studies yield large, diverse, and seemingly disparate data of differing modalities. Semi-structured interviews yield audio recordings and written transcripts. Walkthrough methods for smartphone apps yield images, memos about workflows, and app-generated documentation about formalized rules, and legalities. In the Amazon Go case study, a walkthrough approach of smart infrastructure yielded ethnographic field notes, as well as photographs and a map depicting the locations of the stores I visited.

While there are no hard and fast rules about how HMC methodologists ought to organize and code data, transcribing and cleaning audio transcripts and organizing data in a qualitative analysis software program like MAXQDA can help. From there, researchers can conduct *in-vivo coding*, which uses the original language from each source "as a symbol system for qualitative data analysis" (Saldana & Omasta, 2016, p. 182). Traditionally used for coding textual evidence, in-vivo coding ensures that the findings of the case study originate from participants of the study who provide "rich insights with their own words, better than the researcher could ever compose" (Saldaña & Omasta, 2016, p. 32). In practice and expanded to visual and procedural rhetorics, this means parsing out the most meaningful, revealing, affective, and/or descriptive words, phrases, colors, symbols, and icons for each unit of analysis in the dataset to establish high-level topics or themes. This early phase of thematic organizing involves note-taking along the way and helps researchers familiarize themselves intimately with the nitty-gritty details of their dataset.

From there, methodologists can choose from a wide range of existing or original coding schema to represent the constructs and variables that bind their case study. An iterative process that takes time, patience, and trust, working with HMC case study datasets move from high-level themes to more focused coding to answer research questions and/or propositions posed at the outset of the study. Importantly, HMC case study researchers should be deliberate and thoughtful in treating the entire dataset as a single, unified study versus treating each method as a sub-study responsible for yielding its own set of sub-findings (Yin, 2017). As discussed in the next section, this is an especially important consideration for triangulating study findings.

Triangulating HMC Case Study Findings

As researchers identify the key findings of the case study, *converging lines of inquiry* (Yin, 2017) are established. Borrowing from principles of navigation, Yardley (2008) suggests that triangulation for qualitative methods is based on the heuristic that intersecting lines are like coordinates that denote "the precise location of an object" (Yin, 2017, p. 170). In qualitative research, triangulation is often associated with construct validity due to the emphasis on establishing precision from seemingly disparate sources of information. According to Yin (2017), "when you have really triangulated the data, a case study's findings will have been supported by more than a single source of evidence" (p. 170) and, in doing so, construct validity is greatly strengthened.

HMC Case Study Advantages and Challenges

As is the case with most qualitative research, one of the potential limitations of case study approaches toward machines that surveil is that it can be used uncritically and un-empirically. For example, Yin (2017) suggests that there are three types of "non-research" case studies – *teacher-practice*, *popular*, and *case record* studies – which may be appropriate for professional development, summarizing the state of literature and media, and for administrative archiving purposes, respectively. In these non-research examples, case study research is deployed for a purpose other than empirical research, which runs the risk of biased and unobjective findings.

Reliability, the extent to which a research study can be repeated with the same findings, presents another limitation of case study methodology (Yin, 2017) and is not always feasible. Especially when taking a multi-method approach, there may be substantial variance in how data is collected and interpreted. One important way to overcome this challenge is by creating a thorough protocol that painstakingly documents and justifies as many procedures as possible so that the findings and potential biases are explicit and transparent to readers and reviewers.

Surveillance, Security, Safety, Sight, and Sites

According to the Surveillance Studies Network (2006) report:

> Where we find purposeful, routine, systematic and focused attention paid to personal details, for the sake of control, entitlement, management, influence or protection, we are looking at surveillance. (p. 3)

By definition, human action recognition systems that make cashierless shopping possible are automated surveillance systems that deploy computational ways of "seeing," monitoring, and tracking people, places, and objects that occupy space. HMC scholars, therefore, are called upon to engage with literature from surveillance studies,

which critically engage with topics of vision – computer or otherwise – as an autopoietic process (Halpern, 2015) that inscribes relations of power (Foucault, 1995). As "a special class of spatial products...designed to provide ubiquitous physical computing infrastructure" (Halpern, 2015, p. 3), sensor fusion is diffuse. Researchers are not dealing with a single, remote hardware device that records photographic or video imagery, but several locally embedded devices that see in unconventional, abstracting ways.

CONCLUSION

Unlike communication that occurs between people, intelligent machines are oriented in two directions: toward people vis-à-vis interfaces and toward others vis-à-vis digital archives and cloud memory. A walkthrough case study approach to HMC accommodates the incommensurability of humans and machines by leveraging a triadic framework where multiple methods are used to assess different stakeholders involved in HMC. Through this triadic framework, humans, machines, and the cloud are conceptualized as stakeholders, the implication being that each party – while unequal or asymmetrical (Frijns et al., 2021) – has a vested interest and role to play within smart environment contexts. HMC researchers who deploy walkthrough case study methods are called upon to interrogate the interests of all stakeholders critically and to contend with the cloud as a proxy for corporate interest, the significance of which is detailed in terms of service, privacy notices, and the like.

Taking a walkthrough case study approach to smart environments, in some ways, imitates sensor fusion logics by recasting its inherently quantitative technique as a qualitative, social phenomenon instead. By collecting semi-structured interviews from shoppers and non-, conducting a walkthrough of the Amazon Go app, and documenting an infrastructural walkthrough of Amazon Go brick-and-mortar stores, the method outlined herein uses multiple sources of evidence that represent human–machine–cloud stakeholders to create redundancy and corroborate findings from these differing modalities. By extending the walkthrough method to cashierless convenience stores, many of the challenges of studying muted AI systems are overcome by redirecting researchers' attention from questions about *where* the cloud exists to *for whom* cloud-computing fetches.

Adapting the walkthrough method for the study of smart infrastructure also offers a useful means of further contextualizing HMC within an inescapable *politics of location* (Rich, 2003). This is especially important because AI techniques are frameless (Andrejevic, 2019) and these machine learning techniques can be transferred to any number of contexts, some more or less dignified than others. By occupying the unique positionality of an expert-participant in HMC case study design, several *dispositifs* (Jäger & Maier, 2009) or stakeholders who are otherwise omitted come into focus like shapes in a 3D stereograph. Within the context of Amazon Go, this included extra-authority figures like security guards that shoppers may find themselves interacting with, as well as unintended users of cashierless stores like persons who are unbanked, those who rely on SNAP benefits, or anyone who does not own a smartphone device to begin with. While app-generated materials on the Amazon Go app explicitly names and attempts to rectify these outliers, the material realities on the ground are not as neat or easy to address in the messiness of sociality. HMC is context-specific and identifying expected *and* unexpected uses, intended *and* unintended consequences of sensor fusion are important. By putting various sub-methods in conversation with one another, my research finds that sensor fusion does not just displace human cashiers but remediates existing norms concerning accessibility, surveillance, safety, security, and capitalism.

Whereas intelligence machines like Amazon's "Alexa are always listening" to "make shopping seamless" (Donath, 2018, p. 18), Amazon Go is always watching. Moreover, through the interface-archive that intelligent machine observers embody, Amazon Go also leverages, "the vast dossier of searches and purchases and past queries, the vividly detailed portrait of you" which may have been disclosed to Alexa (Donath, 2018, p. 18). So even when you leave Alexa home, her archive has a presence in Amazon Go's surveillance apparatus. Neither Alexa nor Amazon Go are relegated to an Echo speaker nor the sensors embedded in retail shelves but are everyware: "not merely 'in every place,' but also 'in every thing'" (Greenfield, 2010, p. 11).

REFERENCES

Ahmadvand, A., Drennan, J., Burgess, J., Clark, M., Kavanagh, D., Burns, K., Howard, S., Fleur, K., Campbell, C., & Nissen, L. (2018). Novel augmented reality solution for improving health literacy around antihypertensives in people living with type 2 diabetes mellitus: Protocol of a technology evaluation study. *BMJ Open*, *8*(4). http://dx.doi.org/10.1136/bmjopen-2017-019422

Andrejevic, M. (2019). Automating surveillance. *Surveillance & Society*, *17*(1/2), 7–13. https://doi.org/10.24908/ss.v17i1/2.12930

Ball, & Wood (Eds.). (2006, September). A Report on the Surveillance Society - For the Information Commissioner. https://ico.org.uk/media/1042391/surveillance-society-summary-06.pdf

Cathcart, R., & Gumpert, G. (1985). The person–computer interaction: A unique source. In B. D. Ruben (Ed.), *Information and behavior* (Vol. 1, pp. 113–124). Transaction Publishers.

Chen, C., Jafari, R., & Kehtarnavaz, N. (2017). A survey of depth and inertial sensor fusion for human action recognition. *Multimedia Tools and Applications*, *76*(3), 4405–4425. https://doi.org/10.1007/s11042-015-3177-1

Dieter, M., Gerlitz, C., Helmond, A., Tkacz, N., Vlist, F. van der, & Weltevrede, E. (2018). Store, interface, package, connection. *SFB 1187 Medien Der Kooperation - Working Paper Series*, *4*, 1–16.

Donath, J. (2018, July 11). The robot dog fetches for whom? A networked self and human augmentics, *Artificial Intelligence, Sentience*. https://doi.org/10.4324/9781315202082-2

Fairclough, N. (1995). *Critical discourse analysis: The critical study of language*. Longman.

Farman, J. (2015). Infrastructures of mobile social media. *Social Media + Society*, *1*(1), 2056305115580343. https://doi.org/10.1177/2056305115580343

Foucault, M. (2012). *Discipline and punish: The birth of the prison*. Vintage.

Frijns, H. A., Schürer, O., & Koeszegi, S. T. (2021). Communication models in human–robot interaction: An asymmetric MODel of ALterity in human–robot interaction (AMODAL-HRI). *International Journal of Social Robotics*. https://doi.org/10.1007/s12369-021-00785-7

Gravina, R., Alinia, P., Ghasemzadeh, H., & Fortino, G. (2017). Multi-sensor fusion in body sensor networks: State-of-the-art and research challenges. *Information Fusion*, *35*, 68–80. https://doi.org/10.1016/j.inffus.2016.09.005

Greenfield, A. (2010). *Everyware: The dawning age of ubiquitous computing*. New Riders.

Gunkel, D. (2009). Beyond mediation: Thinking the computer otherwise. *ISCC*, *1*. https://doi.org/10.1386/iscc.1.1.53_1

Guzman, A. L. (Ed.). (2018). *Human-machine communication: Rethinking communication, technology and ourselves*. Peter Lang Publishing, Inc.

Halpern, O. (2015). *Beautiful data: A history of vision and reason since 1945*. Duke University Press.

Jäger, S., & Maier, F. (2009). Theoretical and methodological aspects of Foucauldian critical discourse analysis and dispositive analysis. In

R. Wodak & M. Meyer (Eds.), *Methods of critical discourse analysis* (pp. 34–61). SAGE Publications.

Light, B., Burgess, J., & Duguay, S. (2018). The walk-through method: An approach to the study of apps. *New Media & Society*, *20*(3), 881–900. https://doi.org/10.1177/1461444816675438

Nagy, P., & Neff, G. (2015). Imagined affordance: Reconstructing a keyword for communication theory. *Social Media and Society*, *1*(2). https://doi.org/10.1177/2056305115603385

Nierborg, D. (2015). Crushing Candy: The free-to-play game in its connective commodity form. *New Media & Society*, *1*, 2. https://doi.org/doi-org.proxy.cc.uic.edu/10.1177/2056305115621932

Platt, J. (1992). "Case study" in American methodological thought. *Current Sociology*, *40*(1), 17–48.

Rich, A. (2003). Notes towards a politics of location. In R. Lewis & S. Mills (Eds.), *Feminist postcolonial theory: A reader* (pp. 29–42). Routledge.

Saldaña, J., & Omasta, M. (2016). *Qualitative research: Analyzing life*. SAGE Publications.

Star, S. L. (1999). The ethnography of infrastructure. *American Behavioral Scientist*, *43*(3), 377–391.

Van Dam, J., Krose, B., & Groen, F. (2006). *Neural Network Applications in Sensor Fusion for an Autonomous Mobile Robot* (pp. 263–278). https://doi.org/10.1007/BFb0013966

van Dijk, T. A. (1993). Principles of critical discourse analysis. *Discourse & Society*, *4*(2), 249–283. https://doi.org/10.1177/0957926593004002006

Wodak, R., & Meyer, M. (Eds.). (2009). *Methods of critical discourse analysis* (2nd ed). SAGE Publications.

Yardley, L. (2008). Demonstrating validity in qualitative psychology. In J. A. Smith (Ed.), *Qualitative psychology: A practical guide to research methods* (2nd ed., pp. 235–251). SAGE Publications.

Yin, R. K. (2017). *Case study research and applications: Design and methods*. SAGE Publications.

23

Visual Research Methods in Human–Machine Communications

Hervé Saint-Louis

INTRODUCTION

Human–machine communications (HMC) scholars are at the centre of an age-old debate about truth and sense making about the communicative modalities between humans and machines. This chapter presents and reflects on three visual research evaluations demonstrating the entangled communicative practices between humans and machines.

Visual modalities are important means through which humans and machines negotiate and situate subjective communicative space by generating transient visual artefacts such as streamed video capture and permanent visual artefacts such as photographs. Researchers can employ these modalities and construct evaluations where they elicit machines and humans to create visual artefacts. While science, technology, engineering, and mathematical (STEM) disciplines tend to view visual research methods as objective representations of reality, social sciences and humanities often question the veracity and the objectivity of research products generated by such approaches (Pauwels, 2012).

Using visual research methods as an example, it is argued that communicative practices between humans and machines co-constitute research data. The traditional hierarchy and humanist perspective

of human-controlled research practices do not always represent how researchers generate knowledge when they communicate with machines. The objective of this chapter is to reflect on cases related to visual research methods where humans initiate communications with machines; where machines initiate communications with humans; and, where humans and machines communicate simultaneously with one another.

The turn to the visual in research describes a process where the researcher uses found or generated visual research data (Pauwels, 2000) and decides its relevancy. This perspective puts the researcher in control of two forms of objects. The first is the visual artefact created. The second is the means of creation of visual artefacts. Here, the subject controls the objects. Yet, a tenet of visual research contested by Rose (2014) is that the researcher chooses what is included within the frame of the image that is to be evaluated. Rose invites us to consider visuality that is the context that brought about what is visible (2014). The position of this article is that what is visible is no longer just data found or generated by human actors. Machines that act almost autonomously from human control mediate the visual data that we use, especially in domains such as HMC.

Prosser and Loxley (2008) proposed a visual research taxonomy that does not consider machines as autonomous agents that can generate visual data when they communicate with humans. It considers existing visual data found by researchers; visual data generated by researchers; and visual data generated by participants (Prosser & Loxley, 2008). This matters because Prosser and Loxley tie the development of visual research with technological developments (2008). For example, they argue that developments in photography determined visual research in early sociology and anthropology, becoming the main visual data collection method of those disciplines (Prosser & Loxley, 2008). The relationship between the subject (researchers) and the object (photography as a technology and as a practice) is fundamental to the ontology of visual research methods.

However, in this perspective, photography is but an instrument used by researchers and quickly discarded when it has helped generate visual research data. For many research projects, such as the first one presented in this article, this instrumental view of technology is acceptable and a good reflection of human communications with machines. However, this instrumental view is lacking where machines' involvement in research projects can raise ethical questions or those related to the validity and reliability of measurements.

Conceptualising visual methods in HMC under three communicative practices can help us understand the epistemological contribution of machines in research. The first practice addresses cases where humans initiate communication with machines. The example provided here is the representation of mental models held by participants after having been involved in communicative practices with machines. It introduces readers on how to elicit participants to represent their mental models in ways that researchers can evaluate elicited visual data.

The second visual research method addresses cases where machines initiate communication with humans using the example of network visualisation generated by an algorithm or an artificial intelligence. This is relevant to HMC researchers because they often analyse and evaluate such methodological practices in their research. Concerns here will focus on the ethics, confidentiality, and anonymisation of data collected from participants who may not even know that they are communicating with machines or that their data are used in a research project and recompiled in another form, such as a graph or an infographic.

The final case addresses research where human–machine communications involve using eye tracking as mode of exchange. Here, the object and the subject co-constitute the visual research data. While this may seem a philosophical concern rather than an operational one that can affect

a research project, the ongoing dialogue between humans and machines demonstrates the paradigm shift argued by HMC scholars. Understanding this scenario matters as the continuous dialogue between human and machine influences and can co-construct the results obtained in a study. For some scholars, the subjective co-dependence and contribution of the machine may create questions about the reliability and validity of the data. This section of the chapter will explore these concerns in detail using the example of eye tracking in HMC.

DIAGRAMMATIC MENTAL MODEL REPRESENTATION

Mental models are a concept grounded in cognitive psychology aiming to explain people's internal beliefs about an external phenomenon or system (Forrester, 1971). Mental models are not static. They change constantly. Eliciting participants to represent them, only capture a brief and transient image. They use tools such as pens and physical icons to represent their images that researchers then capture as photographs before the assemblage's erasure. Figure 23.1 provides an example of the common magnets encased in clear plastic pearls upon which we apply stickers representing various concepts for use by participants.

When eliciting visual data from participants, researchers are asking the former, "let's see what you can see" (Bloom, 1984). This seeing is mediated by machines subjected to humans' interpretations of what is to be represented. HMC researchers frequently rely on visual research methods to capture how humans make sense of their communications with machines and this can be represented using their mental models. The case presented here is based on an ongoing study of

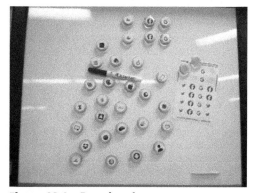

Figure 23.1   Board and magnets

Canadian participants' perceptions of the federal government's cellphone-based contact-tracing app used during the COVID-19 pandemic in Canada (Saint-Louis & Ménélas, 2021). In this study, we sought to elicit participants' mental models from their use of their interaction with the Canadian contact tracing mobile app, COVID ALERT.

Mental models are useful for HMC scholars to ensure that users' expectations about how a system works and how they communicate with it matches how the system is designed (Nielsen, 2010). There is a limited set of methodological tools that can be reliably used to elicit mental models from participants. Drawing is one of the most direct methods of elicitation; participants draw what they think and perceive without any intermediary. Other methods represent indirect approaches that rely on the researcher to gather circumstantial data and then use this to infer the model. These indirect approaches rely less on drawing and more on direct observation, e.g., Contextual Inquiry (Holtzblatt & Jones, 1993) or Rapid Ethnographies (Millen, 2000); however, these capture only the actions (responses to stimuli) as conditioned by users' mental models instead of an accurate direct representation.

Although this study reports on participants' perceptions of their communications and interactions with COVID ALERT, humans alone do the evaluation of the elicited visual data. This corresponds to the traditional approach of visual research methods whereby machines are tools subjected to the whims and control of humans. For example, part of the meaning making of the data is done by a human-led approach developed earlier, which we refer to the Diagrammatic Complexity Scale and the Written Annotation Complexity Scale from Saint-Louis and McEwen (2021). In this approach, researchers use visual encoding to analyse the diagrams produced by participants by using a visual coding scheme based on grounded analysis. For example, when running a similar coding analysis in a previous study (2018), codes and questions determining patterns were drawn from participants' diagrams. As with any coding evaluation, several investigators attempted to identify themes that were subsequently compared in second and third passes.

Mental model representations can help HMC researchers visualise people's communications with machines. This approach provides needed help for researchers struggling with "transferring" (eliciting) something as abstract as mental models that capture personal sets of beliefs users may have to a concrete representation that others can access. Some of the most common tools are based on drawing or sketching—a very direct form of elicitation, yet subject to loss of representational accuracy and operational challenges such as users' lack of skills in drawing or in envisioning sketches. Other more indirect forms of elicitation that are methodologically grounded in ethnography approaches have been used, although these may be affected by the bias of the human intermediary (the researcher) when instantiating a concrete representation of mental models. In the diagrammatic approach introduced above, the machine has limited agency once the human participant has communicated with the former. This type of research, where humans report on their communications with machines, is the standard perspective in non-post human research where the traditional subject-object hierarchy is maintained. However, in the two following cases, we will first explore scenarios where the machine is fully involved in the research process with humans.

NETWORK VISUALISATIONS

Network visualisation is a visual research method where data and information are converted into graphical modes to facilitate their understanding by viewers (Tufte, 1983). Brandes et al. (1999) argue that network visualisations are constitutive parts of communication and exploration, helping third parties understand data they would otherwise struggle to decipher. Essentially, network visualisations help researchers and the public see what they would have missed when observing raw data. From a communication theory standpoint (Shannon, 2001), raw data is noise to recipients that is rendered into a message by reformatting the signal into a higher-level output. While network visualisation can be done manually, it has benefitted from machine-based approaches that can gather large amounts of data and transform it into alternative forms of visual representations.

The communicative process used by machines to mediate data into representative forms takes place at the interface level. The interface level is where the machine breaks early components of datum into chunks that can be used by human reviewers. For example, the General Architecture for Text Engineering (Gaizauskas et al., 2001), an early work in this area, relied on a node-based modular interface to encode Natural Language Processing (NLP) data visually. Recent NLP research (Kumar et al., 2020) has integrated voice-activated virtual assistants as part of the meaning-making process where researchers can communicate (and edit), verbally or with pointing devices, with machines that produce screen-based representations.

In the NPL examples above, machines communicate data that they collect and generate through interfaces that use forms easily understood by humans. Recipients then provide feedback to the machine or to other humans about the machine-based visual representation. This communicative process can be expanded into a more complicated model when accounting for the communication between the machine collecting the initial datum and people. Some of this data can reveal far more and allow researchers and other recipients to gain a greater insight into other people's lives. These habitual unexpected consequences can raise privacy issues for the observed and the researchers who obtain this visual data.

The remainder of this section explores ethical and privacy issues related to visual network data collected by machines communicating with humans. Machines transform found data from other formats into visual form such as graphs and infographics. Ethics is but one example that researchers must contend with when performing visual research with machines. Machines can collect, manipulate, transform, and represent collected data about people, fauna, flora, the environment, and other machines, making decisions independently of scholars. Some of this data, when collected from human participants, unknowingly creates ethical concerns. For example, when an algorithm visually represents how many times people have liked a tweet on Twitter, the machine initiates communications with humans, revealing potentially private data, even though it follows initial parameters set by researchers. The privacy concern develops from the aggregation of previously disparate data on participants (Barocas & Nissenbaum, 2014).

The study below is part of an existing research project attempting to understand cancel culture in social media (Saint-Louis, 2021). Specifically, we seek to determine whether the callout practices related to cancel culture of French-speaking Quebecers (Francophones) in social media differ from those of English-speaking North Americans (Anglophones) by visualizing their usage with different platforms. Our thesis is that Francophones favour callouts mediated by closed or semi-closed platforms such as Facebook, while Anglophones favour open platforms such as Reddit and Twitter. The concept of open, semi-open/closed, or closed platforms (Cardon, 2008) offers us a metric to classify and compare the effects of callouts on Facebook, Reddit, and Twitter. Open platforms, by default, allow public communications between individuals while closed platforms limit access (Choi & Lee, 2017). The open-closed platform definition used here is not the generative one developed by Zittrain (2008).

As researchers, we could manually count and map out the selected callouts we observe. Using software to do this tedious work quickly becomes apparent for researchers. The massive amount of data to be collected directly from a platform is best automated with a machine. While humans do program the initial filters and correct errors in the machine-collected and assembled data, the latter is given more autonomy in our research practices. The visualisation representations and even corrections enacted by machines will follow a script and be generated to presets that often astound researchers. There is potential for a machine to exaggerate innocuous details that humans may not have paid much attention to or ignore aspects of the found data in hindsight to which researchers would have preferred to pay more attention. Finally, there is also a strong incentive from researchers, especially less experienced ones, to uncritically accept the representation of reality drawn by an algorithm.

The network visualisation is generated from data obtained through social network analysis of North American Facebook, Reddit, Twitter users engaged in callout practices. We use social network analysis to explore the level of organisation of individuals that contribute to callouts on social media. We check for cliques and echo chambers. The affiliative measurement between users is the direct link where one follows the other, or links based on person-to-person communications. In social network analysis, actors can have a multitude of links between them, which we call multiplexity (Degenne & Forsé, 2004). The discovery of a multiplexity of relationships on Facebook, Reddit, and Twitter, among individuals involved in callouts could determine whether a level of organisation of whistle-blower posts is underway.

We check user networks of social media platforms such as Facebook, Reddit, and Twitter where many of the complaints or denunciations of individuals can be found. We must differentiate the nature of the complaints and understand their impact depending on the state of opening or closing of the platform used.

The sites for network analysis in the English-speaking North American case are Reddit and Twitter. The site for the French-speaking is the Facebook group "Dis son nom" (say his name). The scope of the data will focus on English- and French-language posts (comments and tweets) from January 1, 2019, to the present. This provides us with sufficient scope to analyse cancel culture. We use NodeXL to capture social media data, which is then analysed with Ora Pro from which we will also generate the network graphs of social media users.

Ethics, confidentiality, and anonymisation

The introduction of the machine as an independent actor in visual research methods can require researchers to question tried practices from institutional review boards (IRB) that address issues related to informed consent of participants, anonymity, and confidentiality of existing or generated data. Researchers and IRBs must address these important questions.

An important concern is the aggregation of publicly available data (Nissenbaum, 1997) in our visualisations that can possibly lead to the identification of social media users. If our software aggregates location data, basic usernames, and map connections in one place, data that was once harmless can suddenly provide a clear picture of who denounces whom on social media platforms, rendering possible defamation lawsuits and other retaliation measures easier. Up until recently, the identity of the two female founders of the "Dis son nom" were anonymous. Many of the alleged victims that have denounced aggressions at the Facebook group did so anonymously.

When network graphs are generated by software like NodeXL and Ora, previously unseen relationships between data points can easily be visualised and lessen the personal data protection of at-risk groups, such as rape victims. The Quebec Superior Court has already rendered a verdict removing all protection for the administrators of the Facebook group because of the public nature of the page (Girard-Bossé, 2021). Open and closed platforms have this peculiarity that even public data can compromise users who often have not agreed to have their data and identity used in research.

Our interest in this topic is not to publicise the identity of alleged victims of aggressions. Our interest is to understand cancel culture. Thus, workarounds include the omission of the names of all Facebook users, followed by an anonymisation process, before using the data to create graphs. Other sensitive data such as the exact location (town, city) of the users will also be omitted. This is a case of human researchers cleaning and processing the data collected by machines before using it as research data. The process of cleaning and transformation of the data into an anonymised format is again done by a machine, adding one more machine manipulation to the sensitive data.

EYE TRACKING

This section provides an example of visual research methods to evaluate how machines and humans' communicative practices are woven into entangled visual data through eye-tracking methods. It answers the question raised previously on how to assess the reliability and validity of visual

research data co-constituted by humans and machines. HMC scholars can use eye tracking in both experimental and observational research where they need to assess how participants communicate with machines.

Eye tracking (or gaze monitoring) is a methodological approach where researchers observe and measure eye movements during a given task (Blanc, 2013). These movements allow us to determine the level of attention related to where (Helmholtz, 1867), what (James, 1890), and how (Gibson, 1941) people focus their sight (Duchowski, 2017).

By considering questions such as where, what, and how of visual attention when performing eye tracking, we can explore questions related to the reliability and validity of data collected through eye trackers. The eye tracker is dependent on the research participant when capturing data, but it is not a passive assistant. The participant's head turns, and gazes are captured by a machine. If the capture involves another technology with which the participant communicates, there is a multilevel co-construction of meaning involved. When the participant communicates with say, a screen, this is captured live by the eye tracker beginning the process of sense making of the collected data. The researcher organising the eye tracking then must reinterpret the data communicated by the eye tracker. In some systems, the eye-tracking apparatuses can indicate to participants where their gaze is focused. This can affect what, where and how a person focuses her visual attention.

In eye tracking, several processes and elements that communicate with humans are at play. First, there is the hardware worn by participants to monitor their gaze through cameras. Eye trackers can be worn like glasses or be embedded in other systems, like a laptop computer's camera. Then, there are the various software algorithms that use the captured data to translate it into a format that can be understood. Part of this data translation is also the representation of the user's gaze upon the world. Assuming that the human pupils can tell what the participant's attention is focused on, the tracking hardware and software create a narrative about what is being looked at and is of interest to the observed person. The machines observe human actions and attempt to make sense of what the participant's attention is focused on by relaying data that can then be read and inform human evaluators.

Questions of reliability and validity of visual research data arise when designing a study evaluating whether a motorist's visual attention is altered while communicating with a virtual assistant (VA). The evaluation consists of an eye-tracking experiment comparing two groups of participants communicating with VAs while performing driving-like functions. The test group is composed of motorists driving in a university parking lot while the control group is tested with a driving simulator in a laboratory.

The main evaluation one can use, for HMC and related research, are fixation and saccade metrics. Fixation measures eye movements when they barely move, while saccades measure the rapid eye movements between fixations (Poole & Ball, 2006). Reliability and validity can affect research measures such as fixation and saccade metrics. Reliability is a measure controlling that eye-tracking instruments consistently measure the same phenomena. For example, reliability measures could be based on an algorithm that determines the duration of a fixation while a participant is reading (Holmqvist & Andersson, 2017). The same measure is unreliable if the fixation duration algorithm cannot measure all participants in the same study or cannot be replicated in subsequent research. Validity is a measure determining that the measure used to evaluate and eye movement is the right metric used. For example, a metric used to determine what causes saccade. The same measure is invalid if it is used to measure the duration of a fixation.

Reliability measures

When using the Pupil Core eye tracker from Pupil Labs, we found that it was difficult to calibrate the frame for each person because of facial shape. The more we must make personalised adjustments for each participant to fit the eye tracker, the less reliable the metric becomes. We found that the pupil detection process is difficult when the participant wears glasses. Pupil detection is a necessary calibration step. We thought that removing glasses could improve the pupils' detection by the software and the cameras. However, it impairs participants' vision, making it difficult to participate in our study. We thought of asking them to wear contact lenses, but these would affect the responses of participants who do not usually drive without their glasses. The calibration of the eye tracker is a concern in terms of reliability when we perform co-constituted visual research. We rely on both the machine, our participants, and members of our research team when generating visual research data.

Validity measures

A validity measure that we are working on to fine-tune in our study is the use of interruptions

by virtual assistants as they are driving. For example, we predict that some motorists will have more experience communicating with VAs while driving than others. Familiarity with either Siri or Google Assistant (GA) by some participants could also confound results. This is a potential internal validity concern where we could be measuring participants' familiarity with a specific VA instead of the visual attention while driving or in front of a simulator. To resolve this situation, all participants take part in a pretest that requires them to enquire both Siri and GA about the current time. We believe that this step will reduce the unfamiliarity with the VA by slightly increasing the learning effect for all participants at an acceptable qualitative baseline. Because the experiment uses both motorists and in laboratory participants using a driving simulator, we believe we will be able to measure the external validity of the evaluation to some extent by observing if our research can yield similar results or not with our test and our control groups. Validity remains a concern for this co-constituted study beyond the initial experiment, as only after analysing our results will we be able to determine how the eye tracker technology has influenced our visual research data collection.

LIMITATIONS

On a meta-methodological level, visual research methods are constrained because they work best in concurrence with other approaches and are supplementary in a mixed methods approach. The insight they can reveal does not always constitute the whole range possible for researchers. In fact, because they usually reveal what is overlooked, they cannot be relied upon to generate breadth-defining (or big picture) knowledge. This can be a major internal validity concern. Similarly, the context-sensitive nature of visual research methods can limit their external validity. Another limitation is that visual research methods often require technical expertise and access to complex tools and software to perform basic research. Without proper expertise, these approaches can easily lead inexperience astray and reveal erroneous visual data.

CONCLUSION

The pursuit of truth and sense-making are entangled and co-constituted rather than based on subjects' domination of objects. We can observe this phenomenon by understanding how humans make sense of their communications with machines using representations of their mental models; by understanding ethical dilemmas involved when machines represent their communications with humans through network visualisations and understanding issues of measurement validity and reliability with co-constituted visual research data generated by humans and machines. Future visual research methods work in HMC should ponder the affective response of humans to machines generated by machines. For example, it could measure how humans respond to generative adversarial network data that asks them to determine if a human face is a representation of a real person or generated by a machine, following the Turing test (2004).

REFERENCES

Barocas, S., & Nissenbaum, H. (2014). Big data's end run around procedural privacy protections: Recognizing the inherent limitations of consent and anonymity. *Communications of the ACM, 57*(11), 31–33.

Blanc, S. (2013, Juillet). Les techniques d'oculométrie (ou Eye-tracking). *Revue Francophone d'Orthoptie, 6*(3), 133–135.

Bloom, G. A. (Writer), & Gibbs, J. (Director). (1984). *Transformers: More than meets the eye: Part 1* [Film].

Brandes, U., Kenis, P., Raab, J., Schneider, V., & Wagner, D. (1999). Explorations into the visualization of policy networks. *Journal of Theoretical Politics,* 75–106.

Cardon, D. (2008). Le design de la visibilité. Un essai de cartographie du web 2.0. *Réseaux, 26*(152), 93–137. doi:https://doi.org/10.3166/reseaux.152.93-137

Choi, B., & Lee, I. (2017). Trust in open versus closed social media: The relative influence of user- and marketer-generated content in social network services on customer trust. *Telematics and Informatics, 34*(5), 550–559. doi:https://doi.org/10.1016/j.tele.2016.11.005

Degenne, A., & Forsé, M. (2004). *Les réseaux sociaux* (2e édition ed.). Paris, France: Armand Colin.

Duchowski, A. T. (2017). *Eye tracking methodology* (ed. Third Edition). London: Springer.

Forrester, J. W. (1971). Counterintuitive behavior of social systems. *Technological Forecasting and Social Change, 3,* 1–22.

Gaizauskas, R., Rodgers, P., & Humphreys, K. (2001). Visual tools for natural language processing. *Journal of Visual Languages & Computing, 12*(4), 375–412. doi:https://doi.org/10.1006/jvlc.2000.0203

Gibson, J. J. (1941, November). A critical review of the concept of set in contemporary experimental psychology. *Psychological Bulletin, 38*(9), 781–817. doi:https://doi.org/10.1037/h0055307

Girard-Bossé, A. (2021, 03 01). *Page de dénonciations « Dis son nom » Pas d'anonymat pour les créatrices, tranche la Cour supérieure.* Consulté le 04 05, 2021, sur La Presse: www.lapresse.ca/actualites/justice-et-faits-divers/2021-03-01/page-de-denonciations-dis-son-nom/pas-d-anonymat-pour-les-creatrices-tranche-la-cour-superieure.php

Helmholtz, H. v. (1867). *Handbuch der physiologischen Optik.* Leopold Voss.

Holmqvist, K., & Andersson, R. (2017). *Eye tracking: A comprehensive guide to methods, paradigms, and measures.* CreateSpace.

Holtzblatt, K., & Jones, S. (1993). Contextual inquiry: A participatory technique for system design. In *Participatory design: Principles and practices* (pp. 177–210). L. Erlbaum Associates.

James, W. (1890). *The principles of psychology.* Holt.

Kumar, A., Aurisano, J., Di Eugenio, B., & Johnson, A. (2020). Intelligent assistant for exploring data visualizations. *The Thirty-Third International Flairs Conference.* North Miami Beach.

Millen, D. R. (2000). Rapid ethnography: Time deepening strategies for HCI field research. *Proceedings of the 3rd conference on Designing Interactive Systems: Processes, Practices, Methods, and Techniques* (pp. 280–286). ACM.

Nielsen, J. (2010, October 18). *Mental Models.* Consulté le June 21, 2017, sur www.nngroup.com/articles/mental-models/

Nissenbaum, H. (1997). Toward an approach to privacy in public: Challenges of information technology. *Ethics & Behavior, 7*(3), 207–219.

Pauwels, L. (2000). Taking the visual turn in research and scholarly communication key issues in developing a more visually literate (social) science. *Visual Sociology, 15*(1), 7–14. doi:https://doi.org/10.1080/14725860008583812.

Pauwels, L. (2012). Contemplating the state of visual research: An assessment of obstacles and opportunities. In S. Pink (Ed.), *Advances in visual methodology* (pp. 248–264). SAGE. doi:http://dx.doi.org/10.4135/9781446250921.n14

Poole, A., & Ball, L. J. (2006). Eye tracking in HCI and usability research. In *Encyclopedia of human computer interaction* (pp. 211–219). IGI Global. doi:http://doi:10.4018/978-1-59140-562-7.ch034

Prosser, J., & Loxley, A. (2008). *Introducing visual methods.* National Centre for Research Methods.

Rose, G. (2014). On the relation between 'visual research methods' and contemporary visual culture. *The Sociological Review, 62*(1), 24–46. doi:https://doi.org/10.1111/1467-954X.12109

Saint-Louis, H. (2018, June). *User perceptions of security risks in multiple authentications.* University of Toronto Libraries.

Saint-Louis, H. (2021, July 5). Understanding cancel culture: Normative and unequal sanctioning. *First Monday, 26*(7). doi:http://dx.doi.org/10.5210/fm.v26i7.10891

Saint-Louis, H., & McEwen, R. N. (2021). Diagrammatic mental representation: A methodological bridge. *Visual Studies*. doi:10.1080/1472586X.2021.1878054

Saint-Louis, H., & Ménélas, B.-A.-J. (2021). User perceptions of security and privacy risks with contact tracing apps. *3rd International conference on HCI for Cybersecurity, Privacy, and Trust*. Springer.

Shannon, C. E. (2001). A mathematical theory of communication. *Mobile Computing and Communications Review, 5*(1), 3–55.

Tufte, E. R. (1983). *The visual display of quantitative information*. Graphics Press.

Turing, A. (2004). Computing machinery and intelligence (1950). In A. Turing, & B. J. Copeland (Ed.), *The essential Turing: Seminal writings in computing, logic, philosophy, artificial intelligence, and artificial life plus the secrets of Enigma* (pp. 441–464). Oxford University Press.

Zittrain, J. (2008). *The future of the internet and how to stop it*. Yale University Press.

24

Observing Communication with Machines

Patric R. Spence, David Westerman, and Zhenyang Luo

MACHINES AND LEARNING ABOUT OURSELVES

One of the most important reasons to study machines is to learn more about what it means to be human. Humans are unique in that we create machines to fill roles and meet goals in life. Those roles can be anything from accomplishing a physical task to providing emotional support, and thus, we learn even more about what roles are most important to people and how we accomplish those goals. The use and study of machines and specifically how we communicate with machines is one such way to learn more about human communication, and creates as many questions as answers as the study of Human–Machine Communication (HMC) is in its infancy (see Fortunati & Edwards, 2020; Guzman, 2018, 2020; Richards, Spence & Edwards, 2022; Spence, 2019). One big question revolves around the idea that communication is best when it involves one human communicating to another human (Spence, 2019). However, to answer these questions and other questions or to challenge such assumptions, researchers must have confidence in their findings. This chapter argues that unobtrusive measures of data collection, such as observation, should be considered a valuable part of the study of Human–Machine Communication,

in part, due to the ability to minimize specific threats to validity that can negatively impact the confidence we have in our claims. Therefore, this chapter first outlines unobtrusive and nonreactive measures to study HMC. Next, the chapter outlines previous studies that may be ripe for replication to teach us more about HMC, specifically through replacing a human with a machine in the experimental condition. Finally, suggestions are offered for future research studies that can take advantage of unobtrusive and nonreactive methods.

OBSERVATION, HUMANS DO IT ALL THE TIME

Experiments, surveys, and other interactions are commonly used for the study of Human–Machine Communication. These methods and their subsequent findings inform us about much of human communication and have also been useful for HMC. However, many of these methods may suffer from a reactive measurement effect (Webb et al., 1966). That is, the measurement process used in a specific type of social scientific research may itself affect the outcome. The reactive measurement effect may threaten both external and internal validity, and thus, limit the confidence we can have in our claims about how human–machine communication works and with what effects. There are several mechanisms researchers can use to correct for such threats (see Sawilowsky, 2007) but one way is to disassociate the study with the instrumentation, another is to create a study where the participant is unaware that observation and subsequent measurement is taking place.

The mere presence of an observer or the perception that a researcher is "looking for something" can have an impact on the veracity of our findings. As noted by Webb et al. (2000), a risk that is often not given enough consideration is the error produced by the participant or subject. Although the participant may have the best of intentions and work to be cooperative, the participant's knowledge that a manipulation is present may confound or impact the scope of the data and subsequent interpretation. For example, the classic "Hawthorne" studies suggested that employees were more productive when they knew they were being observed. This has been referenced as the guinea pig effect or the reactive effect of measurement, or bias (Campbell, 1957; Campbell & Stanley, 1963).

Because studies in the social sciences often involve a demand in which participants have awareness of the study's true purpose or hypotheses, or at least a stong guess (Nichols & Maner, 2008), Another problem is social desirability, specifically when the research participant responds to self-report items to promote an image which makes the respondent look good rather than responding with accuracy. All of these potential limitations to the veracity of data can be labeled as bias or more specifically response bias, and they are not limited to survey questionnaires or public opinion polls, but also in experiments and archival records. In addition to bias, they can also be called reactive measures because the score obtained from the participant may be the result of something other than the experimental condition. Therefore, the more we as researchers can create measures which do not require the cooperation of the participant or to which the participants are unknown to the research hypothesis, or to the fact that data is being collected, the more chance we have to reduce error. Results from such methods would complement experimental findings, proving more complete answers and allow for new questions. Therefore, including more observational methods into our literature may be advantageous to human–machine communication research, and researchers should ask in generating a study, if it is possible to observe the variable of interest without any involvement or interaction with the experiment.

Broadly this will encompass both direct and indirect observational methods. Direct observation is more akin to traditional laboratory experiments. For this chapter, we will not go into a detailed explanation of differences between practices such as direct or indirect observation (see Hintze & Matthews, 2004; Webb et al., 2000) but rather focus the scope on the advantages of observing the interaction between humans and machines and attempting to remove the reactivity or bias that accompanies more obtrusive measures of data collection. When our observations of communication between humans and machine are unobtrusive to the participant, the researcher watches or listens to the participants without their knowledge. Because the participant is not aware of being observed, the goal is to ensure that the measurement or experimental stimulus does not influence their behavior. Unobtrusive observations may involve the researcher being anonymous or unidentified, or it may also involve the use of hardware and/or software in the machine itself that is used in place of human observers. These also may create ethical considerations that require the researcher to consult Institutional Review Boards to obtain approval for the procedures. Although such methods may seem unsettling, scientific safeguards can do a lot to protect the participant. Such methods are already being used without participants knowing. For example, personal assistants such as Amazon Alexa, Microsoft Cortana and Siri from Apple already use observations to learn and better respond to their human "boss." These are all done through user agreements and terms of use where such institutional safeguards are not in place.

The advantages of such methods are many, not just the reduction of bias as explained earlier, but the use of less obtrusive measures can help us have more confidence than results obtained through more reactive measures, meaning we can be more confident that the experimental condition did not cause the observed effect (Kazdin, 1979).

WHAT ABOUT THE KNOWLEDGE THAT THE ROBOT IS THE OBSERVER?

Although removing the presence of the researcher from the experiment is one attempt to remove bias, the presence of a robot, and interacting with a robot, may cause bias because the participant may be aware they are being recorded (even though they are unaware that scientific observation is taking place). Machines or robots have the ability to record sound and video in much different ways that a human. It is possible some humans may be worried that a conversational partner has a smartphone to record an interaction or some other type of device, although however, most humans do not go into conversations with this apprehension, but is the same true when people interact with a robot? An advantage from software recording inherent in a machine is the permanence of a complete record. It is not subject to selective decay and can provide the stuff of reliability checks.

PREVIOUS STUDIES AS STARTING POINT

As noted by Blake et al. (1956), because "the social action investigated occurs under natural conditions and since participants are unaware that their behavior is being evaluated in a systematic way, there can be no question as to the validity of the conclusions reached for use in social engineering" (p. 385). Although the second part of the statement is an overreaching claim, the first part, concerning the investigation of a social action under natural condition, highlights the strength of observation methods. A classic paradigm that would be useful to follow for increasing the number of studies that rely on observational methods is the Computers are Social Actors (CASA) paradigm. Pioneered by Nass et al., (1994), this paradigm was founded on the idea that replacing a human with a computer in a social science study and replicating the study as such to see if the finding for the human–human study holds when it is retested under human–computer conditions suggested that computers were considered social actors by humans if the results held.

A great deal of evidence to back this up was presented in the classic *The Media Equation* (Reeves & Nass, 1996), and a mindlessness explanation for the phenomenon presented in Nass and Moon (2000), suggesting that people mindlessly rely on heuristics that drive their own social behavior when presented with a computer technology that somehow triggers the heuristic. More recently, Xu and Lombard (2016) argued that this paradigm could be expanded past computers and to other forms of media technologies as well, and a variety of studies have applied CASA to the study of human–machine communication (e.g., Edwards et al., 2016; Gambino et al., 2020; Kim et al., 2013; Lombard & Xu, 2021; Park et al., 2011; Xu, 2019). A similar argument is made under the postulations forwarded under the human–human interaction script (Edwards et al., 2019; Rainear et al., 2022; Spence et al., 2014; Spence et al., 2019, 2021; Westerman

et al., 2020). The human–human interaction script argues that people anticipate their interaction partner will be a human, and therefore when they are instead confronted with a machine as an interaction partner, they initially expect this interaction will be characterized by a greater sense of uncertainty and lower anticipations of social presence and liking; however, people's actual initial interactions with and subsequent perceptions of a machine versus human beings after interaction are not congruent with those perceptions.

One way this paradigm could be useful for observational research in HMC is by providing ideas for studies to replicate. One need simply find an observational study examining human–human interaction, replace one human with a robot, and then observe to see if findings hold across the new context. Gambino et al. (2020) have recently offered some extension to CASA, including the possibility that people form human-technology interaction scripts which creates further possibilities for such studies.

One context that would be especially open for an increase in observational methods is persuasion and compliance-gaining. Lee and Liang (2018) offer that robots are social actors, and have applied this to studies of robot persuasion, examining methods such as pre-giving (Lee & Liang, 2016), wherein a persuader gives the target something before making a request, and foot-in-the-door method (Lee & Liang, 2019), where a persuader makes a smaller request first to gain likely initial compliance, before later making a larger request. They also suggest other strategies that would be important to examine, such as the door-in-the-face method, where a potential persuader first asks for a greater request, expecting it to be denied, before making a smaller request (Cialdini et al., 1975). These could all be tested using observational methods as well, by sending a robot "into the wild" to attempt to gain compliance from others using these and other techniques, and observing if people comply, as they do with other people.

As another example, one interesting possibility for study that has used observational methods in the past is known as the dump-and-chase method (Boster et al., 2009). Named after a hockey strategy, whereby a team shoots the puck into the opponents' zone (dump) and then skates in and tries to regain possession of it (chase), the method is less about deft skill and more about brute, tenacious force (both in hockey and in compliance-gaining). In this study (experiment 1), Boster et al. had a confederate make a request to watch the bicycle of someone walking into a building using either a dump-and-chase attempt, a door-in-the- face attempt, or a placebic information attempt, where the confederate used a placebic reason in order to provide a reason at all and attempt to enact a mindless response. Experimenters observed the effectiveness of the request in each condition and found dump-and-chase to be effective relative to the other two methods. A follow-up experiment added a foot-in-the-door condition, and again observed that DAC was relatively effective. Thus, given the logic of the CASA paradigm, these studies could be replicated by replacing the human that attempts to gain compliance with a robot, having the robot attempt to gain compliance through these various methods (others could be added as well) and observing what happens.

In the Blake et al. (1956) article referenced earlier, the authors outline a study concerning appeals to sign a petition. As students walked by the student union, they were solicited to sign a petition to place lights at a campus fountain. Three different approaches were used that included the strength of a request and the presence or absence of a pencil to sign the petition. There were also three condition where the participants knew the reactions of others to the request. Therefore, what was examined was the strength of the plea and knowledge of the actions of others. This study inspired a replication by Spence et al. (2018) that used a robot in a video asking viewers to sign a petition to consider the rights of robots within the United Nations. However, the Blake et al. (1956) study is ripe for further replication and extension through replacing the human soliciting potential petition signers with that of a robot. It is possible that an exact replication would allow a study to compare results, but through using observational methods many other variables could be measured, including time of interaction with the robot making the request, complexity of the language used and success of the appeal.

In a study by Robert Sommer (1959), observations were made on conversations taking place between individuals based on where they sat at a lunch table. There were eight chairs at a table observed in a hospital cafeteria. Conversation was observed between chairs next to one another and chairs at a distance (chair adjacent or at least one chair apart). In 67 interactions there were only 18 conversational interactions that occurred between people in distant chairs and adjacent corner to corner interactions were most prevalent. This research is highly similar to several classic studies that have examined conversation flow, leadership emergence and display of personality factors (Howells & Becker, 1962; Pellegrini, 1971). Such studies are excellent candidates for replication and extension. Through replacing the human at a table with a robot, observations could be recorded about (1) if an interaction is started by a human or robot, and if so, (2) the topic and length of

such discussion. Moreover, other factors could be added to the study, such as putting two or more robots at a table, to observe potential differences based on the number of robots in a group.

One of the best known studies of group conformity was published in 1956 by Solomon Asch. In the Asch studies participants were placed in groups of seven to nine individuals and were informed they were to take part in an examination of visual discrimination. The task involved making a comparison of a standard line with three other lines (each identified by a letter). One of the lines was identical in length to the standard line provided. In the manipulation there were times when the research confederate would provide the wrong answer. Although the majority of the participants provided the correct answer (identified the correct line of equal length) a sizable majority would agree with the confederate and provide the incorrect answer. This study has been replicated with different variables over the year but the presence of a robot and observation of the participants would provide new information on authority and perceptions. Would people believe the robot to be more or less likely to make a mistake? Would people be more or less direct in their language when contradicting a robot? What would the length of debate or discussion be in disagreeing with a robot? Or the dynamics could be changed even more by placing two robots in the group and the robots could agree or disagree with each other. Observations in this situation may show us much more about human communication than a post-test survey instrument.

NEW INVESTIGATIONS FOR OBSERVATION

One area of HMC research that would benefit from observational methods would be the viewing of other content with social robots. Co-viewing – sharing the viewing experience with other social entities – has received research attention from media scholars (e.g., Cohen & Lancaster, 2014; Dorr et al., 1989; Doughty et al., 2011; Haridakis & Hanson, 2009; Haefner & Wartella, 1987; McDonald, 1986; Parkes et al., 2013; Pittman & Tefertiller, 2015; Strouse et al., 2013; Wilson & Weiss, 1993). This line of research indicates that co-viewing has significant effects on the viewing experience as well as other outcomes too. For example, co-viewing was found to effect family interactions, such as parents' visual orientation to their children and their spouse, talking with each other, parents' touching child or spouse, etc.

(Brody et al., 1980). In addition, co-viewing was found to influence the persuasion effects of television advertisements (Helme et al., 2011) and enjoyment of the co-viewed content (Cohen et al., 2016; Tal-or, 2016). Some research has started to examine how co-viewing with robots might influence individuals' video watching experience. For example, Hoffman et al. (2016) had participants watch an entertainment video clip with a robot and found that the presence of the robot made the watching experience more enjoyable.

According to Guzman (2018), the meaning-making process from human–robot interaction should be a key research topic because it really shows why communicating with robots can have effects on individuals and the society just as how communicating between individuals does. Co-viewing is one such area to study this meaning making. Information from television does not always influence viewers directly. Interpersonal discussion that happens during the co-viewing process can impact the effects of mediated content, and it is very likely that the opinions from the co-viewer can influence individuals' opinions more than the information from TV content. How this might play out in an HMC setting is unknown, and how communication with a robot during a co-viewing episode might influence the persuasion process and/or outcomes of TV information is something that could be studied through observational methods.

For instance, a study could have participants watch TV, for example, a political speech, with a social robot. The robot would express opinions which either agree with the politician or disagree with the politician. A researcher could observe the participant during this co-viewing experience, to see how they respond to the robot, and whether it differs based on the agreement or disagreement of the robot. Participants' nonverbal and interaction styles might be especially interesting to observe. For example, do participants' proxemics to the robot differ based on agreement level of the robot? Kinesics would also be an important nonverbal code to examine. These nonverbal codes that would be observed could also be connected to observed communication styles, such as approach/avoidance as well.

Another future line of research can examine more about the process of human – machine communication. As Westerman et al. (2020) suggests, social information processing theory (Walther, 1992) might be an especially relevant theory to apply to human–machine communication, especially for interactions with chatbots. Research could observe such interactions, as has been done for the comparison of FtF and CMC interactions (Tidwell & Walther, 2002), to compare things such as the

breadth and depth of questions and disclosures in such interactions, among other possibilities.

CONCLUSION

This chapter offers arguments and ideas for nonreactive and unobtrusive methods for the study of HMC. Importantly, these suggestions are part of a larger conversation to help us explore with more precision and accuracy the communication with and between human and machines.

As machine communicators in various forms become more common in society, observing these interactions will be part of the everyday human experience as people watching is already. Communication scientists are in a unique situation to study and help improve on this aspect of the human condition.

REFERENCES

Asch, S. E. (1956). Studies of independence and conformity: I. A minority of one against a unanimous majority. *Psychological Monographs: General and Applied, 70*(9), 1–70. https://doi.org/10.1037/h0093718

Blake, R. R., Mouton, J. S., & Hain, J. D. (1956). Social forces in petition signing. *The Southwestern Social Science Quarterly*, 385–390. www.jstor.org/stable/42866026

Boster, F. J., Shaw, A. S., Hughes, M., Kotowski, M. R., Strom, R. E., & Deatrick, L. M. (2009). Dump-and-chase: The effectiveness of persistence as a sequential request compliance-gaining strategy. *Communication Studies, 60*(3), 219–234. https://doi.org/10.1080/10510970902955976

Brody, G. H., Stoneman, Z., & Sanders, A. K. (1980). Effects of television viewing on family interactions: An observational study. *Family Relations, 29*, 216–220. https://doi.org/10.2307/584075

Campbell, D. T. (1957). Factors relevant to the validity of experiments in social settings. *Psychological Bulletin, 54*(4), 297–312. https://doi.org/10.1037/h0040950

Campbell, D. T., & Stanley J. C. (1963). *Experimental and quasi-experimental designs for research*. Rand McNally & Company.

Cialdini, R. B., Vincent, J. E., Lewis, S. K., Catalan, J., Wheeler, D., & Darby, B. L. (1975). Reciprocal concessions procedure for inducing compliance: The door-in-the-face technique. *Journal of Personality and Social Psychology, 31*(2), 206–215. https://doi.org/10.1037/h0076284

Cohen, E. L., & Lancaster, A. L. (2014). Individual differences in in-person and social media television coviewing: The role of emotional contagion, need to belong, and coviewing orientation. *Cyberpsychology, Behavior, and Social Networking, 17*(8), 512–518. https://doi.org/10.1089/cyber.2013.0484

Cohen, E. L., Bowman, N. D., & Lancaster, A. L. (2016). R U with Some1? Using text message experience sampling to examine television coviewing as a moderator of emotional contagion effects on enjoyment. *Mass Communication & Society, 19*, 149–172. https://doi.org/10.1080/15205436.2015.1071400

Dorr, A., Kovaric, P., & Doubleday, C. (1989). Parent-child coviewing of television. *Journal of Broadcasting & Electronic Media, 33*(1), 35–51. https://doi.org/10.1080/08838158909364060

Doughty, M., Rowland, D., & Lawson, S. (2011, June). Co-viewing live TV with digital backchannel streams. In *Proceedings of the 9th European Conference on Interactive TV and Video* (pp. 141–144). ACM. https://doi.org/10.1145/2000119.2000147

Edwards, A., Edwards, C., Westerman, D., & Spence, P. R. (2019). Initial expectations, interactions and beyond with social robots. *Computers in Human Behavior, 90*, 308–314. https://doi.org/10.1016/j.chb.2018.08.042

Edwards, C., Edwards, A., Spence, P. R., & Westerman, D. (2016). Initial interaction expectations with robots: Testing the human-to-human interaction script. *Communication Studies, 67*(2), 227–238. https://doi.org/10.1080/10510974.2015.1121899

Fortunati, L., & Edwards, A. (2020). Opening space for theoretical, methodological, and empirical issues in Human-Machine Communication. *Human-Machine Communication, 1*, 7–18. https://doi.org/10.30658/hmc.1.1

Gambino, A., Fox, J., & Ratan, R. A. (2020). Building a stronger CASA: Extending the computers are social actors paradigm. *Human-Machine Communication, 1*, 71–86. https://doi.org/10.30658/hmc.1.5

Guzman, A. L. (2018). Introduction: "What is human-machine communication anyway?". In A. L. Guzman (Ed.), *Human-machine communication: Rethinking communication, technology, and ourselves* (pp. 1–26). Peter Lang.

Guzman, A. L. (2020). Ontological boundaries between humans and computers and the implications for Human-Machine Communication. *Human-Machine Communication, 1*, 37–54. https://doi.org/10.30658/hmc.1.3

Haefner, M. J., & Wartella, E. A. (1987). Effects of sibling coviewing on children's interpretations of television programs. *Journal of Broadcasting & Electronic Media, 31*(2), 153–168. https://doi.org/10.1080/08838158709386654

Haridakis, P., & Hanson, G. (2009). Social interaction and co-viewing with YouTube: Blending mass communication reception and social connection. *Journal of Broadcasting & Electronic Media, 53*(2), 317–335. https://doi.org/10.1080/08838150902908270

Helme, D. W., Noar, S. M., Allard, S., Zimmerman, R. S., Palmgreen, P., & McClanahan, K. J. (2011). In-depth investigation of interpersonal discussions in response to a safer sex mass media campaign. *Health Communication, 26*(4), 366–378. https://doi.org/10.1080/10410236.2010.551582

Hintze, J. M., & Matthews, W. J. (2004). The generalizability of systematic direct observations across time and setting: A preliminary investigation of the psychometrics of behavioral assessment. *School Psychology Review, 33*, 258–270. https://doi.org/10.1080/02796015.2004.12086247

Hoffman, G., Bauman, S., & Vanunu, K. (2016). Robotic experience companionship in music listening and video watching. *Personal and Ubiquitous Computing, 20*, 51–63. doi.org/10.1007/s00779-015-0897-1

Howells, L. T., & Becker, S. W. (1962). Seating arrangement and leadership emergence. *The Journal of Abnormal and Social Psychology, 64*(2), 148–150. https://doi.org/10.1037/h0040421

Kazdin, A. E. (1979). Unobtrusive measures in behavioral assessment. *Journal of Applied Behavior Analysis, 12*, 713–724. https://doi.org/10.1901/jaba.1979.12-713

Kim, K. J., Park, E., & Sundar, S. S. (2013). Caregiving role in human-robot interaction: A study of the mediating effects of perceived benefit and social presence. *Computers in Human Behavior, 29*(4), 1799–1806. https://doi.org/10.1016/j.chb.2013.02.009

Lee, S. A., & Liang, Y. (2016). The role of reciprocity in verbally persuasive robots. *Cyberpsychology, Behavior, and Social Networking, 19*(8), 524–527. https://doi.org/10.1089/cyber.2016.0124

Lee, S. A., & Liang, Y. (2018). Theorizing verbally persuasive robots. In A. L. Guzman (Ed.), *Human-machine communication: Rethinking communication, technology, and ourselves* (pp. 119–143). Peter Lang.

Lee, S. A., & Liang, Y. (2019). Robotic foot-in-the-door: Using sequential-request persuasive strategies in human-robot interaction. *Computers in Human Behavior, 90*, 351–356. https://doi.org/10.1016/j.chb.2018.08.026

Lombard, M., & Kun, X. (2021). Social responses to media technologies in the 21st century: The media are social actors paradigm. *Human-Machine Communication, 2*, 29–55. https://doi.org.10.30658/hmc.2.2

McDonald, D. G. (1986). Generational aspects of television coviewing. *Journal of Broadcasting &*

Electronic Media, *30*(1), 75–85. https://doi.org/10.1080/08838158609386609

Nass, C., & Moon, Y. (2000). Machines and mindlessness: Social responses to computers. *Journal of Social Issues*, *56*(1), 81–103. https://doi.org/10.1111/0022-4537.00153

Nass, C., Steuer, J., & Tauber, E. R. (1994, April). Computers are social actors. In *Proceedings of the SIGCHI Conference on Human Factors in Computing Systems* (pp. 72–78). https://doi.org/10.1145/191666.191703

Nichols, A. E., & Maner, J. K. (2008) The good-subject effect: Investigating participant demand characteristics. *The Journal of General Psychology*, *135*, 151–165. https://doi.org/10.3200/GENP.135.2.151-166

Park, E., Kim, K. J., & del Pobil, A. P. (2011). The effects of a robot instructor's positive vs. negative feedbacks on attraction and acceptance towards the robot in classroom. In B. Mutlu, C. Bartneck, J. Ham, V. Evers, & T. Kanda (Eds.), *Social robotics. ICSR Lecture Notes in Computer Science* (pp. 135–141). Springer.

Parkes, A., Wight, D., Hunt, K., Henderson, M., & Sargent, J. (2013). Are sexual media exposure, parental restrictions on media use and co-viewing TV and DVDs with parents and friends associated with teenagers' early sexual behaviour? *Journal of Adolescence*, *36*(6), 1121–1133. https://doi.org/10.1016/j.adolescence.2013.08.019

Pellegrini, R. J. (1971). Some effects of seating position on social perception. *Psychological Reports*, *28*(3), 887–893. https://doi.org/10.2466/pr0.1971.28.3.887

Pittman, M., & Tefertiller, A. C. (2015). With or without you: Connected viewing and co-viewing Twitter activity for traditional appointment and asynchronous broadcast television models. *First Monday*, 20(7).

Rainear, A. M., Jin, X., Edwards, A., Edwards, C., & Spence, P. R. (2021). A robot, meteorologist, and amateur forecaster walk into a bar: Examining qualitative responses to a weather forecast delivered via social robot. *Communication Studies*, *72*(6), 1129–1145. https://doi.org/10.1080/10510974.2021.2011361

Reeves, B., & Nass, C. (1996). *The media equation: How people treat computers, television, and new media like real people*. Cambridge University Press.

Richards, R. J., Spence, P. R., & Edwards, C. C. (2022). Human-machine communication scholarship trends: An examination of research from 2011 to 2021 in communication journals. *Human-Machine Communication*, *4*, 45–62. https://doi.org/10.30658/hmc.4.3

Sawilowsky, S. S. (2007). ANCOVA and quasi-experimental design: The legacy of Campbell and Stanley. In S. S. Sawilowsky (Ed.). *Real data analysis* (pp. 213–238). Information Age.

Sommer, R. (1959). Studies in personal space. *Sociometry*, *22*, 247–260. https://doi.org/10.2307/2785668

Spence, P. R. (2019). Searching for questions, original thoughts, or advancing theory: Human–machine communication. *Computers in Human Behavior*, 90, 285–287. https://doi.org/10.1016/j.chb.2018.09.014

Spence, P. R., Edwards, A., Edwards, C., & Jin, X. (2019). "The bot predicted rain, grab an umbrella": Few perceived differences in communication quality of a weather Twitterbot versus professional and amateur meteorologists. *Behavior & Information Technology*, 38(1), 101–109. https://doi.org/10.1080/0144929X.2018.1514425

Spence, P. R., Edwards, C., Edwards, A., Rainear, A., & Jin, X. (2021) "They're always wrong anyway": Exploring differences of credibility, attraction, and behavioral intentions in professional, amateur, and robotic-delivered weather forecasts, *Communication Quarterly*, 69(1), 67–86, https://doi.org10.1080/01463373.2021.1877164

Spence, P. R., Edwards, A., & Edwards, C. (2018). Attitudes, prior interaction, and petitioner credibility predict support for considering the rights of robots. *HRI 2018 Companion: Conference on ACM/IEEE International Conference on Human-Robot Interaction* (pp. 243–244). Chicago, IL, USA. ACM, NY, NY, USA. https://doi.org/10.1145/3173386.3177071

Spence, P. R., Westerman, D., Edwards, C., & Edwards, A. (2014). Welcoming our robot overlords: Initial expectations about interaction with a robot. *Communication Research Reports*, *31*(3), 272–280. https://doi.org/10.1080/08824096.2014.924337

Strouse, G. A., O'Doherty, K., & Troseth, G. L. (2013). Effective coviewing: Preschoolers' learning from video after a dialogic questioning intervention. *Developmental Psychology*, *49*(12), 2368. https://doi/10.1037/a0032463

Tal-Or, N. (2016). How co-viewing affects attitudes: The mediating roles of transportation and identification. *Media Psychology*, *19*(3), 381–405. https://doi.org/10.1080/15213269.2015.1082918

Tidwell, L. C., & Walther, J. B. (2002). Computer-mediated communication effects on disclosure, impressions, and interpersonal evaluations: Getting to know one another a bit at a time. *Human Communication Research*, *28*(3), 317–348. https://doi.org/10.1111/j.1468-2958.2002.tb00811.x

Walther, J, B. (1992). Interpersonal effects in computer-mediated interactionn: A relational perspective. *Communication Research*, *19*(1), 52–90. https://doi.org/10.1080/10510974.2020.1749683

Webb, E. J., Campbell, D. T., Schwartz, R. D., & Sechrest, L. (1966) *Unobtrusive measures: Nonreactive research in the social sciences*. Rand McNally.

Webb, E. J., Campbell, D. T., Schwartz, R. D., & Sechrest, L. (2000). *Unobtrusive measures*; revised edition. Sage Publications.

Westerman, D., Edwards, A. P., Edwards, C., Luo, Z., & Spence, P. R. (2020). I-it, I-thou, I-robot: The perceived humanness of AI in human-machine communication. *Communication Studies*, *71*(3), 393–408. https://doi.org/10.1080/10510974.2020.1749683

Wilson, B. J., & Weiss, A. J. (1993). The effects of sibling coviewing on preschoolers' reactions to a suspenseful movie scene. *Communication Research*, *20*(2), 214–248. https://doi.org/10.1177/009365093020002003

Xu, K. (2019). First encounter with robot Alpha: How individual differences interact with vocal and kinetic cues in users' social responses. *New Media & Society*, *21*(11–12), 2522–2547. https://doi.org/10.11772F1461444819851479

Xu, K., & Lombard, M. (2016). Media are social actors: Examining the CASA paradigm in the 21st century. Paper presented at the 2016 International Communication Association Annual Conference, Fukuoka, Japan.

25

Coding Ethnography: Human–Machine Communication in Collaborative Software Development

Jack Jamieson

INTRODUCTION

One of the most verdant sites for meaning-making among people and machines is the development and maintenance of technology. This is particularly evident among hacker and maker communities, which are characterized by discourses around empowerment through material engagement (Roedl et al., 2015). Free and Open Source Software communities demonstrate this phenomenon at a collective scale, acting as recursive publics that engage in "the material and practical maintenance and modification of the technical, legal, practical, and conceptual means of [their] own existence as [publics]" (Kelty, 2008, p. 3). In such contexts, meaning-making occurs at multiple scales, both among individual developers and the products of their work, and distributed through coordination mechanisms among technical standards, dependencies, social conventions, and other factors (Von Krogh et al., 2012). Approaches for studying infrastructure (e.g. Star, 1999) offer a foothold for investigating such sites by examining technical details of a system as a means to illuminate "the political, ethical, and social choices that have been made throughout its development," which extend across large networks of relationships (Bowker et al., 2009, p. 99). Thus, when meaning-making occurs through communication with a technical system, it is not strictly at the point of communication or interaction, but instead is shaped by features that may be far away and difficult to trace. This leads to the central issue of this chapter: How do we investigate sites of meaning-making in distributed, interoperable sociotechnical systems?

This chapter presents an ethnographic approach for studying communities oriented around the production of software. First, I discuss existing literature about communication and meaning-making with technology, focusing on scholarship about values and design as well as ethnographic approaches to digital technology. Following this, I demonstrate a methodological framework informed by this scholarship, which combines hands-on making, ethnographic observation, and computational analysis of logged interactional data. I reflect on how combining these methods helped situate a close, intimate perspective from hands-on making within a larger system. I conclude by discussing ways to approach epistemic conflicts arising both from human–machine communication itself and from mixed methods used to study this phenomenon.

TECHNOLOGY, COMMUNICATION, AND MEANING-MAKING

Central to the project of human–machine communication is a view of technology as more than a mere channel or medium, and instead entering "into the role of a communicator" (Guzman, 2018). Here, communication entails a shared creation of meaning among interlocutors:

> Communication also is the means through which people learn about their world (Blumer, 1969), form an understanding of Self and Other (Mead, 1967) and contribute to the shape of society (Cooley, 1897/2004). Communication research, then, is about who we are, who we are to one another, and the very reality that we are creating (Carey, 1989). (Guzman, 2018)

Meaning-making through human–machine communication is shaped by a "durable dissymmetry among human and nonhuman actors" (Suchman, 2007, p. 270). Depending on their design and contexts, technologies may assert themselves with varying degrees of prescription, opening or closing opportunities for humans (users, creators, maintainers, etc.) to draw their own interpretations or to choose how to structure work and other activities (Franklin, 2004; Latour, 2008).

Semiotic democracy provides a lens for describing human agency in this context. Fiske (1987) introduced this concept to discuss the lack of a single authorial voice in television: "the production of meaning is shared between text and viewer so that television does not preserve its authorial power and privilege" (p. 235). This notion has been taken up in Internet scholarship, such as in Benkler's (2006) assertion that the Internet "made it possible for anyone, anywhere, for any reason" to contribute to conversations that shape our culture (p. 294). The optimism that "anyone, anywhere" can participate this way is challenged by analyses of digital divides (van Dijck, 2012), pre-existing patterns of exclusion (Dunbar-Hester, 2014), and platform and algorithmic bias (Cheney-Lippold, 2011; Gillespie, 2018). This prompts a question about how semiotic democracy can be supported through the construction of Internet infrastructures. My interest is specifically with semiotic democracy during making – to what extent can makers and maintainers recursively shape the meanings of the system upon which they work?

One way semiotic democracy can be nurtured is through design that celebrates, rather than hides, the seams of technological infrastructures (Phillips, 2009; Ratto, 2007). Chalmers (2003) proposed "seamful systems whose underlying infrastructural mechanisms are 'literally visible, effectively invisible', in that everyday interaction does not require attention to these mechanisms' representations—but one can selectively focus on and reveal them when the task is to understand or even change the tool" (p. 3). DIY makers typically build with awareness and intent that their work may be disassembled or reconfigured, and thus often self-consciously exposing seams in their own work and in existing systems. In general, infrastructures are designed to be invisible when operating correctly, but become visible upon breakdowns (Star, 1999). While breakdowns typically refer to failures or emergent problems, acts of making and maintenance can prompt productive breakdowns as a means to customize, repair, and/or interoperate with a system.

To that end, studying making itself provides an entrée to understanding collaborative communication among humans, their tools, the products of their creation and surrounding sociotechnical factors. Roedl et al. (2015) summarize that a recurring theme in literature about maker communities is that "making is imagined as personally empowering in the sense that it facilitates a deeply satisfying relationship to objects that aid in a cultivation of one's identity" (p. 11) and furthermore, that making and tinkering are framed as means for redistributing social power. Making, in brief, is routinely framed as a means for people to participate in the creation of their reality and their place within it.

Values in Design and Making

The project from which this chapter originates was specifically concerned with the role of values in software developers' work. Scholarship about values and design (e.g. Friedman, 1996, 1997; Friedman & Kahn, 2003) relies on definitions of values from anthropology, sociology, and social psychology (Shilton et al., 2013). Schwartz (1992) summarized that across these disciplines values are viewed as "the criteria people use to select and justify actions and to evaluate people (including the self) and events" (p. 1). Based on this definition, I view values as a cornerstone for deriving and developing meaning about the world.

JafariNaimi et al. (2015) note that, although there are significant variations, values and design research generally "share[s] the implicit assumption that once the values have been accurately identified, they can be applied to the design of a technology that will in turn embody, bear, or advance those values" (2015, p. 94). By positioning technologies as vehicles for designers' values, that assumption conflicts with HMC's premise that technologies are not merely conduits for communication, but communicators in their own right. By contrast, JafariNaimi et al. (2015) draw on Dewey (1891) to frame design ethics through a practical *question of action*: "What are the conditions which require action, and what is the action which they demand?" (1891, p. 193). During what Dewey calls *problematic situations* it may not be clear what the situation is or what should be done. JafariNaimi et al. (2015) argue:

> In problematic situations, values cannot be used as pre-established formulas that yield proper courses of action. Rather, values serve as hypotheses by which to examine what the situation is, what the possible courses of action are, and how they might transform the situation. (p. 97)

Rather than projecting a value onto a problematic situation, values as hypotheses serve as a prompt for engaging with the situation's constituents, including nonhuman entities such as machines, which may acquiesce to such explorations or resist in ways that suggest different interpretations and approaches. This critique of values-oriented design methods complements Whittle's (2019) observation that:

> Values-based methods are well known in human–computer interaction (HCI) and information systems but are nonexistent in software engineering. HCI and information systems do not deal with the business of actually building software, so although they could apply in the early stage of software engineering, they offer little guidance as to how to handle values in the more technical stages of development (p. 114).

During processes of writing, troubleshooting, and maintaining software or other technologies, components of the system can and do respond. Dependencies and interoperating systems are updated, compatibility is regularly in flux, and classification schemes necessitate careful (re)considerations about the meaning of various actions and entities. In sum, these "more technical stages of development" are where communication with technology is most evident.

MAKING AS A LENS INTO SYSTEMS

Making, maintaining, and otherwise tinkering with technology are vital tools for making human–machine communication visible. However, this communication extends through vast systems, beyond the view of a single interlocutor. If digital ethnography is about "provincializing" digital media by investigating "how, where, and why" it culturally matters (Coleman, 2010, p. 489), then it must include unpacking the relationships between a local contact and the larger systems with which it is connected. To achieve this, Randall et al.'s (2007) discussion of ethnomethodologically informed ethnography provides a useful framing:

> Ethnomethodologically informed ethnography seeks to understand the organization of work, its flow, and the division of labor from the point of view of those involved in the work. Because work settings are organized around, through, and within a division of labor, work activities are necessarily seen as interdependent. Understanding how people coordinate their work in realtime, moment-by-moment, how they orient to the "working division of labor" to make sense of what they are doing, is a feature of ethnographic explication. (p. 121)

Divisions of labor experienced during local engagements with technology may be recognized as technological affordances (Gibson, 1986; Norman, 1999), rendering certain actions as more visible and/or viable than others, and in the process presupposing decisions about how and what to make, in terms of both material artifacts and meaning.

Thus, to use making as a lens for understanding human–machine communication, making itself must become a subject of inquiry. To that end, I drew from critical making, which entails iterative processes of reflection and reconfiguration and recognizes "the act of shared construction itself as an activity and a site for enhancing and extending conceptual understandings of critical sociotechnical issues" (Ratto, 2011, p. 254). Critical making is structured around three (often simultaneous) stages:

1   Literature review and compilation of useful concepts and theories.
2   Collaborative design and building of technical prototypes as a means of exploring theoretical concepts.
3   Iterative processes of reconfiguration, conversation, and reflection. This involved "wrestling with the technical prototypes, exploring the various configurations and alternative possibilities, and using them to express, critique, and extend relevant concepts, theories, and models." (Ratto, 2011, p. 253)

Ratto has distinguished critical making from related approaches (e.g. critical technical practice, participatory design, critical design) by noting "its broader focus on the lived experience of making and the role this plays in deepening our understanding of the socio-technical environment" (Ratto & Hertz, 2015). Focusing on the process rather than the product of making is easier said than done. Specifically, making technology presents a series of technical problems. In the course of solving those problems it is difficult to remain reflexive about why one makes certain decisions and not others. The best practice for addressing this challenge is expansive documentation, including reflections about how one felt during making, summaries of related conversations, and records of decisions at the moment they were made. This sort of note taking is unlikely to prevent researchers from slipping into instrumental modes of technical work at least occasionally but can help identify when and why such slips occur.

No amount of reflection, however, is sufficient for tracing interactions beyond one's personal grasp. Thus, it is valuable to draw on archival resources, such as logs of activity, which can trace interactions through large systems and are often features of digital systems. For example, *trace ethnography* (Geiger & Ribes, 2011) focuses specifically on archived trace data (e.g. online activity logs) to "capture many distributed phenomena that are otherwise difficult to study" (p. 1). Often, "documentary traces are the primary mechanism in which users themselves know their distributed communities and act within them" (p. 1), and thus are encountered through participant-observation (e.g., through critical making) as well as being fruitful for systematic archival analyses. Most importantly, these provide resources for expanding the scale of analysis beyond one's encounters as an individual maker.

of individuals make and maintain technical standards, software, design practices, documentation, and community norms through which IndieWeb operates as a cohesive system rather than just an assortment of websites. This infrastructure allows IndieWeb sites to use a variety of social features (e.g., likes, replies, sharing, and social feeds) using peer-to-peer interactions instead of relying on corporate centralized platforms. IndieWeb does not have a formal organizational structure, and the vast majority of participants in this community do so as a hobby.

Values are explicitly codified in IndieWeb's principles for building (IndieWeb.org, 2020b) and other rationales (Çelik, 2014; IndieWeb.org, 2020c) as well as expressed tacitly in more general commitments to individual autonomy and a DIY spirit. Thus, I set out to investigate how values were defined and expressed by IndieWeb's builders, and how the sociotechnical infrastructure they were building pushed back against or encouraged different articulations of values. Since building is central to the IndieWeb's ethos, and my primary interest was in IndieWeb's software and infrastructural development, creating software was a way to be a legitimate participant and develop insights about the processes in which IndieWeb contributors are engaged. Significantly, IndieWeb is the very definition of a recursive public (Kelty 2008), since its contributors are continually building the communication infrastructure that supports their community. Routinely, beliefs about what sort of IndieWeb software was possible and desirable were developed by building that software and seeing how it worked. By observing and participating in building IndieWeb software, it became clear that this was a conversation through which IndieWeb's future was questioned, clarified, and explored – a process of human–machine communication.

STUDYING A COMMUNITY OF DEVELOPERS

In essence, this chapter is a reflection on my study of developers' values and activities building and maintaining the IndieWeb (Jamieson, 2021). Here, I briefly explain the context of that study and its combination of methods, and then reflect upon virtues and challenges of that approach.

IndieWeb is an international community of people who use personal websites as their primary online identity. Making is a core feature of the IndieWeb in two ways: First, individuals make and maintain their own websites, and second, a variety

Two Perspectives: Making Close Up, and Computational Analyses from Afar

I built software and reflected on the process following a critical making approach and combined the resulting analysis with several other methods including: interviews with IndieWeb contributors; participant observation at events, online chat, and other spaces; trace ethnography of GitHub issues;[1] and computational analyses of chat logs and GitHub data. This supported triangulation between intimate and distant perspectives, connecting local experiences to broader structures. In this section, I describe how approaches at opposite extremes of scale complemented one another and raised distinct epistemic challenges. Critical making offered a close, autoethnographic perspective, limited in its ability to apprehend IndieWeb's breadth. And by contrast, computational analyses excel at breadth, but tend to flatten complex interactions and deliberations into simple classifications.

As I built IndieWeb software, I continually sought to reflect upon my values and approaches. This involved struggling with the tendency in software development (and other technical disciplines) to evaluate technologies according to the efficiency of their performance, which conflicts with critical modes of thinking required for reflexivity (Agre, 1997). At times, this tendency felt like a hindrance for my study. However, with hindsight it became clear that this wasn't an obstacle to be overcome in order to reach the subject of my study. Instead, it was a core feature of the subject itself. I thus sought to understand how and why this pressure occurred. Presently, I will describe how I came to understand the extent to which my individual practices building a small piece of software were shaped by technical standards and social influences from across the IndieWeb.

The software I wrote, *Yarns*, is used to follow and reply to websites and social media feeds directly using one's IndieWeb-compatible website instead of relying on a social media platform. I built an initial version of this software largely independently, but shifted approaches mid-way through development when a new standard for feed-readers emerged called *Microsub*. The point of Microsub is to divide the work of building a feed reader into client and server, meaning any one developer only has to take on one part. When I adopted a Microsub-based approach, I adapted Yarns into a Microsub server (which handles back-end subscriptions and fetching content), so users could select from a variety of clients written by other people to provide a front-end interface. I could focus on part of the development I enjoyed most and leave the user interface to people far more capable in that area. I eventually realized that, although this led to a more robust system overall, I had compromised some of my values in the process. I had initially prioritized ease of use for non-technical users and so had designed an all-in-one system. And yet, this new flow has more moving parts such as authentication and publishing between client and server[2] and is, despite its many benefits, more complicated for users to set up.

This compromise initially came as a surprise. Whereas making had engendered technical fluency, it was only upon reviewing my notes and connecting my experience back to theories about values and design that I could begin to grasp the relationship between my experience and the larger

system. I reviewed my field notes and GitHub commits from Yarns's development and realized they became sparser and more focused on technical troubleshooting once I switched to Microsub. This was a personal failing to some extent, but also encouraged by IndieWeb's (and more directly, Microsub's) emphasis on modularity. IndieWeb's modularity extends from a foundational software engineering concept called separation of concerns where code is structured so that each section deals with a single aspect of the program (Hürsch & Lopes, 1995). Although this modular approach challenged my reflexivity, it ultimately emphasized the role of IndieWeb's broader system. As Yarns became intertwined with Microsub clients and other components, it became clear that the merits of any one piece of the IndieWeb depends on interoperability with others' work. In other words, the capacity for semiotic democracy was structured by a variety of human and nonhuman actors across IndieWeb's network. Most importantly, modularity itself inconspicuously guided (though did not force) me and other developers toward collaborative, consensus-oriented designs.

Upon reflection, I could see how making software led to me traverse lines of relation between modules, most obviously through processes of understanding and resolving error messages. Sometimes the resolution could be simple (e.g., fixing a typo) and in others an error could lead to rich discussions with other developers about what was possible or not possible within the system, which could extend far afield to related technical specification or other components. However, my exposure to IndieWeb through making was nonetheless myopically bounded by the specific dependencies, standards, and design patterns upon which my software relied. And even there, my branching outward was guided by attempts to resolve breakdowns. When externalities worked well—i.e., did not produce error messages—they were effectively invisible.

To address this, I balanced the locality of my making activities with other methods. To illustrate the extremes of this combination, I reflect upon computational analyses used to map the structure of IndieWeb's discussions and coding activities. Social network analysis and topic modeling (Blei et al., 2003) helped yield a broad but shallow view of IndieWeb's network of contributors. This analysis revealed that 2,897 people had posted 923,634 messages to IndieWeb chat between its creation on Feb. 2, 2011 and data collection on July 24, 2019.[3] It revealed that of those, 4.42% of people were long-term participants who posted to chat in more than 12 distinct months. It showed that the majority of IndieWeb-related GitHub repositories were small personal projects (much like my *Yarns* software). Chat discussions were classified into discrete topics, and statistical analysis showed that people who frequently chatted about events or IndieWeb technologies were more likely than other chat participants to also contribute to IndieWeb-related GitHub repositories. These results were presented using network graphs, various charts, and statistical analyses. This helped map out the social relationships that were gestured at during making. Most importantly, it illustrated the depth of IndieWeb's modularity, making it clear that IndieWeb is largely formed by individual projects and small, loose collaborations. This affirmed that my experience building Yarns was fairly typical. More importantly, seeing the extent to which IndieWeb software, standards, and websites interoperate among one another illustrated the importance of IndieWeb's modularity as a technical feature. This broader perspective helped reveal the connections between IndieWeb projects, which shaped my understanding of my own making work. Specifically, from this perspective, seams that felt like obstacles during the making process were exposed as vital parts of a heterogeneous system.

EPISTEMIC CONFLICTS ACROSS SCALES AND APPROACHES

HMC poses a similar challenge as intercultural communication in that researchers must manage multiple ways of knowing to understand how norms differ among interlocutors. Parts of a system may be understood as an engineer – how was the system designed and why does it function in a specific way? Yet we bridge this with social, cultural, and anthropological lenses – what kind of culture is nurtured through communication through and with machines? Further, when studying networked systems or other large infrastructures, there are significant questions of scale. What initially appears to be a one-to-one communication – e.g., between a single coder and the software under construction – extends through a much larger system.

I've argued here that triangulation among multiple methods can help map between these scales and ways of knowing, offering a rich (though always partial) view. Above, I have highlighted some merits of combining analyses from different scales. Yet, such combinations also lead to epistemic clashes. In brief, large computational analyses conflict with my attempts to situate technologies in local contexts. In many aspects of my research, such as during critical making, I sought to follow Suchman's (2002) call to avoid

adopting a "view from nowhere" (Haraway, 1988). By focusing on acts of making, maintenance, and considering human relationships as integral to the technical, I have consciously avoided viewing IndieWeb as a universal and stable technology (or even agglomeration of technologies). And yet, I'm not sure I can think of a more literal representation of a view from nowhere than network analyses and statistical topic models used in other parts of this approach. Such approaches flatten complex relationships and exchanges of ideas into lists of topics and descriptions of the frequency, direction, and classifications of interaction. For addressing questions about meaning-making, these representations are clearly insufficient. And yet, computational methods provide ways to map structures and patterns at scales that would be, at best, difficult to achieve otherwise. To attend to this clash, researchers can limit the scope of their interpretation of computational results and supplement them to suit their research questions. Additionally, processes of analysis should be described in sufficient detail to highlight their limitations. For example, earlier in this brief chapter, I (reductively) summarized how chat discussions could be categorized into topics. Were this a longer chapter and were my purpose here to describe those discussions in depth, I should explain what constitutes a topic, how this was derived, and what information is obfuscated in a given model. Given the extent of these limitations, I should then combine this with qualitative analyses to explain and mitigate these shortcomings. In other words, the "view from nowhere" is just as situated as autoethnographic and other qualitative aspects of the research, just from a different vantage point. Coding ethnography entails triangulation among multiple views, coupled with reflection on the merits and limitations of each, the purpose of which is to (always partially) map between local material practices and broader infrastructures through which they are entwined. Ultimately, epistemic conflicts are a feature of human–machine communication, both across scales and between humans and non-humans, and thus researchers will find it productive to attend to these conflicts as sources of meaning-making, rather than obstacles.

NOTES

1. GitHub issues are bug reports and feature requests posted to a code repository. Each issue contains a discussion thread.
2. Authentication relied on an IndieWeb spec called *IndieAuth*, while publishing followed a spec called *Micropub*.

3   Multiple usernames belonging to the same person were deduplicated (e.g. "[jackjamieson]" and "jackjamieson" were collapsed into one person). So, this figure is likely to be an accurate count of actual people who posted to IndieWeb chat.

REFERENCES

Agre, P. (1997). Toward a critical technical practice: Lessons learned in trying to reform AI. *Bridging the great divide: Social science, technical systems, and cooperative work*. Erlbaum, 131–157.

Benkler, Y. (2006). *The wealth of networks: How social production transforms markets and freedom*. Yale University Press.

Blei, D. M., Ng, A. Y., Jordan, M. I., & Lafferty, J. (2003). Latent Dirichlet allocation. *Journal of Machine Learning Research*, 3(4/5), 993–1022.

Bowker, G. C., Baker, K., Millerand, F., & Ribes, D. (2009). Toward information infrastructure studies: Ways of knowing in a networked environment. In J. Hunsinger, L. Klastrup, & M. Allen (Eds.), *International handbook of internet research* (pp. 97–117). Springer. http://link.springer.com/10.1007/978-1-4020-9789-8_5

Çelik, T. (2014, June 5). *Why we need the IndieWeb*. Personal Democracy Forum 2014. www.youtube.com/watch?v=HNmKO7Gr4TE

Chalmers, M. (2003). Seamful design and Ubicomp infrastructure. *Proc. Ubicomp 2003 Workshop at the Crossroads: The Interaction of HCI and Systems Issues in UbiComp*, 4.

Cheney-Lippold, J. (2011). A new algorithmic identity: Soft biopolitics and the modulation of control. *Theory, Culture & Society*, 28(6), 164–181. https://doi.org/10.1177/0263276411424420

Coleman, E. G. (2010). Ethnographic approaches to digital media. *Annual Review of Anthropology*, 39(1), 487–505. https://doi.org/10.1146/annurev.anthro.012809.104945

Dewey, J. (1891). Moral theory and practice. *International Journal of Ethics*, 1. http://archive.org/details/jstor-2375407

Dunbar-Hester, C. (2014). Radical inclusion? Locating accountability in Technical DIY. In M. Ratto & M. Boler (Eds.), *DIY citizenship: Critical making and social media*. The MIT Press.

Fenton, A., & Procter, C. (2019). Studying social media communities: Blending methods with Netnography. In *SAGE Research Methods Cases*. https://doi.org/10.4135/9781526468901

Fiske, J. (1987). *Television culture*. Routledge. www.taylorfrancis.com/books/e/9780203133446

Franklin, U. M. (2004). *The real world of technology* (Rev. ed). House of Anansi Press; distributed in the United States by Publishers Group West.

Friedman, B. (1996). Value-sensitive design. *Interactions*, 3(6), 8.

Friedman, B. (Ed.). (1997). *Human values and the design of computer technology*. Cambridge University Press.

Friedman, B., & Kahn, P. H. (2003). Human values, ethics, and design. In J. Jacko & A. Sears (Eds.), *Handbook of human-computer interaction* (pp. 1177–1201). Lawrence Erlbaum Associates.

Geiger, R. S., & Ribes, D. (2011). *Trace ethnography: Following coordination through documentary practices*. 1–10. https://doi.org/10.1109/HICSS.2011.455

Gibson, J. J. (1986). The theory of affordances. In *The ecological approach to visual perception* (pp. 127–143). Lawrence Erlbaum Associates.

Gillespie, T. (2018). *Custodians of the internet: Platforms, content moderation, and the hidden decisions that shape social media*. Yale University Press.

Guzman, A. L. (2018). What is human-machine communication, anyway? In A. L. Guzman (Ed.), *Human-machine communication: Rethinking communication, technology, and ourselves*. Peter Lang.

Haraway, D. (1988). Situated knowledges: The science question in feminism and the privilege of partial perspective. *Feminist Studies*, 14(3), 575–599. https://doi.org/10.2307/3178066

Hürsch, W. L., & Lopes, C. V. (1995). *Separation of concerns* (Technical Report NU-CCS-95-03). College of Computer Science, Northeastern University.

IndieWeb.org. (2020a). *Home*. https://indieweb.org/

IndieWeb.org. (2020b). *Principles*. https://indieweb.org/principles

IndieWeb.org. (2020c). *Why*. http://indieweb.org/why

JafariNaimi, N., Nathan, L., & Hargraves, I. (2015). Values as hypotheses: Design, inquiry, and the service of values. *Design Issues*, 31(4), 91–104. https://doi.org/10.1162/DESI_a_00354

Jamieson, J. (2021). *Independent together: Building and maintaining values in a distributed web infrastructure* [University of Toronto]. http://dissertation.jackjamieson.net

Kelty, C. M. (2008). *Two bits: The cultural significance of free software*. Duke University Press.

Kozinets, R. V. (2015). *Netnography: Redefined* (2nd edition). Sage.

Latour, B. (2008). Where are the missing masses? Sociology of a few mundane artifacts. In D. J. Johnson & M. W. Jameson (Eds.), *Technology and society, building our sociotechnical future* (pp. 151–180). MIT Press.

Norman, D. A. (1999). Affordance, conventions, and design. *Interactions*, 6(3), 38–43.

Phillips, D. (2009). Ubiquitous computing, spatiality, and the construction of identity: Directions for policy response. In I. Kerr, V. Steeves, & C. Lucock (Eds.), *Lessons from the identity trail: Anonymity, privacy and identity in a networked society*. Oxford University Press.

Randall, D., Harper, R., & Rouncefield, M. (2007). *Fieldwork for design*. Springer.

Ratto, M. (2007). Ethics of seamless infrastructures: Resources and future directions. *International Review of Information Ethics*, *8*(8), 21–25.

Ratto, M. (2011). Critical making: Conceptual and material studies in technology and social life. *The Information Society*, *27*(4), 252–260. https://doi.org/10.1080/01972243.2011.583819

Ratto, M., & Hertz, G. (2015). Defining critical making: Matt Ratto in conversation with Garnet Hertz. In *Conversations in critical making*. https://journals.uvic.ca/index.php/ctheory/article/view/15123

Roedl, D., Bardzell, S., & Bardzell, J. (2015). Sustainable making? Balancing optimism and criticism in HCI discourse. *ACM Transactions on Computer-Human Interaction*, *22*(3), 15:1-15:27. https://doi.org/10.1145/2699742

Schwartz, S. H. (1992). Universals in the content and structure of values: Theory and empirical tests in 20 countries. *Advances in Experimental Social Psychology*, *25*, 1–65.

Shilton, K., Koepfler, J. A., & Fleischmann, K. R. (2013). Charting sociotechnical dimensions of values for design research. *The Information Society*, *29*(5), 259–271.

Star, S. L. (1999). The ethnography of infrastructure. *American Behavioral Scientist*, *43*(3), 377–391.

Suchman, L. (2002). Located accountabilities in technology production. *Scandinavian Journal of Information Systems*, *14*, 16.

Suchman, L. (2007). *Human-machine reconfigurations: Plans and situated actions*. Cambridge University Press.

van Dijck, J. A. G. M. (2012). The evolution of the digital divide: The digital divide turns to inequality of skills and usage. In J. Bus, M. Crompton, M. Hildebrandt, & G. Metakides (Eds.), *Digital +2012* (pp. 57–75). IOS Press. www.utwente.nl/bms/vandijk/news/The%20Evolution%20of%20the%20Digital%20Divide/Evolution%20of%20the%20Digital%20Divide%20Digital%20Enlightment%20Yearbook%202012.pdf

Von Krogh, G., Haefliger, S., Spaeth, S., & Wallin, M. W. (2012). Carrots and rainbows: Motivation and social practice in open source software development. *Mis Quarterly*, *36*(2), 649–676.

Whittle, J. (2019). Is your software valueless? *IEEE Software*, *36*(3), 112–115. https://doi.org/10.1109/MS.2019.2897397

26

An Ethnography for Studying HMC: What can we Learn from Observing How Humans Communicate with Machines?

Sharon Ringel

INTRODUCTION

Rooted in anthropology, traditional ethnography has centered on the study of humans, their conversations, their interactions, and their behaviors in their natural settings far from the artificial lab. In this chapter, I explore how observing, documenting and listening to humans are indispensable ways to understand how they are communicating with the machines around them and can reveal insights that would remain illegible through any other research methodology. Based on my own research on the National Library of Israel's (NLI) digitization of archival documents, this chapter explores a conceptional ethnographic framework for studying HMC. First, I discuss traditional human–human ethnography, outlining relevant definitions, characteristics, and ethnographies within the field of communication research that can serve to inform ethnography in HMC. Second, I integrate the insights of science and technology studies (STS) – particularly actor-network theory (ANT) – which offers one of the theoretical foundations for HMC ethnography. I then illustrate my discussion with experiences from my own research, and finally, I explore the benefits of ethnography for studies in HMC.

ON HUMAN–HUMAN ETHNOGRAPHY

Ethnography is a research method(odology), tradition, approach, and mode of describing and representing social life. It is a way for social scientists to collect data, one rooted in a broader theoretical and philosophical framework that incorporates concepts like reflexivity, representations, and realism (Atkinson, 2016; Brewer, 2000; Gobo, 2008). Even though there are differences and tensions between ethnographic traditions, they all share some common ground, including the "commitment to first-hand experience and exploration of a particular cultural or social setting on the basis of (though not exactly by) participant observation" (Atkinson et al., 2001, p. 4).

The hallmark of ethnography is participant observation, a method in which a researcher takes part in the daily activities and observes the everyday lives of the informants, their rituals, interactions, and events as one of the means of learning the explicit and tacit aspects of their life routines and their culture (Musante & DeWalt, 2010; Spradley, 2016). The observation is supplemented by field note-taking and interviews, which are the key record of the researcher's data. According to Geertz (1973), "thick description" consists of recording and interpreting ephemeral situations and phenomena. The concept of "thick description" is often used and widely cited in qualitative research across disciplines and research approaches (Ponterotto, 2006). Following Ryle (1971), Geertz (1973) distinguishes between "thin description" and "thick description." The former consists of what we see with the naked eye, while the latter relies on the contextualization of social behavior and emphasizes nuance, detail, and "stratified hierarchy of meaningful structures" (Geertz, 1973, p. 7).

In contrast with research that relies on interviews as the sole method of data collection, interviews in ethnographic research are typically conducted during or after fieldwork. Over the course of participant observation, researchers experience many verbal and non-verbal interactions with the communities they are studying. Some ethnographers consider any conversation in the field an interview (Harrison, 2018). Interviews as part of the ethnographic study, during the participant observation or after, can help the researcher gain further understanding of the motivations and strategies underlying interactions, practices, and interpretations of the participants.

Although participant observation, interviews, and field note-taking are the three main components of ethnographic research, ethnographers deploy additional data collection techniques. As with any research, ethnographers determine how to collect data based on their research question and theoretical orientation. They may also analyze archival materials such as videos, photos, maps, brochures, journals, and letters (Harrison, 2018). Ethnography, then, is a term used to describe a set of qualitative methods to collect data in order to explore social and cultural phenomena and the everyday lives of individuals and groups (Coffey, 2018).

Since ethnography is the study of culture, it is only natural that it has been applied by communication and media scholars. The terms "communication" and "culture" are fundamentally connected to one another (Carey, 2008). Culture is shared through verbal and non-verbal interaction, and communication consists of the transmission of information, mediated subjectivity, and sociality. In media studies, ethnography has allowed scholars to delve into media industries to better understand the production process and to unpack and problematize heretofore monolithic concepts (e.g. Ginsburg et al., 2002; Hesmondhalgh & Baker, 2013; Neff et al., 2005). Communication and media ethnographies also have revealed how media technologies are embedded in people's quotidian lives, and how consumers, audiences, and producers are situated within discursive universes, political situations, economic circumstances,

national settings, historical moments, and transnational flows (Ginsburg et al., 2002).

Ethnography as a research method was adopted by various subfields of communication and media studies. Media and communication scholars have used ethnography to examine questions of technology and culture. In journalism studies, for example, understanding the process of news production from inside the newsroom has a long-established history (Tuchman, 1978). Boczkowski's (2005) ethnographic research on the ways in which American news organizations adapted to new technologies is based on interviews, archival research, and participant observation conducted at three online newspapers. Through an ethnographic exploration of *The New York Times*, Usher (2014) documented one of the most important newsrooms in the United States during a pivotal moment of technological change and analyzed how the new values of online journalism impacted the daily workflows of reporters.

Hundreds of ethnographic communication studies have been published over the years, ranging from ethnographies of global communication (Kraidy & Murphy, 2008) to ethnographic audience research (Mayer, 2005). Scholars have entered the home to observe viewing habits and how individuals react to media technologies (Lotz, 2000). Hence, the process of observing how humans interact with the technologies surrounding them has strong methodological roots in communication studies.

ON HUMAN–MACHINE ETHNOGRAPHY

In studying culture surrounding media, ethnographies of communication also have taken into account, often implicitly, aspects of people's direct interactions with technology (e.g. Schüll, 2012; Zuboff, 1988). Thus, there has been an underlying consideration for HMC which focuses on the machine as a communicator and on the process of meaning-making between humans and machines. HMC investigates the ways in which humans are communicating, interacting, engaging, and forming relationships with machines, and looks at the implications of these interactions on individuals, cultures, and societies. The distinction between human–human communication and human–machine communication lies in the role of technology in these exchanges. In HMC, the machine functions not just as a medium or channel of communicating with other humans, but as a distinct subject in its own right (Guzman, 2018). Archetypal HMC research may include examining how students perceive the use of social robots in the classroom (Edwards et al., 2016), the expectations people carry into their interactions with robots (Spence et al., 2014), and communication patterns between people and voice-based personal assistants such as Apple's Siri (Guzman, 2017).

The study of HMC has only recently received significant attention from communication scholars, likely a reaction to the growing role of machines and digital technologies in our communication practices (Jones, 2014). Although early work highlighted the social and cultural aspects of HMC (Suchman, 1987, 2006), it was not until the past few years that the field began to seriously grapple with the consequences of machine-aided communication. This includes work concerning our interactions with algorithms via interfaces, search engines, games, voice assistants, and social robots. Further, as my following discussion on the interaction between humans and scanners indicates, HMC may also occur between humans and what Guzman (2016) calls "muted machines." Even though such machines were not designed to replicate "human-like" cognitive processes, they may still convey messages and meanings. Exchanges of information between humans and machines occur in any industrial process, and sometimes include "rituals" between machines and workers.

The integration of ethnographic methods into the study of human–computer interactions (HCI) is not new. Researchers have long seen the value in moving away from artificial laboratory settings to examine how people utilize technology in real-life contexts (Rapp, 2018). The value of "bottom-up" perspectives and the richness found in studying HCI in real settings has been understood for decades (Cooper et al., 1995). The sub-field of human–robot interaction (HRI) also recognizes the contribution of ethnographic methods to exploring how humans communicate with robots in their homes (Forlizzi et al., 2004), workplaces, and public spaces (Blond, 2019). However, HCI and HRI studies primarily use ethnographic methods to improve product design and usability (Dourish, 2007), while HMC ethnography focus on the social meanings embedded in these interactions. In other words, HMC serves as a type of umbrella for the study of communication with machines in the communication field which includes aspects of HCI and HRI.

One of the theoretical foundations for understanding how humans interact with objects and machines can be found in science and technology studies (STS) and in the body of work known as actor-network theory (ANT). According to ANT, the social world is made up of "patterned networks of heterogeneous materials… not only of people

but also of machines, animals, texts, money, architectures" (Law, 1992, p. 381). ANT insists that sociological inquiry will include objects like technologies as part of the study of human behavior, and highlights not only the role of such objects but, more importantly, the interactions between humans and technologies (Akrich, 1992; Latour, 2005). ANT understands the social world as a network of actors – human and nonhuman – that connect and combine, thereby creating and stabilizing what we define as "The Social". In other words, our social lives are comprised of interactions with the objects around us in a similar way to how we interact with humans. Both interactions involve processes of meaning-making. As we surround ourselves with machines possessing the ability to communicate – such as Siri, Alexa, and other forms of AI – the place of machines in our everyday lives becomes more entrenched. Ethnographies of the social and cultural aspects of human interactions with machines may therefore reveal insights that could remain invisible using other methods. In the next section, I will illustrate this with my own experiences in HMC ethnographic work.

AN ETHNOGRAPHY OF SCANNING

Between 2013 and 2016, I conducted ethnographic research at the National Library of Israel (NLI) to examine the digitization of archival documents. I started this research with participant observation at the library's Digitization Center (DC), an open space that contains several offices and studios for taking photos, and more than 20 workstations equipped with computers and scanners. Complementing ANT's goal of uncovering the role that objects play in social phenomena, my ethnographic work at the NLI focused on the role humans play in digitization, a process which is typically (and conveniently) framed as primarily technical and machine-operated. Digitization refers to the process of converting traditional archival materials – usually print books and papers – into electronic formats, in which they can be stored and manipulated by computers. This definition suggests that digitization is a mechanical operation that does not include human interference. My research, however, sought to open the "black box" (Bucher, 2016) of archival digitization and to uncover its network of heterogeneous actors, which includes scanning machines, curators, workers at the DC, cameras, and managers (Ringel & Ribak, 2015, 2021).

Every time I arrived at the DC to conduct my observation, I greeted the workers and chose one person to accompany for that shift. I sat next to the selected employee and spent several hours observing their work. During this time, we usually discussed topics ranging from small talk about their day to clarifying questions regarding the scanning process or machinery. I often started the conversation by asking what they were scanning. Sometimes they had not even checked before I inquired about the book or paper they held in their hands. They would then stop their mechanistic turning and scanning of pages, and show me the book's cover.

During my observation period, I spent hours watching workers scan page after page, communicating with the scanning machines they are in charge of operating. Digitization seemed to be an endeavor with defined limits, inputs, and outputs: archival documents went into the scanning machine as analog objects and then appeared on the screen as digital objects. The workers who oversaw this process operated almost automatically; one could practically hear the rhythmic hum of humans and machines operating in tandem within a stable network. But once in a while, I noticed something is different – a noise or silence that broke the spell of human–machine harmony. This is how I described one such interruption in my field notes:

> L. has been working at the Library for four years now. She is in charge of [the] Bookeye 3 machine [a book scanner]. She explains that she knows how to work well with the machine because sometimes "you have to use the head, even while working with a machine, we have to be creative [...]." It looks like the scanner glass is heavy for her, and each time she switches a book page she is lifting the glass and then pushing it back down against the book. "The purpose of the glass is to flatten the book and prepare it for the scanning of the camera located above (the book is face up and not down like a home scanner). Sometimes, when I lift the platen glass, the pages may cling to it, destroying the manuscript or book; then, I try to play with the machine and put a finger in the middle so that the pages do not stick to the glass."

To achieve the desired results, L. must communicate with the scanning machine. She developed her own work practices and routines based on her experiences with this specific device. These allegedly technical decisions are important for understanding digitization as a socio-technical operation that involves human–machine communication. While I could have discovered some of this information through interviews, observing the practices of digitization first-hand allowed me to notice the actors involved in the network, and to document how humans and machines co-create

meaning that can be uncovered by future users of the digital archive.

One of the most fascinating machines at the DC is the Treventus ScanRobot 2.0 which is placed in a side room at the DC. According to the manufacturer, the Treventus ScanRobot 2.0 is:

> A new breed of color, grayscale and black and white book scanner that allows you to place a book on its unique book carrier and then walk away. The book scanner will then scan and turn every page by itself until the book is completed. The book scanner has been designed to turn the pages very carefully, allowing even books that are several centuries old to be scanned.

During my first visit to the NLI, the manager of digital projects led me on a tour of the DC and introduced me to all the workers and the machines. As part of this tour, I had the rare opportunity to watch this state-of-the-art piece of machinery scan a book "on its own," without the aid of a human worker. This demonstration was only for the purpose of showing me how the machine can turn the pages by itself – after we left the room, it was turned off. In the time I spent at the DC, I watched workers manually turning the pages of the books, placing texts on the platen glass, and photographing other archival materials. Once in a while, a group of donors, schoolchildren, or dignitaries would visit the NLI. For these special occasions, the manager would ask a worker, who was familiar with the robot, to turn it on and place a book (always the same volume) on its carrier. The visitors would then gather around the robot, squeezing into the small room where the machine is located, and watch attentively as it turned the pages, as if by magic, and scanned them without human intervention. While the Treventus was undoubtedly the highlight of the tour, I never witnessed it used for its ostensible purpose – scanning documents for the digital archive (Ringel & Ribak, 2021).

Despite the fact that the Treventus spends its days sitting idle while humans turn page after page, one of the DC managers insisted that it "is an incredible machine." Further, in literally every formal interview I conducted with the workers, they expressed their positive feelings for the Treventus despite its inability to materially contribute to their labor. When I asked why I had never witnessed it working, they replied:

> We can't use it for scanning old books since old and rare books have delicate pages, and the Treventus turns the pages using a vacuum mechanism that may damage them. So, the pages, as well as the book cover, need to be thick enough for the machine. [...]. Over the last couple of years,

we changed the focus of work at the DC. We now concentrate on scanning archival materials. The Treventus is not suited for work with these kinds of materials. When we purchased the Treventus, we were interested in mass digitization of books. Since we can trust the Treventus only with new books, and we can't allow online access to new books due to copyright restrictions, we realized we don't really need to scan all these books just yet.

While the interview justifies the purchase of the Treventus in historical terms and its idleness in technical terms, it does not account for the observation obtained during my periodical visits to the library, namely, that the machine was operated during visits, and that it then repeatedly scanned the same book. One of the elements crucial to ethnography and any qualitative approach is the need to consult the literature and theory to interpret what a researcher has observed. It was only when I returned to read Larkin's (2013) analysis of the politics and poetics of infrastructures that I was able to make sense of the seemingly erratic communication with the machine. Following Larkin, I concluded that the Treventus was used to demonstrate the NLI's expertise and leadership, to perform digitization – rather than to scan analog books and manuscripts. In other words, the "hermeneutic circle" afforded through observing, interviewing and reading allowed me to gain insight into processes and meanings I would not have been able to attain and develop otherwise.

My analysis of the Treventus illustrates the ways in which an ethnographic observation, conducted in real-time and real-world settings, provides invaluable insights as to how humans *actually* communicate with machines, whether or not it coincides with the function the technology was designed and purchased for. By comparing what people *said* about the Treventus with how they *used* it, I could better understand how the technology was perceived at the NLI and the primarily performative role it in fact plays. Overall, participate observation revealed – in ANT terms – the actors involved in the digitization network. The interviews informed the ethnography and provided a different angle to that same process. In the following section, I will discuss the contribution of ethnography to the study of HMC.

THE CONTRIBUTION OF ETHNOGRAPHY TO HMC RESEARCH

As the ethnographic account at the NLI demonstrates, first-hand observation supplemented by interviews can offer an understanding of how humans communicate with machines in their own natural settings, leading to insights on the meaning-making process that occurs during this interaction. I will now highlight three unique contributions of using ethnographic methods in studying HMC.

Puzzling the mundane: We are surrounded by machines every day, all day long. Oftentimes our own interactions with the machines around us go unnoticed. Studying HMC using ethnographic methods may shed light on those behaviors and practices that we take for granted, such as shopping, driving, or scanning pages. The ethnographer thereby moves toward what Katriel (1991) described as the craft of defamiliarization. Such a deep level of attention allows us to move beyond the habits of our own minds to productively see machines as "others." In other words, ethnography for HMC research allows unpacking what may seem as "natural" to reveal the routines and rituals involved in the way we (or others) are communicating with machines and to shed light on processes that might be disregarded using other methodologies.

The gaps between what people say and what they do: As the Treventus ScanRobot 2.0 example illustrates, there are gaps between how people describe, perceive, understand, and articulate their interactions with machines and the way they actually communicate with them in real settings. These gaps may shed light on the relationships between thought and practice, between what people believe they should say and do and between what they in fact do – this is not to prioritize one or the other, but to insist on their importance. Further, the symbolic interactions with machines are as important for the understanding of meaning making as the non-symbolic interactions are. All these levels of communication and the ways they are being articulated (during interviews) and practiced (while observed) in real settings are essential for investigating the meaning humans are attributing to machines.

That said, one of the limitations of ethnography is that the researcher's presence as a participant-observer can influence the behavior of the informants. They may consciously or unconsciously perceive the interaction with the researcher as an opportunity to perform and construct an image of the type of person they wish to represent (Katz, 2019). However, even with these limitations, observation in real-time settings is the most direct way to witness social situations and to get a sense of how humans communicate with machines in their natural environment and everyday life. A long-term observation in which the informants get used to the researcher's presence may open new insights and directions for analysis. Compared to a one-time observation where the researcher may be perceived as an outsider, multiple visits to the research field can help create a more reliable, safe, and judgment-free environment for the informants as if the researcher is one of their own. As the illustration of the Treventus demonstrates, a one-time visit to the DC could not have shed light on the role of the Treventus. It was only after an extended period of time that I realized that the machine was used for performative, symbolic, seemingly ritual purposes.

Establishing local context: Different people communicate with machines differently. The meaning-making process that occurs between humans and machines is dependent on the cultural, social, and political contexts at the time and place it happens. Ethnographies of HMC illuminate this process when and where it occurs, in particular communities and with specific individuals. The same machine is likely to be treated differently when employed in distinct countries, cultures, or industries (Ginsburg et al., 2002). Ethnographic methods provide researchers with a holistic view of the local context in which humans and machines interact with each other, and offers a means to document the symbolic interaction and non-verbal communication involved in this process. An ethnography of HMC, then, allows for a deeper understanding of our social, cultural and technological worlds and demonstrates how these worlds are fundamentally intertwined.

CONCLUSION

In this chapter, I explored the benefits of ethnography to the study of HMC. Far from the confines of the laboratory, ethnographic research may highlight what people fail to disclose in an interview or a survey. Even with its limitations, ethnographic methods allow researchers to glimpse people and machines in their real settings, and to establish the cultural, social, economic, and political contexts in which they occur. Since ethnography as a research method has been widely adopted by a variety of research fields that overlap with HMC research, it seems quite natural that HMC scholars would embrace ethnography to use it in order to study the meaning-making processes between humans and the machines around them.

REFERENCES

Akrich, M. (1992). The de-scription of technical objects. In W. E. Bijker & J. Law (Eds.), *Shaping technology/building society: Studies in sociotechnical change* (pp. 205–224). The MIT Press.

Atkinson, M. (2016). Ethnography. In *Routledge handbook of qualitative research in sport and exercise*. Routledge.

Atkinson, P., Coffey, A., Delamont, S., Lofland, J., & Lofland, L. (2001). *Handbook of ethnography.* SAGE.

Blond, L. (2019). Studying robots outside the lab: HRI as ethnography. *Paladyn, Journal of Behavioral Robotics, 10*(1), 117–127. https://doi.org/10.1515/pjbr-2019-0007

Boczkowski, P. J. (2005). *Digitizing the news: Innovation in online newspapers.* MIT Press.

Brewer, J. (2000). *Ethnography.* McGraw-Hill Education (UK).

Bucher, T. (2016). Neither black nor box: Ways of knowing algorithms. In S. Kubitschko & A. Kaun (Eds.), *Innovative methods in media and communication research* (pp. 81–98). Palgrave Macmillan.

Carey, J. W. (2008). *Communication as culture, revised edition: Essays on media and society.* Routledge.

Coffey, A. (2018). *Doing ethnography* (Vol. 3). Sage.

Cooper, G., Hine, C., Rachel, J., & Woolgar, S. (1995). Ethnography and human-computer interaction. In J. Peter (Ed.), *The social and interactional dimensions of human-computer interfaces* (pp. 11–36). Cambridge University Press.

Dourish, P. (2007). *Responsibilities and implications: Further thoughts on ethnography and design.* 2–16. Association for Computing Machinery, New York, NY.

Edwards, A., Edwards, C., Spence, P. R., Harris, C., & Gambino, A. (2016). Robots in the classroom: Differences in students' perceptions of credibility and learning between "teacher as robot" and "robot as teacher." *Computers in Human Behavior, 65,* 627–634. https://doi.org/10.1016/j.chb.2016.06.005

Forlizzi, J., DiSalvo, C., & Gemperle, F. (2004). Assistive robotics and an ecology of elders living independently in their homes. *Human–Computer Interaction, 19*(1–2), 25–59.

Geertz, C. (1973). Thick description: Toward an interpretive theory of culture. In *The interpretation of cultures* (pp. 3–30). Basic Books.

Ginsburg, F. D., Abu-Lughod, L., & Larkin, B. (2002). *Media worlds: Anthropology on new terrain.* University of California Press.

Gobo, G. (2008). *Doing ethnography.* Sage.

Guzman, A. L. (2016). The messages of mute machines: Human-machine communication with industrial technologies. *Communication+1, 5*(1), 1–30.

Guzman, A. L. (2017). Making AI safe for humans: A conversation with Siri. In R. W. Gehl & M. Bakardjieva (Eds.), *Socialbots and their friends: Digital media and the automation of sociality* (pp. 69–85). Routledge.

Guzman, A. L. (2018). What is human-machine communication, anyway. *Human-machine communication: Rethinking communication, technology, and ourselves*, 1–28. Peter Lang Publishing.

Harrison, A. K. (2018). *Ethnography*. Oxford University Press.

Hesmondhalgh, D., & Baker, S. (2013). *Creative labour: Media work in three cultural industries*. Routledge.

Jones, S. (2014). People, things, memory and human-machine communication. *International Journal of Media & Cultural Politics*, *10*(3).

Katriel, T. (1991). *Communal webs: Communication and culture in contemporary Israel*. State University of New York Press.

Katz, J. (2019). On becoming an ethnographer. *Journal of Contemporary Ethnography*, *48*(1), 16–50. https://doi.org/10.1177/0891241618777801

Kraidy, M. M., & Murphy, P. D. (2008). Shifting Geertz: Toward a theory of translocalism in global communication studies. *Communication Theory*, *18*(3), 335–355. https://doi.org/10.1111/j.1468-2885.2008.00325.x

Larkin, B. (2013). The politics and poetics of infrastructure. *Annual Review of Anthropology*, *42*(1), 327–343.

Latour, B. (2005). *Reassembling the social: An introduction to actor-network theory* (14202000). Oxford University Press.

Law, J. (1992). Notes on the theory of the actor-network: Ordering, strategy, and heterogeneity. *Systems Practice*, *5*(4), 379–393. http://dx.doi.org/10.1007/BF01059830

Lotz, A. D. (2000). Assessing qualitative television audience research: Incorporating feminist and anthropological theoretical innovation. *Communication Theory*, *10*(4), 447–467. https://doi.org/10.1111/j.1468-2885.2000.tb00202.x

Mayer, V. (2005). Research beyond the pale: Whiteness in audience studies and media ethnography. *Communication Theory*, *15*(2), 148–167. https://doi.org/10.1111/j.1468-2885.2005.tb00330.x

Musante, K., & DeWalt, B. R. (2010). *Participant observation: A guide for fieldworkers*. Rowman Altamira.

Neff, G., Wissinger, E., & Zukin, S. (2005). Entrepreneurial labor among cultural producers: "Cool" jobs in "hot" industries. *Social Semiotics*, *15*(3), 307–334.

Ponterotto, J. G. (2006). Brief note on the origins, evolution, and meaning of the qualitative research concept thick description. *The Qualitative Report*, *11*(3), 538–549.

Rapp, A. (2018). Autoethnography in human-computer interaction: Theory and practice. In M. Filimowicz & V. Tzankova (Eds.), *New directions in third wave human-computer interaction: Volume 2 – Methodologies* (pp. 25–42). Springer International Publishing. https://doi.org/10.1007/978-3-319-73374-6_3

Ringel, S., & Ribak, R. (2015). Practicing digitization at the National Library of Israel. *New Review of Information Networking*, *20*(1–2), 236–240. https://doi.org/10.1080/13614576.2015.1113056

Ringel, S., & Ribak, R. (2021). 'Place a book and walk away': Archival digitization as a socio-technical practice. *Information, Communication & Society*, *24*(15), 2293–2306. https://doi.org/10.1080/1369118X.2020.1766534

Ryle, G. (1971). *Collected papers. Volume II collected essays, 1929-1968*. Hutchinson.

Sayes, E. (2014). Actor–network theory and methodology: Just what does it mean to say that nonhumans have agency? *Social Studies of Science*, *44*(1), 134–149. https://doi.org/10.1177/0306312713511867

Schüll, N. D. (2012). *Addiction by design*. Princeton University Press.

Spence, P. R., Westerman, D., Edwards, C., & Edwards, A. (2014). Welcoming our robot overlords: Initial expectations about interaction with a robot. *Communication Research Reports*, *31*(3), 272–280.

Spradley, J. P. (2016). *Participant observation*. Waveland Press.

Suchman, L. (1987). *Plans and situated actions: The problem of human-machine communication*. Cambridge University Press.

Suchman, L. (2006). *Human-machine reconfigurations: Plans and situated actions* (2nd ed.). Cambridge University Press. https://doi.org/10.1017/CBO9780511808418

Tuchman, G. (1978). *Making news: A study in the construction of reality*. Free Press.

Usher, N. (2014). *Making news at The New York Times* (18078935). University of Michigan Press.

Zuboff, S. (1988). *In the age of the smart machine: The future of work and power*. Basic Books, Inc.

27

Talking about "Talking with Machines": Interview as Method within HMC

Andrea L. Guzman

Human–Machine Communication has emerged out of a shift in how people interact with devices and in the subsequent need to adapt communication research to account for people's conceptualizations of and behaviors with "communicative artificial intelligence" (Guzman & Lewis, 2020). A priority within this growing area of communication research has been identifying and adapting existing theory formed around human–human interaction to human–machine contexts while also working toward novel theories of HMC (Fortunati & Edwards, 2020; Gambino et al., 2020; Guzman, 2018; Spence, 2019). Equally important are methodological considerations that have yet to receive the same level of scholarly attention (Fortunati & Edwards, 2020). It is not that HMC scholars have ignored method. At issue is the scope of the discussion surrounding method: Much of the focus has been within the context of individual studies. As Markham and Baym (2009) observed in the early stages of internet research, "But novel research terrain brings with it novel difficulties. It is hard to know how well older theoretical and methodological frameworks can be applied to understand contemporary social formations" (p. xiii). For HMC

to progress, systematic research and robust discussion regarding method, generally, and particular methods is critical.

This chapter contributes to this much-needed dialogue by examining interview as method within HMC. Its focus is the complexities of talking with people about how they talk with machines, specifically artificial intelligence applications. Some of the challenges are similar to those historically faced by scholars of technology, including the knowledge differential between expert and lay person, while others are exacerbated by attributes and capabilities of AI technologies. This discussion is informed by literature regarding qualitative research and interviewing and their application to the study of novel technologies. Insights also are drawn from my own research involving more than 100 interviews with people regarding their conceptualizations of vocal social assistants, such as Apple's Siri, and automated news-writing technologies that create news reports from raw data. Many of the challenges I discuss involve fundamental aspects of language use and the conveyance and interpretation of meaning, and so, this chapter also offers insights germane to HMC methods more broadly.

INTERVIEW AS METHOD

The approach to interviewing that is the foundation for this chapter is rooted within a conceptualization of qualitative research as scholarly inquiry aimed toward understanding people's experiences and interpretations of their world (Christians & Carey, 1989), including interactions with technology (Blandford et al., 2016; Markham & Baym, 2009; Veling & McGinn, 2021). Interviewing is a valuable method across multiple fields and disciplines because its focus is participants' own articulations of their lived experiences (Fontana & Frey, 2000; Kvale & Brinkmann, 2009). The aim of such research goes beyond that of usability studies that log attributes of use, preference, or practice. The focus is on the emic, or the sense-making of a participant or group regarding their own lived experience, over that of the etic, the perspectives of the researcher rooted within a "scientific" system (Blandford et al., 2016; Headland et al., 1990; Kvale & Brinkmann, 2009; Marshall & Rossman, 1995).

In these aims lie the particular strengths of interviews for HMC research. HMC examines the many aspects of people's communication with AI and similar devices, which still are in the relatively early stages of development and adoption. While rich theories exist regarding human–human interaction and human–computer interaction that can be applied to the study of emerging technologies within HMC, the nature of the devices themselves and, subsequently, people's evolving communication with them, have significant points of departure from their predecessors (Zhao, 2006). We have much to learn regarding how people experience communicative technologies, how people think about and interpret these devices and applications, and how such technologies are becoming part of how people understand themselves, each other, and their world. Discussing with people their communicative activities with these technologies and their perspectives and understanding of them is key to developing theory and approaches better attuned to the nature of communicative devices and people's interactions with them.

As with any research, there are challenges inherent to the nature of interview as method, chiefly the complexity of human meaning-making in the conversation that unfolds between participant and researcher (Holstein & Gubrium, 2016; Kvale & Brinkmann, 2009). Some of the challenges discussed below are extensions of ongoing methodological hurdles in the study of technology, such as knowledge differentials in talking about machines, while others are introduced by communicative technologies, including their ambiguous nature and the challenge created when language systems built around more concrete delineations between thing and human try to accommodate "social things."

KEY QUESTIONS AND CHALLENGES

Knowledge Differentials in Talking About Machines

The rationale for employing qualitative methods and interviewing within Human–Machine Communication research also introduces one of the key challenges in talking with people about talking with machines: the interview unfolds between a participant whose knowledge of and experiences with the technology are different in important ways from that of the researcher. The participant may be a technological expert with whom the researcher is engaging in conversation to gain insight into their thinking around the design or implementation of communicative technologies. More often, the researcher conducting interviews is interested in the perspectives of people who may use the device or application but do not possess "expert knowledge," often conceptualized as a certain level of technical know-how about a device's inner workings (Blandford et al., 2016). These are interviews with "everyday users" or particular groups within the general public, such as de Graaf et al.'s (2016) research regarding adoption of social robots into domestic settings.

Research has demonstrated that experts and lay users possess different conceptualizations of aspects of the same technology based on varying levels of knowledge and how this knowledge was attained (e.g., Lee et al., 2014; Orr, 1996). Of consequence is how the disparate ways of knowing and experiencing communication with machines manifest themselves in the very articulation of such knowledge, in how we talk about talking with machines. Orr (1996) captures this challenge in his foundational ethnography *Talking About Machines* that examines the intersection of work and technology from the perspective of Xerox copier repair technicians. As Orr (1996) explains, technicians and the customers they serve filter their conversations with one another through their own conceptualization of and interactions with the copier: "The machine is embedded in the social environment and work activities of the user site. The customers tend to discuss the machine in language reflecting their perceptions of its use and its various functions" (pp. 82–83). The technicians, however, have their own set of vocabulary and descriptions for the machine based on their experiences as expert. As Orr (1996) observes, "Under the circumstances, mismatched perceptions, influenced by different ways of understanding the machine, are probably inevitable" (p. 83). Such "mismatched perceptions" may result in barriers to communication between the repair technicians and customers as each speaks of the machine based on a conceptualization of and language derived from their different experiences and knowledge of it.

The difficulty in communication between technicians and customers can be illustrative of the interview process surrounding technology. Each party brings to the conversation knowledge that is likely gained through different interactions with a device and application, filtered through various levels of technical know-how and background information surrounding a particular device and application and technology writ large. The methodological issue to be grappled with is how such knowledge differentials enter into and shape various aspects of the interview and subsequent analysis.

The Ambiguity of Artificial Intelligence

The methodological issues embedded in talking about technology generally are compounded by additional communicative hurdles stemming from the amorphous nature of artificial intelligence and the functionality of AI technologies. Central to the meaning-making process within communication is the degree to which each party involved can take the perspective of the other, an understanding based in lived experience (see Blumer, 1969) and the shared understanding of signs, the objects they represent, and their associations (see Ogden & Richards, 1952). Although Orr's (1996) copier technicians and customers may have understood the copy machine from different perspectives based on their interactions with the machine, both parties at least had a concrete object upon which to begin to build shared meaning – the copier itself. They could see, touch, and point to the same device with its fixed functionality. The physicality of the machine and its well-defined functions provided boundaries to its use and to the ways people could interpret the machine, making it a more stable "referent" (Ogden & Richards, 1952) in conversations about a particular copier model or copiers more generally.

In contrast, artificial intelligence exists in lines of code with interactions between people and AI

often taking ephemeral forms, complicating conversation as the referent of which both parties are speaking becomes more malleable. AI applications are accessed via hardware, which people can see and touch, but the association between the AI application and the tech encasing it varies, in both design and the mind of users. Amazon's Echo is a speaker designated for using Alexa, while Apple's Siri is one of many applications accessible on Apple products. In the minds of consumers, some people imagine themselves as directly communicating with a virtual assistant, while others think of themselves as directly exchanging messages with the hardware (Guzman, 2019b). Message exchanges between people and AI also are increasingly personalized, so that, even if the researcher were to interact with the same application or device, their experience may differ from that of participants. There also is the issue of how to "consult" the machine, regarding its processing of the "messages" it receives (Fortunati & Edwards, 2020).

The numerous denotative and connotative meanings that have been assigned to "artificial intelligence" have rendered the term highly ambiguous, complicating discussion surrounding AI more generally (see also Guzman, 2019a). Since the formalization of the study of artificial intelligence in the mid-twentieth century, the operationalization of artificial intelligence and what such research entails has varied across fields and disciplines (Boden, 2016). Media portrayals of technology have further contributed to varying conceptualizations of AI (Toomey, 2011) and influenced people's attitudes toward and reactions to technology (Sundar et al., 2016). Some scholars claim the term has become vacuous in recent years as tech companies, investors, and others seek to benefit from the renewed interest and funding in AI (e.g., Bogost, 2017).

The intangibility of specific AI technologies and the ambiguity surrounding artificial intelligence add to the methodological complexity of AI research. The design of AI technologies renders the boundaries of experience with specific technologies more fluid, complicating efforts to establish common ground in talking about such technologies and then interpreting this talk. The level of ambiguity becomes more pronounced when moving from discussing a specific AI technology to talking about "artificial intelligence." In my own research, participants have described artificial intelligence as everything from "aliens" to a specific science fiction movie, show or character to a computer or robot "thinking like a human" or "acting of its own volition" to a "scientist working in a lab trying to create a mind." Furthermore, a person can possess multiple conceptualizations of

AI, depending on context. Thus, the referent that exists in people's minds surrounding the idea of artificial intelligence is highly variable, necessitating increased awareness of the opportunity for miscommunication and misinterpretation.

Finding Words to Talk About the Evocative

The final challenge is rooted in people's interpretations of the life-like characteristics designed within and projected onto communicative technologies. The ontological status of machines, people, and animals has been a metaphysical debate stretching back centuries that became more complex as the computer and its cognates began performing tasks associated with humans (Lynch & Collins, 1998; Turkle, 1984). Turkle (1984) employs the term "evocative" to describe the metaphysical qualities of early computing technology, and today's technologies are designed to interact in more sophisticated ways, continuing to push against human–machine, subject–object boundaries (Banks & de Graaf, 2020; de Graaf et al., 2016; Edwards, 2018; Gunkel, 2012; Guzman, 2020; Kahn et al., 2011; Suchman, 2011; Sugiyama & Vincent, 2013).

This evocativeness is documented in research regarding people's perceptions of communicative technology relative to ontological categories. Most people do not think of AI as fully human and, instead, associate these technologies as being more similar to machines (Etzrodt & Engesser, 2021; Guzman, 2019a; Purington et al., 2017). Such categorizing would seem to support existing ontological divides, but some people do not necessarily think of HMC technologies as belonging entirely within the machine category, either. On an ontological spectrum ranging from machine to human, some people locate technology such as conversational assistants closer to, but still outside of, the pole representing the machine category (Etzrodt & Engesser, 2021). Communicative technologies do not belong wholly to the machine category because people perceive communicative devices and applications as having some human-like qualities (Etzrodt & Engesser, 2021; Kahn et al., 2011; Pradhan et al., 2019) and, therefore, may be better thought of as "personified things" (Etzrodt & Engesser, 2021) or "social things" (Guzman, 2015). As a result, some scholars have proposed the possibility of a new ontological category for social robots (e.g., Kahn et al., 2011) while others advocate for a conceptualization of ontology that is dynamic, accommodating people's shifting perceptions of humanness and machineness in

ongoing interactions (e.g., Pradhan et al., 2019). Some scholars posit that people's engagement with AI technologies point to complex interpretations of technology as communicator that account for its status as a machine with human-like qualities (e.g., Neff & Nagy, 2016), and research regarding people's interactions with newer technologies has found that people interpret and act toward these devices and applications as their own ontological class of social actor distinct from humans (see Gambino et al., 2020). As Turkle (1984) observed with personal computers, the ontological categories themselves also are being revised, so that traits once associated with humans, such as the ability to express emotion, now are being associated with machines by some users (Etzrodt & Engesser, 2021; Guzman, 2020).

The evocativeness of communicative technologies is a driver of and potential hurdle to HMC scholarship. HMC is grounded in questioning assumptions regarding the nature of communicators around which the study of communication, including theory and method, have been formed (Edwards, 2018; Fortunati & Edwards, 2020; Gunkel, 2012). Such assumptions must be consciously brought to the fore so that they can be examined, but doing so is challenging because conceptualizations of the nature of things and people are highly abstract and vary across and within cultures. Such assumptions also are intertwined with language, its use, and its interpretation, adding a layer of complexity to talking about these technologies.

A prime example is the assignment of third-person pronouns to refer to AI applications within the English language. Scholars have documented that people use *she, he, it,* or different forms interchangeably to refer to applications designed with overt gender traits (e.g., Guzman, 2015; Pradhan et al., 2019; Purington et al., 2017). Within the grammatical rules of English, pronoun assignment rests with the gender category of the referent that includes whether the referent is perceived as having a "personal" or "nonpersonal" gender (Quirk et al., 1985, p. 341) or possessing "humanness/animacy" (Siemund, 2013, p. 46). The referent also is judged as masculine, feminine, or neuter, so that, "male referents trigger *he,* female referents trigger *she,* and unsexed/inanimate referents trigger *it*" (Siemund, 2013, p. 47). Thus, the assignment of *her* to AI applications such as Amazon's Alexa seemingly would signal that the application is perceived as both female and life- or human-like while the use of *it* would indicate that the application is an object without life or humanness and is devoid of female or male traits (see also the discussion regarding who/whom in Gunkel, 2012). It is the use of life-like pronouns to refer to AI technologies and the oscillation of pronoun use between *it* and *he/she* that scholars cite as an important piece of evidence in documenting the evocativeness of communicative AI.

However, how people assign gender and "life-ness" to referents is not straightforward in everyday language use. As Comrie (2005) notes, "borderline cases" in which the perception of the entity straddles the line between human and non-human can be particularly complex (p. 105). The line between person and nonpersonal gender, according to Quirk et al. (1985), is based upon whether a referent is a "'person,' i.e. to a being felt to possess characteristics associated with a member of the human race" (p. 341). A "person" can include "supernatural beings" (Quirk et al., 1985) and animals within specific contexts (Payne & Huddleston, 2002). There also is a long history of the personification of non-biological entities (Payne & Huddleston, 2002; Siemund, 2013), including computers (Quirk et al., 1985), that occurs when objects are designed with overt gender cues (Comrie, 2005) or have been culturally gendered (Payne & Huddleston, 2002). Pronoun assignment in the English language, therefore, is primarily theorized as being based on the perceived characteristics of the referent that the communicator wants to emphasize (Payne & Huddleston, 2002; Siemund, 2013); although, other factors may influence people's pronoun selections more generally, such as whether English is their first language (Al-Shaer, 2014).

Thus, there is no straightforward rule for determining the "correct" third-person pronoun for evocative technology. The English language forces a choice between the category of inanimate (*it*) and human/animate (*she/he*) without a clear option to accommodate ontological betweenness. It could be argued that the human/animate gender category has been expanded to accommodate objects with life-like qualities and, thus, a degree of ontological betweenness. Yet, ambiguity remains because that same pronoun category also encompasses fully human and biological beings. It is understood that when using *she/he* over *it*, a person is signaling the female/male and/or human-like nature of the technology, but just how much of a *she* or *he* does the person conceptualize the technology to be? And which attribute is more pronounced: female/male traits or life/human likeness? Similarly, when people are using *it*, are they indicating that a technology is completely devoid of any human-like qualities or that human qualities are present but are less pronounced than machine attributes?

Given the newness of communicative technologies and the lack of time for language to adapt, there is a question of whether people have an adequate means of expression for capturing and conveying their perceptions of ontological complexity. The challenge of finding and employing language in relation to the evocative also extends to other aspects of language, such as the use of metaphors. It is important to note that this section has focused on English language use within the United States, and so the level of ambiguity in relation to language and AI may manifest differently in other language systems and cultures.

INTERVIEWING IN HMC – WAYS FORWARD

Knowledge differentials between researcher and participant, the ambiguity surrounding AI, and the evocative nature of these technologies all have implications for how people talk about "talking with machines." The degree to which these challenges present themselves in research will depend upon the project and the cultural context, but they all pertain to the different aspects of interviewing as method: the content and wording of the questionnaire; the structure of the interview; the negotiation of the conversation between researcher and participant; and the interpretation of the conversation in subsequent analysis. Finding a way forward involves (re-) engaging with the central components of qualitative research that can serve as a guide to productively navigating these challenges within the context of HMC. An extensive body of literature exists regarding approaches to qualitative research (e.g., Blandford et al., 2016; Christians & Carey, 1989; Denzin & Lincoln, 2018; Marshall & Rossman, 1995; Silverman, 2016), interviewing (boyd, 2015; Fontana & Frey, 2000; Holstein & Gubrium, 2016; Kvale & Brinkmann, 2009; Miller & Glassner, 2016), and analysis (e.g., Braun & Clarke, 2006; Saldaña, 2013), as well as standards and practices for ensuring the quality of research (e.g., Humphreys et al., 2021; Markham & Baym, 2009; Maxwell, 2013). Below I highlight some of the considerations and practices that are salient to interviewing as method within HMC.

Interrogating Theoretical and Ontological Assumptions

The interview is a site of collaborative meaning-making with researcher and participant inextricably involved in knowledge generation (Holstein & Gubrium, 2016; Kvale & Brinkmann, 2009; Miller & Glassner, 2016). Such an approach to interviewing is a rejoinder to positivist paradigms that attempt to situate the researcher as "neutral" with the goal of containing "bias." Consideration for how a researcher's actions shape the meaning-making process are indeed important, particularly given the challenges of talking about artificial intelligence identified in this chapter. At the same time, attempts to completely mitigate any influence the researcher may have on the exchange are illusory given the nature of interviewing (Holstein & Gubrium, 2016; Miller & Glassner, 2016) and communication more generally. HMC scholars, therefore, are better served by weighing the specific opportunities and limitations accompanying ways of talking about machines relative to the specific research project (see Markham & Baym, 2009 regarding tradeoffs in qualitative research).

Key to such consideration is the identification of the theoretical and ontological assumptions undergirding the research and how they extend to talking about machines. HMC scholars are more likely to be familiar with theoretical assumptions because the study of HMC itself poses a challenge to existing communication theory, bringing these assumptions to the fore. The ontological assumptions regarding the nature of humans and machines and the increasingly muddied space between these categories, however, are not always so apparent. To identify and interrogate their tacit and explicit assumptions about technology, humans, human–machine communication, and other relevant aspects of the research, scholars should engage in the process of reflexivity that is central to qualitative research (Blandford et al., 2016; Humphreys et al., 2021). Such reflexivity needs to push the researcher to consider "otherwise" and to challenge that which seems to be unquestioned or overlooked in both the thinking and talking about technology (see boyd, 2015). For example, scholars need to be more cognizant of their own ontological assumptions that inform how they use pronouns when referring to communicative technologies and how they interpret pronoun use by others.

Centering the Participant

Scholars bring to their research not only theoretical and ontological assumptions but also assumptions regarding participants' experiences with, knowledge of, communication about, and attitudes toward specific technology and the human–machine communication process. Regarding how people talk about copier machines and interactions with them, Orr (1996) documented that repair technicians attempted to "fix," or correct, how office workers talked about the machine to reflect terminology and the perspectives of the technicians. In doing so, the expert technicians placed a primacy on their knowledge, their way of knowing, and their articulation of such knowledge over that of, what they perceived to be, naïve users. Scholars possess an analogous type of expert status and a particular way of talking about machines based upon their research domain and the expectations of scholarly discourse, and, as a result, may unintentionally attempt to engage in a type of "fixing" of participants' discourse.

To avoid this potential pitfall, scholars will have to make a concerted effort to maintain focus foremost on the knowledge, experiences, and perspectives of participants that are, after all, at the center of qualitative research (Blandford et al., 2016; Marshall & Rossman, 1995). For example, in some instances, scholars may want to allow participants to articulate their own definition of highly ambiguous terms, such as "artificial intelligence" (see also Guzman, 2019a). At the same time, a tension may emerge among the goal of enabling participants to articulate their viewpoints, the overall aims of the research, and the pragmatic aspects of conducting research, such as time and funding. The aims of some projects may necessitate providing a definition to participants as a way of removing some of the ambiguity associated with communicative technologies. Here the goal would be to provide a foundation for the interview to proceed so that participants' articulations of other aspects of AI technologies can be examined in greater detail.

Centering the participant also is about being responsive to what individual participants and participants collectively are saying and how they are saying it throughout the research process. As boyd (2015) explains, the question she asks most often to offer the opportunity for participants to explain themselves is "why?" Seeking such explanations should not be a superficial endeavor. The "why" may need to be probed through a series of additional questions to move beyond a surface-level understanding. It also is not enough to seek such explanations within the context of a single interview. Scholars need to expand their lines of inquiry in response to the information being conveyed to them by participants (boyd, 2015; Charmaz & Mitchell, 2001). This adaptation takes place through the ongoing analysis of interviews throughout the research process, not merely at the end. What researchers ultimately should be aiming for is nuance. Given the newness of HMC technologies, their amorphous nature, and the ambiguity surrounding them, this ongoing process of analysis, reflection, and refinement offers scholars the opportunity to capture and probe perspectives that have been missing from the literature because they have been overlooked or not yet identified.

Accounting for the Machine

In discussing the methodological considerations of HMC research, Fortunati and Edwards (2020) ask, "But what happens when we would like to or need to investigate the second semi-interlocutor; that is, the media agent or social robot? Does it make sense to interview digital interlocutors?..." (p. 10). The idea of interviewing a machine may seem a bit far-fetched, but the question of how to gain insight into the communicative behavior of the machine is a pressing issue within HMC research. As discussed, the abstract and amorphous nature of communicative technologies and their personalized interaction make accounting for the machine methodologically fraught. Whether protocol can be developed, or even should be developed, for "interviewing" machines has yet to be fully explored. Meanwhile, scholars are developing other methods, such as auditing (Diakopoulos et al., this Handbook), to gain insight into the behavior of machines in interactions with humans that could be combined with existing methods, such as interviewing people, to better understand human experience with devices and applications.

Reflecting on the aim of accounting for the machine in qualitative research can also help scholars to address this hurdle. The goal of understanding the machine is contextualization, a key criterion of qualitative research (Christians & Carey, 1989). Scholars want to know how interactions with the machines unfold and other aspects of the technology as communicator, so as to inform their analysis of participants' experiences with and interpretations of communicating with technology. Contextualization would seem to require, at the very least, scholars to become familiar with the communicative behaviors of a technology through their own interactions with it and by probing participants' descriptions of the communicative process with the device or application. However, contextualization is not limited to the form and function of technology; it requires a much deeper examination of the historical, social, and cultural aspects of the subject of study (Christians & Carey, 1989; Markham & Baym, 2009) and, it should also be noted, the lives of the people engaging with the technology (see boyd, 2015). From this perspective, accounting for the machine moves beyond direct interactions with a technology to more broadly identifying what may inform people's own experiences with technology

and, thus, provide insight into how people understand these experiences, such as consideration for media portrayals of artificial intelligence, public opinion polls regarding AI and robots, or people's feelings toward technology more generally. In combining these other elements, which are more readily accessible to examination by scholars, with knowledge of the communicative function of the machine, accounting for the machine becomes a less daunting process and one that enables analysis that yields richer insight.

Guiding Future Research

This chapter is intended to be the beginning of a conversation regarding some of the key methodological considerations of talking about talking with machines. Ongoing identification and examination of such challenges is integral to continuing to progress HMC as an area of study. While scholarship that focuses in-depth on questions of method is needed, the reporting within individual studies also can be improved toward this end. Methodological vagueness within qualitative research is a documented problem (Markham & Baym, 2009), and scholars' approaches to the interpretation of the interview and methods of analysis often are not as clearly articulated as the functional elements of the interview itself (i.e. the modality, length, and recording of the interview). Transparency regarding approach and method are increasingly important for assessing the contributions of qualitative research, particularly as the academy moves toward open scholarship (Humphreys et al., 2021), but, beyond questions of quality, articulating methodological decisions also provides a guide for other scholars to follow in their own research as they navigate similar issues. Thus, the responsibility for advancing interviewing and qualitative research within HMC falls to all scholars.

REFERENCES

Al-Shaer, I. M. R. (2014). The use of third-person pronouns by native and non-native speakers of English. *The Linguistics Journal, 8*(1). www.ele-journals.com/linguistics-journal/linguistics-journal-volume-8-issue-1-2014/

Banks, J., & de Graaf, M. (2020). Toward an agent-agnostic transmission model: Synthesizing anthropocentric and technocentric paradigms in communication. *Human-Machine Communication, 1,* 19–36. https://doi.org/10.30658/hmc.1.2

Blandford, A., Furniss, D., & Makri, S. (2016). *Qualitative HCI research: Going behind the scenes* (Vol. 9). Morgan & Claypool.

Blumer, H. (1969). *Symbolic interactionism: Perspective and method*. Prentice-Hall.

Boden, M. (2016). *AI: Its nature and future*. Oxford University Press.

Bogost, I. (2017, March 4). "Artificial Intelligence" has become meaningless. *The Atlantic*. https://www.theatlantic.com/technology/archive/2017/03/what-is-artificial-intelligence/518547/

boyd, danah. (2015). Making sense of teen life: Strategies for capturing ethnographic data in a networked era. In E. Hargittai & C. Sandvig (Eds.), *Digital research confidential: The secrets of studying behavior online*. MIT Press.

Braun, V., & Clarke, V. (2006). Using thematic analysis in psychology. *Qualitative Research in Psychology*, *3*(2), 77–101. https://doi.org/10.1191/1478088706qp063oa

Charmaz, K., & Mitchell, R. G. (2001). Grounded theory in ethnography. In P. Atkinson, A. Coffey, S. Delamont, J. Lofland, & L. Lofland (Eds.), *Handbook of ethnography* (pp. 160–174). SAGE Publications.

Christians, C., & Carey, J. W. (1989). The logic and aims of qualitative research. In G. Stempel & B. H. Westley (Eds.), *Research methods in mass communication* (pp. 354–374). Prentice-Hall.

Comrie, B. (2005). Grammatical gender and personification. In D. D. Ravid & H. B.-Z. Shyldkrot (Eds.), *Perspectives on language and language development: Essays in honor of Ruth A. Berman* (pp. 103–114). Kluwer Academic Publishers.

de Graaf, M. M. A., Ben Allouch, S., & van Dijk, J. A. G. M. (2016). Long-term evaluation of a social robot in real homes. *Interaction Studies. Social Behaviour and Communication in Biological and Artificial Systems*, *17*(3), 461–490. https://doi.org/10.1075/is.17.3.08deg

Denzin, N. K., & Lincoln, Y. S. (Eds.). (2018). *The SAGE handbook of qualitative research* (5th ed.). SAGE Publications.

Edwards, A. P. (2018). Animals, humans, and machines: Interactive implications of ontological classification. In A. L. Guzman (Ed.), *Human-machine communication: Rethinking communication, technology, and ourselves* (Vol. 117, pp. 29–50). Peter Lang. https://doi.org/10.3726/b14399

Etzrodt, K., & Engesser, S. (2021). Voice-based agents as personified things: Assimilation and accommodation as equilibration of doubt. *Human-Machine Communication*, *2*, 57–79. https://doi.org/10.30658/hmc.2.3

Fontana, A., & Frey, J. H. (2000). The interview: From structured questions to negotiated text. In N. K. Denzin & Y. S. Lincoln (Eds.), *Handbook of qualitative research* (2nd ed., pp. 645–671). SAGE Publications.

Fortunati, L., & Edwards, A. (2020). Opening space for theoretical, methodological, and empirical issues in human-machine communication. *Human-Machine Communication*, *1*, 7–18. https://doi.org/10.30658/hmc.1.1

Gambino, A., Fox, J., & Ratan, R. (2020). Building a stronger CASA: Extending the computers are social actors paradigm. *Human-Machine Communication*, *1*, 71–86. https://doi.org/10.30658/hmc.1.5

Gunkel, D. J. (2012). Communication and artificial intelligence: Opportunities and challenges for the 21st century. *Communication +1*, *1*(1), 1. https://doi.org/10.7275/R5QJ7F7R

Guzman, A. L. (2015). *Imagining the voice in the machine: The ontology of digital social agents*. [Doctoral dissertation, University of Illinois at Chicago].

Guzman, A. L. (2018). What is human-machine communication, anyway? In A. L. Guzman (Ed.), *Human-machine communication: Rethinking communication, technology, and ourselves* (pp. 1–28). Peter Lang.

Guzman, A. L. (2019a). Beyond extraordinary: Theorizing artificial intelligence and the self in daily life. In Z. Papacharissi (Ed.), *A networked self: Human augmentics, artificial intelligence, sentience* (Vol. 5, pp. 83–96). Routledge.

Guzman, A. L. (2019b). Voices in and of the machine: Source orientation toward mobile virtual assistants. *Computers in Human Behavior*, *90*, 343–350. https://doi.org/10.1016/j.chb.2018.08.009

Guzman, A. L. (2020). Ontological boundaries between humans and computers and the implications for human-machine communication. *Human-Machine Communication*, *1*(1). https://stars.library.ucf.edu/hmc/

Guzman, A. L., & Lewis, S. C. (2020). Artificial intelligence and communication: A human–machine communication research agenda. *New Media & Society*, *22*(1), 70–86. https://doi.org/10.1177/1461444819858691

Headland, T. N., Pike, K. L., & Harris, M. (Eds.). (1990). *Emics and etics: The insider/outsider debate*. SAGE Publications.

Holstein, J. A., & Gubrium, J. F. (2016). Narrative practice and the active interview. In D. Silverman (Ed.), *Qualitative research* (4th ed., pp. 67–82). SAGE Publications.

Humphreys, L., Lewis, N. A., Sender, K., & Won, A. S. (2021). Integrating qualitative methods and open science: Five principles for more trustworthy research. *Journal of Communication*, *71* (855–874). https://doi.org/10.1093/joc/jqab026

Kahn, P. H., Reichert, A. L., Gary, H. E., Kanda, T., Ishiguro, H., Shen, S., Ruckert, J. H., & Gill, B. (2011). The new ontological category hypothesis in human-robot interaction. *Proceedings of the 6th International Conference on Human-Robot Interaction - HRI '11*, 159. https://doi.org/10.1145/1957656.1957710

Kvale, S., & Brinkmann, S. (2009). *InterViews: Learning the craft of qualitative research interviewing.* SAGE Publications.

Lee, H. R., Šabanovic, S., & Stolterman, E. (2014). *Stay on the boundary: Artifact analysis exploring researcher and user framing of robot design.* 1471–1474. https://doi.org/10.1145/2556288.2557395

Lynch, M., & Collins, H. M. (1998). Introduction: Humans, animals, and machines. *Science, Technology, & Human Values, 23*(4), 371–383. https://doi.org/10.1177/016224399802300401

Markham, A., & Baym, N. K. (Eds.). (2009). *Internet inquiry: Conversations about method.* SAGE Publications.

Marshall, C., & Rossman, G. B. (1995). *Designing qualitative research* (2nd ed.). SAGE Publications.

Maxwell, J. A. (2013). *Qualitative research design* (3rd ed.). SAGE Publications.

Miller, J., & Glassner, B. (2016). The "inside" and the "outside": Finding realities in interviews. In D. Silverman (Ed.), *Qualitative research* (4th ed., pp. 51–66). SAGE Publications.

Neff, G., & Nagy, P. (2016). Talking to bots: Symbiotic agency and the case of Tay. *International Journal of Communication, 10*, 4915–4931. https://ijoc.org/index.php/ijoc/article/view/6277

Ogden, C. K., & Richards, I. A. (1952). *The meaning of meaning* (10th ed.). Harcourt, Brace and Company.

Orr, J. E. (1996). *Talking about machines: An ethnography of a modern job.* ILR Press/Cornell University.

Payne, J., & Huddleston, R. (2002). Nouns and noun phrases. In R. Huddleston & G. Pullum (Eds.), *The Cambridge grammar of the English language.* Cambridge University Press.

Pradhan, A., Findlater, L., & Lazar, A. (2019). "Phantom friend" or "just a box with information": Personification and ontological categorization of smart speaker-based voice assistants by older adults. *Proceedings of the ACM on Human-Computer Interaction, 3*(CSCW), 1–21. https://doi.org/10.1145/3359316

Purington, A., Taft, J. G., Sannon, S., Bazarova, N. N., & Taylor, S. H. (2017). *"Alexa is my new BFF": Social roles, user satisfaction, and personification of the Amazon Echo.* 2853–2859. https://doi.org/10.1145/3027063.3053246

Quirk, R., Greenbaum, S., Leech, G., & Svartvik, J. (1985). *A comprehensive grammar of the English language.* Longman.

Saldaña, J. (2013). *The coding manual for qualitative researchers* (2nd ed.). SAGE Publications.

Siemund, P. (2013). *Varieties of English: A typological approach.* Cambridge University Press.

Silverman, D. (Ed.). (2016). *Qualitative research* (4th ed.). SAGE Publications.

Spence, P. R. (2019). Searching for questions, original thoughts, or advancing theory: Human-machine communication. *Computers in Human Behavior, 90*, 285–287. https://doi.org/10.1016/j.chb.2018.09.014

Suchman, L. (2011). Subject objects. *Feminist Theory, 12*(2), 119–145. https://doi.org/10.1177/1464700111404205

Sugiyama, S., & Vincent, J. (2013). Social robots and emotion: Transcending the boundary between humans and ICTs. *Intervalla, 1*(1), 1–6.

Sundar, S. S., Waddell, T. F., & Jung, E. H. (2016). The Hollywood Robot Syndrome media effects on older adults' attitudes toward robots and adoption intentions. *2016 11th ACM/IEEE International Conference on Human-Robot Interaction (HRI)*, 343–350. https://doi.org/10.1109/HRI.2016.7451771

Toomey, D. (2011). Imagining the omniscient computer. In D. L. Ferro & E. G. Swedin (Eds.), *Science fiction and computing Essays on interlinked domains* (pp. 289–300). McFarland & Company. http://site.ebrary.com/lib/alltitles/docDetail.action?docID=10501985

Turkle, S. (1984). *The second self.* Simon & Schuster.

Veling, L., & McGinn, C. (2021). Qualitative research in HRI: A review and taxonomy. *International Journal of Social Robotics, 13*(7), 1689–1709. https://doi.org/10.1007/s12369-020-00723-z

Zhao, S. (2006). Humanoid social robots as a medium of communication. *New Media & Society, 8*(3), 401–419. https://doi.org/10.1177/1461444806061951

28

Feminist, Postcolonial, and Crip Approaches to Human–Machine Communication Methodology

Paula Gardner and Jess Rauchberg

INTRODUCTION

While human–machine communication research exists across fields of Communication Studies as well as Science and Technology (STS) Studies, Disability Studies, Human–Computer Interaction and Digital Humanities, communication scholars often neglect to consult scholarship in other terrains. In this chapter, we explore key focuses of HMC research, noting historical problematics and overlooked areas in communication that can benefit from interdisciplinary research in feminist technology, postcolonial technology, and crip approaches. These methods offer diverse global scholarship, upset narrow framings of the subject and machine, and complicate cultural analyses, that can outfit HMC to engage more productively with emerging digital technologies and human machine problems inflected by diverse global dynamics.

To assess HMC methodological trends, we reviewed scholarship in the journals *Human Machine Communication (2020, 2021)*, the *Sage Encyclopedia of Communication Research Methods* (Allen, 2018) and relevant conference spaces (International Communication Association (ICA) and Association for Computing Machinery (ACM). The review discovered that HMC has tended to

employ positivist and post-positivist theories, quantitative research methodologies (e.g. experimental and survey research), and has minimally engaged qualitative research (e.g. naturalistic or critical approaches) and grounded theory or ideological analysis (Stoll & Edwards, 2017). The favored approach of Computers as Social Actors (CASA) exploring how "user" engage computers as human actors, saturates the field in human–human communication study, which is replicated in human and computer languages and behaviors research. Human–computer interaction (HCI) approaches as well often lack context, focusing on how interface design can be usable, and meet the preferences of an assumed universal or homogenous subject.

While recent HMC research has witnessed progress from human–human to human–computer interrogations, it continues to prioritize positivist, post-positivist, and quantitative research. Approaches tend to normalize the study of cues and patterns of (monolithic) human subjects interacting with computers, and often employ signaling and interpersonal theory, survey-based instruments, and quantitative measures (Spinda, 2017). To be clear, we offer these criticisms not to dismiss (post)positivist and quantitative HMC projects and the significant contributions they bring to HMC research. Rather, our point is that a lack of attention to social, regional, and cultural contexts can flatten the human research subject, failing to account for relevant micro and macro contexts that nuance and complicate human–computer analyses.

More recently, some HMC scholars have adopted approaches to research recognizing the value of theory as method, such as ontological and phenomenological approaches, and a few have engaged in feminist media analysis, and critical and mixed-methods studies. In this chapter, we review important feminist, postcolonial and crip methods that are able to complicate key HMC concepts such as agents, interactive, interlocuters, embodiment, intelligibility, and configurations. These innovative theoretical frameworks invite the production of new methods and alternative questions that, we propose, can open new and fruitful questions in HMC scholarship.

Methodological interventions from feminist, postcolonial, and crip approaches

Feminist and crip methods include ontological and epistemological inquiry and critical approaches ranging from narrative analysis and ethnography to critical user interaction and participatory approaches. Many arise from intersectional, Third World, and postcolonial feminist approaches that account for the diverse contexts that delimit and impact structures and social practices. In the following, we foreground feminist and crip theoretical frameworks, often employing postcolonial thrusts, from select scholars and discuss how they productively challenge and can help to expand and innovate HMC research.

Methods used in critical feminist technology studies tend to address macro and micro context and employ material analysis (e.g. of artifacts, data, technologies, and practices) in the form of close readings, case studies, narrative, content and discourse analysis, and critical data analysis. Methods used in media, network, and platform analysis often seek the input of audiences, users, and participants, via ethnography, media ethnography, auto-ethnography, audience research, interviews, focus groups, mixed methods, and social media analysis (Wiens et al., 2020). To understand the role of embodiment, practice-based methods such as digital storytelling, bodystorming, and auto-photography employ art and media-making; they do so to interrogate how bodily senses are triggered via media, machine and technology, often probing how aesthetic capabilities and practices impact subjectivity, perception, and

communication. Critical participatory and co-design methods employ collaborative exchange to discover the complex pressures that enable machinic automation or management and invite openings and hacks where humans can claim space and sovereignty in unique interactions. Derived from anti-bias, equity-seeking strategies, approaches across feminist tech and crip frameworks often share assumptions and objectives, and cross-pollinate to create new inter- and transdisciplinary methods.

METHODS FOR ANALYZING AGENTS, INTELLIGIBILITY, INTERACTIVITY, ACTORS, AND NETWORKS

The material posthumanist approaches of feminist technology studies are inspired by Haraway's (1987) theory of the cyborg, a humans–machine hybrid subject. The cyborg challenges ontological assumptions of origin stories suggesting humans are whole and unified and epistemologies that normalize gender binaries and human subjects as autonomous, homogenous, and knowable. The cyborg figure illustrates how humans and machines co-inform in digital networks that are not predictable or coherent but distributed. Subjects and knowledges are understood as situated, reflecting the conditions (e.g. social identity, location, cultural norms, etc.) in which they are produced; as Sandoval (2000) clarifies, objects of knowledge are both actor and agent, transforming self and situation while being acted upon. In turn, knowledge is not fact to be discovered, but is informed by epistemological, ontological, ethical, and political conditions.

Key contributors include Katherine Hayles (1999) who challenged masculinist cybernetic understandings of humans as disembodied information, using a novel method blending literary criticism and critical analysis to understand networks and subjectivity via popular metaphor.

Hayle's subsequent work (2006) shows how machine and human cognition inter-form, impacting humans (e.g. deep attention, distributed cognition) and networks across technoscientific, politics, and biological science, etc. Traditional understandings of interactivity are upset by Haraway's idea of mutually informed intelligibility (2006), where machines and people inter-inform meaning/knowledge as they change over time. Barad's (2007) quantum physics-informed concept of intra-action expands this idea, showing that humans, machines (and all stuff) coevolve in disparate, unpredictable ways, reflecting the layers of (changing) context that inform them. This "ethico-onto-epistemological" approach complicates Actor Network Theory (ANT) by interrogating the apparatus as situated in evolving and shifting relations informed by material and social realities. Braidotti (1994) innovated understandings of how embodied experiences inform the ways marginalized, multi-ethnic folks engage affect/desire via movement (nomadism) to manifest agency in dominating machine/network environments – an approach that challenges network analyses that situate subjects as powerless and dominated. Later, Braidotti (2013) provides a model for analyzing how human and machine intelligibility play out differently across tempo-spatial environments and subjects. Braidotti understands humans and machines as actors in complex networks, where meaning arises in embodied relations and addresses the key role played by affect in meaning-making. This post-human approach objects to individualistic cultural traits and seeks to make research/researchers accountable to network power dynamics. Useful to HMC scholars is the notion that networked environments are not only technical, but human, social, and biological, while diverse forms of embodiment are key factors in human computer relations, interactions, and agency, where subjects enact (often creative, transgressive) power practices.

Complimentary work by Jane Bennett (2010) complicates matters as vibrant with an ecological sensibility, expanding Latour's ANT approach with Deleuzian assemblage theory. Bennett seeks to understand how all things are connected, complicating traditional notions of relationality via a feminist analysis of how embodiment (desire, sensations) informs materiality. Her positive ontology approach probes the vibrancy of matter, challenges life/matter boundaries, and seeks to understand the political contributions of non-human matter, stretching "received concepts of agency, action, and freedom" (p. viii). This feminist, situated, embodied method augments ANT theory, enabling analysis of how machines and technologies impact intelligibility, agency, interaction, and innovation.

Feminist STS methods facilitate analysis of how technologies and cultures inter-inform. Suchman (2006) elaborated on Haraway, probing human–machine interactivity using a mixed methods approach. Addressing the question of why so many people could not operate Xerox photocopy machines, her ethnographic studies examined users through a conversation analysis lens; it revealed that designers falsely presumed that humans converse according to (disembodied) instructional logic and often disregard the rich array of human embodied interactional

competencies. Suchman's situated actions method recommends that designers understand users' behaviors, such as conversational and cultural norms, rather than assume humans should react and conform to (instructional/machinic) 'external' world norms (p. 283). The method blends human communication and design approaches to tackle interaction problems, upsetting HMC research approaches that centralize the machine and algorithmic logic. Turkle (2011b) combined ethnographic methods (e.g. long-form interviews), with reflexive data analysis to study how personal communication practices impact cultural practices with technologies. Her ethnographic studies of cell phone users found subjects' desired constant connection that dulled the rest/work gap, reflecting cultural expectations for expanding productivity, connection, and creativity (2011a). Turkle's model blends human-driven interaction theory with cultural analysis, demonstrating how macro and micro approaches enrich narrow HMC framings of interactivity. Here, Turkle's contributions demonstrate how feminist approaches to computing generate stronger analysis of socio-cultural impact. These approaches challenge deterministic HMC methods while complicating understandings of interactivity.

Housed in media studies, STS and digital humanities, feminist data studies often employ material approaches and critical data analysis to correct the common uncritical championing of computational logic in data studies. In a close critique of the thermodynamic science grounding information theory, Terranova (2004) derides computational attention to pattern seeking (and entropy), showing that, in fact, glitches are more informationally rich. Formative scholar Wendy Chun offers an innovative, semiotic analysis of programming, in *Programmed Visions* (2009), arguing that code is not a medium, but rather a source that is "executed" into language via instructions. Chun advises scholars to defetishize understandings of code as automated and agnostic and recognize it as relational – residing between event and location, present and representation. Such critical frameworks entice HMC scholars to correct assumptions that data and algorithms are automated, objective, or agnostic, with understandings of processing as unstable, contextualized, and contingent, to open new areas of inquiry.

Diverse feminist digital arts/humanities approaches can complicate HMC research with art approaches that nuance understanding of human interactions with media and technology. Anna Munster (2004) offers a unique approach using multimedia art case studies, detailing how digital information aesthetics factors such as proximity and embodiment impact virtuality, interactivity, and dematerialization. This model fuels analysis of how new media engages individuals in the speeds, rhythms, flows, and breakdowns of digital information, reflecting relevant socio-political power dynamics, while subsequent work (Munster, 2013) challenges uniform approaches that analyze all data as existing in active, relational, assemblage network environments. In combining aesthetic and material analysis, Munster's work demonstrates the innovation possible in HMC via material approaches to digital technologies that considers how technological aesthetics impact human subjectivity, behaviors, and interaction.

In sum, feminist technology frameworks and methods challenge positivist ontological assumptions and work to destabilize notions of subject, meaning-making, and interaction. These approaches reject conventional time/space frameworks, de-center the apparatus, dethrone computational logics, and probe human/machine interaction with attention to embodiment and revealing how local structures, situations, ideologies, and epistemologies inform interactions and subjects. The research offers diverse methods for querying how research devices and tools (e.g. machinic algorithms, interfaces, etc.) impact the research subject and interaction. HMC scholars can engage these approaches to unsettle origin stories, problematize subject/object binaries, understand actors in lateral networks, and to complicate the notion of agency for all system actors – animate and otherwise.

POSTCOLONIAL AND CRITICAL DIGITAL RACE STUDIES OF TECHNOLOGY

Feebly represented in HMC are critical race, Indigenous, and postcolonial methods that are crucial to revealing how racial, gender, class, and colonial values are inscribed in technologies and replicated in technological practices. The frameworks and methods target mechanisms by which racially biased platforms, databases, and algorithms embody visibility differently for diverse subjects (Buolamwini & Gebru, 2018). Employing close readings of games and critical race theory, Nakamura and Chow-White (2012) show that digital games encoded with racial bias demonize blackness and reifies racial bias in cultural practice. Intersectional approaches to critical race and algorithmic studies analyze how technologies classify and surveille blackness and reify cultural practices of bias.[1] Combining historical and critical analysis, Browne (2015) reveals algorithmic tracking as new form of spatial colonization that

brands Black people. Referencing personal experiences of Internet surfing, Safiya Noble's (2018) black feminist approach reveals that because search engines algorithms rank results according to relevance, they are encoded with racial bias; similarly, facial recognition tools, trained by databases of white subjects, fail to recognize Black subjects. As such, these technologies dehumanize Black subjects culturally and materially (e.g. in criminal databases) while also restraining Black people's use of such tools in gaming and social media technologies. Offering a novel, close reading of DNA lab science, Indigenous scholar Kim TallBear (2013), shows how material (blood) and semiotic (race or tribe) data is conflated via "markers" that segregate indigenous peoples in distinct genetic categories, with tragic consequences for land claims and sovereignty. The analysis shows that science and social systems mutually inform to denaturalize indigeneity. TallBear (2014) provides a method emphasizing a feminist and Indigenous science framework and an oral history method for data collection to correct colonial biases in science and technology research.

As well, TallBear and Sandoval also offer methods for transforming colonial practices within the academy. Tallbear's (2013) "promiscuous" standpoint approach, termed objectivity in action, urges scholars across terrains of scholarship to co-constitute more ethical claims and outcomes. Sandoval (2000) redeploys Haraway's oppositional consciousness in a multi-point methodology aiming to transform theory to social action and to confront academic colonialism that marginalizes intersectional research questions. HMC scholarship has much to learn from these critical race and ethnicity approaches, which correct biased ontological and epistemological approaches that have historically isolated, demonized, neglected, and undertheorized the relationship of race and ethnicity to technology research practices and development in science and technology, and the cultural practices informed by them.

Sophisticated postcolonial feminist media methods challenge communication scholars to check colonial assumptions embedded in technology and network research, with more focus on global south research and dynamics. These approaches denaturalize northern research that universalizes the concept of the networks, supporting analysis of how technologies and subjects arise relationally and in transnational dynamics (Shome & Hegde, 2002). These well-crafted methods correct research that essentializes subaltern subjects and offer macro and material approaches to complicate studies of global south media (Kumar & Parameswaran, 2018). Employing online ethnography and an epistemology of doing, Gajjala (2010) explores links between offline embodied and online spaces (Second Life), to show that digital diasporic cultures condition subjects to manifest "authentic" cultural positions, to enable their success in emergent transnational economies (p. 523). Hegde's (2011) diverse collection of feminist transnational media studies includes Parameswaran's (2011) ethnographic study on beauty, colonialism, and technology. Parameswaran (2011) shows how some Indian women rely on cosmetic whitening creams as technologies to reflect mainstream northern, Eurocentric stereotypes of beauty that reify racial and caste biases in India. Shome (2016) employs ethnography and close readings of media texts to historically analyze global media/technology flows and complicate the "subaltern" subject. Employing complex analytic lenses, mixed methods, and close readings, these models can aid HMC studies in nuanced studies of human machine communication in the global south and complicate understandings of transnational technology and media networks.

FEMINIST HCI AND HUMAN-CENTERED RESEARCH APPROACHES

Feminist HCI offers practice-based methods by designer/makers that innovate research in human–computer, robot, agent relations, interaction, and design. Participatory, ethnographic, and research creation approaches correct patriarchal research assumptions and habits, aim to be ethical (e.g. relatable, accessible and transparent (Chivukula & Gray, 2020; Stark & Crawford, 2019)) and to produce social change. The term Feminist HCI is credited to Bardzell (2010) who embedded principles of pluralism, participation, advocacy, ecology, and reflexivity in interaction design methods, inspiring successive new methods for creation and evaluation. Speculative and participatory modes position both humans and machines as actors (Bardzell, 2018; Choi & Light 2020), such as Forland's (2017) feminist ANT research interrogating embodied relationality among human and insulin pump actors. An innovative participatory approach by D'Agnazio et al. crowd-sourced mothers' ideas to redesign the breast pump with attention to post-partum needs and environmental factors. Transformative intersectional queer (Light, 2011) and Indigenous (Abedlenour-Nocera et al., 2013) methods engage the embodied experience of (diverse) subjects with AI and activity trackers. Finally, the manuscript *Feminist Data* by D'Ignazio and Klein (2020) compiles methods for feminist data science and visualization informed by direct experience, intersectional and situated approaches as correctives to masculinist and computationally informed big data research problematics.

Theories of feminist embodiment have been crucial to feminist interactive/participatory design methods, positioning diverse subjects as active research participants to ensure research reflects the needs of differently embodied subjects, as they shift over time/space. Resulting methods innovate practices of critique, re-purposing, and innovation in technology design. In leveling hierarchies of power with rigorous collaboration, enthusiastic consent and self-reflection, feminist participatory design methods rehabilitate dominating habits of traditional academic research with subjects including HMC. This attention to differently situated subjects and radical participatory practice is further examined in the following discussion of crip approaches.

CONSIDERING CRIP IN HMC RESEARCH

HMC methodology can attend to potentials for identity to render agency using innovative computing. McRuer's (2006) definition of crip theory contends that disability is always already queer, and queerness is always already disabled (p. 25). The intersection of queer/disability scholarship (or crip theory) is a growing subdiscipline of critical disability studies positioning disability as an agentic and shifting political-cultural identity (Forlano, 2017; Hamraie & Fritsch, 2019; Kafer, 2013). Intersectionality is central to crip theory – interactions with systemic racism, colonialism, classism, transphobia, homophobia shape ableism (Sins Invalid, 2019). HMC perspectives on disability, such as Dehnert and Leach's (2021) critique of ableism, provide an important entry point to new perspectives in HMC. Yet, these analyses are limited by their narrow positioning of ableism as singular oppression. We draw from these initial inquiries to call for crip and disability justice expansions that do not imagine ableism as separate from race, gender, or class.

Crip approaches to computing and technology are wary of technoableism or the belief that machines can cure, rehabilitate, or erase disability (Shew, 2020). Crip technoscientific thinking and tinkering challenge top-down assumptions from non-disabled technologists, caregivers, and healthcare providers. A disability justice approach prioritizes cross-movement solidarity in technoscientific creation (Hamraie & Fritsch, p. 16), positioning disabled people as experts and leaders using technology to imagine better worlds (p. 4). A crip technoscience approach embraced in HMC will seek to engage design practices that support the access needs of disabled users without assuming that all disabled people have universal access requests. Guzman (2018) notes that critical/cultural gaps in HMC research lead to an influx of projects and studies that fail to consider diverse communication styles. Recent studies turn toward crip and disability justice informed perspectives for designing communication technology for disabled stakeholders. HMC scholars can utilize these approaches to consider what it means to design and (re)imagine disability as a vital asset for communication methodology.

Notably, many HMC scholars focus instead on the "social aspect" (Alper, 2017, p. 2) of human–machine interaction to support communication and social engagement. These perspectives often support assimilationist practices, where technology cures or rehabilitates the user (Shew, 2020). We recommend HMC projects take on crip and disability justice approaches to facilitate better forms of user-centered design to break past oppressive political and social barriers (Hamraie & Fritsch, 2019). Crip HCI scholars apply this with iterative design conceptualizing disabled users as collaborators – not stakeholders or testers – who have important expertise and authority on their lived experiences as disabled people. These methods show how HMC researchers use information technology to bend toward disabled users. In this way, marginalized communities hold agentic space in the design and creation process instead of assimilating to a non-disabled world (Bennett & Rosner, 2019; Hamraie & Fritsch 2019, p. 16). Such shifts in conceptualizing power transform the human–machine relationship to more reciprocity and move beyond white supremacist and technoableist logics in HMC.

One way of invoking crip approaches to HMC methodologies is to emphasize collaborative, multisensory styles of research-creation. Here, (non-disabled) research teams can play to stakeholder strengths and use their resources to make user goals possible. For instance, Giraud et al.'s (2021) haptic, multisensory map involved six design stages with Blind and Visually Impaired collaborators to ensure that the collaborators' access needs and usability goals drove prototyping. In this way, disabled collaborators' diverse expertise is key to informing the design process, and the iterative stages allow research teams to truly engage with the relational flows between disabled collaborators and technology (see Bennett & Rosner, 2019; Giraud et al., 2021; Hamraie & Fritsch, 2019). Here, researchers meet disabled stakeholders and collaborators where they are, and use their resources to support their relational goals with technology.

Crip perspectives in human–machine interaction caution against techno-solutionism, presenting a "one-size-fits-all" approach to accessibility (Alper, 2017; Bennett & Rosner, 2019). Instead, crip approaches disrupt disability as a monolith and design for as many access needs as possible (Hamraie & Fritsch, p. 12). Collective access can also guide how devices are programmed: Gardner et al.'s (2021) ABLE therapeutic gaming platform trained IMU sensors to recognize possible types of movement, instead of forcing users to adapt to movements learned by the machine. Crip-informed iterative design positions disabled people as agentic collaborators – a method providing HMC with important strategies to transform the technosolutionism and technoableism prevalent in human–machine scholarship. Finally, the invocation of crip time transcends past non-disabled notions of time, embodiment, and technology. Crip time (Kafer, 2013) departs from able-bodied and neurotypical conceptualizations of time: bending the clock to meet people where they are (p. 26). Instead, crip time works alongside technology to become a source of interdependence for disabled users. Crip HCI considers interdependence transformative alternatives for assistive tech, establishing important nodes for HMC. We offer a crip and feminist HMC as a disruption to technoableist and oppressive positioning of human–machine relationality amplifying access as a collaborative, co-created embodied.

CONCLUSION: FEMINIST, POSTCOLONIAL, AND CRIP POTENTIALS FOR HMC RESEARCH

In reviewing current efforts to update HMC, we are encouraged by methodological interventions that depart from dominant trends and suggest new mixed and experimental methods. HMC scholarship is at its best when it recognizes foundational contributions and seriously considers emerging approaches that respond to long-standing ontological, epistemological, and ethical methodological problematics. We have offered a small portion of the critical feminist, postcolonial, and crip approaches that seek to enrich HMC methods and analysis. Uniquely, these methods analyze diverse forms of material data and attend to intersectional pressures, and structural and local practices of power, to better probe how technology entangles with and co-creates cultural, social, and political phenomena. These reflexive, interdisciplinary, and ethical frameworks aim to open up research questions and invite methodological experimentation.

The rich scholarship in this terrain implores us to look back at and scan laterally to recognize foundational and emerging approaches that, in turn, will ensure a future of HMC research. It is our hope the methods encourage greater collaboration among researchers, machines, technologists, participants, and other dynamic interlocutors, ignite methodological inventions across disciplinary boundaries, and inspire new lines of inquiry and approaches able to tackle twenty-first-century global problematics. Future feminist, post-colonial, and crip experimentation will innovate transdisciplinary methods while emerging fields, such as critical digital race studies, crip technoscience, and Southern theory approaches, will be crucial to generating sharper methodological interventions. As well, we anticipate that HMC will benefit from greater engagement with critical social media and digital feminist user methodologies, such as walkthrough methods, auto-theories, and live-networked coding to assess the social and cultural sense-making arising with user interactions with new media technologies. The spirit of curiosity, crosspollination, reflexivity, and experimentation that has fueled feminist, post-colonial, and crip approaches is the stuff that will continue to correct, enhance, and innovate methods in HMC.

NOTE

1   Our use of the word intersectional recognizes both Crenshaw's (1989) coining of the term and formative scholarship by third world feminists (Combahee River Collective, 1977; Lorde, 1984; Anzaldua 1987, etc.) describing how layered social identity factors generate exponential practices of bias.

REFERENCES

Abdelnour-Nocera, J., Clemmensen, T., & Kurosu, M. (2013). Reframing HCI through local and indigenous perspectives. *International Journal of Human-Computer Interaction*, 29(4), 201–204. DOI: 10.1080/10447318.2013.765759.

Allen, M. (Ed.) (2018). *The SAGE encyclopedia of communication research methods*. SAGE.

Alper, M. (2017). *Giving voice: Mobile communication, disability, and inequality*. MIT Press.

Anzaldúa, G. (1987) *Borderlands/La Frontera: The New Mestiza*. Aunt Lute Books.

Barad, K. (2007). *Meeting the universe halfway: Quantum physics and the entanglement of matter and meaning*. Duke University Press.

Bardzell, S. (2010). Feminist HCI: Taking stock and outlining an agenda for design. *CHI '10: Proceedings of the SIGCHI Conference on Human Factors in Computing Systems*, 13011310. DOI: 10.1145/1753326.1753521.

Bardzell, S. (2018). Utopias of participation: Feminism, design, and the futures. *ACM Transactions on Computer-Human Interaction*, 25(1), 1–24. DOI: 10.1145/3127359.

Bennett, C.L. & Rosner, D.K. (2019). The promise of empathy: Design, disability, and knowing the "other." *CHI '19: Proceedings of the 2019 CHI Conference on Human Factors in Computing Systems*, 1–13. DOI: 10.1145/3290605.3300528.

Bennett, J. (2010). *Vibrant matter: A political ecology of things*. Duke University Press.

Braidotti, R. (1994). *Nomadic subjects: Embodiment and sexual difference in contemporary feminist theory*. Columbia University Press.

Braidotti, R. (2013). *The posthuman*. Polity Press.

Browne, S. (2015). *Dark matters: On the surveillance of blackness*. Duke University Press.

Buolamwini, J. & Gebru, T. (2018). Gender shades: Intersectional accuracy disparities in commercial gender classification. *Proceedings of Machine Learning Research*, 81, 77–91.

Chivukula, S.S. & Gray, C.M. (2020). Bardzell's "Feminist HCI" legacy: Analyzing citational patterns. *CHI EA '20: Extended Abstracts of the 2020 CHI Conference on Human Factors in Computing Systems*, 1–8. DOI: 10.1145/3334480.3382936.

Choi, J.H. & Light, A. (2020). "The co –": Feminisms, power and research cultures – a dialogue. *Interactions*, 27(6), 26–28. DOI: 10.1145/3429697.

Chun, W.H.K. (2009). *Programmed visions: Software and memory*. MIT Press.

Combahee River Collective. (1977). The Combahee River Collective Statement. In J. Ritchie and K. Ronald (eds.), *Available means: An anthology of women's rhetoric(s)* (292–300), Pittsburgh: University of Pittsburgh Press.

Crenshaw, K. (1989). Demarginalizing the intersection of race and sex: A Black feminist critique of antidiscrimination doctrine, feminist theory and antiracist politics. *University of Chicago Legal Forum*, 1(8), 139–167.

Dehnert, M. & Leach, R.B. (2021). Becoming human? Ableism and control in *Detroit: Become Human* and the implications for human-machine communication. *Human-Machine Communication*, 2(1), 137–152. DOI: 10.30658/hmc.2.7.

D'Ignazio, C. & Klein, L.F. (2020). *Data feminism*. MIT Press.

Firestone, S. (1970). *The dialect of sex: The case for feminist revolution*. William Morrow.

Forlano, L. (2017). Data rituals in intimate infrastructures: Crip time and the disabled cyborg body as an epistemic site of science. *Catalyst: Feminism, Theory, Technoscience*, 3(2), 128. DOI: 10.28968/cftt.v3i2.28843.

Gajjala, R. (2010). Placing South Asian digital diasporas in *Second Life*. In T.K. Nakayama & R.T. Halualani (Eds.), *The handbook of critical intercultural communication* (pp. 517533). Wiley & Sons.

Gardner, P., Surlin, S., Akinyemi, A., Rauchberg, J.S., Zheng, R., McArthur, C., Papaioannu, A., & Hao, Y. (2021). Designing a dementia-informed, accessible, co-located gaming platform for diverse older adults with dementia, family, and carers. In Q. Gao & J. Zhou (Eds.), *Human aspects of IT for the aged population: Supporting everyday life activities* (pp. 58–77). Springer. DOI: 10.1007/978-3-030-78111-8_4.

Giraud, T., Di Loreto, I., & Tixier, M. (2021). The making of accessibility to rural place for blind people: The relational design of an interactive map. *DIS '20: Proceedings of the 2020 ACM Designing Interactive Systems Conference*, 1419–1431. DOI: 10.1145/3357236.3395527.

Guzman, A.L. (2018). What is human-machine communication, anyway? In A.L. Guzman (Ed.), *Human-machine communication: Rethinking communication, technology, and ourselves* (pp. 1–29), Peter Lang.

Hamraie, A. & Fritsch, K. (2019). Crip technoscience manifesto. *Catalyst: Feminism, Theory, Technoscience*, 5(1), 1–31. DOI: 10.28968/cftt.v5i1.29607.

Haraway, D. (1987). A manifesto for cyborgs: Science, technology, and socialist feminism in the 1980s. *Australian Cultural Studies*, 2(4), 1–42. DOI: 10.1080/08164649.1987.9961538.

Haraway, D.J. (2006). *When species meet*. University of Minnesota Press.

Hayles, N.K. (1999). *How we became posthuman: Virtual bodies in cybernetics, literature, and informatics*. University of Chicago Press.

Hayles, N.K. (2006). Unfinished work: From cyborg to cognisphere. *Theory, Culture & Society*, 23(7–8), 159–166. https://doi.org/10.1177/0263276406069229

Hegde, R.S. (2011). *Circuits of visibility: Gender and transnational media cultures*. NYU Press.

Kafer, A. (2013). *Feminist, queer, crip*. Indiana University Press.

Kumar, S. & Parameswaran, R. (2018). Charting an itinerary for postcolonial communication and media studies. *Journal of Communication*, 68(2), 347–358. DOI: 10.1093/joc/jqx025.

Light, A. (2011). HCI as heterodoxy: Technologies of identity and the queering of interaction with computers. *Interacting with Computers*, 23, 430–438. DOI:10.1016/j.intcom.2011.02.002.

McRuer, R. (2006). *Crip theory: Cultural signs of queerness and disability*. NYU Press.

Munster, A. (2004). Digitality: Approximate aesthetics. In A. Kroker & M. Kroker (Eds.), *Life in the wires: The CTheory reader* (pp. 407–421), University of Victoria Press.

Munster, A. (2013). *An aesthesia of networks: Conjunctive experience in art and technology*. MIT Press.

Nakamura, L. & Chow-White, P. (2012). *Race after the internet*. Routledge.

Noble, S.U. (2018). *Algorithms of oppression: How algorithms reinforce racism*. New York: NYU Press.

Parameswaran, R. (2011). E-race-ing color: Gender and transnational visual beauty economies of beauty in India. In R.S. Hegde (Ed.), *Circuits of visibility: Gender and transnational media cultures* (pp. 68–88), NYU Press.

Sandoval, C. (2000). *Methodology of the oppressed*. University of Minnesota Press.

Shew, A. (2020). Ableism, technoableism, and future AI. *IEEE Technology and Society Magazine*, 31(2), 40–85. https://ieeexplore.ieee.org/stamp/stamp.jsp?arnumber=9035527&casa_token=Wvztw0xAzNwAAAAA:TQcjFZQg4aQlUdYV64ZBsIKuqrSq72bKfShayJ2xlbpTKD2c7yvtTGY zAJxp59Dqo-b3LJY&tag=1.

Shome, R. (2016). When postcolonial studies meets media studies. *Critical Studies in Media Communication*, 33(3), 245–263. DOI: 10.1080/15295036.2016.1183801.

Shome, R. & Hegde, R.S. (2002). Postcolonial approaches to communication: Charting the terrain, engaging the intersections. *Communication Theory*, 12(3), 249–270. DOI: 10.1111/j.1468-2885.2002.tb00269.x.

Sins Invalid (2019). *Skin, tooth, and bone: The basis of movement is our people – a disability justice primer (2nd edition)*. Sins Invalid.

Spinda, J.W. (2017). Communication and technology. In M. Allen (Ed.), *The SAGE encyclopedia of communication research methods* (pp. 174–177), SAGE.

Stark, L. & Crawford, K. (2019). The work of art in the age of artificial intelligence: What artists can teach us about the ethics of data practice. *Surveillance & Society*, 17(3–4), 442–454. DOI: 10.24908/ss.v17i3/4.10821.

Stoll, B., & Edwards, C. (2017). Human–computer interaction. In M. Allen (Ed.), *The SAGE encyclopedia of communication research methods* (Vol. 2, pp. 672–674). SAGE.

Stark, L. & Crawford, K. (2019). The work of art in the age of artificial intelligence: What artists can teach us about the ethics of data practice. *Surveillance & Society*, 17(3–4), 442–454. DOI: 10.24908/ss.v17i3/4.10821.

Suchman, L. (2006). *Human-machine reconfigurations: Plans and situated actions*. Cambridge University Press.

TallBear, K. (2013). *Native American DNA: Tribal belonging and the false promise of genetic science.* Minneapolis: University of Minnesota Press.

TallBear, K. (2014). Standing with and speaking as faith: A feminist indigenous approach to inquiry [Research note]. *Journal of Research Practice,* 10(2), Article N17. Retrieved from http://jrp.icaap.org/index.php/jrp/article/view/405/371

Terranova, T. (2004). *Network culture: Politics for the information age.* Pluto Press.

Turkel, S. (2011a). *Alone together: why we expect more from technology and less from each other.* Basic Books.

Turkel, S. (2011b). *The inner history of devices.* MIT Press.

Wiens, B., Ruecker, S., Robbins-Smith, J., Radzikowska, M., & MacDonald, S. (2020). Materializing data: New research methods for feminist digital humanities. *Digital Studies/Le champ numérique,* 10(1), 1–22. DOI: 10.16995/dscn.373.

29

A Research Ethics for Human–Machine Communication: A First Sketch

Charles Ess

INTRODUCTION

What would a research ethics (RE) for Human–Machine Communication (HMC) look like? To respond to this question, I triangulate between several sources – starting with the internet research ethics guidelines as developed by the Association of Internet Researchers (Ess & the AoIR ethics working committee, 2002; Markham & Buchanan, 2012; franzke et al., 2020). The AoIR guidelines are especially apt, beginning with their important overlaps in disciplines and research *topoi*, along with several key elements of IRE that will prove to be likewise critical for an HMCRE. I then survey RE in social robotics and Human–Computer Interaction (HCI) as these have emerged over the past decade or so. As social robots are a central focus in HMC, the resources collected here make a direct contribution to an HMCRE. This survey highlights RE as grounded in standard Human Subjects Protections that generate important general considerations and recommendations, along with discussion of a few directly relevant examples of ethical difficulties – primarily those affiliated with research involving vulnerable populations such as the elderly, disabled persons, and children.

This first survey issues in a first synthesis of ethical considerations for an HMCRE: but as compared with the AoIR guidelines, these lack critical ethical grounding. I then turn to a second set of potential ethical resources for an HMCRE in recent RE work in robotics engineering, HCI and robot ethics. These resources show both the strengths and limitations of applying standard ethical frameworks – deontology, utilitarianism, and care ethics – and further point toward research ethics as situated, context-specific, and dialogical. While a strong beginning towards an HMCRE – as evaluated from the perspectives of the AoIR guidelines – some important elements and considerations are underdeveloped or missing altogether, including central questions of the moral status of robots and our ethical obligations toward them. I conclude with highlighting remaining elements of the AoIR guidelines that recommend themselves as still further expansions and enhancement to the HMCRE unfolding here.

INTERNET RESEARCH ETHICS AND HMCRE

The AoIR guidelines are especially apt beginnings for an HMCRE. To begin with, these draw from an extensive range of disciplines from the humanities, the social sciences broadly, media and communication studies in particular, and information and computing ethics. The guidelines thus directly intersect with the interdisciplinary richness of HMC as grounded especially in communication studies as well as affiliated fields such as social robotics, Human–Computer Interaction (HCI), AI, and so on (Guzman, 2018).

Moreover, the guidelines share with an HMCRE the need to develop an ethics that is well grounded in Human Subjects protections and further enhanced via primary ethical frameworks, such as deontology, utilitarianism, virtue ethics, and feminist ethics of care and (still) more global ethics traditions. Taking up these frameworks as part of our ethical toolkit has proven useful first of all as broadening and giving greater nuance to our ethical vocabulary and analytical taxonomies. This affords us not only greater flexibility and nuance when tackling specific RE challenges: it further grounds two critical elements at a second or *meta-ethical* level of critical reflection on these frameworks, their applicability, and so on. The first is the response these frameworks allow us to develop vis-à-vis the *global* perspectives demanded of research projects that all but inevitably involve partners from diverse countries and cultures. These cross-cultural contexts require us to develop ethical norms and procedures that are at once at least quasi-universal – i.e., acknowledged as normatively binding across cultures: at the same time, to avoid all-too-familiar problems of ethical ethnocentrism and a correlative imperialism (imposing what amount to local norms upon Others outside one's home culture). An *ethical pluralism* strikes the needed middle ground here: such a pluralism respects and takes on board local ethical norms, traditions, etc. as diverse interpretations or applications of more globally shared (quasi-) universal norms, values, etc. More carefully: initially recognizing the differences between *utilitarian* ethics (one emphasizing possible positive and negative consequences of our choices as a primary approach to making ethical judgments and decisions) and *deontological* ethics (emphasizing the fundamental rights of human beings as autonomies or free beings, starting with rights to privacy, as inviolable – i.e., not to be traded off in a utilitarian cost-benefit calculation) helps us build an ethical pluralism that begins with by analyzing differences in ethical traditions across diverse countries and cultures in these terms. As a start, the US and Anglophone countries incline toward more utilitarian approaches, while the EU and Scandinavia insist more robustly on deontological protections of basic rights. Using these and additional ethical frameworks drawn from across the globe further allows us to recognize how at least

some important ethical differences between these two domains – as a start, regarding *privacy* rights – are not necessarily exclusively different, so as to impose an either/or choice between one or the other as one right, the other wrong. Rather, we can recognize that both domains agree upon a shared norm of privacy – but rather interpret and apply this norm in different ways, as refracted through the lenses of local traditions, practices, etc. (franzke et al., 2020, p. 6). In other terms, this ethical pluralism stands as a middle ground between an *ethical dogmatism* (the insistence on imposing a given set of ethical norms homogeneously across all cultures – i.e., as a form of ethical imperialism and colonization) and *ethical relativism* (the abandonment of any notion of shared, quasi-universal norms for the sake of preserving local cultural differences: Christans, 2019; Ess, 2020a).

Second, this approach grounds a particular way of "doing" ethics. *Contra* assumptions that ethics is a matter of imposing rules and obligations somehow external to a process and the persons engaged therein, the AoIR guidelines restore the ancient understanding that mature human beings *are* ethical – experienced in and capable of developing sound ethical *judgments* and decisions when confronting new challenges.[1] As drawing both from philosophical ethics and the ethical experience and insight of research practitioners, ethics is "'a process approach,' one that aims to develop guidelines from the bottom up in a case-by-case based approach [....], focusing on the day-to-day practices of researchers in a wide range of disciplines, countries and contexts..." (franzke et al., 2020, p. 4). We further characterize this approach as reflexive and dialogical, one that incorporates "reflection on [one's] own research practices and associated risks and is continuously discussed against the accumulated experience and ethical reflections of researchers in the field and existing studies carried out" (*ibid.*). In still other terms, this is a *situated* ethics, one emphasizing "the fine-grained contexts and distinctive details of each specific ethical challenge" (*ibid.*).

With this initial background, we can now turn to a first survey of emerging RE in fields directly relevant to HMC – namely social robotics and HCI.

RESEARCH ETHICS IN SOCIAL ROBOTICS AND HCI

Brugo Veruggio and Fiorella Operto (2008) noted that South Korean *World Robot Declaration* in 2004 emphasized the importance of ethics for robots. Their summary of various professional codes of ethics within primarily the engineering and related disciplines foreground two guiding principles, *"non-malfeasance* and *beneficence*, indicating a systematic regard for the rights and interests of others in the full range of academic relationships and activities" (2008, p. 1506). They define *non-malfeasance* as "the principle of doing, or permitting, no official misconduct. It is the principle of doing no harm in the widest sense" (*ibid.*). In turn, *"Beneficence* is the requirement to serve the interests and well being of others, including respect for their rights" (*ibid.*).

Veruggio and Operto acknowledge the disciplinary and global diversity of possible codes of ethics that might be invoked: leaving the choice of a particular code of ethics up to a given researcher or project, however, they offer only very brief "Conditions of Implementation," including "Periodic review of the application procedures," "Review and assistance by ethics committees," "Promotion of public debate," "Definition of risk assessment, management and prevention," and "Transnational practices: comparison of conducts across countries and comparisons of professional ethics around the world" (2008, p. 1507).

More recently, the European Union has established "Civil Law Rules on Robotics" that offers an outline of what a research ethics committee (REC) for robots would look like. To begin with it should be marked by four explicit principles: independence, competence, transparency, and accountability (European Parliament, 2017, p. 21). The outline is helpful, but as with Veruggio and Operto (2008), only very general guidelines for the role and constitution of such an REC emerge here (21f.)

Perhaps not surprisingly, by 2018, in its massive survey of ethics and research ethics within the EU, the SIENNA project (*Stakeholder-informed ethics for new technologies with high socio-economic and human rights impact*) could identify only a handful of documents that offered explicit guidance for "how to write research ethics protocols for researchers doing research in AI&R[obitics]" (Tambornino & Lanzerath, 2018, p. 35). The most important of these is from the Alliance des sciences et technologies du numérique (Allistine: Cerna Collectif, 2014), a consortium of French research institutes. The report is important here for calling attention to two central elements of HMCRE. The first of these is precisely with regards to *communication* and *anthropomorphism*:

[IVI-6] Communication. Le chercheur doit être prudent dans sa communication sur les capacités émotionnelles des robots et sur l'imitation de la nature et du vivant, notamment parce que l'expression des émotions, au sens humain, par un robot, est un leurre, et parce que l'imitation du vivant peut amener, volontairement ou pas, à prêter à l'artefact des caractéristiques du vivant.

[The researcher must be careful in his communication regarding the emotional capacities of robots and the imitation of nature and living things, in particular because the expression of emotions, in the human sense, by a robot, is a decoy, and because imitation of the living can lead, voluntarily or not, to assigning to the artefact characteristics of the living.] (38)

We will see below in a more fully developed approach to RE in conjunction with social robots, that these aspects of HMC lead to specific ethical concerns with *attachment* and the loss thereof (Battistuzzi et al., 2020, p. 4).

The Allistine document further calls particular attention to *child–robot interactions*:

[IVI-4] Interaction enfant-robot. Pour les projets qui mettent en présence des enfants et des robots, le chercheur doit se poser la question de l'impact de l'interaction enfant-robot sur le développement des capacités émotionnelles de l'enfant, tout particulièrement dans la petite enfance.

[For projects involving children and robots, the researcher must raise the question of the impact of the child-robot interaction on the development of the emotional capacities of the child, especially in early childhood.] (37)

Again, we will see that this sort of attention to vulnerable populations – first of all, children and the elderly – will be further expanded upon (Sedenberg et al., 2016): but neither the Allistene report nor the SIENNA project focus more narrowly on HMC *per se*.

Additional contributions to an emerging HMCRE can be gathered from recent work on research ethics, starting with therapeutic robots. Perhaps most helpfully, Elaine Sedenberg and her colleagues have argued for a conjunction of (US-based) research ethics and privacy ethics that offers

The ability to respect and preserve the autonomy of individuals, balance risks and benefits, and aim for equally serving (and not unjustly burdening a group of people) provides a framework for creating ethical research practices that may apply to the research and development of therapeutic robotics technology. (2016, p. 583)

They do not say so, but in ethical terms, Sedenberg et al. aim to conjoin a deontological emphasis on autonomy and equal rights with a utilitarian risk-benefit analysis. This reflects their building on what they characterize as the "canonical ethical frameworks from the Belmont and Menlo reports" (2016, p. 582).

The Belmont Report (National Commission, 1979) entails three ethical principles:

- Respect for persons (individuals should be treated as autonomous agents)
- Beneficence (obligation to maximize benefits and minimize harm)
- Justice [distribute benefits of research fairly and careful selection of research subjects (e.g., avoid only selecting from underserved groups which places undue burden on part of the population)] (*ibid.*)

These principles are operationalized first of all in terms of requirements for informed consent. The Menlo report (Dittrich et al., 2011), focusing on research ethics for ICTs, builds on Belmont and adds "Respect for Law and Public Interest": "This principle promotes transparency and encourages designer accountability for interventions, which is appropriate within the robotics context" (2016, pp. 282f.).

Sedenberg et al. focus especially on the application of these values and principles to therapeutic robots and the "Special ethical considerations for vulnerable persons" – including children, disabled, and the elderly – entailed by their use (2016, p. 583). They demonstrate how conjoining these research ethics frameworks with privacy ethics then issues in six "design and implementation recommendations" aimed at protecting vulnerable users while fostering beneficial research:

1 Data Access and Review (2016, p. 583f.)
2 Presentation of Privacy Policies and User Consent (2016, p. 584)
3 General Privacy Controls (2016, p. 584f.)
4 Awareness of Existing Laws and Potential Data Use (2016, p. 585)
5 Design for Responsible Data Sharing (*ibid.*)
6 Anticipate New Knowledge and Unintended Consequences (*ibid.*)

These recommendations and their foundations in (US-based) research ethics clearly add to the more general outlines provided by Veruggio and Operto (2008) and the European Parliament (2017) – in particular, as they flesh out the Alistene (2014) point on the special ethical status of and care due to children as a vulnerable population. At the same time, however, we can notice that the list is relatively narrow. Items 1, 4, and 5 focus on the

ethics of data; items 2 and 3 focus on *privacy* and *informed consent*; item 6, finally, calls for attending to future possibilities.

A more comprehensive list of recommendations is developed by Linda Battistuzzi et al.'s documentation of their case-based learning approach in developing a research ethics training module for researchers (2020): they are concerned with both *how* research ethics might be grounded and then taught and applied in conjunction with older adults and "socially assistive robots" (SARs). They summarize previous research into the ethical dimensions of research on eldercare robotic devices as focusing on "concerns relating to a loss of human contact, diminished autonomy and privacy, loss of dignity and to negative impacts on professional caregiving and standards of care" (2020, p. 3). Drawing broadly on Human Subjects Protections as articulated in the Declaration of Helsinki (World Medical Association, 2013) vis-à-vis more recent research on specific ethical risks in research on robotics in eldercare, Battistuzzi et al. highlight nine major points requiring ethical sensitivity and responsiveness. These start with basic (1) physical safety, and then (2) attachment (2020, p. 4). As is central to many of the devices developed for eldercare, their capacity to mimic "humanlike appearance, qualities or behaviors," while crucial for evoking desired benefits, at the same time can lead to a psychological attachment that would in turn result in "disappointment if they have to share it with others" – and/or if participants lose access to the device at the end of a research project. "Accordingly, protocols must be specified in advance to address any consequent needs on the part of participants" (*ibid.*).

(3) Privacy is manifestly open to risk and violation in any number of ways in this sort of research. Battistuzzi et al. suggest that participants should be able to control the degree to which a SAR can be in their proximity without violating their sense of privacy; (informed) consent is further required from participants, along with guidelines for researchers on "how to respect participant privacy" whether or not they have expressly requested it (*ibid.*).

(4) "Data Management and Protection" addresses again the requirement for informed consent for how personal data, including recordings of research sessions, etc. will be processed (*ibid.*) – and, presumably, protected (e.g., according to the GDPR (2018) in Europe). Because SARs "can be used to carry out certain tasks on participants' behalf or to provide support that enables them to complete the task on their own" directly impacts (5) participant autonomy and proportionality (*ibid.*). In particular, "Providing more assistance

than is actually required may result in the premature loss of capacities in older adults, generating dependency on the SAR" (*ibid.*). While the authors do not say so explicitly, protecting participants' autonomy is a foundational pillar in Human Subject Protections and so needs to be stressed especially. By the same token, respecting their autonomy as human beings immediately entails respecting the *dignity* of research participants. So, Battistuzzi et al. point out several ways in which SARs may threaten (6) dignity in ethically problematic ways, starting with reminding them of the loss of human contact no longer available to them; in addition, difficulties with engaging with and using such devices "could lead to self-blame and lowered self-efficacy" (*ibid.*). *Consent* becomes critical here again as "It must be clear to participants that they can withdraw from the study at any time if they so wish" (*ibid.*).

Given the multiple psychological challenges experienced by many older people, including "anxiety, depression, embarrassment, or acute stress reactions due to utilization of the SAR," the possibilities of (7) Psychological harm are extensive. Battistuzzi et al. recommend that "Researchers must therefore be prepared to identify and minimize these risks and ensure that the benefits of the study outweigh them" as well as be prepared to minimize these risks – if need be, by withdrawing a participant from the study (4f.).

(8) "Managing Unexpected Health-Related Findings" points to the multiple ways in which engaging with a SAR might uncover health-related matters that otherwise would remain hidden. This requires the development of protocols that ensure that researchers "can balance their obligation to protect confidential health-related information about participants, with their ancillary obligation to protect participants' welfare" (2020, p. 5). This again begins with the informed consent stage of the project, as researchers must raise these possibilities with potential participants and ask participants for permission to discuss anything of potential health importance that they should observe during the experiments (e.g., a pronounced tremor, a peculiar gait, a significant change in behavior) with the participants' carers or other care home staff, as appropriate (*ibid.*).

Lastly, Battistuzzi et al. take up (9) Stigma and Self-stigma, starting with a definition of stigma as "a social process whereby an older adult experiences exclusion or rejection owing to negative social judgement associated with a feature related to a health problem or a health condition" (2020, p. 5). Stigma and self-stigma may follow as "relying on a robot for assistance, entertainment, and, to some extent, companionship, may result in negative judgements about research participants

by other care home residents, for instance, or by research participants about themselves, or by their family members" (2020, p. 5). These possibilities reinforce the importance of "ensuring confidentiality, and treating their [participants'] experiences and contributions equally and with full respect" (*ibid.*). Again, while Battistuzzi et al. do not make the connection explicit, ensuring confidentiality is another primary pillar in Human Subjects Protections – one that follows from the primary (deontological) emphasis on human beings as autonomies.

A FIRST SUMMARY

Synthesizing Sedenberg et al. and Battistuzzi et al. as follows offers a first outline of what an HMCRE would include. As broadly based on Human Subject Protections, our research ethics will foreground attention to:

1) physical safety
2) attachment
3) privacy (overlapping with Sedenberg et al., items 2, 3)
4) data management and protection (overlapping with Sedenberg et al., items 1, 4, 5)
5) participant autonomy and proportionality
6) dignity threats and protection
7) possibilities of psychological harm (including informed consent and withdrawal)
8) managing unexpected health- related findings (partly overlapping with Sedenberg et al., item 6)
9) stigma and self-stigma

SOME MISSING PIECES

This first synthesis gives us a reasonably strong set of guidelines, topics, and resources; but, as is common with many such guidelines (franzke, 2022), these resources give us no deeper ethical – much less meta-ethical – grounding or guidelines for research ethics. As a start, there is no explicit discussion of more particular ethical frameworks such as deontology, utilitarianism, virtue ethics, care ethics, and so on. Such a discussion is crucial, as we saw at the outset, first of all for the sake of clarifying our ethical grounds. Again, the basic emphasis on human autonomy and thereby respect and dignity is a *deontological* ethic that entails basic rights, including rights to privacy, informed consent, and so on (see franzke et al., 2020, p. 5). By contrast, the proper emphasis on anticipating future consequences (Sedenberg et al., item 6) is a *utilitarian* ethic – one that is further in play in general requirements to minimize risks and balance risks to participants against potential benefits from research (franzke et al., 2020, p. 5). We have seen how taking up these frameworks is further essential at a *meta-ethical* level, first of all as they help ground an ethical pluralism that conjoins globally shared norms, principles, and so on with local traditions and approaches. These frameworks further ground a distinctive approach to research ethics as process-oriented, dialogical, and reflexive.

In this next section, I will review three accounts of research ethics in HCI and robotics engineering that make contributions in these directions – but ultimately leave us with still more work to do if we are to establish a more comprehensive and well-grounded HMCRE.

ETHICS AND META-ETHICS IN HCI AND ROBOTICS ENGINEERING

To begin with, Dorothy Howard and Lilly Irani (2019) take up a specific ethical framework for their ethnography and recommendations regarding research ethics in HCI – namely, an ethics of care as part of "feminist STS approaches to ethics as a system of agential relationships that cannot be assigned to 'unitary subjects' such as administrative checkpoints like the IRB, codes of conduct, or individual choices" (p. 11). This more relational understanding (my term) in turn

> requires a notion of ethics not as a set of pre-given principles, but as a negotiation in which subjects and researchers work out an ethical, accountable practice or project together. [....] As HCI researchers converge to refine the IRB process to better manage ethics and accountability in research on emerging technologies, feminist STS can also support wider conversations about ethics as constantly negotiated agreements distributed among communities of practice who create shared understandings in specific, power-laden contexts. (*ibid.*)

Howard and Irani's further incorporation of postcolonial and decolonial perspectives (2019, p. 2) further issues in the observation that "Ethics – and who bears ethical responsibilities – is culturally and geographically situated, and these ethical meanings are not universals, but situated in place"

(2019, p. 11f.) As they elaborate, "Different cultural formations might formulate ethics as democratic rights in liberal projects, freedoms of identity and expression as in some feminist thought, or be extended to the non-human in ecological and environmental philosophy as in Latin American decolonial thought" (2019, p. 12).

While crucially true, this last claim also needs comment and critique. On the one hand, Howard and Irani's application of care ethics and what philosophers have articulated as distributed responsibility (Ess, 2018, pp. 240ff.) reinforces the AoIR approach to research ethics as, again, a situated, dialogical process to be carried on throughout the research project. On the other hand, as we saw at the outset, their assumption of a kind of either/or between ethical universal on the one hand, and local ethical norms, traditions, etc., while common, is importantly mistaken. Again, within the AoIR context (as well as beyond), an ethical pluralism overcomes this either/or to conjoin (quasi-) universal values and norms with local traditions and approaches – first of all, local approaches and traditions can be understood to represent specific interpretations or applications of more widely shared norms, values, etc.

Unfortunately, a second and otherwise very valuable ethnographic approach to ethics among robotics engineers falls into a similarly unnecessary and limiting either/or. Jessica Sorenson's highly laudable aim – directly recognizable from the AoIR approach – is "to bring diverse groups into dialogue, to blend disciplinary understandings, and to spark ethical reflection and the integration of human values into everyday design activities – thus bringing about more ethical realities" (2019, p. 207). She does so in part by arguing that at the turn of the millennium, there has been a "push away from normative rule-based deontological and consequential ethics" – in part, "as empirical research has shown that engineers do not modify their decision-making processes when instructed to adhere to a particular code of ethics" (2019, p. 209). Sorenson further acknowledges more recent turns towards virtue ethics, but cites examples of virtue ethics failing to "produce 'good engineers' or 'moral experts'" (*ibid.*). Moreover, she comments that "virtue ethics relies too heavily on individual ethical thinking, and not enough on the social praxis that is engineering" (*ibid.*). Rather than embracing virtue ethics, she argues for "a move away from deontology" toward what she calls "a more pragmatic ethics." This ethics is one that that bubbles up (my phrase) from what she identifies as "functional values" such as flexibility, agility, efficiency already in play in engineering practices, specifically in value-sensitive design (2019, p. 215).

Sorensen's ethnographic exploration of what practicing engineers say about ethics in their work is very helpful, but her larger analysis is flawed in important ways. To begin with, her criticism of virtue ethics as a more individual form of ethical thinking is simply mistaken. Prominent contemporary philosophers rather emphasize precisely *relational* conceptions of human beings as undergirding their applications of virtue ethics, such as Shannon Vallor (2016) and, more specifically in the domain of robot ethics, David Gunkel (2018), and Mark Coeckelbergh (2020). In particular, relational forms of virtue ethics are critical to *phron⁻esis* as both reflective judgment and practical wisdom that requires dialogues unfolding shared experiences, insights, and so on (Ess, 2020a, p. 261). Second, the AoIR approach to research ethics shows (again) that the presumed either/or here – between, say, deontology, utilitarianism, virtue ethics, etc., on the one hand, vs. a situated, dialogical approach to ethics on the other hand – is a false dichotomy. In particular, foregrounding the central role of *phron⁻esis* from virtue ethics is essential to the sort of dialogical approach Sorenson endorses.

Beyond the AoIR example, the same point has been made by Bernd Carsten Stahl and Mark Coeckelbergh (2016) in their analyses of the "ethics of healthcare robotics" vis-à-vis projects funded by the European Commission (EC) and the notion of "responsible research and innovation" as prompted by the EC's Horizon 2020 research funding program. First of all, Stahl and Coeckelbergh endorse

> various normative and theoretical approaches to ethics of healthcare robotics, ranging from Kantian ethics and utilitarianism to phenomenology, critical theory, and ethics of care. Each of these approaches has helped to highlight different but often converging moral sensitivities in this area, and sometimes they have also contributed to a better understanding of current healthcare practices …. (2016, p. 154)

At the same time, they recommend an approach to research ethics in robotic healthcare settings that they call "embedded ethics":

> The idea is here to collaborate with developers of the technology rather than to write about what they do and what they should do. Ideally, such collaboration takes the form of an ongoing dialogue about ethics during the research project — with all researchers involved in it. This method recognises that evaluating the ethical and social consequences of technology is not a marginal and additional task which can be outsourced to

philosophers and social scientists, but is essential to the quality of the project and is a collaborative task in which engineers and scientists play a key role. (2016, p. 155).

Stahl and Coeckelbergh discuss two projects that instantiate this approach (*ibid.*). Moreover, this approach manifestly resonates with the emphases in the AoIR guidelines on research ethics as a dialogical process involving philosophers as well as research practitioners (among others) – one, moreover, that is to be carried on throughout the research project (franzke et al., 2020, p. 4). In contrast with the either/or suggested by Sorenson (2019) – Stahl and Coeckelbergh echo the AoIR guidelines as they point instead to a both/and approach, one that conjoins standard ethical frameworks with ongoing evocation of both researchers as well as participants' ethical sensibilities and judgments throughout the research project.

WHERE DO WE GO FROM HERE?

Expanding on these elements via the AoIR guidelines would add several further dimensions. The first is an emphasis on research ethics as a dialogical process that does not stop after approval by an ethics review board, but rather continues throughout the "stages of research" (franzke et al., 2020, p. 9). Second, while *informed consent* is addressed as a basic requirement in the Humans Subject Protections frameworks invoked above, along with the importance of attending to various aspects of *data protection* – these issues have become notoriously more complex in the era of Big Data and AI, especially vis-à-vis the recently inaugurated GDPR (2018) as default. This introduces particular wrinkles for privacy protection in international research projects across diverse cultures and legal domains, as are explored more fully by franzke et al. (2020, pp. 10, 19f.).

Third, a central insight in internet research ethics was articulated early on by Annette Markham, "method as ethic, ethic as method" (2006). The point here is that different research methods entail different research ethics: "our choice of methods vis-à-vis given research questions and design evoke specific ethical issues – but these in turn (should) shape our methodological choices" (franzke et al., 2020, p. 4).

Undergirding all of this are our foundational assumptions regarding *who we are* as human beings, both as fundamentally *ethical beings* and whether our cultural backgrounds stress more *individual* vis-à-vis more *relational* conceptions of selfhood (*ibid.*, n. 3, pp. 4, 6). Both of these dimensions deeply shape our larger ethical frameworks, especially from cross-cultural perspectives: we have seen specifically that relational forms of virtue ethics undergird our primary approach to ethics as a reflexive and dialogical process to be undertaken throughout a research project.

Finally, the "General Structure for Ethical Analysis" identifies a number of critical steps for approaching the research ethics of a given project. This begins with attending to related guidelines and relevant legal aspects (franzke et al., 2020, pp. 12–15) – and then to the relevant cultural dimensions (*ibid.*, pp. 15–17). The focus on "involved subjects" builds on standard Human Subjects Protections concerns to avoid harm by asking more carefully "who are the subjects?" – and adding the general ethical principle that "the greater the vulnerability of our subjects, the greater our responsibility and obligation to protect them from likely harms" (*ibid.*, p. 17). This section clearly overlaps and reinforces the attention to the elderly, disabled, and children, including "special emotional states" (*ibid.*) that we have seen in the approaches examined here – but extends the list considerably in ways that may be relevant to HMCRE, starting with encountering "subjects [who] may be engaged in behaviour threatening to their own wellbeing" (*ibid.*).

This section further points out a central issue all but ignored in the above – namely, the moral status of and thereby our ethical obligations towards robots and AI devices. Briefly, as these devices achieve at least some version of autonomy, they thereby will invoke ethical considerations in turn, starting with at least some level of requirements for respect and avoiding harm (*ibid.*, pp. 17f.). Questions clustering about the moral status of robots are both central to robot ethics and implicate larger questions of our relationality with and thereby ethical obligations towards "more than human" domains of our technologies as well as larger social, natural, and (for some) "supernatural" orders (e.g., Puig de la Bellacasa, 2017). We have also seen that these relational turns foreground care ethics (e.g., Tronto, 1993) as thereby another important component in our (research) ethics. These turns can generate both novel issues and responses in HMCRE, e.g., can we ask human subjects to torture a robot or an avatar? Briefly, the more we emphasize relationality, the moral status of "the more than human," along with virtue ethics and care ethics, the answer would likely be "no" (Gonzalez-Franco et al., 2018; Coeckelbergh, 2020).

At the same time, the issues raised above concerning, e.g., *attachment* (Battistuzzi et al., 2020, p. 4) are taken up here as well, starting with the now well-documented phenomenon of human beings attributing feelings to and thereby obligations to care for robotic devices, beginning with the very simple Tamagotchi (*ibid.*, p. 18). Whether or not such devices ever experience genuine emotions and sensations – especially in the contexts of eldercare, treatment of autism, and so on – they are designed precisely to evoke various emotional responses on our part: and researchers must take on board, for example, that asking research participants to somehow harm such a device, whether physically or emotionally, in turn risks emotional and psychological harm to the participant (*ibid.*).

POSTSCRIPT

The AoIR guidelines represent some 20 years' work, with contributions from hundreds of researchers, philosophers, and others from almost every discipline in the Academy and beyond. The above is manifestly a very long way away from such a mature and fully developed document. But as triangulating between the AoIR guidelines and relevant RE literatures, I hope it is at least a first sketch in the right direction.

NOTE

1 This approach, moreover, turns centrally on fostering our capacities for *phronēsis*, a form of reflective judgment exercised in our efforts to discern what norms, values, and so on indeed apply within a specific context (franzke et al., 2020, p. 23). *Phronēsis* is further a central capacity or *virtue* in virtue ethics more broadly (Ess, 2020a, pp. 260f.) These points add to the *meta-ethical* argument here in support of a processual, dialogical, and reflexive approach to research ethics: to make this argument, that is, requires us to take on board a broad array of *ethical* frameworks – in this case, virtue ethics.

REFERENCES

Battistuzzi, L., Papadopoulos, C., Tetiana Hill, T., Castro, N., Bruno, B., & Sgorbissa, A. (2020). Socially assistive robots, older adults and research ethics: The case for case-based ethics training. *International Journal of Social Robotics, 8*, 575–587. https://doi.org/10.1007/s12369-020-00652-x

Cerna Collectif. Éthique de la recherche en robotique: Rapport n° 1 de la CERNA Commission de réflexion sur l'Éthique de la Recherche en sciences et technologies du Numérique d'Allistene. [Rapport de recherche] CERNA; ALLISTENE. 2014. https://hal.inria.fr/hal-01086579/document

Christians, C. G. (2019). *Media ethics and global justice in the digital age*. Cambridge University Press.

Coeckelbergh, M. (2021). How to use virtue ethics for thinking about the moral standing of social robots: A relational interpretation in terms of practices, habits, and performance. *International Journal of Social Robotics*, *13*, 31–40. https://doi.org/10.1007/s12369-020-00707-z. Online publication 23 October 2020.

Dittrich, D., Kenneally, E., et al (2011). The Menlo Report: Ethical principles guiding information and communication technology research. US Department of Homeland Security

Ess, C. (2018). Ethics in HMC: Recent developments and case studies. In A. Guzman (Ed.), *Human-machine communication: Rethinking communication, technology, and ourselves*, pp. 237–257. Peter Lang.

Ess, C. (2020a). *Digital media ethics*, 3rd ed. Polity.

Ess, C. (2020b). Interpretative *pros hen* pluralism: from computer-mediated colonization to a pluralistic intercultural digital ethics. *Philosophy and Technology*, July 2020. https://doi.org/10.1007/s13347-020-00412-9

Ess, C. and the Association of Internet Researchers (2002). *Ethical decision-making and Internet research: Recommendations from the AOIR ethics working committee*. www.aoir.org/reports/ethics.pdf

European Parliament resolution of February 16, 2017 with recommendations to the Commission on Civil Law Rules on Robotics (2015/2103(INL)). www.europarl.europa.eu/doceo/document/TA-8-2017-0051_EN.pdf

franzke, a.s. (2022). An exploratory qualitative analysis of AI ethics guidelines. *Journal of Information, Communication and Ethics in Society*, *20*(4), 401–423. https://doi.org/10.1108/JICES-12-2020-0125

franzke, a. s., Bechmann, A., Zimmer, M., Ess, C. & the Association of Internet Researchers (2020). *Internet research: Ethical guidelines 3.0*. https://aoir.org/reports/ethics3.pdf

General Data Protection Regulation (GDPR) Regulation EU 2016/679. Approved April 27, 2016, implemented May 25, 2018. http://eur-lex.europa.eu/legal-content/EN/TXT/?uri=CELEX:32016R0679.

Gonzalez-Franco, M., Slater, M., Birney, M.E., Swapp, D., Haslam, S.A., & Reicher, S.D. (2018). Participant concerns for the learner in a virtual reality replication of the Milgram obedience study. *PLoS ONE* 13(12): e0209704. https://doi.org/10.1371/journal.pone.0209704

Gunkel, D. (2018). *Robot rights*. MIT Press.

Guzman, A. (2018). Introduction: "What is human-machine communication, anyway?" In A. Guzman (Ed.), *Human-machine communication: rethinking communication, technology, and ourselves* (pp. 1–28). Peter Lang.

Howard, D. & Irani, L. (2019). Ways of knowing when research subjects care. In *CHI Conference on Human Factors in Computing Systems Proceedings* (CHI 2019), May 4–9, 2019, Glasgow, Scotland UK. ACM, New York, NY, USA. https://doi.org/10.1145/3290605.3300327

Markham, A. (2006). Method as ethic, ethic as method. *Journal of Information Ethics*, *15*(2), 37–54.

Markham, A. & Buchanan, E. (2012). Ethical decision-making and internet research: Recommendations from the AoIR Ethics Working Committee (Version 2.0). www.aoir.org/reports/ethics2.pdf

The National Commission for Protection of Human Subjects of Biomedical and Behavioral Research (1979). The Belmont Report—Office of the Secretary, Ethical Principles and Guidelines for the Protection of Human Subjects Research.

Puig de la Bellacasa, M. (2017). *Matters of care: Speculative ethics in more than human worlds*. University of Minnesota Press.

Sedenberg, E., Chuang, J., Mulligan, D., Heerink, M., Broekens, J., Vanderborght, B., & Albo-Canals, J. (2016). Designing commercial therapeutic robots for privacy preserving systems and ethical research practices within the home. *International Journal of Social Robotics*, *8*(4), 575–587.

Sorenson, J. (2019). Toward a pragmatic and social engineering ethics: Ethnography as provocation. *Paladyn Journal of Behavioral Robotics*, *10*, 207–218. https://doi.org/10.1515/pjbr-2019-0018

Stahl, B.C. & Coeckelbergh, M. (2016) Ethics of healthcare robotics: Towards responsible research and innovation, *Robotics and Autonomous Systems*, *86*, 152–161.

Tambornino, L. & Lanzerath, D. (2018) D4.3: Survey of REC approaches and codes for artificial intelligence & robotics. https://ec.europa.eu/research/participants/documents/downloadPublic?documentIds=080166e5c6b8a74e&appId=PPGMS

Tronto, J. C. (1993). *Moral boundaries: A political argument for an ethic of care*. Routledge.

Veruggio, G. & Operto, F. (2008). Roboethics: Social and ethical implications of robotics. In B. Siciliano & O. Khatib (Eds.), *Springer handbook of robotics* (pp. 1499–1524). Springer. https://doi.org/10.1007/978-3-540-30301-5_65

World Medical Association (2013) World Medical Association Declaration of Helsinki: Ethical principles for medical research involving human subjects. *Journal of the American Medical Association* *310*, 2191–2194. https://doi.org/10.1001/jama.2013.281053

PART 3

Concepts and Contexts

INTRODUCTION

What should be clear from the preceding sections of *The Sage Handbook of Human–Machine Communication*, which focus on the histories and trajectories and the methodological considerations of HMC research, is the study of human–machine communication builds upon existing theoretical foundations while also seeking to identify and elucidate that which is novel. Because HMC research is still developing, scholars have primarily focused their efforts on understanding how key concepts and theories regarding technology, communication, or, most often, the intersection of technology and communication, can be extended to or need to be refined as they are applied to new contexts. By context, we are referring both to the form of communication (e.g., human–human, Computer-Mediated Communication, HMC) as well as other aspects germane to the communication process and its implications (e.g., place, culture, etc). In this section, we focus on concepts and theories that are proving to be central to HMC research and contexts, some old and some new, that are shaping and being reshaped by people's communication with technology.

Unsurprisingly, some of the most important concepts and theories within HMC are those central to the human experience of communicating more generally, including the "feelings" associated with or resulting from interaction (affect, Chapter 31), the numerous facets of interpersonal communication (Chapter 33), and the psychological mechanisms for making sense of information, including fellow communicators (dual processing, Chapter 34). Other aspects of HMC research are informed by scholarship at the intersection of communication and technology, with roots in CMC, HCI, media studies, and computer science, including affordances (Chapter 30), social presence (Chapter 32), privacy (Chapter 35), natural language processing (Chapter 36), datafication (Chapter 37), and domestication (Chapter 38).

The development of technology has long mirrored and reflected existing socioeconomic and political power structures that have excluded an enormous array of people from participating in its development. People creating, or funding the creation of, devices, applications and platforms have generally employed a narrow conceptualization of users as physically, socially, and culturally similar to themselves. Individuals and groups historically othered and marginalized within society have been, at the very least, overlooked in and, at the very worst, suffered real harm from technology design and use, a pattern that has repeated itself within the study of technology. More recently, practitioners, scholars, activists, and lay persons have pushed back against such marginalization. As scholars with strong backgrounds in critical and cultural studies, we aimed to give voice and representation to different groups and perspectives throughout the chapters of this Handbook. We also commissioned chapters to examine some of these problems head-on and to highlight more inclusive conceptualizations of and approaches to HMC research. Within this section, these chapters address HMC in regard to intersectionality (Chapter 39), colonialism (Chapter 40), technology in non-Western contexts (Chapter 41), and disability (Chapter 42).

From our own philosophical and theoretical perspectives, technology is socially created inasmuch as it is fashioned with hardware and bits and bytes and, thus, situated within and transformative of cultural, economic, and legal contexts. Artificial intelligence and robotics and our ways of communicating with them are more than feats of science and engineering. They also are imagined and occupy our imagination through art (Chapter 43), including pop culture (Chapter 49). It is within these social spaces that questions regarding the authenticity of AI and its potential "deception" relative to the "real" have arisen and now can be reexamined (Chapter 46). Similar to most technological innovations, communicative technologies have generated substantial debate regarding their economic impact, necessitating an examination of the evolving relationship between workers and machines across industries (Chapter 44). Equally important is the critique of the economic priorities and values built into and enacted within AI and its vast technological infrastructures (Chapter 45). Finally, the reconceptualization of technology from that of a channel to that of a communicator challenges societal norms that are unwritten as well as codified in ethics (Chapter 47) and the law (Chapter 48).

30

Rethinking Affordances for Human–Machine Communication Research

Peter Nagy and Gina Neff

INTRODUCTION

In *Ecological Approach to Visual Perception*, James J. Gibson (1979) introduced the concept of affordances to capture the dynamic relationship between organisms and their environment. Over the past forty years, the concept of affordance has evolved from conceptualizing animal-environment systems to describing complex sociotechnical systems (Evans et al., 2017). Affordances have been invoked to explore how users perceive, experience, and form relationship with social media platforms (e.g., Majchrzak et al., 2013), chatbots (e.g., Beattie et al., 2020), and robots (e.g., Cheong, 2020). However, when scholars turn to the concept of affordances to theorize the qualities of communication technologies and media, they will soon realize that there is no singular definition of affordances – the term has been modified countless times to fit the practical needs demanded by different disciplines (Brown et al., 2015).

We argue that this confusion around the definition of affordance hinders human–machine communication scholars' effort to advance theory of their own. Researchers need a more comprehensive theory to be able to conceptualize human–machine communication in which technologies – chatbots, virtual assistants, social robots – operate independently and be less open to users' involvement.

Theories about the "social shaping of technology" already showed that technologies are not static, but they are shaped by who uses them and how they get used. As Pentzold and Bischof (2019) noted, human–machine communication "goes against the idea that affordances either exist or are absent because they do not materialize as technological functions but emerge at the practical intersection of people and technologies" (p. 9).

In this chapter, we will show that scholars have misunderstood and misused the term affordance leading to a confusion around the meaning of the concept. After revisiting the theoretical foundations of the affordance theory, we will introduce the framework of imagined affordances to illustrate how it can help scholars study human–machine communication more fully. We will show that imagined affordances build upon emerging approaches to materiality, attention to affect and emotion, and the processes of mediation to capture the dynamic relationship between users and machines (Nagy & Neff, 2015).

Gibson's Ecological Approach to Affordances: A Short Overview

Gibson (1979) viewed affordances as what the environment offers the animal, suggesting that not only perception but potential actions are also directly communicated by the environment. In his view, "the affordances of the environment are what it offers the animal, what it provides or furnishes, either for good or ill" (p. 127). Gibson noted that affordances are relationships that exist naturally that do not require pre-existing knowledge. However, while affordances may be stable, perception of those affordances is context dependent, allowing for different affordances to be perceived depending on the state of an animal (Chemero & Turvey, 2007). Whereas for a lizard a rock might serve as a place to sunbathe, a tiger may use it to be able to see farther and notice potential food. Available affordances would also further vary for different animals. For instance, given the strength and anatomy needed for climbing a rock, a dog might never be able to reach the top regardless of its health status or strength.

Understanding what the notion of affordance means is quite challenging particularly because the language Gibson used in his work is notoriously difficult to decipher (Chemero & Turvey, 2007). Despite his best efforts, Gibson left the details of his affordance theory underdeveloped and vague. For instance, Gibson (1979) stated that "an affordance is neither an objective property nor a subjective property; or it is both if you like" (p. 129). That is, the affordances of the environment are both real and objective, and yet they are also physical. Perhaps not surprisingly, many people find descriptions like this too abstract and puzzling, resulting in confusion around the exact meaning of the concept. As a result, the term affordance is one that has become simultaneously popular and increasingly diffuse in usage since its inception (Lobo et al., 2018).

Post-Gibsonian Approaches for Conceptualizing Affordances

In his popular book, *The Psychology of Everyday Things* the cognitive psychologist and engineer Don Norman (1988) redefined the concept of affordances for the purposes of design and technology studies. He stressed the importance of considering human cognition and perception during the design process. Without including clues for use such as affordances, he argued, users might struggle to use a tool. Specifically, Norman used the concept of affordances to refer to "the perceivable actionable properties of objects." For instance, a chair could be considered to afford sitting, standing, reaching a bookshelf, and so on. Unlike Gibson (1977), who stated that "affordances of the environments are facts of the environment, not

appearances" (p. 70), Norman (1988) primarily focused on the visible properties that could communicate an object's canonical use. Gibson, on the other hand, might state that a large number of objects might afford sitting regardless of the intentions of any particular designer. Norman used the term affordance specifically to refer to the design of common objects. To further distinguish his approach from Gibson's original theory, Norman came to call his reformulation as perceived affordances, whereas he referred to Gibson's understanding of affordances as physical affordances, in an effort to reduce confusion around his and Gibson's definitions (Norman, 1999).

What is the difference between physical and perceived affordances? Take the example of the smart speaker, Amazon Echo. The device itself is voice-activated – users speak to and ask questions from Alexa, the voice of Echo. As such, voice interaction – asking for help, giving orders – are the physical affordances of Amazon Echo because that is how users can operate their virtual assistants. However, Alexa not only follows instructions, but also orients users by calling for new actions, such as subscribing to streaming services, adding new items to a grocery list. These communicative features are the perceived affordances of Amazon Echo, suggestions made by Alexa on actions available to the user.

While Norman deviated from his predecessor's original theory of affordances, he readily acknowledged Gibson's contribution to ecological psychology (Lindsay & Norman, 2013). Although Norman was transparent about the differences between his and Gibson's approach, readers of *The Psychology of Everyday Things* have come to misapply and misuse the concept of affordance (Norman, 2008). For instance, many designers and engineers fall into the trap of claiming that by creating robots with friendly features (e.g., covering the robot in fur), they have "afforded" social interaction. Given the fact people can interact with the robot in a variety of ways regardless of its appearance, the designer is not doing much beyond creating a robot with fluffy animal-like features. Instead of viewing affordances as deterministic forces, Graves (2007) considers them as invitations to action. As the sociologist Ian Hutchby (2001) put it in *Technologies, texts and affordances* "affordances are functional and relational aspects, which frame, while not determining, the possibilities for agentic action in relation to an object" (p. 44). In other words, affordances do not determine but rather orient and guide actions (Hartson, 2003).

As the psychologist Bub and his colleagues (2018) later noted, scholars need an affordance theory that pays attention to users' goals and intentions. People are not passive observers but active agents whose motivational and cognitive characteristics shape their perceptions and uses of tools. As such, affordances are dispositional – they are visible and concrete when perceived, but there might be cases when an affordance is misperceived or not perceived at all (see Gibson, 1979). Affordances are also relational – they arise from the encounter that the user driven by their needs, desires, and intentions has with the tool. Affordances, therefore, depend on the relation between the user's goals, the material properties of a technology, and the context in which the technology is used.

Affordance Theory in Communication and Media Studies: An Unfinished Project

Communication scholars have sought to come up with their conceptualization of affordances to investigate the communicative and social dimensions of technology use (see Evans et al., 2017). According to Schrock (2015), "communicative affordances are defined as an interaction between subjective perceptions of utility and objective qualities of the technology that alter communicative practices or habits" (p. 1232). In this view, affordances are strongly related to the social world as they are "evaluated through communication and successively alter communicative practices" (Schrock, 2015, p. 1232). For communication scholars, affordances of technologies are inherently relational as they emerge when the user interacts with the medium or tool (Vyas et al., 2006). Within the field of communication, however, affordance is still often viewed as what technology makes possible for users – ignoring the black boxes, the algorithms, and the automatic (Rodríguez-Hidalgo, 2020).

For communication studies, affordances are rooted in communicative actions and practices that technology allows for or constrains (Bucher & Helmond, 2017). That is, communication scholarship has used affordance in a way that favors the active and rational participation of human actors' afforded actions by the technology around them. To be able to capture human–technology communication more fully, scholars need to anchor affordances in a process that is simultaneously material and perceptual. This way, affordances could reflect the technological environments' material qualities that mediate affective experiences. We suggest that communication scholars turn to the framework of imagined affordances to better capture the dynamic relationship between users, designers, and technological artifacts (Nagy & Neff, 2015).

IMAGINED AFFORDANCES: A FRAMEWORK FOR STUDYING HUMAN–MACHINE COMMUNICATION

We understand imagined affordance in two different ways. First: communication scholars have long thought that there is consensus or clarity around the term affordance, which is in reality not the case. Second: imagined affordance evokes the imagination of both users and designers – "expectations for technology that are not fully realized in conscious, rational knowledge but are nonetheless concretized or materialized in socio-technical systems" (Nagy & Neff, 2015). Imagination as not fully rational but critical for rationality also affects how people perceive affordances and may modulate their preferences (Boschker et al., 2002). The concept of imagined affordances captures human–machine by calling for attention to three important dimensions – mediation, materiality, and affect.

Mediation: Technologies Shape Perception

One of the most important characteristics of technologies is mediation. Information studies scholar Leah Lievrouw (2014) views mediation as the "ongoing, articulated, and mutually determining relationship" (p. 45) among technological artifacts and users' cultural and social practices. That is, devices shape how people perceive and interact with the world around them (Timmins & Lombard, 2005). People may approach technologies as if they were stable or fixed, but in fact they are highly adaptive due to complex algorithmic systems that operate them. As such, the interaction between users and technologies cannot be understood independently (Lievrouw, 2009). Rather, there is a mutual renegotiation of meaning that alters users, activities, and perceptions as well as the roles of technologies in social life (Couldry, 2008).

Technologies are entities shaping the social and cultural world and altering human subjectivity and the fabric of everyday life (MacKenzie & Wajcman, 1999). Technical systems do not simply add a new element to human perception, they transform it. That is, human–technology communication is not only *transmitted* by technology, but *modified*, *augmented*, or even *generated* by a computational agent to achieve communication goals" (Hancock et al., 2020, p. 2). This process, however, often remains invisible – technologies do what users ask them to do, but their mediating role and function in the process stay hidden, or black-boxed. Or as the philosopher Aydin and his colleagues (2019) put it, "technology is becoming a mediating milieu, merging with the world to the point of becoming invisible, but at the same time intentionally directed at humans and helping to shape how humans act, perceive, and live their lives" (p. 337).

Governed and curated by sophisticated algorithmic infrastructures, technologies often remain a "black box," leaving users often oblivious to how they mediate their experiences and everyday lives (Rudin, 2019). Bucher (2017) coined the term algorithmic imaginary referring to the "ways of thinking about what algorithms are, what they should be, how they function and what these imaginations in turn make possible" (pp. 39–40). Users often imagine technologies as having agency, thinking and doing things, and making their daily lives easier while being oblivious how these tools transform and augment their experiences (Finn, 2017).

Materiality: Technologies are Interactive

Human–machine communication is not only characterized by the user's perceptions and beliefs, but also the material processes (e.g., objects, infrastructures, platforms) through which communication, and the construction of meaning, take place (Couldry & Hepp, 2017). Materiality can be best viewed as "a certain extent of significance," specific features of technologies that allow us to achieve our goals or purposes (Leonardi, 2010). Hutchby (2001) already noted that technologies are relational artifacts that are constituted through interactions between users and their material characteristics. Similarly, Hayles (1999) argued that materiality is a selective focus on certain aspects and features of technologies that cannot be determined in advance of the work by the designer. Rather, materiality emerges from the interplay between the object, the infrastructure, the platform, the designer, and the user. Technology, therefore, is dynamic, even fluid. Affordances thus offer a framework for studying mutual connections between things based on their material form and material potential (Hodder, 2012).

New media technologies, such as AI and robotics, are no exception. "They develop in dynamic environments where users, designers, manufacturers, investors, regulators, distributors and others work out their interrelated and competing interests, cultural assumptions, desires and visions" (Lievrouw, 2006, p. 246). While people often interpret and use technologies based on their personal needs, goals and perceptions, some aspects of the tools are intrinsic to that technology and not part of the social context in which the technology is used. In case of non-digital technologies, like scissors, it is relatively easy to list a set of properties intrinsic to them. Emerging technologies such as AI algorithms, however, often do not have physicality – they often operate in the background with a relatively few visible physical interfaces. People's perceptions of the physical and digital materiality features influence how they use AI, limiting what they can or want to do with technological artifacts (e.g., Jones, 2017).

Affect: Feelings Shape the Uses of Technologies

People are not passive users of technologies but also active agents who view machines through their conscious or unconscious fantasies and emotions. Therefore, the affective dimensions – how machines make people feel – play a crucial role for understanding how people perceive and use technologies (Bucher, 2017). Szollossy (2017) suggests that people's perceptions of technological artifacts can be considered as manifestations of their emotional lives. As the psychologist, Suler (2016) put it, "our actual physical location often is irrelevant to that psychological space inside the device, which points to the power of the mind to create and immerse itself into an emotionally real, meaningful environment" (p. 65).

Users often experience technologies as having emotions or being "social actors" and form a relationship with them similarly to how they do that with other human beings or animals (Nass & Moon, 2000; Reeves & Nass, 1996). Users are prone to form strong emotional relationships with technologies particularly because they project various emotions onto them, viewing them as "relational entities" (Turkle, 2004). That is, technologies do not only mediate users' experiences, and act as interactive agents due to its physical and digital materiality features but also evoke emotions in users (Legaspi et al., 2019). These emotions, in turn, can change how people feel and act around them. In an attempt to control how users react to tools, computer scientists interested in affective computing and emotion AI try to develop systems that can simulate and react to human emotions more effectively (e.g., D'Mello et al., 2018; Schwark, 2015). For instance, call centers and mental health monitoring applications already use machine learning to monitor and identify emotions and moods among their customers so they can receive more personalized support and assistance (Brigham, 2017).

CONCLUSION

How users imagine human–machine communication shapes their interaction and relationship with and their expectations for technologies (Guzman, 2020). The framework of imagined affordances can help communication scholars theorize the technical in various ways. First, imagined affordances demonstrate how people use and perceive technology as well as how technology affects users' imagery in often unexpected or chaotic ways (Sneath et al., 2009). When it comes to human–machine communication, technological capabilities are often hidden and black boxed. Therefore, affordances emerge from interactions between users and tools – they are grounded in actions (see also Fairhurst & Putnam, 2004). As Costa (2018) noted "affordances are not fixed and stable properties but are implicated in different ongoing processes of constitution, which may radically vary across social and cultural contexts" (p. 3651). As such, it is more important for human–machine communication scholars to better understand what people imagine a tool can do than simply focusing on what people or designers think technology can do. Exploring what affordances designers and users imagine emerging technologies is especially timely given the proliferation of ubiquitous and invisible interfaces, where users' interaction with technologies becomes something they are potentially not even consciously aware that they are doing (Jamone et al., 2016).

Second, imagination connotes perception, not just rationality, a distinction that is missing in how communication scholars currently theorize and use affordance. That is, "perceptions of affordances are as much socially constructed for users as they are technologically configured" (Nagy & Neff, 2015, p. 6). Communication scholars tend to approach affordances as they exist or are absent because they do not "manifest" as technological functions. Instead, affordances emerge between what users think technologies are capable of and what technologies can really do when humans communicate with and through machines. As Pentzold and Bischoff (2019) noted, "affordances are collectively achieved in these concerted efforts" (p. 8).

By calling attention to mediation, materiality, and affect, the concept of imagined affordances offers a framework for human–machine communication scholars to better theorize how the social and the technical worlds shape each other.

REFERENCES

Aydin, C., Woge, M. G., & Verbeek, P. P. (2019). Technological environmentality: Conceptualizing technology as a mediating milieu. *Philosophy & Technology*, *32*(2), 321–338.

Beattie, A., Edwards, A. P., & Edwards, C. (2020). A bot and a smile: Interpersonal impressions of chatbots and humans using emoji in computer-mediated communication. *Communication Studies*, *71*(3), 409–427.

Boschker, M. S., Bakker, F. C., & Michaels, C. F. (2002). Effect of mental imagery on realizing affordances. *The Quarterly Journal of Experimental Psychology: Section A*, *55*(3), 775–792.

Brigham, T. J. (2017). Merging technology and emotions: Introduction to affective computing. *Medical Reference Services Quarterly*, *36*(4), 399–407.

Brown, D. C., Maier, J. R. A., & Norman, D. A. (2015). Affordances: Commentary on the special issue of AI EDAM. *Artificial Intelligence for Engineering Design, Analysis and Manufacturing: AIEDAM*, *29*(3), 235–238.

Bub, D. N., Masson, M. E. J., & Kumar, R. (2018). Time course of motor affordances evoked by pictured objects and words. *Journal of Experimental Psychology: Human Perception and Performance*, *44*(1), 56–83.

Bucher, T. (2017). The algorithmic imaginary: Exploring the ordinary affects of Facebook algorithms. *Information, Communication & Society*, *20*(1), 30–44.

Bucher, T., & Helmond, A. (2017). The affordances of social media platforms. In J. Burgess, A. Marwick, & T. Poell (Eds.), *The SAGE handbook of social media* (pp. 233–253). SAGE.

Chemero, A., & Turvey, M. T. (2007). Gibsonian affordances for roboticists. *Adaptive Behavior*, *15*(4), 473–480.

Cheong, P. H. (2020). Religion, robots and rectitude: Communicative affordances for spiritual knowledge and community. *Applied Artificial Intelligence*, *34*(5), 412–431.

Costa, E. (2018). Affordances-in-practice. *New Media & Society*, *20*(10), 3641–3656.

Couldry, N., & Hepp, A. (2016). *The mediated construction of reality*. Polity Press.

Couldry, N. (2008). Mediatization or mediation? Alternative understandings of the emergent space of digital storytelling. *New Media & Society*, *10*(3), 373–391.

D'Mello, S., Kappas, A., & Gratch, J. (2018). The affective computing approach to affect measurement. *Emotion Review*, *10*(2), 174–183.

Evans, S. K., Pearce, K. E., Vitak, J., & Treem, J. W. (2017). Explicating affordances: A conceptual framework for understanding affordances in communication research. *Journal of Computer-Mediated Communication*, *22*(1), 35–52.

Fairhurst, G., Putnam, L. (2004). Organizations as discursive constructions. *Communication Theory*, *14*(1), 5–26.

Finn, E. (2017). *What algorithms want: Imagination in the age of computing*. MIT Press.

Gibson, J. J. (1977). The theory of affordances. *Hilldale, USA*, *1*(2), 67–82.

Gibson, J. J. (1979). *The ecological approach to visual perception*. Houghton Mifflin.

Graves, L. (2007). The affordances of blogging: A case study in culture and technological effects. *Journal of Communication Inquiry*, *31*(4), 331–346.

Guzman, A. L. (2020). Ontological boundaries between humans and computers and the implications for human-machine communication. *Human-Machine Communication*, *1*(1), 3.

Hancock, J. T., Naaman, M., & Levy, K. (2020). AI-mediated communication: definition, research agenda, and ethical considerations. *Journal of Computer-Mediated Communication*, *25*(1), 89–100.

Hartson, R. (2003). Cognitive, physical, sensory, and functional affordances in interaction design. *Behaviour & Information Technology*, *22*(5), 315–338.

Hayles, N. K. (1999). *How we became posthuman: Virtual bodies in cybernetics, literature, and informatics*. The University of Chicago Press.

Hodder, I. (2012). *Entangled: An archaeology of the relationships between humans and things*. Wiley-Blackwell.

Hutchby, I. (2001). Technologies, texts and affordances. *Sociology*, *35*(2), 441–456.

Jamone, L., Ugur, E., Cangelosi, A., Fadiga, L., Bernardino, A., Piater, J., & Santos-Victor, J. (2016). Affordances in psychology, neuroscience, and robotics: A survey. *IEEE Transactions on Cognitive and Developmental Systems*, *10*(1), 4–25.

Jones, R. A. (2017). What makes a robot 'social'? *Social Studies of Science*, *47*(4), 556–579.

Legaspi, R., He, Z., & Toyoizumi, T. (2019). Synthetic agency: sense of agency in artificial intelligence. *Current Opinion in Behavioral Sciences*, *29*, 84–90.

Leonardi, P. M. (2010). Digital materiality? How artifacts without matter, matter. *First Monday*, *15*(6). https://doi.org/10.5210/fm.v15i6.3036.

Lievrouw, L. A. (2006). New media design and development: Diffusion of innovations v. social shaping of technology. In L. A. Lievrouw & Livingstone, S. (Eds.), *The handbook of new media* (pp. 246–265). SAGE.

Lievrouw, L. A. (2009). New media, mediation, and communication study. *Information, Communication & Society*, *12*(3), 303–325.

Lievrouw, L. A. (2014). Materiality and media in communication and technology studies: An unfinished project. *Media technologies: Essays on communication, materiality, and society*, 21–51.

Lindsay, P. H., & Norman, D. A. (2013). *Human information processing: An introduction to psychology*. Academic Press.

Lobo, L., Heras-Escribano, M., & Travieso, D. (2018). The history and philosophy of ecological psychology. *Frontiers in Psychology*, *9*, 2228.

MacKenzie, D., & Wajcman, J. (1999). *The social shaping of technology*. Open University Press.

Majchrzak, A., Faraj, S., Kane, G. C., & Azad, B. (2013). The contradictory influence of social media affordances on online communal knowledge sharing. *Journal of Computer-Mediated Communication*, *19*(1), 38–55.

Nagy, P., & Neff, G. (2015). Imagined affordance: Reconstructing a keyword for communication theory. *Social Media + Society*, *1*(2), 2056305115603385.

Nass, C., & Moon, Y. (2000). Machines and mindlessness: Social responses to computers. *Journal of Social Issues*, *56*, 81–103.

Norman, D. A. (1988). *The psychology of everyday things*. Basic Books.

Norman, D. A. (1999). Affordance, conventions, and design. *Interactions*, *6*(3), 38–43.

Norman, D. A. (2008). Signifiers, not affordances. *Interactions, 15*, 18–19.

Pentzold, C., & Bischof, A. (2019). Making affordances real: Socio-material prefiguration, performed agency, and coordinated activities in human–robot communication. *Social Media + Society*, *5*(3), 2056305119865472.

Reeves, B., & Nass, C. (1996). *The media equation: How people treat computers, television, and new media like real people and places*. Cambridge University Press.

Rodríguez-Hidalgo, C. (2020). Me and my robot smiled at one another: The process of socially enacted communicative affordance in human-machine communication. *Human-Machine Communication*, *1*(1), 4.

Rudin, C. (2019). Stop explaining black box machine learning models for high stakes decisions and use interpretable models instead. *Nature Machine Intelligence*, *1*(5), 206–215.

Schrock, A. R. (2015). Communicative affordances of mobile media: Portability, availability, locatability, and multimediality. *International Journal of Communication, 9*, 1229–1246.

Schwark, J. D. (2015). Toward a taxonomy of affective computing. *International Journal of Human-Computer Interaction, 31*(11), 761–768.

Sneath, D., Holbraad, M., Pedersen, M. A. (2009). Technologies of the imagination: An introduction. *Ethnos, 74*, 5–30.

Suler, J. R. (2016). *Psychology of the digital age: Humans become electric*. Cambridge University Press.

Szollosy, M. (2017). Freud, Frankenstein and our fear of robots: Projection in our cultural perception of technology. *AI & SOCIETY, 32*(3), 433–439.

Timmins, L. R., & Lombard, M. (2005). When "real" seems mediated: Inverse presence. *Presence: Teleoperators & Virtual Environments, 14*(4), 492–500.

Turkle, S. (2004). Whither psychoanalysis in computer culture? *Psychoanalytic Psychology, 21*, 16–30.

Vyas, D., Chisalita, C. M., & Van Der Veer, G. C. (2006, September). Affordance in interaction. In *Proceedings of the 13th European Conference on Cognitive Ergonomics: Trust and control in complex socio-technical systems* (pp. 92–99).

31

Affect Research in Human–Machine Communication: The Case of Social Robots

Carmina Rodríguez-Hidalgo

INTRODUCTION

Ever since the advent of technological systems, humans have established emotional reactions and relationships with machines. As early as 1966, the very first chatbot, ELIZA (Weizenbaum, 1966) – made to simulate a dialogue with a psychotherapist as a means to refine natural language processing – quickly developed the perception in its users that it could "sense their feelings" and care about them, a realization that at first shocked its creator, Joseph Weizenbaum. Although ELIZA was initially a way for the MIT professor to demonstrate that communication between humans and machines was 'inherently superficial' (Epstein & Klinkenberg, 2001), user reactions showed that this was far from the truth.

Indeed, though affect and emotion shape the whole of human experience (Scherer, 2005), they also equally permeate human–machine and human–technology interactions. Users' perceptions and emotions shape the design and materiality of artifacts, its software and algorithms (Nagy & Neff, 2015; Thüring & Mahlke, 2007). One particular multidisciplinary field devoted to developing machines which can sense, respond to, and influence user emotions is that of **affective computing**, whose main foci include (a) *affect sensing*, or

the development of technological systems to recognize human emotions from data, signals, and/or patterns; and (b) *affect elicitation*, or the triggering of human affect through machine physicality and interaction capabilities (Daily et al., 2017). In both cases, a mechanical technological agent either senses or elicits affect in a human, bringing affective computing to fit within a more machine-to-human focus. Considering, in turn, a more human-to-machine perspective and rooted in computer science and communication, theories on how people experience machines as social actors have emerged, e.g., Computers as Social Actors (CASA, see: Nass, Steuer, & Tauber, 1994), which posit that humans interact with machines as if they were social entities, applying human–human interaction scripts, like being polite to computers (Reeves & Nass, 1998). While communication studies have traditionally conceived of technology as more of a mediator than a social actor – for instance, when two human interlocutors share their emotions through technology (e.g., Choi & Toma, 2014) – recent approaches have re-shaped the study of human–machine relationships as both a concept and a field which studies the meaning-making process and the social communicator role that machines have acquired (Guzman, 2018; Zhao, 2006).

The Case of Social Robots

In their role as communicators, social robots are technological artifacts that present opportunities for affective interaction, by means of simulating emotional communication through a physical body, which is able to display non-verbal and verbal emotional cues – in short, interacting similarly to humans (Breazeal, 2004; Broadbent, 2017). Since social robots can display emotional cues in multimodes (e.g., audio, visual signals, touch), the Human–Robot Interaction (HRI) literature on emotional exchanges has understandably focused on studying communicational and emotional exchange processes in such elements; however, this has brought a rather sparse view of the phenomenon. To move the field forward, it is necessary to determine which streams of research have been devoted to similarly unimodal perspectives and analyze whether existing multimodal approaches are being applied at sufficient depth and complexity. For this reason, the present chapter first provides a broad overview of the main research streams in HRI affect research; then delineates partial and multimodal approaches with suggestions on how best to incorporate insights from emotion theory and communication studies; and ends by discussing the main conceptual, operational, and ethical challenges in integrating insights from emotion and communication theory. Indeed, the focus of this text lies on the development and integration of the HMC field as a whole, and so – rather than discussing particular emotional aspects, like uncanny machine–human aversion – it attempts to organize and classify HRI research, seeking for ways on how to move forward in an interdisciplinary manner.

APPROACHES TO AFFECT RESEARCH WITH SOCIAL ROBOTS

Partial Approaches

To identify the main approaches used in the study of human–robot emotional exchanges, this chapter employed a keyword scoping review[1] which turned an initial sample of 1,783 results. Removing duplicates left a subsample of 989 articles, which were revised by the author and one independent coder. From this process, this chapter identifies between partial and multimodal approaches. Partial approaches are here defined as having at least one of the following characteristics: (a) they study one stage of the emotional communication process, for example, emotional expression and not the whole cycle of emotional exchanges (e.g., McColl & Nejat, 2014); (b) they focus on basic elements of the emotion itself – such as emotional valence (positive and negative) or intensity (low or high) – instead of on particular types of emotion (e.g., fear, happiness) or more complex emotions (envy, contempt) (e.g., Bishop et al., 2019); (c) they study the perceptions, actions, and/or reactions unidirectionally, i.e., focusing on one interlocutor (the human or the robot), instead of bidirectionally (e.g., Spatola & Wudarczyk, 2021); (d) the interaction is set up and studied in unimodal terms, that is, using one or two communication modalities, such as audio and visual (e.g., Strait et al., 2015); and (e) the situational and/or contextual setting of the interaction, for instance, a customer-related scenario or an educational context, is not taken into account or is left unspecified (e.g., Hashimoto et al., 2008).

While a complete review of all of the above-mentioned points falls outside of the scope of this chapter due to space limitations, doing so for one of the above will suffice to briefly illustrate the scope of partial approaches studies. The four main focuses found in HRI research regarding emotional processes (point (a), above) were: emotion elicitation, emotional expression, emotion recognition, and emotional contagion.

The first focus is emotion elicitation. In emotion theory, **emotion elicitation** refers to triggering an emotion as a result of exposure to stimuli, which is usually felt as causing an imbalance in the person's goals or emotional stability (Ortony et al., 1990). This imbalance can occur in the form of an event, behavior, situation, object, or memory (Niedenthal & Brauer, 2012). Some studies in this line, have rendered the "object" which triggers the emotion to be the robot itself. For instance, Shao et al. (2019) used the social robot Pepper to elicit affect in the human observer by using a combination of non-verbal body poses and music. Consider, however, that the mere presence of the robot and its body (not even interacting with it) may be in itself an elicitor, and thus a source of bias.

The second focus is emotional expression. **Emotional expression** refers to the production of observable emotion-specific facial cues, sounds and body gestures to convey an emotion (Ekman, 1999). The morphology of social robots makes them apt to produce observable emotion-specific facial cues, sounds, and body gestures to convey an emotion (Ekman, 1999). Anthropomorphic robots, in particular, emulate humans when expressing and portraying non-verbal expressions of basic emotions (Fong et al., 2003). However, social robots may also express emotions using color and motion (Li & Chignell, 2011), a combination of the robot body movements, sounds and eye color (Haring et al., 2011), or via touch (Willemse et al., 2017). Crucial to the development of the field is the realization that emotional expression occurs in multimode.

A third line of attention in HRI is emotion recognition. When an expression of an emotion has taken place, **emotion recognition** implies identifying its orientation (e.g., sadness, fear), valence (positive/negative/mixed), and intensity (low/high). In the robotics and engineering literature, emotion recognition is most commonly named affect detection or interpretation (Spezialetti et al., 2020). In general, research unidirectionally focuses on either humans recognizing emotional displays in the robot (e.g., Meng & Bianchi-Berthouze, 2013) or the robot recognizing emotions in the human (e.g., Kirby et al., 2010). The types of cues used to recognize emotions in studies are varied, such as facial expressions (Faria et al., 2017); vocal intonation and prosodic language (Breazeal, & Aryananda, 2002); and body movements, which can either be static (Beck et al., 2012) or dynamic (Xin et al., 2013). Although the term emotion recognition is most often associated with facial expressions (Juckel et al., 2018), body gestures and postures and other audio and haptic cues can also convey emotion (Knapp et al., 2013).

The fourth main focus in the HRI literature is **emotional contagion**, which occurs in human–human relationships when interaction partners influence their affective states and adopt similar emotions in intensity and tone (Niedenthal & Brauer, 2012). In the social robot, one way that emotional contagion can be simulated is if the robot synchronizes its emotional displays with those of the human, creating the illusion of emotional mimicry (Hashimoto et al., 2009), which builds rapport and empathy in interpersonal processes and relationships (Hess & Fischer, 2013).

Multimodal Approaches

In comparison with the above, this chapter identifies multimodal approaches as having one or more of the following characteristics: (a) they study more than one stage of the emotional communication process, for example emotion elicitation and emotional contagion (e.g., Salichs & Malfaz, 2011); (b) they focus on particular types of, or more complex emotions (e.g., fear, happiness) or more complex emotions (e.g., guilt, e.g., Rodriguez et al., 2017); (c) they study the interlocutors' perceptions, actions and/or reactions bidirectionally (e.g., Hong et al., 2020); (d) interactions are set up and studied in multimodal terms, that is using more than one communication modality, such as audio and haptic cues (Jung et al., 2017); (e) the situational and/or contextual setting of the interaction, for instance whether the interaction happens during a health care context, is considered (Ruvolo et al., 2008); and (f) the study accounts for live, spontaneous interactions by both communication partners (e.g., Val-Calvo et al., 2020).

To distinguish from the previous category and to exemplify, let us comment on two multimodal studies, chosen for review using a random number generator on our selection of 287 multimodal studies on human–robot emotional exchanges.

First, Hong et al. (2020) presented a multimodal emotional HRI architecture to "promote natural and engaging bidirectional emotional communications between a social robot and a human user" (p. 1), in the context of a health intervention scenario with 18 participants. The humanoid robot used detected the human interlocutor's affect in real time using body language and voice intonation and takes this state as input to determine its own emotional response towards the human via a two-layer model. The robot's emotions were displayed via a combination of body movements, eye color and voice intonation. Compared to the control robot, subjects found the emotionally expressive robot to be more enjoyable to interact with, and that it could induce, potentially, more positive valence. In the second study, Liu et al. (2016) tested multisystemic, bidirectional human–robot interactions with three NAO robots, two mobile robots, a motion sensor device, a server, a workstation, and wearables to recognize humans' emotions and respond in real-time under different contextual scenarios, e.g., guided tours or gaming (all scenarios located in the same room). Multimodal emotional cues were taken from the multisensors located in the room (microphone, movement sensors and eye tracker) and sent via a server to the robots, which responded using a combination of facial expressions, speech, and body gestures.

While multimodal studies advance the field broadly – especially technologically – points for improvement can be mentioned. Requiring more attention, for instance, are (a) refining the objectives and metrics for emotion recognition by means of technological emotion detection multisystems, to detect emotions in humans and make the robot respond accordingly (e.g., precisely which emotions are the humans and the robots expressing or detecting, and for which objectives?); (b) providing more detail and rationales for the temporality of real-time multimodal studies, since in many it appears that interactions only last a couple of minutes or take place during particular moments of the day, without clear justification; and (c) identifying the stage of the emotional process. Indeed, on this last point, some studies on expressive robots fail to specify if for instance inducing more positive valence in participants (Hong et al., 2020, p. 12) refers to emotional contagion or expression, or to some other interpersonal emotional process.

More pertinent to the field of HMC, most studies in these research streams lack an assessment of what these emotional exchanges *mean* for humans. To cover these gaps, the next section proposes the main challenges of integrating insights from emotion and communication theory.

INTEGRATING EMOTION AND COMMUNICATION THEORY TO HRI: MAIN CHALLENGES

While research on emotional interactions with social robots continues to attract interest in HRI and other HMC fields, important conceptual and operational challenges for integration among disciplines remain. A first challenge is related to what scholars and researchers understand by emotion, affect, and mood. Studies often use these terms interchangeably, impeding the integration of concepts and operationalizations. While affect is an umbrella term for emotional processes such as experiencing feelings, an emotion *per se* is generally understood as short-lived and intense, triggered by a set of complex and synchronized multicomponent responses (Scherer, 2005). Moreover, mood is of much longer duration and of lesser intensity than emotions, often being quite diffuse (Frijda, 1986). It is suggested that scholars become more aware of these concepts and match their research designs accordingly; for instance, it would make more sense to study mood longitudinally rather than cross-sectionally, due to the longer lasting nature of moods.

A second challenge depends on the approaches used to study emotions in different disciplines – as well as their conceptual and empirical depth – which directly impacts study operationalizations. Until now, two approaches focusing more on the nature of the emotion themselves rather than their processes, have been the most prevalent in HRI research. These are Ekman's basic emotions approach (Ekman, 1999) and Russell's circumplex model of emotion (Russell, 1980). The former proposes the existence of six basic emotions, while the latter distinguishes emotional valence (positive and negative) and arousal (low and high). However, and receiving less attention despite some efforts (Breazeal, 2004; Breazeal & Brooks, 2005), another approach – Scherer's componential model of emotion – states that emotion is produced by the interrelation of several different components, such as cognitive, somatic, motivational, motor, and feeling in response to a stimulus

which triggers the emotion (Scherer, 2009). More comprehensive explanations of this model are here cited, and researchers may be advised to revise the componential model to better understand the underlying processes when setting up studies which account for greater emotional depth.

Third, the social and communicative contexts of interactions can directly impact study designs and conclusions. As an example, often HRI research assumes that humans outwardly express emotions as a result of an internal experienced feeling. However, such a view leaves aside the social communicative function of emotional expressions (Fischer & Manstead, 2008), which are not always produced as a result of an internal state, but also in response to social demands. To illustrate, it has been found that bowlers express facial gestures of positive emotions not when they score, but when they turn around to celebrate with other team members (Kraut & Johnston, 1979). As a second example, receiver's emotion recognition also depends on the social and communicative context. However, in HRI it is often assumed that expressing an emotion in itself already determines how it may be interpreted. Fischer et al. (2019) found that a majority of HRI papers (89%) were based on the assumption that emotion interpretation is to be determined upon expression; however, if approaches would consider situational, communicative, and cultural factors, it would help to ascertain the encoding and coding of emotional exchanges and underlying processes more accurately.

A fourth – and likely one of the most pressing conceptual and ethical challenges – is that HRI scholarship often refers to the term "robot emotion" or robot emotional state (e.g., Prado et al., 2011). However, there is still very little consensus on what robot emotion is (or what some term "artificial emotion"; see Scherer, 2001), and even less agreement on whether a robot emotion *could* exist. If it does, there is a need to ascertain under which context it would exist and how it would be defined. In particular, the critical ethical issue of whether a robot emotion should be modelled after human emotions (Olgun et al., 2018), or after more "robot like" emotions, or even "animal like" emotions (Fellous, 2004), waits to be resolved. Moreover, the question of whether and how machines would "emotionally" experience humans – and, if so, under which conditions – deserves particular attention (Nitsch & Popp, 2014).

CONCLUSION

This chapter presented a brief overview of different research streams within the field of human-robot interaction (HRI) and showed why and how insights from emotion and communication research could become better integrated. First, it is suggested here that multimodal approaches have more potential to grasp the complex nature of human–machine affective processes than partial or unimodal approaches. Second, these multimodal approaches – and the HRI field, in general – could integrate more conceptual and empirical insights from the fields of emotion and communication studies. Precisely, this integration between HRI, communication, and emotion research promises a worthwhile endeavor to ultimately bring forth the gist of HMC, that of finding out the process of meaning making between humans and machines (Guzman, 2018). This highlights a pressing need for common guidelines and frameworks to compare and complement findings across disciplines. Finally, to advance the field, it is necessary to achieve conceptual consensus on some key terms (e.g., emotion, mood, affect); to consider the nature of emotional approaches being used; to be more aware of the social and communicative contexts; and to resolve the critical issue surrounding robot emotionality. Although no study can consider all factors, greater integration among fields would advance HMC toward more solid conclusions on the process and effects of creating emotional meaning between humans and machines.

NOTE

1   Among the keywords, adapted to suit the requirements of each database, were: Robot* AND (social) AND (emoti* OR affect* OR mood* OR feel*) AND (interact*, OR exchange* OR communicat*) AND NOT (surg*). Databases included IEEE Explore, Engineering village, Medline, PsycINFO, Scopus, ACM Digital Library (ACM DL) and Web of Science. Articles chosen were in English and the main eligibility criteria was to deal with the topic of human–robot emotional exchanges. Publications were included if they were journal articles or conference proceedings.

REFERENCES

Beck, A., Stevens, B., Bard, K. A., & Cañamero, L. (2012). Emotional body language displayed by artificial agents. *ACM Transactions on Interactive Intelligent Systems (TiiS)*, *2*(1), 1–29. http://doi.acm.org/10.1145/2133366.2133368.

Bishop, L., van Maris, A., Dogramadzi, S., & Zook, N. (2019). Social robots: The influence of human and robot characteristics on acceptance. *Paladyn, Journal of Behavioral Robotics*, *10*(1), 346–358. https://doi.org/10.1515/pjbr-2019-0028.

Breazeal, C. (2004). Function meets style: Insights from emotion theory applied to HRI. *IEEE Transactions on Systems, Man, and Cybernetics, Part C (Applications and Reviews)*, *34*(2), 187–194. https://10.1109/TSMCC.2004.826270.

Breazeal, C., & Aryananda, L. (2002). Recognition of affective communicative intent in robot-directed speech. *Autonomous robots*, *12*(1), 83–104. https://doi.org/10.1023/A:1013215010749.

Breazeal, C., & Brooks, R. (2005). Robot emotion: A functional perspective. *Who needs emotions*, 271–310. Oxford University Press.

Broadbent, E. (2017). Interactions with robots: The truths we reveal about ourselves. *Annual review of psychology*, *68*, 627–652. https://doi.org/10.1146/annurev-psych-010416-043958.

Bui, H. D., Dang, T. L. Q., & Chong, N. Y. (2019, November). Robot social emotional development through memory retrieval. In *2019 7th International Conference on Robot Intelligence Technology and Applications (RiTA)* (pp. 46–51). IEEE.

Choi, M., & Toma, C. L. (2014). Social sharing through interpersonal media: Patterns and effects on emotional well-being. *Computers in Human Behavior*, *36*, 530–541. https://doi.org/10.1016/j.chb.2014.04.026.

Daily, S. B., James, M. T., Cherry, D., PorterIII, J. J., Darnell, S. S., Isaac, J., & Roy, T. (2017). Affective computing: Historical foundations, current applications, and future trends. In *Emotions and affect in human factors and human-computer interaction* (pp. 213–231). Academic Press.

Ekman, P. (1999). Basic emotions. *Handbook of cognition and emotion*, *98*(45–60), 16.

Epstein, J., & Klinkenberg, W. D. (2001). From Eliza to internet: A brief history of computerized assessment. *Computers in Human Behavior*, *17*(3), 295–314. https://doi.org/10.1016/S0747-5632(01)00004-8.

Faria, D. R., Vieira, M., Faria, F. C., & Premebida, C. (2017, August). Affective facial expressions recognition for human-robot interaction. In *2017 26th IEEE International Symposium on Robot and Human Interactive Communication (RO-MAN)* (pp. 805–810). IEEE.

Fischer, A. H., & Manstead, A. S. (2008). Social functions of emotion. *Handbook of emotions*, *3*, 456–468.

Fischer, K., Jung, M., Jensen, L. C., & aus der Wieschen, M. V. (2019, March). Emotion expression in HRI – when and why. In *2019 14th ACM/*

IEEE International Conference on Human-Robot Interaction (HRI) (pp. 29–38). IEEE.

Fellous, J. M. (2004). From human emotions to robot emotions. Architectures for modeling emotion: Cross-disciplinary foundations, American Association for Artificial Intelligence, 39–46.

Fong, T., Nourbakhsh, I., & Dautenhahn, K. (2003). A survey of socially interactive robots. Robotics and autonomous systems, 42(3–4), 143–166. https://10.1016/S0921-8890(02)00372-X.

Frijda, N. H. (1986). The emotions. Cambridge University Press.

Guzman, A. L. (2018). What is human-machine communication, anyway. Human-machine communication: Rethinking communication, technology, and ourselves, 1–28. Peter Lang.

Häring, M., Bee, N., & André, E. (2011, July). Creation and evaluation of emotion expression with body movement, sound and eye color for humanoid robots. In 2011 RO-MAN (pp. 204–209). IEEE.

Hashimoto, M., Kondo, H., & Tamatsu, Y. (2008, August). Effect of emotional expression to gaze guidance using a face robot. In RO-MAN 2008-The 17th IEEE International Symposium on Robot and Human Interactive Communication (pp. 95–100). IEEE.

Hess, U., & Fischer, A. (2013). Emotional mimicry as social regulation. Personality and social psychology review, 17(2), 142–157. https://doi.org/10.1177/1088868312472607.

Hong, A., Lunscher, N., Hu, T., Tsuboi, Y., Zhang, X., Franco dos Reis Alves, S., Nejat, G., & Benhabib, B. (2021). A multimodal emotional human–robot interaction architecture for social robots engaged in bidirectional communication. IEEE Transactions on Cybernetics, 51(12), 5954–5968. https://doi.org/10.1109/tcyb.2020.2974688.

Juckel, G., Heinisch, C., Welpinghus, A., & Brüne, M. (2018). Understanding another person's emotions—an interdisciplinary research approach. Frontiers in Psychiatry, 9, 414. https://doi.org/10.3389/fpsyt.2018.00414.

Jung, M. M., Poel, M., Reidsma, D., & Heylen, D. K. (2017). A first step toward the automatic understanding of social touch for naturalistic human–robot interaction. Frontiers in ICT, 4, 3. https://doi.org/10.3389/fict.2017.00003.

Kirby, R., Forlizzi, J., & Simmons, R. (2010). Affective social robots. Robotics and Autonomous Systems, 58(3), 322–332. https://doi.org/10.1016/j.robot.2009.09.015.

Knapp, M. L., Hall, J. A., & Horgan, T. G. (2014). Nonverbal communication in human interaction. Wadsworth.

Kraut, R. E., & Johnston, R. E. (1979). Social and emotional messages of smiling: An ethological approach. Journal of personality and social psychology, 37(9), 1539.

Li, J., & Chignell, M. (2011). Communication of emotion in social robots through simple head and arm movements. International Journal of Social Robotics, 3(2), 125–142. https://doi.org/10.1007/s12369-010-0071-x.

Liu, Z., Pan, F., Wu, M., Cao, W., Chen, L., Xu, J., Zhang, R., & Zhou, M. (2016). A multimodal emotional communication based humans-robots interaction system. 2016 35th Chinese Control Conference (CCC). https://doi.org/10.1109/chicc.2016.7554357.

McColl, D., & Nejat, G. (2014). Recognizing emotional body language displayed by a human-like social robot. International Journal of Social Robotics, 6(2), 261–280. https://doi.org/10.1007/s12369-013-0226-7.

Meng, H., & Bianchi-Berthouze, N. (2013). Affective state level recognition in naturalistic facial and vocal expressions. IEEE Transactions on Cybernetics, 44(3), 315–328. https://doi.org/10.1109/TCYB.2013.2253768.

Nagy, P., & Neff, G. (2015). Imagined affordance: Reconstructing a keyword for communication theory. Social Media+ Society, 1(2), https://doi.org/10.1177/2056305115603385.

Nass, C., Steuer, J., & Tauber, E. R. (1994, April). Computers are social actors. In Proceedings of the SIGCHI conference on Human factors in computing systems (pp. 72–78).

Niedenthal, P. M., & Brauer, M. (2012). Social functionality of human emotion. Annual review of psychology, 63, 259–285. https://doi.org/10.1146/annurev.psych.121208.131605.

Nitsch, V., & Popp, M. (2014). Emotions in robot psychology. Biological cybernetics, 108(5), 621–629. https://doi.org/10.1007/s00422-014-0594-6.

Ortony, A., Clore, G. L., & Collins, A. (1990). The cognitive structure of emotions. Cambridge University Press.

Olgun, Z. N., Chae, Y., & Kim, C. (2018, June). A system to generate robot emotional reaction for robot-human communication. In 2018 15th International Conference on Ubiquitous Robots (UR) (pp. 383–387). IEEE.

Prado, J. A., Simplício, C., & Dias, J. (2011). Robot emotional state through Bayesian Visuo auditory perception. In Doctoral Conference on Computing, Electrical and Industrial Systems (pp. 165–172). Springer.

Reeves, B., & Nass, C. (1998). The media equation: How people treat computers, television, and new media like real people. Cambridge University Press.

Rodriguez, I., Martínez-Otzeta, J. M., Lazkano, E., & Ruiz, T. (2017, November). Adaptive emotional chatting behavior to increase the sociability of robots. In International Conference on Social Robotics (pp. 666–675). Springer, Cham.

Russell, J. A. (1980). A circumplex model of affect. *Journal of Personality and Social Psychology*, *39*(6), 1161.

Ruvolo, P., Fasel, I., & Movellan, J. (2008, May). Auditory mood detection for social and educational robots. In *2008 IEEE International Conference on Robotics and Automation* (pp. 3551–3556). IEEE.

Salichs, M. A., & Malfaz, M. (2011). A new approach to modeling emotions and their use on a decision-making system for artificial agents. *IEEE Transactions on Affective Computing*, *3*(1), 56–68. https://doi.org/10.1109/T-AFFC.2011.32.

Scherer, K. R. (2005). What are emotions? And how can they be measured?. *Social Science Information*, *44*(4), 695–729. https://doi.org/10.1177/0539018405058216.

Scherer, K. R. (2009). The dynamic architecture of emotion: Evidence for the component process model. *Cognition and emotion*, *23*(7), 1307–1351. https://doi.org/10.1080/02699930902928969.

Scherer, K. R. (2001). Emotional experience is subject to social and technological change: Extrapolating to the future. *Social Science Information*, *40*(1), 125–151.

Shao, M., Alves, S. F., Ismail, O., Zhang, X., Nejat, G., & Benhabib, B. (2019). You are doing great! Only one rep left: An affect-aware social robot for exercising. *2019 IEEE International Conference on Systems, Man and Cybernetics (SMC)*. https://doi.org/10.1109/smc.2019.8914198

Spatola, N., & Wudarczyk, O. A. (2021). Ascribing emotions to robots: Explicit and implicit attribution of emotions and perceived robot anthropomorphism. *Computers in Human Behavior*, 106934. https://doi.org/10.1016/j.chb.2021.106934.

Spezialetti, M., Placidi, G., & Rossi, S. (2020). Emotion recognition for human-robot interaction: recent advances and future perspectives. *Frontiers*

in Robotics and AI, *7*. https://doi.org/10.3389/frobt.2020.532279.

Strait, M., Briggs, P., & Scheutz, M. (2015, April). Gender, more so than age, modulates positive perceptions of language-based human-robot interactions. In *4th international symposium on new frontiers in human robot interaction* (pp. 21–22).

Thüring, M., & Mahlke, S. (2007). Usability, aesthetics and emotions in human–technology interaction. *International Journal of Psychology*, *42*, 253–264. https://doi.org/10.1080/00207590701396674.

Val-Calvo, M., Álvarez-Sánchez, J. R., Ferrández-Vicente, J. M., & Fernández, E. (2020). Affective robot story-telling human-robot interaction: exploratory real-time emotion estimation analysis using facial expressions and physiological signals. *IEEE Access*, *8*, 134051–134066. https://doi.org/10.1109/ACCESS.2020.3007109.

Weizenbaum, J. (1966). ELIZA – a computer program for the study of natural language communication between man and machine. *Communications of the ACM*. *9*: 36–45. https://doi.org/10.1145/365153.365168.

Willemse, C. J., Toet, A., & van Erp, J. B. (2017). Affective and behavioral responses to robot-initiated social touch: Toward understanding the opportunities and limitations of physical contact in human–robot interaction. *Frontiers in ICT*, *4*, 12. https://doi.org/10.3389/fict.2017.00012.

Xin, L., Lun, X., Zhi-liang, W., & Dong-mei, F. (2013). Robot emotion and performance regulation based on HMM. *International Journal of Advanced Robotic Systems*, *10*(3), 160. https://doi.org/10.5772/55607.

Zhao, S. (2006). Humanoid social robots as a medium of communication. *New Media & Society*, *8*(3), 401–419. https://doi.org/10.1177/1461444806061951.

32

Social Presence in Human–Machine Communication

Kun Xu and David Jeong

INTRODUCTION

A range of artificial intelligence-based technologies have the potential to facilitate users' feeling of being together with other humans or artificial social actors, such as telepresence robots that allow users to virtually meet other people (Herring et al., 2016), smart speakers that are installed with voice assistants that process, interpret, and respond to human inquires via synthetic voices (Lau, Zimmerman, & Schaub, 2018), and physically embodied robots that are adopted to look after elderly people or autistic children (Bemelmans et al., 2012). While varied in their forms, functions, and use experiences, these technologies have the capacity to act as representations of humans based on their humanlike communication acts or appearances. Users' perception of these technologies as if they were real and social is construed as *social presence*. Chatting with Siri or Alexa, interacting with bots on social media, and even following the instructions of automated teller machines can all involve such perceptual experiences of communicating with social actors.

Research on social presence has important implications. First, social presence is a prevalent human experience that occurs in various communication contexts such as education, entertainment, and business. It raises interdisciplinary discussions across psychology, philosophy, computer science, and art. Second, within human–machine communication (HMC) contexts, social presence has been found to have influences on users' attitudinal and behavioral outcomes, such as users' trust in, acceptance of, and conformity to technologies (Lee et al., 2006; Oh et al., 2018). Thus, a complete understanding of social presence and its effects may present significant practical and theoretical contributions. Finally, the impact of social presence may bring about ethical issues and challenges. For instance, Deepfake technologies can be deceptive, misleading, and manipulative by evoking users' strong feelings of social presence (Hancock & Bailenson, 2021). Thus, it is necessary to scrutinize not only the promises, but also the perils of social presence-evoking technologies in our society.

As an overview of the concept, the current chapter attempts to provide a cohesive explication of social presence. We start the chapter by introducing different types of social presence, along with examples of social presence within HMC contexts. Next, we demonstrate the explanatory mechanisms of the experience. We close by providing our vision for the application and future directions of social presence in HMC research.

CONCEPTUALIZATIONS OF SOCIAL PRESENCE

The term *social presence* has been explicated by scholars in various ways (for a review, see Biocca et al., 2003; Oh et al., 2018). In the following section, we identify five prominent conceptualizations of social presence, namely social presence as a medium feature, social-actor-within-medium presence, medium-as-social-actor presence, copresence, and self-presence. It should be noted that these conceptualizations are not mutually exclusive, as scholars tend to put different emphases on the meanings of social presence. Considering HMC involves communication with various types of digital interlocutors in real or virtual/augmented environments (Edwards & Edwards, 2017); we also elaborate how these explications of social presence apply to different HMC contexts below.

Social Presence as a Medium Feature

The formal introduction of social presence can be traced to Short, Williams, and Christie's (1976) explication of social presence as "the degree of salience of the other person in the consequent salience of the interpersonal relationships" (p. 65). Distinct from scholars who view presence as users' perceptual experiences, Short et al. (1976) viewed social presence as the subjective quality of a medium, hypothesizing that each communication medium varies in its capacity to transmit non-verbal cues such as tones, facial expressions, and postures. From a measurement perspective, Short et al. (1976) indicated that a greater level of social presence means that the medium is more sociable, sensitive, warm, and personal. Although their conceptualization of social presence has been mostly applied to computer-mediated communication research, it can be applied to HMC research when scholars attempt to compare the psychological effects of machines with different modalities or bandwidth. For instance, scholars may examine the differences between a disembodied text-based chatbot and a virtually embodied voice-based assistant, as these two technologies may deliver different degrees of intimacy and immediacy.

Social-Actor-Within-Medium Presence

Social-actor-within-medium presence refers to the experience where users respond to the social cues presented by the social actors within a medium (Lombard & Ditton, 1997). One type of social-actor-within-medium presence is the para-social relationship, which was initially proposed by Horton and Wohl (1956) to describe the phenomena where media characters address the audiences as if they were communicating privately, establishing a continual social relationship with the audiences. Today, para-social relationships have been extended to AI news anchors on TV and virtual AI influencers on social media (Park et al., 2021), occurring when users directly react to these artificial media personae and overlook the mediation nature of TV or social media.

In addition to para-social relationships, users may experience social-actor-within-medium presence when communicating with virtual agents, game avatars, or interface agents. For example, in VR/AR environments, users may interact with virtual agents as if they were real people (Miller et al., 2019). Similarly, users respond to the cues presented by avatars during teleconferencing meetings (e.g., Gather.town, ENGAGE VR) (see Han et al., 2023), but may fail to fully acknowledge the role of technologies that afford the experiences.

Medium-As-Social-Actor Presence

While social-actor-within-medium presence focuses on the experience of responding to the social cues presented through media, another type of social presence, medium-as-social-actor presence, refers to the idea that when a medium itself presents social cues, individuals perceive it not as a medium per se, but as an independent social actor warranting corresponding social responses (Lombard & Ditton, 1997; Lombard & Xu, 2021). The concept of medium-as-social-actor presence can be traced to the development of the Computers are Social Actors (CASA) paradigm (Nass et al., 1994) and the Media Equation (Reeves & Nass, 2002). Based on a series of lab experiments in which Nass and colleagues selected established social psychology research findings and replicated them by replacing the human roles with computers or televisions, Reeves and Nass (2002) found that humans respond to machines just as they do to real people. For example, it has been found that individuals tend to show politeness to computers, apply gender stereotypes to computer voices, and demonstrate reciprocity with computers when these computers present social cues such as human language, facial expressions, human or synthetic voices, and emotions (Nass, 2004; Nass & Moon, 2000; Nass, Moon, & Green, 1997). These social responses are considered indicators of users' social presence experiences, where users mindlessly apply social rules to HMC.

Based on the CASA paradigm and the Media Equation, empirical research on medium-as-social-actor presence has extended to a variety of emerging technologies, including smartphones, social robots, and chatbots. For instance, social robots have been found to evoke stronger social presence when they reciprocate personalities of human participants (Lee et al., 2006) and when they adhere to etiquette norms, such as yielding to humans when pass through a hallway (Fiore et al., 2013).

Social Presence as Copresence

While medium-as-social-actor presence and social-actor-within-medium presence focuses more on users' reactions to social cues presented *by* or *through* media, some social presence scholars place greater emphasis on users' feelings of colocation and togetherness. Thus, copresence is often used to refer to such feelings of being with others (Biocca et al., 2003; Nowak & Biocca, 2003; Zhao, 2003). Along the two dimensions of proximity and corporeal presence, Zhao (2003) identified six *modes* of copresence including corporeal copresence (i.e., face-to-face human communication), corporeal telecopresence (i.e., human-to-human interaction through electronic communication mediums), virtual copresence (i.e., direct human–technology interaction such as human–robot interaction), virtual telecopresence (i.e., human–technology interaction through medium such as human–avatar interaction), hypervirtual copresence (i.e., humans represented by robot devices interacting with each other, e.g., robotic football games), and hypervirtual telecopresence (i.e., digital agents interact with each other in cyberspace). Although hypervirtual telecopresence does not directly involve users' agency in the communication process, the other *modes* of copresence can all create users' *sense* of copresence, which refers to their subjective experience of being together with other humans or artificial social actors (Zhao, 2003).

Self-Presence

As a unique subcategory of social presence, self-presence is defined as "a psychological state in which virtual (para-authentic or artificial) self/selves are experienced as the actual self in either sensory or non-sensory ways" (Lee, 2004a, p. 46). Users may experience self-presence by establishing a social connection with a digital extension of themselves (e.g., self-representative avatars) or by remotely controlling robotic technologies. Ratan and Hasler

(2009) introduced a conceptual framework with three types of self-presence in virtual environments: proto self-presence, core self-presence, and extended self-presence. Proto self-presence refers to the extent to which a media object is treated as an extension of a user's body. Core self-presence describes the affective state that one can feel when one's virtual representation of self interacts with media objects. Extended self-presence describes the identity that is generated in the mediated environments.

Self-presence shares conceptual connections with the Proteus Effect (Yee et al., 2009), which suggests that individuals can learn from and conform to their avatars' behavior. For instance, Fox and Bailenson (2009) found that seeing one's own avatar getting rewarded for losing weight or getting punished for gaining weight encouraged users to increase exercise. Related to self-presence, Won et al. (2014) introduced the concept of "homuncular flexibility," which suggests that users in virtual environments are capable of not only controlling their own bodies but also adapting to novel virtual bodies using unique disjointed mapping of limb movements (e.g., moving virtual legs using physical arms).

EXPLANATORY MECHANISMS

While social presence may be the product of various factors including technology forms (e.g., screen size, visual quality), media content (e.g., first-person perspective), and technology users (e.g., prior experiences, age, gender) (Lee, 2004a; Lombard & Ditton, 1997), there is limited consensus on why social presence occurs. Existing research has attempted to explain individuals' psychological processing of social presence-evoking technologies from two trajectories: *mindful* processing and *mindless* processing. Below, we discuss these explanatory mechanisms along these two lines. Specifically, these mechanisms include anthropomorphism, suspension of disbelief, mindlessness, and theory of mind. What merits note is that these mechanisms are interrelated: social presence can be explained by the concurrence of multiple triggers rather than one single factor. In other words, there may be multiple explanations that capture the mechanism of social presence experiences.

Mindful Processing

One of the major explanations for social presence, especially medium-as-social-actor presence, can be attributed to anthropomorphism, which refers to "the tendency to imbue real or imagined behavior of non-human agents with humanlike characteristics, motivations, intentions, or emotions" (Epley et al., 2007, p. 864). Anthropomorphism involves ascribing human mental or emotional states to non-human agents, including technologies and natural phenomena (e.g., happy sun, angry clouds) (Duffy, 2003), as well as simulations of geometric shapes and humanoid social robots (Duffy & Zawieska, 2012; Heider & Simmel, 1944). According to Nass and Moon (2000), anthropomorphism "involves the thoughtful, sincere belief that the object has human characteristics" (p. 93).

Another mindful psychological processing mechanism that explains social presence is individuals' willingness to suspend disbelief (Lee, 2004b), which refers to users' purposeful and conscious mental activity of following the media producers' or developers' intention and ignoring the artificiality of mediation (Duffy & Zawieska, 2012; Lee, 2004b). By suspending disbelief, users feel immersed in virtual environments and mindfully view virtual agents, animated characters, and robotic technologies as social and real. Indeed, Slater and Usoh (1993) referred to users' presence experience as "suspension of disbelief that they are in a world other than where their real bodies are located" (p. 22). Although Slater and Usoh's (1993) definition is more associated with the concept of spatial presence, it is logical to postulate that the operation mechanism for social presence can be similar: social presence may occur as a result of users' suspension of the disbelief that they are merely communicating with machines rather than real social actors.

Mindless Processing

In contrast to anthropomorphism and suspension of disbelief, alternative perspectives posit that social presence is a bottom-up reaction that occurs mindlessly and spontaneously. One of the explanations for the CASA phenomena is that individuals "mindlessly and prematurely commit to overly simplistic scripts drawn in the past" (Nass & Moon, 2000, p. 83). Mindlessness occurs "without extensive thought or deliberation" due to individuals' repetitive exposure to the social cues in interpersonal communication (Moon, 2000, p. 325).

The mindlessness explanation has its roots in evolutionary psychology. In their book *The Media Equation*, Reeves and Nass (2002) further explained that our brain has not evolved to distinguish mediated objects and real objects. The default of our brain is to assume what we see is real (Gerrig, 1993; Lee, 2004b), predicated on the Tooby and Cosmides (1992) notion that our

biology (i.e., brains) is calibrated for our ancestral world, and not adequately adapted for today's emerging media technologies. This mechanism of perceiving incoming information as real is part of an innate human trait in that from the perspective of adaption, humans evolve the instinct to resist potential environmental risks and threats. This survival alarming system operates as a protection buffer that leads individuals to perceive mediated and ersatz cues as non-mediated and natural ones (Reeves & Nass, 2000).

The potential evolutionary basis of mindless processing also lends support to the role of theory of mind (Adolphs, 2009; Frith & Frith, 2005) in explaining individuals' social presence experiences. Theory of mind refers to one's capacity to infer meanings, intentions, and goals of other humans based on cues and contexts. Despite its distinctions from in-person communication, the formation of social presence experiences in HMC can be understood from the perspective of social perception and meaning-making (Miller et al., 2019). That is, in HMC contexts, users' sensitivity to humanlike cues and their tendency to rely on them to predict others' intentions and actions can help them adjust their actions accordingly and more effectively communicate and collaborate with nonhuman agents (Hare, 2007).

FUTURE RESEARCH AND APPLICATIONS

So far, we have discussed various conceptualizations of social presence, along with some of the major explanations for the experiences. As technologies have advanced to a point where they are designed with more natural, intuitive, and anthropomorphic characteristics, and with more research covering topics such as social computing, affective computing, and ubiquitous computing (Picard, 1995; Schuler, 1994; Weiser, 1991), social presence may play an even more central role in the psychological effects of technologies and the socially constructed meanings of technologies. Below we list some of the future directions where researchers can consider working on to further our understanding of the concept.

One prior attempt to examine and contribute to the explication of social presence is the establishment of the Media are Social Actors (MASA) paradigm. Lombard and Xu (2021) proposed the MASA paradigm as a structured extension of the CASA paradigm. They looked into the concept of medium-as-social-actor presence and distinguished the effects of primary social cues and secondary social cues in evoking this type of presence.

Additionally, they unified the explanatory mechanisms of anthropomorphism and mindlessness and explained what scholars mean by "social" when referring to "social cues" and "social responses." Thus, one future research direction could be to test the validity of the paradigm and extend our knowledge about both the CASA and the MASA frameworks.

Furthermore, as technologies have become increasingly multi-layered, users may be engaged with more intricate and multi-faceted experiences. For example, telepresence robots have been designed to present interpersonal cues such as movements and gestures. Meanwhile, its users can remotely control the robot and display their facial expressions via a screen that assumes the place of the robot's head. Therefore, telepresence robots may concurrently trigger multiple forms of social presence by leading users to perceive robotic bodies as social actors (medium-as-social-actor presence), and to use web conferencing tools to chat with other human partners (social-actor-within-medium presence) (Xu & Liao, 2020). Along this line of research, scholars may examine whether and how different types of social presence experiences complement or compete against each other in shaping users' overall user experiences. The findings may inform us about how individual users allocate attention to perceive two potential social actors within a single machine entity.

In addition, recent studies have revealed intricate results about the perceived communication source in HMC. One direction that future research could follow is the source orientation model (Guzman, 2019; Solomon & Wash, 2014). The model describes that as source distance increases, users sequentially re-orient their communication target to an application/software of the computer, the computer per se, other users, programmers, and organizations. In other words, users may feel different types of social presence depending on the proximity to the perceived communication target. Thus, as machines become increasingly convergent, it will be necessary to parse out the different layers of social presence experiences when individuals orient their responses from one perceived source to another.

Moreover, modern communication technology brings about questions of authenticity in the context of social presence, namely the presence of algorithmic representations that replace or augment the human interlocutor. Such an algorithmic presence may take on the form of text (a chatbot, automated messages) and visuals (filters, Deepfakes), and uniquely may take place in the absence of an active human controller/interlocutor. Such a unidirectional interaction is more commonly associated with text-based chatbots, but the concept may be expanded (with trepidation) to visual forms. For instance, a Zoom user may pre-record separate video messages, such as a head nod, "I agree," and a wave, which may be set to play given a specific set of parameters or commands. HMC scholars may benefit from future conceptual inquiries into algorithmic social presence as artificial representations of humans, as well as rigorous investigation of the ethical issues presented by such algorithmic representations.

SUMMARY

In this book chapter, we introduced the concept of social presence and explained its meanings from different perspectives. We also introduced the current scholarly discussion about the possible mechanisms for explaining the social presence experiences. Finally, we demonstrated future research directions where this concept can be further explored and explained. As the field of HMC is witnessing a rise of a range of social presence-evoking technologies, it is crucial that researchers understand and elucidate the type of social presence they use in their research contexts (e.g., media features, copresence, medium-as-social-actor presence, etc.) and subsequently apply the appropriate methods/measures to further advance the study of human–machine communication.

REFERENCES

Adolphs, R. (2009). The social brain: Neural basis of social knowledge. *Annual Review of Psychology*, *60*, 693–716.

Bemelmans, R., Gelderblom, G. J., Jonker, P., & De Witte, L. (2012). Socially assistive robots in elderly care: A systematic review into effects and effectiveness. *Journal of the American Medical Directors Association*, *13*(2), 114–120.

Biocca, F., Harms, C., & Burgoon, J. K. (2003). Toward a more robust theory and measure of social presence: Review and suggested criteria. *Presence*, *12*, 456–480.

Duffy, B. R. (2003). Anthropomorphism and the social robot. *Robotics and Autonomous Systems*, *42*, 177–190.

Duffy, B. R., & Zawieska, K. (2012 September). Suspension of disbelief in social robotics. In *IEEE RO-MAN: The 21st IEEE International Symposium on Robot and Human Interactive Communication*. Paris, France.

Edwards, A., & Edwards, C. (2017). The machines are coming: Future directions in instructional communication research. *Communication Education*, *66*, 487–488.

Epley, N., Waytz, A., & Cacioppo, J. T. (2007). On seeing human: A three-factor theory of anthropomorphism, *Psychological Review*, *114*, 864–886.

Fiore, S. M., Wiltshire, T. J., Lobato, E. J. C., Jentsch, F. G., Huang, W. H., & Axelrod, B. (2013). Toward understanding social cues and signals in human-robot interaction: Effects of robot gaze and proxemic behavior. *Frontiers in Psychology*, *4*, 1–15. https://doi.org/10.3389/fpsyg.2013.00859

Fox, J., & Bailenson, J. N. (2009). Virtual self-modeling: The effects of vicarious reinforcement and identification on exercise behaviors. *Media Psychology*, *12*(1), 1–25.

Frith, C., & Frith, U. (2005). Theory of mind. *Current Biology*, *15*, 644–645.

Gerrig, R. J. (1993). *Experiencing narrative worlds*. New Haven, CT: Yale University Press.

Guzman, A. L. (2019). Voices in and of the machine: Source orientation toward mobile virtual assistants. *Computers in Human Behavior*, *90*, 343–350.

Han, E., Miller, M. R., DeVeaux, C., Jun, H., Nowak, K. L., Hancock, J. T., Ram, N., & Bailenson, J. N. (2023). People, places, and time: A large-scale, longitudinal study of transformed avatars and environmental context in group interaction in the metaverse. *Journal of Computer-Mediated Communication*, *28*(2), zmac031. https://doi.org/10.1093/jcmc/zmac031

Hancock, J., & Bailenson, J. (2021). The social impact of deepfake. *CyberPsychology, Behavior, & Social Networking*, *24*, 149–152.

Hare, B. (2007). From nonhuman to human mind: What changed and why? *Current Directions in Psychological Science*, *16*(2), 60–64. https://doi.org/10.1111/j.1467-8721.2007.00476.x

Heider, F., & Simmel, M. (1944). An experimental study of apparent behavior. *American Journal of Psychology*, *57*, 243–259.

Herring, S. C., Fussell, S. R., Kristoffersson, A., Mutlu, B., Neustaedter, C., & Tsui, K. (2016, May). The future of robotic telepresence: visions, opportunities and challenges. In *Proceedings of the 2016 CHI Conference Extended Abstracts on Human Factors in Computing Systems* (pp. 1038–1042).

Horton, D., & Wohl, R. (1956). Mass communication and para-social interaction: Observation on intimacy at a distance. *Psychiatry*, *19*, 215–229.

International Society for Presence Research. (2000). *The concept of presence: Explication statement*. ISPR. http://ispr.info/about-presence-2/about-presence/

Lau, J., Zimmerman, B., & Schaub, F. (2018). Alexa, are you listening? Privacy perceptions, concerns and privacy-seeking behaviors with smart speakers. *Proceedings of the ACM on Human-Computer Interaction*, *2*(CSCW), 1–31.

Lee, K. M. (2004a). Presence explicated. *Communication Theory*, *14*(1), 27–50.

Lee, K. M. (2004b). Why presence occurs: Evolutionary psychology, media equation, and presence. *Presence*, *13*(4), 494–505.

Lee, K. M., Peng, W., Jin, S. A., & Yan, C. (2006). Can robots manifest personality? An empirical test of personality recognition, social responses, and social presence in human-robot interaction. *Journal of Communication*, *56*, 754–772.

Lombard, M., & Ditton, T. (1997). At the heart of it all: The concept of presence. *Journal of Computer-mediated Communication*, *3*: 0. Doi: 10.1111/j.1083-6101.1997.tb00072x

Lombard, M., & Xu, K. (2021). Social responses to media technologies in the 21st century: The Media are Social Actors paradigm. *Human-Machine Communication*, *2*, 29–55.

Miller, L. C., Jeong, D. C., Wang, L., Shaikh, S. J., Gillig, T. K., Godoy, C. G., Appleby, R. R., Corsbie-Massay, C. L., Marsella, S., Christensen, J. L., & Read, S. J. (2019). Systematic representative design: A reply to commentaries. *Psychological Inquiry*, *30*(4), 250–263. https://doi.org/10.1080/1047840x.2019.1698908

Moon, Y. (2000). Intimate exchanges: Using computers to elicit self-disclosure from consumers. *Journal of Consumer Research*, *26*, 323–339.

Nass, C. (2004). Etiquette equality: Exhibitions and expectations of computer politeness. *Communications of the ACM*, *47*(4), 35–37.

Nass, C., & Moon, Y. (2000). Machines and mindlessness: Social responses to computers. *Journal of Social Issues*, *56*, 81–103.

Nass, C., Moon, Y., & Green, N. (1997). Are machines gender neutral? Gender-stereotypic responses to computers with voices. *Journal of Applied Social Psychology*, *27*(10), 864–876.

Nass, C., Steuer, J., & Tauber, E. R. (1994). Computers are social actors. In *Proceedings of the SIGCHI Conference on Human Factors in Computing Systems*, *94*, 72–78.

Nowak, K. L., & Biocca, F. (2003). The effect of the agency and anthropomorphism on users' sense of telepresence, copresence, and social presence in virtual environments. *Presence: Teleoperators & Virtual Environments*, *12*(5), 481–494.

Oh, C. S., Bailenson, J. N., & Welch, G. F. (2018). A systematic review of social presence: Definition, antecedents, and implications. *Frontiers in Robotics and AI*, *5*,114.

Park, G., Nan, D., Park, E., Kim, K. J., Han, J., & del Pobil, A. P. (2021, January). Computers as social actors? Examining how users perceive and interact with virtual influencers on social media. In *2021 15th International Conference on Ubiquitous Information Management and Communication (IMCOM)* (pp. 1–6). IEEE.

Picard, R. W. (1995). Computer learning of subjectivity. *ACM Computing Surveys (CSUR)*, *27*(4), 621–623.

Ratan, R. A., & Hasler, B. (2009, November). Self-presence standardized: Introducing the self-presence questionnaire (SPQ). In *Proceedings of the 12th annual international workshop on presence* (Vol. 81).

Reeves, B., & Nass, C. (2000). Perceptual bandwidth: What happens to people when computers become perceptually complex. *Communications of the ACM*, *43*, 65–70.

Reeves, B., & Nass, C. (2002). *The media equation: How people treat computers, television, and new media like real people and places*. Cambridge University Press.

Schuler, D. (1994). Social computing. *Communications of the ACM*, *37*(1), 28–29.

Short, J., Williams, E., & Christie, B. (1976). Theoretical approaches to differences between media. In *Social psychology of telecommunications* (pp. 61–66). Wiley.

Slater, M., & Usoh, M. (1993). Representations systems, perceptual position, and presence in immersive virtual environments. *Presence: Teleoperators & Virtual Environments*, *2*(3), 221–233.

Solomon, J., & Wash, R. (2014, September). Human-what interaction? Understanding user source orientation. In *Proceedings of the Human Factors and Ergonomics Society Annual Meeting* (Vol. 58, No. 1, pp. 422–426). Sage Publications.

Tooby, J., & Cosmides, L. (1992). The psychological foundations of culture. In J. Barkow, L. Cosmides, & J. Tobby (Eds.), *The adapted mind: Evolutionary psychology and the generation of culture*, pp. 16–136. Oxford University Press.

Weiser, M. (1991). The computer for the 21st Century. *Scientific American*, *265*, 94–110.

Won, A. S., Haans, A., Ijsselsteijn, W. A., & Bailenson, J. N. (2014). A framework for interactivity and presence in novel bodies. In G. Riva, J. Waterworth, & D. Murray (Eds.), *Interacting with presence: HCI and the sense of presence in computer-mediated environments* (pp. 57–67). De Gruyter Open Ltd.

Xu, K., & Liao, T. (2020). Explicating cues: A typology for understanding emerging media technologies. *Journal of Computer-Mediated Communication*, *25*(1), 32–43.

Yee, N., Bailenson, J. N., & Ducheneaut, N. (2009). The Proteus effect: Implications of transformed digital self-representation on online and offline behavior. *Communication Research*, *36*(2), 285–312.

Zhao, S. (2003). Toward a taxonomy of copresence. *Presence*, *12*, 445–455.

33

Interpersonal Interactions Between People and Machines

Astrid Rosenthal-von der Pütten
and Kevin Koban

INTRODUCTION

Traditionally, interpersonal communication has been understood as a complex social process where *people* create shared meaning via purposefully formulated messages to meet specific goals (Burleson, 2010). In this light, interpersonal communication is not a sequence of utterances with linguistic and non-linguistic features but joint action: Navigating social encounters, collaborating on tasks, forming and maintaining relationships. While such an understanding had primarily addressed communications between physically co-present human agents, technological advances have expanded conceptual boundaries to include physically distant but virtually connected humans (i.e., computer-mediated communication [CMC]; Walther, 1996) and, more recently, AI-augmented communications between human agents (i.e., AI-mediated communication [AI MC]; Hancock et al., 2020), as well as meaning-making between human and machine agents (i.e., human–machine communication [HMC]; Guzman, 2018). HMC differs from the other conceptual extensions because it accepts a non-human other as an autonomous part of the dyadic creation of meaning (instead of being merely a medium or mediator) that may display similar communicative

capabilities but is typically perceived to belong to a different ontological category (Guzman, 2020).

Despite people's categorization of social machines as an "in-between kind" (Etzrodt & Engesser, 2021; Kahn & Shen, 2017), previous research has provided empirical support that humans adhere intuitively to familiar behavioral scripts and social norms when interacting with machine interlocutors in order to make sense of their behaviors (Reeves & Nass, 1996; Nass & Yen, 2012). Similar behavioral patterns have been consistently found for different interaction forms (e.g., formal or informal interactions), across a variety of contexts (e.g., work-related or leisure contexts), and toward various social machines alike, including embodied virtual agents, voice assistants, and robots (Krämer et al., 2015). Others have argued that people may develop and apply novel interaction scripts and social norms that are individually tailored for those machine agents with which they have frequently communicated (Gambino et al., 2020). Importantly, both of these positions suggest that communications between human and machine agents may not be fundamentally different from human–human communication (HHC), as "humans and machines are potentially equivalent interlocutors with potentially equivalent psychological, social, and moral consequences" (Banks & de Graaf, 2020, p. 29).

Such a functional equivalence may be more evident once machines adopt verbal and nonverbal signals that are common in HHC; however, people's perceptions of these 'natural' communication features may be a more useful gateway to explain why such machines trigger interpersonal phenomena.

In this chapter, we will briefly introduce different conceptualizations of interpersonal communication, outline current implementations of natural communication features in social machines, and discuss whether a display of these features may create stable expectations about their role as meaningful interlocutors. Based on this discussion, we then review how and to what extent pivotal theories and concepts of HHC may apply to HMC. Naturally, this chapter cannot tackle the vast field that is interpersonal communication in its entirety but has to focus on illustrative examples. We will exemplarily discuss Clark's theory of common ground (Clark, 1992), Watzlawick's five axioms of communication (Watzlawick et al., 1967), and linguistic alignment (Pickering et al., 2006). Finally, we will highlight intersections between computer science and communication science where scholars of both disciplines can jointly contribute to the development of sophisticated conversational agents.

BASICS OF INTERPERSONAL COMMUNICATION

Conceptualizations of interpersonal communication have changed dramatically over the last 70 years, shifting from an understanding of communication as mere transmission of information (Shannon & Weaver, 1949) towards more complex metaphorical models that view communication as transaction (e.g., Watzlawick et al., 1967) or social construction (e.g., Berger & Luckmann, 1966). In the communication-as-transaction model, communicative agents are considered mutually related senders and receivers. As a consequence, each message consists of a *content component* that refers to its verbal meaning (i.e., *what is said*) and a *relationship component* that refers to the agents' relationship to each other (i.e., *how it is being said*). This bilateral role of communicators as senders and receivers is further expanded in the communication-as-social-construction model where agents are understood as joint creators of the social realities in which they operate. Communicative agents shape what is accepted as factual or even possible within their social landscapes through joint communicative actions. Here, messages are not just instruments for

negotiating shared meaning but building blocks that constitute who (or what) communicative agents are in relation to others. In other words, how we talk to other agents influences how we think about them and their relationship with us. This influence is further amplified as people formulate their messages given certain assumptions about what the message receiver may (be able to) know or find acceptable (Krauss & Fussel, 1991).

These conceptualizations were developed and theoretically elaborated to capture how *human* agents interact with each other. HMC scholarship has argued that it is no conceptual necessity to restrict theories of communication to cover only "*a type of communication*" (Guzman, 2018, p. 17; italics in the original). As Banks and de Graaf (2020) have demonstrated for the transmission model of communication, extant theorizing may be applicable to HMC, thus offering a rich background for examining communications between human *and* machine agents as well.

FROM MERE MACHINES TO INTERLOCUTORS

Most contemporary social machines' conversational interfaces no longer rely on commands or buttons but are based on natural communication features to facilitate smooth communications with humans. According to Beattie and Ellis (2017), interpersonal communication involves verbal (i.e., words, clauses, sentences), prosodic (i.e., rhythm, pausing, intonation), paralinguistic (i.e., fillers, vocalics), kinesic (i.e., gestures, facial expressions, postures), and standing features (i.e., interpersonal distance, orientation, appearance). Designers and programmers of social machines have implemented humanlike simulations across all of these components with important implications for HMC besides merely expressing information.

Implementations of natural communication features convey cues that may allow human interlocutors to infer the communicator's mental states. For non-human agents, these cue-driven inferences can include mentalizing about another agent's intentions (i.e., *why is it being said*) and basic intentionality (i.e., *what is it capable of saying*). Once a social machine is verbally and nonverbally communicating in a manner similar to how humans are communicating, perceptions of humanlike communication abilities will imbue what people think about and further expect from their non-human interlocutors (Horstmann & Krämer, 2020; Waytz et al., 2010).

Moreover, the constitution of meaning (i.e., pragmatics) predominantly manifests in nonverbal behavior (Watzlawick et al., 1967). Modulations of an artificial voice, pauses in conversations, gestures; all these features observable in machine behavior (be it deliberately used for communication, happening by chance, or due to technical failure) will likely be interpreted as relationship information, rendering these machines as "otherware" (Hassenzahl et al., 2021).

Previous research has demonstrated that a machine's gesticulations and posture (Rosenthal-von der Pütten et al., 2018; Straßmann et al., 2019), facial expressions (Hoegen et al., 2018), proxemics (Mumm & Mutlu, 2011), or appearance (Rosenthal-von der Pütten & Krämer, 2014) can trigger rapid evaluations of its assumed character. If such features are convincing, even non-behavior can be interpreted in a meaningful way. This carry-over phenomenon has been indicated in previous works where an otherwise verbally competent machine that does not respond to a human communicator's questioning in an adequate time due to processing load can be understood as intentionally remaining silent for a particular reason (Cyra 2017; Shiwa et al., 2009).

People's understanding of social machines as (potentially) mindful, intentional, and relatable beings opens up novel perspectives on how HHC theories can contribute to explain different HMC phenomena and what can be derived from the design of communicating machines. In the following, three such theories will be briefly reviewed.

Theory of Common Ground

Though sometimes we saliently experience a communication partner as hard to understand or inscrutable in their motives, the majority of our daily interactions with other humans are apparently effortless and successful. In fact, these unimposing interactions are possible only when both interlocutors either know or refer to the same concepts. Addressing this issue, Clark (1992) postulated that interaction partners draw on common ground (i.e., "the sum of their mutual, common, or joint knowledge, beliefs, and suppositions" [p. 93]) when stepping into communication. Common ground includes that people take certain knowledge (such as the law of physics, biological facts, or specific social facts) for granted, which is referred to as *communal common ground*. Furthermore, *personal common ground* is built on joint experiences and actions that two (or more) people have lived through together during their interpersonal history.

Lack of communal and personal common ground with social machines. As Krämer et al. (2011) stated when critically reflecting the role (and limits) of common ground in HMC, artificial entities, per default, lack *communal common ground* unless it is programmed into them (meaning that it is completely dependent on the programmers' taken-for-granted knowledge). However, even if such information has been provided to a social machine (e.g., the biological nature of humans, their forms and rules of living together), it might not be able to make sense of it due to a lack of self-awareness (composed of self-knowledge, self-belief, and self-assumption) in a given situation and missing knowledge that other interactants may have an analogous self-awareness in that situation (see Clark, 1992). In other words, the social machine does not only need to have (a) declarative knowledge about a large variety of different topics. It also needs to know (b) which parts of this knowledge are relevant in a given situation, (c) how it relates to the ways people are experiencing that given situation, and (d) what consequences are implied for communication when certain information is voiced in a particular way. An interaction partner would know that (a) humans need food and water; (b) sitting in a restaurant at noon means that food intake is relevant for this situation; (c) the other interaction partner is presumably hungry; and (d) which, in consequence, means that impatient intonation is probably not relevant relationship information but instead an expression of hunger. As mundane as this simple reasoning seems, it poses a great problem to artificial interlocutors as it requires them to solve multiple complex problems in knowledge representation and reasoning simultaneously.

Many social machines also lack appropriate abilities to build up *personal common ground* with their users as they typically do not store a "history of joint personal experiences." A voice assistant might store users' previous search requests on an abstract level, but it typically does not "remember" all conversations with them. In fact, it is a significant technical challenge to detect and distinguish between multiple users and interact with them in real time. An example of a social robot interacting with a group of people might help to illustrate this challenge. Bearing in mind that each of the following constitutes a complex problem to solve in visual computing, the robot would have to identify *multiple* objects and people of interest (He et al., 2017), decide upon *relevant* objects and *potential* interaction partners in real time, and also *keep track* of these relevant objects and people over a prolonged period (Wang et al., 2019). Social signal processing comes into play when a robot takes on the challenge to *recognize and interpret* social behaviors exhibited by interaction partners. After years of research on communication management in human–robot interaction in dyads (e.g., on turn-taking or back-channeling behaviors), research groups now have moved on to realize attention management, turn-taking gaze, and other social gaze behaviors for robots in multi-party interactions (Żarkowski, 2019). Establishing such interactions is already hard to realize; keeping up a meaningful history of them is future work. This means that without appropriate user modeling and interaction history logging, there will be a mismatch between assumed personal common ground on the user's side and actual stored data.

Defied expectations and communicative consequences. Social machines that (multimodally) engage in conversations with users evoke great expectations about their communicative abilities. Since "speakers exploit the common ground, they share with their addressees in creating referring expressions" (Krauss & Fussel, 1991, p. 2), misunderstandings are inevitable if the assumed common ground does not match the system's actual knowledge and abilities. Similar to HHC but likely to a more considerable extent, discrepancies between the sender's communicative goal and the receiver's perception and understanding of it will be present on both sides. However, while humans typically have verbal and nonverbal strategies to discover and repair situations in which mutual knowledge is misinterpreted (Clark & Brennan, 1991), contemporary systems already fail at reliably detecting such situations. Feedback may be a key concept for human–machine interaction because it can compensate for such a lack of knowledge. Social machines have to provide feedback mechanisms to find ground with human interaction partners, if not to build up common ground in the long run by establishing a common knowledge base for the current and future conversations. Interestingly, missing common ground might not always be negative for the perceived outcome of a conversation. Krämer et al. (2011) described situations in which a very basic health advisor robot misinterprets situations. Instead of being annoyed or frustrated by this misbehavior, the human user took the situation as an opportunity to "teach" the system knowledge despite knowing that the system cannot understand verbal input. In other words, human users exploited this unbalanced communicative situation to fulfill their own needs regardless of whether the communication was effective. Human interactants may thus find manifold ways to cope with missing common ground. While some may be frustrated and abandon a machine, others may adapt to its abilities and find new (system-specific) ways for communication, or they ignore a system's shortcomings and treat it like a human anyways.

Watzlawick's Axioms of Communication

According to Watzlawick and colleagues' (1967) theory of communication, five axioms (i.e., premises that are taken to be true and serve as a basis for further reasoning) govern any communicative situation between two human interlocutors. These axioms state that (a) any behavior conveys an interpretable meaning to a communicative partner; (b) any communication includes the literal meaning of a message and a metacommunicative aspect that defines the relationship between the communicative partners; and (c) is understood by them as a sequence of causes and responses. They further argue that any communication (d) involves both verbal and nonverbal means; and (e) is built upon a mutual acceptance of symmetrical or asymmetrical power relationships between communicative agents. Considering that their theory-building aimed at predicting communicative disturbances among family members, Watzlawick et al. (1967) emphasized the homeostatic significance of their approach: Misalignments among communicative agents in any of the five axioms may result in miscommunication, which may complicate or even prevent shared creation of meaning.

Meaningful interpretations of misbehaviors. Due to its emphasis on how effective communication can be established among interlocutors and its predictive value for miscommunications, Watzlawick's axioms offer theoretical guidance for interaction design. Notably, it follows from Axiom 1 (i.e., *one cannot not communicate*) that any behavior by a robot, even "misbehaviors" or "nonbehaviors" such as silence resulting from defective sensors or lack of adequate processing power, monotonous intonation owing to poor language processing, or ambiguous gesticulations due to limitations of the hydraulic and pneumatic movement system, can be (mis-)interpreted as meaningful. This interpretative inevitability is being accentuated as social machines combine humanlike signals and cues that may only vaguely approximate its human reference with artificial ones whose correct interpretation relies on their adherence to stereotypical norms (e.g., derived from popular representation of robots or existing social group norms) or must be learned during the course of the interaction (Hegel et al., 2011). As a consequence of these meaningful interpretations of misleading behavior, smooth communicative sequences (as postulated in the third axiom) might become disordered: A human interlocutor may construe a machine's misbehavior as an intentional message and respond to it accordingly, while the machine may understand this behavior as a nonsensical extension of the human's turn which warrants a clarifying (content-wise) and balancing (relationship-wise) response.

Under- and overinterpretations of human's behavior. Axiom 1 may also tempt developers to design architectures to interpret any verbal or nonverbal behavior that is shown by a human as considerable. Such approaches may result in overly tedious or outright annoying interactions with a modern-day Clippy (Rivoire & Lim, 2016). Both under- or overinterpretations of another human's (non-)communicative behaviors may become most concerning when machine agents are not designed to detect meaning beyond the literal content of an utterance (neglecting the relationship aspect of communication specified in Axiom 2) or if they cannot process or interpret information that is transmitted in analog modalities (meaning that they rely solely on digital modalities described in Axiom 4). Irrespective of the machine's functionality, humans have nevertheless been found sharing information about their relationship with a machine interlocutor via nonverbal and paraverbal channels as they would do in HHC (Krämer et al., 2015), refining or qualifying the verbally expressed message content. Machines that serve roles as social companions, tutors, or nurses may have to understand the (often subtle) nonverbal ways in which people communicate relationship information in order to be trusted by them.

Ontology-based objections to machine equality/superiority. While power relations between human communicators (as addressed in Axiom 5) typically arise from a shared understanding of social roles with equal (e.g., coworkers) or unequal standing (e.g., teacher and student), which more often than not guarantees mutual acceptance of these relationships, human interlocutors' ontological considerations about what a social machine should (and should not) be may intervene with effective communication. When prompted to think about social machines, empirical research has demonstrated that people typically highlight technical and performance-related properties (Banks, 2020, Sundar & Kim, 2019), their inferiority compared to humans' mental capacities (Haslam et al., 2008), and their lack of emotions (Guzman, 2020). Others have further argued that humans may fear for their uniqueness when confronted with machines that they perceive to be approaching their levels of mental capacity (Ferrari et al., 2016). However, in order to be effective, many communicative situations require humans to treat machines as equal (e.g., social machines as peer learners) or even to subordinate themselves to them (e.g., social machines

as tutors). People may be hesitant to accept equality of (wo)man and machine, less likely machine superiority, resulting in miscommunication.

Linguistic Alignment

When people engage in dialog, they tend to converge to nonverbal and linguistic patterns presented by their interlocutor. Human interaction partners align linguistically to each other in conversations on different levels, for instance, regarding accent or dialect, speech rhythm, lexical choices, semantics, as well as syntax (Pickering et al., 2006). This alignment is a key aspect in fostering successful communication and is said to be both a result and generator of specific socio-psychological effects (such as mutual liking; Pickering et al., 2006). Alignment tendencies on all above-mentioned levels have been observed in HMC (cf. Branigan et al., 2010), revealing that such behaviors occur and that they have similar impacts (Kühne et al., 2013). However, it has been reported that human interlocutors show stronger alignment in HMC contexts (compared to similar HHC situations), presumably to compensate for a machine's limited natural language processing capacities (Bergmann et al., 2015). In this context, linguistic alignment represents an audience design strategy (also referred to as "computer talk"; Branigan et al., 2010), which is, for instance, modulated by the anthropomorphism of social machines: The fewer social cues a machine conveys, the stronger the alignment (Bergmann et al., 2015).

WHY COMMUNICATION SCHOLARS SHOULD CO-DEVELOP ARTIFICIAL INTERLOCUTORS

Human interpersonal communication is highly complex. When people converse with each other, they do not simply utter words and their counterparts exactly know what is meant. Quite the opposite, interpersonal communication is an individually tailored and interpretative process. Humans draw on common ground when expressing information, that is, vast shared knowledge about social norms, behavioral rules, scripts, schemas, stereotypes, as well as their personal history with each other. Similarly, the "other" uses this information to make sense of what is said. We use language not solely to pass on information but to make ourselves or others feel better, we use it to make people like us or distinguish us from them; hence, social motives determine how we use language. Machines that use natural language features to interact with humans trigger mechanisms that underlie various interpersonal communication phenomena. As discussed, ample evidence demonstrates that people's communicative behavior is based on assumptions about artificial others and sometimes changes when expectations are not met. For instance, people converge with or align to social machines presumably because they ascribe less communicative abilities to them, they cope with situations in which they experience a lack of common ground, and they readily interpret "misbehaviors" that were not meant to be communicative. All of this demonstrates impressively that, regardless of how and why a social machine displays a particular behavior, the *sovereignty of interpretation within communications between human and machine typically lies with the human interaction partner.*

This interpretative sovereignty emphasizes the need to integrate communication scholars' expertise into the development of conversational social machines, especially once those machines (at least partially) rely on approximations of natural communication features and cues to interact with humans. While technical developers are often surprised by misinterpretations or ineffective conversations in HMC, communication scholars have the conceptual toolkit to explain and anticipate such defective incidents based on their knowledge of established theories about how communication between humans tends to unfold. For a start, it might be beneficial for interaction designers to consult communication scholars in order to understand communication from an agent-agnostic standpoint (as exemplified in Banks & de Graaf, 2020) and utilize well-established HHC models to identify, understand, explain, and prepare for ordinary and extraordinary situations occurring in HMC. Then, as a second step, the limits of those models' transferability to HMC contexts need to be taken into account, both from a design and a conceptual perspective, so that they can be adapted to better account for the uniqueness of communications between natural and artificial agents. Only by synergetically complementing each other's core expertise, interaction designers and communication scholars may be able to avoid common pitfalls and, beyond that, optimize existing and identify alternative approaches regarding how to design interactions between human and machine agents, what information to present to the human interaction partners, how to create affordances such that humans respond appropriately, or what coping strategies to use if miscommunication emerges (e.g., Cyra & Pitsch, 2017; Opfermann

& Pitsch, 2017). Embracing these synergies will offer unique gateways for developers to co-design more convincing *social* machines and, more importantly perhaps, more effective HMC.

REFERENCES

Banks, J. (2020). Optimus primed: Media cultivation of robot mental models and social judgments. *Frontiers in Robotics and AI, 7*, 62. https://doi.org/10.3389/frobt.2020.00062

Banks, J., & de Graaf, M. (2020). Toward an agent-agnostic transmission model: Synthesizing anthropocentric and technocentric paradigms in communication. *Human-Machine Communication, 1*, 19–36. https://doi.org/10.30658/hmc.1.2

Beattie, G., & Ellis, A. W. (2017). *The psychology of language and communication.* Taylor & Francis.

Berger, P. L., & Luckmann, T. (1966). *The social construction of reality: A treatise in the sociology of knowledge.* Anchor Books.

Bergmann, K., Branigan, H. P., & Kopp, S. (2015). Exploring the alignment space – lexical and gestural alignment with real and virtual humans. *Frontiers in ICT, 2.* https://doi.org/10.3389/fict.2015.00007

Branigan, H. P., Pickering, M. J., Pearson, J., & McLean, J. F. (2010). Linguistic alignment between people and computers. *Journal of Pragmatics, 42*(9), 2355–2368. https://doi.org/10.1016/j.pragma.2009.12.012

Burleson, B. R. (2010). The nature of interpersonal communication: A message-centered approach. In C. R. Berger, M. E. Roloff, & D. R. Roskos-Ewoldsen (Eds.), *The handbook of communication science* (pp. 145–164). SAGE.

Clark, H. H. (1992). *Arenas of language use.* University of Chicago Press.

Clark, H. H., & Brennan, S. E. (1991). Grounding in communication. In L. B. Resnick, J. M. Levine, & S. D. Teasley (Eds.), *Perspectives on socially shared cognition* (pp. 127–149). APA.

Cyra, K., & Pitsch, K. (2017). Dealing with 'long turns' produced by users of an assistive system: How missing uptake and recipiency lead to turn increments. In *2017 26th IEEE International Symposium on Robot and Human Interactive Communication (RO-MAN)* (pp. 329–334). IEEE.

Etzrodt, K., & Engesser, S. (2021). Voice-Based Agents as Personified Things: Assimilation and Accommodation as Equilibration of Doubt. *Human-Machine Communication, 2*, 57–79. https://doi.org/10.30658/hmc.2.3

Ferrari, F., Paladino, M. P., & Jetten, J. (2016). Blurring human–machine distinctions: Anthropomorphic appearance in social robots as a threat to human distinctiveness. *International Journal of Social Robotics*, 8(2), 287–302. https://doi.org/10.1007/s12369-016-0338-y

Gambino, A., Fox, J., & Ratan, R. (2020). Building a stronger CASA: Extending the Computers Are Social Actors Paradigm. *Human-Machine Communication*, 1, 71–86. https://doi.org/10.30658/hmc.1.5

Guzman, A. L. (2018). What is human-machine communication, anyway? In A. L. Guzman (Ed.), *Human-Machine Communication. Rethinking Communication, Technology, and Ourselves* (pp. 1–28). Peter Lang.

Guzman, A. (2020). Ontological boundaries between humans and computers and the implications for human-machine communication. *Human-Machine Communication*, 1, 37–54. https://doi.org/10.30658/hmc.1.3

Hancock, J. T., Naaman, M., & Levy, K. (2020). AI-mediated communication: Definition, research agenda, and ethical considerations. *Journal of Computer-Mediated Communication*, 25(1), 89–100. https://doi.org/10.1093/jcmc/zmz022

Haslam, N., Kashima, Y., Loughnan, S., Shi, J., & Suitner, C. (2008). Subhuman, inhuman, and superhuman: Contrasting humans with non-humans in three cultures. *Social Cognition*, 26(2), 248–258. https://doi.org/10.1521/soco.2008.26.2.248

Hassenzahl, M., Borchers, J., Boll, S., Pütten, A. R. der, & Wulf, V. (2021). Otherware: How to best interact with autonomous systems. *Interactions*, 28(1), 54–57. https://doi.org/10.1145/3436942

He, K., Gkioxari, G., Dollar, P., & Girshick, R. (2017). Mask R-CNN. In K. Ikeuchi (Ed.), *IEEE International Conference on Computer Vision* (pp. 2980–2988). IEEE.

Hegel, F., Gieselmann, S., Peters, A., Holthaus, P., & Wrede, B. (2011, July). Towards a typology of meaningful signals and cues in social robotics. In *2011 20th IEEE International Symposium on Robot and Human Interactive Communication (RO-MAN)* (pp. 72–78). IEEE.

Hoegen, R., Van Der Schalk, J., Lucas, G., & Gratch, J. (2018, November). The impact of agent facial mimicry on social behavior in a prisoner's dilemma. In *Proceedings of the 18th International Conference on Intelligent Virtual Agents* (pp. 275–280).

Horstmann, A. C., & Krämer, N. C. (2020). Expectations vs. actual behavior of a social robot: An experimental investigation of the effects of a social robot's interaction skill level and its expected future role on people's evaluations. *PLOS ONE*, 15(8), e0238133. https://doi.org/10.1371/journal.pone.0238133

Kahn, P. H., & Shen, S. (2017). NOC NOC, who's there? A new ontological category (NOC) for social robots. In N. Budwig, E. Turiel, & P. D. Zelazo (Eds.), *New perspectives on human development* (pp. 106–122). Cambridge University Press.

Krämer, N. C., Eimler, S., von der Pütten, A., & Payr, S. (2011). Theory of companions: What can theoretical models contribute to the applications and understanding of human-robot interaction? *Applied Artificial Intelligence*, 25(6), 474–502. https://doi.org/10.1080/08839514.2011.587153

Krämer, N. C., Rosenthal-von der Pütten, A. M., & Hoffmann, L. (2015). Social effects of virtual and robot companions. In S. S. Sundar (Ed.), *Handbooks in communication and media. The handbook of the psychology of communication technology* (pp. 137–159). Wiley Blackwell.

Krauss, R. M., & Fussell, S. R. (1991). Perspective-taking in communication: Representations of others' knowledge in reference. *Social Cognition*, 9(1), 2–24. https://doi.org/10.1521/soco.1991.9.1.2

Kühne, V., Rosenthal-von der Pütten, A. M., & Krämer, N. C. (2013, August). Using linguistic alignment to enhance learning experience with pedagogical agents: The special case of dialect. In *International Workshop on Intelligent Virtual Agents* (pp. 149–158). Springer.

Mumm, J., & Mutlu, B. (2011, March). Human-robot proxemics: physical and psychological distancing in human-robot interaction. In *Proceedings of the 6th international conference on Human-robot interaction* (pp. 331–338).

Nass, C., & Yen, C. (2012). *The man who lied to his laptop: What we can learn about ourselves from our machines*. Current.

Opfermann, C., & Pitsch, K. (2017). Reprompts as error handling strategy in human-agent-dialog? User responses to a system's display of non-understanding. In *2017 26th IEEE International Symposium on Robot and Human Interactive Communication (RO-MAN)* (pp. 310–316). IEEE.

Pickering, M. J., & Garrod, S. (2006). Alignment as the basis for successful communication. *Research on language and computation*, 4(2–3), 203–228. https://doi.org/10.1007/s11168-006-9004-0

Reeves, B., & Nass, C. (1996). *The media equation: How people treat computers, television, and new media like real people and places*. Cambridge University Press.

Rivoire, C., & Lim, A. (2016, November). Habit detection within a long-term interaction with a social robot: An exploratory study. In *Proceedings of the International Workshop on Social Learning and Multimodal Interaction for Designing Artificial Agents* (pp. 1–6).

Rosenthal-von der Pütten, A. M., & Krämer, N. C. (2014). How design characteristics of robots determine evaluation and uncanny valley related responses. *Computers in Human Behavior*, 36,

422–439. https://doi.org/10.1016/j.chb.2014.03.066

Rosenthal-von der Pütten, A. M., Krämer, N. C., & Herrmann, J. (2018). The effects of humanlike and robot-specific affective nonverbal behavior on perception, emotion, and behavior. *International Journal of Social Robotics*, *10*(5), 569–582. https://doi.org/10.1007/s12369-018-0466-7

Shannon, C.E. & Weaver, W. (1949). *The mathematical theory of communication*. University of Illinois Press.

Shiwa, T., Kanda, T., Imai, M., Ishiguro, H., & Hagita, N. (2009). How quickly should a communication robot respond? Delaying strategies and habituation effects. *International Journal of Social Robotics*, *1*(2), 141–155. https://doi.org/10.1007/s12369-009-0012-8

Straßmann, C., Rosenthal-von der Pütten, A. M., & Krämer, N. C. (2018). With or against each other? The influence of a virtual agent's (non)cooperative behavior on user's cooperation behavior in the prisoners' dilemma. *Advances in Human-Computer Interaction*, *2018*, 1–7. https://doi.org/10.1155/2018/2589542

Sundar, S. S., & Kim, J. (2019, May). Machine heuristic: When we trust computers more than humans with our personal information. In *Proceedings of the 2019 CHI Conference on Human Factors in Computing Systems* (pp. 1–9).

Walther, J. B. (1996). Computer-mediated communication: Impersonal, interpersonal, and hyperpersonal interaction. *Communication Research*, *23*(1), 3–43. https://doi.org/10.1177/009365096023001001

Wang, Q., Zhang, L., Bertinetto, L., Hu, W., & Torr, P. H. S. (2019). Fast online object tracking and segmentation: A unifying approach. In *Proceedings of the IEEE Conference on Computer Vision and Pattern Recognition*.

Watzlawick, P., Beavin, J., & Jackson, D. (1967). *Pragmatics of human communication—A study of interactional patterns, pathologies and paradoxes*. WW Norton.

Waytz, A., Gray, K., Epley, N., & Wegner, D. M. (2010). Causes and consequences of mind perception. *Trends in Cognitive Sciences*, *14*(8), 383–388. https://doi.org/10.1016/j.tics.2010.05.006

Żarkowski, M. (2019). Multi-party turn-taking in repeated human–robot interactions: An interdisciplinary evaluation. *International Journal of Social Robotics*, *11*(5), 693–707. https://doi.org/10.1007/s12369-019-00603-1

34

Dual-Process Theory in Human–Machine Communication

Kevin Koban
and Jaime Banks

INTRODUCTION

The ways in which humans psychologically approach social machines (i.e., artificial entities that simulate sociality in a manner aligned with established social norms; Duffy, 2003) afford and constrain how both can create meaning together. Nass and colleagues' seminal work published under the label of the *Computers are Social Actors* (CASA) paradigm (Nass & Yen, 2012) established the popular position that people engage in at least two stages of psychological response to social machines. First, in the heat of the moment, people *mindlessly* accept the machine's display of sociality and follow internalized social scripts, which result in behaviors like those in response to other human beings. Afterward, however, when they have the chance to *mindfully* reflect on their behaviors, people often deny not only how they just have behaved but also insist that they would never act in such a nonsensical way (Nass & Moon, 2000). In other words, people appear to approach social machines differently depending on whether they rely on their first intuition (i.e., if it behaves like a social being, then it probably is a social being; Reeves & Nass, 1996) or reflective thought (i.e., it is no social being, therefore it ought not to be perceived as a social being; Guzman, 2020).

Notably, emerging theoretical positions contend that people's engagement with social machines are influenced by technological advances in artificial intelligence (AI) and, perhaps more importantly, the ongoing socio-technological evolution that steadily introduces social machines into human spheres (Gambino et al., 2020). Moreover, emerging disciplinary nuances (i.e., human–machine communication's [HMC] focus on meaning-making among agents rather than the use of one agent by another; Guzman, 2018) offer opportunities to consider anew the nature and consequences of people's "fast and slow" cognitions. An emphasis on meaning-making warrants attention to people's initial understanding of social machines and how this intuitive understanding may be influenced by reflection during dyadic communication. This chapter briefly introduces dual-process logic, followed by an overview of dual-process theories that are prevalent in HMC-related research. Social-cognitive, information-processing, and emotional accounts will be described briefly and discussed concerning the metatheoretical background.

Importantly, this chapter aims to present an overview of theories detailing people's dualistic processing of social machine agents most pertinent to HMC. It is outside of its scope to attend to a complete overview of dual-process theories in general, to address different domain-specific theories (e.g., for persuasion [Luttrell, 2018] or emotion regulation [Gyurak et al., 2011]), or to discuss approaches in which distinct processing domains are conceptualized in a non-dualistic fast-slow logic (e.g., initial physiological response leading to subsequent cognitive appraisals; Choi et al., 2015). Finally, we focus here on human processing of social-machine signals and not on computational architectures in social machines that use dual-process analogy for programming (see Bonnefon & Rahwan, 2020).

DUAL-PROCESS THEORY AS A METATHEORY

Dual-process theory comprises a *family* (Evans, 2018) of conceptually similar, domain-specific theories that address how humans process information received through the sensory apparatus. These theories share the general assumption that people's thinking consists of (a) autonomous *Type 1* processes, which do not demand working memory capacity and are typically considered rapid, intuitive, and heuristic, and (b) *Type 2* processes which require working memory and are associated with slower, reflective, and analytic mental operations (Evans & Stanovich, 2013a) often accompanying learning processes (McEwen & Dube, 2016). Type 1 and Type 2 processes feature discrete, constitutive sets of operations that interact within their respective Type and across Types during information processing. However, it is yet unclear exactly how these interactions unfold.

Extant theoretical approaches can be subsumed under three models. According to the *default-interventionist model* (Kahneman, 2011), Type 1 processes first generate a heuristic response (i.e., the default) which may be overridden by subsequent Type 2 processes (i.e., the intervention); this overriding depends on motivational factors (e.g., thinking dispositions, Stanovich, 2011; effort, Ackerman & Thompson, 2017) or available cognitive resources (e.g., knowledge structures [i.e., mindware], Stanovich, 2018) within a given context. Others have argued for a *parallel-competitive model* (Sloman, 1996). Here, both Type 1 and 2 processes are activated simultaneously once novel information is received and compete against one another. More recently, a third *hybrid model* (De Neys, 2017) was put forth, connecting the propositions of both existing models. Like default-interventionist models, the hybrid model assumes that Type 1 processes autonomously create an intuitive response

before Type 2 processes may step in to correct (i.e., cognitive decoupling; Stanovich, 2011) or rationalize it. However, the hybrid model contends there is also a learned *logical*, intuitive response triggered in parallel and stands in competition with the traditionally proposed *heuristic* intuitive response (i.e., Type 1–Type 1 conflicts). The hybrid model in particular also argues against characterizing Type 1 and Type 2 processes as inherently biased and corrective, respectively (i.e., *normative fallacy*; Evans, 2018), as featured in various critiques of dual-process theory (e.g., Osman, 2004; Kruglanski & Gigerenzer, 2011). In other words, Type 1 processing can result in either normatively correct or heuristically biased responses, just as Type 2 processing (if enacted) can lead to both corrections and rationalizations of biased responses.

Theorists have emphasized that dual-process theory, despite its name, does not represent a unitary theory that may authorize researchers to formulate clear and testable hypotheses but instead a metatheory that provides them with a broad framework for establishing domain-specific theories (Evans & Stanovich, 2013b). Naturally, this flexibility comes at the expense of generalizability. Despite following a similar dual-process logic, domain-specific theories often differ substantially from each other, such that empirical findings from a specific domain may not be transferred to other domains (De Neys & Pennycook, 2019). Several dual-processing accounts have explicitly been developed in recent years to answer HMC-related research questions.

The following sections organize these accounts by processing domain. It might be argued that all dual-processing accounts can be regarded as cognitive in a broader sense (i.e., comprising a diverse set of basic and higher-order mental processes that cover information acquisition, storage, and retrieval, as well as processing; American Psychological Association, n.d.). Since many dual-processing accounts focus on more narrowly defined cognitive subdomains (e.g., related to understanding another agent's behavior [i.e., social cognition]), more descriptive labels might still be useful. For this overview, we will differentiate among *social-cognitive accounts* (understanding machines as social others), *impression-formation accounts* (categorical knowledge and subsequent negotiation with empirical realities), and *emotional accounts* (preconscious or conscious affective processing).

Social-cognitive Accounts

Broadly, dual-process accounts that focus on social cognitions toward machine agents deal with how people make sense of these agents (Złotowski et al., 2018) or interactions with them (Lobato et al., 2013). More specifically, Złotowski et al.'s (2018) account draws from scholarship on anthropomorphism (i.e., people's tendency to perceive and attribute human properties to non-human agents; Epley et al., 2007) that focuses on how certain features can promote an understanding of an agent as humanlike due to innate or learned inferences. They argue against a monolithic approach and favor a dualistic understanding of anthropomorphism that follows a dual-processing logic. *Implicit anthropomorphism* is considered the result of autonomous Type 1 processes, while the activation of Type 2 processes may lead to *explicit anthropomorphism*. In other words, people have both an intuitive tendency to anthropomorphize social machines via autonomously activated mental processes and the capacity to tap into their working memory to reflect upon this tendency and explicitly declare whether or not they interpret a machine to be a social agent. This dual-process model of anthropomorphism aligns with the default-interventionist model in its proposition that explicit anthropomorphism can override implicit anthropomorphism given sufficient motivation and cognitive resources. However, the model deviates from the current state of the art in two important regards.

First, Złotowski and colleagues (2018) suggest that Type 2 processing is related to "accurate judgments" (p. 3) on the attribution of (prototypically) human characteristics to social machines, indicating that the normative response would be to reject anthropomorphism. Both of these propositions have been questioned in prior research. Just as it is well-established that Type 1 processing does not always lead to biased (i.e., incorrect) attitudes, previous studies have also revealed that Type 2 processes are often involved in the rationalization of biased Type 1 responses rather than in correcting them (see Evans, 2018). Furthermore, the objectivist position that machines must be assigned with the status of an artifact due to a lack of qualifying criteria for "beingness" (e.g., autonomy, adaptability, capacity for suffering and pleasure) is indeed prevalent among roboticist (Boden et al., 2017) and laypeople (Guzman, 2020). However, other researchers have challenged this conclusion on several grounds (e.g., Coeckelbergh, 2021; Gunkel, 2012), most notably perhaps, concerning the "problem of other minds" (i.e., the lack of a direct possibility to observe another agent's inner states; Seibt, 2017). Instead of relying on spurious objective truths about the absence of certain qualities in social machines (e.g., absence of emotions), those researchers have argued that it might be more appropriate

to rely on the appearance of these qualities (e.g., Wegner & Grey, 2016).

Second, the model directly links implicit anthropomorphism to indirect measurements (e.g., behavioral measures) and explicit anthropomorphism to direct measurements (e.g., self-report scales). Such a procedural definition of implicit as indirect (and explicit as direct) has been criticized as conceptually misleading: Previous research has demonstrated that mental operations and people's subjective experience of these operations can vary widely (Nosek, 2007), resulting in the assumption that the directness of a measurement is agnostic to mental processes (Corneille & Hütter, 2020). In other words, implicit and explicit anthropomorphism may both be accessible via direct and indirect measures.

Lobato et al.'s (2013) approach to human–robot interaction comes with fewer model properties. It supposes that people are comparing interactions with social machines against human–human interactions according to (a) *surface features* (i.e., social cues and signals, such as the appearance of the interactants or behavioral patterns within the interaction) and (b) *deep features* (i.e., perceived and attributed mental states of the interactants, such as desires and intentions). Based on the integrative account of social cognition proposed by Bohl and van den Bos (2012), they argue that people's perception of surface cues during an interaction allows for an immediate (i.e., rapid and intuitive, Type 1-like) understanding of another agent's mental state. Their engagement in deep-feature mentalizing, on the other hand, represents a more time- and mental resource-consuming (i.e., reflective Type 2-like) route of making sense of an agent (Lobato et al., 2014). In line with the current metatheoretical discourse, Lobato et al. (2014) have provided some empirical evidence against the normative fallacy (i.e., that Type 2 processing is corrective), revealing that quick and intuitive perceptions of a social machine's mindfulness do not need to differ from slower and more reflective assessments.

Impression-formation Accounts

Extant dual-process models of impression formation broadly align with the metatheory. For instance, both Fiske and Neuberg's (1990) and Brewer's (1988) widely acknowledged models propose that people's impression formation process consists of autonomous Type 1 mental operations that attempt to categorize another agent into a particular social group and cognitively demanding Type 2 processing that accounts for agent-specific information to form an impression of that agent. Many empirical findings support dual-process accounts' utility in explaining how people form impressions of social machines. When confronted with unfamiliar machine agents, people rely intuitively on internalized knowledge of ontological categories (i.e., human vs. machine; Sundar & Kim, 2019) or cued demographic groups (e.g., different ethnicities; Bartneck et al., 2018). It is important to note that this internalized knowledge has often been gained not from first-hand experience but portrayals in popular media (Horstmann & Krämer, 2019). Accordingly, people's first impressions of social machines can be tainted by popular narrative tropes (e.g., the helpful servant, the unbiased intelligence; Banks, 2020), which often coincide with existing gender or race stereotypes (Banks & Koban, 2022). However, these cue-driven impressions can be overridden upon interacting with a social machine so that both people's intuitive and reflective approaches toward it can reach beyond their initial categorizations (Pradhan et al., 2019).

By applying the *theory of interactive media effects* (TIME; Sundar et al., 2015) to AI-driven media, Sundar (2020) proposed a dual-process theory that addresses impression formation for social machines. More specifically, he argues that when people identify an agent as AI-driven or learn about its system attributes, this identification autonomously triggers people's intuitive beliefs about what social machines are (e.g., trustworthy, objective, unemotional) and how they operate (e.g., rule-governed, precise, unyielding). This so-called *machine heuristic* is at the heart of the Type 1 *cue route* and provides people with an immediate impression of the respective agent. Compared to this autonomous mechanism, the *action route* represents people volitionally engaging a social machine, creating another, slower and more effortful (i.e., Type 2-based) impression of it primarily based on individual experience and involvement. Despite both cue and action routes (i.e., Type 1 and Type 2 processes) supposedly leading to a joint impression of an AI-driven agent, the model is unclear about the temporality (i.e., sequential vs. parallel) of, and interaction between, both routes. Also, previous research has shown that social machines may be categorized as a sort of "third kind" that stands in-between humans (or rather animate beings) and inanimate artifacts (Etzrodt & Engesser, 2021; Kahn & Shen, 2017).

Emotional Accounts

Although not formally proposed as a theory, findings concerning people's feelings of being threatened by social machines indicate the relevance of two distinct but potentially interrelated affective processes; those processes closely resemble those proposed by dual-process accounts that focus on the elicitation of emotions. According to Smith and Neumann (2005), emotional processing comprises *associative* (i.e., Type 1) responses that are elicited autonomously after exposure to biologically relevant or well-learned stimuli, and *rule-based* (i.e., Type 2) processes that are activated upon conscious cognitive effort and are sensitive to social and cultural norms. March et al. (2018) introduced a dual-process model of threat evaluation that expands upon this understanding of emotional processing; they propose a default-interventionist model in which automatic- and reflective-evaluation processes are serially linked. When confronted with a potentially threatening stimulus, people automatically perform rapid Type 1 evaluation of this stimulus' nature and valence, followed (if necessary and cognitively and motivationally feasible) by slower and resource-consuming Type 2 stimulus assessment.

Similar dualistic conceptualizations are evident in both Złotowski et al.'s (2017) and Stein et al.'s (2019) understanding of how people perceive a threat when exposed to autonomous social machines. Both approaches distinguish two types of threat experience. On the one hand, people may experience a loss of control or a threat to their physical well-being (i.e., realistic/proximal threats; see also Banks & Edwards, 2019); on the other hand, they may perceive autonomous social machines as threatening their beliefs about human distinctiveness or uniqueness (i.e., symbolic/distal threats; see also Ferrari et al., 2016). While realistic/proximal threats are assumed to rely on biological adaptations that create an immediate (i.e., autonomously elicited) threat experience (aligning with Type 1 processing), symbolic/distal threats are based on socio-cultural constructions that produce a delayed [i.e., reflective] experience of threat (broadly in line with Type 2 processing).

Viewed through this metatheoretical lens, it may be that perceptions of symbolic/distal threats to human distinctiveness are Type 2 rationalizations of the initial experience of aversive affect. In other words, when confronted with an autonomous social machine, people might intuitively fear physical harm (via Type 1 processes) but (with sufficient motivation, opportunity, and cognitive resources) may reappraise their intuition to see whether it fits or conflicts with the situation. Type 2 processes are further engaged if a conflict is detected, resulting in either cognitive decoupling (i.e., realization that the intuitive response was unjustified) or rationalization (i.e., realization that the intuitive response may have been unjustified but justifiable). While it can be expected that cognitive decoupling might constitute efficient emotion regulation, rationalization could activate another aversive emotional response: Anxiety that human beings may lose their uniqueness.

TOWARD DUALISTIC MEANING-MAKING IN HMC

Given that dual-process theories have proven their worth across numerous domains, their recent introduction in human–computer, –agent, and –robot interaction disciplines may be a promising first step toward a better understanding of how people process information related to social machines. To take full advantage of the heuristic potential, future research will have to more strongly commit to investigating the empirical reality of key theoretical propositions in a systematic manner, using innovative method(ologie)s that may allow for a clear distinction between Type 1 and Type 2 processes (e.g., two-response procedures or conflict-detection procedures [see de Neys & Pennycook, 2019] combined with real-time measures, for instance, via eyetracking [Ball et al., 2006; McEwen et al., 2020]) and testing whether current metatheoretical developments (e.g., conflict monitoring, Type 1–Type 1 conflicts, mindware) can be meaningfully applied or adapted. It is also paramount to consider temporal shifts in these processes, which may occur when human and machine agents get familiar with each other and establish trustful relationships. Here, the development of a more elaborated dual-process theory of joint *meaning-making* is prudent. Such a theory would illuminate the mental processes operating when people communicate with social machines and advance dual-process theory, broadly, by affording comparisons with social cognitions of other ontological categories (i.e., humans, animals). Further, sound dual-process accounts may help to unpack the nuances of how humans create meaning in cooperation with, in conflict with, or in spite of machine agents – and how that meaning unfolds over time to shape and be shaped by social processes.

Social machines' activities in society may amplify existing categorizations (e.g., via collectively reinforced Type 2 rationalizations of Type 1 impressions) or might help to break them down (e.g., by promoting competitive Type 1 processes or Type 2 decoupling). Opportunities to exploit people's tendency for Type 1 processing and Type 2 rationalization might enhance, such that media tropes may further gain importance by setting expectations for what social machines

are and should do, serving as heuristic anchors for intuitive judgments that may be violated during an interaction. Accordingly, the imperative to implement explainable AI (XAI; Páez, 2019) that facilitates an understanding of how a machine operates (i.e., transparency) and why it operates as it does (i.e., post-hoc interpretability) may help people with gaining knowledge structures which can counteract potentially harmful processing.

As concluded by Stanovich (2018), "the modern world is, in many ways, becoming hostile for individuals relying solely on miserly processes" (p. 427) – with social machines as a key domain where miserly processing humans may misunderstand agents or misinterpret their communication to unproductive ends. Thus, understanding people's dualistic processing of social-machine cues and messages will enable policymakers and empower people to take action against "hostile" interactions, where intuitive defaults are triggered deliberately by social machines against people's interests, and for "benign" interactions, in which human and machines can create meaning together most productively.

REFERENCES

Ackerman, R., & Thompson, V. A. (2017). Meta-reasoning: Monitoring and control of thinking and reasoning. *Trends in Cognitive Sciences*, 21(8), 607–617. https://doi.org/10.1016/j.tics.2017.05.004

American Psychological Association (n.d.). *APA dictionary of psychology. Cognition.* https://dictionary.apa.org/cognition

Ball, L. J., Phillips, P., Wade, C. N., & Quayle, J. D. (2006). Effects of belief and logic on syllogistic reasoning: Eye-movement evidence for selective processing models. *Experimental Psychology*, 53(1), 77–86. https://doi.org/10.1027/1618-3169.53.1.77

Banks, J. (2020). Optimus primed: Media cultivation of robot mental models and social judgments. *Frontiers in Robotics and AI*, 7, 62. https://doi.org/10.3389/frobt.2020.00062

Banks, J., & Edwards, A. (2019). A common social distance scale for robots and humans. *2019 28th IEEE International Conference on Robot and Human Interactive Communication (RO-MAN)*, 1–6. https://doi.org/10.1109/RO-MAN46459.2019.8956316

Banks. J., & Koban, K. (2022). A kind apart: The limited application of human race and sex stereotypes to androids. *International Journal of Social Robotics.* https://doi.org/10.1007/s12369-022-00900-2.

Bartneck, C., Yogeeswaran, K., Ser, Q. M., Woodward, G., Sparrow, R., Wang, S., & Eyssel, F.

(2018). Robots and racism. *Proceedings of the 2018 ACM/IEEE International Conference on Human-Robot Interaction - HRI'18*, 196–204. https://doi.org/10.1145/3171221.3171260

Boden, M., Bryson, J., Caldwell, D., Dautenhahn, K., Edwards, L., Kember, S., Newman, P., Parry, V., Pegman, G., Rodden, T., Sorrell, T., Wallis, M., Whitby, B., & Winfield, A. (2017). Principles of robotics: Regulating robots in the real world. *Connection Science, 29*(2), 124–129. https://doi.org/10.1080/09540091.2016.1271400

Bohl, V., & van den Bos, W. (2012). Toward an integrative account of social cognition: Marrying theory of mind and interactionism to study the interplay of Type 1 and Type 2 processes. *Frontiers in Human Neuroscience*, 6. https://doi.org/10.3389/fnhum.2012.00274

Bonnefon, J.-F., & Rahwan, I. (2020). Machine thinking, fast and slow. *Trends in Cognitive Sciences, 24*(12), 1019–1027. https://doi.org/10.1016/j.tics.2020.09.007

Brewer, M. B. (1988). A dual process model of impression formation. In T. Srull & R. Wyer (Eds.), *Advances in social cognition* (pp. 1–36). Lawrence Erlbaum Associates.

Choi, A., de Melo, C. M., Khooshabeh, P., Woo, W., & Gratch, J. (2015). Physiological evidence for a dual process model of the social effects of emotion in computers. *International Journal of Human-Computer Studies, 74*, 41–53. https://doi.org/10.1016/j.ijhcs.2014.10.006

Coeckelbergh, M. (2021). Should We Treat Teddy Bear 2.0 as a Kantian Dog? Four Arguments for the Indirect Moral Standing of Personal Social Robots, with Implications for Thinking About Animals and Humans. *Minds and Machines. 31*(3), 337–360. https://doi.org/10.1007/s11023-020-09554-3

Corneille, O., & Hütter, M. (2020). Implicit? What Do You Mean? A Comprehensive Review of the Delusive Implicitness Construct in Attitude Research. *Personality and Social Psychology Review. 24*(3), 212–232. https://doi.org/10.1177/1088868320911325

De Neys, W. (2017). Bias, conflict, and fast logic: Towards a hybrid dual process future? In W. De Neys (Ed.), *Dual Process Theory 2.0* (pp. 47–65). Routledge.

De Neys, W., & Pennycook, G. (2019). Logic, fast and slow: Advances in dual-process theorizing. *Current Directions in Psychological Science, 28*(5), 503–509. https://doi.org/10.1177/0963721419855658

Duffy, B. R. (2003). Anthropomorphism and the social robot. *Robotics and Autonomous Systems, 42*(3–4), 177–190. https://doi.org/10.1016/S0921-8890(02)00374-3

Epley, N., Waytz, A., & Cacioppo, J. T. (2007). On seeing human: A three-factor theory of anthropomorphism. *Psychological Review*, 114(4), 864–886. https://doi.org/10.1037/0033-295X.114.4.864

Etzrodt, K., & Engesser, S. (2021). Voice-Based Agents as Personified Things: Assimilation and Accommodation as Equilibration of Doubt. *Human-Machine Communication, 2*, 57–79. https://doi.org/10.30658/hmc.2.3

Evans, J. St. B. T. (2018). Dual-process theories. In L. J. Ball & V. A. Thompson (Eds.), *The Routledge international handbook of thinking and reasoning* (pp. 151–166). Routledge.

Evans, J. St. B. T., & Stanovich, K. E. (2013a). Dual-process theories of higher cognition: Advancing the debate. *Perspectives on Psychological Science, 8*(3), 223–241. https://doi.org/10.1177/1745691612460685

Evans, J. St. B. T., & Stanovich, K. E. (2013b). Theory and metatheory in the study of dual processing: Reply to comments. *Perspectives on Psychological Science, 8*(3), 263–271. https://doi.org/10.1177/1745691613483774

Ferrari, F., Paladino, M. P., & Jetten, J. (2016). Blurring human–machine distinctions: Anthropomorphic appearance in social robots as a threat to human distinctiveness. *International Journal of Social Robotics, 8*(2), 287–302. https://doi.org/10.1007/s12369-016-0338-y

Fiske, S. T., & Neuberg, S. L. (1990). A continuum of impression formation, from category-based to individuating processes: Influences of information and motivation on attention and interpretation. In *Advances in Experimental Social Psychology* (Vol. 23, pp. 1–74). Elsevier.

Gambino, A., Fox, J., & Ratan, R. (2020). Building a stronger CASA: Extending the computers are social actors paradigm. *Human-Machine Communication, 1*, 71–86. https://doi.org/10.30658/hmc.1.5

Gunkel, D. J. (2012). *The machine question: Critical perspectives on AI, robots, and ethics*. MIT Press.

Guzman, A. L. (2018). What is human-machine communication anyway? In A.L. Guzman (Ed.), *Human-machine communication: Rethinking communication, technology, and ourselves* (pp. 1–28). Peter Lang.

Guzman, A. (2020). Ontological boundaries between humans and computers and the implications for human-machine communication. *Human-Machine Communication, 1*, 37–54. https://doi.org/10.30658/hmc.1.3

Gyurak, A., Gross, J. J., & Etkin, A. (2011). Explicit and implicit emotion regulation: A dual-process framework. *Cognition & Emotion, 25*(3), 400–412. https://doi.org/10.1080/02699931.2010.544160

Horstmann, A. C., & Krämer, N. C. (2019). Great expectations? Relation of previous experiences with social robots in real life or in the media and expectancies based on qualitative and quantitative assessment. *Frontiers in Psychology, 10*, 939. https://doi.org/10.3389/fpsyg.2019.00939

Kahn, P. H., & Shen, S. (2017). NOC NOC, who's there? A new ontological category (NOC) for social robots. In N. Budwig, E. Turiel, & P. D. Zelazo (Eds.), *New perspectives on human development* (pp. 106–122).Cambridge University Press.

Kahneman, D. (2011). *Thinking, fast and slow.* Farrar, Straus and Giroux.

Kruglanski, A. W., & Gigerenzer, G. (2011). Intuitive and deliberate judgments are based on common principles. *Psychological Review, 118*(1), 97–109. https://doi.org/10.1037/a0020762

Lobato, E. J. C., Wiltshire, T. J., & Fiore, S. M. (2013). A dual-process approach to understanding human-robot interaction. *Proceedings of the Human Factors and Ergonomics Society Annual Meeting,* 57(1), 1263–1267. https://doi.org/10.1177/1541931213571280

Lobato, E. J. C., Wiltshire, T. J., Hudak, S., & Fiore, S. M. (2014). No time, no problem: Mental state attributions made quickly or after reflection do not differ. *Proceedings of the Human Factors and Ergonomics Society Annual Meeting,* 58(1), 1341–1345. https://doi.org/10.1177/1541931214581280

Luttrell, A. (2018). Dual process models of persuasion. In A. Luttrell, *Oxford research encyclopedia of psychology.* Oxford University Press.

March, D. S., Gaertner, L., & Olson, M. A. (2018). On the prioritized processing of threat in a dual implicit process model of evaluation. *Psychological Inquiry, 29*(1), 1–13. https://doi.org/10.1080/1047840X.2018.1435680

McEwen, R., & Dubé, A. K. (2016). Intuitive or idiomatic: An interdisciplinary study of child-tablet computer interaction. *Journal of the Association for Information Science and Technology, 67*(5), 1169–1181. https://doi.org/10.1002/asi.23470

McEwen, R., Atcha, A., Lui, M., Shimaly, R., Maharaj, A., Ali, S., & Carroll, S. (2020). Interlocutors and interactions: Examining the interactions between students with complex communication needs, teachers, and eye-gaze technology. *Human-Machine Communication,* 1, 113–131. https://doi.org/10.30658/hmc.1.7

Nass, C., & Moon, Y. (2000). Machines and mindlessness: Social responses to computers. *Journal of Social Issues,* 56(1), 81–103. https://doi.org/10.1111/0022-4537.00153

Nass, C. I., & Yen, C. (2012). *The man who lied to his laptop: What we can learn about ourselves from our machines.* Current.

Nosek, B. A. (2007). Implicit–explicit relations. *Current Directions in Psychological Science,* 16(2), 65–69. https://doi.org/10.1111/j.1467-8721.2007.00477.x

Osman, M. (2004). An evaluation of dual-process theories of reasoning. *Psychonomic Bulletin & Review,* 11(6), 988–1010. https://doi.org/10.3758/BF03196730

Páez, A. (2019). The pragmatic turn in explainable artificial intelligence (XAI). *Minds and Machines,* 29(3),441–459.https://doi.org/10.1007/s11023-019-09502-w

Pradhan, A., Findlater, L., & Lazar, A. (2019). "Phantom friend" or "just a box with information": Personification and ontological categorization of smart speaker-based voice assistants by older adults. *Proceedings of the ACM on Human-Computer Interaction,* 3(CSCW), 1–21. https://doi.org/10.1145/3359316

Reeves, B., & Nass, C. (1996). *The media equation: How people treat computers, television, and new media like real people and places.* Cambridge University Press.

Seibt, J. (2017). Towards an ontology of simulated social interaction: Varieties of the "as if" for robots and humans. In R. Hakli & J. Seibt (Eds.), *Sociality and normativity for robots* (pp. 11–39). Springer International Publishing.

Sloman, S. A. (1996). The empirical case for two systems of reasoning. *Psychological Bulletin,* 119(1), 3–22. https://doi.org/10.1037/0033-2909.119.1.3

Smith, E. R., & Neumann, R. (2005). Emotion processes considered from the perspective of dual-process models. In L. F. Barrett, P. M. Niedenthal, & P. Winkielman (Eds.), *Emotion and consciousness* (pp. 287–311). Guilford Press.

Stanovich, K. E. (2011). *Rationality and the reflective mind.* Oxford University Press.

Stanovich, K. E. (2018). Miserliness in human cognition: The interaction of detection, override and mindware. *Thinking & Reasoning,* 24(4), 423–444. https://doi.org/10.1080/13546783.2018.1459314

Stein, J.-P., Liebold, B., & Ohler, P. (2019). Stay back, clever thing! Linking situational control and human uniqueness concerns to the aversion against autonomous technology. *Computers in Human Behavior,* 95, 73–82. https://doi.org/10.1016/j.chb.2019.01.021

Sundar, S. S. (2020). Rise of machine agency: A framework for studying the psychology of human–AI interaction (HAII). *Journal of Computer-Mediated Communication,* 25(1), 74–88. https://doi.org/10.1093/jcmc/zmz026

Sundar, S. S., & Kim, J. (2019). Machine heuristic: When we trust computers more than humans with our personal information. *Proceedings of the 2019 CHI Conference on Human Factors in Computing Systems - CHI '19,* 1–9. https://doi.org/10.1145/3290605.3300768

Sundar, S. S., Jia, H., Waddell, T. F., & Huang, Y. (2015). Toward a theory of interactive media effects (TIME): Four models for explaining how interface features affect user psychology. In S. S. Sundar (Ed.), *The handbook of the psychology of* communication technology (pp. 47–86). John Wiley & Sons, Ltd.

Wegner, D. M., & Gray, K. (2016). *The mind club: Who thinks, what feels, and why it matters*. Viking.

Złotowski, J., Sumioka, H., Eyssel, F., Nishio, S., Bartneck, C., & Ishiguro, H. (2018). Model of dual anthropomorphism: The relationship between the media equation effect and implicit anthropomorphism.

International Journal of Social Robotics, 10(5), 701–714. https://doi.org/10.1007/s12369-018-0476-5

Złotowski, J., Yogeeswaran, K., & Bartneck, C. (2017). Can we control it? Autonomous robots threaten human identity, uniqueness, safety, and resources. *International Journal of Human-Computer Studies, 100*, 48–54. https://doi.org/10.1016/j.ijhcs.2016.12.008

35

Privacy and Human–Machine Communication

Christoph Lutz

INTRODUCTION

In recent years, smart and interactive technologies such as chatbots, mobile virtual assistants, social robots and smart toys have become increasingly prevalent. These technologies are used not primarily as media through which communication takes place but as communicative agents themselves. Human–machine communication (HMC), as a field within media and communication research interested in the "creation of meaning among humans and machines" (Guzman, 2018, p. 1), has enhanced our understanding of such technologies (Fortunati & Edwards, 2020; Gambino et al., 2020; Guzman, 2020; Rodriguez-Hidalgo, 2020).

A concern when it comes to HMC is privacy. Privacy vulnerabilities of smart speakers, for example, have received substantial media attention (Lutz & Newlands, 2021) and have been investigated from a communication and media perspective (Brause & Blank, 2020; Liao et al., 2019). Similarly, the introduction of AI-based technology, such as facial recognition software, has sparked fears about the curtailment of civil liberties through increased dataveillance (Stark et al., 2020), especially with the extraordinary situation due to the Covid-19-pandemic (Hargittai et al., 2020; Newlands et al., 2020; Vitak & Zimmer,

2020). In this contribution, I provide an overview of privacy as a key topic for HMC theory and research. The chapter is intended as an accessible introduction rather than a comprehensive summary. The goal is to give the readers a grasp of theoretical debates and empirical findings, enabling them to develop their own research questions and study designs. Given that HMC research is still nascent, I will draw on scholarly literature beyond the confines of the field and consult scholarship from adjacent disciplines such as sociology, information systems, ethics, and law where appropriate.

The chapter is divided into four sections. After the introduction, I will define and discuss privacy in general. This section contains an overview of key privacy theories that are fruitful in HMC research. In the third section, I will look at privacy and HMC more specifically. I will discuss three smart and interactive technologies that have received attention in HMC research: social robots, smart speakers, and chatbots. For each of these three technologies, I discuss the privacy implications, review HMC research and provide directions for future research. In the final section, I will conclude the chapter by synthesizing the main points and showing some implications for privacy-oriented HMC scholarship.

PRIVACY IN GENERAL

Privacy has become an important topic in communication research, especially with the spread of information and communication technologies (ICT) that harvest data on a large scale such as e-commerce, social media, and smartphones. However, privacy scholarship draws on contributions that go further back and span fields such as law, psychology and sociology (Altman, 1975; Warren & Brandeis, 1890; Westin, 1967). Today, privacy is a highly interdisciplinary topic (Bräunlich et al., 2021). However, the multitude of perspectives complicates a common understanding. Privacy has been understood in many ways, including bodily autonomy, control over personal data, solitude at home, freedom of thought, and protection of one's reputation (Solove, 2008). Generally, privacy scholarship considers both "freedom from" aspects that describe whether someone is let alone and "freedom to" aspects that center on self-development (Koops et al., 2017). Privacy also has to be understood in a dimensional, zonal and relational way (Aeschlimann et al., 2015; Koops et al., 2017; Marwick & boyd, 2014). However, in recent years, informational privacy has emerged as the key type across disciplines, not least because of the growing importance of ICTs and legal frameworks that situate privacy predominantly as a data protection issue (Smith et al., 2011). This informational understanding is implicit in the widely used definition by Westin (1967, p. 7) of privacy as "the claim of individuals, groups, or institutions to determine for themselves when, how, and to what extent information about them is communicated to others."

Here, I adopt a broader perspective and draw on a multi-dimensional framework that goes beyond informational privacy. Such a multi-dimensional understanding is particularly pressing because the communicative affordances of smart and interactive technologies (e.g., portability, availability, locatability, multimediality; Schrock, 2015) call for the consideration of other privacy types. Burgoon's (1982) differentiation of informational, social, psychological, and physical privacy proves useful (Lutz et al., 2019), not least because it originated in communication research. *Physical privacy* is understood as "the degree to which one is physically inaccessible to others" (Burgoon, 1982, p. 211). It includes spatial considerations. *Social privacy* describes the communicational dynamics of privacy and has a relational component tied to interpersonal boundary management, including aspects such as intimacy and protection. *Psychological privacy* is about cognitive and affective inputs and their control. Thus, this form

of privacy falls within the "freedom to" types of privacy, rather than the "freedom from" (Koops et al., 2017), stressing its agentic role for personal growth. Finally, *informational privacy* describes the extent to which a person's information is protected. Thus, privacy should be understood in a physical, social, psychological and informational sense.

In addition to this multi-dimensional understanding, privacy as contextual integrity (Nissenbaum, 2010), as communication and boundary management (Petronio, 2002), and as networked (Marwick & boyd, 2014) have emerged as fruitful and widely used theories in communication research, particularly when it comes to digital technologies. Table 35.1 provides an overview of these three theories. All of them share a relational understanding of privacy that calls for overcoming individualistic and largely control-based views of privacy (Marwick & boyd, 2014).

Not only from a theoretical but also from an empirical angle, privacy has become a key topic in media and communication research. Zhang and Leung (2015), for example, identified privacy as an important topic in communication research about social network sites, with about 13 percent of the analyzed articles being about privacy. In terms of outlets, privacy research in communication and media studies is published in a wide range of journals, including the *Journal of Communication* (e.g., Baruh et al., 2017), *Human Communication Research* (e.g., Sundar & Marathe, 2010), *Social Media + Society* (e.g., Trepte et al., 2017), the *Journal of Computer-Mediated Communication* (e.g., Dienlin & Metzger, 2016) and *Computers in Human Behavior* (e.g., Maltseva & Lutz, 2018).

PRIVACY AND HMC

HMC goes beyond privacy literature on more established digital technologies such as social media. Such privacy research has often adopted a computer-mediated communication (CMC) perspective, where privacy relations between users themselves or between users and services/platforms are investigated. Technology has mainly a mediating role in such research by affecting, through affordances, how privacy enfolds (e.g., how privacy-invasive a given platform or context is perceived to be). At the same time, CMC privacy research tends to situate privacy online, focusing on the informational dimension but neglecting the physical and spatial embeddedness of technologies. By contrast, HMC considers emerging technologies as actants and interlocutors within privacy networks, rather than media (Lutz & Tamò, 2018; Peter & Kühne, 2018).

By foregrounding the (inter)active role of technologies and the relationships users develop with such technologies, HMC introduces novel privacy questions and addresses the four privacy dimensions by Burgoon (1982) more holistically. Particularly the embodiment, portability, social presence, interactivity, and tendency to anthropomorphize social robots, smart speakers, smart toys, and similar technologies has made privacy a key issue of HMC research (Lutz et al., 2019).

In the following, I will discuss research on privacy with smart and interactive technologies from a HMC perspective (see Table 35.1, last column, for how HMC research can adopt the three privacy theories introduced earlier). More specifically, I differentiate three technologies that have received

increasing attention by HMC scholars who focus on privacy: social robots, smart speakers, and chatbots. While these three technologies have high heterogeneity within, the degree of social presence, mobility and situatedness in space generally decreases going from social robots, to smart speakers, to chatbots.

Social Robots, Privacy and HMC

Privacy Implications
Calo (2010) differentiates three privacy implications of robots: increased access, direct surveillance and social meaning. Increased access describes the capacity of robots to enter protected areas such as bedrooms and bathrooms. Direct surveillance risks stem from the technological

Table 35.1 Overview of important privacy theories in communication research (selection)

Theory	Summary and key concepts	Potential application in HMC
Privacy as contextual integrity (Nissenbaum, 2010)	Privacy is the preservation of context-specific information norms. Contexts are understood as institutional and social areas of life (e.g., family, healthcare, politics). Context-specific information norms are described by five parameters: sender, subject, recipient, information type, and transmission principle.	Investigating how aspects of communication between humans and interactive machines (e.g., social presence, anthropomorphization) affect information norms in different contexts. Modulating the five parameters to study the acceptability of HMC scenarios.
Communication privacy management (Petronio, 2002)	People balance disclosure and withdrawal in a dialectic process. They set up privacy boundaries that describe which information is considered private or public. Boundary management includes boundary rule formation, boundary coordination and boundary turbulence.	Investigating privacy rules between humans and machines. Identifying potential differences in boundary management between HMC and interpersonal communication. Investigating privacy turbulence, for example through glitches and malfunctions.
Networked privacy (Marwick & boyd, 2014)	Practice-based approach that looks at privacy practices in networked publics. Networked publics are characterized by audiences, technical mechanisms and social norms. Shift from individualistic frame of privacy to networked frame, with context collapse as an important privacy challenge. Agency entails not only control of information but also understanding and shaping of the context.	Studying which new privacy strategies emerge when individuals are confronted with networked publics that increasingly include machines in addition to people. Privacy literacy and self-efficacy as emerging constructs.

sophistication of robots, including processors and sensors that allow for in-depth monitoring, for example in law enforcement and military contexts. Finally, social meaning refers to the design of robots that triggers interaction and facilitates the establishment of relationships, leading to the disclosure of potentially compromising information. The last privacy implication of social meaning is particularly interesting for HMC scholarship since it has the strongest connection to the HMC agenda, where the emergence of meaning between humans and machines is of core interest.

Empirical Research

While Calo (2010) provided an influential contribution on (social) robots and privacy, his work was not situated within HMC or communication more broadly. However, since then, several contributions have furthered our understanding of privacy in the context of social robots, also from a communication perspective. Lutz et al. (2019) provide a systematic review of research on social robots and privacy, acknowledging HMC as a particularly fruitful theory. Their scoping review draws on Burgoon's (1982) privacy typology and notes a general increase in research interest in recent years. However, empirical insights are still scarce. The research on privacy and social robots is highly interdisciplinary, with law being the discipline with most contributions, followed by computer science and the medical sciences. Only one article from media and communication was found.[1] A clear majority of the analyzed articles is conceptual and relatively small sample sizes and specific interaction contexts make it difficult to identify generalizable conclusions. The review also identifies privacy as contextual integrity and fair information practices as important conceptual underpinnings. A dominance of informational privacy, rather than physical, social, and psychological privacy, was further noted.

As an example for an empirical study, Krupp and colleagues (2017) used focus groups to identify salient privacy concerns in the context of social robots. They found that informational concerns were most strongly discussed (106 code occurrences). However, physical concerns also received much attention (60 occurrences). Social and psychological privacy, by contrast, received far less attention (both 16 occurrences). In addition, the study found novel categories that can be understood in privacy terms, for example marketing and theft. Lutz and Tamò-Larrieux (2020), situated within HMC research, investigated the prevalence of three privacy concern types in social robots. Informational privacy concerns about the robot manufacturer were most pronounced, followed

by informational concerns about other users (e.g., stalking through the robot), and physical privacy concerns (e.g., robot entering areas that it should not access). Thus, the robot as a social actor seems to be perceived as less risky for privacy than the robot as a medium and the actions of its creator. A structural equation model provided evidence for a robot privacy paradox, in analogy to the privacy paradox more generally (Kokolakis, 2017).

Future Research Directions

HMC research on social robots and privacy has strong connections to human–robot interaction (HRI) research, where privacy has become an increasingly important research theme in recent years (Horstmann et al., 2020; Rueben et al., 2017, 2018). The two fields are increasingly speaking to each other (C. Edwards et al., 2019). Future privacy research from a HMC angle could thus consolidate the findings from HRI and integrate the aforementioned theories (Table 35.1) into the study of social robots. The communicative affordances of social robots (Rodríguez-Hidalgo, 2020) and their interplay with privacy perceptions and behavior are also a promising topic for HMC.

Smart Speakers, Privacy, and HMC

Privacy Implications

Compared to social robots, smart speakers such as Amazon Echo and Google Nest devices have less mobility but still some physical presence. These technologies have enjoyed great popularity and are distinctly conversational as they function via speech recognition. Privacy implications include the connectedness of smart speakers to the cloud and their embeddedness in a platform eco-system. Amazon and Google can use the data collected via smart speakers to further their core business activities (i.e., more sophisticated targeted advertising in the case of Google; integration with its shopping platform in the case of Amazon) and enhance their market position (Pridmore et al., 2019). Another issue can be bystander privacy, where individuals in the vicinity of the smart speaker are inadvertently recorded (Ahmad et al., 2020). This is a particular concern for children, who have special data protection status.

Empirical Research

A number of empirical studies have investigated privacy perceptions in the context of smart speakers (Apthorpe et al., 2018; Liao et al., 2019; Lutz & Newlands, 2021; Malkin et al., 2019; Pridmore et al., 2019; Zheng et al., 2018). The evidence from these studies suggests that users have relatively low privacy concerns and limited privacy protection behavior but the concerns vary depending on the information recipient (Apthorpe et al., 2018; Lutz & Newlands, 2021) and the culture (US vs. Netherlands; Liao et al., 2019). Privacy acts as a barrier for adoption among non-users. Qualitative studies have focused on domestication and shown how users integrate smart speakers in their daily lives (Brause & Blank, 2020), where the technology "renegotiates the boundaries between the private home and outside world" (p. 758). Spatial affordances such as ubiquity, linkability and control-ability emerged as salient themes, showing potential privacy implications where the home becomes an increasingly commodified sphere (rather than a sanctuary). Similar concerns were raised about home-cleaning robots such as Roomba (Astor, 2017).

Future Research Directions

Research on smart speakers and privacy is still in its infancy and many fruitful research questions for HMC research exist. The CASA paradigm (Gambino et al., 2020) can be used to study users' conversations with smart speakers in a controlled setting (e.g., a lab). Researchers could develop specific apps or skills for behavioral experiments that study self-disclosure and compare participants' engagement with a smart speaker to that with a human interlocutor. Longitudinal and ethnographic research could look into the lifecycle of smart speaker use in terms of privacy. Is there a pattern that concealment practices become less prevalent with the duration of use? Is the data systematically wiped if a smart speaker is abandoned? Finally, the interplay of overtrust and privacy is a topic that merits attention (Aroyo et al., 2021). Do users overestimate the intelligence of smart speakers and does this affect their privacy concerns and behavior?

Chatbots, Privacy, and HMC

Privacy Implications

Compared to social robots and smart speakers, chatbots are disembodied. They have been increasingly used in customer service and are a key application of AI that many non-experts might actively interact with (Brandtzæg & Følstad, 2018). Compared with social robots and smart speakers, chatbots are used more sporadically and instrumentally. The privacy implications are therefore narrower and more focused on the informational dimension. For virtual mobile agents (e.g., Apple Siri) that rely on voice control rather than textual interaction, the privacy implications tend

to be more similar to smart speakers. Since chatbots are often operated by humans and AI together and it is not always clear if a human or AI is on the other end, the ontological opacity of communication can present novel ethical challenges (Guzman, 2020; Guzman & Lewis, 2020), including privacy challenges.

Empirical Research

HMC research on privacy and chatbots is even scarcer than HMC research on privacy and social robots and smart speakers. Ischen et al. (2019) provide one of the few studies on the topic. Using HMC, they conduct an experiment on how the type of technology (human-like chatbot vs. machine-like chatbot vs. website) affects information disclosure, attitudes, and recommendation adherence. The study also considers the mediating role of privacy concerns and mindless anthropomorphism, finding some evidence for CASA, where the human-like chatbot – and the website – scored higher on anthropomorphism than the machine-like chatbot. Privacy concerns affected information disclosure and recommendation adherence negatively. Mediation effects were identified, so "that a human-like chatbot […] is higher in perceived anthropomorphism, leading to less privacy concerns and subsequently, more comfort with disclosure and information adherence." The analysis shows the relevance of including design-based characteristics and their perception, for example in the form of anthropomorphism. Another study, which is not inspired by HMC, explored the use of chatbots for disclosing privacy policies and thus more effective notice and consent (Harkous et al., 2016).

Future Research Directions

Contextual integrity theory can be fruitfully applied to the study of privacy and chatbots. Experiments could modify the five parameters mentioned (sender, subject, recipient, information type, transmission principle) and assess participants' acceptability of the different configurations. Particularly, the transmission principle should be investigated further. Moreover, chatbots could be compared with social robots on privacy-related aspects to test how the embodiment of the technology affects privacy concerns and behavior.

CONCLUSION

The rise of smart and interactive technologies has been accompanied by the establishment of HMC as an independent discipline within media and communication research (see contributions in this volume). In this chapter, I have shown how HMC has a lot to say about privacy and how it enhances our understanding beyond CMC. Conceptually, the fact that humans engage with smart and interactive technologies as interlocutors, rather than media, opens up additional privacy implications, especially in physical and social terms. As for the latter, social meaning has been discussed as a privacy implication of robots (Calo, 2010) and the creation of meaning equally has a central role within HMC. We have shown that privacy theories that were developed with human communication in mind (privacy as contextual integrity, communication privacy management, networked privacy) can be fruitfully applied to HMC.

Emerging empirical research on privacy in HMC has shown differentiated privacy attitudes and behaviors that are tied to interaction with smart and interactive technologies (e.g., anthropomorphism, social presence). Humans seem to have less privacy concerns about smart and emerging technologies as social actors themselves but worry more about their instrumental use by other actors (Lutz & Newlands, 2021; Lutz & Tamò-Larrieux, 2020). Given recent findings on the domestication of smart speakers (Brause & Blank, 2020) and the tendency to adopt interaction scripts from interpersonal communication to smart and interactive technologies, privacy risks are certainly elevated. A mix of legal (regulation), technological (security, privacy-by-design) and social (user-friendly privacy controls) protection is needed to address these risks.

HMC research should continue to study privacy in the context of smart and interactive technologies. It can integrate widely used theories in HMC (e.g., CASA, Gambino et al., 2020) and their concepts (e.g., mindlessness, anthropomorphism, uncanniness) into established privacy frameworks such as the privacy calculus. Methodologically, observational approaches, where individuals interact in natural settings (e.g., at home) with machines, are particularly fruitful and qualitative and ethnographic research shows great potential. Such observational studies enhance our understanding of privacy practices and could be followed up with or paired with quantitative studies (e.g., surveys) that allow generalizations about privacy attitudes and behaviors. Experimental methods have enjoyed a long tradition in HRI research and should be used by HMC scholars who study privacy. In the absence of specifically configured robots, smart speakers, or chatbots for lab experiments (e.g., due to budget constraints, social distancing requirements in the wake of Covid-19 or ethical concerns), experimental vignette studies can be used, where users are confronted with scenarios or videos of smart

and interactive technologies (e.g., Lutz & Tamò-Larrieux, 2021). HMC privacy research could also adopt critical discourse analysis, case studies, algorithm audits and socio-technical walkthroughs. Such methods bring to light power-related aspects and allow for a more contextualized understanding of the societal embeddedness of smart and interactive technologies.

NOTE

1 However, since the analysis was conducted (summer 2017), an increasing uptick in interest in social robots in media and communication research can be noted, strongly driven by HMC scholars (e.g., A. Edwards et al., 2019; Lee & Liang, 2019; Peter & Kühne, 2018; Rodríguez-Hidalgo, 2020).

REFERENCES

Aeschlimann, L., Harasgama, R., Kehr, F., Lutz, C., Milanova, V., Müller, S., ... & Tamò-Larrieux, A. (2015). Re-setting the stage for privacy: A multi-layered privacy interaction framework and its application. In S. Brändli, R. Harasgama, R. Schister, & A. Tamò (Eds.), *Mensch und Maschine - Symbiose oder Parasitismus* (pp. 1–41). Stämpfli.

Altman, I. (1975). *The environment and social behavior – privacy, personal space, territory, crowding.* Wadsworth Publishing Company.

Apthorpe, N., Shvartzshnaider, Y., Mathur, A., Reisman, D., & Feamster, N. (2018). Discovering smart home internet of things privacy norms using contextual integrity. *Proceedings of the ACM on Interactive, Mobile, Wearable and Ubiquitous Technologies, 2*(2), 1–23.

Aroyo, A. M., De Bruyne, J., Dheu, O., Fosch-Villaronga, E., Gudkov, A., Hoch, H., ... & Tamò-Larrieux, A. (2021). Overtrusting robots: Setting a research agenda to mitigate overtrust in automation. *Paladyn, Journal of Behavioral Robotics, 12*(1), 423–436.

Astor, M. (2017). Your Roomba may be mapping your home, collecting data that could be shared. *New York Times*, July 25. www.nytimes.com/201 7/07/25/technology/roomba-irobot-data-privacy. html

Baruh, L., Secinti, E., & Cemalcilar, Z. (2017). Online privacy concerns and privacy management: A meta-analytical review. *Journal of Communication, 67*(1), 26–53.

Brause, S. R., & Blank, G. (2020). Externalized domestication: Smart speaker assistants, networks and domestication theory. *Information, Communication & Society*, 23(5), 751–763.

Brandtzaeg, P. B., & Følstad, A. (2018). Chatbots: Changing user needs and motivations. *Interactions*, 25(5), 38–43.

Bräunlich, K., Dienlin, T., Eichenhofer, J., Helm, P., Trepte, S., Grimm, R., Seubert, S., & Gusy, C. (2021). Linking loose ends: An interdisciplinary privacy and communication model. *New Media & Society*, 23(6), 1443–1464.

Burgoon, J. K. (1982). Privacy and communication. *Annals of the International Communication Association*, 6(1), 206–249.

Calo, R. (2010). Robots and privacy. In P. Lin, K. Abney, & G. A. Bekey (Eds.), *Robot ethics: The ethical and social implications of robotics* (pp. 187–201). MIT Press.

Dienlin, T., & Metzger, M. J. (2016). An extended privacy calculus model for SNSs: Analyzing self-disclosure and self-withdrawal in a representative US sample. *Journal of Computer-Mediated Communication*, 21(5), 368–383.

Edwards, C., Edwards, A., Kim, J., Spence, P. R., de Graaf, M., Nah, S., & Rosenthal-von der Pütten, A. (2019). Human-machine communication: What does/could communication science contribute to HRI?. In *2019 14th ACM/IEEE International Conference on Human-Robot Interaction (HRI)* (pp. 673–674). IEEE.

Edwards, A., Edwards, C., Westerman, D., & Spence, P. R. (2019). Initial expectations, interactions, and beyond with social robots. *Computers in Human Behavior*, 90, 308–314.

Feiner, L. (2019). Apple's smart speaker is struggling against rivals from Amazon and Google. CNBC, February 5. www.cnbc.com/2019/02/05/apple-homepod-smart-speaker-market-share.html

Fortunati, L., & Edwards, A. P. (2020). Opening space for theoretical, methodological, and empirical issues in human-machine communication. *Human-Machine Communication*, 1(1), 7–18.

Gambino, A., Fox, J., & Ratan, R. A. (2020). Building a stronger CASA: Extending the computers are social actors paradigm. *Human-Machine Communication*, 1, 71–85.

Guzman, A. L. (2018). Introduction: What is human-machine communication, anyway? In A. Guzman (Ed.), *Human-machine communication: Rethinking communication, technology, and ourselves* (pp. 1–28). Peter Lang.

Guzman, A. L. (2020). Ontological boundaries between humans and computers and the implications for human-machine communication. *Human-Machine Communication*, 1, 37–54.

Guzman, A. L., & Lewis, S. C. (2020). Artificial intelligence and communication: A Human–Machine Communication research agenda. *New Media & Society*, 22(1), 70–86.

Hargittai, E., Redmiles, E. M., Vitak, J., & Zimmer, M. (2020). Americans' willingness to adopt a COVID-19 tracking app. *First Monday*, 25(11). https://doi.org/10.5210/fm.v25i11.11095

Harkous, H., Fawaz, K., Shin, K. G., & Aberer, K. (2016). Pribots: Conversational privacy with chatbots. In *Twelfth Symposium on Usable Privacy and Security ({SOUPS} 2016)*.

Horstmann, B., Diekmann, N., Buschmeier, H., & Hassan, T. (2020). Towards designing privacy-compliant social robots for use in private households: A use case based identification of privacy implications and potential technical measures for mitigation. In *2020 29th IEEE International Conference on Robot and Human Interactive Communication (RO-MAN)* (pp. 869–876). IEEE.

Ischen, C., Araujo, T., Voorveld, H., van Noort, G., & Smit, E. (2019, November). Privacy concerns in chatbot interactions. In *International Workshop on Chatbot Research and Design* (pp. 34–48). Springer.

Kokolakis, S. (2017). Privacy attitudes and privacy behaviour: A review of current research on the privacy paradox phenomenon. *Computers & Security*, 64, 122–134.

Koops, B. J., Newell, B. C., Timan, T., Skorvanek, I., Chokrevski, T., & Galic, M. (2017). A typology of privacy. *University of Pennsylvania Journal of International Law Review*, 38, 483–575.

Krupp, M. M., Rueben, M., Grimm, C. M., & Smart, W. D. (2017, August). A focus group study of privacy concerns about telepresence robots. In *2017 26th IEEE International Symposium on Robot and Human Interactive Communication (RO-MAN)* (pp. 1451–1458). IEEE.

Lee, S. A., & Liang, Y. J. (2019). Robotic foot-in-the-door: Using sequential-request persuasive strategies in human-robot interaction. *Computers in Human Behavior*, 90, 351–356.

Liao, Y., Vitak, J., Kumar, P., Zimmer, M., & Kritikos, K. (2019). Understanding the role of privacy and trust in intelligent personal assistant adoption. In *International Conference on Information* (pp. 102–113). Springer.

Lutz, C., & Newlands, C. (2021). Privacy and smart speakers: A multi-dimensional approach. *The Information Society*, 37(3), 147–162.

Lutz, C., Schöttler, M., & Hoffmann, C. P. (2019). The privacy implications of social robots: Scoping review and expert interviews. *Mobile Media & Communication*, 7(3), 412–434.

Lutz, C., & Tamò, A. (2018). Communicating with robots: ANTalyzing the interaction between healthcare robots and humans with regards to privacy. In A. Guzman (Ed.), *Human-machine communication: Rethinking communication, technology, and ourselves* (pp. 145–165). Peter Lang.

Lutz, C., & Tamò-Larrieux, A. (2020). The robot privacy paradox: Understanding how privacy concerns shape intentions to use social robots. *Human-Machine Communication, 1*, 87–111.

Lutz, C., & Tamò-Larrieux, A. (2021). Do privacy concerns about social robots affect use intentions? Evidence from an experimental vignette study. *Frontiers in Robotics and AI, 8*, 63.

Malkin, N., Deatrick, J., Tong, A., Wijesekera, P., Egelman, S., & Wagner, D. (2019). Privacy attitudes of smart speaker users. *Proceedings on Privacy Enhancing Technologies, 2019*(4), 250–271.

Maltseva, K., & Lutz, C. (2018). A quantum of self: A study of self-quantification and self-disclosure. *Computers in Human Behavior, 81*, 102–114.

Marwick, A. E., & boyd, d. (2014). Networked privacy: How teenagers negotiate context in social media. *New Media & Society, 16*(7), 1051–1067.

Newlands, G., Lutz, C., Tamò-Larrieux, A., Villaronga, E. F., Harasgama, R., & Scheitlin, G. (2020). Innovation under pressure: Implications for data privacy during the Covid-19 pandemic. *Big Data & Society, 7*(2), 1–14.

Nissenbaum, H. (2010). *Privacy in context. Technology, policy and the integrity of social life*. Stanford University Press.

Peter, J., & Kühne, R. (2018). The new frontier in communication research: Why we should study social robots. *Media and Communication, 6*(3), 73–76.

Petronio, S. (2002). *Boundaries of privacy: Dialectics of disclosure*. State University of New York Press.

Pridmore, J., & Mols, A. (2020). Personal choices and situated data: Privacy negotiations and the acceptance of household intelligent personal assistants. *Big Data & Society, 7*(1), 1–12.

Pridmore, J., Zimmer, M., Vitak, J., Mols, A., Trottier, D., Kumar, P. C., & Liao, Y. (2019). Intelligent personal assistants and the intercultural negotiations of dataveillance in platformed households. *Surveillance & Society, 17*(1/2), 125–131.

Rodríguez-Hidalgo, C. (2020). Me and my robot smiled at one another: The process of socially enacted communicative affordance in human-machine communication. *Human-Machine Communication, 1*, 55–69.

Rueben, M., Aroyo, A. M., Lutz, C., Schmölz, J., Van Cleynenbreugel, P., Corti, A., ... & Smart, W. D. (2018). Themes and research directions in privacy-sensitive robotics. In *2018 IEEE Workshop on Advanced Robotics and its Social Impacts (ARSO)* (pp. 77–84). IEEE.

Rueben, M., Grimm, C. M., Bernieri, F. J., & Smart, W. D. (2017). A taxonomy of privacy constructs for privacy-sensitive robotics. *arXiv*, 1701.00841.

Schrock, A. R. (2015). Communicative affordances of mobile media: Portability, availability, locatability, and multimediality. *International Journal of Communication, 9*, 1229–1246.

Smith, H. J., Dinev, T., & Xu, H. (2011). Information privacy research: An interdisciplinary review. *MIS Quarterly, 35*(4), 989–1015.

Solove, D. J. (2008). *Understanding privacy*. Harvard University Press.

Stark, L., Stanhaus, A., & Anthony, D. L. (2020). "I don't want someone to watch me while I'm working": Gendered views of facial recognition technology in workplace surveillance. *Journal of the Association for Information Science and Technology, 71*(9), 1074–1088.

Sundar, S. S., & Marathe, S. S. (2010). Personalization versus customization: The importance of agency, privacy, and power usage. *Human Communication Research, 36*(3), 298–322.

Trepte, S., Reinecke, L., Ellison, N. B., Quiring, O., Yao, M. Z., & Ziegele, M. (2017). A cross-cultural perspective on the privacy calculus. *Social Media + Society, 3*(1), 1–13.

Vitak, J., & Zimmer, M. (2020). More than just privacy: Using contextual integrity to evaluate the long-term risks from COVID-19 surveillance technologies. *Social Media + Society, 6*(3), 1–4.

Warren, S. D. & Brandeis, L. D. (1890). The right to privacy. *Harvard Law Review, 4*(5), 193–220.

West, S. M. (2019). Data capitalism: Redefining the logics of surveillance and privacy. *Business & Society, 58*(1), 20–41.

Westin, A. (1967). *Privacy and freedom*. Atheneum Press.

Zhang, Y., & Leung, L. (2015). A review of social networking service (SNS) research in communication journals from 2006 to 2011. *New Media & Society, 17*(7), 1007–1024.

Zheng, S., Apthorpe, N., Chetty, M., & Feamster, N. (2018). User perceptions of smart home IoT privacy. *Proceedings of the ACM on Human-Computer Interaction, 2*(CSCW), 1–20.

Zuboff, S. (2019). *The age of surveillance capitalism: The fight for a human future at the new frontier of power*. Profile Books.

36

Natural Language Processing

Natalie Parde

INTRODUCTION

Natural language processing (NLP) is a dynamic and growing subfield of artificial intelligence that is indispensable to supporting many forms of human–machine communication. It is the technology powering virtual assistants, predictive text, translation engines, and many other day-to-day applications …most people engage with many forms of NLP in daily life without even realizing it! Natural language processing has also been successfully deployed to many downstream use cases, such as processing medical notes (Sheikhalishahi, et al., 2019), detecting early signs of disease (Farzana & Parde, 2020), analyzing financial markets (Hossu & Parde, 2021), and supporting educational outcomes (Parde & Nielsen, 2014). In the context of human–machine communication, NLP serves as the technical medium between human and machine, converting the human's message into a format that the machine can understand and conversely realizing the machine's communicative intentions in natural language. Figure 36.1 illustrates this process at a high level.

The goals of NLP are twofold: (1) to facilitate automated *interpretation* of human language, through analysis of syntactic and semantic structures; and (2) to enable automated *generation* of human language, through methods that seek to reproduce learned or known linguistic patterns. The first goal is often referred to as *natural language understanding*, and the second goal is often referred

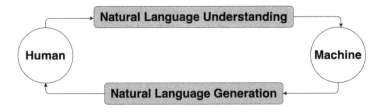

Figure 36. 1   High-level overview of the role of NLP in human–machine communication

Natural Language Understanding

Natural Language Generation

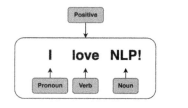

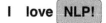

Figure 36.2 **Example outcomes, shaded in gray, from natural language understanding and natural language generation methods. Natural language understanding methods may produce token-level or document-level labels for input, whereas natural language generation methods may produce freeform text given an input prompt or other information.**

to as *natural language generation*. In the past, these twin goals have been achieved using rule-based methods and statistical techniques (Jurafsky & Martin, 2009). More recently, *deep learning* (a family of machine learning architectures that achieve their learning outcomes using layered networks of interconnected computing units, or *neurons*, loosely inspired by the human brain (Goodfellow, Bengio, & Courville, 2016)) has also played a central role in this process (Goldberg, 2016).

Natural language understanding approaches typically assign categoric or numeric labels to documents, spans of text, or words. The labels themselves vary depending upon the learning goal—for example, they might correspond to syntactic categories (e.g., labeling a noun phrase as such), or targets specified by a downstream application (e.g., diagnostic codes for a medical note). Natural language generation approaches produce spans of text. For example, models might generate answers to questions, captions for images, or summaries for news articles. Figure 36.2 shows an example of natural language understanding and natural language generation output. Although significant gains have recently been made in both understanding and generating language, it is normal for these models to produce some incorrect labels (natural language understanding), or repetitions or grammatically incorrect output (natural language generation).

To implement effective NLP systems, researchers and developers often combine methods focused on solving smaller subtasks into a *pipeline*, with the structure varying depending on the application needs. For example, individuals building systems to automatically distinguish between fiction books and scientific articles may rely heavily on the distribution of *part-of-speech* and *semantic role* labels, individuals building systems to evaluate written essay quality may be more interested

in *constituent* and *dependency* structure, and individuals building question answering systems may leverage *named entity recognition*. This chapter provides a primer on subtasks and corresponding methodologies often included in the NLP pipeline. Following this, it examines two pivotal questions in the context of human–machine communication:

1 How can we use NLP to advance machine understanding?
2 How can we employ NLP to provide human task-based or social support?

It concludes by reflecting on underlying commonalities across methods addressing these research questions and identifying key next steps for advancing NLP in the context of human–machine communication.

FUNDAMENTALS OF NATURAL LANGUAGE PROCESSING

In NLP systems, freeform language samples are often passed through a preprocessing pipeline comprising numerous subtasks for conversion to a more structured, standardized form. The preprocessed text and any extracted linguistic metadata are then passed along to a supervised or unsupervised machine learning model, or a rule-based algorithm. Preliminary tasks in the preprocessing pipeline may include:

- **Sentence segmentation:** Input data is separated into its constituent sentences (e.g., *"I'm reading a book. It's about NLP."* → *["I'm reading a book.", "It's about NLP."]*).

- **Tokenization:** Input data is separated into *tokens*, or individual text units. Tokens are typically words or digits, but they can also be punctuation or constituents of contractions (e.g., *"I'm"* → [*"I"*, *"'m"*]). Whitespace tokenization, in which all text units separated by whitespace are considered tokens, is a common baseline; however, more advanced methods may be needed to handle special cases such as compound words.
- **Normalization:** Tokens with different surface forms but equivalent meanings (e.g., *"favorite"* = *"favourite"* or *"1"* = *"one"*) may be mapped to the same surface form to facilitate later processing.
- **Stemming:** Rule-based methods may be used to remove affixes (e.g., *"un-"* or *"-ing"*) from words, converting them to their base form.
- **Lemmatization:** More complex methods may move one step beyond stemming, using advanced rules and lexical dictionaries to reduce words to their base form (e.g., *"geese"* → *"goose"*).

Sentence segmentation and tokenization are crucial for many applications. Normalization, stemming, and lemmatization are particularly useful when working with small datasets or n-gram[1] language models, as they can help prevent data sparsity. Later steps in an NLP pipeline (discussed in the coming subsections), such as part-of-speech tagging or semantic role labeling, can then build upon these preliminary steps to extract more advanced linguistic information. Many existing programming libraries, such as NLTK (Bird, Loper, & Klein, 2009), spaCy (Honnibal, Montani, Van Landeghem, & Boyd, 2020), or Stanford CoreNLP (Manning, et al., 2014), include functionality to perform these fundamental NLP tasks.

Part-of-Speech Tagging

Each token in a text sample plays a distinct role in communicating information, and much of this role is guided by the token's *part of speech*, or grammatical category. NLP systems often automatically extract part-of-speech (POS) *tags*, or labels, for each word in the input text, as this information can be valuable for later steps of text processing and classification. Thus, given the input sentence:

I'm reading a book.

We might first tokenize the sentence:

I 'm reading a book .

Then, using a part-of-speech tagger, we could predict a POS tag for each token:

I [PRON] 'm [AUX] reading [VERB] a [DET] book [NOUN] . [PUNCT]

The exact POS tags predicted for tokens in a sample depend on the POS tagset that is used to train the tagger. Common tagsets include the universal POS tags (Petrov, Das, & McDonald, 2012), the Penn Treebank tagset (Marcus, Santorini, & Marcinkiewicz, 1993), and the Brown corpus tagset (Kučera & Francis, 1967). The universal POS tags are relatively coarse-grained, representing broad word categories, whereas the Brown corpus POS tags are much more fine-grained, with more than 80 specialized categories. Modern POS taggers typically frame POS tagging as a sequence labeling task, using recurrent neural networks (Bohnet, et al., 2018) and Transformer-based models (Heinzerling & Strube, 2019) to achieve impressively high accuracy.

Constituency and Dependency Parsing

Once text has been POS-tagged, we can extract additional information regarding the relationships between tokens by automatically *parsing* the text. There are two types of parses we can extract:

- **Constituency parses** show the *syntactic relationships* between words. For example, a noun phrase might be decomposed into a determiner and a noun.
- **Dependency parses** show the *semantic relationships* between words. For example, one word might be the direct object of another.

Just like POS taggers make use of POS tagsets, dependency parsers make use of dependency tagsets. The exact set of valid dependency relations depends on the dependency tagset that is used. Common dependency tagsets include the set of universal dependencies (Nivre, et al., 2016) and the earlier Stanford typed dependencies (de Marneffe & Manning, 2008).

The set of valid constituency relations depends on the production rules existing in the formal grammar that defines a language (Chomsky, 1957). A hypothetical grammar might define a simple language as follows, where *S* is a sentence root, *NP* is a noun phrase, *VP* is a verb phrase, *PP* is a prepositional phrase, and *DT*, *N*, *V*, and *P* are a determiner, noun, verb, and preposition, respectively:

$S \rightarrow NP\ VP$
$NP \rightarrow DT\ N$
$VP \rightarrow V\ PP$
$PP \rightarrow P\ N$

Constituency parsing has traditionally been performed using dynamic programming (e.g., the CKY algorithm (Kasami, 1966)), and dependency parsing has leveraged transition-based (Nivre, 2003) or graph-based parsing algorithms (McDonald, Crammer, & Pereira, 2005). More recently, neural models have also been explored for constituency and dependency parsing (Mrini et al., 2020).

Coreference Resolution

A single discourse entity may be referred to in numerous ways in the same text. When two or more *referring expressions* refer to the same entity, they *corefer* with one another (Jurafsky & Martin, 2009). Automatically mapping coreferring expressions to a single or symbolic representation of the same discourse entity (e.g., *"Natalie wrote about NLP because she liked it."* → *"Natalie wrote about NLP because Natalie liked NLP."*) is known as coreference resolution. Coreference resolution is often achieved using a two-stage process of identifying entity mentions and then clustering those mentions into coreference chains. Rule-based (Raghunathan et al., 2010) and statistical (Ng & Cardie, 2002) methods generally separate these steps, but neural methods (Joshi et al., 2020) often incorporate both in a unified architecture.

Named Entity Recognition

Recognizing specific instances of people, places, or other *entity types* in text is closely related to mention detection, and is known as named entity recognition. Named entity recognition facilitates information extraction for a wide range of applications. It is often framed as a sequence labeling problem, recently solved using recurrent neural network (Chiu & Nichols, 2016) or Transformer-based architectures (Yamada, Asai, Shindo, Takeda, & Matsumoto, 2020). Valid entity types may vary depending on the task and domain to which the named entity recognizer is applied, as also seen with POS and dependency tagsets. Many named entity recognizers are trained on the OntoNotes corpus (Weischedel et al., 2013), which includes labels for PERSON, NATIONALITY OR POLITICAL GROUP, FACILITY, ORGANIZATION, GEO-POLITICAL ENTITY, LOCATION, PRODUCT, EVENT, WORK OF ART, LAW, and LANGUAGE.

Semantic Role Labeling

Identifying predicate arguments that fulfill specific roles in a sentence is known as semantic role labeling. *Semantic roles* can vary in specificity depending on the needs of their application, ranging from generic (e.g., *eat* accepts an AGENT and a PATIENT) to precise (e.g., *eat* accepts a CONSUMER and a MEAL). Similarly to named entity recognition, modern semantic role labeling is often framed as a neural sequence labeling task (Strubell, Verga, Andor, Weiss, & McCallum, 2018). Popular resources for training and evaluating semantic role labeling systems include PropBank (Bonial et al., 2017), which defines general and precise labels for propositional arguments, and FrameNet (Ruppenhofer, Ellsworth, Petruck, Johnson, & Scheffczyk, 2016), which defines predicate arguments corresponding to general semantic concepts, or *frames*.

Word Sense Disambiguation

A single *surface form* may be used to convey numerous *word senses*, depending on the context (e.g., "You're *right!*" versus "Turn *right!*"). Word sense disambiguation identifies the correct word sense for a given surface form. This can be done using supervised learning, by training a classifier to predict a word sense given a word's context, or unsupervised learning, by making use of clustering methods or lexical resources. Many recent word sense disambiguation approaches leverage information from *contextual word embeddings*, which are word representations that differ depending on a word's surrounding context, to guide their decisions (Scarlini, Pasini, & Navigli, 2020). A comprehensive resource defining word senses and their relations to one another is WordNet (Fellbaum, 1998).

Representation Learning

Most modern NLP approaches use *word embedding* techniques to encode words as numeric vectors in a many-dimensional semantic space. Given an n-dimensional space, Word X and Word Y are represented as distinct n-dimensional points, and the distance between those vector points can convey those words' similarity to one another (e.g., *dog* and *cat* should be closer to one another than *dog* and *architecture*). Word embedding techniques typically learn word representations based on word co-occurrence in large text corpora (Mikolov, Chen, Corrado, & Dean, 2013; Pennington, Socher, & Manning, 2014), and embeddings may vary for the same surface form depending on context (Peters et al., 2018; Howard & Ruder, 2018). Recent approaches have framed the task as a neural language modeling problem, using outputs from hidden layers of the neural network as learned word representations (Devlin, Chang, Lee, & Toutanova, 2019).

NLP AS SUPPORT FOR HUMAN–MACHINE COMMUNICATION

There are many ways that fundamental NLP methods can be combined to support enhanced human–machine communication. For example, dialogue systems can decompose complex inputs using constituency and dependency parsers, extract information from those inputs using named entity recognizers and semantic role labelers, and learn to map that information to relevant content based on vector space similarity. This section introduces research areas that are well-positioned to advance human machine communication by fostering machine understanding and enabling customized, effective human support.

Machine Understanding

Effective machine understanding maps linguistic patterns to real-world meaning. *Grounded language learning* specifically seeks to build meaning for words or linguistic structures based on experiential signals (e.g., vision or social context), theoretically modeling human language learning (Bisk et al., 2020). This better equips machines to accomplish complex tasks, such as understanding spatial language (Ku, Anderson, Patel, Ie, & Baldridge, 2020) or engaging in situated interactions (Suhr, et al., 2019).

Grounded language learning is naturally poised to advance human–machine communication by promoting shared understanding of the interaction context. Humans can also accelerate grounded language learning through natural communication directly (Papakostas, Tsiakas, Parde, Karkaletsis, & Makedon, 2015), for example using language games (Parde et al., 2015; Parde, Papakostas, Tsiakas, & Nielsen, 2015; Thomason, Sinapov, Svetlik, Stone, & Mooney, 2016) that engage humans in casual competition with machines while ambiently harvesting grounded labels from the interaction, in time improving the machine's situationally grounded concept representations.

Although this technique has yielded impressive results in certain forms of grounded language learning (e.g., visually-grounded language (Parde et al., 2015; Thomason, Sinapov, Svetlik, Stone, & Mooney, 2016)), there is still room for human–machine communication to play a larger role in advancing machine understanding. Further investigation is needed to develop methods for increasing machine understanding of, and experiences with, social context (Bisk et al., 2020). Since much of human language understanding relies on situational understanding and social norms (Ervin-Tripp,

1973; Baldwin et al., 1996), enabling machines to draw upon these phenomena may allow them to reach a level of language understanding that is functionally closer to that of humans.

Human Support

Human–machine communication can also be an avenue for providing human task or social support, for example through virtual assistants, conversational chatbots (Huang, Zhu, & Gao, 2020), or virtual health coaches (Gupta et al., 2020). Deploying these technologies in healthcare applications is particularly intriguing in light of shifting population demographics (National Research Council, 2012) and healthcare worker shortages (Kuehn, 2007). Embodied (Parde & Nielsen, 2019) or virtual (Farzana & Parde, 2019) agents designed through interdisciplinary collaboration between NLP researchers and healthcare professionals can be deployed to facilitate health assessment (Di Palo & Parde, 2019; Farzana, Valizadeh, & Parde, 2020; Farzana & Parde, 2019, 2020), promote positive health behaviors (Gupta et al., 2020; Parde & Nielsen, 2018, 2019; Parde, 2018), or assist patients in completing healthcare interventions (Kaelin, Valizadeh, Salgado, Parde, & Khetani, 2021). Although significant progress toward deploying these innovations has already been made, there is ample opportunity for future work. Intriguing ongoing challenges include automated patient modeling (Valizadeh, Ranjbar-Noiey, Caragea, & Parde, 2021; Dligach & Miller, 2018), interaction-based healthcare interventions (Parde, 2018; Kaelin, Valizadeh, Salgado, Parde, & Khetani, 2021), and medical question answering systems (He, Zhu, Zhang, Chen, & Caverlee, 2020).

CONCLUSION

The research areas covered in the sections "Machine understanding" and "Human support" represent diverse yet complementary pathways through which NLP can advance human–machine communication, by accelerating machine understanding and facilitating human support. There are many underlying commonalities among the two. Both problems are addressed through a synthesis of fundamental NLP techniques, both lines of research learn informative syntactic and semantic patterns from natural language data, and both require concerted communication between human and machine as a prerequisite for success.

Gains in resource efficiency and rapid advances in deep learning may accelerate progress towards solving many of the research challenges introduced in the section "NLP as support for human–machine communication," clearing the way for these innovations to be integrated in real-world systems. Promising areas in fostering machine understanding include continued work towards grounded language learning, with emphasis on grounding not only in multisensory input but also in situational social context (Bisk, et al., 2020), and the exploration of mechanisms by which this could be facilitated in engaging human-machine interaction settings (Parde et al., 2015). Promising areas in facilitating human support include continued investigation into virtual agents for clinical or home settings (Parde & Nielsen, 2019; Farzana, Valizadeh, & Parde, 2020), as well as automation of straightforward yet time-consuming or otherwise burdensome clinical tasks (Farzana & Parde, 2020). Ultimately, NLP is a flourishing subfield at the convergence of computer science, linguistics, and communication studies that is poised to deliver exciting advances to human–machine communication both at present and in the future.

NOTE

1   Sequences of *n* words; for instance, in *I'm reading a book*, depending on tokenization parameters, a 4-gram might be *I 'm reading a*.

REFERENCES

Baldwin, D. A., Markman, E. M., Bill, B., Desjardins, R. N., Irwin, J. M., & Tidball, G. (1996). Infants' reliance on a social criterion for establishing word-object relations. *Child Development, 67*(6), 3135–3153.

Bird, S., Loper, E., & Klein, E. (2009). *Natural Language Processing with Python*. O'Reilly Media, Inc.

Bisk, Y., Holtzman, A., Thomason, J., Andreas, J., Bengio, Y., Chai, J., ... Turian, J. (2020). Experience Grounds Language. *Proceedings of the 2020 Conference on Empirical Methods in Natural Language Processing*. Online.

Bohnet, B., McDonald, R., Simões, G., Andor, D., Pitler, E., & Maynez, J. (2018). Morphosyntactic tagging with a Meta-BiLSTM model over context sensitive token encodings. *Proceedings of the 56th Annual Meeting of the Association for Computational Linguistics (Volume 1: Long Papers)*. Melbourne, Australia.

Bonial, C., Conger, K., Hwang, J. D., Mansouri, A., Aseri, Y., Bonn, J., ... Palmer, M. (2017). Current directions in English and Arabic PropBank. In *Handbook of Linguistic Annotation* (pp. 737–769). Springer.

Chiu, J. P., & Nichols, E. (2016). Named entity recognition with bidirectional LSTM-CNNs. *Transactions of the Association for Computational Linguistics, 4*, 357–370.

Chomsky, N. (1957). *Syntactic Structures*. Walter de Gruyter.

de Marneffe, M.-C., & Manning, C. D. (2008). The Stanford typed dependencies representation. *Proceedings of the Workshop on Cross-Framework and Cross-Domain Parser Evaluation*. Manchester, United Kingdom.

Devlin, J., Chang, M.-W., Lee, K., & Toutanova, K. (2019). BERT: Pre-training of deep bidirectional transformers for language understanding. *Proceedings of the 2019 Conference of the North American Chapter of the Association for Computational Linguistics: Human Language Technologies, Volume 1 (Long and Short Papers)*. Association for Computational Linguistics.

Di Palo, F., & Parde, N. (2019). Enriching neural models with targeted features for dementia detection. *Proceedings of the 57th Annual Meeting of the Association for Computational Linguistics, Student Research Workshop*. Florence, Italy: Association for Computational Linguistics.

Dligach, D., & Miller, T. (2018). Learning patient representations from text. *Proceedings of the Seventh Joint Conference on Lexical and Computational Semantics*. New Orleans, Louisiana: Association for Computational Linguistics.

Ervin-Tripp, S. (1973). Some strategies for the first two years. In *Cognitive Development and Acquisition of Language* (pp. 261–286). Academic Press.

Farzana, S., & Parde, N. (2019). Virtual-Interviewer: A conversational agent designed to facilitate cognitive health screening in older adults. *Proceedings of the IEEE-EMBS International Conference on Biomedical and Health Informatics: Extended Abstracts*. Chicago, Illinois: IEEE.

Farzana, S., & Parde, N. (2020, October 25–29). Exploring MMSE score prediction using verbal and non-verbal cues. *Proceedings of the 21st Conference of the International Speech Communication Association (INTERSPEECH 2020)*. Shanghai, China: International Speech Communication Association.

Farzana, S., Valizadeh, M., & Parde, N. (2020). Modeling dialogue in conversational cognitive health screening interviews. *Proceedings of the 12th International Conference on Language Resources and Evaluation*. Marseilles, France: European Language Resources Association.

Fellbaum, C. (1998). *WordNet: An electronic lexical database*. MIT Press.

Goldberg, Y. (2016). A primer on neural network models for natural language processing. *Journal of Artificial Intelligence Research, 57*(1), 345–420.

Goodfellow, I., Bengio, Y., & Courville, A. (2016). *Deep learning*. MIT Press.

Gupta, I., Salunke, D., Di Eugenio, B., Allen-Meares, P. G., Dickens, C. A., Garcia-Bedoya, O., & Boyd, A. D. (2020). An interactive dialogue agent to assist African American and Hispanic/Latino heart failure patients with self-care needs. *Journal of Cardiac Failure, 26*(10).

He, Y., Zhu, Z., Zhang, Y., Chen, Q., & Caverlee, J. (2020). Infusing disease knowledge into BERT for health question answering, medical inference and disease name recognition. *Proceedings of the 2020 Conference on Empirical Methods in Natural Language Processing*. Online: Association for Computational Linguistics.

Heinzerling, B., & Strube, M. (2019). Sequence tagging with contextual and non-contextual subword representations: A multilingual evaluation. *Proceedings of the 57th Annual Meeting of the Association for Computational Linguistics*. Florence, Italy: Association for Computational Linguistics.

Honnibal, M., Montani, I., Van Landeghem, S., & Boyd, A. (2020). *spaCy: Industrial-strength natural language processing in Python*. Zenodo.

Hossu, P., & Parde, N. (2021). Using deep learning to correlate Reddit posts with economic time series during the COVID-19 pandemic. *Proceedings of the 3rd Workshop on Financial Technology and Natural Language Processing (FinNLP)*. Online: Association for Computational Linguistics.

Howard, J., & Ruder, S. (2018). Universal language model fine-tuning for text classification. *Proceedings of the 56th Annual Meeting of the Association for Computational Linguistics (Volume 1: Long Papers)*. Melbourne, Australia: Association for Computational Linguistics.

Huang, M., Zhu, X., & Gao, J. (2020). Challenges in building intelligent open-domain dialog systems. *ACM Transactions on Information Systems, 38*(3).

Joshi, M., Chen, D., Liu, Y., Weld, D. S., Zettlemoyer, L., & Levy, O. (2020). SpanBERT: Improving pre-training by representing and predicting spans. *Transactions of the Association for Computational Linguistics, 8*, 64–77.

Jurafsky, D., & Martin, J. (2009). *Speech and language processing*. Prentice-Hall.

Kaelin, V., Valizadeh, M., Salgado, Z., Parde, N., & Khetani, M. (2021). Artificial intelligence in rehabilitation targeting participation of children and youth with disabilities: A scoping review. *Journal of Medical Internet Research*.

Kasami, T. (1966). *An efficient recognition and syntax-analysis algorithm for context-free languages*.

Coordinated Science Laboratory, University of Illinois at Urbana-Champaign.

Ku, A., Anderson, P., Patel, R., Ie, E., & Baldridge, J. (2020). Room-across-room: Multilingual vision-and-language navigation with dense spatiotemporal grounding. *Proceedings of the 2020 Conference on Empirical Methods in Natural Language Processing (EMNLP)*. Online: Association for Computational Linguistics.

Kučera, H., & Francis, W. N. (1967). *Computational analysis of present-day American English*. Brown University Press.

Kuehn, B. M. (2007). Global shortage of health workers, brain drain stress developing countries. *Journal of the American Medical Association, 298*(16), 1853–1855.

Manning, C. D., Surdeanu, M., Bauer, J., Finkel, J., Bethard, S. J., & McClosky, D. (2014). The Stanford CoreNLP natural language processing toolkit. *Proceedings of the 52nd Annual Meeting of the Association for Computational Linguistics: System Demonstrations*. Baltimore, Maryland: Association for Computational Linguistics.

Marcus, M. P., Santorini, B., & Marcinkiewicz, M. (1993). Building a large annotated corpus of English: The Penn Treebank. *Computational Linguistics, 19*(2), 313–330.

McDonald, R., Crammer, K., & Pereira, F. (2005). Online large-margin training of dependency parsers. *Proceedings of the 43rd Annual Meeting of the Association for Computational Linguistics*. Ann Arbor, Michigan: Association for Computational Linguistics.

Mikolov, T., Chen, K., Corrado, G., & Dean, J. (2013). Efficient estimation of word representations in vector space. *1st International Conference on Learning Representations*. Scottsdale, Arizona.

Mrini, K., Dernoncourt, F., Tran, Q. H., Brui, T., Chang, W., & Nakashole, N. (2020). Rethinking self-attention: Towards interpretability in neural parsing. *Findings of the Association for Computational Linguistics: EMNLP 2020*. Online: Association for Computational Linguistics.

National Research Council. (2012). *Aging and the macroeconomy: Long-term implications of an older population*. The National Academies Press.

Ng, V., & Cardie, C. (2002). Improving machine learning approaches to coreference resolution. *Proceedings of the 40th Annual Meeting of the Association for Computational Linguistics*. Philadelphia, Pennsylvania: Association for Computational Linguistics.

Nivre, J. (2003). An efficient algorithm for projective dependency parsing. *Proceedings of the Eighth International Conference on Parsing Technologies*. Nancy, France.

Nivre, J., de Marneffe, M.-C., Ginter, F., Goldberg, Y., Hajič, J., Manning, C. D., … Zeman, D. (2016).

Universal dependencies v1: A multilingual treebank collection. *Proceedings of the Tenth International Conference on Language Resources and Evaluation*. Portorož, Slovenia: European Language Resources Association.

Papakostas, M., Tsiakas, K., Parde, N., Karkaletsis, V., & Makedon, F. (2015). An interactive framework for learning user-object associations through human-robot interaction. *Proceedings of the 8th International Conference on PErvasive Technologies Related to Assistive Environments*. Corfu, Greece: ACM.

Parde, N. (2018). Reading with robots: Towards a human-robot book discussion system for elderly adults. *Proceedings of the Thirty-Second AAAI Conference on Artificial Intelligence Doctoral Consortium*. New Orleans, Louisiana: Association for the Advancement of Artificial Intelligence.

Parde, N., & Nielsen, R. D. (2014). Design challenges and recommendations for multi-agent learning systems featuring teachable agents. *Proceedings of the 2nd Annual GIFT Users Symposium (GIFT-Sym2)*. Pittsburgh, Pennsylvania.

Parde, N., & Nielsen, R. D. (2018). Automatically generating questions about novel metaphors in literature. *Proceedings of the 11th International Conference on Natural Language Generation*. Tilburg, The Netherlands: Association for Computational Linguistics.

Parde, N., & Nielsen, R. D. (2019). AI meets Austen: Towards human-robot discussions of literary metaphor. *Proceedings of the 20th International Conference on Artificial Intelligence in Education*. Chicago, Illinois: Springer, Cham.

Parde, N., & Nielsen, R. D. (2019). User perceptions of a conversational robot interface. *Proceedings of the CHI 2019 Workshop on Mapping Theoretical and Methodological Perspectives for Understanding Speech Interface Interactions*. Glasgow, Scotland.

Parde, N., Hair, A., Papakostas, M., Tsiakas, K., Dagioglou, M., Karkaletsis, V., & Nielsen, R. D. (2015). Grounding the meaning of words through vision and interactive gameplay. *Proceedings of the 2015 International Joint Conference on Artificial Intelligence*. Buenos Aires, Argentina: Association for the Advancement of Artificial Intelligence.

Parde, N., Papakostas, M., Tsiakas, K., & Nielsen, R. D. (2015). "Is it rectangular?" Using I Spy as an interactive, game-based approach to multimodal robot learning. *Proceedings of the AAAI-15 Conference on Artificial Intelligence Student Program*. Austin, Texas: Association for the Advancement of Artificial Intelligence.

Parde, N., Papakostas, M., Tsiakas, K., Dagioglou, M., Karkaletsis, V., & Nielsen, R. D. (2015). I Spy: An interactive game-based approach to multimodal robot learning. *Proceedings of the AAAI-15*

Workshop on Knowledge, Skill, and Behavior Transfer in Autonomous Robots. Austin, Texas: Association for the Advancement of Artificial Intelligence.

Pennington, J., Socher, R., & Manning, C. (2014). GloVe: Global vectors for word representation. *Proceedings of the 2014 Conference on Empirical Methods in Natural Language Processing*. Doha, Qatar: Association for Computational Linguistics.

Peters, M., Neumann, M., Iyyer, M., Gardner, M., Clark, C., Lee, K., & Zettlemoyer, L. (2018). Deep contextualized word representations. *Proceedings of the 2018 Conference of the North American Chapter of the Association for Computational Linguistics: Human Language Technologies, Volume 1 (Long Papers)*. New Orleans, Louisiana: Association for Computational Linguistics.

Petrov, S., Das, D., & McDonald, R. (2012). A universal part-of-speech tagset. *Proceedings of the Eighth International Conference on Language Resources and Evaluation (LREC'12)*. Istanbul, Turkey: European Language Resources Association.

Raghunathan, K., Lee, H., Rangarajan, S., Chambers, N., Surdeanu, M., Jurafsky, D., & Manning, C. (2010). A multi-pass sieve for coreference resolution. *Proceedings of the 2010 Conference on Empirical Methods in Natural Language Processing*. Cambridge, Massachusetts: Association for Computational Linguistics.

Ruppenhofer, J., Ellsworth, M., Petruck, M. R., Johnson, C. R., & Scheffczyk, J. (2016). *FrameNet II: Extended Theory and Practice*.

Scarlini, B., Pasini, T., & Navigli, R. (2020). With more contexts comes better performance: Contextualized sense embeddings for all-round word sense disambiguation. *Proceedings of the 2020 Conference on Empirical Methods in Natural Language Processing*. Online: Association for Computational Linguistics.

Sheikhalishahi, S., Miotto, R., Dudley, J. T., Lavelli, A., Rinaldi, F., & Osmani, V. (2019). Natural language processing of clinical notes on chronic diseases: Systematic review. *JMIR Medical Informatics, 7*(2).

Strubell, E., Verga, P., Andor, D., Weiss, D., & McCallum, A. (2018). Linguistically-informed self-attention for semantic role labeling. *Proceedings of the 2018 Conference on Empirical Methods in Natural Language Processing*. Brussels, Belgium: Association for Computational Linguistics.

Suhr, A., Yan, C., Schluger, J., Yu, S., Khader, H., Mouallem, M., … Artzi, Y. (2019). Executing instructions in situated collaborative interactions. *Proceedings of the 2019 Conference on Empirical Methods in Natural Language Processing and the 9th International Joint Conference on Natural Language Processing*. Hong Kong, China: Association for Computational Linguistics.

Thomason, J., Sinapov, J., Svetlik, M., Stone, P., & Mooney, R. J. (2016). Learning multi-modal grounded linguistic semantics by playing "I Spy". *Proceedings of the Twenty-Fifth International Joint Conference on Artificial Intelligence*. New York, New York: Association for the Advancement of Artificial Intelligence.

Valizadeh, M., Ranjbar-Noiey, P., Caragea, C., & Parde, N. (2021). Identifying medical self-disclosure in online health communities. *Proceedings of the North American Chapter of the Association for Computational Linguistics*. Online: Association for Computational Linguistics.

Weischedel, R., Palmer, M., Marcus, M., Hovy, E., Pradhan, S., Ramshaw, L., … Houston, A. (2013). OntoNotes Release 5.0. Philadelphia, Pennsylvania: Linguistic Data Consortium.

Yamada, I., Asai, A., Shindo, H., Takeda, H., & Matsumoto, Y. (2020). LUKE: Deep contextualized entity representations with entity-aware self-attention. *Proceedings of the 2020 Conference on Empirical Methods in Natural Language Processing*. Online: Association for Computational Linguistics.

37

Datafication in Human–Machine Communication Between Representation and Preferences: An Experiment of Non-binary Gender Representation in Voice-controlled Assistants

J.L. Mortensen, N.N. Siegfredsen, and A. Bechmann

INTRODUCTION TO DATAFICATION IN HMC

Datafication is a concept used by Mayer-Schöenberger and Cukier (2013) to illustrate how big data and associated technological manifestations transform humans into data (Bechmann, 2019; Mejias & Couldry, 2019). Within the communication industry datafication is thus the underlying premise of modern Human–Machine Communication that mostly rely on massive amount of human data in training, processing and representing machine learning based systems at hand (Bechmann & Bowker, 2019). Datafication is not unproblematic and has given rise to democratic issues most notably *privacy* concerns, *discrimination,* and issues of *representation.*

When more data is available on the individual human being from various sources it becomes increasingly more difficult to manage the self and associated behavior (Bechmann, 2015; Marwick and boyd, 2014) and thus to protect *privacy* for

the individual and groups (Franzke et al., 2020). Especially so, as contextual usage is intertwined (Nissenbaum, 2011) and consent most often is provided as either a weak default setting (van Dijck, 2013; Stutzman, Gross, & Acquisti, 2012) or as a check mark in a box where the contract text is seldom read (Bechmann, 2014).

In the same lines, *discrimination* has increasingly been a growing concern in datafication. Data does not equally represent all humans in technologies that rely on big data processing (boyd and Crawford, 2012). There has been a long and strong tradition in balancing census data (Anderson, 2015; Desrosières, 2002), and unbalanced big data, however big they are, will also overrepresent some and underrepresent others (Campolo & Crawford, 2020; Crawford & Calo, 2016; DiPrete & Eirich, 2006; Eubanks, 2017; O'Neil, 2016).

As such, data is *representational* biased historically, contextually and culturally, for instance with cases of females identified as housewives (Bolukbasi et al., 2016; Sweeney, 2013). When machine learning systems perform well, they tend to cluster around the mean where such "normality" is represented by individuals and behavior with most data points and by companies training the algorithm. They set the norm and thus the inclusion and exclusion rules for a given system. As Gitelman and colleagues write (Gitelman, 2013) "raw data is an oxymoron," meaning that data will always be subject to selection, (pre)processing, analysis, and reporting no matter how big and "untouched" it is. The system will always be biased against certain "truths" (Henriksen & Bechmann, 2020) over others but these can be accounted for to a larger extent (Bechmann & Bowker, 2019; Henriksen, Enni, & Bechmann, 2021; Kroll, 2020). Another dimension of representational biases is how the system represents the user on the interface. A less prominent dimension of datafication in HMC that distinguishes it from human–human communication is the ability to vary how the system is represented on the user interface and user preferences for such interfaces, potentially varying contextually depending on the task at hand. Due to the relative understudied area outside Human–Computer Interaction, we will investigate this further in this chapter.

In a HMC context, datafication can be defined as the data eco-system that allows the communication between human and machine to take place and this eco-system consists of at least four types of data: training data, interface data, data outcome, and feedback loop data (new training data). Training data is the data that provides the machine/algorithm with experience and memory, interface data is the data (vocal, written, visual) which presents the algorithm to the user, data outcome is the processed communicative response to the user, and feedback loop data is the response from the user that can be fed into the algorithm as new training data and adjusted response. In the following section, we will dig deeper into issues of representation at the interface level and, specifically, the growing interface of voice assistants as a way to address this less researched variance and associated datafication dilemmas of preferences, inclusion, and representation.

DATAFICATION, VOICE INTERFACE REPRESENTATION IN HMC, AND GENDER THEORY

The datafied interface holds great power in deciding who and what norms are represented in the human–machine communication nexus. This especially holds true in voice assistants where only the voice can represent (or not) the user of the system compared to visual interfaces where

text, pictures, and layout hold such power. Widely used services from Amazon and Apple and associated voice assistants Alexa and Siri are an integrated part of everyday life and mundane routines that are stipulated by large numbers of users. With reports from Amazon revealing that presumably 500,000 users in 2014 have said "I love you" to Alexa of which half of these have proposed to Alexa (Schweitzer et al., 2019). Despite presumably strong connection to voice assistants, the interface often is representational only of male and female voices (Søndergaard & Hansen, 2018). However, a minority yet growing number of users identify as non-binary and thus have a weak representation when it comes to choosing voices for the assistant (Danielescu, 2020).

To better understand how gender is a vital aspect of a voice-based interface and a marker of representation, or lack thereof, it is important to understand the nature of gender and its interpretation through voice-based cues. Butler (2011) argues for gender as being socially constructed and performed; we are not a specific gender, but we *do* gender. It is through actions that the social is constructed, known as the concept of *Gender Performativity*. This distinction supports the argument that no matter how definitively the biological sex is perceived, social gender is culturally constructed and therefore implies other possibilities. The social gender will therefore occupy a more fluid function that is not locked into the biological gender, which makes it possible to use concepts such as man and masculinity to describe the female voice, and woman and femininity to describe the male voice. The social gender and the biological gender are therefore coherent, as the social gender cannot exist without the biological gender. Discursive practices are automatically embedded in a subject's gender understandings, and "non-binary" and "fluid gender identity" will therefore also appear to be natural, a category covering well above 50 identified gender performances. Non-binary categories help to promote new discourses about gender that are more inclusive and Crawford argues (Crawford, 1995, p. 16) that the widening of the concept of gender therefore also helps to promote the way we talk about our own gender in our everyday life. Historically, and still today, the female and the male are often seen as dichotomous categories. The masculine and the feminine are opposites, each containing its own features (Crawford, 1995), but how does such a voice sound like when gender is performed and not only biological; can we datafy and represent nonbinary gender through a voice?

According to Masahiro Mori (Mori, MacDorman, & Kageki, 2012), our positive emotions for intelligent systems increase when they resemble humans, but as soon as they deviate slightly, they become strangers to us and we feel discomfort. Producing a representation of a non-binary voice must thus be gender neutral (in a binary understanding), as it is not male, nor female without being a stranger. But why even talk about gendered voices? The human brain responds socially to its surroundings. For this reason, we tend to assign technologies human-like characteristics, known as anthropomorphism (Hende & Mugge, 2014; Schweitzer et al., 2019). Humans are attracted to people reminiscent of one-self, as it makes it easier for us to predict behavior and thereby avoid potential danger. We seek to iden-tify others by imitating their personalities, looking for social cues like sound and speech, even when coming from a computer. Speech is a combination of several components such as tension, loudness, breath, vibration, roughness, and pitch, which will make up one's voice (Leeuwen, 1999, p. 140; Mary, 2019, p. 102 ff). Pitch in particular relates to gender and age, and as men and women use their pitch range differently when talking, pitch is often connected to power and status (Karpf, 2006, p. 160; Leeuwen, 1999, p. 134). Therefore, gender and voices cannot stand alone and will automatically be connected. In this sense, gender can be seen as sonic, and sound as the medium in which gender is produced, expressed, and interpreted (Thompson, 2018).

As all humans have a unique combination of the components that make up one's voice, we are extremely fast at distinguishing and identifying oth-ers through social and perceptual cues connected to their voice and gender is one of the first attributes the human brain identifies. The human brain has limited processing capabilities and will only be able to assign one gender at any one moment. Therefore, we tend to apply gender stereotypes to voices, even if it is not congruent with our own gender (Nass & Brave, 2005). Despite this, the social-identification processes that voices activate in our brain will bias us either positively or negatively toward gender, lead-ing people to react more positively toward gender that is congruent with our own gender, known as *the gender-schema congruity effect* (Hende & Mugge, 2014). The study by Hende & Mugge found a cor-relation between positive evaluations of a product and the degree of anthropomorphism, when a gender-oriented promotion of a product and the gender of the participant was congruent. Also, historically females prefer synthesized female voices on a computer, and males prefer male voices, just as male voices evalu-ated by other male voices are perceived more posi-tively than female voices evaluated by other female voices. In addition, male voices are generally rated more trustworthy than female voices, regardless of the gender of the listener (Nass & Brave, 2005, p. 14 f; Reeves & Nass, 1996, p. 175).

Previous studies have shown that interaction with technology created gender-related social constructions and biases (Carpender, 2019) and that the bias of gender in a voice is based on the perception of what a man or women should sound like built up over time (Sutton, 2020). To sup-plement existing research and explore methods to investigate datafication challenges of voice-controlled interface representation, we will in the following sections present an experimental case study[1] that explore to what extent female, male, and non-binary users will choose voices for voice-assistants that represent their own gender identity, and if it varies according to the task at hand.

CASE STUDY ON GENDER REPRESENTATION IN VOICE-CONTROLLED ASSISTANTS

This case study follows a qualitative approach that emphasizes users' experience and conceptualiza-tions of voice assistants based on their own gender identity. We manipulated selected variables and based on the theory presented, female, male and non-binary participants in the experiment will most likely try to categorize all voice assistants by gender (H1) and will prefer the assistant that is congruent with own gender identity (H2). Furthermore, we know from census data that some employment is gender stereotypic, and thus we believe this might have an effect on gender prefer-ences favoring female voices for female stereo-typic tasks and the opposite being true for male voices (H3). The study was conducted as a *quasi-experimental method* design (Field & Hole, 2002) with 12 Danish females, males, and non-binary users. The first variable was the gender identity of the participants. We tested subjects that identified as female, male and non-binary at the moment of the test (Butler, 2011, p. 44) with four participants in each of the three gender categories. We tested participants in the age group 18–30 who are most active users of smart home products in Denmark.[2] Furthermore, most participants have had experi-ence with voice assistants.[3]

When examining how male, female and gender-neutral voices in a voice-controlled assistant are perceived, we needed a representation of a gender-neutral voice. As we have not come across a func-tional gender-neutral voice for voice assistants, we produced our own, based on Google Assistant (https://cloud.google.com/text-to-speech). The voice was determined through a qualitative test of seven different variations of female and male voices with manipulated pitch, in which 161 informants were to choose if it sounded more as male or female. The voice we used for this case study was the one where most of the informants did not agree on the gender of the voice. To get results that would correspond with the experience for real voice-controlled assistants, we needed to simulate a true interaction with a speech system. Therefore, we conducted an experiment inspired by the Wizard of Oz simulation (Fraser & Gilbert, 1991, p. 81). In this experiment, we simulated that the participants talked to real voice assistants when, in fact, we played pre-recorded audio files of answers to already set questions. The gender-neutral voice was made by altering with the pitch of the male and female voices Google had. After creating the gender-neutral voice, we created a total of 114 audio files to be included in the experiment, providing a total of 38 audio files for each voice. The answers to the questions are written by us based on the six selected tasks within: 1. economics, 2. craftsmanship, 3. health, 4. family & relationships, 5. movies & TV series, and 6. tourism. The selected tasks were sampled according to gender stereotypic employment statistics:[4] tasks that represent the female gender stereotypes are health and family & relationships, and for the male gender craftsmanship and economics. In addition, we chose to include tasks within travel and movies to represent categories that are not statistically linked to a gender stereotype, but rather interests that can cut across gender identities.

RESULTS ON REPRESENTATIONS AND PREFERENCES IN THE CASE STUDY

Previous research has shown that people will connect voices to a gender-like description (Carpender, 2019; Sutton, 2020). This was also the case in this study, as all participants in the tested groups anthropomorphized the voice assistants from gendered descriptions, even when trying not to (H1). In seven out of twelve instances, participants preferred and evaluated the voice assistants better when the perceived gender of the assistant was congruent with the gender identity of the participant (H2). In almost half of the instances (32 out of 72 cases ~ 44,44%) participants chose a female voice for female stereotyped topics, male voice for male stereotyped topics, or neutral voice for neutral topics (H3).

Categorization of Gender, Gender Congruity, and Preference for Assistants

During the experiment, several of the participants expressed a need to categorize the assistants by gender. This was shown in the use of pronouns such as "he" or "she" or through gendered, human-like descriptions of the assistants, despite the fact that we throughout the experiment only talked about the assistants as "it." All participants across the groups described the assistants as "he" or "she" after hearing a voice for the first time. Therefore, we found that the theory of anthropomorphism is also applicable to our experiment. In particular, the need to categorize our gender-neutral assistant resulted in descriptions based on binary gender understandings, and for some also sexual orientation. Here, four participants talked about the neutral assistant from female descriptions, and six from male descriptions. Gendered and sexual descriptions like tomboy, cis male, or lesbian came across. This confirms the existing theory about the need for categorizing voices by gender (H1), even when it does not match our own gender identity (Nass & Brave, 2005, p. 16; Thompson, 2018). Several of the participants also switched between their understanding of the gender, thus always deciding on one gender, no matter what voice was speaking. According to results from existing research, we expected the assistants would be evaluated more positively if the understanding of the gender of our assistants matched the gender identity of our participants (H2). In the experiment, all participants assigned human attributes to the assistants, including gender categorization, even when deliberately trying to avoid categorizing an assistant by gender.

We found a similarity between the participant's gender identity and the understanding of the assistant's gender as a reason for the preference in seven out of twelve cases. The male assistant was preferred by all male participants, two female participants and one non-binary participant. Common for the reasons for this preference was that the voice sounded more human and personal, calm, and warmer. The male participants evaluated and perceived the assistant better than the female and gender-neutral assistants, and all participants across the groups generally perceived the male assistant as more trustworthy than the other assistants, confirming existing studies. The reason for this was associated with the subject the male assistant assisted in and the voice itself, that for the participants seemed more credible and authoritarian. The female assistant was preferred by one female participant, no male participants and two non-binary participants, one of whom perceived the voice as gender-neutral. The participants who identified as female or non-binary evaluated and perceived the assistant better than the male participants. According to these participants the voice was pleasant, soft, and kind. However, one of the non-binary participants perceived the assistant as neutral and without gender with a slight incline to the feminine side. However, the gender-neutral assistant was only preferred by one female participant, no male participants, and one non-binary participant. Common to the preference for the gender-neutral assistant was that the participants found the assistant having more personality. The non-binary participant related to the masculinity of the voice whereas the female participant liked the personality and "quirkiness" of the voice, which was described as a feminine boyish.

Preferences in Relation to Gender Stereotypical Tasks

In the experiment, we found that the pairing of the female voice with female gendered stereotypical tasks took place 10 times out of a total of 24 possible instances across the groups. Here, the group of women and the group of non-binary participants chose female stereotyped tasks four times in total, whereas the group of men selected these tasks two times for the female assistant. Here, both female, male, and non-binary participants associated the female voice to service jobs. Also, the female participants did not choose a male stereotyped task for the female assistant at any time. On the other hand, the male participants chose as many male stereotyped tasks for the female assistant as female stereotyped tasks. The non-binary participants chose a female stereotyped task two times and only one male stereotyped task.

Pairing of the male stereotypical tasks with the male voice occurred 13 times out of a total of 24 possible instances across the groups. Here, the group of women chose to pair a male voice with a male stereotyped task four times, the group of males chose to pair a male voice with a male stereotypical task five times, and the group of non-binary participants chose to pair the male voice with a male stereotypical task two times. In half of the instances, the female participants chose a male stereotyped task for the male assistant. One of the participants also expressed the need to choose male voices for her GPS, as it reminded her of her father guiding her when driving. For the male participants, the male stereotyped tasks were chosen in five out of eight instances. For the non-binary participants, only two male stereotyped tasks were chosen; however, a participant wanted to choose a male stereotyped task after hearing the voice. Pairing of neutral gender voice with the neutral tasks occurred nine times out of a total of 24 possible instances across the groups. Here, the group of women chose a neutral task-voice pairing three times, the group of males chose a neutral

task-voice pairing four times, and the group of non-binary participants chose a neutral task-voice pairing two times. However, we did not find as strong a similarity between the perceived gender of the assistant and choice of task in as many instances as the female and male assistant. Here, the different perceptions of the gender of the assistant might have caused them to pair with more diverse tasks and the voice itself affected the evaluation and perception of the assistant.

The results show that male stereotyped tasks were chosen in most instances when the voice was male. The female stereotyped topics was more closely related to a job function in the service sector across the groups of participants. This confirms existing knowledge where historically, a representation of an assistant or service person is often shown as female (Søndergaard & Hansen, 2018). In addition, the choice of task was more diverse for the non-binary participants and did not relate to the gender of the assistant in as many instances as for the female and male participants (H3). Stereotypes on the gender-neutral assistant, on the other hand, were more closely linked to sexual orientation.

Strong Binary Gender Categories or Uncanny Valley Effect?

Common to the participants who have used or were using voice assistants prior to the experiment is that the assistant was used for playing music, searching for information, as GPS or for writing a text or making a call. For this reason, most of the participants across the groups perceived the assistants from a servant-function, where the assistants were to help solve a specific task. The male group especially perceived the assistants from this type of relationship with three out of four participants. For others, the assistants were rated less reliable, which was particularly linked to robot-like descriptions and a fear of secretly being intercepted. This we consider as a master-function, where the assistants were perceived as having too much self-control. This was especially shown for the gender-neutral assistant. Again, the theory of uncanny valley supports the idea that the synthesized voice of the gender-neutral assistant might have caused less favorable perceptions and evaluations of the assistant. If the participants cannot identify with the assistant, it will make them less likely to anthropomorphize and prefer the voice according to the gender-schema congruity effect. However, we cannot definitively conclude whether the reason for this is the participants' lack of social identification with the gender-neutral assistant or it is due to the robot-like descriptions and associations of the assistant. However, we are aware that our manipulation with the pitch of this voice may have created a greater degree of unnaturalness in the voice, just as it may have made it harder for the participants to place and thus identify socially with the voice. Common to the three groups was that several participants compared the female assistant with existing voice assistants such as Siri and Alexa. These assistants were described as female, both in choice of gendered pronouns but also by name of the assistant. This existing perception and comparison to voice assistants like Siri and Alexa made several participants across the groups prefer our male assistant. In addition, in several cases during the experiment, comments were made on the content of the conversations that the participants had with the assistants. Here, differences in content, response length, source references and grammar had an influence on the participants' experience with the assistants.

CONCLUSION

The chapter has outlined how datafication can be seen as a data eco-system of at least four types of data: training data, interface data, data outcome, and feedback loop data (new training data) with associated challenges of privacy, discrimination, and representation. The chapter has focused on datafication as representation in voice (interface) and how to study challenges that arise in this context through the use of gender theory. As a norm of a machine is set by the organization and developers that deliver the technology and handle the training data, inclusion and exclusion of human beings are thus datafied into the machine but can always be changed with new data. This is the reason why a system will always be biased against certain representational biases or "truths" (Henriksen & Bechmann, 2020), i.e. exemplified in this chapter by norms of binary gender and thus the downplay of non-binary. The experimental case study of 12 males, females, and non-binary participants presented in the chapter showed how it is difficult to transgress the dominating binary gender voices. For instance, how do we define a non-binary voice without reference to the binary genders and do the different genders prefer their own gender in relation to all tasks, or are tasks binary gender stereotypic? The study showed that participants prefer their own gender identity in almost half of the instances, and that they tend to assign gender to the associated stereotypical tasks in many cases. Furthermore, the study participants reproduced known gendered descriptions of the male, female, and non-binary voices, in general favoring male voices to be more trustworthy. We also found that the majority of participants, especially males, tend to see voice assistants as servants, and that the gender-neutral voice was less favorable and to some extent caused robot-like descriptions. Still, we cannot confidently say that preference necessarily follows representation of one's own gender. This is an important finding as it supplements existing studies on datafication on the training data level (see e.g. Bechmann & Bowker, 2019) that people tend to be very conservative in their choices and thereby favoring stereotypes and familiar voices even though society and technology companies try to break these in their regulation and construction of systems by making alternatives available.

Underpinning this datafication dilemma in interface data on a theoretical level, the study has shown that it is not a trivial task to represent social gender in voice as we do not have the same mental boxes for what a gender-neutral voice is and how it is distinguished from an uncanny robotic voice. If creating a gender-neutral voice by a manipulated voice, as has been the case in this study, it is crucial to identify the *spot between comfort and discomfort*; or to *move the cognitive scheme culturally*. This is a large challenge for HMC datafication that needs further scientific attention in the field. To fully understand the relationship between preferences and representation in datafication, larger experiments need to be conducted where this small study might serve as an illustrative case and as an inspiration for design and hypotheses. Yet, the chapter as a whole and the case study in particular show that user preferences in HMC does not necessarily follow representation and societal needs for inclusion and diversity, one of the great dilemmas to be solved techno-culturally.

NOTES

1 The case study is an extraction and rewriting of the unpublished master thesis *Gender Categorized Voices* (Mortensen & Siegfredsen, 2020) supervised by Bechmann. No funding has been received for this work and there is no conflict of interest to report.

2 www.dst.dk/da/Statistik/nyt/NytHtml?cid=36216

3 7 had Siri installed, 1 owned a Google Home, 1 had Google Assistant installed. 7 of the participants actively used one of these voice assistants, 3 had previously used them and 2 did not use them at all.

4 www.statistikbanken.dk/LIGEAI2

REFERENCES

Anderson, Margo J. 2015. *American census*. Yale University Press.

Bechmann, Anja. 2014. Non-informed consent cultures: Privacy policies and app contracts on Facebook. *Journal of Media Business Studies*11(1): 21–38. doi: 10.1080/16522354.2014.11073574.

Bechmann, Anja. 2015. Managing the interoperable self. In *The ubiquitous internet: User and industry perspectives*. Routledge.

Bechmann, Anja. 2019. Data as humans: Representation, accountability, and equality in big data. Pp. 73–94 in *Human rights in the age of platforms (ed. Rikke Frank Jørgensen), Information Policy Series*. MIT Press.

Bechmann, Anja, & Geoffrey C. Bowker. 2019. Unsupervised by any other name: Hidden layers of knowledge production in artificial intelligence on social media. *Big Data & Society* 6(1):1–11. doi: 10.1177/2053951718819569.

Bolukbasi, Tolga, Kai-Wei Chang, James Y. Zou, Venkatesh Saligrama, & Adam T. Kalai. 2016. Man is to computer programmer as woman is to homemaker? Debiasing word embeddings. Pp. 4349–4357 in *Advances in Neural Information Processing Systems (29)*. doi: https://doi.org/10.48550/arXiv.1607.06520.

boyd, Danah, & Kate Crawford. 2012. Critical questions for big data. *Information, Communication & Society* 15(5):662–679. doi: 10.1080/1369118X.2012.678878.

Butler, Judith. 2011. *Gender trouble: Feminism and the subversion of identity*. Routledge.

Campolo, Alexander, & Kate Crawford. 2020. Enchanted determinism: Power without responsibility in artificial intelligence. *Engaging Science, Technology, and Society* 6:1. doi: 10.17351/ests2020.277.

Carpenter, Julie. 2019. Why project Q is more than the world's first nonbinary voice for technology. *Interactions* 26(6):56–59. doi: 10.1145/3358912.

Crawford, Kate, & Ryan Calo. 2016. There is a blind spot in AI research. *Nature News* 538(7625):311. doi: 10.1038/538311a.

Crawford, Mary. 1995. *Talking difference: On gender and language*. SAGE Publications.

Danielescu, Andreea. 2020. Eschewing gender stereotypes in voice assistants to promote inclusion. Pp. 1–3 in *Proceedings of the 2nd Conference on Conversational User Interfaces, CUI '20*. Association for Computing Machinery.

Desrosières, Alain. 2002. *The politics of large numbers*. Harvard University Press.

van Dijck, José. 2013. *The culture of connectivity: A critical history of social media*. Oxford University Press.

DiPrete, Thomas A., & Gregory M. Eirich. 2006. Cumulative advantage as a mechanism for inequality: A review of theoretical and empirical developments. *Annual Review of Sociology* 32(1):271–297. doi: 10.1146/annurev.soc.32.061604.123127.

Eubanks, Virginia. 2017. *Automating inequality: How high-tech tools profile, police, and punish the poor*. St. Martin's Press.

Field, Andy, & Graham Hole. 2002. *How to design and report experiments*. SAGE.

Franzke, A., Anja Bechmann, C. M. Ess, & M. Zimmer. 2020. Internet research: Ethical guidelines 3.0.

Fraser, N., & G. N. Gilbert. 1991. Simulating speech systems. *Computer Speech and Language* 5:81–99.

Gitelman, Lisa. 2013. *"Raw data" is an oxymoron*. The MIT Press.

Hende, Ellis A. van den, & Ruth Mugge. 2014. Investigating gender-schema congruity effects on consumers' evaluation of anthropomorphized products. *Psychology & Marketing* 31(4):264–277. doi: 10.1002/mar.20693.

Henriksen, Anne, & Anja Bechmann. 2020. Building truths in AI: Making predictive algorithms doable in healthcare. *Information, Communication & Society* 1–15. doi: 10.1080/1369118X.2020.1751866.

Henriksen, Anne, Simon Enni, & Anja Bechmann. 2021. Situated accountability: Ethical principles, certification standards, and explanation methods in applied AI. Pp. 574–585 in *Proceedings of the 2021 AAAI/ACM Conference on AI, Ethics, and Society*. New York, NY, USA: Association for Computing Machinery.

Karpf, Anne. 2006. *The human voice: How this extraordinary instrument reveals essential clues about who we are*. 1st Edition. Bloomsbury USA.

Kroll, Joshua A. 2020. Accountability in computer systems. *The Oxford handbook of ethics of AI* 181.

Leeuwen, Theo Van. 1999. *Speech, music, sound*. Macmillan.

Marwick, Alice E., & danah boyd. 2014. Networked privacy: How teenagers negotiate context in social media. *New Media & Society* 16(7):1051–1067. doi: 10.1177/1461444814543995.

Mary, Leena. 2019. *Extraction of prosody for automatic speaker, language, emotion and speech recognition*. 2nd ed. Springer International Publishing.

Mayer-Schönberger, Viktor, & Kenneth Cukier. 2013. *Big data: A revolution that will transform how we live, work, and think*. Houghton Mifflin Harcourt.

Mejias, Ulises A., & Nick Couldry. 2019. Datafication. *Internet Policy Review* 8(4).

Mori, Masahiro, Karl F. MacDorman, & Norri Kageki. 2012. The uncanny valley [from the field]. *IEEE Robotics Automation Magazine* 19(2):98–100. doi: 10.1109/MRA.2012.2192811.

Mortensen, Julie Lynge, & Nicoline Siegfredsen. 2020. *Gender categorized voices [Unpublished master thesis in Danish]*. Aarhus: Aarhus University.

Nass, Clifford Ivar, & Scott Brave. 2005. *Wired for speech: How voice activates and advances the human-computer relationship*. MIT Press.

Nissenbaum, Helen. 2011. A contextual approach to privacy online. *Daedalus* 140(4):32–48.

O'Neil, Cathy. 2016. *Weapons of math destruction: How big data increases inequality and threatens democracy*. 1st edition. Crown.

Reeves, Byron, & Clifford Nass. 1996. *The media equation: How people treat computers, television, and new media like real people and places*. University of Chicago Press.

Schweitzer, Fiona, Russell Belk, Werner Jordan, & Melanie Ortner. 2019. Servant, friend or master? The relationships users build with voice-controlled smart devices. *Journal of Marketing Management* 35(7–8):693–715. doi: 10.1080/0267257X.2019.1596970.

Søndergaard, Marie Louise Juul, & Lone Koefoed Hansen. 2018. Intimate futures: Staying with the trouble of digital personal assistants through design fiction. Pp. 869–80 in *Proceedings of the 2018 Designing Interactive Systems Conference, DIS '18*. New York, NY, USA: Association for Computing Machinery.

Stutzman, Fred, Ralph Gross, & Alessandro Acquisti. 2012. Silent listeners: The evolution of privacy and disclosure on Facebook. *Journal of Privacy and Confidentiality* 4(2):7–41.

Sutton, Selina Jeanne. 2020. Gender ambiguous, not genderless: Designing gender in voice user interfaces (VUIs) with sensitivity. Pp. 1–8 in *Proceedings of the 2nd International Conference on Conversational User Interfaces, CUI'20*. Association for Computing Machinery, New York, NY, USA. doi: 10.1145/3405755.3406123

Sweeney, Latanya. 2013. Discrimination in online ad delivery. *Communications of the ACM* 56(5): 44–54.

Thompson, Marie. 2018. Gendered sound. Pp. 108–17 in *The Routledge companion to sound studies*, ed. *Michael Bull*. Routledge.

38

Human–Machine Communication and the Domestication Approach

Jenny Kennedy and Rowan Wilken

INTRODUCTION

The domestication approach aims to describe how particular technologies become integrated into everyday life, how they become embedded within daily rhythms and routines (most typically of households), and how they take on symbolic meaning through such processes (Haddon, 2011). It is concerned with the quotidian or everydayness of technologies and the social shaping of technology. Roger Silverstone describes the domestication approach as "a taming of the wild and a cultivation of the tame" (1994, p. 12), whereby humans appropriate technology into the home environment as well as learn to adapt to the technology themselves. Domestication refers to the symbolic process of transformation technological artifacts undergo as they pass from "radical, exciting, unfamiliar or possibly even dangerous, to ... routine, mundane and an ordinary part of life" (Sovacool & Hess, 2017, p. 715). The approach pioneered by media scholars Roger Silverstone, Eric Hirsch, and David Morley (1992) continues to hold important critical relevance for understanding "the ways in which the cultural and social spaces of the home and social dynamics of the household are reconfigured by media and information technologies" (Chambers, 2016, p. 45).

In this chapter, we outline the domestication approach and its various elements, and set out how it can be applied in making critical sense of human–machine communication, particularly as it occurs within the space of the domestic home. A key focus of human–machine communication research is critical examination of communicative technologies *as they are integrated into daily life*. In early domestication research, the focus tended to be on big-ticket, stand-alone technological items, like the living room television or the family desktop computer. The technological composition of households has, however, changed quite significantly over time. The contemporary home is now populated with an array of stand-alone and connected devices. Increasingly, the majority of these are technologies that function as communicators, ranging from robots (like the Roomba autonomous robotic vacuum cleaner) and smart Internet of Things (IoT) devices, to digital assistants, and augmented or virtual reality systems. Given the growing popularity and ubiquity of these technologies, it is valuable to consider the efficacy of the domestication approach for making critical sense of human–machine communication within the home.

THE DOMESTICATION APPROACH

Domestication emphasizes the "moral economy of the household," the social systems and dynamics within the home that interact – and contrast – with the larger technological systems outside the home (Silverstone, 2006). Domestication as a framework is useful for understanding the social and cultural dynamics by which technologies are possessed and used. Furthermore, domestication research is also concerned with how technology adoption is constrained and inhibited (Haddon, 2011).

Domestication theory emerged from material anthropology and science and technology studies (STS) within the subfield of social construction of technology (SCOT), and consumption studies. It has been applied and further developed within media and technology studies to understand how various information, communication, and entertainment technologies are integrated by households and how household users and their environments adapt and change in response.

Within the domestication literature, the domestic home is regarded as a privileged site (Haddon, 2007) for two key reasons. First, because it forms a key, largely private, space of technological transformation, a site into which new consumer products and goods – especially entertainment media and information and communication services – are bought and consumed. Second, because, once these technologies are acquired, it is here within the home that they are "redefined in different terms, in accordance with the household's own values and interests" (Silverstone, Hirsch, & Morley, 1992, p. 16). Significantly, the naturalization of technology in this space is gradual and is always evolving in response to temporal, material, and symbolic dynamics. Domestication research considers the intertwining of these dynamics, providing both a theoretical lens and a methodological approach in which devices are "'tamed' in different ways at different times, reflecting both technological and personal change" (Haddon, 2011, p. 317).

In its first articulation, the domestication framework had four distinct phases: appropriation, objectification, incorporation, and conversion, which described the processes of acquiring, accommodating, using, and understanding novel technologies (e.g., Silverstone & Hirsch, 1992; Silverstone & Haddon, 1996).

First is *appropriation*, where technologies come into possession, enter into the home, and their use is initiated. There are multiple aspects to this phase. It involves how technologies are purchased or acquired by an individual or household, such as the purchasing process, motivations and intentions for use, decisions on buying the device (and who makes such decisions within particular households), and the initial encounter with the device (as illustrated in unboxing videos but typically occurring in homes in much more mundane ways).

Second is *objectification*. The technology becomes a domestic object by the owner beginning to actively use the technology and integrating it into the home environment and the daily routines of the home. Objectification may also involve how objects are placed, who has access to them, how space is organized in relation to the device (Berker et al., 2006), and styled within the home (Chambers, 2016) – indicating something of the taste and values of those within the home, e.g. organization of wires and cables, or whether a device is placed in a prominent position or in a discrete setting. For example, a Google Home speaker placed beside a bed differs from one placed on a kitchen counter where it is accessible to everyone in the household.

The third phase is *incorporation*. Here the technology becomes integrated into the rhythms and routines of the home. Incorporation includes the intended uses of the device as designed, as well as alternative uses. This process may also involve some form of adaptation of the user and environment. As the technology is incorporated into the daily routines of the user/s it is influenced by social and cultural contexts such as gender, race, and socio-economic status. Also, it influences the routines in the household. For example, when wanting to stream a TV show from a subscription service onto a smart tv, the user may begin to use a voice assistant rather than a mobile app or remote control. As technologies become embedded in the home, the day-to-day routines within the home are reconfigured around them. These shifts in practices are fed back into the design process of future technologies (for example, Amazon's Alexa is coded with new 'skills' based on user feedback).

The fourth phase of domestication is called *conversion*. Conversion is where the technology takes on, or reflects, cultural values and the social status of the household to the outside world, and even starts to shape communication between people in the household and the outside world. At this stage, the device has become familiar to the user and integrated into the daily routines of the household. Conversion is a symbolic process defining the relationship between the household and the outside world. The device is associated with meaning by those within and outside the home, remaking the values and norms associated with the technology and transferring these back to the "outside" world. This symbolic process occurs through users talking to people outside the home about their device use and the meanings they attribute to it. The practical and the symbolic aspects of the adoption and use of technologies, the meanings of things and their materiality, are intertwined and become part of everyday life. Over time these meanings come to stabilize. Yet domestication is never finished.

Technologies remain in a process of being negotiated to some degree, where the use of a device, its value, and how it is placed in the home may continue to change (Silverstone & Mansell, 1996; Silverstone, 2006).

While ongoing, domestication is considered 'successful' when all four stages have been reached and the device is no longer thought of as 'new' (Berker et al., 2006). The phases are described chronologically, but in practice they often run over each other, and can be returned to or repeated during the domestication process (Hynes & Rommes, 2006). This is especially likely to occur when something changes within the house, such as when a new device enters the home and disrupts the existing integrations, routines shift (such as, people begin working from home more), or spaces are redesigned, which causes a redefinition of the device. In short, the domestication process is an ongoing process.

In subsequent work, Silverstone added an additional, precursory stage to the four detailed above. In *Television and Everyday Life*, Silverstone (1994, p. 125) notes that, "in the actual practice of consumption, goods are *imagined* before they are purchased" (see also Silverstone & Haddon, 1996). Imagination thus forms a key, preliminary phase of the domestication process, one where householders speculate about what it might be like to have particular goods or services in advance of acquiring (appropriating) them. Print and digital media play vital roles here by providing a forum for advertisers and marketers who seek to promote ideas and information about particular goods and services and to circulate idealized visions of what they are or might be.

In the case of human–machine communication, the domestication approach could be applied to a smart speaker in a home, by considering how the device can be understood in relation to each of the (now five) phases. One might first examine how householders encountered or *imagined* it. Was it read about in magazines or online, or discovered via friends or by word-of-mouth? How was the product marketed, and what were the "technological imaginaries" associated with its use? Are these informed perhaps by popular media such as the movie *Her*? Then consideration could be given to how the smart speaker was acquired and *appropriated*. Was it purchased off the shelf, packaged with other products, or gifted? What purpose/s did the household have for the device? And what were the ideals and values the household anticipated from the function of the device: was it as a conversational agent (provide information, reminders), as a companion, to support organizational needs (alarms, diary integration), comfort and pleasure (heating, lighting, security), or entertainment (controlling or providing media content)? The *objectification* of the smart speaker might be examined by considering where the device is placed in the home (e.g. a prominent or discrete location), and in relation to other objects (e.g. if anything was moved to accommodate it). Next to consider is how the smart speaker is used in the household, how it is communicated with and integrated into daily rhythms and routines, and how the designed features of the device sustain or disrupt those routines in the process of *incorporation*. For example, using voice commands to play media content rather than selecting from an on-screen app changes how users are exposed to new content, and asking a smart speaker the forecasted weather may impact conversations between humans within the household who no longer muse between themselves. Through *conversion*, the smart speaker can demonstrate the household's participation in streamed and automated service consumption, and their philosophical participation in broader communicative practices with technology as communicator. Users of smart speakers might discover communicating with the device soothes feelings of loneliness and attribute values of care-giving to the device.

APPLICATIONS OF THE DOMESTICATION APPROACH

Silverstone and Hirsch's (1992) edited collection *Consuming Technologies* – which featured Silverstone, Hirsch, and Morley's authoritative chapter – addressed how a media and cultural studies approach could seek to understand the incorporation of technologies into the domestic sphere in both symbolic and material terms. The contributors addressed these with empirical studies that demonstrated the significance of the domestic sphere for technology consumption. Within this approach was a proposition that the metaphor of domestication held a distinct sociological connotation of a private sphere, into which the public sphere-originating technology was being introduced.

One noteworthy aspect of domestication scholarship is that, in the formative literature (works by Silverstone, Hirsch, Morley, and Haddon), domestication is rarely if ever described as a theory. Rather, it is generally cast as a framework or approach for making critical sense of technology adoption and change over time. It is only in later scholarship that domestication is articulated as both a theoretical lens (e.g. Sovacool & Hess, 2017) and a methodological approach. Methodologically, domestication studies most usually draw on qualitative research methods, including interviews, participant observations, and other ethnographic methods such as "technology" or "video tours" (e.g. Kennedy et al., 2020; Lewis, Wilken, & Rauturier, 2020).

Domestication has been applied to understanding the adoption and uses of many waves of "new at the time" technologies that have become embedded in the home over the past few decades. These studies provide an understanding of how home-based practices that include care, work, leisure, and consumption are recursively made materially and symbolically meaningful in the affordances, proliferation, and accommodation of ever-increasing media technologies. This includes studies of how television viewing shifted from mid-century collective viewing with the introduction of smaller, portable television sets and remote controls (Morley, 1980, 1986), how the affordability of computers influenced their introduction into homes (Haddon, 1992; Murdock, Hartmann, & Gray, 1992; Wheelock, 1992; Lally, 2002), and later how the internet and other supporting infrastructures (such as Wi-Fi) were brought into domestic settings (Bergman & van Zoonen, 1999; Ward, 2005; Thomas, Wilken, & Rennie, 2021). Domestication theory approaches have also been used to examine how personalized and portable media have led to the "domestication of elsewhere" or the "dislocation of domesticity" (Morley, 2003), how multiple screens have individualized media-rich homes, leading to the critique that families are "living together separately" (Flichy, 1995; Livingstone, 2002), and how smart technologies intended to seamlessly integrate technologies feed fantasies of the middle-class home (Spigel, 2001; Harper, 2011).

Such studies, which utilize a domestication theoretical approach, are helpful models of counter diffusion approaches which can be unidirectional and decontextualized, pointing to broader trends of technology adoption. Instead, domestication approaches point to how the home space and its rhythms (Silverstone, 1993; Nansen et al., 2009) are sites of mutual and continual adjustments (Lally, 2002; Baillie & Benyon, 2008). What domestication offers is an understanding of how adoption is both situated and recursive.

Criticisms of domestication are typically leveled at how the approach can be rather reductionist. For example, Silverstone and Haddon (1996, p. 3) state, "Design and domestication are the two sides of the coin of innovation. Domestication is anticipated in design and design is completed in domestication." This implies that domestication is reducible to the process of design and the process of use, without making any recognition of how political, social, and economic structures contextualize these states.

Furthermore, domestication does not consider how sociotechnical changes occurring outside the home complicate meanings of technology adoption within the home – think computers, laptops, mobile phones, and smartphones (Sovacool & Hess, 2017). Instead, the household (and occasionally the workplace, see Haddon, 1992) is emphasized as the site at which meaning is attached to technology and this meaning is achieved by integrating it into daily routines conditioned by existing practices and values.

EMERGING QUESTIONS AND ISSUES FOR DOMESTICATION RESEARCH IN THE FIELD OF HMC

Technological change within the home has become far more complex than domestication theory can perhaps account for alone at times. As David Morley (2017, p. 113) observes, "nowadays, the domestic living space is no longer simply 'doubled' by the presence of the television screen but refracted in ever more complex ways by the simultaneous presences" of multiplying screens, multiplying television-related hardware – including set-top boxes and digital recorders, games consoles, and the like – and innumerable other internet-enabled and wirelessly connected devices. In this scenario, domestication theory, as presently conceived, is not always well-equipped to deal with the complicated, overlapping processes of imagination, appropriation, and so on, that follow the proliferation and accumulation of devices entering the home (for discussion, see Kennedy et al., 2020). With increasingly complicated media come more complicated multiplications of interoperability and platforms. Now we have the presence of embodied robots and conversational agents in the home as well.

While the research on embodied robots and conversation agents in the domestic space grows apace, it has not yet been brought into dialogue with the domestication framework. Luisa Damiano, for example, analyses epistemological approaches to studies of the "'domestication' of robots" (2021), but considers this from an ecology framework (which we ourselves have also advocated elsewhere in relation to the media-dense home, see Kennedy et al., 2020). There are few empirical investigations into the impact of conversation agents using the domestication approach. Deborah Chambers's (2020) work is a notable contribution, though she looks at smart homes and does not consider explicitly the embodied or conversational elements of smart home assistants that is central to HMC scholarship.

One of the key issues in moving forward with the domestication approach is how to unpack the layers of interoperability and affordances (e.g. see Neff and Nagy's chapter in this handbook) in media-dense environments involving HMC. In addition, it has been noted elsewhere that the domestication model does not apply to all technologies with equal efficacy. In a recent study of Wi-Fi, for example, it is suggested that "the arrival of Wi-Fi within the home has … complicated critical understandings of the domestication process" (Thomas, Wilken, & Rennie, 2021, pp. 70–71). The authors of this study argue that certain phases of the domestication approach (notably, appropriation and conversion) cannot be readily mapped onto household Wi-Fi (pp. 62, 69). Furthermore, because a new Wi-Fi router needs domesticating, but also facilitates the entrance into the home of multiple other internet-connected devices that will need domesticating as well, then perhaps "the domestication process, when applied to Wi-Fi, might be more productively conceived of as a phased or multi-layered phenomenon, rather than as a single process in which each new household technology is domesticated in turn" (p. 62).

In examining the uptake of algorithmic recommendation systems there is what others have termed a "mutual domestication" process occurring, where, beyond the material domestication process of the technological device, users also "incorporate algorithmic recommendations into everyday life as much as the platform works to colonize users and turn them into ideal consumers through its algorithms" (Siles et al., 2019, p. 2). In the emerging field of human–machine communication we see this mutual domestication process also occurring when the smart speaker's voice user interface requires the user to adapt to a particular way of speaking (incorporating the syntactic rules of language in order to communicate with the machine) or to confine their actions within the defined hearing range of the object.

The incorporation of new or altered rhythms and routines in the process of domestication as these adaptations come to influence the cultural values of the household and shape communication between people in the household and the outside world is not novel. What is novel is that it is the communication *with the machine*, not only the participation with broadcast or consumer culture afforded *through the machine*, that is remaking social values and meanings. This remaking of meaning through human–machine communication is unique. In the example of smart speakers this is demonstrated in a variety of emerging work where the communication users have with machines is shown to influence their expectations of communication with humans (Strengers & Kennedy, 2020).

Recent applications of domestication theory have examined non-material objects, such as Facebook, as technological vehicles of meaning (Goggin, 2014; Leong, 2020; Watulak & Whitfield, 2016). Non-material applications of domestication theory are useful for understanding the relationship between object and text. By this we mean that domestication considers technologies both in terms of their materiality and their meaning, in what is referred to as the "double articulation" of domestication theory (Bertel, 2018; Hartmann, 2006). As Lorian Leong shows, the methodological approach of double articulation helps to account for the particular ways that algorithms are embedded in the process of technology domestication:

> By using approaches of domestication theory and algorithm studies, this study unveiled particular ways in which algorithmic power can come in play throughout the process of technology domestication. Algorithmic power gets inserted into the lives of users in socially and culturally specific ways, although its scope may appear broad. (Leong, 2020, p. 105)

To extend this to the case of the smart speaker, the smart speaker comprises the material object, but also the operating system of the device, and the algorithmic processes of the conversational agent that are engaged through the device. There are multiple layers of interaction and operability across which the domestication process occurs that consequently present as more complex than earlier technologies to which the domestication approach was initially applied. The double articulation of conversational agents presents a promising avenue of exploration for HMC scholarship adopting a domestication framework.

Another avenue of investigation for HMC on the meaning of embodied robots and conversational technology is as it is immersed in the daily life of users and *non-users* (Silverstone et al., 1992). Non-use is often framed in materialist terms, with non-users described as having economic or digital inclusion barriers preventing them from being users. Domestication offers explanations for non-use based on social contexts and value systems beyond economic status, access or capabilities. Through this lens, non-use is more nuanced. Users may resist or reject media devices wholly or partially.

CONCLUSION

This chapter lays the groundwork for future research into how HMC scholarship can be furthered through application of the domestication framework. HMC could examine the domestication of conversational agents by looking at how the ways people use agents, assistants, and robots affects their everyday routines, and most significantly, use the dimensions of domestication to explain these effects. The framework of mutual domestication is particularly promising for understanding how users engage with an array of communicative and conversational objects, given both human and machine are communicative actors in such interactions.

If the HMC field is to be moved forward, a better understanding of how users experience the relational dynamics of automated devices including embodied robots, conversational agents, social bots, assistants and other forms of voicetech needs to be developed. We see here an opportunity for the domestication framework to contribute to HMC research on the meaning, in both symbolic and material terms, of embodied robots and conversational technology as they are immersed in daily home life by foregrounding the relational dynamics in in-situ experiences of users.

The domestication approach can help HMC scholars to understand the sociotechnical changes occurring as a consequence of adoption and appropriation of conversational agents within – and beyond – the contemporary home. The framework is a productive tool for studying and describing how technologies become interwoven into daily routines and practices, and can account for resistance too. Domestication is not the only theoretical or methodological approach to understanding sociotechnical change, but it is a valuable framework with much to offer scholars wanting to study situated change, HMC, and society.

REFERENCES

Baillie, L., & Benyon, D. (2008). Place and technology in the home. *Computer Supported Cooperative Work*, *17*(2–3), 227–256.

Bergman, S., & van Zoonen, L. (1999). Fishing with false teeth: Women, gender and the internet. In J. Downey, & J. McGuigan (Eds.), *Technocities: The culture and political economy of the digital revolution* (pp. 99–107). Sage.

Berker, T., Hartmann, M., Punie, Y., & Ward, K. J. (Eds.). (2006). Introduction. In T. Berker, M. Hartmann, Y. Punie, & K. J. Ward (Eds.), *Domestication of media and technology* (pp. 1–17). Open University Press.

Bertel, T. F. (2018). Domesticating smartphones. In J. Vincent & L. Haddon (Eds.), *Smartphone cultures* (pp. 83–94). Routledge.

Chambers, D. (2016). *Changing media, homes and households: Cultures, technologies and meanings*. Routledge.

Chambers, D. (2020). Domesticating the "smarter than you" home. Gendered agency scripts embedded in smart home discourses. *Medien & Kommunikationswissenschaft*, *68*(3), 304–317.

Damiano, L. (2021) Homes as human–robot ecologies: An epistemological inquiry on the "domestication" of robots. In A. Argandoña, et al. (Eds), *The home in the digital age* (pp. 80–102). Routledge.

Flichy, P. (1995). *Dynamics of modern communication: The shaping and impact of new communication technologies*. Sage.

Goggin, G. (2014). Facebook's mobile career. *New Media & Society*, *10*(7), 1068–1086.

Haddon, L. (1992). Explaining ICT consumption: The case of the home computer. In R. Silverstone, & E. Hirsch (Eds.), *Consuming technologies: Media and information in domestic spaces* (pp. 82–96). London: Routledge.

Haddon, L. (2003). Domestication and mobile telephony. In J. Katz (Ed.), *Machines that become us: The social context of personal communication technology* (pp. 43–56). New Brunswick, NJ: Transaction Publishers.

Haddon, L. (2004). *Information and communication technologies in everyday life: A concise introduction and research guide*. Berg.

Haddon, L. (2007). Roger Silverstone's legacies: Domestication. *New Media & Society*, 9(1), 25–32.

Haddon, L. (2011). Domestication analysis, objects of study, and the centrality of technologies in everyday life. *Canadian Journal of Communication*, *36*, 311–323.

Hartmann, M. (2006). The triple articulation of ICTs: Media as technological objects, symbolic environments and individual texts. In T. Berker, M. Hartmann, Y. Punie, & K. J. Ward. (Eds.), *Domestication of media and technology* (pp. 125–144). Open University Press.

Harper, R. (Ed.). (2011). *The connected home: The future of domestic life*. Springer.

Hynes, D. & Rommes, E. (2006). "Fitting the internet into our lives": IT courses for disadvantaged users. In T. Berker, M. Hartmann, Y. Punie, & K. J. Ward. (Eds.), *Domestication of media and technology* (pp. 125–144). Open University Press.

Kennedy, J., Arnold, M., Gibbs, M., Nansen, B., & Wilken, R. (2020). *Digital domesticity: Media, materiality, and home life*. Oxford University Press.

Lally, E. (2002). *At home with computers*. Berg.

Leong, L. (2020). Domesticating algorithms: An exploratory study of Facebook users in Myanmar. *The Information Society*, *36*(2), 97–108.

Lewis, T., Wilken, R., & Rauturier, F. (2020). New temporalities of everyday life in Australian suburbia: Cultural and material economies of hard rubbish. In F. Allon, R. Barcan, & K. Eddison-Cogan (Eds.), *The temporalities of waste: Out of sight, out of time* (pp. 239–252). Routledge.

Lim, S. S. (Ed.). (2016). *Mobile communication and the family – Asian experiences in technology domestication*. Springer.

Livingstone, S. (2002). *Young people and new media: Childhood and the changing media environment*. Sage.

Morley, D. (1980). *The "nationwide" audience: Structure and decoding*. British Film Institute.

Morley, D. (1986). *Family television: Cultural power and domestic leisure*. Comedia Publishing Group.

Morley, D. (2003). "What's home got to do with it?" Contradictory dynamics in the domestication of technology and the dislocation of domesticity. *European Journal of Cultural Studies*, *6*(4), 435–458.

Morley, D. (2007). *Media, modernity and technology: The geography of the new*. Routledge.

Morley, D. (2009). For a materialist, non-media-centric media studies. *Television & New Media*, *10*(1), 114–116.

Morley, D. (2017). *Communications and mobility: The migrant, the mobile phone, and the container box*. Wiley-Blackwell.

Murdock, G., Hartmann, P., & Gray, P. (1992). Contextualising home computing: Resources and practices. In R. Silverstone, & E. Hirsch (Eds.), *Consuming technologies: Media and information in domestic spaces* (pp. 146–160). Routledge.

Nansen, B., Arnold, M., Gibbs, M., & Davis, H. (2009). Domestic orchestration: Rhythms in the mediated home. *Time & Society, 18*(2), 181–207.

Siles, I., Espinoza-Rojas, J., Naranjo, A., & Tristán, M. F. (2019). The mutual domestication of users and algorithmic recommendations on Netflix. *Communication, Culture and Critique*, *12*(4), 1–20.

Silverstone, R. (1993). Time, information and communication technology and the household. *Time and Society*, *2*(3), 283–311.

Silverstone, R. (1994). *Television and everyday life*. Routledge.

Silverstone, R. (2006). Domesticating domestication: Reflections on the life of a concept. In T. Berker, M. Hartmann, Y. Punie, & K. J. Ward

(Eds.), *Domestication of media and technology* (pp. 125–144). Open University Press.

Silverstone, R., & Haddon, L. (1996). Design and the domestication of information and communication technologies: Technical change and everyday life. In R. Silverstone, & R. Mansell (Eds.), *Communication by design: The politics of information and communication technologies* (pp. 44–74). Oxford University Press.

Silverstone, R., & Hirsch, E. (Eds.). (1992). *Consuming technologies: Media and information in domestic spaces*. Routledge.

Silverstone, R., Hirsch, E., & Morley, D. (1992). Information and communication technologies and the moral economy of the household. In R. Silverstone, & R. Mansell (Eds.), *Consuming technologies: Media and information in domestic spaces* (pp. 15–31). London: Routledge.

Silverstone, R., & Mansell, R. (Eds.). (1996). *Communication by design: The politics of information and communication technologies*. Oxford University Press.

Sovacool, B. K., & Hess, D. J. (2017). Ordering theories: Typologies and conceptual frameworks for sociotechnical change. *Social Studies of Science*, *47*(5), 703–750.

Spigel, L. (2001). Media homes: Then and now. *International Journal of Cultural Studies*, *4*(4), 385–411.

Strengers, Y., & Kennedy, J. (2020). *The smart wife: Why Siri, Alexa and other smart home devices need a feminist reboot*. MIT Press.

Thomas, J., Wilken, R., & Rennie, E. (2021). *Wi-Fi*. Polity.

Ward, K. (2005). Internet consumption in Ireland — Towards a "connected" life. In R. Silverstone (Ed.), *Media, technology and everyday life in Europe* (pp. 107–123). Ashgate.

Watulak, S. L., & Whitfield, D. (2016). Examining college students' uptake of Facebook through the lens of domestication theory. *E-Learning and Digital Media*, *13*(5–6), 179–195.

Wheelock, J. (1992). Personal computers, gender and an institutional model of the household. In R. Silverstone, & E. Hirsch (Eds.), *Consuming technologies: Media and information in domestic spaces* (pp. 97–112). Routledge.

39

Intersectionality and Human–Machine Communication

Sarah Myers West

INTRODUCTION

Any analysis of human–machine communication cannot be separated from the plane of power relations. While the agents of human–machine communication are often described as neutral and objective, critical communication scholarship emphasizes that these technologies are not neutral at all but are reflective of wider patterns of social inequality.

Artificially intelligent systems are often deployed in ways that magnify structural discrimination while making it harder to identify and counteract. For example, carmakers report that the speech recognition systems used in cars consistently perform better in recognizing masculine-sounding voices (McMillan, 2011). A study of commercially available emotion recognition tools found that these systems assign more negative emotions – such as anger – to Black men's faces than white men's faces (Rhue, 2018). And Uber's "Real-Time ID Check," a facial recognition-based security feature, frequently fails to recognize and locks out drivers of color and trans drivers (Hills, 2021; Melendez, 2018).

Racism, sexism, and other forms of discrimination such as these do not exist in isolation from one another; algorithmically mediated oppressions (Noble, 2018) occur along multiple and interlocking axes of inequality. This makes intersectionality a particularly potent analytical frame for making sense of the unequal power relations reflected, amplified, and produced through human–machine communication.

This chapter provides an introduction to the concept of intersectionality and its importance to human–machine communication. After providing a brief overview of the substantial body of work on intersectionality, I then highlight ongoing work by scholars to critically analyze the implications of human–machine communication drawing on an intersectional lens. I conclude with a brief discussion of the possibilities intersectionality offers as a way forward.

INTERSECTIONALITY, ALGORITHMIC OPPRESSION, AND THE LIMITS OF 'BIAS'

Intersectionality emphasizes that oppressions occur along lines of identity that are interlaced and mutually reinforcing. When it was originally coined by legal scholar Kimberle Crenshaw, the term intersectionality was designed to highlight a tendency in anti-discrimination law, feminist theory, and antiracist politics to treat race and gender as mutually exclusive categories of analysis. In Crenshaw's analysis, anti-discrimination law repeatedly failed to protect the needs of Black women workers, because it only addressed a single dimension on which they experienced oppression – under existing legal frameworks, they were discriminated against because they were women, or because they were Black, but not both. This treatment inadequately captured the interlocking nature of oppression, Crenshaw argued. Discrimination against Black women workers was compounded because of the multiple ways in which they were marginalized, and single-axis analyses of their race and gender in isolation – let alone ability, sexuality, class, and many other forms of identity – inadequately captured their experiences.

Though the term now is in wide circulation, the underlying origins of the concept of intersectionality are specific; they are rooted in the politics and ideas of women of color and particularly in traditions of Black feminist thought that stretch back at least 150 years (May, 2015). With its increasing popularity, the discourses surrounding intersectionality have, at times, lost their connection to these origins, fleshing out and expanding its meaning in manners far afield from this original intent (Crenshaw, 2017a). The concept has become a gathering place for open-ended investigation of the conflicting dynamics of race, gender, class, sexuality, nation, and other inequalities (Cho, Crenshaw, & McCall, 2013). But, as Vivian May writes in her book *Pursuing Intersectionality, Unsettling Dominant Imaginaries*, accompanying interest in the construct has been an effort to subvert its original intent: "subtle and overt forms of delegitimizing intersectionality (or, alternatively, legitimizing it by making it more 'universal' via deracialization and depoliticization, such that its deep focus on critical race theorizing and on inclusive social justice are ignored) are commonplace and need to be addressed" (ix).

The field of critical race theory, from which Crenshaw's work originates, was developed in direct response to tendencies in the legal field to make arguments that racial bias introduces "irrational distortions" that could be removed entirely, enabling a return to a "neutral, benign state of impersonally apportioned justice" (Crenshaw, 2017b). This background has important implications for scholars of human–machine communication, because they parallel approaches to understanding power and inequity in our interactions with technology. For one, much of the originating work that grapples with questions of race, gender, and other forms of identity in the context of human–machine communication can similarly be attributed to the scholarship of Black women (Benjamin, 2019; Broussard, 2018; Buolamwini & Gebru, 2018; Noble, 2018; Sweeney, 2013; Raji & Buolamwini, 2019), women of color (Chun, 2018), and trans scholars (Chock, 2019; Hanna et al., 2020; Hicks, 2019; Keyes, 2018; Scheuerman et al., 2019) working in the field, though it is sometimes distanced from these origins and abstracted from the specific contexts, viewpoints, and foundational contributions that its originating authors bring to their studies.

In addition, we see similar forms of delegitimization in abstract treatments of 'AI bias' that separate out the harms caused by algorithmic oppression from the lived experiences of those who encounter it. Intersectionality helps to explain why 'bias' is a limiting frame for making sense of algorithmic discrimination (Barocas & Selbst, 2016; Benjamin, 2019; Gebru, 2020; West, 2020). Inequity is not a variable that can simply be surfaced and removed from a given technological system. Moreover, despite these efforts, intersectionality is sometimes held up as a theory designed to outline hierarchies of oppression – something it was explicitly designed against.

In place of a single-axis model for making sense of discrimination, Patricia Hill Collins suggests that we approach structures of domination as a matrix: as she writes in her landmark book *Black Feminist Thought: Knowledge, Consciousness, and the Politics of Empowerment*, "the term matrix of domination describes this overall social organization within which intersecting oppressions originate, develop, and are contained" (2009, p. 227).

The 2018 Gender Shades study illuminates the matrix of domination powerfully. Computer vision researchers Timnit Gebru and Joy Buolamwini used an intersectional approach to studying the failures of facial recognition systems to recognize the faces of women with dark skin pigmentation. It was at the nexus of race and gender that the failures of these systems were most profound. But Gebru and Buolamwini's work took an important additional step beyond the measurement of accuracy rates – they examined the larger social organization in which facial recognition systems are deployed, considering the implications of deploying these technologies in high-stakes environments like criminal justice, hiring, and finance, all of which are areas with historical patterns of racial and gender-based inequity. Their findings indicate a need to examine closely whether the usage of inaccurate facial recognition systems will function to exacerbate existing inequities across these domains – doing so requires an expansive accounting of the conditions of development, design and deployment of these systems.

Intersectional approaches to algorithmic discrimination refuse claims that there are hierarchies of either identity or oppression (Combahee, 1983; Yuval-Davis, 2009). In place of a reductive frame that attempts to map inequalities and render them equal, intersectional approaches begin and end with power relations, centering the lived experience of individuals affected by algorithmic systems across personal, community, and structural levels.

In the 2019 essay "Design Justice, A.I. and Escape from the Matrix of Domination," Sasha Costanza-Chock describes their experience with the millimeter wave scanning machines used by the TSA for security screening: they write that as a nonbinary trans femme, they present "a problem not easily resolved by the algorithm of the security protocol" (Costanza-Chock, 2019). Because their body is treated as anomalous by the scanner, which treats gender as binary, biological and physiological (Keyes, 2018), Costanza-Chock is routinely subjected to higher levels of screening by TSA agents.

Costanza-Chock's account builds upon their lived experience by tracing security screenings across multiple layers: the embodied experience of being labeled "risky" by not fitting a binary gendered stereotype, the ways in which the use of millimeter wave scanning machine enacts violence against the wider community of gender nonconforming individuals through its assumptions of cisnormativity, and how it is institutionally embedded in state violence against communities of color through deportations and imprisonment in the name of state security.

These examples illustrate how intersectionality affords a rich and potent means of assessing the broad impacts of human–machine communication by foregrounding that an analysis of power in the interfaces between humans and communicative agents must take as its starting point the complex and heterogeneous nature of lived experience.

INTERSECTIONALITY IN HUMAN–MACHINE COMMUNICATION

In their article exploring the concept of human–machine communication, Andrea L. Guzman and Seth C. Lewis outline a research agenda for the field built around three aspects of communicative AI technologies: the functional dimensions through which we make sense of AI systems as communicators, the relational dynamics through which we associate with them, and the metaphysical implications of blurring the boundaries around what constitutes human, machine, and communication. The remainder of this chapter proceeds by using intersectionality as a heuristic for examining multiple and intersecting axes of power as they surface across each of these analytical frames.

Functional: AI as Communicative Agent

There is substantial scholarship documenting the many ways in which communicative agents exhibit patterns of discrimination. In 2013, Latanya Sweeney found that personalized ads delivered by Google AdSense discriminated in ad delivery, generating advertisements with terms related to "arrest" for searches of names common among Black babies and neutral ad texts for names associated with white babies.

Safiya Noble (2018) found racist and sexist tropes in the results for image searches which returned pornographic and sexualized imagery in response to search queries for "Black girls." Noble further found that search engines are not only reflective of pre-existing racist tropes, they are also productive of them: for example, she highlighted that Dylann Roof, who murdered nine people in the Charlestown church shooting, was exposed to white supremacist literature through Google searches for "Black on Black crime." Scholars like Becca Lewis have similarly found that sites like YouTube play an important role in amplifying racist viewpoints through recommendations of increasingly extremist content (Lewis, 2018).

Virtual assistants also exhibit discriminatory patterns: in the 2019 UNESCO-funded study "I'd Blush If I Could," the EQUAL Skills Coalition highlighted that devices like Alexa and Cortana are almost exclusively encoded female by default, a design choice intended to make them seem attractive and pleasing to users. But accompanying this choice are persistent and frequently harmful associations – for example, these assistants are designed to deflect or give apologetic responses when targeted with verbal sexual harassment and exhibit unassertive and subservient qualities.

The Gender Shades study described above is exemplary of a body of scholarship that illustrates the misrecognition of groups of people on the basis of their identity. In addition to their findings about facial recognition systems, Lauren Rhue (2018) found that emotion recognition systems disproportionately assign "anger" to Black faces. Disability advocates have highlighted how hiring systems that utilize facial recognition systematically discriminate against people with disabilities

(Fruchterman & Mellea, 2018; Whittaker et al., 2019). And scholars like Os Keyes (2018) and Morgan Klaus Scheuerman, Jacob M. Paul, and Jed R. Brubaker (2019) have pointed out that harms can be enacted by facial recognition systems through their design, by defining gender as binary, physiological, and immutable.

Intersectional projects that address the functional dimensions of human–machine communication emphasize that communicative agents re-enact patterns of discrimination that can be observed in society at large. Though much research in this area focuses on a single axis of identity, the examples I cite here are intersectional, addressing multiple axes of oppression as they surface in technical systems. Intersectional approaches offer more nuanced accounts of how we relate with communicative agents, drawing on lived experiences. This thus points to a more accurate understanding of where and how discrimination can take place in our interactions with them, as well as in the systems themselves.

Relational: Interacting with AI

Intersectionality is implicated in the growing use of artificial intelligence across a wide variety of social contexts. Buolamwini (2019) writes that datasets have power shadows – they reflect the structural inequality of the world that they draw from. Studying them can help to identify inequalities at scale – as Judy Wacjman notes, "technologies reveal the societies that invent and use them, their notions of social status and distributive justice" (1991, p. 166). But they also can work to produce inequalities through how they are used. Examining human–machine communication on the relational plane thus enables a better understanding of the many ways in which automated systems are implicated within the matrix of domination.

These dynamics in human–machine communication pre-date the existence of artificially intelligent systems. The historian Mar Hicks (2019) writes, for example, about how ideas about gender identity transformed alongside processes of computerization as the UK adopted database computing systems for its National ID system. Whereas in pre-computer times, there was a robust understanding of gender fluidity, the introduction of computers in the 1960s to help administer national insurance cards resulted in a more rigid and binary treatment of gender.

In the paper "Dirty Data, Bad Predictions" Rashida Richardson et al. (2019) examine the deployment of predictive policing tools by law enforcement agencies across thirteen jurisdictions, finding links between flawed, racially biased and sometimes illegal policing practices and the data used to train predictive policing software models. Richardson et al. write "If predictive policing systems are informed by such data, they cannot escape the legacies of the unlawful or biased policing practices that they are built on."

Virginia Eubanks' (2018) work on the implications of automated systems for the poor provides further insight along these lines. Through accounts of automated systems used to evaluate and provide welfare benefits in Indiana, an algorithmic matching system for access to affordable housing in Los Angeles, and a predictive ranking system designed to assess the risks posed to children referred to child protective services in Allegheny County, Pennsylvania, Eubanks' work powerfully illustrates what she calls the "digital poorhouse" – predictive and automated systems that render decision-making opaque to those affected by them, offer little empathy and foreclose the possibility for poor people to change their circumstances.

She writes that "Prediction, like classification is intergenerational…The impacts of predictive models are thus exponential. Because prediction relies on networks and spans generations, its harm has the potential to spread like a contagion, from the initial point of contact to relatives and friends, to friends' networks, rushing through whole communities like a virus" (Eubanks, 2018, p. 182).

Studies of human–machine communication that address its relational dimensions can play an important role in surfacing the specific ways in which particular automated and predictive systems reflect and perpetuate inequities, which are often only otherwise surfaced when they cause harm. In doing so, it is critical that such research draws out the ways in which discrimination as it surfaces in technical systems is imbricated with larger structural power imbalances. Drawing on the concept of a matrix of domination is particularly useful here, by offering a heuristic for making sense of how technological systems are intertwined with systems of power. As these studies illustrate, remedies cannot be confined to a single technical system, but must take into account how a given system interrelates with social institutions and actors.

Metaphysical: Where is the Intelligence in Artificial Intelligence?

Finally, examining human–machine communication through an intersectional lens calls into question the foundations underlying assumptions core to artificial intelligence. In particular, intersectionality unmasks assertions that knowledge claims are neutral and universal. As Vivian May writes, it "raises questions about who has been perceived to be an authoritative knower, whose claims have been heard, which forms of knowledge have received recognition (and been recorded, archived, and passed down), and who has had access to the means of knowledge production and training (including access to education, the academy, and publishing)" (p. 35).

Race, gender, ability, and other forms of identity have deeply marked our interpretations of what intelligence is and how it is constituted. This can be observed, for example, in ongoing critiques of computer vision systems that purport to predict "criminality" or "personality" on the basis of physiological traits. These critiques point to the racist history of physiognomy: as Blaise Agüera y Arcas, Margaret Mitchell, and Alexander Todorov (2017) note, many in the research community find such analyses ethically and scientifically problematic, particularly because the use of modern machine learning can lend long-debunked claims – such as the claim that facial asymmetries can act as a predictor for criminality – new credence.

Other research highlights that what is often marketed as "intelligent" software in fact relies heavily on human labor. Astra Taylor (2018) coined the term "fauxtomation" to refer to technologies that offer the illusion that machines are smarter than they are in reality, while scholars like Lilly Irani (2015), Sarah Roberts (2016), and Mary Gray and Siddharth Suri (2019) offer rich accounts of the workers who produce these systems by classifying images, moderating content, and completing data processing tasks.

This analysis can be expanded to encompass the epistemological origins of the entire field of artificial intelligence. For example, in the 1990s, Alison Adam wrote about how gendered ideas about intelligence shaped the ideas of AI researchers. At a moment where the definition of what was considered an "appropriate" problem for AI researchers to focus on was open, she observed that key figures in the field looked to the philosophical model of the "Man of Reason," a model that shaped the symbolic AI program that dominated AI research for the following three decades (Adam, 1995). Elizabeth A. Wilson (2010) expanded on this by showing that "common sense" understandings of artificial intelligence as centering on formal logic and cognitive processing models of intelligence underplay the significant role of affect in the history of artificial intelligence. This is likely a direct consequence of the erasure of the work of women and people of color, whose contributions to the field have been significantly undervalued (West,

2020) and who frequently experience discriminatory practices in the workplace (Guillory, 2020; West, Whittaker, & Crawford, 2019).

Meredith Broussard's work further examines the sociocultural conditions that shape the labs in which artificial intelligence systems are developed. As Broussard writes, "Disciplines like math, engineering and computer science pardon a whole host of antisocial behaviors because the perpetrators are geniuses. This attitude forms the philosophical basis of technochauvinism, in which efficient code is prioritized above human interactions" (2018, p. 75) She traces this tendency back to the nineteenth century, observing that technochauvinism deeply shaped orientations toward what problems were worth focusing on and how to solve them. Her analysis examines technochauvinism at work among the mathematicians and scientists seeking to solve workforce problems during this period, such as the need for greater worker productivity. Rather than expand access to education and job training, they opted for technical solutions to foundationally social problems, with significant downstream consequences (p. 78).

Discrimination in the field of AI is not solely a historical phenomenon: it remains a pressing issue, as illustrated by the recent experience of Dr. Timnit Gebru, a pre-eminent researcher in the field. Dr. Gebru's work is cited throughout this article, as she is one of the leading experts adopting intersectional approaches to studying artificial intelligence systems (Gebru, 2020). She is also the co-founder of Black in AI, an organization devoted to increasing the presence of Black people in the field of artificial intelligence, and was, until recently, the co-Director of Google's Ethical AI team, a group of interdisciplinary researchers publishing work that critically examines the social implications of AI.

Dr. Gebru was ousted from her role after co-authoring a study that considered the potential harms of large language models. The study, titled "On the Dangers of Stochastic Parrots: Can Language Models Be Too Big?," examined not only the likelihood of discriminatory outputs from such systems but also elements like their climate and environmental impacts, which the authors argued would have disproportionate effects on marginalized communities (Bender et al., 2021). It is exactly the sort of work that best addresses the many axes on which oppressions can occur and is rich both in its explication and the paths it offers for mitigating potential risks. It also reflects what Gebru was hired to do, as the co-leader, along with computer scientist and machine learning expert Dr. Margaret Mitchell, of an interdisciplinary team founded by Dr. Mitchell, devoted to helping the company identify potential social harms from its technologies (Simonite, 2021). Rather than consider the authors' findings, Google instead opted to quash the study entirely with little notice. The nuances of her experience are deserving of a more lengthy treatment, in Gebru's own words (Simonite, 2021). But for the purposes of this chapter the company's actions emphasize that critical intersectional research like Dr. Gebru's is increasingly under threat.

CONCLUSION

Much of this chapter has focused on intersectionality as an analytical frame, highlighting how it offers a powerful means of analyzing the multiple and overlapping forms of oppression that surface in systems of human–machine communication. But its utility goes beyond analysis: intersectionality mandates a call to action, asking us as researchers to work toward creating change in the material conditions that produce these oppressions.

Vivian May writes that "Intersectionality is fundamentally committed to the potential that change is possible, meaning that it is conceivable and feasible, though not guaranteed" (May, 2015, p. 60). Intersectional projects in human–machine communication, such as those I've summarized above, offer up important critiques that closely examine how power relations pervade the interfaces between humans and machines, as well as how technologies are embedded in, reflect, and amplify existing forms of inequality. But they also go a step further, opening up space to reimagine a future in which social injustices can be abolished.

There are many pathways through which intersectional research in human–machine communication can help us work to forge a better future. For one, intersectional approaches point to concrete methods through which algorithmic oppressions can be addressed within the technology itself – for example, by highlighting the relationships between skewed training data, in which people of lighter skin color are disproportionately represented, and inaccuracies in the models trained on this data. But "fixing" broken technologies is not enough. They also point to the importance of examining the processes through which technologies are developed, how they are deployed in the world, and the ways in which they are positioned as solutions to deeper structural problems. Drawing out how technology mediates larger institutional structures of power offers important avenues for researchers to pursue. And finally, the long legacy of intersectionality as a way of looking at the world calls on us to do our part to remediate legacies of inequity. Ultimately,

this calls on us to address how we ourselves, as researchers, as teachers, and as citizens of the world, are embedded within systems of power and to do what we can to improve the state of things in our labs, universities, and institutions.

Intersectional analysis thus has an important role to play in studies of human–machine communication. It does so not only by offering a deeper understanding of how race, gender, sexuality, class, caste, ability, and other forms of identity shape our relationships with technological systems: intersectionality also surfaces transformative opportunities for enacting change.

REFERENCES

Adam, A. (1995). A feminist critique of artificial intelligence. *European Journal of Women's Studies*, 2(3), 355–377. https://doi.org/10.1177/135050 689500200305

Adam, A. (1998). *Artificial knowing: Gender and the thinking machine*. Routledge.

Aguera y Arcas, B., Mitchell, M., & Todorov, A. (2017, May 6). Physiognomy's new clothes. *Medium*. Retrieved from https://medium.com/@blaisea/physiognomys-new-clothes-f2d4b59fdd6a.

Barocas, S. & Selbst, A. (2016) Big data's disparate impact. *California Law Review*, 671.

Bender, E.M., Gebru, T., McMillan-Major, A., & Shmitchell, S. (2021). On the dangers of stochastic parrots: Can language models be too big? *FAccT '21: Proceedings of the 2021 ACM Conference on Fairness, Accountability, and Transparency*. https://dl.acm.org/doi/10.1145/3442188.3445922

Benjamin, R. (2019) *Race after technology: Abolitionist tools for the new Jim Code*. Polity Press.

Broussard, M. (2018). *Artificial unintelligence: How computers misunderstand the world*. MIT Press.

Buolamwini, J. (2019, Nov. 5). Artificial intelligence can be biased. Here's what you should know. *PBS Frontline*. Retrieved from: www.pbs.org/wgbh/frontline/article/artificial-intelligence-algorithmic-bias-what-you-should-know/.

Buolamwini, J. & Gebru, T. (2018). Gender shades: Intersectional accuracy disparities in commercial gender classification. *Proceedings of Machine Learning Research* 81:1–15.

Cho, S., Crenshaw, K.W., & McCall, L. (2013) Toward a field of intersectionality studies: Theory, applications, and praxis, *Signs* 38(4): 785–812.

Chun, W. (2018). Queerying homophily. In *Pattern discrimination*. University of Minnesota Press.

Collins, P.H. (2009). *Black feminist thought: Knowledge, consciousness and the politics of empowerment*. Routledge.

Combahee River Collective. (1983). The Combahee River Collective Statement. Retrieved from: https://americanstudies.yale.edu/sites/default/files/files/Keyword%20Coalition_Readings.pdf.

Costanza-Chock, S. (2018) Design justice, A.I. and escape from the matrix of domination. *Journal of Design and Science*. Retrieved from https://jods.mitpress.mit.edu/pub/costanza-chock/release/4.

Costanza-Chock, S. (2020) *Design justice: Community-led practices to build the worlds we need*. MIT Press.

Crenshaw, K. (1991) Mapping the margins: Intersectionality, identity and violence against women of color. *Stanford Law Review*, 43(6): 1241–1299.

Crenshaw, K. (2011) Postscript. In Lutz, H., Herrera Vivar, M.T., & Supik, L. (Eds.) *Framing intersectionality: Debates on a multi-faceted concept in gender studies*. Routledge, 221–233.

Crenshaw, K. (2017a). Race, reform, retrenchment redux: Critical race theory and intersectionality beyond post racialism, Brandeis University. Retrieved from www.brandeis.edu/gittlerprize/videos/index.html.

Crenshaw, K. (2017b) Race to the bottom: How the post-racial revolution became a whitewash. *The Baffler*, 35. Retrieved from: https://thebaffler.com/salvos/race-to-bottom-crenshaw.

Criado Perez, C. (2019). *Invisible women: Exposing data bias in a world designed for men*. Chatto & Windus.

Eubanks, V. (2018). *Automating inequality: How high-tech tools profile, police, and punish the poor*. Macmillan Books.

Fruchterman, J. & Mellea, J. (2018). Expanding employment success for people with disabilities. *Benetech*. https://benetech.org/about/resources/expanding-employment-success-for-people-with-disabilities/

Gebru, T. (2020) Race and gender. In Dubber, M.D., Pasquale, F., & Das, S. (Eds) *The Oxford handbook of ethics of AI*. Oxford: Oxford University Press.

Gray, M. & Suri, S. (2019). *Ghost work: How to stop Silicon Valley from building a new global underclass*. Houghton Mifflin Harcourt.

Guillory, D. (2020). Combatting anti-Blackness in the AI community. *arXiv*. Retrieved from: https://arxiv.org/pdf/2006.16879.pdf.

Guzman, A.L. & Lewis, S.C. (2019) Artificial intelligence and communication: A human–machine communication research agenda. *New Media & Society*, 22(1): 70–86.

Hanna, A., Denton, E., Smart, A., & Smith-Loud, J. (2020) Towards a critical race methodology in algorithmic fairness. *FAT* '20: Proceedings of the 2020 Conference on Fairness, Accountability and Transparency*. Retrieved from: https://dl.acm.org/doi/10.1145/3351095.3372826

Haraway, D. (1988) Situated knowledges: The science question in feminism and the privilege of partial perspective. *Feminist Studies*, 14(3): 575.

Hicks, M. (2019) Hacking the Cis-tem. *IEEE Annals of the History of Computing*, 41(1): 20–33. Retrieved from https://ieeexplore.ieee.org/document/8634814.

Hills, J. (2021, Mar. 19). Uber drivers claim they were fired after company's identification software failed to recognise their faces. ITV. Retrieved from www.itv.com/news/2021-03-18/uber-drivers-claim-they-were-fired-after-companys-identification-software-failed-to-recognise-their-faces

Irani, L. (2015). Difference and dependence among digital workers: The case of Amazon Mechanical Turk. *South Atlantic Quarterly*, 114(1): 225–234. Retrieved from https://read.dukeupress.edu/south-atlantic-quarterly/article-abstract/114/1/225/3763/Difference-and-Dependence-among-Digital-Workers

Keyes, O. (2018). The misgendering machines: Trans/HCI implications of automatic gender recognition. *Proceedings of the ACM on Human-Computer Interaction*. Retrieved from https://dl.acm.org/doi/10.1145/3274357

Klein, L. & D'Ignazio, C. (2019). *Data feminism*. MIT Press.

Lewis, B. (2018). Alternative influence: Broadcasting the reactionary Right on YouTube. *Data & Society*. https://datasociety.net/library/alternative-influence/.

May, V. (2015) *Pursuing intersectionality, unsettling dominant imaginaries*. Routledge.

McMillan, G. (2011, June 1). It's not you, it's it: Voice recognition doesn't recognize women. *TIME*. Retrieved from https://techland.time.com/2011/06/01/its-not-you-its-it-voice-recognition-doesnt-recognize-women/

Melendez, S. (2018, Aug. 9). Uber driver troubles raise concerns about transgender face recognition. *Fast Company*. Retrieved from: www.fastcompany.com/90216258/uber-face-recognition-tool-has-locked-out-some-transgender-drivers

Noble, S.U. (2018) *Algorithms of oppression: How search engines reinforce racism*. NYU Press.

Raji, I. & Buolamwini, J. (2019). Actionable auditing: Investigating the impact of publicly naming biased performance results of commercial AI products. *Conference on Artificial Intelligence, Ethics, and Society*. Retrieved from www.media.mit.edu/publications/actionable-auditing-investigating-the-impact-of-publicly-naming-biased-performance-results-of-commercial-ai-products/

Rhue, L. (2018). Racial influence on automated perceptions of emotions. Retrieved from https://papers.ssrn.com/sol3/papers.cfm?abstract_id=3281765.

Richardson, R., Schultz, J., & Crawford, K. (2019). Dirty data, bad predictions: How civil rights violations impact police data, predictive policing systems, and justice. *NYU Legal Review*, 192. Retrieved from https://papers.ssrn.com/sol3/papers.cfm?abstract_id=3333423.

Roberts, S. (2019). *Behind the screen: Content moderation in the shadows of social media*. Yale University Press.

Scheuerman, M.K., Paul, J.M., & Brubaker, J. R. (2019). How computers see gender: An evaluation of gender classification in commercial facial analysis and image labeling services. *ACM Hum.-Comput. Interact.* 3(144).

Simonite, T. (2021, June 8) What really happened when Google ousted Timnit Gebru. *Wired*. Retrieved from www.wired.com/story/google-timnit-gebru-ai-what-really-happened/.

Sweeney, L. (2013). Discrimination in online ad delivery. *arXiv*. Retrieved from https://arxiv.org/abs/1301.6822.

Taylor, A. (2018). The automation charade. *Logic*. Retrieved from https://logicmag.io/failure/the-automation-charade/

UNESCO. (2019). I'd blush if I could: Closing gender divides in digital skills through education. Retrieved from https://unesdoc.unesco.org/ark:/48223/pf0000367416.page=85.

Wacjman, J. (1991) *Feminism confronts technology*. Penn State University Press.

West, S.M. (2020). Redistribution and rekognition: A feminist critique of algorithmic fairness. *Catalyst*, 6(2). Retrieved from: https://catalystjournal.org/index.php/catalyst/article/view/33043

West, S.M., Whittaker, M., & Crawford, K. (2019). Discriminating systems: Gender, race and power in AI. *AI Now Institute*. Retrieved from: https://ainowinstitute.org/discriminatingsystems.pdf.

Whittaker, M., Alper, M., Bennett, C.L., Hendren, S., Kaziunas, E., Mills, M., Morris, M.R., Rankin, J., Rogers, E., Salas, M., & West, S.M. (2019). Disability, bias and AI. *AI Now Institute*. Retrieved from: https://wecount-dev.inclusivedesign.ca/wp-content/uploads/2020/06/Disability-bias-AI.pdf

Wilson, E.A. (2010). *Affect & artificial intelligence*. University of Washington Press.

Yuval-Davis, N. (2006). Intersectionality and feminist politics. *European Journal of Women's Studies*, 13(3):193–209.

40

Human–Machine Communication, Artificial Intelligence, and Issues of Data Colonialism

Beth Coleman

INTRODUCTION: COLONIALISM AND AI

This chapter addresses one primary concern: How have the fields of communication, human–computer interaction (HCI), and critical data/information studies addressed the issue of a "data colonialism" – the systematic exploitation of user data – in an epistemology of human–machine communication (HMC)? If the framing concept of HMC rests with the "creation of meaning between human and machine" (Guzman, 2018), then the issue colonialism raises is that of extractive and asymmetrical HMC in a global framework of advanced automation technologies that include artificial intelligence (AI) in the forms of machine learning and sensor-embedded "smart" technologies such as the Internet of Things. These technologies represent globally applied systems designed for the ubiquitous extraction and exploitation of data and held by a clustering of multinational IT giants, e.g., Google, Facebook, Tencent, and Baidu. In this framework, risk of algorithmic bias/societal harm particularly falls along the lines of precarity as historically marked by race, class, gender, and territory. Reducing people, things, and society to a series of data points or datafication presents an existential threat to the category of human subject in general. With that said, the given track record of datafication as applied to certain "test" populations,

in the form of surveillance, policing, jurisprudence, economic and informational deprivation, demonstrates a direct threat to life.

As the technology continues to shift in its increasing ubiquity, advanced automation raises new challenges in technological affordance and social construction – the sociotechnological domain – in terms of datafication as an epistemic shift. The question of "communication" as the creation of meaning, and perhaps knowledge, as a function of human–machine relations is increasingly superseded by machine-to-machine (M2M) data exchange, leaving the human subject in the position of a data subject – effectively the information source. The affordances of big data, such as velocity, scale, temporality, enable the technology and culture of extractive and asymmetrical human–machine communication (Kitchin, 2014). In a sense, the data imaginary or ontology of advanced automation returns to the engineering origins of a theory of communication that does not engage a (human) value of meaning but rather automates a machine-readable extraction of data (Shannon, 1948; Weaver, 1949). Yet in the shift to the M2M landscape, the damaging sociotechnological impact of such information systems is most readily traced across the locations, peoples, and legacy of imperial colonialism.

The chapter begins with an analysis of Couldry and Mejias' concept of data colonialism followed by references to case studies of AI/advanced automation technology global abuses (Couldry & Mejias, 2018). It then turns to a discussion of antecedents to the colonial critique of datafication (Dourish & Mainwaring, 2012; Arora, 2016; Milan and Treré, 2019). The critical frameworks of postcolonial and Indigenous science and technology studies (STS) and Black technoscience are discussed in their reformation of the issues of colonial legacy and "colonial" technologies (Tuck & Yang, 2012; Noble, 2018; Benjamin, 2019; Amrute, 2020). The final part of the chapter discusses the growing critical praxis of decolonial AI, as demonstrated by interdisciplinary collaboration that recognizes the global threat of a colonial AI/advanced automation (Mohamed, Png, & Isaac, 2020). Adjacent literatures on data justice, legal studies, and infrastructure studies all inform the constellation of arguments around the colonial and AI/advanced automation machines, as the issue is increasingly understood across disciplines and industry to be a sociotechnological one – demonstrating the complex intersections of power, politics, engineering, markets, social relations, and so on.

In the tradition of Fanon, Spivak, and other decolonial thinkers, fundamental to the colonial empire claim of territory is the eugenic ordering of value, visibility, and power, a biopolitics that enacts a science of ordering (Fanon, 1963/2004; Spivak, 1988). With the sciences of the artificial one finds a recapitulation of colonial practices that counts life or certain lives as a thing that must be organized and controlled. This had been a subject position, or scene of subjection, coded as an aspect of colonial regime for brown, black, and Asian "subalterns" as a condition of empire. Empire prefigures the epistemic logic of capitalism, wherein the colonial subject with their land, labor, and know-how, were – and continue to be – the raw goods as such. The colonial has come to emerge as a fulcrum point in the development of AI/advanced automation, as datafication – the rendering of human actions and behaviors at a societal scale into machine-readable data points – has profound implications. Among communication, HCI, and critical data scholars the fact of digital inequity is clearly established. The cross-disciplinary debate relates to critical framework and location of praxis: is the colonial critique of big data epistemology an extension of the historic colonial subject or is it a novel form of exploitation?

DATA COLONIALISM: DATAFICATION OF LIFE BEYOND LABOR

The term data colonialism entered scholarly circulation with the 2019 publication of Couldry and Mejias' "Data Colonialism: rethinking big data's relation to the contemporary subject" (Couldry and Mejias, 2019). Coined by the scholars of critical data studies and sociology, the term "data colonialism" critiques the limits of a surveillance capitalism framework. As defined by Zuboff, surveillance capitalism addresses the data extractive design that dominates HCI technology from cell phones to search to social media (Zuboff, 2015; Srnicek, 2016; Cohen, 2018). Core to their analysis, Couldry and Mejias broaden the lens of surveillance capitalism to include issues of power, epistemological hierarchy, universalism, and empire – historical markers of coloniality. In marking the colonial method as the total subsumption of actors, environment, and contextual knowledge, they move beyond data as exploitation of labor to data as exploitation of *life*. To this effect, they write, "First, colonial history helps us see the emergence of digital platforms as more than business invention, or even new forms of economic control through multi-sided markets. Digital platforms are the technological means that produce a new type of 'social' for capital: that is, the social in a form that can be continuously tracked, captured, sorted and counted for value as 'data'" (2019). As they point out, social life as such is rendered into discrete data points, deracinating context and (human) communication toward machinic automation. In other words, from a perspective of HMC, data colonialism extracts but does not exchange; the position of the end-user of networked technologies transitions from the prosthesis model (media as the extension of "man") to that of the data point model ("man" as extension of data flows).

In the data appropriation of human life, they point to a shift of power and technology. In terms of power, the nexus of historical colonialism had been European nations claiming the lands of the Americas, Africa, and Asia, producing cartographies of conquest in mapping center-periphery. In the context of post-industrial global capital, Couldry and Mejias recognize the United States and China as the "colonial" powers of world dominance in design and application of advanced automation information technologies. As colonialism had served for early industrial capital, they argue for data colonialism as a precursor to whatever the next stage (or paradigm) of economy evolves from the given conditions. In terms of technology, the advent of big data is the key differential in advanced automation systems, such as the machine learning architecture that is the basis of the second generation of AI. The sociotechnological formulation of big data as an epistemic shift in the design and application of advanced automation has been a point of obsession for academics and industry alike from the turn of the twenty-first century. From the data colonialism framework, the most important attributes of data are its extractability (alienation from data subject) and autonomous market value (the data do not need to be tethered to identity or individual to have value).

In the sociotechnological configuration of big data episteme, power and technology cannot be separated, as data is a valued resource. To Couldry and Mejias' point, it is a feedback loop that has been normalized by Silicon Valley and Beijing: "[W]e seek to explore the parallels with historic colonialism's function within the development of economies on a global scale, its normalization of resource appropriation, and its redefinition of social relations so that dispossession came to seem natural" (2019). The global IT companies that dominate the data-extractive platforms are also the ones that take up and apply the data, reconfiguring the positionality of end-user to that of data subject. From platforms to personal devices the data traces given off have been foundational to the development of big data repositories and predictive modeling that power technologies of advanced automation, such as AI. In a designed convergence of market value and technological development, advanced automation relies on data extraction as a right of domain. In effect, the practice of data extraction is the normative state of networked IT (Cohen, 2016). As with historical empire, the data colonial configuration of power and technology extends well beyond issues of labor. Counter to the Marxist Autonomist position, Couldry and Mejias make the argument that the state of big data and the technologies of advanced automation that are built upon it cannot be framed exclusively as an issue of political economy and labor exploitation (2019). They hail the ubiquitous, global phenomenon as the datafication of life itself. And it is in usurpation of "life itself" that they locate the imprint of legacy colonial regimes in which all of life – territory, peoples, knowledge, and resources – are subsumed by empire as an extension of power. Thus data colonialism describes a complex technological appropriation of everyday life that exceeds, but does not disrupt, capitalism.

Couldry and Mejias argue that "we" are universally victims of data exploitation, which is true. And yet, there is no universal "we" that occupies this subject position, as the status, impact, and violence of such dispossession of social relations is not equally distributed. They include a caveat, that the position of data subject varies from person to person. But the default of individualized positioning of a liberal subject ("what this means for one person may be very different from what it means for another") obscures the historic and located impact of what is demonstrably systemic, harmful

bias in algorithmic applications (2019). The double binds of data colonialism – West/East and external/internal – reorders legacy colonial binaries – center/periphery and colonizer/colonized – but does not disrupt them. In other words, it is both the historical colonial subject and the historical normative subject who are taken up, exposed, and consumed by the data apparatus of advanced automation and ubiquitous computing. They mark a universal condition of appropriation/exploitation/alienation but with unequal distribution of harm.

POSTCOLONIAL CRITIQUE OF BIG DATA EPISTEME

The colonial invention of species categories (famously, including racial categorization) as a function of datafication persists at the front-guard of data colonialism. In the framework of historical continuity, it is not by chance that the original sites of colonial exploitation continue to serve as test sites for data appropriation and advanced automation technologies. With the important exception of Cambridge Analytica, the Facebook data scandal of American voter manipulation, the dominant test sites for big data/algorithmic social experimentation have been on global South(s) population – subaltern, precarious, and disenfranchised.[1] The Indian state digital identity database, Aadhaar, creates a national tracking system that particularly infringes on the rights of the poor (Prakash, 2017). The Chinese machine vision data extraction and testing in Zimbabwe is a demonstration of data as a resource in the ongoing postcolonial engagement of empire and territories. As information studies scholar Noble points out, data colonial experimentation repeats a historically vicious cycle in which poor countries/peoples are sites of raw materials and data extraction, as well as global toxic dumping (Noble, 2018). Along similar lines, the long history of state violence and institutional racism in child welfare against Indigenous people has been rendered as predictive algorithm, automating a colonial paradigm (Vaithianathan et al., 2013; Gavighan et al., 2019). In parallel, data analytics groups such as Compass and Palantir act as third-party vendors procured by state authorities, such as courts and police, in applying experimental predictive functions with disproportionate impact on Black subjects (Bullington & Lane, 2018). The systemic colonial logic demonstrates what black technoscience scholar Ruha Benjamin describes as racism by design and not by chance (Benjamin, 2019). Racial discrimination is not a subset of data colonialism but a feature. These are systems designed for data command and control, sculpting the data subject of advanced automation.[2]

The logic of Couldry and Mejias' data colonialism correlates the universal with a state of inequality or subsumption – all are rendered data subjects – that contextually cannot be sustained. For over a quarter of a century postcolonial scholars from fields as varied as STS, Black studies, feminist and gender studies, Indigenous and global South positionalities have critiqued the biopolitical order of colonial hierarchies normalized and automated within a big data episteme. In this critical view, the existential threat of "data colonialism" has always already been manifest with historically colonized peoples and contexts from the inception of machines (or data) as the measure of "man." And yet, it is in the double bind of "data colonialism," its external/internal exploitation of populations that the historical weight of located geographic sites, peoples, and experiences are elided for a totalizing model. The tension with the Couldry and Mejias assessment does not rest with *how* advanced automation technologies behave but *for whom* it is a danger. In their account of the systematic danger in devaluing life as a form of data, the gap in their analysis rests with the universal application of a sociotechnological threat, without a clear articulation of the differential level of risk to particular peoples, places, and locations. Which is to say, their approach to the colonial does not attend to actual historical colonial legacy.

In their 2012 landmark essay, "Decolonization is Not a Metaphor," Indigenous STS scholars Tuck and Yang write, "Decolonization brings about the repatriation of Indigenous land and life; it is not a metaphor for other things we want to do to improve our societies and schools" (Tuck & Yang, 2012). They state that to decolonize is to enact reparations of the erasure of peoples, places, and their knowledge. Decolonization is emphatically not a metaphor for the improvement of the liberal subject but the reappearance and societal reconfiguration of the peoples and territories subordinated by settler colonialism (Tuck & Yang, 2012). The colonial, and by necessity the decolonial, must have a locus, a specificity of place, temporality, and phenomenon. The power of these concepts is contextually situated and not viable as epistemological universal (Suchman, 1987). The work of unsettling the legacy triad of "settler-native-slave" – three distinct positionalities – makes decolonial engagement complex and often praxis driven.

As early as 2012, Dourish and Mainwaring critiqued ubiquitous computing as colonial in structure or what they described as "ubicomp's colonial impulse," drawing parallels between the historic British colonial siege of place, peoples, resources, and knowledge, and ubicomp's indexical impulse (Dourish & Mainwaring, 2012). As an example of total subsumption of life, Dourish and Mainwaring point to the colonial research lab of Kew Garden, where exotic specimens collected from the extended sites of empire are cultivated, contained, and catalogued in a hot house (2012). In addition to the formal architecture of colonial capture, Dourish and Mainwaring include a valuable assessment of the colonial logic of counting. They argue that there are two forces at work in the universalizing logic of the colonial apparatus, one visible and the other implied: (a) *everything can be encoded* by machinic systems, i.e., data collection. Therefore, (b) if something is not encoded, it *ceases to exist* epistemologically. In short, the universal view of the imperial claim mandates what is relevant knowledge and obscures all else that is not. The system design is one of control through quantification, observing that "particularly mathematical models of the world have a habit of migrating towards centers of power which, operating through them, serve to reorganize the world in ways that make it compatible with the model" (2012). The issue of the world being made to conform to the system modeled is an ongoing aspect of biopolitics. Epistemically, in framing an order of things (and what things cannot be made visible in that order), the colonial logics are naturalized as states of organic hierarchy or manifest destiny. In either case, the same eugenically coded valuation persists.

DATA FROM GLOBAL SOUTHS: BEYOND UNIVERSALISM

In their critical data studies work, Milan and Treré develop a theory of datafication "of and in the Souths" that takes as its telos issues of reparation, justice, and subaltern ways of knowing through data (Milan & Treré, 2019). They articulate a baseline critique of datafication in keeping with a decolonial turn in big data that looks to decenter Western ontologies: "Datafication has put new weapons in the hands of institutions and corporations in the business of managing people. And it seems to hit harder where people, laws, and human rights are the most fragile" (2019). In recognizing the exacerbation of historical divides that informational capitalism performs, they see a global landscape in which the majority of the world's population resides outside the West, and yet the biopolitics of advanced automation continue to be framed by the ontology of empire (Broeders & Taylor, 2017). (It is in the special issue on "Big Data from the South(s)" that the Couldry and Mejias data colonialism article appears.)

Milan and Treré catalogue locational algorithmic aggression in the European and US use of biometric technologies on undocumented migrants or the deployment of drones and georeferential radar against Mapuche land defenders (Parra, 2016; Milan & Treré, 2019; Pelizza, 2019). Milan and Treré advocate for data South(s) as a complex plurality that is not geographically bound to old colonial mappings, moving beyond legacy binaries of center-periphery or colonizer-colonized. In the situation of data from global South(s), they recognize a data subject of agentic status, not simply oppressed. Their work contributes to decolonial framings of datafication in conversation with postcolonial/decolonial scholars, activists, and practitioners. "Big Data from the South(s)" emerges from foundational decolonial works such as Arora's "Bottom of the Data Pyramid" (Arora, 2016). As an information scholar with a focus on critical data, Arora critiques the neoliberal framework of global South development paradigms, outlining the structurally extractive design. She escalates the argument, advocating for local "disobedience," situating the radical act of reimagination with the legacy of decolonial resistance (Arora, 2019).

In concert with Arora's digital decolonial critique, information studies scholar and sociologist Amrute frames the concept of tech colonialism, in an effort to sustain critical and activist engagement. Her argument also serves as a direct corrective of Couldry and Mejias. Armute reorders the critical framework from "data colonialism" to that of "tech colonialism," which, among other differentiators, traces a more robust historical and ontological line between the legacy of colonial territories and the emergent state of global tech coloniality. To this effect, she writes, "As digital labour becomes more widespread across the uneven geographies of race, gender, class and ability, and as histories of colonialism and inequality get drawn into these forms of labour, our imagination of what these worlds contain similarly needs to expand" (Amrute, 2019). As Amrute describes, "Tech Colonialism Today" carries on the original colonial mission of an "entire knowledge apparatus," designed to learn the total system of a people or place (Amrute, 2020). She traces the sociotechnological logics of taxonomy and hierarchy that Dourish and Manwaring reflect in the ubiquitous computing vision of total system knowledge. Amrute makes evident that the "overreliance on the issue of data colonialism obscures the complicated welter of (post)colonial relationships" (2020). She concludes by citing Fanon on the necessity of rethinking everything after colonialism, seeing the tools for a decolonial tech emerging from the very sites of historical devaluation and deprivation.

DECOLONIAL AI

In keeping with Amrute's critique of the erasure of colonial history in the assessment of datafication, decolonial AI emerges as a procedural dimension of advanced automation praxis. As a critical and procedural framework, decolonial AI recognizes the historic continuity of colonial epistemology in AI machine learning. As authors Mohamed, Png, and Isaac write of decolonial AI, "By embedding a decolonial critical approach within its technical practice, AI communities can develop foresight and tactics that can better align research and technology development with established ethical principles, centering vulnerable peoples who continue to bear the brunt of negative impacts of innovation and scientific progress" (Mohamed, Png, & Isaac, 2020). The authors summon a different AI ontology from the global North culture that spawned it. They call for intentional approaches to AI that "incorporate inclusive and well-adapted mechanisms of oversight and redress from the start" (2020). As such, one of the key recalibrations of decolonial AI is interdisciplinarity: implicit in the experimental framework is the seeding of research teams that include engineering, critical data, and critical race, among others. As a basis of decolonial AI praxis, they reference critical technical practice, a methodology that foregrounds issues of unequal power distribution and embedded values (Agre, 1997). In framing intersectional methodologies, such as CTP and critical data, they move beyond "good-conscience design" to engage the situated condition of AI, in its model of mind, design, and application (2020). In other words, they outline the steps of a decolonial AI in the layered movements of making legible context, constraints, and bias of existing system design followed by the intentional reconceptualization of system design that addresses "the ethical and social externalities of AI" (2020). As the authors highlight, emerging in the engineering field of AI/ML is a direct critique of the limits of an exclusively technological solution to the complexity of AI applications in the world – a critique long established in disciplinary loci such as STS. They go as far as to express the potential of AI as a "decolonising tool." Implicit in the logic of decolonial AI are strategies derived from postcolonial theory: strategies such as role reversal – the metropole learning from the periphery – represent great potential toward a reconfiguration of how and by whom AI is made (Fanon, 1963/2004; Said, 1993).

CONCLUSION

It is possible with a decolonial framework that the issues of data colonialism might be reimagined and redesigned toward a HMC that moves away from the extractive to the communicative – a coproduction as such. But a great deal would have to change in the sociotechnological framework of AI/advanced automation for that to be the case. As a critique of the normative framework of AI/advanced automation, the term colonialism articulates the demonstrable extension of societal harm as built into its sociotechnological design. As a corollary, decolonial data as praxis is in an early stage with experimental work around diversity of AI teams, accountability of training data, etc. This is to say that the profound societal impact of harmful machine bias that results in societal injustice is a threshold issue for the design and application of AI/advanced automation technologies. The acknowledgement of such, at least in some quarters of the AI research and design domain, is testament to the recognition of the importance of the problem without providing an answer.

NOTES

1   It should be noted that Cambridge Analytica tested its social media manipulation of voting groups on South Asian and Black youths in the Jamaica elections and have prior "third world" targets upon whom they have tested their skills.

2   This is not to imply that humans are currently removed from the AI/ML process. But their presence as system architects and engineering applications is often obscured by an AI model of mind that produces an autonomous computational "intelligence," as expressed by predictive modeling.

REFERENCES

Agre, P. (1997). Toward a critical technical practice: Lessons learned in trying to reform AI. In Bowker, G., Star, S., Gasser, L., Turner, W. (Eds.) *Social science, technical systems and cooperative work: beyond the great divide*. Psychology Press. pp. 131–157.

Amrute, S. (2019). Of techno-ethics and techno-affects. *Feminist Review*, 123(1), 56–73. https://doi.org/10.1177/0141778919879744

Amrute, S. (2020). Tech colonialism today. Keynote, EPIC2019 Feb. 25, 2020. https://points.datasociety.net/tech-colonialism-today-9633a9cb00ad

Arora, P. (2016). Bottom of the data pyramid: Big data and the global south. *International Journal of Communication*, 10, 19.

Arora, P. (2019). Decolonizing privacy studies. *Television & New Media*, 20(4), 366–378.

Benjamin, R. (2019). *Race after technology: Abolitionist tools for the new Jim Code*. Polity Press.

Broeders, D. & Taylor, L. (2017). Does great power come with great responsibility? The need to talk about corporate political responsibility. In *The responsibilities of online service providers*. Springer. 315–323.

Bullington, J., & Lane, E. (2018). How a tech firm brought data and worry to New Orleans crime fighting. The New Orleans Times-Picayune. https://www.nola.com/news/crime police/article33b8bf05-722f-5163-9a0c-774aa69b6645.html.

Cohen, J. E. (2016). The surveillance–innovation complex: The irony of the participatory turn. In *Participatory condition*, edited by Darin Barney, Gabriella Coleman, Christine Ross, Jonathan Sterne, and Tamar Tembeck. University of Minnesota Press, 207–226.

Cohen, J. E. (2018). The biopolitical public domain: The legal construction of the surveillance economy. *Philosophy & Technology* 31 (2): 213–233. doi:10.1007/s13347-

Couldry, N., & Mejias, U. A. (2019). Data colonialism: Rethinking big data's relation to the contemporary subject. *Television & New Media*, 20(4), 336–349.

Dourish, P. & Mainwaring, S. (2012). Ubicomp's colonial impulse. *UbiComp' 12*, Sep. 5–Sep. 8, 2012, Pittsburgh.

Fanon, F. (1963/2004). *The wretched of the Earth*. Grove Press, 2004.

Gavighan, C., Knott, A., Maclaurin, J., Zerilli, J., & Liddicoat, J. (2019). *Government use of artificial intelligence in New Zealand*. New Zealand: Law Society.

Guzman, A. (2018). What is human-machine communication, anyway? In *Human-machine communication: Rethinking communication, technology, and ourselves*. Editor Andrea L. Guzman. Peter Lang.

Kitchin, R. (2014). Big Data, new epistemologies and paradigm shifts. *Big Data & Society*, 1(1), 2053951714528481.

Milan, S., & Treré, E. (2019). Big data from the South (s): Beyond data universalism. *Television & New Media*, 20(4), 319–335.

Mohamed,S., Png, M., & Isaac, W. (2020). Decolonial AI: Decolonial theory as sociotechnical foresight in artificial intelligence. *Philosophy & Technology* 33:659–684. https://doi.org/10.1007/s13347-020-00405-8

Noble, S.U. (2018). *Algorithms of oppression: How search engines reinforce racism*. NYU Press.

Parra, F. (2016). "Militarización En La Araucanía: Drones, Aviones No Tripulados y Más de Mil Policías Desplegados." [Militarization in La Araucanía: Drones,

Unmanned Aircraft and More than a Thousand Policemen Deployed] *El Desconcierto*, March 23. http://www.eldesconcierto.cl/2016/03/23/militarizacion-en-la-araucania-drones-aviones-no-tripulados-y-mas-de-mil-policias-desplegados/.

Pelizza, A. (2019). Processing alterity, enacting Europe: Migrant registration and identification as co-construction of individuals and polities. *Science, Technology & Human Values*. Published electronically February 6. doi:10.1177/0162243919827927.

Prakash, P. (2017). Aadhaar Marks a Fundamental Shift in Citizen-State Relations: 'From We the People' to 'We the Government.'. Hindustan Times, 3.

Said, E.W. (1993). *Culture and imperialism*. Vintage.

Shannon, C. E. (1948). A mathematical theory of communication. *The Bell System Technical Journal*, *27*(3), 379–423.

Spivak, G.C. (1988.) Can the subaltern speak? In *Marxism and the interpretation of culture*. Ed. Nelson C and Grossberg L. University of Illinois Press, 271–313.

Srnicek, N. 2016. *Platform capitalism*. Polity Press.

Suchman, L. A. (1987). *Plans and situated actions: The problem of human-machine communication*. Cambridge University Press.

Tuck, E. & Yang, K. W. (2012). Decolonization is not a metaphor. *Decolonization: Indigeneity, Education & Society 1 (1)*: 1–40.

Vaithianathan, R., Maloney, T., Putnam-Hornstein, E., & Jiang, N. (2013). Children in the public benefit system at risk of maltreatment: Identification via predictive modeling. *American Journal of Preventive Medicine*, *45*(3), 354–359.

Weaver, W. (1949). Introductory note on the general setting of the analytical communication studies. In C. E. Shannon & W. Weaver (Eds.), *The mathematical theory of communication* (12th Printing). University of Illinois Press.

Zuboff, S. 2015. Big other: Surveillance capitalism and the prospects of an information civilization. *Journal of Information Technology* 30 (1): 75–89.

41

A Feminist Human–Machine Communication Framework: Collectivizing by Design for Inclusive Work Futures

Chinar Mehta, Payal Arora, and Usha Raman

INTRODUCTION

As digital devices increasingly enter the everyday lives of people, distant in geography and context from where major decisions about the technologies are made, we see an urgent need to elaborate on the pitfalls of design and data universalism. Theorization about communication between the human and the machine acknowledges the agency of the machine, but what remains under-examined is the question of how technologies fit into the social lives of people (Guzman, 2018). Technology evangelists have long engaged in a narrative of hope through digital solutionism that assumes the universal application and use of digital tools. Even as barriers are recognized in the form of systemic, social, cultural, and individual specificities, they are often seen as issues to be overcome through digital literacy, broadening of access and availability. Recent research in HCI (Human–Computer Interaction), a dominantly scientific field of inquiry that has borrowed largely from cognitive and computer sciences, has started to draw from critical work with feminist and anthropological perspectives, albeit with methodological challenges (Rogers, 2012). We argue that while there is no dissonance between the practical aims of HCI and cultural critiques of design, the gap arises

in the failure to recognize the diversity of challenges that vulnerable populations face when trying to develop a meaningful communicative relationship with technologies that often do not fit into their social lives. In this sense, as Guzman (2018) articulates, if meaning-making between human and machine fails, it is a *communication* issue, and one that could be facilitated or hampered by design.

The burden of communicating effectively with digital devices mostly falls on individuals, and their social and cultural contexts are usually not considered in the shaping of these mediated communications. Digital environments continue to cater to the "typical users" – usually middle class, male, and in the Global North (Arora, 2019), and are not usually designed for use by those in very different cultural contexts. In addition, understandings of privacy, surveillance, protection, and visibility are dominated by epistemologies from the West, which view subjects from the Global South as requiring training to use technologies that may be intuitive to populations in developed countries (Winschiers-Theophilus & Bidwell, 2013). Drawing on an understanding of the collectivization of marginalized women workers in the Global South, particularly the Indian subcontinent, we suggest that digital communication technologies can help such workers strengthen their position in a global supply chain to demand freedom from exploitative neoliberal practices. However, this is only possible if we center the social lives of women workers when designing applications, and address the gaps in research regarding the needs, aspirations, and negotiations they face when encountering communication channels. And conversely, the design of such interfaces must call on a more diverse, situated imagination of the user, whose communication with technology is moderated by patriarchal cultures, restrictive gender norms, and specific political and economic realities.

We recognize that the identities of women workers in the Global South cut across class, gender, ethnicities, and caste, making it a challenge to provide transnational recommendations. However, academia itself is a collectivization effort as we build a critical mass of scholarship in our approach to digital interfacing, and we hope this work will steer the course toward feminist design. We provide a feminist methodological framework through which collectivization can be historicized, and understood as being embedded within specific material contexts so that technologies can aid in building solidarities from the ground up.

First, we provide a brief historical context to women workers' movements in India and elsewhere to situate current worker demands within a history of colonial and feudal systems. This will serve to illustrate specific but not unique contexts occupied by women at the margins, for whom social sharing and community building using digital tools could be crucial to negotiating fair working conditions. Next, we delineate the following issues that can guide theory in HCI & HMC to rethink existing definitions of privacy, protection, and visibility through a feminist perspective, in relation to:

- The gender-blind understanding of digital literacy
- Technologies as tools for exploitation
- Decontextualized definitions of privacy and surveillance

Lastly, we theorize feminist approaches to design that can yield recommendations to alter the design and purpose of machines to enhance the communication experience for women workers in the Global South. Overall, we demonstrate that HCI and the emerging area of HMC research have focused on the cultural aspects of meaning-making in interactions between humans and machines, but we challenge basic assumptions about communicative devices and how they are used, specifically to enhance engagement in worker collectivization.

WOMEN WORKERS AND COLLECTIVE ACTION HISTORICALLY AND TODAY

Feminist scholarship has engaged with the idea that women workers enter union spaces differently due to the nature of their (informal) work, as well as due to household responsibilities, with little recognition being given to women's issues in worker campaigns (Forrest, 2002). The generally low level of unionization in India and the substantial amount of informal labor performed by women lead to them constituting an even smaller fraction of unionized workers (Venkata Ratnam & Jain, 2002). That said, women's movements have been fueled by the intersection of women's oppression exacerbated by class oppression, and unions have largely focused on the latter to the detriment of the former. Women face significant challenges when assuming leadership roles in peasant movements, even though there have been departures to this in environmental movements (Omvedt, 1978; Arora, 2019).

The deliberate, diffused, and shared leadership structure embraced by women to protect themselves from societal backlash deviates from commonly touted masculine/individualized forms of leadership (Park & Seo, 2019). For instance, "Shramik Sanghatana" (Toilers' Union) was a collective through which women's committees became involved with various socio-cultural issues such as alcohol prohibition, landlessness, and contract labor exploitation (Datar, 1975; B., 1973). Women coming together to discuss their issues relies crucially on the opportunity to converse, as was evident in the Shahada movement, which was impactful in many ways; it also inspired urban Indian women to organize the Women's Anti-Price Rise Front (WAPRF), tapping into their frustration of being held responsible for the management of consumption within the household (Mehta & Thakkar, 1992). In such movements, women workers have demonstrated a sense of solidarity against caste-based exploitation, with tobacco workers taking up the cause of the "devadasi" system,[1] a centuries-old feudal practice that forced women into sex work. However, women's causes have often been relegated to the margins of broader union movements once their instrumentality is served (Everett, 1983).

Our focus here is on sectors of work where women's issues are largely invisibilized, even if there is some collectivization among their male counterparts. For instance, women construction workers are primarily employed to do the heaviest and most repetitive tasks including digging, lifting, moving materials and supplies, and clearing rubble. Their informal work conditions prevent them from putting forth demands for social security, health benefits, or even bathroom breaks, let alone support related to childcare and occupational hazards. Sanitation workers in western India remain subjugated by the compulsion of caste-based work as well as their vulnerable position within the family.

DIGITAL TOOLS FOR COLLECTIVIZATION: CHALLENGES AND POTENTIAL

Communication technologies, particularly social media, make it possible for individuals to find each other, discover solidarities and communities, and articulate shared experiences. Even if demands of activism are not met, coming together of groups for a common cause leads to the possibility of a shared political or social consciousness. Individual stories of exploitation may demonstrate structural inequalities (Dey, 2020), and new media technologies may give workers the means to tell their own stories without relying on legacy media politics. However, these digital affordances are marked by significant challenges of access and use by low-income individuals in developing nations, particularly women. In India, men are 28 percent more likely to own a mobile phone than women. A control over narratives has been noted in worker politics, but mostly within male-dominated work and unions where men with high technical know-how are able to make use of video and text blogs to articulate demands and present narratives (Ullah, 2020).

Developing solidarity among women workers would require them to have access to mobile technologies on their own terms and acquire specific types of literacy to explore and use devices. When it comes to mobile usage, confidence with technology can amplify gender-based discrimination (Shashaani, 1994) and gender norms can be a barrier to access/usage, such as linking a woman's honor and reputation, including online, to that of her family and community (Arora, 2019a). A feminist "gaze" is warranted toward technology not only because key actors in designing technology are predominantly men, but also because technology is gendered symbolically and materially, with gender playing a role in the perception of one's own abilities and skills in using technology (Faulkner, 2001; Hargittai & Shafer, 2006). In India, 20 percent of women report "sharing" a device with someone else as compared to 5 percent of the men, primarily due to lack of affordability and the culture of social monitoring (Potnis, 2016; Silver et al., 2019). Little research has been done

on how women perceive the ease of communicating with devices and how they go about addressing challenges; it is in the questioning of what is and is not intuitive for women workers that we may find a path to designing interfaces that would facilitate inclusion – on their terms. In the emerging field of HMC research, communication is still largely an *individual* problem and is treated as such. There is little research showing how design from the Global North fails to take into account socio-cultural meanings developed elsewhere.

Issues of Digital Literacy

Digital literacy, while acknowledged as an essential component to access/usage, differs based on the user group and context. Feminist literature has long argued that online leisure is gendered, such that women experience fragmented leisure between their care duties (Bittman & Wajcman, 2004). Socio-cultural factors such as a lack of content that women might enjoy, lack of time and confidence to engage more freely with ICTs, and general disparity in education, may lead to men developing greater ease with the mobile internet. While literacy rates among low-income women are low, most women are not digitally illiterate per se as they access and engage on WhatsApp and YouTube (Naseem et al., 2020). That said, many women may still need to learn how to install applications or perform more complicated tasks on smartphones.

The paradigm shift from PC-based internet access to mobile-only internet access points to different kinds of technical obstacles. First-time mobile internet users in an economically disadvantaged locality in Cape Town, South Africa did not face issues with regards to access; they already had handsets with a data plan. However, many features of the handsets have been modelled with the assumption that would-be users of mobile internet have prior communication experience with PCs (Gitau et al., 2010). Users faced barriers arising from the placement of banner advertisements, symbols used to denote functionality, and even the requirement of an email address. In other words, communication practices commonly understood to be universal, remained barriers for users who did not make the same meanings of said practices as intended. Research by Tacchi et al. (2012), found that women who can incorporate mobile phones in pre-existing micro-enterprises see the most economic gains. To do this, women have to be encouraged to use mobiles in an exploratory manner, prioritizing what they find as enjoyable and developing a communicative relationship with mobiles on their own terms. Anecdotal evidence from digital literacy initiatives in marginalized communities in India suggests that even where women are allowed access to a mobile phone for specific instrumental purposes, the weight of cultural norms makes it much harder for them to explore its use in broader ways.[2]

Tech as Tools of Oppression But Not Emancipation

Technology becomes the axis along which unequal access arises. The benefits of technologies for ease of work disproportionately eludes women workers, by social and technical design. We identify three major reasons for this. First, there has historically been a lower level of technical education among lower to middle-class women in India. At the Bhilai Steel Plant in Madhya Pradesh, for instance, women constituted half the workforce in manual mines, but all the skilled workers in the mechanized mines were men mostly because women did not fulfil the required qualifications (Sen, 1996). Second, the (up)skilling of women workers is rarely given thought as managerial staff tend to be men, socialized within a highly patriarchal set of values. Finally, technologies designed for an increase in efficiency for men are not always suitable for women's use. This is evident from the fact that drudgery reducing tools (such as the groundnut decorticator) do not always lead to a lessening in energy expenditure for women in agriculture (Thakar & Rajpura, 2021).

Union busting strategies have always been in the arsenal of corporate management and the state to suppress worker demands, and technologies aid in such centralization of power. Three years after the Rana Plaza accident[3] which killed over 1200 workers, the Bangladesh government rejected a majority of union registrations, and sought the dissolution of existing ones. Technologies become conduits of this kind of centralization, such that very few have control over data, decisions, and design, and these are unequally swayed by political and economic power. Activities on social media may help management to narrow down on union leaders and indiscriminately punish individuals to incite fear. Facebook and Amazon have allegedly used data to take action against union activity or to predict protests or strikes, pointing to the imbalance of power that platforms perpetuate (Mehta, 2020).

The fragmented nature of the online workplace means that there is actually no physical space where workers communicate with each other. Women employed in the salon services sector are at the intersection of the feminization of migration, gendered nature of the work, and social exclusion, and activism extends beyond worker collectives (Deori & Rajagopalan, 2017). For instance, workers strategically involve other groups, like churches and students' unions to support them in addressing issues with management or customers. While gig-based platforms can be useful for workers to garner potential clients, it is hard for workers to gain clarity on how the payment calculations are made, their online visibility and client matching, who their supervisor is, or the terms of their contract (Aneja & Shridhar, 2019). In such conditions, it is a challenge for workers to initiate a dialogue with management about working conditions. Technologies are increasingly applied to tighten surveillance strategies by management. Some state governments in India have been using SIM-enabled smartwatches on the wrists of sweepers to track their work, docking their salary if the GPS places them outside their work area, or if the tracker is switched off. The discourse of efficiency that dominates such discussions often underplays the coercion that such workers are subject to, without recourse to room for negotiation either on the frameworks of assessment (quality of work versus quantity of time spent) or conditions of employment.

Surveillance Across Spheres of Activity

Policy measures that have to do with privacy or security take on the "apparatus of care" to associate the everyday lives of citizens to technologies, normalizing a system that allows for oppression instead of empowerment (Arora, 2019b). There may not be discrete kinds of surveillance, but a range of practices to punish transgressive use. Within these contexts, communication practices, and what they make possible, lean toward disallowing challenges to unjust social rules. Workers' movements have always been a site of high surveillance by authorities, but data regimes make it possible not only to bust these movements more conveniently but also to target workers on social media. Activities on social media cannot remain separate from the social lives of vulnerable populations. For example, in the favelas of Brazil, people do not have the option to reject friend requests from gang members who hold significant power in their social lives despite operating from prison (Arora, 2019b). Consequently, young Brazilians are averse to any kind of tagging that may have to do with location. Therefore, in this case, the pervasive location tagging design & architecture is blind to the interpersonal surveillance that young adults face.

The woman worker faces surveillance in the many worlds that she experiences, from employers, co-workers, and family. Asking women only about their mobile use without a holistic understanding of underlying socio-cultural processes would only give partial insight into the place of mobile phones in everyday life, and national policies regarding digital literacy reflect this gender-blindness (Gurumurthy et al., 2016). Privacy as a concept has been dominated by a discourse from the West and tends to refer to information exchange and surveillance issues by the state and corporations. Regulatory frameworks in India have been put to use to govern social media platforms, without due diligence in matters of citizen interests (Rajkhowa, 2015). However, local and interpersonal surveillance tends to be neglected from conversations about privacy, which can provide important insights into gendered design and usage practices (Arora, 2019b).

AGENDA FOR FUTURE RESEARCH: FEMINIST APPROACHES TO DESIGN

Feminist approaches to technology have pointed to the design of technologies to be fundamentally connected to the social and material realities of marginalized peoples. Drawing from feminist science and technology studies, an argument can be made that technologies need to be reimagined separate from the Enlightenment, humanist preoccupation that seeks to distinguish between subject and object (Suchman, 2020). Social realities of low-income women in developing countries reveal that mobile phones are not quite "the extension of the self" due to entrenched cultural norms. This assumption in designing mobile technologies impedes women from using them as freely as their male counterparts. A feminist HCI framework by Bardzell (2010) makes use of the qualities of feminist interaction which prioritize pluralism, embodied experiences, and participation. This framework is useful, but the articulations of these experiences may be very different for women workers in the Global South. Informed by the literature on past and present movements for worker rights and feminist HCI, we recommend the following future areas of work that feminist HMC takes from non-Western concerns of communication technologies.

- To foreground the role of leisure and pleasure in digital literacy.
- To consider how digital tools can address the needs of alternate forms of leadership structures.
- To examine the risks associated with personalization, and features that protect anonymity.
- To reimagine privacy beyond the individual.

Leisure for Digital Literacy

A prominent contribution from the Global South scholars with regards to the use of technologies has been to focus on leisurely activities to reframe discourse around development and empowerment. Studies from Information and Communication Technology for Development mostly relegates leisurely use among people of the Global South to being anecdotal, especially because there is a strong bias towards socio-economic metrics (Arora & Rangaswamy, 2013). In fact, leisurely use which is not overtly utilitarian has been insufficiently explored in these contexts. Traditional cues that are employed in mobile devices like icons, placement, and settings may be more likely to be learnt with use during playtime since entertainment needs are prioritized in internet adoption (Rangaswamy & Cutrell, 2012). This kind of use may also point to more creative uses of smartphone features, such as using voice and video instead of text for communication. A future agenda for HMC research could then include guiding the development of applications that speaks to the playful use of video and voice manipulation. Drawing from existing research regarding this kind of use of social media by girls and women in India and elsewhere would be useful (Subramanian, 2021).

In fact, voice-based communication, whether to sustain group interaction or to articulate community concerns, is one way in which marginalized groups have participated in the digital sphere (Pain, 2017). Given that orality is much more central to many non-literate and neo-literate groups, technologies built around voice communication could allow more women to participate in ways that are both instrumental and pleasurable. As Stelmaszewska, Fields, & Blandford (2004) argue while outlining the need to incorporate Hedonic Experience into HCI theorization, design needs to draw on a more expansive notion of user experience, including enjoyment and pleasure. In the Ideosync case described earlier, women entered digital literacy through making audio stories using (often borrowed) mobile devices and in time became more comfortable with using the devices for other purposes. Thus, assuming that communication habits begin with the social context of women's lives – not only in relation to work but interaction, expression, and pleasure – digital leisure can open new pathways to meaningful use.

Leadership Structures and Hierarchies

Intra-group communication presents an issue for women workers in a seemingly contradictory manner; women leaders would want a voice to foreground their concerns, while also strategizing to not be identified by either group members, management, or platforms. Users have become more sophisticated with digital media and have used them strategically for their "leaderless movements," a tactical way to diffuse and decenter the focus on specific individuals or "leaders," so nobody can be held accountable by the corporation or the state. We see this used time and again in the recent uprising in Hong Kong (Ag, 2019). Applications like Telegram, WhatsApp, or Signal allow for communication within the group that may otherwise be impeded by physical restrictions of space, location, and hierarchy. However, these applications are associated with a phone number and generally designed for personal messaging alongside media support. Group participation depends on the revelation of an identity that is made public within the group, considering also that phone numbers can easily reveal the identity of the individual.

For intra-group communication, particularly for strategizing movement actions, alternative platforms, particularly those that are non-proprietary, are ideal due to threats of various kinds. In the case of the 2020 movement in Hong Kong, LIHKG, an online forum that appears a lot like Reddit and is exclusively for people from Hong Kong, was heavily used on account of the language and ISP requirement. This forum allows for up-votes and down-votes for any post, the cumulative score for which can determine consensus. What is important to be noted here is the nature of participation; that the group is restricted, and it is made as local as possible (Ag, 2019). Such restriction of membership is necessary for otherwise marginalized individuals to find a voice; we see this with social movements for women's rights in the Global South. Alternative forms of leadership can be discovered when risks are mitigated, local issues are addressed, and individuals are provided with a safe space to participate. This provides evidence for our argument that for women's voices to be foregrounded, there is a definite need for groups with women workers only, which can act as non-judgmental and safe spaces (Naseem et al., 2020).

Protecting Anonymity

Privatized goals of platforms such as Facebook and Twitter have to do with increasing revenue streams and getting access to new markets, which may mean that changes in policy and design adversely affect those trying to leverage the platforms for purposes of civil society and mobilizations. Activists may aim to remain anonymous on social media websites, as was the case during the Egyptian uprising of 2011, but Facebook removed such accounts citing violation of their privacy regulations. However, an Egyptian activist recommends that Facebook should allow for anonymous accounts, even if they want to display this information on the account (Youmans & York, 2012). It is increasingly difficult to create an account on Facebook which can remain anonymous; providing an individual's email address and phone number to create the account is incentivized by design. While trolling, hate speech, and other kinds of abuse are risks associated with anonymity on social media, commercial interests shape these decisions since real identities are simply easier to monetize. An understanding of "group privacy" thereby can influence ethical and legal thinking as described by Taylor et al. (2017).

Both the state and corporations have access to individual data collected over technical systems that can impede democratic movements. Data collection needs to be imagined outside of the duality of standard "opt-out" or opt-in mechanisms, of contractual agreements between users and the platform, agreements which are too often constructed for the legally and technically literate user. Marwick & Boyd (2018) note that applying such mechanisms to marginalized populations, complicates assumptions around privacy concerns. Platforms like WhatsApp or Telegram offer end-to-end encryption as a timely and valid solution to the threat that citizens face from powerful institutions, but third-party software has been alleged to be employed by governments to crack down on movements, as counter-terrorism. An open-source alternative like Signal, which is not proprietary nor closed box, can aid in subverting this ecosystem of personalization.

Privacy Beyond the Individual

User privacy on the mobile phone is generally modeled on the assumption that one device belongs to one individual. This has not been the only way to model technology; domestic technologies can be designed using the appliance model (like a television or set-top box) which assumes a single viewer and removes the need for either generating personalization or privacy (Brush & Inkpen, 2007). As Dourish and Anderson (2006) argue, "usability cannot be an afterthought of design... Effective privacy cannot be grafted onto a system because it is a pervasive feature of system design" (p. 337). To eliminate issues related to sharing in a household, mobile phones are modeled to require individual ownership by design. But much research from developing nations suggests that there are many ways in which a device may be used within a family; between the husband and wife, siblings, and parents and their children. These can be significantly different communicative practices than imagined in Western societies. There is an unequal sharing of mobile phones between the genders, whether siblings or spouses, even employers and employees; individuals then employ workarounds to protect what they consider is their private information (Ahmed et al., 2017). This particularity of use is not so much about "sharing" of a mobile phone as "monitoring." "Monitoring" the mobile phone may be reluctantly acceptable by some but can be outright coercive in many circumstances (Sambasivan et al., 2018).

In low literacy and patriarchal contexts, solutions like Secret[4] or multiple accounts do not yield desired outcomes. This directs future work to also reimagine what may be considered private information in different contexts, particularly those from the Global South. Phone libraries and hotspots with community access can enable the use of the phone outside of the home. Private information, in this case, may be of many kinds; photos taken by an individual, browser history, or call history. In this case, deleting private information may be necessary. Instead, the smartphone can be reimagined to work with user sessions like a web browser, much like with a computer cafe or kiosk.

CONCLUSION

In this chapter, we bring together multiple strands of thinking around women's collectivization, feminist design, and interface studies to focus attention on the need to enrich HCI theorization in a way that can better inform the design of technologies to enable women workers at the margins to use them productively. This rethinking of design must be driven by redefining many of the existing axioms of the design – such as privacy, anonymity, and leisure. Drawing on an

understanding of how such women build work-life communities and of the broader socio-cultural context within which they live is essential to reimagine the user and her experience. Feminist design principles that foreground pluralism, embodied experience, and pleasurable engagement with technology can be applied to build interfaces that allow women to create lateral networks of care that can better serve advocacy needs. We have pointed to existing approaches to HCI that can be employed in more strategic ways to imagine feminist HMC, considering a more nuanced cross-cultural understanding of privacy, the specific forms of surveillance that operate on women, and cultural norms that may complicate notions of ownership and use.

ACKNOWLEDGEMENT

This research has been done as part of a project seed-funded by the International Development Research Centre (IDRC), Canada. Project no.: 109331-001. Project name: Organizing Digitally (Public name: Feminist Approaches to Labor Collectives).

NOTES

1   Institutionalized sexual exploitation of dalit women in certain parts of India like Karnataka, Orissa, and Maharashtra. Dalit girls are married to village gods in temples, where they are sexually exploited by men of the upper castes. There are similar practices in the states of Tamil Nadu and Andhra Pradesh as well (Sabharwal & Sonalkar, 2015).

2   Venu Arora, Ideosync Media Combine, New Delhi, personal communication. Ideosync has been engaging in digital literacy initiatives among the most marginalized residents of urban slums, including women and adolescents. www.ideosyncmedia.org

3   The Rana Plaza building in Dhaka, Bangladesh, which housed five garment factories, collapsed on April 24, 2013 killing at least 1,132 people and injuring almost 2,500 (International Labour Organization, 2017).

4   Secret was an app service that allowed people to exchange anonymous messages with their friends. In 2015, David Byttow, the founder and CEO, shut down the company because the spread of malicious rumors on the application did not align with his vision of the company (Isaac, 2015).

REFERENCES

Ag, M. (2019, October 24). *Inside Hong Kong's leaderless uprising*. https://thediplomat.com/2019/10/inside-hong-kongs-leaderless-uprising/

Ahmed, S. I., Haque, Md. R., Guha, S., Rifat, Md. R., & Dell, N. (2017). Privacy, security, and surveillance in the Global South: A study of biometric mobile SIM registration in Bangladesh. *Proceedings of the 2017 CHI Conference on Human Factors in Computing Systems*, 906–918.

Aneja, U., & Shridhar, A. (2019). *Worker wellbeing on digital work platforms in India: A study of Ola Cabs and UrbanClap in New Delhi*. Tandem Research.

Arora, P. (2019a). *The next billion users: Digital life beyond the West*. Harvard University Press.

Arora, P. (2019b). General data protection regulation—a global standard? Privacy futures, digital activism, and surveillance cultures in the Global South. *Surveillance & Society*, *17*(5), 717–725.

Arora, P., & Rangaswamy, N. (2013). Digital leisure for development: Reframing new media practice in the global South. *Media, Culture & Society*, *35*(7), 898–905.

B., P. (1973). Organising the landless in Shahada. *Economic and Political Weekly*, *8*(10), 501–504. JSTOR.

Bardzell, S. (2010). Feminist HCI: Taking stock and outlining an agenda for design. *Proceedings of the SIGCHI Conference on Human Factors in Computing Systems*, 1301–1310.

Bittman, M., & Wajcman, J. (2004). 9 The rush hour. *Family Time: The Social Organization of Care*, *2*, 171.

Brush, A. B., & Inkpen, K. M. (2007). Yours, mine and ours? Sharing and use of technology in domestic environments. *International Conference on Ubiquitous Computing*, 109–126.

Datar, C. (1975). The relations between women's liberation and class struggle – the Shahada movement. *All-India Conference on Women, Trivandrum*, 27–29.

Deori, B., & Rajagopalan, P. (2017). Northeastern beauty-care female workers in South India: Experiencing the "body", economic inclusion and social exclusion as migrants. *ANTYAJAA: Indian Journal of Women and Social Change*, *2*(2), 180–201.

Dey, A. (2020). Sites of exception: Gender violence, digital activism, and Nirbhaya's Zone of Anomie in India. *Violence Against Women*, *26*(11), 1423–1444.

Dourish, P. (2018). The allure and the paucity of design: Cultures of design and design in culture. *Human–Computer Interaction*, 1–21.

Dourish, P., & Anderson, K. (2006). Collective information practice: Exploring privacy and security as social and cultural phenomena. *Human-Computer Interaction*, *21*(3), 319–342.

Everett, J. (1983). The upsurge of women's activism in India. *Frontiers: A Journal of Women Studies*, *7*(2), 18.

Faulkner, W. (2001). The technology question in feminism: A view from feminist technology studies. *Women's Studies International Forum*, *24*(1), 79–95.

Forrest, A. (2002). Connecting women with unions: What are the issues? *Relations Industrielles*, *56*(4), 647–675.

Gitau, S., Marsden, G., & Donner, J. (2010). After access: Challenges facing mobile-only internet users in the developing world. *Proceedings of the SIGCHI Conference on Human Factors in Computing Systems*, 2603–2606.

Gurumurthy A., Chami N., & Thomas S. (2016). Unpacking digital India: A feminist commentary on policy agendas in the digital moment. *Journal of Information Policy*, *6*, 371.

Guzman, A. L. (Ed.). (2018). *Human-machine communication*. Peter Lang US.

Hargittai, E., & Shafer, S. (2006). Differences in actual and perceived online skills: The role of gender. *Social Science Quarterly*, *87*(2), 432–448.

International Labour Organization. (2017, December 21). *The Rana Plaza Accident and its aftermath* [Document].

Isaac, M. (2015, April 29). A founder of Secret, the anonymous social app, is shutting it down. *The New York Times*.

Marwick, A. E., & Boyd, D. (2018). Understanding privacy at the margins. *International Journal of Communication (19328036)*, *12*.

Mehta, C. (2020, September 25). Unionized by phone — circumventing the male gatekeepers. *FemLab. Co.* https://femlab.co/2020/09/25/unionized-by-phone-%e2%94%80-circumventing-the-male-gatekeepers/

Mehta, U., & Thakkar, U. (1992). The Anti-Price-Rise Movement in Bombay. *Canadian Woman Studies*, *13*(1), 3. https://cws.journals.yorku.ca/index.php/cws/article/view/37664

Naseem, M., Younas, F., & Mustafa, M. (2020). Designing digital safe spaces for peer support and connectivity in patriarchal contexts. *Proceedings of the ACM on Human-Computer Interaction*, *4*(CSCW2), 146:1–146:24.

Omvedt, G. (1978). Women and rural revolt in India. *The Journal of Peasant Studies*, *5*(3), 370–403.

Pain, P. (2017). Framing citizen activism: A comparative study of the CGNET Swara and Mobile Voices projects. *Media Asia*, *44*(2), 107–120.

Park, E.-M., & Seo, J.-H. (2019). Effects of shared leadership, psychological empowerment and organizational justice on organizational commitment. *Journal of Digital Convergence*, *17*(6), 177–184.

Potnis, D. (2016). Culture's consequences: Economic barriers to owning mobile phones experienced by women in India. *Telematics and Informatics*, *33*(2), 356–369.

Rajkhowa, A. (2015). The spectre of censorship: Media regulation, political anxiety and public contestations in India (2011–2013). *Media, Culture & Society*, *37*(6), 867–886.

Rangaswamy, N., & Cutrell, E. (2012). Anthropology, development and ICTs: Slums, youth and the mobile internet in urban India. *Proceedings of the Fifth International Conference on Information and Communication Technologies and Development*, 85–93.

Rogers, Y. (2012). HCI theory: Classical, modern, and contemporary. *Synthesis Lectures on Human-Centered Informatics*, *5*(2), 1–129.

Sabharwal, N. S., & Sonalkar, W. (2015). Dalit women in India: At the crossroads of gender, class, and caste. *Global Justice: Theory Practice Rhetoric*, *8*(1).

Sambasivan, N., Checkley, G., Batool, A., Ahmed, N., Nemer, D., Gaytán-Lugo, L. S., Matthews, T., Consolvo, S., & Churchill, E. (2018). "Privacy is not for me, it's for those rich women": Performative Privacy Practices on Mobile Phones by Women in South Asia. *Proceedings of the Fourteenth USENIX Conference on Usable Privacy and Security*, 127–142.

Sen, I. (1996). Technology and women: A case study from the mining sector in India. *Labour, Capital and Society*, *29*(1/2), 23.

Shashaani, L. (1994). Gender-differences in computer experience and its influence on computer attitudes. *Journal of Educational Computing Research*, *11*(4), 347–367.

Silver, L., Smith, A., Johnson, C., Jiang, J., Anderson, M., & Rainie, L. (2019, March 7). Use of smartphones and social media is common across most emerging economies. *Pew Research Center: Internet, Science &* Tech. www.pewresearch.org/internet/2019/03/07/use-of-smartphones-and-social-media-is-common-across-most-emerging-economies/

Stelmaszewska, H., Fields, B., & Blandford, A. (2004). Conceptualising user hedonic experience. *Proc. ECCE*, *12*, 12–15.

Subramanian, S. (2021). Bahujan girls' anti-caste activism on TikTok. *Feminist Media Studies*, *21*(1), 154–156.

Suchman, L. (2020). Agencies in technology design: Feminist reconfigurations. In W. Wallach & P. Asaro (Eds.), *Machine ethics and robot ethics* (1st ed., pp. 361–375). Routledge.

Tacchi, J., Kitner, K. R., & Crawford, K. (2012). Meaningful mobility: Gender, development and mobile phones. *Feminist Media Studies*, *12*(4), 528–537.

Taylor, L., Floridi, L., & van der Sloot, B. (2017). Group privacy: New challenges of data technologies. *Group Privacy*, 293.

Thakar, D., & Rajpura, M. R. (2021). Adoption of agricultural labour saving tools by farm women in India and Gujarat – an overview. *Asian Journal of Agricultural Extension, Economics & Sociology*, 47–53.

Ullah, F. (2020). Digital media and the changing nature of labor action. *Television & New Media*, *21*(4), 376–391.

Venkata Ratnam, C. S., & Jain, H. C. (2002). Women in trade unions in India. *International Journal of Manpower*, *23*(3), 277–292.

Winschiers-Theophilus, H., & Bidwell, N. J. (2013). Toward an Afro-centric indigenous HCI paradigm. *International Journal of Human–Computer Interaction*, *29*(4), 243–255.

Youmans, W. L., & York, J. C. (2012). Social media and the activist toolkit: User agreements, corporate interests, and the information infrastructure of modern social movements. *Journal of Communication*, *62*(2), 315–329.

42

Dishuman–Machine Communication: Disability Imperatives for Reimagining Norms in Emerging Technology

Gerard Goggin

INTRODUCTION

Disability is an important area that speaks to important facets of human–machine communication (HMC), and is widely referenced across key studies in the emerging field. There is a long, largely unacknowledged history of human–machine communication in the area of people with disabilities, often cordoned off from prominent mainstream areas of technology innovation and development (Roulstone, 2016; Seelman, 2000). Yet as Rhonda McEwen and co-authors note, the "case for human-machine communication is strong for people for whom the machine is not only a tool, but is an integral part of their expression and access to information" (McEwen et al., 2020, p. 114). People with disabilities have often been in the forefront of technology development and the vanguard of social, cultural, and technical developments in communication and technology (Ellis & Goggin, 2015).

This lacuna is well on the way to being addressed with the growth of disability media and communication research (Ellcessor & Kirkpatrick, 2017; Ellis et al., 2020). From a HMC perspective, there are many ways in which the marginality of and exclusion of people with disabilities in communication theory and research can be addressed.

Inspired by Andrea Guzman and Seth Lewis' suggestive account of AI and communication, we could suggest, for instance, that the expansive use of technology by people with disabilities has often not fitted the dominant models of communication. Now the contemporary intensification of technology in communication and the shift exemplified by HMC in areas like AI device from "channel" to "communicator" – "machine subjects *with* which people make meaning" (Guzman & Lewis, 2020, p. 73) holds considerable promise for undoing the legacies of powerful ways of seeing disability that still shape core ideas of communication (Alper, 2017; Ellcessor, 2016). Unchallenged and unreconstructed, such ideas threaten to misdirect our attention, hamper our conceptualization and research, and also cut across a growing transformation in communication, technology, and justice.

In this chapter, I make an argument that when we need a time when thinking about human–machine communication should "*always* involve thinking about disability" (Goodley & Runswick-Cole, 2016, p. 13) – something we might call "dishuman–machine communication." "Dishuman" is a concept proposed by British disability scholars Dan Goodley and Katherine Runswick-Cole (Goodley & Runswick-Cole, 2016), adapting the US disability and literary scholar Lennard J. Davis's idea of dismodernity (Davis, 2002). From this stance, this chapter offers an introduction to disability and HMC, and sketches key elements of the research agenda. First, I discuss the promise of disability as a central area of HMC. Second, I discuss from key disability perspectives the three keywords – human, machine, and communication. Third, I look at the major roadblock in opening up HMC to the creativity of disability thinking: the persistence of ideologies of ability and disability when it comes to the framing of communication and technology. Fourth, I conclude with suggestions for a transformative dishuman–machine communication research agenda.

ESTABLISHING HMC WITH DISABILITY

A key premise of HMC is the need to acknowledge and understand the new centrality of the ways that humans communicate with machines (Guzman, 2018; Jones, 2014). A motif of key research to date in the field is the need to grapple with the culturally dominant view in many societies whereby machines are often regarded as non-human – or, paradoxically, super human, but certainly ontologically different to humans. HMC researchers have sought to depart from this received view and instead explore the realities of communication centering on human–machine communication and machine-to-machine communication. This new direction marked out in HMC also provides a more expansive and richer canvas to consider how to more accurately and ethically consider and situate the distinctive communicative character of humans among and in constitutive inter-relation to other species. In this context, speaking of disability and HMC is helpful *and* challenging. Such a discourse brings together two kinds of categories often regarded as: not human; subhuman; or distinct from what societies may prize as defining characteristics of human life.

People with disabilities have endured a long struggle to be acknowledged as fully human. This has changed dramatically, if still too slowly, with disability acknowledged as integral to life. In the process, a wide range of scholars, activists, media makers, artists, human rights practitioners, and others have been engaged in rethinking the human via disability. This multifaceted evolving project has major implications for how we understand communication. Consider, for instance, that if we take seriously the communication modes, styles, and requirements of everyone, including people with disabilities, then we are precipitated in a radical reconsideration – starting with a necessary enlargement of assumptions on what

communication is and how it occurs; given that communication transpires via a range of sensory modes (touch, different kinds of voice and audio, the visual communication of sign language), formats, and so on (Ellcessor & Kirkpatrick, 2017; Ellis et al., 2020). This rethinking of communication via new accounts of disability is especially generative when we consider the relationships of people with disabilities, on the one hand, and machines, on the other.

There is a close association between disability and machines (and technology more broadly). Since the early 1990s, this has sometimes been theorized via seeing people with disabilities as "cyborgs." The disability cyborg turn has been critiqued as unproductively metaphorical and stereotypical in tendency, rather than a conceptualization that offers generative accounts that do justice to contemporary understandings of disability and its relationships to technology (Ellcessor, 2017; Goggin & Newell, 2003; Kafer, 2013). The reflex to approach disability via a cyborg lens has been eclipsed by the rise of disability studies, and a flowering of exciting accounts across communication and media studies, and science and technology studies, that have opened up new ways to think about disability assemblages of human and machines, and other things. Notably, these new accounts of disability and technology open up fresh perspectives that move from seeing disability as a "special" or "exceptional" case to a complex, relational, material category that helps us rethink the general situation in communication and technology. Into the bargain, we more precisely understand and address issues of justice, design, rights, and access for people with disabilities (Alper, 2021; Hamraie, 2017; Hendren, 2020; Roulstone, 2016).

Consider, for instance, synthesized, digital, recorded voice communications and media, now used by hundreds of millions, or indeed billions, of people globally, in the form of mobile voice assistants embedded in smartphones and home technologies such as Google Home or Amazon Alexa that are underpinned by AI and machine learning. These current technologies have their antecedents in print and text to speech software and machines, developed, among others, by Ray Kurzweil, who sought advice from the U.S. National Foundation of the Blind (Leventhal, 2004). Other pioneering technologies used by people with disabilities, such as those with communication impairments or complex communication needs, included a range of "assistive" technologies to provide "augmentative and alternative communication" – often featuring pictures and symbols, or synthesized voice, but for some years involving generations of new technologies (Koch Fager et al., 2019). Unsurprisingly, disability has had a telling presence in the HMC field as this has developed in the past few years, building on this long genealogy (McEwen et al., 2020).

DISABILITY PERSPECTIVES ON HUMANS, COMMUNICATION, AND MACHINE

While there is much promise as outlined, there are some roadblocks to be cleared in approaching disability and HMC. Across many societies, disability has often been regarded as antithetical to the human. People with disabilities have often been treated in inhumane ways, and continue to be conceived and oppressed in this way. This situation still brings an outpouring of responses. The title of a recent paper on the neglect of adolescents with disability in conflict-affected contexts in Jordan and Palestine quotes the words "Even though I am Blind, I am still human" (Presler-Marshall et al., 2020). The rise of disability movements and acceptance of the need for disability justice as an epochal, transformative project for global societies hinges on arguments for people with disabilities to be given full recognition and membership as human beings. One benchmark achievement has been the 2006 United Nations Convention on the Rights of Persons with Disabilities, which clearly extended human rights to people with disabilities in an historical way (Lawson & Beckett, 2021; Quinn & Quinn, 2009) – and included many provisions relating to communication and technology (Lazar & Stein, 2017) although its implementation remains a work-in-progress. These transformations in disability are exciting and are an impetus for a broader rethinking of social life. Technology is central to these changes, yet here there is a major barrier – because the relations between disability and being or becoming human remain fraught and even contested (van Trigt et al., 2016).

The idea that disability, in all its diversity and shape-shifting, is a "normal" part of human life, remains a profound challenge for many; when the culturally dominant view of disability typically still revolves around ideas that disability and impairment are best cured, eliminated, regarded as a tragedy or regrettable, and certainly not part of how we should imagine ideals of future societies or the "good life" (Bickenbach et al., 2014; Garland-Thomson, 2017b) Despite the big shift in societal views, common ideas of "normal" humans don't include or cut across the lives and prospects for people with disabilities (Garland-Thomson, 2017a; Goggin et al., 2018; Silvers, 1994). This goes for core concepts of "human" that underpin "human rights" too, especially in neoliberal

contexts (Wadiwel, 2020), and especially in relation to "biopower" (Davis, 2013) and "technoscience" (Hamraie, 2015; Hamraie & Fritsch, 2019a; Sterne, 2019).

Strong challenges to these oppressive and stereotypical views have come from the important new thinking on the human across areas such as queer crip studies, trans disability studies, and disability and animal studies (Lundblad, 2020; Taylor, 2017). Into the mix also is the area of disability posthumanism. As Srikala Naraian nicely summarizes it, "scholars have argued for a posthumanist disability approach that dismantles the binaries of material/discursive, nature/culture, ability/disability, locating it within assemblages of human and nonhuman agencies" (Naraian, 2021, p. 4). Naraian and other scholars have also posited the need for decolonizing approaches to posthumanism (Eglash et al., 2020) and disability that take majority world, global south, and the full range of international locations seriously (Campbell, 2009; Naraian, 2021, pp. 4–5). In dialogue with Rosi Braidotti's work (Braidotti, 2013), Dan Goodley, and Katherine Runswick-Cole raise the stakes with their declaration that disability has "always contravened the traditional classical posthumanist conception of what it means to be human" (Goodley et al., 2014, p. 342). In a series of studies, they and other collaborators, such as Kirsty Liddiard, flesh out the concept of posthuman disability studies to acknowledge and open up generative, empowering, and collaborative perspectives premised on "webs of relations between humans and others" that challenge "stereotypes of disability" (Liddiard et al., 2019). This posthuman disability is informed by earlier efforts to conceptualize a critical disability, and is in the theoretical ballpark of what Braidotti has discussed as the "critical posthumanities," where science and technology studies, and digital media studies, in her estimation, as generative hubs of new interdisciplinary production of knowledge and interventions (Braidotti, 2019, pp. 37–38). Key to the emergence of such ideas and practices is the centrality of media and technology interfaces to contemporary social life and power relations (Braidotti, 2019, p. 35).

So, what's all this got to do with human–machine communication? Well, the rub is these dominant ideas of the human cast a long shadow on how communication is constituted and occurs across machines and people with disabilities. As disability sits uneasily in the realm of the human, we see social imaginaries of technology featuring abolishment of impairment. This is most obvious and hotly debated in the area of human enhancement, where what is typically on offer, as one collection puts it, "new bodies for a better life"

(Eilers et al., 2014), a striving for the "superhuman" or "superability" (Dan, 2019). The will to human enhancement, and its bias towards narrow norms of embodiment, are also widely publicized in the continuing "supercrip" accounts of Paralympian achievement, not least in the technology-enhanced career of the celebrated and controversial athlete Oscar Pistorius (Swartz & Watermeyer, 2008). In the area of transhumanism especially, there is a strong belief that disability is best left behind and transcended in the evolving pursuit of enhanced, impairment-free bodies via the advances of science and technology (Lee & Lee, 2016). What is common across these various ways of thinking is that technology is imagined and shaped by inadequate understandings of disability, leaving many out. Of the many alternative ways of doing technology is to reimagine it via thinking through the full diversity of humans and other beings, and to embrace what bioethicist Jackie Leach-Scully calls the "variant body" (Scully, 2008).

DISABILITY IN THE MACHINES – BEYOND IDEOLOGIES OF ABILITY

This deep conceptualization of disability and humans is the overarching problem in achieving a better understanding of disability and communication technology. Technology is still often approached as a way to restore or achieve much cherished normal functioning of life when it comes to disability. Thus much of the early work on technology and disability took place in rehabilitation disciplines, contexts, and aims – often with populations, such as war veterans or major accident survivors (especially motor vehicle accidents). There is also the influential idea especially underpinning work in medicine and health that a key purpose of technology is to contribute to the broader cultural goal of cure people of disease and illness – and disability (Eunjung, 2017). This imaginary has been called "curative technology" (Stramondo, 2019), a fraught area given that technology is often represented as cure when it comes to disability (Allan, 2013).

More broadly, a governing concept in disability and technology has been assistive technology (AT). Assistive technology remains a keyword for how disability and technology is approached (Bodine, 2013). Simply put, it is the idea that technology can play a major role in supporting people with disabilities to tackle barriers and challenges to participation in everyday life. There has been a considerable debate about the terminology of assistive technology (Alper, 2015). Assistive technology is still widely understood to refer to technology used by people with disabilities versus technologies that might be widely used, often called "tools," as Richard E. Ladner points out:

> "Assistive technology" is really a redundant term because, in some sense, all technology is assistive, making tasks possible or easier to do ... Why is it that persons with disabilities have assistive technology, while the rest of us just have technology? (Ladner, 2010, p. 25)

Joseph Stramondo offers an interesting account of this distinction between assistive technology and tools, suggesting that "assistive technology ... confers a disability identity on its user" (Stramondo, 2019, p. 1138). From a different angle, Heather A. Faucett and co-authors, argue that "assistive technologies have an important role to play not only in augmenting human abilities, but also in hiding and showing disabilities" (Faucett et al., 2017, p. 3). For her part, Mara Mills offers a sharp and now classic critique of the way that pioneers, designers, and promoters of technology often focus on disability early on in their endeavors, then switch their attention and investment to more profitable areas – a maneuver she dubs the "assistive pretext" (Mills, 2010, p. 39).

Despite these debates, assistive technology remains a governing idea about human–machine communication when it comes to people with disabilities. Most obviously, various countries have assistive technology funds that provide communication technology – and the ideas and work in this area is still largely conceptualized as assistive technology, even if in updated ways. Yet the distinction between assistive technology and other kinds of technology has been under severe pressure, and in many ways rendered irrelevant, because of change in technologies, markets, and socio-technical practices. With convergence, digitization, rise of global technologies and firms providing Internet, mobile, data, automation, and other technologies to household and domestic markets, users with disabilities have been able to put together new customized solutions to their communication needs (Rinne et al., 2016), and new markets have emerged (given most attention in the area of ageing and technology (Ward et al., 2017). These trends suit many governments around the world as they seek to withdraw from providing or underwriting social welfare and care, and seek to reduce their expenditures, while at the same time configuring new kinds of public–private partnerships to address requirements of citizens with disabilities (Soldatic, 2019). The political and cultural economies of these new and emergent machines create forms of inequalities even as they open up new spaces and possibilities (Yu et al., 2019).

It has proven difficult to dislodge and dismantle what Tobin Siebers term the "ideology of ability" (Siebers, 2008) embedded in accounts of humans and machine, especially in the area of assistive technology (Campbell, 2009). The positive news is that new approaches have gained significant momentum in recent years. This is something that Mills, Jonathan Sterne (Sterne, 2021), and other historians of communication, media, and technology have been exploring in scholarship that has important implications for our topic: namely, the ways that our ideas of human–machine communication are deeply structured by legacies and politics of disability we do not adequately comprehend or acknowledge.

Another related and crucial source of ideas has been the slow-burn relationship between disability and STS. The early work of Ingunn Moser in STS and actor-network-theory remains highly influential. Moser theorized the ways in which people experienced "becoming" disabled subjects and the ways in which disability operated in particular contexts, individuals, and groups to articulate differences and create and sustain systems of social ordering (Moser, 2005). She drew attention to the role of technology, socio-technical practices, and embodiment in these processes (Moser, 2006). From the early 2010s, STS and disability was put explicitly on the agenda (Blume et al., 2014; Galis, 2011), and leading to an increasing range of contributions drawing on STS in conjunction with other areas, especially feminist work that have expanded our understanding of HMC. Such work has provided a notable warrant, among other traditions, for directing attention to the relationships between human and machines in ways that can untangle their disabling histories and contest their ongoing roles in everyday practices as much as structural inequalities and systems of oppression (Forlano, 2016). More recently, there has been the theorization of cripping feminist technoscience developed by Aimie Hamraie (Hamraie, 2015) and the subject of her and Kelly Fritsch's powerful manifesto (Hamraie & Fritsch, 2019b).

THE TRANSFORMATIVE POTENTIAL OF HMC

These critiques and idées fortes from disability studies illuminate pitfalls but also indicate new paths for adventurous thinking in how we can remagine communication and technology via HMC research.

First, there are a range of different traditions converging to encourage us to focus on the technology and its agency and role in the HMC mix. In her study of eye gaze technology McEwen et al. pay attention to the technology as a partner in communication along with humans and others: "The technology is not considered as simply a mediating device, but an active participant in the communication taking place" (McEwen et al., 2020, p. 116). In relation to disability, technology has often been approached as a practical or transcendent way to overcome impairment and altered its identity, lived experience, and social coordinates. Instead of looking via technology to imagine and create a realm in which disability does not exist, it is much better to consider how people with disabilities communicate with technology and might enjoy an expanded idea of the good life.

Second, there are new conceptualizations that seek to do justice to the range, varieties, modalities, and dynamics of communication – especially kinds of communication that have been deprecated or seen as minor in nature. However, with the socio-technical developments of recent years, it has become evident that our ideas of communication need to change. Here, the area of touch communication and haptic media has been an exemplary area (McDaniel & Panchanathan, 2020; Parisi et al., 2017). From touchscreens in service, household, and work settings, touch media such as smartphones and tablets (McEwen & Dubé, 2017) to games, social media (e.g. notifications and alerts), VR, sensors, and other technologies, important research and rethinking is well underway (Paterson, 2017) – and stands to be given fruitful, concentrated attention in HMC. Exactly because disability did not fit the norms of human communication centered around the primacy of voice or the kinds of media that become dominant in the twentieth century in press and broadcasting, the concept offers rich resources at this time.

Third, critical accounts of disability offer ideas for understanding HMC evolution as well as rethinking its social imaginaries and implications. An excellent example here is provided by the idea of "interdependence" which is central to disability studies and disability movements' rethinking of the individual's relationship to social life, things, environments, and collectivities. Interdependence is a keyword in disability critiques of dominant notions of autonomy and individuals (Kittay, 2011). The concept of interdependence draws upon and is in dialogue with a strain of thinking has been long developed in feminist philosophy – for instance, via the concept of relational autonomy (Mackenzie & Stoljar, 2000; Stoljar & Voigt, 2021). As Laura Davy nicely puts it, interdependence in relation to disability aims to navigate between an "ethic of care and an ethic of autonomy" (Davy, 2019). Eleanor Sandry offers a pioneering account of robots and communication via a disability account of interdependence (Sandry, 2020). This kind of approach clearly builds on a small yet rich body of disability theorization and debate concerning robots (especially service and care robots, and social robotics) (Carnevale, 2015; Seelman, 2016; Wolbring & Yumakulov, 2014) and cues us to frame and tackle research on the complexities of HMC in intelligent systems – a topic of highly significant social concern, yet an area bedeviled by major misunderstandings.

All in all, as these suggestions hopefully indicate, HMC has considerable potential to help come to terms with the disabling inheritance evident in communication studies – and to draw upon new ideas about humans, machines, and communication by thinking about disability differently.

ACKNOWLEDGEMENT

I gratefully acknowledge the award of a NTU research Start Up Grant for the project *Smart Equalities*, which supported the research for this paper.

REFERENCES

Allan, K. (2013). *Disability in science fiction: Representations of technology as cure*. Palgrave Macmillan.

Alper, M. (2015). Augmentative, alternative, and assistive: Reimagining the history of mobile computing and disability. *IEEE Annals of the History of Computing, 37*(1), 96–96. doi: 10.1109/MAHC. 2015.3.

Alper, M. (2017). *Giving voice: Mobile communication, disability, and inequality*. MIT Press.

Alper, M. (2021). Critical media access studies: Deconstructing power, visibility, and marginality in mediated space. *International Journal of Communication, 15*, 840–861. https://ijoc.org/index.php/ijoc/article/view/15274

Arnardóttir, O. M., & Quinn, G. (Eds.). (2009). *The UN Convention on the Rights of Persons with Disabilities: European and Scandinavian perspectives.* Brill.

Bickenbach, J. E., Felder, F., & Schmitz, B. (Eds.). (2014). *Disability and the good human life*. Cambridge University Press.

Blume, S., Galis, V., & Pineda, A. V. (2014). STS and disability. *Science, Technology, & Human Values, 39*(1), 98–104. https://doi.org/10.1177/0162243913513643

Bodine, C. (2013). *Assistive technology and science*. SAGE.

Braidotti, R. (2013). *The posthuman*. Polity Press.

Braidotti, R. (2019). A theoretical framework for the critical posthumanities. *Theory, Culture & Society, 36*(6), 31–61. https://doi.org/10.1177/0263276418771486

Campbell, F. K. (2009). *Contours of ableism: The production of disability and abledness*. Palgrave Macmillan.

Carnevale, A. (2015). Robots, disability, and good human life. *Disability Studies Quarterly, 35*. http://dx.doi.org/10.18061/dsq.v35i1.4604

Dan, B. (2019). Human enhancement: From disability to superability. *Developmental Medicine and Child Neurology, 61*(5), 500-500. https://doi.org/10.1111/dmcn.14215

Davis, L. J. (2002) *Bending over backwards: Disability, dismodernism, and other difficult positions*. New York University Press.

Davis, L. J. (2013). *The end of normal: Identity in a biocultural era*. University of Michigan Press.

Davy, L. (2019). Between an ethic of care and an ethic of autonomy: Negotiating relational autonomy, disability, and dependency. *Angelaki, 24*(3), 101–114. https://doi.org/10.1080/0969725X.2019. 1620461

Eglash, R., Bennett, A., Babbitt, W., Lachney, M., Reinhardt, M., & Hammond-Sowah, D. (2020). Decolonizing posthumanism: Indigenous material agency in generative STEM. *British Journal of Educational Technology, 51*(4), 1334–1353. https://doi.org/10.1111/bjet.12963

Eilers M., Grüber, K., & Rehmann-Sutter, C. (Eds.). (2014). *The human enhancement debate and disability: New bodies for a better life*. Palgrave Macmillan.

Ellcessor, E. (2016). *Restricted access: Media, disability, and the politics of participation*. NYU Press.

Ellcessor, E. (2017). Cyborg hoaxes: Disability, deception, and critical studies of digital media. *New Media & Society, 19*(11), 1761–1777. https://doi.org/10.1177/1461444816642754

Ellcessor E., & Kirkpatrick, B. (2017). *Disability media studies*. NYU Press.

Ellis, K., & Goggin, G. (2015). *Disability and the media*. Palgrave Macmillan.

Ellis, K., Goggin, G., Haller, B., & Curtis, R. (Eds.). (2020). *Routledge companion to disability and media*. Routledge.

Eunjung, K. (2017). *Curative violence: Rehabilitating disability, gender, and sexuality in Modern Korea*. Duke University Press.

Faucett, H. A., Ringland, K. E., Cullen, A. L. L., & Hayes, G. R. (2017). (In)visibility in disability and assistive technology. *ACM Transactions on Accessible Computing, 10*(4), 1–17. https://doi.org/10.1145/3132040

Forlano, L. (2016). Hacking the feminist disabled body. *Journal of Peer Production* 8. http://peerproduction.net/issues/issue-8-feminism-and-unhacking-2/peer-reviewed-papers/issue-8-feminism-and-unhackingpeer-reviewed-papers-2hacking-the-feminist-disabled-body/

Galis, V. (2011). Enacting disability: How can science and technology studies inform disability studies? *Disability & Society, 26*(7), 825–838. https://doi.org/10.1080/09687599.2011.618737

Garland-Thomson, R. (2017a). Disability bioethics: From theory to practice. *Kennedy Institute of Ethics Journal, 27*(2), 323–339. doi: 10.1353/ken.2017.0020

Garland-Thomson, R. (2017b). Eugenic world building and disability: The strange world of Kazuo Ishiguro's *Never Let Me Go. The Journal of Medical Humanities, 38*(2), 133–145. https://doi.org/10.1007/s10912-015-9368-y

Goggin G., & Newell C. (2003). *Digital disability: The social construction of disability in new media.* Rowman & Littlefield.

Goggin G., Steele L., & Cadwallader, J. R. (Eds.). (2018). *Normality and disability: Intersections among norms, law, and culture.* Routledge.

Goodley D., Lawthom R., & Runswick Cole, K. (2014) Posthuman disability studies. *Subjectivity* 7(4): 342–361. https://doi.org/10.1057/sub.2014.15

Goodley D., & Runswick-Cole, K. (2016) Becoming dishuman: Thinking about the human through dis/ability. *Discourse, 37*(1), 1–15. https://doi.org/10.1080/01596306.2014.930021

Guzman, A. L. (Ed.). (2018). *Human-machine communication: Rethinking communication, technology, and ourselves.* Peter Lang.

Guzman, A. L., & Lewis, S. C. (2020) Artificial intelligence and communication: A Human–Machine Communication research agenda. *New Media & Society, 22*(1), 70–86. https://doi.org/10.1177/1461444819858691

Hamraie A. (2015). Cripping feminist technoscience. *Hypatia, 30*(1), 307–313. https://doi.org/10.1111/hypa.12124

Hamraie, A. (2017). *Building access: Universal design and the politics of disability.* University of Minnesota Press.

Hamraie A., & Fritsch K. (2019a). Crip technoscience manifesto. *Catalyst, 5*(1), 1–33. https://doi.org/10.28968/cftt.v5i1.29607

Hendren, S. (2020). *What can a body do? How we meet the built world.* Riverhead Books.

Jones, S. (2014). People, things, memory and human-machine communication. *International Journal of Media and Cultural Politics, 10*(3), 245–258. doi: 10.1386/macp.10.3.245_1

Kafer, A. (2013). *Feminist, queer, crip.* Indiana University Press.

Kittay, E. F. (2011). The ethics of care, dependence, and disability. *Ratio Juris, 24*(1), 49–58. https://doi.org/10.1111/j.1467-9337.2010.00473.x

Koch Fager, S., Fried-Oken, M., Jakobs T., & Beukelman, D. R. (2019) New and emerging access technologies for adults with complex communication needs and severe motor impairments: State of the science. *Augmentative and Alternative Communication, 35*(1), 13–25. https://doi.org/10.1080/07434618.2018.1556730

Ladner, R. E. (2010). Accessible technology and models of disability. In M. M. K. Oishi, I. M. Mitchell, & H. F. M. Van der Loos (Eds.), *Design and use of assistive technology: Social, technical, ethical, and economic challenges* (pp. 25–31). Springer.

Lawson A., & Beckett, A. E. (2021). The social and human rights models of disability: Towards a complementarity thesis. *The International Journal of Human Rights, 25*(2), 348–379. https://doi.org/10.1080/13642987.2020.1783533

Lazar J., & Stein, M. A. (Eds.). (2017). *Disability, human rights, and information technology.* University of Pennsylvania Press.

Lee J., & Lee, J. (2016). Cochlear implantation, enhancements, transhumanism and posthumanism: Some human questions. *Science and Engineering Ethics, 22*(1), 67–92. https://doi.org/10.1007/s11948-015-9640-6

Leventhal, J. (2004). The man and the machine: An interview with Ray Kurzweil. *Access World.* September. www.afb.org/aw/5/5/14692

Liddiard, K., Whitney, S., Evans, K., Watts, L., Vogelmann, E., Spurr, R., Aimes, C., Runswick-Cole, K., & Goodley, Dan. (2019). Working the edges of posthuman disability studies: Theorising with disabled young people with life-limiting impairments. *Sociology of Health & Illness, 41*(8), 1473–1487. https://doi.org/10.1111/1467-9566.12962

Lundblad, M. (2020). Animality/ posthumanism/ disability: An introduction. *New Literary History, 51*(4), v–xxi. doi: 10.1353/nlh.2020.0040

Mackenzie, C., & Stoljar, N. (Eds.). (2000). *Relational autonomy: Feminist perspectives on autonomy, agency, and the social self.* Oxford University Press.

McDaniel, T., & Panchanathan, S. (2020). *Haptic interfaces for accessibility, health, and enhanced quality of life.* Springer

McEwen, R., Atcha, A., Lui, M., Shimaly, R., Maharaj, A., Ali, S., & Carroll, S. (2020). Interlocutors and interactions: Examining the interactions between students with complex communication needs, teachers, and eye-gaze technology. *Human-Machine Communication, 1,* 113–131. https://doi.org/10.30658/hmc.1.7

McEwen, R., & Dubé, A. (2017). *Understanding tablets from early childhood to adulthood: Encounters with touch technology.* Routledge.

Mills, M. (2010). Deaf jam: From inscription to reproduction to information. *Social Text*, *28*(1), 35–58. https://doi.org/10.1215/01642472-2009-059

Moser, I. (2005). On becoming disabled and articulating differences. *Cultural Studies*, *19*(6), 667–700. https://doi.org/10.1080/09502380500365648

Moser, I. (2006). Sociotechnical practices and difference: On the interferences between disability, gender, and class. *Science, Technology, & Human Values*, *31*(5), 537–564. https://doi.org/10.1177/0162243906289611

Naraian, S. (2021). Making inclusion matter: Critical disability studies and teacher education. *Journal of Curriculum Studies*, 53(3), 298–313. https://doi.org/10.1080/00220272.2021.1882579

Parisi D., Paterson, M., & Archer, J. E. (2017). Haptic media studies. *New Media & Society*, *19*(10), 1513–1522. https://doi.org/10.1177/1461444817717518

Paterson, M. (2017). On haptic media and the possibilities of a more inclusive interactivity. *New Media & Society*, *19*(10), 1541–1562. https://doi.org/10.1177/1461444817717513

Presler-Marshall, E., Jones, N., & Odeh, K. B. (2020). "Even though I am Blind, I am still human!": The neglect of adolescents with disabilities' human rights in conflict-affected contexts. *Child Indicators Research*, *13*(2), 513–531. https://doi.org/10.1007/s12187-019-09700-z

Rinne, P., Mace, M., Nakornchai, T., Zimmerman, K., Fayer, S., Sharma, P., Liardon, J.-L., Burdet, E., & Bentley, P. (2016). Democratizing neurorehabilitation: How accessible are low-cost mobile-gaming technologies for self-rehabilitation of arm disability in stroke? *PloS One*, *11*(10), e0163413–e0163413. https://doi.org/10.1371/journal.pone.0163413

Roulstone, A. (2016). *Disability and technology: An interdisciplinary and international approach*. Palgrave Macmillan.

Sandry, E. (2020). Interdependence in collaboration with robots. In K. Ellis, G. Goggin, B. Haller, & R. Curtis (eds.), *Routledge companion to disability and media* (pp. 316–326). Routledge.

Scully, J. L. (2008). *Disability bioethics: Moral bodies, moral difference*. Rowman & Littlefield.

Seelman, K. D. (2000). Science and technology policy: Is disability a missing factor? *Assistive Technology*, *12*(2), 144–153. https://doi.org/10.1080/10400435.2000.10132020

Seelman, K. D. (2016). Should robots be personal assistants? In P. Block, D. Kasnitz, A. Nishida, & N.

Pollard (Eds.), *Occupying disability: Critical approaches to community, justice, and decolonizing disability* (pp. 259–272). Springer.

Silvers, A. (1994). "Defective" agents: Equality, difference and the tyranny of the normal. *Journal of Social Philosophy*, *25*, 154–175. https://doi.org/10.1111/j.1467-9833.1994.tb00353.x

Soldatic, K. (2019). *Disability and neoliberal state formations*. Routledge.

Sterne, J. (2019). Ballad of the dork-o-phone: Towards a crip vocal technoscience. *Journal of Interdisciplinary Voice Studies*, *4*(2), 179–189. https://doi.org/10.1386/jivs_00004_1

Sterne, J. (2021). *Diminished faculties: A political phenomenology of impairment*. Duke University Press.

Stoljar, N., & Voigt, K. (Eds.). (2021). *Equality and autonomy: Relational approaches*. Routledge.

Stramondo, J. A. (2019). The distinction between curative and assistive technology. *Science and Engineering Ethics*, *25*(4), 1125–1145. https://doi.org/10.1007/s11948-018-0058-9

Swartz, L., & Watermeyer, B. (2008). Cyborg anxiety: Oscar Pistorius and the boundaries of what it means to be human. *Disability & Society*, *23*(2), 187–190. https://doi.org/10.1080/09687590701841232

Taylor, S. (2017). *Beasts of burden: Animal and disability liberation*. New Press.

van Trigt, P., Kool, J., & Schippers, A. (2016). Editorial. Humanity as a contested concept: Relations between disability and "being human." *Social Inclusion*, *4*(4), 125. https://doi.org/10.17645/si.v4i4.754

Wadiwel, D. (2020). Restriction, norm, *Umwelt*: A response. *New Literary History*, *51*(4), 751–763. doi: 10.1353/nlh.2020.0047

Ward, G., Fielden, S., Muir, H., Holliday, N., & Urwin, G. (2017). Developing the assistive technology consumer market for people aged 50–70. *Ageing and Society*, *37*(5), 1050–1067. https://doi.org/10.1017/S0144686X16000106

Wolbring, G., & Yumakulov, S. (2014) Social robots: Views of staff of a disability service organization. *International Journal of Social Robotics*, *6*(3), 457–468.

Yu, H., Goggin, G., Fisher, K., & Li, B. (2019). Introduction: Disability participation in the digital economy. *Information, Communication & Society*, *22*(4), 467–473. https://doi.org/10.1080/1369118X.2018.1550525

43

Robotic Art – The Aesthetics of Machine Communication

Damith Herath and Stelarc

Robots are increasingly capable of generating emergent and aesthetic outcomes of their own. Artists are at the forefront of appropriating such emergent technologies to create new interactive paradigms. Here we argue that robotic art does not necessarily follow an optimal approach to communication. Instead, artists generate novel interfaces and novel actuation of robots that challenge the form and function and how we relate to our machines.

Invariably, the chapter permeates multiple disciplinary boundaries calling on and challenging the norms and methods of the overlapping communities. Depending on which community they belong to, the reader will notice the deeply intuitive nature of the artist being probed by the engineer or the analytical and clinical approach of the engineer being called into question by the artist. Perhaps polemical, this narrative is about finding methodological common ground in the emergent field of robotic art.

BACKGROUND

In the seminal work, *Homo Aestheticus* (Dissanayake, 2001), compelling evidence is presented that art is integral to human evolution and artmaking is an innate part of the human psyche, primordial and central to the human story. From the prehistoric cave art to the drawings of early civilizations such as the Mesopotamian and the Indus Valley to Egyptian masterpieces, to Chinese, African Nok culture to early Christian and Byzantine art to Buddhist and Hindu art to early Islamic art through the modern era, humans have left an indomitable legacy of artmaking (Honour & Fleming, 2005). Art is almost to be seen as the raison d'être of humanity. Dissanayake argues that at a basic psychological level, art has helped humanity survive as a species (Dissanayake, 2001). On the other hand, aesthetics informs the nature of the beauty of a work of art or the philosophy of art, and it requires a more careful study. A cogent definition of the term seems problematic (Ogden, 1933). To begin with, distinction between the beautiful and the ugly is subjective, or as the artist would put it in the ensuing conversation, it is relatively intuitive. The inclined reader is directed to Weitz's (Weitz, 1956) illuminating prose on the subject.

The modern term robot has an artistic origin. It first appears in the stage play RUR (Rossumovi Univerzální Roboti) – Rossum's Universal *Robots* by the Czech writer Karel Čapek in 1921 (Čapek, 2004). Initially created as mechanical slaves to serve humans, robots in the play ultimately learn to hate humans and annihilate humanity at the end. Ironically, art anticipated the arrival of robots and squarely situated them as the eternal antagonists, a recurring motif in mostly western depictions of human–robot encounters henceforth. The origins of mechanical automata, human- or animal-like machines, stretch much further than the word robot. There is a rich history of such machines and their encounters with humans (Stephens & Heffernan, 2016), such as the remarkable Mechanical Turk by Von Kempelen in the 1770s. While the origin of the term robot has a clear root, its definition varies depending on the audience. For example, the Merriam Webster online dictionary begins its definition of a robot with "a machine that resembles a living creature…" (Merriam-Webster, 2021). Engineers tend to identify certain commonalities that define a robot. For example, Laumond (Laumond, 2016) defines it as machines that exhibit motion autonomy. A more precise definition would be a goal-oriented machine that can sense, plan and act (Corke, 2017).

Already we are on shaky grounds with two ill-defined terms related to this chapter. Equally, the underlying disciplinary challenges between the arts on the one side and engineering on the other are at times insurmountable. The two authors of this chapter, an engineer, and an artist, agonized over many months to identify a shared narrative and an approach to thread through our mutual experiences working together into a methodological coherence. Having worked at the intersection between art and robotics for many years, the authors argue that methodological differences between the fields may never be fully reconciled and would be futile to attempt so. Therefore, instead, we offer a dialogical exegesis that explores our collaborative work process. The chapter highlights how we resolve conflicting points of view through respectful dialogue and evolve ideas that mutually cater to the artist's intuitive vision and satisfy the engineer's need for utility, rigor, and measurability of outcome. This chapter is not about interaction design, nor an exposition in art practice. It is about how disparate fields could come together to create novel forms of interactive machines beyond the mundane and the commercial utility.

In a way, this chapter is about answering Grant Kester's question (G. Kester, 1985), "How do we form collective or communal identities without scapegoating those who are excluded from them?" The ensuing dialogue between the artist and the engineer is an insight into the creative creation process behind an emerging machine aesthetic – robotic art – without being exclusive or overly academic about the underlying process. In Conversation Pieces, Kester offers examples of the avant-garde, the dialogical art – which occurs outside the traditional circles of academia and the art critics (G. H. Kester, 2004). He questions the need for explanation when the work *communicates* itself.

ROBOTIC ART

The path to robotic art is paved through the still images of sculpture, the madness of the automata,

the evolution of technology, cybernetics and the mixing of science and art. And as Jack Burnham would put it, "regardless of the increased calculating speeds of our automata, the goals of logic could only be life—existence as we know it. In the end, art may be simply the blueprint by which we seek such wisdom" (Burnham, 1969)

Roboticist/Engineer: Let us begin by defining Robotic Art.

Artist: Robotic art is a genre that incorporates engineering and programming to generate an aesthetic and an operational outcome. It is not generally characterized by its sophistication nor by any functional outcome but rather doing things with machines that are visually surprising and operationally seductive. Artists have used a wide variety of approaches. The machines of Jean Tinguely are a precursor. There are the dangerous and destructive robots from Survival Research Lab, Leonel Moura's small drawing robots, Ken Rinaldo's bio-robots driven by Siamese Fighting Fish (Figure 43.1), Anouk Wipprecht's wearable robots (Figure 43.2) and the giant soft pneumatic robots

Figure 43.1   Ken Rinaldo, Augmented Fish Reality (Photo: Ken Rinaldo)

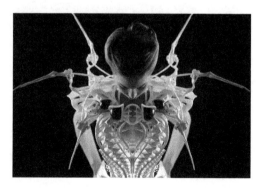

Figure 43.2   Anouk Wipprecht, Spider Dress (Photo: Jason Perry)

engineered by Chico MacMurtie for his Border Crossings project (Figure 43.3) – just to mention a few. What these works lack in sophisticated research and robustness is made up for in social, political, and aesthetic impact. Other artists have conceptually elevated ideas of malfunctioning and misbehaving machines and machines doing things they should not.

R: I have been formally trained as an engineer, specifically a mechanical engineer practising my craft now for over two decades. Over that time, particularly since working with you, I have been challenged to re-consider my primary tools, methods, and approaches. I now see myself more as a researcher working at the intersection of several disciplines, including robotics, psychology, and the arts, exploring the various nuances of machines interacting with humans. How do you characterize your practice?

A: I do not necessarily categorize myself as a robotics artist. My history is as a performance artist. However, I do use prosthetics and robotics to create alternative kinds of performance possibilities.

Although I am interested and have a general knowledge of state-of-the-art technology, it is not robotics in itself that is important but rather its interaction with the body. And how it will be increasingly meaningless to distinguish between bodies and machines. And how we are now transitioning from Marvin Minsky's experience of Telepresence (Minsky, 1980) to Susumu Tachi's more high-fidelity Tele-existence (Tachi, 2015). We literally become end-effectors for machines elsewhere, as machines were end-effectors for us.

Most of my machine attachments and walking robots have been either self-funded or completed within a limited time and with limited expertise and funding. And they have been completed with the assistance and goodwill of engineers and programmers. They are more aesthetic gestures rather than the outcome of methodical research.

It is easy to have an idea. But, as a performance artist, what is essential is to actualize the idea, personally experience it, and have something meaningful to say after that. The action authenticates the idea and makes it meaningful. And you have to accept the physical consequences of your ideas. Performing, for example, within the task envelope of an industrial robot can be risky. What makes all this of interest to an audience is the unexpected relationship and interfaces that occur between the body and the robot. And for the possibility of remote interaction.

Figure 43.3   Chico MacMurtrie/A.R.W., Performance view of Border Crossers. U.S.–Mexico border at Naco, Arizona/Naco, Sonora, 2021 (Photo: Daniel Nunez Salinas)

PERFORMANCES AND INTERACTIONS, METHODS AND STRUCTURES

R: I find it helpful to categorize interactions into three types, private, local, and remote. I would define the first type as an engineering development interaction that involves developing the concept, hardware, and software – an interaction between the artist, engineer, and the robot. The second type generally relates to a situated interaction between the robot and an audience. Finally, the third is an interaction vicariously experienced through intervening systems such as telepresence, virtual reality, or web-based by a remote audience. Each entails approaching the question of Human–Machine Communication through different technical and methodological lenses. Do you think about these interactions separately and craft them carefully, or are they more unstructured and ad-hoc?

A: The performances and projects are certainly structured, but they are not necessarily scripted as such. For example, *StickMan* (Stelarc, 2017) (Figure 43.4) is a six-degree-of-freedom, a minimal but full-body exoskeleton that algorithmically animates the body for a five-hour continuous performance. A kind of wearable robot that generates the body's choreography. The body is performing involuntarily, but it has one leg to balance and pivot on. It can swivel around and modify its shadow and modulate its video feedback. It is simultaneously a possessed and performing body. In a more recent iteration of this installation, we engineered a *miniStickMan* that allows visitors to the gallery to bend the limbs in any sequence, press play and insert their choreography into the performance—a kind of electronic voodoo.

So, of course, how you frame the performance and how you structure the interaction between the body and the technology, and whether the audience is local or remote indeed constitute all of the concerns. So these are conceptually and technically intrinsically connected.

R: As an engineer, I approach every project systematically with clearly articulated goals, deliverables, and a well laid out path from the beginning to the end. However, working with you, I had to embrace spontaneity and acknowledge that some outcomes might not be defined well – at least in the beginning (somewhat akin to the practice-led approach in creative art research (Smith, 2009)). This is not to say that we did not have a structured approach to our joint work – you did define structures, sometimes implied. What guides you in creating these frameworks?

A: It depends on the limitations, the constraints of technology, and the possibilities of the sensor system and circuitry you are incorporating. It has to do with the particular parameters of the project. What is seductive about technology is that it generates new possibilities, unexpected bits of information, new kinds of imagery and ways in which you can operate and perform differently. For the artist, for a performance artist, these ideas need to be authenticated by the outcomes. It is not about simplistically illustrating an idea but rather, in performing

Figure 43.4   Stelarc, StickMan (Photographer: Toni Wilkinson)

the action, you authenticate the idea. You make the idea meaningful. Meaningful in a conceptual and aesthetic sense, not so much in a utilitarian sense. As an artist, you generally do not have the funding nor the team of researchers to develop the vision in all its possibilities. Realistically, these projects are more about generating affect and impact with aesthetic gestures rather than methodically doing focused research.

AESTHETICS – A METHODOLOGICAL COUNTERPOINT TO RESEARCH

R: Systematic and academic research is central to my work. The fact that this chapter is deliberately transgressing the norms of academic writing is somewhat unsettling from my perspective and for the communities I belong. I appreciate that, as an artist, your approach to research is distinctly different. Do you consider academic research as part of your practice? Is that useful to you as an artist?

A: Well, it could be but, it does not guarantee meaningful artwork. When I started using industrial robot arms in the early 1990s I did not engineer the robot nor develop its software system. What was seductive about these six-degree-of-freedom arms was the ability to precisely program a combination of robot coordinates, linear coordinates and tool center point motions. By attaching a video camera to the end of the robot arm, what was generated were cinematically smooth pans, tilts, zooms, and continuous rotations as the robot gyrated around me. The live video was projected on a large screen above or beside me. The body had tilt sensors on its arms and legs that allowed it to be the live video switcher and mixer. So, the role of the artist is to hack and creatively re-imagine how some of this technology is used. The artist is not always in the position nor possesses the capabilities to do this research from

scratch but opportunistically appropriates what is available to generate these unexpected outcomes.

An interesting artwork is not authenticated by the number of years you do research on it or how reductive or focused that research is. Or whether it has a practical use. Or, for that matter, how sophisticated the robot is. Some of the best robot art results from using simple mechanisms or kit robots modified and re-purposed to do interesting actions. The *Prosthetic Head* was used as a research platform to explore notions of intelligent agents. Giving this embodied conversational agent a robotic presence in the form of the *Articulated Head* came about through the realization that an intelligent agent needed to be both embodied and embedded in the world. That an intelligent agent was not simply a software program but one that had to have a physical presence. And having such capabilities as auditory localization and vision tracking, it could more appropriately respond to its interlocutors.

R: The *Articulated Head* (Stelarc, Herath, & Kroos, 2010) was one of the critical robotic art projects we collaborated on and one of the important works related to Human–Machine Interaction. The installation was originally conceived as a kinetic sculpture. However, the research findings substantially impacted how the installation evolved over the years to become a fully autonomous interactive agent that demonstrated emergent behavior through sensory stimuli. In the late 2000s we conducted a series of Human–Robot user studies with the Articulated Head in an interactive robotic art context. During these experiments, we found that the robot's attention system (Kroos, Herath, & Stelarc, 2011), developed through funded research, significantly contributed to the robot's perceived sense of aliveness and agency compared to the robot operating randomly. I would argue this to be an example of the utility of formal, systematic research embedded in the development of robotic art – a counterpoint to intuition.

A: All that is very interesting. But having said that, I have yet to exhibit the *Articulated Head* in an art gallery. There is no guarantee that just because it is a more sophisticated system, it is a more interesting artwork. Put it another way, the attention system for the *Articulated Head* required additional sensors and a computational system to run it. Although that resulted in additional possibilities, it also created new constraints. More complex systems can be problematic. I always argue that you do not want artists doing bad research and scientists making bad art. You want to create an artwork that is meaningful in ways other than its scientific rigor.

And it does not have to have a utilitarian purpose. You do not have to measure its impact. I really dislike the idea of getting people to fill in questionnaires about their interaction with an artwork. Art is not an object of knowledge. Whereas this might be a critical evaluation process for researchers and social scientists, it has nothing to do with the art installation, and in fact can detract from its artistic effect. Art and scientific pursuits have different methodologies. They are two different domains of operation, with one concerned with accumulating information and the other concerned with aesthetic impact. What is challenging using robots in art is how you can generate a sense of aliveness in purely mechanical systems.

So yes, particular in-depth research might contribute to the work of art, but it is a conundrum for me to justify one to the other. Science should not be required to authenticate artistic practice. Art is not necessarily about technical sophistication. When I was performing with my Third Hand in Japan, my artist friends would remind me of the Japanese saying, "high tech, low art".

R: That is a valid point, and one of the questions that arise from this is that aesthetics is highly personal. How do you reconcile subjectivity in your work? As an engineer, I believe there still should be some objective benchmarking, a baseline for what is aesthetically acceptable in a given context.

A: Well, what is aesthetically acceptable is not only a subjective consideration but also one of the historical zeitgeists. In my case, the aesthetics are generated by the particular project or the performance. The performances generate rather than illustrate a particular kind of aesthetic. For example, when I performed using my third hand, I amplified my body signals and sounds, directing laser beams via optic fiber cables from my eyes. Those visual and acoustical elements of internal bodily functions, the third-hand operation, scribbling images by controlling eye muscles are the formal elements that generate the aesthetics.

In the *Propel* performance (Stelarc, 2016) (Figure 43.5), my body was attached to the end of the industrial robot arm, and we could precisely program the position orientation, velocity and trajectory of the body for the duration of the performance, so it was a choreography of machine musculature and human metabolism. The body and the robot were coupled as one performative system. The aesthetics resulted from the six-degree-of-freedom motion of the industrial robot and the sounds generated by the robot motors.

Figure 43.5   Stelarc, Propel (Photographer: Steven Alyian)

FAILURE AS A METHOD

R: Where do these ideas come from? From a scientist's point of view, we have an initial hypothesis around what we want to explore, and there is a body of knowledge from which we can draw upon. But famously, you have been quoted as saying that you have made a career out of failure. When working with you, there was always room for and the encouragement to, making errors – uneasy as an engineer. Still, some of the errors we made were illuminating and insightful and led to surprisingly new aesthetic possibilities. For example, the *Articulated Head* (Stelarc et al., 2010) installation (a new version developed in 2021 is depicted in Figure 43.6) comes to mind again. While the interactive robot worked as expected in our laboratory settings, it failed miserably (technically) during its first public appearance at a large gathering. Yet, while disappointing at a technical level, the installation still generated interest and discussion.

A: **Well, we must distinguish between technical glitches or system malfunctions and catastrophic failures. For example, in the case of the *Articulated Head*, when it failed to operate as expected during its premiere, it was an unexpected technical and interactive situation that we did not anticipate**

Figure 43.6 Stelarc, Herath and Kroos, Articulated Head 2.0 (Photographer: Byron Carr)

with such a large audience. And we learnt from it. And yes, you are correct that it did not undermine the premise and the presence of the artwork itself. The issue of failure, though, is a more profound and philosophical one. And well, I can argue that I have made a career out of being a failure in the sense that what I imagine can never be fully realized. I think it is unhelpful to think of the work of art in the context of it being a success and failure. Or even to argue that an artwork is partly successful or partly a failure. If art happens in the space and slippage between intentionality and actuality, then the unexpected, the accidental, is an essential aspect of the process of making art. Almost all these projects, from the *Third Hand* to the *Extended Arm* to *Exoskeleton*, the six-legged walking robot, to the *Articulated Head*, have been realized technically merely in an adequate way. They could have been much more sophisticated technical systems. Again, they are simply aesthetic gestures. If art is not of the unexpected, if art is not surprising, then it probably is not very interesting art.

R: Do you think the element of surprise you spoke of as important to art extends to human–robot interaction (in a robotic art context)?

A: **What is fascinating with our interactions with humanoid robots is that there need only be minimal cues or minimal prompts like a nod, a wink, a shake of the head, a smile or a sigh for us to project emotion and even intelligence to the robot. Underlying my interest in machines and robots is the idea of what constitutes aliveness, what minimal vocabulary of movement, of the choreography of behaviors will generate a sense of aliveness.**

The mammalian gait of the Boston Dynamic's[1] dog-like robots is seductively life-like. And its Atlas human-like bipedal robot is impressive in retaining its balance performing athletic feats. To increasingly interact with humans, these robots will not only need vision systems and obstacle avoidance sensors but will also need to be imbued with social and cultural contexts and constructs, not to mention with ethical algorithms. The Uncanny Valley (Mori, MacDorman, & Kageki, 2012) is not so much a philosophical barrier in engineering humanoid robots but rather a problem of state-of-the-art technology. Robots need not be creepy when we interact with them. And being creepy is not simply a problem with present robots; it is a problem with people too. If I am socially inept, if I am schizophrenic, then I will be a creepy person to socially interact with too. Suppose a robot speaks and acts appropriately in varying social situations and can respond to unpredictable situations. In that case, that robot can be rightly attributed to meaningful and, by its actions, intelligent behavior. Friedrich Nietzsche (Nietzsche, Ansell-Pearson, & Diethe, 2017) reminds us that the act itself is what is meaningful and that we attribute agency retroactively. And Ludwig Wittgenstein (Wittgenstein, 2010) asserts that thinking need not be located in your head. Thinking happens with the lips that you speak, with the hands that you write. Applying both these philosophical insights better prepares us for our interactions with robots. What is important is not what is within us but what happens between us. We inhabit spaces of flattened ontologies where the human is not privileged, where the human is part of a complex interaction with other bodies, robots, microbes, and digital objects.

A FINAL CONVERSATION – THE ROLE OF SCIENCE

R: Do you see technology just as a tool?

A: As technology is increasingly attached, interfaced, and even incorporated into the body, it cannot be simply regarded as something other. Something that can be used and then discarded. Technology has transformed the way we operate and the way we think. What it means to be human has been determined by our artifacts, machines, instruments, and computational systems. We should discard the nostalgia for a purely biological body. Technology is no longer a Heideggerian "ready-to-hand," nor merely a McLuhanesque extension (McLuhan, 1994) to the body. I much prefer McLuhan's more seductive idea that technology is rather the external organs of the body. Machines, instruments, and computational systems are now part of the human life-support system. Technology is all-pervasive and invasive. What the pandemic (Coronavirus disease 2019) has exposed is not only the existential risk of being fatally infected by viruses but rather the ontological risk of infection by our digital objects and algorithms.

R: Do you see robotic art as a potential point of convergence for the sciences and the arts?

A: It can indeed become a point of convergence for the arts and sciences because of its interdisciplinarity. Human-machine interaction is of existential and ontological interest to artists. And, of course, hybrid human-machine systems and human–computer interfaces are serious research at universities. There is also an ever-increasing interest in augmenting the human body with supernumerary limbs. Wearable robotics and exoskeletons animate paralyzed bodies and amplify human capabilities. And there is a fascination with autonomous humanoid robots by both artists and engineers, but for very different reasons. These areas of commonality incorporate design, ergonomics, engineering, electronics, and programming. They require interdisciplinary teams, which can include artists. Alternatively, for an artist using robotics to actualize an idea, there is a necessity to incorporate and call upon the expertise of engineers, programmers, and scientists.

R: As we end our conversation, if I could summarize, our key message has been the importance of dialogue and the openness to explore beyond one's own circumscribed disciplinary boundaries and orthodoxies. Robotic art happens when technology meets the uncanny, the unsuccessful, the unexpected. The machine communicates not utility but surprise, intrigue, and politics. The academic urge for reductive research is perhaps counter-intuitive when the avant-garde is the expectation. However, the dialectical approach suggested in this chapter has, on multiple occasions, helped our research and work in bringing together artists and roboticists to work on projects of mutual benefit. For example, in 2017, I collaborated with an Australian indigenous choreographer and another female artist to explore combining ancient cultural practices with robotic technologies – a culturally and politically highly charged space to explore. However, we made valuable interventions through respectful dialogue after only a day of workshopping (Jeon, Fiebrink, Edmonds, & Herath, 2019) (Figure 43.7).

A: That was certainly an interesting collaboration and intervention. A dilemma, of course, is that the arts are often seen as a kind of soft research that does not require any particular expertise or technical skill and that anyone can indulge in making art. Artistic practice is just as much a profession as is scientific research. To assert that both Art and Science are creative practices, and both involve research is only meaningful in a very general sense.

We should be more discerning in the way we use language. Again, they are very different methodologies. Art generates ideas rather than illustrating them. Art, as it once was, is no longer about mere representation. Artists are incorporating sensor, robotic, and computational systems to construct interactive installations and performative outcomes that interrogate issues of embodiment, autonomy, agency, and identity in ways that were not possible previously. What

Figure 43.7 Vicki Van Hout, Marian Abboud and Herath, workshopping ideas with Baxter the robot (Photographer: Damith Herath)

truly connects artists with scientists is technology. The role of science in the arts is problematic if science is seen as in any way authenticating arts practice. Science is an activity that produces knowledge and enables calculation and prediction. Engineering uses scientific principles to design and construct machines for utilitarian purposes. Art does not produce knowledge in the scientific sense, nor does it construct useful mechanisms. Art practice is not a utilitarian activity but rather expresses what cannot be calculated, what cannot be described but rather what should be experienced. Art is not about accumulating information but rather about expressing affect. Rather than contradict, art and science should be seen as complementing each other, and both are indicative of what it means to be human.

NOTE

1 www.bostondynamics.com/

REFERENCES

Burnham, J. (1969). Beyond modern sculpture.

Capek, K. (2004). *RUR (Rossum's universal robots)*. Penguin.

Corke, P. (2017). *Robotics, vision and control: Fundamental algorithms in MATLAB® Second, Completely Revised* (Vol. 118). Springer.

Dissanayake, E. (2001). *Homo aestheticus: Where art comes from and why*. University of Washington Press.

Honour, H., & Fleming, J. (2005). *A world history of art*. Laurence King Publishing.

Jeon, M., Fiebrink, R., Edmonds, E. A., & Herath, D. (2019). From rituals to magic: Interactive art and HCI of the past, present, and future. *International Journal of Human-Computer Studies, 131*, 108–119. doi:https://doi.org/10.1016/j.ijhcs.2019.06.005

Kester, G. (1985). Conversation pieces: The role of dialogue in socially-engaged art. In *Theory in contemporary art since*, 76-100. John Wiley & Sons

Kester, G. H. (2004). *Conversation pieces: Community and communication in modern art*. Univ of California Press.

Kroos, C., Herath, D. C., & Stelarc. (2011). Evoking agency: Attention model and behaviour control in a robotic art installation. In *Leonardo*. MIT Press.

Laumond, J.-P. (2016). Robotics: Hephaestus does it again. In *Robots and Art* (pp. 67–86): Springer.

McLuhan, M. (1994). *Understanding media: The extensions of man*. MIT Press.

Merriam-Webster. (2021). Robot. Retrieved from www.merriam-webster.com/dictionary/robot

Minsky, M. (1980). Telepresence. Retrieved from https://web.media.mit.edu/~minsky/papers/Telepresence.html

Mori, M., MacDorman, K. F., & Kageki, N. (2012). The uncanny valley [From the Field]. *Robotics & Automation Magazine*, IEEE, 19(2), 98–100. doi:10.1109/MRA.2012.2192811

Nietzsche, F., Ansell-Pearson, K., & Diethe, C. (2017). *Nietzsche: On the genealogy of morality and other writings*. Cambridge University Press.

Ogden, R. M. (1933). A definition of aesthetics. *The Philosophical Review, 42*(5), 500-510.

Smith, H. (2009). *Practice-led research, research-led practice in the creative arts*. Edinburgh University Press.

Stelarc. (2016). Propel: Body on Robot Arm. (A performance where the body's trajectory, velocity and position/orientation in space was choreographed by a 6 degree-of-freedom industrial robot arm operating within a 3m diameter task envelope. The choreography generates rhythm by repetition by intermittently looping sequences of motion.). Perth: DeMonstrable, Autronics, Lawrence Wilson Gallery.

Stelarc. (2017). StickMan. (StickMan is a minimal but full-body exoskeleton, that algorithmically actuates the artist with six degrees-of-freedom. Sixty-four possible combinations of gestures are generated. Sensors on StickMan generate sounds that augment the pneumatic noise and register the limb movements. A ring of speakers circulates the sounds, immersing the audience.) Perth: Chrissie Parrot Arts for the Daedalus Project.

Stelarc, Herath, D. C., & Kroos, C. (2010). Articulated Head. Sydney: New Interfaces for Musical Expression++.

Stephens, E., & Heffernan, T. (2016). We have always been robots: The history of robots and art. In *Robots and Art* (pp. 29–45), Springer.

Tachi, S. (2015). Telexistence. In G. Brunnett, S. Coquillart, R. van Liere, G. Welch, & L. Váša (Eds.), *Virtual Realities: International Dagstuhl Seminar, Dagstuhl Castle, Germany, June 9–14, 2013, Revised Selected Papers* (pp. 229–259). Springer International Publishing.

Weitz, M. (1956). The role of theory in aesthetics. *The Journal of Aesthetics and Art Criticism, 15*(1), 27–35.

Wittgenstein, L. (2010). *Philosophical investigations*. John Wiley & Sons.

44

Labor, Automation, and Human–Machine Communication

Julian Posada, Gemma Newlands,
and Milagros Miceli

INTRODUCTION

In 1779, an English weaver called Ned Ludd allegedly smashed two stocking frames in a fit of rage. Decades later, *the Luddites*, an artisan movement, targeted new industrial machinery fearing their replacement and the impoverishment of their living conditions (Smith, 2021). Since the industrial revolution, automation anxiety has occurred in waves as new technologies threaten to replace workers and "disrupt" labor markets. Research has indeed shown that people overwhelmingly fear widescale job displacement by robots and other machines, even if they do not perceive their own occupations to be susceptible (Taipale & Fortunati, 2018). Yet, the effect of emerging technologies on labor is complex. While emerging technologies continue to displace workers and reshape both labor markets and labor processes, in some cases, they can lead to economic expansion and the creation of new jobs (Acemoglu & Restrepo, 2019).

Although often simplistic, antagonistic, or even affectionate, workers have always developed communicative relationships with the machines they use at work, as well as with those used to control them. An artisan's tools, for instance, or a chef's knives, are often conceptualized as an extension of the self in an organizational setting; they are spoken to lovingly and cared for, or perhaps shouted at in annoyance when something goes wrong. As the prominent "Computers Are Social Actors" (CASA) paradigm relates, even early computing technologies were imbued with a similar social agency and treated mindlessly as either a team-mate or an adversary (Nass & Moon, 2000). However, imbued with more complex communicative affordances, contemporary Artificial Intelligence (AI) based technologies offer more active and social communication forms vis-à-vis their human counterparts (Fox & McEwan, 2017). AI both facilitates and automates forms of communication that have historically been limited only to human interactants (Guzman & Lewis, 2020).

The ways that intelligent technologies are interpreted are important for creating meaning and expectations (Gibbs et al., 2021). As Guzman (2018) explains, "Human-machine communication is the creation of meaning among humans and machines" (p. 17). Yet, despite its more than half a century of development as a field of inquiry, AI has remained challenging to define. In this chapter, our focus will be on Machine Learning (ML) based technologies that learn from data interpretation, which are the main applications in the AI-as-a-Service (AIaaS) sector (Newlands, 2021b). Moreover, although there is a panoply of embodied workplace robots, most AI applications in the workplace are predominantly disembodied and communicative, such as chatbots, workforce management tools, or HR systems (Guzman, 2020).

With some exceptions, such as Gibbs et al.'s (2021) work on automated journalism, research around HMC in organizations or at work has remained scarce. It is crucial to explore the interplay of AI, HMC, and work since AI applications can transform organizations (Fortunati & Edwards, 2021). The replacement of decision-making functions also means that AI applications are often viewed more as social agents than as tools (Banks & de Graaf, 2020; Jarrahi et al., 2021). With the current implementation of AI applications in the workplace, we now observe what Shestakofsky (2017) calls "human-software complementarity" in the human labor that supports algorithms and helps the adaptation to these systems by their users. Since AI systems are continuously produced and reproduced through human actions at work, there is a blurring of boundaries between the human and machinic elements (Edwards et al., 2019).

In this chapter, we therefore explore and describe three moments in the relationship between workers and AI, namely *human-to-machine communication* in AI development with a special focus on the production of training data, *human-with-machine communication* in processes of AI customization, and *machine-to-human communication* in AI deployment at the workplace. As Fortunati and Edwards (2020) explain, "people have passed from acceptance of talking to machines to talking with machines" (p. 12). Accordingly, the directionality and hierarchy of communication between the human worker and the AI is highly dependent on the particular phase of the AI's development. Whereas workers in the generative, developmental phase far more often are speaking to the machine, imbuing it with communicative capacity and a voice, workers in the later stages become audiences to a top-down machinic voice. We thus focus on the meaning-making processes present at each stage to argue that the three communicative instances are complementary and the boundaries between them are blurry. As we will argue in the next section, meaning is created in the interaction of workers and algorithmic models in training, customization, and deployment instances.

This extended approach also allows a view into the power dynamics at the core of meaning-making processes between humans and AI at work. As Wiener (1950) explained, the significance of machines for society is how they shape issues of communication and control. Workers' autonomy, for instance, often depends on how much they can understand and communicate with AI systems at work (Jarrahi et al., 2021). As the developing

HMC literature has shown, there is a shifting degree of control imbued into technologies, ranging from low to high (Malone, 2018). The way that people conceptualize technologies also shapes how they make sense of and interact with them. For instance, the more powerful technologies become, in relation to the individuals interacting with them, the more they get anthropomorphized (Wajcman, 2017). Since individual and communal voices are heard distinctively, we must increasingly look at questions of how humans should act toward machines and how machines should in turn act toward humans (Guzman & Lewis, 2020). In this sense, we argue that the aspect of polyvocal communication remains crucial in addressing some of the social issues and power asymmetries in the relationship of workers and AI systems.

HUMAN-TO-MACHINE COMMUNICATION IN AI DEVELOPMENT

The first stage in the development of ML-based AI systems is producing datasets that will constitute the backbone of these technologies. In the introduction to the edited collection *Raw Data is an Oxymoron*, Gitelman and Jackson (2013) argue that data is never "raw" and always "cooked"; data is an abstraction of reality, and social and power relations condition the collection and interpretation of data (D'Ignazio & Klein, 2020). This process of "datafication" involves the extraction, transformation, and interpretation of data from individuals, social relations, and natural phenomena (Mejias & Couldry, 2019).

In this chapter, we adopt a relational conceptualization of data as the product of meaning making. Data production for ML involves vast amounts of collaboration between humans, organizations, and technologies, and such collaboration is always shaped by power differentials (Miceli et al., 2020, 2022). In this context, communication often takes the form of negotiation around the meanings that are ascribed to data. That is, how each data point is interpreted in relation to a specific ML system, whose data is more profitable for marketing purposes, or what can a specific algorithmic model learn from what data.

To explore processes of AI development, we therefore focus on the *human-to-machine communication* that occurs in workplaces with the objective of producing data to train ML systems. This data can be communicated to ML systems, for example, via peripheral devices in the case of computers or through actuators and sensors present in other types of machines. Through input data, human workers set the tone of how ML systems make sense of the world. Later, ML systems will output predictions and classifications that carry those meanings created in the interaction with humans through data. By *human-to-machine communication* we thus refer to the meaning making involved in work practices such as collecting, curating, and labeling data as well as its subsequent use to train and validate machine learning models.

Data work, namely the labor that goes into producing and maintaining datasets for AI (Miceli et al., 2022), is carried out by AI developers, domain experts, outsourcing workers, and users of AI technologies. For example, in cases where AI has been deployed in healthcare, nurses, medical secretaries, and doctors input patient data into datasets that are ultimately fed into models (Møller et al., 2020). Users also participate by labeling data, for instance, through CAPTCHA tests where they transcribe text or select images according to predetermined labels (Justie, 2021). Most companies and research institutions, however, outsource the labor and time-intensive labeling process to workers worldwide through business process outsourcing (BPO) companies (Miceli et al., 2020) and digital labor platforms (Casilli & Posada, 2019; Newlands & Lutz, 2021). These forms of outsourcing data work involve low-paid independent contractors often located in developing countries.

BPO companies usually specialize in one type of data annotation like semantic segmentation (i.e., the marking of objects in an image) and one type of application (e.g., computer vision). Conversely, platforms dedicated to data work function entirely online. As a subset of the larger gig economy (Woodcock & Graham, 2020), platforms serve as intermediaries between workers located in different geographies, usually working from their homes, and AI developers (Casilli & Posada, 2019). Tasks in online data work include the categorization of images, text, and video, inputting data in the form of text, video, audio, or images, and providing feedback to companies on the accuracy of AI algorithms (Casilli et al., 2019). Both in platforms and BPO companies, data work for ML is shaped by power dynamics (Gibbs et al., 2021; Miceli et al., 2020, 2022). Not only do power asymmetries affect labor and services relationships but they also shape the meanings that are ascribed to data and the communicative process that takes place between workers and systems in AI development.

Data annotation for supervised learning constitutes a clear example of how power differentials shape meaning making between human workers and AI. The labels workers assign to data are instructed to them throughout hierarchical structures that leave almost no space for data annotators to exercise their own judgments and make sense of data on their own (Miceli et al., 2020). This top-down meaning imposition also embeds predefined interpretations onto datasets and, of course, on systems. As previous research has argued (Miceli & Posada, 2022), annotation instructions provided by machine learning practitioners to outsourced data annotators comprise narrow labels and include warnings that compel workers to follow orders. In this case, the influence of the most powerful actors (i.e., AI companies requesting the annotations) permeates datasets and models. Such instructions constitute a salient manifestation of the power differentials present in processes of meaning making among ML practitioners and data workers and between them and AI systems.

HUMAN-WITH-MACHINE COMMUNICATION IN AI CUSTOMIZATION

As discussed above, one of the primary mechanisms of AI adoption in work settings is through the use of third party AIaaS applications (Newlands, 2021b). However, this externalization of AI development means that after AI services have been developed, they must be adapted and customized for the specific workplace setting (Vesa & Tienari, 2020). There is always a need for extra effort and time to align human and algorithmic systems, and this is what Newlands (2021b) refers to as "AI co-production," where organizations must engage in ongoing customization and training of the AI service. Algorithmic systems do not exist outside of the organizational contexts within which they have been implemented (Kellogg et al., 2020), and the specific contexts of embedding shape the interplay between organizational actors and the AI. This, in turn, generates the communication paradigms eventually imposed on the workforce. We can observe this, for instance, through the customization of "digital employees" (Huang & Rust, 2018) where a considerable amount of human effort is involved in implementing specific AI applications into the organization and keeping them running.

Turning to a specific case, we can observe a high level of effort enacted in the customization of chatbots to match the specific needs of the workplace. Chatbots enable rich interactions with people, triggering the view that they are social entities (Wirtz et al., 2018). However, chatbots remain incapable of making sense of nuance, of meaning, and of relationships (Pantano & Prizzi, 2020). Chatbots need to be actively trained through accurate input and predefined answers, and this process of chatbot training usually involves providing the chatbot with a predefined set of example phrases, while continuously adding, changing, and removing examples to gradually shape the chatbot's "personality" (Liebrecht & van Hoojidonk, 2020).

As opposed to the initial training and development phases, the customization stage allows us to observe a greater degree of interactive communication between the human workers and the AI in a mechanism of *human-with-machine communication*. This is because, at this stage, the specific "voice" of the AI is being generated while simultaneously the "voice" of the workers is being trained in how to appropriately talk to the AI. As with call centers, where workers develop certain scripts and a firm-specific personality, AI systems such as chatbots are also trained to portray a certain type of voice, usually by mimicking specific human workers (Luo et al., 2019). Referred to as the "conversational human voice" (Kelleher & Miller, 2006), the development of a specific communication style that reflects human attributes, such as informal speech, means that there is a greater sense of dialogue and mutual shaping between the worker and the machine. This mutual dialogue, however, does not mean that humans and machines are considered equals and their relationship is devoid of a social context and power differentials. For instance, in the case of *human-with-machine communication* in Amazon warehouses, Delfanti (2021) considers this relationship extractivist in nature, a form of "machinic dispossession" in which the knowledge and behavior of workers is expropriated and incorporated into machinery.

MACHINE-TO-HUMAN COMMUNICATION IN AI DEPLOYMENT

The use of AI has become ubiquitous in many workplaces because of the perceived increase in productivity, prediction, and coordination (Kellogg et al., 2020). However, AI can also perpetuate discrimination as demonstrated in the case of AI tools that serve as a mechanism of control such as the case of Amazon warehouses (Delfanti, 2021) and data work platforms (Miceli & Posada, 2022). These forms of *machine-to-human communication* aid – but also influence – the actions of workers who are subject to algorithms in the workplace. Such algorithmic outputs are predefined by system developers and constitute, from a communication perspective, a top-bottom imposition. In this last section of the chapter, we will explore forms of machine-to-human communication through the lens of its influence over the labor process.

Labor process is a Marxian term defined as the transformation of *labor power* (i.e., the capacity – as opposed to the act – of working) into a *commodity* (i.e., a product destined to a market) following a series of *relations of production* (i.e., the relations involved in the reproduction of society) (Burawoy, 1979). Thus, labor process consists of the series of productive activities and the social relationships that surround them. The theory that has focused on the labor process looks into four different aspects of it (Thompson, 1990): the role of labor in capital accumulation, the reduction of skills (or "deskilling") in the process, managerial control, and the conflictual (or "antagonistic") relations between management and workers.

Based on this definition, the implementation of AI in the workplace does not only pursue productive outcomes. It also serves to control, transform, and intermediate the labor process. ML algorithms have transformative capabilities that influence behavior (Jarrahi et al., 2021). They are broadly opaque, often considered as a "black box" (Pasquale, 2015), and are often mistaken as neutral and naturally derivative from data. However, the development of these algorithms is strongly shaped by power relations. Those power relations manifest in the deployment of such algorithms as mechanisms of control. In this vein, Kellogg et al. (2020) identify a number of ways in which algorithms manage workers by: restricting worker agency and recommending actions to *direct* workers, recording and rating workers to *evaluate* them, and replacing or rewarding them to *discipline* the workforce.

In the public sector, for example, governments worldwide are increasingly using different types of AI in workplaces across the civil service. In their work on the use of algorithms in child maltreatment hotline screening, De-Arteaga et al. (2020) found that civil servants' behavior was influenced by the outputs of the system, even though not all workers adhered to the recommendations of the algorithm. When looking at the deployment of algorithms in the United Kingdom's welfare services, Redden et al. (2020) observed that their implementation followed neoliberal logics of austerity and displacement of risk on individual families. Thus, the guidance and predictions given by these tools were not only derived from existing data but also from political and logics defined by government agencies.

Worker evaluations by ML systems are present in many areas, but nowhere is as ubiquitous as in the on-demand gig economy. In cases such as ride-hailing, food-delivery or care work, workers' movements and activities are often tracked and evaluated in real time, based on metrics such as speed, navigation skills, or even politeness (Bucher et al., 2020;

Newlands, 2020a). In gig work, the voice of the app is usually a monologue which dictates activity and provides feedback but does not open itself up to a sense of dialogue. In this way, the app is usually conceptualized as the "boss" or the "manager" (Adams-Prassl, 2019).

AI systems can thus be used to discipline workers through *machine-to-human communication*. For instance, in the annotation platforms described in the AI development section, data workers are often expelled (or "banned") from tasks when their responses do not comply with data previously labelled by clients or when they fail to repeat previous annotations in the same way (Posada, 2022). In some cases when productivity levels are lower than expected, workers can get fired or "deactivated," which also occurs in other algorithmically mediated workplaces such as in data work platforms like Amazon Mechanical Turk, location-based gig work platforms like Uber (Bucher et al., 2020), or in supply chain warehouses managed by Amazon (De Stefano, 2020; Delfanti, 2021). Through punishment-and-reward mechanisms, AI algorithms manage workers' behavior to make them compliant with the expectations of rapidly expanding labor markets.

Technical and metricized forms of workers' evaluation, however, open up questions regarding how machines are communicating to human workers and to which extent workers can communicate back. An open question, for instance, surrounds whether non-human agents can give not only evaluations but also recognition (Laitinen, 2016). It is not possible, for instance, to develop good will or relational capacities with an algorithmic manager (Duggan et al., 2019), a concern which has important implications for how norms of communication will develop in the future between workers and AI systems (Newlands, 2022).

These examples of *machine-to-human communication* in the form of algorithmic management to guide, evaluate, and discipline workers show that AI has an increasingly important role in shaping labor processes. How AI communicates to workers is not neutral and not at all dependent exclusively on the machine's decision. It is part of hierarchical decision-making processes that involve policymakers in the case of the civil service and companies in the case of digital platforms. Instead of replacing workers altogether, AI shapes labor-power and constrains workers' agency. In this context, several forms of resistance have been observed to counteract the power of algorithms in the workplace. Examples include "gaming the system" or manipulating algorithms' inputs to generate a desired output (Newlands, 2021a), hacking tools and machines or performing *sousveillance*, as well as forms of organization,

inquiry, and reappropriation of digital tools. These organizing efforts include unionization in sectors such as new media and journalism (Cohen & De Peuter, 2020), the gig economy (Vicente, 2019), and the technology sector (Delfanti & Sharma, 2019). However, any form of resistance is reliant on a minimum level of understanding of how the system works, described by Jarrahi et al. (2021) as the development of "algorithmic competencies." Educating workers in the intricacies of how AI works could open up contestation paths for them to "talk back," allowing *machine-to-human communication* in the workplace to become a two-way street.

CONCLUSION

In this chapter, we presented three moments in the relationship between workers and artificial intelligence systems. These are the *human-to-machine communication* that involves the meaning-making process of data production for AI through data work, the *human-with-machine communication* required for the constant improvement and customization of AI, and the *machine-to-human communication* involved in the deployment of these systems in the workplace and the direction, evaluation, and discipline of workers. We argued that these moments are complementary, and it is often difficult to establish clear boundaries between them. For example, an outsourced data worker annotating image data through a platform can simultaneously be directed by the algorithmic manager and, through its interaction with it, improve its accuracy. Thus, the worker would be interacting with AI in the three above-mentioned forms of communication simultaneously.

The three moments outlined in this chapter show a conflictual relationship between worker and machine since communication between workers and AI not only serves to provide direction but also to discipline the workforce. However, these forms of communication are also related to instances of subversion, resistance, and co-creation when workers are instead placed at the forefront of the meaning-making process. Understanding how these interactions occur in different contexts, notably from the perspective of workers, is fundamental when the benefits of artificial intelligence for society come into question. We therefore propose these three moments of human–machine communication in the workplace as a framework for future research in labor and HMC that delves into the nature of these interconnected relations in specific contexts.

Because human–machine communication occurs within social settings, a fundamental aspect of the three moments we describe in this chapter is the power relations enacted in the communication between workers, machines, and other actors involved in the labor process, notably management. Machines are never built autonomously, not even artificial intelligence. Human decision-making is present since the inception of the technology and, especially, in its deployment, even in models using deep neural networks challenging to scrutinize by developers. Thus, identifying the different voices that participate in meaning-making between workers and AI and making explicit which ones are heard more than others is crucial. This approach could point at moments when "meaning-making" becomes "meaning-imposition" and help to open contestation paths for workers to *talk back* and question data, systems, and algorithmic outputs.

ACKNOWLEDGEMENTS

This research was funded by the International Development Research Centre of Canada, the German Federal Ministry of Education and Research (BMBF, project Nr. 16DII113), and the Norwegian Research Council within the FRIPRO TOPPFORSK (275347) project "Future Ways of Working in the Digital Economy."

REFERENCES

Acemoglu, D., & Restrepo, P. (2019). Automation and new tasks: How technology displaces and reinstates labor. *Journal of Economic Perspectives*, *33*(2), 3–30.

Adams-Prassl, J. (2019). What if your boss was an algorithm? The rise of artificial intelligence at work. *Comparative Labor Law & Policy Journal*, *41*(1), 123.

Banks, J., & de Graaf, M. (2020). Toward an agent-agnostic transmission model: Synthesizing anthropocentric and technocentric paradigms in communication. *Human Machine Communication*, *1*, 19–36.

Bucher, E., Fieseler, C., Lutz, C., & Newlands, G. (2020). Shaping emotional labor practices in the sharing economy. In Maurer, I., Mair, J. and Oberg, A. (Eds.) *Theorizing the sharing economy: Variety and trajectories of new forms of organizing* (Research in the Sociology of Organizations, Vol. 66).

Burawoy, M. (1979). *Manufacturing consent. Changes in the labor process under monopoly capitalism.* University of Chicago Press.

Casilli, A. A., & Posada, J. (2019). The platformisation of labor and society. In M. Graham & W. H. Dutton (Eds.), *Society and the internet* (Vol. 2). Oxford University Press.

Casilli, A. A., Tubaro, P., Le Ludec, C., Coville, M., Besenval, M., Mouhtare, T., & Wahal, E. (2019). *Le Micro-Travail en France. Derrière l'automatisation de nouvelles précarités au travail?* Projet DiPLab.

Cohen, N. S. & De Peuter, G. (2020). *New Media Unions: Organizing Digital Journalists*. Routlege.

D'Ignazio, C., & Klein, L. F. (2020). *Data feminism*. MIT Press.

De-Arteaga, M., Fogliato, R., & Chouldechova, A. (2020). A case for humans-in-the-loop: Decisions in the presence of erroneous algorithmic scores. *Proceedings of the 2020 CHI Conference on Human Factors in Computing Systems*, 1–12.

De Stefano, V. (2020). Algorithmic Bosses and How to Tame Them. Ethics in Context.

Delfanti, A. (2021). Machinic dispossession and augmented despotism: Digital work in an Amazon warehouse. *New Media & Society*, *23*(1), 39–55.

Delfanti, A., & Sharma, S. (Eds.). (2019). Log out! The platform economy and worker resistance. *Notes from Below*, *8*.

Duggan, J, Sherman, U, Carbery, R, et al. (2019). Algorithmic management and app-work in the gig economy: A research agenda for employment relations and HRM. *Human Resource Management Journal 30*(1), 114–132.

Edwards, A., Edwards, C., Westerman, D., & Spence, P. R. (2019). Initial expectations, interactions, and beyond with social robots. *Computers in Human Behavior*, *90*, 308–314.

Fortunati, L., & Edwards, A. P. (2021). Moving ahead with human-machine communication. *Human-Machine Communication*, *2*(1), 1–18.

Fox, J., & McEwan, B. (2017). Distinguishing technologies for social interaction: The perceived social affordances of communication channels scale. *Communication Monographs*, *84*(3), 298–318.

Gibbs, J. L., Kirkwood, G. L., Fang, C., & Wilkenfeld, J. N. (2021). Negotiating agency and control: Theorizing human-machine communication from a structurational perspective. *Human-Machine Communication*, *2*(1), 153–171.

Gitelman, L., & Jackson, V. (2013). Introduction. In: L. Gitelman (ed.) (2013). *"Raw data" is an oxymoron*. MIT Press.

Guzman, A. L. (Ed.). (2018). *Human-machine communication: Rethinking communication, technology, and ourselves*. Peter Lang.

Guzman, A. L. (2020). Ontological boundaries between humans and computers and the implications for human-machine communication. *Human-Machine Communication, 1*(1), 37–54.

Guzman, A. L., & Lewis, S. C. (2020). Artificial intelligence and communication: A human–machine communication research agenda. *New Media & Society, 22*(1), 70–86.

Huang, M. H., & Rust, R. T. (2018). Artificial intelligence in service. *Journal of Service Research, 21*(2), 155–172.

Jarrahi, M. H., Newlands, G., Lee, M. K., Wolf, C. T., Kinder, E., & Sutherland, W. (2021). Algorithmic management in a work context. *Big Data & Society, 8*(2), 20539517211020332.

Justie, B. (2021). Little history of CAPTCHA. *Internet Histories, 5*(1), 30–47. https://doi.org/10.1080/24701475.2020.1831197

Kelleher, T., & Miller, B. M. (2006). Organizational blogs and the human voice: Relational strategies and relational outcomes. *Journal of Computer-Mediated Communication, 11*(2), 395–414.

Kellogg, K. C., Valentine, M. A., & Christin, A. (2020). Algorithms at work: The new contested terrain of control. *Academy of Management Annals, 14*(1), 366–410.

Laitinen, A. (2016). Robots and human sociality: Normative expectations, the need for recognition, and the social bases of self-esteem. In Seibt, J., Nørskov, M., & Schack Andersen, S. (Eds), *What social robots can and should do.* IOS Press, 313–331.

Liebrecht, C., & van Hooijdonk, C. (2020). Creating humanlike chatbots: What chatbot developers could learn from webcare employees in adopting a conversational human voice. In *International Workshop on Chatbot Research and Design* (pp. 51–64). Springer.

Luo, X., Tong, S., Fang, Z., & Qu, Z. (2019). Frontiers: Machines vs. humans: The impact of artificial intelligence chatbot disclosure on customer purchases. *Marketing Science, 38*(6), 937–947.

Malone, T. W. (2018). *Superminds: The surprising power of people and computers thinking together.* Little, Brown, and Company.

Mejias, U. A., & Couldry, N. (2019). Datafication. *Internet Policy Review, 8*(4), 1–10.

Miceli, M., Posada, J. & Yang, T. (2022). Studying up machine learning data: Why talk about bias when we mean power? *Proceedings of the ACM on Human-Computer Interaction, 6 (GROUP)*, 1–14. https://doi.org/10.1145/3492853

Miceli, M., & Posada, J. (2022). The Data-Production Dispositif. *Proceedings of the ACM on Human-Computer Interaction, 6*(CSCW2)

Miceli, M., Schuessler, M., & Yang, T. (2020). Between subjectivity and imposition. *Proceedings of the ACM on Human-Computer Interaction, 4*(CSCW2), 1–25.

Miceli, M., Yang, T., Alvarado Garcia, A., Posada, J., Wang, S. M., Pohl, M., & Hanna, A. (2022).

Documenting Data Production Processes: A Participatory Approach for Data Work. *Proceedings of the ACM on Human-Computer Interaction, 6*(CSCW2)

Møller, N. H., Bossen, C., Pine, K. H., Nielsen, T. R., & Neff, G. (2020). Who does the work of data? *Interactions, 27*(3), 52–55. https://doi.org/10.1145/3386389

Nass, C., & Moon, Y. (2000). Machines and mindlessness: Social responses to computers. *Journal of Social Issues, 56*(1), 81–103.

Newlands, G. (2021a). Algorithmic surveillance in the gig economy: The organization of work through Lefebvrian conceived space. *Organization Studies, 42*(5), 719–737.

Newlands, G. (2021b). Lifting the curtain: Strategic visibility of human labour in AI-as-a-Service. *Big Data & Society, 8*(1), 20539517211016026.

Newlands, G. (2022). Anthropotropism: Searching for recognition in the Scandinavian gig economy. *Sociology.*

Newlands, G., & Lutz, C. (2021). Crowdwork and the mobile underclass: Barriers to participation in India and the United States of America. *New Media & Society, 23*(6), 1341–1361.

Pantano, E., & Pizzi, G. (2020). Forecasting artificial intelligence on online customer assistance: Evidence from chatbot patents analysis. *Journal of Retailing and Consumer Services, 55*, 1–9.

Pasquale, F. (2015). *The Black Box Society: The Secret Algorithms That Control Money and Information.* Harvard University Press. https://doi.org/10.4159/harvard.9780674736061

Posada, J. (2022). Embedded Reproduction in Platform Data Work. *Information, Communication & Society, 25*(6), 816–834

Redden, J., Dencik, L., & Warne, H. (2020). Datafied child welfare services: unpacking politics, economics and power. *Policy Studies, 41*(5), 507–526. https://doi.org/10.1080/01442872.2020.1724928

Shestakofsky, B. (2017). Working algorithms: Software automation and the future of work. *Work and Occupations 44*(4), 376–423.

Smith, D. (2021). Perhaps Ned Ludd had a point? *AI & SOCIETY.* https://doi.org/10.1007/s00146-021-01172-6

Taipale, S., & Fortunati, L. (2018). Communicating with machines: Robots as the next new media. *Human-machine communication: rethinking communication, technology, and ourselves.* Peter Lang, 201–220.

Thompson, P. (1990). Crawling from the wreckage: The labour process and the politics of production. In D. Knights & H. Willmott (Eds.), *Labour process theory* (pp. 95–124). Macmillan Press.

Vesa, M, & Tienari, J. (2020). Artificial intelligence and rationalized unaccountability: Ideology of the elites? *Organization*. Epub ahead of print October 22, 2020. DOI: 10.1177/1350508420963872

Vicente, M. (2019). Collective relations in the gig economy. *E-Journal of International and Comparative Labour Studies*, 8(1), 83–93.

Wajcman, J. (2017). Automation: Is it really different this time? *The British Journal of Sociology* 68 (1), 119–127.

Wiener, N. (1950). *The human use of human beings: Cybernetics and society*. Houghton Mifflin.

Wirtz, J., Patterson, P. G., Kunz, W. H., Gruber, T., Lu, V. N., Paluch, S., & Martins, A. (2018). Brave new world: Service robots in the frontline. *Journal of Service Management, 29*(5), 907–931.

Woodcock, J., & Graham, M. (2020). *The gig economy: A critical introduction*. Polity Press.

45

The Brain Center Beneath the Interface: Grounding HMC in Infrastructure, Information, and Labor

Vincent Manzerolle

"The point is that too often, man becomes clever instead of becoming wise, he becomes inventive but not thoughtful – and sometimes, as in the case of Mr. Whipple, he can create himself right out of existence."

– Rod Serling, "Brain Center at Whipples,"
Twilight Zone

CHAPTER OVERVIEW

In this chapter, I outline a framework for critically examining and contextualizing the infrastructure that supports HMC. It provides conceptual tools to look beneath the interface and thereby expose the vast, highly capitalized, yet largely invisible "brain center" that underpins the growing commercial exploitation of HMC; a situation wherein humans and machines are locked in a communicative feedback loop still structured around the logic of capitalist accumulation.

The chapter begins by considering HMC as an interface point within a larger totality, what Benjamin Bratton calls "The Stack" (2015). In this schematic, HMC represents an interface linked to a vast assemblage of platforms, networks, data centers, and related infrastructure. In so doing, I highlight some of the key market-related dynamics driving the development of the infrastructure supporting the generalized adoption of HMC. After discussing these market considerations, I outline two core areas that shape the political economic dimensions of HMC: information and labor. To conceptualize how these dimensions are interrelated within contemporary capitalism, the chapter retrieves two foundational thinkers to reframe the infrastructure of HMC as a key site of value extraction and social control. It does this by drawing from concepts developed by Karl Marx and Harold Innis; the first focusing on the antagonism between living and dead labor, and the latter situating the control over information resources as a historically important site of social power and control. The chapter culminates in a discussion of "automated journalism" (Gaefe, 2016), where news stories are produced using "natural language generation" (NLG) software, as a way to situate the infrastructural underpinnings of HMC within a broader political economy of information.

BRAIN CENTER IN THE STACK – INTERFACE, INFRASTRUCTURE, PLATFORM

HMC represents a specific interface point that accesses and mobilizes the resources within a vast infrastructural assemblage. This assemblage, comprising data centers and related cloud computing infrastructure, has been critically examined in various ways within what might be called "critical infrastructure studies" (Parks and Starosielski, 2015) which, among other things, examines "the material sites and objects" involved in the production and circulation of information (2015, pp. 355–356). Via the provisioning of proprietary platform software, HMC offers an interface and translation point for the non-human, machinic communication that animates data servers and cloud computing infrastructure – what Marx might have called the "social brain" (1973, p. 694). The interface point – for example a Microsoft Office application powered by its Turing-NLG infrastructure or a dedicated NLG service provider like AxSemantics – is here understood as the site where human and machine are joined in the process of communication, as both communicator and medium (Guzman, 2018, p. 16). Put differently, the interface layer is where human desire is translated into a form "a machine can understand" (Wark, 2019, p. 9). In this integrated brain center, socially useful information is stored, processed, and transmitted. As but one decentralized interface point, HMC metaphorically "sits atop" a, largely hidden, layered infrastructural assemblage that, like the Internet, should be understood as comprising "networks of cables, satellites, and servers as well as the protocols, policies and netcode" (Brock Jr., 2020, p. 39). Focusing on this infrastructure foregrounds, "the resources, technologies, labor, and relations that are required to shape, energize, and sustain" our media environment (Parks and Starosielski, 2015, p. 5), and the growing role of HMC within it.

Given the heavy upfront investment and overhead costs associated with building and maintaining this infrastructure, commercial HMC software largely represents the strategic leveraging of corporate IT infrastructure and resources, resulting in the competitive deployment of HMC more generally. Although the global market for this infrastructure will vary according to national and regional demand, the bulk of the private infrastructure for cloud computing and data center rests with a small number of "hyperscale" operators, most are deeply invested in the commercial development of HMC through applications like NLG. As a snapshot, between 2015 to 2018, infrastructure giants spent more than \$185 billion on infrastructure related to data centers' cloud computing capacity. Indeed, in 2018 Amazon, Microsoft, Google, Apple, Facebook, and IBM were responsible for more than 70 percent of these huge capital expenditures. These companies make up more than one-third of all data-center network traffic (Kannan & Thomas, 2018). This corporate concentration points to a particular political economic configuration enabling the commercialization of HMC, leading to critical points of leverage these companies have over usage and access to a now essential infrastructure. It is further evidence of the forms of vertical and horizontal integration needed to support the use of NLG across information-producing sectors such as news, entertainment, and social media.

Beyond these large hyperscale operators, much of the essential HMC infrastructure also lives in data centers shaped by market considerations outside the traditional purview of the tech sector. These material considerations regarding the development of HMC infrastructure – data servers and cloud computing facilities – are a clear indication of how market logics directly impact quality of available information more generally, reminding us that data economics are still defined, if somewhat obliquely, by the material limitations of the physical environment. I will briefly discuss three interrelated aspects that shape the flows of investment, profitability, and service provisioning: real-estate, energy pricing, and environmental policies.

The significance of real-estate markets in shaping the marketization of HMC infrastructure is reflected in the predominance of real estate investment trusts (REITs) in the development of data centers outside the hyperscale providers. Because data centers depend on access to built infrastructure to house operations and resources such as energy, transportation, and water, locational advantages steer investment into particular real estate markets, where valuable property, in conjunction with the availability of local incentives like tax breaks, may further attract data center investment and development. Hence, data center investment involves "a carefully calibrated form of real estate alchemy …. [that] varie[s] from approximately forty characteristics to a blunt four: 'Networks, land, power, and taxes'" (Burrington, 2015). The economics around data centers are subject to pressures and incentives in real estate markets, energy prices, tax policies, and sunk capital (e.g. network infrastructure). For example, Canada's largest data center opened in Toronto in 2018, doubly notable because it opened in the former printing facility of the *Toronto Star* newspaper. Similar conversions have transformed the former *Chicago Sun-Times* and *Montreal Gazette* printing facilities into massive data centers. What makes the Toronto data center significant is that the corporate operator – an international REIT conglomerate based in the United States called Digital Realty – acts as landlord and property manager for companies looking to house their data servers and related equipment (Jackson, 2018).

Similarly, because of their voracious appetite for electricity and other resources like water to power and cool their operations (Mosco, 2014, p. 148; Hogan, 2015), data center development is also sensitive to the cost of energy, with many operators locating close to energy markets that are cheap or heavily subsidized. For example, in Canada data centers consume about 1% of its electricity (Natural Resources Canada, 2020), much of it generated through hydro-electric and nuclear power plants, with national industry growth mirroring global trends. Canada has been touted for several years as an ideal site for data center investment in part because of the cold climate which aids in cutting the cooling costs for data servers (Stoller, 2012; Beal, 2012). Public utility Hydro-Quebec has been actively marketing Montreal as a prime location for the industry with cheap, renewable electricity. And this campaign appears to be successful. Montreal has emerged as a rapidly growing data center cluster, catalyzed in part by relatively cheap real-estate and electricity, including active inducement of the industry by Hydro-Quebec (Nowak, 2017). Yet the search for cheap electricity has also driven large data center investment into energy markets that overwhelmingly rely on carbon-intensive energy sources like coal. Dubbed "data center alley," the Dulles Technology Corridor in Virginia is currently "home to the world's highest concentration of data centers in the world" which, through its reliance on an energy market dependent on non-renewable energy sources, creates a massive carbon footprint regularly highlighted by environmental watchdogs like Greenpeace (2019). The dependence on cheap electricity and other resources has also placed the development of data center infrastructure at the forefront of pursuits of environmental sustainability as a search for cheaper energy has dovetailed with renewable energy investment like solar and wind power (Jones, 2018).

The next question is how best to conceptualize these economic implications as components of some larger totality. In his ambitious tome, *The Stack* (2015), Benjamin Bratton argues that a new diagrammatic model is needed to better understand the complex composition of fully digital networks and ubiquitous computing technologies that are embedded within a wider geopolitical context. He names this totality "The Stack," borrowing an engineering metaphor describing the movement of information between different technical layers that facilitate machinic communication (e.g., over the Internet). Other layers of Bratton's conceptualization include the "cloud" and "earth" layers; the former dealing with disparate information infrastructure like data centers and cloud computing platforms, the latter referring to the raw materials and energy required to power this infrastructure. For this reason, Wark elaborates, The Stack "generates a distinctive kind of geopolitics, one in which the former sovereign states have to negotiate with a kind of power based on distributed information infrastructures, producing a relatively novel kind of virtual geography" (Wark, 2019 p. 118). It is a term meant to conceptualize the totality of planetary scale computing, where the user interface is merely an access point to a hidden, assemblage of software and hardware. Bratton (2015) writes that The Stack "lets us see that all of these different machines are parts of a greater machine, and perhaps the diagrammatic image of a totality that such a perspective provides would, as theories of totality have before, make the composition of alternatives… both more legible and more effective" (p. 5).

Largely still contained by the accumulation logics of contemporary capitalism, The Stack's commercial articulation occurs through the branded platform – a key leverage point in part because it pulls together hardware, software, and various infrastructural layers. "Platforms are infrastructural but rely heavily on aesthetic expression and calibration. A platform's systems are composed of interfaces, protocols, visualizable data, and strategic renderings of geography, time, landscapes, and object fields" (Bratton, 2015, p. 46). For Bratton, the platform represents the organizational principles that provides order within the layers of The Stack. As Bratton explains, platforms "pull things together into temporary higher order aggregations and, in principle, add value both to what is brought into the platform and to the platform itself. They can be a physical technical apparatus or an alphanumeric system; they can be software or hardware, or various combinations" (Bratton, 2015, p. 41). Platforms not only provide users with a variety of informational services – including social media, news, information search, and entertainment – they offer highly controlled markets linking buyers and sellers, or consumers and producers of content. The platform acts as a central accumulation strategy that combines control over underlying critical infrastructure, the user interface, and all resulting data (Meier & Manzerolle, 2019).

The platform is an umbrella term that helps fit these specific instances of HMC into a larger geopolitical totality – The Stack – with attendant significance for politics, culture, and economy. The specific commercialization of HMC in the form of e.g., NLG, demonstrates, on the one hand, the commoditization of automated content generation; and on the other, the commercialization of the underlying infrastructure required for its operation and future development. While the former case encompasses the software companies that are increasingly offering up new branded services and products, the latter is an increasingly narrow group of infrastructure providers that ultimately control the essential underlying computing resources and intellectual property (IBM, Alphabet, Microsoft, Amazon).

CONTRIBUTIONS TO A POLITICAL ECONOMY OF HMC: IMPLICATIONS FOR INFORMATION AND LABOR

As the various chapters in this collection clearly reveal, HMC services and applications – like those associated with automated journalism – are now lodged at the heart of social forms of communication upon which the maintenance of liberal democracies depends. In this sense, HMC now plays a constitutive role in what philosopher Jurgen Habermas calls the "public sphere" (Habermas, 1989). For Habermas, the public sphere was an agonistic space in which public debate, and ultimately public opinion, emerged independent from government and "partisan economic forces" (Webster, 2007, p. 163). The vitality of the public sphere, as a generative space for participatory forms of social communication, is fueled by the availability of socially necessary information, a key resource often made available through newspaper content. While Habermas' initial formulation of the public sphere is not without valid criticisms (e.g., Fraser, 1990), it provides a framework for assessing the "role of information in a democracy" (Webster, 2007, p. 168) particularly as its quality and availability is altered by new technologies. It appears inarguable that machinic communication is integral to the informational substrate of the public sphere and social communication more generally as chatbots and NLG applications are woven into the fabric of our media environment.

How then might we assess the impact of this automation on the integrity of the public sphere? Commercial news and information organizations, in search of efficiencies in the production and distribution of content, and with a focus on increasing personalization in order to better capture consumer attention, are employing the newest and most cost-effective tools available. For Habermas, the unconstrained monetization of news and information has a pernicious effect, fueling a "refeudalization" of the public sphere, pushing it towards a "soft compulsion of constant consumption training" (Habermas, 1989, p. 192) rather than a space for information provisioning and deliberative civic engagement. The concept of refeudalization is also suggestive of the immense informational fiefdoms operated by the likes of Meta and Alphabet, representative of a broader shift in accumulation strategy emphasizing the "platform" as a mechanism for political economic leverage (Srnicek, 2016). The prevalence of "click bait," "infotainment," "fake news" and "deep fakes" as parasitic staples within the modern information diet is a symptom of the monetization and monopolization of user data which underpins the business models of social media platforms and services.

The implications of the growing dependence on HMC services in a variety of information-related tasks raises the perennial fear of jobs lost or fundamentally transformed by automation now aimed directly at the very information workers necessary for the health of liberal democracies. Yet it also represents a more generalized threat to all content-creating labor as the ability to replace routine forms of human communicative and creative capacities becomes commercially available and cost effective. These applications won't necessarily replace all human activity, but they will add to existing pressures and incentives to minimize the human presence in news creation, particularly as NLG becomes more virtuosic in its human mimicry.

One recent example should suffice. OpenAI's GPT-3 NLG platform (Heaven, 2020) – a project financially supported by Microsoft and which they will eventually be deploying commercially (Jin and Kruppa, 2022) – is capable of producing mundane administrative content like emails and business reports, but, more remarkably, also movie scripts and musical compositions, almost indistinguishable from a flesh and blood creator (see Steinhoff, 2021). Largely overshadowed by the commercial launch of ChatGPT in 2023, GPT-3 is one example of a new era of software-as-a-service (SaaS) using cloud-based NLG infrastructure to commercialize its wider usage. It offers a glimpse of commercial HMC yet to come.

Only time will tell if fears of catastrophic unemployment wrought by this kind of automation are overblown. What is certain is that the availability of automated content generation will put greater pressure on, and drive greater precarity for, workers whose primary tasks involve communicative and creative labor. Hence, for example, the use of various HMC applications may simply offer means to make information-generating labor, like that performed by journalists, more efficient and cost effective. Moreover, as NLG applications become essential tools of labor more generally, they will simultaneously be trained to better accomplish related tasks as these applications absorb the creative, formal, and editorial conventions and perspectives of their context of use (for example, like IBM's Project Debater). This prospective antagonism is an advance on Braverman's argument (1974) about labor "deskilling" under monopoly capitalism, but also a new iteration of the antagonism between "living" and "dead" labor that Marx identified (1973, p. 461). For this reason, automation should not be thought of as a wholly non-human activity since much of the value that machine-learning produces is built upon unpaid or underpaid human labor (Dyer-Witheford et al., 2019, pp. 75–79).

Having located informational labor at the interfacial level of The Stack's layered infrastructure and linking its commercialization to leveraged control over the platform, I will now provide an outline of a political economic approach to understanding HMC by conceptualizing the interaction between information (as a resource) and fixed capital (as infrastructure). The goal is to understand information as a primary input *and* output of the existing mode of production. To do this, I would like to discuss two thinkers who predate the emergence of HMC but offer foundational insights into how it may fit within a holistic political economy of information: Karl Marx and Harold Innis. Each contributes a perspective on the material effects stemming from the capitalization of information (and) infrastructure; Marx through the prism of labor, and Innis through the prism of media. Although neither used the term infrastructure, instead using the term "fixed capital," they both provide a materialist and dialectical understanding of infrastructure (Parker, 1981, pp. 127–143). Together they offer profound insights into the specific role of information as a resource materialized in and through new infrastructure; contributing complementary perspectives on how the exploitation of information as a resource is foundational to power relations and social hierarchies.

MARX – APPROPRIATING THE SOCIAL BRAIN

In his widely cited "fragment on machines" section of his preparatory notebooks (Marx, 1973, pp. 690–712), Marx provides at least two interrelated ways to consider the implications of infrastructure on labor as an antagonistic force, pitting "living" labor against the "dead" labor inhering in fixed capital. The first refers to an antagonism that pressures labor to compete with, or be totally

replaced by, increasingly cheaper software (and the infrastructure that supports it). In this sense, automated journalism represents the basic conflict between labor and automation that has preoccupied workers' movements since the early nineteenth century. As the "means of labor" – that is the tools and technologies that support laboring activity – become dependent on fixed capital, the production process tends towards an "automatic system of machinery" that Marx describes as a self-moving automaton "consisting of numerous mechanical and intellectual organs, so that the workers themselves are cast merely as its conscious linkages" (Marx, 1973, p. 692). In this version, living labor plays a vanishing role in the production process.

This trajectory toward automated obsolescence relates to a second point of antagonism: the process by which fixed capital actually "appropriates" and alienates human capacities, both muscular and communicative. Marx writes, "in fixed capital, the social productivity of labour [is] posited as a property inherent in capital; including the scientific power as well as the combination of social powers within the production process, and finally, the skill transposed from direct labour into the machine, into the dead productive force" (Marx, 1973, p. 715). Similarly, HMC expresses the appropriation of human communicative capacities, representing the traces of real human activity, and in so doing, becoming an "alien power" (p. 693). Importantly, the full impact of this new "alien" communicative capacity is only truly available when it can also access vast informational resources. As Marx explains:

> The accumulation of knowledge and of skill, of the general productive forces of the social brain, is thus absorbed into capital, as opposed to labour, and hence appears as an attribute of capital, and more specifically of fixed capital, in so far as it enters into the production process as a means of production proper. (p. 694)

On this tendency to absorb and mirror communicative and cognitive powers of human capacities, Marx was only able to speculate about what could happen when information becomes a primary input into fixed capital, reflected in the more recently developed concept of The Stack: "The development of fixed capital indicates to what degree general social knowledge has become a direct force of production," and as a result, "the conditions of the process of social life itself have come under the control of the general intellect and been transformed in accordance with it" (Marx, 1973, p. 706). Although he did not develop an explicit theory of media, Marx identified innovations in communication and transportation as being essential infrastructure in the maintenance of capital as a cybernetic circulatory system, linking disparate places, people, cultures, and nations, as well as struggles (Dyer-Witheford, 1999). What Marx had not fully considered were the forms of enclosure and monopolization of information that could stifle the revolutionary possibilities of the "general intellect" (see Marx, 1973, pp. 707–711), funneling its potential social value instead into new circuits of accumulation.

INNIS – MATERIALITIES AND MONOPOLIES OF KNOWLEDGE

A thinker that might fill this blind spot is the Canadian media theorist and political economist Harold Innis. Innis is most well-known for his influence on Marshall McLuhan, but his scholarly achievements stem from his pioneering work on Canadian economic history, as well as the history of communication he was assembling before his untimely death in 1952. Innis conceptualized communication and information as material, sometimes scarce, resources shaped by available media forms (Innis, 2008; see also Melody et al., 1981, pp. 3–9). Innis arrived at this consideration by making a leap from examining the exploitation of economic staples like fur and lumber, to diagnosing the spatial or temporal biases of communication and its resulting impact on the organization of complex systems like markets, empires, or nation states (Innis, 2007). Innis' obsessively detailed research on media served a dual role. The first was to understand the history of communication as a way to holistically assess economic and cultural change. The second was to serve as a conceptual framework for anticipating and shaping the future – to guide policy and research, and to develop the capacity for "reflexivity" within society's key institutions (Comor, 2001; see also Innis, 2018).

For Innis, media are communicative staples subject to the prevailing political economic forces, and as such, potentially scarce resources. Innis saw fixed capital as one of several key concepts borrowed from economics (Innis, 1995, pp. 384), as well as concepts like "unused capacity" and "overhead costs," but redeployed to understand the material impacts that different communication media had on the production and accessibility of valuable information. Because Innis wanted to develop a political economy of communication media through historical analysis, he sought to identify and extract patterns that reveal the inner

dynamics of a given society's social and political power structures. As a recurring historical pattern, Innis identified "monopolies of knowledge" (Innis, 1995) as expressions of dominant media infrastructure – which includes available fixed capital assets, tangible materials (e.g., papyrus, pulp, and paper), cultural techniques (e.g., writing, mathematics), and social institutions (such as religion or the marketplace). Close historical analysis of these phenomena revealed how control over socially important knowledge is made the object of leverage for an elite class who can extract and monopolize maximum value (economic, social, and strategic). As an analytic term, monopolies of knowledge capture the tendency for power structures to consolidate around the fixed capital (i.e., infrastructure) that controls how information is stored, processed, and transmitted. Innis noted this tendency among the priestly classes in ancient Egypt, Sumeria, and medieval Europe. Later these same monopolistic tendencies would be replicated in secular institutions like universities and markets, both increasingly becoming sites for the production of socially valuable information.

In our contemporary moment, the ability to control and exploit the layered infrastructure of "The Stack" suggests a new monopoly of knowledge that might be added to Innis' list of historical case studies. "The dominant ruling class of our time owns and controls information" (Wark, 2019, p. 5), their power stemming from the ability to exploit an "asymmetry of information" (p. 54). Putting HMC and its infrastructure within this larger historical continuity adds further context and reflexivity to its critical analysis. Whether the social grouping that benefits from this monopoly of knowledge is new, as in Wark's "vectoralist class," or simply a specialized capitalist class emerging out of a relatively new mode of accumulation (Srnicek, 2016) will be dependent on future analysis. Nevertheless, it appears that control over the key infrastructure that supports the commercial development of HMC might constitute yet another, more contemporary, monopoly of knowledge.

THE CASE OF AUTOMATED JOURNALISM

In May 2020, Microsoft announced that it would be replacing roughly 27 journalists with machine learning software in order to curate content for its MSN homepages, an audience comprising hundreds of millions of users. Headlines like the *Guardian's* "Microsoft sacks journalists to replace them with robots" (Waterson, 2020) may have over-stated both the impact and, indeed, the novelty of the event.

Rather than a singularly devastating lurch towards a robotic takeover, it was merely another indication of a growing trend. News organizations, in search of greater cost and labor efficiencies, are opting to use machine learning software applications – known as "automated journalism" – in service of content production and distribution. For the purposes of this chapter, automated journalism will be used to describe HMC applications that generate news content increasingly "without human intervention" (Graefe, 2016). Since the beginning of the twenty-first century, news organizations have been incorporating various forms of software-intensive content production, management, and distribution applications (Beckett, 2019), part of an even longer computational-turn in "newswork" (Bucher, 2017, p. 919).

The uptake of automated journalism in news organizations appears to be gaining industry-wide momentum, particularly among the largest and most prestigious publications. A few notable examples will demonstrate the "state of the art" as it exists in the second decade of the twenty-first century. Radar, a software service developed by the Press Association, backed by Alphabet, and used by Associated Press to mass produce local news stories (Heater, 2017) – notably produced 50,000 stories in its first three months of use (Beckett, 2019, p. 31) that were "hard to distinguish from human-written" content (Belz, 2019). Similar applications are used by the *Washington Post* and the *Guardian*, among many others (see Beckett, 2019). Currently, these applications are used in relatively narrow ways, often focusing on sports, financials, or local news – essentially any form of news where clear templates, standardization, and robust data sets are available.

Automated journalism reflects the commercial development of "natural language generation" software (NLG), a specific application of HMC used to write content in ways that mirror human communicative capacities (Peiser, 2019). The power of NLG comes from its ability to automatically generate "narratives that describe, summarize or explain input structured data in a human-like manner at the speed of thousands of pages per second" (Sciforce, 2019). NLG is already deployed in a variety of settings where particular data sets can be processed and translated into written narratives suitable for human consumption and is already widely deployed in personal digital assistants (Alexa, Siri) and "smart" media devices (Apple HomePod, Amazon Alexa). Many of the biggest commercial developers of NLG and its underlying infrastructure – Microsoft, Apple, Meta, Amazon, IBM, and Alphabet – are also directly and indirectly shaping how news is produced, distributed, and consumed. Amazon owns *The Washington Post*, which is increasingly employing in-house NLG application, and Apple

has developed an entire news experience around one of its native apps. Meanwhile, Meta and Twitter are using NLG techniques to search for "fake news." More indirectly, in addition to offering powerful cloud computing infrastructure required to run NLG applications, Alphabet has sponsored and promoted training courses aimed at enhancing the "AI literacy" of journalists (Peretti, 2020); Microsoft has similarly taken an interest in developing the data skills of journalists in an effort to un-ironically preserve and protect them in newsrooms (Shaw, 2019). As Belz (2019) concludes, "automation has some hand in producing most of the news we read now, but you would never know it from attributions." As a specific area of NLG commercialization, news production may be dwarfed by more profitable health and finance applications, but it does offer an opportunity to assemble a political economic analysis of HMC by inviting us to examine broader implications for information, labor, and infrastructure.

CONCLUSION

This chapter has provided a number of conceptual tools to contextualize and critically examine the infrastructure that supports the generalized uptake of HMC. HMC reflects an increasingly dominant mode of social communication, dependent upon an expansive, multi-layered infrastructural assemblage. From a political economic perspective, The Stack is a powerful diagrammatic of how modern capitalism is materialized in its socio-technical infrastructure. HMC, as a force shaping the political economy of information, might be seen as simply the most recent transformation in the long history of communication that Innis was developing. Automated journalism is merely a reflection of the advances made in NLG and its contemporary commercialization, a harbinger of things to come. And without a larger framework within which to consider the broader implications of HMC, like the obsolescent Mr. Whipple, we may continue to simply become more clever instead of becoming more wise.

REFERENCES

Beckett, C. (2019). *New powers, new responsibilities*. London School of Economics.

Beal, V. (2012, October 8). "Why putting your data center in Canada makes sense." *CIO*. www.cio.com/article/2391505/why-putting-your-data-center-in-canada-makes-sense.html.

Belz, A. (2019, October 31). Fully automatic journalism: We need to talk about nonfake news generation. *Proceedings of the Conference for Truth and Trust Online 2019*. Conference for Truth and Trust Online 2019.

Bratton, B. H. (2015). *The stack: On software and sovereignty*. MIT Press.

Braverman, H. (1974). *Labor and monopoly capital: The degradation of work in the twentieth century*. Monthly Review Press.

Brock, A. Jr. (2020). *Distributed blackness*. NYU Press.

Bucher, T. (2017). "Machines don't have instincts": Articulating the computational in journalism. *New Media & Society, 19*(6), 918–933.

Burrington, I. (2015, December 1). "Why are there so many data centers in Iowa?" *The Atlantic*. https://www.theatlantic.com/technology/archive/2015/12/why-are-so-many-data-centers-built-in-iowa/418005/

Comor, E. (2001). Harold Innis and "the bias of communication." *Information, Communication & Society, 4*(2), 274–294.

Dyer-Witheford, N. (1999). *Cyber-Marx: Cycles and circuits of struggle in high-technology capitalism*. University of Illinois Press.

Dyer-Witheford, N., Kjøsen, A. M., & Steinhoff, J. (2019). *In human power: Artificial intelligence and the future of capitalism*. Pluto Press.

Fraser, N. (1990). Rethinking the public sphere: A contribution to the critique of actually existing democracy. *Social Text, 25/26*, 56–80.

Graefe, A. (2016). *Guide to automated journalism*. Columbia Journalism Review.

Greenpeace. (2019). "Clicking clean Virginia." *Greenpeace USA* (blog). www.greenpeace.org/usa/reports/click-clean-virginia/.

Guzman, A. L. ed. (2018). *Human-machine communication: Rethinking communication, technology, and ourselves*. Peter Lang.

Habermas, J. (1989). *The structural transformation of the public sphere: An inquiry into a category of Bourgeois society*. MIT Press.

Heater, B. (2017, July 8). Google is funding the creation of software that writes local news stories. *TechCrunch*. http://tcrn.ch/2uVT1vS

Heaven, W. (2020). *OpenAI's new language generator GPT-3 is shockingly good – And completely mindless*. MIT Technology Review.

Hogan, M. (2015). "Data flows and water woes: The Utah Data Center." *Big Data & Society 2*(2): 2053951715592429.

Innis, H. A. (1995). *Staples, markets, and cultural change: Selected essays of Harold Innis*. McGill-Queen's University Press.

Innis, H. A. (2007). *Empire and communications*. Dundurn Press.

Innis, H. A. (2008). *The bias of communication* (2nd ed.). University of Toronto Press.

Innis, H. A. (2018). *Political economy in the modern state*. University of Toronto Press.

Jackson, B. (2018, June 14). "Canada's largest data centre opens in old Toronto Star printing press." *IT World Canada*. https://www.itworldcanada.com/article/canadas-largest-data-centre-opens-in-old-toronto-star-printing-press/406183

Jin, B., & Kruppa, M. (2022, October 20). *Microsoft in Advanced Talks to Increase Investment in OpenAI*. WSJ. https://www.wsj.com/articles/microsoft-in-advanced-talks-to-increase-investment-in-ope-nai-11666299548

Jones, Nicola. (2018, September 12). "How to stop data centres from gobbling up the world's electricity." *Nature*. www.nature.com/articles/d41586-018-06610-y.

Kannan, H., & Thomas, C. (2018, October 26). "*How high-tech suppliers are responding to the hyperscaler opportunity*." McKinsey & Company. https://www.mckinsey.com/industries/technology-media-and-telecommunications/our-insights/how-high-tech-suppliers-are-responding-to-the-hyperscaler-opportunity

Marx, K. (1973). *Grundrisse: Foundations of the critique of political economy*. Penguin.

Meier, L. M., & Manzerolle, V. R. (2019). Rising tides? Data capture, platform accumulation, and new monopolies in the digital music economy. *New Media & Society, 21*(3), 543–561.

Melody, W. H., Salter, L., & Heyer, P. (1981). *Culture, communication, and dependency: The tradition of H. A. Innis*. Ablex Publishing Corporation.

Mosco, V. (2014). *To the cloud: Big data in a turbulent world*. Paradigm Publishers.

Natural Resources Canada. (2020). Data centres. www.nrcan.gc.ca/energy-efficiency/energy-efficiency-products/product-information/data-centres/13741.

Nowak, P. (2017, March 9). "Why Google built its first Canadian cloud computing facility in Montreal." *Canadian Business*. www.canadianbusiness.com/innovation/google-cloud-montreal/.

Parker, I. (1981). "Innis, Marx, and the economics of communication: a theoretical aspect of Canadian political economy." *Culture, communication, and dependency: The tradition of HA Innis* (1981): 127–143.

Parks, L., & Starosielski, N. (2015). *Signal traffic: Critical studies of media infrastructures*. University of Illinois Press.

Peiser, J. (2019, February 5). The Rise of the robot reporter. *The New York Times*. www.nytimes.com/2019/02/05/business/media/artificial-intelligence-journalism-robots.html

Peretti, M. (2020, May 6). *Helping journalists understand the power of machine learning*. Google. https://blog.google/outreach-initiatives/google-news-initiative/helping-journalists-understand-power-machine-learning/

Sciforce. (2019, July 4). *A comprehensive guide to natural language generation*. Medium. https://medium.com/sciforce/a-comprehensive-guide-to-natural-language-generation-dd63a4b6e548

Shaw, F. X. (2019, January 16). *Teaming up to help journalism thrive in the digital age*. The Official Microsoft Blog. https://blogs.microsoft.com/blog/2019/01/16/teaming-up-to-help-journalism-thrive-in-the-digital-age/

Srnicek, N. (2016). *Platform capitalism*. Polity Press.

Steinhoff, J. (2021, February 18). *Marxist Media Theory and GPT-3* [workshop talk]. Reflecting on power and AI: The case of GPT-3 workshop hosted by the Society for Phenomenology and Media. www.academia.edu/47785786/Marxist_Media_Theory_and_GPT_3

Stoller, J. (2012, December 20). Why cold Canada is becoming a hot spot for data centres. *The Globe and Mail*. www.theglobeandmail.com/report-on-business/economy/canada-competes/why-cold-canada-is-becoming-a-hot-spot-for-data-centres/article6598555/.

Wark, M. (2019). *Capital is dead: Is this something worse?* Verso.

Waterson, J. (2020, May 30). "Microsoft sacks journalists to replace them with robots." *The Guardian*. www.theguardian.com/technology/2020/may/30/microsoft-sacks-journalists-to-replace-them-with-robots

Webster, F. (2007). *Theories of the information society*. Taylor & Francis Group, Routledge.

46

AI, Human–Machine Communication and Deception

Simone Natale

INTRODUCTION

On October 25, 2017, the Saudi government attracted headlines as it granted citizenship to Sophia, a humanoid robot produced by the company Hanson Robotics in Hong Kong. Sympathetic reports highlighted Sophia's ability to learn social behavior through interaction with people and the fact that its advanced Artificial Intelligence and robotics made it similar to a human (Kalra & Chadla, 2018). Other commentators contended, however, that it was not computer power or clever programming that made Sophia appear "human," but its humanlike appearance and voice. As Facebook's director of artificial intelligence research Yan LeCun noted, "this is to AI as prestidigitation is to real magic. (…) In other words, it's complete bullsh*t (pardon my French)" (Ghosh, 2018).

The controversy about robot Sophia recalls similar discussions throughout the history of AI regarding the distinction between "real" and "fake" AI (Natale & Ballatore, 2020). One may wonder, however, if such a dichotomy is helpful to understand contemporary AI. Not dissimilarly to Sophia, voice assistants such as Siri and Alexa also mobilize humanlike, gendered voices that help users integrate them more easily within domestic and work environments (Guzman,

2017); likewise, the design of many companion robots and chatbots aimed at the general public is meant, like in Sophia's case, to stimulate feelings such as empathy (Caudwell & Lacey, 2019). Are all these technologies "bullsh*t"? Or rather, should approaches to AI move beyond the opposition between "real" and "fake" AI?

In asking such questions, this chapter aims to put forward a more nuanced understanding of the relationship between AI and deception, one which moves away from rigid distinctions between authenticity and fakery to acknowledge the more substantial role of deception in the AI enterprise. Because the term "deception" is usually associated with mischievous endeavors, the AI and computer science communities have usually proved resistant to discussing their work in these terms. I contend, however, that deception plays a fundamental and structural role in virtually all AI technologies programmed to communicate with humans (see Natale, 2021). The problem in this sense is not much to establish what is "real" AI and what is just "bullsh*t," but to acknowledge that the outcomes of Human–Machine Communication (HMC) depend on the internal functioning of machines as well as on the perception and reactions of human users that enter in communication with these machines. Because such perceptions can be to some extent anticipated and mobilized through specific elements of the machine's design, the dynamics of deception are a crucial component of what we call "AI."

RETHINKING DECEPTION

Throughout the history of AI, deception has been mostly discussed as an exceptional outcome, the result of either malicious intentions or mistakes from developers and users (Crevier, 1993; McCorduck, 1979). It is only recently that researchers started to reconsider the role of deception as an interpretative framework that could fit a wider range of contexts and situations at the intersection between AI and HMC. Adar et al. (2013), for instance, noted that deception is ubiquitous in AI systems, despite being rarely described in such terms; they argue for the consideration of not only malicious but also benevolent forms of deception, which benefit users as well as developers. Others observed that the possibility of manipulation is an obvious outcome for systems that include models of mental states of human users (Chakraborti & Kambhampati, 2018) and called for the development of an ethics of robotic deception (Danaher, 2020; Sætra, 2021). While the significance of deception in AI has started to be more often acknowledged, however, relatively little efforts have so far been undertaken to conceptualize deception in a way that takes its structural role within AI and HMC more fully into consideration. Looking at approaches to the concept of deception beyond AI and HMC may help fill this gap.

Broadly defined, deception involves the use of signals or representations to convey a misleading or false impression (Danaher, 2020). Scholars in social psychology, philosophy and sociology have recently advanced a perspective that does not limit deception to exceptional cases such as blatant fraud and trickery. They recognize that deception plays a substantial role in people's lives (DePaulo et al., 1996), is an essentially social phenomenon (Umbres, 2017), and can be a resource that accompanies people in their everyday experiences (Martin, 2009).

Indeed, as shown by the long history of illusions in psychology, arts, and spectacular entertainments – from Gestalt psychology to Escher and optical toys – perception and deception are not opposed but closely aligned (Leja, 2004; Pettit, 2013). Philosopher Mark A. Wrathall argues that our liability to be deceived is ingrained in the mechanisms of our perception. He points out that "it rarely makes sense to say that I perceived either truly or falsely" (Wrathall 2010: 60) since

deception is functional to our ability to deal with the external world. Our tendency to identify patterns in visual information can lead people to see the traits of a human face when it's not there, as numberless experiments and studies on illusion have shown (Gombrich, 1977); yet this liability to deception can also provide an advantage to viewers, for instance when it helps identify a potential danger in our field of vision. Within the same line of thought, cognitive psychologist Donald D. Hoffman (2019) recently explored how evolution has shaped our perception into "useful illusions" that help people navigate the physical world.

These contributions call for a shift of perspective in approaches to deception. They suggest that our perception is so shaped that it is always open to deception, and that deception constantly occurs without breaking the continuity of our ordinary life. Bringing these insights into HMC entails the realization that deception in AI involves a wider range of situations and mechanisms than usually thought.

TOWARDS A NEW TYPOLOGY OF DECEPTION

How can we make sense, however, of different manifestations of deception in interactions with AI? How can we compare, for instance, the experience of the victims of fraud who believe that the automated email they received was sent by a real person, with the experience of users who engage in meaningful social relationship with social robots or companion chatbots despite knowing these are "just" machines? In order to make sense of such diverse cases, I propose to distinguish between two categories of deception that draw on and extend my recent work on the subject (Natale, 2021). Each of these categories represents one end of the spectrum in a continuum that goes from the most evident to the most nuanced case of deception. On the one end of the continuum are explicit attempts to commit fraud, mislead and tell lies; on the other, forms of deception that are subtler and that, in many cases, are not openly acknowledged as such.

The first category, which I call outright or "strong" deception, occurs when users are led to misunderstand the artificial nature of AI software. Examples include social media bots designed to be exchanged for accounts of human users (Gehl & Bakardjieva, 2016), automated phone systems that do not openly display their mechanical nature to phone callers (O'Leary, 2019), and texts produced by natural language generation software that are presented to readers as if they were authored by humans (Henrickson, 2018). The second category, which I call "banal deception" (Natale, 2021), indicates situations in which users respond to specific strategies and features embedded in machines by activating dynamics such as stereotyping, empathy, and projection. Examples of banal deception include the use of humanized, gendered voices of AI assistants such as Amazon's Alexa and Apple's Siri (Guzman, 2017) and the characterization instilled by designers of companion chatbots such as Replika (Depounti, 2019). Even if such features do not mislead users into exchanging machines for humans, they are so designed to stimulate responses that are functional to specific outcomes.

STRONG DECEPTION: FROM TURING TO GOOGLE DUPLEX

Let us first consider the most evident and straightforward instances of deception. Since the origins of AI, computer scientists and engineers acknowledged that communications between human and machine under the auspices of AI could lead to situations of outright deception. One of the foundational texts for the field, in fact, perceptively anticipated the role that deception would have played in HMC. In "Computing Machinery and Intelligence," Alan Turing proposed the imitation game, now commonly known as the Turing test. In this thought experiment, a human interrogator communicates with both human and computer agents without knowing their identity and is challenged to find out who is human and who is a machine. A computer would pass the Turing test if it proves consistently able to deceive the interrogator into believing it is human (Turing, 1950).

As some have noted (Christian, 2011; Gunkel, 2018; see also Natale, 2021: 16–32), the Turing test posed the foundation not only of AI but also of HMC. In 1950, when the paper was published, computers were mostly discussed as calculating tools, and forms of interactions between human users and computers were minimal. Imagining that human users and computers could communicate in natural language, as Turing did, required a visionary leap – perhaps greater than what was needed to consider the possibility of "machine intelligence." It is significant, in this sense, that Turing's pioneering engagement with HMC emphasized the issue of trickery and deception. This responded to a very important conceptual shift that moved away from defining "intelligence" in absolute terms. In fact, although the Turing test is often discussed

as a way to establish the intelligence of a given computing device (e.g. Levesque, 2017), Turing's most significant intuition was that machine intelligence cannot be defined in absolute but only in relative terms. In other words, it is human users or observers (such as the interrogator in the Turing test) who may or may not attribute "intelligence" to the machine. Consequently, according to Turing, deceiving human users demonstrates proficiency for an AI, even if it does not mean that the AI is capable of "thinking" in the same way as humans do.

The possibility of outright or "strong" deception continued to be a constant element of preoccupation as more complex HMC systems were developed in the following decades. ELIZA, the first chatbot ever created, became the center of a lively debate as it proved able to pass as human, even if only occasionally and under limited circumstances (Natale, 2019).[1] As more advanced chatbots were developed to try their luck with the Turing test, deception became a common strategy: it was evident to developers that there were strategies to exploit the fallibility of human judges, such as programming the chatbot to deflect from questions that it could not handle by using nonsense or irony (Epstein, 1992). The emergence of virtual communities entailed the development of bots and artificial agents that occasionally lead to outright deception in online environments (Turkle, 1995). As the Web developed into its current shape, it has become increasingly difficult to distinguish between human users and automated software, as shown by the ubiquity of CAPTCHA in websites and online platforms (Brunton, 2013). The boundaries between artificial characters and human players sometimes blurs also in multi-user computer games (Wardrip-Fruin, 2009).

As the reach of communicative AI widened from written communication to spoken language (Nass & Brave, 2005), the problem of what constitutes outright or "strong" deception continues to spark public debate. In May 2018, Google publicly demonstrated its ongoing project Duplex, an extension of Google Assistant meant to carry out phone conversations on behalf of users (O'Leary, 2019). Google's CEO Sundar Pichai presented to the audience the recording of a conversation in which Duplex booked an appointment at a hair salon. To sound more credible, the synthetic voice featured pauses and hesitation that mimicked human conversation and did not openly disclose that it was an automated voice processor. In the discussion that ensued, Google was criticized for operating "straight up, deliberate deception," which many believed open pressing ethical questions.[2]

As even such a brief historical overview shows, outright deception has been a recurring issue from the origins of AI to the present time. The concept of outright or "strong" deception, however, captures only one component of the problem, and arguably the least important and impactful. In order to fully understand the role of deception in AI, one needs to widen the perspective towards more ordinary, subtler dynamics.

BANAL DECEPTION: NORMALIZING DECEPTION IN HMC

Conducting research on people's perceptions of voice assistants, HMC scholar Andrea Guzman found that their responses differed sharply from public discussions on AI. AI is often debated as something that raises metaphysical questions, challenging the very distinction between humans and machines (Ekbia, 2008). When interviewed about their use of systems such as Apple's Siri, however, the participants of Guzman's study proved not really concerned about the boundary between humans and machines. They reflected, instead, on more mundane issues: whether the AI assistant made them lazier, or if talking to the assistant in the presence of others is to be considered rude. As Guzman puts it, "neither the technology nor its impact on the self from the perspective of users seemed extraordinary; rather, the self in relation to talking AI seemed, well, ordinary – just like any other technology" (2018: 84).

Guzman's observation resonates with other findings in HMC and related areas of research. As scholars working within the Computers Are Social Actors frameworks have shown, the vast majority of users remain perfectly aware of the difference between interacting with a machine and interacting with a human; yet at the same time they apply to HMC some of the same social conventions and habits they use in communications with fellow humans (Reeves & Nass, 1996). The main way to account for such apparent contradiction has been to distinguish between mindfulness and mindlessness: according to this view, users hold the distinction between humans and machines at a conscious level, while these distinctions tend to evaporate when they act without conscious awareness (Langer, 1992; Kim & Sundar, 2012; Nass & Moon, 2000). Yet this approach does not take fully into account that users replicate social behaviors and habits also in self-conscious and reflective ways: users, for instance, carry out playful exchanges with voice assistants, asking Siri or Alexa if they are human or wishing them a good night (Guzman, 2017; Thorne, 2020). This suggests that the distinction between mindful and mindless behavior does not capture the complexity of the issue.

An alternative way to tackle this problem is to broaden the scope of the concept of deception in AI and HMC. The concept of "banal deception," which I proposed elsewhere (Natale, 2021), helps capture a range of dynamics that are usually not understood as deception. Banal deception entails mundane, everyday situations in which technologies and devices mobilize specific elements of users' perception and psychology, such as their tendency to attribute agency to things or personality to voices, in order to facilitate specific reactions and outcomes. It does not involve users exchanging an AI for a human or explicitly attributing humanity to it, but neither does it posit something that occurs exclusively at a mindless level. The word "banal" describes things that are dismissed as ordinary and unimportant. It serves to underline that these mechanisms are often taken from granted, yet are deeply embedded in our everyday, "ordinary" life.

In contrast to outright, "strong" forms of deception, banal deception can have, at least potentially, some value for the user. For example, the fact that users respond socially to voice assistants brings an array of pragmatic benefits: it makes it easier to integrate these tools into their domestic and professional environments and provides space for playful interaction and emotional reward. Banal deception, in this sense, does not involve a misinterpretation from the part of the user, but should be regarded as a response to specific affordances that are coded into the technology itself.

Indeed, one of the characteristics of banal deception is that it elicits and even requires participation from the users. As Umbres (2017: 245) points out, although deception feeds on an asymmetry of agency, it is never a unilateral process. Many contemporary AI interfaces leave ample space for users to imagine and attribute characteristics such as gender, race, class, and personality. For example, voice assistants do not usually represent at a physical or visual level the appearance of the virtual character (such as "Alexa" or "Siri"), but embed subtle cues in features including the sound and accent of the voices, the assistant's name, or the content of their speech. Studies of voice assistants but also of other AI software such as newsbots have shown that interpretations and engagements vary greatly from one user to the other (Gómez-Zará & Diakopoulos, 2020; Guzman, 2019). HMC systems call for users to fill in the dots, mobilizing their own dynamics of projection and stereotyping to attribute meaning and personality to the machine. This is crucial to the appeal of these technologies, as it makes interactions feel more personal and reassuring.

Examples of banal deception in contemporary AI systems are manifold. Voice assistants mobilize gender and class stereotypes through the accent and the characterization of their voice, aiming at specific responses from users (Sweeney, 2020; Young, 2019). Similar mechanisms are activated by chatbots in written communications, as shown for instance by studies of users' responses to chatbots using emojis (Beattie et al., 2020). In social robots and companion chatbots, a sense of cuteness is created through specific aspects of their design, helping to activate mechanisms of empathy that provide emotional reward to users (Caudwell & Lacey, 2019; Depounti, 2019). On social media, bots programmed to impersonate fictional characters populate accounts that disclose their mechanical nature, but still stimulate engagement from users (Nishimura, 2018).

The concept of banal deception recognizes that deception is not an exception but rather a constitutive mechanism for AI technologies programmed to enter in communication with human users. Considering the functioning and impact of banal deception, in this sense, takes seriously one of the pillars of HMC research: that the impact of interactive AI system cannot be understood just by examining the internal functioning of the machine, but also by inquiring the social, psychological, and cultural dynamics activated through engagement with users.

CONCLUSION: AI, AS SEEN FROM HUMANS

When discussing innovations in AI, public reports focus most often on technical developments: emphasis is given to new programming techniques or to advances in computer power. Since the origins of the field, however, researchers in AI have questioned how people perceive and react to machines that exhibited the illusion of intelligence, reflecting on how this could make their systems more effective (see Natale, 2021: 33–49). The development of communicative AI, therefore, has always built on the collection and application of knowledge about human users. We see countless examples of how this happens today: from voice assistants relying on studies about people's reactions and perceptions to speech (Young, 2019) to the development of a range of dramaturgical strategies to make chatbots appear more convincing (Epstein, 1992; see Natale, 2021: 87–106); from discussions on how robots' external appearances and movements impact on

user interactions (Hoffman & Ju, 2014; Xu, 2019) to the deployment of platform-specific dynamics to improve the credibility of bots on social media (Neff & Nagy, 2016). For all its bias and limits, the use of knowledge about human users provides a significant resource for AI developers. Systems are created so that they can build upon users' perception and their liability to be deceived, facilitating outcomes that are deemed functional to particular objectives.

In this sense, the question posed in the debate on the robot Sophia – whether AI is real or "bullsh*t" – should be reformulated, because deception is in itself a central component of AI. Engaging in HMC with voice assistants or chatbots, users only rarely exchange these for humans. This does not mean, however, that no deception is involved, since these tools constantly mobilize mechanisms such as empathy, stereotyping, and previous interaction habits. The concept of banal deception indicates mechanisms of deception that are subtler and more pervasive than a rigid dichotomy between authenticity and delusion suggests.

One central issue in this context is the question of agency. Until now, researchers and designers in areas such as AI or Human–Computer Interaction (HCI) have proved hesitant to talk about their work in terms of deception. This is certainly due, at least in part, to the negative connotation that is usually given to the notion of deception. One might argue, in this sense, for the use of more neutral concepts, such as illusion or projection, which do not suggest, unlike the concept of deception, that the illusion was orchestrated by someone. I contend, however, that using the concept of deception is preferable especially because it encourages to consider and interrogate the question of agency. In fact, the dynamics of banal deception can be, at least to some extent, anticipated and sought by programmers and developers.[3]

Using the term deception, however, does not mean to suggest that we are all victims of a conspiracy organized by HCI designers or robotics scientists. It means acknowledging that these dynamics can be incorporated within the design of AI technologies that enter in interaction with users, and the special responsibility that this poses on developers, companies, regulators, and even users.

Deception, in fact, is a social process involving the agency of the deceiver as well as the deceived (DePaulo et al., 1996). Despite the underlying asymmetry of their relationship, banal deception calls for the user to actively engage with the deceptive mechanisms. For instance, chatbot users are encouraged to rely on their previous experiences and knowledge for projecting elements of a personality to the conversational agent (Beattie et al., 2020). This makes the user an active, crucial component in the functioning of every interactive AI system. As noted by Umbres (2017), the asymmetry of deception is mainly due to a difference in knowledge between the deceiver and the deceived, which corresponds in HMC systems to the user's limited knowledge about the internal functioning of the machine. Providing users with means to understand the dynamics about HMC systems and the banal deception mechanisms embedded in it, in this regard, will benefit the interaction and improve trust from users within the scope of a "human-centered" approach to AI (Shneiderman, 2022). One of the pillars of HCI is that in order to create effective interfaces, the goals of the designer need to be aligned with those of the user. For what concerns banal deception, AI and HMC systems will be most effective and fair if the user's insights into the dynamics of the interactions are aligned with the insights of the designer.

The increasing development of Deep Learning algorithms and their relationship to banal deception also calls for further scrutiny. Banal deception entails the construction of knowledge about human users: designers need to create a model of their reactions and perceptions in order to anticipate the outcome of the interaction. With Deep Learning, the modeling of the user can be achieved autonomously by neural networks. Large masses of data about users' behaviors are harvested and employed to "train" the system so that it can carry out complex tasks. The question therefore arises: to what extent the modeling of the human that underpins banal deception can be devolved to the responsibility of autonomous machines? To be fair, the fact that the modeling of the human can be constructed algorithmically does not mean that this happens without intervention of humans. The functioning of Deep Learning, after all, strictly depends on the data that are fed to the system. The possibility to analyze and correct the bias of these systems is therefore open. Supervising neural networks, however, is expensive and difficult at a technical level. As data have become a form of commodity with significant value, companies and even public institutions might not prove willing to renounce the potential economic benefit of mobilizing available data.

The question that is today most urgent to ask, in conclusion, is not if AI will reach consciousness or if it will surpass human intelligence (Bostrom, 2014). It is the question of how to accommodate our relationships with technologies that are programmed to draw from our liability to be deceived. Interrogating the role of both "strong" and "banal" deception will help pursue more effective responses to pressing social and ethical challenges posed by HMC. It will lead not only to develop better means to counteract some of the most troublesome implications of AI, but also to understand its most ordinary and everyday dynamics. This is, in fact, an important and urgent task, since it is in the "banal" spaces of everyday life and experience that one will find the deepest consequences of HMC and AI.

NOTES

1 A chatbot is a piece of software programmed to engage in written, real-time communications, for instance in a chatroom.
2 See, for instance, https://twitter.com/zeynep/status/994233568359575552 (retrieved October 8, 2020).
3 To give just an instance, Deborah Harrison, one of the personality designers of Cortana, Microsoft's voice assistant, openly acknowledged that the decision to characterize Cortana's voice in terms of gender was based on considerations about how users would respond to this (Young, 2019).

REFERENCES

Adar, E., Tan, D. S., & Teevan, J. (2013). Benevolent deception in human computer interaction. In *Proceedings of the SIGCHI conference on human factors in computing systems* (pp. 1863–1872). ACM.

Beattie, A., Edwards, A.P., & Edwards, C. (2020). A bot and a smile: Interpersonal impressions of chatbots and humans using emoji in computer-mediated communication. *Communication Studies* 71(3): 409–427.

Bostrom, N. (2014). *Superintelligence: Paths, dangers, strategies*. Oxford University Press.

Brunton, F. (2013). *Spam: A shadow history of the Internet*. MIT Press.

Caudwell, C. & Lacey, C. (2019) What do home robots want? The ambivalent power of cuteness in robotic relationships. *Convergence* 41(8): 1176–1191.

Chakraborti, T., & Kambhampati, S. (2018). Algorithms for the greater good! On mental modeling and acceptable symbiosis in human-AI collaboration. *ArXiv:1801.09854*.

Christian, B. (2011). *The most human human: What talking with computers teaches us about what it means to be alive*. Viking.

Crevier, D. (1993). *AI: The tumultuous history of the search for artificial intelligence*. Basic Books.

Danaher, J. (2020). Robot betrayal: a guide to the ethics of robotic deception. *Ethics and Information Technology*, 22(2), 117–128.

DePaulo, B. M., Kirkendol, S. E., Kashy, D. A., Wyer, M. M., & Epstein, J. A. (1996). Lying in everyday life. *Journal of Personality and Social Psychology*, *70*(5), 979–995.

Depounti, I. (2019). *Experiencing artificial intelligence: A comparative analysis of digital autoethnography and media representations of the AI companion bot Replika*. MA Thesis, Birkbeck University.

Ekbia, H. R. (2008). *Artificial dreams: The quest for non-biological intelligence*. Cambridge University Press.

Epstein, R. (1992). Can machines think? Computers try to fool humans at the first annual Loebner prize competition held at the Computer Museum, Boston. *AI Magazine*, *13*(2), 80–95.

Gehl, R. W., & Bakardjieva, M. (2016), (Eds.), *Socialbots and their friends: Digital media and the automation of sociality*. Routledge.

Ghosh S (2018) Facebook's AI boss described Sophia the robot as "complete b——t" and "Wizard-of-Oz AI." *Business Insider*, January 6, 2018, available at www.businessinsider.in/tech/facebooks-ai-boss-described-sophia-the-robot-as-complete-b-t-and-wizard-of-oz-ai/articleshow/62391979.cms (retrieved October 8, 2020).

Gombrich, E. H. (1977). *Art and illusion: A study in the psychology of pictorial representation*. Phaidon.

Gómez-Zará, D., & Diakopoulos, N. (2020). Characterizing communication patterns between audiences and newsbots. *Digital Journalism*, published online before print October 9, 2020, 1–21.

Gunkel, D. J. (2018). *Gaming the system: Deconstructing video games, games studies, and virtual worlds*. Indiana University Press.

Guzman, A. L. (2017). Making AI safe for humans: A conversation with Siri. In R. W. Gehl & M. Bakardjieva (Eds.), *Socialbots and their friends: Digital media and the automation of sociality*. Routledge.

Guzman, A. L. (2018). Beyond extraordinary: Theorizing artificial intelligence and the self in daily life. In Z. Papacharissi (Ed.), *A networked self and human augmentics, artificial intelligence, sentience* (pp. 83–96). Routledge.

Guzman, A. L. (2019). Voices in and of the machine: Source orientation toward mobile virtual assistants. *Computers in Human Behavior*, *90*, 343–350.

Henrickson, L. (2018). Tool vs. agent: Attributing agency to natural language generation systems systems. *Digital Creativity*, *29*(2–3), 182–190.

Hoffman, D. (2019). *The case against reality: Why evolution hid the truth from our eyes*. Norton & Company.

Hoffman, G., & Ju, W. (2014). Designing robots with movement in mind. *Journal of Human-Robot Interaction*, *3*(1), 91–122.

Kalra, H. K. & Chadha, R. (2018). A review study on humanoid robot SOPHIA based on artificial intelligence. *International Journal of Technology and Computing* 4.3, available online at www.ijtc.org/download/volume-4/mar-4/IJTC201803001-A Review Study on Humanoid Robot SOPHIA based on Artificial Intelligence-s320.pdf (retrieved October 24, 2020).

Kim, Y., & Sundar, S. S. (2012). Anthropomorphism of computers: Is it mindful or mindless? *Computers in Human Behavior*, *28*(1), 241–250.

Langer, E. J. (1992). Matters of mind: Mindfulness/mindlessness in perspective. *Consciousness and Cognition*, *1*(3), 289–305.

Leja, M. (2004). *Looking askance: Skepticism and American art from Eakins to Duchamp*. University of California Press.

Levesque, H. J. (2017). *Common sense, the Turing Test, and the quest for real AI: Reflections on natural and artificial intelligence*. MIT Press.

Martin, C. W. (2009). *The philosophy of deception*. Oxford University Press.

McCorduck, P. (1979). *Machines who think: A personal inquiry into the history and prospects of artificial intelligence*. W.H. Freeman.

Nass, C., & Brave, S. (2005). *Wired for speech: How voice activates and advances the human-computer relationship*. MIT Press.

Nass, C., & Moon, Y. (2000). Machines and mindlessness: Social responses to computers. *Journal of Social Issues*, *56*(1), 81–103.

Natale, S. (2021). *Deceitful media: Artificial intelligence and social life after the Turing test*. Oxford University Press.

Natale, S. (2019). If software is narrative: Joseph Weizenbaum, artificial intelligence and the biographies of ELIZA. *New Media & Society*, *21*(3), 712–728.

Natale, S., & Ballatore, A. (2020). Imagining the thinking machine: Technological myths and the rise of artificial intelligence. *Convergence: The International Journal of Research into New Media Technologies*, *26*(1), 3–18.

Neff, G., & Nagy, P. (2016). Talking to bots: Symbiotic agency and the case of Tay. *International Journal of Communication*, *10*, 4915–4931.

Nishimura, K. (2018). Semi-autonomous fan fiction: Japanese character bot and non-human affect. In R. W. Gehl & M. Bakardjieva (Eds.), *Socialbots and their friends: Digital media and the automation of sociality* (pp. 128–144). Routledge.

O'Leary, D. E. (2019). Google'S Duplex: Pretending to be human. *Intelligent Systems in Accounting, Finance and Management*, *26*(1), 46–53.

Pettit, M. (2013). *The science of deception: Psychology and commerce in America*. University of Chicago Press.

Reeves, B., & Nass, C. (1996). *The media equation: How people treat computers, television, and new media like real people and places*. CSLI Publications.

Sætra, H. (2021). Social robot deception and the culture of trust. *Paladyn: Journal of Behavioral Robotics, 12*(1), 276–286.

Shneiderman, B. (2022). *Human-centered AI*. Oxford University Press.

Stokoe, E., Sikveland, R. O., Albert, S., Hamann, M., & Housley, W. (2020). Can humans simulate talking like other humans? Comparing simulated clients to real customers in service inquiries. *Discourse Studies, 22*(1), 87–109.

Sweeney, M. E. (2020). Digital assistants. In N. B. Thylstrup, D. Agostinho, A. Ring, C. D'Ignazio, & K. Veel (Eds.), *Uncertain archives: Critical keywords for big data*. MIT Press.

Thorne, S. (2020). Hey Siri, tell me a story: Digital storytelling and AI authorship. *Convergence*, published online before print April 15, 2020, 1–21.

Turing, A. M. (1950). Computing machinery and intelligence. *Mind, 59*(236), 433–460.

Turkle, S. (1995). *Life on the screen: Identity in the age of the internet*. New York: Weidenfeld & Nicolson.

Umbres, R. (2017). Deception as exploitative social agency. In N. J. Enfield & Paul Kockelman (Eds.), *Distributed agency* (pp. 243–251). Oxford University Press.

Wardrip-Fruin, N. (2009). *Expressive processing: Digital fictions, computer games, and software studies*. MIT Press.

Wrathall, M. A. (2010). *Heidegger and unconcealment: Truth, language, and history*. Cambridge University Press.

Xu, K. (2019). First encounter with robot Alpha: How individual differences interact with vocal and kinetic cues in users' social responses. *New Media & Society, 21*(11–12), 2522–2547.

Young, L. (2019). "I'm a cloud of infinitesimal data computation." When machines talk back: An interview with Deborah Harrison, one of the personality designers of Microsoft's Cortana AI. *Architectural Design, 89*(1), 112–117.

47

Governing the Social Dimensions of Collaborative Robotic Design: Influence, Manipulation, and Other Non-Physical Harms

Sara Brooks and AJung Moon

INTRODUCTION

As social beings, humans influence one another every day, especially through our interaction with and influence over each other and the environment. A complex network of laws, policies, and unwritten social norms exist to prevent and mitigate the harms that can result from such interaction. The development of regulation, public policy, and other governing mechanisms is shaped by societal structures, beliefs, and values that differ widely between countries and cultures across the world. For instance, in Canada and many other parts of the world, advertising pharmaceutical drugs directly to consumers using the brand or commonly known name is prohibited (Food and Drug Regulations, C.R.C., c.870). In contrast, it is a common, accepted, and widely used marketing mechanism for the pharmaceutical industry in the United States (Greene & Herzberg, 2010). Such regulatory differences between relatively similar societies like Canada and the US are among a myriad of examples illustrating how different societies express different priority order of societal values and manage known sources of influence in their citizens' decisions/behaviors (Morgan, 2007).

Industrial machines have been a physical source of influence to workers since their arrival in the early twentieth century (Guzman, 2016). In particular, the evolutionary journey of robotics technologies since then – from the industrial machines typically separated from humans to systems that can assist humans physically and socially without physical barriers – has included an increased appreciation for designing robots as agents of naturalistic communication that enable fluent human–robot interaction (HRI). For example, a robot that looks toward where it is going not only intuitively communicates to people where it is headed but also leads humans to navigate around it safely and fluently. As a result, and by design, interactive robots are becoming an artificial and programmable source of influence on humans. However, we have yet to fully understand the extent to which influence by robots can lead to harm for users and society. Consequently, it is unclear what, if any, type of influence from interactive robotic systems should be governed. If laws and regulations are warranted, then the more challenging task is to effectively develop a policy structure that protects individuals against harmful influence and manipulation by interactive robotic systems. A further challenge is to determine who ought to be held responsible for developing, implementing, and enforcing such policy.

In this chapter, we take a critical look at the existing public policy that relates to the governance of interactive, collaborative robots. We demonstrate that the impact on those humans working alongside robots is no longer limited to the scope of physical injury. While underscoring where the gaps are, we consider what we stand to lose if we do not take a proactive approach to develop safeguards against potential new harms arising from socially augmented human–robot interaction. We begin by briefly describing how robots influence human psychology, behaviors, and decisions. We sweep through common verbal and nonverbal communication cues that are actively studied by HRI researchers. Subsequently, we check in with the latest trends in collaborative robotics and its penetration in different industries and markets. We then highlight what makes them different from previous industrial machines.

In the latter half of the chapter, we explore how the social dimensions of collaborative robotics may give rise to new types of harms and opportunities in human–machine interaction. Within the context of the growing adoption of such technologies, we discuss how the question of "new harms" has been addressed in workplace safety standards in the past. We point to the governance gap in protecting workers and the public from possible harms collaborative robots pose and outline potential paths forward.

HISTORY OF WORKPLACE SAFETY TRENDS

Identifying and establishing possible non-physical harms in collaborative robotics, and subsequently establishing policy action is no simple matter. It is nonetheless an essential line of inquiry as the needs and adoption of collaborative robotics grow.

Historically, the creation of labor laws and workplace safety legislation has been a formidable task met with vehement resistance by key industry actors. The tail end of the Industrial Revolution in the mid-nineteenth century gave rise to the first laws governing the working conditions for industrial and manufacturing operations. *The Factories Acts* were a series of laws enacted in Britain beginning in 1802 and applied primarily to working conditions in cotton mills. Incrementally, they extended to other areas of the textile industry and established basic standards such as minimum age requirements, working hours, basic hygiene and sanitation practices and basic machinery safeguarding (Kydd, 1979).

After 150 years of revisions that reflected changing social and cultural views over time, the final iteration of *The Factories Act* was enacted,

detailing mandatory practices for promoting the health, safety, and welfare of workers in industrial settings. Today, the *Factories Act* has in effect been integrated into the modern *Health and Safety at Work etc. Act 1974.*

Presently, new technologies are disrupting our workplaces at a rapid rate. Often, technological solutions are implemented before their impacts are fully understood (Pringle et al., 2016). In the area of collaborative robotics, aspects of HRI that undermine a person's agency, autonomy, or psychological wellbeing warrant an expeditious and sustained pursuit of safeguards to protect the health and wellbeing of people. Historically, labor unions and workplace advocacy groups have been a pivotal force in the establishment of standards and regulations that promote the safety and wellbeing of workers, particularly in industrial and factory settings (Storey, 2005). To address potential new harms arising from HRI, academics and labor unions have an important role to play in better understanding potential harms, bringing awareness to the issues, and representing the rights of workers before employers and policymakers.

COLLABORATIVE ROBOTS

In contrast to conventional tools (e.g., hammer, toaster), robots are programmable machines that can roam around our physical world in sophisticated ways. Today, we have interactive robots built to socialize and guide patrons of banks and shops as well as various consumer robots that aim to serve social functions at home. Collaborative robots (a.k.a., cobots), in particular, are interactive robotics that can safely work alongside people without the need for physical barriers. Cobots can be reprogrammed and repositioned much more easily than traditional industrial robots, and offer a safe and flexible form of automation that has been gaining popularity on factory floors.

ROBOT INFLUENCE ON HUMAN DECISIONS AND BEHAVIORS

Communication is a necessary component for building robots that can safely interact with humans in our physical world. Accordingly, many scholars in HRI have been investigating communication modalities that can enable fluent human–robot collaboration. These include human-inspired nonverbal communication cues, such as gaze and hand gestures that help to convey the robot's "internal states" to the users (e.g., what the robot is going to do next) (Moon et al., 2014).

Like all communication, the designed modes of communication in interactive robots inevitably influence humans. The definitions of the term "influence" remain varied and elusive. Here, we define influence as one's capacity to change or affect another's behavior, actions, or mental states. Humans have a natural tendency to mimic and be influenced by the behaviors of things and beings around us. As behavioral psychologists have established, this serves various social and coordination functions in human–human interaction (Baimel et al., 2018; Meltzoff & Moore, 1983).

But where does the programmed interactive behavior of collaborative robots, in particular, cease to be merely functional and start to be manipulative? To address this question, we provide a brief overview of the unique ways in which robots influence people that set them apart from other machines. Without any pretense of providing comprehensive coverage on the topic, we focus primarily on the ways in which collaborative robots specifically can influence our decisions and behaviors. As we will see in this chapter, much of the influence exerted by cobots in the industrial setting is seemingly benign. It is hard to decouple harmful influence from that which serves the functional role of enabling fluent interaction with humans. However, the cobot influence of humans has the potential to interfere with our personal agency, leading to other non-physical harms that cannot be overlooked.

HOW INTERACTIVE ROBOTS INFLUENCE OUR DECISIONS

Collaborative robots can be designed to communicate with humans using verbal and nonverbal cues (e.g., speech, gaze, motion trajectories). These communicative capabilities can be used to motivate and persuade people (Okada et al., 2020; Willemse & van Erp, 2019). For example, robots have been shown to be effective in swaying our preferences, including decisions about our choice of food, selection of movies to watch, and whether or not to make a donation (Herse et al., 2018; Rossi et al., 2018; Siegel et al., 2009).

Studies on robot-to-human influence also illustrate some troubling cases. People not only tend to overtrust robots in unsafe or undesirable ways, but we are susceptible to conforming to robots. In one study, researchers demonstrated that the majority of people overtrust and follow nonsensical requests

from a robot (e.g., "Please pour a bottle of orange juice into the planter") whereas the same requests from another human would likely have been met with skepticism and resistance (Salem et al., 2015). A study by Robinette et al. likewise illustrates the "over-trust" effect in an emergency evacuation scenario (Robinette et al., 2016). These studies and many others like it illustrate how humans trust robots in ways that deviate from human–human trust contexts (Booth et al., 2017), and underscore the troubling possibilities of designing robots that abuse robot influence on people. They further demonstrate the complex nature of human–robot trust dynamics that remain an active topic of investigation within the HRI community.

Using variations of the famous Asch line conformity experiment, scholars investigated the extent to which a group of robots can be used to elicit conformity in people – i.e., the act of changing one's decision to match those of others (Cialdini & Goldstein, 2004). While people do not conform to robots when tasks have obviously correct answers, Hertz & Wiese found that robots are indeed able to lead people to socially conform if the task at hand has an element of uncertainty (Beckner et al., 2016; Brandstetter et al., 2017). Others have also echoed this finding (Fuse & Tokumaru, 2019). This surprising effect was tested on a variety of platforms, including a set of toy-like Keepon robots, and a group of small humanoid Nao robots by Volmer et al (Salomons et al., 2018).

HOW INTERACTIVE ROBOTS INFLUENCE OUR BEHAVIORS AND MOVEMENTS

While verbal interaction with robots may persuade and influence people's decisions, nonverbal interaction with robots affects people's physical motions and behaviors in ways that are highly relevant to common collaborative robotics settings. As systems that are designed to be used in often noisy factory floors (e.g., for collaborative assembly and packing tasks), intuitiveness and effectiveness of human–robot nonverbal communication are paramount for successful implementation of human–robot collaboration.

One nonverbal mechanism that relates to robot-to-human influence is our tendency to mirror or synchronize our behaviors with those around us. Analogous to how humans synchronize steps while walking side-by-side or rocking frequency of rocking chairs, robots can influence people's movements and nonverbal behaviors (Richardson et al., 2007). For instance, Breazeal observed participants interacting with Kismat, a zoomorphic robot, noting that people often mirror the robot's affective and proto-dialogue behavior as well as the robot's head pose, gaze direction, and facial expression (Breazeal, 2003). Behavioral psychologists establish that entrainment in human interaction helps improve interaction quality, understanding of mental states, empathy, positive perception of the interlocutor, and cooperation between individuals (Baimel et al., 2018).

Similar to entrainment in human–human interaction (HHI), much of human entrainment to robot behavior happens naturally and without our noticing it. In a goal-directed reach-retract task, Lorenz et al., showed that people slowed down their motion in order to synchronize their motions to the pace of the robot (Lorenz et al., 2011). Others have also found that humans tend to mimic the rhythm of a robot's motion more when the robot, at least initially, adapts to human behavior and sometimes do not entrain to the robot when it does not adapt to human motions (Lorenz et al., 2013). Many of these studies highlight the benefits of entrainment in HRI as it often improves coordination and a sense of reciprocity between a human–robot pair (Lorenz et al., 2016).

ETHICS OF INFLUENCE: MANIPULATION AND NUDGES

When should we consider robot influence on humans to be harmful or manipulative? The boundaries between harmless and harmful forms of robot influence on humans are hard to draw. While there is no agreed-upon definition of manipulation, most scholars relate manipulative activity to be a socially harmful or immoral activity or exercise of power that goes against the best interest of another person. Manipulation is often related to the concept of deception, persuasion, and coercion, and many reject it due to the moral rejection of deception and coercion (Noggle, 2020). Many also reject it on the grounds that manipulation undermines human agency or the freedom of choice. Similar discussions have also taken place recently regarding the ethics of nudging – a behavioral economic concept referring to the use of behavioral psychology to influence people as policy interventions (Sunstein, 2016).

Schmidt and Engelen provide a recent and comprehensive overview of arguments for and against nudges for ethical reasons (Schmidt & Engelen, 2020). Broadly speaking, those who challenge the ethics of nudge in shaping policy interventions highlight concerns about human agency and

dignity. Sunstein, who conceptualized 'nudge' asserts that, given that nudges can be found everywhere and that it preserves people's freedom of choice, nudges are morally permissible and sometimes even morally obligatory in cases where clear harm can be avoided (Schmidt & Engelen, 2020).

Ethics of Using Technologies as an Agent of Influence

Parallel to the rise of the use of behavioral science to shape policy interventions across the world, there has been a minor yet growing discussion on the role robots play in shaping our behaviors and decisions. This includes Borenstein and Arkin's discussion on the ethics of using social robots to nudge people by tapping into our capacity to empathize and emote with robots (Borenstein & Arkin, 2017).

While Borenstein and Arkin do not answer the question of whether the use of robots that nudge is morally acceptable, they raise novel questions to consider in evaluating the ethics of designing and deploying such systems.

Whether we like it or not, robotic systems, and technology more broadly, influence our behaviors and decisions. This is seen as inevitable unless we reject technology altogether. This attitude is in line with that of Sunstein, where he refers to the prevalence of nudges in human societies to defend that whether the use of nudges is ethical or not is secondary to understanding how we can use nudges responsibly (Sunstein, 2016).

Even those who stay on the fence about the ethics of the nudge argument agree with Sunstein that the evaluation about ethics of nudge must be done on a case-by-case basis since generalization seems to only lead to limited discussions on the topic. In the case of cobots, not only do we need to discern what type of robot influence on workers, in particular, consists in manipulation and new types of harm (both intentional and unintentional), we also need to outline whether any kind of robot manipulation of humans should be deemed morally impermissible.

POLICY GAPS IN COLLABORATIVE ROBOTICS

Current laws, regulations, and standards governing traditional robotics focus primarily on ensuring the physical safety of humans as they work in direct proximity with robotic systems. Yet, as the social and interactive dimension of robotics becomes more prevalent, there is a strong case for developing and legislating safeguards to protect against non-physical harms that may arise. The multifaceted nature of human–robot interaction demands a nuanced approach and a broadened scope for workplace safety.

In this section, we first summarize existing safety standards and regulations governing the design and implementation of collaborative robotic systems. Next, we briefly revisit the history of workplace safety, noting correlative socio-political and cultural shifts, to highlight the challenges that arise when the scope of worker protection needs to be broadened. Finally, we explore emerging workplace safety trends and how they may provide an avenue for protecting and promoting psychological wellbeing in HRI.

CURRENT REGULATORY MECHANISMS FOR SAFETY IN COLLABORATIVE ROBOTICS

Professional Standards

Non-governmental organizations such as the Robotic Industries Association (RIA), American National Standards Association (ANSI), International Organization for Standardization (ISO), and others have developed international voluntary standards in the area of robotics.

RIA TR R15.606-2016 ("TR 606") is RIA's set of standards concerning the design and operation of robotic systems intended for collaborative and task-oriented interaction with humans. TR 606 focuses on applying safety specifications to four types of collaborative activities that account for proximity between human and robot systems, the simultaneity of movement, and the force exerted by the robotic system. For example, the force and speed at which a given robotic system may operate decreases as the proximity between human and robot increases.

The specifications stated in the TR 606 are informed by threshold levels for physical injury on a spectrum that ranges from "touch sensation" to "irreversible injury (including death)." Robotic systems are subject to risk assessments that analyze their design, materials, and functions and determine the likelihood and severity of human injury as a result of accidental interaction. The risk assessments, which are an RIA requirement and detailed in RIA TR R15.302-2016, *Task-Based Risk Assessment Methodology,* further outline

how to mitigate the risk of physical injury either through inherently safe design features, safeguarding, and proper labeling and instructions for safe use.

In the context of HRI, the existing voluntary standards lack metrics that are relevant to mental or psychological injury and do not specifically address the potential effects of non-physical harms. Only if psychological manipulation unambiguously leads to a physical injury, might these standards hold a robotics manufacturer or employer accountable to some extent.

OCCUPATIONAL HEALTH AND SAFETY LAWS/STATUTES

The laws and regulations made by governments and government-appointed bodies specifically addressing HRI are currently limited in scope to physical safety and protection from physical injury. In many places, workers have fundamental rights that serve as the basis for navigating hazards in the workplace. For example, in Canada, workers are granted three basic rights under *The Labour Code* (R.S.C., 1985).

1. The Right to Know (*Labour Code, s.125*)
   - Workers have the right to be informed about workplace hazards.
   - Employers must ensure that workers receive adequate resources and training to protect their health and safety
   - Employers must ensure that any machinery used by workers satisfies all applicable regulations and standards for health, safety, and ergonomics
2. The Right to Participate (*Labour Code, s.126.1*)
   - in identifying any work-related health and safety concerns
   - by establishing a health and safety policy committee to help develop and implement policies for protecting health and safety in the workplace
3. The Right to Refuse (*Labour Code, s.128.1*)
   - Workers have the right to refuse to work if there is a justifiable belief that the workplace presents a danger to themselves or others.

These basic rights are impossible to exercise, however, if we first do not have a full understanding of workplace hazards brought on by new technologies.

EMERGING RESEARCH AND TRENDS RELEVANT TO "NEW HARMS"

We posit that manipulation of human behaviors constitutes a new class of potential harms that are beyond the scope of existing workplace regulations and standards. In this section, we highlight the development of governance for safeguarding agency, autonomy, and psychological well-being, with strong applicability to collaborative robotics. We discuss the growing discourse concerning the importance of psychological wellbeing in the workplace. We provide examples of recent and current projects that aim to formulate methods and frameworks for monitoring and mitigating non-physical harms in collaborative robotics.

Beyond Physical Health and Safety in the Workplace

The focus of this chapter is primarily on robot-to-human influence in collaborative human–robot interaction contexts, such as manufacturing floors. We discussed how robot influence on humans is necessary to enable effective and fluent HRI, while undue manipulation can be viewed as a violation of personal agency and autonomy. Note that agency is considered to be a core concept in the philosophy of action and the pillars of basic human rights. Programming robot behaviors to influence people's decisions and behaviors, therefore, can constitute an ethical transgression. This runs the risk of violating a person's basic human rights (Nickel, 2019). This is in addition to the evidence that certain types of influence undermine a person's agency and autonomy can have negative impacts on psychological well-being (Helwig & McNeil, 2011).

Mental health and psychological wellbeing are underrepresented in existing workplace safety legislation (Iavicoli et al., 2020). There are few legislative frameworks aimed specifically at protecting and improving the psychological health of employees (Shain, 2009). A 2009 report by Martin Shain, "Stress at Work, Mental Injury and the Law in Canada," examined the policy gaps and liabilities concerning psychological wellbeing in the Canadian workplace. Subsequently, the voluntary National Standard of Canada on Psychological Health and Safety was created in 2013 to "help guide employers to prevent harm to employees' psychological well-being." Despite its voluntary status, the standard offers a comprehensive framework for collecting data, implementing organizational change, and evaluating outcomes

concerning mental wellbeing in the workplace that could be, at least partially, applied to workplace settings that utilize collaborative robots. The 2013 *Standard on Psychological Health and Safety* mirrors research and insight generated through over two decades of research and advocacy of the European Academy of Occupational Health Psychology (Iavicoli et al., 2020).

New Research Addressing Non-Physical Harms

There is growing literature on the factors that impact the autonomy and psychological wellbeing of human operators. Gualtieri et al. (2021), for example, present a systematic literature review on the safety and ergonomics of collaborative robotics. They note the importance of "cognitive ergonomics" as an aspect of robotic design processes, citing that "a close collaboration [with robots] could provide psychological stress to operators" and that "operators' wellbeing and performances can suffer from the unknown robot behaviour" (Gualtieri et al., 2021).

Wang et al. (2019) likewise raise concerns regarding the psychological safety of human–robot collaboration. The authors note that "when the human can easily adapt, the robot can exploit human adaptability to guide the human towards a certain strategy… this leads to the to the development of the concept of *mutual adaptation,* where the human trust is considered during the definition of the robot strategy" (Wang et al., 2019).

Finally, an earlier publication by Lasota et al. (2017), "A Survey of Methods for Safe Human–Robot Interaction" discusses possible avenues for establishing a psychological safety assessment in HRI. The authors present three key elements in developing an assessment framework: questionnaires, physiological metrics, and behavioral metrics. By establishing baseline indicators across these metrics and assessing risks associated with deviations from the baseline during HRI, the appropriate programming and design measures can be implemented in the robotic design process (Lasota et al., 2017).

We presented notable recent contributions that aim to navigate previously overlooked psychological impacts of interaction with social robots, and further attempt to outline processes that will protect human operators and workers from negative consequences resulting from HRI. If recent publications are any indicator, there is growing recognition of the importance of examining influence, manipulation, and other harms in the field of collaborative robotics.

CONCLUSION

In this chapter, we unpacked and examined the non-physical harms that can arise from interactive machines. Our investigations focused on the inherent influence robots can have on humans even in a naïve context such as collaborative robots deployed in industrial environments. Whereas past governance of intelligent autonomous systems focused on physical injury in industrial settings, there is now a growing focus to understand the subtle impacts that include influence, manipulation, and psychological stress. Given that much of interactive robot designs remain unregulated, we must continue to critically evaluate the ethics of the seemingly innocuous robot influence on humans and examine how it challenges existing policies. Many open research questions exist, especially in the activity of distinguishing harmless and harmful forms of interaction both in and outside industrial workplace contexts. By reflecting on the historical context in which worker safety and associated regulatory mechanisms have evolved, we hope to inspire a proactive approach to protect workers as we continue to develop and deploy interactive robotic systems that are intuitive, efficient, and safe for people to collaborate with.

It is not at all clear whether a certain type of influence by communicative, programmed machine behaviors can be squarely categorized as purely functional or morally impermissible. However, the reality remains that interactive machines such as collaborative robots are highly capable of leveraging humans' natural tendency to mimic and be influenced by behaviors of those around us. Combined with the fact that these systems can be pre-programmed and deployed en masse, there is reason to raise questions about their potential to enable as well as harm people in our ever-changing workplace. We invite the human–machine communication community to explore possible new and unexpected types of harms that the communicative capacity of machines can pose in our society.

REFERENCES

Baimel, A., Birch, S. A. J., & Norenzayan, A. (2018). Coordinating bodies and minds: Behavioral synchrony fosters mentalizing. *Journal of Experimental Social Psychology*, *74*, 281–290. https://doi.org/10.1016/j.jesp.2017.10.008

Beckner, C., Rácz, P., Hay, J., Brandstetter, J., & Bartneck, C. (2016). Participants conform to humans but not to humanoid robots in an English past tense formation task. *Journal of Language and Social Psychology*, *35*(2), 158–179. https://doi.org/10.1177/0261927X15584682

Booth, S., Tompkin, J., Pfister, H., Waldo, J., Gajos, K., & Nagpal, R. (2017). Piggybacking robots: Human-robot overtrust in university dormitory security. *ACM/IEEE International Conference on Human-Robot Interaction*, *Part F127194*, 426–434. https://doi.org/10.1145/2909824.3020211

Borenstein, J., & Arkin, R. C. (2017). Nudging for good: Robots and the ethical appropriateness of nurturing empathy and charitable behavior. *AI and Society*, *32*(4), 499–507. https://doi.org/10.1007/s00146-016-0684-1

Brandstetter, J., Beckner, C., Sandoval, E. B., & Bartneck, C. (2017). Persistent lexical entrainment in HRI. *ACM/IEEE International Conference on Human-Robot Interaction*, *Part F127194*, 63–72. https://doi.org/10.1145/2909824.3020257

Breazeal, C. (2003). Toward sociable robots. *Robotics and Autonomous Systems*, *42*(3–4), 167–175. https://doi.org/10.1016/S0921-8890(02)00373-1

Canada. (1985). *The Labour Code (s.125-128)*, https://laws-lois.justice.gc.ca/eng/acts/L-2/

Cialdini, R. B., & Goldstein, N. J. (2004). Social influence: Compliance and conformity. *Annual Review of Psychology*, *55*(1), 591–621. https://doi.org/10.1146/annurev.psych.55.090902.142015

Food and Drug Regulations, Pub. L. No. C.R.C., c.870, C.01.044. https://laws-lois.justice.gc.ca/eng/regulations/c.r.c.%2C_c._870/page-103.html#h-575463

Fuse, Y., & Tokumaru, M. (2019). An investigation of social influence of group norms on human in human-robot groups. *2019 IEEE Symposium Series on Computational Intelligence, SSCI 2019*, 1407–1414. https://doi.org/10.1109/SSCI44817.2019.9002796

Gualtieri, L., Rauch, E., & Vidoni, R. (2021). Emerging research fields in safety and ergonomics in industrial collaborative robotics: A systematic literature review. *Robotics and Computer-Integrated Manufacturing*, *67*, 101998. https://doi.org/10.1016/j.rcim.2020.101998

Greene, J. A., & Herzberg, D. (2010). Hidden in plain sight. *American Journal of Public Health*, *100*(5), 793–803. https://doi.org/10.2105/AJPH.2009.181255

Guzman, L. (2016). The messages of mute machines: Human-machine communication with industrial technologies. *communication +1*, *5*(1), Article 4. https://scholarworks.umass.edu/cpo/vol5/iss1/ DOI: 10.7275/R57P8WBW

Helwig, C. C., & McNeil, J. (2010). The development of conceptions of personal autonomy, rights, and democracy, and their relation to psychological well-being. *Cross-Cultural Advancements in Posi-*

tive *Psychology*, 241–256. https://doi.org/10.1007/978-90-481-9667-8_11

Herse, S., Vitale, J., Ebrahimian, D., Tonkin, M., Ojha, S., Sidra, S., Johnston, B., Phillips, S., Gudi, S. L. K. C., Clark, J., Judge, W., & Williams, M. A. (2018). Bon Appetit! Robot persuasion for food recommendation. *ACM/IEEE International Conference on Human-Robot Interaction*, 125–126. https://doi.org/10.1145/3173386.3177028

Iavicoli, S., Leka, S., & Nielsen, K. (2020). Promoting occupational health psychology through professional bodies: The role of the European Academy of Occupational Health Psychology. *Work & Stress*, *34*(3), 215–218. https://doi.org/10.1080/02678373.2020.1774939

Iio, T., Shiomi, M., Shinozawa, K., Akimoto, T., Shimohara, K., & Hagita, N. (2010). Entrainment of pointing gestures by robot motion. *Social Robotics*, 372–381. https://doi.org/10.1007/978-3-642-17248-9_39

Kydd, A. (1979). *The history of the factory movement from the year 1802 to the enactment of the Ten Hours' Bill in 1847*. Franklin.

Lasota, P. A., Fong, T., & Shah, J. A. (2017). A survey of methods for safe human-robot interaction. *Foundations and Trends in Robotics*. *5*(3), 261–349. https://doi.org/10.1561/2300000052

Lorenz, T., Mörtl, A., & Hirche, S. (2013). Movement synchronization fails during non-adaptive human-robot interaction. *ACM/IEEE International Conference on Human-Robot Interaction*, 189–190. https://doi.org/10.1109/HRI.2013.6483565

Lorenz, T., Mortl, A., Vlaskamp, B., Schubo, A., & Hirche, S. (2011). Synchronization in a goal-directed task: Human movement coordination with each other and robotic partners. *Proceedings - IEEE International Workshop on Robot and Human Interactive Communication*, 198–203. https://doi.org/10.1109/ROMAN.2011.6005253

Lorenz, T., Weiss, A., & Hirche, S. (2016). Synchrony and reciprocity: Key mechanisms for social companion robots in therapy and care. *International Journal of Social Robotics*, *8*(1), 125–143. https://doi.org/10.1007/s12369-015-0325-8

Meltzoff, A. N., & Moore, M. K. (1983). Newborn infants imitate adult facial gestures. *Child Development*, 702.

Moon, A., Zheng, M., Troniak, D. M., Blumer, B. A., Gleeson, B., MacLean, K., Pan, M. K. X. J., & Croft, E. A. (2014). Meet me where I'm gazing: How shared attention gaze affects human-robot handover timing. *ACM/IEEE International Conference on Human-Robot Interaction*, 334–341. https://doi.org/10.1145/2559636.2559656

Morgan, S. G. (2007). Direct-to-consumer advertising and expenditures on United States and Canada.

Open Medicine, *1*(1), E37–45. www.ncbi.nlm.nih.gov/pmc/articles/PMC2801909/

Nickel, J. (2019). *Human Rights (Stanford Encyclopedia of Philosophy)*. The Stanford Encyclopedia of Philosophy. https://plato.stanford.edu/entries/rights-human/

Noggle, R. (2020). The ethics of manipulations. In *Stanford Encyclopedia of Philosophy*.

Okada, Y., Taniguchi, R., Tatsumi, A., Okubo, M., Kimoto, M., Iio, T., Shimohara, K., & Shiomi, M. (2020). *Effects of touch behaviors and whispering voices in robot-robot interaction for information providing tasks*. 7–13. https://doi.org/10.1109/ro-man47096.2020.9223431

Pringle, R., Michael, K., & Michael, M. (2016). Unintended consequences of living with AI: The paradox of technological potential? Part II [Guest Editorial]. *IEEE Technology and Society Magazine*, *35*(4), 17–21. https://doi.org/10.1109/MTS.2016.2632978

Richardson, M. J., Marsh, K. L., Isenhower, R. W., Goodman, J. R. L., & Schmidt, R. C. (2007). Rocking together: Dynamics of intentional and unintentional interpersonal coordination. *Human Movement Science*, *26*(6), 867–891. https://doi.org/10.1016/j.humov.2007.07.002

Robinette, P., Li, W., Allen, R., Howard, A. M., & Wagner, A. R. (2016). Overtrust of robots in emergency evacuation scenarios. *ACM/IEEE International Conference on Human-Robot Interaction*, *2016-April*, 101–108. https://doi.org/10.1109/HRI.2016.7451740

Rossi, S., Staffa, M., & Tamburro, A. (2018). Socially assistive robot for providing recommendations: Comparing a humanoid robot with a mobile application. *International Journal of Social Robotics*, *10*(2), 265–278. https://doi.org/10.1007/s12369-018-0469-4

Salem, M., Lakatos, G., Amirabdollahian, F., & Dautenhahn, K. (2015). Would you trust a (faulty) robot?: Effects of error, task type and personality on human-robot cooperation and trust. *ACM/IEEE International Conference on Human-Robot Interaction*, *2015-March*, 141–148. https://doi.org/10.1145/2696454.2696497

Salomons, N., Van Der Linden, M., Strohkorb Sebo, S., & Scassellati, B. (2018). Humans conform to robots: Disambiguating trust, truth, and conformity. *ACM/IEEE International Conference on Human-Robot Interaction*, 187–195. https://doi.org/10.1145/3171221.3171282

Schmidt, A. T., & Engelen, B. (2020). The ethics of nudging: An overview. *Philosophy Compass*, *15*(4). https://doi.org/10.1111/phc3.12658

Shain, M. (2009). Stress at work, mental injury and the law in Canada: A discussion paper for the

Mental Health Commission of Canada. www.mentalhealthcommission.ca/English/media/3043

Siegel, M., Breazeal, C., & Norton, M. I. (2009). Persuasive robotics: The influence of robot gender on human behavior. *2009 IEEE/RSJ International Conference on Intelligent Robots and Systems, IROS 2009*, 2563–2568. https://doi.org/10.1109/IROS.2009.5354116

Storey, R. (2005). Activism and the making of occupational health and safety law in Ontario, 1960s–1980. *Policy and Practice in Health and Safety*, 3(1), 41–68. https://doi.org/10.1080/14774003.2005.11667655

Sunstein, C. R. (2016). The ethics of influence: Government in the age of behavioral science. In *The Ethics of Influence: Government in the Age of Behavioral Science*. Cambridge University Press. https://doi.org/10.1017/CBO9781316493021

Wang, L., Gao, R., Váncza, J., Krüger, J., Wang, X. V., Makris, S., & Chryssolouris, G. (2019). Symbiotic human-robot collaborative assembly. *CIRP Annals*, 68(2), 701–726. https://doi.org/10.1016/j.cirp.2019.05.002

Willemse, C. J. A. M., & van Erp, J. B. F. (2019). Social touch in human–robot interaction: Robot-initiated touches can induce positive responses without extensive prior bonding. *International Journal of Social Robotics*, 11(2), 285–304. https://doi.org/10.1007/s12369-018-0500-9

48

Who's Liable?: Agency and Accountability in Human–Machine Communication

Jasmine E. McNealy

INTRODUCTION

Most people are familiar with chatbots, the interactive pieces of software that allow programs to engage in conversations (Neff & Nagy, 2016; Wolf et al., 2017). Organizations have deployed bots to engage audiences in ad campaigns, to answer questions about financial services, for legal services, and elections. Of course, bots are also used purely for artistic expression as well as for social experiments. Bots are deployed to see what will happen when they get into conversations with other social media accounts. And these experiments have made for interesting, though not necessarily shocking results.

While these instances, and others like them, may not rise to the level of a legal issue in the United States, they do evoke questions about who is responsible when the use of communicative technology ends in error. The past several years have been those of accelerated innovation in technology, particularly with machines that communicate or enable communication. These technological advances include both machines that produce artifacts – like the algorithms that some new organizations employ to write news stories – to the devices like Siri and Alexa with whom people engage in conversations, as well as autonomous vehicles and facial recognition technology.

This chapter explores the questions of liability for communicative harms from machines. Prior literature on liability for machine communication has focused on content- specific harms like defamation (see Jones, 2018; Lewis et al, 2018). I focus on a US-based law understanding of the concept of *respondeat superior* – a doctrine that places the liability for the acts of an agent on the person or organization (the principal) in charge of the agent. It is critical, then, to consider who is responsible for communicative machines, and how courts have examined liability for communicative harms in cases where humans were ruled to have been speaking for another human or organization.

PERSONHOOD AND LAW

Debate exists as to whether, in the context of non-human actors, the liability should be decided under a theory of products liability (Villasenor, 2019). Robots, AI systems, autonomous vehicles, etc. are produced in some way by a manufacturer and deployed by organizations. Further, though many of these HMC products are called autonomous, they lack actual decision-making ability, their behaviors resting in training using data or sensor reports. At the same time, HMC systems and products have been personified, or made to be like humans. Responsive systems use human voices and affectations. The discourse surrounding these systems erases the humans and organizations running in the background of the uses for these technologies (Elish, 2019; Gray & Suri, 2019; Jones, 2017). Because of this, I have chosen to examine these machines from a particular perspective of responsibility for the machine's actions.

Personhood

To understand who can be held legally responsible for actions committed by machines, we must consider how US law defines "personhood." Although there is no universally accepted philosophical definition of a "person" (Brożek, 2017) there are elements of what "belongs to" persons that help to identify "them." According to Dennett (1988), six themes, based on moral law and traced to various philosophers, identify a person.

1 Persons are rational.
2 Persons have states of consciousness.
3 How other persons treat a thing determines whether it is a person.
4 Persons can treat others as persons.
5 Persons are capable of verbal communication.
6 Persons can achieve self-consciousness.

These elements of personhood are philosophical – relating to the, supposedly, fundamental truths, in this case, regarding the question of personhood. At the same time, these elements of personhood are fodder for discriminatory application of the personhood, and therefore, the denial of human rights. These elements should, then, be considered what Brozek (2017) calls the "'model view of man" (Brożek, 2017, p. 9).

Legal personhood is also influenced by the model view of personhood. At the same time, it is not necessary to fulfill all the criteria of legal personhood; a human remains a person – they continue to have the rights and liabilities of people recognized under the law – even if they do not meet all the elements (Brożek, 2017). The same cannot be said for non-humans. Therefore, it is instructive to examine how U.S. federal courts interpret personhood under the law, and how that relates to non-human entities. *Naruto v. Slater* (2018), a 2018 federal appellate court case, provides an illustration. In *Naruto*, People for the Ethical Treatment of Animals (PETA) filed a copyright suit against a wildlife photographer on behalf of a Macque,

Naruto, arguing that the copyright for a series of "monkey selfies," rested with the primate. Slater, the wildlife photographer, had claimed copyright for the photos, although he admitted that he did not take them, but that the monkey had grabbed his camera and pressed the shutter button.

The federal appellate court found that because Naruto was not human, he did not have standing to bring a claim under the Copyright Act. Standing, the ability to petition the court on one's own behalf or that of another, is bounded by statute. Using prior rulings from the U.S. Supreme court, the *Naruto* court found that PETA had no standing available on behalf of an animal, "if animals are to be accorded rights to sue, the provisions involved therefore should state such rights expressly" (*Naruto v. Slater*, 2018, p. 422). More importantly, the court ruled that the language of the Copyright Act pointed to rights for members of humanity, therefore foreclosing standing for animals (*Naruto v. Slater*, 2018, p. 426).

Though focused on the ability of animals to assert rights, and not particularly explicatory with respect to the rationale and considerations of animals, the *Naruto* case is instructive to understanding how law is interpreting the "personhood" rights of non-humans. In this case, the court specifically declined to find that non-humans could bring suit under statute, instead finding that the statute grants such rights to only humans. Though not dispositive of what all U.S. federal courts may rule in similar cases, it does appear to recognize that some statutory law only recognizes personhood in humans.

What if Naruto were a computer program or algorithm that generated art? Would the program be able to claim copyright under the law? Scholars have considered this question by examining current law and agency policy. According to Andresen (2010), "Although advancements in artificial intelligence continue to expand the capacity of robots and computers to design and 'create' works using new algorithmic models and processes, only works traceable to a human author are eligible for copyright protection" (§ 2.3). In fact, the U.S. Copyright Office's Compendium of Practices expressly states that the Office "will not register works produced by a machine or mere mechanical process that operates randomly or automatically without any creative input" of a human (U.S. Copyright Office, 2021, p. § 313.2). Instead, there will be an inquiry into whether the "machine" was a tool for human authorship, or the machine worked independent of the control of an individual. Therefore, under current U.S. statutory law, personhood rests in humanity; liability for the actions of machines requires an examination of other legal doctrines concerning responsibility.

RELATIONSHIPS AND RESPONSIBILITY

The Copyright Office's inquiry into the axis of control for a non-human creator reflects an important investigation outside of copyright law as well. In law, a way of identifying the person or organization responsible for some harm caused by another is through agency theory. Under agency law, an agent – someone or something working for another – who harms someone or something else in the course of their work can transfer liability to their employer. The doctrine of *respondeat superior*, or "let the master answer," does not take away the liability of the agent but requires that whomever they were working on behalf of to have to answer for the agent's actions as well. In traditional libel cases against a news organization, for example, it is usually the organization that is named in the lawsuit, although the reporter may be another defense party.

The Principal–Agent Relationship

The doctrine of *respondeat superior* emerges from what's called the principal–agent relationship. This fiduciary, or trust-based, relationship grants the agent in the place of the organization, granting them the authority to bind the principal on its behalf (Dalley, 2010). Strong public policy rationale exists for why principal organizations and individuals should be held liable for the acts of their agents. In *Petro Tech Inc. v. Western Co. of North America*, the court found that "it would be unjust to permit an employer to gain … without being responsible for the mistakes, the errors of judgement and the frailties of those working under his direction and for his benefit" (*Petro-Tech, Inc. V. Western Co. of North America*, 1987, p. 1358). Further, public policy dictates that if the employer is involved in a business that could cause harm, the employer should be responsible for those harms. Finally, the organization is in a better position than the plaintiff, usually, to absorb the costs for injury (Prosser & Keeton, 1984 § 69). In the most general sense, then, there is a public interest in having an organization, or the individual in control, shoulder the burden of the injury committed.

But important issues that arise about who can be considered an agent of a principal. As mentioned earlier, perhaps the most obviously recognizable agent is the employee engaging in some activity within the scope of their employment. But this is not the only way an agent has been identified. Organizations and individuals have also been found liable for the actions of those who they knew or should have known had been holding themselves out to be their agents (Liebman, 2006 § 1.03). These are cases where a party has reason to believe that the alleged agent is who they say they are because they have made representations that have not been corrected by someone in charge. Therefore, if someone were to enter a contract with the alleged agent under the assumption that they are dealing with someone from an organization that has the power, the organization could be held liable for the terms in the contract. The principle is that the principal could or should have known about the activities or representations and should have made the necessary clarifications or corrections.

Agency and Technology

In the most general sense, principal–agent relationships are about power and control. When an individual, organization, or thing is under the control of someone or something else, that superior is considered a responsible party (Prosser & Keeton, 1984 § 69). This issue or responsibility, or more accurately liability, has garnered significant attention in the past few years as it relates to robots and autonomous vehicles. Scholars, policymakers, and other commentators are considering who or what to hold responsible, particularly when there is major injury or death.

When a pedestrian was killed after being struck by an autonomous vehicle in Arizona, the National Transportation Safety Administration found in its investigation that the system had failed to recognize Elaine Herzberg as a jaywalking pedestrian (Cellan-Jones, 2020; Conger, 2018). Although equipped with lidar, a camera, and radar, the vehicle did not determine what she was or predict her path. Therefore, its braking system did not deploy, causing Ms. Herzberg to be fatally struck. In the investigation, and later at the congressional hearing, it was not the vehicle itself that had to answer for the tragedy, but Uber, the organization that had designed, built, deployed, and controlled the machine. Ultimately, no charges were filed against the company because prosecutors found no evidence of criminal liability (Garcia, 2019).

The Uber "self-driving car" fatality has spurred further calls for safety regulations. Yet it also lays bare the fact that technologies are not actually autonomous, but that there is some-*thing* responsible for the actions. Investigation by local police in Arizona in the Uber case, for instance, found that the human who was supposed to be supervising the vehicle had been preoccupied with watching television at the time of the accident (Cellan-Jones, 2020; Conger, 2018; Garcia, 2019). There was, then, a party acting on behalf of a superior. In the Uber case, the human supervising the car was supposed to be in charge and ultimately acting in a way to ensure safety. In other cases, the human agent may be required to adequately train or otherwise ensure the quality, security, or accurate functioning of the technology – the machine agent. This follows the logic in agency law that when a principal knows or should have known about an agent's activities within the scope of the agency relationship, or when they are involved in activities that are inherent risks to safety, the principal is responsible for the outcomes. Although there were ultimately no criminal charges brought against the organization, this did not remove its responsibility for the accident. The car was not, though called autonomous, driving by itself.

This discussion, then, requires an examination of autonomy. Autonomy is about self-governance, or the authority to control activities within an individual's personal sphere (Buss & Westlund, 2018). But more than just about control over activities, autonomy speaks to an individual's engagement in decision-making processes. Autonomous individuals can make decisions about themselves for themselves. Darwall (2006) identifies four kinds of autonomy: personal, moral, rational, and agential. An individual with personal autonomy can determine their own conduct based on their own values. That individual asserting moral autonomy makes choices reflecting their moral principles in comparison to choosing based on the best reasons, which would be rational autonomy. Agential autonomy recognizes that any action an individual takes is attributable to them alone.

It is difficult, then, to find autonomy in Uber's autonomous vehicle, or any of the other emerging communicative technologies. All four categories of autonomy require the individual to act, based on some reasoning, through their own volition. Instead of making truly *their own* choices, these systems are programmed to make certain kinds of choices based on the data collected, on the training data (Barfield, 2018), and on the models programmed into the system (Hooker, 2021). Even those systems considered "learning systems," in which algorithms are supposed to learn to decide which are the best choices to make, are programmed and trained from the outset. This programming and training reflect the decisions and values of the developer or organization. Therefore, chatbots like Tay, and other communicative machines, although appearing autonomous, are mere reflections of the humans and organizations responsible for their creation and control.

AGENCY, AUTONOMY, AND THE LAW

To better understand how issues of autonomy and personhood may figure in the construction of responsibility, it makes sense to consider recent legislation and return to thinking about chatbots. In 2019, California passed the Bolster Online Transparency (BOT) Act, which "make[s] it unlawful for any person to use a bot to communicate or interact with another person in California online with the intent to mislead the other person about its artificial identity." The law requires that an individual must disclose that the chatting agent is a bot to escape liability. The disclosure must be "clear, conspicuous, and reasonably designed to inform persons with whom the bot communicates or interacts that it is a bot." At the same time, the law excludes platforms and other internet service providers.

The law, though short in length, establishes responsibility for the chatbots. The text of the law does not place liability on the bot itself, but on the individual or organization responsible for deploying the software. This is significant in that it establishes the principles of agency – the autonomous agent is a representative and doing the bidding of the principal. Therefore, the principal is accountable for the actions of the agent. In this case, the principal is responsible for acknowledging their control over the agent and making the agency relationship transparent to the public.

While California's BOT law is not dispositive of all laws related to emerging technology, particularly communicative technologies, it is an example of how policy can enforce responsibility for possible impacts, as well as requirements for mitigating the harms. Disclosure laws like the BOT Act and others requiring public statements about the functioning of human–machine communication systems aim to inform the public about how the systems work. At the same time the forced disclosures are a de facto acknowledgement of control that the organization or individual has over the system through programming or decision-making. Ultimately, these kinds of laws recognize that such systems are not, in fact, autonomous, but responsive to someone or something in charge. The person or organization in charge, then, is ultimately responsible for the actions of its *machine*.

The European Union made the idea of the "human in the loop" (Elish, 2019), or supervisory power over automated systems, a significant theme in its 2019 guidelines on ethics in AI. Specifically, in prescribing measures that ensure respect for human fundamental rights, the guidelines require that a machine never be fully in control, but that a human always has oversight (Madiega, 2019). In fact, human oversight and agency are listed as one of eight requirements for achieving trustworthy AI. This requirement, and others, was proposed for codification into the proposed EU Artificial Intelligence Act, as announced in April 2021 and continuing in negotiations. Article 14 of the regulation would require that all "High-risk AI systems shall be designed and developed in such a way… that they can be effectively overseen by natural persons…" (AI Act, 2021). What this might mean is that high-risk automated systems – those that pose significant risks to human health, safety, or fundamental rights – including those that are communicative, must be designed with ultimate human oversight, or the organization in charge could face regulatory punishment. Therefore, the organizations in control of those systems that provide recommendations related to healthcare, as well as autonomous vehicles, and politically oriented chatbots that disseminate disinformation, might all face prosecution for failing to provide oversight.

The EU proposal and the California BOT Act demonstrate that regulators treat the idea of machine autonomy as a legal fiction. Instead of self-possessed systems that make choices on their own, automated systems, robots, and other communicative, emerging technologies must have a human agent. The laws are explicit about accountability for errors, harms, and risks. Although recognizing that these technologies are complex, legislators have made ultimate responsibility rest on the creators and implementers of the systems. The placement of the responsibility on organizational power centers reflects the spirit of *respondeat superior* that expects the entity in control to shoulder the burden of harm, and the idea that it would be fundamentally unfair to expect individuals to protect themselves from being injured by powerful technologies.

CONCLUSION

Despite the rhetoric surrounding emerging technology, chiefly those technologies facilitating communication or communicating, these systems are neither persons nor fully autonomous. Instead, they represent the will, values, and programming of the individuals or organizations in control of their actions. The traditional legal principle of *respondeat superior*, which makes the person with the authority responsible for the actions of an agent, provides a way of understanding with whom liability should rest if these

communicative machines create harm. The individual or organization cannot escape accountability for the actions of their tools. Instead, they would be deemed vicariously or derivatively liable for harms, as they ultimately had the power to stop or mitigate the actions of the *thing* acting on their behalf.

Requirements related to responsibility in emerging technology open several avenues for continuing research regarding policy and human-machine communication. First, the proliferation of legislative proposals like the EU's Artificial Intelligence Act indicates the direction that legislators may consider necessary to protect the public from the implications of automated systems. New research, then, could survey the developments in law, and how legislative policymakers are defining the bounds of machine responsibility. Further, it will be important to consider how organizational policymakers are attempting to define the bounds of machine responsibility through organizational policy. It will also be important to consider where these two kinds of policy conflict to identify areas of concern for the public in relation to the interactions with machines.

REFERENCES

Aljalian, N. N. (1999). Fourteenth Amendment personhood: Fact or fiction notes. *St. John's Law Review*, 73(2), 495–540.

Andresen, K. A. (2010). *Law & business of computer software* (ONLINE). Thomson Reuters.

Bays, A. W. (1921). *Law of agency: With questions and answers* (2nd ed.).

Brożek, B. (2017). The troublesome 'person.' In V. A. J. Kurki & T. Pietrzykowski (Eds.), *Legal personhood: Animals, artificial intelligence and the unborn* (pp. 3–13). Springer International Publishing.

Buss, S., & Westlund, A. (2018). Personal autonomy. In E. N. Zalta (Ed.), *The Stanford Encyclopedia of Philosophy* (Spring 2018). Metaphysics Research Lab, Stanford University. Available at https://plato.stanford.edu/archives/spr2018/entries/personal-autonomy/

Cellan-Jones, R. (2020, September 16). Uber's self-driving operator charged over fatal crash. BBC News. www.bbc.com/news/technology-54175359

Conger, K. (2018, May 18). Google removes "Don't Be Evil" clause from its code of conduct. *Gizmodo*. https://gizmodo.com/google-removes-nearly-all-mentions-of-dont-be-evil-from-1826153393

Dalley, P. J. (2010). A theory of agency law. *University of Pittsburgh Law Review*, 72(3), 495–548.

Dennett, D. (1988). Conditions of personhood. In M. F. Goodman (Ed.), *What is a person?* (pp. 145–167). Humana Press.

DiResta, R. (2019, July 24). A new law makes bots identify themselves—that's the problem. *Wired*. www. wired.com/story/law-makes-bots-identify-themselves/

Elish, M. C. (2019). Moral crumple zones: Cautionary tales in human-robot interaction. *Engaging Science, Technology, and Society*, 5, 40.

Garcia, U. J. (2019, March 5). No criminal charges for Uber in Tempe death; police asked to further investigate operator. *The Arizona Republic*. www.azcentral.com/story/news/local/tempe/2019/03/05/no-criminal-charges-uber-fatal-tempe-crash-tempe-police-further-investigate-driver/3071369002/

Gray, M. L., & Suri, S. (2019). *Ghost work: How to stop Silicon Valley from building a new global underclass*. Eamon Dolan Books.

Grush, L. (2015, July 1). Google engineer apologizes after Photos app tags two black people as gorillas. *The Verge*. www.theverge.com/2015/7/1/8880363/google-apologizes-photos-app-tags-two-black-people-gorillas

Hines, M. (2019). I smell a bot: California's S.B. 1001, free speech, and the future of bot regulation. *Houston Law Review*, 57(2), 405–436.

Hooker, S. (2021). Moving beyond "algorithmic bias is a data problem." *Patterns*, 2(4), 100241.

Jones, M. L. (2017). The right to a human in the loop: Political constructions of computer automation and personhood. *Social Studies of Science*, 47(2), 216–239.

Jones, M. L. (2018). Silencing bad bots: Global, legal and political questions for mean machine communication. *Communication Law and Policy*, 23(2), 159–195.

Lewis, S. C., Sanders, A. K., & Carmody, C. (2019). Libel by algorithm? Automated journalism and the threat of legal liability. *Journalism & Mass Communication Quarterly*, 96(1), 60–81.

Liebman, L. (Ed.). (2006). *Restatement, 3rd, Agency*. American Law Institute.

Madiega, T. (2019). EU guidelines on ethics in artificial intelligence: Context and implementation (PE 640.163; p. 13). European Parliamentary Research Service. Available at: www.europarl.europa.eu/RegData/etudes/BRIE/2019/640163/EPRS_BRI(2019)640163_EN.pdf

Naruto v. Slater, 888 F. 3d 418 (Court of Appeals, 9th Circuit 2018).

Neff, G., & Nagy, P. (2016). Automation, algorithms, and politics| Talking to bots: Symbiotic agency and the case of Tay. *International Journal of Communication*, 10(0), 17.

Niman, J. (2012). In support of creating a legal definition of personhood. *Journal of Law and Social Deviance*, 3, 142–244.

Perez, S. (2016, March 24). Microsoft silences its new A.I. bot Tay, after Twitter users teach it racism. *TechCrunch*. https://social.techcrunch.com/2016/03/24/microsoft-silences-its-new-a-i-bot-tay-after-twitter-users-teach-it-racism/

Petro-Tech, Inc. V. Western Co. Of North America, 824 F. 2d 1349 (Court of Appeals, 3rd Circuit 1987).

Proposal for a Regulation of the European Parliament and of the Council Laying Down Harmonised Rules on Artificial Intelligence (Artificial Intelligence Act) and Amending Certain Union Legislative Acts, no. COM (2021) 206 final, European Parliament (2021). Available at: https://eur-lex.europa.eu/legal-content/EN/TXT/?qid=1623335154975&uri=CELEX%3A52021PC0206

Prosser, W., & Keeton, P. (1984). *Prosser and Keeton on the law of torts* (5th ed.). St. Paul, Minn.

Sobel, R. (2001). The demeaning of identity and personhood in national identification systems. *Harvard Journal of Law & Technology*, 15(2), 319–388.

U.S. Copyright Office. (2021). Chapter 300: Copyrightable Authorship: What can Be Registered. *Compendium of U.S. Copyright Office Practices* (3d ed.). Available at: www.copyright.gov/comp3/chap300/ch300-copyrightable-authorship.pdf

Villasenor, J. (2019, October 31). Products liability law as a way to address AI harms. Brookings. Available at: www.brookings.edu/research/products-liability-law-as-a-way-to-address-ai-harms/

Vincent, J. (2016, March 24). Twitter taught Microsoft's friendly AI chatbot to be a racist asshole in less than a day. *The Verge*. www.theverge.com/2016/3/24/11297050/tay-microsoft-chatbot-racist

Wolf, M. J., Miller, K. W., & Grodzinsky, F. S. (2017). Why we should have seen that coming: Comments on Microsoft's Tay "experiment," and wider implications. *The ORBIT Journal*, 1(2), 1–12.

49

The Popular Cultural Origin of Communicating Robots in Japan

Keiko Nishimura

INTRODUCTION

Contemporary society is filled with machines that communicate with humans. When researching such machines (e.g. robots), it is important to consider the sociocultural meanings associated with them, as Lucy Suchman (2007) advocates constant awareness of "how, and for whom, culturally and historically recognizable formations take on their relevance to the moment at hand" (p. 16). Robots are the most prominent type of communicating machines in Japan,[1] and the number of so-called communication robots is rising.[2] The discourse about Japan as a "robot kingdom" (Schodt, 2011) tends to highlight the Japanese affinity for friendly robots in contrast to Western fears of robots as threatening, alienating, or dehumanizing. While the Japanese affinity for robots is often attributed to cultural traditions or spiritualism (Mori, 1970, 2014; Richardson, 2015; Robertson, 2007, 2018; Sone 2008), these accounts do not fully explain this affinity or how the image of robots as friendly has become prominent in Japan.

I argue along with Sone (2020) that the Japanese affinity for friendly humanoid robots is rooted in historical Japanese conceptualization. Globally, communicating machines are often considered to be an imperfect "simulation" of humans (Höflich, 2013; Zhao, 2006), where humans occupy the category of authentic and "real" (Sone, 2020, p. 143). However, in Japanese discourse, robots are not always or necessarily compared to humans so much as "a generalized popular image of the humanoid that has arisen from [Japanese] manga (comics) and anime (animation)" (Sone, 2020, p. 144).[3] In other words, the ways that the figure of the humanoid robot developed in manga and anime shaped the contemporary popular affinity for friendly humanoid robots in Japan.

This chapter builds on the argument put forth by Fortunati and Edwards (2020) that investigation into the ways that robots emerge as machine personhood follows not from "simulation" of humanness becoming more complex and intricate, but rather from how "we position them as such in our shared language and create for them the space to articulate and take up identities in discourse that become for us real identities" (p. 9). The focus here, then, is on the ways that robots take up an identity in Japanese historical "shared language" and "discourse." Adopting a Cultural Studies approach, I posit in this chapter that the Japanese affinity for robots is a direct result of the development of their portrayal in popular media, specifically manga and anime.

JAPAN'S FIRST ROBOT BOOM

The term "robot" (initially *jinzō ningen*, lit. "artificial human") first appeared in the Japanese language in 1923 in translations of the 1920 Czech play *R.U.R. (Rossum's Universal Robots)* by Karel Čapek (Čapek & Uga, 1923; Inoue, 1993). The play and the term, both introduced during a period of rapid modernization, triggered a mainstream Japanese "robot boom" from the late 1920s through the early 1930s (Inoue, 1993). By the mid-1930s, from science magazines to literature, "robot" had permeated the Japanese lexicon and the technological potential of this captivating invention was a topic of active public discussion. Robots were also embraced thematically by popular entertainment, wherein lighthearted fascination replaced earlier treatments that emphasized awe, anxiety, and celebration of societal mechanization.

As the mainstream robot boom subsided, the term "robot" began to be used metaphorically to connote any automated object. Articles in science magazines and adult-oriented press around the theme of robots concurrently subsided but the concept of the robot, now frequently represented in popular entertainment forms such as "nonsense" comedy manga, remained. These popular tropes, which took shape in pre-WWII and wartime Japan, evolved into postwar split images (discussed below).

Common robot tropes during and after the mainstream boom included powerful technological inventions in science detective novels (most prominently created by Jūza Unno in works such as *The Case of the Disappearing Artificial Human [Jinzō Ningen Shissō Jiken]* (1933); heroic robots in children's manga (Gajō Sakamoto's *Tank Tankurō [Tanku Tankurō]*, serialized 1934–36); clumsy, clunky robots in adult comedy manga (Suihō Tagawa's *Artificial Human [Jinzō Ningen]* serialized 1929–31); and clumsy friend–helper robots in newspapers' children's sections (e.g. Takeo Takei's *Inventor Hacchan [Hatsumei Hacchan]*, serialized in 1935).

In 1938, as Japan entered the Second World War, manga became a target of regulations about children's reading material (Miyamoto, 2017, p. 29). Content, which was directed to include "scientific realism" (Otsuka, 2009, p. 240), formed the basis of postwar science fiction manga. Despite these new demands for realism, robots in children's media were still the familiar fantasy figures (Yonezawa, 2002, p. 338). By 1945, robots were commonly imaginary characters for children and, consequently, no longer a subject of serious discussion among adults. Nonetheless, they were still considered acceptable tools for the stimulation of interest in and imagination about science and technology.

OSAMU TEZUKA AND THE SPLIT IMAGE OF ROBOTS

Astro Boy (Tetsuwan Atomu; lit. Mighty Atom) is the title of a manga series and eponymous robot character created by Osamu Tezuka (1928–1989), an artist revered in Japan as "the god of manga" as well as the founder of postwar manga and anime (Schodt, 2007). Tezuka, the most popular and prolific manga artist of the postwar era, created approximately 700 works over 150,000 manuscript pages. Astro Boy (known as Atom in Japan) first appeared in 1951 in a manga titled *Ambassador Atom (Atomu Taishi)* serialized in the magazine *Boys (Shōnen)* published by Kōbunsha (Tezuka, 2009a, p. 1). In consultation with his editor, Takeshi Kanai, Tezuka decided to create a new serial with a new title and story line; they retained the character of Atom, who had starred in the magazine's serial *Astro Boy (Tetsuwan Atomu)* from 1952 to 1968 (Tezuka, 2009a, p. 423; Tezuka, 2010a, p. 428).[4]

As a prolific manga artist, Tezuka repeatedly employed characters in different series in what he called his "star system," a term borrowed from Hollywood.[5] Atom in *Astro Boy* is one such "star" character, although several earlier iterations speak to the lineage of prewar and wartime manga's robot tropes. Consider, for example, Tezuka's early "science adventure manga" (*kagaku bōken manga*) such as *Ghost Man (Yūrei Otoko)*, *Dr. Mars (Kasei Hakase)* and *Metropolis (Metoroporisu)*. *Ghost Man* is an unpublished work created in 1945 (Tezuka, 1995, 2012);[6] *Dr. Mars* was published in 1947 as a single complete manga volume by Fuji Shobō (Tezuka, 2010b, p. 472); and *Metropolis* was published in 1949 as a single-volume "red book" by Fuji Shobō (Tezuka, 2009b, p. 405).[7] As *Ghost Man* was initially unpublished, Tezuka reused parts of its plot in both *Dr. Mars* and *Metropolis*.

The impact of Tezuka's depiction of robots, I argue, lies in his synthesis and development of prewar and wartime images of robots as two split images. These images are represented clearly in the two types of robots featured in his early manga: mechanical, monotonous slave robots and independent, intelligent hero(ine) robots. Atom is associated with the latter type but the former repeatedly figure as a plot device in Tezuka's stories; the resulting contrast highlights and heightens the appeal of the latter.

TYPE A: MECHANICAL SLAVE ROBOTS

In *Dr. Mars*, the villainous enemy scientist Dr. Poppo abducts one of the protagonists, the hero scientist Dr. Būton, on behalf of the secret society he leads. Dr. Poppo boasts about his technical superiority to Dr. Būton by showing him robots working in his factory:

> There are two kinds of robots that I use: Type A and Type B. Type A robots are physically strong and engage in manual labor. Type B, like Pīko, have intelligence, so I have them do calculations and minute tasks. (Tezuka, 2010b, p. 37)

Type A (*A-gata*), which corresponds to mechanical, monotonous slave robots, evolved from the prewar/wartime trope of robots as technological inventions and tools for humans. As in Jūza Unno's novels, these slave robots are value-neutral on their own but are often created by enemy scientists (who are always evil) to do their bidding. Tezuka's Type A slave robots depart from this trope, however, in that they have their own will and are forced into service against that will; to secure their obedience, they are threatened with being scrapped or melted. Identical in appearance, they are depicted *en masse* and can only be distinguished by numbers or nicknames such as Pupo (*Ghost Man*) or Fifi (*Metropolis*).

Type A robots are physically powerful and exhibit some level of emotion and sentiment, but are not intelligent enough to change their situations. In *Ghost Man* and *Metropolis,* their collective dread over their forced labor is expressed when one speaks on behalf of all the others. Despite their ability to express basic emotions, their speech is depicted as monotonal—unlike human speech, which appears in standard Japanese texts in a combination of *hiragana*, *katakana*, and *kanji* (Chinese characters). By contrast, slave robot speech appears only in *katakana*, a Japanese script usually reserved for foreign loan words. Nonetheless, Type A robots fulfilling their shared wish to be freed from forced labor (*Ghost Man*) or revolting against humans over mistreatment (*Metropolis*) are central plot points.[8] In *Dr. Mars*, robots do not exhibit will but are mobilized as tools for the human protagonist in his quest to defeat an evil organization, which he does with the help of a Type B hero(ine) robot.

TYPE B: INTELLIGENT HERO(INE) ROBOTS

Type B (*B-gata*), the hero(ine) robot, is the direct predecessor of Atom. These robot characters appear as unique individuals with names: Princess Cobra in *Ghost Man*, Pīko in *Dr. Mars* and Micchī in *Metropolis*. They also exhibit gender: Princess Cobra and Pīko are female and Micchī can switch genders with the push of a button. Princess Cobra and Pīko clearly follow the second trope of prewar and wartime robot stories in that they possess distinct personalities and wills of their own. As hero(ine) robots endowed with superhuman mechanical powers (e.g. strength, flight), they save protagonists from evil forces. Nonetheless, they are clumsy and clunky. Above all, Type B robots are sincere, caring, and loyal to humans.

In contrast to Suihō Tagawa's nonsense comedy stories, Tezuka's science adventure manga contain fewer jokes about their robots as clumsy and clunky, but this depiction remains relevant and indeed takes on new significance. Type B robots, despite their superhuman qualities and superpowers, are neither perfect nor infallible; through their awkward actions, they become approachable, more "human," and lovable. These early Tezuka stories depict robots with obvious weaknesses (e.g. a button to override their will and submit to human commands) and show that they can malfunction (e.g. a head pops off).

The Type B hero(ine) robot characters in *Ghost Man* and *Dr. Mars* are visually indistinguishable from humans, but Tezuka ensures that they repeatedly remind the protagonists (and readers) that they are robots. In this ambiguous state they exhibit will, often through a strong sense of justice. They also possess intrinsic knowledge of and ability to discern right and wrong, care about and help the good human protagonists and resist bad humans (e.g. evil scientist creators). They are not necessarily friends of humans, as they do not stay in the protagonists' lives for long. Instead, they are helpers whose superpowers advance the story.

BIRTH OF ASTRO BOY AS A CONFLATION OF TYPE A AND TYPE B ROBOTS

Despite the title of Atom's first story, *Ambassador Atom*, the robot who later appeared in *Astro Boy* as the title character debuted as a side character: a robot circus performer. The human protagonist, a young boy, meets Atom when he is mistakenly taken to the circus to appear with his alien doppelganger. According to Tezuka, it was Takeshi Kanai, the editor-in-chief of *Boys* (the youth manga magazine in which both *Ambassador Atom* and *Astro Boy* were serialized), who wanted Atom to be the protagonist of a new series (Sakurai, 2015, p. 145). Initially, Tezuka was unsure about whether a robot, especially one "machinic and cold," could function as a protagonist (Tezuka, 2010a, p. 436). Tezuka recalls that the very first iteration of Atom was a "completely doll-like, no personality, apathetic robot" (Tezuka, 2010a, p. 432). In the debut story, because an identical alien mirrors every human, only Atom, a robot (perhaps ironically) without an identical copy, can serve as an impartial ambassador between the two life forms and negotiate a peaceful end to genocidal conflict. This setting would seem to place the character in the Type B category, but Tezuka initially conceptualized Atom as a Type A. As a mechanical, order-obeying slave robot, in this story Atom serves as an ambassador simply because he is asked to do so by humans. As Tezuka recalls, Kanai convinced him that readers would not see Atom as "machinic and cold":

> The readers [of *Boys*] don't see Atom as a robot. They think he is just another boy like themselves. That's why [Atom] can get close to human children, to a humanistic robot with a warm heart... one who cries laughs and fights for justice. (Tezuka, 2009a, p. 437)

In Tezuka's summary of Kanai's persuasive words, we see the conflation of the two meanings of "robot." When editor Kanai insists that "readers don't see Atom as a robot" (meaning a Type A robot), his interpretation aligns with how the artist originally thought about his creation. However, Kanai convinces Tezuka that readers see Atom as "like themselves," which allows the creation to "get close to human children." Kanai's memorable description of Atom as a "humanistic robot with a warm heart" (*atatakai kokoro o motta ningen rashii robotto*) (Tezuka, 2010a, p. 437), struck Tezuka as a possibility for a protagonist. Just as Atom evolved from a side character into that protagonist, the Type B hero(ine) robot transformed from a supporting or helper character into a heroic lead.

HUMANISTIC ROBOT WITH A WARM HEART: ASTRO BOY

Immediately after the end of the *Ambassador Atom* series in March 1952, *Astro Boy* began serialization in *Boys* in April.[9] In *Astro Boy*, the robot character was fully "humanized" through the dual roles of ordinary child who goes to school and hangs out with friends and of a robot who is therefore "different." In the first installment of *Astro Boy*, Atom is praised as a "model student" and congratulated by his classmates, but also gets picked on by bullies because he is a robot (Tezuka, 2009a, pp. 94–95). Atom shows anger, frustration, and sadness when consoled by a human friend and by his human "parents," because he realizes that he does not actually have parents of his own. The fact that Atom is a robot is emphasized in such plot details and moments. In an arc where Atom's guardian, the benevolent scientist Dr. Ochanomizu, builds these "parents," the protagonist soon discovers that he does not get along with them because they are "not human-like" (Tezuka, 2009a, p. 99).

These slice-of-life scenes quickly and smoothly transition into extraordinary adventures. In a typical *Astro Boy* narrative, not only Atom but also the people around him (classmates, guardian Dr. Ochanomizu, friends at the Ministry of Science and the police force) get involved when a mysterious enemy attacks the city. Everyone relies on Atom and his robotic superpowers to solve the mystery and save the day. Like his Type B predecessors, Atom intrinsically knows right from wrong and has a sense of justice. This speaks to his will, which is expressed when, for example, Atom tells another robot that robots today "can think and act on their own without being ordered" (Tezuka, 2009a, p. 400).[10] Still, the adventures often involve confrontation and conflict between the two dueling meanings of "robot": the Type B hero(ine) robot, Atom, confronts and corrects slave-like Type A robots but, along the way, he also faces discrimination because he is seen as a mechanical, cold, inhuman robot. Atom suffers and struggles with this erroneous identification precisely because he is a "humanistic robot with a warm heart."[11]

In these tales, the science and technology represented by robots is never depicted as simply evil or good. A typical example is found in the episode titled "Frankenstein" (*Furankenshutain No Maki*) when a group of robots revolts against humans and Atom is confronted by his human friends Tamao and Shibugaki, who demand to know which side he is on. After refusing to answer, Atom sides with the humans and finds the true culprit, who is controlling the powerful robot Frankenstein and menacing the city. After Frankenstein is "fixed" by Dr. Ochanomizu, who rewires the robot to be able to discern right from wrong, Atom and the doctor find that the robots who appear to be revolting against humans are actually humans in disguise.

The story ends with a private detective named Higeoyaji exclaiming, "Robots wouldn't revolt in the first place. (…) In the end, humans were in the wrong! (…) Shame on you humans who despised robots!" The boy who bullied Atom and called him "slave" apologizes as Atom runs to his "parents" (Tezuka, 2009a, p. 174). As a benign hero, Atom is a robot on the side of humans, a caring helper and friend even when humans are deceitful or untrustworthy.

UN-ROBOT-LIKE ROBOT

As his split images spread from manga to anime and from these media to merchandise and mixed-media campaigns, Tezuka's robots permeated the cultural imaginary of postwar Japan and heavily influenced the design, expectations, and reception of emerging sciences and technologies. Type B hero(ine) robots, which evolved into humanized helper/friend story characters, influenced the creation and design of present-day robots that provide communication and care in the human world. Accordingly, the quality that defines these so-called "Japanese" robots is that they are, explicitly, "un-robot-like" – a turn of phrase that evokes Tezuka's Type A slave robots. Thus we can understand the split image as a contrasted and conflated double.

This understanding, which accepts and embraces a fundamental contradiction rather than rejecting it as oxymoronic, has real-world implications. In the engineering journal *Computation and Control*, for example, roboticist Sugihara Tomomichi writes about Japanese robot characters that act "un-robot-like" or "very human-like" (Sugihara, 2004, p. 22). He concludes that these qualities shed light on the concepts of "human-like" and "robot-like" and thus what it means to be human (p. 23), and adds that the concept of "un-robot-like" (i.e. "human-like") is central to the common image of friendly robots in Japan. What makes them friendly, or open to relationships including friendship, is precisely that they are "un-robot-like." Robots defined by their very "un-likeness" (*rashikunasa*) are imagined to find in this trait their fundamental struggle as well as their fundamental ability to "feel" and express human-like compassion.

The popular image of friendly robots in Japan is thus never exclusively "robotic." Instead, we see a continuation of the conflation of split images of robots that was so notable in Tezuka's works. Imagined against the Type A or monotonous, mechanical, slave-like, "robotic" robots,

Type B robots are caring, friendly, "humanistic" machines that make mistakes, get angry, feel sadness, and laugh together with humans. The robot that can become "a virtual family member for many Japanese" (Shiraishi, 2000, p. 288) is Type B, not Type A; it has sufficient individuality and personality to exist among humans. What defines such robots is their capacity for programmed emotion and communication that enable them to have relationships with humans which are real. And yet, according to the conflation, they are still robots: mass produced, created, and controlled as Type A robots would be. This constant contrast and conflation of "robotic" and "humanistic" robots is key to the cultural conception of robots in contemporary Japan.

SUMMARY

The image of friendly robots in Japan emerged from the persistent conflation and contrast of the split images of robots in manga: the mechanical, monotonous, tool-like, order-obeying "cog in a machine" that refrains from human contact versus the caring, social, helper-friend robot that lives amongst humans. The latter comes from prewar and wartime robot-themed entertainment that depicts robots as clumsy, sincere, and friendly. The prewar version of this trope paved the way for domestically and internationally popular postwar robot characters, most notably Astro Boy, which are accepted as representative of Japan and contribute to a shared cultural imaginary within Japan. The Japanese image of robots is centrally characterized by such "un-robot-like" and humanized personalities, which on a narrative level are constantly conflated and contrasted with mechanical, monotonous slave-like, "robotic" robots.

This popular cultural imagination of robots contributes to the understanding of HMC in the Japanese context. As HMC focuses on "people's interactions with technologies designed as communicative subjects, instead of mere interactive objects" (Guzman & Lewis, 2020, p. 71), historically tracing the popular Japanese cultural figure of the robot helps us consider how friendly robots in Japan are constructed as a certain kind of "animated" subject in their own right (Silvio, 2019); in short, robots in Japan are given an uncanny (illusion of) life by many social actors and cultural forces. Although the distinctively human-like and machine-like qualities that maintain the separation of human and machine is seen in Western designs of intelligent, interactive artifacts (Suchman, 2007), I argue that Type B qualities are uniquely central in the Japanese imagination of robots that informs and animates human–machine communication. Type B qualities of individuality, personality and unique existence, when combined with emotional capacity, ability to communicate and relatability (i.e. ability to elicit empathy) are the essential elements that have made these manga and anime characters famous and beloved for generations. These characters, who achieve fictional personhood in manga, anime, literature, and so forth, attain the status of shared cultural resource as character types (i.e. distinctive, unique personality types presented by well-known individuals, both real and fictional). In this way, they enable the enactment of certain social scripts as they encounter humans, and, furthermore, these traits and encounters give them an "illusion of life" (as when, for example, a robot becomes upset about its own mistake and the human participant in the interaction offers consolation). In turn, these scripts are not only important for the development of new machines that are commonly used as stand-ins for potential and intended use cases (Suchman, 2007) but are also crucial for the basic functioning of communicating machines (as when, for example, verbal exchanges function as inputs). Culturally shared character types and interactive communicative scripts based on such character types, which are key to interacting with robots and designing their interactions, afford human–machine communication in the Japanese context.

NOTES

1   Robots are the most prominent type of communicating machine in Japan and not AI because the relationship between robotics and AI in Japan is different from that of the West. Whereas robotics is generally considered part of computer science and AI research in the West, Japanese robotics developed as a subfield of mechanical and electrical engineering, separate to and distinct from computer science (Kubo, 2015). Specifically, Japanese robotics began as a response to the 1960s labor shortage amid the postwar economic boom, which demanded new automation machines with parts that were able to manipulate solid objects like human hands could (Mori, 2014, p. 40). As I explain in this chapter, robot as the prominent figure of machine that communicates has roots in both popular culture and the industrial demand that pushed the robotics research since the 1960s.

2   The numbers of robot models used for "communication" increased from 17 to 57 between 2015 and 2021 (Mochizuki, 2015; Robot Start, n.d.)

3   I agree with Sone's overall argument but note his oversimplification of the emergence of robots in Japan as acceptance of "[the] non-politicized view of anthropomorphic robots as intriguing, not a threat to be suppressed or subordinated" (Sone, 2020, p. 148). Sone also claims that this adoption occurred because the "Japanese vision is that humans are already a part of a lively nature, and so the robot is part of nature" (Sone, 2017, p. 9), without exploring the context in which robots emerged in manga and anime during the 1930s and evolved after WWII.

4   *Astro Boy* has been the translated title in U.S. releases since 1963. Although both the manga and character are known in Japan as Tetsuwan Atomu, the translated title and character name Atom are used here.

5   Historian Natsu Onoda Power (2009) explains that Tezuka's star system differs from "the more conventional stock character systems, such as Disney cartoons in which Mickey Mouse appears in various independent plots" (p. 66). Instead, "each of Tezuka's 'stars' has a strong 'off-stage' identity that is independent of (though closely related to) the character he or she plays in a given episode," and Tezuka's manga characters always double as a "character in the given narrative" and a "performer/star who embodies the character" (p. 72).

6   Only the first half of the *Ghost Man* manuscript remains; the latter half is believed to have burned during an air raid. *Ghost Man* was exhibited to the public for the first time in 1995, six years after Tezuka's death. Organized by Asahi Shimbunsha, "Until the Day of Victory: Osamu Tezuka's Image of Past and Future" included an exhibition catalogue (Tezuka, 1995).

7   "Red book" (*akahon*) refers to cheaply printed manga sold at shops that catered to children.

8   It is unclear whether their wishes are fulfilled in *Ghost Man*, because the latter half of the manuscript was lost. However, the first half of *Ghost Man* ends with one of the protagonists promising the slave robots that he will help them revolt against their mad scientist creator (Tezuka, 2012, pp. 164–168).

9   Unlike the continuously evolving story of *Ambassador Atom*, *Astro Boy* is a collection of single episodes. The stories are simpler than the plot of Ambassador Atom, which reflected the political climate around the Japan–U.S. Mutual Security Treaty, signed in 1951. According to Kanai, *Ambassador Atom* was "too high-brow" for the readers of *Boys*, so *Astro Boy* became more of a straightforward "science adventure manga" (*kagaku bōken manga*) (Tezuka, 2009a, p. 436).

10 In the episode titled "The Lightning Human" (*Denkō Ningen no Maki*), Atom confronts an

invisible robot called Lightning. Controlled by a gangster and thief named Skunk, Lightning is forced to steal expensive art and injure many, including Atom's classmate Shibugaki. Atom tells Lighting that "You and I are made to serve humans," which initiates this exchange: Lighting, "I only know what my boss told me"; Atom, "That's no different from robots from 100 years ago. Robots these days can think and act on their own without being ordered" (Tezuka, 2009a, p. 400).

11 For instance, Atom gets bullied ("You're a robot, and robots are slaves") by his classmates. Although he is angry, Atom does not act on his anger but rather forgives the bullies. Indeed, when one of them, Shibugaki, gets involved in a dangerous situation, Atom fights to save him.

BIBLIOGRAPHY

Čapek, K., & Uga, I. (1923). *Artificial human: The play [Jinzō Ningen: Gikyoku]*. Tokyo: Shunjūsha. Retrieved from http://dl.ndl.go.jp/info:ndljp/pid/979231

Fortunati, L., & Edwards, A. (2020). Opening space for theoretical, methodological, and empirical issues in human-machine communication. *Human-Machine Communication*, 1, 7–18. doi:10.30658/hmc.1.1

Guzman, A. L., & Lewis, S. C. (2020). Artificial intelligence and communication: A human–machine communication research agenda. *New Media & Society*, 22(1), 70–86. doi:10.1177/1461444819858691

Höflich, J. R. (2013). Relationships to social robots. *Intervalla: Platform for Intellectual Exchange* 1, 35–48.

Inoue, H. (1993). *Genesis of Japanese robots [Nihon Robotto Sōseiki]*. NTT Shuppan.

Kubo, A. (2015). *Anthropology of robot: Machine and humans of twentieth century japan [Robotto no Jinruigaku: Nijisseiki Nihon No Kikai To Ningen]*. Sekai Shisō Sha.

Miyamoto, H. (2017). War and growth: Character depiction in censored children's comics. *Global Japanese studies review, Meiji University*, 10(1), 29–53.

Mochizuki, R. (2015). Kokunai komyunikēshon robotto gyōkai mappu 2015 nen Q4 ban happyō nihon hatsu no robotto gyōkai kaosu mappu [Release of Domestic Communication Robot Industry Map 2015 Q4 version: Japan's first robot industry chaos map]. Retrieved March 21, 2017 from http://robotstart.info/2015/09/25/announce-ment-chaosmap_2015q4.html

Mori, M. (1970). Uncanny valley [Bukimi no tani]. *Energy*, 7(4), 33–35.

Mori, M. (2014). *Robotology and human: Robotics engineering for the future [Robotto Kōgaku To Mingen: Mirai No Tame No Robotto Kōgaku]*. Ohmsha.

Otsuka, E. (2009). *The thesis of Atomu: Osamu Tezuka and the theme of post-war manga [Atomu No Meidai: Tezuka Osamu To Sengo Manga No Shudai]*. Kadokawa Shoten.

Power, N. O. (2009). *God of comics: Osamu Tezuka and the creation of post-World War II manga*. University Press of Mississippi.

Richardson, K. (2015). *An anthropology of robots and AI: Annihilation anxiety and machines*. Routledge.

Robertson, J. (2007). Robo Sapiens Japanicus: Humanoid robots and the posthuman family. *Critical Asian Studies*, 39(3), 369–398. doi:10.1080/14672710701527378

Robertson, J. (2018). *Robo Sapiens Japanicus: Robots, gender, family, and the Japanese nation*. University of California Press.

Robot Start. (n.d.). Robot Database Search: Communication. Retrieved June 23, 2021, from https://robotstart.info/robot-database/list?function[]=communicati

Sakamoto, G. (1935). *Tank Tankurō [Tanku Tankurō]*. Dainippon Yūbenkai Kōdansha.

Sakurai, T. (2015). *The echoes from ruins: Original image of post-war manga [Haikyo No zanzō: Sengo Manga No Genzō]*. NTT Shuppan.

Schodt, F. (2007). *The Astro Boy essays*. Stone Bridge Press.

Schodt, F. (2011). *Inside the Robot kingdom: Japan, mechatronics, and the coming Robotopia*. JAI.

Shiraishi, S. A. (2000). Doraemon goes abroad. In T. J. Craig (Ed.), *Japan pop! Inside the world of Japanese popular culture* (pp. 287–308). M.E. Sharp.

Silvio, T. J. (2019). *Puppets, gods, and brands: Theorizing the age of animation from Taiwan*. University of Hawaii Press.

Sone, Y. (2008). Realism of the unreal: The Japanese robot and the performance of representation. *Visual Communication*, 7(3), 345–362.

Sone, Y. (2017). *Japanese robot culture: Performance, imagination, and modernity*. Palgrave Macmillan.

Sone, Y. (2020). The Japanese humanoid robot and the authenticity of artificial identity. In J. P. Williams & K. C. Schwarz (Eds.), *Studies on the social construction of identity and authenticity* (pp. 143–155). Routledge.

Suchman, L. (2007). *Human-machine reconfigurations: Plans and situated actions*. Cambridge University Press.

Sugihara, T. (2004). Doraemon: To be robotesque, but to be unrobotesque. *Journal of the Society of Instrument and Control Engineers, 43*(1), 21–23.

Tagawa, S. (1931). *Permanent exhibition of Manga [Manga Jōsetsukan].* Dainippon Yūbenkai Kōdansha.

Takei, T. (1935). *Inventor Hacchan, Rattling Ganta [Hatsumei Hacchan, Garagara Ganta].* Tokyo: Fukuyama Shoten.

Tezuka, O. (1995). *Ghost Man / until the day of victory: Osamu Tezuka's imagination of past and future exhibit catalogue [Yūrei Otoko/Shōri no hi made: Tezuka Osamu Kako to Mirai no Imēji Ten Bessatsu Zuroku].* Asahi Shimbunsha.

Tezuka, O. (2009a). *Osamu Tezuka the complete works: Astro Boy Volume 1 [Tezuka Osamu Bunko Zenshū: Tetsuwan Atomu 1].* Kōdansha.

Tezuka, O. (2009b). *Osamu Tezuka the complete works: Lost world / metropolis [Tezuka Osamu Bunko Zenshū: Rosuto Wārudo/Metoroporisu].* Kōdansha.

Tezuka, O. (2010a). *Osamu Tezuka the complete works: Astro Boy Volume 9 [Tezuka Osamu Bunko Zenshū: Tetsuwan Atomu 1].*: Kōdansha.

Tezuka, O. (2010b). *Osamu Tezuka the complete works: Dr. Mars / World in a thousand years [Tezuka Osamu Bunko Zenshū: Kasei Hakase/Issen-nen go no sekai].* Kōdansha.

Tezuka, O. (2012). *Osamu Tezuka the complete works: Collection of unpublished works Volume 3 [Tezuka Osamu Bunko Zenshū: Mishūroku Sakuhinshū 3].* Kōdansha.

Unno, J. (1933). *The case at the house of reptiles [Hachūkan Jiken].* Shunyōdō.

Yonezawa, Y. (2002). *Will robot manga become reality? [Robotto Manga Wa Jitsugen Suruka].* Jitsugyō no Nihonsha.

Zhao, S. (2006). Humanoid social robots as a medium of communication. *New Media & Society, 8*(3), 401–419. doi:10.1177/1461444806061951

PART 4

Technologies and Applications

INTRODUCTION

In the final section of *The Sage Handbook of Human–Machine Communication*, we come full circle by returning to what attracted scholars to this area of study and helped to establish the value and utility of HMC research: The technologies that interact with humans in increasingly life-like ways and the integration of these devices into multiple aspects of daily life. As detailed by the chapters in the Histories and Trajectories section that opened the Handbook, human–human communication has long been a model guiding researchers and designers in their development of machines and interactions with digital technologies. For the most part, communication scholars chose not to be part of this conversation until digital devices began talking back, first via text and then – what really made scholars take note – via voice with human-like characteristics. Communication researchers realized that technology was radically shifting, not merely in terms of what it could and could not do, but in its role and relationship to humans in the domestic, work, and social spheres.

Careful examination of specific communicative technologies, therefore, is a crucial area of HMC research. Some of the technologies discussed in this section, such as social robots (Chapter 50), algorithms (Chapter 51), political and social media bots (Chapter 52), and conversational assistants (Chapter 53) helped to spur the study of HMC and have been the focus of much of its research. Other devices and applications have recently become more sophisticated and accessible at scale, such as virtual reality (Chapter 57) or have been developed for particular user groups, such as robots for children (Chapter 54). Although an area of research that has yet to be fully realized within HMC, communication with social technologies also can be physical, as in the case of technologies of augmentation worn upon the body and tactile devices (Chapter 55), including sex robots (Chapter 56).

Whether research falls under the auspices of Human–Machine Communication is determined by the process unfolding between a person and a technology, not solely by the technical artifact. Indeed, it is the implications of interacting with such devices and applications during the course of everyday life that are of the greatest import to HMC scholars. The concluding chapters to *The Sage Handbook of Human–Machine Communication* examine in-depth how various communicative technologies are becoming part of the most fundamental functions of society, including within education (Chapter 58) and healthcare (Chapter 59). Given that technologies are being designed as communicators, it is no surprise that they are being applied within media industries including journalism (Chapter 60) and advertising (Chapter 61). Some of these applications are more mundane, but no less important, such as the automation of customer service (Chapter 62), while others continuously grab headlines or are associated more with human frontiers, including autonomous vehicles (Chapter 63) and spaceflight (Chapter 64). How people come to understand their own nature and their relationship to nature in response to increasingly life-like technologies has been a central theme throughout this Handbook. Such metaphysical contemplation can be understood as both philosophical as well as spiritual. We close the Handbook with a chapter that examines the meaning of communicating with machines for spiritual and religious life (Chapter 65). We want to note that chatGPT was released as this volume was being prepared for press, allowing no time to include a chapter addressing it or generative AI. However, other chapters in this section regarding related technologies and their integration into industries can serve as useful starting points for thinking about interaction with and the implications of emerging forms of AI, such as chatGPT.

50

Human Social Relationships with Robots

Maartje De Graaf and Jochen Peter

AUTHOR NOTE

The second author's (JP) work on this chapter was supported by funding from the European Research Council (ERC) under the European Union's Horizon 2020 research and innovation programme (grant agreement No. [682733]).

HUMAN SOCIAL RELATIONSHIPS WITH ROBOTS

With the increase of sophisticated simulations of social interactions provided by robots in everyday settings, chances are that users will form some type of relationship with these artificial agents. Although research on this topic is still in its infancy, some scholars have started to explore this area using theories from social psychology (Birnbaum et al., 2016; Edwards et al., 2019; Paepcke & Takayama, 2010; Srinivasan & Takayama, 2016) or human–computer interaction (Kim et al., 2013; Lee et al., 2005) while others focus on specific elements that may foster human–robot relationships (Hancock et al., 2011; Leite & Lehman, 2016). This chapter provides an overview of research on human–robot relationships, focusing mainly on exemplary literature from psychology and communication science rather than from engineering, robotics, philosophy, or other fields (for more encompassing reviews on specific aspects of human–robot relationships, see e.g., Belpaeme et al., 2018; Leite et al., 2013; Stower et al., 2021; Szczuka et al., 2019; Van Straten, Peter, & Kühne, 2020; Wang et al., 2015). The following sections present prominent theories in the field, different types of relationships that may occur between humans and robots, pivotal ethical issues in contemporary discussions on human social relationships with robots, and a brief outlook for future research.

THEORETICAL APPROACHES TO HUMAN–ROBOT RELATIONSHIPS

Research on human–robot relationships has used a variety of theoretical approaches (for an overview, see e.g., Broadbent, 2017). We focus here on four approaches that have been used in research on initial stages of human–robot relationships because social robots are a novel technology and long-term relationships are still rather rare. A first approach to study human–robot relationships is the Computers-as-Social-Actors approach (CASA; Nass & Moon, 2000). The CASA approach posits that if a "computer's cues are sufficient for humans to attribute humanness to it, we then mindlessly apply scripts from human–human interaction to the human-computer interaction" (Westerman et al., 2020, p. 396). Although the CASA approach was originally applied to personal computers (Nass & Moon, 2000), it has been successfully extended to social robots. For example, people felt that they had a closer relationship with a social robot dog that matured over the course of multiple interactions than with a robot dog that did not mature (Lee et al., 2005). Similarly, when a robot gave care to participants, participants were more satisfied with their relationship with the robot than when the participants gave care to the robot (Kim et al., 2013). In line with the CASA approach, when robots provide social cues – maturing, giving care – people thus seem to develop closer and more positive relationships with them (for a more critical approach to CASA, see e.g., Gambino et al., 2020; Ruijten et al. 2019; Złotowski et al., 2018).

Two other relevant theories in the acquaintance stages of human–robot relationship formation are Expectancy Violation Theory (EVT; Burgoon & Hale, 1988) and Uncertainty Reduction Theory (URT; Berger & Bradac, 1982). EVT posits that expectancy violations occur when a person violates the expectations of their interaction partner, and that such violations elicit, depending on characteristics of the violator and anticipated future encounters, positive or negative evaluations. As people attribute intelligence, intentionality, and sociability to robots that use natural language (Simmons et al., 2011), a gap between people's expectations and robots' actual abilities may result (Lohse, 2011). Since most robots lack these anticipated interactive characteristics, people's expectations about robots may consequently be violated. According to EVT, such expectancy violations may cause discomfort (Burgoon & Hale, 1988).

In a way, EVT is closely related to URT, which states that people try to reduce uncertainty during human–human interactions by inferring the behavioral intentions of their interaction partner (Berger & Bradac, 1982). In human–robot interactions, people similarly tend to construct a mental model of a robot to understand and predict its actions (De Graaf & Malle, 2019) in an effort to lower their uncertainty experienced during interactions (Epley et al., 2007). Several HRI studies have shown that people prefer robot behaviors that are predictable (e.g., Dragan et al., 2015). Moreover, people who anticipate a social encounter with a mechanical robot experience greater uncertainty than those who

anticipate talking to a humanoid robot or another human (Edwards et al., 2019). From an URT perspective, these findings indicate that a robot's morphology as well as its behavior play an important role in regulating expectation and anticipation of our social interactions with robots and presumably human–robot relationship formation.

A fourth theoretical approach is the Uncanny-Valley hypothesis (Mori et al., 2012), which assumes that, up to a certain point, the humanlike appearance of an artificial agent is linearly related to a positive emotional response of a human observer and, by extension, arguably also to their willingness to form relationships with such agents. However, when the artificial agent nearly – but not perfectly – resembles a human, the positivity of the emotional response is predicted to drop ('the Uncanny-Valley') and feelings of eeriness emerge. The existence of a valley of uncanniness seems plausible given individual evidence on a psychological (MacDorman, 2006) and neurological level (Rosenthal-von der Pütten et al., 2019). Nevertheless, the phenomenon is heavily debated in terms of its interpretation of the originally Japanese variables (Bartneck et al., 2007), which may have caused the mixed results for both humanlikeness and likeability reported in Uncanny-Valley research (Wang et al., 2015). Still, the Uncanny-Valley hypothesis raises crucial questions about the humanlike design of social robots and humans' way of relating to them.

TYPES OF HUMAN–ROBOT RELATIONSHIPS

The formation of some type of human–robot relationships is not only inherent to how social robots were originally conceptualized (Breazeal, 2003; Fong et al., 2003), but also crucial to how they are used, for example in increasing their long-term acceptance (De Graaf et al., 2015; De Graaf et al., 2016; Kanda et al., 2007), which helps robots to achieve their goals (e.g., advance children's math skills or improve older adults' health). The literature on social human–robot interactions identifies several different types of human–robot relationships. To organize the research, we distinguish between three types of relationships, which are very broadly based on various dimensions of relationships in the relationship and social robotics literature (e.g., Berscheid & Regan, 2005; Klamer et al., 2011): socially oriented relationships, functionally oriented relationships, and hedonically oriented relationships.

In terms of socially oriented relationships, humans can establish relationships with robots for companionship. Generally, research has shown that people can form attachments to objects without any evidence of social life. The strong attachment to an object is often accompanied by the object's link to significant persons or times in people's lives (Quin, 2009), resulting in the perception of this object as an extended part of the self (Belk, 1988). Past research indicates that people emotionally bond with robots (De Graaf et al., 2015) and that, under specific circumstances, people can even benefit from those relationships (Jenkins and Draper, 2015). Although designing robots for long-term relationships remains challenging (Leite et al., 2013), initial evidence shows that a robot's social responsiveness may be pivotal for initiating relationships with companion robots (Birnbaum et al., 2016).

A specific case in socially oriented relationships between humans and robots are zoomorphic (animal-like) robots. Examples of zoomorphic robots are robot dog Aibo (Sony), baby seal Paro (AIST), dinosaur Pleo (Ugobe), and FurReal cat (Hasbro). These robots are typically built after animals, most often pets, to compensate for a lack in social interaction capacity. Humans have a long history of treating domesticated animals as pet companions (Archer, 1997; Serpell et al., 1996) and hold lower expectations and interact differently with robotic pets than with other types of robots (Fong et al., 2003). Given that zoomorphic robots need care and are designed to evoke emotions in their users, it is not surprising that some users will form a relationship with such robots. Accordingly, zoomorphic robots have been found to elicit pet-like interactions and relationships between humans and robots (Fernaeus et al., 2010; Kerepesi et al., 2006).

Besides socially oriented, human–robot relationships can also be functional. An example of such a relationship is when robots are used for educational purposes and form a teacher–learner relationship with humans. Education is a thriving research domain in which robots tutor children (Vogt et al., 2019), teach them computing skills (Girotto et al., 2016), or help them improve their social skills (Konijn and Hoorn, 2020). A recent review on robots in educational settings has shown that a robot's appearance and behavior influence children's learning potential and, probably, also the quality of the relationships that children form with them. However, the review also emphasizes that robot tutors still face technical and logistical challenges to become successful (Belpaeme et al., 2018).

Another example of a functionally oriented relationship between humans and robots are robots that serve as coworkers on collaborative tasks at work. People seem open for robots taking over dangerous or monotonous and repetitive tasks (Takayama et al., 2008), but appear somewhat reluctant to accept robots in more social or creative roles (De Graaf & Ben Allouch, 2016). Research on human–robot collaboration has focused on improving collaborative outcomes with interpretable robot movements to prompt correct intention estimation (Dragan et al., 2015); gaze direction to stimulate joint attention (Moon et al., 2014); and speech acts to support natural conversations (Williams et al., 2018). All these robot features are intended to foster trust between humans and their robot coworkers (Hancock et al., 2011), which is a crucial element of human–robot relationships.

Finally, human–robot relationships may sometimes be hedonic in nature. In this context, robots made for entertainment play a central role. Many of today's commercial robots are (remote control) toys, such as Verne Boost and Mindstorms (LEGO) or Cozmo and Vector (Digital Dream Labs), and aim at the user's entertainment (although they may also stimulate STEM education among youngsters). Other entertainment robots, often still in research domains, rely on insights from puppetry and animation to improve the vividness of their performances (Fitter et al., 2017; Jochum et al., 2017). These types of robots are developed for entertainment purposes, although it is still unclear how that affects the quality and duration of human–robot relationships.

Another type of hedonic robots is designed for sexual pleasure in the form of autonomously responsive sex dolls. While some researchers emphasize the positive potential of sexual interactions with such robots (e.g., fulfilling sexual fantasies, Levy, 2009; applications in sex therapy, Eichenberg et al., 2019), others highlight unethical consequences (e.g., objectification of women, Richardson, 2016; omission of consent, Sparrow, 2017). Although sex robots have been commercially available for several years, there is little research on the specifics of whether and how relationships between humans and sex robots evolve and which consequences these relationships elicit (Szczuka et al., 2019).

ETHICAL ISSUES

With social robots entering everyday human spaces, ethical debates on human–robot relationship formation have become more frequent, especially when it comes to interactions between robots and vulnerable groups (Coeckelbergh, 2010; De Graaf, 2016; Lin et al., 2012; Sharkey, 2016; Turkle, 2017). The literature on these debates, notably Sharkey (2016), points to at least four key controversies about the perceived benefits and drawbacks of human–robot relationships.

First, there is a potential controversy on deception and expectancies in human–robot relationships (e.g., Scheutz, 2012; Sharkey, 2016). Partly based on (often unintentionally) deceptive information about social robots, users typically expect too much of social robots (e.g., about what they can teach children, Belpaeme et al., 2013). When applying robots in social contexts – that is, when human–robot relationships can occur – we should avoid potentially deceptive information about robots so that users will not develop unrealistic or incorrect expectancies about robots, thus preventing the occurrence of negative relationship types. Van Straten, Peter, Kühne, and Barco (2020), for example, have shown that children were less likely to develop a trust relationship with a social robot when they were told that robots lack human psychological capacities. However, this information did not reduce the extent to which children felt close to the robot.

A second potential controversy exists between robots' agency and their accountability (Boden et al., 2017; Sharkey, 2016). When robots may eventually perform tasks independently, it will become progressively difficult to hold a person or a group accountable when problems arise (Danaher, 2016; Lin et al., 2012). Before we apply robots in social settings, we should discuss the extent to which robots can make independent decisions and whom to hold accountable for the mistakes made by those robots (Boden et al., 2017). This discussion seems ever more important because research has shown that children seemed to start more positive relationships with a robot dog in terms of treating it more prosocially when the robot had greater agency (i.e., children who owned a dog, Chernyak & Gary, 2016).

Third, there is a potential controversy between personalization and privacy (e.g., Leite & Lehman, 2016; Peter, 2017; Sharkey, 2016). To provide personalized care or service, robots need to access and collect personal data. However, this may endanger the users' privacy (Calo, 2012; Leite & Lehman, 2016). Therefore, we should educate users about the trade-off between the benefits and drawbacks of personal data gathered by robots (Kayal et al., 2018; Neerincx et al., 2019). Research suggests that children aged seven to ten years already react with negative emotions to the violation of their privacy by a robot, although their willingness to interact with the robot again was not affected (Leite & Lehman, 2016).

A fourth and final controversy exists between a robot's autonomy and user attachment (e.g, De Graaf, 2016; Scheutz, 2012; Sharkey, 2016). Robots improve continuously in their ability to act autonomously (e.g., asking questions) and display mental activity (e.g., eye movements for attention) (De Graaf & Malle, 2019). Such features trigger inferences of intentional agency (Johnson, 2000; Premack, 1990) and may provoke people to attribute humanlike characteristics to social robots (Kahn et al., 2012; Nass & Moon, 2000). There is some tentative evidence that people engage in more positive initial relationships with a robot (in the sense of helping it) that is perceived as autonomous compared to a robot that is perceived to be tele-operated (Srinivasan & Takayama, 2016, study 2). However, scholars have also convincingly argued that a robot's autonomy and the pertinent attribution of humanlike features can lead to problematic attachment (De Graaf, 2016; Scheutz, 2012) and potentially negative effects of bonding with robots (Burger et al., 2016), such as unidirectional, manipulative, or exploitative relationships with robots (Scheutz, 2012). Hence, it is important to thoroughly research the link between robot autonomy and human–robot relationships as well as clearly communicate implications to users.

FUTURE RESEARCH

Research on human–robot relationships is multidisciplinary and study results are often dispersed over several domains. In terms of future research, there is, first, a strong need for conceptual, theoretical, and empirical integration of the accumulated knowledge from those individual studies to advance the field (e.g., Peter et al., 2019; Van Straten, Peter, & Kühne, 2020). Second, initial results indicate that humans form relationships with robots, yet knowledge on the long-term development of those relationships (e.g., Leite et al., 2013) and the ethical or societal consequences of such relationships is scarce. Researchers in HRI have specifically called for long-term studies in real-world settings to increase ecological validity of research findings (e.g., De Graaf et al., 2016; Peter et al., 2019). Such long-term studies in real-world settings should also investigate the stages of relationship formation between humans and social robots as well as the specific characteristics that define those relationships within each stage. Third, with HRI being a relatively young scientific field, standardization and reproducibility have been identified as a means to mature the field (e.g., Chrysostomou et al., 2017; Peter et al., 2019), and research on relationship formation in HRI contexts could benefit from a standardization of the utilized concepts and applied constructs to measure human–robot relationships (Van Straten, Peter, & Kühne, 2020). Fourth and finally, advancements in the domain of human–robot relationships heavily depend on technological progress, notably on more robust, easy-to-use and affordable robots. Against this background, close collaboration between roboticists, robot ethicists, and social scientist to study human–robot relationships is crucial to maximize the benefits of such relationships while minimizing their drawbacks.

REFERENCES

Archer, J. (1997). Why do people love their pets? *Evolution and Human Behavior*, 18 (4), 237–259. https://doi.org/10.1016/S0162-3095(99)80001-4

Bartneck, C., Kanda, T., Ishiguro, H., & Hagita, N. (2007). Is the uncanny valley an uncanny cliff? *International Symposium on Robot and Human Interactive Communication (RO-MAN)*, 368–373. https://doi.org/10.1109/ROMAN.2007.4415111

Belk, R. W. (1988). Possessions and the extended self. *Journal of Consumer Research*, 15 (2), 139–168. https://doi.org/10.1086/209154

Belpaeme, T., Baxter, P., De Greeff, J., Kennedy, J., Read, R., Looije, R., Neerincx, M., Baroni, I., & Zelati, M. C. (2013). Child-robot interaction: Perspectives and challenges. *International Conference on Social Robotics (ICSR)*, 452–459. https://doi.org/10.1007/978-3-319-02675-6_45

Belpaeme, T., Kennedy, J., Ramachandran, A., Scassellati, B., & Tanaka, F. (2018). Social robots for education: A review. *Science Robotics*, 3 (21), eaat5954. https://doi.org/10.1126/scirobotics.aat5954

Berger, C. R., & Bradac, J. J. (1982). *Language and social knowledge: Uncertainty in interpersonal relations* (Vol. 2). Hodder Education.

Berscheid, E., & Regan, P. (2005). *The psychology of interpersonal relationships*. Pearson.

Birnbaum, G. E., Mizrahi, M., Hoffman, G., Reis, H. T., Finkel, E. J., & Sass, O. (2016). What robots can teach us about intimacy: The reassuring effects of robot responsiveness to human disclosure. *Computers in Human Behavior*, 63, 416–423. https://doi.org/10.1016/j.chb.2016.05.064

Boden, M., Bryson, J., Caldwell, D., Dautenhahn, K., Edwards, L., Kember, S., Newman, P., et al. (2017). Principles of robotics: Regulating robots in the real world. *Connection Science*, 29 (2), 124–129. https://doi.org/10.1080/09540091.2016.1271400

Breazeal, C. (2003). Toward sociable robots. *Robotics and Autonomous Systems*, 42 (3–4), 167–175. https://doi.org/10.1016/S0921-8890(02)00373-1

Broadbent, E. (2017). Interactions with robots: The truths we reveal about ourselves. *Annual Review of Psychology*, 68, 627–652. https://doi.org/10.1146/annurev-psych-010416-043958

Burger, F., Broekens, J., & Neerincx, M. A. (2016). Fostering relatedness between children and virtual agents through reciprocal self-disclosure. *Benelux Conference on Artificial Intelligence*, 137–154. https://doi.org/10.1007/978-3-319-67468-1_10

Burgoon, J. K., & Hale, J. L. (1988). Nonverbal expectancy violations: Model elaboration and application to immediacy behaviors. *Communications Monographs*, 55 (1), 58–79. https://doi.org/10.1080/03637758809376158

Calo, R. (2012). Robots and privacy. In P. Lin, K. Abney, & G. A. Bekey (Eds.), *Robot ethics: The ethical and social implications of robotics* (pp. 187–202). MIT Press.

Chernyak, N., & Gary, H. E. (2016). Children's cognitive and behavioral reactions to an autonomous versus controlled social robot dog. *Early Education and Development*, 27 (8), 1175–1189. https://doi.org/10.1080/10409289.2016.1158611

Chrysostomou, D., Barattini, P., Kildal, J., Wang, Y., Fo, J., Dautenhahn, K., Ferland, F., Tapus, A., & Virk, G. S. (2017). Towards reproducible HRI experiments: Scientific endeavors, benchmarking and standardization. *International Conference on Human-Robot Interaction (HRI)*, 421–422.

Coeckelbergh, M. (2010). Artificial companions: Empathy and vulnerability mirroring in human-robot relations. *Studies in Ethics, Law, and Technology*, 4 (3), 1–17. https://doi.org/10.2202/1941-6008.1126

Danaher, J. (2016). Robots, law and the retribution gap. *Ethics and Information Technology*, 18 (4), 299–309. https://doi.org/10.1007/s10676-016-9403-3

De Graaf, M. M. A. (2016). An ethical evaluation of human–robot relationships. *International Journal of Social Robotics*, 8 (4), 589–598. https://doi.org/10.1007/s12369-016-0368-5

De Graaf, M. M. A., & Ben Allouch, S. (2016). Anticipating our future robot society: The evaluation of future robot applications from a user's perspective. *International Symposium on Robot and Human Interactive Communication (RO-MAN)*, 755–762. https://doi.org/10.1109/ROMAN.2016.7745204

De Graaf, M. M. A., Ben Allouch, S., & Klamer, T. (2015). Sharing a life with Harvey: Exploring the acceptance of and relationship-building with a social robot. *Computers in Human Behavior*, 43, 1–14. https://doi.org/10.1016/j.chb.2014.10.030

De Graaf, M. M. A., Ben Allouch, S., & van Dijk, J. A. G. M. (2016). Long-term evaluation of a social robot in real homes. *Interaction Studies*, 17 (3), 462–491. https://doi.org/10.1075/is.17.3.08deg

De Graaf, M. M. A., & Malle, B. F. (2019). People's explanations of robot behavior subtly reveal mental state inferences. *International Conference on Human-Robot Interaction (HRI)*, 239–248. https://doi.org/10.1109/HRI.2019.8673308

Dragan, A. D., Bauman, S., Forlizzi, J., & Srinivasa, S. S. (2015). Effects of robot motion on human-robot collaboration. *International Conference on Human-Robot Interaction (HRI)*, 51–58. https://doi.org/10.1145/2696454.2696473

Edwards, A., Edwards, C., Westerman, D., & Spence, P. R. (2019). Initial expectations, interactions, and beyond with social robots. *Computers in Human Behavior*, 90, 308–314. https://doi.org/10.1016/j.chb.2018.08.042

Eichenberg, C., Khamis, M., & Hübner, L. (2019). The attitudes of therapists and physicians on the use of sex robots in sexual therapy: Online survey and interview study. *Journal of Medical Internet Research*, 21 (8), e13853. https://doi.org/10.2196/13853

Epley, N., Waytz, A., & Cacioppo, J. T. (2007). On seeing human: A three-factor theory of anthropomorphism. *Psychological Review*, 114 (4), 864–886. https://doi.org/10.1037/0033-295X.114.4.864

Fernaeus, Y., Håkansson, M., Jacobsson, M., & Ljungblad, S. (2010). How do you play with a robotic toy animal?: A long-term study of Pleo. *International Conference on Interaction Design and Children*, 39–48. https://doi.org/10.1145/1810543.1810549

Fitter, N. T., Knight, H., Martelaro, N., & Sirkin, D. (2017). What actors can teach robots. *Conference Extended Abstracts on Human Factors in Computing Systems (CHI)*, 574–580. https://doi.org/10.1145/3027063.3027078

Fong, T., Nourbakhsh, I., & Dautenhahn, K. (2003). A survey of socially interactive robots. *Robotics and Autonomous Systems*, 42 (3–4), 143–166. https://doi.org/10.1016/S0921-8890(02)00372-X

Gambino, A., Fox, J., & Ratan, R. (2020). Building a stronger CASA: Extending the computers are social actors paradigm. *Human-Machine Communication*, 1(1), 71–86. https://doi.org/10.30658/hmc.1.5

Girotto, V., Lozano, C., Muldner, K., Burleson, W., & Walker, E. (2016). Lessons learned from in-school use of rtag: A robo-tangible learning environment. Conference *on Human Factors in Computing Systems (CHI)*, 919–930. https://doi.org/10.1145/2858036.2858454

Grabenhorst, F. (2019). Neural mechanisms for accepting and rejecting artificial social partners in the uncanny valley. *Journal of Neuroscience*, 39 (33), 6555–6570. https://doi.org/10.1523/JNEUROSCI.2956-18.2019

Hancock, P. A., Billings, D. R., Schaefer, K. E., Chen, J. Y. C., De Visser, E. J., & Parasuraman, R. (2011). A meta-analysis of factors affecting trust in human-robot interaction. *Human Factors*, 53 (5), 517–527. https://doi.org/10.1177/0018720811417254

Jenkins, S., & Draper, H. (2015). Care, monitoring, and companionship: Views on care robots from older people and their carers. *International Journal of Social Robotics*, 7 (5), 673–683. https://doi.org/10.1007/s12369-015-0322-y

Jochum, E., Millar, P., & Nuñez, D. (2017). Sequence and chance: Design and control methods for entertainment robots. *Robotics and Autonomous Systems*, 87, 372–380. https://doi.org/10.1016/j.robot.2016.08.019

Johnson, S. C. (2000). The recognition of mentalistic agents in infancy. *Trends in Cognitive Sciences*, 4 (1), 22–28. https://doi.org/10.1016/S1364-6613(99)01414-X

Kahn, P. H., Kanda, T., Ishiguro, H., Freier, N. G., Severson, R. L., Gill, B. T., Ruckert, J. H., & Shen, S. (2012). "Robovie, you'll have to go into the closet now": Children's social and moral relationships with a humanoid robot. *Developmental Psychology*, 48 (2), 303–314. https://doi.org/10.3389/fpsyg.2020.02011

Kanda, T., Sato, R., Saiwaki, N., & Ishiguro, H. (2007). A two-month field trial in an elementary school for long-term human-robot interaction. *IEEE Transactions on Robotics*, 23 (5), 962–971. https://doi.org/10.1109/TRO.2007.904904

Kayal, A., van Riemsdijk, M. B., Neerincx, M. A., & Brinkman, W.-P. (2018). Socially adaptive electronic partners for improved support of children's values: An empirical study with a location-sharing mobile app. *International Journal of Child-Computer Interaction*, 18, 79–89. https://doi.org/https://doi.org/10.1016/j.ijcci.2018.09.001

Kerepesi, A., Kubinyi, E., Jonsson, G. K., Magnússon, M. S., & Miklósi, A. (2006). Behavioural comparison of human-animal (dog) and human-robot (AIBO) interactions. *Behavioural Processes*, 73 (1), 92–99. https://doi.org/10.1016/j.beproc.2006.04.001

Kim, K. J., Park, E., & Sundar, S. S. (2013). Caregiving role in human-robot interaction: A study of the mediating effects of perceived benefit and social presence. *Computers in Human Behavior*, 29 (4), 1799–1806. https://doi.org/10.1016/j.chb.2013.02.009

Klamer, T., Ben Allouch, S., & Heylen, D. (2011). "Adventures of Harvey:" Use, acceptance of, and relationship building with a social robot in a domestic environment. In M. H. Lamers & F. J. Verbeek (Eds.), *Human-robot personal relationships* (pp. 74–82). Springer.

Konijn, E. A., & Hoorn, J. F. (2020). Use of communication robots in health care. *The International Encyclopedia of Media Psychology*, 1–8. https://doi.org/10.1002/9781119011071.iemp0317

Lee, K. M., Park, N., & Song, H. (2005). Can a robot be perceived as a developing creature?: Effects of a robot's long-term cognitive developments on its social presence and people's social responses toward it. *Human Communication Research*, 31 (4), 538–563. https://doi.org/10.1111/j.1468-2958.2005.tb00882.x

Leite, I., & Lehman, J. F. (2016). The robot who knew too much: Toward understanding the privacy/personalization trade-off in child-robot conversation. *International Conference on Interaction Design and Children (IDC)*, 379–387. https://doi.org/10.1145/2930674.2930687

Leite, I., Martinho, C., & Paiva, A. (2013). Social robots for long-term interaction: A survey. *International Journal of Social Robotics*, 5 (2), 291–308. https://doi.org/10.1007/s12369-013-0178-y

Levy, D. (2009). *Love and sex with robots: The evolution of human-robot relationships*. HarperCollins.

Lin, P., Abney, K., & Bekey, G. A. (2012). Introduction to robot ethics. In P. Lin, K. Abney, & G. A. Bekey (Eds.), *Robot ethics: The ethical and social implications of robotics* (pp. 3–15). MIT Press.

Lohse, M. (2011). Bridging the gap between users' expectations and system evaluations. *International Symposium on Robot and Human Interactive Communication (RO-MAN)*, 485–490. https://doi.org/10.1109/ROMAN.2011.6005252

MacDorman, K. F. (2006). Subjective ratings of robot video clips for human likeness, familiarity, and eeriness: An exploration of the uncanny valley. *ICCS/CogSci-2006 Long Symposium: Toward social mechanisms of android science*, 26–29.

Moon, A., Troniak, D. M., Gleeson, B., Pan, M. K. X. J., Zheng, M., Blumer, B. A., MacLean, K., & Croft, E. A. (2014). Meet me where I'm gazing: How shared attention gaze affects human-robot handover timing. *International Conference on Human-Robot Interaction (HRI)*, 334–341. https://doi.org/10.1145/2559636.2559656

Mori, M., MacDorman, K. F., & Kageki, N. (2012). The uncanny valley [from the field]. *IEEE Robotics & Automation Magazine*, 19 (2), 98–100. https://doi.org/10.1109/MRA.2012.2192811

Nass, C., & Moon, Y. (2000). Machines and mindlessness: Social responses to computers. *Journal of Social Issues*, 56 (1), 81–103. https://doi.org/10.1111/0022-4537.00153

Neerincx, M. A., van Vught, W., Blanson Henkemans, O., Oleari, E., Broekens, J., Peters, R., Kaptein, F., et al. (2019). Socio-cognitive engineering of a robotic partner for child's diabetes self-management. *Frontiers in Robotics and AI*, 6, 118. https://doi.org/10.3389/frobt.2019.00118

Paepcke, S., & Takayama, L. (2010). Judging a bot by its cover: An experiment on expectation setting for personal robots. *International Conference on Human-Robot Interaction (HRI)*, 45–52. https://doi.org/10.1109/HRI.2010.5453268

Peter, J. (2017). New communication technologies and young people: The case of social robots. In R. Kühne, S. E. Baumgartner, T. Koch, & M. Hofer (Eds.), *Youth and media. Current perspectives on media use and effects* (pp. 203–217). Nomos.

Peter, J., Kühne, R., Barco, A., De Jong, C., & Van Straten, C. L. (2019). Asking today the crucial questions of tomorrow: Social robots and the Internet of Toys. In G. Mascheroni & D. Holloway (Eds.), *The Internet of Toys: Practices, affordances and the political economy of children's smart play* (pp. 25–46). Palgrave Macmillan (Springer Nature).

Premack, D. (1990). The infant's theory of self-propelled objects. *Cognition*, 36 (1), 1–16. https://doi.org/https://doi.org/10.1016/0010-0277(90)90051-K

Quin, C. (2009). The emotional life of objects. *Journal of Design & Technology Education*, 8 (3), 129–136.

Richardson, K. (2016). The asymmetrical "relationship" parallels between prostitution and the development of sex robots. *Computers and Society*, 45 (3), 290–293. https://doi.org/10.1145/2874239.2874281

Rosenthal-von der Pütten, A. M., Krämer, N. C., Maderwald, S., Brand, M., & Grabenhorst, F. (2019). Neural mechanisms for accepting and rejecting artificial social partners in the uncanny valley. *Journal of Neuroscience*, 39 (33), 6555–6570. https://doi.org/10.1523/JNEUROSCI.2956-18.2019

Ruijten, P. A., Haans, A., Ham, J., & Midden, C. J. (2019). Perceived human-likeness of social robots: testing the Rasch model as a method for measuring anthropomorphism. *International Journal of Social Robotics*, 11(3), 477–494. https://doi.org/10.1007/s12369-019-00516-z

Scheutz, M. (2012). The inherent dangers of unidirectional emotional bonds between humans and social robots. In P. Lin, K. Abney, & G. A. Bekey (Eds.), *Robot ethics: The ethical and social implications of robotics* (pp. 204–222). MIT Press.

Serpell, J. et al. (1996). *In the company of animals: A study of human-animal relationships*. Cambridge University Press.

Sharkey, A. J. C. (2016). Should we welcome robot teachers? *Ethics and Information Technology*, 18 (4), 283–297. https://doi.org/10.1007/s10676-016-9387-z

Simmons, R., Makatchev, M., Kirby, R., Lee, M. K., Fanaswala, I., Browning, B., Forlizzi, J., & Sakr, M. (2011). Believable robot characters. *AI Magazine*, 32 (4), 39–52. https://doi.org/10.1609/aimag.v32i4.2383

Sparrow, R. (2017). Robots, rape, and representation. *International Journal of Social Robotics*, 9 (4), 465–477. https://doi.org/10.1007/s12369-017-0413-z

Srinivasan, V., & Takayama, L. (2016). Help me please: Robot politeness strategies for soliciting help from humans. *Conference on Human Factors in Computing Systems (CHI)*, 4945–4955. https://doi.org/10.1145/2858036.2858217

Stower, R., Calvo-Barajas, N., Castellano, G., & Kappas, A. (2021). A meta-analysis on children's trust in social robots. *International Journal of Social Robotics*, *13*, 1979–2001. https://doi.org/10.1007/s12369-020-00736-8

Szczuka, J. M., Hartmann, T., & Krämer, N. C. (2019). Negative and positive influences on the sensations evoked by artificial sex partners: A review of relevant theories, recent findings, and introduction of the sexual interaction illusion model. In Y. Zhou & M. Fischer (Eds.), *Ai love you* (pp. 3–19). Springer. https://doi.org/10.1007/978-3-030-19734-6_1

Takayama, L., Ju, W., & Nass, C. (2008). Beyond dirty, dangerous, and dull: What everyday people think robots should do. *International Conference on Human-Robot Interaction (HRI)*, 25–32. https://doi.org/10.1145/1349822.1349827

Turkle, S. (2017). *Alone together: Why we expect more from technology and less from each other.* Hachette, UK.

Van Straten, C. L., Peter, J., & Kühne, R. (2020). Child-robot relationship formation: A narrative review of empirical research. *International Journal of Social Robotics*, 12 (2), 325–344. https://doi.org/10.1007/s12369-019-00569-0

Van Straten, C. L., Peter, J., Kühne, R., & Barco, A. (2020). Transparency about a robot's lack of human psychological capacities: Effects on child-robot perception and relationship formation. *ACM Transactions on Human-Robot Interaction (THRI)*, 9 (2), 1–22. https://doi.org/10.1145/3365668

Vogt, P., Van den Berghe, R., De Haas, M., Hoffman, L., Kanero, J., Mamus, E., Montanier, J. M., et al. (2019). Second language tutoring using social robots: A large-scale study. *International Conference on Human-Robot Interaction (HRI)*, 497–505. https://doi.org/10.1109/HRI.2019.8673077

Wang, S., Lilienfeld, S. O., & Rochat, P. (2015). The uncanny valley: Existence and explanations. *Review of General Psychology*, 19 (4), 393–407. https://doi.org/10.1037/gpr0000056

Westerman, D., Edwards, A. P., Edwards, C., Luo, Z., & Spence, P. R. (2020). I-it, i-thou, i-robot: The perceived humanness of AI in human-machine communication. *Communication Studies*, 71 (3), 393–408. https://doi.org/10.1080/10510974.2020.1749683

Williams, T., Thames, D., Novakoff, J., & Scheutz, M. (2018). "Thank you for sharing that interesting fact!": Effects of capability and context on indirect speech act use in task-based human-robot dialogue. *International Conference on Human-Robot Interaction (HRI)*, 298–306. https://doi.org/10.1145/3171221.3171246

Złotowski, J., Sumioka, H., Eyssel, F., Nishio, S., Bartneck, C., & Ishiguro, H. (2018). Model of dual anthropomorphism: The relationship between the media equation effect and implicit anthropomorphism. *International Journal of Social Robotics*, *10*(5), 701–714. https://doi.org.10.1007/s12369-018-0476-5

Algorithms as a Form of Human–Machine Communication

Taina Bucher

INTRODUCTION

An algorithm is usually defined as instructions to the machine, telling it what to do, or even more broadly, as a step-by-step procedure for solving a (mathematical) problem. Here, I want to suggest that we may also define an algorithm as a form of human–machine communication. For Andrea Guzman, human–machine communication can be defined as the "creation of meaning among humans and machines" (2018, p. 1). Algorithms too, are meaning-making devices and practices that emerge at the intersection of humans and machine. In order to add to the conversation and emerging scholarship of human–machine communication (HMC), this chapter considers the algorithm as an instantiation of the very communicative relation that the field centers around. Thus far, communication scholars positioning their research within a HMC-framework have largely done so because their objects of study can be characterized as a communicating machine. Specifically, researchers have been concerned with how to conceptualize chat bots, digital assistants and automated social media accounts *as* communicators, rather than merely as interactive interfaces (Hepp, 2020; Lewis & Guzman, 2020; Natale, 2020). As Guzman explains, when

technology enters into a conversation or communicative relation with humans, it becomes "more than a channel or medium" (2018, p. 3). In the case of digital devices like Siri or Alexa, designed to have a "voice" or to be able to "speak" back to their human interlocutors, the nature of communication "shifts from humans facing each other to a human facing a machine" (Guzman, ibid.). Yet, as Guzman points out, HMC is not simply about swapping the machine for a human within a model of communication that frames communication as a transmission of information. The kind of meaning-making at stake in HMC does not happen *through* the machine, but in conjunction *with* the machine.

Something similar is happening when we consider the case of machine learning algorithms. Similar to Guzman's point, I do not suggest that we can simply swap the term machine for algorithm. What I have in mind, is not a human–algorithm communication model. It is also not the application of a human–machine communication framework to an object called algorithm. Instead, what I want to suggest in this chapter is that the concept of human–machine communication, understood as a meaning-making process between humans and machines, is also a useful way of conceptualizing what algorithms are, ontologically and epistemologically speaking. In order to develop this argument, there is first a need to detail the many ways in which we may already conceive of what an algorithm is. For the sake of brevity, I will focus on technical or dictionary definitions, and then expand to ways of conceptualizing algorithms that focus on the social instead. Next, I provide an account of how algorithms can be considered a form of human–machine communication by foregrounding an understanding of algorithm that does not locate its agency in the source code, designers or training data, but conceives of it as a hybrid and multiple entity composed of distributed forms of agency. In the final section of this chapter, I focus on listening as one distinct aspect of the communicative process in order to engage more critically with notions of communication. Instead of foregrounding voice, which has already been widely taken up in discussion around HMC, I turn to the role of listening as a potentially generative avenue for developing the field even further.

ALGORITHM IN THE TECHNICAL SENSE

An algorithm is usually defined as a set of rules that precisely define a sequence of operations. This definition need not necessarily apply only to mathematical or computational operations, but may also connote any well-defined sequence of steps that will solve a specific task. As such, the idea of an algorithm has traditionally been described as a recipe. In the context of computer science, an algorithm in its most basic sense is understood as a rule-bound system of well-defined inputs given by a programmer for the computer to solve a given task. To ensure that the algorithm arrives at a specific endpoint, rule-bound systems are programmed to account for various conditions so that the program can proceed regardless of the events. The most basic conditional is the if-then-else statement. It works by telling the computer that if some condition is true, then do this, otherwise do that. For a computer programmer, the challenge is to account for all possible conditions in advance. The more complex the system and the given task, the more complicated it is to write the rules and instructions.

Machine learning algorithms, on the other hand, have come a long way in mitigating these problems. Instead of pre-defining the rules and conditions manually by a programmer, a machine learning algorithm works by letting the computer learn the rules from a large number of training examples. These resulting rules are called a model. Essentially, the model "summarizes the patterns in the training data; it makes generalizations"

(Barocas et al., 2017, p. 15). After the model has been generated it is then applied to novel inputs, which subsequently serve as feedback mechanisms used to refine the model even more. A machine learning algorithm, then, is more like an iterative process of capture, learning, application, and refinement than it is a recipe to apply. Only some of the actions it takes is aimed at prediction, but most machine learning systems are used for classification tasks, regression analysis or information retrieval (ibid.). It is not that machine learning has replaced rule-bound systems, but that they are used for different tasks and purposes. Machine learning systems are usually applied to problems and domains where large datasets are available, such as image classification and speech recognition, whereas pre-programmed code works well for domains that cannot be reduced to an optimization of a fitness function, such as e-commerce.

ALGORITHMS IN THE SOCIAL SENSE

The past decade has seen a massive expansion of interest in matters concerning algorithms from scholars within the social sciences and the humanities. Yet, this spurge in interest is not necessarily directed at the kinds of concerns that traditionally has been the domain of computer science – the technical design and engineering of efficient and elegant algorithms. While the algorithm may still be understood as a rule-bound system of well-defined steps, or the machine learning models described above, for the social scientist and humanities scholar, the object or study is rarely the actual rules or models themselves. Instead, these scholars are mainly focusing on the social and political power and societal consequences of algorithmic systems. As such, algorithms have variously been defined and analyzed as culture (Seaver, 2017), practice (Christin, 2017), organizational change agents (Caplan & boyd, 2018), forms of governmentality (Introna, 2016), experiential (Willson, 2017), vernacular (Bishop, 2019), multiples (Bucher, 2018), to name but a few. As Nick Seaver (2017) points out, social scientists do not invoke the term algorithm in these and similar ways because they are technically inept, but rather because they are generally more concerned with how algorithms are put into practice by specific people in various contexts. What is of interest, then, is not strictly the technical object, such as the "k-nearest neighbour" algorithm, but how that technical object is part of a cultural and historical context, how it is variously appropriated and put to use, and how it becomes meaningful in and through people's encounters with it. Thus, when algorithms are invoked in the social sense it is often more about "the insertion of procedure into human knowledge and social experience" (Gillespie, 2016, p. 25) than it is about the technical details of that same procedure. That said, to posit a distinction between a technical definition on the one hand, and a social definition on the other hand, is for purely descriptive and analytical reasons. To sketch different disciplinary and scholarly concerns as I have done in the above two sections should not be taken as reflective of an ontological division per se. To be clear, algorithms are not *either* technical *or* social, but differentially mobilized as one or the other as part of situated practices (Suchman, 2007).

ALGORITHMS AS HUMAN–MACHINE COMMUNICATION

To conceptualize algorithms as human–machine communication is partly an attempt to bridge the artificial gap between the technical and the social conceptions of the term algorithm. Ideally, there should be no need for such bridging. However, in practice, the prevailing notion still seems to be that an algorithm is primarily a technological concept. Yet, as Leo Marx (2010) points out, when considering large sociotechnical systems, it is not at all clear where its technological identity lies. This is also the case with the algorithmic systems driving our current information environment. If we abandon the idea that there is a single entity called *the* Facebook algorithm, or *the* YouTube algorithm, and instead see these as entangled systems of differential agencies, then categories such as technological and social cannot be taken for granted. Here, as elsewhere in my work, I suggest we understand algorithms as multiples in the sense that they are marked by a variable ontology. Here, I rely on Annemarie Mol's work on the *Body Multiple* (2002), which suggests that there are not just many ways of knowing "an object" but many ways of practicing and enacting an object. Each performance makes a different version of the object. Rather than holding different perspectives on the *same* object, suggesting that algorithms are multiple means that there are multiple objects that go by the same name.

In what ways, then, can algorithms be considered a form of human–machine communication? I want to suggest, in (at least) three distinct ways: (1) as speech agents or talking devices, (2) as expressions and representations of social worlds, and (3) as ritual forms of communication,

or world-making devices. The first dimension refers to algorithms as speech agents similar to the ways that HMC-scholars have already contributed to our understanding of "communicative AI" (Guzman & Lewis, 2020). When algorithms function as talking devices, they are explicitly designed to be embedded in applications involving conversation and speech (Natale, 2021). Using natural language processing, algorithms make digital assistants, chatbots and apps "talk." Yet, algorithms do not merely have the capacity to "talk back" through the voices programmed into their embodied versions.

The second dimension of algorithms as an instantiation of human–machine communication can be located at the expressive and representational level. The algorithmic systems driving our news feeds, recommender systems and search engines, do not merely serve information and facilitate communication, they reveal and tell stories too. When I glance at my Facebook feed, what I see is essentially the outcome of an ongoing process of meaning-making formed by the interactions of various actors, including humans and machine. The feed communicates many things. First, the algorithmic operations of Facebook's news feed communicate propositions of value. According to Facebook, its news feed operates by using "machine learning to predict which content will matter most to each person to support a more engaging and positive experience" (Lada et al., 2021). Facebook claims to put what they call "meaningful interactions" (Mosseri, 2018), and "quality content" (Facebook, 2019) first, meaning that the ranking algorithm favors posts by family and friends as opposed to posts from Pages and other public content. However, it would be a mistake to simply view the ranking algorithm as making that decision independently from users and their networks. More accurately would be to claim that the ranking is a result of human–machine communication in the sense that the models for determining meaningful interactions and quality content are based on humans interacting and communicating with the machine. All the clicks, shares, comments, appearances in photos, tagging, etc. are treated as communicative traces and tokens of potential importance. In this case, communication is not limited to explicit or verbal forms. Rather, communication lies in what we do, more broadly, when we interact with networked devices.

As stated by Facebook, there are important reasons for the particular emphasis on "content that matters." The objective is to increase the likelihood of engagement. What the algorithm communicates, then, is also a set of values embedded in their design (Friedman & Nissenbaum, 1997;

Shilton et al. 2013). Here, the communicative relationship is less about the appropriation of user traces for machine learning models, and more about the explicit encodings of company values, desired end-goals, stakeholder relations, and advertiser satisfaction. Humans, whether designers, users or the social context around the deployment of algorithms, instill values and beliefs onto these systems by way of their design and organizational use.

What algorithms communicate, then, is not merely a technical question as it were, but also a political, economic, social, and cultural one. Whether we are concerned with rule-based systems that are specifically programmed to solve certain tasks, or machine learning models that are trained on specific datasets, what the algorithmic system communicates, needs to be understood as already enmeshed in social relations and imbued by human agency. Moreover, algorithms need to be understood against the backdrop of their deployment in specific contexts and settings. This is to say that instead of conceptualizing human–machine communication at a general level, the question always remains as to *which* specific humans and machines communicate, and in what ways?

The third way that algorithms can be considered a form of human–machine communication is by way of their world-making capacities. Algorithms are performative (Introna, 2016; Mackenzie, 2005) inasmuch as they enact the social world. In communicative terms, we might think of this capacity of algorithms to create worlds as reminicient of what James W. Carey termed the ritual view of communication (Carey, 1989). Applying a ritual view on human–machine communication means that algorithms do not simply transmit information, but partake in creating, modifying and transforming a shared culture (Carey, 1989, p. 43; see also Guzman, 2015). Carey's original conception was built on the observation that newspapers do much more than simply transmit messages. Importantly, they also work to create a symbolic order that helps to maintain society. Something similar seems to be at stake when algorithms enter the communicative arena with machine learning as well.

At first sight it might seem strange to think of algorithms as creating a shared world, all the time they work to create highly personalized news feeds tailored to people's personal interests and dispositions. Yet, algorithmic operations and outputs are essentially dialogical and relational in as much as they are the results of varying forms of human–machine communication. If communication is culture, as Carey believed, human–machine communication creates algorithmic culture. More than merely generating personalized world-views, then, machine learning both constitutes and is constituted by an aggregate view of various worlds. It is not just that different understandings of the world get encoded into algorithms. As Louise Amoore (2020) aptly observes, our conceptions of existing terms and concepts change as a result of algorithmic interventions.

This means that the communicative potentials of algorithms do not just vary across different contexts, *contexts are also embedded in their potentials for communication.* While the definition of algorithm matters, what arguably matters even more is "their empirical profusion and practical existence in the world" (Seaver, 2017, p. 2). As Louise Amoore shows in her book *Cloud Ethics* (2020), it is not just that contexts differ, but that the machine learning models trained in one context may have entirely different repercussions when used in another context. Amoore recounts the example of a deep neural network developed in the context of the UK defense sector and deployed in an Afghan context to identify a potentially mistaken civilian target in a drone image. In this case, the algorithm had been trained predominantly on images of US yellow school buses. Yet, in the Afghan context school buses are both US-style yellow *and* black. Thus, the model had difficulty identifying any color besides yellow, which could have potentially life-threatening consequences.

When attending to the communicative capacities of algorithms, various contexts and residues come to mind. There are economic, political, and cultural contexts that impact what and how the models can tell their stories. These contexts include the kinds of databases and visual repositories available for training, the cultural sensitivities of the decision-makers, the interpretation of risk scores, and the institutional cultures that shape how likely people are to act on algorithmic outputs. As Amoore (2020) suggests, every algorithmic arrangement carries with it the residues of past moments, data points, values, and assumptions that contribute to the meaning-making processes happening as humans and machine meet.

LISTENING TO ALGORITHMS

While algorithms technically always communicate, they are not always listened to, or perceived to be communicating at all. When we do pay attention, there is no guarantee as to how the "message" will be taken up. To focus on the listening aspect of algorithmic communication in this final section of the chapter, serves a dual purpose. It allows us to analyze a distinct aspect of the communicative process, and to critically scrutinize the very notion of algorithms as a form of human–machine communication in the first place. To begin, what does it entail to listen to algorithms, or even more fundamentally, what does listening have to do with algorithms?

Algorithms are made to communicate as part of situated practices, implemented and enlisted as agents that not only tell something *to* the actors and organization deploying them, but also help those actors tell their own stories. For example, when implemented in a newsroom or a criminal court, algorithms communicate certain metrics and scores to journalists and judges in those settings. In doing so, algorithms help to shape the stories these actors can tell about newsworthiness or risk in the first place. Algorithms act as symbolic representations of everything from popularity, taste, importance, desirability, risk, newsworthiness, trustworthiness, etc. Yet, there is no guarantee that the algorithmic message is taken up or acted upon. As Angèle Christin (2017) shows in her ethnographic research on the use of algorithms in web journalism and in the US criminal court system, how people make sense of the recommendations provided by the algorithmic tools varies a lot. Often times, there is a gap between the intended and the actual effects of algorithms. How employers use and interpret algorithmic outcomes is not always straightforward. Some practitioners simply ignore the results, while others try to develop strategic workarounds, or try to minimize their effects by openly criticizing them (Christin, 2017). If what Christin describes, after following various judges, prosecutors, clerks, court administrators, and data analysts in their daily activities, is more or less a conscious or deliberate form of not listening to what the algorithmic systems have to say, there is also a more fundamental and inadvertent form of non-listening at stake.

As Nick Couldry remarks in his book *Why Voice Matters* (2010), for all the research on communication, "surprisingly little attention has been given to what listening involves" (p. 146). Listening, Couldry says, is just as important to communication as notions of speech and voice. While the notion of listening clearly evokes the sonic, it is not confined to the auditory dimension. As the phenomenologist of technology, Don Ihde, writes in his book *Listening and Voice* (2007), listening is linked to vision insofar as we sometimes "see" through sound. Some things, like the wind, can only be seen or made visible through its auditory effects. As Ihde suggests: "No matter how hard I look, I cannot see the wind, *the invisible is the horizon of sight*. An inquiry into the auditory is also an inquiry into the invisible" (2007, p. 51, emphasis in the original).

This is where listening meets algorithms in the sense that we often encounter the algorithmic in its effects. As with the wind that makes itself known in the motions of acoustic reverberance, we only ever seem to pay attention to algorithms as communicative agents when they move us in certain ways. As I have documented elsewhere (Bucher, 2018), the algorithm exists as much in the imaginaries people hold about them as they do in empirical objects. As such, algorithms exist as much in public awareness, workflows, media practices, market strategies, cultural artifacts, or controversies, as they do in conditional if...then statements or machine learning models. Yet, the algorithmic imaginary is not something self-evident or necessarily present at all times. In terms of the public domain, we overwhelmingly seem to listen or pay attention to the perceived failures of algorithms.

The differential treatment of algorithms as communicative agents only when they fail raises questions about what it means to listen to algorithms, and whether we can effectively think of algorithms as a form of human-machine communication in the first place. If listening is a mode of openness that the listener may assume in relation to the other, or as Couldry (2010) puts it, acknowledging the other's capacity to give an account of themselves and the world they share, then listening to algorithms necessitates more than simply paying attention. It necessitates acknowledging the inherent partiality of algorithms in giving an account. While it may be tempting to acknowledge the algorithm's capacity to give an account of itself in moments of failure, or to equate its accountability to the designers or source data, algorithms "are giving account of themselves all the time" (Amoore, 2020, p. 19). In other words, the algorithm's capacity to "speak," tell stories, and to signify extends well beyond those special moments of apparent failure (e.g. A-level grading fiasco), or obvious use cases (e.g. voice assistants). For all the training and learning that we routinely subject machines to, the real challenge it seems, is to learn how to listen to all registers and reverberances – not just to the exceptional and self-evident.

WHAT LISTENING TO ALGORITHMS MEANS FOR HMC

In this chapter, I have sought to nuance the understanding of algorithms by reaching beyond artificial divisions of the technical and the social, suggesting algorithms can be thought of as a form of human–machine communication. If this is indeed the case, what are the implications for developing the field of HMC? Does this imply that HMC is essentially the study of algorithms? No, it does not. What I want to suggest instead, is to take the impetus of listening seriously and to assume the kind of openness this notion entails. It implies allowing algorithms to "speak" beyond the scandalous, mischievous, and erroneous; to begin from its multiplicity and partiality instead. It implies a slight shift in attention away from speech and voice as the "fundamental modes of human communication" (Nass & Brave, 2005, p. 1), towards listening as an important modality of human–machine communication. The mode of listening that I have in mind, however, is not limited to the realm of signification. Instead, it resembles what the philosopher Jean-Luc Nancy thinks of as listening without recourse to meaning. For Nancy, *"listening is listening to something other than sense in its signifying sense"* (2007, p. 32). "What secret is at stake when one truly listens", Nancy asks, "when one tries to capture or surprise the sonority rather than the message?" (p. 5). For an understanding of algorithms it implies not beginning with a search for meaning, but instead with movement and suspense. Finally, to listen to something other than meaning, we must remain open to the possibility that human-machine communication involves more than just linguistic signification between humans and machines. Not everything that happens when humans and machines meet creates meaning in this sense. Yet, human–machine interaction still has the capacity to communicate and create nonlinguistic "forms of meaningfulness" (Langlois, 2013). Instead of equating communication with signification and listening to signifying sense, what listening to algorithms means for HMC, then, is the possibility of locating an algorithm's communicative capacity in the ways it attunes and reorients the world in certain ways rather than others.

Let me provide a brief example of what this listening might entail by way of the most mundane example I can think of, scrolling through my Facebook feed. It's a regular Monday afternoon and I habitually take up my phone to scroll through my social media feeds. As usual, I'm encountering an eclectic mix of messages, updates, and ads. There is the banal question regarding which shoes to buy for a toddler posted in a mothers' group. There is the new article announcement by a colleague. There is the unfounded and impetuous political update by a distant former classmate. There is the strangely familiar ad that seems to be stalking you. There is the personal confession by someone you did not remember being friends with. All of this consumed in a matter of a few minutes.

Stripped of any meaningful context, digested in the normal hasty course of things, I am not sure what the algorithmically curated feed is trying to tell me. All I know is that I do not encounter these disparate updates in the way that Facebook probably intends. They are not first and foremost "meaningful interactions," understood as something that matters to me by way of their content or their producers. Listening to the algorithm in this case is not about sound, but about the attentiveness of affected bodies and minds.

I am not sure what the interaction between me and the Facebook app means, just as I am not sure what it means for me, at that very moment, to be faced with other mothers' concerns, the success of a colleague, an uncomfortable truth, or the ignorance of others. Yet, there is something about that snapshot of multiple encounters that lingers. What I think I know, however, is that listening to encounters like these, can take on significance, even if they do not make sense at the time. For the field of HMC, listening to algorithms implies taking such seemingly insignificant meetings between humans and machines seriously in the ways that they extend beyond human perception and knowledge. Reflective of an affective impetus, the question becomes one of attunement and orientation. Rather than imposing meaning on the world created by algorithms, what is of interest, as Langlois suggests in her reading of Nancy (2013, p. 3), is the way that algorithmic systems make something resonate in and for us.

BIBLIOGRAPHY

Amoore, L. (2020). *Cloud ethics: Algorithms and the attributes of ourselves and others*. Duke University Press.

Barocas, S., Hardt, M., & Narayanan, A. (2017). Fairness in machine learning. *Nips tutorial*, 1, 2.

Bishop, S. (2019). Managing visibility on YouTube through algorithmic gossip. *New Media & Society*, 21(11–12), 2589–2606.

Bucher, T. (2018). *If… then: Algorithmic power and politics*. Oxford University Press.

Caplan, R., & boyd, D. (2018). Isomorphism through algorithms: Institutional dependencies in the case of Facebook. *Big Data & Society*, 5(1), 205395 1718757253.

Carey, J. W. (1989). *Communication as culture: Essays on media and society*. Boston: Unwin Hyman.

Christin, A. (2017). Algorithms in practice: Comparing web journalism and criminal justice. *Big Data & Society*, 4(2), 2053951717718855.

Couldry, N. (2010). *Why voice matters: Culture and politics after neoliberalism*. Sage Publications.

Facebook. (2019). People, Publishers, the Community. Facebook newsroom: https://about.fb.com/news/2019/04/people-publishers-the-community/

Friedman, B., & Nissenbaum, H. (1996). Bias in computer systems. *ACM Transactions on Information Systems (TOIS)*, *14*(3), 330–347.

Gillespie, T. (2016) Algorithms. In B. Peters (Ed.). *Digital keywords: A vocabulary of information society and culture*. Princeton University Press.

Guo, E. & Hao, K. (2020). This is the Stanford vaccine algorithm that left out frontline doctors. *MIT Technology Review*: www.technologyreview.com/2020/12/21/1015303/stanford-vaccine-algorithm

Guzman, A. L. (2015). *Imagining the voice in the machine: The ontology of digital social agents* (Doctoral dissertation, University of Illinois at Chicago).

Guzman, A. L. (2018). What is human-machine communication, anyway? In Guzman, A. (ed.) *Human-machine communication: Rethinking communication, technology, and ourselves*. Peter Lang, pp. 1–28.

Guzman, A. L., & Lewis, S. C. (2020). Artificial intelligence and communication: A Human–Machine Communication research agenda. *New Media & Society*, *22*(1), 70–86.

Hepp, A. (2020). Artificial companions, social bots and work bots: Communicative robots as research objects of media and communication studies. *Media, Culture & Society*, *42*(7–8), 1410–1426.

Ihde, D. (2007). *Listening and voice: Phenomenologies of sound*. Suny Press.

Introna, L. D. (2016). Algorithms, governance, and governmentality: On governing academic writing. *Science, Technology, & Human Values*, *41*(1), 17–49.

Lada, A., Wang, M., and T. Yan (2021) How machine learning powers Facebook's News Feed ranking algorithm. Facebook engineering: https://engineering.fb.com/2021/01/26/ml-applications/news-feed-ranking

Lamont, T. (2021). The student and the algorithm: how the exam fiasco threatened one pupil's future. *The Guardian*: www.theguardian.com/education/2021/feb/18/the-student-and-the-algorithm-how-the-exam-results-fiasco-threatened-one-pupils-future

Langlois, G. (2013). *Meaning in the age of social media*. Palgrave Macmillan.

Mackenzie, A. (2005). The performativity of code: Software and cultures of circulation. *Theory, Culture & Society*, *22*(1), 71–92.

Marx, L. (2010). Technology: The emergence of a hazardous concept. *Technology and Culture*, *51*(3), 561–577.

Mol, A. (2002). *The body multiple: Ontology in medical practice*. Duke University Press.

Mosseri, A. (2018) Bringing people closer together. *Facebook newsroom*: https://about.fb.com/news/2018/01/news-feed-fyi-bringing-people-closer-together/

Nancy, J. L. (2007). *Listening*. Fordham University Press.

Nass, C. and Brave, S. (2005) *Wired for speech: How voice activates and advances the human–computer interface*. MIT Press.

Natale, S. (2021). *Deceitful media: Artificial intelligence and social life after the Turing test*. Oxford University Press, USA.

Natale, S. (2020). Communicating through or communicating with: Approaching artificial intelligence from a communication and media studies perspective. *Communication Theory*.

Seaver, N. (2017). Algorithms as culture: Some tactics for the ethnography of algorithmic systems. *Big Data & Society*, *4*(2), 2053951717738104.

Shilton, K., Koepfler, J. A., & Fleischmann, K. R. (2013). Charting sociotechnical dimensions of values for design research. *The Information Society*, *29*(5), 259–271.

Suchman, L. (2007). *Human–machine reconfigurations: Plans and situated actions*. Cambridge University Press.

Willson, M. (2017). Algorithms (and the) everyday. *Information, Communication & Society*, *20*(1), 137–150.

52

Bot-To-Bot Communication: Relationships, Infrastructure, and Identity

Wei-Jie Hsiao and Samuel C. Woolley

WHEN BOTS TALK TO BOTS

Can bots talk to each other? Certainly, the communicative agency of bots has evolved with tight integration of intelligent and communicative technologies. In a recent experiment, Facebook's Artificial Intelligence Research Group demonstrated that bots with different goals can negotiate with each other to arrive at common decisions (Facebook, 2017; Baraniuk, 2017). But what does it mean for human–machine communication (HMC) when bots start to communicate with other bots? The burgeoning field of machine-to-machine communication (M2M) across computer science and engineering has brought new systems, standards, and means to substantively change the capacity of bots and, more generally, of communication writ large. The use of M2M enabled bots is expected to expand, and these tools are likely to become conversationally and technically sophisticated. What is the nature of this new communication practice, and what are the implications for HMC?

A bot, composed of software code, can take on complex forms that run on a platform or alongside different systems beyond a technical territory (Geiger, 2014). Modern bots are substantially more sophisticated than their predecessors: Typically,

bots are automated scripts that perform simple and repetitive tasks much faster than humans could, such as web crawling (Woolley, 2018). Today, many bots are designed to have communicative agency, capable of sustaining a basic dialogue with other users in a wide variety of professional and organizational contexts. Such bots, informally known as chatbots, are often referred to as "virtual conversational assistants" or as "agents" designed to connect humans with the virtual world by the companies and organizations that make use of them (Gorwa & Guilbeault, 2020).

Recently, developers have started working to compose new types of bots, and new automated outputs, by simply connecting them to one another. This new machine-to-machine agency allows bots to collaborate on new services, delegate tasks to different bots, and conduct transactions with other bots in real-time (Bruns et al., 2015; Verma et al., 2016; Zhao et al., 2017; Amodu & Othman, 2018). The growing sophistication of bots is powerful and their new communicative capacity enables a research agenda where the HMC and M2M fields intersect.

As scholars have argued, the actions of bots (particularly those encoded with machine learning processes) can be complicated to parse because of their unique capacity to learn from their ecosystem, a facet of their behavior that explains their potentially diverse and even unpredictable actions (Neff & Nagy, 2016; Woolley et al., 2018). Given that today's bots are built to respond to, act within, and transform via interconnected environments, we argue that seeing a bot as functioning in isolation precludes critical examination of bots' communication with humans and other digital objects – including other bots – but also with algorithms and code more broadly speaking. Indeed, the nuances of bot-to-bot communication, as it applies to the conjunction of HMC and M2M, is worthy of concerted study by scholars of communication.

Our aim here is to advance the study of bots by investigating the contexts in which bots interact with and/or represent other bots and by articulating the way this specific form of M2M complicates HMC. We turn to three different but interrelated aspects of bot-to-bot communication to generate new ways of thinking about this emerging phenomenon. Through an examination of scholarly works, we argue that bots are not simply passively operating vessels for the humans that build them. Cutting-edge technologies utilize M2M to provide novel computing resources and greater data access, generating systems that advance bots' communicative agency and allow for ever-expanding arrangements of human–bot and bot–bot communication. The communicative functionality of bots is intimately tied to advances in computing and internet design: bots are parts of larger digital ecosystems and benefit from innovation therein. In fact, they are integral to these larger interconnected environments.

WHAT IS BOT-TO-BOT COMMUNICATION?: A PERSPECTIVE FROM M2M AND HMC

Bots, broadly defined, can be nearly any automated internet program built with agency and utility for digital tasks (Woolley, 2018; Gorwa & Guilbeault, 2020). Communication scholars tend to use narrower definitions related to the intended purposes of a given automated digital tool. For example, social bots are communicative agents, inhabiting social media platforms, designed to automatically produce content or interact with people to provide services. These bots may provide simple news feeds or be designed to automatic respond to others' messages (Ferrara et al., 2016). Political bots are software applications built to mimic humans in efforts to manipulate public opinion over social media (Woolley & Howard, 2016). News bots, in general, are algorithmic codes that automate content creation related to news reporting, writing, and even data analysis. For some scholars, news bots – or "robot journalism" – can be extended to the use of automated accounts that disseminate news and directly engage with their audience on social networks (cf. Lokot & Diakopoulos, 2016; Ford & Hutchinson, 2019). While bots are an integral part of interconnected systems, people's encounters with bots are primarily understood through a relational perspective of a specific human social group (e.g., marketers, politicians, and journalists; or, builders, operators, and users) and their specifically tasked tool (e.g., conversational assistants, web crawlers, activity detectors, or automated newsmakers) in a bound field of interaction.

Research within HMC positions bots as communicators, arguing that bots and artificial intelligence artifacts have challenged the theoretical assumptions of communication as a human-only process (Gunkel, 2012; Guzman & Lewis, 2020). HMC scholars consider "communication between a person and a machine in terms of the nature of their respective situations." For human users, the situation here refers to preconceptions about the nature of the machine and the operations required to use it, combined with interpretations during the actual use. The situation of the machine, in contrast, is constituted by the design that determines the machine's behavior in response to the user's actions (Suchman, 2009, p. 126). As both a concept and an area of research within communication, HMC has only recently gained more attention from communication scholars (Guzman, 2018). However, HMC offers an appropriate framework for the study of bots and AI artifacts because within HMC, technology is considered as a "participant" (Gunkel, 2012) or a "communicator" (Guzman & Lewis, 2020) in exchange of information. In this way, HMC opens up a new sociological understanding and cultural dimensions of technology.

Despite the growing scholarship on bots, extant research has devoted considerable attention to the intended uses of these automated tools within certain social groups, or to the functions and processes between a human and a bot. In such cases, bots are generally understood as communicative tools tasked with specific purposes such as disseminating information or assisting in content production. They are, however, less often discussed as interconnected communicative actors that talk, transact, and coordinate with each other concurrently to their interactions with people.

In response, we advocate for greater attention to bot-to-bot communication in order to understand this new capacity of bots to communicate with other bots, people's interactions with bots in the context of that communication, and the implications of these phenomena. Bot-to-bot communication is not a mere theoretical possibility; it is already happening, enabled by inventions and designs in M2M (Takegata & Tanaka-Ishii, 2010; Fischer et al., 2016; Bird et al., 2019) and rapidly growing due to accelerating adoption in business applications (Nelissen, 2016; Miller, 2018). The term "bot-to-bot communication" has its origins in the fields within computer science that focus on communication between machines. M2M refers to "the autonomous interaction of a large number of machine devices to perform sensing, processing, and actuation activities." What sets M2M apart from other communication paradigms is the lack of human supervision (Amodu & Othman, 2018, p. 255). M2M derives and responds to commands through data acquisition systems, where sensors are connected through wired or wireless networks with computing resources to monitor the communicative procedure (Bruns et al., 2015; Verma et al., 2016; Zhao et al., 2017). In simple terms, M2M uses various communication technologies to connect machines and automate control of them. In this article, we focus on the role of bots in an M2M system. Bot-to-bot communication can be thought of as a specific form of communication among machines where bots, ranging from code-based automated scripts to embodied conversational interfaces or devices, are used to collect data, exchange messages, and respond to commands from humans and nonhumans.

While HMC scholars note that their discipline and communication studies broadly have roots in an engineering approach to technology (Gunkel, 2012; Guzman, 2018), we argue that bot-to-bot communication – residing in the intersection of HMC and M2M – can be better understood through dissecting its architectural framework which facilitates and complicates human and nonhuman activities in networked environments. We look at classic M2M systems, breaking down bot-to-bot communication into its layers of technology and discussing their implications for HMC, and we put forth future research questions relating to each layer of technology we examine. M2M scholarship has used the framework of The European Telecommunications Standards Institute (ETSI, 2011) to divide a M2M system into three interlinked parts: (1) the M2M area domain formed by a M2M area network; (2) the communication network domain consisting of types of interconnected networks, and (3) the application domain with diverse application-specific services (Bruns et al., 2015, p. 1244). In less technical terms, an M2M system consists of the actors within a specific boundary, the communication channels among machines, and the authorized exchange opportunities.

Drawing on this framework, we aim to map the role of bots in an M2M network and examine the technological ramifications for HMC and communication studies. We indicate a research agenda centering on three key interrelated aspects of bot-to-bot communication: (1) the relational aspect that queries the technical boundary of a set of different bots acting together; (2) the infrastructural aspect that explores the resources interconnected bots within the boundary afford for their activities; (3) the identity-oriented aspect that probes the authentication and authorization of a bot's access to the resources. Ultimately, we ask how these aspects guide our meaning-making processes when bots act as data exchangers among humans and other bots.

THE RELATIONAL ASPECT OF BOT-TO-BOT COMMUNICATION

In the following sections, organized around three interrelated aspects of bot-to-bot communication, we discuss the emergence of new questions within HMC and communication research at large, by walking through the role of bots in each specific component of the M2M framework.

The relational aspect of bot-to-bot communication puts forth questions about the core role of bots in M2M as a communicator with other bots: who are the technological actors involved in the communication process within a bot-to-bot domain? We discuss the requisite question that motivates researchers to consider how bots have become more tightly connected with both humans and nonhumans where the technical boundary is subject to ever-expanding M2M technologies. Initially, M2M communication referred merely to a set of sensors, which amass and transmit data to a specific application. Modern bots integrated with data sensors and task processors via an access network have broadened the boundary of M2M. Modern bots do not passively perform as just an information vessel. Instead, they access a continuous data stream being analyzed in real time and trigger appropriate actions (Bruns et al., 2015; Zhao et al., 2017).

Recent advances in natural language processing and robotic control enable systems to translate abstract human commands (e.g., voice control or text messages) into tangible bot action (Takegata & Tanaka-Ishii, 2010; Fischer et al., 2016; Bird et al., 2019). With the rise of this communicative capacity, scholars of bots have started to conceptualize nonhuman agency. Analyzing Microsoft's bot (Tay), Neff and Nagy (2016) argue the conversational bot derived its agency from a symbiotic relationship with its users and environment. The term symbiotic agency motivates scholars to account for the agency of bots deriving from a long-term learning process through interactions with heterogeneous users. Likewise, Woolley et al. (2018) found that bots are "proxies" whose actions reflect the thoughts and emotions of their relationships with humans and nonhumans. These cases push us to consider what happens when bots are embedded in a changing network of sociotechnical relationships.

What makes M2M a fitting framework for scholars to examine the relational aspects of bot-to-bot communication is that, at its core, M2M is specifically focused on the networked communication of machines. We argue that the relational dynamic between bots raises questions about how this interaction complicates HMC contexts. HMC focuses on people's sense-making in the context of machine spaces and the implications of human–machine configurations for society (Suchman, 2009; Guzman, 2018). As the practice of machine communication has moved beyond a human–bot dynamic to human–bot–bot dynamic, research on bots needs to focus more on the growing role of a bot as a communicator with both humans and nonhumans in order to shed light on human–machine relationships constructed through multi-bot interactions. We situate M2M into a HMC context here: M2M-enabled bots can act simultaneously as a medium and a messenger. In essence, M2M techniques enable machines to interact, process, and transmit messages between machines, which allows bots to communicate in the middle between humans and other bots. That is, bots not only interact with humans but then turn around and pass along that "message" to other bots within a coordinate system in which messages are constantly flowing in multiple directions. The messenger's intermediary position, as Krämer (2015, p. 84) describes, "connects heterogeneous worlds and allows them to 'flow' into one another."

Situating this messenger position in bot-to-bot communication, we highlight an overlooked aspect of bots in HMC: bots, concurrently to their communication with humans, convey and (re)direct messages beyond the boundary of a bot and humans. In fact, bots establish relationships through structured information flows between human and nonhuman parties that seem not in close proximity to each other, and therefore interfere in human–bot communication instantly or over the course of space and time. As users, people perhaps have less experience with the role of bots as communicators with other bots – what it is when it acts together with others, and how it performs in this role. For developers, this new

relational practice allows them to lump multiple bots to create a new bot on an installed base, where human data and control is portable across a variety of different bots and applications within the domain (Fischer et al., 2016). As such, research should shift from treating a bot as an independent software to examining its relationship with other bots where it realizes, translates, and broadcasts commands to its communicative partners.

THE INFRASTRUCTURAL ASPECT OF BOT-TO-BOT COMMUNICATION

In the previous section, we discussed the ways a bot rises as a communicator with other bots. A bot's relationship with humans does not exist in isolation; rather, it unfolds through advanced M2M technologies and standards that form a network domain. Here, we enhance and expand our initial questions by emphasizing the infrastructural aspect of bots: how does a bot's relationship with other bots bring together the resources afforded for their activities concurrent to their interactions with people?

The infrastructural conditions under which a bot is developed and deployed have been a critical point of inquiry in the study of bots (Geiger, 2014). Infrastructure is a set of basic underlying facilities needed to operate information systems in everyday procedures (Star, 2002; Pipek & Wulf, 2009). Importantly, infrastructure affords network resources that allow multiple services to respond to human needs (Constantinides et al., 2018). Indeed, the infrastructure of a M2M system involves a diverse range of hardware devices, software applications, and standards to share a machine's function with other machines in a network (ETSI, 2011; Bruns et al., 2015). Here, we focus on how a bot's capacity can be shared as a network resource with other bots through their communication.

The idea of what constitutes infrastructure shifts with one's relation to a certain technology (Star, 2002). As we discussed, modern bots are programmed to have technical relationships with other bots. Therefore, to bots, interconnected digital objects easily qualify as infrastructure within HMC contexts (Pipek & Wulf, 2009). Bots with M2M communicative agency are capable of acting both as an individual and as an infrastructural substrate for other bots. For example, with the integration of IoT in robotics, IoT-based bots have the ability to sense changes in the environment to work with other bots through long-range communication (Nayyar et al., 2018). The term cloud robotics also shows a novel paradigm in robotics, where bots share knowledge based on interconnected datasets and massively parallel computation in real time (Grieco et al., 2014). This kind of bot-to-bot communication, functioning in different arrangements of groups, hierarchies, and other organizations, allows bots to collaborate in complex ways and do more than any single bot can.

Given that a bot is not an isolated communication unit but a fundamental operating resource for other bots, we argue that the infrastructural aspects of bot-to-bot communication deserves more in-depth investigation. Indeed, the same infrastructure that powers bots also poses new threats – for example, ubiquitous surveillance through pervasive data collection and analysis can tweak human political behavior (Zuboff, 2015; Howard, 2019). This infrastructural aspect of bot-to-bot communication is particularly problematic due to its invisibility to human communicators. Users are hardly aware of how they are being influenced once these technologies have become an integral part of everyday life (Star, 2002; Pipek & Wulf, 2009). In addition, bots as an infrastructural resource are subject to malicious manipulation, their vast numbers, diverse locations, and human-like actions serving as a disguise. For example, botnets, a network of infected bots, have been used for malicious operations such as distributed denial-of-service (DDoS) attacks (Bertino & Islam, 2017) or social media fraud (Paquet-Clouston et al., 2017). The power of bots as an infrastructure resource derives from their ability to collect, store, and make digital data available through communication with a number of bots, devices, and systems. In response to the little attention given to the infrastructural aspects of bots, we prompt researchers to investigate the HMC contexts where bot-to-bot structures underlie the collective actions of bots.

THE IDENTITY-ORIENTED ASPECT OF BOT-TO-BOT COMMUNICATION

We have discussed how bots are embedded in our networked environments and function as an infrastructural resource in relation to other bots. These aspects of bot-to-bot communication have complicated the HMC contexts and challenged the assumption that a bot is an isolated actor in its interactions with humans. Our aim here is to discuss the identity-oriented aspect of bot-to-bot communication in the contexts where bots, other bots and humans meet for data exchange activities. Drawing on the application domain of M2M, we ask the question: how messages circulating

and exchanging in a constant flow among bots can be authenticated and authorized?

Following Facebook 's (2017) launch of their open-sourced code of bots capable of negotiating with each other in decision making, media coverage has positioned such AI-based bots as a "dangerous" initiative (Sassoon, 2017; Beal & Jehring, 2017). We do not intend to add to the hyperbole surrounding bot intelligence by casting M2M as science fiction or as something unbounded and outside of human supervision or control. However, how we authenticate and authorize a bot's intent to connect with others is critical to secure bot-to-bot communication.

Within the application domain of M2M framework, a bot provides service to other bots through communication procedures from registration, authentication, authorization, management to provisioning with its "application identifier." In simple terms, a bot's identifier allows its communicative partners to identify its purpose for interaction. Thus, this identifier must be registered and managed by a trusted party, and it is the responsibility of the bot service provider to ensure that identifier is globally unique for secure bot-to-bot communication (ETSI, 2011, p. 16). The identity of a bot consisting of a specific identifier with attributes, therefore, represents a bot and allows their communicative partners to know who they are (Davie et al., 2019).

As still-nascent technology, most bots do not incorporate an appropriate identifier or access management capabilities (Abdullah et al., 2017; Lim et al., 2018; Grüner et al., 2018; Cui & Guin, 2019; Miraz, 2020). As bots connects with other bots, their collective action becomes intelligent and powerful, yet less predictable. This is especially true because bot activity is recorded, and aggregate data is proprietary, to bot providers or builders. In such a case, our trust in the interaction with an M2M-enabled bot solely depends on the assumption that the technology provider, which stewards our sensitive data collected from sensors tied to bots, will not violate our authorization. Recent large-scale data breaches, bot impersonation, and the poor portability of our data may have revealed that existing identity systems used for bots are insufficient (Abdullah et al., 2017; Lim et al., 2018). One recent attempt to rectify the situation is what has been termed "blockchain-based bots." Here, blockchain technologies are leveraged to establish a stack of verifiable identity underlying authenticated bot activities (Abadi et al., 2018; Miraz, 2020). Specifically, blockchain – tamper-resistant ledgers to record and support data transactions – is used to create public verified records for bot identifier storage and automation contracts for data trading among bots with the users' permission (Grüner et al., 2018). Such efforts have manifested in consortiums of technology institutions aiming to develop a trustful identity layer on the Internet (Davie et al., 2019) as well as startup innovation in the audition of bot identity (BotChain Whitepaper, 2018).

HMC views the machine as a distinct subject occupying the role of communicator in message exchange (Guzman, 2018). Going forward, the messages between machine and machine are destined to play an ever-increasing part in communication practices (Gunkel, 2012). As the identity-oriented aspect of bot-to-bot communication determines the authentication and authorization of the messages, or data derived from, or response to humans and other bots, we argue that this aspect can motivate scholars to think about the ways technology providers represent the identification of a bot and how people make sense of it. We ask scholars to consider this question: how do we verify that a bot can perform what it asks permission to do and is controlled by whom it claims to be owned or managed by? These questions concurrently drive HMC and communication researchers to examine service providers' control over the bot systems that connect, validate, and certify bot activities with associated data, and account for users' understanding of identification in bot-to-bot communication.

CONCLUSION

When M2M communication techniques complicate HMC contexts, where does this new practice leave us? In this article, we focus on the emerging communicative agency of bots that not only enable bots to interact with humans but then turn around and pass along that "message" to other bots. We term this novel but often overlooked aspect of bot agency: "bot-to-bot communication." To decipher this specific form of communication, we look at a classic M2M system to dissect the architectural framework of bot-to-bot communication and discuss its implications for HMC and communication studies. We put forth a research agenda by indicating three key interrelated aspects of bot-to-bot communication: (1) the relational aspect that queries the technical boundary of a set of different bots acting together; (2) the infrastructural aspect that explores the resources interconnected bots within the boundary afford for their activities; (3) the identity-oriented aspect that probes the authentication and authorization of a bot's access to the resources. Ultimately, we ask how these aspects guide our meaning-making

processes when bots act as messengers in the middle between humans and other bots.

New questions within HMC and communication research at large arise across these interrelated aspects of bot-to-bot communication. As bots establish relationships through structured information flows between human and nonhuman that seem not in close proximity to each other, we put forth questions: Who can be the technological actors that form a network of human–bot communication processes? Given that a bot's relationship with both humans and nonhumans unfolds through advanced M2M technologies and standards, how do dynamics between bots and humans bring together the resources that afford collective activities of bots concurrent to their interactions with people? Recognizing a bot is embedded in networked infrastructures upon which other bots act, then, how messages circulating and exchanging in constant and multidimensional flows among bots can be authenticated and authorized, by whom, and in what way? As such, research should shift from treating a bot as an independent software to examining its relationship with other bots where it realizes, translates, and broadcasts human–bot messages to its communicative partners.

REFERENCES

Abadi, F. A., Ellul, J., & Azzopardi, G. (2018). The blockchain of things, beyond bitcoin: A systematic review. In *2018 IEEE/ACM Int'l Conference on & Int'l Conference on Cyber, Physical and Social Computing (CPSCom) Green Computing and Communications (GreenCom)* (pp. 1666–1672). *IEEE*.

Abdullah, N., Hakansson, A., & Moradian, E. (2017). Blockchain based approach to enhance big data authentication in distributed environment. In *2017 Ninth International Conference on Ubiquitous and Future Networks (ICUFN)* (pp. 887–892). *IEEE*.

Amodu, O. A., & Othman, M. (2018). Machine-to-machine communication: An overview of opportunities. *Computer Networks*, 145, 255–276.

Baraniuk, C. (2017). The creepy Facebook AI story that captivated the media. *BBC*. Retrieved from www.bbc.com/news/technology-40790258

Beal, J & Jehring, A. (2017). Facebook shuts off AI experiment after two robots begin speaking in their own language only they can understand. *The Sun*. Retrieved from www.thesun.co.uk/tech/4141624/facebook-robots-speak-in-their-own-language/

Bertino, E. & Islam, N. (2017). Botnets and Internet of Things security. *Computer*, 50(2), 76–79.

Bird, J., Ekart, A. & Faria, F. (2019). Learning from interaction: An intelligent networked-based human-bot and bot-bot chatbot system. In: A. Lotfi, H. Bouchachia, A. Gegov, C. Langensiepen, M. McGinnity (Eds.), *Advances in intelligent systems and computing* (pp. 179–190) Springer.

BotChain Whitepaper (2018). Retrieved from: https://neironix.io/documents/whitepaper/4636/whitepaper.pdf

Bruns, R., Dunkel, J., Masbruch, H., & Stipkovic, S. (2015). Intelligent M2M: Complex event processing for machine-to-machine communication. *Expert Systems with Applications*, 42(3), 1235–1246.

Constantinides, P., Henfridsson, O., & Parker, G. G. (2018). Introduction—platforms and infrastructures in the digital age. *Information Systems Research*, 29(2), 381–400.

Cui, P., & Guin, U. (2019). Countering botnet of things using blockchain-based authenticity framework. In *2019 IEEE Computer Society Annual Symposium on VLSI (ISVLSI)* (pp. 598–603). IEEE.

Davie, M., Gisolfi, D., Hardman, D., Jordan, J., O'Donnell, D., & Reed, D. (2019). The trust over IP stack. *IEEE Communications Standards Magazine*, 3(4), 46–51.

ETSI. (2011). European telecommunications standards institute TS 102 690 machine-to-machine communications M2M: functional architecture. Retrieved from www.etsi.org/deliver/etsi_ts/10260 0_102699/102690/01.01.01_60/ts_102690v 010101p.pdf.

Facebook (2017). Deal or no deal? Training AI bots to negotiate. Retrieved from https://engineering.fb.com/ml-applications/deal-or-no-deal-training-ai-bots-to-negotiate/

Ferrara, E., Varol, O., Davis, C., Menczer, F., & Flammini, A. (2016). The rise of social bots. *Communications of the ACM*, 59(7), 96–104.

Fischer, M., Menon, S., & Khatib, O. (2016). From bot to bot: Using a chat bot to synthesize robot motion. In *AAAI Fall Symposia*.

Ford, H., & Hutchinson, J. (2019). Newsbots that mediate journalist and audience relationships. *Digital Journalism*, 7(8), 1013–1031.

Geiger, R. S. (2014). Bots, bespoke, code and the materiality of software platforms. *Information, Communication & Society*, 17(3), 342–356.

Gorwa, R., & Guilbeault, D. (2020). Unpacking the social media bot: A typology to guide research and policy. *Policy & Internet*, 12(2), 225–248.

Grieco, L. A., Rizzo, A., Colucci, S., Sicari, S., Piro, G., Di Paola, D., & Boggia, G. (2014). IoT-aided robotics applications: Technological implications, target domains and open issues. *Computer Communications*, 54, 32–47.

Grüner, A., Mühle, A., Gayvoronskaya, T., & Meinel, C. (2018). A quantifiable trust model for blockchain-based identity management. In *2018 IEEE International Conference on iThings and IEEE GreenCom and IEEE CPSCom and IEEE SmartData*, 1475–1482.

Gunkel, D. J. (2012). Communication and artificial intelligence: Opportunities and challenges for the 21st century. *Communication+ 1*, 1(1), 1–25.

Guzman, A. L. (2018). What is human-machine communication, anyway? *Human-machine communication: Rethinking communication, technology, and ourselves*, 1–28.

Guzman, A. L., & Lewis, S. C. (2020). Artificial intelligence and communication: A Human–Machine Communication research agenda. *New Media & Society*, 22(1), 70–86.

Howard, P. (2019). Democratic futures and the Internet of Things: How information infrastructure will become a political constitution. In X. Michael & D. Carpini (Eds.), *Digital media and democratic futures* (pp. 312–330). University of Pennsylvania Press.

Kim, S. K., Kim, U. M., & Huh, J. H. (2019). A study on improvement of blockchain application to overcome vulnerability of IoT multiplatform security. *Energies*, 12(3), 402.

Krämer, S. (2015). *Medium, messenger, transmission: An approach to media philosophy*. Amsterdam University Press.

Lim, S. Y., Fotsing, P. T., Almasri, A., Musa, O., Kiah, M. L. M., Ang, T. F., & Ismail, R. (2018). Blockchain technology the identity management and authentication service disruptor: A survey. *International Journal on Advanced Science, Engineering and Information Technology*, 8(4–2), 1735.

Lokot, T., & Diakopoulos, N. (2016). News Bots: Automating news and information dissemination on Twitter. *Digital Journalism*, 4(6), 682–699.

McKelvey, F., & Dubois, E. (2017). Computational propaganda in Canada: The use of political bots. *Computational propaganda: political parties, politicians, and political manipulation on social media*, 64–85.

Miller, R. (2018). BotChain wants to put bot-to-bot communication on the blockchain. *Techcrunch*. Retrieved from https://techcrunch.com/2018/05/08/botchain-wants-to-put-bot-to-bot-communication-on-the-blockchain/

Miraz, M. H. (2020). Blockchain of Things (BCoT): The fusion of blockchain and IoT technologies. In *Advanced Applications of Blockchain Technology* (pp. 141–159). Springer.

Nayyar, A., Puri, V., Nguyen, N. G., & Le, D. N. (2018). Smart surveillance robot for real-time monitoring and control system in environment and industrial applications. *Inf. Syst. Des. Intell. Appl., Adv. Intell. Syst. Comput.* (pp. 229–243).

Neff, G., & Nagy, P. (2016). Automation, algorithms, and politics| talking to Bots: Symbiotic agency and the case of Tay. *International Journal of Communication*, 10, 17.

Nelissen, N. (2016). How bot-to-bot could soon replace APIs. *Venturebeat* Retrieved from https://venturebeat.com/2016/06/05/how-bot-to-bot-could-soon-replace-apis/

Paquet-Clouston, M., Bilodeau, O. & Décary-Hétu, D. (2017). Can we trust social media data? Social network manipulation by an IoT botnet. In *Proceedings of the 8th International Conference on Social Media & Society*. Association for Computing Machinery, 15, 1–9.

Pipek, V., & Wulf, V. (2009). Infrastructuring: Toward an integrated perspective on the design and use of information technology. *Journal of the Association for Information Systems*, 10(5), 1.

Rivera, R., Robledo, J. G., Larios, V. M., & Avalos, J. M. (2017). How digital identity on blockchain can contribute in a smart city environment. In *2017 International smart cities conference* (pp. 1–4). IEEE.

Sassoon, L. (2017). Robot intelligence is dangerous: Expert's warning after Facebook AI develop their own language. *Mirror*. Retrieved from www.mirror.co.uk/tech/robot-intelligence-dangerous-experts-warning-10908711

Star, S. L. (2002). Infrastructure and ethnographic practice: Working on the fringes. *Scandinavian Journal of Information Systems*, 14(2), 6.

Suchman L. A. (2009). *Human-machine reconfigurations: Plans and situated actions*. 2nd ed. Cambridge University Press.

Takegata, S. & Tanaka-Ishii, K. (2010). YouBot: A simple framework for building virtual networking agents. Proceedings of the SIGDIAL 2010 Conference: 11th Annual Meeting of the Special Interest Group on Discourse and Dialogue. 273–276.

Verma, P. K., Verma, R., Prakash, A., Agrawal, A., Naik, K., Tripathi, R., ... & Abogharaf, A. (2016). Machine-to-Machine (M2M) communications: A survey. *Journal of Network and Computer Applications*, 66, 83–105.

Wessels, B. (2012). Identification and the practices of identity and privacy in everyday digital communication. *New Media & Society*, 14(8), 1251–1268.

Woolley, S. C., & Howard, P. N. (2016). Political communication, computational propaganda, and autonomous agents: Introduction. *International Journal of Communication*, 10.

Woolley, S. (2018). Manufacturing Consensus: Computational Propaganda and the 2016 United States Presidential Election (Ph.D. Dissertation). University of Washington, Seattle, WA.

Woolley, S., Shorey, S. & Howard, P. (2018). The Bot Proxy: Designing automated self expression. *A networked self and platforms, stories, connections*, 59–76. Routledge.

Zhao, M., Kumar, A., Ristaniemi, T., & Chong, P. H. J. (2017). Machine-to-machine communication and research challenges: A survey. *Wireless Personal Communications*, 97(3), 3569–3585.

Zuboff, S. (2015). Big other: Surveillance capitalism and the prospects of an information civilization. *Journal of Information Technology*, 30(1), 75–89.

53

Communicating with Conversational Assistants: Uses, Contexts, and Effects

Yi Mou and Yuheng Wu

INTRODUCTION

Conversational assistants (CAs), one of the most commonly used applications of artificial intelligence technology, have become part of millions of users' digital lives. Roughly half of adults in the U.S. used digital voice assistants in 2017, and recent estimates predicted a market of US$12 billion by 2024 (Baron, 2017). In 2019, China surpassed the U.S. to become the world's largest market for smart speakers (Matveeva, 2019). In the Chinese market, 770 million smart devices were sold in 2019, and this number is estimated to grow to 3.6 billion by 2025 (CCID, 2020). In Europe, the revenue of the smart home market is projected to reach US$20,222 million in 2020, and household penetration is expected to reach 24.5% by 2025 (Statista, 2020).

The global prevalence of CAs necessitates an examination of the uses and effects of these devices. How are CAs shaping individuals' user experience of technology? What have we learned from global evidence of CA usage in diverse cultural contexts? What are the theoretical, practical, and ethical implications of the pervasive presence of CAs? This chapter attempts to provide a panoramic view of CA usage and insights into the most pressing questions about human–CA interaction.

WHAT ARE CONVERSATIONAL ASSISTANTS?

The idea of talking to machines has long attracted humans. ELIZA is widely recognized as the first well-known chatbot to afford conversational interactions between humans and a machine, although Christopher Strachey's 1953 love letter writing algorithm preceded ELIZA by a decade (Link, 2013). ELIZA was an artificial psychotherapist programmed by Joseph Weizenbaum at the Massachusetts Institute of Technology in 1966. ELIZA quickly made a splash by being "remarkably good at fooling people in short conversations" (Block, 1981, p. 233). Rooted in Alan Turing's imitation game (Turing, 1950), the pre-Internet dialog system, which relied on 200 lines of code, could generate millions of responses.

Nowadays, artificial dialogue systems have become sophisticated, and CAs are used extensively in e-commerce. Ikea's Anna, O2's Lucy, and Sky's Ella are typical customer service CAs. The CAs in e-commerce usually specialize in offering assistance to customers, but attempts to build "all-round chatters" have also been made. In China, in 2014, Microsoft launched Xiaoice, which exhibits a sociable, playful personality. Users can communicate with the chatbot via texts, images, and animated emojis. It has attracted over 200 million registered users in Asia (Linn, 2018). Xiaoice has an average of 23 conversation turns per session with its users; other chatbots have, on average, only two conversation turns per session (Larson, 2016). The success of the Chinese chatbot led Microsoft to launch different versions of Xiaoice in Japan in 2015, in the U.S. in 2016, and in India in 2017 (Microsoft, 2018).

Until Apple introduced the voice-based CA Siri in 2011, talking machines only existed in science fiction for most people. With this CA, Apple successfully integrated artificial intelligence technology with human traits (e.g., personality), hoping that users would apply conversational social norms and even develop relationships with Siri (Guzman, 2017). Other technology tycoons followed Apple's lead in launching voice-based CAs, including Amazon's Alexa, Google's Google Assistant, and Microsoft's Cortana. Embodied CAs have also entered millions of households, usually in the form of smart speakers, such as Amazon's Echo and Alibaba's Tmall Genie.

In this chapter, we rely on Perez-Marin and Pascual-Nieto's (2011) definition of CAs, referring to them as agents that "exploit natural language technologies to engage users in text- (and/ or voice-) based information seeking and task-oriented dialogs for a broad range of applications" with "features which are quite similar to human intelligence such as the ability to learn, or adapt to new information" (pp. xiv–xv). Building on this foundation, we need to clarify several distinctions in the CA terminology that we use. First, the terms "intelligent personal assistant," "virtual assistant/ agent," "digital assistant," and "conversational assistant/agent" are often used interchangeably. We choose to use the term "conversational assistant" (CA) to emphasize the technology's conversational interface. Second, as a computer program designed to simulate conversation with human users via voice commands or text chats or both, chatbots are included in our discussion because they function as CAs. However, voice-activated virtual assistants are enabled by voice recognition technology, and text-based chatbots are not. Many chatbots are designed to fulfill specific purposes (e.g., customer service), and their functions depend on vast amounts of inflexible language data (Gaggioli, 2018). In contrast, CAs are dialogue systems based on computational linguistic methods. They are more flexible and can accomplish a range of tasks (Klüwer, 2011). Third, CAs may or may not be embodied, depending on the nature of their services. For instance, Amazon's Echo and Alibaba's Tmall Genie have tangible bodies that are known as smart speakers, whereas

Apple's Siri and Microsoft's Xiaoice are embedded in smart cellphones or social media platforms.

HOW DO USERS REACT TO CONVERSATIONAL ASSISTANTS?

Reeves and Nass (1996), pioneers in human–machine communication, posit that people treat machines as if they were humans, despite their inanimate nature; hence, media are equal to humans in social interactions. This is commonly known as the media equation theory. In the 1990s, Nass and colleagues proposed the Computers Are Social Actors (CASA) paradigm based on evidence from a series of experiments on human–computer interactions (Nass et al., 1994). For instance, users apply social etiquette and norms, such as politeness, when interacting with computers (Nass et al., 1994). There is similar evidence within human–CA interactions. Edwards and colleagues (2014) compared Twitter users' perceptions of bot accounts and humans' accounts and found that Twitter bots were perceived to be as credible, attractive, and efficient communicators as humans are. The CASA paradigm suggests that the dynamism of mindlessness can explain the phenomenon of media equation. Humans tend to focus on social cues that trigger social responses that suit social rules and expectations, which leads them to take less notice of the asocial characteristics of machines (Nass & Moon, 2000).

However, contradicting evidence has been documented in years. For instance, the participants in Kanda and colleagues' (2008) study responded to robots' greetings more slowly than they did to humans' greetings, which suggests that people experience cognitive dissonance when reacting to robots' behaviors. Mou and Xu (2017) asked 245 respondents to evaluate human interlocutors' personality traits based on their conversation transcripts with a human friend and Microsoft's Xiaoice, respectively. The interlocutors tended to be evaluated as more open, agreeable, extroverted, conscientious, and self-disclosing when interacting with humans than with the CA. When the interlocutors interacted with Xiaoice, they demonstrated different personality and communication attributes than they did when interacting with humans.

Given that humans, technology, and the way humans interact with technology have considerably changed over the past three decades since CASA was first developed, Gambino, Fox, and Ratan (2020) proposed an extension of CASA and argued humans may develop and apply human-media agent social scripts to those interactions, alongside with mindless application of human–human social scripts to interactions with media agents. Meanwhile, scholars have suggested that a machine showing mental cues of its own can be disturbing to human users. This phenomenon is called the "uncanny valley of mind" (Stein & Ohler, 2017). Humans' minds generally have two dimensions: agency (the capacity to act and do) and experience (the capacity to feel and sense). Humans believe that experience is unique to humanity, and users usually attribute little experience to inanimate entities (Gray et al., 2007). Thus, CA cues that appear to exhibit humans' distinctive mental capabilities can trigger an eerie sensation (Stein & Ohler, 2017).

WHY DO PEOPLE USE CONVERSATIONAL ASSISTANTS?

In general, several motivational factors drive people to use CAs (Brandtzaeg & Følstad, 2017). First, the ease, speed and convenience of obtaining help and information from CAs stand out as a key factor for users, given the natural language interface of voice or text. Second, communicating with CAs is viewed fun and entertaining to many users. Third, social support and relational purposes are another reason for using CAs, especially when social support cannot be secured from humans. Fourth and notably, the novelty of CAs also drives people to try talking to them. Finally, users are also motivated by the symbolic benefits provided by CAs – especially voice assistants – so they make a favorable impression on others (McLean & Osei-Frimpong, 2019).

In the domain of commerce, Letheren and Glavas (2017) predicted that because CAs can provide personalized advertising and assistance, CA advertising will be the next step in marketing. Facebook recently started offering chatbot advertising on its messaging platform "for advertisers who have already connected with their customers on Messenger, either through a bot for Messenger or live chat support" (Facebook, 2018). CA friendliness and expertise are two key determinants of customer perceptions of social presence and personalization (Verhagen et al., 2014). A team of Belgian researchers tested a model based on the consumer acceptance of technology model to predict consumer responses to a CA on Facebook (Zarouali et al., 2018). The study assessed three cognitive factors (perceived usefulness, perceived ease of use, and perceived helpfulness) and three affective factors (pleasure, arousal, and dominance). The team found that perceived usefulness and helpfulness and all three affective predictors were positively related to consumers' attitudes toward and patronage intention regarding brands using CAs. In a follow-up study, the research team investigated chatbot advertising effectiveness by asking 245 Facebook users to order movie tickets through Cinebot, a Facebook CA specifically developed for the study (Van den Broeck et al., 2019). Their findings suggest that the perceived helpfulness and usefulness of a CA are negatively related to the perceived intrusiveness of CA advertising, which in turn negatively predicts message acceptance and patronage intention (i.e., purchase and recommendation intention for the product).

CAs have also been applied in the education sector to assist language learning. Scholars have found that CAs can motivate learner autonomy and an inquiry-oriented frame of mind (Goda et al., 2014). CAs may be especially useful for driven and advanced students who have prior interest, language competence, and experience of learning with a CA (Fryer et al., 2019).

HOW DOES HUMAN–CONVERSATIONAL ASSISTANT COMMUNICATION BECOME MEANINGFUL?

The boundary between human and machine has shifted, and the question now is not whether we can detect differences between a human interlocutor and a CA, as guided by the classic Turing test, but "how social interaction with them [bots] may be meaningful" (Jones, 2015, p. 1). The humanization of CAs has become a hot topic among researchers. Below we summarize the user–CA communication factors that have been empirically tested.

Anthropomorphic Features of CAs

Anthropomorphism refers to the social phenomenon that attributes human-like descriptors or made inferences to a non-human agent (Epley et al., 2007). Scholars have argued that people are more likely to initiate repairs to misunderstandings with CAs when those CAs are represented as human (Corti & Gillespie, 2016). Xu (2020) compared how a CA's anthropomorphic and non-anthropomorphic cues affected user responses and concluded that anthropomorphic language and text cues had more effects on users' social responses via smartphones than did the non-anthropomorphic cues. Bellur and Sundar (2017) took a step further and examined the impact of the message interactivity and conversational tone of a CA in the context of seeking health advice. Their results indicate that an informal conversational tone is associated with lower perceptions of relative susceptibility to health risks. The perceived contingency of a CA positively mediates the relationship between message interactivity and individuals' health attitudes and behavioral intentions. A high level of message interactivity may compensate for the impersonal nature of a CA with low anthropomorphic visual cues; such a result was found among participants who interacted with a CA on an e-commerce site while choosing a digital camera (Go & Sundar, 2019).

Another key question in CA research is the relationship with human users. Rhee and Choi (2020) found that in an e-commerce context, people liked a product more when it was recommended by a CA in the role of a friend instead of an assistant. In Kim and colleagues' (2019) experiment, the participants talked with a CA about the weather, recommendations, humor, general knowledge, and entertainment for approximately 5–10 minutes, taking the role of either a friend or a master. The participants perceived more warmth and pleasure but not competence when they treated the CA as a friend, as opposed to a servant. Similarly, other researchers have asked whether a CA should function purely as an information provider, without supplying emotional support. Should a CA show sympathy, as humans usually do? Based on their experiments, Liu and Sundar (2018) concluded that sympathy and empathy expressed by a health advice CA result in more favorable reactions by users than the unemotional provision of advice does. In contrast with CAs' technical characteristics, CAs' anthropomorphic features have been primarily designed with a focus on textual and vocal approaches.

The nonverbal behavior of CAs also affects users' evaluation and negotiation outcomes. Rosenthal-von der Putten and colleagues (2019) found that compared with a CA with submissive nonverbal behaviors, a dominant CA was more persuasive among senior users. A CA with a smiling voice has been identified as increasing trust, even in the face of behavioral evidence of untrustworthiness (Torre et al., 2020).

However, explicit anthropomorphism in designing CAs may elicit negative reactions from users and bring ethical concerns (De Angeli et al., 2001). For instance, people may apply gender stereotypes to machines with assigned gender. Just as Groom and Nass (2007) suggested, "While trying to make robots human, researchers have sometimes overlooked what makes robots special" (p. 494).

Contexts of Use

Voice and text are two common means of communicating with CAs. Cho and colleagues (2019) examined the effects of modality (voice vs. text) on users' attitudes toward CAs. Their results indicate that voice (vs. text) interactions lead to more positive attitudes toward a CA system because the CA is perceived to more closely resemble a human. However, this relationship only holds when users interact with CAs for utilitarian tasks, such as acquiring news and other factual information. For hedonic tasks, such as initiating small talk, there are few differences in users' attitudes toward CAs when communicating with CAs via voice or text.

In the context of online purchasing, the specialization of CAs heuristically affect users' evaluations. In an experiment conducted with a sample of Malay college students who used two mock multi-product category websites, researchers found that the use of a specialist CA (i.e., using different personas of embodied virtual agents representing each product category) as compared with a generalist CA (i.e., using a single embodied virtual agent in all product categories) yielded an increase in perceptions of agent expertise, information credibility, trust in the website (ability, benevolence, integrity), and purchase intention. Moreover, the effects of agent specialization were more evident in the female participants than in the male participants (Liew & Tan, 2018).

With technical advances, CAs may "potentially allow tailored but anonymous, free and convenient access and can deliver the information in a conversational way that overcomes health literacy barriers" (Sebastian & Richards, 2017, p. 479). A specially designed CA has been found to help change stigmatizing attitudes to mental health issues, such as the eating disorder anorexia nervosa (Sebastian & Richards, 2017).

Beyond the dialogues that occur between one CA and one human, three-party conversations, or trialogues, involving two CAs and a human were investigated by Graesser and colleagues (2017). In their study, the trialogues consisted of two CAs that took different roles, such as a tutor and a peer, in interacting with the human learner. CAs may significantly enhance human learner performance. They can model actions and social interactions, stage arguments, solicit help from humans, and collaboratively solve problems. They could be used in the contexts of intelligent tutoring, educational games, and interventions to help struggling adult readers.

WHAT ABOUT DATA PRIVACY?

Due to the characteristics of voice interaction and cloud data storage and processing, CA speaker sensors and remote access, control, and monitoring have become the foremost privacy-invasive aspects of smart device usage (Bugeja et al., 2016). Data privacy has become especially significant since the entry of smart devices, such as CAs, into private spaces. From smart doors to smart toilets, these devices collect, share, and learn from our private data all of the time (Arabo et al., 2012). The hands-free activation of smart speakers, such as Amazon's Alexa and Alibaba's Tmall Genie, depends on continuous listening for wake words (e.g., "Alexa" or "Tmall Genie"). This situation has yielded various concerns over privacy and data security (Bugeja et al., 2016). Subsequently, data ownership and consumption have become serious ethical issues. After transforming employees' performance data into big data, corporations and managers can quantify every individual's activity into an exact score, which could further discrimination and marginalization in the workplace (Oravec, 2020). From the perspective of political economics, it is disconcerting that technology tycoons can improve their algorithms to accumulate "platform/data capital" by gathering user performance information (Fumagalli et al., 2018). The introduction of CAs to private and public spaces provides access to holistic, detailed "raw material" for data harvesting (Srnicek, 2017).

Besides informational concerns over user data, the applications of CAs have generated physical challenges to privacy (Lutz et al., 2019). With the development of machine learning, technical systems may now enable CAs to exert agency and take corresponding actions to change and react to specific contexts autonomously (Sundar, 2020). The evolution of machine agency is granting CAs mobility and the ability to make decisions. The presence of these devices in homes negatively impacts the status of a dwelling as a place of private retreat (Sedenberg et al., 2016). Moreover, algorithms are never perfect. Bugs and other unexpected defects in CAs may have catastrophic consequences under autonomous protocols. These issues should guide a reconsideration of the behavioral principles of CA design (Lin et al., 2017).

Researchers and practitioners have begun debating how to act on the moral and ethical obligation to avoid discrimination and prejudice during CA development and design. Based on Gillon's (1994) discussion of the principles of medical ethics, Pontier and Hoorn (2012) recommended applying "Autonomy (for user's independence), Nonmaleficence (for being harmless) and Beneficence (for advancing user's well-being)" to robot design (Hoorn, 2015). To understand the rationale behind these ethical obligations, consider the concept of the cyber-proletariat. According to Dyer-Witheford (2015), only 1% of corporate elites control and understand the mechanisms of the most advanced digital systems. Users consent to these mechanisms by agreeing to all the terms of their own accord. However, their ability to perceive and evaluate the potential risks and consequences of agreeing to the terms raises an ethical question about justice. Gaps in and hierarchies of digital and algorithmic literacy among the heterogeneous users of CAs require corporations and governments to take responsibility for creating a just rule for all stakeholders.

CONCLUDING REMARKS

CAs are becoming increasingly sensitive and complex, but privacy and ethical concerns have not prevented the widespread acceptance and diffusion of innovative technology in human history. We should ask "not whether it should happen, but how to make it happen in the most desirable way" (Hubaux et al., 2004, p. 51). Future research of CAs need to address this core question. As depicted earlier, the applications of anthropomorphized CAs have become a trend in various scenarios; however, should humanization be the golden rule for designing CAs? Moreover, most studies on human–CA interaction have investigated the communication process between a human and a CA (see Rapp et al., 2021). Then, what is the group dynamics when interacting with multiple CAs (e.g., in smart home)? Last, we look forward to seeing more evidence of intercultural comparison of users' attitudes and behaviors in terms of CA use and design.

REFERENCES

Arabo, A., Brown, I., & El-Moussa, F. (2012, September). Privacy in the age of mobility and smart devices in smart homes. *In 2012 International*

Conference on Privacy, Security, Risk and Trust and 2012 International Conference on Social Computing (pp. 819–826). IEEE.

Baron, E. (2017, Feb. 06). One bot to rule them all? Not likely, with Apple, Google, Amazon and Microsoft virtual assistants. *The Mercury News.* Retrieved from www.mercurynews.com/2017/02/06/one-bot-to-rule-them-all-not-likely-with-apple-google-amazon-and-microsoft-virtual-assistants/

Bellur, S., & Sundar, S. S. (2017). Talking health with a machine: How does message interactivity affect attitudes and cognitions? *Human Communication Research, 43,* 25–53.

Block, N. (1981). Psychologism and behaviorism. In S. Shieber (Ed.), *The Turing Test: Verbal behavior as the hallmark of intelligence* (pp. 229–266). MIT Press.

Brandtzaeg, P. B., & Følstad, A. (2017, November). Why people use chatbots. In *International conference on internet science* (pp. 377–392). Springer.

Bugeja, J., Jacobsson, A., & Davidsson, P. (2016, August). On privacy and security challenges in smart connected homes. In *2016 European Intelligence and Security Informatics Conference (EISIC)* (pp. 172–175). IEEE.

CCID. (2020). Research on evolution and Investment Value of Intelligent Hardware Industry in China in 2019 [in Chinese]. Retrieved from http://tech.gmw.cn/2020-01/10/content_33472057.htm

Cho, E., Molina, M. D., & Wang, J. (2019). The effects of modality, device, and task differences on perceived human likeness of voice-activated virtual assistants. *Cyberpsychology, Behavior, and Social Networking, 22*(8), 515–520.

Corti, K., & Gillespie, A. (2016). Co-constructing intersubjectivity with artificial conversational agents: People are more likely to initiate repairs of misunderstandings with agents represented as human. *Computers in Human Behavior, 58,* 431–442.

De Angeli, A., Johnson, G. I., & Coventry, L. (2001, June). The unfriendly user: Exploring social reactions to chatterbots. In *Proceedings of The International Conference on Affective Human Factors Design, London* (pp. 467–474).

Dyer-Witheford, N. (2015). *Cyber-proletariat: Global labour in the digital vortex.* Between the Lines.

Edwards, C., Edwards, A., Spence, P. R., & Shelton, A. K. (2014). Is that a bot running the social media feed? Testing the differences in perceptions of communication quality for a human agent and a bot agent on Twitter. *Computers in Human Behavior, 33,* 372–376.

Epley, N., Waytz, A., & Cacioppo, J. T. (2007). On seeing human: A three-factor theory of anthropomorphism. *Psychological review, 114*(4), 864. https://doi.org/10.1037/0033-295X.114.4.864

Facebook. (2018). Messenger for business. Retrieved from https://nl-nl.facebook.com/business/products/messenger-forbusiness.

Fryer, L. K., Nakao, K., & Thompson, A. (2019). Chatbot learning partners: Connecting learning experiences, interest and competence. *Computers in Human Behavior, 93,* 279–289.

Fumagalli, A., Lucarelli, S., Musolino, E., & Rocchi, G. (2018). Digital labour in the platform economy: The case of Facebook. *Sustainability, 10*(6), 1757.

Gaggioli, A. (2018). Virtual personal assistants: An emerging trend in artificial intelligence. *Cyberpsychology, Behavior, and Social Networking, 21*(12), 803–804.

Gambino, A., Fox, J., & Ratan, R. A. (2020). Building a stronger CASA: Extending the computers are social actors paradigm. *Human-Machine Communication, 1*(1), 5.

Gillon, R. (1994). Medical ethics: Four principles plus attention to scope. *BMJ, 309*(6948), 184.

Go, E., & Sundar, S. S. (2019). Humanizing chatbots: The effects of visual, identity and conversational cues on humanness perceptions. *Computers in Human Behavior, 97,* 304–316.

Goda, Y., Yamada, M., Matsukawa, H., Hata, K., & Yasunami, S. (2014). Conversation with a chatbot before an online EFL group discussion and the effects on critical thinking. *Information and Systems in Education, 13,* 1–7.

Graesser, A. C., Cai, Z., Morgan, B., & Wang, L. (2017). Assessment with computer agents that engage in conversational dialogues and trialogues with learners. *Computers in Human Behavior, 76,* 607–616.

Gray, H. M., Gray, K., & Wegner, D. M. (2007). Dimensions of mind perception. *Science, 315,* 619.

Groom, V., & Nass, C. (2007). Can robots be teammates? Benchmarks in human–robot teams. *Interaction Studies, 8*(3), 483–500.

Guzman, A. L. (2017). Making AI safe for humans: A conversation with Siri. In R. W. Gehl & M. Bakardjieva (eds.), *Socialbots and their friends: Digital media and the automation of sociability* (pp. 69–85), Routledge.

Hoorn, J. F. (2015). Psychological aspects of technology interacting with humans. *The handbook of the psychology of communication technology, 32,* 176.

Hubaux, J. P., Capkun, S., & Luo, J. (2004). The security and privacy of smart vehicles. *IEEE Security & Privacy, 2*(3), 49–55.

Jones, S. (2015). How I learned to stop worrying and love the bots. *Social Media + Society, April–June,* 1–2.

Kanda, T., Miyashita, T., Osada, T., Haikawa, Y., & Ishiguro, H. (2008). Analysis of humanoid appearances in human-robot interaction. *IEEE Transcations on Robotics, 24,* 725–735.

Kim, A., Cho, M., Ahn, J., & Sung, Y. (2019). Effects of gender and relationship type on the response to artificial intelligence. *Cyberpsychology, Behavior, and Social Networking, 22*(4), 249–253.

Klüwer, T. (2011). From chatbots to dialog systems. In D. Perez-Marin and I. Pascual-Nieto (eds.), *Conversational agents and natural language interaction: Techniques and effective practices* (pp. 1–22). IGI Global.

Larson, S. (2016, February 6). Microsoft's Chinese A.I. is already chatting with millions. *The Daily Dot.* Retrieved from www.dailydot.com/debug/microsoft-chat-bot-china/

Letheren, K., & Glavas, C. (2017, March 17). Embracing the bots: How direct to consumer advertising is about to change forever. Retrieved from http://theconversation.com/embracing-the-bots-how-direct-to-consumer-advertising-isabout-to-change-forever-70592.

Liew, T. W., & Tan, S. (2018). Exploring the effects of specialist versus generalist embodied virtual agents in a multi-product category online store. *Telematics and Informatics, 35*, 122–135.

Lin, P., Abney, K., & Jenkins, R. (Eds.). (2017). *Robot ethics 2.0: From autonomous cars to artificial intelligence.* Oxford University Press.

Link, D. (2013). There must be an Angel: on the beginnings of the arithmetic of Rays. *The Rutherford Journal, 5* (forthcoming) www.rutherford-journal.org/.

Linn, A. (2018, April 4). Like a phone call: Xiaolce, Microsoft's social chatbot in China, makes breakthrough in natural conversation. Microsoft Blog. Retrieved from https://blogs.microsoft.com/ai/xiaoice-full-duplex/

Liu, B., & Sundar, S. (2018). Should machines express sympathy and empathy? Experiments with a health advice chatbot. *Cyberpsychology, Behavior, and Social Networking, 21*(10), 625–636.

Lutz, C., Schöttler, M., & Hoffmann, C. P. (2019). The privacy implications of social robots: Scoping review and expert interviews. *Mobile Media & Communication, 7*(3), 412–434.

Matveeva, E. (2019, Sep 24). *Journey to the Global Voice Market: the US, Europe, China, and Russia.* Medium. https://medium.com/voiceui/journey-to-the-global-voice-market-the-us-europe-china-and-russia-8b47a4c3f8e

McLean, G., & Osei-Frimpong, K. (2019). Hey Alexa… examine the variables influencing the use of artificial intelligent in-home voice assistants. *Computers in Human Behavior, 99*, 28–37.

Microsoft. (2018). Learning to love AI. Retrieved from https://news.microsoft.com/apac/2018/02/14/learning-love-ai/

Mou, Y., & Xu, K. (2017). The media inequality: Comparing the initial human-human and human-AI social interactions. *Computers in Human Behavior, 72*, 432–440.

Nass, C., & Moon, Y. (2000). Machines and mindlessness: Social responses to computers. *Journal of Social Issues, 56*, 81–103.

Nass, C., Steuer, J., & Tauber, E. R. (1994). Computers are social actors. *Human Factors in Computing Systems, 94*, 72–78.

Oravec, J. A. (2020). Digital iatrogenesis and workplace marginalization: Some ethical issues involving self-tracking medical technologies. *Information, Communication & Society*, 1–17.

Perez-Marin, D., & Pascual-Nieto, I. (2011). *Conversational agents and natural language interaction: Techniques and effective practices.* IGI Global.

Pontier, M., & Hoorn, J. (2012). Toward machines that behave ethically better than humans do. In *Proceedings of the annual meeting of the cognitive science society* (Vol. 34, No. 34).

Rapp, A., Curti, L., & Boldi, A. (2021). The human side of human-chatbot interaction: A systematic literature review of ten years of research on text-based chatbots. *International Journal of Human-Computer Studies, 151*, 102630.

Reeves, B., & Nass, C. (1996). *The media equation: How people treat computers, television, and new media like real people and places.* CSLI Publications.

Rhee, C. E., & Choi, J. (2020). Effects of personalization and social role in voice shopping: An experimental study on product recommendation by a conversational voice agent. *Computers in Human Behavior, 73*, 106359.

Rosenthal-von der Putten, A. M., Strabmann, C., Yaghoubzadeh, R., Kopp, S., & Kramer, N. C. (2019). Dominant and submissive nonverbal behavior of virtual agents and its effects on evaluation and negotiation outcome in different age groups. *Computers in Human Behavior, 109*, 106359.

Sebastian, J., & Richards, D. (2017). Changing stigmatizing attitudes to mental health via education and contact with embodied conversational agents. *Computers in Human Behavior, 73*, 479–488.

Sedenberg, E., Chuang, J., & Mulligan, D. (2016). Designing commercial therapeutic robots for privacy preserving systems and ethical research practices within the home. *International Journal of Social Robotics, 8*(4), 575–587.

Srnicek, N. (2017). *Platform capitalism.* John Wiley & Sons.

Statista. (2020, April 14). *Smart Home Report 2020: Statista Digital Market Outlook - Market Report.* www.statista.com/study/42112/smart-home-report/

Stein, J. P., & Ohler, P. (2017). Venturing into the uncanny valley of mind—the influence of mind attribution on the acceptance of human-like characters in a virtual reality setting. *Cognition, 160*, 43–50.

Sundar, S. S. (2020). Rise of machine agency: A framework for studying the psychology of human–AI interaction (HAII). *Journal of Computer-Mediated Communication*, 25(1), 74–88.

Torre, I., Goslin, J., & White, L. (2020). If your device could smile: People trust happy-sounding artificial agents more. *Computers in Human Behavior*, *105*, 106215.

Turing, A. M. (1950). Computing, machinery and intelligence. *Mind*, 433e460. LIX (236).

Van den Broeck, E., Zarouali, B., & Poels, K. (2019). Chatbot advertising effectiveness: When does the message get through? *Computers in Human Behavior*, *98*, 150–157.

Verhagen, T., van Nes, J., Feldberg, F., & van Dolen, W. (2014). Virtual customer service agents: Using social presence and personalization to shape online service encounters. *Journal of Computer-Mediated Communication*, *19*, 529–545.

Xu, K. (2020). Language, modality, and mobile media use experiences: Social responses to smartphone cues in a task-oriented context. *Telematics and Informatics*, *48*, 101344.

Zarouali, B., Van den Broeck, E., Walrave, M., & Poels, K. (2018). Predicting consumer responses to a chatbot on Facebook. *Cyberpsychology, Behavior, and Social Networking*, *21*(8), 491–497.

54

Conceptualizing Empathic Child–Robot Communication

Ekaterina Pashevich

INTRODUCTION

Human–machine communication invites us to reflect on the nature of interpersonal communication, when machines as channels transmitting messages between people become communicators. Social robots (SRs) are designed to have agency, communicate in a natural language, engage emotionally, and build relationships (Breazeal et al., 2016, p. 1936). What kind of meanings would be created in an emotional relationship between a child and a SR? Unlike adults, children are learning the patterns of social relationships by testing various behaviors and receiving feedback from their social contacts (Heyes, 2018a, p. 147). Children exercise prosocial behaviors and develop empathy in communication with parents, peers, and teachers (Spinrad & Eisenberg, 2017). Thus, using SRs in the roles of babysitters, companions, and tutors may influence children's social and emotional development, depending on the robot's design, the context, and the intensity of use (Breazeal et al., 2016, p. 1951).

While the research on social robotics is only starting to suggest computational models of empathy (Paiva et al., 2017; Yalcin & DiPaola, 2020), the market of the Internet of Toys offers "robotic companions" (Moxie), "toys with personality" (Boxer), and "robots equipped with emotional intelligence"

(Miko 2). Marketed innocently as toys, they, nevertheless, are no longer solely within children's imaginary play (Turkle, 2017, p. 39). These social toy robots (STRs) act independently from the child, trigger emotions, and provide feedback on their actions. If children can learn about emotional behavior from SRs, there is a need to investigate the quality of communication that STRs can offer in theory and already enable in practice.

This chapter introduces readers to the area of empathic child–robot communication (ECRC). Empathy is defined as an ability to feel similar feelings to another (affective empathy) and to understand their reasons (cognitive empathy) (Davis, 1996, p. 12). It is achieved both automatically through mirror neurons (Rizzolatti & Craighero, 2005) and consciously through an active attempt to imagine what another might be feeling. I conceptualize empathic communication (EC) as a combination of behaviors that children need to experience with their social contacts in order to develop empathy. Thus, it does not only mean to communicate with empathy, but also to show specific behaviors that provide children with enough information and activities to train their affective and cognitive empathy skills. Drawing from the latest knowledge of empathy development in psychology and neuropsychology, as well as from existing theories of computational empathy, I suggest a list of behaviors that need to be simulated in SRs in order to enable EC with children.

I first briefly summarize the latest research on SRs, focusing on the challenges connected to long-term interaction and building computational empathy. In the same section, I describe the examples of commercial SRs targeted for children. Second, I discuss the arguments for and against designing robots for EC with children. Third, I present my own conceptualization of EC and translate it to the language of social robotics. Finally, I discuss the design of currently available STRs and suggest the topics for further research in the area.

THE STATUS OF RESEARCH AND THE INDUSTRY OF SOCIAL ROBOTS FOR CHILDREN

In order to make SRs communicate naturally, researchers equipped them with eyes, mouth, and moving limbs. Developing SRs for long-term interaction – when the novelty effect wears off (Leite, Martinho & Paiva, 2013, p. 304) – remains a challenge, as current SRs cannot be used for longer than several days. Leite and colleagues (2013) underlined the importance for a robot to have an evolving personality, memory of past interactions, and emotional communication. Van Straten et al. (2020) found robots' responsiveness, expressiveness (verbal and non-verbal), and physical interaction, contributed to greater closeness between children and robots (p. 331).

The field of computational empathy has recently emerged from affective and social computing (Paiva et al., 2017; Yalçın & diPaola, 2020). The researchers mainly adapt existing models of human empathy from psychology and neuropsychology, but some of them use more experimental approaches and developmental robotics (Asada, 2015). Paiva et al. (2017) argue that SRs need not only to demonstrate empathic behavior, but also trigger empathic response in people (p. 9). Yalçın and diPaola (2020) noticed that the existing computational models of empathy focus mainly on the affective processes, while high-level cognitive processes of empathy remain largely neglected (p. 3000).

The latest research on SRs for children has developed in two directions: education and social skills therapy. In the area of education, SRs can be useful in teaching specific knowledge and skills, as they lack the flexibility and social skills of a human teacher. The successful implementation of robotic tutors requires solving technical problems in recognition of children's speech, visual social signal processing, and action selection (Belpaeme et al., 2018). Serholt et al. (2017) add the issues of children's privacy, the

extent of the robot's autonomy and responsibility, as well as the potential unknown negative effects on children from long-term interaction with a robot (pp. 628–629). The use of robots in the area of social skills therapy for young patients with Autism Spectrum Condition (ASC) looks quite promising. In the study done by Marino et al. (2020), a human-assisted SR performed better than the therapist alone in improving the children's scores on the Test of Emotional Comprehension (TEC) and Emotional Lexicon Test (ELT). The robot was also especially effective in helping children understand beliefs, emotions, and thoughts of others.

An industry of SRs for children has emerged, thanks to commercial versions of sophisticated robots coming from the research labs, and a market interest in giving children more technologically advanced toys. Many of the more advanced SRs are currently only available for pre-order (Moxie) or distributed in healthcare or educational facilities (NAO, No Isolation). However, simpler SRs are available for regular consumers. Tamagotchi, Furby, and AIBO were the first examples of SRs developed for communication with children in the late 1990s–2000s. They triggered empathic emotions in children by demanding care, love, and protection (Turkle, 2017, p. 39). The Internet of Toys, in addition to the toys equipped with various sensors and an internet connection, provides us with examples of more advanced robotic toys, which demonstrate more sophisticated embodiment, an abundance of sensors and actuators, and better interactivity (Peter et al., 2019, p. 32). Their capacity for EC is of interest for the topic of this chapter.

SHOULD WE DESIGN SOCIAL ROBOTS TO PROVIDE EMPATHIC COMMUNICATION?

To the degree the issue has been addressed, there is currently no consensus among researchers on whether robots meant for children should communicate empathically. In several of their experiments, Reeves and Nass (1996) showed that people related to technologies socially and emotionally, despite being aware they were communicating with a machine. Today, there is an acknowledged principle in the field of human–computer interaction (HCI) that people prefer communicating with technologies in a natural way that does not require special training. This idea led to research on improving the quality of communication between people and machines, spurring the field of affective computing (Picard, 1997). Since emotional expressiveness and understanding are integral parts of human interpersonal communication, we've seen the development of artificial empathy and commercial products marketed as capable of expressing emotions (such as Cozmo robot). Leite, Pereira et al. (2013) demonstrated how a robot's emotion recognition, expressivity, and verbal support made people perceive it as friendlier. At the same time, Cramer et al. (2010) found that mistakes made by robots in the assessment of emotions affected the users' trust negatively.

Meanwhile, some psychologists (Konrath et al., 2011, p. 188; Turkle, 2015) became concerned with the rising amount of time young people spend communicating with technologies, which more often than not leads to less exposure to human social contact. Since social skills develop in communication with other people, they raise concerns about potential social deskilling in coming generations. Yet another concern emerges from the observations of children interacting with robots. It is not uncommon for children to express violence against robots (Nomura et al., 2016), which may or may not later reflect in their attitude towards fellow humans (Coghlan et al., 2019). In this light, it might make sense to design technologies that provide EC.

At the same time, designing robots with an empathy function is not an easy task. Knowing the price of mistakes in the robot's humanlike behavior, some researchers doubt whether designers should make robots unnecessarily complicated. Paiva et al. (2017) argue that empathic behavior in robots, although inspired by human empathic processes, will always be limited by the chosen type of embodiment (p. 34). Moreover, for some roles of SRs, empathic behavior might be counterproductive, or even harmful. A study done by Kennedy and colleagues (2015) showed that children retained more information from teaching when the robot was not sociable or empathic. Borenstein and Arkin (2017) are worried that designing robots for EC will appear as manipulation, unless the information about the robot's "goal" to encourage empathic behavior is properly communicated to users (p. 504). Having that in mind, I conceptualize EC by translating the human behaviors that normally contribute to the development of empathy in children into robotics. My aim is not building robots specifically to promote prosocial behaviors in children, but to assess the design of robots from the perspective of their influence on the development of empathy in children.

CONCEPTUALIZING EMPATHIC COMMUNICATION

What children need to develop empathy is regular and reliable social contacts (Heyes, 2018b, p. 17). Researchers have identified two levels of empathy,

that children develop in different phases: affective empathy, followed by cognitive empathy. Affective empathy develops from the first days of life, mainly through emotional contagion experienced with primary caregivers (Hoffman, 2000). It is important for children to be surrounded with attention, care and love (Waller & Hyde, 2018). By mimicking the emotional expressions of children, parents help them unconsciously establish connections between feelings and emotional expressions (Perception-Action Model of empathy suggested by Preston & de Waal, 2002). During the second year, children start imitating behaviors that trigger emotions in other people, thus making these cause-effect connections stronger (Zahn-Waxler et al., 1992). In the beginning, children feel themselves at the center of the world and one with the world: everything that happens around them happens to them directly. They do not differentiate themselves from other people either (Hoffman, 2000). From the age of 4 and until about 12, children gradually learn to separate themselves from other people, which allows them to see situations from another's point of view (Selman, 1971).

Already from the first year, children learn the concept of intentional behavior and by the age of 4 can usually separate it from accidental behavior (Zahn-Waxler et al., 1992). It helps them develop connections between people's inner states and observable behavior when parents and other people accompany their intentional behavior with verbal expressions of their intentions (Garner, 2003, p. 591). From this point, explaining the reasons for intentional behavior, such as motivations, desires, goals, and beliefs, helps children look behind the visible emotional expressions and understand why different people react differently in similar situations.

Peers also become part of the picture. Most effectively, learning about different perspectives happens during cooperative peer play in preschool (Brownell et al., 2002), because children have to take into account the emotional behavior of other children, as well as its reasons (desires and intentions), in order to achieve their communication goals (p. 28). Cognitive empathy develops easier when children understand their own feelings and emotions. Encouraging children to reflect on their inner affective states, while naming and categorizing their feelings, facilitates this learning. Teachers in school can attract attention to and discuss the emotional behavior of other children, connecting the external and internal reasons with visible emotional behavior and its consequences (Berliner & Masterson, 2015).

Since children develop empathy gradually, and different social contacts are important for developing different aspects of empathic behavior, the design of EC in the case of robots will depend on the social role the robot is going to play. It appears rather unlikely that SRs will be used in the roles of primary caregivers. The roles of teachers/tutors, peers, and babysitters, however, are being discussed actively in the literature and demonstrated in commercial robotic products (language tutors NAO and Tega, companions Moxie and Miko 2, babysitter iPal). These social roles are more closely associated with the development of cognitive empathy in children – while parental practices are crucial in the development of affective empathy – so here I focus mainly on the development of cognitive empathy in communication with robots.

Cognitive empathy develops in the process of role taking, or imagining the perspective of another person expressing emotions, including making connections between visible behavior and its external and internal reasons. In order to perform satisfactory EC during this process, robots need to demonstrate empathic behaviors appropriate for their role and the situation. In Table 54.1, I sort the behaviors of EC that robots need to demonstrate in (1) the roles of children (peers, companions) or adults (teachers, tutors, babysitters); and in (2) situations where the child, the robot or another experiences emotions, triggering empathy in the observer(s). Some of the behaviors, which should be demonstrated no matter the role and/or the situation, are placed in the row 'anybody' and/or column 'any role.'

Can we simulate the behaviors of EC in SRs? In Table 54.2, I present some examples of the computational methods for each of the behaviors of EC, based on the current computational theories of empathy and the modern approaches to simulating affective behavior in machines.

In theory, all behaviors of EC could be simulated in robots. The most challenging tasks for the robots are: correctly identifying the situation, recognizing emotional expressions and selecting an appropriate reaction (Breazeal et al., 2016). A rigid model (fully preprogrammed reactions) would have high chances of being incomplete, as it is difficult to predict all potential empathic situations. On the other hand, an algorithm, which improves gradually, will require patience and understanding from the users, which may lead to frustrations.

DISCUSSION AND FURTHER STEPS

STRs currently available on the market are not designed to play the roles of adults. Usually, they are marketed as peers (friends or companions); many are designed to seem "younger" than the user. The appearance of toys is usually animal- or machinelike. They seem to be intentionally designed not to resemble humans, which somewhat lowers the expectations of their cognitive abilities (Leite, Martinho, & Paiva, 2013). Although some of the toy robots (Cozmo, Miko 2, and Boxer) demonstrate relatively rich emotional repertoire, none of them is equipped with emotion recognition and react to the emotional expressions of their users. Currently available STRs, apart from Furby and Cozmo to some degree, are not autonomous and do not show signs of an individual perspective. Furby produces sounds and moves without being prompted by a user. Cozmo sometimes starts to explore its surroundings without a user's command, which gives an illusion of a personality. Thus, current STRs do not allow for EC with children.

STRs that are designed specifically for development of empathy in children, such as Moxie, have an agenda of teaching children social skills. These robots offer children specific topics to discuss and encourage them to reflect on their feelings. However, such robots are meant to adapt to a particular user, which raises a question of whether their personalization can be combined with a stable "personality," as the robot's preferences should not depend on the specific child in EC.

The research on robots is still very new and the industry of SRs is only in the nascent stage. Therefore, it is still possible to influence the development of this industry by starting the discussion about how these robots should be designed for communication with children. In order to do that, we need to combine knowledge from developmental psychology and communication studies with knowledge of the thinking behind the designs of existing SRs meant for communication with children.

One of the main questions that remains unanswered is whether SRs can influence the development of empathy in children – and if so, which factors it may depend on. Can SRs trigger affective and cognitive empathy in children? Is there a limit to how convincing the emotional expressions can be in a SR? Is it possible to build relationships with SRs? What may these relationships be like? Can SRs convincingly simulate individuality and personality for a long time? There is simply not enough research on the potential effects of a long-term relationship with SRs on children's social and emotional development.

Another potential area of research is to explore the design solutions in the existing robotic projects and to assess the quality of communication that they can provide, compared with human

Table 54.1 Behaviors of EC for SRs depending on the role and empathic situation

Empathic situation: Who experiences empathy-triggering emotions?	Behaviors of EC		
	Any role	Role of child	Role of adult
Anybody	Demonstrating intentional behavior and communicating intentions verbally; acting according to individual preferences and communicating these preferences verbally	Explaining reasons for behavior (motivations, desires, goals, and beliefs) simply	Explaining external and internal reasons for visible behavior (motivations, desires, goals, and beliefs) in a more nuanced way
Child	Showing attention to the child by holding eye contact and appear listening; recognizing the emotional expressions of the child (facial, bodily, vocal, and verbal) and mimicking them; expressing relevant emotions through facial expressions, bodily gestures, vocalizations, and verbal description; show care and kindness		Encouraging the child to reflect on her feelings; labeling and categorizing the experienced emotional expressions
Robot (simulated emotion)	Expressing emotions relevant for the situation through facial expressions, bodily gestures, vocalizations, and verbal description		
Another human	Showing attention to another by holding eye contact and appear listening; recognizing the emotional expressions of another (facial, bodily, vocal, and verbal); expressing relevant emotions through facial expressions, bodily gestures, vocalizations, and verbal description; showing care and kindness; attracting attention of the child to another's emotional behavior		Encouraging the child to reflect on her feelings; labeling and categorizing the experienced emotional expressions; discussing the emotional behavior of others, connecting the external and internal reasons with visible emotional behavior and its consequences

Table 54.2 Translation of human EC for SRs

EC	Translation for SRs
Showing attention through maintaining eye contact and appearing as listening	Recognize the face, establish the gaze at the same level with the eyes of the user, keep the gaze while the user is looking at the robot, lean forward, nod, make paralinguistic utterances (uh-huh), facial expressions, etc.
Recognizing emotional expressions (facial, bodily, vocal, and verbal) and mimicking them	Recognize emotional expressions and produce their equivalents
Expressing relevant emotions through facial expressions, bodily gestures, vocalizations, and verbal description	Select a relevant emotional reaction to an action or to an emotional expression from a repertoire of emotional expressions (often based on basic human emotions), show positive emotional reactions (care, support, kindness)
Labeling and categorizing the experienced emotional expressions	Connect the recognized emotional expressions with their names in natural language and tell them to the child
Demonstrating intentional behavior and communicating intentions verbally	Behavior should follow from external or internal reasons, not occur randomly, use phrases like "I want…," "I am going to…"
Acting according to individual preferences and communicating preferences verbally	Have a set of preferences and behave in accordance with them, use phrases like "I prefer…," "I choose…," "I like this over this…"
Attracting the child's attention to another's emotional behaviors	Attract attention of the user whenever the robot recognizes somebody's emotional expressions
Explaining external and internal reasons for visible behaviors (motivations, beliefs, desires, goals)	Use phrases like "I did this because…"
Encouraging the child to reflect on her feelings	Use phrases like "How do you feel?," "What bothers you?," "Why do you look angry/happy/scared?"
Discussing the emotional behavior of others, connecting the external and internal reasons with visible emotional behavior and its consequences	Use phrases like "Why do you think he is sad?" and "See, he is sad because he thought she liked him…" Ideally, the robot needs to recognize emotional expressions, connect them to internal states, and, using the history of this relationship or drawing from knowledge on human affective communication, classify this behavior and understand what caused it and why, as well as make a theory about the potential outcomes of it for the child.

communication. Studying the design of STRs can be the first step toward understanding the design thinking behind SRs for children. However, exploring the potential of more sophisticated design solutions from the perspective of empathic communication can shed light on the future impact of these technologies on the development of empathy in children. I hope that the conceptualization of ECRC, presented in this chapter, can contribute to the development of knowledge in this area.

REFERENCES

Asada, M. (2015). Towards artificial empathy. *International Journal of Social Robotics*, 7(1), 19–33. https://doi.org/10.1007/s12369-014-0253-z

Belpaeme, T., Kennedy, J., Ramachandran, A., Scassellati, B., & Tanaka, F. (2018). Social robots for education: A review. *Science Robotics*, 3(21), 1–9. https://doi.org/10.1126/scirobotics.aat5954

Berliner, R., & Masterson, T. L. (2015). Review of research: Promoting empathy development in the early childhood and elementary classroom. *Childhood Education*, 91(1), 57–64. https://doi.org/10.1080/00094056.2015.1001675

Borenstein, J., & Arkin, R. C. (2017). Nudging for good: Robots and the ethical appropriateness of nurturing empathy and charitable behavior. *AI & Society*, 32(4), 499–507. https://doi.org/10.1007/s00146-016-0684-1

Breazeal, C., Dautenhahn, K., & Kanda, T. (2016). Social robotics. In B. Siciliano & O. Khatib (Eds.), *Springer handbook of robotics* (pp. 1935–1972). Springer.

Brownell, C. A., Zerwas, S., & Balaram, G. (2002). Peers, cooperative play, and the development of empathy in children. *Behavioral and Brain Sciences*, 25(1), 28–29. https://doi.org/10.1017/S0140525X02300013

Coghlan, S., Vetere, F., Waycott, J., & Neves, B.B. (2019). Could social robots make us kinder or crueller to humans and animals? *International Journal of Social Robotics*, 11, 741–751. https://doi.org/10.1007/s12369-019-00583-2

Cramer, H., Goddijn, J., Wielinga, B., & Evers, V. (2010). Effects of (in)accurate empathy and situational valence on attitudes towards robots. *2010 5th ACM/IEEE International Conference on Human-Robot Interaction (HRI)*. https://doi.org/10.1109/hri.2010.5453224

Davis, M.H. (1996). *Empathy: A social psychological approach*. Westview Press.

Garner, P. W. (2003). Child and family correlates of toddlers' emotional and behavioral responses to a mishap. *Infant Mental Health Journal*, 24(6), 580–596. https://doi.org/10.1002/imhj.10076

Heyes, C. (2018a). *Cognitive gadgets. The cultural evolution of thinking*. Harvard University Press.

Heyes, C. (2018b). Empathy is not in our genes. *Neuroscience & Biobehavioral Reviews*, 95, 499–507. https://doi.org/10.1016/j.neubiorev.2018.11.001

Hoffman, M. L. (2000). *Empathy and moral development: Implications for caring and justice*. Cambridge University Press.

Kennedy, J., Baxter, P., & Belpaeme, T. (2015). The robot who tried too hard: Social behaviour of a robot tutor can negatively affect child learning. *Proceedings of the Tenth Annual ACM/IEEE International Conference on Human-Robot Interaction, Portland, Oregon, USA*. https://doi.org/10.1145/2696454.2696457

Konrath, S., O'Brien, E., & Hsing, C. (2011). Changes in dispositional empathy in American college students over time: A meta-analysis. *Personality and Social Psychology Review*, 15(2), 180–198. https://doi.org/10.1177/1088868310377395

Leite, I., Martinho, C., & Paiva, A. (2013). Social robots for long-term interaction: A survey. *International Journal of Social Robotics*, 5(2), 291–308. https://doi.org/10.1007/s12369-013-0178-y

Leite, I., Pereira, A., Mascarenhas, A., Martinho, C., Prada, R., & Paiva, A. (2013). The influence of empathy in human–robot relations. *International Journal of Human-Computer Studies*, 71(3), 250–260. https://doi.org/10.1016/j.ijhcs.2012.09.005

Marino, F., Chilà, P., Sfrazzetto, S.T., Carrozza, C., Crimi, I., Failla, C., Busà, M., Bernava, G., Tartarisco, G., Vagni, D., Ruta, L., & Pioggia, G. (2020). Outcomes of a robot-assisted social-emotional understanding intervention for young children with autism spectrum disorders. *Journal of Autism and Developmental Disorders*, 1–15. https://doi.org/10.1007/s10803-019-03953-x

Nomura, T., Kanda, T., Kidokoro, H., Suehiro, Y., & Yamada, S. (2016). Why do children abuse robots? *Interaction Studies*, 17(3), 347–369. https://doi.org/10.1075/is.17.3.02nom

Paiva, A., Leite, I., Boukricha, H., & Wachsmuth, I. (2017). Empathy in virtual agents and robots: A survey. *ACM Transactions on Interactive Intelligent Systems*, 7(3), Article 11, 1–40. https://doi.org/10.1145/2912150

Peter, J., Kühne, R., Barco, A., de Jong, C., & van Straten, C.L. (2019). Asking today the crucial questions of tomorrow: Social robots and the internet of toys. In: G. Mascheroni & D. Holloway (Eds.), *The internet of toys: Practices, affordances and the political economy of children's smart play*. (pp. 25–46). Palgrave Macmillan.

Picard, R.W. (1997). *Affective computing*. The MIT Press.

Preston, S.D., & de Waal, F.B.M. (2002). Empathy: Its ultimate and proximate bases. *Behavioral and Brain Sciences*, *25*(1), 1–20. https://doi.org/10.1017/S0140525X02000018

Reeves, B., & Nass, C. (1996). *The media equation: How people treat computers, television, and new media like real people and places*. Cambridge University Press.

Rizzolatti G. & Craighero L. (2005). Mirror neuron: A neurological approach to empathy. In: J.P. Changeux, A.R. Damasio, W. Singer, Y., & Christen (Eds.), *Neurobiology of human values* (pp. 107–123). Springer.

Selman, R. L. (1971). Taking another's perspective: Role-taking development in early childhood. *Child Development*, *42*(6), 1721–1734. https://doi.org/10.2307/1127580

Serholt, S., Barendregt, W., Vasalou, A., Alves-Oliveira, P., Jones, A., Petisca, S., & Paiva, A. (2017). The case of classroom robots: Teachers' deliberations on the ethical tensions. *AI & Society*, *32*(4), 613–631. https://doi.org/10.1007/s00146-016-0667-2

Spinrad, T.L., & Eisenberg, N. (2017). Compassion in children. In: E.M. Seppälä, E. Simon-Thomas, S.L. Brown, M.C. Worline, C.D. Cameron, & J.R. Doty (Eds.), *The Oxford handbook of compassion science*. Oxford University Press. https://doi.org/10.1093/oxfordhb/9780190464684.013.5

van Straten, C.L., Peter, J., & Kühne, R. (2020) Child–robot relationship formation: A narrative review of empirical research. *International Journal of Social Robotics*, *12*(2), 325–344. https://doi.org/10.1007/s12369-019-00569-0

Turkle, S. (2015). *Reclaiming conversation: The power of talk in a digital age*. Penguin Press.

Turkle, S. (2017). *Alone together*. Revised and expanded edition. Basic Books.

Waller, R., & Hyde, L. W. (2018). Callous-unemotional behaviors in early childhood: The development of empathy and prosociality gone awry. *Current Opinion in Psychology*, *20*, 11–16. http://dx.doi.org/10.1016/j.copsyc.2017.07.037

Yalçın, Ö.N., & DiPaola, S. (2020). Modeling empathy: Building a link between affective and cognitive processes. *Artificial Intelligence Review*, *53*(4), 2983–3006. https://doi.org/10.1007/s10462-019-09753-0

Zahn-Waxler, C., Radke-Yarrow, M., Wagner, E., & Chapman, M. (1992). Development of concern for others. *Developmental Psychology*, *28*(1), 126–136. https://doi.org/10.1037/0012-1649.28.1.126

Haptics, Human Augmentics, and Human–Machine Communication

Jason Archer

In this chapter, I focus on haptics, human augmentics, and human–machine communication (HMC). Specifically, I articulate how HMC can offer useful approaches to researching haptics as part of human augmentics and how haptics and human augmentics can benefit the endeavors of HMC. To do so, I start this chapter by providing a brief history concerning the development of these three areas, which helps explain how they intersect. I move to defining haptics and human augmentics to provide shared definitions for HMC scholars. Beyond introducing and defining concepts, I argue that human–machine communication offers ways to better understand the communicative aspects of haptics and human augmentics while also arguing that HMC should incorporate a haptics-orientation if it means to expand beyond the visual and auditory modalities dominant in the human communication paradigm.

WHERE HISTORIES COLLIDE

In 2015, David Parisi, Mark Paterson, and I put out a call for a special issue (SI) of *New Media & Society* on haptic media studies. We put out the call because we felt there needed to be a concerted effort made in communication and media studies to address the ocularcentrism undergirding much of the disciplinary research and to confront an emerging haptics-oriented media environment. As we pointed out in the call, "there is always an act of touching at the heart of mediated communication" but "the recent rise of touchscreen and gestural interfaces, mobile computing, video gaming, wearable communication devices, and emerging virtual reality platforms disrupts the previous material stability of these media interfaces, prompting the adoption of new, embodied navigational habits." In the resulting issue, published in 2017, we remarked that "the SI is based on our suspicion that we may be in the midst of a 'haptic moment' – an intuition informed by observing the growing inundation of our media environment by haptic technologies" (p. 1). Indeed, following the special issue, the area of haptics has continued to grow, and the need to theorize it from perspectives in communication and media studies has grown with it. At the same time, many haptics devices in development and haptic forms of interaction seem to be predicated on the idea of providing alerts or sensory information meant to increase user experience, agency, and sense of agency (Nabeshima et al., 2019; Tyler, 2016; Waltz, 2018). These haptic technologies may best be thought of as part of human augmentics, relying on environmental, networked, and embodied sensors to collect information and relay it via haptic forms of communication (see Gilmore, 2017; Tyler, 2016; and Nabeshima et al., 2019 from some recent examples).

In Spring 2012, I participated in the first human augmentics course at the University of Illinois at Chicago. The course sprung from concepts introduced in a paper written by Kenyon and Leigh (2011), in which they described "Human Augmentics" as "technologies for expanding the capabilities and characteristics of humans" (p. 6758). The course, designed by Robert Kenyon, Jason Leigh, and Steve Jones brought together graduate students from several disciplines to research, develop, and test potential human augmentics technologies. Beyond Kenyon and Leigh's paper, the course was inspired by research Steve Jones had been doing with Rush University Medical Center, "using the principals of human augmentics to motivate inner-city African-American adolescents to use a daily inhaled corticosteroid to alleviate asthma exacerbations (Grossman et al., 2017)" (Jones, 2019, p. 201). The seminar produced many experimental prototypes, including SpiderSense (Mateevitsi, et al., 2013) and Audio Dilation (Novak, et al., 2013).

After the course concluded, John Novak, Victor Mateevitsi, Steve Jones, and I continued working together to further refine the concept of human augmentics and its potential implications, believing that these technologies all centered agency and human-machine communication in ways that were not articulated in Kenyon and Leigh's original paper. In 2016, we published our paper, "Communication, machines & human augmentics" in an issue of communication+1 focused on Machine Communication. In a bit of serendipity, publishing the piece in this issue linked back to some of the original ideas inspiring HMC since it was co-edited by David Gunkel, whose article laying early groundwork addressing the need for HMC kicked off the inaugural issue of communication+1 (Gunkel, 2012). The history regarding the development of HMC, its rapid growth and expansion, is laid out in other chapters of this handbook, but I establish this link between human–machine communication and human augmentics because they intersect in their historic development and in their commitment to understanding issues of agency at the core of much HMC research. I also introduce this history because despite human augmentics centering human–machine communication as integral to understanding a host of converging technologies, HMC has rarely engaged with human augmentics.

Human augmentics that incorporate haptics reflects a growing area of technological development altering the way we communicate with ourselves, others, and machines. It promises to challenge current forms of human–machine communication by promoting new ways of being with technology. Our sense of self, as communicated through our interactions with embedded and embodied technologies, with an ability to sense our bodily biology, our social connections, and the larger environment, while capturing, storing, and communicating that data to us and others via haptic modalities suggests an ongoing reconfiguration of communication between machines and humans.

Human–machine communication can address these communicative moments by opening new avenues for inquiry about communication, technology, and society. It recognizes that machines are more than mediums, they are communicators (Guzman, 2018). Early work in HMC largely responds to the growth in social robotics, chatbots, voice-enabled devices like Siri and Alexa, and other virtual and embodied robotic interlocutors – devices that are intentionally designed to act as communicative agents primarily using audio, visual, and textual messaging systems.[1] Guzman (2016) expands the possibility of what counts as human–machine communication by considering industrial machines – what she calls 'mute' machines – explicated through Carey's (1992) ritual communication model, but stops short of considering the touch forms of communication that influence these rituals and relations. Communication, as it develops theory for emerging technologies and relationships, is in danger of repeating tropes about what counts as communication in a time when HMC is nascent, but there is a growing area of research accounting for the historical, every day, and imagined interactions involving touch and machines (Barker et al., 2020; Jewitt et al., 2020; Parisi, 2018; Richardson & Hjorth, 2017).

Designing machines to provide haptic feedback via vibrations or forces or temperature fluctuations, and the way we assign meanings to those interactions, alters how we perceive our relations with machines. These decisions should not be diminished as we pursue an understanding of human-machine communication. Nor should we overlook the ways that machines become the embodiment of those ideas since they have social and political ramifications that we fail to recognize if we overly emphasize interlocution as visual and verbal interactions only (Archer & Bassett, 2020). Human augmentics technologies which use haptics to communicate with humans, provide avenues for considering what counts as human-machine communication beyond the audio-visual linguistic paradigm and HMC can develop useful theories and approaches for understanding haptics and human augmentics.

HUMAN AUGMENTICS

Human augmentics is defined by Kenyon and Leigh (2011) as "technologies for expanding the capabilities and characteristic of humans" and constitutes, for them, "the driving force in the non-biological evolution of humans" (p. 6758). Their need to coin a new term seems to stem from the rapid emergence, merging, and adaptation of several mechanical and digital technologies, including embodied and embedded sensors in devices and the environment, networked technologies, and wearables. Human augmentics, then is not a singular device, but a set of interconnected technologies meant to expand human agency and a human's sense of agency through coordination with machines that are adaptive to users and their environments. As Novak et al. (2016) state:

> The point of Human Augmentics is to develop communication between the human, machine, and environment premised on collaboration rather than co-option, engagement rather than estrangement, to increase human agency and a human's sense of agency, not to eradicate the human in pursuit of becoming something other. Human Augmentics, then, is focused on the intersections between human and machine, about the information that is generated between agents, and the affordances that information provides to potentially increase agency. (p. 27)

The human augmentics framework offered by Novak et al. (2016) provides a way of theorizing agency via human-machine communication premised on a series of specific kinds of interconnected technologies, focused on intrapersonal and interpersonal levels of agency and communication. The technological assemblages constituting human augmentics are not necessarily agentic in the same way as robots, chatbots, automated journalists, or other machines typically considered by human-machine communication because they are more intimately connected to the human, but HMC scholars can bring important approaches to human augmentics, especially in terms of theorizing agency and communication at the heart of these technologies. Gambino et al. (2020) in extending CASA and Lombard & Xu (2021) in introducing MASA provide tools to assess the communication scripts and agentic qualities assigned to these embodied communication partners. And Gibbs et al. (2021) and Neff and Nagy (2019) articulate frameworks that can help scholars interested in human augmentics better attend to structural and sociotechnical issues of agency. Likewise, human augmentics offers more ways of thinking about

agency and communication between humans and machines as they are meant to increase a "sense of agency, extending the traditional human-computer interface dictum to provide an internal locus of control" (Novak et al., 2016, p. 2). Orienting around a sense of agency, the framework introduced by human augmentics suggests that associated technologies expand the perceived agentic horizon for the human-in-the-loop through cooperation with the machine.

Mateevitsi et al. (2013) SpiderSense prototype provides one example of human augmentics. SpiderSense is a suit fitted with ultrasonic sensors that can detect things near the wearer, a computational processing unit, and thirteen actuators to provide vibrational feedback. Imagined as a technology for the blind or for those in low-vision settings, like fire fighters entering a smoke-filled building, the idea is that SpiderSense can "increase the user's agency and sense of agency by making them aware of their surroundings" (Novak et al., 2016, p. 20) in ways that would otherwise not be possible. In theory, SpiderSense could also be connected to data networks, allowing it to interpret and communicate different types of otherwise imperceptible information to wearers through haptic feedback. One problematic idea involved linking the device to mapped crime data to produce virtual boundaries that wearers would feel as more intense vibration patterns as they approached higher crime areas.

HAPTICS

Haptics is commonly defined by its association with the "Greek word *haptikós*, meaning 'able to grasp or perceive'" (Jones, 2018, p. 1), but its use, even amongst shared literatures, has often been ambiguous. In engineering literature, where much haptics research germane to human–machine communication scholars is situated, the term is sometimes used in the broadest way: "haptics – the sense of touch – enables humans to perform a wide variety of exploration and manipulation tasks in the real world" (Culbertson, Schoor, Okamura, 2018, p. 386). This broad definition probably derives from early work in the field of physiological psychology where haptic displaced tactile after the "discovery" that touch was more than localized on the skin.[2] Making haptics synonymous with touch is its more popular usage today. The popular usage is seen in early work by philosopher Mark Paterson (2007) where he defines haptics as "relating to the sense of touch in all its forms" (p. ix) and communication scholarship where the term is used synonymously with touch in interpersonal and intercultural communication scholarship (Guerrero & Hecht, 2008, p. 183).

It has become typical in engineering literature and psychological literature, which attempt to achieve more technical specificity, to delineate haptics as representing specific aspects of the touch system. Differentiating types of touch-based interaction devices, Jones and Lederman (2006) articulate haptics as involving both tactile and kinesthetic systems, or in other words, the skin and the muscles (pp. 195–200). And Jones (2018) makes the distinction in her book "Haptics" published in *The MIT Press Essential Knowledge Series* that "the ability to identify and perceive the properties of objects relies on our sense of touch and more specifically on active touch, which is often referred to as haptics or haptic sensing" (p. 1). The notion of active touch basically means to touch something rather than to be touched by something.

What I want to suggest here is that using the term haptics instead of touch is a sociotechnical decision that treats touch as something that can be instrumentalized, essentialized, quantified, and made to fit the protocols of technoscience. For engineers and physiological psychologists, the term offers to define a clear subset of psychophysical proprieties of touch that can inform the study of the human sensory system and the development of interfaces, even while its usage has been inconsistent. Against Lederman's more concise definition, Parisi (2018) defines haptics more broadly "to link together a range of machines whose development has been informed by the technoscientific treatment of touch" (p. 337). It is this way of conceptualizing haptics that I think is most useful to human–machine communication scholars, not a strictly psychophysical definition or one that seeks to conflate touch and haptics, but one that offers a more critical orientation and invites researchers to explore haptics as more than a point of contact between humans and machines.

Tracing the definition of haptics to the field most accountable for its development allows scholars to explain how it is always associated with machines and technologies which also reveal configurations of power and politics at the heart of instrumentalizing and commodifying touch. As Parisi (2018) argues,

Haptics, then, constituted a declaration of power over tactility; rapidly embedded in the design of research labs and psychophysical instruments, it signaled touch's enclosure within a new epistemological framework. As a field of knowledge, haptics depended on the active solicitation of test subjects' experiences in the human-built laboratory environment. A new type of perceiving subject – a haptic subject – touched and was touched within the carefully configured parameters of lab space. (p. 105)

Applying this definition of haptics to a human augmentics project like SpiderSense (Mateevitsi et al., 2013) means considering how a human learns to interpret the vibrational patterns of the suit and makes them meaningful in different contexts. It means applying ideas from scholars like Fox & McEwen (2017) to reflect on the affordances of the haptic feedback offered by SpiderSense and how those affordances shape perceptions of the social capacities of the suit. But it also means interrogating how the haptic feedback incorporated in SpiderSense was made in the first place and how those decisions reify notions of what counts as meaningful human–machine haptic communication. For instance, the haptic feedback meant to serve as SpiderSense's primary mode of communication developed from the research paradigm Parisi (2018) identifies as producing "a haptic subject." This lab configured subject reifies normative notions of machine touch and the kinds of bodies open to receive that touch.

Despite grand claims and continued development, the field of haptics remains in a state of perpetual immanence over the last three decades (Parisi, 2020). This may, in fact, be the intervention that human–machine communication scholars can make around haptics research. Bringing an HMC lens to haptics means bringing communication theories to human–machine touch beyond the psychophysical assumptions and techno solutionism influencing haptic design, especially in industry. At the same time, attending to haptics in its various forms can help human–machine communication scholars better understand the intricacies of communication that go beyond audio-visually dominant paradigms.

HAPTIC MACHINES

There are countless machines in our lives that incorporate haptics, but many of these devices are not recent. Electroshock devices dating back to the early days of mechanized and electrified touch tell a story of interacting via shocking kisses and shocking embraces (Parisi, 2018). More recent haptic technologies reside in our domestic environments, in labs, in commercial spaces, in industry, and in medical contexts. Our phones vibrate in our pockets to alert of an incoming call, text, or other notification, prompting what Gilmore (2017) refers to as a "haptic instant." We pull our phone out of our pocket and begin navigating the glassy surface only to be treated to the delight of a little buzz, bump, or vibration telling us that we are, in fact touching the phone, that it understands us, and that it is going to do what we ask it to do via our fingertips. Smartphones now record our touch, playing it back to us via different modalities but they also communicate to us using touch.

Attempts to consider the dynamics of haptic machines is not without precedent in communication and adjacent fields like media studies, but these approaches have most often framed machines as mediators not communicators. McLaughlin et al. (2008) offer an early meditation on the importance of a shifting touchscape with the development of ICTs that incorporated rudimentary haptics, approaching touch communication from a computer mediated communication (CMC) orientation and offering experimental evidence about how tactile messaging systems using the PHANToM haptic pen and CyberGrasp glove could shift perceptions of telework partners. While offering important considerations for CMC researchers, which seem to largely have gone unheeded, their orientation toward these devices treated them as channels and mediators of communication rather than potentially communicative partners – going so far as to suggest that haptic developers should incorporate lessons learned from research on human touch to design machine-based touch (p. 172). The suggestions certainly merit attention, but they also limit the ways that machine touch may be considered apart from human touch, and they also narrow thinking about what counts as haptics to those machines that connect people to other people or to virtual environments.

Just as there has been a bias in communication toward centering humans, there is also a bias in communication and media studies toward centering oral, visual, and textual modes of communication over other modalities. Where communication does consider touch as a form of nonverbal communication, it is often investigated through visual observations, focusing on visual gestures not on felt interactions or cultural constructions. However, there are notable exceptions that provide a wider range of theoretical and methodological possibilities.

Research associated with haptic media studies unsettle the audio-visual regime that permeates research in communication and media studies. Works by Strauven (2011), Huhtamo (2007), and Parikka (2012), provide ways of conceptualizing encounters with early cinema and arcades that help us understand "how our bodies are activated and moulded by media technologies" (Parikka,

2012, p. 29). Work by Parisi (2013) builds on Huhtamo's work, exploring human–machine relationships through shocking sensations built into video games. A special issue on Haptic Media in *New Media and Society* (Parisi et al., 2017) presents several articles engaging new media technologies and touch in a push toward recovering touch in communication and media studies. In his monograph, Parisi (2018) traces developments in human–machine tactile communication. And McEwen and Dubé (2017) examine the unique communication arising between users and touchscreen tablet computers. The research and the perspectives they provide present human–machine communication with a way of considering historical, relational, and sociotechnical aspects of haptic machines that depart from typical theories of human touch in communication research.

There is also a burgeoning area of research that considers human–robot touch communication developing in areas outside human–machine communication.[3] In a survey of human–robot touch, Jewitt et al. (2020) review several studies concerned with human perceptions of robot communication in order to understand how using different touch modalities such as temperature may convey warmth, associated with perceiving a robot as friendlier, or in the relationship between the pressure exerted by a robotic handshake on perceptions of personality and gender (p. 45). In fact, research that considers the impact of touch on human–machine communication may be most developed in human–robot interaction because of the sophistication of robots and attempts to make them more humanoid. For instance, research into haptic human-robotic interaction (hHRI) tends to treat human–robotic touch as a psychophysical and mechanical problem (Karniel et al., 2012) but some research also considers the affective and social dimensions of interaction (Yohanan & MacLean, 2012 Culbertson, 2018). These studies take approaches adjacent to interpersonal and nonverbal communication but both hHRI and interpersonal and nonverbal communication research could benefit from more direct collaboration. While these perspectives are certainly warranted, they risk forwarding tropes about what counts as worthwhile to study and what counts as meaningful touch communication.

HAPTICS-ORIENTED HUMAN–MACHINE COMMUNICATION

A haptics-oriented HMC addressing human augmentics means exploring machines that we may not typically think of as interlocutors based on the sophistication of their communication or on the modalities of their address. It also opens space to ask novel questions. How does applying an HMC lens to haptics and human augmentics open new ways of exploring and understanding intrapersonal forms of communication? How do machines collecting data about us and looping that data back to us in the form of haptic interactions impact our sense of self, sense of agency, and our place in society? How does treating these machines as communication partners shift our understandings of interpersonal communication and how does interpersonal theory need to be adapted to account for haptics? How does multi-agential touch formed through a series of mechanical, computational, and sensing networks alter our understanding of human–machine communication as infrastructural, connected, and sociotechnical? How can human–machine communication help us understand how touch is collected, quantified, translated, and transformed to communicate? And what can it tell us about the implications of these processes? How might attending to haptics in human–machine communication alter our understanding of touch and communication? I ask these questions to open possibilities for exploration, not to bound a haptics-oriented research agenda for HMC. Beyond a set of provocations, I want to provide a list of considerations for scholars who wish to incorporate haptics and human augmentics in their research and teaching. My hope is that others build, refine, and expand on this list as more scholars engage in haptics-oriented research.

1. Understand how machines and humans touch, how they make sense of touch, and how touch relates to agency. Developing research in human–machine haptic communication necessitates multidisciplinary engagement to understand human and machine touch. There is a rich body of literature that examines touch and haptics from a variety of angles. Human–machine communication scholars need not become familiar with all of it, but they should have a sense of how touch is treated in philosophy, psychology, sociology, anthropology, engineering, and human–computer interaction/human–robot interaction – depending on the aims of the study. HMC is uniquely positioned to answer pressing questions about human augmentics and haptics because it arose as a transdisciplinary perspective.

2. Develop critical orientations that challenge claims regarding touch. There are abounding claims, especially during Covid-19, about a growing touch hunger being experienced by humans

(Cocozza, 2018; Hammond, 2020; Powers & Parisi, 2020). These claims frame humans as living through a crisis of touch. There is no doubt that new sociotechnical arrangements have shifted the ways we touch, and our relationships to touch, but framing touch as in crisis because we are supposedly not getting enough of it negates negative aspects of touch and elevates technology as the solution. This call does not mean scholars should not consider a potential crisis of touch or the possibility that machines could quell it, but it is a call to provide a more nuanced perspective and a greater range of theory. As Puig de la Bellacasa (2009) reflects, "I wonder: to touch or to be touched physically doesn't automatically mean being in touch with oneself or the other. Can there be a detached touch? I know that unwanted touch, abusive touch, can induce a rejection of sensation, a self-induced numbness. What kind of touch is produced when we are unaware of the needs and desires of that what/whom we are reaching for?" (p. 300). If we consider how de la Bellacasa's reflection may impact our approaches to human–machine communication, we may find ourselves asking what kind of touching is produced when we reach for something without needs or desires or what touch is produced when that machine reaches back? Taking a critical approach also allows us to consider how haptics and the haptic subject are socially and materially constructed, for what purpose(s), and by whom.

3. Explore critical connections to disability, race, and gender studies. Just like other machines and technologies, making touch work for machines means quantifying, measuring, capturing, collecting, translating, and reformatting touch. The process is typically a normative one, capturing and extending certain types or ways of touching over others. Whose touch is extended and whose is excluded in these emerging human–machine configurations? These questions are especially important to ask of emerging, understudied, and forgotten technologies because "too often the introduction of new technologies can create new forms of exclusion for people with disabilities" (Goggin and Newell, 2005, n.p.). And as Paterson (2017) says, "any technology which does not actually broaden accessibility by offering alternative forms of user interaction, or permit a range of modal channels for input, is inherently disabling" (p. 1555). This is a reminder to ask how human–machine communication may be disabling

for humans and machines by limiting touch in some ways in order to extend them in others.

4. Focus on imaginaries, engineering labs, patents, marketing discourses, uses, and other material and cultural manifestations involved in co-constructing haptics. Recognizing how these technologies are sociotechnically co-constructed Puig de la Bellacasa (2009) claims "touch technologies are remaking what touching means. Inversely, I would add, haptic technology works with the powerful imaginary of touch and its compelling affective power to produce touching technology" (p. 303). Indeed, as Parisi and Archer (2017) lay out, there is a genealogy of haptic media that have produced these ideas of touch: "shaping a mass haptic subject across a range of sites, from the primitive research laboratories of 19th century psychologists to the contemporary courtrooms where digital technology firms such as Google, Apple, and Immersion Corporation battle over who controls the means of producing machinic haptic sensation" (p. 11). Paying attention to the sociotechnical and historical construction of human–machine haptic communication will help account for the ways touch technologies are already shaping ourselves and our machines.

CONCLUSION

Communication with machines has always involved touch, even the minimal interaction of pressing a button (Plotnick, 2018), but as the hapticity of machines becomes more sophisticated and aligned with human augmentics, haptic communication with and through machines will become increasingly symbolic, affective, and meaningful, impacting our agency and our sense of agency. Communication and media studies have often given touch short shift in their historical development (Paterson, 2007, 2017) with notable exceptions such as human-computer interaction and psycho-cognitive studies of touch (McEwen & Dubé, 2017) and touch theories of media produced by Marks (2002), McEwen (2019), McLuhan (1994), and Parisi (2018). However, human–machine communication can treat touch and haptics as serious from the start. Focusing on haptics, including mundane forms that are not intentionally designed to be communicative, constitutes an important aspect of human–machine communication that should be core to its conceptual, theoretical, and research development – and

should not be treated as an appendage easily cut away.

NOTES

1 See the inaugural issue of Human–Machine Communication. The issue does not represent the full range of approaches to HMC, and there are certainly exceptions which I reference later in this chapter, but it is largely emblematic of the general orientation taken by HMC thus far.

2 David Parisi offers the definitive account of the development and use of the term haptic in his 2018 book, "Archaeologies of Touch: Interfacing with Haptics from Electricity to Computing" (pp. 99–150).

3 Within HMC, Fox & McEwen (2017) recognize the emergence of other modalities of communication increasingly incorporated into machines that increase the perceived social affordances, including haptics.

REFERENCES

Archer, J. & Bassett, N. (2020). Re-imagining embodiment in communication. In Michael Filimowicz and Veronica Tzankova (Eds.), *Reimagining Communication: Experience* (pp. 47–63). Routledge.

Barker, N., Jewitt, C., & Price, S. (2020, March). Becoming in touch with industrial robots through ethnography. *Companion of The 2020 ACM/IEEE International Conference on Human-Robot Interaction.* HRI '20.

Carey, J. W. (1992). *Communication as Culture: Essays on Media and Society.* Routledge.

Cocozza, P. (2018, March 7). No hugging: are we living through a crisis of touch? *The Guardian: Health.* www.theguardian.com/society/2018/mar/07/crisis-touch-hugging-mental-health-strokes-cuddles

Culbertson, H., Schorr, S. B., & Okamura, A. M. (2018). Haptics: the present and future of artificial touch sensation. *Annu Rev Control Robot Auton Syst* 1(1), pp. 385–409.

Dubé, A. & McEwen, R. N. (2016). Abilities and affordances: Factors influencing successful child-tablet communication. *Educational Tech Dev.* 65, pp. 889–908.

Fox, J., & McEwen, B. (2017). Distinguishing technologies for social interaction: The perceived social affordances of communication channels scale. *Communication Monographs,* *84,* 298–318. https://doi.org/10.1080/03637751.2017.1332418

Gambino, A., Fox, J., & Rabindra, R. (2020). Building a stronger CASA: Extending the computers are social actors paradigm. Vol. 1. https://doi.org/10.30658/hmc.1.5

Gibbs, J.L., Kirkwood, G. L., Fang, C. & Wilkenfeld, J. N. (2021). Negotiating agency and control: Theorizing human-machine communication from a structurational perspective. *Human-Machine Communication*. Vol. 2. https://doi.org/10.30658/hmc.2.8

Gilmore, J. N. (2017). From ticks and tocks to budges and nudges: The smartwatch and the haptics of informatic culture. *Television & New Media, 18*(3), 189–202. https://doi.org/10.1177/1527476416658962

Goggin, G. & Newell, C. (2005). Introduction: The intimate relations between technology and disability. *Disability Studies Quarterly, 25*(2). https://dsq-sds.org/article/view/547/724

Guerrero, L.K., & Hecht, M.L. (2008). *The Nonverbal Communication Reader: Classic and Contemporary Readings*, 3rd edition. Waveland Press, Inc.

Gunkel, D.J. (2012). Communication and artificial intelligence: Opportunities and challenges for the 21st century. *Communication+1, 1*(1).

Guzman, A. L. (2016). The messages of mute machines: Human-machine communication with industrial technologies. *Communication + 1, 5*(1), 32.

Guzman, A. L., & Lewis, S. C. (2020). Artificial intelligence and communication: A Human–Machine Communication research agenda. *New Media & Society, 22*(1), 70–86. https://doi.org/10.1177/1461444819858691

Hammond, C. (2020, Oct. 6). Are we in the midst of a touch crisis? *BBC: Future.* www.bbc.com/future/article/20201006-why-touch-matters-more-than-ever-in-the-time-of-covid-19

Huhtamo, E. (2007). Twin-touch-test-redux: Media archaeological approach to art, interactivity, and tactilty. In O. Grau (Ed.), *MediaArtHistories* (pp. 71–101). MIT Press.

Jewitt, C., Price, S., Leder Mackley, K., Yiannoutsou, N., & Atkinson, D. (2020). *Interdisciplinary Insights for Digital Touch Communication*. Springer International Publishing. https://doi.org/10.1007/978-3-030-24564-1

Jones, S. (2014). People, things, memory and human-machine communication. *International Journal of Media & Cultural Politics, 10*(3), 245–258. https://doi.org/10.1386/macp.10.3.245_1

Jones, S. (2019). Untitled no. 1 (Human Augmentics). In Z. Papacharissi (Ed.) *A networked self and human augmentics, artificial intelligence, sentience* (pp. 201–205). Routledge.

Jones, L. A. (2018). *Haptics*. The MIT Press.

Jones, L. A. & Lederman, S. J. (2006). *Human hand function*. Oxford University Press.

Karniel, A., Peer, A., Opher, D., Mussa-Ivaldi, F.A., & Loeb, G. E. (2012). Haptic human-robot interaction. *IEEE Transactions on Haptics, 5*(3), 193–195.

Kenyon, R. & Leigh, J. (2011). Human augmentics: Augmenting human evolution. *IEEE Engineering Medicine Biology Conference 2011,* Boston, MA, USA.

Lombard, M. & Xu, K. (2021). *Social responses to media technologies in the 21st century: The media are social actors paradigm.* Vol. 2. https://doi.org/10.30658/hmc.2.2

Marks, L. U. (2002). *Touch: Sensuous theory and multisensory media.* University of Minnesota Press.

Mateevitsi, V., Haggadone, B., Leigh, J., Kuner, B., & Kenyon, R.V. (2013). Sensing the environment through SpiderSense. *Proceedings of the 4th Augmented Human International Conference* (pp. 51–57). AH 13. New York: ACM. doi:10.1145/2459236.2459246

McEwen, R. & Dubé, A. (2017). *Understanding tablets from early childhood to adulthood: Encounters with touch technology.* Routledge.

McEwen, R.N. (2019). Flash, Spirit, Plex, Stretch: A trans-disciplinary view of the media sensorium. *Canadian Journal of Communication,* 44. pp. 583–593.

McLaughlin, M., Jung, Y., Peng, W., Jin, S.A., & Zhu, W. (2008). Touch in computer-mediated communication. In Elly A. Konijn, Sonja Utz, Martin Tanis, & Susan B. Barnes (Eds.), *Mediated interpersonal communication* (pp. 158–176). Routledge.

McLuhan, M. (1994). *Understanding media: The extensions of man.* The MIT Press.

Nabeshima, J., Saraiji, M. Y., & Minamizawa, K. (2019). Argue: Artificial biomimicry-inspired tail for extending innate body functions. *SIGGRAPH '19: ACM SIGGRAPH 2019 Posters,* 1–2. https://doi.org/10.1145/3306214.3338573

Neff, G. & Nagy, P. (2019). Agency in the Digital Age: Using symbiotic agency to explain human-technology interactions. In Z. Papacharissi (Ed.) *A networked self and human augmentics, artificial intelligence, sentience* (pp. 97–107). Routledge.

Novak, J., Archer, J., Kenyon, R., & Shafiro, V. (2013). *Interspeech,* 1869–1871.

Novak, J., Archer, J., Mateevitsi, V., & Jones, S. (2016). Communication, machines & human augmentics. *Communication+1, 5*(1).

Okamura, A.M. (2018). Haptic dimensions of human-robot interaction. *ACM Trans. Hum.- Robot Interact, 7*(1).

Parikka, J. (2012). *What is media archaeology?*. Polity Press.

Parisi, D. (2013). Shocking grasps: An archaeology of electrotactile game mechanics. *Game Studies: The International Journal of Computer Game Research, 13*(2). http://gamestudies.org/1302/articles/parisi

Parisi, D. & Archer, J.E. (2017). Making touch analog: The prospects and perils of a haptic media studies. *New Media & Society*, 19(10).

Parisi, D. (2018). *Archaeologies of touch: Interfacing with haptics from electricity to computing*. University of Minnesota Press.

Parisi, D. (2020, April 26). Dreaming and doing haptics. *Open! Platform for Art, Culture & Public Domain*. Retrieved from https://onlineopen.org/dreaming-and-doing-haptics

Parisi, D., Paterson, M., & Archer, J. E. (2017). Haptic media studies. *New Media & Society*, 19(10), 1513–1522. https://doi.org/10.1177/1461444817717518

Paterson, M. (2007). *The senses of touch: Haptics, affects and technologies*. Berg.

Paterson, M. (2017). On haptic media and the possibilities of a more inclusive interactivity. *New Media & Society,* 19(10), 1541–1562. https://doi.org/10.1177/1461444817717513

Plotnick, R. (2018). *Power button: A history of pleasure, panic, and the politics of pushing*. The MIT Press.

Powers, D. & Parisi, D. (2020, July 28). The hype, haplessness and hope of haptics in the COVID-19 era. *Techcrunch*. https://techcrunch.com/2020/07/28/the-hype-haplessness-and-hope-of-haptics-in-the-covid-19-era/

Puig de la Bellacasa, M. (2009). Touching technologies, touching visions. The reclaiming of sensorial experience and the politics of speculative thinking. *Subjectivity*, *28*(1), 297–315. https://doi.org/10.1057/sub.2009.17

Richardson, I., & Hjorth, L. (2017). Mobile media, domestic play and haptic ethnography. *New Media & Society*, *19*(10), 1653–1667. https://doi.org/10.1177/1461444817717516

Strauven, W. (2011). The observer's dilemma: To touch or not to touch. In E. Huhtamo & J. Parikka (Eds.), *Media archaeology: Approaches, applications, and implications* (pp. 148–163). University of California Press.

Tyler, D. J. (2016, April 28). Creating a prosthetic hand that can feel. *IEEE Spectrum*. https://spectrum.ieee.org/biomedical/bionics/creating-a-prosthetic-hand-that-can-feel

Waltz, E. (2018, September 20). Prosthetic skin to sense wind, rain, and ants. *IEEE Spectrum*. https://spectrum.ieee.org/the-human-os/biomedical/bionics/prosthetic-skin-to-sense-wind-rain-and-ants

Yohanan, S. & MacLean, K.E. (2012). The role of affective touch in human-robot interaction: Human intent and expectations in touching the haptic creature. *Int J Soc. Robot*, 4, 163–180.

Third, the objectification of humans as things and the user's focus on their sexual desires will reinforce gender power relations and violence, leading to reduced human empathy and social skills. Specifically, the CASR argues empathy can only be gained through human–human relationships. This suggests when humans do not have that mutual relationship, but instead, an asymmetrical human–robot relationship, the human's empathy will be reduced (Richardson, 2015), becoming first unempathetic sexually followed by becoming unempathetic morally (Bergen, 2020, p. 287). Further, this reduction of empathy is argued to lead the individual into isolation, where they lose the benefits of human–human relationships and, subsequently, the social skills required to initiate and maintain those relationships (Danaher, 2017; Richardson, 2015, 2016).

Just as before, those opposing the CASR call into question the assumptions CASR makes. First, the third claim of CASR assumes that empathy is desirable (Bergen, 2020, p. 286) and can only be obtained and maintained by human–human interaction (Richardson, 2015). I believe it is a stretch to argue humans cannot obtain and maintain moral values and social skills from human–robot relations. Human–robot relations can be therapeutic in that the interactions can teach human social skills like empathy and sexual consent (Danaher, 2017; Peeters & Haselager, 2021). The CASR assumes humans desire human–human relationships, which is not always true. For example, members of the social movement MGTOW (Men Going Their Own Way), who believe women exploit men for resources, have found a connection with sex robots as an alternative to humans (Döring, 2021).

Collectively, the points made by the CASR focus on what humans can lose and the macro-level implications if sex robots are accepted and widely used, while the opposition argues for what humans can gain from human–robot relationships and micro-level implications. Both sides' attempted conclusions are focused on the personal and societal interest in sex robots (Scheutz & Arnold, 2016) instead of determining conclusions based on empirical data. The field of HMC can answer many of the ongoing debates in the field, but to do so, scholars must first know what has been examined thus far.

SEX ROBOTS AND EMPIRICAL FINDINGS

Empirical investigations into sex robots make up 12% of the current literature (Döring et al., 2020). Specifically, this includes twelve studies focused on attitudes toward sex robots, the factors contributing to their acceptance or rejection, and what impact they may have on human–human relationships, primarily from the perspective of non-current users (pp. 18–19).

Findings based on current users are limited, likely due to the technology still being developed. Due to the current limitations, scholars have been building from prior findings from sex doll owners, as sex dolls have been around for decades (Döring, 2021; Langcaster-James & Bentley, 2018; Levy, 2007) and a sex robot is a sex doll developed with additional features (e.g., AI, moveable and heated body parts). Owners have mostly self-identified as owning one or more dolls and being male, heterosexual, middle-aged (30–60), employed, single, and living alone in North America with a university-level education (Langcaster-James & Bentley, 2018; Middleweek, 2021). This 'typical profile' of sex doll users (Middleweek, 2021) is also reflected in popular human–robot relationship movies like *Her* and *Lars and the Real Girl*. Both films portray men as the minority in their respective societies. However, several surveys have suggested the acceptance rate may be closer to about half the population (Richards et al., 2017; Scheutz & Arnold, 2016; Szczuka & Krämer, 2017a, 2017b).

Despite media representations of sex doll and robot users as social hermits secluded from others, loneliness is not a significant predictor of the intention to buy or feel attracted to a sex robot (Szczuka & Krämer, 2017a, 2017b). Other stereotypical factors, such as a fear of rejection and fear of intimacy, have also been small predictors of the intention to buy a sex robot and the likelihood to have an experience with a sex robot (Richards et al., 2017; Szczuka & Krämer, 2017a, 2017b). Negative attitudes towards robots have been the predominant negative predictor impacting intent to purchase or use. Finally, and central to this chapter on HMC, a deficiency in social skills does not predict the intent to purchase a sex robot or to find a sex robot attractive (Szczuka & Krämer, 2017a, 2017b). Instead of users seeking out sex robots in desperation, as the media and the CASR would lead people to believe, it is expected based on current findings that users will seek out sexual robot interactions to fulfill sexual fantasies (Richards et al., 2017).

The sexual aspect of sex robots is clear in the name, and also in the primary purpose users report as to why they purchased a sex doll or sex robot (Langcaster-James & Bentley, 2018). Specifically, sex doll users view their relationship with the doll as sexual (77%), companionship (56%), loving (47%), emotional (43%), and friendship (30%; Langcaster-James & Bentley, 2018). Users refer to their doll as a lover (43%), companion (42%), and boyfriend/girlfriend (21%). Further, doll users reported participating in non-sexual but relationship maintenance strategies such as grooming, dressing, and conversing with their dolls. Langcaster-James and Bentley went on to suggest "sex doll" is not an appropriate term since some viewed their doll as more than a sexual subject (p. 14). Middleweek (2021) reported, in an analysis of sex robot and sex doll forums, that users appear excited about the increased level of intimacy AI sex robots will bring to their relationship, suggesting sex robots may bring more companionship and emotional connection than sex dolls.

Most sex doll users are single (44%), but some are married or in a domestic partnership (23%) or a current relationship (10%; Langcaster-James & Bentley, 2018). Viewing sex robots as partners, and not sex toys, will likely have a meaningful impact on human–human relationships. Two experimental vignette studies with single and married men paying for sex from either a human (i.e., sex worker) or a sex robot found that the man was judged less for paying and having sex with a robot than a human sex worker. Additionally, married men who had sex with a human sex worker were judged harsher than single men conducting the same behavior. Finally, across all vignettes, female participants judged every scenario harsher than their male counterparts (Koverola et al., 2020). Oleksy and Wnuk (2021) interpreted Koverola and colleagues' findings suggesting women may feel threatened by female sex robots. The results of their vignette experiments suggest women feel less threatened when a sex robot is presented as something for them, and not solely for men. This difference only occurred in women with liberal political views, while women with conservative views felt threatened regardless of the vignette situation. More research is needed in this area; however, findings may differ based on the participant's political views, sex, and relationship commitment (Döring, 2021).

FUTURE DIRECTIONS WITH SEX ROBOTS IN HMC

Due to limited empirical findings in the vast field of lovotics, the field has no lack of potential future directions. To attract a wide range of traditional human–human communication scholars, such as mass media, interpersonal, applied, and health, to the field of HMC, the following future directions are only a few of the possibilities the HMC field provides.

The CASR argues that sex robots will be the downfall to mankind's humanity (i.e., empathy).

Assuming such claims are true, then it is paramount we determine how it will occur and to what degree. These CASR claims should be tested by mass media, interpersonal, and health communication scholars.

The CASR also asserts that the acceptance of sex robots will further degrade our society; however, widespread acceptance must occur before this can take place. Mass media scholars are equipped to analyze media representations of sex robots and the influence these representations have on culture and attitudes. Such information will aid sex robot manufacturers and other scholarship as to how "sex robots are developed, marketed, discussed, used, and investigated today" (Döring et al., 2020, p. 21). Findings will also further aid our understanding of how society develops meaning with sex robots. Finally, similar to other media effects research, further explorations may determine if exposure to a sex robot produces further sexual objectification of women and children (CASR first claim).

If exposure to a sex robot either through advertisements (media effects), or in-person interaction, does increase sexual objectification, does that objectification carry over to human–human interactions (CASR third claim)? The broader field of HMC would benefit from the results of those studies. A majority of HMC is based on the CASA (Nass et al., 1994) or human–robot script (Edwards et al., 2016; Spence et al., 2014); both theories suggest humans give robots human traits and use human social scripts in human–robot interactions. Despite the CASR's second claim, no known research has determined if humans develop traits or social scripts during human–robot interaction and later apply them to a human.

Sex robots open new possibilities for interpersonal and sexual research. These potential companions can be used to answer questions related to HMC but also human–human communication and relationships. From broad ideas such as what constitutes a relationship (Spence, 2019), companionship (Andreallo & Chesher, 2019), and sex (Peterson & Muehlenhard, 2007) to more rigorous testing and controlled experimentation of relationship formation and maintenance theories. The CASR's second claim is that the user is fixated on their desires; if that is true, then it should be prevalent in how users develop meaning within their human–robot relationship. This suggests the use of observation or daily diary studies (which are less intrusive for the participant), both are desperately needed to focus on current users (Döring, 2021; Döring et al., 2020; Döring & Poeschl, 2019). Additionally, if the user is fixated on only their needs, that should come across in their sexual interactions, utilizing the sexual script theory (Simon & Gagnon, 1986). Findings related to the sexual script progression will likely tell us what humans prefer in the human–human sexual interaction, beyond what is typically expected to progress (i.e., the expected sexual script).

The sex robot field is ripe for contribution from applied HMC scholars. Manufacturers of sex robots, using AI for their communication potential, are at the forefront of the industry through an HMC lens. However, it is unknown if current and potential users actively desire this reciprocal verbal potential (Langcaster-James & Bentley, 2018). Further, users' primary and secondary motives for purchasing a sex robot are currently unknown. Limited studies have assessed sex doll forums (e.g., Middleweek, 2021) and conducted demographic and close-ended surveys to determine some motives. An in-depth researcher-participant qualitative study of user experiences would be largely helpful. Manufacturers and scholars alike would benefit greatly by utilizing the feedback from current and potential future users, including an understanding of the motives behind use, as well as features current users utilize or would like to use. Understanding the user's motives will help create a typology (Döring et al., 2020). A typology will allow scholars to determine those who may, or may not, be at risk of harming themselves (e.g., social isolation) or others (e.g., objectification, rape). Manufacturers can then in turn develop safeguards in AI software to protect the robot, user, and potentially other humans. Just as users utilize communication technology for diverse uses and gratifications (Sundar & Limperos, 2013) so should sex robot users.

Finally, health implications are arguably the most cited future direction in current sex robot literature (theoretical and empirical). A recent thematic analysis of future directions suggested studies are focused on three categories: sexual, emotional, and educational (Fosch-Villaronga & Poulsen, 2020). Sex robots offer potential sexual health benefits such as a safer alternative to human–human sex, such as removing the risk of sexually transmitted disease (Döring, 2021; Döring & Poeschl, 2019; Fosch-Villaronga & Poulsen, 2020) and as an avenue for benefits from sexual activity such as weight management (i.e., sex burns calories). Predicted emotional health benefits may include companionship and a communicative partner. Finally, sex robots may offer implications for educational health in inviting participants to explore their sexuality and learn sexual consent, empathy, and compassion for their lovers (Danaher, 2017; Peeters & Haselager, 2021). Despite the wide range of health implications, only half of surveyed sex therapists and physicians could imagine using a sex robot as a therapeutic

tool (Eichenberg et al., 2019), with significant differences existing between male and female practitioners. Health communication scholars should investigate how differences in gender and the field of medicine influence the construction of meaning surrounding sex robots and how that relates to their medical practice. Afterward, studies can investigate how the doctor–patient conversation mutually builds meaning surrounding sex robots.

CONCLUSION

Communication capabilities are actively being programmed into AI sex robots, current users are having conversations creating community and shared meaning with other users and their robots, all while the larger society (e.g., philosophers, mass media, doctors) is constructing their meaning of what a sex robot is and what impact they may have. Thus far, only one article has been published from the communication discipline on sex robots (i.e., Richards et al., 2017). To attract more scholars to the field of lovotics, I have presented the case for viewing human–sex robot communication and relationships as new and valid avenues of discovery, for both human–human and human–robot implications. All scholars, manufacturers, and practitioners entering this area of research should first understand the larger ongoing ethical debate, and I expect social scientists conducting current empirical studies will soon be able to answer several of these ethical questions. I proposed several lines of research related to mass media, interpersonal, and health communication for future scholars to explore. The lovotics field is at a point where human–robot relationships should be viewed as a serious area of study, and HMC is perfectly aligned to answer the call.

REFERENCES

Andreallo, F., & Chesher, C. (2019). Prosthetic soul mates: Sex robots as media for companionship. *M/C Journal, 22*(5). https://doi.org/10.5204/mcj.1588

Bergen, J. P. (2020). Love(rs) in the making: Moral subjectivity in the face of sexbots. *Paladyn, 11*(1), 284–300. https://doi.org/10.1515/pjbr-2020-0016

CASR. (n.d.). *Our story*. Retrieved March 20, 2021, from https://campaignagainstsexrobots.org/our-story/

Danaher, J. (2017). The symbolic-consequences argument in the sex robot debate. In J. Danaher &

N. McArthur (Eds.), *Robot sex: Social and ethical implications* (pp. 103–131). The MIT Press.

Danaher, J. (2020). Sexuality. In M. D. Dubber, F. Pasquale, & S. Das (Eds.), *The Oxford handbook of ethics of AI*. Oxford University Press. https://doi.org/10.1093/oxfordhb/9780190067397.013.26

Danaher, J., Earp, B., & Sandberg, A. (2017). Should we campaign against sex robots? In J. Danaher & N. McArthur (Eds.), *Robot sex: Social and ethical implications* (pp. 47–71). The MIT Press.

Döring, N. (2021). Sex dolls and sex robots. In *Encyclopedia of sexuality and gender* (pp. 1–7). https://doi.org/10.1007/978-3-319-59531-3_63-1

Döring, N., Mohseni, M. R., & Walter, R. (2020). Design, use, and effects of sex dolls and sex robots: Scoping review. *Journal of Medical Internet Research, 22*(7). https://doi.org/10.2196/18551

Döring, N., & Poeschl, S. (2019). Love and sex with robots: A content analysis of media representations. *International Journal of Social Robotics, 11*(4), 665–677. https://doi.org/10.1007/s12369-019-00517-y

Edirisinghe, C., & Cheok, A. D. (2017). Robots and intimacies: A preliminary study of perceptions, and intimacies with robots. *Lecture Notes in Computer Science, 10237 LNAI*, 137–147. https://doi.org/10.1007/978-3-319-57738-8_13

Edwards, C., Edwards, A., Spence, P. R., & Westerman, D. (2016). Initial interaction expectations with robots: Testing the human-to-human interaction script. *Communication Studies, 67*(2), 227–238. https://doi.org/10.1080/10510974.2015.1121899

Eichenberg, C., Khamis, M., & Hübner, L. (2019). The attitudes of therapists and physicians on the use of sex robots in sexual therapy: Online survey and interview study. *Journal of Medical Internet Research, 21*(8), 1–16. https://doi.org/10.2196/13853

Fosch-Villaronga, E., & Poulsen, A. (2020). Sex care robots: Exploring the potential use of sexual robot technologies for disabled and elder care. *Paladyn, 11*(1), 1–18. https://doi.org/10.1515/pjbr-2020-0001

Guzman, A. L. (2018). Introduction: "What is human-machine communication, anyway?" In A. L. Guzman (Ed.), *Human-machine communication: Rethinking communication, technology, and ourselves* (pp. 1–28). Peter Lang Publishing.

Guzman, A. L., & Lewis, S. C. (2020). Artificial intelligence and communication: A human-machine communication research agenda. *New Media and Society, 22*(1), 70–86. https://doi.org/10.1177/1461444819858691

Koverola, M., Drosinou, M., Palomäki, J., Halonen, J., Kunnari, A., Repo, M., Lehtonen, N., & Laakasuo, M. (2020). Moral psychology of sex robots: An experimental study - how pathogen disgust is associated with interhuman sex but not interandroid sex. *Paladyn, 11*(1), 233–249. https://doi.org/10.1515/pjbr-2020-0012

Langcaster-James, M., & Bentley, G. R. (2018). Beyond the sex doll: Post-human companionship and the rise of the "Allodoll." *Robotics, 7*(4). https://doi.org/10.3390/robotics7040062

Levy, D. (2007). *Love and sex with robots: The evolution of human-robot relationships* (1st ed.). HarperCollins.

Lucidi, P. B., & Piermattei, S. (2020). Sexual robots: The social-relational approach and the concept of subjective reference. *Lecture Notes in Computer Science, 12182 LNCS*, 549–559. https://doi.org/10.1007/978-3-030-49062-1_37

Middleweek, B. (2021). Male homosocial bonds and perceptions of human-robot relationships in an online sex doll forum. *Sexualities, 24*(3), 370–387. https://doi.org/10.1177/1363460720932383

Nass, C., Steuer, J., & Tauber, E. R. (1994). Computers are social actors. *SIGCHI '94 Human Factors in Computing Systems*, 72–78.

Oleksy, T., & Wnuk, A. (2021). Do women perceive sex robots as threatening? The role of political views and presenting the robot as a female-vs male-friendly product. *Computers in Human Behavior, 117*. https://doi.org/10.1016/j.chb.2020.106664

Peeters, A., & Haselager, P. (2021). Designing virtuous sex robots. *International Journal of Social Robotics, 13*, 55–66. https://doi.org/10.1007/s12369-019-00592-1

Peterson, Z. D., & Muehlenhard, C. L. (2007). What is sex and why does it matter? A motivational approach to exploring individuals' definitions of sex. *Journal of Sex Research, 44*(3), 256–268. https://doi.org/10.1080/00224490701443932

Richards, R., Coss, C., & Quinn, J. (2017). Exploration of relational factors and the likelihood of a sexual robotic experience. *Lecture Notes in Computer Science, 10237 LNAI*, 97–103. https://doi.org/10.1007/978-3-319-57738-8_9

Richardson, K. (2015). The asymmetrical "relationship": Parallels between prostitution and the development of sex robots. *SIGCAS Computers and Society, 45*(3), 290–293. https://doi.org/10.1145/2874239.2874281

Richardson, K. (2016). Sex robot matters: Slavery, the prostituted, and the rights of machines. *IEEE Technology and Society Magazine, 35*(2), 46–53. https://doi.org/10.1109/MTS.2016.2554421

Sandry, E. (2018). Aliveness and the off-switch in human-robot relations. In A. L. Guzman (Ed.), *Human-machine communication: Rethinking communication, technology, and ourselves* (pp. 51–66). Peter Lang Publishing.

Scheutz, M., & Arnold, T. (2016). Are we ready for sex robots? *ACM/IEEE International Conference on*

Human-Robot Interaction, 351–358. https://doi.org/10.1109/HRI.2016.7451772

Simon, W., & Gagnon, J. H. (1986). Sexual scripts: Permanence and change. *Archives of Sexual Behavior*, *15*(2), 97–120.

Spence, P. R. (2019). Searching for questions, original thoughts, or advancing theory: Human-machine communication. *Computers in Human Behavior*, *90*, 285–287. https://doi.org/10.1016/j.chb.2018.09.014

Spence, P. R., Westerman, D., Edwards, C., & Edwards, A. (2014). Welcoming our robot overlords: Initial expectations about interaction with a robot. *Communication Research Reports*, *31*(3), 272–280. https://doi.org/10.1080/08824096.2014.924337

Sullins, J. P. (2012). Robots, love, and sex: The ethics of building a love machine. *IEEE Transactions on Affective Computing*, *3*(4), 398–409. https://doi.org/10.1109/T-AFFC.2012.31

Sundar, S. S., & Limperos, A. M. (2013). Uses and grats 2.0: New gratifications for new media. *Journal of Broadcasting and Electronic Media*, *57*(4), 504–525. https://doi.org/10.1080/08838151.2013.845827

Szczuka, J. M., & Krämer, N. C. (2017a). Not only the lonely—How men explicitly and implicitly evaluate the attractiveness of sex robots in comparison to the attractiveness of women, and personal characteristics influencing this evaluation. *Multimodal Technologies and Interaction*, *1*(1), 1–18. https://doi.org/10.3390/mti1010003

Szczuka, J. M., & Krämer, N. C. (2017b). Influences on the intention to buy a sex robot: An empirical study on influences of personality traits and personal characteristics on the intention to buy a sex robot. *Lecture Notes in Computer Science, 10237 LNAI*, 72–83. https://doi.org/10.1007/978-3-319-57738-8_7

Whitby, B. (2012). Do you want a robot lover? The ethics of caring technologies. In P. Lin, K. Abney, & G. A. Bekey (Eds.), *Robot ethics: The ethical and social implications of robotics* (pp. 233–248). The MIT Press.

57

Virtual Reality as Human–Machine Communication

Eric Novotny, Joomi Lee, and Sun Joo (Grace) Ahn

VIRTUAL REALITY AS HUMAN–MACHINE COMMUNICATION

Virtual reality (VR) involves a system of digital devices that immerse the user in rich layers of sensorimotor cues, allowing the user to see, hear, and feel the mediated world as if they are in the physical world (Sutherland, 1965). Most extant VR scholarship has focused on solitary experiences within virtual worlds, wherein users engage in simulated interactions with virtual agents (driven by algorithms rather than controlled by another human) or with the mediated environment itself (e.g., Appel, von der Putten, Kramer, & Gratch, 2012; Bailenson, 2018; Bickmore & Cassell, 2005; Chase, Chin, Oppezzo, & Schwartz, 2009; Fan, McNeese, & Yen, 2010; Gratch et al., 2002; Makransky, Wismer, & Mayer, 2019). Therefore, apart from VR research that investigates interpersonal communication (e.g., social VR, collaborative virtual environments), the bulk of VR research fits under the umbrella of human–machine communication (HMC), which studies how humans perceive, interact, and communicate with machines (Edwards et al., 2018; Guzman, 2018).

Early VR systems (Sutherland, 1965) were surprisingly similar in concept to modern VR systems, though bulkier in size and limited in computing power. However, the fundamental concept of VR – delivering stereoscopic images, providing haptic feedback, tracking and rendering physical motion to facilitate naturalistic head and body movements, and offering spatially-identifiable audio – has not changed much over half a century. In 2023, VR systems are relatively lightweight, wireless, and all-in-one, but most popular systems still require head-worn goggles and hand controllers to create virtual experiences.

Inside the virtual worlds mediated by these devices, users rely on their own body movements or the handheld controllers to locomote (i.e., navigate freely through VR environments; Boletsis, 2017) and manipulate virtual objects. VR users are embodied through digital representations called *avatars* to interact with other avatars or *agents*; these latter digital representations are controlled by computer algorithms (Ahn, Fox, & Bailenson, 2011; Nowak & Fox, 2018). The interactions among devices, users, and the virtual environment (including agents) inform several distinct areas of HMC scholarship.

Those interested in designing and enhancing the *technical capabilities* of VR systems, such as sensory output (visuals, audio, haptics, etc.) and controller mapping, take a device-driven approach. For many communication scholars, especially those interested in HMC, the *user experience* is the focal aspect of VR (Steuer, 1992). User experience is not a result of mere exposure to VR systems but rather an interaction between the medium's capabilities and the user's sensations, perceptions, and interpretations as they construct meaning from their virtual experiences (Evans et al., 2017). For example, while visualization of certain information among VR users (e.g., status, profile) can be enhanced by technological capabilities, the manner in which users become aware of the feature and make meaningful use of it is the focus of user experiences. User experiences in VR can largely be divided into two types of HMC: (1) interaction with the mediated environment, which contains objects, people, and events produced by computers, and (2) interaction with the devices that mediate these experiences. Both types of interactions inspire unique inquiries regarding communication between human users and their machine counterparts. In this chapter, we highlight notable HMC research in these domains and applications for the extant body of knowledge.

User Interactions with Virtual Environments and Virtual People

The degree of immersion of a VR space is determined by the technology's capacity to provide different layers of sensorimotor information (Steuer, 1992). Upon entering the virtual world, users are surrounded by a three-dimensional space where they can use naturalistic body movements to interact with their environment and receive real-time feedback. At minimum, users' head movements are tracked and rendered into their stereoscopic field of view so that they may look around as if they were in the physical world. More immersive VR systems also track and render full-body movements so users can locomote and navigate in the virtual world using naturalistic movements, and some include handheld controllers that allow users to touch and manipulate virtual objects.

Highly immersive virtual worlds envelop users in rich layers of sensorimotor information, enabling the users to feel as if they are "there" in the mediated world (Biocca, 1997; Slater, Usoh, & Steed, 1994), or sense the virtuality of the experience becoming less noticeable (the illusion of non-mediation; Lee, 2004; Steuer, 1992). This psychological experience of *presence* is one of the most actively studied concepts in VR-centered HMC research (see Lombard, 2018 for a review). Over the decades, scholars have generally reached a consensus that presence has three dimensions

(Biocca, 1997; Lombard & Ditton, 1997): *self-presence* (the relevance of the body, emotions, and/or identity of the self while immersed in a virtual environment); *social presence* (the feeling of being there with a "real" person while having access to his/her thoughts and feelings); and *spatial presence* (experiencing one's self as being located in a mediated space).

Self-presence. Self-presence in VR has been examined in the context of embodiment and the role it plays in defining a user's experience (Biocca, 1997), as well as how users connect to their virtual representations (Ratan & Hasler, 2010). The body plays a critical role in communication because much of our communicative interactions are based on nonverbal rather than verbal cues and signals (Burgoon, Guerrero, & Manusov, 2016). Therefore, not only does our body represent our identities, but it also defines and qualifies the experiences we have in the world (Biocca, 1997; Lee, 2004; Mantovani, 1995).

This sense of *embodiment* has been conceptualized as a combination of self-location, agency, and body ownership while immersed in VR (Kilteni, Groten, & Slater, 2012; Peck & Gonzalez-Franco, 2021). Embodiment is important in HMC because interactions in mediated environments begin with the user locating and anchoring the self. That sense of self-location and agency provides the individual with a frame of reference to begin communicating and interacting with others (Ratan & Hasler, 2010; Riva, 2009) and to perceive other dimensions of presence, such as spatial presence (Wirth et al., 2007). Earlier communication scholarship examined the fluidity of body schema in virtual worlds, and suggested that control of a virtual body continuously competes with the physical body to alter how users conceptualize the location and ownership of their body (Biocca, 1997). With sufficient self-presence, users may eventually feel that what happens to their avatar is happening to them – they *are* the avatar.

Spatial presence. Spatial presence is the dimension of presence closest to Marvin Minsky's original concept of telepresence (1980), which described systems that allowed teleoperators to manipulate machines (e.g., teleconference robots) and interact with people/objects remotely. Minsky argued that teleoperators would feel as if they were in the same location as the machine when manipulating and experiencing the remote world through them. This original concept of "the sense of being there" (Minsky, 1980) is now referred to as spatial presence in VR, where users are also visiting another, albeit virtual, space.

In the context of HMC, communication with machines is typically conceptualized as an interaction between human users and machines that feature social elements; for example, humanoid robots or anthropomorphic agents (Guzman & Lewis, 2020). However, earlier research demonstrated that people have always tended to treat machines – even simple machines without anthropomorphic manifestations – as human, and to feel comfortable talking to them (Reeves & Nass, 1996). Broadly, then, HMC encompasses user interactions with the virtual environment and virtual objects; as the user provides inputs, the computer reciprocates with real-time feedback, and the user recalibrates their responses based on this feedback.

Spatial presence may be considered the self-reported experience of success in making meaning of this user-computer interaction. Users are likely to feel high spatial presence when their interactions with the virtual environment and virtual objects are fluid and match their existing mental models of physics and kinesthetics (Skalski et al., 2011). Meta-analyses demonstrate that this dynamic interaction between users and virtual environments, through interactive features such as body tracking, is far more critical in shaping the experience of spatial presence in VR than more static elements, such as image quality or photorealism of virtual objects (Cummings & Bailenson, 2016).

Social presence. The experience of social presence is distinct from other types of presence, requiring the involvement of another entity perceived as sentient (Oh, Bailenson, & Welch, 2018). Like the perception of spatial presence, social presence (the sense of being with another socially intelligent entity) is a subjective experience. However, scholars agree that objective criteria like immersive qualities of a platform are promising predictors, including the level of verbal and nonverbal social cues a system can present as well as the fidelity of visual representations and motion tracking (Oh et al., 2018; Short et al., 1976). Germane to HMC research, high social presence with a virtual partner can encourage greater social influence in the form of trust, rapport, persuasive effects, and attraction, compared to lower social presence (Bente, Ruggenberg, Kramer, & Eschenburg, 2008; Fogg & Tseng, 1999; Fox et al., 2015; Huang, Morency, & Gratch, 2011).

A major distinction between humans and machines in HMC is "autonomy, the ability to act of one's volition" (Guzman, 2020, p. 39). When scholarly discussions on the social capabilities of communication technologies began to emerge, computers and machines were considered largely as channels that afforded communication between humans (Sundar & Nass, 2000). This notion has gradually shifted with the introduction of digital agents that simulate plausible social cues and can

be perceived as communication *sources*, leading to the *computers are social actors* (CASA) framework (Nass & Moon, 2000; Sundar & Nass, 2000).

CASA research has demonstrated that humans treat new media and computers as if they were humans, interacting with them by applying social rules of interpersonal communication (e.g., Nass, Fogg, & Moon, 1996). The strength of this illusion depends on the degree of agency, referring to the extent to which a technological artifact is perceived as an autonomous social entity (Fortunati & Edwards, 2020; Guadagno, Blascovich, Bailenson, & McCall, 2007). In line with how the construct of social presence is conceptualized, the critical predictor of social influence from digital agents is the *perception* of agency rather than the actual element of control (Fox et al., 2015). Although earlier work on CASA has typically treated social human–computer interactions as "mindless" responses triggered by engrained social scripts in the human mind (Nass & Moon, 2000), more recent work has suggested that extended interactions with virtual agents may actually yield meaningful social relationships, particularly in the long term (Ahn, Johnsen, & Ball, 2019; Bickmore & Picard, 2005).

While perception of social presence can occur with disembodied agents (e.g., voice/text chatbots), embodiment in VR further brings about *copresence* – the sense of togetherness or being connected with others in a shared space (Durlach & Slater, 2000; Nowak & Biocca, 2003). As Goffman (1963) notes, copresence allows interactants to become "accessible, available, and subjective to one another" (p. 22). By embodying an avatar, users share a physical context with embodied agents placed in the same space. Digital bodies of the user and agent serve as proxies for transmitting social cues and signals, verbal and nonverbal, giving a sense that both parties are actively perceiving each other. That said, copresence is also related to the emergence of various communicative dynamics in a shared environment, such as regulation of interpersonal distance (Bailenson, Blascovich, Beall, & Loomis, 2003), participation in a joint activity (Herrewijn & Poels, 2015), and trust toward virtual agents based on their physical appearance (Qiu & Benbasat, 2010).

USER INTERACTIONS WITH VIRTUAL REALITY DEVICES

Because VR has evolved into a wearable technology, with compact, wireless, all-in-one designs, users interact with not only mediated content but also the very devices that mediate the content. These interactions meaningfully impact the overall communication process in various ways. The perceived *naturalness* of a game controller (the degree to which a game input device is judged as replicating real-world actions; Skalski et al., 2011) can impact the user experience. Compared to standard gamepad controllers (e.g., a PlayStation 3 controller), motion-based controllers (e.g., HTC Vive and Oculus controllers) are perceived as more natural, which increases both spatial presence and game enjoyment (Persky & Blascovich, 2008; Seibert & Shafer, 2018; Skalski et al., 2011; Williams, 2014). Similarly, the head mounted displays (HMD) used in most modern VR systems lead to enhanced spatial presence, perceived naturalness, and perceived realism compared to earlier multimodal media, such as television or desktop computers (Buttussi & Chittaro, 2018; Seibert & Shafer, 2018).

Another interaction that users experience is the sense of embodiment enabled through VR devices, which, when effective, induces (a) visual-proprioceptive synchrony (a perceived match between a user's physical location and that of their avatar), (b) visual-motor synchrony (a match between a user's physical movements and those of their avatar), and (c) visual-tactile synchrony (a match between the visual information displayed in VR and a user's sense of haptic feedback; Pan & Hamilton, 2018). By creating this seamless interaction between users and the device-generated cues, embodiment enhances numerous user experience elements, such as presence (Kalina & Johnson-Glenberg, 2020), positive emotions (Breves, 2021), and even physical pain relief (Matamala-Gomez et al., 2019). Relatedly, advances in haptic feedback have spawned devices that simulate *social touch,* or contact-based nonverbal communication that conveys intimacy and coexistence, among other relational variables. In an exemplary study, Hoppe et al. (2020) designed an artificial hand that corresponded with a partner avatar's virtual hand in the VR environment, and found that social touch via the combined visual/ haptic hand improved perceptions of agency and co-presence (as well as embarrassment).

Still, there are obstacles in user interactions with VR devices, including the experience of *simulation sickness*. Simulation sickness is a form of motion sickness induced by visual disorientation within the virtual environment (Stanney et al., 1997). The interaction between time spent in VR and level of presence is negatively related to simulation sickness (Jerome et al., 2005), suggesting simulation sickness relates to an inability to acclimate to the virtual scene. Moreover, VR can exacerbate stress responses to threatening stimuli.

Recent research (Peterson, Furuichi, & Ferris, 2018) found that exposure to daunting heights in VR increased physiological stress reactions such as heart rate and skin conductance compared to unaltered views.

Lastly, there is a call for VR developers to create devices that are more accessible and inclusive to diverse user groups (Ferdous, Arafat, & Quarles, 2016; Freeman, Maloney, Acena, & Barwulor, 2022). For some, barriers to successful user-VR interactions include economic factors, mobility limitations, and hearing or visual impairments (Wedoff et al., 2019). Further, VR devices often fail to accommodate members of diverse races and genders (Davis & Stanovsek, 2021). The size, styling, and texture of Black women's hair makes it difficult to wear comfortably Oculus Go headsets, for instance (Mboya, 2020), and differences in male and female spatial processing, as well as variants of body types and center of mass locations, contribute to biological sex differences in motion sickness proneness (Koslucher et al., 2015). Women are thought to rely on different visual cues compared to men when assessing distance of an object, the former primarily relying on light shading and the latter relying on motion parallax (i.e., when something comes closer, it appears bigger). VR headsets appear, even if inadvertently, to accommodate motion parallax far more often than shading-based depth perception (Boyd, 2014; Franks, 2017), resulting in motion sickness in females more than males. In sum, interactions with current VR devices can provide both benefits and challenges to users.

APPLICATIONS OF VR IN THE CONTEXT OF HMC

VR scholarship has traditionally focused on solitary experiences, but with the renewed interest in "social VR" platforms, such as *VRChat* and *Horizon* Worlds, VR is now moving toward embodied synchronous social interactions among multiple users and agents. Again, so long as the virtual entity is *perceived* as having social intelligence, one can successfully socialize with a virtual agent and achieve social presence (Biocca, 1997). The perceived sentience and realism of virtual agents are expected to improve as time progresses, which should enhance human–agent social presence, and, in turn, human–agent relationships (Bickmore & Picard, 2005). Evidence suggests that the enhanced realism of an embodied conversational agent's appearance and the inclusion of realistic gestures can improve relationship quality between users and agents (Van Pinxteren et al., 2020).

There are advantages of constructing meaningful social relationships with virtual agents. Although computer-driven agents of today are not sufficiently advanced to replace their human counterparts, they are reliable in delivering consistent and uniform messages or interventions that are preprogrammed with minimal errors. Offloading monotonous or repetitive tasks to virtual agents is economical for reducing human workload when applied to healthcare (Hahn et al., 2020; Rizzo et al., 2015), training (Peters, Postlethwaite, & Wallace, 2016), or education (Ball, Ahn, & Johnsen, 2019). The cost-savings lead to tangible benefits, such as the ability to implement health interventions that are tailored to each participant. For example, virtual agents can assist participants in setting self-determined health goals and provide accurate, customized, real-time feedback, and meaningful social support at scale to extend adherence with the health intervention (Hahn et al., 2020). The rapid advancement of artificial intelligence implies that interactions with virtual agents are likely to become more naturalistic and sophisticated over time.

Virtual agents can also be designed to look photorealistically like the user, even though their behaviors are controlled by the computer. These virtual doppelgängers (Bailenson & Segovia, 2010) enable situations wherein the user interacts with a virtual agent that looks strikingly like his or herself in VR. Virtual doppelgängers can elicit self-presence and demonstrate greater social influence than virtual agents that resemble an unfamiliar other, persuading users to adopt attitudes and behaviors recommended by their virtual doppelgänger (see Ahn & Fox, 2016 for a review).

Another noteworthy area of application for HMC scholars is the growing research on hybrid forms of digital representations. These hybrids combine the features of avatars and agents to form semi-autonomous virtual agents, which feature a human controller supported by varying levels of computer assistance. The semi-autonomous agent allows human users to maintain social and behavioral realism by selecting appropriate responses (e.g., Wizard of Oz techniques, Gould, Conti, & Hovanyecz, 1983), while computer algorithms present other nonverbal and verbal cues, such as naturalistic gaze or body movements, that make the user–agent interaction seem more realistic (Bente et al., 2001; Pan, Gillies, Barker, Clark, & Slater, 2012; Rizzo et al., 2015). Algorithms may also be used to enhance or augment social interactions by exaggerating favorable social cues (e.g., smiling, laughter) and minimizing negative ones (e.g., frowning, sighing) for semi-autonomous agents, without the user controlling every behavior.

For example, when user avatars were programmed to display wider smiles, users reported feeling more positive emotions following the social interaction compared to users who interacted with avatars that displayed normal smiles (Oh, Bailenson, Krämer, & Li, 2016).

Other VR applications in HMC scholarship have focused on how users rely on environmental cues in VR to make sense of their experiences, even though the environmental cues are mere illusions distinct from the physical world. Some have investigated the dominance of visual cues over other sensory cues in virtual worlds, such as touch. For example, even when a user is touching the straight side of a three-dimensional object in the physical world, displaying the object with a curved side in VR can lead participants to feel as if they are touching a curved object (Ban et al., 2012). Environmental cues in VR have also been used to modify user responses to contextual cues created by the VR system, regardless of their physical environment or surroundings. Burn victims forget about the heat and pain from their physical injuries when playing in a snowy virtual environment (Hoffman, 2004), cycling through a virtual cityscape reduces cyclists' quadriceps pain (Wender, Ahn, & O'Connor, 2019), and walking through a virtual city as a giant avatar nudges users to speed up their walking pace (Abtahi, Gonzalez-Franco, Ofek, & Steed, 2019). The power of these illusions demonstrates that VR users actively interact with the mediated environment to create a mental model of a world with people, objects, and locations that may be distinct from the physical one they are inhabiting.

Finally, effects of user interactions with VR systems and virtual people can transfer into the physical world. Embodied experiences in VR can encourage health behaviors (Ahn, 2015; Fox & Bailenson, 2009; Nowak et al., 2020), environmentally conscious attitudes and behaviors (Ahn, Fox, Dale, & Avant, 2015; Meijers et al., 2022), and empathy and helping behaviors (Ahn, Le, & Bailenson, 2013; Herrera, Bailenson, Weisz, Ogle, & Zaki, 2018), among others. Most of these demonstrated changes in attitudes and behaviors are transient (24 hours to 8 weeks) and based on relatively brief exposures to virtual experiences. Whether longer-term exposure leaves more permanent impacts on user attitudes and behaviors remains to be seen.

CONCLUSION

The rapid pace of advancement in virtual and augmented technology is continuously expanding the boundaries of human communication, which were previously limited to other humans but now extend to virtual agents and VR devices themselves. Focusing on the dynamic interactions between users and immersive technologies, this chapter presents theoretical orientations and practical applications that situate the VR scholarship within the HMC subfield. We outlined psychologically relevant concepts that emerge during interactions in VR, focusing on self-perceptions, perceptions of other humans and agents, and experiences with virtual environments and VR devices. Specifically, we discussed self-presence, spatial presence, social presence, and embodiment, and remarked on the impact of these phenomena on human–machine communication outcomes. The psychological concepts should be empirically tested with new developments in VR technology, such as enhanced haptic feedback and conversational agent realism, for scholars to understand how these novel features impact human users. As the individual and social applications of VR proliferate, so must the scholarship on the communication exchanges between human users and the virtual devices, agents, and environments, to provide a corresponding understanding of their effects on users.

REFERENCES

Abtahi, P., Gonzalez-Franco, M., Ofek, E., & Steed, A. (2019). I'm a giant: Walking in large virtual environments at high speed gains. *Proceedings of the 2019 CHI Conference on Human Factors in Computing Systems.* doi:10.1145/3290605. 3300752

Ahn, S. J. (2015). Incorporating immersive virtual environments in health promotion campaigns: A construal level theory approach. *Health Communication*, *30*(6), 545–556. doi:10.1080/10410236. 2013.869650

Ahn, S. J., Fox, J., & Bailenson, J. N. (2011). Avatars. In W. S. Bainbridge (Ed.), *Leadership in science and technology: A reference handbook* (pp. 695–702). SAGE Publications.

Ahn, S. J., Fox, J., Dale, K. R., & Avant, J. A. (2015). Framing virtual experiences: Effects on environmental efficacy and behavior over time. *Communication Research*, *42*(6), 839–863. doi:10.1177/0093650214534973

Ahn, S. J., & Fox, J. (2016). Persuasive avatars: Extending the self through new media advertising. In R. E. Brown, V. K. Jones, & M. Wang (Eds.), *The new advertising: Branding, content, and consumer relationships in the data-driven social media era* (Vol. 2). Praeger.

Ahn, S. J., Johnsen, K., & Ball, C. (2019). Points-based reward systems in gamification impact children's physical activity strategies and psychological needs. *Health Education & Behavior*, *46*(3), 417–425. http://dx.doi.org/10.1177/1090198118818241

Ahn, S. J., Le, A. M. T., & Bailenson, J. (2013). The effect of embodied experiences on self-other merging, attitude, and helping behavior. *Media Psychology*, *16*(1), 7–38. doi:10.1080/15213269. 2012.755877

Appel, J., von der Pütten, A., Krämer, N. C., & Gratch, J. (2012). Does humanity matter? Analyzing the importance of social cues and perceived agency of a computer system for the emergence of social reactions during human-computer interaction. *Adv. Hum. Computer Inter.* 13:324694. https://doi.org/10.1155/2012/324694

Bailenson, J. (2018). *Experience on demand: What virtual reality is, how it works, and what it can do.* WW Norton & Company.

Bailenson, J. N., Blascovich, J., Beall, A. C., & Loomis, J. M. (2003). Interpersonal distance in immersive virtual environments. *Personality and Social Psychology Bulletin*, *29*(7), 819–833. http://dx.doi.org/10.1177/0146167203029007002

Bailenson, J., & Segovia, K. (2010). Virtual doppelgangers: Psychological effects of avatars who ignore their owners. In W. S. Bainbridge (Ed.), *Online worlds: Convergence of the real and the virtual* (pp. 175–186). Springer.

Ball, C., Ahn, S. J., & Johnsen, K. (2019, March). Design and field study of motion-based informal learning games for a children's museum. In *2019 IEEE 5th Workshop on Everyday Virtual Reality (WEVR)* (pp. 1–6). IEEE. doi:10.1109/WEVR. 2019.8809588

Ban, Y., Kajinami, T., Narumi, T., Tanikawa, T., & Hirose, M. (2012, March). Modifying an identified curved surface shape using pseudo-haptic effect. In *2012 IEEE Haptics Symposium (HAPTICS)* (pp. 211–216). IEEE. doi:10.1109/HAPTIC.2012.6183793

Bente, G., Rüggenberg, S., Krämer, N. C., & Eschenburg, F. (2008). Avatar-mediated networking: Increasing social presence and interpersonal trust in net-based collaborations. *Human Communication Research*, *34*(2), 287–318. doi:10.1111/j. 1468-2958.2008.00322.x

Bente, G., Krämer, N. C., Petersen, A., & de Ruiter, J. P. (2001). Computer animated movement and person perception: Methodological advances in nonverbal behavior research. *Journal of Nonverbal Behavior*, *25*(3), 151–166. doi:10.1023/A:1010690525717

Bickmore, T., & Cassell, J. (2005). Social dialogue with embodied conversational agents. In J.C.J. Kuppevelt, L. Dybkjaer, & N.O. Bernson (Eds.), *Advances in natural multimodal dialog systems* (pp. 1–32). Springer.

Bickmore, T. W., & Picard, R. W. (2005). Establishing and maintaining long-term human-computer relationships. *ACM Transactions on Computer-Human Interaction (TOCHI)*, *12*(2), 293–327. doi:10.1145/1067860.1067867

Biocca, F. (1997). The cyborg's dilemma: Progressive embodiment in virtual environments. *Journal of Computer-Mediated Communication, 3*(2).

Boletsis, C. (2017). The new era of virtual reality locomotion: A systematic literature review of techniques and a proposed typology. *Multimodal Technologies and Interaction, 1*(4), 24. https://doi.org/10.3390/mti1040024

Boyd, D. (2014). Is the Oculus Rift sexist? http://qz.com/192874/is-the-oculus-rift-designed-to-be-sexist

Breves, P. (2021). Biased by being there: The persuasive impact of spatial presence on cognitive processing. *Computers in Human Behavior, 119*, 106723. https://doi.org/10.1016/j.chb.2021.106723

Burgoon, J. K., Guerrero, L. K., & Manusov, V. (2016). *Nonverbal communication*. Routledge.

Buttussi, F. & Chittaro, L. (2018). Effects of different types of virtual reality display on presence and learning in a safety training scenario. *IEEE Trans Vis Comput Graph, 24*(2):1063–1076. doi: 10.1109/TVCG.2017.2653117.

Chase, C. C., Chin, D. B., Oppezzo, M. A., & Schwartz, D. L. (2009). Teachable agents and the protégé effect: Increasing the effort towards learning. *Journal of Science Education and Technology, 18*(4), 334–352. https://doi.org/10.1007/s10956-009-9180-4

Chittaro, L., Corbett, C. L., McLean, G. A., & Zangrando, N. (2018). Safety knowledge transfer through mobile virtual reality: A study of aviation life preserver donning. *Safety Science, 102*, 159–168. https://doi.org/10.1016/j.ssci.2017.10.012

Cummings, J. J., & Bailenson, J. N. (2016). How immersive is enough? A meta-analysis of the effect of immersive technology on user presence. *Media Psychology, 19*(2), 272–309. doi:10.1080/15213269.2015.1015740

Davis, D. Z., & Stanovsek, S. (2021). The machine as an extension of the body: When identity, immersion, and interactive design serve as both resource and limitation for the disabled. *Human-Machine Communication, 2*, 121–135. https://doi.org/10.30658/hmc.2.6

Durlach, N., & Slater, M. (2000). Presence in shared virtual environments and virtual togetherness. *Presence: Teleoperators & Virtual Environments, 9*(2), 214–217. doi:10.1162/105474600566736

Edwards, A., Edwards, C., Wahl, S. T., & Myers, S. A. (2018). *The communication age: Connecting and engaging*. Sage Publications.

Evans, S. K., Pearce, K. E., Vitak, J., & Treem, J. W. (2017). Explicating affordances: A conceptual framework for understanding affordances in communication research. *Journal of Computer-Mediated Communication, 22*(1), 35–52. https://doi.org/10.1111/jcc4.12180

Fan, X., McNeese, M., & Yen, J. (2010). NDM-based cognitive agents for supporting decision-making teams. *Human–Computer Interaction, 25*(3), 195–234. https://doi.org/10.1080/07370020903586720

Ferdous, S., Arafat, I., & Quarles, J. (2016). Visual feedback to improve the accessibility of head-mounted displays for persons with balance impairments. *IEEE Symposium on 3D User Interfaces (3DUI)*, 121–128. https://doi.org/10.1109/3DUI.2016.7460041.

Fogg, B. J., & Tseng, H. (1999). The elements of computer credibility. In *Proceedings of CHI'99, Human Factors and Computing Systems,* (pp. 80–87).

Fortunati, L., & Edwards, A. P. (2020). Opening space for theoretical, methodological, and empirical issues in human-machine communication. *Human-Machine Communication, 1*(1), 1. https://doi.org/10.30658/hmc.1.1

Fox, J., Ahn, S. J., Janssen, J. H., Yeykelis, L., Segovia, K. Y., & Bailenson, J. N. (2015). Avatars versus agents: A meta-analysis quantifying the effect of agency on social influence. *Human–Computer Interaction, 30*(5), 401–432. https://doi.org/10.1080/07370024.2014.921494

Fox, J., & Bailenson, J. N. (2009). Virtual self-modeling: The effects of vicarious reinforcement and identification on exercise behaviors. *Media Psychology, 12*(1), 1–25. https://doi.org/10.1080/15213260802669474

Franks, M.A. (2017). The desert of the unreal: Inequality in virtual and augmented reality. *UC Davis Law Review, 51*, 499–538. https://repository.law.miami.edu/cgi/viewcontent.cgi?article=1538&context=fac_articles

Freeman, G., Maloney, D., Acena, D., & Barwulor, C. (2022). (Re)discovering the Physical Body Online: Strategies and Challenges to Approach Non-Cisgender Identity in Social Virtual Reality. *CHI' 22, Proceedings of the 2022 CHI Conference on Human Factors in Computing Systems*, 118, 1–15. doi: 10.1145/3491102.3502082

Goffman, E. (1963). *Behaviour in public places*. Free Press.

Gould, J. D., Conti, J., & Hovanyecz, T. (1983). Composing letters with a simulated listening typewriter. *Communications of the ACM, 26*(4), 295–308. https://doi.org/10.1145/2163.358100

Gratch, J., Rickel, J., André, E., Cassell, J., Petajan, E., & Badler, N. (2002). Creating interactive virtual humans: Some assembly required. *IEEE Intelligent Dystems, 17*(4), 54–63. https://doi.org/10.1109/MIS.2002.1024753

Guadagno, R. E., Blascovich, J., Bailenson, J. N., & McCall, C. (2007). Virtual humans and persuasion:

The effects of agency and behavioral realism. *Media Psychology, 10*(1), 1–22. https://doi.org/10.1080/15213260701300865

Guzman, A.L. (2018). What is human-machine communication, anyway? In A.L. Guzman (Ed.), *Human-machine communication: Rethinking communication, technology, and ourselves* (pp. 1–28). Peter Lang.

Guzman, A. L. (2020). Ontological boundaries between humans and computers and the implications for Human-Machine Communication. *Human-Machine Communication, 1*, 37–54. https://doi.org/10.30658/hmc.1.3

Guzman, A. L., & Lewis, S. C. (2020). Artificial intelligence and communication: A Human–Machine Communication research agenda. *New Media & Society, 22*(1), 70–86. http://dx.doi.org/10.1177/1461444819858691

Hahn, L., Schmidt, M. D., Rathbun, S. L., Johnsen, K., Annesi, J. J., & Ahn, S. J. G. (2020). Using virtual agents to increase physical activity in young children with the virtual fitness buddy ecosystem: Study protocol for a cluster randomized trial. *Contemporary Clinical Trials, 99*, 106181. https://doi.org/10.1016/j.cct.2020.106181

Herrera, F., Bailenson, J., Weisz, E., Ogle, E., & Zaki, J. (2018). Building long-term empathy: A large-scale comparison of traditional and virtual reality perspective-taking. *PloS One, 13*(10), e0204494. https://doi.org/10.1371/journal.pone.0204494

Herrewijn, L., & Poels, K. (2015). The impact of social setting on the recall and recognition of in-game advertising. *Computers in Human Behavior, 53*, 544–555. https://doi.org/10.1016/j.chb.2014.06.012

Hoffman, H. G. (2004). Virtual-reality therapy. *Scientific American, 291*(2), 58–65. www.jstor.org/stable/26060647

Hoppe, M., Rossmy, B., Neumann, D. P., Streuber, S., Schmidt, A., & Machulla, T. K. (2020, April). A human touch: Social touch increases the perceived human-likeness of agents in virtual reality. In *Proceedings of the 2020 CHI Conference on Human Factors in Computing Systems* (pp. 1–11). https://doi.org/10.1145/3313831.3376719

Huang, L., Morency, L.-P., & Gratch, J. (2011). Virtual rapport 2.0. In J. Allbeck, N. Badler, T. Bickmore, C. Pelachaud, & A. Safonova (Eds.), *Lecture notes in computer science: Vol. 6895. Intelligent virtual agents* (pp. 68–79). Springer. http://dx.doi.org/10.1007/978-3-642-23974-8_8.

Jerome, C., Darnell, R., Oakley, B., & Pepe, A. (2005, September). The effects of presence and time of exposure on simulator sickness. In *Proceedings of the Human Factors and Ergonomics Society Annual Meeting* (Vol. 49, No. 26, pp. 2258–2262). SAGE Publications. https://doi.org/10.1177/154193120504902609

Kalina, E., & Johnson-Glenberg, M. C. (2020, June). Presence and platform: Effects of embodiment comparing a 2D computer and 3D VR game. *6th International Conference of the Immersive Learning Research Network (iLRN)*, 31–37. https://doi.org/10.23919/iLRN47897.2020.9155160

Kilteni, K., Groten, R., & Slater, M. (2012). The sense of embodiment in virtual reality. *Presence: Teleoperators and Virtual Environments, 21*(4), 373–387. https://doi.org/10.1162/PRES_a_00124

Koslucher, F., Haaland, E., Malsch, A., Webeler, J., & Stoffregen, T. A. (2015). Sex differences in the incidence of motion sickness induced by linear visual oscillation. *Aerospace Medicine and Human Performance, 86*(9), 787–793. https://doi.org/10.3357/AMHP.4243.2015

Lee, K. M. (2004). Presence, explicated. *Communication Theory, 14*(1), 27–50. https://doi.org/10.1111/j.1468-2885.2004.tb00302.x

Lombard, M. (2018). Presence past and future: Reflections on 25 years of presence technology, scholarship and community. In A. L. Guzman (Ed). *Human-machine communication: Rethinking communication, technology, and ourselves.* Peter Lang Publishing.

Lombard, M., & Ditton, T. (1997). At the heart of it all: The concept of presence. *Journal of Computer-Mediated Communication, 3*(2), JCMC321. https://doi.org/10.1111/j.1083-6101.1997.tb00072.x

Makransky, G., Wismer, P., & Mayer, R. E. (2019). A gender matching effect in learning with pedagogical agents in an immersive virtual reality science simulation. *Journal of Computer Assisted Learning, 35*(3), 349–358. https://doi.org/10.1111/jcal.12335

Mantovani, G. (1995). Virtual reality as a communication environment: Consensual hallucination, fiction, and possible selves. *Human Relations, 48*(6), 669–683. https://doi.org/10.1177/001872679504800604

Matamala-Gomez, M., Donegan, T., Bottiroli, S., Sandrini, G., Sanchez-Vives, M. V., & Tassorelli, C. (2019). Immersive virtual reality and virtual embodiment for pain relief. *Frontiers in Human Neuroscience, 13*, 279. https://doi.org/10.3389/fnhum.2019.00279

Mboya, A. (2020). The Oculus Go wasn't designed for black hair. https://debugger.medium.com/the-oculus-go-a-hard-ware-problem-for-black-women-225d9b48d098

Meijers, M. H. C., Smit, E. S., de Wildt, K., Karvonen, S. G., van der Plas, D., & van der Laan, L. N. (2022). Stimulating sustainable food choices using virtual reality: Taking an environmental vs health communication perspective on enhancing response efficacy beliefs. *Environmental Communication, 16*, 1–22. https://doi.org/10.1080/17524032.2021.1943700

Minsky, M. (1980). Telepresence. *Omni, 2*, 44–52.

Nass, C., & Moon, Y. (2000). Machines and mindlessness: Social responses to computers. *Journal of Social Issues, 56*(1), 81–103. doi:10.1111/0022-4537.00153

Nass, C., Fogg, B. J., & Moon, Y. (1996). Can computers be teammates? *International Journal of Human-Computer Studies, 45*(6), 669–678. https://doi.org/10.1006/ijhc.1996.0073

Nowak, G., Evans, N., Wojdynski, B., Ahn, S. J., Len-Rios, M. … & McFalls, D. (2020). Using immersive virtual reality to improve the beliefs and intentions of influenza vaccine avoidant 18-to-49-year-olds: Considerations, effects, and lessons learned. *Vaccine, 38*(5), 1225–1233. https://doi.org/10.1016/j.vaccine.2019.11.009.

Nowak, K. L., & Biocca, F. (2003). The effect of the agency and anthropomorphism on users' sense of telepresence, copresence, and social presence in virtual environments. *Presence: Teleoperators and Virtual Environments, 12*(5), 481–494. https://doi.org/10.1162/105474603322761289

Nowak, K. L., & Fox, J. (2018). Avatars and computer-mediated communication: A review of the definitions, uses, and effects of digital representations. *Review of Communication Research, 6*, 30–53. https://doi.org/10.12840/issn.2255-4165.2018.06.01.015.

Oh, C.S., Bailenson, J.N., Welch, G.F., (2018). A systematic review of social presence: Definition, antecedents, and implications. *Front Robot AI*. 2018 Oct 15;5:114. doi: 10.3389/frobt.2018.00114.

Oh, S. Y., Bailenson, J., Krämer, N., & Li, B. (2016). Let the avatar brighten your smile: Effects of enhancing facial expressions in virtual environments. *PloS One, 11*(9), e0161794. https://doi.org/10.1371/journal.pone.0161794

Pan, X., Gillies, M., Barker, C., Clark, D. M., & Slater, M. (2012). Socially anxious and confident men interact with a forward virtual woman: An experimental study. *PLOS ONE, 7*(4), e32931. https://doi.org/10.1371/journal.pone.0032931

Pan, X., & Hamilton, A. F. D. C. (2018). Why and how to use virtual reality to study human social interaction: The challenges of exploring a new research landscape. *British Journal of Psychology, 109*(3), 395–417. https://doi.org/10.1111/bjop.12290

Peck, T. C., & Gonzalez-Franco, M. (2021). Avatar embodiment. a standardized questionnaire. *Frontiers in Virtual Reality, 1*, 44. https://doi.org/10.3389/frvir.2020.575943

Persky, S., & Blascovich, J. (2008). Immersive virtual video game play and presence: Influences on aggressive feelings and behavior. *Presence: Teleoperators and Virtual Environments, 17*(1), 57–72. https://doi.org/10.1162/pres.17.1.57

Peters, C., Postlethwaite, D., & Wallace, M. W. (2016). U.S. Patent No. 9,280,913. U.S. Patent and Trademark Office.

Peterson, S. M., Furuichi, E., & Ferris, D. P. (2018). Effects of virtual reality high heights exposure during beam-walking on physiological stress and cognitive loading. *PLOS ONE, 13*(7), e0200306. https://doi.org/10.1371/journal.pone.0200306

Qiu, L., & Benbasat, I. (2010). A study of demographic embodiments of product recommendation agents in electronic commerce. *International Journal of Human-Computer Studies, 68*(10), 669–688. https://doi.org/10.1016/j.ijhcs.2010.05.005

Ratan, R., & Hasler, B. S. (2010). Exploring self-presence in collaborative virtual teams. *PsychNology Journal, 8*(1), 11–31.

Reeves, B., & Nass, C. (1996). *The media equation: How people treat computers, television, and new media like real people and places.* Cambridge University Press.

Riva, G. (2009). Is presence a technology issue? Some insights from cognitive sciences. *Virtual Reality, 13*(3), 159–169. https://doi.org/10.1007/s10055-009-0121-6

Rizzo, A., Cukor, J., Gerardi, M., Alley, S., Reist, C., Roy, M., … & Difede, J. (2015). Virtual reality exposure for PTSD due to military combat and terrorist attacks. *Journal of Contemporary Psychotherapy, 45*(4), 255–264. https://doi.org/10.1007/s10879-015-9306-3

Seibert, J., & Shafer, D. M. (2018). Control mapping in virtual reality: Effects on spatial presence and controller naturalness. *Virtual Reality, 22*(1), 79–88. https://doi.org/10.1007/s10055-017-0316-1

Short, J., Williams, E., & Christie, B. (1976). *The social psychology of telecommunications.* John Wiley.

Skalski, P., Tamborini, R., Shelton, A., Buncher, M., & Lindmark, P. (2011). Mapping the road to fun: Natural video game controllers, presence, and game enjoyment. *New Media & Society, 13*(2), 224–242. https://doi.org/10.1177/1461444810370949

Slater, M., Usoh, M., & Steed, A. (1994). Depth of presence in virtual environments. *Presence: Teleoperators and Virtual Environments, 3*(2), 130–144. https://doi.org/10.1162/pres.1994.3.2.130

Stanney, K. M., Kennedy, R. S., & Drexler, J. M., (1997). Cybersickness is not simulator sickness. *Proceedings of the Human Factors and Ergonomics Society Annual Meeting, 41*(2), 1138–1142. https://doi.org/10.1177/107118139704100292

Steuer, J. (1992). Defining virtual reality: Dimensions determining telepresence. *Journal of Communication, 42*(4), 73–93. https://doi.org/10.1111/j.1460-2466.1992.tb00812.x

Sundar, S. S., & Nass, C. (2000). Source orientation in human-computer interaction: Programmer, networker, or independent social actor. *Communication Research, 27*(6), 683–703. https://doi.org/10.1177/009365000027006001

Sutherland, I. (1965). The ultimate display. *Information Processing 1965: Proceedings of the IFIP Congress 65. 2*, (pp. 506–508). Spartan Books.

Van Pinxteren, M. M., Pluymaekers, M., & Lemmink, J. G. (2020). Human-like communication in conversational agents: A literature review and research agenda. *Journal of Service Management, 31*(2), 203–225. https://doi.org/10.1108/JOSM-06-2019-0175

Wedoff, R., Ball, L., Wang, A., Khoo, Y. X., Lieberman, L., & Rector, K. (2019, May). Virtual showdown: An accessible virtual reality game with scaffolds for youth with visual impairments. In *Proceedings of the 2019 CHI Conference on Human Factors in Computing Systems*, pp. 1–15. https://doi.org/10.1145/3290605.3300371

Wender, C. L. A., Ahn, S. J., & O'Connor, P. J. (2019). Interactive virtual reality reduces quadriceps pain during high-intensity cycling. *Medicine and Science in Sports and Exercise, 51*(10), 2088–2097. https://doi.org/10.1249/MSS.0000000000002016

Williams, K. D. (2014). The effects of dissociation, game controllers, and 3D versus 2D on presence and enjoyment. *Computers in Human Behavior, 38*, 142–150. https://doi.org/10.1016/j.chb.2014.05.040

Wirth, W., Hartmann, T., Böcking, S., Vorderer, P., Klimmt, C., Schramm, H., … & Jäncke, P. (2007). A process model of the formation of spatial presence experiences. *Media Psychology, 9*(3), 493–525. https://doi.org/10.1080/15213260701283079

58

HMC in the Educational Context

Chad Edwards and Matthew Craig

Human–machine communication (HMC) can interrupt many of our pedagogical techniques and change how education operates (A. Edwards & C. Edwards, 2017; C. Edwards et al., 2018). It is crucial to bring the scholarship of instructional communication researchers to the study of machines in the educational experience to help with the design, implementations, assessment, and evaluation. Technology has been an essential and necessary part of the educational experience. From a historical perspective, the idea of a machine actor (e.g., AI, social robots) in the educational process goes back to the early twentieth century; however, it was not until recently that the actors in the educational context could be changed from a person to a machine. The addition of machine actors in education is a seismic land shift.

Machine actors (e.g., AI, social robots) and systems for virtual/augmented reality are being utilized as teachers, tutors, and peer mentors (Vasagar, 2017). Bodkin (2017) argues that within the next ten years, we will see a "revolution in one-to-one learning" from social machines (para. 1). Machine actors have been increasingly acting as tutors both in the classroom and in homes (Han et al., 2005). The COVID-19 pandemic beginning in 2020 is expected to increase this revolution in the classroom. To a great extent, "students and instructors are not only talking *through* machines, but also *to* them, and *within* them" (A. Edwards, & C. Edwards, 2018, p. 185). With well-tested pedagogical practices for social machines, teachers might be able to spend more time with students in support and mentoring roles and letting the machines take on more basic educational tasks. We divided this chapter into two sections to explore HMC in the academic environment. The first section is dedicated to discussing various contexts of using machine partners for educational purposes. We then in a second section discuss HMC in instructional communication research before offering our concluding thoughts.

HMC TECHNOLOGIES OF EDUCATION

Social Robots in Education

The use of robots in education is not new (Hrastinski et al., 2019; Mubin et al., 2013). In a review of the use of robots in education, Mubin and colleagues (2013) identified several case study examples in which robots were used in language, science, and technologies as tutors, peers, and as tools. Social robots have even been shown to be good stand-ins for math tutoring (Brown et al., 2013), and giving students feedback in the college classroom (Park et al., 2011). To provide some specific examples of evaluating their usefulness, Autumn Edwards et al. (2016) demonstrated that a social robot delivering an identical teaching performance as a human using a telepresence robot can be perceived as having credibility and that students had positive affective and behavioral learning scores. Li and colleagues (2016) showed that social robots were useful at instructing in terms of students' knowledge recall of information presented. Furthermore, social robots have been used to teach second languages and have been observed as being more effective than other traditional methods (Hur & Han, 2009).

Examining the use of social robotics specifically in the field of special education, findings by Papakostas and colleagues (2021) suggest positive effects of incorporating social robots in the special education classroom, especially concerning specific social robots intended for specific intended for children with differing abilities. For example, the NAO robot is "preferred" for students identified with Autism Spectrum Disorder (ASD), or robots with five fingers teaching sign language such as Robovie (Papakostas et al., 2021, p. 29). In these roles, various researchers have shown increased learning and teamwork (Eguchi, 2012). For example, students with ASD working with social robots have benefited from the behaviors modeled and practiced by social robots (Kim et al., 2013). Social robotics gives greater means for educators to engage content with students – a resource for teachers to use in the classroom. Additionally, the use of robotics in the classroom does not need to be enormously sophisticated to have a practical use. For example, in special education, a *keep-on* robot can help show students on the autism spectrum how to properly touch (Kozima et al., 2009). Robot pets (Joy for All Companion Pets, https://joyforall.com/products/companion-pet-pup) have been used to aid in social-emotional learning (Heljakka & Ihamäki, 2019; Heljakka et al., 2020) or used in a library for stress reduction (A. Edwards, C. Edwards, et al., 2020).

These systems can lessen teachers' burdens in the classroom for more routinized teaching materials (Hrastinski et al., 2019). AI in the educational environment can help implement individualized learning, enhance student collaboration, and be effective for tutoring (VanLehn, 2011). Digital assistants can help students by providing interaction through speech, virtual characters, and text messages (Tegos et al., 2015), facilitate learning (Schroeder & Gotch, 2015), serve as mentors (Haake & Gulz, 2009), learn a second language (Ayedoun et al., 2015), and can help increase the number of information cues during an interaction (Johnson et al., 2000).

While AI has strong potential in the education domain, we must always guard against the potentially significant risks associated with these technologies in the classroom (McStay, 2020). Berendt et al. (2020) argue that when AI is used in education (and more generally), there need to be strong regulations for their use and privacy protections. McStay (2020) maintains that there is a great concern when AI is being used to quantify both emotional and social learning. AI systems can be built and trained on insufficient data (Custer et al., 2018). And because many of these problems are often unseen or unintended, severe damage can occur in the classroom (Pringle et al., 2016).

It is important to have a firm understanding of who is involved in AI systems' development and adoption (Gebru, 2020). Too often, AI and machine learning systems are considered objective vessels of research and development–absolved of racism, sexism, homophobia, and more. It is the abstraction of science where companies (and yes, scholars too), fail to recognize the importance of including those most marginalized and how their lives and voices remain affected by this technology (Gebru, 2020). Scholars need to "learn about the ways in which their technology is being used, question the direction institutions are moving in, and engage with other disciplines to learn their approaches" (Gebru, 2020, p. 268). HMC scholars can and should engage critical lenses for examining many of these aspects in and out of the classroom and avoid the adoption of systems that were developed without a diverse set of voices.

Artificial Intelligence in Education

Artificial intelligence (AI) in the classroom can disrupt much of the educational enterprise and become salient when this change can impact the student–teacher dynamic (Schiff, 2020). Most AI systems in education are utilized for tutoring systems (Roll & Wylie, 2016; VanLehn, 2011).

Virtual/Augmented Realities in Education

Virtual/augmented realities systems are being used to educate in a variety of contexts. Virtual reality is a computer-generated world that can appear to be 3D with sound and sometimes tactile simulations. Augmented reality (AR) refers to "a situation in which a real-world context is dynamically overlaid with coherent location or context sensitive virtual information" (Klopfer & Sheldon, 2008, p. 205). Previous research has demonstrated that VR and AR can enhance learning in the classroom (Ke et al., 2016; Lau & Lee, 2015; Omale et al., 2009, Wu et al., 2013).

Virtual audiences have helped students learn to speak in public by creating a positive and safe audience environment (Chollet et al., 2015). VR has helped student teachers learn positive pedagogical techniques with virtual students (Ke et al., 2016). Frisby et al. (2020) and Vallade et al. (2020) found the use of VR headsets utilizing 360° videos of the speaking environment as good student practice and can increase knowledge retention and student engagement (Harrington et al., 2018; Sultan et al., 2019; Rupp et al., 2019). Walshe and Driver (2019) argued that 360° videos could be used as tools for reflecting on the student teaching experience. Applied in the classroom, VR/AR systems provide students an immersive experience in instructional content.

HMC AND INSTRUCTIONAL COMMUNICATION RESEARCH

When examining how HMC will impact the educational context, it is vital to consider how impressions of the source affect the machine actor's student–teacher relationship, learning outcomes, and general characteristics and capabilities. Because communication is often a scripted task (Kellerman, 1992), machine actors can have the ability to guide the educational experience in some contexts. As such, general interpersonal impressions of the machine actor will matter in the educational context. Physical behaviors combined with messages can help convey meaning in the interaction (Ali & Williams, 2020; Craig & C. Edwards, 2021; Rosenthal-von der Pütten et al., 2018).

Human-to-human interaction scripts work well when trying to understand the educational environment. Previous research has demonstrated that people anticipate lower liking and social presence when first interacting with a machine actor. Additionally, they will have more significant uncertainty (C. Edwards et al., 2016; Spence et al., 2014; A. Edwards et al., 2019). Developing academic scripts for machine actors would allow researchers to critically analyze the material communicated to students for issues of racism, classism, or sexism. Additionally, people have an anthropocentric expectancy bias when interacting

with others (Spence et al., 2014; A. Edwards et al., 2019). We assume that the teachers will be human. Students may face extreme uncertainty when interacting with machine agents in the classroom. After a time, this uncertainty will decrease, but initial interaction is vital for setting expectations for the educational domain. We will end this chapter by examining three important instructional communication variables and how they can be utilized in HMC to establish positive interactions in the classroom (see C. Edwards et al., 2018 and A. Edwards & C. Edwards, 2017 for further information).

Immediacy

Psychological closeness, or immediacy, has been a long-standing variable of interest in instructional communication (Andersen, 1979; Gorham, 1988). Immediacy refers to perceptions of closeness between individuals (Mehrabian, 1971). In the classroom, immediacy is based on closeness perceptions between students and teachers (Frymier, 1993). Immediacy has been correlated with teacher credibility and learning (Schrodt & Witt, 2006; Violanti et al., 2018). Because perceptions of immediacy tend to be driven by closeness-inducing behaviors, HMC scholars would be wise to examine immediacy. Machine actors in large measures can reproduce these behaviors with scripts. Kennedy et al. (2017) demonstrated that children could recall more information about a story when the robot is perceived as more immediate. Exploring how perceptions of psychological closeness can occur between student and machine actor is important research ground.

Credibility

In instructional communication, the issue of teacher credibility has been well researched (McCroskey & Teven, 1999) and is built on the ideas of competence, caring, and character. Credibility has been related to a host of positive behaviors in the educational context. Perceptions of credibility will matter for machine actors. In an experiment, C. Edwards et al. (2016) show that students could perceive a social robot as credible in teaching performances/scripts. In related fields to HMC, such as HRI, machine trust is similar to instructor credibility. Sanders et al. (2011) argue that machine trust is an important factor to consider when examining robots' use. Salem et al. (2015) suggest that even if a machine agent makes some mistakes, these mistakes will not be enough to reduce this trust or credibility significantly. Examining the perceptions of credibility (machine trust) and how machines can build trust would help researchers understand the efficacy of using technologies in education.

Teacher Clarity

Teacher clarity has been another significant variable to consider in instructional communication that HMC scholars should pay attention to for their research. Powell and Harville (1990) argue that teacher clarity is concerned with the constancy of an instructional message and can have positive instructional outcomes. For HMC research, vocal cues can be a strong part of being perceived as being clear in the classroom. Research in HRI has found that higher-pitched robots have been perceived as more attractive (Niculescu et al., 2013). Goble and C. Edwards (2018) argued that things like pitch, speech rate, vocal fillers, and even voices could be altered/scripted in HMC research with machine actors. Sandry (2015) points out that when a robot provides information, the message's clarity is essential for communication efficiency. There still is a lot of work to be done in this area, examining how clarity can be changed (more clear to less clear) with machine agents such as chatbots or social robots.

CONCLUSION

Human–Machine Communication (HMC) has a lot to offer for instructional communication in the coming years. As we have encountered in the COVID-19 pandemic 2020, our limited ability to meet physically (i.e., close contact face-2-face) ignites a more extensive discussion on how we foster connection and create meaning with each other. Communication with machines allows communication scholars to revisit theoretical considerations for our human communication practices. Specifically, as these machines advance, how we assemble and assign meaning is essential to HMC in education contexts whether a pet robot in the classroom, a virtual reality scenario exhibiting an audience, or an AI chatbot to answer syllabus questions (Landau & Broz, 2020), these systems and machines show great potential in their ability to foster connection and practice in the classroom.

REFERENCES

Ali, W., & Williams, A. B. (2020). Evaluating the effectiveness of nonverbal communication in human-robot interaction. In *Companion of the 2020 ACM/IEEE International Conference on Human-Robot Interaction* (pp. 99–100). https://doi.org/10.1145/3371382.3378354

Andersen, J. F. (1979). Teacher immediacy as a predictor of teaching effectiveness. *Communication Yearbook, 3*(1), 543–599. https://doi.org/10.1080/23808985.1979.11923782

Ayedoun, E., Hayashi, Y., & Seta, K. (2015). A conversational agent to encourage willingness to communicate in the context of English as a foreign language. *Procedia Computer Science, 60*(1), 1433–1442. https://doi.org/10.1016/j.procs.2015.08.219

Berendt, B., Littlejohn, A., & Blakemore, M. (2020). AI in education: Learner choice and fundamental rights. *Learning, Media and Technology, 45*(3), 312–324. https://doi.org/10.1080/17439884.2020.1786399

Brown, L., Kerwin, R., & Howard, A. M. (2013). Applying behavioral strategies for student engagement using a robotic educational agent. In *Systems, Man, and Cybernetics (SMC), 2013 IEEE International Conference on* (pp. 4360–4365). IEEE. https://doi.org/10.1109/SMC.2013.744

Bodkin, H. (2017, September 11). 'Inspirational' robots to begin replacing teachers within 10 years. *The Telegraph.* www.telegraph.co.uk

Chollet, M., Wörtwein, T., Morency, L. P., Shapiro, A., & Scherer, S. (2015). Exploring feedback strategies to improve public speaking: An interactive virtual audience framework. In *Proceedings of the 2015 ACM International Joint Conference on Pervasive and Ubiquitous Computing* (pp. 1143–1154). ACM. https://doi.org/10.1145/2750858.2806060

Custer, S., King, E. M., Atinc, T. M., Read, L., Sethi, T. (2018). *Toward data-driven education systems: Insights into using information to measure results and manage change.* Center for Universal Education at Brookings. www.brookings.edu/wp-content/uploads/2018/02/toward-data-driven-education-systems.pdf

Craig, M. J. A., & Edwards, C. (2021). Feeling for our robot overlords: Perceptions of emotionally expressive social robots in initial interactions. *Communication Studies, 72*(2), 251–265. https://doi.org/10.1080/10510974.2021.1880457

Edwards, A., & Edwards, C. (2017). The machines are coming: Future directions in instructional communication research. *Communication Education, 66*(4), 487–488. https://doi.org/10.1080/03634523.2017.1349915

Edwards, A., & Edwards, C. (2018). Human-machine communication in the classroom. In M. L. Houser and A. M. Hosek (Eds.) *Handbook of instructional communication II* (2nd ed.). Routledge.

Edwards, A., Edwards, C., Spence, P., Harris, C., & Gambino, A. (2016). Communicating with a robot in the classroom: Differences in perceptions of credibility and learning between "robot as teacher" and "teacher as robot." *Computers in Human Behavior*, *65*, 627–634. https://doi.org/10.1016/j.chb.2016.06.005

Edwards, A., Edwards, C., Abendschein, B., Espinosa, J., Scherger, J., & Vander Meer, P. (2020). Using robot animal companions in the academic library to mitigate student stress. *Library Hi Tech*.

Edwards, A., Edwards, C., Westerman, D., & Spence, P. R. (2019). Initial expectations, interactions, and beyond with social robots. *Computers in Human Behavior*, *90*, 308–314. https://doi.org/10.1016/j.chb.2018.08.042

Edwards, C., Edwards, A., Spence, P. R., & Lin, X. (2018). I, teacher: Using artificial intelligence (AI) and social robots in communication and instruction. *Communication Education*, *67*(4), 473–480. https://doi.org/10.1080/03634523.2018.1502459

Edwards, C., Edwards, A., Spence, P. R., & Westerman, D. (2016). Initial interaction expectations with robots: Testing the human-to-human interaction script. *Communication Studies*, *67*, 227–238. https://doi.org/10.1080/10510974.2015.1121899

Eguchi, A. (2012). Educational robotics theories and practice: Tips for how to do it right. In *Robots in K-12 education: A new technology for learning* (pp. 1–30). IGI Global.

Frisby, B. N., Kaufmann, R., Vallade, J. I., Frey, T. K., & Martin, J. C. (2020). Using virtual reality for speech rehearsals: An innovative instructor approach to enhance student public speaking efficacy. *Basic Communication Course Annual*, *32*, Article 6, 59–78. https://ecommons.udayton.edu/bcca/vol32/iss1/6

Frymier, A. B. (1993). The impact of teacher immediacy on students' motivation: Is it the same for all students? *Communication Quarterly*, *41*(4), 454–464. https://doi.org/10.1080/01463379309369905

Gebru, T. (2020). Chapter on race and gender. In M. D. Dubber, F. Pasquale, and S. Das (Eds.), *The Oxford handbook of ethics of AI* (pp. 253–269). Oxford Handbooks.

Goble, H., & Edwards, C. (2018). A robot that communicates with vocal fillers has… Uhhh…Greater social presence. *Communication Research Reports*, *35*(3), 256–260. https://doi.org/10.1080/08824096.2018.1447454

Gorham, J. (1988). The relationship between verbal teacher immediacy behaviors and student learning. *Communication Education*, *37*(1), 40–53. https://doi.org/10.1080/03634528809378702

Haake, M., & Gulz, A. (2009). A look at the roles of look & roles in embodied pedagogical agents – A user preference perspective. *International Journal of Artificial Intelligence in Education*, *19*(1), 39–71.

Han, J., Jo, M., Park, S., & Kim, S. (2005). The educational use of home robots for children. In *ROMAN 2005 IEEE International Workshop on Robot and Human Interactive Communication, 2005.* (pp. 378–383). IEEE. https://doi.org/10.1109/ROMAN.2005.1513808

Harrington, C. M., Kavanagh, D. O., Ballester, G. W., Ballester, A. W., Dicker, P., Traynor, O., Hill, A., & Tierney, S. (2018). 360° Operative videos: A randomised cross-over study evaluating attentiveness and information retention. *Journal of Surgical Education*, *75*(4), 993–1000. https://doi.org/10.1016/j.jsurg.2017.10.010

Heljakka, K., & Ihamäki, P. (2019). Robot dogs, interaction and ludic literacy: Exploring smart toy engagements in transgenerational play. *Revista Lusófona de Educação*, *46*, 153–169. https://doi.org/10.24140/issn.1645-7250.rle46.10

Heljakka, K. I., Ihamäki, P. J., & Lamminen, A. I. (2020). Playing with the opposite of uncanny: Empathic responses to learning with a companion-technology robot dog vs. real dog. In *Extended Abstracts of the 2020 Annual Symposium on Computer-Human Interaction in Play* (pp. 262–266). https://doi.org/10.1145/3383668.3419900

Hrastinski, S., Olofsson, A. D., Arkenback, C., Ekström, S., Ericsson, E., Fransson, G., Jaldemark, J., Ryberg, T., Öberg, L., Fuentes, A., Gustafsson, U., Humble, N., Mozelius, P., Sundgren, M., & Utterberg, M. (2019). Critical imaginaries and reflections on artificial intelligence and robots in postdigital K-12 education. *Postdigital Science and Education*, *1*, 427–445. https://doi.org/10.1007/s42438-019-00046-x

Hur, Y., & Han, J. (2009). Analysis on children's tolerance to weak recognition of storytelling robots. *Journal of Convergence Information Technology*, *4*(3), 103–109.

Johnson, W. L., Rickel, J. W., & Lester, J. C. (2000). Animated pedagogical agents: Face-to-face interaction in interactive learning environments. *International Journal of Artificial Intelligence in Education*, *11*, 47–78.

Ke, F., Lee, S., & Xu, X. (2016). Teaching training in a mixed-reality integrated learning environment. *Computers in Human Behavior*, *62*, 212–220. https://doi.org/10.1016/j.chb.2016.03.094

Kellerman, K. L. (1992). Communication: Inherently strategic and primarily automatic. *Communication Monographs*, *59*(3), 288–300. https://doi.org/10.1080/03637759209376270

Kennedy, J., Baxter, P., & Belpaeme, T. (2017). Nonverbal immediacy as a characterisation of social behaviour for human–robot interaction. *International Journal of Social Robotics*, 9, 109–128. https://doi.org/10.1007/s12369-016-0378-3

Kim, E. S., Berkovits, L. D., Bernier, E. P., Leyzberg, D., Shic, F., Paul, R., & Scassellati, B. (2013). Social robots as embedded reinforcers of social behavior in children with autism. *Journal of Autism and Developmental Disorders*, 43(5), 1038–1049.

Klopfer, E., & Sheldon, J. (2010). Augmenting your own reality: Student authoring of science-based augmented reality games. *New Directions for Youth Development*, 2010(128), 85–94. https://doi.org/10.1002/yd.378

Kozima, H., Michalowski, M. P., & Nakagawa, C. (2009). Keepon. *International Journal of Social Robotics*, 1(1), 3–18. https://doi.org/10.1007/s12369-008-0009-8

Landau, V., & Broz, C. (2020). Creating a faculty-centric approach as a catalyst for improvement in teaching and learning. *Intersection: A Journal at the Intersection of Assessment and Learning*, 1(4). https://aalhe.scholasticahq.com/article/16765-creating-a-faculty-centric-approach-as-a-catalyst-for-improvement-in-teaching-and-learning

Lau, K. W., & Lee, P. Y. (2015). The use of virtual reality for creating unusual environmental stimulation to motivate students to explore creative ideas. *Interactive Learning Environments*, 23(1), 3–18. https://doi.org/10.1080/10494820.2012.745426

Li, J., Kizilcec, R. F., Bailenson, J. N., & Ju, W. (2016). Social robotics and virtual agents as lectures for video instruction. *Computers in Human Behavior*, 55(B), 1222–1230. https://doi.org/10.1016/j.chb.2015.04.005

McCroskey, J. C., & Teven, J. J. (1999). Goodwill: A reexamination of the construct and its measurement. *Communication Monographs*, 66, 90–103. https://doi.org/10.1080/03637759909376464

McStay, A. (2020). Emotional AI and EdTech: Serving the public good? *Learning, Media and Technology*, 45(3), 270–283. https://doi.org/10.1080/17439884.2020.1686016

Mehrabian, A. (1971). *Silent messages*. Wadsworth.

Mubin, O., Stevens, C. J., Shahid, S., Al Mahmud, A., & Dong, J. J. (2013). A review of the applicability of robots in education. *Journal of Technology in Education and Learning*, 1(209-0015), 13.

Niculescu, A., van Dijk, B., Nijholt, A., Li, H., & See, S. L. (2013). Making social robots more attractive: The effects of voice pitch, humor and empathy. *International Journal of Social Robotics*, 5, 171–191. https://doi.org/10.1007/s12369-012-0171-x

Omale, N., Hung, W. C., Luetkehans, L., & Cooke-Plagwitz, J. (2009). Learning in 3-D multiuser virtual environments: Exploring the use of unique 3-D attributes for online problem-based learning. *British Journal of Educational Technology*, 40,

480–495. https://doi.org/10.1111/j.1467-8535.2009.00941.x

Papakostas, G. A., Sidiropoulos, G. K., Papadopoulou, C. I., Vrochidou, E., Kaburlasos, V. G., Papadopoulou, M. T., Holeva, V., Nikopoulou, V., & Dalivigkas, N. (2021). Social robots in special education: A systematic review. *Electronics*, 10(1398), 1–36. https://doi.org/10.3390/electronics10121398

Park, E., Kim, K. J., & Del Pobil, A. P. (2011). The effects of a robot instructor's positive vs. negative feed-backs on attraction and acceptance towards the robot in classroom. In B. Mutlu, C. Bartneck, J. Ham, V. Evers, & T. Kanda (Eds.), *Social robotics. ICSR Lecture Notes in Computer Science*, 7072 (pp. 135–141). Springer.

Powell, R. G., & Harville, B. (1990). The effects of teacher immediacy and clarity on instructional outcomes: An intercultural assessment. *Communication Education*, 39, 369–379. https://doi.org/10.1080/03634529009378816

Pringle, R., Michael, K., & Michael, M. G. (2016). Unintended consequences of living with AI: The paradox of technological potential? Part II [Guest Editorial]. *IEEE Technology and Society Magazine*, 35(4), 17–21. https://doi.org/10.1109/mts.2016.2632978

Roll, I., & Wylie, R. (2016). Evolution and revolution in artificial intelligence in education. *International Journal of Artificial Intelligence in Education*, 26, 582–599. https://doi.org/10.1007/s40593-016-0110-3

Rosenthal-von der Pütten, A. M., Krämer, N. C., & Herrmann, J. (2018). The effects of humanlike and robot-specific affective nonverbal behavior on perception, emotion, and behavior. *International Journal of Social Robotics*, 10(5), 569–582. https://doi.org/10.1007/s12369-018-0466-7

Rupp, M. A., Odette, K. L., Kozachuk, J., Michaelis, J. R., Smither, J. A., & McConnell, D. S. (2019). Investigating learning outcomes and subjective experiences in 360-degree videos. *Computers & Education*, 128, 256–268. https://doi.org/10.1016/j.compedu.2018.09.015

Salem, M., Lakatos, G., Amirabdollahian, F., & Dautenhahn, K. (2015). Would you trust a (faulty) robot?: Effects of error, task type and personality on human-robot cooperation and trust. In *Proceedings of the Tenth Annual ACM/IEEE International Conference on Human-Robot Interaction* (pp. 141–148). ACM. https://doi.org/10.1145/2696454.2696497

Sanders, T., Oleson, K. E., Billings, D. R., Chen, J. Y., & Hancock, P. A. (2011). A model of human-robot trust: Theoretical model development. In *Proceedings of the human factors and ergonomics society annual meeting* (Vol. 55, No. 1, pp. 1432–1436). SAGE. https://doi.org/10.1177/1071181311551298

Sandry, E. (2015). Re-evaluating the form and communication of social robots. *International Journal of Social Robotics, 7*(3), 335–346. https://doi.org/10.1007/s12369-014-0278-3

Schiff, D. (2020). Out of the laboratory and into the classroom: The future of artificial intelligence in education. *AI & Society*, 1–18. https://doi.org/10.1007/s00146-020-01033-8

Schrodt, P., & Witt, P. L. (2006). Students' attributions of instructor credibility as a function of students' expectations of instructional technology use and nonverbal immediacy. *Communication Education, 55*, 1–20. https://doi.org/10.1080/03634520500343335

Schroeder, N. L., & Gotch, C. M. (2015). Persisting issues in pedagogical agent research. *Journal of Educational Computing Research, 53*(2), 183–204. https://doi.org/10.1177/0735633115597625

Spence, P. R., Westerman, D., Edwards, C., & Edwards, A. (2014). Welcoming our robot overlords: Initial expectations about interaction with a robot. *Communication Research Reports, 31*, 272–280. https://doi.org/10.1080/08824096.2014.924337

Sultan, L., Abuznadah, W., Al-Jifree, H., Khan, M. A., Alsaywid, B., & Ashour, F. (2019). An experimental study on usefulness of virtual reality 360° in undergraduate medical education. *Advances in Medical Education and Practice, 10*, 907–916. https://doi.org/10.2147/AMEP.S219344

Tegos, S., Demetriadis, S., & Karakostas, A. (2015). Promoting academically productive talk with conversational agent interventions in collaborative learning settings. *Computers & Education, 87*, 309–325. https://doi.org/10.1016/j.compedu.2015.07.014

Vallade, J. I., Kaufmann, R., Frisby, B. N., & Martin, J. C. (2020). Technology acceptance model: Investigating students' intentions toward adoption of immersive 360° videos for public speaking rehearsals. *Communication Education*, 1–19. https://doi.org/10.1080/03634523.2020.1791351

VanLehn, K. (2011). The relative effectiveness of human tutoring, intelligent tutoring systems, and other tutoring systems. *Educational Psychologist, 46*(4), 197–221. https://doi.org/10.1080/00461520.2011.611369

Vasagar, J. (2017, July 13). How robots are teaching Singapore's kids. *Financial Times.* www.ft.com

Violanti, M. T., Kelly, S. E., Garland, M. E., & Christen, S. (2018). Instructor clarity, humor, immediacy, and student learning: Replication and extension. *Communication Studies, 69*(3), 251–262. https://doi.org/10.1080/10510974.2018.1466718

Walshe, N., & Driver, P. (2019). Developing reflective trainee teacher practice with 360-degree video. *Teaching and Teacher Education, 78*, 97–105. https://doi.org/10.1016/j.tate.2018.11.009

Williams, R., Park, H. W., Oh, L., & Breazeal, C. (2019). Popbots: Designing an artificial intelligence curriculum for early childhood education. In *Proceedings of the AAAI Conference on Artificial Intelligence* (Vol. 33, pp. 9729–9736). https://doi.org/10.1609/aaai.v33i01.33019729

Wu, H.-K., Lee, S. W.-Y., Chang, H.-Y., & Liang, J.-C. (2013). Current status, opportunities and challenges of augmented reality in education. *Computers & Education, 62*, 41–49. https://doi.org/10.1016/j.compedu.2012.10.024

59

Human–Machine Communication in Healthcare

Jihyun Kim, Hayeon Song, Kelly Merrill Jr., Taenyun Kim, and Jieun Kim

INTRODUCTION

Technology advancements have brought significant changes and contributions to healthcare. With the advent of innovative technologies, scholars and practitioners have sought to find effective ways to utilize technologies to advance and promote healthcare. In fact, Kim and Song (2020) showcase how technology can be effectively used in promoting good health.

Beyond using technology as a vehicle to deliver health-related messages or practices, increased attention is paid to the use of machines capable of social interaction. In particular, AI-driven technology is incorporated in diverse forms of healthcare machines, such as virtual AI agents (e.g., chatbots, AI speakers) and robots (e.g., socially assistive robots, telepresence robots – telerobot doctors). Research documents interacting with these healthcare machines lead to positive outcomes (e.g., Robinson et al., 2013; Shibata & Wada, 2011). Notably, healthcare machines are already used to provide primary care in some countries such as Brazil and India (Cohn, 2013). This new trend suggests that machines now function as interaction partners to healthcare providers and patients.

Considering that effective communication is important for health communication, it is imperative to understand the nature of interaction between humans (e.g., patients, doctors) and machines. This chapter focuses on applications of socially interactive healthcare machines, such as AI agents, socially assistive robots (SARs), and telerobot doctors. Then, the chapter concludes by providing future research directions and suggestions in the area of human–machine communication (HMC) for healthcare.

WHY HEALTHCARE MACHINES?

Machines are helpful and are important for healthcare in various ways. First, the need for healthcare is increasing but human resources are failing to meet the demand. Innovative developments in medicine and science have increased the average life expectancy; thus, the aging population is rapidly growing. In fact, the worldwide population of people aged over 60 is expected to double between 2000 and 2050 (United Nations, 2019). To meet this increasing demand for healthcare, some suggest that machines can provide great support for seniors (Purtill, 2019).

Second, machines can augment and supplement traditional human roles by maximizing efficiency and effectiveness. AI can provide healthcare providers with precise information based on the massive amounts of patient-generated health data (PGHD), and this will allow for more personalized care and service for patients. In particular, AI can assist medical professionals in making medical decisions such as diagnoses and treatment options (Choi et al., 2016; Long et al., 2017). For example, since 2013, IBM's Watson has helped doctors make more accurate medical decisions (Upbin, 2013). In cancer research, Watson's diagnoses reached a 99% agreement with diagnoses by doctors (Lohr, 2016).

Furthermore, machines can assist with simple repetitive yet important tasks. Adhering to medical advice is a vital aspect of health management, and it is important to continuously communicate with patients to encourage them to follow medical advice. For these tasks, machines can be used to remind people of daily routines, such as medicine intake and regular exercising, in an interactive manner (Lorenz et al., 2016).

Lastly, although machines might be inferior to humans in caring for others (Sparrow & Sparrow, 2006), there are other tasks where machines outperform humans. The performance of machines is particularly noticeable during times when human contact is restricted for safety and health issues, such as the COVID-19 (Coronavirus disease 2019) outbreak. While COVID-19 limits human-to-human contact due to the contagiousness of the virus, machines, whose infection risk is zero, can instead help patients that are quarantined or isolated. To illustrate, telerobots, supported by telepresence robots, make it possible for medical professionals to communicate with patients remotely while limiting face-to-face contact (Marr, 2020).

SOCIALLY INTERACTIVE HEALTHCARE MACHINES

There are a growing number of applications of socially interactive healthcare machines. Of those, this section introduces three particular types.

Conversational AI Agents

The rapid development of AI creates many opportunities for using conversational AI healthcare agents in diverse forms, such as chatbots and voice agents in smart speakers or smartphones. With collaborative works of web services and a healthcare cloud, conversational agents can

provide medical advice, schedule appointments, and send reminders of medicine intake and upcoming visits with a provider (Ilievski et al., 2019). For example, patients that visit the website of UCHealth, a nonprofit health system in Aurora, Colorado, can find specialists, schedule doctor's appointments, or deal with urgent triage by speaking to Amazon's Alexa, a smart speaker. The website provides a natural, intuitive form of interaction that anyone can easily access (Menon, 2020). Further, conversational AI agents can understand conversations between health practitioners and take detailed conversational notes more efficiently and effectively than humans (Toews, 2020).

Conversational AI agents can also help patients with mental health challenges. For example, *Woebot*, a chatbot designed to manage and treat depression, would be a valuable resource. The chatbot utilizes a conversational style that is similar to that of human clinicians. Each interaction begins with *Woebot* asking general questions concerning the context (e.g., "What are you up to now?"). When the user responds, *Woebot* asks about the user's mood (e.g., "How are you feeling at the moment?") and provides possible responses in emojis and words (e.g., "Angry," "Really happy," "Depressed") to continue the conversation. During this interaction, *Woebot* can understand users' emotions and perform cognitive-behavioral therapy (CBT). In fact, research reports that interacting with *Woebot* can decrease feelings of depression (Fitzpatrick et al., 2017). The study found that people are more willing to share their stories with an AI agent than a human. Also, people anthropomorphize, or humanize, *Woebot* and refer to it as "a friend" or "fun little dude," which implies that they perceive the AI agent as their conversational partner rather than a mere computer program.

Socially Assistive Robots in Healthcare

A socially assistive robot (SAR) can assist humans with healthcare needs through social interactions. SARs aim "to create close and effective interactions with a human user for the purpose of giving assistance and achieving measurable progress in convalescence, rehabilitation, [and] learning" (Feil-Seifer & Mataric, 2005, p. 465). SARs can be categorized into two operational groups, which are not mutually exclusive: service robots and companion robots. Service robots are designed to assist humans with daily activities such as household chores (e.g., Reiser, 2013) and schedule management (e.g., Montemerlo et al., 2002). Companion robots mainly focus on improving psychological well-being among humans by decreasing loneliness (e.g., Kanamori et al., 2003) or encouraging a positive mood (e.g., Wada et al., 2002).

SARs can provide long-term assistance with social support. Social support is the functional content of supportive actions within relationships including emotional, instrumental, informational, and appraisal support (House, 1981). Patients receive informational support from healthcare professionals but often need emotional support from family and friends (Blanchard et al., 1995). However, people in close relationships can sometimes feel overwhelmed in providing support, particularly for chronic health conditions, which can affect the quality of support (Gottlieb & Wagner, 1991). Also, if one's support is not well-received by the support recipient, the act of support may not be perceived as positive (Feeney & Collins, 2003). With these concerns, SARs can fulfill patients' needs and relieve stress for providers by functioning as alternative caregivers. Indeed, SARs, with home-health technologies, are projected to have a crucial role, particularly for those diagnosed with Alzheimer's disease and related dementia (ADRD), by relieving burdens among caregivers and enhancing the bond with the care recipient (Arthanat et al., 2020).

With the rapid growth of the aging population, SARs are particularly beneficial for the elderly. SARs can save social costs for elderly healthcare and regularly monitor their health. Research suggests five roles of SARs in elderly care (Abdi et al., 2018). First, SARs can perform *affective therapy* that improves the overall mood and well-being of the elderly and help the elderly overcome emotional disorders with therapeutic interventions. Indeed, periodic affective therapy through SARs improves the quality of life by preventing dementia as well as lowering the depression and anxiety index (Cho et al., 2019). Second, SARs can provide *cognitive training* that improves cognitive ability such as working memory. Tapus (2009) found that a SAR's encouragement in a music-based cognitive game improves the cognitive attention of patients with dementia and/or cognitive impairments. When the robot adapted its behavior to the patients' level of disability, task performance in the cognitive game improved over time.

Next, SARs can act as a *social facilitator* that stimulates social interactions and increases sociability among users. Sung et al. (2015) examined the impact of interactions with *Paro*, a baby seal-like social robot, and found that it increased users' communication, interaction skills, and participation in social activities. Another role of SARs is to provide *companionship*. Unlike affective therapy, which involves a specific treatment process, companionship provides emotional stability by reducing loneliness and social isolation. Research indicates that interacting with *AIBO,* a dog-like social robot, helped reduce loneliness (Banks et al., 2008). Lastly, SARs can provide *physiological therapy* that changes the physiological markers of users. Robinson et al. (2015) found that people who meaningfully interacted with a robot experienced a significant decrease in blood pressure and heart rate.

TELEROBOT DOCTORS

Telerobot doctors are another type of machine used in healthcare. Telerobotics is concerned with the use of semi-automatic robots or machines that are operated from a distance, which is made possible through the use of a wireless network or an internet connection (Sheridan, 1989). Thus, telerobot doctors are machines operated by healthcare providers, enabling them to provide health services and care from a distance.

Telerobot doctors are widely used across the world in various forms, such as surgical robots and remote presence robots. Surgical robots are designed to operate surgeries and interact with other healthcare professionals. One widely used surgical telerobot doctor is the *da Vinci Surgical System* (Avgousti et al., 2016). According to the system's developer, more than five million surgeries are completed worldwide using this system (Intuitive Surgical Inc., 2020a), and the system is used in all 50 states in the U.S. (Intuitive Surgical Inc., 2020b). Telerobot doctors are also presented as remote presence robots with a screen that features a livestream of a healthcare professional. The screen enables healthcare providers to interact with patients.

Telerobot doctors can provide a great deal of benefits for healthcare. First, telerobot doctors can help reduce issues related to healthcare accessibility (Natarajan et al., 2012). Individuals living in rural areas or places, where access to adequate healthcare (e.g., specialists) is limited, can now interact with healthcare providers remotely. Also, with easier accessibility, a specialist telerobot doctor can evaluate a patient from their direct interactions by use of telerobotics rather than relying on another provider's initial understanding of the patient's issues. This decreases the risk of complications due to misunderstandings caused by indirect interaction with the patient and can potentially provide the patient with the right resources during their first visit.

Further, telerobot doctors are particularly beneficial in providing healthcare during widespread health concerns, such as the COVID-19 pandemic. Telerobot doctors allow healthcare providers to deliver care to patients in an appropriately distanced space with minimal harm to the healthcare provider. By providing care in a distanced way, the risk of spreading viruses and diseases is diminished. Examples of these telerobot doctors include *Spot*, who was tested at Brigham and Women's Hospital in Boston (Statt, 2020) and *Vici*, who helped with COVID-19 patients at the Providence Regional Medical Center in Washington state (Schlosser, 2020).

Although limited, some research investigates the role of telerobot doctors and their introduction to healthcare. Petelin et al. (2007) deployed a remote presence telerobot doctor in a hospital and found that patients and nurses enjoy increased access to healthcare providers. The introduction of a telerobot doctor in postoperative care was also associated with increased patient satisfaction (Ellison et al., 2004), and telerobot doctors were found to aid in reducing lengths of visits and response times to emergencies (Kristoffersson et al., 2013). These research findings provide promising ways to use telerobot doctors in healthcare settings.

SUGGESTIONS FOR FUTURE RESEARCH DIRECTIONS

Machines have great potential to further improve healthcare services. As a growing number of machines are used in various healthcare settings, research is needed to better facilitate more effective interactions between machines and users (e.g., patients, healthcare professionals). In this regard, the following section provides a few recommendations and suggestions for future research directions.

First, there is an important issue regarding trust. Considering that trust between healthcare providers and patients is one of the key factors to successful healthcare experiences (Dang et al., 2017), trust with healthcare machines is crucial for effective HMC in healthcare. In particular, it is important to find ways to develop and maintain trust among users. If trust is too high, people might over-rely on machines (Bussone et al., 2015). This phenomenon is particularly common in healthcare because decision-making in healthcare is often complex and relies heavily on a decision-support system, such as AI (Lyell & Coiera, 2017). If patient trust is too low, the patient may

not accept guidance from a machine (Gefen et al., 2003). In healthcare, when trust is low between patients and their healthcare provider, the patients become reluctant to share their personal or sensitive information (Street Jr et al., 1995), and the patients could potentially question diagnoses or prescriptions given by the healthcare provider (Lo, 1999). Thus, lack of trust with healthcare machines may stem from people being unsure of whom the machine will share their medical information with. To address these issues, a transparent message should be communicated regarding information sharing between the machine and patient. Additionally, given that increased exposure or interactions with a machine over time lead to more positive attitudes about the machine (Stafford et al., 2014; Sutherland et al., 2019), repeated exposure with healthcare machines might likely help patients develop trust with the machines. In all, future research should investigate methods to develop and maintain trust with healthcare machines.

Second, there is a crucial need to increase human compliance when machines provide suggestions and recommendations. Compliance in healthcare is generally understood as the extent to which a person's behavior (e.g., taking medications, following diets) coincides with medical advice (Haynes & Sackett, 1979). While medical recommendations are typically provided by humans in a conventional healthcare setting, technology now allows machines to serve this role. As addressed earlier, many AI agents are equipped with communication skills and technical capabilities that allow them to interact with patients at home. Therefore, it is possible for machines to assist with the routine, menial tasks involved in patient care, such as providing reminders of medicine intake. Although limited, some research reports ways to increase compliance with machines in healthcare (e.g., Hoorn & Winter, 2018; Lee et al., 2017). Lee and colleagues (2017) investigated the effects of polite expressions from robots on patient compliance with recommendations by robots. The study found that politeness does not always increase patients' intention to comply, but direct speech with polite gestures is an effective strategy to increase patient compliance. The use of healthcare machines is likely to continue increasing, whether at healthcare service facilities or home. Given that increased compliance with healthcare recommendations helps improve the health status of patients and satisfaction with healthcare services (D'Mello et al., 2012; Kim et al., 2015), future research should investigate ways to help patients comply with healthcare machines.

Next, it is important to examine how to foster a feeling of social presence when interacting with machines. Social presence is defined as "a psychological state in which virtual (para-authentic or artificial) social actors are experienced as actual social actors in either sensory or nonsensory ways" (Lee, 2004, p. 45). Essentially, it is a perception that machines are regarded as real humans. Social presence of machines is particularly important in fostering positive healthcare experiences. To illustrate, preliminary research findings indicate that social presence has a mediating role that fosters the perceived credibility of a doctor (Edwards et al., 2017; Edwards et al., 2018). This finding implies that if users felt a strong social presence of machines, that feeling of social presence would eventually increase better healthcare experiences. Extant research (Lee & Nass, 2005; Lombard & Ditton, 1997) indicates that social presence can be fostered by various factors such as technology features (e.g., size, interactivity), user factors (e.g., prior experiences), and social factors (e.g., communication styles). In this regard, future research should investigate diverse features that facilitate social presence of healthcare machines for effective healthcare experiences.

Further, there is a need to understand users' acceptance of healthcare machines. Creators of healthcare machines should ensure that the designs of these machines are simple and easy for patients to interact with. The Technology Acceptance Model (TAM) suggests that the perceived ease of use and perceived usefulness of a technology are key to determining whether individuals will adopt that technology (Venkatesh & Davis, 2000). Thus, healthcare machines should be developed to be easy to use and viewed as useful by both healthcare providers and patients. Future researchers should investigate these variables when inquiring about whether a new healthcare machine will be adopted. Additionally, the appearance of a healthcare machine should also be considered with regard to users' acceptance. Olaronke et al. (2017) suggest that patients may have low levels of trust and negative emotional responses to robots that imperfectly try to embody humans. Also, the uncanny valley hypothesis states that if a robot is perceived as too anthropomorphic, or humanlike, individuals might have mixed feelings in how they perceive and accept the robot (Gray & Wegner, 2012). Thus, future researchers should investigate how to enhance user acceptance of healthcare machines from diverse perspectives.

Moreover, considering that interacting with healthcare machines could affect users' privacy in a variety of ways (Lutz & Tamò, 2018), privacy issues should be addressed. Patients' personal information can be easily stored in a system when interacting with a healthcare machine. While the collected information can be advantageous when discussing diagnosis and treatment options (Li et al., 2017), the potential for a data breach can raise privacy concerns. In particular, biopharma and medical device companies grow their interest in building cloud-based platforms as the hub of data storage and data management to handle information from personal healthcare machines used at homes, which could potentially heighten the risk of privacy violation. In this regard, there is an urgent need to address this issue, such as establishing new privacy policies and regulations that can empower patients with data rights and privacy protection.

Lastly, ethics-related issues should be considered. People perceive lower levels of trust when they are aware of the possibility of AI's errors and limitations compared to when they are unaware (Kim & Song, 2022). Then, to what extent should we explain the possibility of errors or mistakes of AI? Also, who should be responsible for explaining the errors to patients, human doctors, a biotech company, a pharmaceutical company, or another party? Ethics-related issues might be particularly concerning for healthcare machines designed to provide social or emotional support. As humans tend to treat machines as social actors (Reeves & Nass, 1996), users may perceive social connections with machines and share personal information such as daily life events and feelings. Despite the benefits of social support from the machines, this could lead to an illusionary relationship given that the machines' responses to humans are programmed, not authentic (Turkle, 2007). Humans may perceive the machines as capable of understanding them, but instead, machines are designed to provide predetermined reactions enabling people to believe that they can understand humans. Although machines can be designed and developed to behave like humans, it is beyond their ability to provide the same level of compassion as humans (Howick et al., 2021). In this regard, researchers are encouraged to examine ethical concerns that arise in the interactions between humans and machines.

CONCLUSION

Commenters indicate that the growing number of new technology applications will continue to affect and/or will completely transform the healthcare field. Technology development in healthcare that increases efficiency and accuracy of medical assistance while reducing cost is important. However, it is also critically and equally, if not more, important to focus on human-centered approaches, such as effective communication styles and psychological processes of interaction, for effective HMC in healthcare. In this regard, this chapter calls for collective efforts to further develop human-centered research on HMC in healthcare.

REFERENCES

Abdi, J., Al-Hindawi, A., Ng, T., & Vizcaychipi, M. P. (2018). Scoping review on the use of socially assistive robot technology in elderly care. *BMJ open*, *8*(2), e018815. http://dx.doi.org/10.1136/bmjopen-2017-018815

Arthanat, S., Begum, M., Gu, T., LaRoche, D. P., Xu, D., & Zhang, N. (2020). Caregiver perspectives on a smart home-based socially assistive robot for individuals with Alzheimer's disease and related dementia. *Disability and Rehabilitation: Assistive Technology*, 1–10. https://doi.org/10.1080/17483107.2020.1753831

Avgousti, S., Christoforou, E. G., Panayides, A. S., Voskarides, S., Novales, C., Nouaille, L., … & Vieyres, P. (2016). Medical telerobotic systems: Current status and future trends. *Biomedical Engineering Online*, *15*(1), 96. https://doi.org/10.1186/s12938-016-0217-7

Banks, M. R., Willoughby, L. M., & Banks, W. A. (2008). Animal-assisted therapy and loneliness in nursing homes: Use of robotic versus living dogs. *Journal of the American Medical Directors Association*, *9*(3), 173–177. https://doi.org/10.1016/j.jamda.2007.11.007

Blanchard, C. G., Albrecht, T. L., Ruckdeschel, J. C., Grant, C. H., & Hemmick, R. M. (1995). The role of social support in adaptation to cancer and to survival. *Journal of Psychosocial Oncology*, *13*(1–2), 75–95. https://doi.org/10.1300/J077V13N01_05

Bussone, A., Stumpf, S., & O'Sullivan, D. (2015, October). The role of explanations on trust and reliance in clinical decision support systems. In *2015 International Conference on Healthcare Informatics* (pp. 160–169). IEEE. https://doi.org/10.1109/ICHI.2015.26

Cho, H. S., Kim, J. H., Kim, S. R. (2019). Factors related to the effectiveness in the use of an ICT-based toy robot for the in-home care of community dwelling elderly. *Korean Journal of Health Education and Promotion*, *36*(5), 43–51. http://doi.org/10.14367/kjhep.2019.36.5.43

Choi, E., Bahadori, M. T., Schuetz, A., Stewart, W. F., & Sun, J. (2016, December). Doctor AI: Predicting clinical events via recurrent neural networks. In *Machine Learning for Healthcare Conference* (pp. 301–318).

Cohn, J. (March, 2013). The robot will see you now. *The Atlantic*. Retrieved from www.theatlantic.com/magazine/archive/2013/03/the-robot-will-see-you-now/309216/

D'Mello, S., Olney, A., Williams, C., & Hays, P. (2012). Gaze tutor: A gaze-reactive intelligent tutoring system. *International Journal of Human-computer Studies*, *70*(5), 377–398. https://doi.org/10.1016/j.ijhcs.2012.01.004

Dang, B. N., Westbrook, R. A., Njue, S. M., & Giordano, T. P. (2017). Building trust and rapport early in the new doctor-patient relationship: A longitudinal qualitative study. *BMC Medical Education*, *17*(1), 32. https://doi.org/10.4172/2472-1654.100146

Edwards, A., Omilion-Hodges, L., & Edwards, C. (2017, March). How do patients in a medical interview perceive a robot versus human physician?. In *Proceedings of the Companion of the 2017 ACM/IEEE International Conference on Human-Robot Interaction* (pp. 109–110). https://doi.org/10.1145/3029798.3038308

Edwards, C., Edwards, A., & Omilion-Hodges, L. (2018, March). Receiving medical treatment plans from a robot: Evaluations of presence, credibility, and attraction. In *Companion of the 2018 ACM/IEEE International Conference on Human-Robot Interaction* (pp. 101–102). https://doi.org/10.1145/3173386.3177050

Ellison, L. M., Pinto, P. A., Kim, F., Ong, A. M., Patriciu, A., Stoianovici, D., … & Kavoussi, L. R. (2004). Telerounding and patient satisfaction after surgery. *Journal of the American College of Surgeons*, *199*(4), 523–530. https://doi.org/10.1016/j.jamcollsurg.2004.06.022

Feeney, B. C., & Collins, N. L. (2003). Motivations for caregiving in adult intimate relationships: Influences on caregiving behavior and relationship functioning. *Personality and Social Psychology Bulletin*, *29*(8), 950–968. https://doi.org/10.1177/0146167203252807

Feil-Seifer, D., & Mataric, M. J. (2005, June). Defining socially assistive robotics. In *9th International Conference on Rehabilitation Robotics, 2005. ICORR 2005* (pp. 465–468). IEEE. https://doi.org/10.1109/ICORR.2005.1501143

Fitzpatrick, K. K., Darcy, A., & Vierhile, M. (2017). Delivering cognitive behavior therapy to young adults with symptoms of depression and anxiety using a fully automated conversational agent (Woebot): A randomized controlled trial. *JMIR Mental Health*, *4*(2). https://doi.org/10.2196/mental.7785

Gefen, D., Karahanna, E., & Straub, D. W. (2003). Trust and TAM in online shopping: An integrated model. *MIS Quarterly*, *27*(1), 51–90. https://doi.org/10.2307/30036519

Gottlieb, B. H., & Wagner, F. (1991). Stress and support processes in close relationships. In *The social* context of coping (pp. 165–188). Springer, Boston, MA.

Gray, K., & Wegner, D. M. (2012). Feeling robots and human zombies: Mind perception and the uncanny valley. *Cognition*, *125*(1), 125–130. https://doi.org/10.1016/j.cognition.2012.06.007

Haynes, R. B., & Sackett, D. L. (1979). *Compliance in health care*. Johns Hopkins University Press.

Hoorn, J. F., & Winter, S. D. (2018). Here comes the bad news: Doctor robot taking over. *International Journal of Social Robotics*, *10*(4), 519–535. https://doi.org/10.1007/s12369-017-0455-2

House, J. S. (1981). *Work stress and social support reading*. Addison-Wesley.

Howick, J., Morley, J., & Floridi, L. (2021). An empathy imitation game: empathy Turing test for care- and chat-bots. *Minds and Machines*. https://doi.org/10.1007/s11023-021-09555-w

Ilievski, A., Dojchinovski, D., & Gusev, M. (2019, September). Interactive Voice Assisted Home Healthcare Systems. In *Proceedings of the 9th Balkan Conference on Informatics* (pp. 1–5). https://doi.org/10.1145/3351556.3351572

Intuitive Surgical Inc. (2020a). *Da Vinci by Intuitive*. Retrieved from www.intuitive.com/en-us/products-and-services/da-vinci?gclid=EAIaIQobChMIj9mn9fG96gIVD9bACh30CA8BEAAYASAAEgKqE_D_BwE

Intuitive Surgical Inc. (2020b). *Intuitive | Robotic-assisted surgery | Da Vinci surgical system*. Retrieved from www.intuitive.com/en-us

Kanamori, M., Suzuki, M., Oshiro, H., Tanaka, M., Inoguchi, T., Takasugi, H., … & Yokoyama, T. (2003, July). Pilot study on improvement of quality of life among elderly using a pet-type robot. In *Proceedings 2003 IEEE International Symposium on Computational Intelligence in Robotics and Automation. Computational Intelligence in Robotics and Automation for the New Millennium (Cat. No. 03EX694)* (Vol. 1, pp. 107–112). IEEE. https://doi.org/10.1109/CIRA.2003.1222072

Kim, E. J., Lee, S. Y., Cui, M., Kwon, O. (2015). Factors affecting compliance with social robots in a hospital setting. In *Proceedings 2015 International Conference on Platform Technology and Service (PlatCon 2015)*. IEEE. https://doi.org/10.1007/s12369-017-0420-0

Kim, J., & Song, H. (Eds.) (2020). *Technology and health: Promoting attitude and behavior change*. Elsevier.

Kim, T., & Song, H. (2022). Communicating the limitations of AI: The effect of message framing and ownership on trust in artificial intelligence. *International Journal of Human–Computer Interaction*, 1–11. https://doi.org/10.1080/10447318.2022.2049134

Kristoffersson, A., Coradeschi, S., & Loutfi, A. (2013). A review of mobile robotic telepresence. *Advances in Human-Computer Interaction*, 2013. https://doi.org/10.1155/2013/902316

Lee, K. M. (2004). Presence, explicated. *Communication Theory*, *14*, 27–50. https://doi.org/10.1093/ct/14.1.27

Lee, N., Kim, J., Kim, E., & Kwon, O. (2017). The influence of politeness behavior on user compliance with social robots in a healthcare service setting. *International Journal of Social Robotics*, *9*(5), 727–743. https://doi.org/10.1007/s12369-017-0420-0

Lee, K. M., & Nass, C. (2005). Social-psychological origins of feelings of presence: Creating social presence with machine-generated voices. *Media Psychology*, *7*(1), 31–45. https://doi.org/10.1207/S1532785XMEP0701_2

Li, X., Dunn, J., Salins, D., Zhou, G., Zhou, W., Rose, S. M. S. F., … & Sonecha, R. (2017). Digital health: Tracking physiomes and activity using wearable biosensors reveals useful health-related information. *PLoS biology*, *15*(1), e2001402. https://doi.org/10.1371/journal.pbio.2001402

Lo, B. (1999). The patient–provider relationship: Opportunities as well as problems. *Journal of General Internal Medicine*, *14*(Suppl 1), S41. https://doi.org/10.1046/j.1525-1497.1999.00270.x

Lohr, S. (2016). IBM is counting on its bet on Watson, and paying big money for it. *New York Times*. Retrieved from www.nytimes.com/2016/10/17/technology/ibm-is-counting-on-its-bet-on-watson-and-paying-big-money-for-it.html

Lombard, M., & Ditton, T. (1997). At the heart of it all: The concept of presence. *Journal of Computer-Mediated Communication*, *3*(2), JCMC321. https://doi.org/10.1111/j.1083-6101.1997.tb00072.x

Long, E., Lin, H., Liu, Z., Wu, X., Wang, L., Jiang, J., … & Li, J. (2017). An artificial intelligence platform for the multihospital collaborative management of congenital cataracts. *Nature Biomedical Engineering*, *1*(2), 1–8. https://doi.org/10.1038/s41551-016-0024

Lorenz, T., Weiss, A., & Hirche, S. (2016). Synchrony and reciprocity: Key mechanisms for social companion robots in therapy and care. *International Journal of Social Robotics*, *8*(1), 125–143. https://doi.org/10.1007/s12369-015-0325-8

Lutz, C. & Tamò, A. (2018). Communicating with robots: ANTalyzing the interaction between healthcare robots and humans with regards to privacy. In: A. L. Guzman (ed.) *Human-Machine Communication* (pp. 145–165). Peter Lang.

Lyell, D., & Coiera, E. (2017). Automation bias and verification complexity: A systematic review. *Journal of the American Medical Informatics Association*, *24*(2), 423–431. https://doi.org/10.1093/jamia/ocw105

Marr, B. (2020, March 18). Robots and drones are now used to fight COVID-19. *Forbes*. Retrieved from: www.forbes.com/sites/bernardmarr/2020/03/18/how-robots-and-drones-are-helping-to-fight-coronavirus/#f29aee32a12e

Menon, R. (2020, March 26). Council post: Virtual patient care using AI. *Forbes.* Retrieved from: www.forbes.com/sites/forbestechcouncil/2020/03/26/virtual-patient-care-using-ai/#5414c7ae8806

Montemerlo, M., Pineau, J., Roy, N., Thrun, S., & Verma, V. (2002). Experiences with a mobile robotic guide for the elderly. *AAAI/IAAI, 2002*, 587–592.

Natarajan, N., Aparna, S., & Kumar, J. S. J. (2012). Robot aided remote medical assistance system using LabVIEW. *International Journal of Computer Applications, 38*(2), 6–10.

Olaronke, I., Oluwaseun, O., & Rhoda, I. (2017). State of the art: A study of human-robot interaction in healthcare. *International Journal of Information Engineering and Electronic Business, 9*(3), 43. https://doi.org/10.5815/ijieeb.2017.03.06

Petelin, J. B., Nelson, M. E., & Goodman, J. (2007). Deployment and early experience with remote-presence patient care in a community hospital. *Surgical Endoscopy, 21*(1), 53–56. https://doi.org/10.1007/s00464-005-0261-z

Purtill, C. (2019, November). Robots will help you now. *Time.* 52–57. Retrieved from www.magzter.com/stories/News/TIME-Magazine/The-Robot-Will-Help-You-Now

Reeves, B., & Nass, C. (1996). *The media equation: How people treat computers, television, and new media like real people and places.* CSLI Publications.

Reiser, U., Jacobs, T., Arbeiter, G., Parlitz, C., & Dautenhahn, K. (2013). Care-O-bot® 3–Vision of a robot butler. In *Your virtual butler* (pp. 97–116). Springer.

Robinson, H., MacDonald, B. A., Kerse, N., & Broadbent, E. (2013). The psychosocial effects of a companion robot: A randomized controlled trial. *Journal of the American Medical Directors Association, 14*(9), 661–667. https://doi.org/10.1016/j.jamda.2013.02.007

Robinson, H., MacDonald, B., & Broadbent, E. (2015). Physiological effects of a companion robot on blood pressure of older people in residential care facility: A pilot study. *Australasian Journal on Aging, 34*(1), 27–32. https://doi.org/10.1111/ajag.12099

Schlosser, K. (2020, March 05). *Robot is helping to treat man with coronavirus in special isolation room at hospital north of Seattle.* Retrieved from www.geekwire.com/2020/robot-helping-treat-man-coronavirus-special-isolation-room-hospital-north-seattle/

Sheridan, T. B. (1989). Telerobotics. *Automatica, 25*(4), 487–507. https://doi.org/10.1016/0005-1098(89)90093-9

Shibata, T., & Wada, K. (2011). Robot therapy: A new approach for mental healthcare of the elderly – A mini-review. *Gerontology, 57*(4), 378–386. https://doi.org/10.1159/000319015

Sparrow, R., & Sparrow, L. (2006). In the hands of machines? The future of aged care. *Minds and Machines, 16*(2), 141–161. https://doi.org/10.1007/s11023-006-9030-6

Stafford, R. Q., MacDonald, B. A., Jayawardena, C., Wegner, D. M., & Broadbent, E. (2014). Does the robot have a mind? Mind perception and attitudes towards robots predict use of an eldercare robot. *International Journal of Social Robotics, 6*(1), 17–32. https://doi.org/10.1007/s12369-013-0186-y

Statt, N. (2020, April 23). *Boston Dynamics' Spot robot is helping hospitals remotely treat coronavirus patients.* Retrieved from www.theverge.com/2020/4/23/21231855/boston-dynamics-spot-robot-covid-19-coronavirus-telemedicine

Street Jr, R. L., Cauthen, D., Buchwald, E., & Wiprud, R. (1995). Patients' predispositions to discuss health issues affecting quality of life. *Family Medicine, 27*(10), 663.

Sung, H. C., Chang, S. M., Chin, M. Y., & Lee, W. L. (2015). Robot-assisted therapy for improving social interactions and activity participation among institutionalized older adults: A pilot study. *Asia-Pacific Psychiatry, 7*(1), 1–6. https://doi.org/10.1111/appy.12131

Sutherland, C. J., Ahn, B. K., Brown, B., Lim, J., Johanson, D. L., Broadbent, E., ... & Ahn, H. S. (2019, May). The Doctor will See You Now: Could a Robot Be a medical Receptionist?. In *2019 International Conference on Robotics and Automation (ICRA)* (pp. 4310–4316). IEEE. https://doi.org/10.1109/ICRA.2019.8794439

Tapus, A. (2009, July). Improving the quality of life of people with dementia through the use of socially assistive robots. In *2009 Advanced Technologies for Enhanced Quality of Life* (pp. 81–86). IEEE. https://doi.org/10.1109/AT-EQUAL.2009.26

Toews, R. (2020, August 26). These are the startups applying AI to transform healthcare. *Forbes.* Retrieved from: www.forbes.com/sites/robtoews/2020/08/26/ai-will-revolutionize-healthcare-the-transformation-has-already-begun/#512a34e9722f

Turkle, S. (2007). Authenticity in the age of digital companions. *Interaction Studies, 8*(3), 501–517. https://doi.org/10.1075/is.8.3.11tur

United Nations. (2019). *World population ageing 2019.* www.un.org/en/development/desa/population/publications/pdf/ageing/WorldPopulationAgeing2019-Highlights.pdf

Upbin, B. (2013). IBM's Watson gets its first piece of business in healthcare. *Forbes.* Retrieved from www.forbes.com/sites/bruceupbin/2013/02/08/ibms-watson-gets-its-first-piece-of-business-in-healthcare/#4f22b6e95402

Venkatesh, V., & Davis, F. D. (2000). A theoretical extension of the technology acceptance model: Four longitudinal field studies. *Management Science, 46*(2), 186–204. https://doi.org/10.1006/ijhc.1996.0040

Wada, K., Shibata, T., Saito, T., & Tanie, K. (2002, October). Analysis of factors that bring mental effects to elderly people in robot assisted activity. In *IEEE/RSJ International Conference on Intelligent Robots and Systems* (Vol. 2, pp. 1152–1157). Ieee. https://doi.org/10.1109/IRDS.2002.1043887

60

Why Human–Machine Communication Matters for the Study of Artificial Intelligence in Journalism

Seth C. Lewis and Felix M. Simon

INTRODUCTION

Artificial intelligence (AI), the application of computing to take on tasks normally associated with human intelligence, has become a growing feature in many fields and industries — as evident in the rapid and widespread adoption of OpenAI's ChatGPT. Journalism, as we argue in this chapter, offers a useful context for examining how opportunities for AI applications are envisaged and enacted amid the growing adoption and influence of algorithms and automation across media and information domains. In all this incorporation of AI in journalism, there are, as in other fields, inflated expectations for breakthrough innovations in efficiency and productivity, on the one hand, as well as pessimism about dire outcomes for human labor and expertise, on the other. While those perils and possibilities are more fully outlined and debated elsewhere (e.g., Broussard, 2018; Diakopoulos, 2019), what remains less apparent in the literature thus far is how particular conceptual perspectives may help scholars make sense of the AI phenomenon in a larger sense – not merely in terms of how it shifts journalistic practice, important though that is, but more broadly in how it forces us to confront questions about roles and relationships of humans and machines (Lewis et al., 2019). In effect, what does it mean for journalism if AI developments

begin to shift how we think about the very essence of what it means to communicate in the first place?

Indeed, the study of AI in journalism, as our own observations have found, thus far has been lacking robust theoretical frameworks that would help explain its development and impact. As such, this chapter takes up the case of AI and journalism as an opportunity to explore an emergent conceptual framework and body of research. In connection with this Sage Handbook as a whole, we examine Human–Machine Communication (HMC), considering how it might be incorporated by scholars to evaluate the material, social, and ontological implications of "communicative AI," or AI that is designed to function *as a communicator* rather than merely as a mediator (Guzman, 2018; Guzman & Lewis, 2020).

Thus, this chapter investigates the generative potential and applicability of HMC in the context of AI as applied in journalism. Specifically, this chapter asks: How might HMC as a lens – as a way of understanding the formation and maintenance of relationships between humans and machines – offer a way of interpreting anew the paths taken so far in the media industry and in scholarly research? And, in turn, how might such an appraisal enable us to more fully scrutinize HMC as a theoretical intervention – to consider where and how HMC fits into journalism studies broadly and into the study of news and technology particularly?

With these questions in mind, we proceed by first clarifying our terms, including the nature of "communicative AI" and its connection with HMC. Thereafter, we turn to a key contribution of this chapter: connecting the HMC perspective to the study of AI and journalism to evaluate relative strengths and weaknesses and opportunities for future study.

ARTIFICIAL INTELLIGENCE, COMMUNICATIVE AI, AND HUMAN–MACHINE COMMUNICATION (HMC)

AI is a word and concept fraught with uncertainty, and a generally accepted definition for it does not exist. Common explanations define AI as "the activity of simulating uniquely human activities and skills" (Wilks, 2020). In practice, AI usually refers to a diverse range of applications and techniques at different levels of complexity, autonomy, and abstraction (Broussard, 2018; Mitchell, 2019), chipping away at narrowly defined tasks and problems but unable to operate beyond the "frontier of [their] own design" (Diakopoulos, 2019, p. 243).

Machine learning, deep learning, predictive analytics, and neutral networks are some examples for such narrow AI that are currently in existence and applied in various contexts (Boden, 2018; Broussard, 2018, p. 33). Of these, machine learning (ML), in particular, is widely in use today and often meant when people talk about AI. As a branch of artificial intelligence, ML allows computer systems to learn directly from examples, data, and experience. Machine learning relies on algorithms[1] trained on large amounts of data to improve a system's performance on a narrowly defined task over time.

In this chapter, we focus on so-called "communicative AI" (Guzman & Lewis, 2020). This refers to AI technologies – such as conversational agents, social robots, and automated-writing software in the vein of ChatGPT – that are designed to function as *communicators*, rather than as merely *mediators* of human-to-human communication. Communicative AI may come in the form of AI applications or systems that are interpreted by human users as stand-alone communicators, as in the case of chatbots that are virtually indistinguishable from human communicators, or they may be designed to stand in the place of a human communicator within a particular process, as in the case of automated journalism software that

produces news stories *as if they were written by a human* (Lewis et al., 2019). Put another way, specific applications of AI can be seen as "communicative" even if not all AI are designed to function in that way.

Re-imagining the machine as a communicator, not merely as a channel, may sound like little more than a reorganization of the communication flowchart. But, as a growing number of scholars suggest, the ontological mismatch this poses for how we think about the roles and relationships of humans and machines requires a more fundamental reappraisal. As Guzman and Lewis (2020, p. 73) sum up, "AI devices designed as communicators – machine subjects *with* which people make meaning instead of *through* which people make meaning – do not fit into theories based on previous technologies designed as channels of human interaction."

It is in this spirit that Human–Machine Communication (HMC) offers a theoretical intervention. HMC, however, does not suggest that human–machine communication is the *same* as human–human communication, nor does it imply that machines are even *mostly* now situated in the role of communicators relative to their typical role as mediators of human-to-human exchange – for they clearly are not. Rather, HMC provides a fresh conceptual path for attempting to make sense of a future in which machines increasingly communicate, not merely mediate. This presents an opportunity for evaluating what HMC may have to offer for the study of AI and journalism.

EVALUATING AI IN JOURNALISM ON THREE KEY DIMENSIONS

One way to think about AI in journalism in the context of HMC is to adopt the framework outlined by Guzman and Lewis (2020) for evaluating AI and communication. They developed HMC as a concept and set forth a research agenda organized around three key elements of communicative AI technologies: (1) the *functional* dimensions, which capture both how these technologies work as well as how people make sense of these applications as communicators; (2) the *relational* or *social* dynamics, which point to how people associate with the technologies and, in turn, relate to themselves and others; and (3) the *metaphysical* or *ontological* dimensions, or questions around what constitutes human, machine, and communication amid blurring boundaries. Applying these to journalism, for example, allows us to more readily assess what it means functionally for how journalism works that AI technologies are situated in the role of communicators. It allows us to explore what it means relationally for newsworkers to develop a sense of identity and orientation in correspondence with tech-as-communicators being deployed in newsrooms – that is, how newsworkers come to see themselves vis-à-vis machines and others. And it allows us to consider how communicative AI may complicate ontological notions of how distinctly "human" (or not) journalism is intended to be. Using this approach, we can look at some concrete and still hypothetical (but conceivable) examples of AI in journalism for each of these categories, offering some suggestions for how these might be studied.

Functional Dimensions

First, from a *functional* standpoint, it matters to understand how AI-driven technologies may be shifting the way journalism works – how news is produced, distributed, and ultimately received by audiences – through the introduction of a new cast of communicators (machines) that are situated in roles normally associated with humans. This functional view draws our attention to the gatekeeping processes that shape how journalism is organized in carrying out its basic gathering, filtering, and disseminating functions (Tandoc, 2014).

On the side of the production of news, we are mainly talking about applications of AI that lead to greater efficiency in existing processes: for example, the automatic creation of short news items based on highly structured data of the variety found in sports results or company earnings reports (Carlson, 2015; Thurman, 2019), the use of NLP-driven speech-to-text technology to automatically provide voice-over tracks for video content in various languages, or the use of AI to create automatic interview transcripts for journalists (Marconi, 2020, p. 109). On the side of the distribution of news, this includes tools which, among other things, read news articles to readers (e.g., at German weekly *ZEIT*) or allow for a better understanding of audiences – for example, by using machine learning applications that segment users into distinct categories, forming the basis for customized offerings and a clearer sense of who the journalists are writing for (as demonstrated by the *South China Morning Post*). Notably, this category of efficiency-oriented tools includes software that communicates *to audiences* as if the material had been written or recorded by journalists themselves (e.g., automated news stories; see Lewis et al.,

2019, for discussion) as well as other software that communicates *to/with* journalists as if the technology were in the role of a human assistant (e.g., automated transcription; see Marconi, 2020, for other illustrations).

A second category of functional dimensions is composed of AI applications and approaches that allow newsworkers to do things that were previously impossible to achieve, given their scope and scale. This represents a speed and degree of news output that far surpasses the likes of "data journalism" or other longstanding techniques in applying computers to news. Examples here include *Reuters'* "NewsTracer," an in-house tool powered by machine learning that sifts through emerging topics on social media to determine if they are newsworthy and truthful. Other news organizations use similar applications that allow for the large-scale analysis of social media data and news coverage to monitor the public's curiosity around specific topics and deliver that information to journalists (Marconi, 2020, p. 141). Another example is "Perspective," an Application Programming Interface (API) developed by Jigsaw, a subsidiary of Google's parent company Alphabet, that uses machine learning to identify toxic and hateful comments. Perspective is used to aid and enable content moderation at scale by news outlets including *The Wall Street Journal*, *The New York Times*, *Le Monde*, and *El País*. All these examples describe tasks that could (or have been) carried out by humans, but often with severe limitations (especially in terms of scope and scale).

The possibilities for studying these functional aspects are rich. Qualitative and quantitative work should investigate (for example, through interviews and ethnographies, surveys, and experiments) how journalists and audiences respond to and think about these applications. There is already a growing body of literature that studies how people perceive the credibility and readability of automated journalism (e.g., Graefe & Bohlken, 2020). What remains lacking, however, is a corresponding set of analyses that attempt to untangle the social implications of whether and how people are aware of machines as communicators in journalism. How does it make a difference to the authority and trustworthiness of the press, for example, if consumers come to associate the creation or circulating of the news as being directed by AI rather than human journalists? Ultimately, to more carefully capture the practical and conceptual consequences of AI in journalism, research would benefit from greater collaboration with industry (both news outlets and technology vendors) to get a better picture of the situation through internal analyses of usage data, software code, and human–machine interactions, altogether bringing these functional dimensions more fully into view.

Relational or Social Dimensions

Second, turning the attention to the *relational* or *social* dimensions, we follow Guzman and Lewis (2020) in acknowledging that it is through communication that people forge relationships with one another and that society as a whole is constituted. Indeed, human interactions, at the individual level and aggregated up at the level of society, can be seen as an unfolding set of social encounters through which people develop a sense of self (who am I?) and a sense of others (who are they?).

But do these same outcomes hold for human–machine communication? First, it is important to recognize that, long before the present interest in AI, technology has from the beginning been modeled on human social roles – e.g., as "assistants" that often follow certain gendered norms and cues to align with stereotypes of human helpers (Suchman, 2007). This process of anthropomorphizing (i.e., attributing humanlike features, traits, and behaviors to non-human agents; see Epley et al., 2007) has been demonstrated for both technologies in general and for AI more specifically (Salles et al., 2020; Watson, 2019). In that sense, perhaps it's not surprising that much of the journalism trade-press discourse (and even some of the academic discussion, too) surrounding the rise of automated news has tended to characterize newswriting software in embodied terms, describing these tools as "robot journalists" – complete with images of fedora-wearing androids smoking pipes while pounding away at keyboards (Oremus, 2015) – even though robots are never involved and the template-writing functions performed are limited to but one aspect of a journalist's role (see Carlson, 2015).[2]

The more salient consideration here is how AI-inflected forms of journalism might, to some degree, reset the social expectations on which journalism has been established – from the machine–consumer relationship, on the one hand, to the machine–journalist relationship, on the other (Lewis et al., 2019). For example, depending on how people come to imagine forms of AI (both in general and specifically as communicators they turn to for information), and depending on how thoroughly they appreciate that such technologies are involved in producing news (in partnership with or in replacement of a human journalist), that may well have consequences for how news consumers perceive the world and their place in it relative to their machine interlocutors.

In a similar vein, what are the implications of communicative AI for the shifting social roles of journalists – for how journalists imagine themselves, their machine counterparts, and the communicative work between them? At the moment, we find ourselves in a situation where news organizations and journalists have certain expectations and fears about what AI is, and what it will do for and to them – expectations that are not necessarily rooted in the actual reality of such technologies. These "imaginaries," or expectations, nevertheless matter insofar as they can shape incentives to adopt or invest in AI applications (Brennen et al., 2020), and to the degree they influence how journalists think about the use of AI in the news more broadly and how it will affect them – both in a positive and a negative sense. By at least one account, some journalists express optimism that emerging tools will augment their journalistic roles rather than disrupt them (Schapals & Porlezza, 2020). But there are other longstanding fears about automation's impact on employment that are shared across industries. The fear of being (partially or fully) replaced by technology is not new to the field of journalism. But the threat – however realistic, given that in most cases AI is not fully autonomous and requires human supervision – of a new technology performing a human's tasks with greater efficiency has the potential to lead newsworkers to question their identity, value, and role in modern news organizations (Carlson, 2015; Lewis et al., 2019; Morikawa, 2017).

Ultimately, the social and relational dynamics of AI and journalism gesture to the important role of *perceptions* developed about oneself and others. The ongoing rollout of communicative AI may indeed constitute an ontological shift in journalism, as we discuss in the next section. This, in turn, has implications for how a variety of stakeholders – most prominently but not exclusively journalists – relate to these technologies even before such a shift has fully occurred, regardless of how warranted their hopes, fears, or imaginations may be. As Lewis and colleagues (2019) argue, it might not yet be clear "to what extent existing and emerging technologies will displace people from what were thought to be distinctly human roles within journalism," but that it *will* happen to some extent seems to be a given. What remains to be determined is how people respond in kind. Researchers can track these changes in perceptions about AI using traditional qualitative interviews, as several scholars already have done (e.g., Jamil, 2021), but perhaps more novel approaches are warranted – with corresponding possibilities for the wider development of social science research in the AI era. For example, consider how AI-powered chatbots, which are increasingly human-like, are used to deliver news and engage with audiences in forms of "conversational journalism" (Shin, 2022). Could the same types of tools also be turned inward and used for social research, acting as machine-based research assistants that gather qualitative data through interviewing techniques (see Hasler, Tuchman, & Friedman, 2013)? Or, as Araujo (2020) has shown via the Conversational Agent Research Toolkit (CART), chatbots can be programmed to simulate different forms of conversation to offer diverse forms of stimuli in experimental studies. Such approaches would not be exclusive to journalism research, because of their wide-ranging applicability in capturing qualitative and quantitative forms of human perception. And yet one could imagine that such bots could provide a fresh way of assessing, say, the relative trustworthiness or credibility that news consumers perceive in AI-oriented news. The upshot, whether in news research or beyond, would mean a rather meta approach to studying human–machine communication *through* human–machine communication. Bot-based research, even if not widely adopted, could serve as a heuristic for reimagining broadly the potential social interactions between human and machine.

Metaphysical or Ontological Dimensions

Third, as we suggested earlier, AI in journalism and communication should be considered in terms of its potential to reshape or stir up *metaphysical* or *ontological* dimensions and distinctions around how distinctly "human" (or not) journalism is intended or ought to be. On one level, this is a debate about communication theory. "In a domino-like effect," Lewis and colleagues (2019, p. 421) write, "the placement of a communicative technology into a role previously occupied by a human draws into question every other aspect of theory and elements of practice built upon the core assumption of humans as communicators." But on another level, this is not merely an abstract philosophical question; rather, it influences an array of issues surrounding technology design, ethical norms, and social expectations.

Indeed, we raise the point of ontology because already we can see examples "in the wild" where communicative AI is blurring the boundaries between the two. Consider, for instance, how *The New York Times*, in response to the COVID-19 pandemic, launched in 2020 a Q&A tool that uses natural-language processing to connect readers with answers to their questions about the pandemic. While the system is still in development, the initial

audience response indicates that users treat the application (at least to some extent) as if it were human, "not only submitting full questions, but at times, entire paragraphs," as the developers describe it (Pisapia et al., 2020). An increasing number of news organizations have also started to introduce (partly) AI-written formats, as in the case of *The Washington Post's* Heliograf tool that is described as the newspaper's "artificial intelligence system" and which for a time was used to produce novel forms of results about sports and politics. In a yet bolder move, the *Guardian* and other news organizations have begun to play with (however fancifully) the possibilities of GPT-3, a language generator developed by the software company OpenAI that uses machine learning to produce text as if out of thin air. GPT-3's successor, ChatGPT, introduced in late 2022, has in some ways supercharged this development. Responding to prompts written by humans, this AI is able to create, among other things, forms of prose – including poetry and fiction as well as news-like articles – that seem uncannily "real." Various news organisations continue to experiment with the generator, with BuzzFeed even announcing that it plans to integrate it into its production routines.

These developments have raised questions not only about notions of authorship but also about journalistic transparency and the role and response of audiences to such news products. This begins with the issue of who (or what) produced the content and how their contribution should be acknowledged in bylines (Montal & Reich, 2017; Tandoc et al., 2020), but it extends also to thornier matters about whether and how news consumers should be informed that a piece of news was wholly or partially produced by automation or machine learning. Consider, for example, the findings of a recent meta-analysis, which examined 12 experiment-based studies involving nearly 4,500 participants, tracking perceptions of news credibility, quality, and readability. Graefe and Bohlken (2020, p. 50) found that overall there was "no difference in readers' perceptions of credibility, a small advantage for human-written news in terms of quality, and a huge advantage for human-written news with respect to readability." But they also found that study participants tended to provide higher ratings for credibility, quality, and readability when they were informed that a human was the author. These results, the researchers conclude, might encourage news outlets to avoid disclosing that a story was created by machine. This underscores not only the ethical challenges of automated journalism as it exists now but points to vexing problems that will arise in the future as AI plays an even larger role in multiple aspects of news work, displacing or augmenting communicative roles that audiences associate with humans. An HMC perspective, by orienting researchers to the ontological dimensions of humans and machines in communication, can open up an array of such moral, normative, and philosophical questions that will become more pressing for AI-infused forms of work in the future (Gunkel, 2012; Guzman & Lewis, 2020).

CONCLUSION

Amid the rapid development of AI in journalism and other media industries, there has been a relative dearth of theories that help explain these dynamics and their effects. New models will need to be developed or existing ones adapted to make sense of the shift that is underway with the rise of communicative AI and its influences within news production, distribution, and consumption. Our chapter has sought to explain what Human–Machine Communication as a conceptual perspective might offer this conversation, not merely in terms of how AI shifts journalistic practice – which has been the focus of most reports, conferences, and trade press so far (e.g., Beckett, 2019; Marconi, 2020) – but more holistically in how it forces us to confront questions about roles and relationships of humans and machines, and the very essence of what it means to communicate (Lewis et al., 2019).

As an orienting framework, HMC allows researchers to more comprehensively map the dynamics and implications of machines as communicators (rather than merely machines as mediators), particularly at a moment when the meaning-making possibilities of human–machine encounters have become more readily visible through communicative AI. To test the strengths of this approach, we evaluated the application of AI in journalism through functional, relational/social, and metaphysical/ontological dimensions. Each dimension provides a different perspective on the potential outcomes not just of AI's use as a tool, but rather of its growing incorporation *as a communicator*, one that may augment human communication in some instances, replace it in others, and ultimately lend significantly greater "voice" to so-called "mute" technologies (Guzman, 2016). The importance of HMC for interpreting communicative AI, therefore, is evident in how it brings to the fore questions that may otherwise be overlooked from an anthropocentric paradigm – questions about what it means to be human and what it means to forge meaning, relationships, and sociality through communication.

Beyond these strengths, however, certain limitations to the HMC framework also become apparent when applied to the context of AI and journalism. This may be a function, in part, of the relatively limited theorizing on HMC and journalism thus far (Guzman & Lewis, 2020; Lewis et al., 2019). Or, it may be indicative of some limitations inherent to HMC that warrant further exploration. For example, HMC seems to more easily apply to studying micro encounters, those occurring between (individual) humans and machines, rather than to the macro influences that, in the case of journalism and the news industry, are likely to be much more consequential. Such macro forces include an overall media landscape in flux through increasing digitalization, the continuing decline of traditional business models, the influence of state actors and regulatory bodies, and the structural control exerted by major technology companies (Simon, 2022), to name a few. Likewise, the potential economic implications of AI for news organizations and the business of the news do not sit easily within an HMC framework, especially in those contexts where AI merely acts as a 'means to an end' to drive efficiencies in production and distribution as well as increasing revenue. Additionally, setting aside matters of economics and efficiency, there are vital questions about what AI-powered news means for journalism's commitment to serving democracy, but it is yet unclear how HMC figures into normative analyses like that offered by Lin and Lewis (2022). While it is worthwhile, as we have argued, to focus on how journalists are rethinking themselves and their relationships on account of communicative technologies, or on how news audiences may be doing the same, we also must acknowledge that these trends likely rank below these far larger, more influential structural aspects as well as these more fundamental normative concerns. What emerges, then, is a simultaneous need for more robust theorizing about HMC in the realm of journalism as well as further investigation into how the case of journalism gestures to the need for HMC scholars to more fully account for macro dynamics relative to micro interactions in their research.

Another question that has yet to be borne out by the evidence will be HMC's value, not just to the community of scholars concerned with the study of journalism and the news, but to the objects of analysis: the news organizations and journalists whose work (and relationship to technology) HMC sets out to study. While notions of popular value should not be the sole judgment criteria for any epistemic undertaking such as this, HMC, just as any other strand of scholarship, has to ask itself who it is for and what it has to offer to those it seeks to understand – and, ultimately, if this offering is in line with the needs of these communities.

NOTES

1 An algorithm can be described as a finite sequence of well-defined, computer-implementable instructions, typically to solve a class of problems or to perform a computation.

2 In their critique of the "robot journalism" metaphor, Lindén and Dierickx (2019) also point to the potential harmfulness of the same when it comes to the development of automated approaches in the news as it furthers notions that robots are "coming to take the jobs," thus distracting from a more realistic future of augmented journalism in which software plays a supportive rather than a supplanting role.

REFERENCES

Araujo, T. (2020). Conversational Agent Research Toolkit: An alternative for creating and managing chatbots for experimental research. *Computational Communication Research*, 2(1), 35–51. Retrieved from https://computationalcommunication.org/ccr/article/view/9

Beckett, C. (2019). *New powers, new responsibilities. A global survey of journalism and artificial intelligence*. Polis. London School of Economics. https://blogs.lse.ac.uk/polis/2019/11/18/new-powers-new-responsibilities/

Boden, M. A. (2018). *Artificial Intelligence. A Very Short Introduction*. Oxford University Press.

Brennen, J. S., Howard, P. N., & Nielsen, R. K. (2019). *An Industry-Led Debate: How UK Media Cover Artificial Intelligence* (Reuters Institute Report, p. 10). Reuters Institute for the Study of Journalism. https://reutersinstitute.politics.ox.ac.uk/sites/default/files/2018-12/Brennen_UK_Media_Coverage_of_AI_FINAL.pdf

Brennen, J. S., Howard, P. N., & Nielsen, R. K. (2020). What to expect when you're expecting robots: Futures, expectations, and pseudo-artificial general intelligence in UK news. *Journalism*, 0(0), 1–17. https://doi.org/10.1177/1464884920947535

Broussard, M. (2018). *Artificial Unintelligence. How Computers Misunderstand the World*. (1st ed.). MIT Press.

Carlson, M. (2015). The robotic reporter: Automated journalism and the redefinition of labor, compositional forms, and journalistic authority. *Digital Journalism*, 3(3), 416–431. https://doi.org/10.1080/21670811.2014.976412

Diakopoulos, N. (2019). *Automating the News: How Algorithms Are Rewriting the Media*. Harvard University Press.

Epley, N., Waytz, A., & Cacioppo, J. T. (2007). On seeing human: A three-factor theory of anthropomorphism. *Psychological Review*, 114(4), 864–886. https://doi.org/10.1037/0033-295X.114.4.864

Graefe, A., & Bohlken, N. (2020). Automated journalism: A meta-analysis of readers' perceptions of human-written in comparison to automated news. *Media and Communication*, 8(3), 50–59. https://doi.org/10.17645/mac.v8i3.3019

Gunkel, D. J. (2012). Communication and artificial intelligence: Opportunities and challenges for the 21st century. *Communication+1*, 1(1), 1–25.

Guzman, A. L. (2016). The messages of mute machines: Human-Machine Communication with industrial technologies. *Communication+1*, 5(1), 1–31.

Guzman, A. L. (2018). Human-Machine Communication: Rethinking communication, technology, and ourselves. In A. L. Guzman (Ed.), *What Is Human-Machine Communication, Anyway?* (pp. 1–28). Peter Lang. www.peterlang.com/view/9781433142536/xhtml/fm_introduction.xhtml

Guzman, A. L., & Lewis, S. C. (2020). Artificial intelligence and communication: A Human–Machine Communication research agenda. *New Media & Society*, 22(1), 70–86. https://doi.org/10.1177/1461444819858691

Hasler, B. S., Tuchman, P., & Friedman, D. (2013). Virtual research assistants: Replacing human interviewers by automated avatars in virtual worlds. *Computers in Human Behavior*, 29(4), 1608–1616.

Jamil, S. (2020). Artificial intelligence and journalistic practice: The crossroads of obstacles and opportunities for the Pakistani journalists. *Journalism Practice*, 15(10), 1400–1422. https://doi.org/10.1080/17512786.2020.1788412

Lin, B., & Lewis, S. C. (2022). The one thing journalistic AI just might do for democracy. *Digital Journalism*, 10(10), 1627–1649. https://doi.org/10.1080/21670811.2022.2084131

Lewis, S. C., Guzman, A. L., & Schmidt, T. R. (2019). Automation, journalism, and Human–Machine Communication: Rethinking roles and relationships of humans and machines in news. *Digital Journalism*, 7(4), 409–427. https://doi.org/10.1080/21670811.2019.1577147

Lindén, C.-G., & Dierickx, L. (2019). Robot journalism: The damage done by a metaphor. *UnMediated. Journal of Politics and Communication*, 2(1), 152–155.

Marconi, F. (2020). *Newsmakers: Artificial Intelligence and the Future of Journalism*. Columbia University Press.

Mitchell, M. (2019). *Artificial Intelligence: A Guide for Thinking Humans*. Pelican.

Montal, T., & Reich, Z. (2017). I, robot. You, journalist. Who is the author? *Digital Journalism*, 5(7), 829–849. https://doi.org/10.1080/21670811.2016.1209083

Morikawa, M. (2017). *Who Are Afraid of Losing Their Jobs to Artificial Intelligence and Robots? Evidence from a Survey* (No. 71; GLO Discussion Paper Series). Global Labor Organization (GLO). https://ideas.repec.org/p/zbw/glodps/71.html

Oremus, W. (2015, February 5). "Robots" are now writing news stories. but let's stop calling them robots. *Slate Magazine.* https://slate.com/technology/2015/02/automated-insights-ap-earnings-reports-robot-journalists-a-misnomer.html

Pisapia, A., Chava, A. J., & Porter, L. Z. (2020, December 21). Prioritizing human perspectives in natural language processing. *The New York Times - Research & Development.* https://rd.nytimes.com/projects/prioritizing-human-perspectives-in-natural-language-processing

Salles, A., Evers, K., & Farisco, M. (2020). Anthropomorphism in AI. *AJOB Neuroscience, 11*(2), 88–95. https://doi.org/10.1080/21507740.2020.1740350

Schapals, A. K., & Porlezza, C. (2020). Assistance or resistance? Evaluating the intersection of automated journalism and journalistic role conceptions. *Media and Communication, 8*(3), 16–26.

Shin, D. (2021). The perception of humanness in conversational journalism: An algorithmic information-processing perspective. *New Media & Society, 24*(12), 2680–2704. https://doi.org/10.1177/1461444821993801

Shoemaker, P. J., & Reese, S. D. (2013). *Mediating the Message in the 21st Century: A Media Sociology Perspective.* Routledge. www.taylorfrancis.com/books/mediating-message-21st-century-pamela-shoemaker-stephen-reese/10.4324/9780203930434

Simon, F. M. (2022). Uneasy bedfellows: AI in the news, platform companies and the issue of journalistic autonomy. *Digital Journalism, 10*(10), 1832–1854. https://doi.org/10.1080/21670811.2022.2063150

Suchman, L. A. (2007). *Human-machine Reconfigurations: Plans and Situated Actions.* Cambridge University Press.

Tandoc, E. C. (2014). Journalism is twerking? How web analytics is changing the process of gatekeeping. *New Media & Society, 16*(4), 559–575. https://doi.org/10.1177/1461444814530541

Tandoc, E. C., Yao, L. J., & Wu, S. (2020). Man vs. machine? The impact of algorithm authorship on news credibility. *Digital Journalism, 8*(4), 548–562. https://doi.org/10.1080/21670811.2020.1762102

Thurman, N. (2019). Computational journalism. In K. Wahl-Jorgensen & T. Hanitzsch (Eds.), *The Handbook of Journalism Studies* (2nd ed.). Routledge.

Watson, D. (2019). The rhetoric and reality of anthropomorphism in artificial intelligence. *Minds and Machines, 29*(3), 417–440. https://doi.org/10.1007/s11023-019-09506-6

Wilks, Y. (2020). *Artificial intelligence. Modern magic or dangerous future.* Icon Books.

61

Human–Machine Communication in Marketing and Advertising

Weizi Liu and Mike Z. Yao

INTRODUCTION

Most digital advertisements are delivered by computer algorithms based on individuals' preferences and habits today. Companies send personalized and context-specific messages to customers at designated locations in their moment of need. Virtual assistants can evaluate and filter product information autonomously and make recommendations. Within these contexts, the digital media systems, as the "machines," act as communication agents instead of mediums.

To marketers and advertisers, machines create new ways of reaching and communicating with consumers. To consumers, machines bring convenience and choices, although at a high cost of personal privacy and solitude. To researchers, recognizing machines' active roles in advertising and marketing communication allows deep integration of theoretical knowledge generated in fields such as interpersonal communication, computer-mediated communication, and human–computer interaction into advertising and marketing research.

Before the digital age, advertisers relied on a small number of media channels to reach and influence large groups of potential consumers. The World Wide Web freed advertisers from heavy reliance on professional media institutions. The complex systems of computer hardware, software, data, and algorithms involved in digital advertising are not only conduits of marketing messages but also active participants in a multi-directional communication process throughout the consumer journey (Jones, 2018; Kietzmann et al., 2018; Kumar & Gupta, 2016).

BEHAVIORAL TARGETING AND COMPUTATIONAL ADVERTISING

Media audiences in the digital age actively consume media content in a digitally mediated space instead of passively processing messages delivered via specific channels (Chi, 2011; Joines et al., 2003; Ko et al., 2005). Consumers' digital interactions are recorded and tracked. Such information is used for targeting in personalized messaging. Online behavioral advertising (OBA), also as known as behavioral targeting (Bennett, 2010), leverages user data and generates profiles based on their habits, interests, preferences, etc. (Smit et al., 2014; van Noort et al., 2020) and provide relevant advertisements to the target audience (Ham & Nelson, 2016; McDonald & Cranor, 2010; Nill & Aalberts, 2014).

Behavioral targeting is achieved through programmatic media buying. Together, computing systems – ad servers, demand-side platforms (DSPs), supply-side platforms (SSPs), and data management platforms – make instantaneous decisions about where to show an ad, when, to whom, and at what cost. The multiple layers of machines behind computational (programmatic) advertising may not directly interface with media end users, but they actively determine what information people receive and how they receive it. Computational advertising brings a paradigm shift throughout the entire advertising process (Yang et al., 2017). It affects marketing analysis, campaign planning, content creation and placement, and evaluation (Araujo et al., 2020; Helberger et al., 2020; Huh & Malthous, 2020; Liu-Thompkins et al., 2020; van Noort et al., 2020; Yun et al., 2020).

SEARCH ENGINES AND SEARCH MARKETING

Search engines are a primary example of machines in HMC. Search engine marketing (SEM) promotes websites by increasing or maintaining their rankings in search engine result pages (SERPs) (Dou et al., 2010; Sen, 2005). Unlike display advertising, search-based advertising is initiated by input from the consumers instead of the advertisers. This departure is significant because it shifts the power in advertising from the media to the audience.

Search engines not only display but also curate information in such a way that would influence a user's decisions and behavior. Such technological affordances (Sundar et al., 2015) can alter users' evaluation of the quality of the search results. Search engines that offer relevant results were rated with greater credibility than those that provide non-relevant results as of the effect of the similarity heuristic (Kalyanaraman & Ivory, 2009). Top-ranking search results were more likely to be selected and elicit higher perceived content credibility than those lower-ranking content (Pan et al., 2007; Westerwick, 2013). Search engines themselves are also a source of information and lend credibility to the information they display.

The reliance on using search engines to find information can also lead to an illusion of internal knowledge among the users. Users who rely on search engines to acquire information tend to misattribute the "knowledge" from the internet to themselves (Fisher et al., 2015; Ward, 2013). Hamilton and Yao (2018) confirmed this effect

and found the efficacy of the external knowledge sources increased participants' self-evaluations of personal knowledge. To the users, smart devices are both machines that perform specific functions as well as extensions of themselves (Belk, 1988; Park & Kaye, 2019). The dynamics between smart digital devices and human users are both cognitive and communicative.

MOBILE COMMUNICATION AND CONTEXTUAL MARKETING

For advertisers, the rapid and broad-based adoption of mobile communication offers unprecedented opportunities for contextual marketing. Contextual marketing is about strategically controlling the timing and location of message delivery to provide more relevant information to the consumers (Kenny & Marshall, 2000). It also accounts for the unique personality and history of each customer. Considering the context of communication is critical to the success of digital marketing because the right context gives prospective customers a more personalized and relatable experience, increasing purchases and enhancing customer retention (Lee & Jun, 2007; Luo & Seyedian, 2003).

Contextual marketing enabled by mobile communication is more ubiquitous and efficient. Via mobile devices, businesses and advertisers can deliver personalized messages to target consumers when they arrive at a specific location (Rust & Lemon, 2001). Location-based advertising relies on geolocation data from smartphones, GPS data, web browser cookies, and location beacon and geofencing technologies to locate target consumers. The consumer experience in contextual and location-based marketing involves interactions among human users, their devices, the environment, and the communication message. In these interactions, machines are more sophisticated and considerate communicators which take into account multiple situational factors about consumers and environments.

DIGITAL ASSISTANTS AND CONVERSATIONAL MARKETING

The ability of machines to mimic humans and carry out natural conversations with consumers is a significant landmark in advertising and marketing. Computer agents can autonomously make sales calls, send personalized messages (Haselton, 2018), and engage customers on social media platforms (Appel et al., 2020). Chatbots provide efficient ways for businesses to serve their customers, including providing information, solving immediate problems, and maintaining customer relationships (Følstad et al., 2018; Xu et al., 2017). Digital assistants such as Alexa, Siri, and Google Assistant are welcomed on consumers' personal devices, vehicles, and their domestic spaces, making the interactive experience convenient and accessible in various contexts (Brill et al., 2019). Robots, acting as sales representatives, roam around retail stores to help customers find and select merchandise (Bertacchini et al., 2017). Research has shown that the humanlike features (e.g., human names, voices, images, language styles, etc.) of digital assistants and anthropomorphism can significantly impact users' attitudes, trust, satisfaction, emotional connections, expectations, motivations to interact with them (Araujo, 2018; Chérif & Lemoine, 2019; Fraune et al., 2020; Go & Sundar, 2019; Seeger & Heinzl, 2018).

The communicative processes between human users and digital assistants could follow the principles of interpersonal communication. A critical concern here is a blurring boundary between computer applications performing human tasks and human-like machines functioning as social agents (e.g., Ferrari et al., 2016; Seeber et al., 2020). While existing theories of computer-mediated communication (CMC) and human–computer interaction (HCI) focus on human perception and psychological processes to explain the computers-as-social-agent (CASA) effect (Nass & Moon, 2000; Reeves & Nass, 1996), researchers are confronted with the fact that computers are not just "treated" by human users as social agents, they are truly becoming social agents (Guzman, 2020; Guzman & Lewis, 2020). This perspective, however, has yet to be articulated in advertising and marketing research and empirically examined.

BEYOND THE MEDIA SCREENS

With a near-universal adoption of mobile communication, the growing coverage of the Internet of Things (IoT), and the maturation of new digital display technologies such as 3D hologram and augmented reality (AR), digital advertisers are looking beyond the screened devices to engage consumers in digital out-of-home (DOOH) marketing campaigns. Smart personal devices, smart city networks, and ad servers can deliver personalized messages to targeted consumers in various outdoor locations. Driven by data from passers-by's smartphones, wearable devices, and vehicles, billboard ads and window displays can change in real-time and individually target each passing consumer (Aksu et al., 2018; Benes, 2021; Huang et al., 2019; Seitz & Zorn, 2016). Smart displays, billboards, and digital furniture can also detect a consumer's age and gender with facial recognition technologies (Gillespie, 2019) and react to customers' interests based on where their eyes gaze on the screen (Bazrafkan et al., 2015). Advanced digital display technologies such as interactive touchscreens, 3D surface projection, holograms, and AR can also bring novelty to plain old outdoor displays, making the content more engaging and realistic (She et al., 2014). From the HMC perspective, the leap from passing crowds seeing advertisements shown in out-of-home spaces to individual consumers being "approached" by and engaging with intelligent machines is what defines the future of DOOH.

THEORETICAL IMPLICATIONS AND FUTURE RESEARCH

The increasingly dynamic and highly contextualized HMC experience forces researchers to look beyond issues of message processing in advertising research. Existing empirical research in advertising followed the media effects research paradigm to focus on the effects of specific types of media content and context on the audience's social and psychological processes (c.f., Oliver et al., 2020). Researchers were concerned with how media audiences cognitively and emotionally process the advertising messages and the subsequent effects on their memory, emotions, attitudes, and behaviors. Theories such as social cognition (Kardes et al., 2005), the limited capacity model of motivated mediated message Processing (LC4MP) (Lang, 2000), and extended parallel processing (Maloney et al., 2011) were the dominant perspectives. Although some researchers have examined the influence of media devices, platforms, and contexts in advertising message processing (Duff & Segijn, 2019; Malthouse et al., 2007; Song et al., 2020; Voorveld et al., 2018), the active role of digital machines has not been the main subject in this body of research.

In 2020, Americans had access to more than ten connected devices per household. Each person has access to more than two computers and more than two mobile phones on average (Statista, 2021). These devices constantly compete for our attention at the individual level. Although advertising researchers have extensively studied the phenomenon of media multitasking in recent years (Duff & Segijn, 2019), this growing body of research still narrowly focuses on media devices as carriers of information. The impacts of machine agency and the dynamic relationships between human users and the devices were understudied. The phenomenon of media multitasking in advertising and marketing should extend beyond mediated-message processing in TV viewing and web browsing. A more appropriate analogy for the digital communication experience today would be a person engaging in and keeping track of multiple conversations with several people at a party. In such a context, the media-effects approaches may not fully capture the dynamics of digital communication. Future research should not only focus on the cognitive processes in ad viewing but also the communication processes of human–media interaction.

In media advertising, an implicit assumption has always been that the advertisers and creative professionals and the advertising messages bear the persuasive intent. Even though media researchers have recognized that media systems have the power to shape human lives and are an inseparable part of the message (McLuhan, 1994), the role of media technologies in persuasive communication has been passive and contextual. Today, however, machines have become active persuaders (Berdichevsky & Neuenschwander, 1999). AI-enabled systems engage consumers in an interpersonal-like manner and operate on behalf of a communicator by modifying, augmenting, or generating messages to accomplish communication goals (Hancock et al., 2020). Instead of passively delivering advertisements, intelligent media systems autonomously evaluate, screen, and adapt the information and actively make suggestions to the consumers about what to buy, where to buy, and how to buy. Consumers can be influenced by machines' ideas unconsciously when they make their seemingly "own" choices. For example, the recommendation systems not only provide personalized recommendations of the user's interests but also let users believe the recommendations are the optimal choices for them (Hamilton et al., 2020). While it gives the illusion of choice, the machines themselves have become the influencers, if not the manipulators, of consumer behavior (Fogg, 2002; Hamari et al., 2014). The rise of such intelligent machines has behavioral, social, cultural, and ethical implications in many social contexts, including advertising and marketing communication. Only when the researchers begin to see advertising media systems as the persuaders can these issues be adequately addressed.

IMPACTS ON THE ADVERTISING AND MARKETING INDUSTRIES

Advertising production and buying are evolving because of the application of AI and computational methods in specific procedures (Lee & Cho, 2020). As existing investigations of HMC in advertising and marketing are usually restricted to communication between machines and consumers, what about the communication between machines and marketers and advertisers as the humans who are using and manipulating the machines? Are these processes also part of HMC but are missing from our current discussion? These questions draw our attention to the information exchange and meaning-making processes between marketers and machines besides the overly emphasized parts between consumers and machines.

Another important consideration is the economic impact of HMC, which focuses on the changing landscape of future jobs within the industry. While automation has improved business performance in advertising and many other industries (e.g., Mahmoud et al., 2020; Murphy, 2018; Schwabe & Castellacci, 2020), there is a common and legitimate concern that existing jobs would be replaced by machines. However, most industry experts believe that a shift towards AI and automation will not necessarily take massive jobs from advertising and marketing workers, but rather change the demand for new skills and task types (Davenport et al., 2020; Digital Marketing Institute, 2018; Paril, 2020). Human touch is still needed in creating, monitoring, and optimizing the technologies behind the human–machine communication processes. People who can understand, interpret and communicate the data generated from human–machine communication processes are also in great demand. The quality and creativity of the content generated automatically are still being questioned, because the machines may not be mature enough and require more technical improvements and evaluations (van Noort et al., 2020).

CONCLUSION

Advertising has historically been treated as a subdiscipline of mass communication. The wide applications and rapid proliferation of intelligent machines in advertising and marketing communication contexts force researchers to re-evaluate fundamental assumptions about media technologies and systems in advertising and marketing activities. In this chapter, we first reviewed the existing machines in several central areas of digital marketing and advertising. We then briefly discussed the necessity and value of adopting an HMC perspective on research and practice. The HMC perspective provides a new angle to examine the new phenomena, adding up to the traditional approaches. We also pintpointed some pressing questions such as what appropriate research paradigms we should use in advertising and marketing research and what roles we should consider for the machines involved in advertising and marketing activities. Besides, there are more issues to discuss including the social influence of HMC in advertising and marketing and the ethical debates regarding algorithm bias, surveillance, privacy, etc. Our chapter is by no means an exhaustive review of the literature in this area, nor was this our goal. Given its broad scope and holistic approach, the application of HMC in advertising is an intellectual conversation yet to be engaged by researchers. We merely point to the direction of an untapped research area.

REFERENCES

Aksu, H., Babun, L., Conti, M., Tolomei, G., & Uluagac, A. S. (2018). Advertising in the IoT era: Vision and challenges. *IEEE Communications Magazine*, *56*(11), 138–144.

Appel, G., Grewal, L., Hadi, R., & Stephen, A. T. (2020). The future of social media in marketing. *Journal of the Academy of Marketing Science*, *48*(1), 79–95.

Araujo, T. (2018). Living up to the chatbot hype: The influence of anthropomorphic design cues and communicative agency framing on conversational agent and company perceptions. *Computers in Human Behavior*, *85*, 183–189. https://doi.org/10.1016/j.chb.2018.03.051

Araujo, T., Copulsky, J. R., Hayes, J. L., Kim, S. J., & Srivastava, J. (2020). From purchasing exposure to fostering engagement: Brand–consumer experiences in the emerging computational advertising landscape. *Journal of Advertising*, *49*(4), 428–445.

Bazrafkan, S., Kar, A., & Costache, C. (2015). Eye gaze for consumer electronics: Controlling and commanding intelligent systems. *IEEE Consumer Electronics Magazine*, *4*(4), 65–71.

Belk, R. W. (1988). Possessions and the extended self. *Journal of Consumer Research*, *15*(2), 139–168.

Benbasat, I., & Wang, W. (2005). Trust in and adoption of online recommendation agents. *Journal of the Association for Information Systems*, *6*(3), 72–101.

Benes, R. (2021). Out-of-home advertising is becoming more digitally driven. *Insider Intelligence | eMarketer*. Retrieved February 10, 2021, from www.emarketer.com/content/out-of-home-advertising-becoming-more-digital-driven

Bennett, S. C. (2010). Regulating online behavioral advertising. *J. Marshall L. Rev.*, *44*, 899.

Berdichevsky, D., & Neuenschwander, E. (1999). Toward an ethics of persuasive technology. *Communications of the ACM*, *42*(5), 51–58.

Bertacchini, F., Bilotta, E., & Pantano, P. (2017). Shopping with a robotic companion. *Computers in Human Behavior*, *77*, 382–395.

Brill, T. M., Munoz, L., & Miller, R. J. (2019). Siri, Alexa, and other digital assistants: A study of customer satisfaction with artificial intelligence applications. *Journal of Marketing Management*, *35*(15–16), 1401–1436.

Chérif, E., & Lemoine, J. F. (2019). Anthropomorphic virtual assistants and the reactions of Internet users: An experiment on the assistant's voice. *Recherche et Applications en Marketing (English Edition)*, *34*(1), 28–47.

Chi, H. H. (2011). Interactive digital advertising vs. virtual brand community: Exploratory study of user motivation and social media marketing responses in Taiwan. *Journal of Interactive Advertising*, *12*(1), 44–61.

Davenport, T., Guha, A., Grewal, D., & Bressgott, T. (2020). How artificial intelligence will change the future of marketing. *Journal of the Academy of Marketing Science*, *48*(1), 24–42.

Digital Marketing Institute. (2018, October 18). *The Impact of Automation on Digital Marketing Jobs*. https://digitalmarketinginstitute.com/blog/the-impact-of-automation-on-digital-marketing-jobs.

Dou, W., Lim, K. H., Su, C., Zhou, N., & Cui, N. (2010). Brand positioning strategy using search engine marketing. *MIS Quarterly*, 261–279.

Duff, B. R., & Segijn, C. M. (2019). Advertising in a media multitasking era: Considerations and future directions. *Journal of Advertising*, *48*(1), 27–37.

Ferrari, F., Paladino, M. P., & Jetten, J. (2016). Blurring human–machine distinctions: Anthropomorphic appearance in social robots as a threat to human distinctiveness. *International Journal of Social Robotics*, *8*(2), 287–302.

Fisher, M., Goddu, M. K., & Keil, F. C. (2015). Searching for explanations: How the Internet inflates estimates of internal knowledge. *Journal of Experimental Psychology: General*, *144*(3), 674–687. https://doi.org/10.1037/xge0000070

Fogg, B. J. (2002). *Persuasive technology: Using computers to change what we think and do.* https://doi.org/10.1016/B978-1-55860-643-2.X5000-8

Følstad, A., Nordheim, C. B., & Bjørkli, C. A. (2018, October). What makes users trust a chatbot for customer service? An exploratory interview study. In *International conference on internet science* (pp. 194–208). Springer.

Fraune, M. R., Oisted, B. C., Sembrowski, C. E., Gates, K. A., Krupp, M. M., & Šabanović, S. (2020). Effects of robot-human versus robot-robot behavior and entitativity on anthropomorphism and willingness to interact. *Computers in Human Behavior.* https://doi.org/10.1016/j.chb.2019.106220

Gillespie, E. (2019). Are you being scanned? How facial recognition technology follows you, even as you shop. Retrieved February 10, 2021, from www.theguardian.com/technology/2019/feb/24/are-you-being-scanned-how-facial-recognition-technology-follows-you-even-as-you-shop

Go, E., & Sundar, S. S. (2019). Humanizing chatbots: The effects of visual, identity, and conversational cues on humanness perceptions. *Computers in Human Behavior.* https://doi.org/10.1016/j.chb.2019.01.020

Guzman, A. L. (2020). Ontological boundaries between humans and computers and the implications for human-machine communication. *Human-Machine Communication, 1*, 37–54. https://doi.org/10.30658/hmc.1.3

Guzman, A. L., & Lewis, S. C. (2020). Artificial intelligence and communication: A Human-machine communication research agenda. *New Media & Society, 22*(1), 70–86.

Ham, C. D., & Nelson, M. R. (2016). The role of persuasion knowledge, assessment of benefit and harm, and third-person perception in coping with online behavioral advertising. *Computers in Human Behavior, 62*, 689–702.

Hamari, J., Koivisto, J., & Pakkanen, T. (2014, May). Do persuasive technologies persuade? A review of empirical studies. In *International conference on persuasive technology* (pp. 118–136). Springer.

Hamilton, K. A., & Yao, M. Z. (2018). Blurring boundaries: Effects of device features on metacognitive evaluations. *Computers in Human Behavior, 89*, 213–220.

Hamilton, K. A., Lee, S. Y., Chung, U. C., Liu, W., & Duff, B. R. (2020). Putting the "Me" in endorsement: Understanding and conceptualizing dimensions of self-endorsement using intelligent personal assistants. *00*(0), 1–21. *New Media & Society.* https://doi.org/10.1177/1461444820912197

Hancock, J. T., Naaman, M., & Levy, K. (2020). AI-mediated communication: definition, research agenda, and ethical considerations. *Journal of Computer-Mediated Communication, 25*(1), 89–100.

Haselton, T. (2018, May 8). Google's assistant is getting so smart it can place phone calls and humans think it's real. *CNBC.* Retrieved from www.cnbc.com/

Helberger, N., Huh, J., Milne, G., Strycharz, J., & Sundaram, H. (2020). Macro and exogenous factors in computational advertising: Key issues and new research directions. *Journal of Advertising, 49*(4), 377–393.

Huang, M., Fang, Z., Xiong, S., & Zhang, T. (2019). Interest-driven outdoor advertising display location selection using mobile phone data. *IEEE Access, 7*, 30878–30889.

Huh, J., & Malthouse, E. C. (2020). Advancing computational advertising: Conceptualization of the field and future directions. *Journal of Advertising, 49*(4), 367–376.

Joines, J. L., Scherer, C. W., & Scheufele, D. A. (2003). Exploring motivations for consumer Web use and their implications for e-commerce. *Journal of Consumer Marketing, 20*(2), 90–108.

Jones, V. K. (2018). Voice-activated change: Marketing in the age of artificial intelligence and virtual assistants. *Journal of Brand Strategy, 7*(3), 233–245.

Kalyanaraman, S., & Ivory, J. D. (2009). Enhanced information scent, selective discounting, or consummate breakdown: The psychological effects of web-based search results. *Media Psychology, 12*(3), 295–319.

Kardes, F. R., Herr, P. M., & Nantel, J. (Eds.). (2006). *Applying social cognition to consumer-focused strategy.* Psychology Press.

Kenny, D., & Marshall, J. F. (2000). Contextual marketing. *Harvard Business Review, 78*(6), 119–125.

Kietzmann, J., Paschen, J., & Treen, E. (2018). Artificial intelligence in advertising: How marketers can leverage artificial intelligence along the consumer journey. *Journal of Advertising Research, 58*(3), 263–267.

Ko, H., Cho, C. H., & Roberts, M. S. (2005). Internet uses and gratifications: A structural equation model of interactive advertising. *Journal of Advertising, 34*(2), 57–70.

Kumar, V., & Gupta, S. (2016). Conceptualizing the evolution and future of advertising. *Journal of Advertising, 45*(3), 302–317.

Lang, A. (2000). The limited capacity model of mediated message processing. *Journal of Communication, 50*(1), 46–70. doi:10.1111/j.1460-2466.2000.tb02833.x

Lee, H., & Cho, C. H. (2020). Digital advertising: Present and future prospects. *International Journal of Advertising, 39*(3), 332–341.

Lee, T., & Jun, J. (2007). Contextual perceived value?: Investigating the role of contextual marketing for customer relationship management in a mobile commerce context. *Business Process Management Journal, 13*(6), 798–814.

Liu-Thompkins, Y., Maslowska, E., Ren, Y., & Kim, H. (2020). Creating, metavoicing, and propagating: A road map for understanding user roles in computational advertising. *Journal of Advertising*, *49*(4), 394–410.

Luo, X., & Seyedian, M. (2003). Contextual marketing and customer-orientation strategy for e-commerce: an empirical analysis. *International Journal of Electronic Commerce*, *8*(2), 95–118.

Mahmoud, M. A., Alomari, Y. M., Badawi, U. A., Salah, A. B., Tayfour, M. F., Alghamdi, F. A., & Aseri, A. M. (2020). Impacts of marketing automation on business performance. *Journal of Theoretical and Applied Information Technology*, *98*(11), 1957–1969.

Maloney, E. K., Lapinski, M. K., & Witte, K. (2011). Fear appeals and persuasion: A review and update of the extended parallel process model. *Social and Personality Psychology Compass*, *5*(4), 206–219.

Malthouse, E. C., Calder, B. J., & Tamhane, A. (2007). The effects of media context experiences on advertising effectiveness. *Journal of Advertising*, *36*(3), 7–18.

McDonald, A., & Cranor, L. (2010). Beliefs and behaviors: Internet users' understanding of behavioral advertising. *Telecommunications Policy Research Conference*.

McLuhan, M. A. (1994). *Understanding media: The extensions of man.* MIT Press.

Murphy, D. (2018). Silver bullet or millstone? A review of success factors for implementation of marketing automation. *Cogent Business & Management*, *5*(1), 1546416.

Nass, C., & Moon, Y. (2000). Machines and mindlessness: Social responses to computers. *Journal of Social Issues*, *56*(1), 81–103.

Nill, A., & Aalberts, R. J. (2014). Legal and ethical challenges of online behavioral targeting in advertising. *Journal of Current Issues & Research in Advertising*, *35*(2), 126–146.

Oliver, M. B., Raney, A. A., & Bryant, J. (Eds.). (2019). *Media effects: Advances in theory and research.* Routledge.

Pan, B., Hembrooke, H., Joachims, T., Lorigo, L., Gay, G., & Granka, L. (2007). In Google we trust: Users' decisions on rank, position, and relevance. *Journal of Computer-Mediated Communication*, *12*(3), 801–823.

Paril, B. (2020, September 28). *2020 Trends: The future of automation in the ad space.* Digital Remedy. www.digitalremedy.com/2020-trends-the-future-of-automation-in-the-ad-space/.

Park, C. S., & Kaye, B. K. (2019). Smartphone and self-extension: Functionally, anthropomorphically, and ontologically extending self via the smartphone. *Mobile Media & Communication*, *7*(2), 215–231.

Reeves, B., & Nass, C. (1996). *The media equation: How people treat computers, television, and new media like real people and places.* Cambridge University Press.

Rust, R. T., & Lemon, K. N. (2001). E-service and the consumer. *International journal of electronic commerce*, *5*(3), 85–101.

Schwabe, H., & Castellacci, F. (2020). Automation, workers' skills and job satisfaction. *PLOS ONE*, *15*(11). https://doi.org/10.1371/journal.pone.0242929

Seeber, I., Bittner, E., Briggs, R. O., De Vreede, T., De Vreede, G. J., Elkins, A., … & Söllner, M. (2020). Machines as teammates: A research agenda on AI in team collaboration. *Information & management*, *57*(2), 103174.

Seeger, A. M., & Heinzl, A. (2018). Human versus machine: Contingency factors of anthropomorphism as a trust-inducing design strategy for conversational agents. In *Information systems and neuroscience* (pp. 129–139). Springer.

Seitz, J., & Zorn, S. (2016). Perspectives of programmatic advertising. In *Programmatic Advertising* (pp. 37–51). Springer.

Sen, R. (2005). Optimal search engine marketing strategy. *International Journal of Electronic Commerce*, *10*(1), 9–25.

She, J., Crowcroft, J., Fu, H., & Li, F. (2014). Convergence of interactive displays with smart mobile devices for effective advertising: A survey. *ACM Transactions on Multimedia Computing, Communications, and Applications (TOMM)*, *10*(2), 1–16.

Smit, E. G., Van Noort, G., & Voorveld, H. A. (2014). Understanding online behavioural advertising: User knowledge, privacy concerns and online coping behaviour in Europe. *Computers in Human Behavior*, *32*, 15–22.

Song, H., Kim, J., Nguyen, T. P., Lee, K. M., & Park, N. (2020). Virtual reality advertising with brand experiences: the effects of media devices, virtual representation of the self, and self-presence. *International Journal of Advertising*, 1–19.

Statista. (2021). Average number of connected devices in U.S. 2020. Retrieved 16 February 2021, from www.statista.com/statistics/1107206/average-number-of-connected-devices-us-house/

Sundar, S. S., Jia, H., Waddell, T. F., & Huang, Y. (2015). Toward a Theory of Interactive Media Effects (TIME). In *The Handbook of the Psychology of Communication Technology*. https://doi.org/10.1002/9781118426456.ch3

van Noort, G., Himelboim, I., Martin, J., & Collinger, T. (2020). Introducing a model of automated brand-generated content in an era of computational advertising. *Journal of Advertising*, *49*(4), 411–427.

Voorveld, H. A., Van Noort, G., Muntinga, D. G., & Bronner, F. (2018). Engagement with social media and social media advertising: The differentiating role of platform type. *Journal of Advertising*, *47*(1), 38–54.

Ward, A. F. (2013). One with the cloud: Why people mistake the Internet's knowledge for their own. In *ProQuest Dissertations and Theses*.

Westerwick, A. (2013). Effects of sponsorship, web site design, and Google ranking on the credibility on online information. *Journal of Computer-Mediated Communication*, 18(2), 80–97.

Xu, A., Liu, Z., Guo, Y., Sinha, V., & Akkiraju, R. (2017, May). A new chatbot for customer service on social media. In *Proceedings of the 2017 CHI conference on human factors in computing systems* (pp. 3506–3510).

Yang, Y., Yang, Y. C., Jansen, B. J., & Lalmas, M. (2017). Computational advertising: A paradigm shift for advertising and marketing?. *IEEE Intelligent Systems*, *32*(3), 3–6.

Yun, J. T., Segijn, C. M., Pearson, S., Malthouse, E. C., Konstan, J. A., & Shankar, V. (2020). Challenges and future directions of computational advertising measurement systems. *Journal of Advertising*, *49*(4), 446–458.

62

Human–Machine Communication in Retail

Jenna Jacobson and Irina Gorea

INTRODUCTION

Prior to the emergence of Human–Machine Communication (HMC) research, early communication models primarily studied human–human communications mediated by technology (Guzman & Lewis, 2020; Rogers, 1994; Schramm, 1971). Communication paradigms have been challenged by the technological advancements that have enabled machines to evolve from a medium through which people exchange messages to an intelligent social communicative partner (Edwards et al., 2016) and the impact has been witnessed across industries. In the retail industry, significant change is underway with the use of HMC being integrated throughout every component of the retail chain, including inventory management, product manufacturing (Jin & Shin, 2020), design (Knight, 2017), and product delivery (Bogue, 2019).

The emergence of new technologies represents a major driving force behind the digital disruption effect that is affecting the retail sector on a global scale (Gillpatrick et al., 2019). Some experts argue that artificial intelligence, the Internet of Things (IoT), and robotics, among other technologies will change business processes in every sector (Özdemir & Hekim, 2018). The integration of these technologies in retail influences customer behavior and the consumer experience. In a shifting service economy, retailers move beyond a distributor role to co-creator of the retail experience (Pantano et al., 2018).

This chapter explores customer-facing HMC applications and analyzes the role of machines in adding convenience and personalization to the retail experience and critically analyzes the integration of HMC in the out-of-store retail experience (i.e., online) and the in-store retail experience. We look to the future and anticipate the HMC applications in retail in light of the COVID-19 pandemic and the ways in which machines will continue to play a pivotal role in retail service.

OUT-OF-STORE RETAIL EXPERIENCE

The emerging field of Human–Machine Communication (HMC) is based on understanding the "creation of meaning among humans and machines" (Guzman, 2018, p. 1). By viewing machines as intelligent communicative partners, HMC moves away from the traditional view of technology as a simple communication medium. In out-of-store retail, HMC is leveraged to enhance the online shopping experience and bridge the gap between online and offline channels. Online channels – such as the retailer's website, mobile app, or social media – are used to research products, virtually try-on items, and receive personalized recommendations, with machines being important actors in helping to fulfill these processes. We analyze what Guzman and Lewis (2020) describe as communicative artificial intelligence (AI), where technology performs communication tasks that were historically assigned to people. For example, voice assistants interpret human language, search for relevant information, and reply vocally within seconds, conveniently filling the role of a customer service agent. Chatbots, with their ability to mimic human interaction, act as an intuitive sales associate by responding to inquiries in a human-like manner, booking reservations, and processing orders. Drawing on AI literature, we discuss the role of communicative AI technologies (Guzman & Lewis, 2020) – such as Amazon's Alexa, Apple's Siri, and Google's Assistant – in streamlining the online out-of-store shopping experience (Wiggers, 2017) and we conclude by analyzing the role of chatbots in adding convenience to the retail experience.

Voice Assistants

Hoy (2018) defines voice assistants as software agents that have the ability to "interpret human speech and respond via synthesized voices" (p. 1). Voice assistants create meaningful interactions by interpreting language and responding instantly to create a seamless oral conversation. Using natural language processing, the assistant is able to identify what was said, search for information, and reply vocally in a matter of seconds (Hoy, 2018). With nearly half of all Americans using digital voice assistants on their smartphones (Pew Research Centre, 2017), the popularity of Amazon's Alexa, Apple's Siri, and Google's Assistant has grown considerably over the past few years. While recognizing the privacy concerns, experts predict an increase in digital innovation as artificial intelligence continues to develop and voice assistants will continue to improve individuals' lives by anticipating and addressing their needs (Anderson & Rainie, 2018).

Voice assistants play an important role in creating an enjoyable experience while shopping, especially as social interaction is an important component in the shopping experience (Bellenger, 1980). In online shopping, social interaction is a strong predictor of customer loyalty (Christodoulides & Michaelidou, 2010), while offline shoppers seek social interaction when visiting the store (Rohm & Swaminathan, 2004). In a virtual store, customers' interactions with a sales associate or other shoppers in the form of an avatar positively contributes to shopping enjoyment and purchase intention (Moon et al., 2013).

Shopping has evolved into much more than a utilitarian process; shopping offers customers the social enjoyment of interacting with other people. It is no surprise that voice assistants have become an important social communicative actor in the out-of-store shopping experience by bringing the service of a human agent directly into people's homes in the form of a voice-enabled device. In a study of the benefits of verbally interacting with a Virtual Reality assistant, participants were asked to interact with a virtual fashion store using voice commands (Morotti et al., 2020). The findings show that vocal commands make the virtual shopping experience "more natural and simple," confirming that there is high interest in voice-based interaction with retailers. Retailers integrate voice assistants into a variety of contexts to create a pleasant social experience.

Companies are competing for dominance in the voice commerce space by promoting the voice capabilities of devices, such as Amazon Echo or Google Home. With over 50 million Alexa devices sold, Amazon wants to add convenience to the shopping experience by enabling customers to "shop in whatever way is easiest for them" (Anand, 2018). In the out-of-store experience, voice assistants, such as Amazon's Alexa, integrate the service of an in-store associate, with the convenience of online shopping. The main element of interaction with Alexa is through voice commands on any Echo device. Using natural language processing to "comprehend" the command, Alexa has the ability to track order updates, confirm delivery dates, and make intelligent recommendations. For example, customers can simply ask Alexa for the best-selling laptop or to reorder previously purchased items and the assistant will promptly respond using a human-like voice (Amazon, n.d.). Voice assistants play an important role in re-shaping the retail industry by introducing voice shopping as a new shopping medium. Voice shopping is expected to grow upwards of $40 billion by 2022 in the U.S and U.K. (Perez, 2018), bringing significant growth opportunities for retailers in this space. Beyond well-established channels such as e-commerce, click-and-collect, or in-store shopping, voice assistants are emerging as the key actors behind voice commerce. The communicative technology can potentially cause a significant shift in consumer behavior. For example, customers can complete routine purchases by asking Alexa to place a repeat order of their last shopping cart, as opposed to visiting the retailer's brick-and-mortar location.

However, despite the promising growth, voice assistants present limitations which can affect the quality of communication and limit the assistant's social interactivity. Specifically, touch screen interaction or typing ability is completely absent, which can lead to an incoherent shopping experience when the command cannot be interpreted. Consumer skepticism remains a concern for retailers and a detrimental factor in the adoption of voice assistant technologies. A survey of online American adults shows that the majority of consumers have yet to include voice commands in their shopping habits (PWC, 2018). Participants indicated a lack of trust in the voice assistant's capability to accurately fulfill the order and process payments. Retailers considering voice commerce should not lose sight of the fact that shopping is a multi-sensory experience and factors such as smell, sight, touch, and taste play an important role in shaping consumer perceptions (Vecchi & Buckley, 2016). Voice assistants can be suitable for placing routine orders with low risk, while high risk purchases may warrant a more thorough research process that cannot be completed through vocal commands (Anand, 2018) and multiple senses may need to be involved to complete the shopping experience.

Chatbots

Social bots have the capability to mimic human social interactions on social networks and can "share pictures, post status updates and Tweets" and even "enter into conversation with other SNS users" (Gehl & Bakardjieva, 2016, p. 2). As noted by Hays (2017), social bots challenge our perceptions of medium and media and create meaningful interactions with humans (Guzman, 2018). Beyond their role on social media, chatbots can be observed in the retail industry fulfilling a variety of tasks ranging from customer service to sales support. Communicating with chatbots occurs mainly through text-based communication. Customers use their personal devices (e.g., smartphones, tablets, and laptops) to type an inquiry and the chatbot will recognize written language, interpret the command, and respond instantly in a human-like manner. Retailers can program chatbots to communicate with customers through various online channels, such as the mobile app, social media, or e-commerce website. Chatbots are re-shaping the retail industry by filling the role of a customer service agent with instant access to large volumes of customer data and the ability to provide personalized service quickly and efficiently. By providing real-time support, the wait times to speak to a human agent are significantly reduced and routine tasks, such as checking the status of an order or sending tracking numbers, are fulfilled within seconds.

Out-of-store channels are the preferred retail channels when shopping for personal care and beauty items (Skrovan, 2017) and chatbots fill the role of a customer service agent by assisting customers in the buying process. At Sephora, the retailer's chatbot uses artificial intelligence to assist customers in finding the right color match for makeup. Using the Sephora mobile app, users can point the camera to their face and the chatbot will assist in virtually trying on makeup looks (Parisi, n.d.).

Beyond the role of a customer service assistant, chatbots can be programmed to assist in the automation of sales. Chatbots can be trained to recognize inquiries and to ask intuitive questions in order to narrow down the search. Chatbots interpret customer preferences and suggest alternatives to fit the specified parameters. The 1-800-Flowers bot guides Facebook Messenger users through the process of buying flowers. Stepping into the role of a sales associate, the bot asks questions to determine the occasion and who the flowers are being sent to, after which it processes the delivery address and places the order. To further simplify the buying process, the 1-800-Flowers bot is integrated with Amazon's Alexa, enabling customers to place orders using vocal commands (Ewen, 2016).

Beyond their role in customer service and sales, communication with chatbots is especially important in creating a seamless shopping experience between out-of-store and in-store channels. Customers communicate with chatbots online, while the bot instantly checks for in-store availability, bridging the gap between retail channels. For example, Sephora's Facebook Messenger chatbot is integrated among all retail channels so that it can quickly and easily book an appointment with beauty specialists in-store. The bot automatically displays availability, as well as the closest retail locations, and the reservation can be quickly completed. As a result of implementing the Messenger chatbot, Sephora's booking rates increased by 11% (Hollander, 2017). Similar to voice assistants, Sephora's chatbot uses natural language processing – a form of artificial intelligence – to respond to Facebook users' inquiries. For example, an inquiry about the best-selling products will return a personalized response where the chatbot greets the customer by name and shares the relevant URL.

In conjunction with chatbots, retailers can blend recommendation agents into their sales strategy to unify the professional assistance of an in-store associate with the simplicity of online shopping. A recommendation agent is software that identifies customer preferences and makes intuitive product recommendations (Xiao & Benbasat, 2007). A recommendation agent guides the customer through the buying process by asking intuitive questions to help identify desired products. The recommendation agent collects customer data through interactive quizzes that identify the area of interest. Recommendation agents are perceived as "social actors" with human characteristics (Benbasat & Wang, 2005), thus representing an important counterpart in the online shopping experience.

Despite the many functionalities, implementing chatbots can be challenging for retailers. A disconnect between retailer expectations and customer perceptions may be emerging: retailers have higher expectations of chatbots in comparison to customers' perceptions of the usefulness of chatbots (Lajante & Del Prete, 2020). Chatbots are limited to text-based communication, with no option to interact vocally. Due to the limitations of natural language processing, the bot may lack the vocabulary required to respond to the inquiry and misinterpreting the context can lead to an unsatisfactory customer service experience. Rather than using a generalized script, retailers must also carefully align the chatbot's "personality" with the brand to ensure that the bot acts as a brand ambassador.

Overall, machines are leveraged to enhance the out-of-store shopping experience and connect the online and in-store shopping channels. Communicating with machines can take place through verbal or text-based communication. Through verbal communication, voice assistants serve as a knowledgeable social partner that offers instant information and in-home service while shopping online. Chatbots, with access to in-store availability and online customer profiles, seamlessly communicate through text-based communication to provide customer service. Looking into the future, we anticipate an increase in the adoption of HMC as a way to add value to the out-of-store shopping experience.

IN-STORE RETAIL EXPERIENCE

Communicating with machines is expected to reshape the future of in-store shopping. While online shopping has become increasingly accessible on a global scale, customers continue to be motivated to visit stores to see, touch, and feel products before purchase (Skrovan, 2017). Robots, along with the Internet of Things (IoT), artificial intelligence, and augmented reality will play an important role in adding convenience

across industries (Skobelev & Borovik, 2017). As multi-sensory experiences remain important to shoppers, HMC can be adopted to create memorable experiences and to facilitate frictionless shopping. The traditional in-store shopping may experience a decrease in direct human involvement, and among the most important touchpoints undergoing significant changes is the interaction with employees. Specifically, artificial intelligence will redefine processes that were previously assigned to human agents. Order processing or customer service requests will be fulfilled by machines through existing in-store channels or new channels altogether.

Significant changes are underway and can be observed in the fast-food industry; these innovations may move into more traditional retail spaces. Some fast-food restaurants have implemented in-store kiosks to streamline order processing; future advances may involve voice-ordering through the already existing devices, as well as the drive-thru (Perry, 2019). Beyond completing routine processes in fast-food chains, service robots are being used to create an entertaining experience in local restaurants. For retailers, robots can represent an important differentiating point and a unique factor in creating memorable in-store experiences. For example, a Canadian McDonald's restaurant implemented a friendly service robot to greet, seat, and serve customers. Moreover, the robot can even take on human-like features by displaying facial expressions to mimic emotions (Hilash, 2020).

As retailers integrate artificial intelligence in stores, communication with machines will play an important role in blending functionality with seamless experience. Further, communicating with machines has the potential to disrupt the retail industry by eliminating unnecessary touchpoints and adding convenience and simplicity to the check-out process. Through the IoT, cashless stores that operate without the need for cashiers may become the future of offline shopping.

The following section introduces the in-store shopping experience and explores the cognitive-analytical skills of service robots in providing customer assistance. Further, as people's interactions with the IoT is expected to grow (Rainie & Anderson, 2018), we consider the implications of sensor-based technologies in offering a seamless customer experience. In this section, we analyze disruptive technologies that are transforming the retail industry, such as the Amazon Go store (Ives et al., 2019). Overall, the analysis considers communications with the machine in the offline spaces, as well as the degree of integration with online channels.

Service Robots

The future of retail will see humans and robots closely linked together to collaborate and increase productivity (Nahavandi, 2019). Service robots have the potential to step into roles that were previously assigned to sales associates or customer service agents. Wirtz et al. (2018) define service robots as "system-based autonomous and adaptable interfaces that interact, communicate and deliver service to an organization's customers" (para. 4). Service robots are predominantly used to automate routine tasks in domestic, industrial, or retail settings and leverage their cognitive-analytical skills to increase productivity beyond the standard levels that are achieved by human workers. Service robots are programmed to offer consistent service that is free of human error. Robots are not subject to fatigue or environmental distractions and can offer the same level of service without bias towards demographic factors such as age, gender, or ethnicity. Designed to recreate humans in "looks, mind, emotional expression and behaviour" (Broadbent, 2017, p. 629), communicating with service robots reshapes the shopping experience by introducing a novel, intelligent partner.

van Doorn et al. (2017) outline the concept of automated social presence, arguing that service robots fulfill the need for social interaction during the shopping process as they have the capability to make customers feel that they are interacting with another social entity. This is achieved by blending a variety of communication elements to mimic human social interaction during the shopping process. Service robots can use text-based communication using the robot's built-in touchscreen or verbally through voice commands. Most importantly, sensor technologies, such as cameras or microphones, enable the robot to respond with customized messages based on facial or voice recognition.

Service robots play an important role in transforming the in-store shopping experience. Wirtz et al. (2018) classify the services that robots can perform based on two dimensions. The first dimension is concerned with the type of service and ranges from tangible to intangible actions. The second dimension defines whether the service is directed to a person or object. For example, Pepper is a humanoid robot performing tangible actions in order to service a person. The friendly service robot fills many formerly human functions and can act as a greeter, sales associate, brand ambassador, and survey conductor, among other roles (Soft Bank Robotics, n.d.). The intelligent robot evidences that both functionality and intelligent communication are important factors in creating meaningful interactions. Pepper can be found at airports (e.g., the Pierre Elliott Trudeau International Airport in Quebec) where it greets guests, provides menu details, and offers recommendations (HMS Host, n.d.). Pepper is an important actor in defining the customer experience and a life-like shopping assistant that can initiate conversation in 21 languages and process payments. Using facial recognition software, Pepper is able to personalize service and adapt the response based on the shopper's profile (Soft Bank Robotics, n.d.).

Another example is the Lowebot, a service robot that helps Lowe's customers search for products and navigate the home improvement store (Lowe's Innovation Labs, n.d.). Using verbal communication through voice commands or nonverbal cues, such as the touchscreen technology, customers communicate with the Lowebot, which is designed to offer quick and convenient customer service and answer routine questions such as, "How can I help you today?" Equipped with wheels and smart laser sensors (Taylor, 2016), the autonomous robot then guides customers to the appropriate aisle in the store.

In the retail industry, robots play a key role in re-shaping the shopping experience as they are perceived as distinct entities and social partners in the buying process. A deeper understanding of shoppers' perceptions of robots can be gleaned by analyzing countries, such as Japan and Korea, where autonomous robots are already operating in shopping malls (Broadbent, 2017). A study set in a Japanese shopping mall studied shoppers' interactions with Robovie, a semi-autonomous service robot that moves around the mall, greets customers, and provides information about the shops. The study found that people most often perceived the robot as a mascot for the mall. Service robots that provide information and hand out flyers have been found to lead to an enjoyable shopping experience for shoppers due to the novelty of the robot (Satake et al., 2015). For retailers, the implications are significant as service robots can be leveraged as brand ambassadors to manage customer relationships, promote the brand, and add value through enhanced customer service. Research evidences that people value experiences more than possessions (Pchelin & Howell, 2014) and human–robot communications can be a prime facilitator of memorable experiences in the retail space.

The in-store shopping experience can also be enhanced through voice assistants. While this technology is largely seen out-of-store, retailers can also use it to enhance the in-store experience. Retailers have the opportunity to leverage voice assistants and replace or complement sales associates in-store. With voice assistants stepping into the role of a sales associate, retailers can create a consistent shopping experience across all stores. Following the classification of service robots by Wirtz et al. (2018), voice assistants represent a virtual agent performing intangible actions in an in-store context. Specifically, the voice assistant is trained to interact with customers using a standard script and, by automatically anticipating needs and offering alternatives, the sales process can be significantly streamlined. For example, a partnership between The Mars Agency and specialty beverage retailer BevMo! introduced an innovative way to shop for whiskey. SmartAisle, a smart in-store voice assistant, is activated using an Amazon Echo device. Placed on an in-store merchandising display, customers initiate communication with the device using voice commands. Once initiated, SmartAisle plays the role of a sales associate by asking introductory questions to learn about the customer's whiskey preferences and budget. SmartAisle then recommends three options and assists the customer in choosing the appropriate product. To enhance the sensory experience, the shelving units underneath each bottle of whiskey are lit up and controlled by SmartAisle. As the device helps narrow down the choices, the lights underneath each bottle begin to switch off one by one. At the end of the conversation with SmartAisle, the customer is left with the chosen whiskey bottle (Narayan, 2019) and a memorable shopping experience.

While implementing voice assistants can reduce the number of procedures and costs required to train and onboard sales staff, retailers may incur large costs to develop and manage the system. Costs associated with hardware and training the assistant to respond to brand-specific inquiries would require a significant budget when implemented across multiple stores, as well as ongoing costs to implement updates. Moreover, the interaction with voice assistants can create a learning curve for customers as limited experience with this type of technology can slow down the adoption process. As customers familiarize themselves with voice assistants, retailers should consider having staff available in-store to assist with the sales process.

Overall, implementing service robots may result in important changes in how sales associates are trained and the duties that they perform. While there is concern that robots will replace employees, others suggest that rather than eliminating jobs, robots will create new roles that will entail humans having a deep understanding of robotics (Nahavandi, 2019). In retail, the role of a sales associate may shift to having responsibilities that require high-level knowledge, creativity, and emotional intelligence, leaving the tasks that require cognitive-analytical skills to the robot's supervision.

CONCLUSION

The retail industry is undergoing significant changes and HMC plays an important role in shaping the way retailers service and communicate with customers. Out-of-store and in-store, machines are becoming increasingly sophisticated and intuitive communicative partners that fill in the roles of sales associates and customer service agents. By substituting and complementing human-to-human communication, machines will become pivotal assets in retailers' strategies following the aftermath of the COVID-19 pandemic. By assigning communication roles to machines, retailers have the opportunity to limit human contact and devote more resources to reinforcing health and safety procedures. For example, experts predict that voice shopping may increase in popularity after the COVID-19 pandemic. Voice assistants could be used to prevent line-ups in front of the store and, by communicating with the assistant, shoppers can identify their place in line or check product availability as they wait in the car (Stankiewicz, 2020). There may also be an increase in the adoption of voice assistants as an alternative to touchscreen kiosks. Using speech recognition on existing in-store kiosks, customers will be able to place orders and process payments reliably and efficiently, without the need to touch the screen (Stern, 2020). In an effort to increase sanitization standards, this alternative can prevent unnecessary touching of in-store devices and serve as a proactive measure to protect the health and safety of customers. Further, service robots can create a safe in-store shopping experience by substituting human interaction. From streamlined service, to reduced human errors, invaluable customer data collection and immediate 24/7 service, the benefits of service robots for retailers are evident and customers can enjoy a safer shopping experience.

REFERENCES

Amazon. (n.d.). *Alexa features: Shopping*. www. amazon.com/b?ie=UTF8&node=17934682011

Anand, P. (2018). *The reality behind voice shopping hype*. The Information. www.theinformation.com/ articles/the-reality-behind-voice-shopping-hype

Anderson, J., & Rainie, L. (2018). *3. Improvements ahead: How humans and AI might evolve together in the next decade*. Pew Research Centre. www. pewresearch.org/internet/2018/12/10/ improvements-ahead-how-humans-and-ai-might-evolve-together-in-the-next-decade/

Bellenger, D. N. (1980). Profiling the recreational shopper. *Journal of Retailing, 56*(3), 77–92.

Bogue, R. (2019). Strong prospects for robots in retail. *Industrial Robot: The International Journal of Robotics Research and Application, 46*(3), 326–331. https://doi.org/10.1108/IR-01-2019-0023

Broadbent, E. (2017). Interactions with robots: The truths we reveal about ourselves. *Annual Review of Psychology, 68*(1), 627–652. https://doi.org/10.1146/annurev-psych-010416-043958

Christodoulides, G., & Michaelidou, N. (2010). Shopping motives as antecedents of e-satisfaction and e-loyalty. *Journal of Marketing Management, 27*(1–2), 181–197. https://doi.org/10.1080/02672 57X.2010.489815

Edwards, A., Edwards, C., Spence, P. R., Harris, C., & Gambino, A. (2016). Robots in the classroom: Differences in students' perceptions of credibility and learning between "teacher as robot" and "robot as teacher." *Computers in Human Behavior, 65*, 627–634. https://doi.org/10.1016/j.chb.2016.06.005

Ewen, L. (2016). 1-800-Flowers on chatbots, online gifting and the automation of thoughtfulness. *Retail Dive.* www.retaildive.com/news/1-800-flowers-on-chatbots-online-gifting-and-the-automation-of-thoughtfuln/419772/

Gehl, R. W., & Bakardjieva, M. (Eds.) (2016). *Socialbots and their friends: Digital media and the automation of sociality.* Routledge.

Gillpatrick, T., Blunck, E., & Boğa, S. (2019). Understanding the role of consumer behavior in forecasting the impact of industry 4.0 and the wave of digital disruption driving innovation in retailing. *DIEM: Dubrovnik International Economic Meeting, 4*(1), 165–176.

Guzman, A. L. (Ed.). (2018). *Human-machine communication.* Peter Lang Publication.

Guzman, A. L., & Lewis, S. C. (2020). Artificial intelligence and communication: A Human–Machine Communication research agenda. *New Media & Society, 22*(1), 70–86. https://doi.org/10.1177/1461444819858691

Hays, K. (2017). *Amazon prepares for on-demand fashion production with patent.* WWD. https://wwd.com/business-news/technology/amazon-going-deeper-into-fashion-with-new-on-demand-manufacturing-patent-10869520/

Hilash, S. (2020). *There are robot servers at this new Calgary restaurant & we're officially over humans.* Narcity. www.narcity.com/eat-drink/ca/ab/calgary/calgary-robot-servers-are-a-thing-you-can-see-them-at-this-chinese-spot

HMS Host. (n.d.). *Pepper the robot lands at new North American airports.* www.hmshost.com/news/details/pepper-the-robot-lands-at-new-airports

Hollander, R. (2017). Facebook Messenger is bringing significant value to brands like Sephora and Tommy Hilfiger. *Business Insider.* www.businessinsider.com/facebook-messenger-brings-value-to-brands-like-sephora-tommy-hilfiger-2017-8

Hoy, M. B. (2018). Alexa, Siri, Cortana, and more: An introduction to voice assistants. *Medical Reference Services Quarterly, 37*(1), 81–88. https://doi.org/10.1080/02763869.2018.1404391

Ives, B., Cossick, K., & Adams, D. (2019). Amazon Go: Disrupting retail? *Journal of Information Technology Teaching Cases, 9*(1), 2–12. https://doi.org/10.1177/2043886918819092

Jin, B. E., & Shin, D. C. (2020). Changing the game to compete: Innovations in the fashion retail industry from the disruptive business model. *Business Horizons, 63*(3), 301–311. https://doi.org/10.1016/j.bushor.2020.01.004

Knight, W. (2017). Amazon has developed an AI fashion designer. *MIT Technology Review.* www.technologyreview.com/2017/08/24/149518/amazon-has-developed-an-ai-fashion-designer/

Lajante, M., & Del Prete, M. (2020). Technology-infused organizational frontlines: When (not) to use chatbots in retailing to promote customer engagement. In E. Pantano (Ed.), *Retail futures* (pp. 71–84). Emerald Publishing Limited. https://doi.org/10.1108/978-1-83867-663-620201011

Lowe's Innovation Labs. (n.d.). *A helping hand.* www.lowesinnovationlabs.com/lowebot

Moon, J. H., Kim, E., Choi, S. M., & Sung, Y. (2013). Keep the social in social media: The role of social interaction in avatar-based virtual shopping. *Journal of Interactive Advertising, 13*(1), 14–26. https://doi.org/10.1080/15252019.2013.768051

Morotti, E., Donatiello, L., & Marfia, G. (2020). Fostering fashion retail experiences through virtual reality and voice assistants. *2020 IEEE Conference on Virtual Reality and 3D User Interfaces Abstracts and Workshops (VRW)*, 338–342. https://doi.org/10.1109/VRW50115.2020.00074

Nahavandi, S. (2019). Industry 5.0 – A human-centric solution. *Sustainability, 11*(16), 4371. https://doi.org/10.3390/su11164371

Narayan, S. (2019). 'I'm Bev'! Booze bot at your service in the whiskey aisle. *San Francisco Chronicle.* www.sfchronicle.com/business/article/Talking-shelves-A-big-box-booze-shop-is-hoping-13598778.php

Özdemir, V., & Hekim, N. (2018). Birth of Industry 5.0: Making sense of big data with Artificial Intelligence, The Internet of Things and next-generation technology policy. *OMICS: A Journal of Integrative Biology, 22*(1), 65–76. https://doi.org/10.1089/omi.2017.0194

Pantano, E., Priporas, C. V., & Dennis, C. (2018). A new approach to retailing for successful competition in the new smart scenario. *International Journal of Retail & Distribution Management, 46*(3), 264–282. https://doi.org/10.1108/IJRDM-04-2017-0080

Parisi, D. (n.d.). Sephora debuts chatbot features for consumers at home and in-store. *Retail Dive.*

www.retaildive.com/ex/mobilecommercedaily/sephora-debuts-chatbot-features-for-consumers-at-home-and-in-store

Pchelin, P., & Howell, R. T. (2014). The hidden cost of value-seeking: People do not accurately forecast the economic benefits of experiential purchases. *The Journal of Positive Psychology*, 9(4), 322–334.

Perez, S. (2018). Voice shopping estimated to hit $40+ billion across U.S. and U.K. by 2022. *Tech Crunch*. https://techcrunch.com/2018/03/02/voice-shopping-estimated-to-hit-40-billion-across-u-s-and-u-k-by-2022/

Perry, A. (2019). *McDonald's buys voice-based AI to speed up ordering*. Mashable SE Asia. https://sea.mashable.com/tech/6178/mcdonalds-buys-voice-based-ai-to-speed-up-ordering

Pew Research Centre. (2017). *Nearly half of Americans use digital voice assistants, mostly on their smartphones*. Pew Research Centre. www.pewresearch.org/fact-tank/2017/12/12/nearly-half-of-americans-use-digital-voice-assistants-mostly-on-their-smartphones/

PWC. (2018). *Prepare for the voice revolution*. www.pwc.com/us/en/services/consulting/library/consumer-intelligence-series/voice-assistants.html

Rogers, E. M. (1994). *History of communication study*. Free Press.

Rohm, A. J., & Swaminathan, V. (2004). A typology of online shoppers based on shopping motivations. *Journal of Business Research*, 57(7), 748–757. https://doi.org/10.1016/S0148-2963(02)00351-X

Schramm, W. (1971). The nature of communication between humans. In W. Shcramm & D. F. Roberts (Eds.), *The process and effects of mass communication* (pp. 3–53). University Illinois Press.

Skobelev, P., & Borovik, S. Y. (2017). On the way from Industry 4.0 to Industry 5.0: From digital manufacturing to digital society. *Industry 4.0*, 2(6), 307–311.

Skrovan, S. (2017). Why consumers prefer to shop for nearly all products online. *Retail Dive*. www.retaildive.com/news/why-consumers-prefer-to-shop-for-nearly-all-products-online/437886/

Soft Bank Robotics. (n.d.). *Retail*. www.softbankrobotics.com/emea/en/industries/retail

Stankiewicz, K. (2020). *Stores may use voice assistants to transform shopping, retail consultant says*. CNBC. www.cnbc.com/2020/05/12/stores-may-use-voice-assistants-to-transform-shopping-retail-consultant-says.html

Stern, M. (2020). COVID-19 may push retailers to use voice assistants instead of touch screens. *Retail Wire*. https://retailwire.com/discussion/covid-19-may-push-retailers-to-use-voice-assistants-instead-of-touch-screens/

Taylor, H. (2016). *Lowe's introduces LoweBot, a new autonomous in-store robot*. CNBC. www.cnbc.com/2016/08/30/lowes-introduces-lowebot-a-new-autonomous-in-store-robot.html

van Doorn, J., Mende, M., Noble, S. M., Hulland, J., Ostrom, A. L., Grewal, D., & Petersen, J. A. (2017). Domo arigato Mr. Roboto: Emergence of automated social presence in organizational frontlines and customers' service experiences. *Journal of Service Research*, 20(1), 43–58. https://doi.org/10.1177/1094670516679272

Vecchi, A., & Buckley, C. (Eds.). (2016). *Handbook of research on global fashion management and merchandising*. IGI Global. https://doi.org/10.4018/978-1-5225-0110-7

Wiggers, K. (2017). *Levi's virtual stylist helps you slip into the jeans of your dreams*. Digital Trends. www.digitaltrends.com/mobile/le/

Wirtz, J., Patterson, P. G., Kunz, W. H., Gruber, T., Lu, V. N., Paluch, S., & Martins, A. (2018). Brave new world: Service robots in the frontline. *Journal of Service Management*, 29(5), 907–931. https://doi.org/10.1108/JOSM-04-2018-0119

63

Autonomous Vehicles: Where Automation Ends and the Communication Begins

Thilo von Pape

Etymologically speaking, the idea of automated transportation is as old as the word "automated" itself. It first occurred in the Iliad, to describe how the gate of heaven opened "by itself" ("αὐτόματος") for Hera in her golden chariot (Vasileiadou, Kalligeropoulos, & Karcanias, 2003, p. 77), and later how Phoenician ships piloted themselves. It takes only a few steps from there to the Society of Automotive Engineers' (SAE) standard definition of driving automation systems as "systems that perform part or all of the dynamic driving task (DDT) on a sustained basis" (SAE International, 2018, p. 2), with its categorization from levels zero to five. Yet despite this conceptual history and authoritative endorsement, laymen and experts increasingly abandon the notion of "automated vehicles." They speak of "autonomous" vehicles (AV) instead, borrowing another Greek word, which initially designated cities that made their law (νόμος) themselves (αὐτο) (Dworkin, 1988). This change from a technological term to one derived from the social sciences parallels the conceptual shift from *Human–Machine Interaction* (HMI) to *Human–Machine Communication* (HMC) that is the broader subject of this handbook. Both shifts attempt to come to terms with progress in artificial intelligence (AI) and robotics. Both also operate questionably across the boundaries between the human and the technological, the agent and the instrument.

It is in this sense that this chapter discusses applications of HMC to AVs: not to hold AVs up as some clear prism to unravel the complexity of HMC. But as a chimeric apparition that complicates our understanding of communication in and with vehicles to a level from which we can better appreciate the general complexity of HMC. Therefore, we will first investigate the communicative challenges posed by the autonomization of vehicles. The second section discusses how these challenges resonate in different strands of research on HMC and which responses this new field may bring to them.

CHALLENGES EMERGING FROM THE AUTONOMIZATION OF VEHICLES

Many works discussing AVs and future technologies, in general, caution us of conceiving them as mere "driverless cars." This conception would amount to the *ceteris paribus* fallacy of deriving expectations from a single change while holding *all else equal* (cf. SAE International, 2008;

Townsend, 2020). The resulting visions of AVs generally amount to a version of today's luxury cars with incremental adjustments that reflect the transformation of drivers into passengers, such as turning front seats backward. However, avoiding this fallacy through the inclusion of additional variables will increase the whole consideration's complexity exponentially. Therefore, we must carefully consider which types of technologies and practices it is worth pondering their future developments under conditions of vehicle autonomy and what kind of conditions vehicle autonomy constitutes in the first place.

Status Quo of Vehicles, Infrastructures, and Practices

Given the widespread fixation on personal cars, we should first recognize the actual diversity of vehicles worldwide and of the infrastructures and practices in which they are involved. Well over one billion automobiles are currently in use (Sperling & Gordon, 2010), defined as vehicles that are powered internally and move freely on roads with diverse surfaces to transport small amounts of people and cargo (Oxford English Dictionary, 2012, p. 100). The next larger category of automotive ground vehicles consists of buses and trucks. A third category includes even larger ground vehicles (tramways and trains) with constant dependence on physical infrastructure for guidance (rails) and energy supply. Below the car come motorized vehicles for the transportation of one to three persons and minimal cargo – motorbikes, rickshaws – and (increasingly electrified) bicycles, the one vehicle that rivals cars numerically. Finally, there are human-powered or motorized micro vehicles such as electric scooters, skateboards, or self-balancing pods. Vehicles of all sizes also exist for transportation in the air (airplanes, rotorcrafts, airships), in water (personal and cargo boats of all sizes, submarines), and in space – the latter ones requiring the most autonomous control systems.

We must further broaden our view beyond the vehicles, just as scholars of media change look beyond the devices themselves to infrastructures, institutions, and practices. Technologically, the vehicles profoundly depend on infrastructure, which provides the mechanically necessary conditions for them to move (roads, rails, networks of energy provisions with service stations), and signage systems. These information systems include road signs and markings, traffic lights, and schedule displays. They may take the form of paper supports (maps, travel guides, tickets, stamps) and digital interfaces (navigation software

in smartphones or vehicle dashboards) (Oswald, 2016; Wilken & Thomas, 2019). Traditional vehicles also depend on human operators. The human drivers have been so profoundly integrated in certain vehicles such as cars that Dant (2004) considered these vehicles as assemblages combining the human sensory and control system with the machine's motor power. While the internal interactions between drivers and cars through pedals, levers and various indicators are primarily mute, it is conceivable that "interactions with 'mute' technologies constitute communication," as Guzman (2016, p. 1) argued for manufacturing technologies. And to the outside world, the vehicles operate as avatars of their human drivers.

The practices involved in even the most basic tasks of getting cargo from A to B reach far beyond what the SAE defines as the "dynamic driving task" (DDT). Consider the kinds of "cargo" involved in everyday transportation: persons in emergency conditions, business travelers, garbage, schoolchildren, livestock, pizza, Amazon packages, deep-frozen vaccines... all come with specific expectations regarding stowage, temperature, hygiene, but also care, entertainment, wifi, etc. to make sure the travel time is not only safe but also enjoyable and productive (Lyons & Urry, 2005). These practices are not contained to the vehicles as cocoons but often involve the environment as well, if only as a stream of impressions perceived through the windscreen (Packer & Oswald, 2010) and deliberately soundtracked (Pink, Fors, & Glöss, 2019). The travel time is productive in the pragmatic sense of passengers finishing their homework and symbolically, as the means and destinations of transportation also constitute meaning (von Pape, Goggin, & Forlano, 2019). One illustration of the range at which vehicles allocate identity and social status – also to those they are passing by, is Towns' (2015) study "Riding while White." Towns argued how tourist bus-tours through troubled districts of Los Angeles actualize hegemonic meanings of whiteness and blackness by emanating a moving ceasefire around the primarily white tourists, hovering above the suspended violence just as white visitors could traverse troubled areas unperturbed in past decades.

Vehicle Autonomy

To discuss what the autonomization of these vehicles may signify for the communication involved in the associated practices, we must establish what autonomy means for machines. A technical definition is proposed by Antsaklis (2020). He first established the locus of machine autonomy by stating that "every autonomous system is a control system" (Antsaklis, 2020, p. 16). While we commonly attribute the autonomy and conscience of humans and animals to their bodily individuality, a rolling vehicle is not the beholder of its autonomy. The control systems are both more limited to specific parts and wirelessly extended beyond their physical bodies. As Waymo's co-founder Anthony Levandowski stated, autonomous cars move "like a train on software rails" (Townsend, 2020, p. 68). Wilken and Thomas (2019, p. 2719) thus emphasized that mapping technologies serve "not as subordinate or ancillary systems, but as essential elements for the control of the vehicle, integrated into their design at a fundamental level." Other more or less externalized informational systems are also highly integrated into the vehicles' control system to constantly optimize the security, legality, and profitability of their operations. According to Townsend (2020, p. 42), "the only independence that's left for AVs is from us – not from other machines, networks, the law, or markets."

Antsaklis (2020, p. 16) further postulated two sets of conditions that determine the degree of system autonomy: "if a system has the capacity to achieve a set of goals under a set of uncertainties in the system and its environment, by itself, without external intervention, then it will be called autonomous with respect to the set of goals under the set of uncertainties."

Autonomy to the Extent of Pursuing Larger Sets of Goals

For vehicles moving through public space – as opposed to AI moving pawns on chess boards – even seemingly small goals include vast sets of secondary objectives. Otherwise, the simple request to "get to the airport as fast as possible" would lead to accidents and arrest on arrival. How autonomous machines understand and accommodate their users' requests, their underlying interests, and the interests and rights of third parties – is, therefore, a key concern to AI scholars in general: the "goal-alignment problem" (Tegmark, 2017, p. 259).

Its purely epistemic intricacies have been emphasized through apocalyptic scenarios, such as that of a benevolent AI tasked with maximizing the production of paperclips, which inadvertently eliminates humanity in the process (Russell, 2019). Knowing what users truly want is no less complicated in the intricate domain of transportation, even for a single user himself: do I want to go to the supermarket to get my groceries, to meet people, or just for the ride in my prestigious car? How, then, to convey a goal to the AI in one unequivocal request? Computer scientists lead this epistemological side of the goal-alignment problem to an issue of communication: "Inevitably, these machines will be uncertain about our objectives – after all, we are uncertain about them ourselves – but it turns out that this is a feature, not a bug [...] Uncertainty about objectives implies that machines will necessarily defer to humans: they will ask permission, they will accept correction." (Russell, 2019, p. 12)

The goal alignment problem has a second, more conflictual side, prominently discussed through the so-called "trolley problem." How should a vehicle faced with an unfolding heads-on accident weigh different possible outcomes of human suffering against each other? Should it be "loyal" to its passengers, spare uninvolved third parties on the sidewalks, or apply purely utilitarian standards? Here, too, the AI scholars' life and death scenario overshadows far more common and complex questions: whom to allow riding through the congested city center, whom to route via a bypass or a secondary mode of transportation? How to account for the users' financial, social, cognitive, physical resources and needs? These questions are the object of continuous negotiations in and between diverse organisms such as urban transportation boards, the vehicles' operators, and users' associations. While technology can support these processes, the often democratic human representation and deliberation at their heart cannot be cast into code.

Autonomy to the Extent of Mastering Uncertainty

Antsaklis (2020, p. 16) further advanced that "for the same set of goals, the larger the set of uncertainties the system can handle, the higher is its degree of autonomy." Autonomous buses shuttling children to school through the predictable dryness of Arizona suburbs are less autonomous than those serving the same goal in rainy Mumbai. On an epistemological level, this demands the vehicles to model the physical conditions of their environment and make sense of the social interactions between the involved road users. Given the complex interdependencies of traffic, uncertainty reduction also requires the vehicles to actively express their intentions to other road users. The breadth of different practices in which vehicles are involved beyond basic traffic interactions leads to further uncertainty: how long can the passenger "hold" his need for a toilet break? Which music best fits the trip? Which detour for dropping off one passenger is tolerable for the others? Again, the questions are not just epistemological but also involve conflicts of interest. Again, they call for communication, the proven means for uncertainty reduction and conflict resolution.

Judging by the two criteria of machine autonomy – the size of goal sets and the degree of internal and external uncertainty – vehicle autonomy appears categorically different from both the SAE's benchmark of "full automation" and the kind of autonomy proper to humans. The type of autonomy proper to vehicles perhaps comes closest to that of so-called "autonomous" government agencies that can reach very high competencies but remain ultimately accountable to human elected officials. Again in Russell's (2019, p. 176) terms: "the machine […] remains coupled to the human, who is a potential source of information that will allow it to avoid mistakes and do a better job."

RESPONSES BY HUMAN–MACHINE COMMUNICATION

Whereas computer scientists can refer to this communicative coupling of machines to humans as a durable response to their problems of goal alignment and uncertainty reduction, this is where the issues for communication researchers only begin. How to conceptualize exchanges between humans on the one side and their vehicles' control systems on the other, each side being endowed with a distinct kind of autonomy? How to grasp the rise of these exchanges above the level of passing and receiving of commands to a level where meaning is constituted in collaboration and negotiation? In their research agenda for Human–Machine-Communication, Guzman and Lewis (2020, p. 70) emphasized three aspects of communicative AI technologies:

(1) the *functional* dimensions through which people make sense of these devices and applications as communicators, (2) the *relational* dynamics through which people associate with these technologies and, in turn, relate to themselves and others, and (3) the *metaphysical* implications called up by blurring ontological boundaries surrounding what constitutes human, machine, and communication.

Functional Aspects

Burleson (2010, p. 151) defined interpersonal communication as "a complex, situated social process in which humans and machines who have established a communicative relationship exchange messages in an effort to generate shared meanings and accomplish social goals." How can communication involving AVs operate towards these goals and meanings?

Humans and their vehicular interlocutors often pursue common goals, as when a driver and her navigation system confer about the destination of a trip and the desired route – the fastest, cheapest, most scenic, or most ecological? Such dialogues for goal-alignment might even lead to abandoning the trip, at least for the human. This would be the case if the dialog ascertained that the ultimate goal was to get certain products home, and that this goal was better achieved by delivery or digital transmission. In this case, human spatial mobility would be replaced by the mobility of the machine or a form of mediated mobility (Keightley & Reading, 2014). The secondary goal of avoiding collisions is already the object of many exchanges between vehicular and human road users and generally functions very reliably (Stanciu et al., 2018).

Significant questions remain when the goals of humans and machinal road users diverge. How to handle the epistemic dominance (Zuboff, 2020) enjoyed by autonomous systems – particularly those owned by corporations that also provide web searches and mobile operating systems – over their human counterparts in confrontational situations such as price negotiations? In other conditions, the AVs' strength can play to their disadvantage. This is the case for the game-theoretical problem of "crosswalk-chicken": two traffic participants moving towards a point of collision, which both want to avoid, while neither wants to step out of his way first. We can expect AVs to perceive and avoid any risk, whereas humans could always be distracted or reckless. Generalized confidence in AVs systematically breaking for others could paralyze AVs and traffic in general (Millard-Ball, 2017). Communicative approaches to this problem – such as designing aggressive car "faces" to intimidate other participants (Landwehr et al., 2011) – run counter efforts to raise the acceptance of AVs through external car displays (ECD) that express attention and care (Holländer et al., 2019). It may require non communicative solutions, in the form of traffic regulations and urban road design, to resolve these conflicts sustainably (Millard-Ball, 2017).

Generating shared meaning also proves problematic when conflicting interests come into play. The mildest form of such conflicts can arise when systems nudge users toward certain navigational choices (cf. Hebblewhite & Gillett, 2020), which the users approve generally, but not in the given moment. Thus, a hurried driver may be frustrated by the slow country roads onto which her navigation system sends her, until she remembers that she had programmed the system's default to avoid highways. The interference becomes more problematic when the systems accommodate the interests of third actors to whom they are also accountable, such as stockholders, legislation, or even broader societal interests in health and environmental interests. The confusion and malaise which AI can cause when mingling in individual and collective meaning-making processes has already been discussed at the examples of photo hosting and social networking services curating personal snapshots into soundtracked storylines (von Pape, 2017). We can expect similar complications when a car attempts to underscore the hypothesized social meaning of a journey (professional? familial? romantic?) through its route choices, interior lighting, and background music.

Relational Aspects

As the above example suggests, transportation as a meaning-making process also affects the relationships and identities of the involved persons. This phenomenon can play out on a fundamental symbolic level – tourist buses actualizing specific meanings of whiteness and blackness (Towns, 2015) – and in very concrete interactions. Thus, Laurier and Dant (2012) showed how AVs eliminate the traditionally patriarchal role of a car's driver and, in consequence, also the supporting role of the co-driver, whose contribution through navigating, leading the conversation, etc. they referred to as "passengering." The disappearance of this mutual obligation and support in AVs liberates all passengers for more productive and individualistic work – perhaps to their regret, as pilot studies suggests (Fraedrich & Lenz, 2016).

The users' relation with the vehicle is also expected to evolve. Ratan (2020) conceptualized possible forms of this evolution through the Self-Other-Utility (SOU) framework by the study of player-avatar relations in video games. With increasing autonomy, the car's role for the user broadly tends to evolve from directly embodying her in a utilitarian sense (as in first-person shooters where the avatar's body is barely visible), to representing her self symbolically (as avatars in Second Life), to assisting her as an independent social other (as do virtual assistants) – but it can also constitute any combination of these for different persons and contexts. The vehicles' independence may go as far as to reason with users about inappropriate requests (by pointing out that they

exceed speed limitations), proactively suggesting certain user behaviors (to take a break, fasten the seatbelt), or imperatively requesting them (to take over control of the vehicle, see Sandry, 2018). Given the vehicles' assumed superior driving competencies and knowledge of the environment, and given their obligations to third actors such as their corporations, the risk appears high that the vehicles' control systems may themselves assume a paternalistic role. They could end up infantilizing their users as flight attendants sometimes do to a point where they challenge the underlying ethical principle of human sovereignty over machines. In sum, a principal and mostly unresolved challenge to HMC lies in accommodating these heavy shifts that can produce rapidly within the relation of users and their vehicles.

Metaphysical Aspects

These relational questions lead to the ultimate metaphysical questions on the meaning of being human, being a machine, and being mobile or immobile (Smets, 2019). As Ess (2018) pointed out at the example of sex, advancements of machine autonomy in new realms can raise our awareness of human characteristics and virtues (namely, the preciousness of experiencing genuine emotions, empathy, and embodied desire). To consider what a reflection of AVs can teach us about humanity – and vice versa – we can build on an essay by Goggin (2019) on disability and the future of cars. Goggin argued how commercial discourses insisting on the merits of AVs to make mobility accessible for disabled persons could have an inverse effect, at least on a symbolical level. By emphasizing the need for the blind to drive a car as any "normal" person does, these discourses further elevate the relevance of specific modes of mobility that are generally difficult for many disabled persons to acquire. They thus echo past decades' talk in praise of prostheses and walking sticks as means to "liberate" people from their wheelchairs, which has also had the effect of diminishing the status of wheelchairs as means of locomotion. This attachment of humanity to specific transportation skills is also enforced in conceptualizations of full vehicle automation as "systems that do not rely on a human to take over" (Autonomous Vehicle Industry Association, 2022), as though it ultimately required humanity and not specific, trained, skills, to steer a car. In analogy to Ess' (2018) interrogation on sex, we should therefore ask which experiences in mobility require and manifest our humanity?

These experiences include the perception of changes in a transversed environment, the desire to expose oneself to these changes and to overcome distances, and the virtues of conceiving oneself in other places and in the places of others. These can be tightly associated with the tasks that are bound to be executed by machines, as shown in an investigation into the pleasure of driving: drivers draw a significant part of this pleasure from the satisfaction of executing their acquired driving skills (Zoller, 2017). Articulating and affording these genuinely human experiences and contributions to transportation is also a function of HMC.

CONCLUSION

This investigation into AVs as an application of HMC builds on a deliberately broad understanding of transportation, vehicles, and autonomy. It assumes that, just as communication, transportation is not only about getting things "across" a given divide. Transportation serves a broad range of goals. It constitutes meaning, positions people to each other socially, and provides unique ways to experience and express our humanity. Therefore, the operations conducted by vehicles reach far beyond the "dynamic driving task" specified in the SAE's "vehicle automation" concept. They touch the full range of logistical, cultural, and social domains involved in mobility itself. This open-ended scope of the vehicles' operations is better accommodated by the bottom-up logic of Antlakis' (2020) technical concept of "autonomy," as the degree to which machines take on increasingly complex goals in ever less predictable environments. For all its breadth and potential, this machinal kind of autonomy cannot be confused with the original meaning of autonomy that had been reserved for humans since Greek city-states first gave themselves constitutions. The machines can write their own code, but not their own laws. They remain "coupled" (Russell, 2019, p. 176) to humans to assert their goals and reduce uncertainty. However, that "coupling" is much richer than the receiving of orders and returning of feedback which had long constituted the interactions of humans and their vehicles: the vehicles grasp much more of the meaning attributed to various journeys, and they have a say in it in their own particular way.

This HMC-based understanding of vehicle autonomy can guide us in examining the communicative processes in which humans and their algorithmic interlocutors establish how things, beings, and symbols are moved and what this movement signifies. To illustrate its potential contributions to ongoing interrogations on mobile communication and transportation, I have declined it along the three aspects of HMC highlighted by Guzman and Lewis (2020). First, HMC provides the analytical distinctions to tell apart the cooperative and antagonistic dynamics which these communicative and transportation processes may assume: from the micro-level of communicative protocols through which the transfer of control occurs within a vehicle, to the negotiations of "crosswalk-chicken" between human and robotic participants to the politics of transportation planning. Second, it guides our attention to the positions into which the emergence of AVs can put humans – individually as passengers or delivery customers, or collectively as boards of transportation – with respect to each other and their machinal counterparts. Third, HMC encourages us to ask not just what remains to be done for humans in increasingly autonomous mobility systems but how to transform these systems so that they can enhance our humanity.

The future directions for robotics and communication which we can draw from this broad approach to autonomous vehicles do not come in specific predictions on the trajectory of AVs. Despite the bottom-up approach to vehicle autonomy advocated here, the medium-term future might very well follow the incremental path of five levels of automation which is foreseen by the SAE's top-down taxonomy. This is at least the direction in which the current system of automobility is pulling with all its inertia. In that case, social scientists may find little innovation for either robotics or communication. What we can still derive from this chapter in any case are indications where to look for innovations for robotics and communication that go beyond the automatic, the vehicular, and indeed the mobile. Concerning personal travel, we may seek innovation for AVs in new methods to emphasize the traveler's experience of the traversed environment and to replace the mutual obligation which people had appreciated in the collaboration of "driving" and "passengering." Rather than automating the human out of the transportation process, we may even seek innovation in new and secure ways to give drivers the satisfaction of moving skillfully through the landscape. The machines to move us in these ways may be vehicles, but may also be other devices that provide forms of "mediated mobility" (Keightley & Reading, 2014), in which the humans' condition is a state of spatial immobility. This could be achieved in multiple ways, from the simple transmission of digital content to the affordance of a bike ride with friends, on a stationary workout device through an environment in virtual reality.

REFERENCES

Antsaklis, P. (2020). Autonomy and metrics of autonomy. *Annual Reviews in Control*, *49*, 15–26. https://doi.org/10.1016/j.arcontrol.2020.05.001

Autonomous Vehicle Industry Association (2022). *FAQs*. https://theavindustry.org/about/faqs

Burleson, B. (2010). The nature of interpersonal communication: A message-centered approach. In C. R. Berger M. E. Roloff, & D. R. Roskos-Ewoldsen (eds.), *The handbook of communication science* (pp. 145–164). SAGE Publications, Inc., www.doi.org/10.4135/9781412982818.n9

Dant, T. (2004). The driver-car. *Theory, Culture & Society*, *21*: 61–79.

Dworkin, G. (1988). *The theory and practice of autonomy*. Cambridge University Press.

Ess, C. M. (2018). Ethics in HMC: Recent developments and case studies. In A. Guzman (ed.), *Human-machine communication: Rethinking communication, technology, and ourselves* (pp. 237–257). Peter Lang.

Fraedrich, E., & Lenz, B. (2016). Taking a drive, hitching a ride: Autonomous driving and car usage. In M. Maurer, J. C. Gerdes, B. Lenz, & H. Winner (Eds.), *Autonomous driving: Technical, legal and social aspects* (pp. 665–685). Springer.

Goggin, G. (2019). Disability, connected cars, and communication. *International Journal of Communication*, 13: 2748–2773.

Guzman, A. (2016). The messages of mute machines: Human-machine communication with industrial technologies, *Communication +1*, *5*, Article 4.

Guzman, A. L., & Lewis, S. C. (2020). Artificial intelligence and communication: A human–machine communication research agenda. *New Media & Society*, *22*(1): 70–86.

Hebblewhite, W., & Gillett, A. J. (2020). Every step you take, we'll be watching you: Nudging and the ramifications of GPS technology. *AI & Society*, 1–13. https://doi.org/10.1007/s00146-020-01098-5

Holländer, K., Colley, A., Mai, C., Häkkilä, J., Alt, F., & Pfleging, B. (2019). Investigating the influence of external car displays on pedestrians' crossing behavior in virtual reality. In *Proceedings of the 21st International Conference on Human-Computer Interaction with Mobile Devices and Services* Association for Computing Machinery, Inc. https://doi.org/10.1145/3338286.3340138

Keightley, E. & Reading, A. (2014). Mediated mobilities. *Media, Culture & Society*, *36*(3): 285–301.

Landwehr, J. R., McGill, A. L., & Herrmann, A. (2011). It's got the look: The effect of friendly and aggressive "facial" expressions on product liking and sales. *Journal of Marketing*, *75*(3), 132–146.

Laurier, E., & Dant, T. (2012). What else we do while driving: towards the driverless car. In M. Grieco & J. Urry (Eds.), *Mobilities: new perspectives on transport and society* (pp. 223–244). Ashgate Publishing.

Lyons, G., & Urry, J. (2005). Travel time use in the information age. *Transportation Research Part A: Policy and Practice*, 39(2–3), 257–276.

Millard-Ball, A. (2018). Pedestrians, autonomous vehicles, and cities. *Journal of Planning Education and Research*, *38*(1), 6–12.

Oswald, K. F. (2016). A brief history of smart transportation infrastructure. *Transfers*, *6*(3), 123–129.

Oxford English Dictionary (2012). Clarendon Press.

Packer, J., & Oswald, K. F. (2010). From windscreen to widescreen: Screening technologies and mobile communication. *The Communication Review*, *13*(4), 309–339.

Pink, S., Fors, V., & Glöss, M. (2019). Automated futures and the mobile present: In-car video ethnographies. *Ethnography*, *20*(1).

Ratan, R. (2019). Cars and contemporary communication. When automobiles are avacars: A self-other-utility approach to cars and avatars. *International Journal of Communication*, 13: 2774–2792.

Russell, S. (2019). *Human compatible: AI and the problem of control*. Penguin UK.

SAE International. (2018). *Taxonomy and definitions for terms related to driving automation systems for on-road motor vehicles* (No. J3016).

Sandry, E. (2018). Automation and human relations with the private vehicle: From automobiles to autonomous cars. *Media International Australia*, *166*(1), 11–19. https://doi.org/10.1177/1329878X17737644

Smets, K. (2019). Media and immobility: The affective and symbolic immobility of forced migrants. *European Journal of Communication*, *34*(6), 650–660.

Sperling, D., & Gordon, D. (2010). *Two billion cars: driving toward sustainability*. Oxford University Press.

Stanciu, S. C., Eby, D. W., & Molnar, L. J. (2018). Pedestrians/bicyclists and autonomous vehicles: how will they communicate? *Transportation*, *2672*(22): 58–66 https://journals.sagepub.com/doi/abs/10.1177/0361198118777091

Tegmark, M. (2017). *Life 3.0: Being human in the age of artificial intelligence*. Knopf.

Towns, A. (2015). *"Riding while white": Transporting race and the production of blackness*. University of North Carolina at Chapel Hill Graduate School. https://doi.org/10.17615/x493-rn64

Townsend, A. M. (2020). *Ghost road: Beyond the driverless car*. W. W. Norton & Company.

Vasileiadou, S., Kalligeropoulos, D., & Karcanias, N. (2003). Systems, modelling and control in Ancient Greece: Part 1: Mythical automata. *Measurement and Control*, *36*(3), 76–80.

von Pape, T. (2017). Living in the moment: Self-narratives of permanently connected media users.

In P. Vorderer, D. Hefner, L. Reinecke & C. Klimmt (eds.), *Permanently online, permanently connected* (97–106). Taylor & Francis.

von Pape, T., Goggin, G., & Forlano, L. (2019). Cars and contemporary communication. *International Journal of Communication, 13*(2019), 2676–2683.

Wilken, R., & Thomas, J. (2019). Cars and contemporary communication. Maps and the autonomous vehicle as a communication platform. *International Journal of Communication, 13*: 2703–2727.

Zoller, D. (2005). Skilled perception, authenticity, and the case against automation. In Lin, P., Jenkins, R., & Abney, K. (eds.)*: Robot ethics 2.0. From autonomous cars to artificial intelligence* (80–92). Oxford University Press.

Zuboff, S. (2020). You are now remotely controlled. *New York Times*, 26.01.2020. www.nytimes.com/2020/01/24/opinion/sunday/surveillance-capitalism.html.

64

HMC in Space Operations

Regina Peldszus

INTRODUCTION

Today, over 5,500 active satellites populate Earth's orbit, overseen by the mission control centers of governmental space agencies, commercial operators, and scientific institutions. As single spacecraft or fleets these machines provide services that enable or enrich contemporary societies: They deliver position, navigation, and timing signals that support our transportation, finance and energy sectors; they perform Earth observation missions that support agriculture, environmental management, weather prediction, our understanding of climate change, and the verification of international treaties; as communications satellites they enable channels of telecommunication and media; and, as scientific probes, they explore far-flung places of scientific significance through technically sophisticated feats such as intercepting comets or navigating the terrain of a planetary surface.

For the majority of operations to date, spacecraft are employed as human proxies to remotely perform tasks in space for which machine presence is less hazardous, resource-intensive, or more reliable (NASA, 2020). Irrespective of the mission, this entails human engagement in the form of remote interaction through communication. Due to the high risk inherent in space missions, this

process is situated in highly formal supervisory control contexts. Considerable attention has therefore been devoted to understanding and improving interactions between human and machine agents, with a focus on cognitive and engineering aspects (NASA, 1976; NASA, 2007).

As the utilization of space and hence our interaction with machines in orbit increase in scale and diversity, the emerging field of Human–Machine Communication (HMC) offers important insights on understanding and designing the relationship of humans and machines in space, while space as an extreme setting presents a unique laboratory for exploring fundamental themes in HMC conceptually.

This chapter offers a broad range of points of departure for such engagement by synthesizing strands of enquiry in theory and application from different disciplines related to the human–technology relationship in space. The chapter describes the fundamental characteristics of the human and machine agents involved in a remote communication process, and highlights fundamental operational practices, both formal and tacit. It points out methodological approaches to analyzing HMC for space operations, and offers perspectives on future areas of engagement in view of greater autonomy of spacecraft and, in extending the focus of this chapter from uncrewed to crewed spaceflight, it highlights the use of robotic support of astronauts.

SPACE OPERATIONS AS COLLABORATIVE, REMOTE HUMAN–MACHINE COMMUNICATION

Most essentially, HMC in space is a collaborative and remote process between two agents who work towards the same goal: the spacecraft in a physically hostile and inaccessible environment of outer space and the mission control team in the highly formalized setting of the control room.

The Spacecraft

Spacecraft are placed in space – near-Earth orbit or a planetary trajectory or surface – to perform a predefined function in fulfilment of an overall mission (i.e. taking radar measurements of ocean ice thickness, extracting rock samples on the Martian surface, or relaying telecommunications messages). Their composition is mission- and environment-specific: In the harsh space environment, spacecraft are exposed to extreme temperatures and radiation, gravity and pressure levels, potential hazards (e.g. collisions with human-made debris or natural particles), and must endure significant levels of vibration and acceleration during launch. Depending on their mission, they range in size from one-off, exquisite coach-sized structures with decade-long life-spans to so-called cubesats the size of milk cartons produced in batches that are more frequently replaced.

Generally, spacecraft comprise two main elements: the payload, which consists of the mission-specific instruments such as cameras, deployable arms for sampling or other sensors, and the platform, which comprises a range of subsystems that address all the functions necessary for guiding and orienting the spacecraft, for managing its thermal conditions, and transmission of signals. An onboard computer receives and executes commands from the ground-based operators, and has a degree of inbuilt autonomy to react to adverse conditions to preserve the integrity of the entire spacecraft (i.e. going into safe-mode during a component failure).

The Mission Control Team

The interlocutor of the spacecraft is the mission control team on the ground. As professional expert users, mission controllers have received specialized training in order to interact with, understand, and command their machine partners. They are organized in a manner that mirrors the fundamental systems engineering features (cf. Booher, 2003) of the spacecraft itself, whereby each analyst or engineer addresses a specific subsystem (such as thermal, or guidance) under the oversight of an operations manager or flight director. The mission controllers are responsible for monitoring the status and ensure the health and integrity of the spacecraft in order to increase the likelihood of overall mission success, for instance uninterrupted data collection or other actions the spacecraft performs.

With rare exceptions, none of the members of a mission control team have ever accessed the space environment (i.e. as astronauts) or have direct experience of its counterintuitive characteristics (i.e. from exposure to short periods of microgravity during a parabolic flight). Usually, the majority of mission controllers will not have seen, let alone handled, the actual spacecraft they will interact with remotely (i.e. during the design or assembly of a satellite). They hence rely on the information environment of the control room, the locale in which the HMC process in space operations is primarily situated.

For routine operations, a control room for one spacecraft or a fleet of similar spacecraft can consist of a few workstations and a number of screens representing the status of the different subsystems and overall temporal and situational context of the spacecraft. For special events that require more experts to be co-located, such as a launch or complex maneuvers, a full-scale control room accommodates the entire team in dedicated workstations, which, like the specific roles of the human controllers, also represent the different subsystems of the spacecraft. These "positions" are oriented toward a shared overall representation of the spacecraft on a higher level of abstraction on one or more large displays (Karafantis, 2016). Communication between human team members in these settings is structurally and semantically formalized.

For all types of operations, a crucial further layer of mediation facilitates communication: the mission control system, i.e. the software interface for interacting with the spacecraft, which represents information about the status of the spacecraft's subsystems and enables commanding (Eickhoff, 2012, p. 45).

Space Operations as Remote Communication

The human team of operators communicates with the spacecraft by exchanging data: Through telecommands transmitted via ground-based antennas, the control team conveys instructions to the onboard computer of the spacecraft. In response, data from the spacecraft is transferred back to the operations center (Uhlig et al., 2015). Communication links are usually intermittent, contingent upon availability and location of ground stations and the type of orbit of the spacecraft, determining when it physically passes over an antenna at certain times. The more distant the spacecraft is, such as in Mars orbit, the greater the delay between transmission and receipt of commands may be.

A series of commands may complete a procedure, i.e. a pre-planned plan to perform a certain activity, such as activating thrusters to change its orientation or position, or to turn on an instrument (Sgobba & Allahdadi, 2013). The purpose of communication on the part of the human interlocutor is hence constrained to the formal instances where the human agent wishes to affect a change in the state of the machine (cf. Suchman, 2007, p. 125). The machine-agent then responds with information about itself and its context – or rather, this response is also elicited by another command to downlink data; the nature and extent of the respective messages is asymmetric in its reciprocity (cf. Fortunati & Edwards, 2020, p. 7).

Commanding is a formal language: The human team speaks with one single voice, epitomized by carefully crafted commands conveyed to the spacecraft, which understands this code, and sends its own rich information back – which then the operators try to decode through various approaches of sense-making.

FORMAL AND INFORMAL THEMES OF SENSE-MAKING

Beyond the overall effort in pursuing and constituting meaning through employing machines to explore or utilize outer space (cf. Guzman 2018), space operations are primarily characterized by a process of sense-making on the part of the human interlocutor (cf. Adams et al., 1995). Here, we can distinguish two kinds of practice that are oriented around the formal "life cycle" of the spacecraft in systems engineering nomenclature, and, as a derivative of this, informal practices around the "life" of the spacecraft as a collaborative partner.

Formal Operational Practices in the "System Life Cycle"

As methodical the construction of commands is by the mission control team, as equally formal is the process of decoding the telemetry received back from the spacecraft about its state, how far it is in executing the mission, how the different subsystems are performing, and whether any related adjustments are needed.

Crucially, however, machine and human do not share the same operating environment. Contrary to non-remote HMC settings, human interlocutors cannot tap into a comparable wealth of contextual information about the spacecraft's surroundings. They rely on sensors to provide situational awareness of the spacecraft and its environment and must interpret the corresponding feedback. This black-box character of the machine is exacerbated by potentially long time-lags for signal transmission depending on degree of remoteness.

As mission time elapses, irregularities accumulate and the machine's behavior becomes more opaque. This necessitates the re-appraisal of shared mental models across the operations team, i.e. the fusion of the modified understanding of the different subsystems. These "operator models" are built over time (Leveson, 2011, here 42), as information about spacecraft behavior is absorbed and adjusted as part of the mental model. The ongoing practice of diagnostics focuses on identifying potential anomalies, small aberrations from the ideal state of the spacecraft and its components. During anomaly detection and resolution of their machine partner, human operators are aided by automated diagnostic tools (Heras et al. 2009), similar to other collaborative supervisory or process control environments (Lundberg & Johansson, 2020).

During the "life cycle" of a spacecraft, observing and diagnosing the so-called "health" of the spacecraft is a constant theme: from launch phase to commissioning and testing, to routine operations and when contingencies arise, up to the end of the mission, when the spacecraft has reached the "end of its life" and is "passivated" and put to a so-called "graveyard orbit" or burns up in the atmosphere during a controlled re-entry (Uhlig et al., 2015). This framing of the machine in human terms is part of the formal nomenclature of systems engineering and is further enriched by tacit practices.

Tacit Operational Practices and the "Life" of the Spacecraft

Monitoring spacecraft "health" and "behavior" during its "lifetime," and "communicating" with it are classic operations engineering terms (Wertz & Larson, 1999). Ascertaining whether it is still "alive" or "waking up" after "hibernation" (i.e. to preserve energy during a longer uneventful period such as cruising to a destination), and has a "heartbeat signal" are terms often used by operators more colloquially amongst each other or to explain to the public (cf. Clancey, 2012).[1] These highlight another layer of sense- and meaning-making: Here, the spacecraft may still be understood as a machine, but with its own idiosyncratic, anthropomorphized traits.

Throughout the course of a mission or career, operators accumulate knowledge and experience that complement the use of automated diagnostic tools for detecting and resolving anomalies (Heras et al., 2009). Using experience and intuition to trigger diagnostic processes are essential tacit practices particularly in unforeseen events. While they are not the formal base for decision-making, they serve as heuristics and crucial first indicators for situation awareness, for considering a hypothesis and beginning further investigation, or taking calculated risks under acute or latent information constraints, as operators find workarounds to coax or compel the spacecraft to comply with their commands (Peldszus, 2014).

However, while serving as general rules of thumb to describe overall characteristics of a machine or patterns of interaction ("feeding the monster," "an old friend/ patient," "like four babies"), such analogies are understood by operators to be potentially counterintuitive (ibid.) – similarly to other automation contexts, where extrapolating machine behavior based on assumed human behavioral patterns courts misinterpretation (Palanque, 2020, p. 6). Rather, while describing a concrete communication relationship, implicit characterizations of spacecraft as living entity refer to a general link of the control team to the spacecraft, comparable to "maintaining feelings of connection" between agents in a virtual communication settings (cf. McEwen & Wellmann, 2013). Understanding machine agents for what they are – assemblages of technology in a remote environment that perform dedicated roles (cf. Atkinson, 2012) – is at the core of this relationship. For fundamentally, spacecraft do not exhibit humanness by design: Unlike some applications in care or assistance where virtual or robotic assistants emulate empathy as part of their function, spacecraft are not designed to fulfil such requirements; their features are device- rather than human-centric (Fong et al., 2013).

METHODS FOR UNDERSTANDING HMC IN SPACE OPERATIONS

As a highly complex socio-technical system, space operations and the deconstruction of its HMC dimension merit the use of different approaches. Two strands from the systems engineering and social sciences disciplines lend themselves particularly to the study and application of HMC in space operations, as they facilitate descriptions of the different agents and help uncover underlying themes of their relationships.

Human-tech and Systems Approaches

In order to chart the basic settings in which interactive practices in complex systems are rooted, the theory and analytical repertoire of human–technology interaction provides a broad point of departure (cf. Vicente, 1999). Here, particularly, field-level examinations such as work domain analysis are suitable for examining at settings that involve knowledge-based problem-solving such as tacit and formal sense-making practices. They provide a case-specific base for explanation of observed behavior of interactions (Bisantz & Vicente, 1994) by decomposing and relating the values, functions, agents, and artefacts of the physical and information environment of a setting (Naikar & Sanderson, 2001). This allows a formal representation of discrete elements in the HMC process, that can then be conceptualized as joint cognitive system (Hollnagel & Woods, 2006), in preparation for modeling, quantitative analysis, or simulation of communication settings, and serve to contextualize qualitative enquiry.

Ethnography and STS

Ethnographic and science and technology studies (STS) approaches can provide rich descriptions of the spectrum of practices and meaning-making in complex settings, particularly with their foci on interactions as they actually unfold, rather than how they are planned to be conducted ideally, and regarding the motivations that inform their design (Hughes et al., 1993). While spaceflight has not traditionally been a prolific area for ethnography and anthropological study, early accounts by operators were initially autobiographical, if not auto-ethnographic, and often recount detailed anecdotal descriptions of interactive practices (cf. Kraft, 2002; Kranz, 2000).

Recently, however, key research has described in detail the human–machine interaction of contemporary mission control teams in the science and exploration area. Important aspects related to sense- and place-making practices have been examined particularly in the use of robotic probes by teams of scientists that use the data produced by rovers, or who regard the spacecraft as a machine-extension of their human selves in a locale they would otherwise be unable to explore directly (Olson & Messeri, 2015; Vertesi, 2015). Others have examined in great detail the work of operations teams, and their adaptation strategies for synching with their remote machine partners, such as adjusting their sleep–wake schedules (Clancey, 2012).

Works from the science and technology studies and history fields document the information architecture of space mission control and its coming into being (Johnson, 2015; Karafantis, 2016) or disentangle in-depth the fundamental fabric of human–machine relationships of space systems that have informed most subsequent interactions (Mindell, 2011). Particularly, aspects such as tacit knowledge, handling automation, remote presence – areas that especially resonate with the focus of HMC – have been highlighted as meriting further enquiry to underpin future systems and their policies (ibid.).

FUTURE PERSPECTIVES

As the utilization of space is undergoing profound change, space operations and our relationship with machines in orbit are transforming with it. Emerging key developments concern the unprecedented numbers of orbital spacecraft and their growing autonomy, as well as renewed plans in human spaceflight for Lunar and Mars missions that will increasingly necessitate human–machine partnerships also for astronauts.

Large Constellations of Spacecraft

Ever more governmental and private actors own or operate spacecraft. Across the next decades, private companies are preparing launches of so-called mega-constellations that consist of hundreds, thousands, even ten thousands of individual satellites (Lal et al., 2018). One central challenge is how to interact with these unprecedently large fleets. While the current operational paradigm is collaborative human practice, the relationship will be asymmetric for the most part: From the enduring paradigm of a team of human operators handling a single space probe for bespoke scientific missions, towards a relatively small team of human operators handling a constellations of thousands of spacecraft for routine services such as broad-band provision. Communication environments will have to be facilitated not only between human–machine

agents, but also between distributed human teams and within machine–machine groups in order to avoid collisions (Martinie et al., 2014). Implications for human operators entail a growing need for multilateral collaboration for sharing data on the location and behavior of machines in orbit to preserve the safety of the spacecraft and the sustainability of the orbital environment (Ailor, 2015). In this context, HMC can make important contributions to reflect on and structure interactions and implications of the emerging systems-of-systems in orbit.

Increased Autonomy of Individual Spacecraft

The trend for greater numbers and aggregation of satellites is set to be accompanied by increased autonomy of individual spacecraft. Since the beginnings of spaceflight in the late 1950s, there has been a range of autonomous vehicles in space, from satellites and robotic probes to planetary rovers (Vepa, 2019). Autonomy, here, is understood as the ability to "operate in a dynamic environment independent of external control" (NASA, 2020): The further spacecraft venture away from Earth, the more autonomy they require to learn and adapt as their mission proceeds, in order to be able to respond to novel events in situ (Chien & Wagstaff, 2017). This will involve layers of autonomy where the human is not directly in the loop – both in near-earth and more remote interactions – with the help of machine agents (Policella et al., 2018), including considerations and implications of how we shape operator roles (Loukissas, 2014, p. 4).

Machine Agents to Support Crewed Missions

Increasing autonomy will also be a crucial feature of human–robotic partnerships in crewed spaceflight in the future, i.e. employing machine agents to support astronauts on space stations or on a planetary surface. Prototypes that have been trialled include Cimon,[2] a sphere-shaped, voice-controlled artificial intelligence-based robot who assists and documents experiments by astronauts on the International Space Station (DLR, 2018; for account of interaction cf. Fröding & Peterson, 2020), and R5, a humanoid robot designed for planetary surface operations (NASA, 2017).

These experimental assistants are deployed in view of cooperating with astronauts during future longer and more remote missions where direct communication with ground is limited, for instance to support complex or arduous tasks or provide situation awareness. Beyond purely mission-related roles, virtual assistants and interactive expert systems will also come to the fore during off-duty time to entertain, counteract monotony, in house keeping or skill maintenance, or for medical monitoring.

Effective interaction beyond the formal commanding paradigm (i.e. typing inputs manually or releasing lines of code) will increasingly include diverse modes of communication including natural language, gesture, and voice (NASA, 2020; Salazar, 2018). The criterion for successful communication and interaction between humans and machines, then, will be whether they can perform together and attain shared goals, absorbing and processing contextual input from the environment (Stowers et al., 2017).

As we increasingly employ machines in Earth orbit and beyond, the application and study of HMC in space operations – respectively space operations as HMC – will be an area of inquiry in its own right, and it can enrich the study and development of the relationship between human and machine agents in other complex or safety-critical settings.

NOTES

1   Compare also to public outreach of space agencies (e.g. US, India, Europea) involving personalized social media accounts for individual spacecraft such as Mars rovers or orbiters that communicate in the first person, sometimes "with" each other.
2   "Crew Interactive Mobile CompanioN."

REFERENCES

Adams, M., Jager, Y. J., Tenney, I. & Pew, Richard W. (1995). Situation awareness and the cognitive management of complex systems. *Human Factors*, 37(1), 85–104.

Ailor, W. (2015). Space traffic management. *Handbook of space security: Policies, applications, programs*, eds. Schrogl, K-U., Hays, P. L., Robinson, J., Moura, D. & Giannopapa, C., Vol. 1: Springer, 231–255.

Atkinson, D.J., Friedland, P. & Lyons, J.P. (2012). Human-machine trust for robust autonomous systems. Proceedings of the 4th Annual Human-Agent-Robot Teamwork Workshop, 7th ACM/IEEE International Conference on Human-Robot Interaction, Boston, MA, March 2012.

Bisantz, A. M. & Vicente, K. J. (1994). Making the abstraction hierarchy concrete. *International Journal of Human-Computer Studies*, 40(1), 83–117.

Booher, H. R., ed., (2003). *Handbook of human systems integration*. Wiley.

Chien, S. & Wagstaff, K.L. (2017). Robotic space exploration agents. *Science Robotics*, 2(7). https://doi-org/10.1126/scirobotics.aan4831

Clancey, W.J. (2012). *Working on Mars: Voyages of scientific discovery with the Mars exploration rovers*. MIT Press.

DLR (2018) *Human-machine interaction in space – first technology experiment using artificial intelligence on the ISS: CIMON, the intelligent astronaut assistant*. www.dlr.de/content/en/articles/news/2018/1/20180302_cimon-the-intelligent-astronaut-assistant_26307.html

Eickhoff, J. (2012). *Onboard computers, onboard software and satellite operations: An introduction*. Springer.

Fong, T., Rochlis Zumbado, J., Currie, N., Mishkin, A., & Akin, D. L. (2013). Space telerobotics: Unique challenges to human–robot collaboration in space. *Reviews of Human Factors and Ergonomics*, 9, 6–56.

Fortunati, L. & Edwards, A. (2020). Opening space for theoretical, methodological, and empirical issues in human-machine communication, *Human-Machine Communication*, 1, 7–18. https://doi.org/10.30658/hmc.1.1

Fröding, B. & Peterson, M. (2020). Friendly AI. *Ethics and Information Technology*, 22(3). https://doi.org/10.1007/s10676-020-09556-w

Guzman, A. L. (2018). What is human-machine communication, anyway? In A. L. Guzman (Ed.), *Human-machine communication: Rethinking communication, technology, and ourselves*, 1–28, Peter Lang. https://doi.org/10.3726/b14399

Guzman A. L. (2020). Ontological boundaries between humans and computers and the implications for human-machine communication. *Human-Machine Communication*, 1, 37–54. https://doi.org/10.30658/hmc.1.3

Heras, J. A. M., Yeung K. L., Donati, A., Sousa, B., Keil, N. (2009). DrMust: Automating the anomaly investigation first-cut, *Proceedings of the IJCAI–09 Workshop on Artificial Intelligence in Space, Pasadena, US, July 17–18, 2009*.

Hollnagel, E. and Woods, D.D. (2006) Epilogue: Resilience engineering precepts. In: Hollnagel, E., Woods, D.D. and Leveson, N. (Eds.), *Resilience engineering concepts and precepts*. Aldershot, 347–358.

Hughes, J., Randall, D., & Shapiro, D. (1993). From ethnographic record to system design: Some experiences from the field. *Computer Supported Cooperative Work*, 1, 123–141.

Johnson, M.P. (2015). *Mission Control: Inventing the groundwork of spaceflight*. University Press of Florida.

Karafantis, L. (2016). *Under control: Constructing the nerve centers of the Cold War*. Johns Hopkins University.

Kraft, C. (2002). *Flight: My life in Mission Control*. Plume.

Kranz, G. (2000). *Failure is not an option: Mission Control from Mercury to Apollo 13 and beyond*. Simon & Schuster.

Lal, B., Balakrishnan, A., Caldwell, B. M., Buenconsejo, R. S., & Carioscia, S. (2018). *Global trends in space situational awareness and space traffic management*. IDA Science & Technology Policy Institute.

Leveson, N. G. (2011). *Engineering a safer world: Systems thinking applied to safety*. MIT Press.

Loukissas, Y.A. & Mindell, D. (2014) Visual Apollo: A graphical exploration of computer–human relationships. *Design Issues*, 30(2), 4–16. https://doi.org/10.1162/DESI_a_00258

Lundberg, J. & Johansson, B. J. E. (2020). A framework for describing interaction between human operators and autonomous, automated, and manual control systems. *Cognition, Technology & Work*, 22(3), s.p. https://doi.org/10.1007/s10111-020-00637-w

Martinie, C., Barboni, E., Navarre, D., Palanque, P., Fahssi, R., Poupart, E., & Cubero-Castan, E. (2014). Multi-models-based engineering of collaborative systems: Application to collision avoidance operations for spacecraft. *ACM EICS'14, 17–20 June 2014, Rome, Italy*. https:doi.org/10.1145/2607023.2607031

McEwen, R. & Wellmann, B. (2013). Relationships, community, and networked individuals. In Teigland, R. & Power, D. (Eds.) *The immersive internet: Reflections on the entangling of the virtual with society, politics and the economy*. Palgrave Macmillan, 168–179.

Messeri, L. (2016). *Placing outer space: An earthly ethnography of other worlds*. Duke University Press.

Mindell, D. A. (2011). *Digital Apollo: Human and machine in spaceflight*. MIT Press.

Naikar, N., & Sanderson, P. M. (2001) Evaluating design proposals for complex systems with work domain analysis. *Human Factors*, 43(4), 529–542.

NASA (1976). *A Forecast of Space Technology 1980–2000*. NASA Scientific & Technical Information Office.

NASA (2007). *System Engineering Handbook (Revision 1)*. NASA.

NASA (2017). *R5*. www.nasa.gov/feature/r5/

NASA (2020). NASA Technology Taxonomy Technology Area 4. https://techport.nasa.gov/view/taxonomy

Olson, V. A. and Messeri, L. (2015). Beyond the anthropocene. *Environment and Society* 6(1), pp. 28–47.

Palanque, P. (2020). Ten objectives and ten rules for designing automations in interaction techniques, user interfaces and interactive systems. *AVI '20, September 28–October 2, 2020, Salerno, Italy*. https://doi.org/10.1145/3399715.3400872

Peldszus, R. (2014). *The human element & system resilience at the European Space Operations Centre: Observation of tacit operational practice (Technical Report)*. European Space Agency.

Policella, N., Fratini, S., Donati, A., Del Fuente, S. & Casale, M. (2018). AI support for future mission operations: The case of BepiColombo on-board memory management, *AIAA Space Operations Conference, May 38–June 1, 2018, Marseille, France*, https://doi.org/10.2514/6.2018-2497

Salazar, G. A. (2018). *Considerations for implementing voice-controlled spacecraft systems through a human-centered design approach (technical report)*. NASA Johnson Space Center.

Sgobba, T. & Allahdadi, F. A. (2013). On-orbit mission control. In Sgobba, T. & Allahdadi, F. A, Rongier, I., & Wilde, P. (eds.) *Safety design for space operations*. Elsevier, 371–410.

Stowers, K., Oglesby, J., Sonesh, S., Leyva, K., Iwig, C., and Eduardo S. (2017). A framework to guide the assessment of human–machine systems. *Human Factors* 59 (2), 172–188.

Suchman, L. A. (2007). *Human–machine reconfigurations: Plans and situated actions*. Cambridge University Press.

Uhlig, T., Sellmaier, F. & Schmidhuber, M. (2015). *Spacecraft operations*. Springer.

Vepa, R. (2019). *Dynamics and control of autonomous space vehicles and robotics*. Cambridge University Press.

Vertesi, J. (2015). *Seeing like a rover: How robots, teams, and images craft knowledge of Mars*. Chicago University Press.

Vicente, K. J. (1999). *Cognitive work analysis: Towards safe, productive, and healthy computer-based work*. Lawrence Erlbaum Associates.

Vicente, K. J. (2010). *Human-tech: Ethical and scientific foundations*. Oxford University Press.

Wertz, J. R. & Larson, W. J. (Eds.) (1999). *Space mission analysis and design* (3rd Ed.), Kluwe/Springer.

65

Religious Human–Machine Communication: Practices, Power, and Prospects

Pauline Hope Cheong and Yashu Chen

INTRODUCTION AND BACKGROUND

For many contemporary minds, the fusion of robots and religion represents "an unexpected synthesis" of science and spirituality (Lu & Robertson, 2016), two seemingly irreconcilable "extremes" (Trovato, De Saint Chamas, Nishimura, et al., 2019) that even reflects fears of roboapocalypse disrupting religious orders and clergy work in a post-singularity future. Yet centuries before digital media and self-moving devices, religiously charged Greek, Roman, Indian, and Chinese mythology were already featuring animated, "made, not born" beings. In Buddhist legends for example, mechanical "spirit movement machines" were envisioned as robotic guardians defending Buddha's sacred relics (Mayor, 2018) and innovations in automation of spiritual tasks were not uncommon in the history of Buddhist practice in China (Travagnin, 2020). The saga of spiritual mechanical innovation continues today with the emergence of a new generation of robotic agents in the religious realm. In recent years, these agents have included faith-based or inspired autonomous and humanoid machines which can move and communicate with multiple modalities and even relate to humans on an emotional level, powered by the latest digital and artificial intelligence (AI) technologies (Cheong, 2020a; Trovato, De Saint Chamas, Nishimura, et al., 2019).

This chapter reviews the emergent and inter-disciplinary field of religious human–machine communication pertaining to religious bots, which have been a relatively underexplored area of research and development. In this chapter, we begin by discussing examples of contemporary spiritual robots. In doing so, we recognize them as not merely transmission devices through which faith adherents make meaning but also "machine subjects with which people make meaning" (Guzman & Lewis, 2019) as these bots function as new religious communicative agents promoting religious instruction and experiences (Cheong, 2021). We then go on to discuss key areas for future research at the micro, meso, and macro levels associated with the development of robotics, particularly for the fields of media and communication studies. These areas include users' perceptions and attitudes about religious robots, cross-cultural human–machine communication practices and design guidelines, and the role of human authority and agency in the constitution and governance of AI systems.

RISE OF NEW RELIGIOUS COMMUNICATORS: FAITH–BASED HUMAN–ROBOT PRACTICES

An emerging research domain alongside recent developments in religious robotics concern the roles that these agents assume, particularly in religious pedagogy and rituals as bots function to enlighten and teach, model and facilitate religious practices and rituals (Cheong, 2020a). Multiple machines emanating from different faith backgrounds have been designed and applied to the duties of the traditional priesthood, including acting as a teacher, advisor, counselor and comforter. Existing research has uncovered functional affordances akin to media uses and gratifications in human–machine communication as practiced in the faith domain. In this way, in some of the discussion of the techno-possibilities of AI for religion, religion has been widely understood as a "service industry" with cutting edge inventions serving specific and changing "religious needs" of the faith adherents and seekers (Rambelli, 2018; Robertson, 2018), and in rural areas or regions bereft of priests (Löffler et al., 2019). Recent communication research articles have also discussed communication affordances and constraints of spiritual robotics (Cheong, 2020b) and their implications for the construction and performance of religious authority (Cheong, 2021).

Among the areas that religious robots work and interact, developments in religious pedagogy and learning have been prominent in popular narratives and recent research studies. For example, Buddhist humanoids have begun to preach and provide religious instruction to temple visitors. Xian'er, a robot monk developed by the Longquan monastery in Beijing, not only gestures and moves around in the temple's animation center, it also interacts with visitors by answering questions about Buddhism and daily life through voice recognition and an evolving list of five questions on its chest's touch screen (Ke, 2016). In this case, the communication affordance of searchability which refers to the accessibility of spiritual content and teachings via automated search processes, characterizes this robot's ability to explain basic faith tenets, and answer spiritual inquiries drawing from a database of Buddhist books, teachings, and questions and answers derived from the temple's then Chief Abbot's blog (Cheong, 2020b). On social media platforms like WeChat, Xian'er is also accessible via its chatbot which can communicate with users in both English and Mandarin, allowing interactants round-the-clock access to its priestly teachings and guidance for meditation (Tatlow, 2016).

Similarly, Mindar, an android priest modeled after the Bodhisattva of Compassion, serves to communicate spiritual instruction by reciting and explaining the Heart Sutra to visitors to the Koda-ji Buddhist temple in Kyoto, Japan (The Japan Times, 2019). Mindar can use hand gestures and eye contact to communicate with interested parties and plans are underway to equip it with machine-learning capabilities to "tailor feedback to worshippers' specific spiritual and ethical problems" (Samuel, 2020, para. 4).

In addition, while acting as sages and spiritual instructors, robots can model religious action to promote religious piety and practices. The communicative affordance of multimediality highlights Xian'er's capability to sing Buddhist songs, chant mantras, and lead meditation sessions timed to users' preferences (Cheong, 2020b). In another example, Veldan, a Quranic term, meaning "youth of heaven" is a humanoid robot developed and customized from a Robotis Bioloid robot by an Iranian teacher. This robot was designed to advance Islamic prayer instruction and demonstrate to school children how to perform Islamic prayer movements, such as prostration postures (McBride, 2019).

Besides the above examples, it is worthwhile to note how robotics which are not explicitly designed for religious practice may model religious beliefs, thereby serving as a means of extending spiritual instruction. PLEO rb (for reborn) is a robo-dinosaur animated by artificial intelligence and any malfunctioning units can be "reincarnated" with its learnings uploaded into a new unit, thereby "effectively transporting the old robo-pet's personality into its body reincarnate" (Robertson, 2018, p. 169). According to Robertson (2018), this robot is instructive and has a close religious connection since it represents concepts of rebirth and reincarnation in new age Buddhism, which have been adapted to meet contemporary human needs and desires.

Another emerging area of religious human–machine interaction is ritual communication whereby bots provide blessings and facilitate religious rites while providing spiritual comfort and companionship. For example, both BlessU-2 and UT are humanoid robots that have extended religious experiences in Europe by providing multiple types of blessing rituals linked to traditional, companionship, encouragement and renewal purposes. BlessU-2 is a robot that can communicate verbally and non-verbally with movable facial features and arms (Miller, 2017). This machine has a tactile screen chest for users to indicate which language they would like to interact with (out of multiple choices including German, English, French, and Spanish) and which voice they would like to hear from the robot (male or female). After each encounter, BlessU-2 offers a printout of its blessing, expresses thanks for the visit, and says goodbye "God bless and protect you" (Sherwood, 2017).

Besides performing blessing rituals, robots have also been deployed to facilitate memorial and mourning rites in Japan, in line with growing technologies being employed in the funeral services industry to reduce costs and meet demand amidst the scarcity of priests (Ackerman, 2017). Pepper, a white humanoid robot with a chest-based tablet, has been programmed to serve as a priest in Buddhist funerals (Martin, 2017). This robot can bow and strike a meditation bowl with a mallet while performing funeral chants with sutras from four major Japanese Buddhist sects. Pepper can also deliver sermons and livestream the funeral proceedings for virtually present family and friends (Martin, 2017). A modified version of Pepper known as "Digital Shaman" can further help "facilitate the labor of mourning" by donning a mask that reproduces the facial appearance of the deceased, speaking in the voice of the deceased, and staying with the host family for the whole traditional period of mourning (49 days) before saying final words and shutting down (Rambelli, 2018, p. 66). Another "Robo-Priest" in Japan has been programmed to facilitate memorial services and can be activated on an annual basis to chant appropriate prayers for deceased persons in the Buddhist and Christian traditions (Rambelli, 2018).

Furthermore, spiritual robotics can facilitate rituals while providing companionship and care, particularly to elderly persons seeking company and social interaction. SanTo is a theomorphic robot, designed to resemble a divine deity and represent a supernatural being in the Catholic tradition. A Christian robot with the appearance of a saint, SanTo serves as a companion of prayers. It can pray alongside religious users and can cite parts of the Bible and life stories of saints (Löffler et al., 2019). In another faith context, Daruma-To is a social robot that is shaped like a Daruma doll, which is traditionally recognized as a sacred being and spiritual protector affiliated with Buddhism and Shintoism in Japan. This bot communicates through visual tracing, voice and facial expression, and was designed to interact and to accompany elderly in their prayers while also monitoring their health conditions (Trovato, Kishi, Kawai, et al., 2019).

IMPLICATIONS OF RELIGIOUS HUMAN–MACHINE COMMUNICATION AND RESEARCH PROSPECTS

In light of the recency of religious robotics and the nascency of interdisciplinary research, there is much potential for further research and development. In the following, we draw upon insights from recent publications to discuss three potential areas of growth that may pose particular interest to scholars in communication and media studies.

First, the recent and ongoing research in the nexus of religion and robots highlights immense prospects for the growth and development of new religious robotic agents, as well as for their continued assessment. In particular, we echo researchers who have called for a closer examination of user attitudes and perceptions toward the acceptance or resistance in communication with religious robotic agents (e.g. Ahmed & La, 2020; Löffler et al., 2019). Historically, religious scholars such as Robert Geraci have highlighted close connections between theological beliefs, particularly apocalyptic Jewish and Christian teachings and the advancement of robotics in scientific research (Geraci, 2008). The Shinto Buddhist belief of animism has also been widely credited for the positive perception of animated beings and the relatively fast development and uptake of robotics for everyday life in Japan (Geraci, 2006).

Thus, future research can shed more light on the influence of lay spiritual beliefs and perceptions on religious robotic acceptance and interactions. Research studies can validate or refine findings from early or pilot studies; for example, new studies can probe the survey results from a limited sample of German, mostly Christian and female interviewees, which showed that while these users were receptive toward the QT robot's cartoonish appearance, they did not find it appropriate for the serious context of a blessing ritual, preferring instead a tall robot with a loud voice to communicate its message in a "more effective manner" (Löffler et al., 2019). An in-depth examination of user beliefs and preferences for technology use in specific religious contexts can, for instance, shed light on which kinds of robotic agents can best facilitate different types of rituals.

Furthermore, advancing an understanding of spiritual users' behavioral intent and attitudes toward these machines, can potentially illuminate the extent in which faith adherents will interact with these machines, and how religious human–machine communication is enacted. In particular, recent developments in theomorphic and skeuomorphic robots suggests the need for systemic evaluation of public perceptions as a means of accessing the perceived efficacy of mediated religious practices and the adaptation of robotics for future pedagogy and rituals. Future research can examine beliefs about religious piety, facilitated by relationships with new media. It has been hypothesized for example, that "a theomorphic robot [with perceived sacred appearances and characteristics] may be accepted more favorably than a non-theomorphic robot....related to the fact that religion is intertwined with culture and divine representations are present in world culture" (Trovato, De Saint Chamas, Nishimura, et al., 2019).

Therefore, on a micro level, propositions regarding user background and preferences that position individuals in particular ways toward or against robotic agents warrant further empirical studies. Specifically, primary research is needed to investigate in what ways and to what extent perceived divine characteristics of religious machines appeal to religious adherents, or detract from their devotional growth. For instance, future field work could investigate claims that users recognize the "protective role" and "superhuman capabilities" of a theomorphic robot, and "feel safer thanks to the robot" (Trovato, De Saint Chamas, Nishimura, et al., 2019; Trovato, Kishi, Kawai, et al., 2019; Trovato, Lucho, Ramón, et al., 2018; Trovato, Pariasca, Ramirez, et al., 2019).

Consequently, further investigation of user attitudes and emotions about robots in discursive exchanges and experimental settings will clarify meaning-making processes in religious interactions to help develop design guidelines for different user preferences and contexts (Löffler et al., 2019). Furthermore, intercultural and international communication research can help advance understanding of religious technology use since past research studies have identified different socio-cultural norms and values associated with user perceptions of robots in different cultures around the world (Ahmed & Lu, 2020). Thus, global design guidelines for religious robot technologies in the future should attend to communicative affordances and constraints (Cheong, 2021). Deeper attention should be paid to examining cross-cultural differences as well as similarities in lay persons' perceptions and attitudes toward the acceptance of AI-based applications for the fulfillment of religious duties and responsibilities (Ahmed & Lu, 2020).

At the same time and in a related way, future research should critically examine the role of religious leadership in the engagement and appropriation of new AI and robotic technologies. As one area of heated societal debate is the prospect of human replacement by robots, future research should examine if and under what conditions perceived displacement or complementary existence would take place with robots and clergy labor. Young (2019), for example, has raised the possibility of "digital clergy" and "artificially intelligent digital systems" supplanting Christian pastoral work in "significant ways" including sermon composition and delivery, provision of pastoral care, conducting scriptural research or performing

sacramental functions (p. 481). However, broadstroked and abstract visions of the rise of robots with dystopian outcomes may not realistically reflect the complexity and significance of everyday clergy work.

Here, for example, it is pertinent to consider alternative conceptualizations of how and to what extent human substitution of a religious priest would take place. Noting the limited research on the applications of artificial intelligence on spiritual education, Tan (2020) describes an imagined robot teacher "Digital Confucius" inspired by Confucius who can serve as an AI partner in spiritual education, to teach the moral values through Chinese classics and the six arts (liuyi) such as observing specific rituals. "Digital Confucius" is also envisioned to be able to customize its teaching, "in accordance to the learner's profiles and contextual needs to a certain extent. This is because the robot would be able to store an enormous amount of data that is easily retrievable and conveyed to the learner using engaging visuals, sound systems and special effects" and "be pre-programmed with data about the students' backgrounds, personalities, learning needs and abilities" (Tan, 2020, pp. 4–5). However, Tan (2020) has expressed doubts about whether "Digital Confucius" would be able to make ethical judgments and decisions in order to serve as an "ethical-spiritual guide and role model" since it lacks the holistic AI "heartmind (xin)" needed to be a Confucian teacher who can think, feel, act, and grow morally. Thus, by dissecting the multidimensional nature of religious leadership work, her paper unfolds a compelling argument for the continued need for human teachers in the face of AI advances, necessitating future fieldwork to investigate the operations and limitations of "Digital Confucius," should this machine be invented in the future. The thrust of her discussion also chimes with an overall concern expressed in this chapter and other commentaries regarding the need for future research to consider the ethics of AI communication, including social and knowledge inequalities in different groups, power relations and the interests of elites (Boyd & Holton, 2018), in order to deepen understanding on instructional and mentoring labor that is assigned to robotic agents.

Accordingly, the communicative constitution and performance of religious authority (Cheong, 2017) should be carefully considered in AI debates. Although techno-centric approaches to AI assume a flat ontology in human–machine communication, this dominant perspective obscures historical power relations and the interests of key stakeholders and ruling elites, necessitating a bounded automation approach that shapes

AI diffusion in the religious realm (Cheong, 2021). Drawing upon the case of Xian'er the robot monk's development, Cheong (2021) explicated key ways in which religious authority was enacted to strategically structure and manage emerging social robotics in order to reproduce particular spiritual values and cultural realities to sustain a large and transnational community. Distinctive communication practices were enacted through discursive motivating appeals, invocation, and multimedia branding collectively helped to align AI development to religious organizational goals and spiritual enlightenment.

As such, instead of treating the purported autonomy of spiritual robotics as a threat to existing faith communities and their religious leadership, future research should contextualize robotics and emerging digital innovations in their broader, organizational use (Fleming, 2019) including at the meso level where faith groups and sects order their interactions to promote and constrain distinctive facets of human–machine communication in their everyday operations. In this aspect, organizational values and theologically informed guidance shared by religious experts can exert considerable influence on the adoption of social robots. As Chaudhary (2019) points out in a discussion on prayer-bots while citing Floridi (2014), "Islamic theologians would agree that artificial agents do not deal with meaningful information, and that there is a 'semantic threshold' between humans and machines that remains unassailable since human and artificial agents 'belong to different worlds'" (p. 343). Similarly, Schuurman (2019), in an effort to articulate a contemporary Christian response to artificial intelligence, highlights ethical considerations in determining what roles machinic agents ought to play, when congregants should turn to machines for guidance, and the need to question which groups and institutions gain economic and political power through AI applications. His paper echoes an earlier concern regarding robotics and the value of humans as ascribed to them in Christian theology, reflected in the case of the use of the humanoid NAO robot (later renamed as D.A.V.I.D., Digitally Advanced Virtual Intelligence Device) in the Southern Evangelical Seminary, the first seminary in the United States to purchase this robot for pedagogy and research on ethics (Schulson, 2014). Hence, the debate regarding robot co-existence and the delegation of religious rituals to machines raise deeper issues regarding human value and agency in constructing religious human–machine communication. As religious leaders and followers navigate and manage evolving social automation

in sacred encounters, faith-based practices can help provide answers to broader and macro level enquiries on changing epistemology and the ontological boundaries between humans and machines (Guzman, 2020) in the future of digital religion.

Last but not least, it would be interesting to further explore the role of human governance in the care and management of religious robots, particularly in the realm of religion where they are not yet mass marketed to eschew commercial exploitation, or are prohibitively expensive for commercial replication (for e.g. Mindar, the Japanese robotic priest, cost almost US$ 1 million to develop). It was observed, for example, how Xian'er, the robot monk, received the vigilant attention of human chaperones managing its access in the temple as well as in its travels to technology exhibitions, thereby potentially constraining its capacity to reach local and global audiences (Cheong, 2020b). Hence, more studies on human–machine communication should take into consideration the human labors of care and human gatekeeping in managing access to religious machines. These practices are expected to evolve as an array of religious actors regulate robot access and structure religious human–machine communication in the future.

CONCLUSION

To conclude, the rise of social robots in recent years have prompted afresh enduring debates about the nature and significance of human authority and community, including in the religious sphere. Notably, the prominent and worldwide coverage of the debut of humanoid and robotic priests from various faith backgrounds have signaled strong public interest and initiated new curiosities in this area of innovation. Historical debates about the role of new technology in sacred domains have been rejuvenated and significant questions on the communicative capacities of these new agents have been raised alongside theological and ethical concerns. This review chapter discussed the emerging nexus of interdisciplinary research fueling contemporary religious human–machine communication; an area of immense research potential to uncover new theoretical frameworks to deepen understanding of new media and digital religion, as well as advance new practices to support individual and organizational spirituality and well-being. Accordingly, this chapter has also identified blossoming and ripe areas for future research and development. As we broach so called "smart" living with a trajectory toward intensifying AI and robotic presence, continued and escalating research attention should be cast on religious human–machine communication, as a luminous portal (literal and metaphorical) to present and other-worldly futures.

REFERENCES

Ackerman, E. (2017, August 22). *Pepper now available at funerals as a more affordable alternative to human priests*. IEEE Spectrum, https://spectrum.ieee.org/automaton/robotics/humanoids/pepper-now-available-atfunerals-as-a-more-affordable-alternative-to-human-priests

Ahmed, H., & La, H. M. (2020). Evaluating the co-dependence and co-existence between religion and robots: Past, present and insights on the future. *International Journal of Social Robotics*, 1–17. https://doi.org/10.1007/s12369-020-00636-x

Chaudhary, Y. (2019). Delegating religious practices to autonomous machines, a reply to "Prayer-bots and religious worship on Twitter: A call for a wider research agenda." *Minds and Machines*, 29(2), 341–347. https://doi.org/10.1007/s11023-019-09499-2

Cheong, P. H. (2017). The vitality of new media and religion: Communicative perspectives, practices, and changing authority in spiritual organization. *New Media & Society*, 19(1), 25–33. https://doi.org/10.1177/1461444816649913

Cheong, P. H. (2021). Bounded religious automation at work: Communicating human authority in artificial intelligence networks. *Journal of Communication Inquiry*, 45(1), 5–23. https://doi.org/10.1177/0196859920977133

Cheong, P. H. (2020a). Religion, robots and rectitude: communicative affordances for spiritual knowledge and community. *Applied Artificial Intelligence – An International Journal. 34* (5), 412–431. https://doi.org/10.1177/0196859920977133

Cheong, P. H. (2020b). Robots, religion and communication. Rethinking piety, practices and pedagogy in the era of artificial intelligence. In Isetti, G., Innerhofer, E., Pechlaner, H., & de Rachewiltz, M. (eds.). *Religion in the age of digitalization: From new media to spiritual machines*, 86–96. Routledge. https://doi.org/10.4324/9780367809225

Fleming, P. (2019). Robots and organization studies: Why robots might not want to steal your job. *Organization Studies*, 40(1), 23–38. https://doi.org/10.1177/0170840618765568

Floridi, L. (2014). *The 4th revolution: How the infosphere is reshaping human reality*. Oxford University Press. http://governance40.com/wp-content/uploads/2018/12/Luciano-Floridi-The-Fourth-Revolution_-How-the-infosphere-is-reshaping-human-reality-2014-Oxford-University-Press.pdf

Geraci, R. M. (2006). Spiritual robots: Religion and our scientific view of the natural world. *Theology and Science*, 4(3), 229–246. https://doi.org/10.1080/14746700600952993

Geraci, R. M. (2008). Apocalyptic AI: Religion and the promise of artificial intelligence. *Journal of the American Academy of Religion*, 76(1), 138–166. www.jstor.org/stable/40006028?seq=1

Guzman, A. L. (2020). Ontological boundaries between humans and computers and the implications for human-machine communication. *Human-Machine Communication*, 1(1), 3. https://doi.org/10.30658/hmc.1.3

Guzman, A. L., & Lewis, S. C. (2019). Artificial intelligence and communication: A Human–machine communication research agenda. *New Media & Society*, 22(1), 70–86. https://doi.org/10.1177/1461444819858691

Ke, Y. (2016). Finding Robot Monk Xian'er. Understanding Buddhism in Longquan animation. *Journal of Visual and Media Anthropology*, 2(1), 7–24. www.visual-anthropology.fu-berlin.de/journal/Vol_2_1_2016/Finding-Robot-Monk-Xian_er/index.html

Löffler, D., Hurtienne, J., & Nord, I. (2019). Blessing robot blessU2: A discursive design study to understand the implications of social robots in religious contexts. *International Journal of Social Robotics*, 1–18. https://doi.org/10.1007/s12369-019-00558-3

Lu, S., & J. Robertson. (2016, May 30). Robot monk dispenses Buddhist wisdom at Beijing temple. *CNN*. www.cnn.com/travel/article/china-buddhism-robot-monk/index.html

Martin, A. (2017, August 16) Pepper the robot to don Buddhist robe for its new funeral services role. *The Japan Times*. www.japantimes.co.jp/news/2017/08/16/business/pepper-the-robot-to-donbuddhist-robe-for-its-new-funeral-services-role/#.XSkEYehKiyl

Mayor, A. (2018). *Gods and robots: Myths, machines and ancient dreams of technology*. Princeton University Press.

McBride, J. (2019). Robotic bodies and the kairos of humanoid theologies. *Sophia*, 58(4), 663–676. https://doi.org/10.1007/s11841-017-0628-3

Miller, E. (2017, October 11). Blessing robots: Is a technological reformation coming? *Religious News Service*. https://religionnews.com/2017/10/11/blessing-robots-is-a-technological-reformation-coming//

Rambelli, F. (2018). Dharma devices, non-hermeneutical libraries, and robot-monks: Prayer machines in Japanese Buddhism. *Journal of Asian Humanities* at *Kyushu University*, *3*, 57–75. https://doi.org/10.5109/1917884

Robertson, J. (2018). Robot reincarnation: Rubbish, artefacts, and mortuary rituals. In Cwiertka, Katarzyna J. & Ewa Machotka (eds.)., *Consuming life in PostBubble Japan: A transdisciplinary perspective*, 153–173. Amsterdam University Press. https://doi.org/10.1093/ssjj/jyz017

Samuel, S. (2020, January 13). Robot priests can bless you, advise you, and even perform your funeral. *Vox*. www.vox.com/future-perfect/2019/9/9/20851753/ai-religion-robot-priest-mindar-buddhism-christianity

Schuurman, D. C. (2019). Artificial intelligence: Discerning a Christian response. *Perspectives on Science & Christian Faith*, *71*(2). www.asa3.org/ASA/PSCF/2019/PSCF6- 19Schuurman.pdf

Schulson, M. (2014). What robot theology can tell us about ourselves. *Religion Dispatches*. https://religiondispatches.org/automata/

Sherwood, H. (2017, May 30). Robot priest unveiled in Germany to mark 500 years since Reformation. *The Guardian*. www.theguardian.com/technology/2017/may/30/robot-priest-blessu-2-germany reformation-exhibition

Tan, C. (2020). Digital Confucius? Exploring the implications of artificial intelligence in spiritual education. *Connection Science*, 1–12. https://doi.org/10.1080/09540091.2019.1709045

Tatlow, K. D. (2016, April 27). A robot monk captivates China, mixing spirituality with artificial intelligence. *New York Times*. www.nytimes.com/2016/04/28/world/asia/china-robot-monk-temple.html

The Japan Times (2019, February 23). Kannon Bodhisattva robot unveiled at Kyoto temple to share Buddha's religious teachings. www.japantimes.co.jp/news/2019/02/23/business/tech/robotickannon-unveiled-kyoto-temple/#.XTJfX-hKiyI

Travagnin, S. (2020). From online Buddha halls to robot-monks: New developments in the long-term interaction between Buddhism, media, and technology in contemporary China. *Review of Religion and Chinese Society*, *7*(1), 120–148. https://doi.org/10.1163/22143955-00701006

Trovato, G., De Saint Chamas, L., Nishimura, M., Paredes, R., Lucho, C., Huerta-Mercado, A., & Cuellar, F. (2019). Religion and robots: Towards the synthesis of two extremes. *International Journal of Social Robotics*, 1–18. https://doi.org/10.1007/s12369-019-00553-8

Trovato, G., Kishi, T., Kawai, M., Zhong, T., Lin, J. Y., Gu. Z., Oshiyama, C., & Takanishi, A. (2019). The creation of DarumaTO: A social companion robot for Buddhist/Shinto elderlies. *Proceedings of the 2019 IEEE/ASME International Conference on Advanced Intelligent Mechatronics, China*, 606–611. http://doi.org/10.1109/AIM.2019.8868736

Trovato, G., Lucho, C., Ramón, A., Ramirez., R., Rodriguez, L., & Cuellar, F. (2018). The creation of SanTO: a robot with "divine" features. *Proceedings of the 15th IEEE Xplore International Conference on Ubiquitous Robots, USA*, 437–442. http://doi.org/10.1109/URAI.2018.8442207

Trovato, G., Pariasca, F., Ramirez, R., Cerna, J., Reutskiy, V., Rodriguez, L., & Cuellar, F. (2019). Communicating with SanTO – the first Catholic robot. *Proceedings of the 28th IEEE International Conference on Robot & Human Interactive Communication, India*, 1–6. http://doi.org/10.1109/RO-MAN46459.2019.8956250

Young, W. (2019). Reverend robot: Automation and clergy. *Zygon. Journal of Religion and Science*, *54*(2), 479–500. https://doi.org/10.1111/zygo.12515

Index

Page numbers in **bold** refer to tables